UNDERSTANDING EVIDENCE

Paul C. Giannelli

Albert J. Weatherhead III and Richard W. Weatherhead
Professor of Law
Case Western Reserve University

LexisNexis™
Matthew Bender®

ISBN#: 0820553034

Library of Congress Cataloging-in-Publication Data

Giannelli, Paul C.
    Understanding evidence / Paul C. Giannelli
      p. cm. --(Understanding)
    Includes index.
    ISBN 0-8205-5303-4
      1. Evidence(Law)--United States. 2. United States. Federal Rules of Evidence. I. Title.
II. Understanding series (New York, N.Y.)

KF8935 .G52 2002
347.73'6—dc21

                       2002040695

Editorial Offices
744 Broad Street, Newark, NJ 07102 (973) 820-2000
201 Mission St., San Francisco, CA 94105-1831 (415) 908-3200
701 East Water Street, Charlottesville, VA 22902-7587 (804) 972-7600
www.lexis.com

PREFACE

This book is written for students in evidence and trial practice courses. The focus is on the Federal Rules of Evidence, which have been adopted in one form or another in over forty jurisdictions.

In nearly 30 years of teaching, one's debt to past scholars is immense. Morgan, Wigmore, McCormick, Ladd, and Maguire immediately come to mind. The debt is no less to current scholars: Weinstein, Berger, Imwinkelried, Park, Mueller, Ken Graham, and Michael Graham to name but a few.

I owe a special debt of gratitude to my editor, Leslie Levin, whose efforts substantially improved the text, and to Jackie Braunstein of Brooklyn Law School for making valuable suggestions. Barbara Snyder of Ohio State, as usual, provided important insights. Of course, my wife Sue has always been there for me. I should also thank my sons, Mike and Adam, whose tuition payments inspired this book.

Suggestions for improvements and the identification of any errors are welcome: pcg@po.cwru.edu.

Paul C. Giannelli
January, 2003

SUMMARY TABLE OF CONTENTS

Part D: Real & Demonstrative Evidence

Part E: Writings

Part F: Hearsay

Part G: Privileges

Part H: Substitutes for Evidence

TABLE OF CONTENTS

Page

Page

Part D: Real & Demonstrative Evidence

Page

Part E: Writings

**Chapter 28 AUTHENTICATION OF WRITINGS: FRE
901–903** **375**

Part F: Hearsay

Chapter 31 HEARSAY RULE: FRE 801(a)-(c), 805, 806 . . . 405

Page

Part G: Privileges

Chapter 38 ATTORNEY-CLIENT PRIVILEGE **549**

Page

Chapter 1

OVERVIEW OF EVIDENCE LAW

§ 1.01 Introduction

Lee Harvey Oswald either shot President Kennedy or he did not. This is an important question, but for trial lawyers, the question is whether a party — here, the prosecution — could have proved Oswald's guilt at a trial. This is where the rules of evidence come into play. They govern how we go about the task of attempting to determine what occurred in the past, often under circumstances of uncertainty. What if there were no eyewitnesses to a crime? What if there were two eyewitnesses, but they disagreed?

This chapter introduces the subject of "proof" at trial and then examines one way to classify the rules of evidence. Next, the Federal Rules of Evidence — their enactment and interpretation — are considered. Finally, some basic themes in evidence law are briefly explored.

§ 1.02 Proof at Trial

There are some basic issues that any system of proof would need to confront. We, of course, will focus on the adversarial system used in this country.[1]

Burdens of proof. A fundamental issue involves the allocation of burdens of proof: the burden of persuasion and the burden of production.[2] What if the evidence adduced at trial is insufficiently persuasive under some defined standard? Who should lose the case? Moreover, in defining the burden of persuasion do we want to favor one party over another by placing a thumb on the scales of justice, so to speak? There are two types of errors that can be made in a criminal case: (1) false positives — convicting the innocent, and (2) false negatives — acquitting the guilty. As a policy matter, we want to avoid the former more than the latter, and thus, we use a higher standard in criminal cases, *i.e.,* proof beyond a reasonable doubt. The same policy issue is absent in civil litigation. Thus, a preponderance of evidence standard is used because the system is expensive and we do not want a tie at the end of a one week, one month, or one year trial. Special procedural rules, called presumptions, assist parties in meeting their burdens of proof.[3]

---

[1] Our system of proof is very different from the system used in civil law countries in Europe and elsewhere. *See* Damaska, *Presentation of Evidence and Factfinding Precision*, 123 U. Pa. L. Rev. 1083 (1975); Langbein, *The German Advantage in Civil Procedure*, 52 U. Chi. L. Rev. 823 (1985); Van Kessel, *Adversary Excesses in the American Criminal Trial*, 67 Notre Dame L. Rev. 403 (1992).

[2] *See infra* chapter 4 (burdens of proof).

[3] Fed. R. Evid. 301. *See infra* chapter 5 (presumptions & inferences).

1

"Housekeeping" rules. We also need some "housekeeping" rules. In offering evidence, who should go first? Who goes second and does the first party have a right to rebut? The order of trial is: (1) plaintiff (prosecution) case-in-chief, (2) defense case-in-chief, (3) plaintiff rebuttal, and (4) defense surrebuttal.[4] The party with the burden of production goes first because if that party fails to meet that burden, the trial can end with a directed verdict right then. In examining witnesses, the same issues arise: who examines first, second, and should there be any further examination? The answer: (1) direct examination, (2) cross-examination, (3) redirect examination, and (4) recross examination.[5]

Testimonial proof. In the common law system, proof typically comes in the form of witness testimony. The first issue is who should be considered a *competent* witness.[6] Another issue is the *credibility* of witnesses, *i.e.,* their worthiness of belief.[7] Some witnesses lie, but more often witnesses are inaccurate for other reasons, such as poor eyesight, unconscious bias, or a poor opportunity to observe. Efforts to diminish a witness's credibility fall under the rubric of "impeachment."

Lay witnesses. Evidence law makes a distinction between ordinary witnesses (called "lay" or "fact" witnesses) and experts.[8] As for lay witnesses, the primary rule is that they testify based on their personal observations — the "firsthand knowledge" rule.[9] For example, persons who were not physically present at a bank robbery should not testify about how the bank was robbed based merely on their speculation. We want an eyewitness.

Hearsay. If the eyewitness from the bank robbery tells another person about the robbery, should that other person be allowed to testify about the robbery as a mere conduit? The hearsay rule says "no." We need to be able to cross-examine the eyewitness about what that person saw. For present purposes, hearsay may be defined as an out-of-court statement offered for the truth of its assertion. Oh, yes, there really are 29 exceptions, but you need to know only about a dozen major exceptions.[10]

Documentary evidence. In addition to testimony, proof may consist of documentary evidence. The use of writings at trial produced several rules. The first deals with *authentication*, which requires the offering party to establish that a document is what that party says it is.[11] Assume the accused has signed a written confession in a criminal case. Evidence law typically rejects *self-authentication, i.e.,* letting the document speak for itself. Thus, the prosecution would need to put a witness on the stand to

---

[4] *See infra* chapter 3 (stages of trial).

[5] *See infra* chapter 20 (examination of witnesses).

[6] *See infra* chapter 18 (witness competency).

[7] *See infra* chapter 22 (credibility of witnesses).

[8] *See infra* chapter 23 (lay witnesses); chapter 24 (expert testimony).

[9] Fed. R. Evid. 602.

[10] *See infra* chapters 31–35 (hearsay rule & a bunch of exceptions).

[11] Fed. R. Evid. 901. *See infra* chapter 28 (authentication of writings).

authenticate the confession — here, the detective who obtained the confession could testify that the accused signed the confession in the detective's presence.[12] In addition, a person sufficiently familiar with the accused's signature could identify that signature. Other methods of authentication include the "ancient document" rule[13] and the "reply rule."[14] We also permit an expert or the jury to compare a document with known exemplars. In contrast, certain types of documents such as public records are self-authenticating, and the Federal Rules has expanded this category to include newspapers, trademarks, commercial paper, and so forth.[15]

A second rule, known as the *rule of completeness*, allows a party to introduce a part of writing (or recording) immediately in order to place the writing in context if the other side has introduced a different part of the writing.[16] A third rule comes into play when a party tries to prove the contents of a writing, which might be important in a contract dispute or will contest. Although the phrase original document rule is the more apt description, this rule is typically called the *"best evidence"* rule.[17] In short, sometimes we want the original produced.

Real evidence. Another type of proof is referred to as "real" evidence.[18] An example would be a murder weapon, such as a gun, knife, or baseball bat. Perhaps the prosecution wants to trace the murder weapon back to the accused. If so, the prosecutor would have to show that the gun seized at the murder scene was the same weapon the prosecutor was attempting to admit at trial, at which time a witness could identify it as the defendant's gun. One way to do this is to establish the *chain of custody* for the gun.[19]

Photographs. Typically, photographs are taken at a murder scene, and courts have long admitted them into evidence, provided a witness to the crime scene can testify that the photographs are an "accurate and fair representation" of the scene.[20] The witness, who has firsthand knowledge of the scene, in effect, adopts the photograph as her testimony. This is known as the *pictorial communication* theory of admissibility. If this method is not possible (*e.g.,* surveillance camera in an empty store), the pictures can be admitted through the testimony of a person familiar with

---

[12] The prosecution could not call the accused to authenticate the confession because of the Fifth Amendment privilege against compulsory self-incrimination. *See infra* § 43.05 (accused's privilege at trial).

[13] "Ancient" here means 20 years. *See* Fed. R. 803(16); Fed. R. 901(b)(8). *See infra* § 28.07 (ancient documents).

[14] For example, I send you a letter and you reply. That's it. *See infra* § 28.5[A] (reply rule).

[15] Fed. R. Evid. 902.

[16] Fed. R. Evid. 106. *See infra* chapter 29.

[17] Fed. R. Evid. 1002. *See infra* chapter 30.

[18] *See infra* chapter 26.

[19] Fed. R. Evid. 901 covers real evidence as well as documentary evidence. Moreover, a chain of custody is not the only way to identify real evidence. For example, if the police officer who recovered the gun at the crime scene placed her initials on the weapon, the gun would be "readily identifiable" and thus admissible under most circumstances.

[20] *See infra* chapter 27 (photographs, videos, computer simulations).

the operation of the surveillance system (the *"silent witness"* theory). Comparable rules were developed for movies and later applied to videotapes.

Demonstrations, models, etc. Models, blackboards, and charts may be used to illustrate testimony.[21] In some cases, a witness may exhibit a scar or amputated arm to show the jury the result of an accident (*in-court exhibition*), or, perhaps demonstrate how she can no longer walk without a limp (*in-court demonstration*). Computer animations are now used for such illustrative purposes, although they can also be used for other purposes.

Judge & jury functions. In this system, we also need to allocate responsibility between the judge and jury.[22] The jury decides the "facts," which includes the credibility of witnesses. The judge decides the admissibility of evidence (once an objection is raised) and generally runs the trial.[23]

§ 1.03 Law of Evidence

When first approached, evidence law can appear to be just a "bunch of rules" — and it is that. But there are several ways to classify the rules of evidence that may be of assistance.[24] One way is by type of proof — testimonial, documentary, real, and so forth, as was done in the preceding section. Another way is to divide the subject into three major categories: (1) rules governing the substantive content of evidence, (2) rules governing witnesses, and (3) substitutes for evidence.

[A] Rules Governing the Content of Evidence

There are two main categories of evidentiary rules concerning the substantive content of evidence: *relevance rules* and *competence rules*.

[1] Relevance Rules

All evidence must be relevant. Irrelevant evidence is always inadmissible.[25] Stated another way — relevancy is the threshold issue in deciding the admissibility of all evidence. There are an almost infinite variety of relevancy problems. Some situations have come before the courts so often that "rules of thumb" on admissibility have developed — *e.g.,* "similar happenings," "adverse inferences," and "out-of-court experiments."[26] In other situations, categorical rules have resulted. For instance, character

---

[21] *See infra* chapter 26 (real & demonstrative evidence).

[22] *See infra* chapter 2 (roles of judge & jury).

[23] *See infra* chapter 6 (objections & offers of proof); chapter 7 (preliminary questions of admissibility).

[24] The organization of the Federal Rules of Evidence is set forth *infra* § 1.04[D].

[25] Fed. R. Evid. 402.

[26] *See infra* chapter 9 (relevancy & its counterparts).

evidence is generally prohibited, although there are exceptions.[27] Other relevance rules govern habit[28] and insurance evidence.[29]

[2] Competence Rules

Relevancy, however, is not enough. Relevant evidence may be excluded for various reasons. These reasons are found in competency rules, which can be divided into two subcategories.

[a] Rules Based on Reliability Concerns

Sometimes we exclude evidence because it is believed to be unreliable. The hearsay[30] and "best evidence" rules are examples.[31] Here, relevant evidence is inadmissible due to another evidentiary rule.

[b] Rules Based on External Policies

Competency rules may also be based on some policy extrinsic to the trial process — *i.e.,* rules of privilege. We exclude communications between client and lawyer because we want to encourage such communications. Other common privileges include communications between spouses, doctors-patients, psychotherapists-patients, and clergy-communicants.[32] Here, we exclude evidence that may be both relevant and reliable.

[B] Rules Governing Witnesses

Rules relating to witnesses can be divided into several categories: (1) competency of witnesses, (2) examination of witnesses, (3) types of witnesses (lay and expert), and (4) credibility of witnesses. These were briefly touched upon in the previous section.

[1] Competency of Witnesses

The competency of a witness (as opposed to the competence of the evidence discussed above) refers to the mental capacity of the witness to observe, recall, and relate what that witness has seen and the moral capacity to recognize the obligation to testify truthfully. At common law, competency rules excluded any person with an interest in the case (including the parties), children, the insane, and so forth. For the most part, these

---

[27] Rules 404, 405, and 412–15 deal explicitly with character. *See infra* chapters 10–11.

[28] Fed. R. Evid. 406. *See infra* chapter 12 (habit & routine practice).

[29] Fed. R. Evid. 411. *See infra* chapter 17 (insurance). Another set of relevance rules are based on ancillary policies. Rules 407– 410 all involve the exclusion of relevant evidence based on policy reasons external to the truth-seeking function of the trial. For example, subsequent remedial measures (Rule 407) are excluded in order to encourage people to make repairs after accidents. *See infra* chapters 13–16. The federal drafters placed these rules in Article IV, which is the relevancy article. However, these rules function as competence rules.

[30] *See infra* chapters 31–35 (hearsay rule & exceptions).

[31] *See infra* chapter 30 (best evidence rule).

[32] *See infra* chapters 37–43 on privileges.

rules have been transformed into credibility rules. Indeed, Federal Rule 601 states that everyone is competent to testify. Nevertheless, a few problems remain.[33] Will a two-year old child be permitted to testify?

[2] Examination of Witnesses

As noted in the previous section, there are housekeeping rules governing the order of evidence presentation at trial and the order of witness examination (direct, cross, redirect, and recross).[34] There, are additional rules. For example, "leading questions" are generally prohibited on direct examination but are allowed on cross-examination.[35] Moreover, witnesses forget stuff, so we let them refresh their recollections with documents.[36]

[3] Types of Witnesses

Evidence law divides witnesses into two categories — experts and lay witnesses; the latter are often called fact witnesses.

[a] Lay Witnesses

There are two principal rules relating to lay witnesses. First, lay witness testimony must be based on personal observations — *i.e.,* "firsthand knowledge" rule.[37] Second, we prefer witnesses to testify in terms of their primary sensory impressions rather than to opinions, inferences, or conclusions drawn from those perceptions. If possible, we prefer the witness to testify that the defendant drew a pistol, aimed it at the bank teller, and then fired the pistol, rather than: "The teller was killed in cold blood." This is the much misunderstood "opinion rule."[38]

[b] Expert Witnesses

Some topics are beyond the common understanding of most lay jurors, and in such situations, we use expert witnesses to educate the jurors.[39] For example, had the victim already died from a heart attack before the defendant negligently ran over the victim who was lying in the middle of the street? Here, a physician could provide the jury with helpful information. The use of experts requires a standard for defining the proper *subject matter* of expert testimony[40] and a rule on who *qualifies* as an expert in

---

[33] *See infra* chapter 18 (witness competency). There is still an oath requirement (Rule 603) and we don't want the judge or jurors testifying in the case. Rules 605 and 606(a).

[34] *See infra* chapter 3 (stages of trial) & chapter 20 (examination of witnesses).

[35] Fed. R. Evid. 611(c).

[36] Fed. R. Evid. 612. *See infra* chapter 21 (refreshing recollection).

[37] Fed. R. Evid. 602. *See infra* § 23.02 (firsthand knowledge rule).

[38] Fed. R. Evid. 701. *See infra* § 23.03 (opinion rule).

[39] *See infra* chapter 24 (expert testimony).

[40] The subject matter of expert testimony raises two issue. Some types of evidence, such as the polygraph, may be considered too unreliable for courtroom use. The second issue involves testimony that is so common that a lay juror can handle the issue without the assistance of

that subject matter.[41] In order to take advantage of the witness's expertise, the common law permitted an expert to testify in the form of an opinion, *e.g.*, "In my opinion, the victim died of a heart attack."

In addition, a rule on the *bases* of expert testimony is required.[42] Clearly, an expert with firsthand knowledge should be allowed to testify, *i.e.*, the physician who performed the autopsy. But what about a physician who was not present at the autopsy? Here, the common law dispensed with the firsthand knowledge requirement and provided the expert with the facts through the use of a *hypothetical question*, provided all the facts were established by other witnesses (facts in the record). The federal drafters went beyond the common law, permitting an expert to testify based on facts provided outside of court (nonrecord facts) if these facts are the type reasonably relied upon by experts in the field.[43]

[4] Credibility

Credibility is simply a witness's worthiness of belief.[44] Credibility may be viewed in three stages: (1) bolstering, (2) impeachment, and (3) rehabilitation. Credibility issues most often involve *impeachment, i.e.,* attempts to diminish or attack a witness's credibility.

There are five main lines of attack: bias, untruthful character,[45] sensory or mental defect, prior inconsistent statements (self-contradiction),[46] and specific contradiction.[47] There are no specific Federal Rules on bias or sensory-mental defect impeachment, but they are recognized in the cases.[48] In addition, the common law had a special impeachment rule for experts — the "learned treatise" rule.[49]

Bolstering and rehabilitation refer to attempts to support a witness's credibility; the difference is one of timing — bolstering comes before, impeachment and rehabilitation after.

---

an expert. For instance, we do not need expert testimony on the laws of gravity in a homicide case in which the accused is charged with throwing a large rock from a highway overpass, killing the occupants of a car traveling on the highway below.

[41] Fed. R. Evid. 702.

[42] *See infra* chapter 25 (bases of expert testimony).

[43] Fed. R. Evid. 703.

[44] *See infra* chapter 22 (credibility).

[45] There are several different ways to prove untruthful character: (1) reputation or opinion evidence, Rule 608(a), (2) prior conviction, Rule 609, and (3) specific instances reflecting untruthful character that have not resulted in a conviction, Rule 608(b).

[46] Fed. R. Evid. 613.

[47] A prior inconsistent statement involves self-contradiction by one witness — *i.e.*, the prior statement is inconsistent with the witness's trial testimony. Specific contradiction involves two different witnesses, *e.g.*, Smith testifies that the accused shot the victim, while Jones testifies that somebody else shot the victim.

[48] There are other rules on impeachment. Rule 610 prohibits the impeachment use of a witness's religious beliefs.

[49] Fed. R. Evid. 803(18). *See infra* § 33.16 (learned treatise hearsay exception).

[C] Substitutes for Evidence

The party with the burden of production is obligated to introduce evidence to satisfy that burden. This obligation is excused in two circumstances: (1) where the judge takes judicial notice of a fact[50] and (2) where the parties stipulate (agree) to a fact.[51]

§ 1.04 Federal Rules of Evidence

Before the Federal Rules were enacted in 1975, evidence law was basically a common law subject. There were, of course, a few exceptions; the law of privilege was mostly statutory, and most jurisdictions had codified hearsay exceptions for business and official records.

Several efforts at codification had been attempted. In 1942, the American Law Institute promulgated the Model Code of Evidence.[52] The Model Code, however, was considered so radical by the practicing bar that it was never adopted by any state. In 1953, the Commissioners on Uniform State Laws threw their hat into the ring, promulgating the Uniform Rules of Evidence.[53] Although not as radical as the Model Rules, the Uniform Rules were adopted by only a few jurisdictions. In 1967, California ventured out on its own and enacted an Evidence Code, which continues to this day.

[A] Drafting the Rules

In 1961, a committee appointed by Chief Justice Earl Warren recommended the adoption of uniform Federal Rules of Evidence.[54] Following the recommendation of this committee, the Chief Justice appointed an Advisory Committee to draft the Federal Rules in 1965.[55] The Advisory Committee published a preliminary draft in 1969[56] and a revised draft in 1971.[57] The

---

[50] See infra chapter 44 (judicial notice).

[51] See infra chapter 45 (stipulations).

[52] Model Code of Evidence (1942). When the ALI undertook the task of clarifying the common law through its Restatement of Law project, the law of evidence was considered. The ALI abandoned this project because "however much that law needs clarification in order to produce reasonable certainty in its application, the Rules themselves in numerous and important instances are so defective that instead of being the means of developing truth, they operate to suppress it." Id. at viii.

[53] See Uniform Rules of Evidence (1953). After the Federal Rules of Evidence were drafted, a new version, promulgated in 1974, was adopted; this version was patterned on the Federal Rules. The present version, which continues to follow the Federal Rules, was promulgated in 1999.

[54] See A Preliminary Report on the Advisability and Feasibility of Developing Uniform Rules of Evidence for the United States District Courts, 30 F.R.D. 73 (1962).

[55] See 36 F.R.D. 128 (1965).

[56] See Preliminary Draft of Proposed Rules of Evidence for the United States District Courts and Magistrates, 46 F.R.D. 161 (1969).

[57] See Revised Draft of Proposed Rules of Evidence for the United States Courts and Magistrates, 51 F.R.D. 315 (1971).

Federal Rules were promulgated by the Supreme Court in November 1972 and transmitted to Congress in February 1973.[58]

[B] Congressional Intervention

Congress reacted by enacting legislation that deferred the effective date of the Federal Rules,[59] and extensive hearings on the rules were held by both the House and Senate Judiciary Committees.[60] In 1975, the Federal Rules emerged from Congress in statutory form.[61] Congress had amended the Court-promulgated rules in a number of significant respects.[62] The legislative history of these amendments is found in the various committee reports[63] and in the Congressional Record.[64]

[C] Amendment of the Rules

The Federal Rules have been amended numerous times since their adoption. There are two ways in which the Rules may be amended: (1) an act of Congress, and (2) promulgation by the Supreme Court through its statutory rulemaking authority, which is subject to congressional supervision. Both vehicles have been used to make amendments.[65]

[D] Structure of Federal Rules

The Federal Rules are organized by Article:

Article I	General Provisions (objections, offers of proof, etc.)
Article II	Judicial Notice
Article III	Presumptions
Article IV	Relevancy (character, habit, remedial measures, etc.)
Article V	Privileges
Article VI	Witnesses (competency, impeachment, examination)
Article VII	Opinions (lay opinions, expert testimony)
Article VIII	Hearsay

---

[58] *See Rules of Evidence for United States Courts and Magistrates*, 56 F.R.D. 183 (1973).

[59] Act of March 30, 1973, Pub. L. No. 93-12, 87 Stat. 9. *See also* H.R. Rep. No. 93-52, 93d Cong., 1st Sess. (1973).

[60] *See Proposed Rules of Evidence: Hearings Before the Special Subcommittee on Reform of Federal Criminal Laws of the Committee on the Judiciary, House of Representatives*, 93d Cong., 1st Sess. (1973); *Federal Rules of Evidence: Hearings Before the Committee on the Judiciary*, U.S. Senate, 93d Cong., 2d Sess. (1974).

[61] Act of January 2, 1975, Pub. L. No. 93-595, 88 Stat. 1926.

[62] The single most important example was the rejection of Article V, which contained thirteen rules of privilege. *See infra* § 37.02 (Federal Rule 501).

[63] *See* H.R. Rep. No. 650, 93d Cong., 1st Sess. (1973), reprinted in 1974 U.S.C.C.A.N. 7075; S. Rep. No. 1277, 93d Cong., 2d Sess. (1974), reprinted in 1974 U.S.C.C.A.N. 7051; H.R. Rep. No. 1597, 93d Cong., 2d Sess, (1974), reprinted in 1974 U.S.C.C.A.N. 7098 (conference report).

[64] For a detailed history of the adoption of the Federal Rules, *see* 21 Wright & Graham, Federal Practice and Procedure § 5006 (1977).

[65] *See* Capra, *A Recipe for Confusion: Congress and the Federal Rules of Evidence*, 55 U. Miami L. Rev. 691 (2001).

Article IX   Authentication (documents, real evidence, etc.)
Article X   Original Document Rule ("best evidence rule")
Article XI   Miscellaneous Rules (excepting certain proceedings such as grand juries from the Rules of Evidence)[66]

§ 1.05   State Adoptions of the Federal Rules

Even before the Federal Rules of Evidence were adopted, some states enacted or promulgated evidence rules based on the preliminary and revised drafts of the Federal Rules. After the Federal Rules were proposed, a new version of the Uniform Rules of Evidence was promulgated (1974); this version was patterned on the Federal Rules and has been revised (1999). As of today, over forty jurisdictions, including the military, have rules patterned after the Federal Rules. Most states have made changes in the Federal Rules when adopting them; sometimes the changes have been extensive.

Even jurisdictions that have not adopted the Federal Rules in toto have sometimes accepted a single rule as part of that state's common law.[67] For example, in *Daye v. Commonwealth*,[68] the Massachusetts Supreme Judicial Court adopted Federal Rule 801(d)(1)(A) on prior inconsistent statements as a matter of state common law.

As a federal statute not intended to preempt state law, the Federal Rules are not binding on the states. Thus, a state court is not required to interpret a state evidence rule, even one identical to its federal counterpart, in the same way that the federal rule is construed. For example, the Arizona Supreme Court declined to follow the Supreme Court's decision in *Daubert v. Merrell Dow Pharm., Inc.*[69] That case involved an interpretation of Rule 702, which governs the admissibility of expert testimony. The state court noted that it was "not bound by the United States Supreme Court's non-constitutional construction of the Federal Rules of Evidence when we construe the Arizona Rules of Evidence."[70] The court also remarked: "Our rules . . . are court-enacted. While the United States Supreme Court considers congressional purpose, this court when construing a rule we have adopted must rely on text and our own intent in adopting or amending the rule in the first instance."[71]

---

[66] The numbering of each rule corresponds to this framework. Because Article VIII governs hearsay, all the hearsay rules begin with the number 8 — for example, Rule 801 defines hearsay and Rules 803, 804, and 807 contain the hearsay exceptions.

[67] The following states have not adopted the Federal Rules: Connecticut, Georgia, Illinois, Kansas, Massachusetts, Missouri, New York, and Virginia. California has its own code.

[68] 469 N.E.2d 483 (Mass. 1984).

[69] 509 U.S. 579 (1993).

[70] State v. Bible, 858 P.2d 1152, 1183 (Ariz. 1993).

[71] *Id.*

§ 1.06   Interpreting the Federal Rules: The "Plain Meaning" Debate

Federal Rule 102, the "purpose and construction" provision, provides: "These rules shall be construed to secure fairness in administration, elimination of unjustifiable expense and delay, and promotion of growth and development of the law of evidence to the end that the truth may be ascertained and proceedings justly determined." The goals set out in this rule (there are 5 or 6) often serve cross-purposes. Consequently, the rule is not particularly helpful.[72]

The principal problem concerns the relationship between the Rules and the common law. This raises two distinct issues. The first concerns "gaps" in the Rules, *i.e.,* evidence issues not addressed by any rule. The second issue concerns the use of the common law in interpreting specific rules.

The "gap" problem. The Federal Rules were not intended to be a complete codification of all evidentiary rules. Professor Cleary, the Reporter for the Rules, wrote that Rule 102 indicates "one thing of importance: the answers to all questions that may arise under the Rules may not be found in specific terms in the Rules."[73] For example, no provision in the Rules governs the use of bias as a method of impeachment. Nevertheless, when the issue came before the Supreme Court in *United States v. Abel,*[74] the Court held that impeachment of a witness for bias was proper. According to the Court, "the lesson to be drawn is that it is permissible to impeach a witness by showing his bias under the Federal Rules of Evidence just as it was permissible to do so before their adoption."[75]

The second issue concerns interpreting specific rules. There are numerous examples of the need to resort to the common law when interpreting the Rules of Evidence. For example, Rule 301 governs presumptions but does not define that term; the common law must be consulted.[76] Rule 406 governs habit evidence but does not define what habit is; again the common law must be consulted.[77] Rule 613 governs impeachment by prior inconsistent statements but provides no elaboration of the "inconsistency" requirement; there is a substantial body of evidence case law on this point.[78] As Judge Becker and Professor Orenstein have commented: "Unquestionably, the Federal Rules coexist with unstated common law assumptions that were

---

[72] (Nevertheless, it is good to have a Rule 102 to fill the gap between Rules 101 and 103.)

[73] Cleary, *Preliminary Notes on Reading the Rules of Evidence,* 57 Neb. L. Rev. 908, 908 (1978).

[74] 469 U.S. 45 (1984).

[75] *Id.* at 51. As one court noted, "It is clear that in enacting the Federal Rules of Evidence Congress did not intend to wipe out the years of common-law development in the field of evidence, indeed the contrary is true. The new rules contain many gaps or omissions and in order to answer these unresolved questions, courts certainly should rely on common-law precedent." Werner v. Upjohn Co., 628 F.2d 848, 856 (4th Cir. 1980).

[76] *See infra* § 5.02 (presumptions defined).

[77] *See infra* § 12.02 (habit defined).

[78] *See infra* § 22.10[B] (inconsistency requirement).

never formally incorporated into the corpus of the Rules. The special relationship of the Federal Rules to the common law and the special expertise of the bench in evidentiary matters affect how the Rules should be interpreted."[79]

The Supreme Court, however, has not seen it that way. It has often, but not always, espoused an almost mechanical "plain meaning" approach in construing the Rules of Evidence, treating the Federal Rules as any other statute. In one case, the Court wrote: "We interpret the legislatively enacted Federal Rules of Evidence as we would any statute."[80] This approach has proved controversial. In a different case, Justice Blackmun criticized the Court for "espous[ing] an overly rigid interpretive approach; a more complete analysis casts significant and substantial doubt on the Court's 'plain meaning' easy solution."[81] Commentators' critiques are far stronger.[82]

The Supreme Court in 1995 indicated an intent to place greater reliance on the common law as a source of guidance in interpreting the Federal Rules. In *Tome v. United States*,[83] a case involving the admissibility of a prior consistent statement under Rule 801(d)(1)(B), the Court concluded that the Rule preserved the common-law requirement that the statement had to predate the motive to fabricate. In reaching its conclusion, the Court relied upon the intent of the Advisory Committee: "The [Advisory Committee's] Notes disclose a purpose to adhere to the common law in the

---

[79] Becker & Orenstein, *The Federal Rules of Evidence After Sixteen Years — The Effect of "Plain Meaning" Jurisprudence, the Need for an Advisory Committee on the Rules of Evidence, and Suggestions for Selective Revision of the Rules*, 60 Geo. Wash. L. Rev. 857, 868 (1992).

[80] Daubert v. Merrell Dow Pharm., 509 U.S. 579, 587 (1993). To support its position, the Supreme Court has cited an article by Professor Cleary, the principal drafter. Cleary wrote: "In principle, under the Federal Rules of Evidence no common law of evidence remains. 'All relevant evidence is admissible, except as otherwise provided.' In reality, of course, the body of common law knowledge continues to exist, though in the somewhat altered form of a source of guidance in the exercise of delegated powers." Cleary, *supra* note 72, at 915. However, other parts of Cleary's article point in a different direction: "If what is meant is that meaning is to be ascertained by reading the statute with the aid only of a dictionary and such aphorisms of construction as noscitur a sociis and ejusdem generis as may be suitable, then it must be discarded as unrealistic." *Id.* at 911.

[81] Bourjaily v. United States, 483 U.S. 171, 187–88 (1987) (Blackmun, J., dissenting).

[82] *See* Jonakait, *Text, Texts, or Ad Hoc Determinations: Interpretation of the Federal Rules of Evidence*, 71 Ind. L.J. 551, 571 (1996) ("Sometimes we must look beyond the words of the Rules to understand evidentiary doctrine. We must do so when the Rules are not definitive or are ambiguous . . . but sometimes even when the text is clear."); Jonakait, *The Supreme Court, Plain Meaning, and the Changed Rules of Evidence*, 68 Tex. L. Rev. 745, 786 (1990) ("Inevitably, the plain-meaning standard will produce worse evidence law by freezing evidence into a literalistic mold, by eliminating its dynamism, and by mandating results without any attempt to satisfy the policy goals of evidence law."); Weissenberger, *The Supreme Court and the Interpretation of the Federal Rules of Evidence*, 53 Ohio St. L. J. 1307, 1338 (1992) (The Court's approach "has recast the method of interpreting evidentiary principles in a manner that ignores the wisdom of the common-law history of the Federal Rules of Evidence and the capability of enlightened growth."). *But see* Imwinkelried, *A Brief Defense of the Supreme Court's Approach to the Interpretation of the Federal Rules of Evidence*, 27 Ind. L. Rev. 267 (1993).

[83] 513 U.S. 150 (1995).

application of evidentiary principles, absent express provisions to the contrary. Where the Rules did depart from their common-law antecedents, in general the Committee said so."[84] The Court also acknowledged that the "common law of evidence was the background against which the Federal Rules were drafted."[85]

§ 1.07 Themes in the Federal Rules

One of the purposes listed in Federal Rule 102, the "purpose and construction" provision, is the ascertainment of truth.[86] Although the truth-seeking function of the trial can be considered its main goal, it is not the only one. The law of privileges, for example, precludes the admissibility of evidence that may be both relevant and reliable.[87] Practical considerations such as the consumption of time is also a counterweight.[88]

Admissibility favored. Even when the ascertainment of truth is the goal, how to achieve that goal is often a matter about which reasonable people may disagree. Here, the federal drafters adopted several guiding principles. First, the Federal Rules are biased in favor of admissibility. When the drafters came to a split in the common law cases, they typically adopted the approach that was more permissive, even if it was the minority view.[89] At other times, the drafters adopted both a majority and minority position.[90] This theme is most pronounced in the rules on hearsay and expert testimony. This position is based on a view that juries are capable of dealing

---

[84] *Id.* at 160-61.

[85] *Id.* at 157.

[86] *See also* Portuondo v. Agard, 529 U.S. 61, 80 (2000) (dissenting opinion) ("truth-finding function of trials"); Tennessee v. Street, 471 U.S. 409, 415 (1985) ("there were no alternatives that would have . . . assured the integrity of the trial's truth-seeking function"); Funk v. United States, 290 U.S. 371, 381 (1933) ("And, since experience is of all teachers the most dependable, and since experience also is a continuous process, it follows that a rule of evidence at one time thought necessary to the ascertainment of truth should yield to the experience of a succeeding generation whenever that experience has clearly demonstrated the fallacy or unwisdom of the old rule.").

[87] *See infra* § 37.03 (rationale for privileges).

[88] *See* Fed. R. Evid. 403 (relevant evidence may be excluded if its probative value is substantially outweighed by waste of time, undue delay, needless presentation of cumulative evidence); Fed. R. Evid. 611(a). Even Rule 102 recognizes other values: "These rules shall be construed to secure fairness in administration, elimination of unjustifiable expense and delay, and promotion of growth and development of the law of evidence to the end that the truth may be ascertained and proceedings justly determined."

[89] *See* Fed. R. Evid. 803(4) (hearsay exception for statements made for medical treatment or diagnosis); Fed. R. Evid. 804(b)(3) (declarations against penal interests).

[90] Several hearsay exceptions are illustrative. The drafters adopted both a present sense impression exception and excited utterance exception. Fed. R. Evid. 803(1) & (2). The Rules also contain a hearsay exemption for authorized admission and agent-servant admissions. Fed. R. Evid. 801(d)(2)(C) & (D).

with most types of evidence and would reach better decisions with more, rather than less, information.[91]

Trial judge discretion. Another theme is judicial discretion. Although many trial lawyers want fixed rules, which they argue make evidence law more predictable, the drafters believed that too many unforeseen contingencies can arise at trial, and therefore the judge must be given leeway to shape the rules of evidence to deal with them. Rule 807, which recognizes a residual hearsay exception, is perhaps the best example.

Another issue worth considering is the conventional wisdom that much of the law of evidence is designed to keep information from the jury. This position can be traced to Professor Thayer, who wrote his classic text at the turn of the 20th Century.[92] Professor Nance has challenged this view, arguing that many evidence rules are designed to force attorneys to introduce the "best evidence." In short, attorney-control, not jury-control, is the underlying principle.[93]

§ 1.08   Criminal & Civil Trials

Although the Rules of Evidence apply to both criminal and civil cases, a number of rules recognize a distinction between civil and criminal trials — explicitly or by implication. Several rules apply only to criminal proceedings. For example, Rule 104(c) requires an out-of-court hearing to determine the admissibility of a confession. Rule 404(a) recognizes three exceptions to the rule prohibiting the use of character evidence; two of the three exceptions apply only in criminal cases.[94] Similarly, Rule 609(a) requires a special balancing test when a prior felony conviction is offered to impeach a criminal defendant; in all civil cases and for witnesses other than an accused in criminal cases, a prior felony conviction is admissible subject to a different balancing analysis (Rule 403). In effect, there is a higher threshold requirement when evidence of prior convictions is offered to impeach the accused. Another example is found in Rule 803(8), which contains a special limitation on the use of public records in criminal prosecutions.

On the other hand, a number of rules, due to their subject matter, apply only in civil cases — for example, Rule 407 (subsequent remedial measures) and Rule 411 (liability insurance).

Constitutional issues. In criminal prosecutions, application of the Rules must be consistent with constitutional provisions that bear on evidentiary

---

[91] *See* Weinstein, *Rule 702 of the Federal Rules of Evidence is Sound; It Should Not Be Amended,* 138 F.R.D. 631, 631 (1991) ("The Rules were designed to depend primarily upon lawyer-adversaries and sensible triers of fact to evaluate conflicts."). Judge Weinstein was on the drafting committee of the Federal Rules.

[92] Thayer, A Preliminary Treatise on Evidence at the Common Law (1898).

[93] Nance, *The Best Evidence Principle,* 73 Iowa L. Rev. 227 (1988).

[94] Fed. R. Evid. P. 404(a)(1) (an accused may offer evidence of her own character); Fed. R. Evid. P. 404(a)(2) (an accused may offer evidence of the victim's character in some circumstances).

matters. For example, the Confrontation Clause may require the exclusion of hearsay statements even if a statement falls within a recognized hearsay exception. [95]

§ 1.09 Key Points

The Federal Rules of Evidence were enacted in 1975, and over forty jurisdictions, including the military, have rules patterned after the Federal Rules. As a federal statute not intended to preempt state law, the Federal Rules are not binding on the states. Thus, a state court is not required to interpret a state evidence rule, even one identical to its federal counterpart, in the same way that the federal rule is construed.

The paramount goal of a trial is truth-seeking, but that is not the only goal. The law of privileges, for example, precludes the admissibility of evidence that may be both relevant and reliable. Even when the ascertainment of truth is the goal, how to achieve that goal is often a matter about which reasonable people may disagree. Here, the federal drafters adopted several guiding principles. First, the Federal Rules are *biased in favor of admissibility*. Another theme is *judicial discretion*. Although many trial lawyers want fixed rules, which they argue are predictable, the drafters believed that too many contingencies can arise, and therefore the trial judge must be given leeway to shape the rules of evidence to deal with them.

Civil & criminal cases. Although the Rules of Evidence apply to both criminal and civil cases, a number of rules recognize a distinction between civil and criminal trials — explicitly or by implication. A number of rules, due to their subject matter, apply only in civil cases — for example, Rule 407 (subsequent remedial measures), and Rule 411 (liability insurance). Further differences in applicability in criminal and civil proceedings arise due to constitutional principles — *e.g.*, right of confrontation.

Classification of Evidence Law

Evidence law may be divided into three major categories: (1) rules governing the substantive content of evidence, (2) rules governing witnesses, and (3) substitutes for evidence.

    I.   Rules Governing the Content of Evidence
        A.   Relevance Rules
            1.   Character evidence
            2.   Other acts evidence
            3.   Habit evidence
            4.   Insurance evidence

---

[95] *See infra* chapter 36 (right of confrontation). *See also* Davis v. Alaska, 415 U.S. 308 (1974) (Confrontation Clause requires cross-examination on prior juvenile adjudication notwithstanding state exclusionary rule); Chambers v. Mississippi, 410 U.S. 284 (1973) (due process requires admission of reliable hearsay evidence); Bruton v. United States, 391 U.S. 123 (1968) (Confrontation Clause requires exclusion of confession implicating codefendant in joint trial).

    B.   Competence Rules
        1.   Rules Based on Reliability Concerns
            a.   Hearsay rule
            b.   "Best evidence" rule
        2.   Rules Based on External Policies
            a.   Privileges (*e.g.,* attorney-client)
            b.   Quasi privileges
                (1)   Subsequent remedial measures
                (2)   Offers of compromise
                (3)   Payment of medical expenses
II.   Rules Governing Witnesses
    A.   Competency of Witnesses
    B.   Examination of Witnesses
        1.   Order of examination (direct, cross, redirect, recross)
        2.   Leading questions
        3.   Refreshing recollections
    C.   Types of Witnesses
        1.   Lay witnesses
            a.   Firsthand knowledge rule
            b.   Opinion rule
        2.   Expert witnesses
            a.   Subject matter requirement
            b.   Qualifications requirement
            c.   Bases of expert opinions
    D.   Credibility of witnesses
        1.   Bolstering
        2.   Impeachment
            a.   Bias
            b.   Untruthful character
            c.   Sensory or mental defect
            d.   Prior inconsistent statements
            e.   Specific contradiction
        3.   Rehabilitation
III.   Substitutes for evidence
    A.   Judicial notice of fact
    B.   Stipulations

Chapter 2

ROLES OF JUDGE & JURY: FRE 614

§ 2.01 Introduction

The allocation of responsibilities between the judge and the jury plays a central role in the law of evidence. The judge decides the admissibility of evidence; the jury decides its "weight."[1] The jury also decides the credibility of witnesses. The judge is the "law-giver"; the jury is the fact-finder.

The jury system frequently comes under attack. In the United Kingdom, juries are not used in civil litigation, and in some civil law systems in Europe and elsewhere, a professional judge with two lay judges decide cases. A written opinion supporting the judgment is required.[2] However, most trial attorneys and trial judges in this country believe in the jury system.

§ 2.02 Role of the Judge

The Supreme Court has written: "In a trial by jury in a federal court, the judge is not a mere moderator, but is the governor of the trial."[3] Nevertheless, by comparison with civil law countries, the American judge's role is passive, not active. In the civil law system, the judge conducts the investigation and is the first to ask questions of witnesses. In our system, the lawyers are the fact-gatherers and are responsible for presenting the facts to the jury.

---

[1] Thus, Rule 104(a) provides that "[p]reliminary questions concerning the qualification of a person to be a witness, the existence of a privilege, or the admissibility of evidence shall be determined by the court." Rule 104(e), entitled "weight and credibility," states that the judge's decision on admissibility "does not limit the right of a party to introduce before the jury evidence relevant to weight or credibility."

[2] See Langbein, *Mixed Court and Jury Court: Could the Continental Alternative Fill the American Need?*, 1981 Am. B. Found. Res. J. 195, 202 ("The Anglo-American jury system, by isolating the laymen, complicates the task of safeguarding against the dangers of ignorance and bias that inhere in any attempt to use laymen in adjudication. Because the jury deliberates without professional participation and decides without giving reasons, there is virtually no opportunity to provide learned guidance to the jurors during deliberations, and the means of detecting and relieving against errors after verdict are quite limited.").

[3] Quercia v. United States, 289 U.S. 466, 469 (1933). *See also* United States v. Martin, 189 F.3d 547, 553 (7th Cir. 1999) ("Along with other circuits, we have frequently reminded litigants that the function of a federal trial judge is not that of an umpire or of a moderator at a town meeting. Rather than simply being a silent spectator, intelligent questioning by the trial judge is his prerogative. The occasional questioning of witnesses is one means a judge may use to assist a jury in understanding the evidence. Thus, a trial judge may ask those questions he deems necessary in order to clarify an important issue, as long as he remains impartial.") (citations omitted).

This is not to say that the trial judge cannot influence the outcome of a trial. A judge's decisions and attitude often affect the conduct of a trial. While some of the judge's authority is found in explicit rules such as those recognizing the court's power to call and question witnesses, most of it evolves from the many issues that arise during the course of a trial which the judge must decide. Rule 611(a) recognizes the court's general authority to control the conduct of trial,[4] and the judge's power to regulate the order of proof and the presentation of evidence is discussed in other chapters.[5] This chapter examines the calling and questioning of witnesses, as well as commenting on the evidence.

§ 2.03   Court-Called Witnesses

Federal Rule 614(a), in accordance with the common law, recognizes the authority of the trial court to call witnesses on its own motion or at the behest of one of the parties.[6] The exercise of this authority is rare, however.[7] The authority to call witnesses includes the authority to appoint expert witnesses.[8] The federal drafters justified the rule by noting that the "tendency of juries to associate a witness with the party calling him, regardless of technical aspects of vouching, is avoided" and the "judge is not imprisoned within the case as made by the parties."[9]

All parties are entitled to cross-examine a court-called witness, and the jury should be instructed that the witness is not to be considered more credible simply because called by the court.[10] Indeed, the witness may have been called by the judge because neither party wanted to be associated with

---

[4] Fed. R. Evid. 611(a) ("The court shall exercise reasonable control over the mode and order of interrogating witnesses and presenting evidence. . . .").

[5] *See infra* § 3.05 (order of proceedings at trial); § 20.02 (judicial control of trial).

[6] *See* United States v. Karnes, 531 F.2d 214, 216 (4th Cir. 1976) ("[O]rdinarily the utilization of court witnesses is a matter within the discretion of the trial judge. . . . The power to call and to interrogate court witnesses is said to be derived from the judicial system's basic functions of disclosing truth and administering justice. . . . A trial judge is not captive within the case as made by the parties. He has the authority, if not the duty, to call witnesses who possess relevant information affecting the outcome of the issues when the parties decline to call them."). *See generally* Saltzburg, *The Unnecessarily Expanding Role of the American Trial Judge*, 64 Va. L. Rev. 1 (1978).

[7] *See* United States v. Cochran, 955 F.2d 1116, 1122 (7th Cir. 1992) ("Although authorized by the Federal Rules of Evidence, the use of a court's witness is rare. We are unable to find, and counsel has not cited, a single example of a reversal because of a trial court's decision not to call a witness for the court.").

[8] Fed. R. Evid. 706. *See infra* § 24.06 (court-appointed experts).

[9] Fed. R. Evid. 614 advisory committee's note.

[10] *See* United States v. Karnes, 531 F.2d 214, 217 (4th Cir. 1976) ("[T]he jury was never told why the witnesses were called as court witnesses and the jury was not instructed that these witnesses were entitled to no greater credibility because they had been called by the court. The jury, thus, may well have afforded them greater credibility than if they had been called as government witnesses. The jury's determination of credibility of witnesses may therefore have been unfairly, albeit unintentionally, influenced and the government's case thereby strengthened.").

an unsavory witness whose credibility was questionable. Objections to the calling of witnesses by the court may be made at the time the witness is called or at the next available opportunity when the jury is absent.[11]

§ 2.04   Court Questioning of Witnesses

Federal Rule 614(b) recognizes the trial court's authority to question witnesses. It permits the judge to examine witnesses in order to develop facts germane to the issues and to clear up doubts that may arise from the testimony. Nevertheless, the questioning of witnesses generally is the job of the parties. In the adversary system, the parties develop the facts. The ABA Civil Trial Practice Standards comment: "Generally, the court should not question a witness about subject matter not raised by any party with that witness, unless the court has provided the parties an opportunity, outside the hearing of the jury, to explain the omission. If the court believes that questioning on the subject is necessary, the court should afford the parties an opportunity to develop the subject on further examination prior to questioning the witness itself."[12] The Standards go on to state: "Except in unusual circumstances, the court should not seek to impeach or to rehabilitate a witness, nor seek to emphasize or de-emphasize the importance of any witness or testimony."[13]

Impartiality. An impartiality requirement is implicit in the federal rule.[14] In a criminal case, a trial court's lack of impartiality raises due process concerns.[15] The danger is that the jury might infer the judge's opinion of a witness through the persistence, tenor, range, or intensity of the judge's questions.[16]

---

[11] Fed. R. Evid. 614(c).

[12] ABA Civil Trial Practice Standard 10(a).

[13] ABA Civil Trial Practice Standard 10(c).

[14] *See* Fed. R. Evid. 614 advisory committee's note ("The authority is, of course, abused when the judge abandons his proper role and assumes that of advocate."). *See also* United States v. Tilgman, 134 F.3d 414, 416 (D.C. Cir. 1998) ("Because juries, not judges, decide whether witnesses are telling the truth, and because judges wield enormous influence over juries, judges may not ask questions that signal their belief or disbelief of witnesses."); United States v. Filani, 74 F.3d 378, 385 (2d Cir. 1996) ("[T]hese [judicial] inquiries targeted the defendant's credibility and challenged his story more in the manner of a prosecutor than an impartial judge."); United States v. Beaty, 722 F.2d 1090, 1096-97 (3d Cir. 1983) ("[T]he judge asked Mrs. Axelson again and again how she had come to be a witness in the case. This lengthy cross-examination, which occupies four pages in the trial transcript, was a frontal attack on her credibility. The jury could not have helped but conclude that the judge simply did not believe Mrs. Axelson."); United States v. Michienzi, 630 F.2d 455, 456 (6th Cir. 1980) (conviction reversed because, after an important government witness's testimony, the judge shook his hand and told the jury he was an old friend).

[15] *See* 5 LaFave, Israel & King, Criminal Procedure § 22.4(a) (2d ed. 1999) (right to impartial judge).

[16] *See* Judge Frankel, *The Search for Truth: An Umpireal View*, 123 U. Pa. L. Rev. 1031, 1043 (1975) ("We should be candid, moreover, in recognizing that juries are probably correct, most of the time if they glean a point of view from the judge's interpolations. Introspecting, I think I have usually put my penetrating questions to witnesses I thought were lying,

Objections. Rule 614(c) provides that objections to the questioning of witnesses by the court may be made at the time the witness is questioned or at the next available opportunity that the jury is absent. This provision modifies Rule 103(a)(1), which requires objections to be "timely," that is, without delay.[17] Rule 614(c) "is designed to relieve counsel of the embarrassment attendant upon objecting to questions by the judge in the presence of the jury, while at the same time assuring that objections are made in apt time to afford the opportunity to take possible corrective measures."[18]

§ 2.05 Judicial Commenting on Evidence

Unlike most state judges, federal trial judges have long had the authority to *comment* on the evidence.[19] As proposed, the Federal Rules had a provision on this practice: "After the close of the evidence and arguments of counsel, the judge may fairly and impartially sum up the evidence and comment to the jury upon the weight of the evidence and the credibility of the witnesses, if he also instructs the jury that they are to determine for themselves the weight of the evidence and the credit to be given to the witnesses and that they are not bound by the judge's summation or comment."[20] Although this provision was deleted by Congress, it did not change federal practice.[21]

There are, however, limits to the practice. The judge "may not assume the role of a witness. He may analyze and dissect the evidence, but he may

---

exaggerating, or obscuring the facts. Less frequently, I have intruded to rescue a witness from questions that seemed unfairly to put the testimony in a bad light or to confuse its import."). *See also* Bursten v. United States, 395 F.2d 976, 983 (5th Cir. 1968) ("It is well known, as a matter of judicial notice, that juries are highly sensitive to every utterance by the trial judge, the trial arbiter, and that some comments may be so highly prejudicial that even a strong admonition by the judge to the jury, that they are not bound by the judge's views, will not cure the error.").

[17] *See infra* § 6.02[D] (timeliness of objections).

[18] Fed. R. Evid. 614 advisory committee's note.

[19] *See* Quercia v. United States, 289 U.S. 466, 469 (1933) ("In charging the jury, the trial judge is not limited to instructions of an abstract sort. It is within his province, whenever he thinks it necessary, to assist the jury in arriving at a just conclusion by explaining and commenting upon the evidence, by drawing their attention to the parts of it which he thinks important, and he may express his opinion upon the facts, provided he makes it clear to the jury that all matters of fact are submitted to their determination."); Vicksburg & M.R. Co. v. Putnam, 118 U.S. 545, 553 (1886) (In submitting a case to the jury, the trial judge may "comment upon the evidence, call their attention to parts of it which he thinks important, and express his opinion upon the facts.").

[20] Proposed Fed. R. Evid. 105, 56 F.R.D. 183 (1973).

[21] *See* H.R. Rep. No. 650, 93d Cong., 1st Sess. (1973) ("Rule 105 as submitted by the Supreme Court concerned the issue of summing up and comment by the judge. . . . The Committee recognized that the Rule as submitted is consistent with long standing and current federal practice. However, the aspect of the Rule dealing with the authority of a judge to comment on the weight of the evidence and the credibility of witnesses — an authority not granted to judges in most State courts — was highly controversial. After much debate the Committee determined to delete the entire Rule, intending that its action be understood as reflecting no conclusion as to the merits of the proposed Rule and that the subject should be left for separate consideration at another time."), reprinted in 1974 U.S.C.C.A.N. 7075, 7078-79.

not either distort it or add to it. . . . [T]he trial judge [must] use great care that an expression of opinion upon the evidence 'should be so given as not to mislead, and especially that it should not be one-sided'; that 'deductions and theories not warranted by the evidence should be studiously avoided.'"[22]

§ 2.06 Jury Questioning of Witnesses

Empirical research has sparked interest in permitting greater jury participation in trials.[23] One way to increase jury engagement is to permit questions by the jurors. This may result in enhanced juror attentiveness and alert the attorneys to any misunderstood issues.[24] There is no Federal Rule on jury questioning, but the cases recognize the trial court's discretion on this issue.[25] There are, however, a number of dangers in the practice:

Witness questioning by jurors is fraught with risks. If permitted to go too far, examination by jurors may convert the jurors to advocates, compromising their neutrality. Jurors also may begin premature deliberation. Further, the practice "will often impale attorneys on the horns of a dilemma." Attorneys are faced with objecting to questions proffered by the arbiters that the attorneys are attempting to influence. The risk that an objection will alienate a jury is rather obvious. In cases such as this

[22] Quercia v. United States, 289 U.S. 466, 470 (1933). *See also* United States v. Murdock, 290 U.S. 384, 394 (1933) ("In the circumstances we think the trial judge erred in stating the opinion that the respondent was guilty beyond a reasonable doubt. A federal judge may analyze the evidence, comment upon it, and express his views with regard to the testimony of witnesses. He may advise the jury in respect of the facts, but the decision of issues of fact must be fairly left to the jury."); Hickory v. United States, 160 U.S. 408, 423 (1896) ("The statement that no one who was conscious of innocence would resort to concealment was substantially an instruction that all men who did so were necessarily guilty, thus ignoring the fundamental truth, evolved from the experience of mankind, that the innocent do often conceal through fear or other emotion.").

[23] *See* Penrod & Heuer, *Tweaking Commonsense: Assessing Aids to Jury Decision Making*, 3 Psychol. Pub. Pol'y & L. 259 (1997); Heuer & Penrod, *Increasing Jurors' Participation in Trials: A Field Experiment with Jury Notetaking and Question Asking*, 12 Law & Hum. Behav. 231 (1988); Sand & Reiss, *A Report on Seven Experiments Conducted by District Court Judges in the Second Circuit*, 60 N.Y.U. L. Rev. 423 (1985).

[24] *See* United States v. Richardson, 233 F.2d 1285, 1289–90 (11th Cir. 2000) ("The underlying rationale for the practice of permitting jurors to ask questions is that it helps jurors clarify and understand factual issues, especially in complex or lengthy trials that involve expert witness testimony or financial or technical evidence."); United States v. Sutton, 970 F.2d 1001, 1005 n. 3 (1st Cir. 1992) ("Juror-inspired questions may serve to advance the search for truth by alleviating uncertainties in the jurors' minds, clearing up confusion, or alerting the attorneys to points that bear further elaboration."); United States v. Callahan, 588 F.2d 1078, 1086 (5th Cir. 1979) (If there is confusion, "it makes good common sense to allow a question to be asked about it.").

[25] *E.g.,* United States v. Richardson, 233 F.3d 1285, 1288 (11th Cir. 2000) ("[E]very circuit to consider the practice has permitted it, [and] the decision to allow juror questioning rests within the discretion of the trial judge."); United States v. Feinberg, 89 F.3d 333, 336 (7th Cir. 1996) ("Every circuit to consider the practice has found it permissible in some circumstances."); United States v. Sutton, 970 F.2d 1001, 1005 (1st Cir. 1992). *But see* Morrison v. State, 845 S.W.2d 882 (Tex. Crim. App. 1992) (juror questioning disallowed in criminal cases).

one, where jurors are permitted to blurt out their questions, the district court almost invites a mistrial. The district court leaves open the possibility that a juror will ask an impermissibly prejudicial question to which the witness responds before the judge is able to intervene. In the event of such a mishap, the entire trial may be rendered nothing more than a lesson in futility[26]

If jury questioning is permitted, jurors should be required to submit written questions so that the judge has the opportunity to review the propriety of questions. If a question is unobjectionable, the judge puts it to the witness. The Second Circuit has outlined a series of protections: "(1) jurors should be instructed to submit their questions in writing to the judge; (2) outside the presence of the jury, the judge should review the questions with counsel, who may then object; and (3) the court itself should put the approved questions to the witnesses."[27]

§ 2.07 Key Points

Court-called witnesses. Rule 614(a) recognizes the authority of the trial court to call witnesses on its own motion or at the behest of one of the parties. The exercise of this authority is rare, however. The authority to call witnesses includes the authority to appoint expert witnesses (Rule 706).

Court questioning of witnesses. Rule 614(b) recognizes the trial court's authority to question witnesses. It permits the judge to examine witnesses in order to develop facts germane to the issues and to clear up doubts that may arise from the testimony. An impartiality requirement is implicit in the federal rule. The danger is that the jury might infer the judge's opinion of a witness through the persistence, tenor, range, or intensity of the judge's questions. Rule 614(c) provides that objections to the questioning of witnesses by the court may be made at the time the witness is questioned or at the next available opportunity that the jury is absent.

Jury questioning of witnesses. There is no Federal Rule on questioning by jurors, but the cases recognize the trial court's discretion on this issue. There are a number of dangers in the practice. If jury questioning is permitted, jurors should be required to submit written questions so that the judge has the opportunity to review the propriety of questions. If a question is unobjectionable, the judge puts it to the witness.

---

[26] United States v. Feinberg, 89 F.3d 333, 336–37 (7th Cir. 1996) (citations omitted).

[27] United States v. Bush, 47 F.3d 511, 516 (2d Cir. 1995). *See also* United States v. Cassiere, 4 F.3d 1006, 1018 (1st Cir. 1993); ABA Civil Trial Practice Standard 4 (setting forth procedure and jury instructions for juror questioning).

Chapter 3

STAGES OF TRIAL

§ 3.01 Introduction

Most students have taken a course in civil procedure before they take the evidence course. The same cannot be said for criminal procedure. Thus, this chapter briefly summarizes some of the initial steps before trial, with more background information provided for criminal litigation.

Several provisions of the Rules of Evidence explicitly refer to the Civil and Criminal Rules. For example, Rule 402 provides that relevant evidence is admissible unless there is a rule of exclusion, listing, inter alia, other rules prescribed by the Supreme Court.[1] Thus, the testimony of an expert witness could be excluded as a discovery sanction.[2] The hearsay rule, Rule 802, is similar, recognizing exceptions based on "other rules" prescribed by the Supreme Court.[3] The deposition requirements found in the civil and criminal rules are illustrative of such rules.[4]

§ 3.02 Pretrial Stages: Civil Cases

[A] Pleadings

The Rules of Civil Procedure use "notice" pleadings,[5] which require only a short and plain statement of the claim.[6] A civil suit begins with the filing

---

[1] Fed. R. Evid. 402 ("All relevant evidence is admissible, except as otherwise provided by the Constitution of the United States, by Act of Congress, by these rules, or *by other rules prescribed by the Supreme Court pursuant to statutory authority.* Evidence which is not relevant is not admissible.") (emphasis added).

[2] Fed. R. Civ. P. 37(b)(2)(B) ("prohibiting [a] party from introducing designated matters in evidence" is one available sanction).

[3] Fed. R. Evid. 802 ("Hearsay is not admissible except as provided by these rules or by other rules prescribed by the Supreme Court pursuant to statutory authority or by Act of Congress.").

[4] Fed. R. Crim. P. 15(e) ("At the trial or upon any hearing, a part or all of a deposition, so far as otherwise admissible under the rules of evidence, may be used as substantive evidence if the witness is unavailable, as unavailability is defined in Rule 804(a) of the Federal Rules of Evidence, or the witness gives testimony at the trial or hearing inconsistent with that witness' deposition. Any deposition may also be used by any party for the purpose of contradicting or impeaching the testimony of the deponent as a witness. If only a part of a deposition is offered in evidence by a party, an adverse party may require the offering of all of it which is relevant to the part offered and any party may offer other parts."); Fed. R. Civ. P. 32.

[5] *See generally* Shreve & Raven-Hansen, Understanding Civil Procedure § 8.04 (3d ed. 2002).

[6] Fed. R. Civ. P. 8(a) ("A pleading which sets forth a claim for relief, whether an original claim, counterclaim, cross-claim, or third-party claim, shall contain (1) a short and plain

23

of a complaint.[7] A summons along with the complaint is then served on the defendant,[8] who is required to respond with an answer.[9] Unless the party is unsure, the answer must either admit or deny the averments in the complaint.[10] Failure to deny may result in an admission.[11] Affirmative defenses must also be set forth in the answer,[12] and a counterclaim may also be required.[13]

The pleadings can affect the admissibility of evidence. Rule 401 requires evidence to be relevant to a "fact that is of consequence to the determination of the action."[14] Claims not asserted in the pleadings or waived are *not* issues in the case and therefore evidence directed toward those issues is not relevant under Rule 401.

Once the pleadings are closed, a party may move for a judgment on the pleadings.[15] If the case proceeds, a pretrial conference will be scheduled.

[B] Pretrial Conference

Pretrial conferences often have a significant impact on evidentiary matters. First, the conference may be used to obtain (1) admissions that

---

statement of the grounds upon which the court's jurisdiction depends, unless the court already has jurisdiction and the claim needs no new grounds of jurisdiction to support it, (2) a short and plain statement of the claim showing that the pleader is entitled to relief, and (3) a demand for judgment for the relief the pleader seeks. Relief in the alternative or of several different types may be demanded.").

[7] Fed. R. Civ. P. 3 ("A civil action is commenced by filing a complaint with the court.").

[8] Fed. R. Civ. P. 4 (service within 120 days generally required).

[9] Fed. R. Civ. P. 12(a)(1) (generally within 20 days).

[10] Fed. R. Civ. P. 8(b) ("If a party is without knowledge or information sufficient to form a belief as to the truth of an averment, the party shall so state and this has the effect of a denial.").

[11] Fed. R. Civ. P.8 (d) ("Averments in a pleading to which a responsive pleading is required, other than those as to the amount of damage, are admitted when not denied in the responsive pleading. Averments in a pleading to which no responsive pleading is required or permitted shall be taken as denied or avoided.").

[12] Fed. R. Civ. P. 8(c) ("In pleading to a preceding pleading, a party shall set forth affirmatively accord and satisfaction, arbitration and award, assumption of risk, contributory negligence, discharge in bankruptcy, duress, estoppel, failure of consideration, fraud, illegality, injury by fellow servant, laches, license, payment, release, res judicata, statute of frauds, statute of limitations, waiver, and any other matter constituting an avoidance or affirmative defense.").

[13] Fed. R. Civ. P. 13(a) ("A pleading shall state as a counterclaim any claim which at the time of serving the pleading the pleader has against any opposing party, if it arises out of the transaction or occurrence that is the subject matter of the opposing party's claim and does not require for its adjudication the presence of third parties of whom the court cannot acquire jurisdiction.").

[14] Fed. R. Evid. 401 (" 'Relevant evidence' means evidence having any tendency to make the existence of any fact that is of consequence to the determination of the action more probable or less probable than it would be without the evidence.").

[15] Fed. R. Civ. P. 12(c) ("If, on a motion for judgment on the pleadings, matters outside the pleadings are presented to and not excluded by the court, the motion shall be treated as one for summary judgment and disposed of as provided in Rule 56, and all parties shall be given reasonable opportunity to present all material made pertinent to such a motion by Rule 56.").

will avoid unnecessary proof, (2) stipulations regarding the authenticity of documents, and (3) advance rulings on the admissibility of evidence.[16] Second, restrictions on the use of expert testimony under Rule 702, which governs the admissibility of expert evidence, may be imposed.[17] Third, orders directing a party to present evidence early in the trial with respect to a manageable issue that could, on the evidence, be the basis for a judgment as a matter of law under Rule 50(a) or a judgment on partial findings under Rule 52(c) may be issued.[18] Finally, orders establishing reasonable limits on the time allowed for presenting evidence may be issued.[19] This is where the judge can have a significant impact on evidentiary issues. Suppose the judge requests that all the exhibits be marked for identification and then says, "I will admit them all unless there is an objection." Failure to object is a waiver.[20]

[C] Discovery

The overall purpose of pretrial discovery is to produce a fair trial. It accomplishes this objective by preventing trial by ambush. In addition, pretrial discovery sharpens the issues, which may reduce the length of the trial. It also may induce more settlements, always a goal in pretrial litigation. Information subject to discovery is not limited to admissible evidence.

Compared to criminal cases, discovery in civil litigation is quite extensive. Rule 26(a) provides for the initial disclosure of (1) the names, addresses, and telephone numbers of persons likely to possess discoverable information (unless solely for impeachment); (2) the inspection of documents and tangible things in the party's control; (3) the computation of damages including supporting documentation; and (4) the inspection of insurance agreements.[21]

Additional discovery is obtained through interrogatories,[22] the inspection of documents and tangible items,[23] and physical examinations.[24] In terms of evidence law, depositions and requests for admissions, as well as provisions on expert witnesses, are the most important forms of discovery.

---

[16] Fed. R. Civ. P. 16(c)(3).

[17] Fed. R. Civ. P. 16(c)(4).

[18] Fed. R. Civ. P. 16(c)(14).

[19] Fed. R. Civ. P. 16(c)(15).

[20] *See infra* chapter 6 (objections & offers of proof).

[21] Evidence of liability insurance is generally inadmissible under Rule 411. *See infra* chapter 17 (insurance).

[22] Fed. R. Civ. P. 33.

[23] Fed. R. Civ. P. 34.

[24] Fed. R. Civ. P. 35.

[1] Depositions

Depositions upon oral examination are governed by Civil Rule 30.[25] They are taken under oath or affirmation and recorded. The rule states: "Examination and cross-examination of witnesses may proceed as permitted at the trial under the provisions of the Federal Rules of Evidence except Rules 103 and 615."[26] Rule 615 governs the exclusion of witnesses from trial while other witnesses are testifying.[27] Witnesses can be separated during discovery as well.[28] Rule 103(a) requires that objections be made in a timely fashion at trial. Civil Rule 30 has its own provision on objections.[29] The more important provision is found in Rule 32, which deals with the waiver of certain objections by failing to make them at the deposition.[30] Objections that might have been obviated if made at the time of the deposition cannot be raised at trial. The rationale is fairness. Had the objection been made at the deposition, the opposing party may have been able to rephrase the question and elicit admissible evidence. That opportunity may now be foregone.

Trial use of depositions. Rule 32 specifies the conditions under which depositions may be used at trial. There are several. First, a deposition could be used to impeach a witness with a prior inconsistent statement.[31] There are two evidence rules governing this type of impeachment.[32] A second use would be as former testimony, an exception to the hearsay rule, if the deponent is unavailable at trial.[33] Third, any statement of a party or an

---

[25] *See also* Fed. R. Civ. P. 27 (depositions before action or pending appeal); Fed. R. Civ. P. 28 (persons before whom depositions may be taken); Fed. R. Civ. P. 31 (depositions upon written questions).

[26] Fed. R. Civ. P. 30(c).

[27] *See infra* chapter 19 (sequestration of witnesses).

[28] Fed. R. Civ. P. 26(c)(5) (protective orders may include "that discovery be conducted with no one present except persons designated by the court").

[29] Fed. R. Civ. P. 30(c) ("All objections made at the time of the examination to the qualifications of the officer taking the deposition, to the manner of taking it, to the evidence presented, to the conduct of any party, or to any other aspect of the proceedings shall be noted by the officer upon the record of the deposition; but the examination shall proceed, with the testimony being taken subject to the objections.").

[30] Fed. R. Civ. P. 32(d)(3)(A) ("Objections to the competency of a witness or to the competency, relevancy, or materiality of testimony are not waived by failure to make them before or during the taking of the deposition, unless the ground of the objection is one which might have been obviated or removed if presented at that time.").

[31] Fed. R. Civ. P. 32(a)(1) ("Any deposition may be used by any party for the purpose of contradicting or impeaching the testimony of deponent as a witness, or for any other purpose permitted by the Federal Rules of Evidence.").

[32] *See* Fed. R. Evid. 613 (admissible only for impeachment); Fed. R. Evid. 801(d)(1)(A) (prior inconsistent statements made under oath and subject to penalty for perjury at a deposition or other proceeding are admissible as substantive evidence).

[33] Rule 804(b)(1), which governs the admissibility of former testimony, specifies that testimony given "in a deposition taken in compliance with the law in the course of the same or another proceeding" may be admissible. *See also* Fed. R. Civ. P. 32(a)(3) ("The deposition of a witness, whether or not a party, may be used by any party for any purpose if the court finds: (A) that the witness is dead; or (B) that the witness is at a greater distance than 100 miles

agent of a party made at a deposition may be admitted against that party as an admission of a party opponent; admissions are exempted from the hearsay rule.[34] Fourth, a deposition could be used to refresh a witness's recollection.[35]

[2] Experts

Another significant part of discovery involves expert witnesses, which includes the initial identity of experts and their reports:[36]

> The report shall contain a complete statement of all opinions to be expressed and the basis and reasons therefor; the data or other information considered by the witness in forming the opinions; any exhibits to be used as a summary of or support for the opinions; the qualifications of the witness, including a list of all publications authored by the witness within the preceding ten years; the compensation to be paid for the study and testimony; and a listing of any other cases in which the witness has testified as an expert at trial or by deposition within the preceding four years.[37]

This provision anticipates several evidentiary issues. The most obvious is Rule 702, which requires experts to be qualified as a prerequisite to testifying.[38] In addition, Rule 703 permits experts to testify based on information supplied to the expert before trial (*i.e.*, hearsay) under certain conditions,[39] and Rule 705 allows the expert to give an opinion without first disclosing the underlying bases for that opinion. This rule is workable only if there is extensive pretrial discovery.[40] The other information —

---

from the place of trial or hearing, or is out of the United States, unless it appears that the absence of the witness was procured by the party offering the deposition; or (C) that the witness is unable to attend or testify because of age, illness, infirmity, or imprisonment; or (D) that the party offering the deposition has been unable to procure the attendance of the witness by subpoena; or (E) upon application and notice, that such exceptional circumstances exist as to make it desirable, in the interest of justice and with due regard to the importance of presenting the testimony of witnesses orally in open court, to allow the deposition to be used.").

[34] Admissions of party-opponents are generally admissible. *See* Fed. R. Evid. 801(d)(2)(A) (individual admission); Fed. R. Evid. 801(d)(2)(C) (authorized admission); Fed. R. Evid. 801(d)(2)(D) (agent or employee admission). *See also* Fed. R. Civ. P. 32(a)(2) ("The deposition of a party or of anyone who at the time of taking the deposition was an officer, director, or managing agent, or a person designated under Rule 30(b)(6) or 31(a) to testify on behalf of a public or private corporation, partnership or association or governmental agency which is a party may be used by an adverse party for any purpose.").

[35] Fed. R. Evid. 612 (refreshing recollection).

[36] Fed. R. Civ. P. 26(a)(2) ("Disclosure of Expert Testimony. (A) . . .[A] party shall disclose to other parties the identity of any person who may be used at trial to present evidence under Rules 702, 703, or 705 of the Federal Rules of Evidence.").

[37] Fed. R. Civ. P. 26(a)(B) ("[T]his disclosure shall, with respect to a witness who is retained or specially employed to provide expert testimony in the case or whose duties as an employee of the party regularly involve giving expert testimony, be accompanied by a written report prepared and signed by the witness.").

[38] *See infra* chapter 24 (expert testimony).

[39] *See infra* chapter 25 (bases of expert testimony).

[40] *See* Fed. R. Evid. 705 advisory committee's note ("If the objection is made that leaving

compensation, publications, and testimony in other cases — may be used for impeachment in some cases.[41]

The Civil Rules also contain a special deposition provision for experts.[42]

[3] Requests for Admissions

Another procedural rule that often has a significant impact on evidentiary issues is Rule 36, which governs requests for admissions. Requests may relate to "statements or opinions of fact" including "the genuineness of any documents." Any fact that is admitted is no longer subject to dispute at trial. These are considered judicial admissions, which are binding.[43] In addition, Rule 36, in large part, eliminates the need to authenticate documents in civil cases.[44] In discussing Rule 901, the principal provision on the authentication of documents, the federal drafters noted: "Today, such available procedures as requests to admit and pretrial conference afford the means of eliminating much of the need for authentication or identification."[45]

[D] Summary Judgment

A motion for summary judgment obviously has important ramifications for trial. Indeed, there may be no trial if the court grants the motion.[46]

---

it to the cross-examiner to bring out the supporting data is essentially unfair, the answer is that he is under no compulsion to bring out any facts or data except those unfavorable to the opinion. The answer assumes that the cross-examiner has the advance knowledge which is essential for effective cross-examination. This advance knowledge has been afforded, though imperfectly, by the traditional foundation requirement. Rule 26(b)(4) of the Rules of Civil Procedure, as revised, provides for substantial discovery in this area, obviating in large measure the obstacles which have been raised in some instances to discovery of findings, underlying data, and even the identity of the experts.").

[41] Compensation and testimony in other cases could be used to show bias. The expert's publications could be used for impeachment by prior inconsistent statements. Fed. R. Evid. 613. They may also be admissible as learned treatises if shown to be standard works in the field. Fed. R. Evid. 803(18).

[42] Fed. R. Civ. P. 26(b)(4)(A) ("A party may depose any person who has been identified as an expert whose opinions may be presented at trial. If a report from the expert is required under subdivision (a)(2)(B), the deposition shall not be conducted until after the report is provided."); Fed. R. Civ. P. 26(b)(4)(B) ("A party may, through interrogatories or by deposition, discover facts known or opinions held by an expert who has been retained or specially employed by another party in anticipation of litigation or preparation for trial and who is not expected to be called as a witness at trial, only as provided in Rule 35(b) or upon a showing of exceptional circumstances under which it is impracticable for the party seeking discovery to obtain facts or opinions on the same subject by other means.").

[43] See infra § 32.05[B] (evidential & judicial admissions distinguished).

[44] See infra chapter 28 (authentication of writings).

[45] Fed. R. Evid. 901 advisory committee's note.

[46] See Fed. R. Civ. P. 56(c) ("The motion shall be served at least 10 days before the time fixed for the hearing. The adverse party prior to the day of hearing may serve opposing affidavits. The judgment sought shall be rendered forthwith if the pleadings, depositions, answers to interrogatories, and admissions on file, together with the affidavits, if any, show that there is no genuine issue as to any material fact and that the moving party is entitled to a judgment as a matter of law. A summary judgment, interlocutory in character, may be rendered on the issue of liability alone although there is a genuine issue as to the amount of damages.").

This is a real possibility with expert testimony in some cases. Under the Supreme Court's interpretation of Rule 702, the case may end if the trial judge rules that proffered expert testimony on causation is inadmissible.[47] In *Weisgram v. Marley Co.*,[48] which involved summary judgment in a wrongful death action against the manufacturer of an allegedly defective baseboard heater, the Court wrote: "Since *Daubert*, moreover, parties relying on expert evidence have had notice of the exacting standards of reliability such evidence must meet."[49]

§ 3.03　Pretrial Stages: Criminal Cases

[A]　Charging Instruments

Criminal cases may commence with the filing of a complaint or an arrest, which is then followed by a complaint.[50] (As discussed below, the process may also start with a grand jury indictment.) Once there is an arrest, the arrestee must be brought before a judge or magistrate. This is known as the initial appearance in federal practice and the "arraignment" in many states.[51] This procedure serves several purposes. First, the judge must inform the defendant of the charges. The second objective is to explain to the defendant various rights, including the right to remain silent. The accused is also informed of right to counsel and to a reasonable continuance to secure the services of an attorney or to the appointment of an attorney if the accused is indigent.[52] In addition, an accused charged with a felony is informed of the right to a preliminary hearing, except if the appearance is pursuant to an indictment. Third, the court must set bail if the defendant is charged with a bailable offense.[53] A fourth objective arises in misdemeanor cases, where the defendant is required to enter a plea.

Unlike civil practice, there is no "answer" in criminal practice. There are only pleas.[54] Consequently, if a defendant wishes to remove an issue from trial, it must be done by stipulation, which the prosecution is not obligated to accept.[55]

---

[47] *See* Berger, *Procedural Paradigms for Applying the Daubert Test*, 78 Minn. L. Rev. 1345 (1994).

[48] 528 U.S. 440 (2000).

[49] *Id.* at 445 (citing Daubert v. Merrell Dow Pharm., Inc., 509 U.S. 579 (1993)).

[50] The complaint is the initial charging instrument in felony cases and the final charging instrument in misdemeanor cases. The purpose of a complaint is to inform the accused of the crime charged. It also forms the basis of the court's jurisdiction. *See* Fed. R. Crim. P. 3 ("The complaint is a written statement of the essential facts constituting the offense charged. It shall be made upon oath before a magistrate judge.").

[51] Fed. R. Crim. P. 5(c).

[52] Fed. R. Crim. P. 44.

[53] Fed. R. Crim. P. 46.

[54] Fed. R. Crim. P. 11(a)(1) ("A defendant may plead guilty, not guilty, or nolo contendere. If a defendant refuses to plead, or if a defendant organization, as defined in 18 U.S.C. § 18, fails to appear, the court shall enter a plea of not guilty.").

[55] *See infra* chapter 45 (stipulations).

[B] Preliminary Hearing

The next step in the process is the preliminary hearing,[56] which is a screening device, much the same as the grand jury is a screening device, designed to insure that persons are not made to stand trial for a felony in the absence of "probable cause." Unlike the initial appearance, the preliminary hearing is an adversarial proceeding. In *Coleman v. Alabama*,[57] the Supreme Court held that an indigent defendant has a Sixth Amendment right to appointed counsel at a preliminary hearing. The Court concluded that the preliminary hearing is a "critical stage" in the criminal process and the presence of counsel at the hearing was "necessary to preserve the defendant's basic right to a fair trial as affected by his right meaningfully to cross-examine the witness against him and to have effective assistance of counsel at the trial itself."[58]

The defendant also has the right to present evidence. Unless there is some compelling reason (and there won't be), it is inadvisable to present any defense evidence at the hearing. The defense cannot really "win" at the preliminary hearing. All the prosecutor needs to show is probable cause. Even if the magistrate dismisses the charge, the prosecution can still seek a grand jury indictment or come back with more evidence or try a different magistrate. The defense's goal at the preliminary hearing is discovery — to learn as much as possible about the prosecution's case. The Federal Rules of Evidence do not apply at the preliminary hearing.[59] Since hearsay is admissible at the hearing, the real witnesses may not even testify; instead, a detective may set forth the government's case. If eyewitnesses testify, the defense faces a dilemma. On one hand, a searching cross-examination may give away the defense's case and prepare the witness for trial. On the other hand, failing to cross-examine may result in the admission of the unchallenged preliminary hearing testimony at trial in the event the witness is unavailable at that time. Admissibility would be based on the former testimony exception to the hearsay rule, Rule 804(b)(1).

Trial uses. There are several ways in which preliminary hearing testimony may be used at a subsequent trial. The transcript may be used to refresh a witness's memory at trial.[60] If the defendant testifies at the preliminary hearing, that testimony is admissible against the defendant at trial as a party admission.[61] So the defendant should not testify.[62] The

---

[56] Fed. R. Crim. P. 5.l(a) ("If from the evidence it appears that there is probable cause to believe that an offense has been committed and that the defendant committed it, the federal magistrate judge shall forthwith hold the defendant to answer in district court. The finding of probable cause may be based upon hearsay evidence in whole or in part. The defendant may cross-examine adverse witnesses and may introduce evidence.").

[57] 399 U.S. 1 (1970).

[58] *Id.* at 7.

[59] Fed. R. Evid. 1001(d)(3) (other than privileges, Federal Rules do not apply in preliminary examinations in criminal cases).

[60] Fed. R. Evid. 612 (refreshing recollection).

[61] Fed. R. Evid. 801(d)(2)(A) (individual admission).

[62] The privilege against self-incrimination precludes the prosecution from calling the accused as a witness. *See infra* chapter 43.

transcript may also be used to impeach a witness whose preliminary hearing testimony is inconsistent with her trial testimony.[63]

The most common use of preliminary hearing testimony involves the hearsay exception for former testimony.[64] The admissibility of the preliminary hearing testimony of prosecution witnesses, under the former testimony exception, raises Sixth Amendment right of confrontation concerns.[65]

[C] Grand Jury

The Fifth Amendment provides that "no person shall be held to answer for a capital, or otherwise infamous crime, unless on presentment or indictment of a grand jury."[66] However, the Grand Jury Clause does not apply to the states.[67] Consequently, state law governs indictment issues. Approximately two-thirds of the states do not require grand jury indictment for felonies. The rules of evidence are generally inapplicable to grand jury proceedings.[68]

Functions of grand jury. The grand jury has two very distinct functions: to charge and to investigate. The charging or screening role of the grand jury is the more common role in state practice.[69] In its investigative role, the grand jury serves as a law enforcement tool; it is a means for the prosecution to gather evidence.[70] To carry out this investigative function,

---

[63] Fed. R. Evid. 613; Fed. R. Evid. 801(d)(1)(A) (prior inconsistent statements made under oath and subject to penalty for perjury at a deposition or other proceeding).

[64] Fed. R. Evid. 804(b)(1).

[65] *See infra* § 36.05 (confrontation & hearsay).

[66] *See also* Fed. R. Crim. P. 7(a) ("An offense which may be punished by death shall be prosecuted by indictment. An offense which may be punished by imprisonment for a term exceeding one year or at hard labor shall be prosecuted by indictment or, if indictment is waived, it may be prosecuted by information. Any other offense may be prosecuted by indictment or by information. An information may be filed without leave of court.").

[67] *See* Hurtado v. California, 110 U.S. 516 (1884); Beck v. Washington, 369 U.S. 541 (1962) (no constitutional requirement for grand jury indictment in state prosecutions).

[68] Fed. R. Evid. 1001(d)(2) (other than privileges, Federal Rules do not apply in "[p]roceedings before grand juries"). In Costello v. United States, 350 U.S. 359 (1956), the defendant was indicted for income tax evasion. Although 368 exhibits were introduced and 144 witnesses testified at trial, only three investigating officers testified before the grand jury. Costello challenged the indictment due to the extensive use of hearsay in the grand jury proceeding. The Supreme Court rejected this attack, noting that to apply the hearsay rule "would run counter to the whole history of the grand jury institution, in which laymen conduct their inquiries unfettered by technical rules." The Court went on to state: "An indictment returned by a legally constituted and unbiased grand jury . . ., if valid on its face, is enough to call for trial of the charges on the merits." *Id.* at 364. A later case states that a grand jury "is unrestrained by the technical, procedural and evidentiary rules governing the conduct of criminal trials." United States v. Calandra, 414 U.S. 338, 343 (1974).

[69] Historically, the grand jury evolved as a protective device to shield innocent persons from malicious prosecution by the English Crown. Whether the grand jury serves this function today is debatable. The nonadversarial nature of grand jury proceedings and the prosecutor's considerable influence undermine this function.

[70] In *Calandra*, the Supreme Court gave a concise definition of the role of a grand jury: "[It] is [to conduct] an ex parte investigation to determine whether a crime has been committed and whether criminal proceedings should be instituted against any person." 414 U.S. at 343.

grand juries have the power to (1) compel the attendance of witnesses through the issuance of subpoenas ad testificandum, (2) require the production of evidence through subpoenas duces tecum, and (3) obtain testimony through an offer of immunity.

Presence at hearing. Although the court controls many aspects of grand jury procedure,[71] the judge is not present at the hearing itself.[72] The prosecutor presents the evidence before the grand jury. The power of the prosecutor is significant not only because the prosecutor is the only party permitted to present evidence, but also because the prosecutor exercises significant control over the entire indictment process, even though the grand jury makes the ultimate decision. In contrast to a preliminary hearing, grand jury proceedings are *nonadversarial.* The prosecutor, the witnesses, and the grand jurors are present, but suspects and targets have no right to attend the proceedings, offer evidence, or testify in most jurisdictions.[73] Because of the extensive prosecution control over the process, defense counsel like to say that any decent prosecutor could get a grand jury to indict a ham sandwich.

Trial use. Grand jury testimony may be used at trial for a number of purposes. If later indicted, a suspect's testimony is admissible as a party admission when offered by the prosecution.[74] Thus, suspects typically invoke the privilege against self-incrimination if subpoenaed to testify. Moreover, a witness who testifies at trial, including the accused, may be impeached with grand jury testimony if it is inconsistent with that witness's trial testimony.[75] In addition, Rule 801(d)(1)(A) provides for the substantive use of prior inconsistent testimony under specified conditions, which includes grand jury testimony.[76] In addition, grand jury testimony is often

---

[71] The court summons the grand jury, and the court discharges the grand jury. Once impaneled, the court instructs the grand jury on its responsibilities. Other judicial duties involve determining the validity of a claim of privilege and the imposition of contempt.

[72] Fed. R. Crim. P. 6(d) ("(1) While Grand Jury is in Session. Attorneys for the government, the witness under examination, interpreters when needed and, for the purpose of taking the evidence, a stenographer or operator of a recording device may be present while the grand jury is in session. (2) During Deliberations and Voting. No person other than the jurors, and any interpreter necessary to assist a juror who is hearing or speech impaired, may be present while the grand jury is deliberating or voting.").

[73] Witnesses subpoenaed by the grand jury are accorded certain rights. Witnesses may assert the privilege against compulsory incrimination. *See infra* § 43.03 ("criminal liability" requirement). However, witnesses do not have a right to counsel while testifying in most jurisdictions. Counsel is permitted to remain outside and may be consulted.

[74] Fed. R. Evid. 801(d)(2)(A) (individual admission).

[75] Fed. R. Evid. 613 (impeachment by prior inconsistent statement).

[76] The rule requires that the statement be taken under oath and subject to penalty for perjury. Grand jury testimony does not qualify as former testimony under Rule 804(b)(1) if offered against the accused because the defendant had no opportunity to examine the grand jury witnesses. If the evidence is offered against the prosecution, it may or may not be admissible. The prosecution has the opportunity to cross-examine but the motive to do so may not have been the same as at trial. *See infra* § 34.03[D] (similar motive requirement).

admitted under the residual hearsay exception.[77] It may also be used to refresh the recollection of the witness.[78]

[D] Discovery

Traditionally, criminal discovery has been far more limited than civil discovery. Opponents of liberal discovery argue that criminal discovery will encourage perjury, lead to the intimidation of witnesses, and, because of the Fifth Amendment, be a one-way street. There is little empirical evidence to support the first claim. Witness intimidation is a problem in some cases but not most. And it is difficult to understand how these claims would affect certain types of discovery, such as expert testimony.[79] Moreover, only in a very narrow sense is discovery a one-way street. The state has substantial resources and can gather evidence through searches and grand jury proceedings. In addition, the police investigate and take statements from witnesses. Also, the prosecution has access to crime laboratories and crime scenes. This evidence-gathering capability often produces compelling evidence before a defendant is even arrested, long before any discovery mechanism can be triggered. Finally, the self-incrimination clause as presently interpreted by the Supreme Court presents little impediment to prosecution discovery.

Criminal Rule 16 is the principal discovery rule in federal practice, although other rules cover related topics.[80] Discoverable evidence is limited to (1) defendant's statements,[81] (2) defendant's criminal record,[82] (3) documents and tangible evidence,[83] and (4) reports of examinations and tests.[84] In addition, a summary of an expert's testimony is required upon

---

[77] Fed. R. Evid. 807. *See infra* chapter 35.

[78] Fed. R. Evid. 612.

[79] For example, the first argument fails when applied to scientific evidence because "it is virtually impossible for evidence or information of this kind to be distorted or misused because of its advance disclosure." ABA Standards Relating to Discovery 67 (1968).

[80] *See* Fed. R. Crim. P. 7(e) (provides for bills of particulars).

[81] *See* Fed. R. Crim. P. 16(a)(1)(A). Any statement made by the defendant is an admission of a party-opponent and can be admitted against the accused at trial. Fed. R. Evid. 801(d)(2)(A). Of course, constitutional safeguards, such as *Miranda* warnings, may also affect admissibility.

[82] *See* Fed. R. Crim. P. 16(a)(1)(B). The record may or may not be admissible to impeach the defendant under Rule 609. *See infra* § 22.08 (impeachment by prior convictions).

[83] *See* Fed. R. Crim. P. 16(a)(1)(C) ("Upon request of the defendant the government shall permit the defendant to inspect and copy or photograph books, papers, documents, photographs, tangible objects, buildings or places, or copies or portions thereof, which are within the possession, custody or control of the government, and which are material to the preparation of the defendant's defense or are intended for use by the government as evidence in chief at the trial, or were obtained from or belong to the defendant.").

[84] *See* Fed. R. Crim. P. 16(a)(1)(D) ("Upon request of a defendant the government shall permit the defendant to inspect and copy or photograph any results or reports of physical or mental examinations, and of scientific tests or experiments, or copies thereof, which are within the possession, custody, or control of the government, the existence of which is known, or by the exercise of due diligence may become known, to the attorney for the government, and which are material to the preparation of the defense or are intended for use by the government as evidence in chief at the trial.").

demand.[85] A defense discovery request triggers the prosecution's right to reciprocal discovery.[86]

Note what is missing. There is no requirement for a witness list, although some state discovery rules provide for one. There is no requirement for witness statements. The Jencks Act and Rule 26 provide for disclosure of witness statements *at trial* after direct examination. Finally, there are no discovery depositions or interrogatories in the overwhelming majority of jurisdictions. Depositions in criminal practice are limited to the preservation of testimony and not discovery.[87] In other words, you can depose your own witnesses but not the other side's.

Constitutional issues. The Supreme Court has written that "[t]here is no general constitutional right to discovery in a criminal case."[88] Nevertheless, constitutional considerations play an important role in this area of law. The Court has recognized a limited due process right (*Brady* rule) to the disclosure of exculpatory evidence.[89]

§ 3.04 Jury Selection & Voir Dire

The examination of prospective jurors (voir dire) is conducted to determine whether challenges are warranted. There are two types of challenges: (1) for cause[90] and (2) peremptory.[91] Challenges for cause are based on

---

[85] *See* Fed. R. Crim. P. 16(a)(1)(E) ("At the defendant's request, the government shall disclose to the defendant a written summary of testimony that the government intends to use under Rules 702, 703, or 705 of the Federal Rules of Evidence during its case-in-chief at trial. If the government requests discovery under subdivision (b)(1)(C)(ii) of this rule and the defendant complies, the government shall, at the defendant's request, disclose to the defendant a written summary of testimony the government intends to use under Rules 702, 703, or 705 as evidence at trial on the issue of the defendant's mental condition. The summary provided under this subdivision shall describe the witnesses' opinions, the bases and the reasons for those opinions, and the witnesses' qualifications.").

[86] Fed. R. Crim. P. 16(b).

[87] *See* Fed. R. Crim. P. 15 (a) ("Whenever due to exceptional circumstances of the case it is in the interest of justice that the testimony of a prospective witness of a party be taken and preserved for use at trial, the court may upon motion of such party and notice to the parties order that testimony of such witness be taken by deposition and that any designated book, paper, document, record, recording, or other material not privileged, be produced at the same time and place.").

[88] Weatherford v. Bursey, 429 U.S. 545, 559 (1977).

[89] Brady v. Maryland, 373 U.S. 83 (1963).

[90] 28 U.S.C. § 1870 ("All challenges for cause or favor, whether to the array or panel or to individual jurors, shall be determined by the court."); Fed. R. Civ. P. 47(c) ("Excuse. The court may for good cause excuse a juror from service during trial or deliberation.").

[91] Fed. R. Civ. P. 47(b) ("The court shall allow the number of peremptory challenges provided by 28 U.S.C. § 1870."); 28 U.S. C. § 1870 ("In civil cases, each party shall be entitled to three peremptory challenges. Several defendants or several plaintiffs may be considered as a single party for the purposes of making challenges, or the court may allow additional peremptory challenges and permit them to be exercised separately or jointly."); Fed. R. Crim. P. 24(b) ("If the offense charged is punishable by death, each side is entitled to 20 peremptory challenges. If the offense charged is punishable by imprisonment for more than one year, the government is entitled to 6 peremptory challenges and the defendant or defendants jointly to 10 peremptory

statutory provisions that typically contain age, citizenship, and other disqualifications such as a felony conviction or some relationship with one of the parties. The impartiality of jurors, of course, is required. Thus, evidence of personal bias is a grounds for challenge. In criminal cases it is a due process requirement.[92] A peremptory challenge can be exercised for any reason, except peremptory strikes may not be based on race or gender,[93] a rule that also applies in civil cases.[94]

The voir dire may be conducted by the judge or the attorneys depending on the jurisdiction. In federal practice, the judge conducts the voir dire.[95] The opposite is usually the case in state practice, which is why voir dire can take days in state proceedings.

§ 3.05 Order of Trial Proceedings

Neither the procedural rules nor the evidence rules specify the order of proof at a federal trial. Civil Rule 43(a) provides that "the testimony of witnesses shall be taken in open court, unless a federal law, these rules, the Federal Rules of Evidence, or other rules adopted by the Supreme Court provide otherwise." It also provides that for good cause in compelling circumstances testimony may be presented by contemporaneous transmission from a different location — provided there are "appropriate safeguards." The Criminal Rules also provide for testimony in open court.[96]

---

challenges. If the offense charged is punishable by imprisonment for not more than one year or by fine or both, each side is entitled to 3 peremptory challenges. If there is more than one defendant, the court may allow the defendants additional peremptory challenges and permit them to be exercised separately or jointly.").

[92] The Supreme Court held long ago that a juror will not be disqualified, despite having formed a general impression about a case, where the juror states under oath that she can fairly and impartially render a verdict according to the law. Spies v. Illinois, 123 U.S. 131 (1887). See also Smith v. Phillips, 405 U.S. 209 (1982) (challenge to juror who applied for investigator job in prosecutor's office during trial; no violation); Dennis v. United States, 339 U.S. 162 (1950) (challenge to government employees where the defendant is charged with contempt of House Committee on Un-American Activities; no violation).

[93] See Batson v. Kentucky, 476 U.S. 79, 89 (1986) ("Although a prosecutor ordinarily is entitled to exercise peremptory challenges for any reason, . . . the Equal Protection Clause forbids the prosecutor to challenge potential jurors solely on account of their race or on the assumption that black jurors as a group will be unable impartially to consider the State's case against a black defendant."); J.E.B. v. Alabama ex rel. T.B., 511 U.S. 127 (1994) (gender).

[94] See Edmonson v. Leesville Concrete Co., Inc., 500 U.S. 614 (1991) (extending *Batson* to civil litigation).

[95] Fed. R. Civ. P. 47(a) ("The court may permit the parties or their attorneys to conduct the examination of prospective jurors or may itself conduct the examination. In the latter event, the court shall permit the parties or their attorneys to supplement the examination by such further inquiry as it deems proper or shall itself submit to the prospective jurors such additional questions of the parties or their attorneys as it deems proper."); Fed. R. Crim. P. 24(a) (same).

[96] Fed. R. Crim. P. 26 ("In all trials the testimony of witnesses shall be taken orally in open court, unless otherwise provided by an Act of Congress or by these rules, the Federal Rules of Evidence, or other rules adopted by the Supreme Court.").

Nevertheless, both the procedural and evidence rules implicitly assume the traditional order of proceedings:[97]

(1)   Opening statements
(2)   Plaintiff (prosecution) case-in-chief
(3)   Defense case-in-chief
(4)   Plaintiff (prosecution) rebuttal
(5)   Defense surrebuttal
(6)   Closing arguments
(7)   Jury instructions
(8)   Jury deliberations

[A] Opening Statement

The case formally begins with opening statements. Its purpose is to outline the case to the jury — informing the jury of the issues involved and the evidence that will be introduced. It is black letter law that an opening statement, unlike closing argument, is not suppose to be used to "argue" the evidence, which, of course, has yet to be introduced. Nevertheless, a good attorney will use the opening statement as an opportunity to influence the course of the trial. In some jurisdictions, the defense has the option to defer its opening statement until after the plaintiff (prosecution) has completed its case-in-chief and rested. Don't do it. The jury will begin to make up its mind the first day of trial, and the opening statement should be used to attempt to convince the jury not to rush to judgment.[98]

[B] Case-in-Chief

The case-in-chief is when evidence is first introduced: testimonial, documentary, or real evidence. The plaintiff (prosecution), as the party with the burden of production, goes first because if that burden is not met, the trial can end with a directed verdict for the other side. The defense case-in-chief follows. A defense attorney will attempt to introduce affirmative defenses through the other side's witnesses. If this is not possible, this evidence along with impeachment evidence will be proffered in the defense case-in-chief.

The trial court has inherent authority to alter the order of proceedings.[99] For example, the trial judge is authorized to change the order in which

---

[97] For example, the discovery rules on documents-tangible items and expert reports use the following phrase: "evidence in chief at the trial." Fed. R. Crim. P. 16(a)(1)(C) & (D).

[98] See McElhaney's Trial Notebook 88 (2d ed. 1987) ("The uncomfortable fact is that juries often make up their minds on hearing opening statements. And thoughtful trial lawyers have known for a long time that when juries makeup their minds, it is difficult to change them. It means that the opening statement is so important that it should almost never be waived, and that it is nearly unforgivable (in the absence of a contrary rule) merely to read the pleading to the jury instead of making an opening statement.").

[99] See Huddleston v. United States, 485 U.S. 681, 690 (1988) ("The trial court has tradition-ally exercised the broadest sort of discretion in controlling the order of proof at trial, and we see nothing in the Rules of Evidence that would change this practice."); Fed. R. Evid. 611(a)

witnesses testify, subject only to abuse-of-discretion review.[100] This discretion may be abused if the judge refuses to grant a party the opportunity to present crucial witnesses out of the customary order.[101] There are also constitutional constraints on this authority. In *Brooks v. Tennessee*,[102] the Supreme Court held that requiring a criminal defendant to testify prior to other defense witnesses violated the Compulsory Self-incrimination and Due Process Clauses.

Recalling witnesses. The court's authority to alter the order of proof also includes the authority to permit a witness to be recalled.[103]

[C] Rebuttal & Surrebuttal

Rebuttal is usually confined to refutation of evidence introduced in the defense case-in-chief, and surrebuttal is similarly confined to refutation of evidence admitted during rebuttal.[104] The court's authority to alter the order of proof, however, also includes controlling the extent of rebuttal evidence. There are, of course, limits to this discretion. For example, a party has a right to present rebuttal testimony on matters raised for the first time on redirect.

("The court shall exercise reasonable control over the mode and order of interrogating witnesses and presenting evidence. . . .").

[100] *See* Loinaz v. EG & G, Inc., 910 F.2d 1, 9 (1st Cir. 1990) ("[T]he general rule is that a party should be able to present his case and order that case as he sees fit. However, Rule 611 has carved out an exception to this general rule and requires the trial judge to control the presentation of evidence in the interest of ascertaining truth. The dynamics of a party's presentation may be compromised when the testimony of an opposing witness is allowed to interrupt that presentation, but Rule 611 recognizes that such an alteration in order may be necessary at times."); 6 Wigmore, Evidence § 1867 (Chadbourn rev. 1976) ("It is obvious that, while a usual order for introducing topics of evidence and witnesses is a desirable thing, a variation from that order, which if often equally desirable, will not necessarily cause direct harm; it can do so only where it tends to confuse the jury, or where it misleads the opponent or finds him unprepared to meet it.").

[101] *E.g., id.* at 9 (trial court refused to permit defense to present witness during plaintiff's case due to surgery of witness's wife; defendant forced to use deposition: "The denial of the Rule 611 motion by the trial judge in this case resulted in severe prejudice to the defendant in that neither Buckner nor Francisco, the two principal witnesses who could rebut the testimony of the plaintiff Diego Loinaz, was able to testify at the trial. Because of the decision, the defendant could not present to the jury a person who would rebut the plaintiffs' version of the facts, a person whom the jury could evaluate in the same manner they had Diego and Mary Loinaz.").

[102] 406 U.S. 605, 613 (1972) (Defendant "was deprived of his constitutional rights when the trial court excluded him from the stand for failing to testify first" as required by statute.).

[103] *See* United States v. Puckett, 147 F.3d 765, 770 (8th Cir. 1998) ("The witnesses testified about different subject matter each time they were called to the stand, the defendants were free to cross examine them about any of their testimony, and there is no indication that the government recalled the witnesses to bolster their credibility. While it may be preferable to have witnesses testify in a less interrupted manner, we cannot say the district court abused its discretion.").

[104] *See* United States v. Gaines, 170 F.3d 72, 83 (1st Cir. 1999) ("The trial court has great discretion over the permissible scope of testimony in surrebuttal. . . . Ordinarily, surrebuttal should be allowed 'only to explain away new facts brought forward by the proponent in rebuttal, or evidence to impeach witnesses who testified in rebuttal[.]'") (citation omitted).

Reopening the case. The court's authority to alter the order of proof extends to reopening a case for further testimony. The relevant factors for determining whether to reopen include: "(1) timeliness of the motion, (2) whether a proffer is made, (3) the character of the proffered testimony, (4) the effect of granting the motion, (5) existence of an explanation for failing to present the evidence during the movant's case-in-chief, (6) whether the explanation is reasonable, and (7) whether the proffer is relevant, admissible, technically adequate, and helpful to the jury in ascertaining the guilt or innocence of the accused."[105] If the case is reopened, the opposing side must be given an opportunity to offer rebuttal evidence.

[D]   Closing Argument

Closing arguments are obviously a critical part of the trial. Indeed, in *Herring v. New York*,[106] the Supreme Court held that a denial of the opportunity for final summation in a nonjury trial deprived the accused of the basic right to make his defense as guaranteed by the Sixth Amendment right to counsel.

Closing arguments typically involve three stages, with the plaintiff (prosecutor) going first and last.[107] The reason for this arrangement is that these parties have the burden of persuasion. The arguments of counsel are not evidence, and the jury is so instructed.[108] Moreover, the trial court has discretion in controlling the propriety and duration of final arguments.[109]

There is a "law of closing arguments."[110] First, the argument must be based on the evidence adduced at trial.[111] Here, however, the attorneys

---

[105] United States v. Rodriguez, 43 F.3d 117, 125 (5th Cir. 1995).

[106] 422 U.S. 853, 858 (1975) ("There can be no doubt that closing argument for the defense is a basic element of the adversary fact-finding process in a criminal trial. Accordingly, it has universally been held that counsel for the defense has a right to make closing summation to the jury, no matter how strong the case of the prosecution may appear to the presiding judge.").

[107] Fed. R. Crim. P. 29.1 ("After the closing of evidence the prosecution shall open the argument. The defense shall be permitted to reply. The prosecution shall then be permitted to reply in rebuttal.").

[108] *See* Darden v. Wainwright, 477 U.S. 168, 182 (1986) ("The trial court instructed the jurors several times that their decision was to be made on the basis of the evidence alone, and that the arguments of counsel were not evidence.").

[109] *See Herring*, 422 U.S. at 862 ("This is not say that closing arguments in a criminal case must be uncontrolled or even unrestrained. The presiding judge must be and is given great latitude in controlling duration and limiting the scope of closing summations. He may limit counsel to a reasonable time and may terminate argument when continuation would be repetitious or redundant. He may ensure that argument does not stray unduly from the mark, or otherwise impede the fair and orderly conduct of the trial. In all these respects he must have broad discretion.").

[110] *See* McElhaney's Trial Notebook 479 (2d ed. 1987) (During closing argument, the attorneys may not: (1) misstate the law or evidence, (2) argue facts not in evidence, (3) state a personal belief in the justness of their cause, (4) personally vouch for the credibility of witnesses, (5) appeal to passion or prejudice, or (6) urge an irrelevant use of evidence).

[111] *See Darden*, 477 U.S. at 182 ("The prosecutors' argument did not manipulate or misstate the evidence, nor did it implicate other specific rights of the accused such as the right to counsel or the right to remain silent.").

are given great latitude in drawing inferences from that evidence in order to present their most convincing positions.

Second, attorneys are prohibited from stating their personal opinions in closing argument.[112] "Improper suggestions, insinuation and, especially, assertions of personal knowledge are apt to carry much weight against the accused when they should properly carry none."[113] Implying that the prosecutor had person knowledge of litigated facts is also improper.[114]

A prosecutor's improper comments during closing argument may violate due process.[115] In *Berger v. United States*,[116] the Supreme Court condemned a prosecutor's summation, commenting:

> The United States attorney is the representative not of an ordinary party to a controversy, but of a sovereignty whose obligation to govern impartially is as compelling as its obligation to govern at all; and whose interest, therefore, in a criminal prosecution is not that it shall win a case, but that justice shall be done. As such, he is in a peculiar and very definite sense a servant of the law, the two fold aim of which is that guilt shall not escape or innocent suffer. He may prosecute with earnestness and vigor — indeed, he should do so. But while he may strike hard blows, he is not at liberty to strike foul ones. It is as much his duty to refrain from improper methods calculated to provide a wrongful conviction as it is to use every legitimate means to bring about a just one.[117]

The Court went on to find that the "prosecuting attorney's argument to the jury was undignified and intemperate, containing improper insinuations and assertions calculated to mislead the jury."[118]

---

[112] *See* Model Rule 3.4 ("A lawyer shall not: . . . (e) in trial, allude to any matter that the lawyer does not reasonably believe is relevant or that will not be supported by admissible evidence, assert personal knowledge of facts in issue except when testifying as a witness, or state a person opinion as to the justness of a cause, the credibility of a witness, the culpability of a civil litigant or the guilt or innocence of an accused.").

[113] Berger v. United States, 295 U.S. 78, 88 (1935).

[114] *Id.* at 89.

[115] *See* Donnelly v. DeChristoforo, 416 U.S. 637, 643 (1974) (due process violated if prosecutor's argument "so infected the trial with unfairness as to make the resulting conviction a denial of due process"). *See generally* Alschuler, *Courtroom Misconduct by Prosecutors and Trial Judges*, 50 Tex. L. Rev. 629 (1972); Balske, *Prosecutorial Misconduct During Closing Argument*, 37 Mercer L. Rev. 1033 (1986); Carlson, *Argument to the Jury: Passion, Persuasion, and Legal Controls*, 33 St. Louis U. L.J. 787 (1989).

[116] 295 U.S. 78 (1935).

[117] *Id.* at 88. The prosecutor also acted improperly during the trial. "He was guilty of misstating the facts in his cross-examination of witnesses; of putting into the mouths of such witnesses things which they had not said; of suggesting by his questions that statements had been made to him personally out of court, in respect of which no proof was offered; of pretending to understand that a witness had said something which he had not said and persistently cross-examining the witness upon this basis; of assuming prejudicial facts not in evidence; of bullying and arguing with witnesses; and in general, conducting himself in a thoroughly indecorous and improper manner." *Id.* at 84.

[118] *Id.* at 85.

Appeal to emotions. A prosecutor's argument intended to inflame the passions or prejudices of the jury, is improper and may violate due process. Describing the defendant as a "maggot" is "unprofessional and is deserving of a stern admonition."[119] The terms "thugs" and "goons" are also improper.[120] Labeling the defendant an "animal", however, is not per se improper,[121] and referring to the accused "as a sociopath or psychopath was a fair inference based on the evidence."[122] As one court observed: "Realism compels us to recognize that criminal trials cannot be squeezed dry of all feeling."[123]

In determining the impropriety of final argument, courts look at the entire argument.[124] The Supreme Court has noted, "If every remark made by counsel outside of the testimony were grounds for a reversal, comparatively few verdicts would stand, since in the ardor of advocacy, and in the excitement of trial, even the most experienced counsel are occasionally carried away by this temptation."[125] Moreover, isolated comments are not to be taken out of context and given their most damaging meaning.[126] Other relevant factors include whether (1) the trial court gave a curative instruction,[127] (2) the argument was an invited response to something said by the defense,[128] and (3) there is evidence of overwhelming guilt.[129]

---

[119] State v. Chandler, 483 N.E.2d 192, 195 (Ohio App.1984).

[120] State v. Liberatore, 433 N.E.2d 561, 566–67 (Ohio 1982).

[121] State v. Keenan, 613 N.E.2d 203, 208 (Ohio 1993) ("Such invective is not unfair per se. . . .") (citing Darden v. Wainwright, 477 U.S. 168, 180–81 (1986)).

[122] State v. Richey, 595 N.E.2d 915, 924 (Ohio 1992).

[123] State v. Keenan, 613 N.E.2d 203, 209 (Ohio 1993).

[124] *See* Darden v. Wainwright, 477 U.S. 168, 181–82 (1986); Donnelly v. DeChristoforeo, 416 U.S. 637, 643–45 (1974).

[125] Dunlop v. United States, 165 U.S. 486, 498 (1897).

[126] *See* Donnelly v. DeChristoforeo, 416 U.S. 637, 645 (1974) ("one moment in an extended trial"); Berger v. United States, 295 U.S. 78, 89 (1935) ("[W]e have not here a case where the misconduct of the prosecuting attorney was slight or confined to a single instance, but one where such misconduct was pronounced and persistent, with a probable cumulative effect upon the jury which cannot be disregarded as inconsequential.").

[127] *See Donnelly*, 416 U.S. at 644 ("[T]he trial court took special pains to correct any impression that the jury could consider the prosecutor's statements as evidence in the case. . . . [T]he judge directed the jury's attention to the remark particularly challenged here, declared it to be unsupported, and admonished the jury to ignore it.").

[128] *Darden*, 477 U.S. at 182 ("Much of the objectionable content was invited by or was responsive to the opening summation of the defense."); United States v. Young, 470 U.S. 1, 12 (1985) ("In retrospect, perhaps the idea of 'invited response' has evolved in a way not contemplated. . . . [T]he earlier cases . . . should not be read as suggesting judicial approval or — encouragement — of response-in-kind that inevitably exacerbate the tensions inherent in the adversary process. . . . [T]he issue is not the prosecutor's license to make otherwise improper arguments, but whether the prosecutor's 'invited response,' taken in context, unfairly prejudiced the defendant.").

[129] *Darden*, 477 U.S. at 182.

[E] Jury Instructions

Before the case is submitted to the jury, the trial judge must instruct the jury on the law.[130] The instructions must cover the substantive law that the jury is required to apply — *i.e.,* the elements of a cause of action or crime and the elements of any affirmative defense. In criminal cases, instructions on lesser-included-offenses are common. The judge must also instruction on the burden of persuasion.

As far as evidentiary issues are concerned, the instruction will invariably contain statements concerning the credibility of witnesses — *i.e,* the jury is the sole judge of credibility. Cautionary instructions, limiting the purpose for which evidence may be used under Rule 105 are frequently given. If there are multiple parties, Rule 105 may also require an instruction that evidence may be used against one party but not another.

A hearing or conference to decide on the wording of instructions is typically held before the instructions or closing argument is given. Judges often use pattern instruction that are available in every jurisdiction.

§ 3.06   Jury Deliberation, Verdicts & Postrial Motions

[A] Exhibits in Jury Room

The practice of permitting tangible exhibits and documents into the jury room during deliberations is firmly established, although the trial judge has discretion in this context. However, the Rules of Evidence specify that learned treatises[131] and statements admitted as recorded recollection[132] may be read to the jury but not taken into the jury room. Illustrative evidence (*e.g.,* models) is often not sent to the jury room.[133] Jury experimentation with the exhibits may be a problem if the jury does *more* than inspect and examine the exhibits as they were used at trial.

---

[130] *See* Fed. R. Crim. P. 30 ("At the close of the evidence or at such earlier time during the trial as the court reasonably directs, any party may file written requests that the court instruct the jury on the law as set forth in the requests. At the same time copies of such requests shall be furnished to all parties. The court shall inform counsel of its proposed action upon the requests prior to their arguments to the jury. The court may instruct the jury before or after the arguments are completed or at both times. No party may assign as error any portion of the charge or omission therefrom unless that party objects thereto before the jury retires to consider its verdict, stating distinctly the matter to which that party objects and the grounds of the objection. Opportunity shall be given to make the objection out of the hearing of the jury and, on request of any party, out of the presence of the jury."); Fed. R. Civ. P. 51.

[131] Fed. R. Evid. 803(18). *See* Graham v. Wyeth Labs., 906 F.2d 1399, 1414 (10th Cir. 1990) (permitting treatise in jury room raises danger that jurors will be unduly impressed by treatise). *See also infra* § 33.16 (learned treatises).

[132] Fed. R. Evid. 803(5). This provision is intended to avoid the risk that the record will be given undue weight. *See also infra* § 33.09 (recorded recollection).

[133] *See* United States v. Wood, 943 F.2d 1048, 1053 (9th Cir. 1991) ("[P]edagogical devices should be used only as a testimonial aid, and should not be admitted into evidence or otherwise be used by the jury during deliberations.").

[B]　Post-Verdict Hearings & Motions

When the jury returns its verdict and it is read in open court, losing counsel may ask for the jury to be individually polled.[134] A motion for a directed verdict may also be made at this time,[135] as well as a motion for a new trial.[136] If there is a conviction in a criminal case, a sentencing hearing will be scheduled for sometime after a presentence investigation and report is completed.[137] The next step is meeting the deadline for perfecting an appeal.[138]

§ 3.07　Key Points

Trial order. Evidence is first presented in the plaintiff (prosecution) case-in-chief, which is followed by the defense case-in-chief, plaintiff rebuttal, and defense surrebutal. The judge has the discretionary authority to alter this scheme — *e.g.,* permit (1) a witness to testify out of order, (2) a witness to be recalled, or (3) a party to reopen its case.

Rebuttal & surrebuttal. Rebuttal is usually confined to refutation of evidence introduced in the defense case-in-chief, and surrebuttal is similarly confined to refutation of evidence admitted during rebuttal.

Closing arguments. Final arguments typically involve three stages, with the plaintiff (prosecutor) going first and last. The reason for this arrangement is that these parties have the burden of persuasion. The arguments of counsel are not evidence, and the jury is so instructed. During closing argument, the attorneys may not: (1) misstate the law or evidence, (2) argue facts not in evidence, (3) state a personal belief in the justness of their cause, (4) personally vouch for the credibility of witnesses, (5) appeal to passion or prejudice, or (6) urge an irrelevant use of evidence.

---

[134] *See* Fed. R. Crim. P. 31(d) ("After a verdict is returned but before the jury is discharged, the court shall, on a party's request, or may on its own motion, poll the jurors individually. If the poll reveals a lack of unanimity, the court may direct the jury to deliberate further or may declare a mistrial and discharge the jury.").

[135] *See* Fed. R. Crim. P. 29(c) ("If the jury returns a verdict of guilty or is discharged without having returned a verdict, a motion for judgment of acquittal may be made or renewed within 7 days after the jury is discharged or within such further time as the court may fix during the 7-day period. If a verdict of guilty is returned the court may on such motion set aside the verdict and enter judgment of acquittal. If no verdict is returned the court may enter judgment of acquittal. It shall not be necessary to the making of such a motion that a similar motion has been made prior to the submission of the case to the jury.").

[136] *See* Fed. R. Crim. P. 33 ("On a defendant's motion, the court may grant a new trial to that defendant if the interests of justice so require. If trial was by the court without a jury, the court may — on defendant's motion for new trial — vacate the judgment, take additional testimony, and direct the entry of a new judgment. A motion for new trial based on newly discovered evidence may be made only within three years after the verdict or finding of guilty. But if an appeal is pending, the court may grant the motion only on remand of the case. A motion for a new trial based on any other grounds may be made only within 7 days after the verdict or finding of guilty or within such further time as the court may fix during the 7-day period.").

[137] Fed. R. Crim. P. 32.

[138] Fed. R. App. P. 4.

Chapter 4

BURDENS OF PROOF

§ 4.01 Introduction

Burdens of proof are used all the time in every day affairs. In the instant replay in professional football, the referee's decision on the field stands unless there is convincing evidence of an incorrect call when the videotape is reviewed. Thus, the burden of persuasion is allocated to the party challenging the on-field decision. But why? Why allocate the burden to one party and not the other? Why choose "clear evidence" (what lawyers would probably call the "clear and convincing evidence" standard), rather than a mere preponderance of evidence? There are policy reasons underlying these decisions. Similarly, in the political arena, the nomination of a Supreme Court Justice will raise a comparable issue. Is there an assumption in favor of the President's choice? This would place the burden of proof on those who oppose a nomination. Or, is the burden on the President to make the case to the Senate that a nominee is qualified? And by what standard? What are the policy arguments for either position?

Allocating the burden of proof is often determinative. Take the question of capital punishment. Is it a deterrent to murder? Given the uncertain empirical research, the party with the burden of proof will lose. As this example illustrates, burdens of proof can be powerful instruments in situations of uncertainty. And, by their very nature, trials frequently deal with the uncertainties of proof.

The term "burden of proof" is often confusing because there are two distinct burdens of proof: (1) the "burden of persuasion" and (2) the "burden of production." The *burden of persuasion* refers to the convincing force of the evidence. In contrast, the *burden of production*, sometimes called the "burden of going forward with evidence," refers to a party's responsibility to introduce evidence at trial. In every case, these two burdens are allocated, at least initially,[1] to one of the parties on *every* issue in the case. However, the two burdens do not have to be allocated to the same party, even on the same issue.

§ 4.02 Allocation of Burdens

Burdens of proof are allocated based on the three "P"s — policy, possession of evidence, and probabilities.[2] Convenience is often added as a fourth

---

[1] In civil cases, a presumption will shift the burden of production to the other party. *See infra* § 5.02 (presumptions defined).

[2] *See* Cleary, *Presuming and Pleading: An Essay on Juristic Immaturity*, 12 Stand. L. Rev. 5 (1959).

factor. "Possession of the evidence" refers to one party's greater access to information. This is illustrated by affirmative defenses such as self-defense and insanity. In both situations, the accused is in a better position to come forward with the evidence because of superior access to proof — *i.e.*, possession of the evidence. "Probabilities," as used here, means a rough estimate of how things work in the world — *i.e.*, most people are sane, not insane.

In addition, policy reasons often underlie the allocation of burdens of proof. For example, in federal cases the prosecution has the burden of persuasion ("beyond a reasonable doubt") in self-defense cases, even though the burden of production is on the defense. In contrast, in insanity cases, a federal defendant must establish insanity by "clear and convincing evidence."[3] Thus, in federal practice the prosecution is allocated the burden of persuasion for the affirmative defense of self-defense but not the affirmative defense of insanity. In addition, the standards are different: "beyond a reasonable doubt" in self-defense cases and "clear and convincing evidence" in insanity cases. There is a policy decision underlying these rules — one obviously disfavoring the insanity defense.

§ 4.03 Burden of Persuasion

The burden of persuasion refers to the convincing force of the evidence. Technically, it is the "risk of nonpersuasion" that we are talking about. Three common standards of proof are used to define the legally required persuasive force of the evidence: (1) "proof beyond a reasonable doubt" (the highest standard); (2) "clear and convincing evidence" (an intermediate standard); and (3) "preponderance of evidence" (more probable than not).

These standards are used for the ultimate issues in a case, which are decided by the trier of fact (most often the jury).[4] However, they are also used for issues other than the ultimate issues. For example, in evidence law, someone has to have the burden of persuasion on admissibility issues: Once there is an objection to evidence at trial, the offering party has the burden of persuading the trial judge that the item of evidence is admissible by a preponderance of evidence — *e.g.*, that a hearsay statement fits within a recognized exception to the hearsay rule.[5]

[A] "Preponderance of Evidence" Standard

The term "preponderance of evidence" means "more likely than not" or a probability of 51 percent.[6] The term "preponderance" is misleading

---

[3] 18 U.S.C. § 17(a).

[4] The ultimate issues are the elements of a crime, cause of action, or affirmative defense as defined by the substantive law. For example, proof beyond a reasonable doubt of all essential elements of the offense in criminal cases, and preponderance of evidence for all elements of a cause of action in most civil cases.

[5] *See infra* § 7.02[B] (burden of proof on preliminary questions of admissibility.).

[6] *See* Bourjaily v. United States, 483 U.S. 171, 175 (1987) (preponderance standard means "more likely than not").

because it implies a reference to the quantity of evidence. The burden of persuasion, however, does not concern the amount of evidence, only its convincing force. For example, a party could satisfy this standard with the testimony of one convincing witness, even though the opposing party introduced the testimony of five less convincing witnesses.

[B] "Clear & Convincing Evidence" Standard

The "clear and convincing evidence" standard is an intermediate standard, requiring more convincing force than the "preponderance of evidence" standard but less than the "beyond a reasonable doubt" standard. The term "highly probable" is as good as we can probably do in describing this standard.[7] This standard is sometimes used in civil fraud cases[8] and is constitutionally required in some contexts. For example, in *Santosky v. Kramer*,[9] the Supreme Court held that the preponderance-of-evidence standard did not satisfy due process in Juvenile Court neglect proceedings involving the permanent termination of parental rights: "In parental rights termination proceedings, the private interest affected is commanding; the risk of error from using a preponderance standard is substantial; and the countervailing governmental interest favoring that standard is comparatively slight."[10] Similarly, in *Addington v. Texas*,[11] the Supreme Court ruled that a person committed to a mental institution in a civil proceeding must be shown to be dangerous by clear and convincing evidence. The bottom line is that this standard is used when the stakes are greater than in the typical civil case.

---

[7] *See* Riley Hill General Contractor, Inc. v. Tandy Corp., 737 P.2d 595 (Or. 1987). The Supreme Court has commented:

> The intermediate standard, which usually employs some combination of the words "clear," "cogent," "unequivocal," and "convincing," is less commonly used, but nonetheless "is no stranger to the civil law." . . . Candor suggests that, to a degree, efforts to analyze what lay jurors understand concerning the differences among these three tests or the nuances of a judge's instructions on the law may well be largely an academic exercise; there are no directly relevant empirical studies. Indeed, the ultimate truth as to how the standards of proof affect decisionmaking may well be unknowable, given that factfinding is a process shared by countless thousands of individuals throughout the country. We probably can assume no more than that the difference between a preponderance of the evidence and proof beyond a reasonable doubt probably is better understood than either of them in relation to the intermediate standard of clear and convincing evidence. Nonetheless, even if the particular standard-of-proof catchwords do not always make a great difference in a particular case, adopting a "standard of proof is more than an empty semantic exercise."

Addington v. Texas, 441 U.S. 418, 424–25 (1979).

[8] *See also* 8 U.S.C. § 17(a) (clear and convincing proof required for insanity defense acquittal in federal trials).

[9] 455 U.S. 745 (1982).

[10] *Id.* at 758.

[11] 441 U.S. 418, 433 (1979). *See also* Woodby v. INS, 385 U.S. 276, 285 (1966) (clear and convincing standard applied in deportation hearings); Chaunt v. United States, 364 U.S. 350, 353 (1960) (denaturalization hearings).

[C] "Beyond a Reasonable Doubt" Standard

The "beyond a reasonable doubt" standard is the most difficult standard to satisfy and is used almost exclusively in criminal cases. In *In re Winship*,[12] the Supreme Court held that the Due Process Clause protects "against conviction except upon proof beyond a reasonable doubt of every fact necessary to constitute the crime . . . charged."[13] This standard, according to the Court, protects against erroneous convictions and assures community respect and confidence in the criminal process.[14] In a concurring opinion, Justice Harlan noted that two types of error arc possible at trial: (1) the conviction of an innocent person and (2) the release of a guilty person through a "not guilty" verdict. The same types of error are also possible in civil litigation: (1) the plaintiff prevails when the defendant should have, and (2) visa versa. Nevertheless, the frequency of one type of error, as opposed to the other, raises different issues in civil and criminal cases:

> In a civil suit between two private parties for money damages, for example, we view it as no more serious in general for there to be an erroneous verdict in the defendant's favor than for there to be an erroneous verdict in the plaintiff's favor. A preponderance of the evidence standard therefore seems peculiarly appropriate. . . .
>
> . . . In a criminal case, on the other hand, we do not view the social disutility of convicting an innocent man as equivalent to the disutility of acquitting someone who is guilty. . . . In this context, I view the requirement of proof beyond a reasonable doubt in a criminal case as bottomed on a fundamental value determination of our society that it is far worse to convict an innocent man than to let a guilty man go free.[15]

The Supreme Court has decided several cases involving jury instructions that defined the phrase "beyond a reasonable doubt." Although due process requires the prosecution to prove the essential elements of the charged offense beyond a reasonable doubt, it does not require that any particular words be used to convey this standard — so long as "taken as a whole, the instructions correctly conve[y] the concept of reasonable doubt."[16] The Court, however, has acknowledged that "[a]ttempts to explain the term

---

[12] 397 U.S. 358 (1970).

[13] *Id.* at 364. In addition, the Court ruled that this standard applied in Juvenile Court delinquency proceedings as well as in criminal trials.

[14] The standard embraces a fundamental tenet of American criminal law. *See* Taylor v. Kentucky, 436 U.S. 478 (1978).

[15] 397 U.S. at 371–72. *See also* Speiser v. Randall, 357 U.S. 513, 525–26 (1958) ("There is always in litigation a margin of error, representing error in factfinding, which both parties must take into account. Where one party has at stake an interest of transcending value — as a criminal defendant his liberty — this margin of error is reduced as to him by the process of placing on the other party the burden . . . of persuading the factfinder at the conclusion of the trial of his guilt beyond a reasonable doubt.").

[16] Holland v. United States, 348 U.S. 121, 140 (1954).

'reasonable doubt' do not usually result in making it any clearer to the minds of the jury."[17] In *Cage v. Louisiana*,[18] the Court ruled a jury instruction unconstitutional that included the following passages describing the reasonable doubt standard:

(1) "It must be such doubt as would give rise to a grave uncertainty."

(2) "It is an actual substantial doubt."

(3) "What is required is not an absolute or mathematical certainty, but a moral certainty."

According to the Court, these passages watered-down the constitutional standard. The Court wrote:

It is plain to us that the words "substantial" and "grave," as they are commonly understood, suggest a higher degree of doubt than that is required for acquittal under the reasonable doubt standard. When those statements are then considered with the references to "moral certainty," rather than evidentiary certainty, it becomes clear that a reasonable juror could have interpreted the instruction to allow a finding of guilt based on a degree of proof below that required by the Due Process Clause.[19]

---

[17] Miles v. United States, 103 U.S. 304, 312 (1881). *See also* Hopt v. Utah, 120 U.S. 430, 440–41 (1887) ("The rule may be, and often is, rendered obscure by attempts at definition, which serve to create doubts instead of removing them.").

[18] 498 U.S. 39 (1990).

[19] *Id.* at 41. In Victor v. Nebraska, 511 U.S. 1 (1994), the Court reviewed two cases involving jury instructions on the "beyond a reasonable doubt" standard. One case involved a California instruction. The defendant challenged several passages: "It is not a mere possible doubt; because everything relating to human affairs, and depending on moral evidence, is open to some possible or imaginary doubt." Another passage used the phrase "moral certainty." The defendant challenged the terms "moral certainty" and "moral evidence." These terms had specific meanings, which were often equated with proof beyond a reasonable doubt, when they were adopted in the 19th Century. The question was whether a 20th Century jury would understand 19th Century terms.

The Court found the term "moral evidence" unproblematic because it was explained in the instruction. The jury was told to decide the case on the trial evidence and not from any other source. They were also informed that evidence consisted of the testimony of witnesses, writings, material objects, and anything offered to prove a fact. The term "moral certainty" was more troublesome. The Court was willing to concede that the term, standing alone, "might not be recognized by modern jurors as a synonym for proof beyond a reasonable doubt." *Id.* at 14. Nevertheless, the instruction as a whole sufficiently informed the jury of the constitutional requirement.

The companion case, from Nebraska, contained the following contested passages: "You may find an accused guilty upon the strong probabilities of the case, provided such probabilities are strong enough to exclude any doubt of his guilt that is reasonable. A reasonable doubt is an actual and substantial doubt arising from the evidence . . . as distinguished from a doubt arising from mere possibility, from bare imagination, or from fanciful conjecture."

The defendant argued that the phrase "beyond a substantial doubt" created a lower standard than "beyond a reasonable doubt." Here, again, the Court found the phrase "somewhat problematic" but nevertheless upheld the conviction. Other parts of the instruction provided an alternative definition: a reasonable doubt is one that would cause a reasonable person to hesitate to act. This formulation had been approved repeatedly by the Court. Holland v. United States, 348 U.S. 121, 140 (1954).

[D] Affirmative Defenses

The burden of persuasion on all affirmative defenses must be determined in order to instruct the jury.[20] Constitutional questions concerning the allocation of the burden of persuasion on affirmative defenses have arisen in criminal litigation. For example, in *Mullaney v. Wilbur*,[21] the Supreme Court ruled that allocating the burden of proving "heat of passion" to a homicide defendant violated *Winship*. The Court viewed the "heat of passion" issue as an element of the crime as defined in Maine.[22] Two years later, however, in *Patterson v. New York*,[23] the Court ruled that a New York law that allocated the burden of proving an "extreme emotional disturbance" to a homicide defendant did not violate due process. These two cases are difficult to reconcile. The "extreme emotional disturbance" requirement is a modern formulation of the "heat of passion" rule; it reduces murder to manslaughter. The Court distinguished *Wilbur* on the grounds that Maine, but not New York, had defined "malice aforethought" as an element of murder. As such, *Winship* prohibited shifting the burden of persuasion on this element to the accused. Nevertheless, a state can define crimes in ways to avoid the *Mullaney* result and thus the distinction between *Winship* and *Patterson*, as a practical matter, is rather insignificant.

Ten years later the issue once again came before the Court in *Martin v. Ohio*,[24] which involved the constitutionality of allocating the burden of persuasion on self-defense to the defendant. An Ohio statute specified that the burden of persuasion rested on the defendant.[25] Martin argued that placing on her the burden of proving self-defense violated due process. The Court rejected this argument. According to the Court, *Patterson* controlled. The jury had been instructed that the prosecution had to establish the essential elements of aggravated murder beyond a reasonable doubt. An affirmative defense, whether self-defense or insanity, was not an essential element of the charged crime and, thus, the burden of persuasion could be allocated to the defendant. It did not matter that only a few states followed this rule.

The Court has also upheld the allocation of the burden of persuasion of other affirmative defenses to the accused — for example, the insanity

---

[20] As explained in the next section, the burden of production for any affirmative defense — by definition — is on the defense. Non-affirmative defenses negate one or more of the elements of the crime, which the prosecution must proved beyond a reasonable doubt. Thus, the burden of production and persuasion can never be allocated to the accused for this type of defense. The following defenses fit into this category: alibi, accident, and mistake of fact.

[21] 421 U.S. 684 (1975).

[22] Under Maine law, if the prosecution proved the homicide was both intentional and unlawful, "malice aforethought" was conclusively implied — unless the accused proved by a preponderance of the evidence that he acted in the heat of passion on sudden provocation, which could reduce the crime to manslaughter.

[23] 432 U.S. 197 (1977).

[24] 480 U.S. 228 (1987).

[25] Ohio Rev. Code § 2901.05(A) ("The burden of going forward with the evidence of an affirmative defense, and the burden of proof, by a preponderance of the evidence, for an affirmative defense, is upon the accused.").

defense.[26] Moreover, the Court has ruled that due process does not prohibit a state from allocating the burden of persuasion on the issue of mental competency to stand trial to the accused.[27] These cases involve the burden of persuasion. The Court has long upheld placing the burden of production for affirmative defenses on the accused, as discussed in the next section.

§ 4.04   Burden of Production

The burden of production, sometimes called the "burden of going forward with evidence," refers to a party's responsibility to introduce evidence at trial. Technically, it is the risk of nonproduction that is at issue. The judge (never the jury) determines whether this burden has been satisfied. There are two possible adverse consequences if a party fails to satisfy its burden of production: (1) the party may suffer a directed verdict on that issue, or (2) in the case of an affirmative defense, the jury will not be instructed on the defense. Both consequences take the issue away from the jury.

[A]   Directed Verdicts in Civil Cases

In civil cases, the burden of production typically is on the plaintiff with respect to the elements of the cause of action.[28] Either party can suffer a directed verdict (judgment of law).[29] In deciding a motion for judgment as a matter of law, the trial court reviews all the evidence in the record.

> In doing so, however, the court must draw all reasonable inferences in favor of the nonmoving party, and it may not make credibility determinations or weigh the evidence. "Credibility determinations,

---

[26] In Patterson v. New York, 432 U.S. 197, 206 (1977), the Court wrote: "[O]nce the facts constituting a crime are established beyond a reasonable doubt, based on all the evidence including the evidence of the defendant's mental state, the State may refuse to sustain the affirmative defense of insanity unless demonstrated by a preponderance of the evidence." *See also* Rivera v. State, 351 A.2d 561 (Del. 1976), appeal dismissed, 429 U.S. 877 (1976) (dismissing an appeal challenging the allocation of proving insanity to an accused as not presenting a substantial federal question); Leland v. Oregon, 343 U.S. 790 (1952) (due process not violated even though Oregon was the only state that required an accused to prove insanity beyond a reasonable doubt).

[27] Medina v. California, 505 U.S. 437, 449 (1992) ("Once a State provides a defendant access to procedures for making a competency evaluation . . . we perceive no basis for holding that due process further requires the State to assume the burden of vindicating the defendant's constitutional right by persuading the trier of fact that the defendant is competent to stand trial.").

[28] *See* Shreve & Raven-Hansen, Understanding Civil Procedure § 12.09 (3d ed. 2002).

[29] Fed. R. Civ. P. 50(a) ("Judgment as a Matter of Law. (1) If during a trial by jury a party has been fully heard on an issue and there is no legally sufficient evidentiary basis for a reasonable jury to find for that party on that issue, the court may determine the issue against that party and may grant a motion for judgment as a matter of law against that party with respect to a claim or defense that cannot under the controlling law be maintained or defeated without a favorable finding on that issue. (2) Motions for judgment as a matter of law may be made at any time before submission of the case to the jury. Such a motion shall specify the judgment sought and the law and the facts on which the moving party is entitled to the judgment.").

the weighing of the evidence, and the drawing of legitimate inferences from the facts are jury functions, not those of a judge." Thus, although the court should review the record as a whole, it must disregard all evidence favorable to the moving party that the jury is not required to believe. That is, the court should give credence to the evidence favoring the nonmovant as well as that "evidence supporting the moving party that is uncontradicted and unimpeached, at least to the extent that that evidence comes from disinterested witnesses."[30]

"Physical facts" rule. Typically, direct evidence on the elements of a cause of action suffices to satisfy a party's burden of production.[31] An exception is the "physical facts" rule.[32] "It is generally agreed by all courts that the jury will not be permitted to believe testimony that is contradicted by physical facts. Were a witness to testify that the sun rose at midnight in Chicago, no one would argue that the jury might believe him. This is the sort of 'physical fact' that is within the realm of judicial notice. The difficult questions arise when the physical facts must be established in some other way."[33]

[B] Directed Verdicts in Criminal Cases

In criminal cases, the prosecutor has the burden of production as well as the burden of persuasion on the elements of the crime.[34] If the prosecutor fails to present sufficient evidence on any element, the prosecutor has failed to satisfy its burden of production and the judge should enter a "directed verdict" (motion for judgment of acquittal). Criminal Rule 29, the governing provision, does not specify the standard by which the evidence is to be evaluated.[35] Nevertheless, the trial court must determine whether there

---

[30] Reeves v. Sanderson Plumbing Products, Inc., 530 U.S. 133, 151 (2000) (quoting 9A Wright & Miller, Federal Practice and Procedure 299 (2d ed. 1995) (citations omitted).

[31] *See* Cal. Evid. Code § 411 ("Except where additional evidence is required by statute, the direct evidence of one witness who is entitled to full credit is sufficient for proof of any fact.").

[32] *See* McDonald v. Ford Motor Co., 326 N.E.2d 252, 255 (Ohio 1975) (" 'The palpable untruthfulness' of plaintiff's testimony requiring a trial court to take a case from the jury under the physical facts rule 'must be (1) inherent in the rejected testimony, so that it contradicts itself, or (2) irreconcilable with facts of which, under recognized rules, the court takes judicial knowledge, or (3) is obviously inconsistent with, [or] contradicted by, undisputed physical facts.' Each of these formulations strikes a balance between, on the one hand, the common sense notion that physical facts and evidence can be so conclusive and demonstrative that no reasonable person could accept the truth of contrary testimony, and, on the other hand, the need for courts to be wary of treating a party's theory of a case as 'fact,' when a different theory is also possible in the case.") (citations omitted).

[33] Dow, *Judicial Determination of Credibility*, 38 Neb. L. Rev. 835, 854–55 (1959).

[34] There can never be a directed verdict against a criminal defendant on the elements of the crime because such a verdict would violate the right to a jury trial.

[35] Fed. R. Crim. P. 29(a) ("Motion Before Submission to Jury. Motions for directed verdict are abolished and motions for judgment of acquittal shall be used in their place. The court on motion of a defendant or of its own motion shall order the entry of judgment of acquittal of one or more offenses charged in the indictment or information after the evidence on either

is sufficient evidence on each element of the charged crime from which a reasonable jury could find each element beyond a reasonable doubt. [36]

This standard is constitutionally required. In *Thompson v. Louisville*, [37] the Supreme Court set forth the standard for judging the sufficiency of evidence in federal habeas corpus proceedings. Under that standard, a federal court could reverse a state conviction only if there was *no evidence* to support the conviction. After *Winship*, however, the Court revisited the issue in *Jackson v. Virginia*. [38] The Court held that *Winship* compelled the overruling of the no-evidence standard: "After *Winship* the critical inquiry on review of the sufficiency of the evidence to support a criminal conviction must be not simply to determine whether the jury was properly instructed, but to determine whether the record evidence would reasonably support a finding of guilt beyond a reasonable doubt." [39] The import of *Jackson* goes beyond the context of federal habeas review. The arguments advanced by the Court apply with equal force to directed verdict determinations.

[C]   Affirmative Defenses

By definition, the burden of production on an affirmative defense is allocated to the defense, in both civil and criminal cases. [40] The defendant's failure to satisfy this burden by introducing evidence means the jury will not be instructed on the defense. In effect, the judge is taking the issue away from the jury. If this burden is satisfied, the burden of persuasion on that issue must be allocated to one of the parties and the standard of proof (*e.g.*, preponderance or clear and convincing evidence) determined. [41]

---

side is closed if the evidence is insufficient to sustain a conviction of such offense or offenses. If a defendant's motion for judgment of acquittal at the close of the evidence offered by the government is not granted, the defendant may offer evidence without having reserved the right.").

[36] *See* Jackson v. Virginia, 443 U.S. 307, 318 (1979) ("whether the record evidence could reasonably support a finding of guilt beyond a reasonable doubt").

[37] 362 U.S. 199 (1960).

[38] 443 U.S. 307 (1979).

[39] *Id.* at 318.

[40] Affirmative defenses represent more than a mere denial of an element of a cause of action or a crime. They are a "confession" and "avoidance" — *i.e.*, "I did it, but. . . ." In other words, the defendant's conduct and mental state satisfy all the elements of the crime, but the defendant claims a justification or excuse. The term non-affirmative defense typically refers to a defense that negates an element of a crime. One commentator refers to these as "failure of proof" defenses. *See* 1 Robinson, Criminal Law Defenses § 22, 72–73 (1994) ("General defenses differ conceptually from failure of proof defenses in that the former bar conviction even if all elements of the offense are satisfied, whereas the latter prevent conviction by negating a required element of the offense."). Mistake of fact, accident, and intoxication negate the required mental state for some crimes; the prosecution must prove that mental state beyond a reasonable doubt. Alibi negates the actus reus of the crime; here, again, the prosecution must prove that the accused committed the crime (or was an accomplice) beyond a reasonable doubt.

[41] *See supra* § 4.03[D] (burden of persuasion: affirmative defenses).

The Supreme Court has long upheld placing the burden of production for affirmative defenses on the accused.[42]

§ 4.05 Key Points

The term "burden of proof" is often confusing because there are two distinct burdens of proof: (1) the "burden of persuasion" and (2) the "burden of production." These two burdens are allocated, at least initially, to one of the parties on *every* issue in the case. They, however, do not have to be allocated to the same party, even on the same issue. For example, in some jurisdictions the burden of production on self-defense in a criminal case is allocated to the accused, but once that burden is satisfied, the burden of persuasion rests with the prosecution to disprove self-defense.

Burden of persuasion. The burden of persuasion refers to the *convincing force* of the evidence. Technically, it is the "risk of nonpersuasion." Three common standards of proof are used to define the legally required persuasive force of the evidence: (1) "proof beyond a reasonable doubt" (the highest standard); (2) "clear and convincing evidence" (an intermediate standard); and (3) "preponderance of evidence" (more probable than not).

Burden of production. The burden of production, sometimes called the "burden of going forward with evidence," refers to a party's responsibility to introduce evidence at trial. Technically, it is the risk of nonproduction that is at issue. The judge (never the jury) determines whether this burden has been satisfied. There are two possible adverse consequences if a party fails to satisfy its burden of production: (1) the party may suffer a directed verdict, or (2) in the case of an affirmative defense, the jury will not be instructed on the defense. Both consequences take the issue away from the jury.

---

[42] *See* Patterson v. New York, 432 U.S. 197, 230–31 (1977) (Powell, J., dissenting) ("The State normally may shift to the defendant the burden of production, that is, the burden of going forward with sufficient evidence."); Simopoulos v. Virginia, 462 U.S. 506 (1983) (defense of medical necessity in abortion case, burden of production allocated to accused); United States v. Bailey, 444 U.S. 394 (1980) (necessity and duress defenses, burden of production allocated to accused); Davis v. United States, 160 U.S. 469 (1895) (insanity).

Chapter 5

PRESUMPTIONS & INFERENCES: FRE 301

§ 5.01 Introduction

The law governing presumptions is one of the most difficult areas of evidence law for students and practitioners alike. Some of the problems are caused by inconsistent terminology, which must be understood before endeavoring to go any further.[1] Another problem arises because major scholars in the field (Thayer and Morgan) disagreed about the effect presumptions should have. Moreover, the courts have added their own, and often inconsistent, nuances to this area of law. Finally, because of constitutional considerations, criminal presumptions differ from civil presumptions.

Federal Rule 301 is the principal provision on presumptions. Rule 302 governs the applicability of state presumptions in federal cases in which state law supplies the rule of decision (*e.g.*, diversity cases).

Rule 301 covers *rebuttable* presumptions in *civil* cases. There is no rule dealing with criminal presumptions in the Rules of Evidence.[2] Although the application of Rule 301 depends on an understanding of the terms "presumption" and "burden of proof," neither term is defined in the rule.[3] Rule 301 does not create any presumptions; it merely governs their effect. The rule further limits its own reach by explicitly recognizing legislative authority over the effect of presumptions. The introductory language restricts the rule's application to "civil actions and proceedings not otherwise provided for by Act of Congress."

§ 5.02 Definitions of Presumptions & Inferences

Much of the confusion surrounding the law of presumptions arises from a lack of precise terminology.

Conclusive presumptions. Rule 301 governs only rebuttable presumptions. Conclusive or irrebuttable presumptions are actually substantive rules of law and are therefore beyond the scope of the Rules of Evidence. For example, the common law rule that a child under seven years is conclusively presumed incapable of committing a crime is a substantive rule of criminal law, which the parties may not rebut. To call this rule a presumption serves no purpose, except perhaps to confuse.[4]

---

[1] *See infra* § 5.02 (definitions).

[2] *See infra* § 5.09 (criminal presumptions).

[3] The rule does recognize, but only implicitly, two distinct burdens of proof. For a discussion of burdens of proof, see *supra* chapter 4.

[4] *See* Morgan, Basic Problems of Evidence 31 (1963) ("This is merely a way of expressing the rule of substantive law that a person under seven years of age cannot be legally convicted of a felony.").

Rebuttable presumptions. A "presumption is not evidence."[5] Rather, a presumption, as that term is used in Rule 301, is a procedural rule that defines the relationship between two facts — a basic fact and a presumed fact.[6] If the basic fact is proved, the presumed fact must be accepted as established unless and until rebutted. For example, if a letter is properly addressed and mailed (basic facts), it must be accepted that the letter was received (presumed fact), unless sufficient evidence has been introduced to rebut the presumed fact.[7]

Inferences. A presumption is mandatory. The presumed fact must be accepted once the basic fact is established. In contrast, an inference, which also involves a relationship between two facts, is permissive. For example, the doctrine of res ipsa loquitur usually involves an inference of negligence.[8] Establishment of the basic facts permits, but does not compel, a conclusion of negligence. Nevertheless, such a standardized inference does serve the purpose of satisfying a plaintiff's burden of production on the issue of negligence.

Other terms. Various labels have been used to describe presumptions — for example, "mandatory inferences" and "presumptions of law." Similarly, inferences have been called "permissive presumptions" and "presumptions of fact." These alternative terms add nothing but confusion and should be avoided.

Prima facie. The term "prima facie" evidence, frequently encountered in this context, is often ambiguous, and care must be taken to discern exactly how it is being used in a particular case. Perhaps the term is most often used to describe the burden of production; a party that has "made out a prima facie case" has satisfied its burden of production and therefore should not suffer a directed verdict.

§ 5.03 Rationale for Presumptions

Presumptions are created for a number of reasons: (1) policy, (2) fairness (possession of evidence), and (3) probability. These are often called the three "Ps." Possession of the evidence" refers to one party's greater access to

---

[5] A.C. Aukerman Co. v. R.L. Chaides Const. Co., 960 F.2d 1020, 1037 (Fed. Cir. 1992).

[6] Unlike Federal Rule 301, Uniform Rule 301 defines the term: A presumption "means that when a basic fact is found to exist, the presumed fact is assumed to exist until the nonexistence of the presumed fact is determined as provided in rules 302 and 303." A basic fact "means a fact or group of facts that give rise to a presumption." A presumed fact "means a fact that is assumed upon the finding of a basic fact."

[7] *See* Schikore v. BankAmerica Supplemental, Retirement Plan, 269 F.3d 956, 961 (9th Cir. 2001) ("The mailbox rule provides that the proper and timely mailing of a document raises a rebuttable presumption that the document has been received by the addressee in the usual time. It is a settled feature of the federal common law.") (citing Hagner v. United States, 285 U.S. 427, 430 (1932)); Nunley v. City of Los Angeles, 52 F.3d 792, 796 (9th Cir. 1995) ("Under the common law mailbox rule, proper and timely mailing of a document raises a rebuttable presumption that it is received by the addressee.").

[8] *See* Diamond, Levine & Madden, Understanding Torts § 5.04 (1996).

information. "Probabilities," as used here, means a rough estimate of how things work in the world.

Different reasons underlie different presumptions, and in many instances several reasons may support a particular presumption.[9] The presumption of due delivery of properly posted mail (mailbox rule) is based on probabilities (most letters are delivered) as well as the difficulty, on the part of the mailer, of proving receipt.[10] In contrast, the presumption of undue influence when a lawyer is named a beneficiary under a will prepared by that lawyer is based on policy.[11] Lawyers are fiduciaries; they are suppose to assist their clients, not take advantage of them.

§ 5.04 Effect of Presumptions

There are two principal views on the effect of presumptions in civil cases: (1) Thayer theory, and (2) Morgan theory.

[A] Thayer Theory of Presumptions

Burden of production shifts. Under the Thayer view, sometimes known as the "bursting bubble" theory, a presumption shifts only the burden of production or going forward with the evidence; it does not shift the burden of persuasion.[12] Thus, proof of the basic fact (*e.g.*, letter mailed) automatically establishes the presumed fact (*e.g.*, letter received) and shifts the burden of producing evidence rebutting the presumed fact to the other party. If the opposing party fails to offer sufficient evidence to rebut the presumed fact, that party has failed to satisfy its burden of production and suffers a directed verdict on that issue. If the case goes to the jury, the jury will be instructed that it must find the presumed fact (*e.g.*, letter received). There is no need to mention the term "presumption" in the jury instruction.

---

[9] *See* Morgan, Basic Problems of Evidence 32–34 (1963).

[10] In some circumstances, a presumption may be tied to a substantive policy. *See* Schikore v. BankAmerica Supplemental, Retirement Plan, 269 F.3d 956, 963 (9th Cir. 2001) ("This case exemplifies the reason for the common law's application of the mailbox rule. The evidence is inconclusive: Schikore claims that she mailed the form, and the Plan claims that the form is not contained in its files. As the district court reasoned, the presumption of receipt established by the mailbox rule applied 'precisely to avoid the type of swearing contest in which the parties are presently involved.' In the absence of such a rule, plan participants could easily be disadvantaged and their rights made wholly dependent on the choice that plan administrators would be forced to make between unproved assertions by the participant and similarly unproved assertions by the plan they administer. Permitting such arbitrary decisionmaking would be directly contrary to the purpose of ERISA to 'protect the interests of participants in employee benefit plans and their beneficiaries.' 29 U.S.C. § 1001(b) (congressional findings and declaration of ERISA policy).").

[11] A presumption of undue influence arises when (1) the relationship of attorney and client exists between a testator and an attorney, (2) the attorney is named as a beneficiary in the will, (3) the attorney/beneficiary is not related by blood or marriage to the testator, and (4) the attorney/beneficiary actively participates in the preparation of the will. *See* Krischbaum v. Dillon, 567 N.E.2d 1291 (Ohio 1991).

[12] *See* Thayer, A Preliminary Treatise on Evidence at the Common Law ch 8. (1898); 9 Wigmore, Evidence § 2491(2) (3d ed. 1940).

Rebuttal evidence proffered. If, however, the opposing party offers sufficient evidence to rebut the presumed fact, the presumption *disappears* —
"bursts."[13] It has performed its function of shifting the burden of production, and since that burden has been satisfied by the introduction of rebuttal
evidence, no further function remains to be served. The burden of persuasion remains with the party to whom it was originally allocated. Again,
there is no need to mention the presumption to the jury.[14] Nevertheless,
an inference often continues after rebuttal, and a jury may consider it in
reaching a decision.[15]

Basic fact controverted. If the opposing party introduces sufficient evidence challenging the basic fact (*e.g.*, evidence that the letter was not mailed),
the jury must decide whether the basic fact has been established. In such
a case, the jurors should be instructed that if they find the basic fact, they
must find the presumed fact. Although the basic fact presents a jury issue,
the presumption remains mandatory once the basic fact is established.
Thus, the conditional instruction is required.

[B]   Morgan Theory of Presumptions

A different view was expressed by Morgan.

Burden of production shifts. As with Thayer's theory, a Morgan presumption shifts the burden of production or going forward with the evidence,
and if the opponent fails to offer rebuttal evidence, a directed verdict
results. Thus, initially, there is no difference between Thayer and Morgan.

The difference is that under the Morgan approach a presumption shifts
the burden of *persuasion* as well as the burden of production.[16] Morgan
argued that the Thayer theory failed to support adequately the reasons
underlying the creation of presumptions. According to Morgan, if "a policy
is strong enough to call a presumption into existence, it is hard to imagine
it so weak as to be satisfied by the bare recital of words on the witness
stand or the reception in evidence of a writing."[17] For example, the
presumption of undue influence when a lawyer becomes a beneficiary under

---

[13] *See* Nunley v. City of Los Angeles, 52 F.3d 792, 796 (9th Cir. 1995) ("Under the so-called
'bursting bubble' approach to presumptions, a presumption disappears where rebuttal evidence
is presented.").

[14] Recall, however, that a presumption has an important effect in addition to shifting the
burden of production. As explained earlier, a presumption also enables the proponent to satisfy
its initial burden of production and thus survive a motion for a directed verdict.

[15] *See* Nunley v. City of Los Angeles, 52 F.3d 792, 796 (9th Cir. 1995) ("Even after the 'bubble'
of presumption has 'burst,' the factual question of receipt remains and may be decided in favor
of receipt by a fact finder who may choose to draw inferences of receipt from the evidence of
mailing, in spite of contrary evidence.").

[16] *See* Morgan, *Some Observations Concerning Presumptions*, 44 Harv. L. Rev. 906 (1931);
Morgan, *Instructing the Jury Upon Presumptions and Burden of Proof*, 47 Harv. L. Rev. 59
(1933).

[17] Morgan, *Instructing the Jury Upon Presumptions and Burden of Proof*, 47 Harv. L. Rev.
59, 82 (1933).

a will prepared by that lawyer is based on policy.[18] We do not want this presumption to disappear ("burst") based merely on the lawyer's testimonial assertion that no undue influence was involved. In short, a presumption under the Morgan theory has more "teeth."

Under this theory, there is no need to mention the presumption in the jury instruction; the jury need only be instructed that the opposing party has the burden of persuading the jury (preponderance of evidence) of the nonexistence of the presumed fact.[19]

[C]　Other Approaches

Many courts reject the Morgan theory, but do not adopt the "pure" Thayer view either. Under the Thayer theory, the rebuttal evidence need only be sufficient to permit a reasonable jury to find the nonexistence of the presumed fact. The courts, however, have used a variety of different standards to describe the quantum of proof needed to rebut a presumption. Some have required "substantial evidence" of the nonexistence of the presumed fact; others have demanded that the nonexistence of the presumed fact be as probable as the existence of the presumed fact before the presumption is rebutted.[20] California has both Thayer and Morgan presumptions, depending on the underlying policy for the presumption.[21]

§ 5.05　Federal Rule 301

As originally proposed by the Supreme Court, Rule 301 embraced the Morgan view of presumptions.[22] This rule, however, was subsequently amended by Congress. Although it is clear that Federal Rule 301, as enacted, rejected the Morgan view, it was not as clear that it adopted the Thayer view.[23] Nevertheless, courts[24] and commentators believe that

---

[18] See supra note 10.

[19] The Uniform Rules adopt the Morgan position. See Unif. R. Evid. 302(a) ("In a civil action or proceeding, unless otherwise proved by statute, judicial decision, or these rules, a presumption imposes on the party against whom it is directed the burden of proving that the nonexistence of the presumed fact is more probable than its existence.").

[20] See Morgan, Basic Problems of Evidence 34–36 (1963).

[21] Cal. Evid. Code § 630-47 (presumptions affecting burden of production); § 660-669.5 (presumptions affecting burden of proof).

[22] "In all cases not otherwise provided for by Act of Congress or by these rules a presumption imposes on the party against whom it is directed the burden of proving that the nonexistence of the presumed fact is more probable than its existence." 56 F.R.D. 208 (1973).

[23] The source of the confusion stems from the Conference Report, which reads in part: "[i]f the adverse party offers *no evidence* contradicting the presumed fact, the court will instruct the jury that if it finds the basic facts, it may presume the existence of the presumed fact." H. Rep. No. 1597, 93d Cong., 2d Sess., reprinted in [1974] U.S.C.C.A.N. 7098, 7099 (emphasis added). Under the Thayer view, if "no evidence contradicting the presumed fact" is offered, the adverse party has not satisfied its burden of production and suffers a directed verdict on the issue. In short, there is no reason to instruct the jury that it "may presume" anything. See 21 Wright & Graham, Federal Practice and Procedure § 5122, at 570–73, § 5126, at 607 (1977).

Congress "settled in Rule 301 on what is essentially the *Thayer* view."[25]

Nevertheless, the rule does not specify the standard for determining the sufficiency of rebuttal evidence. Nor does it specify how the jury should be instructed. The presumption is rebutted if sufficient evidence is introduced from which a reasonable jury could find the nonexistence of the presumed fact.[26]

Exceptions. Not all presumptions, however, should require the same quantum of rebuttal evidence. This makes sense because the policy rationales are different for different presumptions. Accordingly, the more important presumptions should have greater effect than less important presumptions. In short, Congress or the courts can create Morgan presumptions.[27]

§ 5.06   Conflicting Presumptions

On occasion, two presumptions may conflict. Under a pure Thayerian view, both presumptions would disappear if rebutted, and the evidence would be considered for its worth by the jury; often the basic fact would be circumstantial proof of the presumed fact. Another approach would look to the underlying rationale for the two presumptions and the presumption with the stronger policy basis would trump the other presumption. The Uniform Rules (1999) take this position.[28]

§ 5.07   State Presumptions in Federal Civil Cases

Federal Rule 302 provides: "In civil actions and proceedings, the effect of a presumption respecting a fact which is an element of a claim or defense as to which State law supplies the rule of decision is determined in

---

[24] *E.g.,* St. Mary's Honor Center v. Hicks, 509 U.S. 502, 503 (1993) (a "fundamental principle of Rule 301 [is] that a presumption does not shift the burden of proof"); A.C. Aukerman Co. v. R.L. Chaides Const. Co., 960 F.2d 1020, 1037 (Fed. Cir. 1992) ("As finally adopted after much scholarly debate, Rule 301 embodies what is known as the 'bursting bubble' theory of presumptions. Under this theory, a presumption is not merely rebuttable but completely vanishes upon the introduction of evidence sufficient to support a finding of the nonexistence of the presumed fact.").

[25] ABA Section of Litigation, Emerging Problems Under the Federal Rules of Evidence, Rule 301, at 37 (3d ed. 1998).

[26] *See St. Mary's Honor Center,* 509 U.S. at 507 (" '[T]he defendant must clearly set forth, through the introduction of admissible evidence,' reasons for its actions which, *if believed by the trier of fact,* would support a finding that unlawful discrimination was not the cause of the employment action."); Texas Dept. of Community Affairs v. Burdine, 450 U.S. 248, 256 (1981); A.C. Aukerman Co. v. R.L. Chaides Const. Co., 960 F.2d 1020, 1037 (Fed. Cir. 1992) ("Under this theory, a presumption is not merely rebuttable but completely vanishes upon the introduction of evidence sufficient to support a finding of the nonexistence of the presumed fact.").

[27] *See supra* note 10.

[28] Unif. R. Evid. 301(b) (rev. 1999) ("If presumptions are inconsistent, the presumption applies that is founded upon weightier considerations of policy. If considerations of policy are of equal weight neither presumption applies.").

accordance with State law." The rule is important in federal courts because the Supreme Court has held that, under the doctrine of *Erie R.R. Co. v. Tompkins*,[29] state law with respect to burdens of proof involving substantive elements of a claim or defense controls if the rule of decision is determined by state law.[30]

An analogous issue may arise in state courts when the cause of action is based upon federal law — for example, a claim arising under the Federal Employers' Liability Act.[31] Uniform Rule 302(c) provides: "In civil actions and proceedings, the effect of a presumption respecting a fact which is an element of a claim or defense as to which federal law supplies the rule of decision is determined in accordance with federal law."[32] A similar "reverse Erie" issue arises with privileges.[33]

§ 5.08 Selected Presumptions

There are numerous presumptions. These are a sample:

Agency: (1) a vehicle identified by the name of the carrier on its side and operating on its regular route presumed driven by an agent of the carrier acting within the scope of employment; (2) driver of a car occupied by its owner presumed an agent of the owner; and (3) automobile driven by servant presumed operated within scope of employment.

Bailments: (1) failure of bailee to return property presumed negligent; and (2) delivery of goods in good condition to a carrier and subsequent return in damaged condition presumed negligent.

Competency: (1) presumption of continuing incompetency; and (2) presumption of incompetency arises after appointment of guardian.

Consent: person driving an automobile presumed to have owner's consent.

Continuation of condition: (1) once a condition is shown to exist, its continuance presumed; (2) continuation of insanity after adjudication of not guilty by reason of insanity; (3) continuation of seaworthiness of a ship; (4) continuation of ownership of property; and (5) continuation of contract.

Death: person missing for seven years presumed dead.

Legitimacy: (1) birth of child during marriage presumed right to inherit property through the father; (2) child conceived during marriage presumed legitimate; and (3) man who marries a pregnant woman presumed to be father of the child.

---

[29] 304 U.S. 64 (1938).

[30] *See* Dick v. New York Life Ins. Co., 359 U.S. 437 (1959); Palmer v. Hoffman, 318 U.S. 109 (1943); Cities Service Oil Co v. Dunlap, 308 U.S. 208 (1939).

[31] 45 U.S.C. 51 et seq.

[32] *See* St. Louis Southwestern Railway Co. v. Dickerson, 470 U.S. 409, 411 (1985) ("FELA cases adjudicated in state courts are subject to state procedural rules, but the substantive law governing them is federal."); Wright, Law of Federal Courts § 45 (5th ed. 1994).

[33] *See infra* § 37.06 (choice of law).

Marriage: (1) presumption of continuation of first marriage; (2) man and woman with different surnames presumed not married; (3) marriage, solemnized in due form, presumed lawful; (4) presumption of continuation of marriage, and (5) presumption that marital property includes all property acquired during marriage or assets produced or earned as a result of mutual effort of both parties.

Property. (1) acceptance by donee of a gift is presumed; (2) where title is put in name of member of purchaser's family, a gift is presumed; (3) where a document of title to real estate lists more than one person as owner, parties presumed to have equal shares; (4) possession raises presumption of ownership; (5) the sale price is presumed to reflect the true value of property.

Suicide: death caused by violent external means presumed accidental.

Wills: (1) will drawn by an attorney, properly executed and attested, presumed valid; and (2) where attorney who drafts will is a named beneficiary, undue influence presumed.

§ 5.09   Criminal Presumptions

Neither Rule 301 nor any other rule of evidence governs presumptions in criminal cases. The Supreme Court proposed a rule on criminal presumptions (proposed Federal Rule 303), but it was not enacted by Congress.[34] The Uniform Rules of Evidence contain a provision based on the Supreme Court proposal, including a rule on jury instructions.[35]

[A]   Criminal Presumptions Defined

As with presumptions in civil cases, confusing terminology is responsible for many of the problems involving presumptions in criminal cases.

Presumption of innocence. For example, the presumption of innocence is not a true presumption; the accused is not required to prove any basic fact in order to trigger the presumption of innocence. Rather, the "presumption of innocence" is the traditional way of stating that the burden of persuasion is on the prosecution.[36]

Presumption of sanity. Another example of confusing terminology is the so-called "presumption of sanity." Again, this is not a true presumption; there is no basic fact that must be proved. The "presumption of sanity" is merely a way of allocating to the accused the initial burden of producing evidence of insanity, which is an affirmative defense.[37] Commentators have

---

[34] The text of proposed Federal Rule 303 and the accompanying Advisory Committee's Note are found at 56 F.R.D. 212–14 (1972).

[35] Unif. R. Evid. 303 (rev. 1999).

[36] *See* Bell v. Wolfish, 441 U.S. 520 (1979).

[37] *See* Ohio Rev. Code § 2901.05(A) ("The burden of going forward with the evidence of an affirmative defense . . . is upon the accused.").

argued that rules that allocate burdens of proof, such as the presumptions of innocence and sanity, should be labeled "assumptions."[38]

Civil-criminal distinction. Even if "assumptions" are distinguished from presumptions, problems of terminology remain. Although the term "presumption" is used in both criminal and civil cases, a presumption operates differently in the criminal context than in a civil case. The difference arises from constitutional limitations on the allocation of the burden of proof. The common law presumption concerning possession of recently stolen property illustrates this point. In a civil case, establishment of the basic fact (possession of recently stolen property) would automatically establish the presumed fact (possessor stole the property), unless rebutted. The effect of the presumption would be to shift, at the very least, the burden of production to the opposing party. If that party failed to satisfy its burden of production, a directed verdict on that issue would follow. In a criminal case, however, an accused cannot constitutionally suffer a directed verdict.[39] Thus, although the term presumption is often used in criminal cases, the effect of such a presumption generally is only that of an inference; the jury should be instructed only that it *may* find the inferred fact without any mention of the words presume or presumption.

[B]　Constitutionality of Criminal Presumptions

A second difference between criminal and civil presumptions involves the test for reviewing the constitutionality of presumptions. In *Tot v. United States*,[40] the Supreme Court held that in a criminal case a "presumption cannot be sustained if there be no rational connection between the fact proved and the ultimate fact presumed."[41] The rational connection test was further defined by the Court in *Leary v. United States*:[42] "[U]nless it can at least be said with substantial assurance that the presumed fact is more likely than not to flow from the proved fact on which it is made to depend," the presumption violates due process.[43] In *Leary*, the Court raised, but did not decide, the issue of whether a criminal presumption that involves an essential element of the offense must also satisfy the "beyond the reasonable doubt" standard.[44] In two subsequent cases, the Court was able to

---

[38] *See* 21 Wright & Graham, Federal Practice and Procedure § 5124, at 589–91 (1977).

[39] *See* Unif. R. Evid. 303(b) (rev. 1999) ("The court is not authorized to direct the jury to find a presumed fact against the accused.").

[40] 319 U.S. 463, 466 (1943) (possession of firearm by convicted violent felon raised statutory presumption that firearm received by interstate or foreign commerce).

[41] *Id.* at 467. *Accord* United States v. Romano, 382 U.S. 136 (1965) (statutory presumption that unexplained presence at illegal distillery site sufficient for conviction of "possession, custody, or control" of illegal distilled spirits held unconstitutional); United States v. Gainey, 380 U.S. 63 (1965) (same statute as in *Romano*; different provision regarding "carrying on" (any involvement) in illegal distilled spirits business held constitutional).

[42] 395 U.S. 6 (1969) (statutory presumption that unexplained possession of marihuana sufficient to convict for knowledge of and participation in the illegal importation of marihuana; "knowledge" aspect unconstitutional).

[43] *Id.* at 36.

[44] *Id.* at 36 n.64.

avoid deciding this issue because the presumptions in question either satisfied the more stringent "beyond a reasonable doubt" test or failed to meet the "more likely than not" test of *Leary*.[45]

In *Ulster County Court v. Allen* ,[46] the Court changed direction, recognizing two types of criminal presumptions: mandatory and permissive. The police stopped an automobile, in which three male adults and a 16-year-old girl were riding, for a speeding violation. Two handguns were spotted in the girl's handbag, and a subsequent search of the trunk revealed a machinegun and heroin. All occupants were charged with illegal possession of weapons and heroin. The state's case was buttressed by a New York statute which provided, with certain exceptions, that the presence of a firearm in an automobile is presumptive evidence of its illegal possession by all persons then occupying the vehicle.

The Court upheld the presumption as applied to the facts of the case. *Allen* represents a departure from the Court's prior decisions. As noted above, the Court had appeared to have established two principles concerning the prosecution's use of a presumption that relates to an element of the charged offense. First, notwithstanding the label, a criminal presumption could have only the effect of a permissive inference. Second, there must be a rational connection between the fact proved and the ultimate fact presumed, although this test awaited further clarification. The *Allen* majority reworked both principles. It recognized two types of presumptions: mandatory and permissive. The constitutionality of permissive presumptions, as in *Allen*, are to be examined as applied in a particular case; the "more likely than not" standard controls.[47] In contrast, the constitutionality of mandatory presumptions are to be examined facially; the beyond reasonable doubt standard controls. The majority's "novel approach," as described by the dissent,[48] seemed to introduce more confusion into an area already permeated with confusion.[49]

---

[45] *See* Barnes v. United States, 412 U.S. 837 (1973) (common law presumption of knowledge from possession of recently stolen property did not violate due process; sufficient evidence for rational juror to find inferred fact beyond a reasonable doubt); Turner v. United States, 396 U.S. 398 (1970) (statutory presumption that unexplained possession of narcotics is sufficient to convict for trafficking was valid for heroin but not cocaine).

[46] 442 U.S. 140 (1979).

[47] *Id.* at 157 ("Because this permissive presumption leaves the trier of fact free to credit or reject the inference and does not shift the burden of proof, it affects the application of the 'beyond a reasonable doubt' standard only if, under the facts of the case, there is no rational way the trier could make the connection permitted by the inference. For only in that situation is there any risk that an explanation of the permissible inference to a jury, or its use by a jury, has caused the presumptively rational factfinder to make an erroneous factual determination.").

[48] *Id.* at 176 (Powell, J., dissenting).

[49] For example, a mandatory presumption in a civil case shifts, at least, the burden of production. Thus, if no evidence controverting the presumed fact is offered, the party in whose favor the presumption operates is entitled to a directed verdict on that issue. In the criminal context, however, a defendant cannot suffer a directed verdict. Thus, although mandatory presumptions are recognized by the *Allen* majority, their meaning and effect remains clouded.

In a subsequent case, *Sandstrom v. Montana*,[50] the Court struck down a jury instruction which provided that the "law presumes that a person intends the ordinary consequences of his voluntary acts." The Court found that the jury could have construed the instruction so as to violate constitutional principles. "First, a reasonable jury could well have interpreted the presumption as 'conclusive,' that is, not technically as a presumption at all, but rather as an irrebuttable direction by the court to find intent once convinced of the facts triggering the presumption."[51] This interpretation would have relieved the prosecution of establishing guilt beyond a reasonable doubt in violation of *Winship*.[52] "Alternatively, the jury may have interpreted the instruction as a direction to find intent upon proof of the defendant's voluntary actions . . . unless the defendant proved the contrary by some quantum of proof . . . thus effectively shifting the burden of persuasion on the element of intent."[53]

In *Francis v. Franklin*,[54] the Court again considered the constitutionality of a criminal presumption. During an escape from custody, Franklin ran to the home of the victim and demanded car keys. The victim slammed the door, Franklin's gun discharged, and the victim died from the gunshot wound. At trial, Franklin claimed the gun discharged accidentally. Thus, the critical issue was his intent to kill. On this issue the trial court instructed the jury as follows: "The acts of a person of sound mind and discretion are presumed to be the product of the person's will, but the presumption may be rebutted. A person of sound mind and discretion is presumed to intend the natural and probable consequences of his acts but the presumption may be rebutted."[55]

The Court found that the instruction could have been interpreted by a reasonable juror to create a mandatory presumption that shifted to the defendant the burden of persuasion on the element of intent. Consequently, the instruction violated due process.

The defendant in *Carella v. California*[56] was convicted of grand theft for failure to return a rental car. The jury instructions adopted two statutory presumptions. One required the jury to find intent to commit theft by fraud if a rental car is not returned within 20 days after a demand is made by the owner. The other presumption required the jury to return a finding of embezzlement if a rental car is not returned within five days of the

---

[50] 442 U.S. 510, 514 (1979) (deliberate homicide).

[51] *Id.* at 517.

[52] *See supra* § 4.03[C] (beyond reasonable doubt).

[53] *Sandstrom*, 442 U.S. at 517. This interpretation would have violated *Mullaney. See supra* § 4.03[D] (burden of persuasion: Affirmative defenses).

[54] 471 U.S. 307 (1985).

[55] *Id.* at 309 (quotation marks omitted). *See also* Rose v. Clark, 478 U.S. 570, 573 (1986) (applying harmless error rule to an unconstitutional presumption) ("All homicides are presumed to be malicious in the absence of evidence which would rebut the implied presumption.").

[56] 491 U.S. 263 (1989) (per curiam).

expiration of the lease. The Supreme Court found these instructions unconstitutional. Due process requires the state to establish guilt beyond a reasonable doubt. Jury instructions that relieve the state of this burden are constitutionally suspect. "Such directions subvert the presumption of innocence accorded to accused persons and also invade the truth-finding task assigned solely to juries in criminal cases."[57] Since the instructions in question were mandatory directives to the jury, they "directly foreclosed independent jury consideration of whether the facts proved established certain elements of the offenses," and they "also relieved the State of its burden of proof articulated in *Winship*, namely, proving by evidence every essential element of Carella's crime beyond a reasonable doubt."[58]

In sum, these cases indicate that terms such as "presumption," "presumed fact," and "prima facie case" should not be used in jury instructions because they may mislead the jury. In addition, the so-called presumption should be given only the effect of a permissive inference; the jury may, but is not required to, find the inferred fact.[59]

§ 5.10　Key Points

Rule 301 covers *rebuttable* presumptions in *civil* cases. There is no rule dealing with criminal presumptions in the Rules of Evidence. Rule 301 does not create any presumptions; it merely governs their effect. The rule further limits its own reach by explicitly recognizing legislative authority over the effect of presumptions. The introductory language restricts the rule's application to "civil actions and proceedings not otherwise provided for by Act of Congress."

Civil Presumptions

Much of the confusion surrounding the law of presumptions arises from a lack of precise terminology.

Conclusive presumptions. Rule 301 governs only rebuttable presumptions. Conclusive or irrebuttable presumptions are actually substantive rules of law and are therefore beyond the scope of the Rules of Evidence.

Rebuttable presumptions. A presumption, as that term is used in Rule 301, is a procedural rule that defines the relationship between two facts — a basic fact and a presumed fact. If the basic fact is proved, the presumed fact must be accepted as established unless and until rebutted. For example, if a letter is properly addressed and mailed (basic facts), it must be

---

[57] *Id.* at 265.

[58] *Id.* at 266.

[59] *See* Unif. R. Evid. 303(c) (rev. 1999) ("At the time the existence of a presumed fact against the accused is submitted to the jury, the court shall instruct the jury that it may regard the basic facts as sufficient evidence of the presumed fact but is not required to do so. In addition, if a presumed fact establishes guilty, is an element of he offense, or negates a defense, the court shall instruct the jury that its existence, on all the evidence, must proved beyond a reasonable doubt.").

accepted that the letter was received (presumed fact), unless sufficient evidence has been introduced to rebut the presumed fact.

Inferences. A presumption is mandatory. The presumed fact must be accepted once the basic fact is established. In contrast, an inference, which also involves a relationship between two facts, is permissive. For example, the doctrine of res ipsa loquitur involves an inference of negligence. Establishment of the basic facts permits, but does not compel, a conclusion of negligence. Nevertheless, such a recognized inference does serve the purpose of satisfying the plaintiff's burden of production on the issue of negligence.

Two theories. There are two principal views on the effect of presumptions in civil cases: (1) Thayer theory, and (2) Morgan theory. Under both theories, the presumption shifts the burden of production or going forward with the evidence and if the opponent fails to offer rebuttal evidence, a directed verdict results. The difference concerns the quantum of proof necessary to rebut. Under the Morgan approach, a presumption shifts the burden of persuasion as well as the burden of production. Thus, a presumption under the Morgan theory has more teeth. Rule 301 follows the Thayer approach.

Criminal Presumptions

Neither Rule 301 nor any other rule of evidence governs presumptions in criminal cases. As with presumptions in civil cases, confusing terminology is responsible for many of the problems involving presumptions in criminal cases.

Presumption of innocence. For example, the presumption of innocence is not a true presumption; the accused is not required to prove any basic fact in order to trigger the presumption of innocence. Rather, the "presumption of innocence" is the traditional way of stating that the burden of persuasion is on the prosecution.

Civil–criminal distinction. Although the term "presumption" is used in both criminal and civil cases, a presumption operates differently in the criminal context than in a civil case. The difference arises from constitutional limitations. In a criminal case, an accused cannot constitutionally suffer a directed verdict. Thus, although the term presumption is often used in criminal cases, the effect of such a presumption generally is only that of an inference; the jury should be instructed only that it *may* find the inferred fact.

Chapter 6

OBJECTIONS & OFFERS OF PROOF: FRE 103

§ 6.01 Introduction

"Objection. Sustained." "Objection. Overruled." If you have not observed this dialogue at a trial, you have seen it in countless movies or TV shows. An *objection* or *motion to strike* evidence is used to exclude information an attorney believes is inadmissible. Even if overruled, it must be made to preserve a challenge to the admissibility of that evidence on appeal. In contrast, when an attorney's proffer of evidence has been excluded by a trial judge's ruling, an *offer of proof* is required to preserve the issue for appeal. In other words, objections (and motions to strike) are used to contest the *admissibility* of evidence, while offers of proof are used to contest the *exclusion* of evidence.

To be precise, this requirement is a forfeiture, rather than a waiver, rule: "Whereas forfeiture is the failure to make the timely assertion of a right, waiver is the 'intentional relinquishment or abandonment of a known right.'"[1] Nevertheless, most courts and lawyers do not make this distinction, and failure to object or make an offer of proof is usually called a "waiver."

Federal Rule 103 governs the procedures for evidentiary rulings. It covers such matters as objections, offers of proof, plain and harmless error, and out-of-court hearings for admissibility determinations.

§ 6.02 Objections: Rule 103(a)(1)

Under Rule 103(a)(1), an objection or motion to strike must be made to preserve a challenge to the admissibility of evidence on appeal.[2] This rule is subject to the *plain error* doctrine.[3] The objection must be *timely* and

---

[1] United States v. Olano, 507 U.S. 725, 733 (1993) (quoting Johnson v. Zerbst, 304 U.S. 458, 464 (1938)).

[2] *See also* ABA Section of Litigation, Emerging Problems Under the Federal Rules of Evidence 10 (3d ed. 1998) ("In multiple party cases, the Rule does not indicate to what extent each party must join in an objection raised by one of the parties in order to preserve an issue for appeal."); United States v. Church, 970 F.2d 401, 409 (7th Cir. 1992) ("Church does not point to any understanding on the record with the trial judge as to whether an objection by counsel for one defendant applies to the other two defendants. Nevertheless, we will treat Surry's objection as preserving the issue for Church.") (citations omitted); Loose v. Offshore Navigation, Inc., 670 F.2d 493, 496–97 (5th Cir. 1982) ("[I]t would seem both dilatory and fatuous for each of the parties to stand in turn and voice its 'me-too.'").

[3] *See infra* § 6.11 (plain error rule).

specific. Another consequence of failing to object is that the admitted evidence becomes part of the trial record and may be considered by the jury in its deliberations, by the trial court in ruling on motions (*i.e.*, directed verdicts), and by a reviewing court determining the sufficiency of the evidence. [4] For example, evidence that could have been excluded as hearsay may be considered for whatever probative value it may possess in the absence of an objection.

Rationale. The objection requirement serves two purposes. First, the objection alerts the trial judge to the nature of the claim of error, thus facilitating a ruling on the objection. [5] Under the adversary system, counsel are presumed to be better acquainted with the facts and issues in the case than is the trial judge, and thus the burden of objecting is cast on the parties through counsel. The judge may not appreciate the irrelevance of an item of evidence when first introduced; counsel should. Second, an objection affords opposing counsel an opportunity to take corrective measures. In response to an objection, for instance, opposing counsel might be able to rephrase the question in unobjectionable terms or withdraw the question and present unobjectionable evidence through another witness.

[A] Specificity: Grounds

Rule 103 requires *specific* objections; that is, a statement of the grounds upon which the objection is based must accompany the objection unless the grounds are apparent from the context. [6] For instance, "objection, hearsay" is a specific objection. In contrast, an objection that is not sufficiently specific is called a *general objection*. Statements such as "I object," "Objection, inadmissible," and "Objection, incompetent" are general objections. They do not highlight the issue for the trial judge. An objection on the ground that evidence is "incompetent, irrelevant, and immaterial" is also a general objection [7] and thus insufficiently specific because virtually every provision of the Rules of Evidence falls under one of these terms. One lawyer even objected "on all the grounds ever known or heard of." [8]

---

[4] *E.g.*, Hastings v. Bonner, 578 F.2d 136, 142–43 (5th Cir. 1978); United States v. Johnson, 577 F.2d 1304, 1312 (5th Cir. 1978); United States v. Jamerson, 549 F.2d 1263, 1266–67 (9th Cir. 1977).

[5] Wilson v. Williams, 182 F.3d 562, 566 (7th Cir. 1999) (en banc) ("Objections alert the judge at critical junctures so that errors may be averted.").

[6] *See* Noonan v. Caledonia Mining Co., 121 U.S. 393, 400 (1887) ("The rule is universal, that where an objection is so general as not to indicate the specific grounds upon which it is made, it is unavailing on appeal . . . . Objections to the admission of evidence must be of such a specific character as to indicate distinctly the grounds upon which the party relies, so as to give the other side full opportunity to obviate them at the time, if, under any circumstances, that can be done.").

[7] *See* Hafner Mfg. Co. v. City of St. Louis, 172 S.W. 28, 31 (Mo. 1914) ("We think the time has come when, for the convenience of apt designation, this stereotyped objection may, without lowering the dignity of our case, be termed the '3 *i's*.' On a similar ground we may say these '*i's*,' like the mere germinating eyes of the potato, see not, and are of little or no sensible use in the administration of justice.").

[8] Johnston v. Clements, 25 Kan. 376, 379 (1881).

All grounds for objection should be specified at the time the objection is made.[9] Generally, a party who has made a specific objection waives all other grounds and therefore cannot assert those grounds in the appellate court. For example, a party who objects on relevance grounds cannot raise hearsay issues on appeal.[10]

"Speaking objections." Some trial judges refuse to permit "speaking objections." Because trial counsel do not want to appear as if they are trying to hide something from the jury, counsel often like to object in a way that the jury understands — for example, "objection, your honor, counsel is putting words in the witness's mouth. This is leading."[11] Sometimes counsel go further, making mini-speeches through this technique. If a judge does not permit reasons for objections to be given, counsel still must get the specific grounds for objection into the record at the first opportunity.

"Apparent from the record." Under Rule 103(a), stating the specific ground for an objection is not necessary if the ground is apparent from the context. However, the risk of relying on an appellate court to find that the ground was obvious from the context is substantial. Trial counsel can never assume that an appellate court will later find that the grounds are "apparent."

[B]　Specificity: Parts of Documents

Although not explicitly stated in Rule 103, the specificity requirement further demands that counsel indicate which particular portion of evidence is objectionable.[12] This aspect of the specificity requirement is rarely important with testimonial evidence because counsel is required to object immediately, but it arises frequently with documentary evidence — for example, only one page of a ten-page document may contain inadmissible hearsay.[13]

---

[9] *See* United States v. Gomez-Norena, 908 F.2d 497, 500 (9th Cir. 1990) ("[A] party fails to preserve an evidentiary issue for appeal not only by failing to make a specific objection, but also by making the *wrong* specific objection . . . .") (citations omitted).

[10] There is a division of authority where the objection is sustained on the wrong grounds. *See* Morgan, Basic Problems of Evidence 54 (1962) ("If a specific objection is sustained and the specified defect does not exist but other defects do exist, there is a conflict in the decisions as to whether the ruling calls for reversal. If the other defect is incurable, there is general agreement that it would be absurd to reverse, for on a new trial the appropriate objection would be made and the court would have to sustain it.").

[11] *Speaking Objections*, McElhaney's Trial Notebook 227 (2d ed. 1987) ("Objection, your honor, the jury cannot tell if someone who is not a witness was telling the truth. This is hearsay.").

[12] *See* Dente v. Riddell, Inc., 664 F.2d 1, 2 n. 1 (1st Cir. 1981) ("Dente at no point specifically objected to, or even identified, the other references which he now contends fell within the court's ruling."); State v. Fox, 12 N.E.2d 413, 417 (Ohio 1938) ("Whenever evidence is offered which is only partially objectionable, the complaining party must point out the objectionable portion specifically.").

[13] *Cf.* Old Chief v. United States, 519 U.S. 172, 179 n. 4 (1997) ("We see no impediment in general to a district court's determination, after objection, that some sections of a document are relevant within the meaning of Rule 401, and others irrelevant and inadmissible under Rule 402.").

[C] "Continuing" or "Running" Objections

Many jurisdictions recognize "continuing objections," which remove the need to object repeatedly to a line of testimony after an adverse ruling on an earlier objection based on the same issue. If the trial judge, for instance, overrules an objection to fingerprint testimony from one expert, it often seems both a waste of time and unnecessarily disruptive to make the same objection to a second fingerprint expert.

Caution, however, demands periodic statements on the record that the prior objection still pertains; otherwise, counsel runs the risk that an appellate court may construe a continuing failure to object as a waiver.[14] Moreover, continuing objections do not work when resolution of the issue depends on the specific context of each part of the testimony. As one court has observed: "At times, a continuing objection is enough to preserve error. However, it was not sufficient in this case. The existence of the marital privilege turns on the specific circumstances surrounding each allegedly privileged communication, *e.g.*, whether a third party was present. Thus, appellant had to object specifically so the circumstances could be determined."[15]

[D] Timeliness of Objections

Rule 103(a)(1) requires that objections be *timely*. If a question is improper, an objection should be made with reasonable promptness — perhaps, the term "immediately" is a more accurate description of this requirement.[16] With documentary evidence, the objection should be made when the document is proffered as an exhibit.[17] The rationale for this rule is that counsel should not be permitted to wait and see whether the answer is favorable before raising an objection.

---

[14] The scope of the continuing objection is limited to that of the initial objection. *See* United States v. Gomez-Norena, 908 F.2d 497, 501 n. 2 (9th Cir. 1990) ("A continuing objection serves only to obviate repeated objections to evidence admitted within the scope of the court's specific evidentiary ruling.").

[15] State v. Henness, 679 N.E.2d 686, 693 (Ohio 1997) (citation omitted).

[16] Although some courts suggest that this rule is not rigid, in the run-of-the-mill cases, the objection needs to be nearly contemporaneous. *See* Jones v. Lincoln Elec. Co., 188 F.3d 709, 727 (7th Cir. 1999) ("[W]e do not believe it to always be the case that an objection has to be perfectly contemporaneous with the challenged testimony in order to satisfy Rule 103(a) and be considered 'timely.' Instead, an objection can still be deemed 'timely' if it is raised within a sufficient time after the proffer of testimony so as to allow the district court an adequate opportunity to correct any error. . . . [P]etitioning the court to strike testimony offered by a witness at the close of that witness's testimony or prior to the start of the proceedings on the very next day when the witness was the last to testify on the preceding day, is a much closer question. In such a situation, the district court can certainly correct any error by issuing a limiting or curative instruction while the testimony is still relatively fresh in the mind of the jurors."); Hutchinson v. Groskin, 927 F.2d 722, 725 (2d Cir. 1991) ("Although an objection should be made after the question has been asked but before an answer has been given, this rule is not inflexible.").

[17] *See* United States v. Benavente Gomez, 921 F.2d 378, 385 (1st Cir. 1990) ("Cerda did not object to the toll record at the time it was admitted.").

[1] Motions to Strike

In some instances, a witness may answer before counsel can object, or a question's tendency to elicit an objectionable response will not become apparent until the response is given. For example, if the prosecutor asks a witness in a homicide prosecution if that witness knows the accused (a typical preliminary question) and the witness replies: "Sure, I know that lying killer," a motion to strike should be made.[18] If a motion to strike is granted, the court should *instruct* the jury to disregard the evidence. Even though the jury has heard the answer, it is nevertheless important to ask the trial judge to strike the response because such a ruling precludes opposing counsel from referring to the stricken material in closing argument. If the objectionable material is so prejudicial (as in the above example), counsel may also ask for a mistrial.[19]

[2] "Connecting up"

Sometimes evidence is admitted *conditionally*. This would typically occur if several witnesses are needed to lay a proper foundation for admissibility. Obviously, only one witness can testify at a time.[20] If a trial court conditionally admits evidence subject to its being "connected up" later in the trial, a motion to strike is required to remove the evidence from jury consideration in the event the "connecting up" evidence is never introduced. In *Huddleston v. United States*,[21] the Supreme Court observed: "Often the trial court may decide to allow the proponent to introduce evidence concerning a similar act, and at a later point in the trial assess whether sufficient evidence has been offered to permit the jury to make the requisite finding. If the proponent has failed to meet this minimal standard of proof, the trial court must instruct the jury to disregard the evidence."[22] Here again, the burden is on the opponent to raise the objection at the close of the other side's case.

---

[18] If a motion to strike is sustained by the trial judge, the stricken material *remains* in the transcript, but it cannot be used by the jury. Stated another way, the material is stricken from jury consideration but not physically from the record. Every word of the trial should be in the record. Judges sometimes go "off the record" to discuss scheduling and other issues, but counsel must assure that important issues are in fact made part of the record. Otherwise, there may be no basis for an appeal.

[19] Under the Double Jeopardy Clause, a mistrial based on a defense request does not preclude the prosecution from retrying the accused. Only if the prosecution takes prejudicial action with the intent to provoke a request for a mistrial is a subsequent trial prohibited. *See generally* Dressler, Understanding Criminal Procedure § 32[C] (3d ed. 2002).

[20] For example, three police officers who sequentially handled a murder weapon from the crime scene may be needed to establish a chain of custody. The foundation for admissibility would not be complete until the third officer testified. Thus, although the weapon should be marked for identification and identified by the first two officers, it would not be admitted as an *exhibit* until the final officer testified. Or, the court could *conditionally* admit it during the testimony of the first officer, subject to later "connecting up." *See infra* § 26.02[C] (chain of custody).

[21] 485 U.S. 681 (1988).

[22] *Id.* at 690.

[3] Motions to Suppress

For some purposes, "timeliness" requires that an objection be made prior to trial. For example, objections in criminal cases based on violations of constitutional rights must often be made in the form of pretrial motions to suppress. Confessions allegedly obtained in violation of *Miranda* are an example.[23] Identifications made at lineups, showups (one-on-one confrontations), or photographic displays, if challenged on right to counsel[24] and due process[25] grounds, are another illustration, as are the fruits of an unconstitutional search or seizure in violation of Fourth Amendment rights.[26] The Rules of Criminal Procedure require that motions to suppress illegally obtained evidence be made prior to trial.[27]

[4] Depositions

Objections to deposition testimony are also subject to special timeliness requirements. The Rules of Civil Procedure provide that objections which might have been obviated if made at the time of the deposition cannot be raised later.[28] The rationale is fairness. Had the objection been made at the deposition, the opposing party may have been able to rephrase the question and elicit admissible evidence. That opportunity may now be gone.

§ 6.03   Offers of Proof: Rule 103(a)(2)

When evidence has been *excluded* by a trial court ruling, Rule 103(a)(2) requires an offer of proof to preserve the issue for appeal.[29] Without an offer of proof in the trial record, an appellate court cannot determine whether or not the action of the trial court was erroneous.[30] Unlike the

---

[23] Miranda v. Arizona, 384 U.S. 436 (1966). Other constitutional grounds for challenging the admissibility of confessions include due process and the right to counsel under the Sixth Amendment. *See* Brewer v. Williams, 430 U.S. 387 (1977).

[24] Moore v. Illinois, 434 U.S. 220 (1977); Kirby v. Illinois, 406 U.S. 682 (1972).

[25] Manson v. Brathwaite, 432 U.S. 98 (1977); Neil v. Biggers, 409 U.S. 188 (1972).

[26] Mapp v. Ohio, 367 U.S. 643 (1961).

[27] Fed. R. Crim. P. 12(b)(3) (motions to suppress); Fed. R. Crim. P. 12(f) ("Effect of Failure To Raise Defenses or Objections. Failure by a party to raise defenses or objections or to make requests which must be made prior to trial, at the time set by the court pursuant to subdivision (c), or prior to any extension thereof made by the court, shall constitute waiver thereof, but the court for cause shown may grant relief from the waiver.").

[28] Fed. R. Civ. P. 32(d)(3)(A) ("Objections to the competency of a witness or to the competency, relevancy, or materiality of testimony are not waived by failure to make them before or during the taking of the deposition, unless the ground of the objection is one which might have been obviated or removed if presented at that time.").

[29] *See* Inselman v. S & J Operating Co., 44 F.3d 894, 896 (10th Cir. 1995) ("Error may not be based on a ruling excluding evidence unless 'the substance of the evidence was made known to the court by offer [of proof] or was apparent from the context within which questions were asked.'") (citation omitted).

[30] *See* United States v. Adams, 271 F.3d 1236, 1241 (10th Cir. 2001) ("A twofold purpose underlies these required showings. First, an effective offer of proof enables the trial judge to make informed decisions based on the substance of the evidence. Second, an effective offer

situation involved with objections, here there is simply nothing in the record.[31] In addition, counsel must state the theory of admissibility as well as the content of the excluded evidence.[32]

The offer of proof should be made out of the hearing of the jury because an offer in front of the jury informs the jury of the nature of excluded evidence, thus defeating the purpose underlying the judge's decision to exclude. A sidebar conference at the judge's bench or a hearing in the jury's absence may be used for this purpose.[33] Although the trial judge may control *when* an offer of proof may be made (*e.g.*, at a hearing without the jury), a party cannot be precluded from making an offer of proof. Counsel who is prevented from making an offer of proof orally at trial should submit a written motion as soon as possible in order to make a record.

[A] Form of Offer of Proof

An offer of proof may take several forms. First, an offer of *testimonial* evidence often takes the form of a statement by counsel as to the expected content of the excluded testimony. There is, however, a real danger that such an offer will be inadequate.[34] Second, the trial court may require or be asked to take the "offer" by an examination of the witness, including cross-examination.[35] For example, some of the early DNA evidence cases involved several weeks of expert testimony before a decision on admissibility was made.[36] Third, an affidavit (which requires an oath) summarizing

---

of proof creates a clear record that an appellate court can review to determine whether there was reversible error in excluding the [testimony].") (citations and internal quotation marks omitted).

[31] When an objection is overruled, the contested evidence is in the record; it simply needs to be identified by a specific objection for the appellate court to review.

[32] *See Adams*, 271 F.3d at 1241 ("In order to qualify as an adequate offer of proof, the proponent must, first, describe the evidence and what it tends to show and, second, identify the grounds for admitting the evidence."); Porter-Cooper v. Dalkon Shield Claimants Trust, 49 F.3d 1285, 1287 (8th Cir. 1995) ("Such a statement is not an adequate offer of proof. An offer of proof is inadequate if '[t]here is nothing in the offer that would apprise the district court that the proffered testimony was anything but cumulative.'") (citation omitted).

[33] *See infra* § 6.10 (hearings outside jury's presence).

[34] *See Adams*, 271 F.3d at 1241–42 ("On numerous occasions we have held that merely telling the court the content of . . . proposed testimony is not an offer of proof. . . . In this case, the colloquy between counsel and the district court was so lacking in detail that it is difficult to decipher why exclusion of the evidence might be error. . . . An offer of proof of testimony by counsel is the least favored method because of its potential to fall short of the standard required by the rules of evidence. . . .") (citations and internal quotation marks omitted).

[35] *See* Fed. R. Evid. 103(b) (Trial court "may direct the making of an offer in question and answer form."). *See also Adams*, 271 F.3d at 1241 ("The question and answer method necessitates excusing a jury, but this concern is not present when the offer of proof is made, as here, at a pretrial motion hearing.").

[36] *See* United States v. Yee, 134 F.R.D. 161, 168 (N.D. Ohio 1991) ("hearings were held for approximately six weeks"); People v. Castro, 545 N.Y.S.2d 985, 986 (Sup. Ct. 1989) ("This hearing took place over a twelve week period producing a transcript of approximately five thousand pages.").

the witness's expected testimony and signed by the witness is another way to make an offer of proof.[37] Finally, excluded *documentary* evidence should be "marked for identification" and appended to the record of trial.[38]

[B] Exceptions to Offer-of-Proof Requirement

There are several exceptions to the offer of proof requirement. First, an offer is not necessary when the substance of the excluded evidence is "apparent from the context within which questions were asked."[39] However, trial counsel can never assume that an appellate court will later find that the substance of the offer is obvious from the context; counsel must make the record. Second, although not explicitly stated in Rule 103, more leeway is typically given to the cross-examiner. Frequently, a cross-examiner, conducting a proper but exploratory examination, will be unable to state what the witness would have said if permitted to answer.[40] In such cases, to require an offer of proof would be impracticable and unfair.[41] Third, the offer of proof requirement is subject to the plain error doctrine.[42]

§ 6.04 Motions in Limine

The term motion in limine means "at the threshold."[43] It is a *pretrial* request for a preliminary decision on an objection or offer of proof. Although the Federal Rules do not explicitly mention motions in limine, their use

---

[37] *See Adams*, 271 F.3d at 1242.

[38] Every document or item of real evidence (*e.g.*, murder weapon) should be marked for identification (*e.g.*, "prosecution exhibit 1 for identification" or "defense exhibit A for identification") as soon as it is used at trial so that an appellate court may ascertain the nature of the exhibit, even if the exhibit is excluded as evidence. A copy of the document or a picture of real evidence is typically appended to the record of trial. If the item is later admitted into evidence, the phrase "for identification" is deleted, and it may be referred to as "prosecution exhibit 1" or "defense exhibit A."

[39] Fed. R. Evid. 103(a)(2). *See* Beech Aircraft v. Rainey, 488 U.S. 153, 174 & n. 22 (1988) ("Although, as is frequently the case in the heat of a trial, counsel did not explain the evidentiary basis of his argument as thoroughly as might ideally be desired, we are satisfied that he substantially satisfied the requirement of putting the court on notice as to his concern."; "Surely the degree of precision with which counsel is required to argue must be judged, among other things, in accordance with the leeway the court affords him in advancing his argument.").

[40] *See* Alford v. United States, 282 U.S. 687, 692 (1931) ("Counsel often cannot know in advance what pertinent facts may be elicited on cross-examination. For that reason it is necessarily exploratory; and the rule that the examiner must indicate the purpose of his inquiry does not, in general, apply.").

[41] *See* Cal. Evid. Code § 354(c) (not requiring objection and offer of proof when the "evidence was sought by questions asked during cross-examination").

[42] *See infra* § 6.11 (plain error rule).

[43] *See* Luce v. United States, 469 U.S. 38, 40 n. 2 (1984) ("'In limine' has been defined as '[o]n or at the threshold; at the very beginning; preliminarily.' Black's Law Dictionary 708 (5th ed. 1979). We use the term in a broad sense to refer to any motion, whether made before or during trial, to exclude anticipated prejudicial evidence before the evidence is actually offered.").

is now common.[44] The trial court's authority to consider these motions is found in Rule 611(a), which recognizes the court's general authority to control the presentation of evidence.[45] Moreover, the 2000 amendment to Rule 103 (definitive ruling "either at or *before* trial") implicitly recognizes motions in limine.[46] Whether the trial court decides to make a pretrial ruling or postpone a ruling until trial is a matter of discretion. The ruling may also be tentative.[47]

"Conclusive pretrial rulings on evidence . . . permit the parties to adjust their trial strategy in light of the court's decisions."[48] Moreover, even if a ruling on a motion in limine is postponed until trial, it serves an important function. The motion may prohibit opposing counsel from attempting to introduce the evidence or from referring to it in the opening statement until the trial court has ruled finally on its admissibility.

[A] "Definitive" Rulings

Rule 103(a) was amended in 2000 to include the following statement: "Once the court makes a definitive ruling on the record admitting or excluding evidence, either at or before trial, a party need not renew an objection or offer of proof to preserve a claim of error for appeal."[49] The amendment makes clear that if a trial judge makes a definitive ruling in response to a motion in limine, a party need not object or make an offer of proof *at trial*.[50] According to the federal drafters, "When the ruling is

---

[44] *See* Ohler v. United States, 529 U.S. 753, 754 (2000); Luce v. United States, 469 U.S. 38, 41 n. 4 (1984) ("Although the Federal Rules of Evidence do not explicitly authorize in limine rulings, the practice has developed pursuant to the district court's inherent authority to manage the course of trials.").

[45] Fed. R. Evid. 611(a) ("The court shall exercise reasonable control over the mode and order of interrogating witnesses and presenting evidence . . . .").

[46] *See* Fed. R. Evid. 103 advisory committee's note (2000) ("The amendment applies to all rulings on evidence whether they occur at or before trial, including so-called '*in limine*' rulings.").

[47] *See* Wilson v. Williams, 182 F.3d 562, 565–66 (7th Cir. 1999) (en banc) ("[I]f the judge's pretrial ruling is tentative — if, for example, the judge says that certain evidence will be admitted unless it would be unduly prejudicial given the way the trial develops — then later events may lead to reconsideration, and the litigant adversely affected by the ruling must raise the subject later so that the judge may decide whether intervening events affect the ruling. An appeal in such a case without an objection at trial would bushwhack both the judge and the opponent. Objections alert the judge at critical junctures so that errors may be averted. When a judge has made a conditional, contingent, or tentative ruling, it remains possible to avert error by revisiting the subject.").

[48] *Id.* at 566.

[49] Fed. R. Evid. 103(a) (last paragraph).

[50] *See Wilson*, 182 F.3d at 566 ("Definitive rulings, however, do not invite reconsideration. When the judge makes a decision that does not depend on how the trial proceeds, then an objection will not serve the function of ensuring focused consideration at the time when decision is best made. A judge who rules definitively before trial sends the message that the right time has come and gone. An objection is unnecessary to prevent error, and it may do little other than slow down the trial. Sometimes an objection or offer of proof will alert the jury to the very thing that should be concealed. . . . Motions *in limine* are designed to avoid the delay

definitive, a renewed objection or offer of proof at the time the evidence is offered is more a formalism than a necessity."[51]

Not all states follow this practice. Some require the party to renew the objection or offer of proof at trial. Failure to do so results in forfeiting the issue on appeal.

[B] Motions to Suppress Compared

Motions in limine are *somewhat* like motions to suppress in criminal cases, except they are not mandatory, whereas motions to suppress typically are.[52] As noted above, suppression motions are usually associated with challenges to the admissibility of evidence on *constitutional* grounds. If a motion to suppress is not made pretrial, the issue is forfeited. In contrast, failure to move in limine does not preclude an objection or offer of proof at trial.

§ 6.05 Required Testimony: *Luce v. United States*

The Supreme Court has engrafted additional requirements onto Rule 103. In *Luce v. United States*,[53] a drug defendant moved in limine to prevent the prosecution from using his prior conviction to impeach him under Rule 609(a).[54] The trial court denied the motion but indicated that the content of Luce's trial testimony might affect its ruling. Luce, who did not testify at trial, was convicted and appealed. The Supreme Court ruled that Luce had not preserved the issue for appeal because he had failed to testify.[55]

The Court gave two reasons for its ruling. First, Rule 609(a) requires the trial court to balance the probative value of the prior conviction for impeachment purposes against its prejudicial effect. Such an evaluation, in the Court's view, is impossible without knowing the precise nature of the defendant's testimony. Second, if the trial court's decision to admit the evidence is erroneous, an appellate court is handicapped in making the required *harmless error* determination without knowing the nature of the defendant's testimony.[56] Consequently, if the motion in limine is denied,

---

and occasional prejudice caused by objections and offers of proof at trial; they are more useful if they can serve these purposes, which they do only if objections (and offers of proof) can be foregone safely.").

[51] Fed. R. Evid. 103 advisory committee's note (2000). The drafters also noted that the burden is "on counsel to clarify whether an in limine or other evidentiary ruling is definitive when there is doubt on that point." *Id.*

[52] *See supra* note 27.

[53] 469 U.S. 38 (1984).

[54] Impeachment by prior conviction is one type of untruthful character impeachment. *See infra* § 22.08 (prior conviction).

[55] 469 U.S. at 43 ("We hold that to raise and preserve for review the claim of improper impeachment with a prior conviction, a defendant must testify.").

[56] *See infra* § 6.12 (harmless error).

the defendant must testify (and be impeached with the prior conviction) to preserve the issue for appeal.[57]

Lower courts have extended the *Luce* requirement to other evidentiary objections in addition to those based on Rule 609.[58]

§ 6.06   "Drawing the Sting": *Ohler v. United States*

A common trial tactic, known as "drawing the sting," involves bringing out adverse information during direct examination if counsel knows that it will be introduced by the opponent during cross-examination. This tactic is designed to reduce the impact of the adverse evidence on the jury; acknowledgment of such evidence on direct examination makes counsel appear more forthright, and preemptive disclosure is better than providing the cross-examiner with a dramatic opportunity to introduce it.

In *Ohler v. United States*,[59] the Supreme Court put a high price on this tactic. In that case, the prosecution filed a motion in limine seeking to use the defendant's prior conviction for impeachment. The district court ruled that, if the defendant testified, her prior conviction would be admissible to impeach under Rule 609(a). The defendant testified and during direct examination acknowledged her prior conviction. On appeal, the defendant argued that the trial court erred in allowing the prior conviction to be used for impeachment. The Supreme Court began its opinion with the observation that "[g]enerally, a party introducing evidence cannot complain on appeal that the evidence was erroneously admitted."[60] The Court found that Rule 103 did not change this result. "The Rule does not purport to determine when a party waives a prior objection, and it is silent with respect to the effect of introducing evidence on direct examination, and later

---

[57] The federal drafters made clear that the 2000 amendment to Rule 103 does not affect the rule in *Luce*. *See* Fed. R. Evid. 103 advisory committee's note (2000) ("Nothing in this amendment is intended to affect the rule set forth in *Luce v. United States* . . . and its progeny. The amendment provides that an objection or offer of proof need not be renewed to preserve a claim of error with respect to a definitive pretrial ruling. *Luce* answers affirmatively a separate question: whether a criminal defendant must testify at trial in order to preserve a claim of error predicated upon a trial court's decision to admit the defendant's prior conviction for impeachment.").

[58] *See* United States v. Bond, 87 F.3d 695, 700 (5th Cir. 1996) ("Bond also attacks the magistrate judge's statements from the bench, in effect a ruling on a motion in limine, that if Bond took the stand to testify regarding the terms of his plea bargain, he would waive his privilege against self-incrimination with regard to all grounds asserted in his motion to withdraw. We hold that Bond has failed to preserve this issue for appellate review. . . . This case does not involve Rule 609(a), but courts have refused to limit *Luce* to Rule 609(a) cases and have instead applied its principles to analogous contexts."); United States v. Goldman, 41 F.3d 785, 788 (1st Cir. 1994) ("Although *Luce* involved impeachment by conviction under Rule 609, the reasons given by the Supreme Court for requiring the defendant to testify apply with full force to the kind of Rule 403 and 404 objections that are advanced by Goldman in this case."); United States v. Weichert, 783 F.2d 23, 25 (2d Cir. 1986) (*Luce* analysis bars review of alleged error permitting impeachment with "bad acts" under Rule 608(b) because defendant never testified).

[59] 529 U.S. 753 (2000).

[60] *Id.* at 755.

assigning its admission as error on appeal."[61] The Court also noted that "both the Government and the defendant in a criminal trial must make choices as the trial progresses," and one example is that "[t]he defendant must choose whether to introduce the conviction on direct examination and remove the sting or take her chances with the prosecutor's possible elicitation of the conviction on cross-examination."[62] Moreover, any possible harm flowing from a district court's *in limine* ruling permitting impeachment by a prior conviction is speculative until "the Government exercises its option to elicit the testimony."[63]

As noted above, the Supreme Court stated that the prosecution also must make choices, *i.e.*, whether or not to introduce a certain item of evidence. However, unlike the defense, the prosecutor must consider two critical factors. First, the prosecution has a very high burden of proof and, in most jurisdictions, must obtain a unanimous verdict from twelve jurors. Many defense counsel consider a hung jury, even though it will result in a mistrial and possible retrial, a victory. Second, the prosecution will be foreclosed from appealing an acquittal due to the Supreme Court's double jeopardy jurisprudence. In contrast, a conviction and reversal on appeal does not preclude a retrial. Thus, all the incentives for the prosecution point to introducing all available evidence. There are, of course, exceptions. A prosecutor may forego introducing evidence for tactical reasons, *e.g.*, to make the case more understandable. Or, when there are numerous witnesses on an issue, the best witnesses may be selected. Nevertheless, the incentive structure pressures the prosecutor to introduce all its evidence, especially in this context.

§ 6.07 Invited Error Rule

The "invited error" doctrine is another waiver rule.[64] This rule prohibits a party who induces error in the trial court from taking advantage of the error on appeal.[65] For example, if counsel elicits testimony, over objection, she cannot complain that it is hearsay on appeal. Similarly, if counsel brings out polygraph results when questioning a witness, counsel will not be permitted to object that polygraph evidence is inadmissible. However, as one has noted, "invited error must be more than mere 'acquiesence in the trial judge's erroneous conclusion.'"[66]

---

[61] *Id.* at 756.

[62] *Id.* at 758.

[63] *Id.* at 759.

[64] *Ohler* is a type of "invited error" case. In that case, however, the defense did not offer the evidence until after it had tried unsuccessfully to have it excluded via the motion in limine.

[65] *See* All American Life and Cas. Co. v. Oceanic Trade Alliance Council Int'l, Inc., 756 F.2d 474, 479 (6th Cir. 1985) ("Under the 'invited error' doctrine, it is an accepted matter of law that where the injection of allegedly inadmissible evidence is attributable to the action of the party seeking to exclude that evidence, its introduction does not constitute reversible error.").

[66] State v. Campbell, 738 N.E.2d 1178, 1188 (Ohio 2000).

§ 6.08 Meeting "Fire with Fire"

Sometimes one party introduces irrelevant or incompetent evidence.[67] Should the other side be permitted to answer "in kind"? ("Fighting fire with fire" is the metaphor often employed in this context.) The question here is whether such a response should be considered a waiver of any objection that had been raised. For example, should cross-examination on a subject to which the cross-examiner had previously objected waive the objection? If waiver results, the objecting party is put to a difficult and unfair choice between preserving the alleged error for appeal or cross-examining the witness. In addition, such a rule may not serve judicial economy. To preserve the issue for appeal, a party may forego cross-examining the witness. If the cross-examination would have succeeded in destroying the credibility of the witness, the need for an appeal might have been obviated.[68]

"Opening the door." A related but distinct notion is sometimes known as "opening-the-door." Here, however, no impermissible conduct is involved. For example, a general rule prohibits the prosecution from introducing evidence of the accused's character, but Rule 404(a)(1) explicitly permits the defendant to introduce evidence of her character.[69] However, once the defense offers character evidence, the prosecution may offer rebuttal evidence. The defense has "opened the door" to character evidence.

§ 6.09 Record of Offer & Ruling: FRE 103(b)

Making the record is one of trial counsel's most important responsibilities. If the court does not make a decision, it is assumed that the court overruled an objection. It is counsel's responsibility to ensure that all objections and offers of proof are recorded. Off–the–record objections are typically insufficient.[70] Failure to request that all pretrial conferences, sidebars, or hearings without the jury be recorded precludes the defendant from asserting that the record is inadequate for appellate review.[71]

Rule 103(b) permits the trial court to add to the record any further statement about an objection, offer of proof, or the court's ruling. According to the federal drafters, the purpose of this provision is "to reproduce for an

---

[67] The other side may have failed to object or the judge may have overruled the objection.

[68] 1 Wigmore, Evidence § 18, at 838 n. 37 (Tillers rev. 1983).

[69] *See infra* § 10.04 (accused's character).

[70] *See* United States v. Johnson, 542 F.2d 230, 234 n.8 (5th Cir. 1976) ("Appellant's manner of preserving the point for appeal was irregular. No objection was ever made on the record. Instead, the objection was made and overruled in chambers with the court reporter absent. . . . If it is necessary to hear an objection outside the presence of the jury, this can be done without depriving this court of a record upon which to base its holding.").

[71] *See* State v. Goodwin, 703 N.E.2d 1251, 1260 (Ohio 1999) ("[The defendant] did not make a pretrial motion to record all sidebars, nor does the record show that counsel for [the defendant] requested that all pretrial or bench conferences be recorded. In the absence of such a request, any possible error is waived."); State v. Keenan, 689 N.E.2d 929, 938 (Ohio 1998) (17 unrecorded sidebars). Appellate Rule 10 provides a method of reconstructing an unrecorded or unavailable record.

appellate court, insofar as possible, a true reflection of what occurred in the trial court."[72] In some cases, trial judges decline to explain a ruling. In *United States v. Dwyer*,[73] for example, the judge refused to provide reasons for excluding evidence. The Second Circuit reversed, stating: "The trial judge's refusal, despite repeated requests, to put his reasons for exclusion on the record substantially impairs our ability to ascertain the source of the 'prejudice' to which he referred in his ruling."[74]

§ 6.10 Hearings Out of the Jury's Presence: FRE 103(c)

As previously noted, the underlying purpose of an exclusionary rule of evidence may be defeated if the jury is exposed to the excluded evidence through an offer of proof or by argument of counsel. Thus, Rule 103(c) requires that discussions involving the admissibility of evidence be held outside the hearing of the jury whenever practicable.[75] The trial judge has discretion to require either a side-bar conference or a hearing without the jury. In addition, evidentiary issues may be raised prior to trial, either at a pretrial conference[76] or by means of a motion in limine.[77]

§ 6.11 Plain Error Rule: FRE 103(d)

Federal Rule 103(d) recognizes the plain error doctrine, under which an appellate court may consider an evidentiary error despite a party's failure to make an objection, a motion to strike, or an offer of proof at trial.[78] The purpose of this doctrine is to safeguard the right to a fair trial, notwithstanding counsel's failure to object. In short, some errors are simply too great to tolerate — even in the absence of an objection. Criminal Rule 52 specifically recognizes the plain error doctrine in criminal cases.[79] The doctrine has also been applied, although rarely, to civil cases.[80]

Attempts to define the doctrine further have not been particularly helpful — perhaps because no formulae can adequately cover all situations.[81] A

---

[72] Fed. R. Evid. 103 advisory committee's note.

[73] 539 F.2d 924 (2d Cir. 1976).

[74] *Id.* at 928.

[75] *See also* Fed. R. Evid. 104(c) (containing a comparable provision).

[76] Fed. R. Civ. P. 16(c); Fed. R. Crim. P. 17.1. *See supra* 3.02[B] (pretrial conferences).

[77] *See supra* § 6.04 (motions in limine).

[78] As the federal drafters noted, "the application of the plain error rule will be more likely with respect to the admission of evidence than to exclusion, since failure to comply with normal requirements of offers of proof is likely to produce a record which simply does not disclose the error." Fed. R. Evid. 103 advisory committee's note.

[79] Fed. R. Crim. P. 52(b) ("Plain errors or defects affecting substantial rights may be noticed although they were not brought to the attention of the court.").

[80] *See* Fed. R. Evid. 103 advisory committee's note.

[81] *See* United States v. Olano, 507 U.S. 725, 732 (1993) ("Rule 52(b) leaves the decision to correct the forfeited error within the sound discretion of the court of appeals, and the court should not exercise that discretion unless the error seriously affect[s] the fairness, integrity or public reputation of judicial proceedings.") (internal quotation marks omitted).

student once put it this way: "It has got to knock your socks off." The Fifth Circuit was more elaborate, if not more informative, when it wrote: "There are four prerequisites to a finding that the district court committed plain error in admitting specified evidence: (1) an error; (2) that is clear and obvious under current law; (3) that affects the defendant's substantial rights; and (4) that would seriously affect the fairness, integrity or public reputation of judicial proceedings if left uncorrected."[82] Moreover, the Supreme Court has noted that, "because relief on plain-error review is in the discretion of the reviewing court, a defendant has the further burden to persuade the court that the error seriously affected the fairness, integrity or public reputation of judicial proceedings."[83]

In criminal cases, plain error will often come close to ineffective assistance of counsel under the Sixth Amendment right to counsel.[84]

§ 6.12 Harmless Error

In determining whether to reverse a trial court judgment, appellate courts must decide whether an evidentiary error is harmless or prejudicial (reversible). Rule 103(a) provides that a case will not be reversed on appeal because of an erroneous evidentiary ruling unless the ruling involves a "substantial right" and the other procedural requirements of Rule 103, such as timely objection, have been satisfied.[85] The term "substantial right" is not defined in the rule, but it refers to the harmless error doctrine.[86]

Rationale. The harmless error doctrine is based on the common sense acknowledgment that a trial without error is not humanly possible; a trial judge has to make too many decisions, often at the spur of the moment. If the judge erroneously admits a hearsay statement in the third week of a ten-week trial, should the defendant automatically be entitled to a new trial? We simply do not have the resources to insist upon errorless trials. As the Supreme Court has noted in criminal cases, the defendant is entitled to fair trial, not a perfect trial.[87] That is not to say, however, that the rules

---

[82] Tompkins v. Cyr, 202 F.3d 770, 779 (5th Cir. 2000).

[83] United States v. Vonn, 122 S. Ct. 1043, 1048 (2002) (citations and internal quotation marks omitted).

[84] The Supreme Court has long held that the right to counsel includes the right to the effective assistance of counsel.

[85] Plain error, as discussed in the preceding section, must be distinguished from harmless error. Even if there is an objection at trial and thus no need to resort to the plain error doctrine, an appellate court must still determine whether an error is harmless.

[86] *See also* Fed. R. Crim. P. 52(a) ("Any error, defect, irregularity, or variance which does not affect substantial rights shall be disregarded."); Fed. R. Civ. P. 61 ("No error in either the admission or the exclusion of evidence and no error or defect in any ruling or order or in anything done or omitted by the court or by any of the parties is ground for granting a new trial or for setting aside a verdict or for vacating, modifying, or otherwise disturbing a judgment or order, unless refusal to take such action appears to the court inconsistent with substantial justice. The court at every stage of the proceeding must disregard any error or defect in the proceeding which does not affect the substantial rights of the parties.").

[87] Delaware v. Van Arsdall, 475 U.S. 673, 681 (1986) ("As we have stressed on more than one occasion, the Constitution entitles a criminal defendant to a fair trial, not a perfect one.").

governing harmless error are without problems.[88] Anyone reading the appellate opinions on evidentiary issues will quickly come to the conclusion that "reversible error" is a very rare commodity, even in some egregious cases.

Standards. Different harmless error tests are used in criminal and civil cases. In criminal trials, errors involving constitutional rights are judged by a high standard — proof "beyond a reasonable doubt that the error complained of did not contribute to the verdict obtained."[89] The Supreme Court has applied this test in numerous cases.[90] However, some rights are considered "structural" (*e.g.*, right to counsel) and therefore not subject to harmless error analysis. Non-constitutional errors in criminal cases are supposed to be judged by a lower standard.[91] Civil cases have used somewhat different formulations.[92]

One court explained it this way: "A number of factors have guided the courts in their determinations of whether error is harmless, including (1) whether erroneously admitted evidence was the primary evidence relied upon, (2) whether the aggrieved party was nonetheless able to present the substance of its claim, (3) the existence and usefulness of curative jury instructions, (4) the extent of jury argument based on tainted evidence, (5) whether erroneously admitted evidence was merely cumulative, and (6) whether other evidence was overwhelming."[93]

§ 6.13 Appellate Review of Admissibility Decisions

Appellate courts use two different standards in reviewing evidentiary decisions. Frequently, appellate courts use an abuse-of-discretion standard

---

[88] *See* Field, *Assessing the Harmlessness of Federal Constitutional Error — A Process in Need of a Rationale*, 125 U. Pa. L. Rev. 15 (1976); Saltzburg, *The Harm of Harmless Error*, 59 Va. L. Rev. 988 (1973).

[89] Chapman v. California, 386 U.S. 18, 24 (1967). *See generally* Dressler, Understanding Criminal Procedure § 4.03 (3d ed. 2002).

[90] *E.g.*, Delaware v. Van Arsdall, 475 U.S. 673 (1986); Brown v. United States, 411 U.S. 223 (1973).

[91] *See* Kotteakos v. United Staes, 328 U.S. 750, 764–65 (1946) ("If, when all is said and done, the conviction is sure that the error did not influence the jury, or had but very slight effect, the verdict and the judgment should stand, except perhaps where the departure is from a constitutional norm or a specific command of Congress. But if one cannot say, with fair assurance, after pondering all that happened without stripping the erroneous action from the whole, that the judgment was not substantially swayed by the error, it is impossible to conclude that substantial rights were not affected. The inquiry cannot be merely whether there was enough to support the result, apart from the phase affected by the error. It is rather, even so, whether the error itself had substantial influence. If so, or if one is left in grave doubt, the conviction cannot stand.").

[92] *See* ATD Corp. v. Lydall, Inc., 159 F.3d 534, 549 (Fed. Cir. 1998) ("Circuit Courts in civil cases not involving constitutional error have articulated the standard in different ways, *e.g.*, whether it is 'highly probable' that the erroneous admission did not affect the jury verdict, and whether it is 'more probable than not' that the erroneous admission did not affect the jury verdict.") (citing Weinstein's Evidence).

[93] *Id.* at 549-50.

when reviewing a trial court's *application* of an evidentiary rule.[94] For example, in *General Elec. Co. v. Joiner*,[95] the Supreme Court adopted an abuse-of-discretion standard for reviewing a trial court's admissibility decision relating to scientific evidence under Rule 702. The trial court had excluded the evidence, but the abuse-of-discretion standard would have also applied had the evidence been admitted. Indeed, the Court cited a prior decision that had admitted evidence[96] and one that had excluded evidence both were upheld under the abuse-of-discretion standard.[97] Under this standard, a reviewing court may not substitute its judgment for that of the trial court. Consequently, the trial court's decision is rarely reversed on appeal.

Questions concerning the interpretation of an evidence rule, rather than its application in a particular case, are different. This involves a de novo review. In addition, factual decisions are reviewed under a "clearly erroneous" standard.[98]

§ 6.14 Bench Trials

The Rules of Evidence apply in bench trials as well as in jury trials. Nevertheless, appellate courts often recognize a difference between bench and jury trials when it comes to *reviewing* evidentiary decisions.[99] For example, in an early case the Supreme Court wrote:

> In some unimportant particulars, the evidence objected to was not admissible. But where the court decides the fact and the law without the intervention of a jury, the admission of illegal testimony, even if material, is not of itself a ground for reversing the judgment, nor is it properly the subject of a bill of exceptions. If evidence appears to have been improperly admitted, the appellate court will reject it, and proceed to decide the case as if it was not in the record.[100]

---

[94] *See* Old Chief v. United States, 519 U.S. 172 (1997); United States v. Abel, 469 U.S. 45 (1984). *See also* Congress & Empire Spring Co v. Edgar, 99 U.S. 645, 658 (1878) ("Cases arise where it is very much a matter of discretion with the court whether to receive or exclude the evidence; but the appellate court will not reverse in such a case, unless the ruling is manifestly erroneous.").

[95] 522 U.S. 136 (1997).

[96] United States v. Abel, 469 U.S. 45 (1984).

[97] Beech Aircraft Corp. v. Rainey, 488 U.S. 153 (1988).

[98] *E.g.,* Estate of Gryder v. Comm'r, 705 F.2d 336, 338 (8th Cir. 1983) ("[T]he Commissioner was unable to produce the originals of many corporate records, including journals and check-stub books. These records were destroyed by employees of the Internal Revenue Service after Cordial's criminal trial. The Tax Court's finding that these documents were destroyed negligently but not in bad faith is not clearly erroneous; thus, the Commissioner could seek to prove their contents by secondary evidence.").

[99] *See generally* Levin & Cohen, *The Exclusionary Rules in Nonjury Criminal Cases*, 119 U. Pa. L. Rev. 905 (1971); Davis, *An Approach to Rules of Evidence for Nonjury Cases*, 50 A.B.A.J. 723 (1964).

[100] United States v. King, 48 U.S. 833, 854–55 (1849). *See also* Sinclair v. United States, 279 U.S. 749, 767 (1929).

The more fundamental issue is whether the rules of evidence ought to apply in bench trials, if the law of evidence is the product of the jury system.[101] Professor Nance has challenged this view, arguing that many rules are designed to force attorneys to introduce the "best evidence." In short, attorney-control, not jury-control, is the underlying principle.[102] Note also that Civil Rule 52(a) requires findings of fact and conclusions of law in a bench trial.[103]

§ 6.15   Common Law "Exceptions" to Evidence

At common law, objecting to evidence was not sufficient to preserve an issue for appeal. In addition, the party had to "except" after the judge made her ruling.[104] This was at a time when verbatim transcripts were not used and counsel was required to prepare a bill of exceptions for appeal.

By omitting any reference to the common law requirement of "excepting" to the trial court's ruling, Rule 103 follows Criminal Rule 51, which provides: "An exception, at any stage or step of the case or matter, is unnecessary to lay a foundation for review, whenever a matter has been called to the attention of the court by objection, motion, or otherwise, and the court has ruled thereon." A similar provision is found in Civil Rule 46.[105]

§ 6.16   Key Points

Objections. The objection requirement serves two purposes. First, the objection alerts the trial judge to the nature of the claim of error, thus

---

[101] *See* McCormick, *Law and the Future*, 51 Nw. U. L. Rev. 218, 225 (1956) ("[T]here is another great field of litigation in which the vitality of the exclusionary rule is already being drained away. This is the great and ever-growing field of trials by judges without a jury. Here it is true that nominally the jury trial rules of evidence are in effect. Actually, however, they are applied so loosely that they lose much of their restrictive force. The atmosphere of such trials discourages objections. Many experienced judges will admit all evidence, though objected to, if admissibility is debated, with the announcement that questions of admissibility will be reserved until all the evidence is in.").

[102] Nance, *The Best Evidence Principle*, 73 Iowa L. Rev. 227 (1988).

[103] *See also* Fed. R. Crim. P. 23(c) ("In a case tried without a jury the court shall make a general finding and shall in addition, on request made before the general finding, find the facts specially. Such findings may be oral. If an opinion or memorandum of decision is filed, it will be sufficient if the findings of fact appear therein.").

[104] *See* Morgan, Basic Problems of Evidence 54–55 (1962) ("At common law a ruling on evidence is not subject to review on writ of error unless an exception is noted and included in a bill of exceptions.").

[105] Fed. R. Civ. P. 46 ("Formal exceptions to rulings or orders of the court are unnecessary; but for all purposes for which an exception has heretofore been necessary it is sufficient that a party, at the time the ruling or order of the court is made or sought, makes known to the court the action which the party desires the court to take or the party's objection to the action of the court and the grounds therefor; and, if a party has no opportunity to object to a ruling or order at the time it is made, the absence of an objection does not thereafter prejudice the party.").

facilitating a ruling on the objection. Second, an objection affords opposing counsel an opportunity to take corrective measures. In response to an objection, for instance, opposing counsel might be able to rephrase the question in unobjectionable terms or withdraw the question and present unobjectionable evidence through another witness.

Failure to make a *timely* and *specific* objection forfeits the right to raise the issue on appeal. Another consequence of failing to object is that the admitted evidence becomes part of the trial record and may be considered by the jury in its deliberations, by the trial court in ruling on motions (*i.e.*, directed verdicts), and by a reviewing court determining the sufficiency of the evidence.

Specific objections. Rule 103 requires *specific* objections; that is, a statement of the grounds upon which the objection is based must accompany the objection unless the grounds are apparent from the context. For instance, "objection, hearsay" is a specific objection. In contrast, an objection that is not sufficiently specific is called a *general objection*. Statements such as "I object," "Objection, inadmissible," and "Objection, incompetent" are general objections. They do not highlight the issue for the trial judge. There is an exception to the objection requirement in the case of plain error.

Motions to strike. A motion to strike is used when a witness answers before counsel can object, or when a question's tendency to elicit an objectionable response does not become apparent until the response is given. If a motion to strike is granted, the court should *instruct* the jury to disregard the evidence. Even though the jury has heard the answer, it is nevertheless important to ask the trial judge to strike the response because such a ruling precludes opposing counsel from referring to the stricken material in closing argument.

Offers of proof. When evidence has been *excluded* by the trial court, Rule 103(a)(2) requires an offer of proof to preserve the issue for appeal. Without an offer of proof in the trial record, an appellate court cannot determine whether or not the action of the trial court was errorroneous. An offer is not required if there is plain error or when the content of the offer is apparent from the record.

Form of offer of proof. An offer of proof may take several forms. First, an offer of *testimonial* evidence often takes the form of a statement by counsel as to the expected content of the excluded testimony. Second, the trial court may require or be asked to take the "offer" by an examination of the witness, including cross-examination. Third, an affidavit (which requires an oath) summarizing the witness's expected testimony and signed by the witness is another way to make an offer of proof. Finally, excluded *documentary* evidence should be "marked for identification" and appended to the record of trial.

Motions in limine. The term *motion in limine* means "at the threshold." It is a *pretrial* request for a preliminary decision on an objection or offer of proof. Although the Federal Rules do not explicitly mention motions in limine, their use is common. Whether the trial court decides to make a pretrial ruling or postpone a ruling until trial is a matter of discretion, and the ruling may be tentative. However, Rule 103(a) provides: "Once the court makes a definitive ruling on the record admitting or excluding evidence, either at or before trial, a party need not renew an objection or offer of proof to preserve a claim of error for appeal."

In *Luce v. United States*,[106] the Supreme Court ruled that an accused who fails to testify may not appeal a decision to permit impeachment under Rule 609 (prior convictions). Other courts have extended *Luce* to other evidentiary contexts.

In *Ohler v. United States*,[107] the Supreme Court held that an accused who brought out her prior conviction on direct examination ("drawing the sting") may not challenge the admissibility of that evidence on appeal.

"Invited error" is another waiver rule. It prohibits a party who induces error in the trial court from taking advantage of the error on appeal.

Making the record is one of trial counsel's most important responsibilities. If the court does not make a decision, it is assumed that the court overruled an objection. It is counsel's responsibility to ensure that all objections and offers of proof are recorded. Off-the-record objections are typically insufficient.

Plain error. Rule 103(d) recognizes the plain error doctrine, under which an appellate court may consider an evidentiary error despite a party's failure to make an objection, a motion to strike, or an offer of proof at trial. The purpose of this doctrine is to safeguard the right to a fair trial, notwithstanding counsel's failure to object.

Harmless error. In determining whether to reverse a trial court judgment, appellate courts must decide whether an evidentiary error is harmless or prejudicial (reversible). Rule 103(a) provides that a case will not be reversed on appeal because of an erroneous evidentiary ruling unless the ruling involves a "substantial right" and the other procedural requirements of Rule 103, such as timely objection, have been satisfied. The term "substantial right" is not defined in the rule, but it refers to the harmless error doctrine.

Plain error must be distinguished from harmless error. Even if there is an objection at trial and thus no need to resort to the plain error doctrine, the appellate court must still determine whether an evidentiary error is harmless.

Appellate review. Questions concerning the interpretation of an evidence rule rather than its application in a particular case are treated differently. The former involve de novo review, while the latter are reviewed under an abuse-of-discretion standard.

---

[106] 469 U.S. 38 (1984).

[107] 529 U.S. 753 (2000).

Chapter 7

PRELIMINARY QUESTIONS OF ADMISSIBILITY: FRE 104

§ 7.01 Introduction

Once there's an objection, somebody has to determine whether the evidence is admissible or inadmissible. That task falls to the trial judge, and this subject is known as *preliminary questions* of admissibility. Federal Rule 104(a) follows the traditional practice of allocating to the trial judge the responsibility for determining admissibility. Rule 104(b), however, modifies this principle somewhat with respect to preliminary questions involving issues of "conditional relevancy," a topic discussed below.[1]

§ 7.02 Preliminary Questions: General Rule: FRE 104(a)

Pursuant to Rule 104(a), the trial judge decides as a preliminary matter questions concerning the qualifications of a person to be a witness, including the competency of lay witnesses and the qualifications of experts.[2] The court also decides the "existence of a privilege,"[3] whether a statement is hearsay, and whether an exception to the hearsay rule applies.[4] In short, the rule entrusts all decisions concerning the application of evidentiary rules exclusively to the trial court, unless Rule 104(b) applies.[5]

Factual matters. In some instances, a preliminary question concerning admissibility requires either a factual determination or the application of a legal standard. In other instances, the admissibility question requires both. For example, the admissibility of statements falling within the hearsay exception for declarations against interest[6] depends upon the

---

[1] *See infra* § 7.03 (conditional relevancy).

[2] *See also* Daubert v. Merrell Dow Pharm., Inc., 509 U.S. 579, 597 (1993) ("[T]he Rules of Evidence — especially Rule 702 — assign to the trial judge the task of ensuring that an expert's testimony both rests on a reliable foundation and is relevant to the task at hand.").

[3] *See* United States v. Zolin, 491 U.S. 554, 566–68 (1989) (discussing application of Fed. R. Evid. 104(a) in determining whether a communication falls within the crime-fraud exception to the attorney-client privilege).

[4] *See* Bourjaily v. United States, 483 U.S. 171, 175 (1987) ("Petitioner and the Government agree that the existence of a conspiracy and petitioner's involvement in it are preliminary questions of fact that, under Rule 104, must be resolved by the court."; coconspirator exemption to hearsay rule).

[5] *See generally* Morgan, *Functions of Judge and Jury in the Determination of Preliminary Questions of Fact*, 43 Harv. L. Rev. 165 (1929); Maguire & Epstein, *Preliminary Questions of Fact in Determining the Admissibility of Evidence*, 40 Harv. L. Rev. 392 (1927).

[6] Fed. R. Evid. 804(b)(3).

unavailability of the declarant — a question of fact if unavailability is based on the death of the declarant. Admissibility also depends upon whether the statement "possesses the required against-interest characteristics" — the application of a legal standard.[7] Thus, the adage that "the jury decides the facts and the judge decides the law" needs modification; if an admissibility decision turns on a factual issue, the judge decides that issue.

[A]   Application of Evidence Rules

Under Rule 104(a), the trial court is "not bound by the rules of evidence except those with respect to privileges" when ruling on the admissibility of evidence.[8] Accordingly, the judge may consider affidavits and other hearsay information. Several arguments support dispensing with evidentiary rules in this context. First, the rules of evidence are designed principally for jury trials. Second, practical considerations support suspension of the rules. In deciding whether a statement falls within the hearsay exception for declarations against interest, the court must consider the content of the statement (*e.g.*, "I shot Jones") to determine if it is against the declarant's interest.[9]

Privileges. Privileges are treated differently under Rule 104(a); they apply when courts decide preliminary questions.[10] Disclosure of privileged information at any stage would defeat the policy underlying the privilege. However, the Supreme Court rejected a reading of Rule 104(a) that would have precluded the trial judge from examining in camera materials asserted to be protected by the attorney-client privilege to determine whether the crime-fraud exception to the privilege applied.[11]

---

[7] Fed. R. Evid. 104 advisory committee's note.

[8] *See Bourjaily*, 483 U.S. at 181 (The trial court "in making a preliminary factual determination . . . may examine the hearsay statements sought to be admitted."); United States v. Raddatz, 447 U.S. 667, 679 (1980) ("At a suppression hearing, the court may rely on hearsay and other evidence, even though that evidence would not be admissible at trial."); United States v. Matlock, 415 U.S. 164, 172–73 (1974) ("[T]he rules of evidence normally applicable in criminal trials do not operate with full force at hearings before the judge to determine the admissibility of evidence.").

[9] *See* Fed. R. Evid. 104 advisory committee's note ("An item, offered and objected to, may itself be considered in ruling on admissibility, though not yet admitted in evidence. Thus the content of an asserted declaration against interest must be considered in ruling whether it is against interest. Again, common practice calls for considering the testimony of a witness, particularly a child, in determining competency."). *See generally* Maguire & Epstein, *Rules of Evidence in Preliminary Controversies as to Admissibility*, 36 Yale L. J. 1101 (1927).

[10] *See also* Fed. R. Evid. 1101(c) ("The rule with respect to privileges applies at all stages of all actions, cases, and proceedings.").

[11] United States v. Zolin, 491 U.S. 554, 565 (1989) ("We conclude that no express provision of the Federal Rules of Evidence bars such use of *in camera* review, and that it would be unwise to prohibit it in all instances as a matter of federal common law."). *See infra* § 38.11 [A] (crime-fraud exception).

[B] Burden of Proof on Preliminary Issues

Rule 104(a) specifies neither the allocation of the burden of proof on preliminary questions nor the applicable standard of proof. As a general rule, the party offering evidence has the burden of persuasion on preliminary issues. Wigmore stated it this way: "The opponent merely invokes the law; the proponent must make the evidence satisfy the law."[12]

Moreover, as a general rule, the "preponderance of evidence" standard applies.[13] There are, however, exceptions — especially in criminal cases.[14] For example, in lineup cases, the prosecution has the burden to establish that an in-court identification is not tainted by an unconstitutional out-of-court identification. The "clear and convincing" evidence standard applies.[15]

§ 7.03 Conditional Relevancy: FRE 104(b)

Rule 104(b), governing preliminary questions of conditional relevancy, operates as an exception to Rule 104(a).[16] Here, the trial court's function is more limited than under Rule 104(a). The court does not decide such questions using the preponderance-of-evidence standard, as under Rule 104(a). Rather, the trial court determines only if sufficient evidence has been introduced "to support a finding of the fulfillment of the condition." In effect, this is a *prima facie* standard.

---

[12] 1 Wigmore, Evidence § 18, at 841 (Tillers rev. 1983). However, the person asserting a privilege has the burden of persuasion.

[13] Interpreting Rule 104, the Supreme Court has commented:

> We have traditionally required that these preliminary matters be established by a preponderance of proof. Evidence is placed before the jury when it satisfies the technical requirements of the evidentiary Rules, which embody certain legal and policy determinations. The inquiry made by a court concerned with these matters is not whether the proponent of the evidence wins or loses his case on the merits, but whether the evidentiary Rules have been satisfied. Thus, the evidentiary standard is unrelated to the burden of proof on the substantive issues, be it a criminal case or a civil case. The preponderance standard ensures that before admitting evidence, the court will have found it more likely than not that the technical issues and policy concerns addressed by the Federal Rules of Evidence have been afforded due consideration.

Bourjaily, 483 U.S. at 175. *See also* Daubert v. Merrell Dow Pharm., Inc., 509 U.S. 579, 593 n. 10 (1993) (preponderance of evidence standard applies to the admissibility of expert testimony under Fed. R. Evid. 104(a)).

[14] *See generally* Saltzburg, *Standards of Proof and Preliminary Questions of Fact*, 27 Stan. L. Rev. 271 (1975).

[15] United States v. Wade, 388 U.S. 218, 250-51 (1967).

[16] *See* Fed. R. Evid. 104 advisory committee's note ("In some situations, the relevancy of an item of evidence, in the large sense, depends upon the existence of a particular preliminary fact. Thus when a spoken statement is relied upon to prove notice to X, it is without probative value unless X heard it. Or if a letter purporting to be from Y is relied upon to establish an admission by him, it has no probative value unless Y wrote or authorized it. Relevance in this sense has been labeled 'conditional relevancy.' ").

The difference is between a preponderance of evidence and *evidence sufficient for a jury to find a fact by a preponderance of evidence*, a rather subtle difference especially for students encountering it for the first time. For example, if a witness testifies that she could identify a person who was 600 feet away (two football fields), the trial judge would *not* determine that the witness had firsthand knowledge under Rule 602 (a conditional relevance rule). Instead, the judge would determine only if there was sufficient evidence (prima facie) from which reasonable jurors could find firsthand knowledge by a preponderance of evidence. If this lower standard is satisfied, the evidence is admitted for the jury's consideration. The judge does not assess the credibility of the evidence; that is a job for the jury.[17]

Rationale. The allocation of functions between the court and jury that is embodied in the concept of conditional relevancy is based on the concern that entrusting some preliminary questions to the trial judge under the preponderance-of-evidence standard will interfere with the jury's proper role. The federal drafters commented: "If preliminary questions of conditional relevancy were determined solely by the judge, as provided in subdivision (a), the functioning of the jury as a trier of fact would be greatly restricted and in some cases virtually destroyed. These are appropriate questions for juries."[18] Thus, the thrust of the rule is to expand the jury's role with a corresponding modest restriction of the judge's role.

Moreover, unlike rules of competence such as the hearsay rule, there is little danger in permitting the jury to decide such issues. For example, if the jury finds that a witness does not have firsthand knowledge, the jury will disregard the evidence. In contrast, the hearsay rule is far too technical for the jury to apply. Moreover, the hearsay rule is intended to keep unreliable evidence from the jury. Thus, the admissibility of hearsay involves a Rule 104(a) issue.

Examples. Rule 104(b) is a provision of general applicability. Several specific rules represent specialized applications of the conditional relevancy concept. As discussed above, the firsthand knowledge rule is one.[19] Similarly, when ruling on the authentication of a document, the trial court does not decide whether the proffered document is genuine; the court's decision is limited to determining whether there is "evidence sufficient to support a finding that the matter in question is what its proponent claims."[20]

---

[17] *See* United States v. Platero, 72 F.3d 806, 815 (10th Cir. 1995) ("We examine this evidence without weighing its credibility, and conclude that Platero clearly presented sufficient evidence such that 'the jury could reasonably find the conditional fact . . . by a preponderance of the evidence.'") (citation omitted).

[18] Fed. R. Evid. 104 advisory committee's note.

[19] Fed. R. Evid. 602. The trial court does not decide whether a witness has firsthand knowledge; the court decides only whether sufficient evidence has been introduced "to support a finding that the witness has personal knowledge of the matter."

[20] Fed. R. Evid. 901(a). *See infra* § 28.02[A] (authentication). *See also* Ricketts v. City of Hartford, 74 F.3d 1397, 1411 (2d Cir. 1996) ("The district court's determination that it 'was not satisfied that the voice on the tape was that of Davis,' is inconsistent with [Rule 104(b).] So long as a jury is entitled to reach a contrary conclusion, it must be given the opportunity to do so.").

Rule 1008, which defines the functions of the court and jury in applying the best evidence rule, is another example of the conditional relevancy principle. In most instances the trial court, pursuant to Rule 104(a), decides the applicability of the best evidence rule.[21] However, Rule 1008 provides that "when an issue is raised (a) whether the asserted writing ever existed, or (b) whether another writing, recording, or photograph produced at the trial is the original, or (c) whether other evidence of contents correctly reflects the contents, the issue is for the trier of fact to determine as in the case of other issues of fact."

Many conditional relevancy issues are not explicitly addressed in specific rules. For example, the Supreme Court in *Huddleston v. United States*[22] applied Rule 104(b) to determine the accused's involvement in other-acts evidence under Rule 404(b).[23]

The drafters of the Federal Rules specifically noted that problems of conditional relevancy "are to be distinguished from problems of logical relevancy."[24] For example, the written confession of a murder defendant is logically relevant; it has probative value in establishing the identity of the person who committed the murder. The relevancy of the confession, however, depends upon a fact — that the accused wrote or signed the confession, an authentication issue. The issue of logical relevancy is decided by the trial court under Rule 401. In contrast, the authentication issue (genuineness of the document) involves a conditional relevancy issue, and the court's role is somewhat limited; a prima facie standard applies.[25]

"Connecting up." The conditional relevancy concept is also sometimes associated with what litigators refer to as "connecting up." Sometimes the foundation for the admissibility of an item of evidence cannot be laid through the testimony of one witness. In such cases, the trial court will often permit the jury to hear the evidence on the condition that the foundation be laid ("connected up") through later witnesses.[26]

---

[21] See Fed. R. Evid. 1001–1007.

[22] 485 U.S. 681, 690 (1988) ("In determining whether the Government has introduced sufficient evidence to meet Rule 104(b), the trial court neither weighs credibility nor makes a finding that the Government has proved the conditional fact by a preponderance of the evidence. The court simply examines all the evidence in the case and decides whether the jury could reasonably find the conditional fact — here, that the televisions were stolen — by a preponderance of the evidence.").

[23] Thus, in federal trials this issue is treated as an issue of conditional evidence and a prima-facie-evidence standard applies. *See infra* § 11.05 (defendant's participation in the "other act"). Other jurisdictions, however, have not followed this approach. Instead, they require "substantial proof." *See also* Minn. R. Evid. 404(b) (1989) ("such evidence shall not be admitted unless the other crime, wrong, or act and the participation in it by a relevant person are proven by clear and convincing evidence").

[24] Fed. R. Evid. 104 advisory committee's note.

[25] *See* Fed. R. Evid. 901(a).

[26] *See Huddleston*, 485 U.S. at 690 ("Often the trial court may decide to allow the proponent to introduce evidence, and at a later point in the trial assess whether sufficient evidence has been offered to permit the jury to make the requisite finding. If the proponent has failed to meet this minimal standard of proof, the trial court must instruct the jury to disregard the evidence."). *See supra* § 6.02|D||2| ("connecting up").

§ 7.04   Hearing of Jury: FRE 104(c)

[A]   Confessions

Rule 104(c) requires the trial judge to hold a hearing out of the presence of the jury when ruling on the admissibility of a confession. The rule is constitutionally mandated as a result of the Supreme Court's decision in *Jackson v. Denno*.[27] This provision should be invoked rarely because Criminal Rule 12 requires that constitutional challenges to the admissibility of confessions be raised prior to trial by a motion to suppress.[28]

[B]   Other Preliminary Matters

Rule 104(c) also provides that hearings "on other preliminary matters shall also be conducted out of the hearing of the jury when the interests of justice require, or when an accused is a witness and so requests."[29] The language concerning a defense request was added by the House Judiciary Committee because it "believed that a proper regard for the right of an accused not to testify generally in the case dictates that he be given an option to testify out of the presence of the jury on preliminary matters."[30]

§ 7.05   Testimony by Accused: FRE 104(d)

[A]   Scope of Cross-examination

Rule 104(d) limits the scope of cross-examination when a criminal defendant testifies on a preliminary matter; such testimony does not subject the defendant to cross-examination about other issues in the case. "The limitation upon cross-examination is designed to encourage participation by the accused in the determination of preliminary matters. He may testify concerning them without exposing himself to cross-examination generally."[31]

[B]   Trial Use

However, as the drafters indicated, Rule 104(d) does not address the issue of whether the accused's testimony on a preliminary matter may be used

---

[27] 378 U.S. 368, 391 (1964) (Due process requires procedures that are "fully adequate to insure a reliable and clear-cut determination of the voluntariness of the confession, including the resolution of disputed facts upon which the voluntariness issue may depend.").

[28] Fed. R. Crim. P. 12(b)(3)(C).

[29] A similar provision is found in Rule 103(c). That provision, however, does not use the interests-of-justice standard; rather, it requires out-of-court hearings whenever "practicable."

[30] H.R. Rep. No. 650, 93d Cong., 1st Sess. (1973), reprinted in 1974 U.S.C.C.A.N. 7075, 7080.

[31] Fed. R. Evid. 104 advisory committee's note. Rule 611(b) is a trial rule on the scope of cross-examination; it provides: "(b) Scope of cross-examination. Cross-examination should be limited to the subject matter of the direct examination and matters affecting the credibility of the witness."

subsequently at trial. In *Simmons v. United States*,[32] the Supreme Court held that suppression hearing testimony given by a defendant to establish standing to object to illegally seized evidence could not be used against the defendant at trial on the issue of guilt.[33] The Court did not believe that the defendant should have to give up the Fifth Amendment privilege (which is waived by testifying) in order to assert Fourth Amendment rights. Whether the *Simmons* rule extends to the *impeachment* use of suppression hearing testimony has not yet been decided; the Court specifically reserved that question in *United States v. Salvucci*.[34]

In other contexts, the Court has recognized impeachment exceptions. In *Harris v. New York*,[35] the Court held that statements obtained in violation of *Miranda v. Arizona*[36] could be used to impeach a defendant who testifies at trial. Similarly, the Court has permitted the impeachment use of evidence seized in violation of Fourth Amendment[37] and Sixth Amendment rights.[38]

§ 7.06   Weight & Credibility: FRE 104(e)

A basic axiom of trial practice is that the trial judge decides issues of admissibility and the jury decides questions of the *weight* of the evidence and the *credibility* of witnesses. Rule 104(e) makes clear that a court's admissibility ruling does not curtail the right of a party to dispute the reliability of admitted evidence before the jury.

In *Crane v. Kentucky*,[39] the defendant moved to suppress a confession on the grounds that it had been coerced in violation of due process.[40] The trial court determined that the confession was voluntary and denied the motion. At trial, the defendant sought to introduce evidence concerning the psychological and physical environment in which the confession was obtained to show its unreliability. The trial court excluded the evidence because it related to the due process voluntariness issue. Citing Federal Rule 104(e), the Supreme Court stated that the circumstances surrounding the taking of a confession may be relevant to two separate issues, one legal

---

[32] 390 U.S. 377 (1968). *See infra* § 22.10[H] (constitutional issues).

[33] *See also* Brown v. United States, 411 U.S. 223 (1973).

[34] 448 U.S. 83 (1980). *See* ABA Section of Litigation, Emerging Problems Under the Federal Rules of Evidence 17 (3d ed. 1998) ("[M]ost lower courts have held that the accused's preliminary hearing testimony can be used to impeach him should he take the stand at trial.").

[35] 401 U.S. 222 (1971).

[36] 384 U.S. 436 (1966).

[37] *See* United States v. Havens, 446 U.S. 620 (1980); Walder v. United States, 347 U.S. 62 (1954).

[38] *E.g.,* Michigan v. Harvey, 494 U.S. 344 (1990) (right to counsel). *See infra* § 22.10[H] (constitutional issues).

[39] 476 U.S. 683 (1986).

[40] The Supreme Court has long held that involuntary (coercive) confessions violate due process. Although this issue has been overshadowed by *Miranda*, it is still a viable grounds for excluding a confession.

and one factual. The legal issue concerns the constitutional issue of voluntariness, which the court must decide. The factual issue concerns the reliability of the confession, a jury issue. According to the Court, the preclusion of evidence on the latter issue deprived the defendant of a fair trial: "Whether rooted directly in the Due Process Clause of the Fourteenth Amendment, or in the Compulsory Process or Confrontation clauses of the Sixth Amendment, the Constitution guarantees criminal defendants 'a meaningful opportunity to present a complete defense.' "[41]

Similarly, if the trial court finds the existence of a conspiracy, as required by Rule 801(d)(2)(E) to support a ruling on the admissibility of a co-conspirator admission, a conspiracy defendant still may introduce evidence before the jury challenging the existence of the conspiracy.[42] The trial court decides the preliminary question of admissibility using the preponderance of evidence standard. There is no reason to inform the jury of this decision; the jury simply hears the evidence. The jury must apply the beyond-a-reasonable-doubt standard when deciding whether the accused has committed the crime of conspiracy.[43]

§ 7.07 Key Points

Federal Rule 104(a) follows the traditional practice of allocating to the trial judge the responsibility for determining the admissibility of evidence. Rule 104(b), however, modifies this principle somewhat with respect to preliminary questions involving issues of "conditional relevancy."

Factual matters. In some instances, a preliminary question of admissibility requires either a factual determination or the application of a legal standard. In other instances, the admissibility question requires both. For example, the admissibility of statements falling within the hearsay exception for declarations against interest[44] depends upon the unavailability of the declarant — a question of fact if unavailability is based on the death of the declarant. Admissibility also depends upon whether the statement "possesses the required against-interest characteristics" — the application of a legal standard.

Rules of evidence. Under Rule 104(a), the trial court is "not bound by the rules of evidence except those with respect to privileges" when ruling on the admissibility of evidence. Accordingly, the judge may consider affidavits and other hearsay information.

---

[41] 476 U.S. at 690 (citations omitted) (quoting California v. Trombetta, 467 U.S. 479, 485 (1984)).

[42] *See infra* § 32.10 (coconspirator admissions).

[43] *See* ABA Section of Litigation, *Emerging Problems Under the Federal Rules of Evidence* 19 (3d ed. 1998) ("Both judge and jury may use the same evidence and reach different results on different issues. The judge must decide whether the prosecution's evidence satisfies the hearsay exception's requirements, while the jury must decide whether a criminal conspiracy existed.").

[44] Fed. R. Evid. 804(b)(3).

Burden of proof. As a general rule, the party offering evidence has the burden of persuasion on preliminary issues once an objection has been raised. Also as a general rule, the "preponderance of evidence" standard applies.

Conditional relevance. The trial court does not decide such questions using the preponderance-of-evidence standard, as under Rule 104(a). Rather, the trial court determines only if sufficient evidence has been introduced "to support a finding of the fulfillment of the condition." In effect, this is a *prima facie* standard. The difference is between a preponderance of evidence and *evidence sufficient for a jury to find a fact by a preponderance of evidence*, a rather subtle difference.

Weight & credibility. A basic axiom of trial practice is that the trial judge decides issues of admissibility and the jury decides questions of weight and credibility. Rule 104(e) makes clear that a court's admissibility ruling does not curtail the right of a party to dispute the reliability of admitted evidence before the jury.

Chapter 8

LIMITED ADMISSIBILITY: FRE 105

§ 8.01 Introduction

This chapter discusses *"multiple admissibility"* and *"limited admissibility."* In many instances, an item of evidence could be used for multiple purposes. In some cases this is proper. For example, a party's prior inconsistent statement may be admitted for impeachment as a prior inconsistent statement if the party testifies[1] and as substantive evidence as a party admission.[2] Hence, the phrase *"multiple admissibility."*

Frequently, however, evidence may be admissible for one purpose but inadmissible for another purpose. Evidence also may be admissible against one party but not against another party. Both these situations involve *"limited admissibility."* In other words, the evidence is admissible for a limited purpose. In such cases, Federal Rule 105 applies, and the court must, upon request, instruct the jury as to the limited purpose of the evidence.[3] The trial court may also give a *limiting instruction* sua sponte.

Whether a limiting instruction is effective — *i.e.*, whether the jury will be either willing or able to abide by the instruction is often questionable. It is somewhat like trying to unring a bell.[4]

§ 8.02 Evidence Admissible for One Purpose

The concept of limited admissibility is ingrained in evidence law. In *United States v. Abel*,[5] the Supreme Court wrote that "there is no rule of evidence which provides that testimony admissible for one purpose and inadmissible for another purpose is thereby rendered inadmissible; quite the contrary

---

[1] Fed. R. Evid. 613.

[2] Fed. R. Evid. 801(d)(2)(A).

[3] *See* 1 Wigmore, Evidence § 13, at 300 (3d ed. 1940) ("When an evidentiary fact is offered for one purpose, and becomes admissible by satisfying all the rules applicable to it in that capacity, it is not inadmissible because it does not satisfy the rules applicable to it in some other capacity, and because the jury might improperly consider it in the latter capacity. This doctrine, although involving certain risks, is indispensible as a practical rule.").

[4] *See* United States v. Nace, 561 F.2d 763, 768 (9th Cir. 1977) ("The government can argue that the cautionary instructions, running as they did in favor of both defendants, gave Warren more than he was entitled to, and Nace can argue that the cautionary instructions gave him less, as they merely attempted to 'unring a bell' to his real or imaginary prejudice. In the context in which the matter was presented to the court, however, the cautionary instructions were, if not perfect, adequate."). *See infra* § 8.06 (effectiveness of limiting instructions).

[5] 469 U.S. 45 (1984).

is the case."[6] The Federal Rules explicitly address some issues of limited admissibility. Examples include:

Other-acts evidence. Rule 404(b) provides that evidence of other crimes, wrongs, or acts may be admissible for several purposes, including proof of motive, opportunity, intent, or identity. Such evidence, however, "is not admissible to prove the character of a person in order to show action in conformity therewith." A limiting instruction is mandatory upon the request of a party.

Subsequent repairs. Similarly, Rule 407 prohibits the use of evidence of subsequent remedial measures if offered to prove negligence or culpable conduct. The prohibition, however, does not extend to the use of the same evidence "when offered for another purpose, such as proving ownership, control, or feasibility of precautionary measures, if controverted, or impeachment."[7]

Prior inconsistent statements. The doctrine of limited admissibility also applies in many situations that the Federal Rules do not explicitly address. For example, prior inconsistent statements are generally admissible only for the purpose of impeachment.[8] When offered for this purpose, the statement is relevant only because it was made and is inconsistent with the witnesses in-court testimony, not because it was true. If the jury uses the statement for the truth of its content, the hearsay rule is violated. Accordingly, an instruction limiting the jury's use of prior inconsistent statements to impeachment is required if requested.

§ 8.03 Evidence Admissible Against One Party

Under Rule 105, when evidence is admissible against one party, but not another party, a limiting instruction must be given upon request, directing the jury to use the evidence against the proper party. This issue most often arises in joint trials in criminal cases and may raise confrontation issues.[9] For example, suppose upon arrest Schmedlap told the police that "Me and Botz killed Jones." Schmedlap's statements would be admissible against Schmedlap but not Botz.[10]

In *Bruton v. United States,*[11] the Supreme Court ruled that a limiting instruction in a joint trial was insufficient to protect against improper jury

---

[6] *Id.* at 56.

[7] Comparable provisions are found in Fed. R. Evid. 408 (compromises & offers to compromise) and Fed. R. Evid. 411 (liability insurance).

[8] There is an exception for prior inconsistent statements that satisfy the requirements of Rule 801(d)(1)(A).

[9] *See infra* chapter 36 (right of confrontation).

[10] As we will see in the hearsay material, Schmedlap's statement is admissible against Schmedlap as an individual admission under Rule 801(d)(2)(A). However, Schmedlap's statement, if offered for the truth, is hearsay as to Botz. It is not a coconspirator admission because it was made after, not during, the conspiracy. Rule 801(d)(2)(E). Moreover, the part about Botz's involvement in the killing is not against Schmedlap's penal interest and thus not admissible as a declaration against interest. Rule 804(b)(3).

[11] 391 U.S. 123 (1968).

use of one defendant's confession that implicated a codefendant. According to the Court,

> there are some contexts in which the risk that the jury will not, or cannot, follow instructions is so great, and the consequences of failure so vital to the defendant, that the practical and human limitations of the jury system cannot be ignored. Such a context is presented here, where the powerfully incriminating extrajudicial statements of a codefendant, who stands accused side-by-side with the defendant, are deliberately spread before the jury in a joint trial.[12]

Once the Court concluded that there existed a "substantial risk that the jury, despite instructions to the contrary, looked to the incriminating extrajudicial statements in determining Bruton's guilt,"[13] it held that Bruton had been denied his Sixth Amendment right to confrontation because his right to cross-examine the codefendant about the statement had been foreclosed.[14]

There are several ways in which the *Bruton* issue can be obviated.

[A] Severance

First, separate trials avoid the problem raised in *Bruton*. If the codefendants have been properly joined for trial under Criminal Rule 8(b),[15] the proper remedy is a motion to sever for prejudice pursuant to Criminal Rule 14.[16] The trial court has discretion to grant such a motion.[17]

[B] Redaction

Second, the prosecution can delete (redact) all references in the confession that relate to the codefendant.[18] The Supreme Court sanctioned the

---

[12] *Id.* at 135–36.

[13] *Id.* at 126.

[14] In subsequent decisions, the Court held *Bruton* applicable to state trials, Roberts v. Russell, 392 U.S. 293 (1968), and subject to the harmless error doctrine. Harrington v. California, 395 U.S. 250 (1969).

[15] Fed. R. Crim. P. 8(b) ("The indictment or information may charge 2 or more defendants if they are alleged to have participated in the same act or transaction, or in the same series of acts or transactions, constituting an offense or offenses. The defendants may be charged in one or more counts together or separately. All defendants need not be charged in each count.").

[16] Fed. R. Crim. P. 14 ("If it appears that a defendant or the government is prejudiced by a joinder of offenses or of defendants in an indictment or information or by such joinder for trial together, the court may order an election or separate trials of counts, grant a severance of defendants or provide whatever other relief justice requires. In ruling on a motion by a defendant for severance the court may order the attorney for the government to deliver to the court for inspection in camera any statements or confessions made by the defendants which the government intends to introduce in evidence at the trial.").

[17] If codefendants have been improperly joined under Criminal Rule 8(b), the proper remedy is a motion for severance for misjoinder pursuant to Criminal Rules 8 and 12(b)(2). In such cases, the defendant need not show prejudice, and the trial judge must sever.

[18] *See Bruton*, 391 U.S. at 134 n.10.

redaction procedure in *Richardson v. Marsh*.[19] Redaction, however, is not always effective. "There are, of course, instances in which such editing is not possible; the references to the codefendant may be so frequent or so closely interrelated with references to the maker's conduct that little would be left of the statement after editing."[20] For example, in *Gray v. Maryland*,[21] a codefendant's confession in a joint trial had been edited by replacing Gray's name with a blank space or the word "deleted." The Supreme Court found a *Bruton* violation, holding that the revisions were transparent. By using the word "deleted" and by asking the detectives if Gray's arrest was based on the confession, the content of the deletions became clear. "Redactions that simply replace a name with an obvious blank space or a word such as 'deleted' or a symbol or other similarly obvious indications of alteration leave statements that, considered as a class, so closely resemble Bruton's unredacted statements that, in our view, the law must require the same result."[22]

[C] Codefendant's Testimony

Third, the *Bruton* problem is avoided, at least in most instances, if the codefendant testifies at trial. Under these circumstances, the defendant has the opportunity to cross-examine the codefendant on the accuracy of the out-of-court statement, thereby obviating the confrontation issue. The Supreme Court took this position in *Nelson v. O'Neil*.[23] The *Nelson* rationale is inapplicable where both defendants are represented by the same attorney because in such a case cross-examination of the testifying codefendant would present a conflict of interests.[24]

[D] Recognized Hearsay Exception

Finally, the codefendant's confession in *Bruton* was clearly inadmissible under the hearsay as to Bruton.[25] In contrast, if a codefendant's statement

---

[19] 481 U.S. 200, 211 (1987) ("We hold that the Confrontation Clause is not violated by the admission of a nontestifying codefendant's confession with a proper limiting instruction when, as here, the confession is redacted to eliminate not only the defendant's name, but any reference to his or her existence."). *See also* United States v. Tutino, 883 F.2d 1125, 1135 (2d Cir. 1989) ("[A] redacted statement in which the names of co-defendants are replaced by neutral pronouns, with no indication to the jury that the original statement contained actual names, and where the statement standing alone does not otherwise connect co-defendants to the crimes, may be admitted without violating a co-defendant's *Bruton* rights.").

[20] ABA Standards Relating to Joinder and Severance 38 (1967).

[21] 523 U.S. 185 (1998).

[22] *Id.* at 186.

[23] 402 U.S. 622, 629–30 (1971) ("We conclude that where a codefendant takes the stand in his own defense, denies making an alleged out-of-court statement implicating the defendant, and proceeds to testify favorably to the defendant concerning the underlying facts, the defendant has been denied no rights protected by the Sixth and Fourteenth Amendments.").

[24] *See* Courtney v. United States, 486 F.2d 1108 (9th Cir. 1973); Holland v. Henderson, 460 F.2d 978 (5th Cir. 1972).

[25] *Bruton*, 391 U.S. at 128 n.3.

falls within a recognized hearsay exception, such as the conspirator exemption,[26] there is no confrontation violation. The Supreme Court has upheld the constitutionality of this rule.[27] The same result occurs with other hearsay exception.[28]

[E] Other *Bruton* Issues

The Supreme Court has decided several other *Bruton* issues. In *Cruz v. New York*,[29] the Court held that *Bruton* applied to "interlocking confessions" — *i.e.* situations in which both defendants make confessions that are admissible against the speaker.

In *Tennessee v. Street*,[30] one burglary-murder defendant claimed that he was forced to sign a confession that mirrored the confession of his codefendant. The prosecution was allowed to admit the codefendant's confession for the nonhearsay purpose of illustrating the dissimilarities between the two confessions and thus to discredit the defendant's claim: "In short, the State's rebuttal witness against the defendant was not his accomplice, but the sheriff."[31]

§ 8.04   Restricting Evidence to its "Proper Scope"

Rule 105 not only directs the court to give a limiting instruction upon request, it also requires the courts to "restrict the evidence to its proper scope." One purpose of this phrase is to limit counsel's use of the evidence to its proper purpose during closing argument.[32] The argument must be based on evidence adduced at trial.[33]

This provision would also apply to a bench trial, where the court is required to limit its use of the evidence to its proper purposes but where no instruction is given.[34]

---

[26] Fed. R. Evid. 801(d)(2)(E).

[27] Bourjaily v. United States, 483 U.S. 171 (1987); United States v. Inadi, 475 U.S. 387 (1986).

[28] *See* United States v. Vasquez, 857 F.2d 857, 864 (1st Cir. 1988) ("We already have held that *Bruton* does not present an obstacle to admission of a statement otherwise admissible as a spontaneous exclamation [excited utterance].").

[29] 481 U.S. 186 (1987).

[30] 471 U.S. 409 (1985).

[31] *Id.* at 414. Chief Justice Burger concluded that the limiting instruction adequately protected the defendant's legitimate interest in ensuring that the confession was not misused by the jury, and "unlike the situation in *Bruton*, there were no alternatives that would have both assured the integrity of the trial's truth-seeking function and eliminated the risk of the jury's improper use of evidence." *Id.* at 415. Since the sheriff who took both statements was available at trial for questioning, the Court held that a *Bruton* issue was not involved.

[32] *See* United States v. Gross, 511 F.2d 910, 919 (3d Cir. 1975).

[33] *See supra* § 3.05[D].

[34] *See* 21 Wright & Graham, Federal Practice and Procedure § 5067 (1977).

§ 8.05 Procedural Issues

[A] Mandatory & Discretionary Instructions

If Rule 105 applies, the trial court must, upon request of a party, instruct the jury as to the limited purpose of the evidence. Because the rule is written in mandatory language,[35] refusal to instruct is error.[36] A party, however, waives the right to a limiting instruction if the request is not "specific and timely."[37] The trial court may also give a limiting instruction sua sponte.

[B] Timing of Instructions

A limiting instruction may be given either at the time the evidence is admitted or at the close of the case. The language of Rule 105 seems to require that the instruction be given at the time the evidence is introduced.[38] This interpretation is further supported by the rationale underlying Rule 105; the instruction will be more effective at the time of admission. The federal cases, however, have not accepted this reading of the rule: "Although there is some support for the proposition that Rule 105 mandates a contemporaneous limiting instruction when any type of evidence is admitted for a limited purpose, the weight of authority is to the contrary. The timing of Rule 105 limiting instructions with regard to physical evidence is best left to the trial court's discretion."[39]

[C] Failure to Request Instructions

Failure to request a limiting instruction constitutes a waiver of the issue, except in those rare instances in which the plain error rule, Rule 103(d), applies.[40] Moreover, in some situations, the failure to request a limiting instruction is a deliberate tactic employed to avoid overemphasizing

---

[35] *See* Beech Aircraft Corp. v. Rainey, 488 U.S. 153, 173 n. 17 (1988) ("The defendants would, of course, have been entitled to a limiting instruction pursuant to Rule 105 had they requested it.").

[36] *See* Frederick v. Kirby Tankships, Inc., 205 F.3d 1277, 1285 (11th Cir. 2000) ("Under Rule 105, a court must give a limiting instruction when requested where evidence is admissible for one purpose and not another."); United States v. Washington, 592 F.2d 680 (2d Cir. 1979).

[37] United States v. Thirion, 813 F.2d 146, 155 (8th Cir. 1987).

[38] Fed. R. Evid. 105 ("*When evidence is admitted*, the court, upon request of a party, shall instruct the jury.") (emphasis added).

[39] United States v. Garcia, 848 F.2d 1324, 1334–35 (2d Cir. 1988) (citations omitted), *rev'd on other grounds*, 490 U.S. 858 (1989). *See also* United States v. Weil, 561 F.2d 1109, 1111 (4th Cir. 1977); United States v. Papia, 560 F.2d 827, 839–40 (7th Cir. 1977); United States v. Campanale, 518 F.2d 352, 362 (9th Cir. 1975).

[40] *See* United States v. Liefer, 778 F.2d 1236, 1244 (7th Cir. 1985); United States v. Regner, 677 F.2d 754, 757 (9th Cir. 1982); United States v. Vitale, 596 F.2d 688, 689 (5th Cir. 1979); United States v. Sangrey, 586 F.2d 1312, 1315 (9th Cir. 1978); United States v. Sisto, 534 F.2d 616, 622–26 (5th Cir. 1976). *See supra* § 6.11 (plain error).

adverse evidence.[41] If competent counsel chooses this course of action, the plain error rule should not apply.[42]

§ 8.06 Effectiveness of Limiting Instructions

Like most courts, the Supreme Court has assumed, almost as an article of faith, that jurors follow instructions. The Court has written that a "crucial assumption underlying the criminal trial system is that juries will follow the instructions given them by the trial judge. Were this not so, it would be pointless for a trial court to instruct a jury, and even more pointless for an appellate court to reverse a criminal conviction because the jury was improperly instructed."[43] On occasion, however, judicial disquiet surfaces. For example, Justice Jackson once commented: "The naive assumption that prejudicial effects can be overcome by instructions to the jury, all practicing lawyers know to be unmitigated fiction."[44] Another judge stated it more colorfully: "[I]f you throw a skunk into the jury box, you can't instruct the jury not to smell it."[45]

As noted above, the Court's decision in *Bruton* turns on the Court's acknowledgment that "the risk that the jury will not, or cannot, follow instructions is so great, and the consequences of failure so vital to the defendant, that the practical and human limitations of the jury system cannot be ignored."[46] This is one of the few instances where the Court rejected the maxim that juries follow instructions.

Perhaps not surprisingly, most studies on the topic question the effectiveness of limiting instructions.[47]

---

[41] *See* United States v. Johnson, 46 F.3d 1166, 1171 (D.C. Cir. 1995) ("Johnson requested no such instruction. Moreover, such instruction might in fact be inconsistent with a defendant's deliberate trial strategy to minimize the jury's recollection of the unfavorable evidence."); United States v. Barnes, 586 F.2d 1052, 1059 (5th Cir. 1978) ("Counsel may refrain from requesting an instruction in order not to emphasize potentially damaging evidence.").

[42] *See* Sherman v. Burke Contracting, Inc., 891 F.2d 1527, 1534 (11th Cir. 1990) ("We have found no civil case in which a federal appellate court has labelled as plain error a trial judge's failure to give a limiting instruction with respect to evidence that is admissible for some purpose."); United States v. Bradshaw, 719 F.2d 907, 920 (7th Cir. 1983) ("It appears to us that the defendant's attorney merely made a tactical decision in declining to ask that this statement be struck and a limiting instruction be given. Such a tactical decision should not increase the defendant's chances of obtaining a reversal.").

[43] Parker v. Randolph, 442 U.S. 62, 73 (1979).

[44] Krulewitch v. United States, 336 U.S. 440, 453 (1949) (concurring). Another example is Shepard v. United States, 290 U.S. 96 (1933), in which the prosecution argued on appeal that a murder victim's statement ("Dr. Shepard has poisoned me") was admissible for a nonhearsay purpose and not for the truth of the assertion. In rejecting this argument, Justice Cardozo responded: "Discrimination so subtle is a feat beyond the compass of ordinary minds. The reverberating clang of those accusatory words would drown all weaker sounds. It is for ordinary minds, and not for psychoanalysts, that our rules of evidence are framed." *Id.* at 104.

[45] Dunn v. United States, 307 F.2d 883, 886 (5th Cir. 1962).

[46] 391 U.S. at 135–36.

[47] *See* Kalven & Zeisel, The American Jury 1159–61 (1971) (jury knowledge of accused's

§ 8.07 Key Points

Multiple admissibility. Sometimes an item of evidence may properly be used for multiple purposes. For example, a party's prior inconsistent statement may be admitted for impeachment as a prior inconsistent statement if the party testifies[48] and as substantive evidence as a party admission.[49]

Limited admissibility. Frequently, however, evidence may be admissible for one purpose but inadmissible for another purpose. Evidence also may be admissible against one party but not against another party. In other words, the evidence is admissible for a limited purpose. In such cases, Rule 105 applies, and the court must, upon request, instruct the jury as to the limited purpose of the evidence. Numerous examples of limited admissibility occur throughout the law of evidence. Sometimes a rule explicitly recognizes this principle[50] and sometimes not (*e.g.,* hearsay context).[51]

Different parties. When evidence is admissible against one party, but not another party, a limiting instruction must be given upon request, directing the jury to use the evidence against the proper party. This issue most often arises in joint trials in criminal cases and may raise confrontation issues under *Bruton v. United States.*[52] The *Bruton* issue can be avoided if separate trials are ordered, the defendant's name is redacted, or the codefendant testifies. There is no *Bruton* issue if the statement falls within a recognized hearsay exception.

Procedural issues. A limiting instruction may be given either at the time the evidence is admitted or at the close of the case. A limiting instruction is mandatory upon request; the trial court may also give a limiting instruction sua sponte. Failure to request an instruction constitutes a waiver.

---

record has substantial impact on verdict); Wrightsman, *Psychology and the Legal System* (5th ed. 2002); Pickel, *Inducing Jurors to Disregard Inadmissible Evidence: A Legal Explanation Does Not Help,* 19 Law & Human Behav. 407 (1995); Wissler & Saks, *On the Inefficacy of Limiting Instructions: When Jurors Use Prior Conviction Evidence to Decide on Guilt,* 9 Law & Human Behav. 37 (1985).

[48] Fed. R. Evid. 613.

[49] Fed. R. Evid. 801(d)(2)(A).

[50] *See* Fed. R. Evid. 404(b) (other-acts evidence); Fed. R. Evid. 407 (subsequent remedial measures); Fed. R. Evid. 408 (compromises & offers to compromise); Fed. R. Evid. 411 (liability insurance).

[51] For example, prior inconsistent statements are generally admissible only for the purpose of impeachment and not for the truth. There is an exception for prior inconsistent statements that satisfy the requirements of Rule 801(d)(1)(A).

[52] 391 U.S. 123 (1968).

Chapter 9

RELEVANCY & ITS COUNTERPARTS: FRE 401 — 403

§ 9.01 Overview of Relevancy Rules

Relevancy is the most pervasive concept in evidence law. It is the threshold issue for all evidence. If the evidence is not relevant, it is excluded.[1] Period. End of matter. If the evidence is relevant, then the next step focuses on whether some other evidentiary rule requires exclusion. For example, relevant evidence may be excluded because it contravenes the hearsay rule or the best evidence rule. Thus, relevancy is a necessary but (sometimes) not a sufficient condition of admissibility.

Basic relevance rules. Federal Rule 401 defines relevant evidence (probative value). Rule 402 makes relevant evidence admissible in the absence of a rule of exclusion. Rule 403 specifies the circumstances under which a trial court is permitted to exclude relevant evidence. These three rules set forth the general provisions governing of relevancy.

There are an almost infinite variety of relevancy problems. Often precedent is of little help because the issues arise in slightly different circumstances. There are, however, some situations that are "repeat players." Some of these, such as "similar happenings," "adverse inferences," and "out-of-court experiments," are discussed later in this chapter.

Special relevance rules. In other situations an issue recurs so frequently that the courts develop categorical rules. For instance, character evidence is generally prohibited, although there are exceptions. Rules 404, 405, and 412–15 deal explicitly with character.[2] Rule 406 governs habit evidence.[3] Similarly, evidence of liability insurance is generally inadmissible; Rule 411 covers that subject.[4]

Ancillary rules based on policy. Rules 407– 410 are relevance rules of a different kind. They all involve the exclusion of relevant evidence based on policy reasons external to the truth-seeking function of the trial. For example, subsequent remedial measures (Rule 407) are excluded in order to encourage people to make repairs after accidents.[5]

---

[1] Fed. R. Evid. 402 ("Evidence which is not relevant is not admissible.").

[2] *See infra* chapters 10–11.

[3] *See infra* chapter 12.

[4] *See infra* chapter 17.

[5] Offers to compromise are excluded under Rule 408 (civil cases) and Rule 410 (criminal cases) in order to encourage parties to settle law suits. The evidence of the payment of medical expenses is excluded under Rule 409 in order to encourage people to pay such expenses after accidents (Good Samaritan rule). *See infra* chapters 13–16.

§ 9.02   Consequential ("material") Facts Defined

Rule 401 embraces two concepts: *relevancy* and *materiality.* To be admissible, evidence must be both relevant and material. However, instead of the term "material fact," Rule 401 uses the phrase "fact that is of consequence to the determination of the action,"[6] which can be shortened to *consequential fact.*

"Relevancy" describes the *relationship* between an item of evidence and the proposition it is offered to prove. In contrast, "materiality" describes the *relationship* between that proposition and the issues in the case — *i.e.,* the consequential or material facts.

Substantive law. With the exception of the credibility of witnesses,[7] the "consequential facts" in a particular case are a matter of substantive law — (1) the elements of the charged crime, (2) the elements of a cause of action, (3) the elements of an affirmative defense, and (4) damages in civil cases. The pleadings may remove some of these elements; for example, if the complaint alleges negligence and the answer does not deny negligence but asserts contributory negligence as a defense, negligence is off-the-table; it is no longer an issue in the case.[8]

Example. Is voluntary intoxication a defense in a homicide case? Is the evidence "material" under Rule 401 in a first degree murder prosecution. (Second degree murder?) Under the substantive criminal law, voluntary intoxication is typically a "defense" to first degree murder because, if believed by the jury, it could negate premeditation and thus reduce the offense to second degree murder. Thus, evidence of an elevated blood-alcohol concentration is both "relevant" and "material." In contrast, this defense is *immaterial* in a second degree murder prosecution because, under the substantive law, premeditation is not an element of that crime.

---

[6] The federal drafters explained this change in terminology: "The rule uses the phrase 'fact that is of consequence to the determination of the action' to describe the kind of fact to which proof may properly be directed. The language is that of California Evidence Code § 210; it has the advantage of avoiding the loosely used and ambiguous word 'material.' " Fed. R. Evid. 401 advisory committee's note.

[7] The credibility of witnesses, although not part of the substantive law, is always considered a consequential or material fact. *See* United States v. Abel, 469 U.S. 45, 52 (1984) ("Proof of bias is almost always relevant because the jury, as finder of fact and weigher of credibility, has historically been entitled to assess all evidence which might bear on the accuracy and truth of a witness' testimony.").

[8] *See supra* § 3.02[A] (pleadings).

FIGURE 9-1

First degree murder

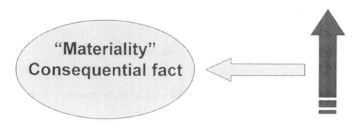

Voluntary intoxication [proposition]

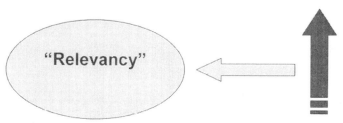

Blood-alcohol test results [evidence]

Example. In a rape prosecution, assume the accused proffers evidence tending to show the alleged victim consented. Because "lack of consent" is an element of common law rape,[9] the evidence relates to a consequential (material) fact. In contrast, the same evidence would not be material in a statutory rape prosecution because lack of consent is not an element of statutory rape.[10]

Example. Suppose in raising an insanity defense, the accused proffers psychiatric testimony concerning her inability to control her conduct (volitional component) due to a mental disease. In some jurisdictions, the definition of insanity contains a volitional component,[11] and thus this evidence would be material. A 1984 statute, however, redefined the insanity defense for federal crimes — specifically eliminating any volitional component. Consequently, any evidence about lack of control is no longer material in federal criminal trials.[12]

---

[9] At common law rape was defined as carnal knowledge of a woman, by a man who was not her husband, and *without her consent*. *See* Dressler, Understanding Criminal Law ch. 33 (3d ed. 2002).

[10] Statutory rape cover situations where the victim was below the age of consent (*e.g.*, age 13, 14, or 15). Unlike common law rape, lack of consent is not an element; even if the female consented, the crime occurs. *Id.*

[11] *See* Model Penal Code § 4.01.

[12] *A related example*: Expert psychiatric testimony may be relevant to establish "diminished capacity," which would reduce premeditated murder (first degree) to second degree murder.

In the above examples, the determinative consideration was the substantive law, not the law of evidence.[13]

§ 9.03   "Relevancy" Defined

The terms relevance and probative value are used synonymously in evidence law. The following questions address relevancy: Does the evidence further the inquiry? Does it advance the resolution of trial issues? Does the evidence throw light on these issues? However, the Federal Rules use a precise definition of relevancy. Rule 401 defines "relevant evidence" as evidence having any tendency to make the existence of a material or consequential fact "more probable or less probable than it would be without the evidence."[14]

Rule 401's standard does *not* require that the evidence make a consequential (material) fact "more probable than not" (preponderance of evidence), but only that the material fact be more probable with the evidence *than without the evidence.* For example, in a homicide case the prosecution may proffer evidence showing a motive (*e.g.,* defendant had an affair with the victim's spouse). Such evidence, by itself, does not establish that it is more probable than not that the defendant committed the crime. It does, however, satisfy the standard of Rule 401; it is more probable that the defendant committed the crime with the motive evidence *than without it.*

Example: Suppose fresh blood is found at a murder scene that shows signs of a violent struggle. The blood type at the scene is "AB", and the victim's type was "O." In ABO system, the blood types by population are:

However, "diminished capacity" is not recognized as a defense under the substantive criminal law of many jurisdictions. Thus, although relevant, this testimony is inadmissible because it does not relate to a consequential (material) fact.

[13] *Torts example:* While contributory negligence is a defense in some jurisdictions, the law in worker's compensation cases does not recognize this defense. Thus, evidence of contributory negligence is "immaterial" in the latter cases.

[14] The federal drafters cited James, *Relevancy, Probability and the Law*, 29 Cal. L. Rev. 689, 690–91 (1941), which includes the following explanation:

> Relevancy, as the word itself indicates, is not an inherent characteristic of any item of evidence but exists as a relation between an item of evidence and a proposition sought to be proved. If an item of evidence tends to prove or to disprove any proposition, it is relevant to that proposition. If the proposition itself is one provable in the case at bar, or if it in turn forms a further link in a chain of proof the final proposition of which is provable in the case at bar, then the offered item of evidence has probative value in the case. Whether the immediate or ultimate proposition sought to be proved is provable in the case at bar is determined by the pleadings, by the procedural rules applicable thereto, and by the substantive law governing the case. . . . But because relevancy . . . means tendency to prove a proposition properly provable in the case, an offered item of evidence may be excluded as "irrelevant" for either of these two quite distinct reasons: because it is not probative of the proposition at which it is directed [relevancy], or because that proposition is not provable in the case [materiality].

A = 42 %

B = 10 %

AB = 3 %

0 = 45 %

FIGURE 9-2

Murder prosecution

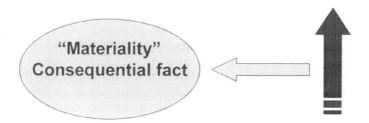

Identity of perpetrator [proposition]

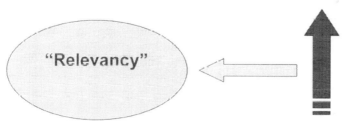

Blood type [evidence]

Is the evidence relevant — *i.e.*, more probative with the evidence *than without it*? Yes. If the population were one million, there would be 30,000 people with AB. Yet, the evidence is still relevant. Even if the crime scene blood type was "O" (victim was A), the evidence is relevant. The evidence excludes a large number of people as the possible assailant (those with types A, B, or AB), even though we are still left with a large group (type O). Stated in Rule 401 terms: The blood type evidence *tends* to make the existence of a consequential (material) fact, *i.e.,* the murderer's identity, more probable with the evidence than without the evidence.

Lax standard. Rule 401 embraces a *very low* standard. For instance, if we know that a bank robber was a white male, each of those facts individually is relevant under Rule 401. By excluding females, we advance the inquiry. By excluding non-Caucasians, we advance the inquiry. As we will discuss below, however, the probative value of some evidence may be so marginal that we will exclude it under Rule 403, even though it satisfies Rule 401's standard.

[A] Admissibility vs. Sufficiency

As the above discussion suggests, there is a difference between relevancy (admissibility) and sufficiency.[15] Although the evidence as a whole must be sufficient to satisfy a party's burden of production and thus send the issue to the trier of fact,[16] each item of evidence need only advance the inquiry.[17] Think of it this way: You can only call one witness at a time, and each witness need not hit a home run; you can score sometimes by hitting three singles or a double and a single.

The federal drafters cited McCormick's metaphor to capture this point: "A brick is not a wall."[18] Assume a murder prosecution (e.g., victim shot in his bedroom) in which the prosecution introduces the following evidence one item at a time: (1) motive (e.g., affair with victim's spouse), (2) accused observed near murder scene at the approximate time of death (i.e., opportunity), (3) accused threatened the victim a week before the crime, (4) accused bought a gun two days prior to the murder, and (5) accused's fingerprints were found in the bedroom. Motive (item 1) is relevant but by itself would not be sufficient to convict beyond a reasonable doubt. However, the fingerprints (item 5) might be sufficient if we could determine when they were left or if the accused claims that he has never been in the bedroom. This illustrates another point: each "brick" is not the same size. Some items of evidence are more probative than others. A good prosecutor will introduce it all because under the Double Jeopardy Clause the government gets only one shot at a conviction.[19] In a civil case, the "wall" is not as high.

---

[15] *See* Bourjaily v. United States, 483 U.S. 171, 179–80 (1987) ("Individual pieces of evidence, insufficient in themselves to prove a point, may in cumulation prove it. The sum of an evidentiary presentation may well be greater than its constituent parts.").

[16] In other words, to avoid a directed verdict. *See supra* § 4.04 (burden of production).

[17] *See* Insurance Co. v. Weide, 78 U.S. (11 Wall.) 438, 440 (1870) ("It is well settled that if the evidence offered conduces in any reasonable degree to establish the probability or improbability of the fact in controversy, it should go to the jury.").

[18] McCormick, Evidence § 152, at 137 (1954).

[19] Once there is an acquittal, the case is over. The accused cannot be tried again for that offense, and the prosecution cannot appeal. If a conviction is overturned on appeal, generally the accused may be retried. The one exception is a reversal based on the insufficiency of the evidence. *See generally* Dressler, Understanding Criminal Procedure ch. 33 (3d ed. 2002).

FIGURE 9-3

Difference between "admissibility" and "sufficiency": McCormick's "wall"

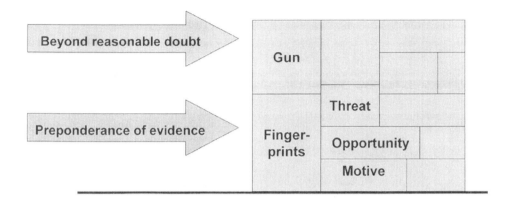

[B]   Basis for Relevancy Determination

In determining relevancy, the trial judge must rely on logic as informed by experience or science.[20] In assessing the relevance of "motive," the judge depends on her life-experiences. Of course, different judges have different life experiences, and sometimes counsel, through argument or an offer of proof, will need to educate the judge on why the evidence is relevant.

The reference to "science" takes account of situations in which a court must rely on expert testimony to discern the relevance of proffered evidence. For example, evidence that a defendant's blood type matches the type found at the crime scene is relevant only because scientific research has demonstrated that the general population can be classified according to ABO blood types.

The judge does not consider the credibility of witnesses when making relevancy determinations. The judge determines probative value of the evidence as *"if true."*[21]

[C]   Direct & Circumstantial Evidence

Problems of relevancy typically involve circumstantial rather than direct evidence. The distinction turns on the manner in which an item of evidence

---

[20] *See* Fed. R. Evid. 401 advisory committee's note (The decision is based on "experience or science, applied logically to the situation at hand.").

[21] Ballou v. Henri Studios, Inc., 656 F.2d 1147, 1154 (5th Cir. 1981)(emphasis added). *See also* United States v. Welsh, 774 F.2d 670, 672 (4th Cir. 1985) ("[T]he credibility of a witness has nothing to do with whether or not his testimony is probative with respect to the fact it seeks to prove. . . . [T]he law does not consider credibility as a component to relevance."). This may seem counterintuitive because, in one sense, unreliable evidence cannot have probative value. However, evidence law assigns credibility determinations to the jury, not the judge.

relates to the material issues in the case. "Footprints in the snow" is a common example. If you see the paperboy deliver the newspaper to your house in the morning, you have *direct* evidence of delivery. In contrast, if you look out your window in the early morning and observe footprints in the snow, you have *circumstantial* evidence of delivery. You must draw a further inference to reach the conclusion that the newspaper has been delivered.

Another example: Testimony in a homicide case that the witness saw the defendant shoot the victim would be direct evidence of the perpetrator's identity. From such testimony, it could be directly concluded that the defendant committed the charged offense. The only issue would be the credibility of the witness, an issue entrusted to the jury. Direct evidence requires no process of inference drawing to go from the item of evidence to a material (consequential) fact (identity of the murderer). If, on the other hand, the witness testifies that she saw the defendant flee from the crime scene after hearing a gunshot, the testimony is only circumstantial evidence of the murderer's identity (albeit "direct" evidence of flight).[22] It could not be directly concluded that the defendant was the person who committed the offense; the defendant may have fled in order to escape being also shot by the real perpetrator. Nevertheless, the evidence could serve as part of a chain of reasoning which might lead the jury to infer that the defendant and the murderer were the same person. Perhaps, the term "circumstantial case" is a better description.[23]

Many people might believe that direct evidence is better than circumstantial evidence. In many instances, however, that is not true.[24] Direct evidence, for instance, an eyewitness account of a bank robbery, comes with credibility problems. The eyewitness may not have gotten a good look at the robber, may not have been wearing his glasses, may hate the defendant,

---

[22] *See infra* § 9.07[A] (admissions by conduct).

[23] Morgan gives the following example to illustrate the series of inferences necessary to use "motive" evidence:

> Assume that X has met his death by violence; the proposition to be proved is that Y killed him; the offered item of evidence is a love letter written by Y to X's wife. The series of inferences is about as follows: From Y's letter, (A), to Y's love of X's wife, (B), to Y's desire for the exclusive possession of X's wife, (C), to Y's desire to get rid of X, (D), to Y's plan to get rid of X, (E), to Y's execution of the plan by killing X, (F). The unarticulated premise, (M), conjoined with (A) is, "A man who writes a love letter to a woman is probably in love with her"; that, (N), conjoined with (B) is, "A man who loves a woman probably desires her for himself alone"; that, (O) conjoined with (C) is, "A man who loves a married woman and desires her for himself alone desires to get rid of her husband"; that, (P), conjoined with (D) is, "A man who desires to get rid of the husband of the woman he loves probably plans to do so"; and that, (Q), conjoined with (E) is, "A man who plans to get rid of the husband of the woman he loves is probably the man who killed him."

Morgan, Basic Problems of Evidence 185–86 (1962).

[24] *See* Holland v. United States, 348 U.S. 121, 140 (1954) ("Circumstantial evidence in this respect is intrinsically no different from testimonial evidence. Admittedly, circumstantial evidence may in some cases point to a wholly incorrect result. Yet this is equally true of testimonial evidence.").

and so forth. In contrast, fingerprints are a type of circumstantial evidence because an expert usually cannot tell when they were left; thus, an inference concerning the time the fingerprints were deposited is required.

Special rule. Nevertheless, some courts employ a special rule to evaluate the sufficiency of circumstantial evidence in criminal cases — *i.e.,* that "circumstantial evidence relied upon to prove an essential element of a crime must be *irreconcilable* with any reasonable theory of an accused's innocence in order to support a finding of guilt."[25] This position has been criticized as more misleading than helpful. For example, the Supreme Court rejected this rule for federal trials: "[T]he better rule is that where the jury is properly instructed on the standards for reasonable doubt, such an additional instruction on circumstantial evidence is confusing and incorrect."[26] It is not unusual to rely on circumstantial evidence to support a murder conviction, even in the absence of the victim's body.[27]

[D] "Inference upon Inference" Rule

Some cases state that an inference cannot be stacked upon another inference,[28] a rule Wigmore vigorously attacked: "There is no such orthodox rule; nor can there be. If there were, hardly a single trial could be adequately prosecuted. All departments of reasoning, all scientific work, every day's life and every day's trials proceed upon such data."[29] It is difficult to see what the "inference upon inference" rule accomplishes. Rules governing the sufficiency of the evidence address adequately the problems of circumstantial proof.[30] Nevertheless, the rule continues to surface in the cases.

[E] "Background" Evidence

All evidence need not involve a disputed issue. The federal drafters specifically approved of the admission of "background" evidence: "A rule limiting admissibility to evidence directed to a controversial point would invite the exclusion of this helpful evidence, or at least the raising of endless questions over its admission."[31] As examples, the drafters cited charts, photographs, views of real estate, and murder weapons.[32]

---

[25] State v. Kulig, 309 N.E.2d 897, 897 (Ohio 1974) (emphasis added).

[26] Holland v. United States, 348 U.S. 121, 139–40 (1954).

[27] *E.g.,* State v. Nicely, 529 N.E.2d 1236, 1239 (Ohio 1988) ("It is well-established that murder can be proven in the absence of a body."). *See also* Perkins, *The Corpus Delicti of Murder,* 48 Va. L. Rev. 173 (1962).

[28] *See* Morgan, Basic Problems of Evidence 188 (1962) ("This is usually taken to mean that if the existence of one fact is found by inference from the existence of another, the inferred fact cannot be used as a basis for inferring still another fact. . . . It is used commonly to express a result without the troublesome process of careful analysis.").

[29] 1A Wigmore, Evidence § 41, at 1111 (Tillers rev. 1983).

[30] *See supra* § 4.04 (burden of production).

[31] *See* Fed. R. Evid. 401 advisory committee's note ("Evidence which is essentially background in nature is universally offered and admitted as an aid to understanding.").

[32] *See* Government of Virgin Islands v. Grant, 775 F.2d 508, 513 (3d Cir. 1985) ("[T]he

This reasoning supports admission of a certain amount of personal history for an accused.[33]

§ 9.04   Admissibility of Relevant Evidence: Rule 402

Rule 402 is the general provision governing the admissibility of evidence: relevant evidence is admissible in the absence of a rule of exclusion, and irrelevant evidence is inadmissible. For present purposes, the most important part of Rule 402 is the phrase "by these rules." This language allows relevant evidence to be excluded by operation of some other rule of evidence. A number of exclusionary rules are found elsewhere in the Rules of Evidence. For example, Rule 403 requires the exclusion of evidence whose probative value is substantially outweighed by the risk of unfair prejudice, confusion of issues, or misleading the jury. Other illustrations found in Article 4 of the Rules include evidence of subsequent remedial measures,[34] offers of compromise,[35] payment of medical expenses,[36] certain types of pleas and offers to plead guilty in criminal cases,[37] and liability insurance.[38] Examples in other Articles include rules on privilege,[39] competency,[40] firsthand knowledge,[41] hearsay,[42] authentication,[43] and best evidence.[44]

In sum, evidence may meet the relevancy standard of Rule 401 but nevertheless be inadmissible because it fails to satisfy the requirements of some other provision of the Rules of Evidence.

---

jurisprudence of 'background evidence' is essentially undeveloped. 'Background' or 'preliminary' evidence is not mentioned in the evidence codes, nor has it received attention in the treatises.").

[33] *E.g.,* United States v. Blackwell, 853 F.2d 86, 88 (2d Cir. 1988) ("The testimony concerning Blackwell's service in the Marine Corps and his completion of two years of college was properly received as background. It told the jury something about the defendant as a person, and his experience in life."); *Grant,* 775 F.2d at 513 ("During the course of a trial, it is customary for the defendant to introduce evidence concerning his background, such as information about his education and employment. Such evidence is routinely admitted without objection, and testimony that an accused has never been arrested is commonly admitted as part of this background evidence.").

[34] Fed. R. Evid. 407.

[35] Fed. R. Evid. 408.

[36] Fed. R. Evid. 409.

[37] Fed. R. Evid. 410.

[38] Fed. R. Evid. 411.

[39] Fed. R. Evid. 501.

[40] Fed. R. Evid. 601.

[41] Fed. R. Evid. 602.

[42] Fed. R. Evid. 802.

[43] Fed. R. Evid. 901.

[44] Fed. R. Evid. 1002.

[A] United States Constitution

Many constitutional rights are enforced through judicially created exclusionary rules. For example, evidence seized in violation of the Fourth Amendment[45] or the Due Process Clause is subject to exclusion.[46] Similarly, statements obtained from criminal defendants in violation of the privilege against self-incrimination,[47] the right to counsel,[48] or due process[49] are subject to exclusion. Evidence of pretrial identifications obtained in violation of constitutional rights may also be excluded; these rights include the right to counsel[50] and due process.[51] Moreover, the Sixth Amendment right of confrontation may preclude the admission of otherwise admissible evidence — for example, hearsay evidence.[52]

Incorporation doctrine. These exclusionary rules also apply in state trials. In a series of decisions during the 1960s, the Supreme Court applied most of the criminal procedure provisions of the federal Bill of Rights to the states through the Due Process Clause of the Fourteenth Amendment.[53] The Fourth Amendment exclusionary rule was extended to state trials,[54] as was the Fifth Amendment's privilege against self incrimination[55] and Double Jeopardy Clause.[56] All the Sixth Amendment protections were made applicable: right to a jury trial,[57] right of confrontation,[58] right to compulsory process,[59] the right to a speedy trial[60] by an impartial jury,[61] and the right to counsel.[62] Finally, the Cruel and Unusual Punishment Clause of the Eighth Amendment was applied to state trials.[63]

---

[45] Mapp v Ohio, 367 U.S. 643 (1961).

[46] Rochin v. California, 342 U.S. 165 (1952).

[47] Miranda v. Arizona, 384 U.S. 436 (1966).

[48] Brewer v Williams, 430 U.S. 387 (1977).

[49] Mincey v. Arizona, 437 U.S. 385 (1978).

[50] Moore v. Illinois, 434 U.S. 220 (1977); Kirby v. Illinois, 406 U.S. 682 (1972).

[51] Manson v. Brathwaite, 432 U.S. 98 (1977); Neil v. Biggers, 409 U.S. 188 (1972).

[52] *E.g.,* Barber v. Page, 390 U.S. 719 (1968). *See infra* § 36.05 (confrontation & hearsay.)

[53] Prior to the 1960s, federal law played but a small role in state criminal trials. Historically, the Supreme Court deferred to the states on matters of criminal procedure because "the problems of criminal law enforcement vary widely from state to state," because state courts generally have greater familiarity and expertise in criminal matters, and because criminal rules should be developed by those who bear the burden of enforcing them. Note, *Stepping Into the Breach: Basing Defendants' Rights on State Rather than Federal Law*, 15 Am. Crim. L. Rev. 339, 339 (1978). *See generally* Dressler, Understanding Criminal Procedure ch. 3 (3d ed. 2002).

[54] Mapp v. Ohio, 367 U.S. 643 (1961).

[55] Malloy v. Hogan, 378 U.S. 1 (1964).

[56] Benton v. Maryland, 395 U.S. 784 (1969).

[57] Duncan v. Louisiana, 391 U.S. 145 (1968).

[58] Pointer v. Texas, 380 U.S. 400 (1965).

[59] Washington v. Texas, 388 U.S. 14 (1967).

[60] Klopfer v. North Carolina, 386 U.S. 213 (1967).

[61] Parker v. Gladden, 385 U.S. 363 (1966).

[62] Gideon v. Wainwright, 372 U.S. 335 (1963).

[63] Robinson v. California, 370 U.S. 660 (1962).

The only two provisions that were not "incorporated" through the Fourteenth Amendment were the right to grand jury indictment and the prohibition against excessive bail. The Court, however, in *Schilb v. Kuebel*[64] commented: "Bail, of course, is basic to our system of law and the Eighth Amendment's proscription of excessive bail has been assumed to have application to the States through the Fourteenth Amendment."[65] Thus, the application of federal constitutional law in state criminal cases has become commonplace.

The Supreme Court has also recognized a constitutional right to introduce defense evidence under limited circumstances. In *Washington v. Texas*,[66] the Court struck down a witness disqualification rule as violative of the Sixth Amendment right to compulsory process: "The right to offer the testimony of witnesses, and to compel their attendance, if necessary, is in plain terms the right to present a defense, the right to present the defendant's version of the facts as well as the prosecution's to the jury so it may decide where the truth lies."[67] In *Chambers v. Mississippi*,[68] the Court held that the combined effect of Mississippi's voucher rule and hearsay rule precluded the admission of critical and reliable defense evidence and thus violated due process.[69]

The United States Supreme Court, however, has no authority to review state evidentiary rules in the absence of a federal constitutional or statutory issue.[70]

[B] Federal Statutes

Some federal statutes exclude evidence.[71] For example, the federal wiretap and eavesdropping statute explicitly states that evidence obtained

---

[64] 404 U.S. 357 (1971).

[65] *Id.* at 365.

[66] 388 U.S. 14 (1967).

[67] *Id.* at 19. *See also* Crane v. Kentucky, 476 U.S. 683, 690 (1986) ("Whether rooted directly in the Due Process Clause of the Fourteenth Amendment, or in the Compulsory Process or Confrontation Clauses of the Sixth Amendment, the Constitution guarantees criminal defendants 'a meaningful opportunity to present a complete defense.'") (citations omitted).

[68] 410 U.S. 284, 293 (1973). *See infra* § 31.08 (constitutional issues).

[69] *See also* United States v. Scheffer, 523 U.S. 303, 308 (1998) ("A defendant's right to present relevant evidence is not unlimited, but rather is subject to reasonable restrictions." Evidence "rules do not abridge an accused's right to present a defense so long as they are not 'arbitrary' or 'disproportionate to the purposes they are designed to serve.' Moreover, we have found the exclusion of evidence to be unconstitutionally arbitrary or disproportionate only where it has infringed upon a weighty interest of the accused.") (citations omitted).

[70] *See* Estelle v. McGuire, 502 U.S. 62, 72 (1991) ("Nor do our habeas powers allow us to reverse McGuire's conviction based on a belief that the trial judge incorrectly interpreted the California Evidence Code in ruling that the prior injury evidence was admissible as bad acts evidence in this case."); Marshall v. Lonberger, 459 U.S. 422, 438 n.6 (1983) ("[T]he Due Process Clause does not permit the federal courts to engage in a finely tuned review of the wisdom of state evidentiary rules.").

[71] *See* Fed. R. Evid. 402 advisory committee's note (listing statutes).

in violation of that statute is inadmissible in any court, state or federal.[72]

[C] Other Procedural Rules

Relevant evidence may also be inadmissible due to "other rules prescribed by the Supreme Court." Other rules include the Rules of Civil and Criminal Procedure, some of which contain provisions relating to the admissibility of evidence. For example, both Civil Rule 32 and Criminal Rule 15 specify the evidentiary uses of depositions. The requirements imposed by these provisions must be satisfied. Moreover, exclusion of evidence as a sanction for a discovery violation is permitted.[73] For example, in *Taylor v. Illinois*,[74] the Supreme Court held that the exclusion of defense evidence as a sanction for a discovery violation in a criminal case is constitutional under certain circumstances, *i.e.,* a willful and blatant violation of a discovery order.

§ 9.05   Rule 403 "Balancing"

Rule 403 specifies the conditions under which a trial court is permitted to exclude relevant evidence.[75] It is the *most important* rule in evidence law because every item of evidence raises a Rule 403 problem — at least in theory. It confers no authority to admit irrelevant evidence; Rule 402 mandates the exclusion of irrelevant evidence.

The application of Rule 403 requires a three-step process. First, the judge must determine the probative value of the proffered evidence. Second, the court must identify the presence of any of the enumerated dangers (unfair prejudice, confusion of issues, or misleading the jury) or considerations (undue delay, waste of time, or needless presentation of cumulative evidence). Finally, the court must balance the probative value against the identified dangers or considerations. If the enumerated dangers or considerations *substantially* outweigh the probative value of the evidence, exclusion is discretionary. The word "substantially" is significant; it makes Rule 403 biased in favor of admissibility.

There is a difference between the "dangers" and the "considerations" enumerated in Rule 403. Evidence that carries a risk of unfair prejudice, confusion of issues, or misleading the jury is excluded because we are concerned that the jury may be incapable of rationally evaluating such

---

[72] 18 U.S.C. § 2515 ("Whenever any wire or oral communication has been intercepted, no part of the contents of such communication and no evidence derived therefrom may be received in evidence in any trial, hearing, or other proceeding in or before any court, grand jury, department, officer, agency, regulatory body, legislative committee, or other authority of the United States, a State, or a political subdivision thereof if the disclosure of that information would be in violation of this chapter.").

[73] Fed. R. Civ. P. 37(b)(2)(A); Fed. R. Crim. P. 16(d).

[74] 484 U.S. 400 (1988).

[75] Rule 403 balancing is sometimes referred to as a "legal relevance" analysis. *See* Rozier v. Ford Motor Co., 573 F.2d 1332, 1347 (5th Cir. 1978). The term "legal relevance" has several meanings and therefore is not used in this text.

evidence. In contrast, the exclusion of evidence that entails undue delay, waste of time, or needless presentation of cumulative evidence rests on different grounds — conservation of judicial time. In short, the "dangers" affect the integrity of the factfinding process; the "considerations" affect only the efficiency of the courts.

[A] Estimating Probative Value

Assessing the probative value of proffered evidence is the first step in applying Rule 403. As we have seen, Rule 401 sets forth a low standard in defining relevant evidence. In applying Rule 403, however, it is not enough for the trial court to determine that the evidence is relevant under Rule 401. Because the court is required under Rule 403 to balance the probative value against the specified dangers or considerations, the court must estimate how much probative worth the evidence has. Every item of evidence does not have the same probative value. In a murder prosecution, for example, fingerprint evidence is generally more probative of identity than motive evidence. In the "wall" metaphor used above, some bricks are larger than others.

Remoteness. Cases often use the term "remoteness" in this context.[76] This usually means remote in time, although it could also mean geographically remote. For example, a threat to kill the victim a day before the murder is far more probative than a threat made a year earlier. Remoteness by itself typically does not extinguish probative value but, by reducing probative value, it may play a part in the exclusion of evidence under Rule 403.

[B] Rule 403 "Dangers"

[1] Unfair Prejudice

Under Rule 403, relevant evidence may be excluded if the risk of unfair prejudice substantially outweighs its probative value. The rule requires exclusion only in the case of *unfair* prejudice. Most evidence introduced by one party is "prejudicial" to the other side in the sense that it damages that party's position at trial. This is *not* the concern of Rule 403. Otherwise, the most probative evidence (*e.g.,* a confession) would be excluded as the most "prejudicial." In other words, there is a difference between being unfavorable and being *unfairly* prejudicial.[77]

Rule 403 comes into play only if the evidence is prejudicial in the sense that the jury cannot rationally evaluate it. The federal drafters described

---

[76] *E.g.,* United States v. Ellzey, 936 F.2d 492, 497 (10th Cir. 1991) (evidence excluded under Rule 403 because "remote and tenuous").

[77] *See* In re Air Crash Disaster, 86 F.3d 498, 538 (6th Cir. 1996) ("Rule 403 does not exclude evidence because it is strongly persuasive or compellingly relevant — the rule only applies when it is likely that the jury will be moved by a piece of evidence in a manner that is somehow unfair or inappropriate. The truth may hurt, but Rule 403 does not make it inadmissible on that account.").

unfair prejudice as "an undue tendency to suggest decision on an improper basis, commonly, though not necessarily, an emotional one."[78] A classic example is the admissibility of gruesome photographs in a homicide case. Sometimes crime scene photographs are charged with such immediacy and emotional impact that the risk of unfair prejudice is disproportionately enhanced. This is not to say that such photographs are automatically inadmissible. Quite the contrary is true, but it does mean the judge may limit the number of photographs and the jury's exposure to them.[79]

Limiting evidence to its proper purpose. In addition to an appeal to emotion, unfair prejudice may involve the risk that a jury will use evidence improperly despite a limiting instruction. For example, Rule 404(b) provides that evidence of other crimes may be admissible to prove motive, opportunity, intent, or preparation. Such evidence, however, is inadmissible if offered to prove character. If the jury uses the evidence to infer character (the improper purpose), the defendant will be unfairly prejudiced. Thus, if a court concludes that the risk of improper use is great, notwithstanding a limiting instruction, the probative value of the evidence for its proper use may be substantially outweighed by the risk of its improper use.[80] The same analysis applies with hearsay. When the risk that the jury will use an extrajudicial statement for the prohibited hearsay inference rather than for the non-hearsay purpose that is offered as the rationale for admissibility, it may be excluded.[81]

[2] Confusion of Issues

Evidence may also be excluded due to the risk of confusion of issues.[82] Suppose, for instance, a plaintiff in a building-collapse case wants to introduce evidence of a prior collapse of another building, which was also constructed by the defendant. The reason for the prior collapse is disputed, and the resolution of this dispute would require numerous witnesses by each side. Here, we will have a "trial within a trial," and there is a risk that the jury will confuse the facts of one collapse with the other. This does not mean that the evidence will be automatically excluded under Rule 403. That would depend on the weighing analysis.[83]

---

[78] Fed. R. Evid. 403 advisory committee's note. *See also* Old Chief v. United States, 519 U.S. 172, 180 (1997) ("The term 'unfair prejudice,' as to a criminal defendant, speaks to the capacity of some concededly relevant evidence to lure the factfinder into declaring guilt on a ground different from proof specific to the offense charged.").

[79] Any number of factors could properly influence the trial court's decision on admissibility. If the photographs show powder burns on the victim's back and the defendant claims self-defense, the probative value of the photograph increases because powder burns indicate an entrance wound, and their presence on the victim's back is therefore inconsistent with a self-defense claim. If, on the other hand, the prosecution alleges that the defendant was the driver of the getaway car and there is no controversy that a homicide occurred, then the need for the photographs decreases. *See infra* § 27.02[F] (gruesome photographs).

[80] *See infra* § 11.04 (determining admissibility of other-act evidence under Rule 403).

[81] *See infra* § 31.06 (statements offered for truth of assertion).

[82] *See* Shepard v. United States, 290 U.S. 96, 104 (1933) ("When the risk of confusion is so great as to upset the balance of advantage, the evidence goes out.").

[83] *See infra* § 9.06 (similar happenings & other accidents).

Collateral matters. Sometimes the term "collateral matters" is used in this context. It is an ambiguous term. It could refer to facts that are totally unrelated to any issue in the case. If used in this sense, the facts are immaterial under Rule 401, and the evidence must be excluded under Rule 402. On the other hand, a fact may be circumstantially relevant to a material issue, but proof of that fact would introduce the danger of confusion of issues.[84] If that danger substantially outweighs probative value, the evidence may be excluded under Rule 403.[85]

[3] Misleading the Jury

Rule 403 also identifies "misleading the jury" as a danger. Frequently, the dangers of "confusion of issues" and "misleading the jury" overlap. If the jury is confused, it can be misled. On the other hand, all misleading evidence may not result in confusion of issues. Scientific evidence is often cited for its potential to mislead the jury because it may "assume a posture of mystic infallibility in the eyes of a jury of laymen."[86] Accordingly, "an exaggerated popular opinion of the accuracy of a particular technique may make its use prejudicial or likely to mislead the jury."[87]

If not properly presented, statistical evidence may also cause problems on this score. As one court has held, "[M]athematical odds are not admissible as evidence to identify a defendant in a criminal proceeding so long as the odds are based on estimates, the validity of which has not been demonstrated."[88]

---

[84] *See* United States v. Scheffer, 523 U.S. 303, 314 (1998) ("[C]ollateral litigation prolongs criminal trials and threatens to distract the jury from its central function of determining guilt or innocence.").

[85] In the impeachment context, the term "collateral matter" has a specific meaning concerning the admissibility of *extrinsic* evidence. *E.g.,* Fed. R. Evid. 608(b) (extrinsic evidence not admissible when impeachment is by prior acts reflecting untruthful character; only cross-examination permitted). Here, again, the term "collateral" does not assist in either identifying or resolving the issue. A third usage is found in an exception to the best evidence rule, where the term means "unimportant." *E.g.,* Fed. Rule 1004(4) ("Collateral matters. The writing, recording, or photograph is not closely related to a controlling issue.").

[86] United States v. Addison, 498 F.2d 741, 744 (D.C. Cir. 1974). *See also* Daubert v. Merrell Dow Pharm., Inc., 509 U.S. 579, 595 (1993) ("Expert evidence can be both powerful and quite misleading because of the difficulty in evaluating it. Because of this risk, the judge in weighing possible prejudice against probative force under Rule 403 of the present rules exercises more control over experts than over lay witnesses.") (quoting Weinstein, *Rule 702 of the Federal Rules of Evidence is Sound; It Should Not Be Amended,* 138 F.R.D. 631, 632 (1991)); People v. King, 72 Cal. Rptr. 478, 493 (Cal. App. 1968) ("[J]urors must not be misled by an 'aura of certainty' which often envelops a new scientific process, obscuring its currently experimental nature.'").

[87] United States v. Baller, 519 F.2d 463, 466 (4th Cir. 1975) (referring to polygraph evidence). *See also* United States v. Alexander, 526 F.2d 161, 168 (8th Cir. 1975) ("When polygraph evidence is offered, it is likely to be shrouded with an aura of near infallibility, akin to the ancient oracle of Delphi.").

[88] State v. Sneed, 414 P.2d 858, 862 (N.M. 1966). *See also* People v. Collins, 438 P.2d 33 (Cal. 1968) (error to admit mathematician's testimony that the chances were one in twelve million that a robbery had been committed by a couple other than the defendants which shared all of the distinctive traits possessed by the defendants and attributed to the perpetrators of the robbery by witnesses).

[4]   Surprise

Common law cases often cited "unfair surprise" as a ground for excluding relevant evidence. This factor, however, is not specified in Rule 403. The federal drafters explained: "The rule does not enumerate surprise as a ground for exclusion, in this respect following Wigmore's view of the common law. While it can scarcely be doubted that claims of unfair surprise may still be justified despite procedural requirements of notice and instrumentalities of discovery, the granting of a continuance is a more appropriate remedy than exclusion of the evidence."[89]

Despite this position, the factor of unfair surprise may enter into Rule 403 determinations through the back door. If a party objects to the admissibility of evidence because of unfair surprise, the trial court has the option of granting a continuance. A continuance, however, may cause "undue delay," which is enumerated in Rule 403 as a factor justifying the exclusion of the evidence. In addition, if one party is surprised because the other party failed to comply with a discovery request, evidence could be excluded on that basis.[90]

[C]   Rule 403 "Considerations"

Rule 403 permits exclusion based on undue delay, waste of time, or needless presentation of cumulative evidence.[91] In contrast to the dangers enumerated in Rule 403, these factors are not intended to protect the integrity of the factfinding process. Instead, they are designed to conserve judicial resources. Justice Holmes put it this way: "So far as the introduction of collateral issues goes, that objection is a purely practical one — a concession to the shortness of life."[92]

For example, taking the jury to the scene of the crime, known as a jury view, is a very time-consuming process, and most trial judge's will not authorize one in an ordinary case, such as the typical bank robbery.[93] Virtually all jurors have been in banks, and unless there is something special about the case, a jury view would constitute undue delay.

Constitutional issue. Limitations on the amount of evidence or the number of witnesses offered by an accused in a criminal case must also be evaluated in light of the constitutional right to present a defense. For example, in *Washington v. Texas*,[94] the Supreme Court commented: "The right

---

[89] Fed. R. Evid. 403 advisory committee's note (citation omitted).

[90] *See supra* § 9.04[C].

[91] *See also* Fed. R. Evid. 611(a) ("The court shall exercise reasonable control over the mode and order of interrogating witnesses and presenting evidence so as to . . . (2) avoid needless consumption of time.").

[92] Reeve v. Dennett, 11 N.E. 938, 943-44 (Mass. 1887). *See also* United States v. Socony-Vacuum Oil Co., 310 U.S. 150, 230 (1940) ("Terminal points are necessary even in a conspiracy trial involving intricate business facts and legal issues.").

[93] *See infra* § 26.06 (jury views).

[94] 388 U.S. 14 (1967).

to offer the testimony of witnesses, and to compel their attendance, if necessary, is in plain terms the right to present a defense, the right to present the defendant's version of the facts. The defendant has the right to present his own witnesses to establish a defense. This right is a fundamental element of due process of law."[95] Accordingly, a trial court should exercise its discretion more cautiously when excluding evidence proffered by the accused in a criminal case.

However, Rule 403 speaks only of the *needless* presentation of cumulative evidence.[96] A court will not exclude a third (or fifth) eyewitness to a murder case in which the identity of the perpetrator is the contested issue.

[D]   Probative Value vs. Dangers & Considerations

If the probative value of proffered evidence is substantially outweighed by the dangers or considerations discussed above, exclusion is discretionary. Significantly, the rule manifests a definite bias in favor of admissibility; the dangers or considerations must *substantially* outweigh probative value before evidence should be excluded. Thus, courts often note that Rule 403 "is an extraordinary measure that should be used sparingly"[97] and the "balance . . . should be struck in favor of admissibility."[98] Anyone who has observed a trial, however, may see multiple examples of these "rare events" in any half-hour space of time.

It has been suggested that the trial judge should view "the evidence in a light most favorable to its proponent, maximizing its probative value and minimizing its prejudicial effect."[99] In contrast, a commentator has argued that judges should "resolve all doubts concerning the balance between probative value and prejudice in favor of prejudice."[100] Still others have advocated an intermediate position: maximum *reasonable* probative force balanced against *likely* prejudicial impact.[101]

[1]   Jury Instructions

Although not specified in the rule itself, the federal drafters indicated that practical factors, such as limiting instructions and alternative means of proof, should also play a part in Rule 403 decisions: "In reaching a decision whether to exclude on grounds of unfair prejudice, consideration

---

[95] *Id.* at 19.

[96] *See* McLaurin v. Fischer, 768 F.2d 98, 104 (6th Cir. 1985) ("Finally, before the eleventh witness was called the district court held that Dr. McLaurin would have to show cause as to why any additional witnesses should be allowed to testify. Since plaintiff's counsel was unable to demonstrate cause, the district court prohibited four proposed witnesses from testifying.").

[97] United States v. Morris, 79 F.3d 409, 412 (5th Cir. 1996).

[98] United States v. Terado-Madruga, 897 F.2d 1099, 1117 (11th Cir. 1990).

[99] United States v. Brady, 595 F.2d 359, 361 (6th Cir. 1979).

[100] Dolan, *Rule 403: The Prejudice Rule in Evidence*, 49 S. Cal. L. Rev. 220, 233 (1976).

[101] 1 Saltzburg, Martin & Capra, Federal Rules of Evidence Manual 403-9 (8th ed. 2002).

should be given to the probable effectiveness or lack of effectiveness of a limiting instruction."[102] A carefully worded and forcefully delivered instruction may reduce the potential of unfair prejudice or confusion of issues.[103] Nevertheless, the efficacy of limiting instructions is often debatable.[104]

[2] Alternative Proof

Alternate means of proof may also obviate the need for the introduction of unfairly prejudicial evidence.[105] For example, if two witnesses can prove a point and one of them is the defendant's probation officer, this would be a valid factor in determining admissibility; probationary status means prior crimes, an extremely prejudicial factor. Here, the judge may require proof through the other witness.[106] The Supreme Court has commented that the "mere fact that two pieces of evidence might go to the same point would not, of course, necessarily mean that only one of them might come in. It would only mean that a judge applying Rule 403 could reasonably apply some discount to the probative value of an item of evidence when faced with less risky alternative proof going to the same point."[107]

[3] Stipulations

Stipulations are often used to avoid the dangers associated with proffered evidence, such as other-crimes evidence.[108] As one federal court has stated: "In achieving this balance under Rule 403, the court has the power to require the government to accept a tendered stipulation in whole or in part as well as to permit it to reject the offer to stipulate in its entirety."[109] Nevertheless, there are practical limitations that must be recognized. According to Wigmore, "[a] colorless admission by the opponent may sometimes have the effect of depriving the party of the legitimate moral force of his evidence."[110]

---

[102] See Fed. R. Evid. 403 advisory committee's note.

[103] See United States v. Morris, 79 F.3d 409, 412 (5th Cir. 1996) ("Despite the Government's assertion that a proper instruction could be formulated to aid the jury in distinguishing between the substantive act and the conspiracy, the record provides no indication that it ever offered such an instruction to the district court. . . . The Government correctly asserts that courts often rely on limiting instructions to resolve problems under Rule 403.").

[104] See supra § 8.06 (effectiveness of limiting instructions).

[105] See Old Chief v. United States, 519 U.S. 172, 184 (1997) ("what counts as the Rule 403 'probative value' of an item of evidence may be calculated by comparing evidentiary alternatives"); Fed. R. Evid. 403 advisory committee's note (rule requires "balancing the probative value of and *need* for the evidence")(emphasis added).

[106] Because the parties control the order of proof, however, the judge may not know of the alternate evidence at the time the probation officer testifies. The judge however, could also preclude the officer from disclosing her occupation.

[107] Old Chief v. United States, 519 U.S. 172, 183 (1997).

[108] See infra § 11.04 (determining admissibility under Rule 403).

[109] United States v. Grassi, 602 F.2d 1192, 1197 (5th Cir. 1979), *vacated on other grounds*, 448 U.S. 902 (1980).

[110] 9 Wigmore, Evidence § 2591, at 824 (Chadbourn rev. 1981). *See also* 2 Imwinkelried, Giannelli, Gilligan & Lederer, Courtroom Criminal Evidence ch. 31 (3d ed. 1998) (stipulations).

The Supreme Court considered the issue in *Old Chief v. United States*.[111] The accused was charged with possession of a firearm by anyone with a prior felony conviction. His previous conviction was for assault causing serious bodily harm. To prevent the jury from hearing the nature of the previous offense, Old Chief offered to stipulate that he had been convicted of a felony. He feared undue prejudice if the jury heard the nature of his prior offense, and he claimed that his offer to stipulate rendered evidence of the nature of his prior offense inadmissible under Rule 403. The prosecution refused to stipulate and the jury found Old Chief guilty.

The Supreme Court reversed, concluding that the "risk of unfair prejudice did substantially outweigh the discounted probative value of the record of convictions, and it was an abuse of discretion to admit the record when an admission was available."[112] In this case, the prosecution lost nothing in accepting the stipulation, while the name of the offense did risk unfair prejudice.

While at first blush, *Old Chief* looks like a strong case for the defense, it is a double edged sword in that the conviction was an element of the offense, and the prior crime was not otherwise connected to the charged offense. In other situations, the Court made clear that the prosecution need not accept an offer to stipulate. The Court wrote:

> The "fair and legitimate weight" of conventional evidence showing individual thoughts and acts amounting to a crime reflects the fact that making a case with testimony and tangible things not only satisfies the formal definition of an offense, but tells a colorful story with descriptive richness. Unlike an abstract premise, whose force depends on going precisely to a particular step in a course of reasoning, a piece of evidence may address any number of separate elements, striking hard just because it shows so much at once; the account of a shooting that establishes capacity and causation may tell just as much about the triggerman's motive and intent. Evidence thus has force beyond any linear scheme of reasoning, and as its pieces come together a narrative gains momentum, with power not only to support conclusions but to sustain the willingness of jurors to draw the inferences, whatever they may be, necessary to reach an honest verdict. This persuasive power of the concrete and particular is often essential to the capacity of jurors to satisfy the obligations that the law places on them.[113]

---

[111] 519 U.S. 172 (1997).

[112] *Id.* at 191.

[113] *Id.* at 187. The Court also wrote:

> In sum, the accepted rule that the prosecution is entitled to prove its case free from any defendant's option to stipulate the evidence away rests on good sense. A syllogism is not a story, and a naked proposition in a courtroom may be no match for the robust evidence that would be used to prove it. People who hear a story interrupted by gaps of abstraction may be puzzled at the missing chapters, and jurors asked to rest a momentous decision on the story's truth can feel put upon at being asked to take

[E] Appellate Review

Appellate courts employ an abuse-of-discretion rule in reviewing a trial court's Rule 403 decisions.[114] Deference to the trial judge's discretion is usually justified on two grounds. First, because the factors which must be balanced are never the same in any two cases,[115] Rule 403 operates in an area of "indefinability" or "nonamenability to fixed legal rules."[116] As one court has recognized: "Many hundreds of potential relevancy issues pass before the trial judge. It is neither desirable nor possible for this court to lay down any general rule that will serve as a solution for every issue, for it is a different question of experience and common sense in each instance."[117] Second, the trial court's vantage point is superior to that of an appellate court reviewing a cold transcript. The trial judge observes the demeanor of witnesses and gets a feel for the trial.[118]

Entrusting discretion to the trial court, however, does not mean that the court is permitted to act arbitrarily. In *United States v. Dwyer*,[119] the trial court refused to provide reasons for excluding evidence. The Second Circuit reversed, stating: "The trial judge's refusal, despite repeated requests, to put his reasons for exclusion on the record substantially impairs our ability to ascertain the source of the 'prejudice' to which he referred in his ruling."[120]

§ 9.06 Similar Happenings; Other Accidents

Frequently, similar events are offered in evidence. This usually presents a problem of circumstantial proof, and the issue becomes how probative are

---

responsibility knowing that more could be said than they have heard. A convincing tale can be told with economy, but when economy becomes a break in the natural sequence of narrative evidence, an assurance that the missing link is really there is never more than second best.

Id. at 189.

[114] *E.g.,* United States v. Abel, 469 U.S. 45, 54 (1984) ("A district court is accorded a wide discretion in determining the admissibility of evidence under the Federal Rules.").

[115] *See* United States v. Morris, 79 F.3d 409, 412 (5th Cir. 1966) ("The admission in other cases, however, does not render erroneous the district court's exclusion of the evidence in the instant cause. To conclude otherwise would eviscerate a district court's discretion to determine admissibility based on the unique facts of each case.").

[116] Rosenberg, *Judicial Discretion*, 38 Ohio Bar 819, 824 (1965).

[117] State v. Anderson, 169 S.E.2d 706, 712 (S.C. 1969).

[118] *See* Espeaignnette v. Gene Tierney Co., Inc., 43 F.3d 1, 5 (1st Cir. 1994) ("Only rarely — and in extraordinarily compelling circumstances — will we, from the vista of a cold appellate record, reverse a district court's on-the-spot judgment concerning the relative weighing of probative value and unfair effect.") (internal quotation marks omitted).

[119] United States v. Dwyer, 539 F.2d 924 (2d Cir. 1976).

[120] *Id.* at 928 (quoting United States v. Robinson, 530 F.2d 1076, 1081 (D.C. Cir. 1976)). The court also wrote: "We find it difficult to comprehend the district judge's adamant refusal to respond to defense counsel's inquiries. The spirit of Rule 403 would have been better served had the judge 'confronted the problem explicitly, acknowledging and weighing both the prejudice and the probative worth' of the proffered testimony." *Id.*

incidents that differ as to parties, times, places, or circumstances from the event involved in the litigation.[121] Rules 401 and 403 govern in this context, unless the evidence involves character.[122] The test is often stated as whether there is *substantial similarity* between the other happening and the present litigation.[123] Nevertheless, the issue involves a classic Rule 403 analysis: Is the probative value (which often depends on similarity) substantially outweighed by the danger of confusing the jury and the consumption of time.[124]

Notice. Sometimes prior occurrences are relevant because they tend to show that a party knew or had a reasonable opportunity to know of a dangerous condition.[125]

Dangerousness. Other incidents may also be admissible to prove the existence of a dangerous condition. The weight of authority supports

---

[121] *See* Kelsay v. Consolidated Rail Corp., 749 F.2d 437 (7th Cir. 1984) (evidence of prior railroad crossing accidents excluded as too remote and dissimilar); Morris, *Proof of Safety History in Negligence Cases*, 61 Harv. L. Rev. 205 (1948).

[122] For example, prior accidents offered to prove a civil defendant is an incompetent driver are inadmissible character evidence. *See infra* § 10.08 (character evidence in civil cases). "Character in issue" is different; in a negligent entrustment suit, incompetence is an element of the cause of action and must be proved. *See infra* § 10.09 (character as an element). *See also infra* § 12.02 (habit & character distinguished).

[123] *See* Lovett ex rel. Lovett v. Union Pacific R.R., 201 F.3d 1074, 1080 (8th Cir. 2000) ("The district court excluded the evidence because the incidents were not 'substantially similar' to Lovett's accident, noting that none: (1) involved a 1985 Cherokee, (2) involved a collision with a locomotive, (3) occurred at a railroad crossing, (4) resulted in the Cherokee rolling over, (5) occurred in a similar topographical area, and (6) involved similar speeds."); First Sec. Bank v. Union Pacific R.R., 152 F.3d 877, 880 (8th Cir. 1998) ("In one of the three excluded accidents, the automobile's collision with the train was alleged to have been due to an apparent malfunction of the warning lights. In the two other accidents, the vehicles involved were traveling westward rather than eastward, giving the drivers an entirely different perspective of the crossing. In one of those accidents, the driver was traveling directly into the late afternoon sunlight when the collision occurred. Accordingly, we conclude that the district court committed no clear and prejudicial abuse of discretion in ruling that the three excluded accidents were not substantially similar to the collision involving Ms. Johnston.").

[124] *See Lovett*, 201 F.3d at 1081 ("[A]dmitting similar-incident evidence also threatens to raise extraneous controversial issues, confuse the issues, and be more prejudicial than probative. For these reasons, the facts and circumstances of the other incidents must be 'substantially similar' to the case at bar to be admissible. Based on our review of the record and the district court's reasoning, we are satisfied that the incidents were not 'substantially similar' to Lovett's accident and that the district court correctly excluded them.").

[125] *See* First Sec. Bank v. Union Pacific R.R., 152 F.3d 877, 879 (8th Cir 1998) ("prove notice of the existence of defects"); Benedi v. McNeil-P.P.C., Inc., 66 F.3d 1378, 1386 (4th Cir. 1995) ("The probative value of these reports was not outweighed by the danger of unfair prejudice, because the reports were highly probative on the issue of notice and because McNeil was free to, and did, offer testimony rebutting the significance of these reports."); Young v. Illinois Cent. Gulf R.R., 618 F.2d 332, 339 (5th Cir. 1980) (evidence of recent prior accidents admissible to show notice of an arguably dangerous railroad crossing without a "trial of the details and circumstances of those prior accidents").

admissibility — provided the former accidents occurred under substantially similar circumstances. [126]

Additional examples include other claims, misrepresentations, contracts, and business transactions, as well as sales of similar property as evidence of value.

Absence of other happenings. The lack of other accidents (good safety history) may be admissible to show the absence of a dangerous condition. [127] Showing probative value, however, is far more difficult here. It depends, first, on whether the relevant condition remained constant over time and, second, on whether any accidents would have been reported.

§ 9.07   Adverse Inferences

An adverse inference can often be drawn from conduct. Such conduct is sometimes known as an "implied admission." [128] Different aspects of this issue are discussed in this section.

[A]   Admissions by Conduct — Flight, Alias, etc.

Conduct of a party, such as intimidating witnesses, may be used circumstantially to draw an adverse inference. [129] Other examples include evidence of false statements, [130] escape, [131] offers to bribe witnesses, [132] refusal

---

[126] *See* Kinser v. Gehl Co., 184 F.3d 1259, 1273 (10th Cir. 1999) ("Both federal and Kansas law permit the introduction of similar accidents in product liability actions to prove 'notice, the existence of a defect, or to refute testimony given by a defense witness that a given product was designed without safety hazzards.' As a prerequisite to admitting such evidence, the proponent must demonstrate 'the circumstances surrounding the other accidents were substantially similar to the accident involved in the present case.' ") (citations omitted); Nachtsheim v. Beech Aircraft Corp., 847 F.2d 1261, 1268 (7th Cir. 1988) ("Evidence of other accidents in products liability cases is relevant to show notice to the defendant of the danger, to show existence of the danger, and to show the cause of the accident.") (citing numerous cases).

[127] *E.g.,* Pandit v. American Honda Motor Co., Inc., 82 F.3d 376, 380 (10th Cir. 1996) ("Evidence of the absence of prior similar claims will not be admitted unless it relates to a substantially similar product. . . ."); Hines v. Joy Mfg. Co., 850 F.2d 1146, 1153–54 (6th Cir. 1988) (evidence of lack of prior claims admissible "to show lack of defective design and lack of notice of any defect"); Jones v. Pak-Mor Mfg. Co., 700 P.2d 819, 824 (Ariz. 1985) ("There is little logic in the proposition that the trial court may admit evidence of other accidents but may never admit evidence of their absence.").

[128] Most "admissions by conduct" cases do not present hearsay problems because the conduct is not intended to be an assertion and therefore falls outside the definition of a "statement" in Rule 801(a) (sometimes known as "implied assertions"). In any event, party admissions are exempted from the hearsay rule under Rule 801(d)(2).

[129] *See also* Gorelick, Marzen & Solum, Destruction of Evidence (1989); Maguire & Vincent, *Admissions Implied from Spoliation or Related Conduct,* 45 Yale L. J. 226 (1935).

[130] *E.g.,* Wilson v. United States, 162 U.S. 613, 621 (1896) ("[F]alse statements in explanation or defense, made or procured to be made, are in themselves tending to show guilt. The destruction, suppression, or fabrication of evidence undoubtedly gives rise to a presumption inference of guilt, to be dealt with by the jury.").

[131] *E.g.,* United States v. Hankins, 931 F.2d 1256, 1262 (8th Cir. 1991) (evidence of escape

to provide handwriting exemplars,[133] and use of an alias.[134] Silence following the reading of *Miranda* warnings is another illustration, but one that raises constitutional issues.[135]

Similarly, flight from justice may indicate consciousness of guilt. As the proverb says: "The wicked flee, even when no man pursueth; but the righteous are bold as a lion."[136] Nevertheless, the relevance of this type of evidence is often questioned by courts[137] because evidence of flight "as circumstantial evidence of guilt depends upon the degree of confidence with which four inferences can be drawn: (1) from the defendant's behavior to flight; (2) from flight to consciousness of guilt; (3) from consciousness of guilt to consciousness of guilt concerning the crime charged; and (4) from consciousness of guilt concerning the crime charged to actual guilt of the crime charged."[138] In any event, such evidence often satisfies the relevancy requirements of Rule 401.[139]

The Federal Rules implicitly recognize this type of inference because a number of rules of exclusion assume that admissions by conduct are admissible. For example, Rule 407 makes subsequent remedial measures

---

admitted on facts but noting "the often marginally probative value of evidence of flight or escape"); United States v. Guerrero, 756 F.2d 1342, 1347 (9th Cir. 1984) ("The fact that the escape took place the day before defendants were to be arraigned on the charges involved in this case strongly suggests that the escape was motivated by the considerations related to this case.").

[132] *E.g.,* United States v. Mendez-Oritz, 810 F.2d 76, 79 (6th Cir. 1986) ("Though not listed in Rule 404(b), spoliation evidence, including evidence that defendant attempted to bribe and threatened a witness, is admissible to show consciousness of guilt.").

[133] *E.g.,* United States v. Jackson, 886 F.2d 838, 846 (7th Cir. 1989) ("[E]vidence of the defendant's refusal to furnish writing exemplars, like evidence of flight and concealment, is probative of consciousness of guilt.").

[134] *E.g.,* United States v. Valencia-Lucena, 925 F.2d 506, 513 (1st Cir. 1991) (Defendant "demonstrated a consciousness of guilt by twice assuming a pseudonym."); United States v. Boyle, 675 F.2d 430, 432 (1st Cir. 1982) ("The use of a false name after the commission of a crime is commonly accepted as being relevant on the issue of consciousness of guilt.").

[135] This inference is inadmissible on constitutional, not evidentiary, grounds. *See infra* § 22.10[H] (constitutional issues).

[136] Proverbs 28:1.

[137] *See* Wong Sun v. United States, 371 U.S. 471, 483 n. 10 (1963) ("[W]e have consistently doubted the probative value in criminal trials of evidence that the accused fled the scene of an actual or supposed crime."); Alberty v. United States, 162 U.S. 499, 511 (1896) ("[I]t is a matter of common knowledge that men who are entirely innocent do sometimes fly from the scene of a crime through fear of being apprehended as the guilty parties, or from an unwillingness to appear as witnesses. The criticism to be made upon this charge is that it lays too much stress upon the fact of flight.").

[138] United States v. Myers, 550 F.2d 1036, 1049 (5th Cir. 1977). *Accord* United States v. Murphy, 996 F.2d 94, 96 (5th Cir. 1993); United States v. Dillon, 870 F.2d 1125, 1127 (6th Cir. 1989).

[139] *See* United States v. Zanghi, 189 F.3d 71, 83 (1st Cir. 1999) ("Evidence of an accused's flight may be admitted at trial as indicative of a guilty mind, so long as there is an adequate factual predicate for the inference that the defendant's movement was indicative of a guilty conscience, and not normal travel.").

or repairs inadmissible if offered to prove negligence; without this exclusionary rule, the repair might be admissible as an admission by conduct.[140]

[B] Destruction of Evidence (spoliation)

Spoliation involves the destruction of evidence. The concept is captured in a legal maxim: "all things are presumed against a wrongdoer." It is a type of circumstantial evidence, an implicit admission of the weakness of a party's case: "A court and a jury are entitled to presume that documents destroyed in bad faith while litigation is pending would be unfavorable to the party that has destroyed the documents."[141] Documents destroyed in good faith pursuant to a valid record retention policy should not be subject to this inference.[142]

There are other remedies in addition to the adverse inference, including criminal prohibitions,[143] exclusion of witnesses, discovery sanctions,[144] and tort remedies.[145]

[C] Failure to Produce Evidence

Sometimes a party's failure to produce evidence may be used to draw an adverse inference.[146] Perhaps the most familiar instance is an accused's

---

[140] *See also* Fed. R. Evid. 408 (offers to compromise); Fed. R. Evid. 409 (medical payments).

[141] Brown & Williamson Tobacco Corp. v. Jacobson, 827 F.2d 1119, 1134 (7th Cir. 1987) (intentional destruction). *Accord* A.C. Becken Co. v. Gemex Corp., 314 F.2d 839, 841 (7th Cir. 1963) ("The law is well settled that these circumstances give rise to an inference that the records destroyed would have been unfavorable to plaintiff.").

[142] Lewy v. Remington Arms Co., 836 F.2d 1104, 1111–12 (8th Cir. 1988) (destruction of documents); Coates v. Johnson & Johnson, 756 F.2d 524, 551 (7th Cir. 1985) (The "documents were destroyed under routine procedures, not in bad faith, and thus cannot sustain the inference that defendants' agents were conscious of a weak case.").

[143] Obstructing justice and tampering with evidence.

[144] Fed. R. Civ. P. 37. *See also* Carlucci v. Piper Aircraft Corp., 102 F.R.D. 472, 486 (S.D. Fla. 1984) (default judgment entered due to destruction of documents).

[145] The leading case is Smith v. Superior Court, 198 Cal. Rptr. 829 (App. Ct. 1984). *See generally* Solum & Marzen, *Truth and Uncertainty: Legal Control of the Destruction of Evidence*, 36 Emory L. J. 1085 (1987); Stipancich, *The Negligent Spoliation of Evidence: An Independent Tort Action May Be the Only Acceptable Alternative*, 53 Ohio St. L.J. 1135 (1992).

[146] *E.g.*, Jewell v. Holzer Hospital Foundation, Inc., 899 F.2d 1507, 1514 (6th Cir. 1990) ("Under Ohio law, there is a general rule that a jury may draw a negative inference from a party's failure to produce, or failure to explain the omission of, relevant evidence within his control and not equally available to the opposing party."); S.C. Johnson & Son, Inc. v. Louisville & Nashville R.R., 695 F.2d 253, 259 (7th Cir. 1982) ("It is elementary that if a party has evidence in its control and fails to produce it, an inference may be warranted that the document would have been unfavorable. *However . . . it must appear that the party had some reason to suppose that non-production would justify the inference . . . the totality of the circumstances must bring home to the non-producing party notice that the inference may be drawn.*") (quoting from Commercial Ins. Co. Newark v. Gonzalez, 512 F.2d 1307, 1314 (1st Cir. 1975). *See generally* Kaye, *Do We Need A Calculus of Weight to Understand Proof Beyond a Reasonable Doubt?*, 66 B.U. L. Rev. 657 (1986); Saltzburg, *A Special Aspect of Relevance: Countering Negative Inferences Associated with the Absence of Evidence*, 66 Cal. L. Rev. 1011 (1978).

failure to testify. Commenting on an accused's failure to testify is prohibited on constitutional, not evidentiary, grounds.[147] This prohibition, of course, does not apply in civil cases.

[D] "Missing Witness" Rule

Similarly, a party's failure to call a presumably favorable witness may give rise to an adverse inference. Known as the "missing witness rule,"[148] this inference was mentioned by the Supreme Court in an 1889 case, *Graves v. United States*.[149] Nevertheless, the inference is often troublesome, especially in criminal cases.[150] The rule applies only when one party has superior "access" to a witness, and this is often not clear cut. In addition, issues of surprise as well as the consumption of time entailed in bringing in witnesses to counter the inference point toward exclusion of this type of evidence.

§ 9.08 Out-of-court Experiments

Expert testimony is often based on out-of-court experiments. Admissibility depends on whether the experiment was conducted under *substantially similar circumstances* as those involved in the case. Rule 403 governs the admissibility of out-of-court experiments. Note, however, that the "substantially similar standard is a flexible one which, even when construed strictly, does not require that all variables be controlled."[151]

For example, the results of shotgun tests conducted to determine muzzle-to-target distance have been admitted in evidence.[152] When a shot shell

---

[147] *See* Griffin v. California, 380 U.S. 609, 614 (1965) (accused's failure to testify cannot be the subject of comment by the court or prosecutor). *See infra* § 43.05[A] (comment on failure to testify).

[148] *See* 2 Wigmore, Evidence § 286 (Chadbourn rev. 1981); Lindley & Eggleston, *The Problem of the Missing Evidence*, 99 Law Q. Rev. 86 (1983); McDonald, *Drawing an Inference from the Failure to Produce a Knowledgeable Witness: Evidentiary and Constitutional Considerations*, 61 Cal. L. Rev. 1422 (1973); Stier, *Revisiting the Missing Witness Inference — Quieting the Loud Voice from the Empty Chair*, 44 Md. L. Rev. 137 (1985).

[149] Graves v. United States, 150 U.S. 118, 121 (1893) ("[I]f a party has it peculiarly within his power to produce witnesses whose testimony would elucidate the transaction, the fact that he does not do it creates the presumption inference that the testimony, if produced, would be unfavorable.").

[150] *See* State v. Brewer, 505 A.2d 774, 777 (Me. 1985) ("To allow the missing-witness inference in a criminal case is particularly inappropriate since it distorts the allocation of the burden of proving the defendant's guilt.").

[151] United States v. Metzger, 778 F.2d 1195, 1204 (6th Cir. 1985). *See also* Persian Galleries, Inc. v. Transcontinental Ins. Co., 38 F.3d 253, 258 (6th Cir. 1994) ("Because the videotaped experiment was substantially similar to the actual conditions at the burglary scene, the district court did not abuse its discretion . . ."); Cowens v. Siemens-Elema AB, 837 F.2d 817, 820 (8th Cir. 1988).

[152] *E.g.*, Andrews v. State, 555 P.2d 1079, 1083 (Okla. Crim. App. 1976) ("The results of tests to determine the distance from which a weapon had been fired are admissible into evidence provided the test was conducted under conditions sufficiently similar to the actual conditions involved in the case that they can be fairly said to have probative value and will enlighten, not confuse, the jury.").

is fired, the pellets generally emerge from the muzzle grouped together and then disperse in an ever-increasing pattern as the distance from the muzzle increases. The closer the shotgun is to the target, the smaller the dispersion pattern. By firing a shotgun at different distances, the dispersion pattern for a particular distance may be ascertained and compared to the dispersion pattern present at the crime scene. The relevancy of these experiments depends on the extent to which the conditions existing at the crime can be replicated in the experiment. Because the dispersion pattern differs for different shotguns and different types of ammunition, the identical weapon and the same type of ammunition used in the crime typically are required for this type of test. If the conditions are not substantially similar, the results are not admissible.[153]

Courts often distinguish between experiments offered as a *reconstruction* of the accident and those that merely *illustrate* general scientific principles: "[E]xperiments which purport to recreate an accident must be conducted under conditions similar to that accident, while experiments which demonstrate general principles used in forming an expert's opinion are not required to adhere strictly to the conditions of the accident."[154] This distinction is sometimes difficult to draw:

> [E]xperimental evidence falls on a spectrum and the foundational standard for its admissibility is determined by whether the evidence is closer to simulating the accident or to demonstrating abstract scientific principles. The closer the experiment gets to simulating the accident, the more similar the conditions of the experiment must be to the accident conditions.[155]

§ 9.09 Demonstrative Evidence

The use of demonstrative evidence often raises Rule 403 issues. Diagrams, maps, models, jury views, and in-court exhibitions and demonstrations are considered in chapter 25. Photographs, videotapes, sound recordings, as well as computer animations and simulations, are examined in chapter 26.

§ 9.10 Key Points

Relevancy is the most pervasive concept in evidence law. It is the threshold issue for all evidence. If the evidence is not relevant, it is excluded.

---

[153] *E.g.,* Miller v. State, 236 N.E.2d 585 (Ind. 1968); Roberts v. State, 35 S.W.2d 175, 178 (Tex. Crim. 1931).

[154] Gilbert v. Cosco, Inc., 989 F.2d 399, 402 (10th Cir. 1993).

[155] McKnight v. Johnson Controls, Inc., 36 F.3d 1396, 1402 (8th Cir. 1994).

Rule 401

Rule 401 embraces two concepts: *relevancy* and *materiality*. To be admissible, evidence must be both relevant and material. However, instead of the term "material fact," Rule 401 uses the phrase "fact that is of consequence to the determination of the action," which can be shortened to *consequential fact*. "Relevancy" describes the *relationship* between an item of evidence and the proposition it is offered to prove. In contrast, "materiality" describes the *relationship* between that proposition and the issues in the case — *i.e.,* the consequential or material facts.

Materiality. With the exception of the credibility of witnesses,[156] the "consequential facts" in a particular case are a matter of substantive law — (1) the elements of the charged crime, (2) the elements of a cause of action, (3) the elements of an affirmative defense, and (4) damages in civil cases. The pleadings may remove some of these elements; for example, if the complaint alleges negligence and the answer does not deny negligence but asserts contributory negligence as a defense, negligence is off-the-table; it is no longer an issue in this case.

Relevancy. Rule 401 defines "relevant evidence" as evidence having any tendency to make the existence of a material or consequential fact "more probable or less probable than it would be without the evidence." Rule 401's standard does *not* require that the evidence make a consequential (material) fact "more probable than not" (preponderance of evidence), but only that the material fact be more probable with the evidence *than without the evidence*. Rule 401 embraces a *very low* standard.

Admissibility vs. sufficiency. There is a difference between relevancy (admissibility) and sufficiency. Although the evidence as a whole must be sufficient to satisfy a party's burden of production and thus send the issue to the trier of fact, each item of evidence need only advance the inquiry. You can only call one witness at a time, and each witness need not hit a home run; you can score sometimes by hitting three singles or a double and a single. The federal drafters cited McCormick's metaphor to capture this point: "A brick is not a wall."

Direct & circumstantial evidence. Problems of relevancy typically involve circumstantial rather than direct evidence. The distinction turns on the manner in which an item of evidence relates to the material issues in the case. "Footprints in the snow" is a common example. If you see the paperboy deliver the newspaper to your house in the morning, you have *direct* evidence of delivery. In contrast, if you look out your window in the early morning and observe footprints in the snow, you have *circumstantial* evidence of delivery. You must draw a *further inference* to reach the conclusion that the newspaper has been delivered. Direct evidence is not necessarily better than circumstantial evidence.

---

[156] The credibility of witnesses, although not part of the substantive law, is always considered a consequential or material fact.

"Inference upon inference" rule. Some cases state that an inference cannot be stacked upon another inference. This rule makes no sense; reasoning requires inferences upon inferences.

"Background" evidence. All evidence need not involve a disputed issue. The federal drafters specifically approved of the admission of "background" evidence: "A rule limiting admissibility to evidence directed to a controversial point would invite the exclusion of this helpful evidence, or at least the raising of endless questions over its admission." As examples, the drafters cited charts, photographs, views of real estate, and murder weapons.

Rule 402

Rule 402 is the general provision governing the admissibility of evidence: relevant evidence is admissible in the absence of a rule of exclusion, and irrelevant evidence is inadmissible. For present purposes, the most important part of Rule 402 is the phrase "by these rules." This language allows relevant evidence to be excluded by operation of some other rule of evidence. A number of exclusionary rules are found elsewhere in the Rules of Evidence. Rule 403 is an illustration. Examples in other Articles include rules on privilege, competency, firsthand knowledge, hearsay, authentication, and best evidence. In sum, evidence may meet the relevancy standard of Rule 401 but be nevertheless inadmissible because it fails to satisfy the requirements of some other provision of the Rules of Evidence.

Relevant evidence may also be excluded due to the Constitution, federal statutes, or the Civil and Criminal Rules of Procedure.

Rule 403

Rule 403 is the *most important* rule in evidence law because every item of evidence raises a Rule 403 problem — at least in theory. It confers no authority to admit irrelevant evidence; Rule 402 mandates the exclusion of irrelevant evidence.

The application of Rule 403 requires a three-step process. First, the judge must determine the probative value of the proffered evidence. Second, the court must identify the presence of any of the enumerated dangers (unfair prejudice, confusion of issues, or misleading the jury) or considerations (undue delay, waste of time, or needless presentation of cumulative evidence). Finally, the court must balance the probative value against the identified dangers or considerations. If the enumerated dangers or considerations *substantially* outweigh the probative value of the evidence, exclusion is discretionary. The word "substantially" is significant; it makes Rule 403 biased in favor of admissibility.

Although not explicitly stated in Rule 403, the judge should consider (1) the effect of cautionary jury instructions, (2) the availability of alternative proof, and (3) the possibility of stipulations to reduce unfair prejudice in making the balancing determination. The Supreme Court's decision in *Old Chief* is a double edged sword in terms of stipulations.

Unfair prejudice. Rule 403 requires exclusion only in the case of *unfair* prejudice. Most evidence introduced by one party is "prejudicial" to the other side in the sense that it damages that party's position at trial. This is *not* the concern of Rule 403. Otherwise, the most probative evidence *(e.g.,* a confession) would be excluded as the most "prejudicial." In other words, there is a difference between being unfavorable and being *unfairly* prejudicial.

Appellate review. Courts of appeals employ an abuse-of-discretion rule in reviewing a trial court's Rule 403 decisions.

Similar Happenings; Other Accidents

Frequently, similar events are offered in evidence. This usually presents a problem of circumstantial proof, and the issue becomes how probative are incidents that differ as to parties, times, places, or circumstances from the event involved in the litigation. Rules 401 and 403 govern in this context, unless the evidence involves character. The test is often stated as whether there is *substantial similarity* between the other happening and the present litigation. Nevertheless, the issue involves a classic Rule 403 analysis: Is the probative value (which often depends on similarity) substantially outweighed by the danger of confusing the jury and the consumption of time.

Notice & dangerous conditions. Prior occurrences are sometimes admissible to show notice or a dangerous condition. Additional examples include other claims, misrepresentations, contracts, and business transactions, as well as sales of similar property as evidence of value.

Absence of other happenings. The lack of other accidents (good safety history) may be admissible to show the absence of a dangerous condition. Showing probative value, however, is far more difficult here. It depends, first, on whether the relevant condition remained constant over time and, second, on whether any accidents would have been reported.

Adverse Inferences

In some cases an adverse inference can be drawn from conduct. This is sometimes characterized as an "implied admission."

Admissions by conduct — flight, alias, etc. Conduct of a party, such as intimidating witnesses, may be used circumstantially to draw an adverse inference. Other examples include evidence of false statements, escape, offers to bribe witnesses, refusal to provide handwriting exemplars, and use of an alias.

Destruction of evidence (spoliation). Spoliation involves the destruction of evidence. It is a type of circumstantial evidence, an implicit admission of the weakness of a party's case. Documents destroyed in good faith pursuant to a valid record retention policy should not be subject to this inference.

"Missing witness" rule. A party's failure to call a presumably favorable witness may give rise to an adverse inference. The inference is often troublesome, especially in criminal cases. The rule applies only when one party has superior "access" to a witness, and this is often not clear cut. In addition, issues of surprise as well as the consumption of time entailed in bringing in witnesses to counter the inference point toward exclusion.

Out-of-Court Experiments

Expert testimony is often based on out-of-court experiments. Admissibility depends on whether the experiment was conducted under *substantially similar circumstances* as those involved in the case. Rule 403 governs. Courts often distinguish between experiments offered as a *reconstruction* of the accident and those that merely *illustrate* general scientific principles. The former generally must be conducted under circumstances closer to the conditions existing at the time of the event which is the subject of the litigation.

Chapter 10

CHARACTER EVIDENCE: FRE 404, 405, 412-15

§ 10.01 Introduction

The saying, "Once a thief, always a thief," captures the notion of *propensity* or *disposition* proof, better known as character evidence. Federal Rule 404(a) governs the circumstantial use of character evidence, *i.e.*, the admissibility of evidence of a character trait to prove that a person acted in conformity with that trait on a particular occasion (character-as-proof-of-conduct). For example, a person's character for honesty may be circumstantially relevant to a theft charge because it could be argued that a person with an honest character tends to act in conformity with that character and thus would be less likely to steal. Similarly, it could be argued that a dishonest person tends to act in conformity with that character and thus is more likely to steal.

General prohibition. Although character evidence may be probative, at least in some cases, it is generally inadmissible. Both Rule 404(a)[1] and Rule 404(b)[2] prohibit character-as-proof-of-conduct. Recent amendments drastically change this rule in sex offense cases (Rules 413–15).

Exceptions. Much of the prejudice inherent in the use of character disappears when an accused offers evidence of her own character or that of a victim. Accordingly, Rule 404(a) recognizes exceptions for (1) a criminal defendant's character and (2) a victim's character in self-defense cases when offered by the accused. Rule 412, the rape shield law, is a special provision limiting the use of the victim's character in sex offense cases. A third exception in Rule 404(a) involves a witness's character and is limited to impeachment (*i.e.*, character for truthfulness), a topic discussed in chapter 22.

Methods of proof. Rule 404(a) specifies the conditions under which character evidence is admissible. The rule does not specify the methods of proof that may be used to establish character. Rule 405(a) governs the methods of proof. Generally, only opinion and reputation evidence (not specific acts) are permitted to prove character when a Rule 404(a) exception applies.

"Character in issue." There is a second use of character evidence. It involves those rare cases in which character is an element of a cause of action, a crime, or a defense. Rule 404(a) does not cover this use of character. Rule

---

[1] Fed. R. Evid. 404(a) (character evidence "not admissible for the purpose of proving that a person acted in conformity therewith on a particular occasion").

[2] Fed. R. Evid. 404(b) ("Evidence of other crimes, wrongs, or acts is not admissible to prove the character of a person in order to show action in conformity therewith.").

405(b), however, specifies the methods of proof when character is "in is-sue."[3] In this situation, specific instances of conduct may be used to estab-lish character.

Other-acts evidence. Rule 404(b) provides that evidence of other crimes, wrongs, or acts, although not admissible to prove character, may be admissible for some other purpose, such as proof of motive, opportunity, intent, preparation, plan, knowledge, identity, or absence of mistake or accident. Other-acts evidence is discussed in the next chapter.

Habit evidence. Rule 406 governs the admissibility of evidence of habit; in some instances, character and habit may be difficult to distinguish.[4] The difference, however, is important because character evidence is generally inadmissible while the opposite is true for habit evidence.

§ 10.02   Rationale for Prohibiting Character Evidence

Although character evidence may be probative, at least in some cases, it is generally excluded because it is extremely prejudicial. There is a concern that the jury will overvalue the evidence and convict the accused for who he is rather than for what he has done. The jury might conclude that the defendant may not be guilty of the charged crime, but he must have gotten away with other crimes.[5]

The accused's character may be improperly introduced in a variety of ways, *e.g.*, "mug" shots, rap sheets, and prior arrests as well as profile[6] or syndrome evidence.[7]

§ 10.03   Methods of Proof: FRE 405

Rule 405 specifies the permissible methods of proving character. It governs how character may be proved but not when character may be proved. In theory, there are three methods of proof: (1) reputation, (2) opinion, and (3) specific acts. For example, if you wanted to determine somebody's honest character at law school, you could ask about that

---

[3] *See infra* § 10.09 (character as element of a cause of action).

[4] *See infra* § 12.02 (habit & character distinguished).

[5] One court put it this way: "(1) The overstrong tendency to believe the defendant guilty of the charge merely because he is a person likely to do such acts; (2) the tendency to condemn not because he is believed guilty of the present charge but because he has escaped punishment from other offenses; (3) the injustice of attacking one who is not prepared to demonstrate the attacking evidence is fabricated; and (4) the confusion of issues which might result from bringing in evidence of other crimes." Whitty v. State, 149 N.W.2d 557, 563 (Wis. 1967).

[6] *See* State v. McMillan, 590 N.E.2d 23, 32 (Ohio 1990) (profile of sex abusers improper "group character evidence").

[7] *See* State v. Pargeon, 582 N.E.2d 665 (Ohio App. 1991) (In a domestic violence prosecution, evidence that the accused's wife is a battered woman "really serves as evidence of the prior bad acts from which the inference may be drawn that appellant has the propensity to beat his wife and that he beat her on this particular occasion. This is precisely the prohibited inference that is excluded. . . .").

person's reputation for honesty, ask someone who knows that person well (opinion), or ask about that person's conduct — *e.g*, person found a wallet filled with money and returned it to the owner. There is a hierarchy working here. Because of numerous *specific acts*, other people form *opinions*, and collective opinions become *reputation*. Although specific acts may be the most probative, this method of proof takes the most time and carries with it the potential for distraction. If a party contests the specific act, there may be counterproof and a "trial within a trial." For this reason, it is generally prohibited.

[A] Reputation Evidence

If character is admissible pursuant to Rule 404(a)(1) (accused's character) or Rule 404(a)(2) (victim's character), Rule 405(a) provides that reputation evidence may be used to prove that character. Reputation is not synonymous with character; it is only one method of proving character.[8]

Foundational requirements. The offering party must lay an adequate foundation, establishing the witness's qualifications to testify about a person's reputation in the community — *i.e.*, where that person lives, works, or goes to school.[9] Furthermore, it is knowledge of the accused's or victim's reputation at the time of the charged offense (not the time of trial) that is relevant for this purpose.[10]

[B] Opinion Evidence

If character is admissible pursuant to Rule 404(a)(1) or 404(a)(2), opinion evidence may also be used to prove that character. Thus, a witness who is sufficiently acquainted with the accused or the victim may give a personal opinion about that person's character. This expands the common law, which permitted only reputation evidence.[11]

---

[8] Rule 803(21) recognizes a hearsay exception for reputation evidence concerning character.

[9] The foundation typically includes eliciting how long the witness has been part of the community, how long the defendant or victim has been part of the community, whether the witness has discussed the defendant or victim with others in the community, and whether, based on these discussions, the witness has an opinion concerning the reputation.

[10] *See* United States v. Curtis, 644 F.2d 263, 268–69 (3d Cir. 1981) ("In dealing with community reputation for a trait of character, moreover, it has long been settled that reputation reasonably contemporaneous with the acts charged is relevant, but that reputation after the criminal charge under consideration is not. The reason for this limitation on relevancy is that the accused's reputation could well be affected by the gossip which accompanies an indictment, and thus might not be a fair reflection of his character.") (citations omitted).

[11] Fed. R. Evid. 405 advisory committee's note ("In recognizing opinion as a means of proving character, the rule departs from usual contemporary practice in favor of that of an earlier day. See 7 Wigmore § 1986, pointing out that the earlier practice permitted opinion and arguing strongly for evidence based on personal knowledge and belief as contrasted with 'the secondhand, irresponsible product of multiplied guesses and gossip which we term "reputation."' It seems likely that the persistence of reputation evidence is due to its largely being opinion in disguise. If character is defined as the kind of person one is, then account must be taken of varying ways of arriving at the estimate. These may range from the opinion of the employer who has found the man honest to the opinion of the psychiatrist based upon examination and testing.").

Foundational requirements. As with reputation evidence, the offering party must qualify the character witness by laying a foundation showing that the witness is sufficiently acquainted with the accused or victim to have formed an opinion about that person's character. With opinion evidence, familiarity with the person herself rather than with that person's reputation is determinative.

Expert testimony. The federal advisory note refers to the "opinion of the psychiatrist based upon examination and testing." The federal courts, however, are divided over the admissibility of this type of evidence. In one case, the Fourth Circuit held that it was not an abuse of discretion to exclude psychiatric testimony that the defendant possessed a personality configuration inconsistent with the outrageous and senseless murders of his family for which he was charged.[12] In contrast, the Seventh Circuit has held that a psychologist's testimony concerning the nonaggressive character of a defendant should have been admitted.[13]

[C] Specific Instances Reflecting Untruthful Conduct

Evidence of specific instances of conduct could be an effective means of proving character. For example, evidence that a person stole money on a previous occasion would be relevant in ascertaining that person's character for honesty. Although this type of evidence may be the strongest evidence of character, Rule 405(a) prohibits its use when character is admitted under Rule 404(a)(1) or (2).[14] As noted above, this type of proof is time-consuming and risks distracting the jury from the issues in the case. This is one of many compromises found in this area of law.

Specific instances, however, may be the subject of cross-examination, a topic discussed in the next section. In addition, Rule 405(b) permits the use of specific instances of conduct, as well as reputation and opinion evidence, to prove character when character is "in issue," that is, when character is an essential element of a charge, claim, or defense.[15]

§ 10.04 Accused's Character: FRE 404(a)(1)

In a criminal case, the accused may offer evidence of a pertinent trait of his character.[16] Once the accused introduces such evidence, the

---

[12] United States v. MacDonald, 688 F.2d 224, 227–28 (4th Cir. 1982).

[13] United States v. Staggs, 553 F.2d 1073, 1075–76 (7th Cir. 1977). *See also* United States v. Roberts, 887 F.2d 534, 536 (5th Cir. 1989); United States v. Hill, 655 F.2d 512, 515–17 (3d Cir. 1981).

[14] *See* United States v. Bautista, 145 F.3d 1140, 1152 (10th Cir. 1998) ("[E]vidence of the victim's aggressive character may be admissible . . . , to establish that the victim was the aggressor. Federal Rule of Evidence 404(a)(2) permits the use. . . . However, Fed.R.Evid. 405 limits the type of character evidence to reputation or opinion evidence. . . . Therefore, Bautista could have introduced evidence of Carrillo's reputation for aggressiveness, but he could not introduce specific instances of aggressive conduct.").

[15] *See infra* § 10.09 (character as element of a cause of action).

[16] *See* Edgington v. United States, 164 U.S. 361, 363 (1896) ("It is not necessary to cite

prosecution may cross-examine the defense character witness on the issue and offer rebuttal character evidence.

There are several limitations. First, it is the defendant's character at the time of the charged offense that is relevant. Second, Rule 405(a) limits the methods by which the accused may introduce character evidence. Under that provision only opinion and reputation evidence, and not specific instances of conduct, may be used. Third, in sex offense cases, Rules 412–15 preempt Rule 404.

Jury instructions. In some cases, evidence of good character offered by the accused may have a significant impact. As the Supreme Court has noted: "The circumstances may be such that an established reputation for good character, if it is relevant to the issue, would alone create a reasonable doubt, although, without it, the other evidence would be convincing."[17] Most federal courts hold that the "standing alone-reasonable doubt" instruction need not be given.[18] Some courts, however, take a different view — at least under certain circumstances.[19]

Personal history. Typically, an accused introduces evidence of good character through the testimony of character witnesses. Sometimes, however, character evidence or positive aspects of the accused's background is brought out by the defense during the examination of the accused or other defense witness.[20] This is often a risky tactic. Once the issue is injected into the trial in a significant way, the prosecution's right to rebut may be

---

authorities to show that, in criminal prosecutions, the accused will be allowed to call witnesses to show that his character was such as would make it unlikely that he would be guilty of the particular crime with which he is charged.").

[17] *Id.* at 366. *Accord* Michelson v. United States, 335 U.S. 469, 476 (1948) ("Such testimony alone, in some circumstances, may be enough to raise a reasonable doubt of guilt.").

[18] *E.g.,* United States v. Pujana-Mena, 949 F.2d 24, 28 n. 2 (2d Cir. 1991).

[19] *E.g.,* United States v. Foley, 598 F.2d 1323, 1336-37 (4th Cir. 1979); United States v. Lewis, 482 F.2d 632, 637 (D.C. Cir. 1973) (whenever the accused offers character evidence); Oertle v. United States, 370 F.2d 719, 726–27 (10th Cir. 1966).

[20] For example, in United States v. Castillo, 181 F.3d 1129, 1132 (9th Cir. 1999), a drug prosecution, the trial court initially ruled that the defendant's prior arrest for cocaine possession was inadmissible:

> On direct examination, Castillo testified that he worked with disadvantaged children, and would not have smuggled drugs "for a million dollars." Castillo portrayed himself as an anti-drug counselor who taught kids to "stay away from drugs." He added that he had never used drugs and would not touch them. Castillo's sweeping denial of any association with drugs was volunteered and often not responsive to questions posed by his lawyer. After hearing Castillo's testimony, the district court advised the parties it was reconsidering its earlier ruling excluding evidence of the 1997 arrest for cocaine possession. . . . Explaining that Castillo had portrayed himself as a "paragon of virtue" and "quintessential model citizen" who would never have anything to do with drugs, the district court concluded that the 1997 cocaine arrest "bears directly on [Castillo's] credibility" and admitted extrinsic evidence concerning the earlier arrest to impeach Castillo.

triggered.[21] The prosecution, however, may not insinuate the subject into evidence on cross-examination and then attempt to rebut it.[22]

[A] Pertinent Trait

The exception recognized in Rule 404(a)(1) permits the accused to introduce only evidence of a *pertinent* trait of character. In other words, the character trait must be relevant to the crimes charged — *e.g.*, peaceful character in crimes of violence; honest character for theft; and truthful character for perjury. The federal cases also permit "law-abiding" character.[23] The introduction of "law-abiding" character, however, is a two-edged sword. The prosecution rebuttal evidence for the character trait of *honesty* should be limited to *dishonesty*; the accused's character for violence is not relevant as rebuttal evidence. But if the accused introduces evidence of law-abiding character, the prosecution may rebut with any evidence of unlawful conduct — *e.g.,* convictions for assault or possession of drugs.[24]

[B] Prosecution Rebuttal Character Evidence

Once the accused has introduced evidence of a pertinent character trait, the prosecution may offer character evidence in rebuttal. The same limitations that apply to defense character evidence also apply to the prosecution. First, the character trait subject to rebuttal must be "pertinent" to the crime charged. For example, in a theft case the defense character witnesses should testify about the defendant's character for honesty. Accordingly, the rebuttal witnesses' testimony should be limited to the same trait, *i.e.*, dishonesty. Second, Rule 405(a) specifies the methods of proof. Thus, the prosecution, like the accused, is limited to opinion or reputation evidence.

[C] Prosecution Cross-examination

The prosecution also may challenge defense character evidence through the cross-examination of the character witnesses. Rule 405(a) provides: "On cross-examination, inquiry is allowable into relevant *specific instances* of conduct." Thus, a reputation or opinion witness may be asked on cross-examination "if she has heard" or "if she knows" of specific acts that reflect

---

[21] *Id.* at 1133–34 ("Courts are more willing to permit, and commentators more willing to endorse, impeachment by contradiction where . . . testimony is volunteered on direct examination. The distinction between direct and cross-examination recognizes that opposing counsel may manipulate questions to trap an unwary witness into 'volunteering' statements on cross-examination. . . . The distinction also recognizes that, as a practical matter, it is often difficult to determine whether testimony is invited or whether it is volunteered on cross-examination.").

[22] *See* United States v. Gilliland, 586 F.2d 1384 (10th Cir. 1978) (prosecution could not convert defense eyewitness into character witness by asking what kind of man defendant was).

[23] *E.g.,* United States v. Angelini, 678 F.2d 380 (1st Cir. 1982) (accused's character as law-abiding citizen always admissible); United States v. Hewitt, 634 F.2d 277 (5th Cir. 1981) (same).

[24] *E.g.,* United States v. Diaz, 961 F.2d 1417, 1419–20 (9th Cir. 1992) (being prone to criminal activity).

upon the character trait addressed by that witness. The cross-examiner "must take the witness's answer;" that is, extrinsic evidence of the specific act is not admissible.

Although decided before the enactment of the Federal Rules, *Michelson v. United States*[25] is the leading case on this subject. Michelson, charged with bribery of an IRS agent, called witnesses who testified about his good character for truth and honesty. The Supreme Court upheld the prosecutor's right to ask these witnesses whether they "had heard" about Michelson's 20-year-old *conviction* for a trademark violation and 27-year-old *arrest* for receiving stolen property. The justification for this type of cross-examination is that the prosecution has the right to test the basis for the character witness's testimony. A character witness who is unaware of a defendant's prior arrests and convictions would not appear to be very well informed about the defendant's reputation.[26] If the witness is informed but ignores such information, the witness's standards for assessing reputation are drawn into question. In *Michelson*, Justice Jackson used the following illustration:

> A classic example in the books is a character witness in a trial for murder. She testified she grew up with defendant, knew his reputation for peace and quiet, and that it was good. On cross-examination she was asked if she had heard that the defendant had shot anybody and, if so, how many. She answered, "Three or four," and gave the names of two but could not recall the names of the others. She still insisted, however, that he was of "good character." The jury seems to have valued her information more highly than her judgment and convicted.[27]

Good faith basis-in-fact requirement. The risk that the jury will use this information for an improper purpose — to infer character — is great notwithstanding a limiting instruction.[28] Moreover, the practice possesses the potential for abuse. As Wigmore observed: "This method of inquiry or cross-examination is frequently resorted to by counsel for the very purpose of injuring by indirection a character which they are forbidden directly to attack in that way; they rely upon the mere putting of the question (not caring that it is answered negatively) to convey their covert insinuation."[29] Consequently, courts have required that this type of cross-examination be

---

[25] 335 U.S. 469 (1948).

[26] *Id.* at 483 ("The inquiry as to an arrest is permissible also because the prosecution has a right to test the qualifications of the witness to bespeak the community opinion. If one never heard the speculations and rumors in which even one's friends indulge upon his arrest, the jury may doubt whether he is capable of giving any very reliable conclusions as to his reputation.").

[27] *Id.* at 479 n.16.

[28] *See* Fed. R. Evid. 105 (limiting instructions).

[29] 3A Wigmore, Evidence § 988, at 921 (Chadbourn rev. 1970).

conducted in good faith, *i.e.*, that the prosecutor have a basis in fact for asking the question.[30]

Pertinent trait. Only acts which bear some relationship to the particular character trait offered by the defendant can properly be raised on cross-examination. For example, if the character witness testifies about the defendant's character for honesty, the witness cannot be cross-examined about violent acts.[31]

Remoteness. Acts which are too remote are not the proper subject of cross-examination. The question concerning the 27-year-old arrest was permitted in *Michelson* only because "two of the character witnesses dated their acquaintance with defendant as commencing thirty years before the trial."[32]

Effect of current charge. Cross-examination of defense character witnesses concerning the effect of the current charges on the defendant's reputation or on the witness's opinion are improper because the question asks the witness to indulge in a hypothetical assumption of the defendant's guilt.[33]

Opinion evidence. While the "have you heard" form is proper when used with the cross-examination of a reputation witness, "did you know" is the proper form for an opinion witness.

[D] Self-defense Cases

If the accused introduces evidence of a victim's violent character (*see infra*), the prosecution may respond with evidence of the accused's violent character.[34]

---

[30] The *Michelson* Court recognized that this type of cross-examination placed a "heavy responsibility on trial courts to protect the practice from any misuse." 335 U.S. at 480. The Court went on to point out that the trial judge in that case "took pains to ascertain, out of presence of the jury, that the target of the question was an actual event, which would probably result in some comment among acquaintances if not injury to defendant's reputation. He satisfied himself that counsel was not merely taking a random shot at a reputation imprudently exposed or asking a groundless question to waft an unwarranted innuendo into the jury box." *Id.* at 481.

[31] *Id.* at 483–84.

[32] *Id.* at 484.

[33] *See* United States v. Guzman, 167 F.3d 1350, 1352 (11th Cir. 1999) ("The government may not, however, pose hypothetical questions that assume the guilt of the accused in the very case at bar. 'These [guilt-assuming] hypotheticals [strike] at the very heart of the presumption of innocence which is fundamental to Anglo-Saxon concepts of fair trial.'") (citations omitted); United States v. Mason, 993 F.2d 406, 409 (4th Cir. 1993) (question improper; citing numerous cases).

[34] A 2000 amendment added the following phrase "or if evidence of a trait of character of the alleged victim of the crime is offered by an accused and admitted under Rule 404(a)(2), evidence of the same trait of character of the accused [may be] offered by the prosecution." Rule 404(a)(1).

§ 10.05   Accused's Character in Sex Offense Cases: FRE 413–15

As part of the 1994 Violent Crime Control and Law Enforcement Act, Congress enacted Rules 413, 414, and 415, which govern the admissibility of evidence of an accused's character in sexual assault and child molestation cases, both criminal and civil.[35] These Rules brought about a fundamental change in evidence law.[36] They "were extraordinarily controversial at the time of their passage,"[37] and only a few states have comparable provisions.[38]

[A]   Sex Offense Cases

These rules raise several issues.

---

[35] *See* Duane, *The New Federal Rules of Evidence on Prior Acts of Accused Sex Offenders: A Poorly Drafted Version of a Very Bad Idea*, 157 F.R.D. 95 (1994); Ojala, *Propensity Evidence Under Rule 413: The Need for Balance*, 77 Wash. U. L.Q. 947 (1999); Symposium, *Perspectives on Proposed Federal rules of Evidence 413–15*, 22 Fordham Urban L.J. 265 (1995); Sheft, *Federal Rule of Evidence 413: A Dangerous New Frontier*, 33 Am. Crim. L. Rev. 57 (1995).

[36] *See* United States v. LeCompte, 131 F.3d 767, 768 (8th Cir. 1997) ("The admissibility of T.T.'s testimony has been considered by this Court once before. In LeCompte's first trial, the government offered the evidence under Rule 404(b). It was not then able to offer the evidence under Rule 414 because of its failure to provide timely notice of the offer, as required by Rule 414. The District Court admitted the evidence, and the jury convicted LeCompte. On appeal, this Court held that the District Court's admission of the evidence under Rule 404(b) was improper, and reversed LeCompte's conviction. United States v. LeCompte, 99 F.3d 274 (8th Cir. 1996). We now consider the admissibility of T.T.'s testimony in LeCompte's retrial, under Rule 414, the government having given timely notice the second time around.") (evidence admitted).

[37] United States v. LeMay, 260 F.3d 1018, 1032 (9th Cir. 2001) (concurring opinion). The congressional enactment of Rules 413–415 was delayed for 150 days in order to permit the Judicial Conference to submit recommendations. The Conference urged Congress to reconsider these rules: "[T]he new rules, which are not supported by empirical evidence, could diminish significantly the protections that have safeguarded persons accused in criminal cases and parties in civil cases against undue prejudice. These protections form a fundamental part of American jurisprudence and have evolved under long-standing rules and case law. A significant concern identified by the [Standing] committee was the danger of convicting a criminal defendant for past, as opposed to charged, behavior or for being a bad person. In addition, . . . because prior bad acts would be admissible even though not the subject of a conviction, mini-trials within trials concerning those acts would result when a defendant seeks to rebut such evidence." *Report of the Judicial Conference on the Admission of Character Evidence in Certain Sexual Misconduct Cases*, 159 F.R.D. 51, 53 (1994). Congress by inaction rejected this position.

[38] *See* Alaska Evid. R. 404(b)(3) ("In a prosecution for a crime of sexual assault in any degree, evidence of other sexual assaults or attempted sexual assaults by the defendant against the same or another person is admissible if the defendant relies on a defense of consent. In a prosecution for a crime of attempt to commit sexual assault in any degree, evidence of other sexual assaults or attempted sexual assaults by the defendant against the same or another person is admissible."); State v. Kennedy, 803 So. 2d 916, 921 (La. 2001) ("[W]e have consistently restricted this judicially-recognized 'lustful disposition' exception . . . to evidence of other sexual crimes committed by the defendant against the same prosecuting victim, whether child or adult.").

Rule 403. A critical issue is whether Rule 403 applies, giving the trial judge the authority to exclude this type of evidence in certain cases. The cases uniformly apply Rule 403. A number of factors are considered relevant to this analysis:

> [1] how clearly the prior act has been proved; [2] how probative the evidence is of the material fact it is admitted to prove; [3] how seriously disputed the material fact is; [4] whether the government can avail itself of any less prejudicial evidence[;] . . . [5] how likely it is such evidence will contribute to an improperly-based jury verdict; [6] the extent to which such evidence will distract the jury from the central issues of the trial; and [7] how time consuming it will be to prove the prior conduct.[39]

Although the remoteness of the evidence diminishes its probative value, some cases have admitted evidence of conduct 16–20 years earlier.[40] Courts have differed on how the Rule 403 balance should be struck[41] and whether a record of Rule 403 balancing is required.[42]

Due process. Since these provisions effect a breathtaking change in a long-established principle of Anglo-American law, they have been challenged on due process grounds. The courts have rejected this argument.[43] In effect,

---

[39] United States v. Enjady, 134 F.3d 1427, 1433 (10th Cir. 1998). *See also* United States v. LeMay, 260 F.3d 1018, 1028 (9th Cir. 2001) ((1) similarity of the prior acts to the acts charged, (2) closeness in time to the acts charged, (3) frequency of the prior acts, (4) presence or lack of intervening circumstances, and (5) necessity of the evidence beyond the testimony already offered at trial).

[40] *See* United States v. Larson, 112 F.3d 600, 605 (2d Cir. 1997) ("Stevens testimony covered events 16–20 years prior to trial. Those events closely paralleled the events complained of by Furs, taking place in the same geographic locations, with Larson using the same enticements for both boys, plying both with alcohol, and engaging both in similar progressions of sexual acts. The similarity of the events clearly demonstrated the Stevens testimony's relevance."); United States v. LeCompte, 131 F.3d 767, 770 (8th Cir. 1997) ("The sexual offenses committed against T.T. were substantially similar to those allegedly committed against C.D. By comparison, the differences were small. In particular, the District Court itself acknowledged that the time lapse between incidents 'may not be as significant as it appears at first glance, because defendant was imprisoned for a portion of the time between 1987 and 1995, which deprived defendant of the opportunity to abuse any children.' ").

[41] *Compare* United States v. Guardia, 135 F.3d 1326, 1331 (10th Cir. 1998) (Rule 413 "contains no language that supports an especially lenient application of Rule 403."), *with* United States v. Meacham, 115 F.3d 1488, 1492 (10th Cir. 1997) ("Rule 403 balancing is still applicable, . . . but clearly under Rule 414 the courts are to 'liberally' admit evidence of prior uncharged sex offenses.").

[42] *See* United States v. Castillo, 140 F.3d 874, 884 (10th Cir. 1998) ("As we said in a similar case: '[T]he district court's summary disposition of this issue renders it impossible for us to review the propriety of its decision. . . . Without any reasoned elaboration by the district court we have no way of understanding the basis of its decision. . . . As an appellate court, we are in no position to speculate about the possible considerations which might have informed the district court's judgment. Instead, we require an on the record decision by the court explaining its reasoning in detail.' ").

[43] *See* United States v. Enjay, 134 F.3d 1427, 1433 (10th Cir. 1998) ("Considering the safeguards of Rule 403, we conclude that Rule 413 is not unconstitutional on its face as a violation of the Due Process Clause."); *Castillo*, 140 F.3d at 883 ("The due process violation that the

the federal cases read Rule 403 into these provisions and then use it to parry the due process argument.

Equal Protection. One criticism of these rules is the disparate treatment between sex and other crimes. Empirical support for such treatment is lacking. [44] However, the courts, using "rational basis" scrutiny, [45] have rejected equal protection attacks on this basis. [46]

Consent issue. Another issue is whether the change should have been limited to the issue of consent in rape cases — *i.e.*, date rape. Arguably, there is a greater need for character evidence in these cases. [47]

Method of proof. Unlike Rule 405(a), the methods of proof are not limited to reputation and opinion evidence. Specific instances are admissible. [48] Convictions are not required. [49]

Notice. Fifteen-day notice is required. It must include statements of witnesses or a summary of the substance of expected testimony. [50]

[B]　Child Molestation Cases

The molestation provision, Rule 414, has an age requirement — the alleged victim must have been under 14 years at the time of the offense. [51] Otherwise the issues are essentially the same as those discussed above.

---

defendant alleges here is that Rule 414 evidence is so prejudicial that it violates the defendant's fundamental right to a fair trial. Application of Rule 403, however, should always result in the exclusion of evidence that has such a prejudicial effect.").

[44] *See* Report, *supra* note 37 ("[T]he new rules . . . are not supported by empirical evidence . . ."). *See also* Baker, *Once a Rapist? Motivational Evidence and Relevancy in Rape Law*, 110 Harv. L. Rev. 563 (1997).

[45] *See Castillo*, 140 F.3d at 883 ("While the rule does treat those accused of child molestation differently than other criminal defendants, such a classification is not subject to a heightened standard of review. . . . Therefore, we ask only whether Rule 414 has a rational basis.").

[46] *E.g.*, United States v. Mound, 149 F.3d 799, 801 (8th Cir. 1998) ("Promoting the effective prosecution of sex offenses is a legitimate end. The legislative history of Rule 413 indicates good reasons why Congress believed that the rule was 'justified by the distinctive characteristics of the cases it will affect.' . . . These characteristics included the reliance of sex offense cases on difficult credibility determinations that 'would otherwise become unresolvable swearing matches,' as well as, in the case of child sexual abuse, the 'exceptionally probative' value of a defendant's sexual interest in children.").

[47] *See* Bryden & Park, *Other Crimes Evidence in Sex Offense Cases*, 78 Minn. L. Rev. 529 (1994).

[48] *See* United States v. Enjay, 134 F.3d 1427, 1434 (10th Cir. 1998) ("But here the government established that B had filed a contemporaneous police report and it presented the investigating officer's testimony about why the alleged rape of B was not prosecuted.").

[49] United States v. LeMay, 260 F.3d 1018, 1029 (9th Cir. 2001) (public record of a delinquency adjudication).

[50] *Enjay*, 134 F.3d at 1433. ("Rule 413(b) requires that the government disclose to defendant the similar crimes evidence to be offered no later than fifteen days before trial (unless shortened by court order). This notice period protects against surprise and allows the defendant to investigate and prepare cross-examination. It permits the defendant to counter uncharged crimes evidence with rebuttal evidence and full assistance of counsel.").

[51] Fed. R. Evid. 414(c). *See* United States v. Larson, 112 F.3d 600, 604 (2d Cir. 1997) ("We

[C] Civil Suits

Rule 415 governs the admissibility of evidence of an accused's other sex offenses in civil cases. For example, in *Johnson v. Elk Lake School Dist.*,[52] the plaintiff claimed that her guidance counselor had sexually harassed and abused her when she was in high school. The Third Circuit ruled that admissibility was governed by Rule 104(b)'s prima facie standard[53] and Rule 403.[54] The court went on to uphold the exclusion of the evidence:

> [T]he uncertainty of the testimony regarding intentionality, the dissimilarities between the similar and alleged acts, and the iso-lated nature of the Radwanski incident reduced significantly the probative value of Radwanski's testimony. Given this reduced probative value, any presumption in favor of admissibility was unwarranted, and the District Court's exclusion of the evidence can be justified on grounds that its introduction might have prejudiced Stevens unfairly, misled the jury, confused the issues, and wasted valuable trial time.[55]

§ 10.06 Victim's Character in Self-Defense Cases: FRE 404(a)(2)

At common law, a victim's character was considered relevant in two types of prosecutions: (1) on the issue of self-defense in homicide and assault cases, and (2) on the issue of consent in rape cases. In the latter cases, the rape-shield statute (Rule 412) rather than Rule 404 now controls. That rule is discussed in the next section. Consequently, Rule 404(a)(2) is applicable only when self-defense is raised.

The rule is limited to criminal cases. The prosecution is prohibited from introducing evidence of the victim's character until the defense "opens the door." The fear is that the prosecutor will paint the victim in glowing terms, which is irrelevant.

First aggressor issue. In a homicide or assault case, the defendant may introduce evidence of the victim's violent character to show that the victim

---

note that where, as here, a witness would testify to acts of molestation that began before the witness was 14 and continued after that age, analysis under Rule 404(b) in addition to Rule 414 will be necessary because the latter Rule, by its terms, authorizes the admission of evidence of molestation only of persons under the age of 14.").

[52] 283 F.3d 138 (3d Cir. 2002).

[53] *Id.* at 154–55 ("As such, a trial court considering evidence offered under Rule 415 must decide under Rule 104(b) whether a reasonable jury could find by a preponderance of the evidence that the past act was an 'offense of sexual assault' under Rule 413(d)'s definition and that it was committed by the defendant.").

[54] *Id.* at 155 ("It appears from the legislative history of Rules 413–15, however, that despite the seemingly absolutist tone of the 'is admissible' language, Congress did not intend for the admission of past sexual offense evidence to be mandatory; rather, Congress contemplated that Rule 403 would apply to Rules 413–15.").

[55] *Id.* at 159.

was the first aggressor, thereby establishing one element of self-defense.[56] Once evidence of the victim's character is introduced by the accused, the prosecution may introduce rebuttal evidence of the *victim's* character for peacefulness. Moreover, the prosecution may respond with evidence of the *accused's* violent character.[57] (This is not the rule in many states).

Both the defense and prosecution are limited by Rule 405(a), which permits reputation and opinion evidence but not evidence of specific acts to prove character.[58]

[A] Special Rule in Homicide Cases

There is a special rule in homicide cases. *Any* evidence that the victim was the first aggressor in a homicide (but not an assault) case triggers the prosecution's right to introduce rebuttal evidence of the victim's peaceful character. For example, if the accused testifies that the victim was the first aggressor, but does not introduce character evidence on this issue, the prosecution may nevertheless introduce evidence of the victim's peaceful character in rebuttal. The disparate treatment in homicide vis-a-vis assault cases is based on the fact that the victim will not be available to contradict the defendant's version of events in a homicide.

[B] "Communicated" Character Distinguished

There is a second use of the victim's violent character that is also relevant to self-defense, *i.e.*, to show its effect on the accused's state of mind.[59] Because this use does not involve character-as-proof-of-conduct, neither Rule 404(a) nor Rule 405(a), limiting the methods of proof to reputation and opinion, apply. Instead, this issue falls under the general relevance rules, Rules 401 and 403. This theory of relevancy obviously depends on whether the accused knew of the victim's character, including knowledge of the victim's reputation or specific acts of violence.[60]

---

[56] *See generally* Dressler, Understanding Criminal Law § 18.02[B] (3d ed. 2001).

[57] A 2000 amendment added the following phrase to Rule 404(a)(1): "or if evidence of a trait of character of the alleged victim of the crime is offered by an accused and admitted under Rule 404(a)(2), evidence of the same trait of character of the accused [may be] offered by the prosecution."

[58] *E.g.*, United States v. Bautista, 145 F.3d 114, 1152 (10th Cir. 1998) ("[E]vidence of the victim's aggressive character may be admissible . . . to establish that the victim was the aggressor. Federal Rule of Evidence 404(a)(2) permits the use. . . . However, Fed. R. Evid. 405 limits the type of character evidence to reputation or opinion evidence unless the character or trait of character is an essential element of the charge, claim, or defense. . . . Therefore, Bautista could have introduced evidence of Carrillo's reputation for aggressiveness, but he could not introduce specific instances of aggressive conduct.").

[59] The reasonable belief issue is a distinct element of self-defense; it differs from the first-aggressor issue. *See generally* Dressler, Understanding Criminal Law § 18.05[A] (3d ed. 2001).

[60] The evidence is not hearsay because it is not offered for the truth (*i.e.*, that the victim was a violent person) but rather to show its effect on the accused. *See infra* § 31.06[A] (show effect on listener).

In contrast, if character evidence is introduced to show that the victim acted in conformity with that character and was therefore the first aggressor, the accused's awareness of the victim's character is not relevant.[61]

§ 10.07   Rape Shield Law: FRE 412

Rule 404(a)'s exception for evidence of the victim's character is subject to Rule 412, the "rape shield law." In effect, Rule 412 trumps Rule 404(a).[62]

At common law, an accused charged with rape was permitted to introduce evidence of the victim's *unchaste* character as circumstantial proof of consent. This rule rested on the dubious assumption that a woman who had consented to premarital or extramarital intercourse was more likely to consent than a woman who had not consented to such past intercourse.[63] Beginning in the 1970s, this assumption, along with other aspects of rape prosecutions, came under vigorous attack by the feminist movement.[64] Virtually all states responded by enacting "shield" laws, which limit the admissibility of evidence of the victim's character. Adopted in 1978, Rule 412 is the federal version.[65]

---

[61] *See* 1A Wigmore, Evidence § 63, at 1369 (Tillers rev. 1983) ("The additional element of communication is unnecessary, for the question is what the deceased probably did, not what the accused probably thought the deceased was going to do. The inquiry is one of objective occurrence, not of subjective belief.").

[62] Rape is a crime of violence. A felony at common law, rape was defined as carnal knowledge of a woman, by a man who was not her husband, without her consent. *See generally* Dressler, Understanding Criminal Law ch. 33 (3d ed. 2001).

[63] Wigmore went even further:

> There is, however, at least one situation in which chastity may have a direct connection with veracity, viz. when a woman or young girl testifies as complainant against a man charged with a sexual crime. . . . Modern psychiatrists have amply studied the behavior of errant young girls and women coming before the courts in all sorts of cases. Their psychic complexes are multifarious, distorted partly by inherent defects, partly by diseased derangements or abnormal instincts, partly by bad social environment, partly by temporary physiological or emotional conditions. One form taken by these complexes is that of contriving false charges of sexual offenses by men. The unchaste (let us call it) mentality finds incidental but direct expression in the narration of imaginary sex incidents of which the narrator is the heroine or the victim. The real victim, however, too often in such cases is the innocent man; for the respect and sympathy naturally felt by any tribunal for a wronged female helps to give easy credit to such a plausible tale.

3A Wigmore, Evidence § 924a, at 736 (Chadbourn rev. 1970). *See also* Bienen, *A Question of Credibility: John Henry Wigmore's Use of Scientific Authority in Section 924(a) of the Treatise on Evidence,* 19 Cal. W. L. Rev. 235 (1983) (criticizing Wigmore).

[64] *See generally* Althouse, *Thelma and Louise and the Law: Do Rape Shield Rules Matter,* 25 Loy. L.A. L. Rev. 757 (1992); Berger, *Man's Trial, Woman's Tribulation: Rape Cases in the Courtroom,* 77 Colum. L. Rev. 1 (1977); Curcio, *Rule 412 Laid Bare,* 67 U. Cin. L. Rev. 125, 155–56 (1998); Galvin, *Shielding Rape Victims in the State and Federal Courts: A Proposal for the Second Decade,* 70 Minn. L. Rev. 763 (1986); Ordover, *Admissibility of Patterns of Similar Sexual Conduct: The Unlamented Death of Character for Chastity,* 63 Cornell L. Rev. 90 (1977); Spector & Foster, *Rule 412 and the Doe Case: The Fourth Circuit Turns Back the Clock,* 35 Okla. L. Rev. 87 (1982).

[65] Federal criminal jurisdiction over the crime of rape is quite limited. The cases arise from federal jurisdiction over Native American Reservations and military enclaves.

Rationale. Rape Shield Laws are designed to protect the complainant's sexual privacy by discouraging the tendency in rape cases to try the victim rather than the defendant. They may also encourage the reporting of rape. Finally, by excluding evidence that is unduly inflammatory, they are intended to aid in the truth-finding process.[66]

The critical point, however, is that the evidence is simply not relevant.[67] The common law rule never took account of the fact that the prior sexual incidents were *not* followed by an accusation of rape, making them fundamentally different from the charged offense. In addition, the issue of whether there is such a thing as "unchaste character" is brought into question. The answer is no.

Scope of statute. The rape shield law, which applies in civil cases as well, excludes evidence of the victim's other sexual behavior and sexual disposition unless an exception applies.[68] For example, the following evidence was excluded in one case: (1) the victim's "general reputation in and around the Army post"; (2) the victim's "habit of calling out to the barracks to speak to various and sundry soldiers"; (3) the victim's "habit of coming to the post to meet people and of her habit of being at the barracks at the snack bar"; (4) the victim's former landlord's "experience with her" alleged promiscuous behavior; and (5) evidence of what a social worker learned of the victim.[69]

Several exceptions are recognized.

[A] Exception: Origin of Semen, Pregnancy or Disease

Rule 412(b)(1)(A) excepts evidence of specific instances offered to show that another person was the source of semen, injury or other physical evidence (*e.g.*, pregnancy or disease).[70] This exception does not involve

---

[66] *See* United States v. Rouse, 111 F.3d 561, 569 (8th Cir. 1997) ("Rule 412 limits the admissibility of such evidence to protect the victims of rape and sexual abuse."); United States v. Saunders, 943 F.2d 388, 390 (4th Cir. 1991) ("The rule manifests the policy that it is unreasonable for a defendant to base his belief of consent on the victim's past sexual experiences with third persons, since it is intolerable to suggest that because the victim is a prostitute, she automatically is assumed to have consented with anyone at any time. If we were to require admission of Smith's testimony about his affair with Duckett, we would eviscerate the clear intent of the rule to protect victims of rape from being exposed at trial to harassing or irrelevant inquiry into their past sexual behavior, an inquiry that, prior to the adoption of the rule, had the tendency to shield defendants from their illegal conduct by discouraging victims from testifying.").

[67] *See* United States v. Kasto, 584 F.2d 268, 271–72 (8th Cir. 1978) ("[E]vidence of a rape victim's unchastity, whether in the form of testimony concerning her general reputation or direct or cross-examination testimony concerning specific acts with persons other than the defendant, is ordinarily insufficiently probative either of her general credibility as a witness or of her consent to intercourse with the defendant on the particular occasion . . . to outweigh its highly prejudicial effect.").

[68] Rule 412 was amended in 1994 to extend the rule to (1) all criminal cases (*e.g.*, kidnapping); (2) impeachment; and (3) civil cases (such as sexual harassment).

[69] Doe v. United States, 666 F.2d 43, 47 (4th Cir. 1981).

[70] Note the method of proof for this exception. By excluding reputation and opinion evidence, Rule 412 differs from Rule 405(a). Indeed, they are opposites.

character as proof-of-conduct. It is sometimes called the "Scottsboro rebuttal."[71] The infamous *Scottsboro* case involved a group of African-American men and teenagers charged with raping two white women on a freight train in Alabama during the Depression. The prosecutor offered evidence of semen to establish intercourse. The defense attempted to introduce evidence that the women had sex the night before in a hobo jungle in Chattanooga. (The rape charges were unsubstantiated. Indeed, one of the woman recanted).[72] Evidence offered under this exception is not automatically admissible.[73]

[B]   Exception: Past Sexual Activity with Accused

Rule 412(b)(1)(B) excepts evidence of specific instances of sexual behavior between the accused and the alleged victim. Typically, this exception is limited to the issue of consent.[74] The probative value of past incidents is no more probative here than it is with third parties. Nevertheless, it would be nearly impossible to ask the jury to decide the case without knowing the relationship between the accused and accuser. Even here, the evidence is not automatically admissible.[75]

[C]   Exception: Constitutionally-Required

Rule 412(b)(1)(C) recognizes a "constitutional exception." Because rape shield laws preclude evidence that is arguably exculpatory, their constitutionality has been questioned.[76] Two Supreme Court cases, *Davis v. Alaska*[77] and *Chambers v. Mississippi*,[78] are usually cited in support of the defendant's right to introduce evidence of the victim's character, at least in some circumstances. In *Davis*, the Court held that a state statute excluding evidence of a juvenile adjudication (a type of shield law) violated

---

[71] 23 Wright & Graham, Federal Practice and Procedure § 5388 (1980).

[72] *See* Carter, Scottsboro: A Tragedy of the American South (rev. ed. 1979). The case went to the Supreme Court several times. *See* Norris v. Alabama, 294 U.S. 587 (1935) (systematic exclusion of African Americans from jury pool); Powell v. Alabama, 287 U.S. 74 (1932) (right to counsel).

[73] *See* United States v. Azure, 845 F.2d 1503, 1506 (8th Cir. 1988) ("We believe the district court properly excluded this evidence as irrelevant to the source of the three centimeter laceration on Wendy's vaginal wall.").

[74] *See* United States v. Saunders, 943 F.2d 388, 392 (4th Cir. 1991) ("When consent is the issue, however, [Fed. R. 412](b)(1)(B) permits only evidence of the defendant's past experience with the victim.").

[75] *See* United States v. Romone, 218 F.3d 1229, 1238 (10th Cir. 2000) (aggravated assault and aggravated sexual abuse, the court commented: "[I]t is difficult to discern what relevance the testimony could have to Ramone's consent defense. We can not agree with the defendant that evidence of prior consensual use of inanimate objects during sex is probative of whether sex after a brutal beating was consensual.").

[76] *See generally* Tanford & Bocchino, *Rape Victim Shield Laws and the Sixth Amendment*, 128 U. Pa. L. Rev. 544 (1980). *See also* authorities cited in note 64 *supra*.

[77] 415 U.S. 308 (1974). *See infra* § 36.04[A] (discussing *Davis*).

[78] 410 U.S. 284 (1973). *See infra* § 31.08 (discussing *Chambers*).

the defendant's Sixth Amendment right of confrontation. In *Chambers*, the Court held that the application of state evidentiary rules that excluded critical and reliable defense evidence violated due process. Neither case involved a rape shield statute and both required the defense evidence to be reliable and probative. Thus, it is not surprising that the shield laws have survived constitutional scrutiny when attacked on their face.

In contrast, individual cases are sometimes a different matter. For example, in *State v. Jalo*,[79] the accused argued that the victim accused him of rape after he had threatened to tell her parents of her sexual conduct with his son. This involved past sexual history but not character-as-proof-of-conduct; consent was not the issue. The court held the evidence was admissible. Application of the shield law in this case precluded the defendant from establishing the complainant's motive to accuse him falsely, the core of his defense.

In *Olden v. Kentucky*,[80] the Supreme Court held that an accused had the right to introduce evidence of the complainant's relationship with another person to show motive for a false accusation. An alleged rape victim testified that Olden had tricked her into leaving a bar, raped her, and then drove her to the house of Bill Russell, where she was released. Russell, also a prosecution witness, testified that he had seen the victim leave Olden's car and that she had immediately complained of rape. The defense claimed consent, arguing that the victim and Russell were involved in an extramarital relationship and that the victim fabricated the rape story to explain to Russell why she was in the defendant's car. By the time of trial, the victim and Russell were living together, but the trial judge refused to permit cross-examination on this fact.[81] The Supreme Court reversed per curiam. Olden had consistently maintained that the alleged victim lied because she feared jeopardizing her relationship with Russell. Thus, her current living arrangement with Russell was relevant to impeachment (bias), and the foreclosure of this line of inquiry violated the right of confrontation.

Prior false accusations. A number of cases have involved a defendant's attempt to introduce evidence of prior false accusations of rape. A rape accusation could be false in two different ways: (1) where there has never been sexual intercourse, and (2) where there has been intercourse but it was consensual. The latter situation may fall within the purview of a rape shield law. False accusations involve truthful character,[82] not unchaste character. The probative value of this type of impeachment depends on the accusations being false.[83] Moreover, most courts require the evidence to

---

[79] 557 P.2d 1359 (Or. App. 1976).

[80] 488 U.S. 227 (1988) (per curiam).

[81] The trial judge believed that this information would prejudice the jury against the victim because she was white and Russell was African American.

[82] *See* Fed. R. Evid. 608(b). *See also infra* § 22.09 (specific instances reflecting untruthful character).

[83] *See* State v. West, 24 P.3d 648, 656 (Haw. 2001) ("[N]early every jurisdiction addressing this question has consistently required a preliminary determination of falsity prior to the

be offered under a *bias* theory, as in *Jalo* and *Olden*, rather than a more generalized attack on untruthful character.[84] Bias is considered a far more potent method of impeachment.

Alternate sources of knowledge. Another situation in which a constitutional argument may be viable involves evidence showing an alternative source of knowledge for a child victim's "sophisticated" sexual knowledge.[85] This is analogous to rebuttal evidence on source of semen or injury. The argument for admissibility is stronger on rebuttal because the prosecution has now injected the issue into the case.

Mens rea. Sometimes evidence of prior sexual behavior is offered on the issue of mens rea — *i.e.*, relevant to the reasonableness of the defendant's belief concerning consent.[86] This issue involves a different element of the crime of rape — not consent, but the mens rea for the element of consent.[87] In effect, this is a "mistake of fact" defense, which is not an affirmative defense; it is simply an assertion that the defendant did not have the requisite mens rea, which the prosecution must prove beyond a reasonable doubt.[88] A problem arises because legislatures often fail to specify the mens rea for the consent element.[89] Another problem is that mens rea will always

---

admission of allegedly false statements of unrelated sexual assaults. . . . Furthermore, as some courts have explained, where the truth or falsity of a statement regarding an unrelated sexual assault is unknown, it falls within the purview of the rape shield statute and must be analyzed accordingly.").

[84] *See* Redmond v. Kingston, 240 F.3d 590, 592 (7th Cir. 2001) (alleged victim had admittedly fabricated an elaborate story of a rape incident in the past year to get her mother's attention); Boggs v. Collins, 226 F.3d 728, 739 (6th Cir. 2000) ("[W]e must reject Boggs's primary argument because it improperly blurs the precise distinctions drawn in Confrontation Clause jurisprudence. Not having articulated an argument sounding in motive, bias or prejudice, Boggs instead seeks to elevate his purpose — attacking Berman's general credibility — into a constitutionally mandated right. . . . No matter how central an accuser's credibility is to a case—indeed, her credibility will almost always be the cornerstone of a rape or sexual assault case, even if there is physical evidence — the Constitution does not *require* that a defendant be given the opportunity to wage a general attack on credibility by pointing to individual instances of past conduct."). *See also* Bopst, *Rape Shield Laws and Prior False Accusations of Rape: The Need for Meaningful Legislative Reform*, 24 J. Legis. 125, 141 (1998) (noting that whether an alleged false accusation of rape must be admitted under the Confrontation Clause turns on the distinction between proving bias or prejudice and proving general credibility).

[85] *See* LaJoie v. Thompson, 217 F.3d 663, 673 (9th Cir. 2000) (constitution required admissibility of evidence of prior rape to show that victim could have learned about sexual acts and male genitalia from source other than defendant); State v. Rolon, 777 A.2d 604 (Conn. 2001) (exclusion violated right of confrontation); State v. Grovenstein, 530 S.E.2d 406, 410 (S.C. App. 2000) ("Other jurisdictions have concluded that evidence of a young victim's sexual history is relevant where the defendant seeks to admit the evidence to show a source for the victim's sexual knowledge. Specifically, these courts found the evidence relevant to rebut the inference that a child victim could not describe the sexual acts unless the defendant had committed the alleged acts.").

[86] *See* United States v. Doe, 666 F.2d 43, 47 (4th Cir. 1981) (the defendant's "state of mind as a result of what he knew of her reputation and what she had said to him").

[87] It is somewhat similar to the "communicated character" issue raised in the self-defense context.

[88] *See* Dressler, Understanding Criminal Law § 33.05 (3d ed. 2001).

[89] Under the Model Penal Code, "recklessness" is the default mens rea if no mens rea is

be an element, and thus the possibility of introducing sexual history through the "backdoor" looms large in this context.[90]

[D] Procedure

Rule 412(c) sets forth the procedures for determining admissibility. It provides for 14-day notice and an in-chambers resolution of the issues,[91] as well as the alleged victim's right to participate. The notice and in camera hearing provisions may be the most important safeguards in the statute; the defense cannot introduce sexual history on any pretense, which had been the former practice, until the court rules. Here, the defense must convince the judge at a separate hearing.

Sanctions. In *Michigan v. Lucas,*[92] the Supreme Court ruled that the exclusion of defense evidence for failing to comply with the notice provision of a rape shield statute was not per se unconstitutional. The Court indicated, however, that exclusion in a particular case may be unconstitutional.

[E] Civil Cases

Rule 412 was amended in 1994 to extend the rule to civil cases such as sexual harassment.[93] The rule sets forth a stringent balancing test — the probative value must substantially outweigh the danger of harm to the

---

specified. An Alaska statute defines first degree sexual assault as requiring evidence that the defendant (1) knowingly engaged in sexual intercourse, and (2) recklessly disregarded the victim's lack of consent. *See* Velez v. State, 762 P.2d 1297, 1303 (Alaska App. 1988)

[90] *See* United States v. Saunders, 943 F.2d 388, 390 (4th Cir. 1991) ("The rule manifests the policy that it is unreasonable for a defendant to base his belief of consent on the victim's past sexual experiences with third persons, since it is intolerable to suggest that because the victim is a prostitute, she automatically is assumed to have consented with anyone at any time. If we were to require admission of Smith's testimony about his affair with Duckett, we would eviscerate the clear intent of the rule to protect victims of rape from being exposed at trial to harassing or irrelevant inquiry into their past sexual behavior, an inquiry that, prior to the adoption of the rule, had the tendency to shield defendants from their illegal conduct by discouraging victims from testifying.").

[91] *See* United States v. Rouse, 111 F.3d 561, 569 (8th Cir. 1997) ("The Rule has strict procedural requirements, including a timely offer of proof delineating what evidence will be offered and for what purpose, and an *in camera* hearing at which the victim may respond. Defendants' vague notice fell far short of complying with the Rule, and the district court properly excluded this evidence.").

[92] 500 U.S. 145 (1991).

[93] *See* Truong v. Smith, 183 F.R.D. 273, 275 (D.C. Colo. 1998) (civil sexual assault) ("Both of defendant's requests concern information regarding plaintiff's 'history of extramarital affairs' which defendant maintains are relevant to his defenses of consensual relationship and initiation of contact by plaintiff."; "Rule 412(a) expressly states that evidence of a victim's past sexual behavior is irrelevant to the credibility of her testimony, and that her prior sexual activity with third parties has no bearing on the issue of whether she consented to the sexual violence charged. From a plain reading of the Rule, it appears that Congress performed its own balancing test and adopted a per se rule that evidence of a victim's past sexual behavior with third parties is never more probative than prejudicial on the issue of consent.").

victim and unfair prejudice to a party. This is a "reverse" Rule 403 analysis, biased in favor of exclusion rather than admission. The rule also precludes reputation evidence unless placed in issue by the alleged victim.

§ 10.08   Character Evidence in Civil Cases

Assume that you are in a traffic accident and the other driver says, "That is the fifth accident that I have been in this year." That statement is inadmissible if offered against the driver. The first two exceptions in Rule 404(a) appear to apply only in criminal cases because the drafters used the term "accused" and the committee note supports this position.[94] A small minority of federal courts, however, have carved out an exception in civil cases when a central issue is criminal in nature.[95]

However, Rule 404(a)'s prohibition does not apply when character is an element of a cause of action, such as in a negligent hiring or entrustment suit, or an affirmative defense, a topic discussed in the next section.

§ 10.09   Character as Element of a Cause of Action or Defense

If character is an element of a crime, cause of action, or affirmative defense ("character in issue"), the prohibition of Rule 404(a) does not apply.[96] "Character in issue" presents a fundamentally different use of character evidence than the circumstantial use of character. If character is an element, it must be proved. Unfortunately, the phrase "character in issue" can be misleading because courtroom parlance frequently refers to the exceptions in Rule 404(a) as "opening the door" or "putting the accused's character in issue." This is not the same thing. Even if an accused introduces honest character in a theft prosecution, honest character is *not* an element of theft.

"Character in issue" is rare. Probably the most important example is a *negligent entrustment*, hiring, or supervising case.[97] Defamation suits also

---

[94] Fed. R. Evid. 404 advisory committee's note ("Character evidence is of slight probative value and may be very prejudicial. It tends to distract the trier of fact from the main question of what actually happened on the particular occasion. It subtly permits the trier of fact to reward the good man and to punish the bad man because of their respective characters despite what the evidence in the case shows actually happened.").

[95] *E.g.,* Bolton v. Tesoro Petroleum Corp., 871 F.2d 1266, 1277 (5th Cir. 1989); Perrin v. Anderson, 784 F.2d 1040, 1044 (10th Cir. 1986); Carson v. Polley, 689 F.2d 562 (5th Cir. 1982); Crumpton v. Confederation Life Ins. Co., 672 F.2d 1248, 1253 (5th Cir. 1982). *See also* Palmquist v. Selvick, 111 F.3d 1332, 1342 (7th Cir. 1997) (assuming admissibility).

[96] Fed. R. Evid. 404 advisory committee's note ("Character may itself be an element of a crime, claim, or defense. A situation of this kind is commonly referred to as 'character in issue.' Illustrations are: the chastity of the victim under a statute specifying her chastity as an element of the crime of seduction, or the competency of the driver in an action for negligently entrusting a motor vehicle to an incompetent driver. No problem of the general relevancy of character evidence is involved, and the present rule therefore has no provision on the subject.").

[97] *E.g.,* Parrish v. Luckie, 963 F.2d 201, 205 (8th Cir. 1992) (civil rights action against officer

illustrate this issue. If a plaintiff sues for defamation because the defendant called the plaintiff a "liar," the defendant can raise "truth" as a defense. In such a case, the plaintiff's character for truthfulness is an element of the defense.

§ 10.10 Key Points

Character evidence is a difficult subject because of the complexity of the rules and not because the concept is hard to learn.

General prohibition. Although character-as-proof-of-conduct may be probative, at least in some cases, it is generally inadmissible. However, recent amendments drastically change this rule in sex offense cases (Rules 413–15).

Methods of proof. Rule 405(a) governs the methods of proof. Generally, only opinion and reputation evidence (not specific acts) are permitted to prove character when a Rule 404(a) exception applies.

Accused's Character

The accused's character may be introduce in the following circumstances:

First, the accused may choose to offer evidence of a *pertinent* character trait (but only through reputation or opinion evidence) under Rule 404(a), in which case the prosecution may respond by cross-examining the character witnesses on specific acts to test the witness's qualifications, or by proffering rebuttal character witnesses.

Second, in sex offense cases, the prosecution (plaintiff) may offer evidence of the accused's character under Rule 413 (sex offenses), Rule 413 (child molestation cases), and Rule 415 (civil cases).

Third, if the accused introduces evidence of a victim's violent character in a self-defense case, the prosecution may respond with evidence of the accused's violent character.

Victim's Character

Self-defense cases. The accused may offer evidence of a victim's violent character (but only through reputation or opinion evidence) on the

---

and police chief; prior acts of violence by officer admitted to prove chief's knowledge of officer's violent character); In re Aircrash in Bali, Indonesia, 684 F.2d 1301, 1314–15 (9th Cir. 1982) (gist of cause of action is entrusting an incompetent employee with a dangerous instrumentality; incompetence — character trait — is an element of the cause of action); Guedon v. Rooney, 87 P.2d 209 (Ore. 1939) ("In cases in which it is sought to hold the owner of an automobile liable on the theory that his negligence in lending a car to an incompetent driver was in fact the cause of injury to the plaintiff, the better rule is to require such incompetence of the driver to be shown by specific acts of carelessness and recklessness committed by him. The car owner's knowledge of the driver's incompetence may be shown either by evidence that he in fact knew of such acts or by evidence tending to show that the driver's incompetence was generally known in the community."); Woods, *Negligent Entrustment: Evaluation of a Frequently Overlooked Source of Additional Liability*, 20 Ark. L. Rev. 101, 105–06 (1966).

first-aggressor issue. Note that there is a different use of character in self-defense cases — *communicated* character — on the issue of reasonable fear. Because this is not character-as-proof-of-conduct, Rules 404(a) and 405 do not apply. Instead, Rules 401–403 control.

Rape Cases. Rule 412, the rape shield law, generally precludes evidence of a victim's character in sex offense cases. There are three exceptions: (1) to show source of semen, pregnancy or disease, (2) to show the victim's past sexual activity with the accused, and (3) when constitutionally required. In addition, notice and in-chambers procedures are mandated.

Witness's Character

A third exception in Rule 404(a) involves a witness's character and is limited to impeachment (*i.e.*, character for truthfulness), a topic discussed in chapter 22.

Other Rules

"Character in issue." There is a second use of character evidence. It involves those rare cases in which character is an element of a cause of action, a crime, or a defense — *e.g.*, negligent entrustment suits. Rule 404(a) does not cover this use of character. Rule 405(b), however, specifies the methods of proof when character is "in issue."

Other-acts evidence. Rule 404(b) provides that evidence of other crimes, wrongs, or acts, although not admissible to prove character, may be admissible for some other purpose, such as proof of motive, opportunity, intent, preparation, plan, knowledge, identity, or absence of mistake or accident. Other-acts evidence is discussed in the next chapter.

Habit evidence. Rule 406 governs the admissibility of evidence of habit; in some instances, character and habit may be difficult to distinguish. Unlike character, habit evidence is admissible. See chapter 12.

Chapter 11

OTHER ACTS EVIDENCE: FRE 404(b)

§ 11.01 Introduction

"Other acts" evidence is the most litigated provision in the Rules of Evidence.[1] Also known as prior crimes or uncharged misconduct, the subject has vexed courts and lawyers for years. Long ago, Wigmore noted the "bewildering variances of rulings in the different jurisdictions and even in the same jurisdiction."[2] Unfortunately, the adoption of the Rules of Evidence has not appreciably changed this picture.[3]

Federal Rule 404(b) provides that evidence of other crimes, wrongs, or acts, although not admissible to prove character, may be admissible for some other purpose, such as proof of motive, opportunity, intent, preparation, plan, knowledge, identity, or absence of mistake or accident. Rule 404(b) must be read along with Rule 404(a). In effect, Rule 404(b) is a clarification provision. Rule 404(a) prohibits *only* the circumstantial use of character evidence (character-as-proof-of-conduct). When evidence of other crimes, wrongs, or acts is *not* offered for that purpose, Rule 404(a) simply does not apply. For example, if a person steals a gun and later uses that weapon to commit a murder, the theft may be relevant in the homicide prosecution to show the identity of the murderer. Thus, although evidence of the theft incidentally shows larcenous character, it is not being offered for that purpose, and thus Rule 404(a) does not prohibit its admission.

[A] Common Misconceptions

Several aspects of Rule 404(b) have caused unnecessary problems. The terms "similar act" or "prior crime" are frequently used to describe this subject matter; these terms are misleading.

Noncriminal conduct. Although often used to admit criminal acts, by its own terms, Rule 404(b) is not limited to crimes; it embraces "wrongs" and

---

[1] *See* Imwinkelried, Uncharged Misconduct Evidence viii (1994) ("The numbers alone tell the story: In most jurisdictions, alleged errors in the admission of uncharged misconduct are the most frequent ground for appeal in criminal cases; in many states, such errors are the most common ground for reversal; and the Federal Rule in point, Rule 404(b), has generated more reported cases than any other subsection of the rules.").

[2] 2 Wigmore, Evidence § 302, at 246 (Chadbourn rev. 1979).

[3] *See* 22 Wright & Graham, Federal Practice and Procedure § 5239, at 427 (1978) ("Rule 404(b) is a good illustration of Wigmore's Rule of Codification: the 'always conceded principle should frequently be found solemnly enacted, while the important controversies are ignored and left without solution.'").

"acts" as well.[4] As an example, consider a murder case in which the prosecution's theory is that the defendant killed the victim because he wanted to marry the victim's wife. Proof of an affair between the defendant and the victim's wife (the other-act) may be admissible to establish motive and ultimately identity.

Dissimilar acts. As the above example shows, the other-act need not be "similar" to the charged offense. (However, under some theories of admissibility, such as modus operandi, remarkable similarity is the theory of admissibility.[5])

Subsequent acts. The other-act need not have occurred prior to the charged offense; evidence of a subsequent act may be admissible.[6] For example, if a robbery defendant threatens a witness the day before trial, evidence of the threat may be admissible to show consciousness of guilt, even though it occurred *after* the charged offence.[7] Or, if after a robbery, the accused used credit cards belonging to the victim, this subsequent act could be used to show identity by connecting the defendant to the robbery.

Offered by accused. The accused may offer evidence under Rule 404(b) in an attempt to show another person committed the charged crime.[8]

Civil cases. Rule 404(b) is not limited to criminal cases; it applies in civil litigation as well.[9]

§ 11.02 Rule 404(b) Analysis

The application of the rule requires three steps:

(1) Rule 401 — identify a material issue (other than character) for which the evidence is being offered to prove (*i.e.*, identity of perpetrator, mens rea, corpus delicti);

(2) Rule 403 — balance the probative value of the evidence against the risk that the jury will ignore the limiting instruction and make the prohibited character inference (unfair prejudice); and

---

[4] *See* United States v. Brooke, 4 F.3d 1480,1483 (9th Cir. 1993) (other-act was feigning terminal cancer); United States v. Rubio-Gonzalez, 674 F.2d 1067, 1075 (5th Cir. 1982) ("Rule 404(b) authorizes the admission of prior 'acts' as well as 'crimes' and 'wrongs.'").

[5] *See infra* § 11.03[A] (proof of identity; modus operandi).

[6] *E.g.,* United States v. Dickerson, 248 F.3d 1036, 1046 (11th Cir. 2001) ("It is well-settled in this circuit that 'the principles governing what is commonly referred to as other crimes evidence are the same whether the conduct occurs before or after the offense charged, and regardless of whether the activity might give rise to criminal liability.'"; cocaine distribution almost two years after last overt act in alleged conspiracy) (citation omitted); United States v. Germosen, 139 F.3d 120, 128 (2d Cir. 1998) ("The fact that the evidence involved a subsequent rather than prior act is of no moment."); United States v. Miller, 959 F.2d 1535, 1538 (11th Cir. 1992) ("At the trial for the January offense, the government introduced the subsequent extrinsic September transaction.").

[7] *See supra* § 9.07[A] (admissions by conduct).

[8] *See infra* § 11.06 (other-acts evidence offered by the accused).

[9] *See infra* § 11.11 (other-acts evidence in civil cases).

(3) Rule 104(b) — determine whether there is prima facie evidence of the accused's involvement in the other act.

These three steps are discussed in the following sections.

§ 11.03   Determining "Materiality" Under Rule 401

Other-acts evidence must tend to prove a consequential (material) fact under Rule 401, *i.e.*, facts proving essential elements of the charged offense. Some of the "purposes" specified in Rule 404(b), such as identity, intent, and knowledge, name essential elements of crimes; thus, evidence relevant to one of these purposes is usually material.[10] Other listed "purposes," however, are not typically elements of crimes. For example, motive, opportunity, and plan are rarely essential elements. If other-acts evidence is offered for one of these purposes, the prosecutor must establish a relationship between the "purpose" and an essential element of the charged offense.

Deletion of the listed purposes in Rule 404(b) would probably be an improvement because "a frequent source of difficulty under Rule 404(b) is the tendency of prosecutors . . . to rely on a 'laundry list' of purposes."[11] Moreover, this tactic is often a subterfuge for sneaking character evidence before the jury.[12]

Typically, other-acts evidence is admitted as proof of one of three essential elements: (1) to show that the accused was the actor (identity issue); (2) to show that the accused possessed the requisite mental state (mens rea issue); or (3) to show that a crime has been committed (actus reus or corpus delicti issue).[13] In addition, it is sometimes impossible to separate the charged offense and the other-act. This is often referred to as "interrelated" acts or res gestae.[14] Finally, the entrapment defense raises further issues.[15]

---

[10] The list of purposes enumerated in Rule 404(b) is not exhaustive. The federal courts follow what is known as the "inclusionary," rather than an "exclusionary," approach. *See* United States v. Jones, 990 F.2d 1047, 1050 (8th Cir. 1993). Stated another way, other-act evidence may be offered for any purpose *other than character*.

[11] ABA Section of Litigation, Emerging Problems Under the Federal Rules of Evidence, Rule 404, at 58 (3d ed. 1998). *See also* People v. Golochowicz, 319 N.W.2d 518, 523–24 (Mich. 1982) ("The prosecutor's first duty is to identify, with specificity, the purpose for which the evidence is admissible. Prosecutors often loose a 'shotgun' fusillade of reasons which typically include most, if not all, of the purposes named in the statute."); 22 Wright & Graham, Federal Practice and Procedure § 5240, at 479 (1978) ("Particularly to be deplored is what might be called the 'smorgasbord' approach to analysis of other crimes evidence in which the court simply serves up a long list of permissible uses without any attempt to show how any of them are applicable to the case at hand.").

[12] *See* United States v. Sampson, 980 F.2d 883, 886 (3d Cir. 1992) ("Although the government will hardly admit it, the reasons proffered to admit prior bad act evidence may often be potemkin village, because the motive, we suspect, is often mixed between an urge to show some other consequential fact as well as to impugn the defendant's character."); People v. Tassell, 679 P.2d 1, 8 (Cal. 1984) (Prosecutor's argument that other-acts evidence was admissible as a "common plan or scheme" was "merely a euphemism for 'disposition.' ").

[13] 22 Wright & Graham, Federal Practice and Procedure § 5239, at 460 (1979).

[14] *See infra* § 11.03[D] (interrelated acts).

[15] *See infra* § 11.07 (entrapment cases).

[A] Proof of Identity; Modus Operandi

The identity of the person who committed the charged offense is always an essential element, and therefore always constitutes a consequential (material) fact. "Identity" is specifically listed in Rule 404(b). Moreover, several of the other listed "purposes" specified in the rule, such as motive, opportunity, or preparation may be relevant to prove identity.

Other-acts evidence may show identity in a number of ways. For example: (1) In a murder case, evidence of the defendant's affair with the victim's wife (the other-act) may be admissible to establish *motive*, and motive is probative of identity. (2) In a murder case in which the victim was killed by a bomb, evidence that the defendant had used a bomb in a prior offense may be admissible to establish the defendant's technical know-how with explosives, and this capacity (*opportunity*) is probative of identity. (3) In a bank robbery case, evidence that the defendant had previously stolen a car that was later identified as the robbery getaway car may be admissible to establish *preparation* and is probative of identity.

Modus operandi. Another way to prove identity is through what is known as modus operandi evidence, *i.e.*, the similarity between the other-act and the crime charged is so *striking* that the same person probably committed both offenses. The commission of two robberies with a weapon, however, is not sufficent.[16] There must be, as one court put it, a "behavioral fingerprint."[17]

Joinder & severance of offenses. Sometimes the admissibility of other-acts evidence is raised in cases considering whether to grant a motion for severance of offenses. If evidence of crimes in the other counts of an indictment are admissible under Rule 404(b), the argument for severance of offenses under Criminal Rule 14 is undercut because the evidence would be admissible even if the motion is granted.

Rule 403. Identifying the material issue, such as identity, is only the first step in determining admissibility. The evidence is still subject to exclusion under Rule 403.

---

[16] *See* United States v. Robinson, 161 F.3d 463, 468 (7th Cir. 1998) ("clearly distinctive from the thousands of the other bank robberies committed each year"); United States v. Shumway, 112 F.3d 1413, 1420 (10th Cir. 1997) ("signature quality" includes geographic location, the unusual quality of the crime, the skill necessary to commit the acts, or use of a distinctive device); United States v. Luna, 21 F.3d 874, 881 (9th Cir. 1994) (generic "takeover" bank robberies not sufficiently distinctive); People v. Haston, 444 P.2d 91, 99 (Cal. 1968) ("It is apparent that the indicated inference does not arise from the mere fact that the charged and uncharged offenses share certain marks of similarity, for it may be that the marks in question are of such common occurrence that they are shared not only by the charged crime and defendant's prior offenses, but also by numerous other crimes committed by persons other than defendant.").

[17] State v. Bey, 709 N.E.2d 484, 492 (Ohio 1999) ("The 'other act' evidence established a 'behavioral fingerprint' linking the [defendant] to the other crime due to the common features shared by the [prior] homicide and the [present] homicide. The deaths of the [two victims] occurred under practically identical circumstances."). *See also* State v. Smith, 551 N.E.2d 190, 194 (Ohio 1990) (accused charged with murder by administering an overdose of morphine to an overnight guest; evidence that another overnight guest also died from a morphine overdose admitted).

[B] Proof of Mens Rea: Intent, Knowledge

Other-acts evidence is often used to show that the accused possessed the requisite mental state for the charged offense, *i.e.*, to establish the mens rea.[18] Two of the listed "purposes" in Rule 404(b) — intent and knowledge — frequently are mens rea elements of crimes, and other-acts evidence may be relevant to prove these mental states. Motive and preparation, which are also listed, may relate to these elements. For example, a defendant's illicit affair with a homicide victim's wife is an other act which tends to show "motive," and a person with a motive is more likely to have intentionally killed than a person without a motive. Similarly, evidence that the defendant stole a gun the day before a homicide may show "preparation," and thus is probative of premeditation in a first degree murder case.

Lack of mistake or accident. The defenses of mistake and accident also relate to mens rea.[19] Neither is an affirmative defense; both involve a claim that the defendant lacked the requisite mens rea of the charged offense. For example, a defendant charged with murder who testifies that the weapon discharged "accidently" because he was unfamiliar with firearms is raising a defense of accident, which tends to negate the mens rea element of a purposeful killing. To rebut this claim, evidence that the defendant had used a weapon during a prior robbery may be admissible. Similarly, a defendant who claims she made a mistake about the nature of a controlled substance is asserting a lack of mens rea, *i.e.*, knowledge that the substance was heroin. Accordingly, her prior heroin transactions may be admissible to show that she is familiar with heroin and thus a "mistake" is unlikely.

Evidence of absence of mistake or accident is typically admitted in *rebuttal* rather than in the prosecution's case-in-chief because the issue is often raised for the first time during the defense's case-in-chief.[20]

Rule 403. Identifying the material issue, such as mens rea, is only the first step in determining admissibility. The evidence is still subject to exclusion under Rule 403.

[C] Proof of Corpus Delicti

Although not as common as the identity and mens rea examples cited above, other-acts evidence may be used to show that a crime has been committed, *i.e.*, to establish the corpus delicti or actus reus of the crime.[21] The famous "Brides in the Bath" case[22] illustrates this use. The defendant

---

[18] *See* 1 Imwinkelried, Uncharged Misconduct Evidence ch. 5 (rev. 1999) (mens rea).

[19] *See* Dressler, Understanding Criminal Law ch. 12 (3d ed. 2001).

[20] The issue, of course, could be raised by the defense during opening statements or through the cross-examination of prosecution witnesses, in which case the prosecution should be permitted to introduce this type of evidence in its case-in-chief. In general, however, the prosecution should not be permitted to introduce other-acts evidence to prove lack of mistake or accident unless mistake or accident is somehow raised by the defendant.

[21] *See* 1 Imwinkelried, Uncharged Misconduct Evidence ch. 4 (rev. 1999) (actus reus).

[22] Rex v. Smith, 11 Crim. App. 229, 84 L.J.K.B. 2153 (1915).

was accused of murdering his wife, who had been found drowned in a bath tub. The prosecution introduced evidence showing that his two other wives had also drowned while taking baths. The evidence was relevant to show that the death in the charged offense was homicidal and not accidental. A similar issue arose in *United States v. Woods,* [23] where the defendant was charged with the murder of an adopted child. A critical issue was whether the death was homicidal or natural. The prosecution offered evidence showing that nine other young children had died or been hospitalized while in the defendant's care.

Perhaps these examples could be classified as "absence of accident" cases. As discussed in the preceding section, however, evidence showing an absence of mistake or accident is admissible to rebut a defendant's claim of lack of mens rea. As such, the evidence typically should be admitted in rebuttal. The "Brides in the Bath" and *Woods* cases are different. The other-acts evidence had to be introduced in the prosecution's case-in-chief to prove that a crime had been committed. Otherwise, the case could have been terminated by a directed verdict for the defense. [24]

As explained earlier, identifying the material issue, such as corpus delicti, is only the first step in determining admissibility. The evidence is still subject to exclusion under Rule 403.

[D] Interrelated Acts ("Res gestae")

In some cases, it is impossible to exclude evidence of other acts that are interwoven ("inextricably interrelated") with the charged offense, even though such acts are not material to an essential element of the charged offense. [25] If two crimes are committed together, the prosecutor typically joins both in the same trial. [26] Sometimes that is not possible — for example,

---

[23] 84 F.2d 127, 133 (4th Cir. 1973) ("Thus, with regard to no single child was there any legally sufficient proof that defendant has done any act which the law forbids. Only when all of the evidence concerning the nine other children and Paul is considered collectively is the conclusion impelled that the probability that some or all of the other deaths, cyanotic seizures, and respiratory deficiencies were accidental or attributable to natural causes was so remote, the truth must be that Paul and some or all of the other children died at the hands of the defendant.").

[24] Fed. R. Crim. P. 29(a) (motion for judgment of acquittal).

[25] *See* United States v. Viscarra-Martinez, 66 F.3d 1006, 1012–13 (9th Cir. 1995) ("There are generally two categories of cases in which we have concluded that 'other act' evidence is inextricably intertwined with the crime with which the defendant is charged and therefore need not meet the requirements of Rule 404(b). First, we have sometimes allowed evidence to be admitted because it constitutes a part of the transaction that serves as the basis for the criminal charge. . . . Second, we have allowed 'other act' evidence to be admitted when it was necessary to do so in order to permit the prosecutor to offer a coherent and comprehensible story regarding the commission of the crime; it is obviously necessary in certain cases for the government to explain either the circumstances under which particular evidence was obtained or the events surrounding the commission of the crime. This exception to Rule 404(b) is most often invoked in cases in which the defendant is charged with being a felon in possession of a firearm.").

[26] *See* Fed. R. Crim. P. 8 (joinder of offenses).

a federal bank robbery prosecution in which the perpetrators steal a car (state crime) to make their getaway, and the federal prosecutor wants to use the stolen vehicle to connect them to the robbery.

This situation is sometimes described as evidence of "res gestae," a phrase that often confuses more than helps.[27] Furthermore, some federal cases hold that this situation is not governed by Rule 404(b) because the interrelated act is not an "other" or "extrinsic" act; rather it is an "intrinsic" act and thus part of the charged crime.[28] Under any view, however, the critical issue remains the same: How much of the other-act need be admitted to provide necessary context?

§ 11.04   Determining Admissibility Under Rule 403

Under Rule 403, relevant evidence may be excluded if its probative value is *substantially* outweighed by the dangers of unfair prejudice, confusion of issues, or misleading the jury. Other-acts evidence presents all three of these dangers, especially the risk of unfair prejudice because the jury may use the evidence for the impermissible purpose of inferring character.[29]

[A]   Disputed Issues

Even if "other acts" evidence is probative of an essential element of the charged offense, the evidence should not be admissible unless that element is a disputed issue in the particular case. This approach is especially important when other-acts evidence is offered on "mens rea." Consequently, the Second Circuit has stated that "other crimes evidence is inadmissible to prove intent when that issue is not really in dispute."[30] Although some

---

[27] The term "res gestae" is also misused in the hearsay context. *See infra* § 31.13 (res gestae).

[28] *E.g.,* United States v. Williams, 900 F.2d 823, 825 (5th Cir. 1990); United States v. Williford, 764 F.2d 1493, 1499 (11th Cir. 1985); United States v. Weeks, 716 F.2d 830, 832 (11th Cir. 1983) ("Evidence of criminal activity other than the charged offense is not considered extrinsic evidence within the proscription of Rule 404(b) of the Federal Rules of Evidence, [1] if it is an uncharged offense which arose out of the same transaction or series of transactions as the charged offense, [2] if it was inextricably intertwined with the evidence regarding the charged offense, or [3] if it is necessary to complete the story of the crime of trial.") (citations omitted). *But see* United States v. Levy, 731 F.2d 997, 1003 (2d Cir. 1984) (Rules 404(b) and 403 govern the admissibility of evidence of uncharged crimes that are inextricably interwoven with the charged offense).

[29] *See* Fed. R. Evid. 404(b) advisory committee's note ("No mechanical solution is offered. The determination must be made whether the danger of undue prejudice outweighs the probative value of the evidence in view of the availability of other means of proof and other factors appropriate for making decisions of this kind under Rule 403.").

[30] United States v. Williams, 577 F.2d 188, 191 (2d Cir. 1978). *See also* United States v. Oritz, 857 F.2d 900, 903 (2d Cir. 1988) (stating that if the other-acts evidence is offered to prove intent, the accused can avoid introduction of the evidence if his defense is that he did not distribute drugs at all and makes it clear that intent is not disputed; if, however, he claims that he distributed a substance without knowledge that the substance was a drug, other-acts evidence is admissible). Frequently, the offer of other-acts evidence should await the conclusion of the defendant's case and be aimed at a specifically identified issue. The prosecution should rest its case, "reserving, out of the presence of the jury, the right to reopen to present such

courts reject the "genuine dispute" requirement,[31] their view unnecessarily opens the door to highly prejudicial evidence: "The mere theory that a plea of not guilty puts everything material in issue is not enough. . . . The prosecution cannot credit the accused with fancy defenses in order to rebut them at the outset with some damning piece of prejudice."[32]

[B] Stipulations

Frequently, a stipulation will eliminate a dispute and thus should preclude the need for other-acts evidence.[33] The stipulation, however, "must be comprehensive and unreserved, completely eliminating the government's need to prove the point."[34] However, in *Old Chief v. United States*,[35] the Supreme Court indicated that a stipulation need not be routinely accepted in this context. This suggestion has not gone unnoticed and an offer to stipulate is no longer determinative.[36]

[C] Jury Instructions

It may be possible to reduce the prejudicial effect of other-acts evidence through instructions informing the jury that such evidence may not be used to infer character.[37] One court stated that the trial judge "must carefully

---

evidence in the event the defendants rest without introducing evidence." United States v. Figueroa, 618 F.2d 934, 939 n. 1 (2d Cir. 1980).

[31] *E.g.,* United States v. Miller, 725 F.2d 462, 466 (8th Cir. 1984) (prosecution need not await the defendant's denial of intent before offering evidence of similar acts).

[32] Thompson v. Rex, 1918 App. C. 221, 232 (1918).

[33] *E.g.,* United States v. Jenkins, 7 F.3d 803, 807 (8th Cir. 1993); United States v. Garcia, 983 F.2d 1160, 1173–75 (1st Cir. 1993) (stipulation insufficient because accused insisted he lacked knowledge); State v. Glodgett, 749 A.2d 283, 286 (N.H. 2000) ("Where the defendant's intent is a required element of the charged offenses, intent is sufficiently at issue to require some evidence of intent, even if the defendant does not contest intent at trial. If, however, the defendant concedes intent, the charged *mens rea* is not sufficiently disputed to justify the admission of other bad acts to prove intent.") (citations omitted). *See also* 2 Imwinkelried, Uncharged Misconduct Evidence § 8.11, at 26 (rev. 1999) ("Once the defendant offers to stipulate, there is little or no bona fide prosecution need for the uncharged misconduct evidence.").

[34] United States v. Jema, 126 F.3d 1267, 1274 (3d Cir. 1994).

[35] 519 U.S. 172, 190 (1997) (if there is "a justification for receiving evidence of the nature of prior acts on some issue other than status (*i.e.,* to prove 'motive, opportunity, intent, preparation, plan, knowledge, identity, or absence of mistake or accident'), Rule 404(b) guarantees the opportunity to seek its admission") (citation and internal quotation marks omitted).

[36] *See* United States v. Williams, 238 F.3d 871, 876 (7th Cir. 2001) ("[A]s the other circuits to consider this issue after *Old Chief* have held, we believe that *Old Chief* counsels that a defendant's offer to stipulate unequivocally to an element of an offense, such as those demonstrating knowledge or intent, does not render the Government's evidence of prior crimes that are relevant to those elements inadmissible under Rule 404(b)."; intent to distribute cocaine).

[37] *See* Huddleston v. United States, 485 U.S. 681, 691–92 (1988) (Protection from unfair prejudice emanates in part "from Federal Rule of Evidence 105, which provides that the trial court shall, upon request, instruct the jury that the similar acts evidence is to be considered only for the proper purpose for which it was admitted.").

identify, in its instructions to the jury, the specific factor named in the rule that is relied upon to justify admission of the other acts evidence, explain why that factor is material, and warn the jurors against using the evidence to draw the inferences expressly forbidden in the first sentence of Rule 404(b)."[38]

The effectiveness of a limiting instruction is doubtful. "To tell a jury to ignore the defendant's prior convictions in determining whether he or she committed the offense being tried is to ask human beings to act well beyond mortal capacities."[39] Indeed, by unduly emphasizing the evidence, the instruction may be more harmful than helpful.[40] Perhaps for this reason, a trial court is generally not required to instruct on other-acts evidence sua sponte.[41]

§ 11.05   Accused's Participation in Other Act: FRE 104(b)

For other-acts evidence to be relevant, the prosecution must offer some evidence tending to show that the defendant committed the other act.[42] Common law courts employed a variety of standards to describe the requisite burden of proof in this context: "preponderance," "substantial proof," or "clear and convincing evidence."

In *Huddleston v. United States*,[43] the Supreme Court rejected all of these approaches. Instead, the Court, based on Rule 104(b), adopted a *prima facie* evidence standard.[44] This is a very lax standard. The Court explained:

> In determining whether the Government has introduced sufficient evidence to meet Rule 104(b), the trial court neither weighs credibility nor makes a finding that the Government has proved the conditional fact by a preponderance of the evidence. The court simply examines all the evidence in the case and decides whether the jury could reasonably find the conditional fact — here, that the televisions were stolen — by a preponderance of the evidence.[45]

---

[38] United States v. Spikes, 158 F.3d 913, 929 (6th Cir. 1998). *See also* United States v. Gilbert, 152 F.3d 152, 159–60 (1st Cir. 1999) (quoting an "admirable instruction").

[39] United States v. Daniels, 770 F.2d 1111, 1118 (D.C. Cir. 1985). *See also* Government of Virgin Islands v. Toto, 529 F.2d 278, 283 (3d Cir. 1976) ("A drop of ink cannot be removed from a glass of milk.").

[40] *See* United States v. Barnes, 586 F.2d 1052, 1059 (5th Cir. 1978) ("Counsel may refrain from requesting an instruction in order not to emphasize potentially damaging evidence.").

[41] *See* 2 Imwinkelried, Uncharged Misconduct Evidence ch. 9 (rev. 1999).

[42] *See* Huddleston v. United States, 485 U.S. 681, 689 (1988) ("In the Rule 404(b) context, similar act evidence is relevant only if the jury can reasonably conclude that the act occurred and that the defendant was the actor.").

[43] 485 U.S. 681 (1988).

[44] *See supra* § 7.03 (conditional relevancy).

[45] *Huddleston*, 485 U.S. at 690.

§ 11.06 Others-act Evidence Offered by the Accused

Rule 404(b) is typically used by the prosecution. For example, evidence of similarity between the other-act and the crime charged is frequently offered to prove identity — *i.e.*, the modus operandi of both crimes is so similar that the same person probably committed both offenses. The probative value of modus operandi to show identity, however, is the same when offered by the defense, sometimes referred to as a "reverse 404(b)" issue. [46]

In this context, the defense is attempting to show that another person, using a distinctive modus operandi, committed the earlier robberies and, since the same modus operandi was used in the charged offense, that person also committed it. [47] Indeed, the argument for admissibility is stronger in this context because the risk of unfair prejudice to the defendant is not present. [48]

§ 11.07 Entrapment Cases

A majority of jurisdictions follow the "origin of intent" test or subjective theory of entrapment. [49] Under this test, entrapment occurs "when the criminal design originates with the officials of the government, and they implant in the mind of an innocent person the *disposition* to commit the alleged offense and induce its commission in order that they may prosecute." [50] Under this view, the defendant's predisposition (propensity) is a material

---

[46] *See* United States v. Stevens, 935 F.2d 1380, 1401–06 (3d Cir. 1991) (extensive review of cases). *See generally* McCord, *"But Perry Mason Made It Look So Easy!": The Admissibility of Evidence Offered by a Criminal Defendant to Suggest That Someone Else is Guilty*, 63 Tenn. L. Rev. 917, 936 (1996).

[47] *See* People v. Hall, 718 P.2d 99, 104 (Cal. 1986) (noting that "courts should simply treat third-party culpability evidence like any other evidence"); State v. Garfole, 388 A.2d 587, 591 (N.J. 1978) ("It is well established that a defendant may use similar other-crimes evidence defensively."); State v. Bock, 39 N.W.2d 887, 892 (Minn. 1949) (The accused should "have the right to show that crimes of a similar nature have been committed by some other person when the acts of such other person are so closely connected in point of time and method of operation."); People v. Primo, 753 N.E.2d 164, 168 (N.Y. 2001) ("The better approach . . . is to review the admissibility of third-party culpability evidence under the general balancing analysis that governs the admissibility of all evidence."; two months after shooting a person present at shooting used the same gun in an unrelated crime).

[48] *See* United States v. Aboumoussallem, 726 F.2d 906, 911 (2d Cir. 1984) (standard of admissibility when other-acts are offered by the defense is not as restrictive as in cases in which the evidence is offered by the prosecution). *See also* United States v. McCourt, 925 F.2d 1229, 1232 (9th Cir. 1991) ("Under Rule 404(b), 'other crimes' evidence may be offered by any party for a purpose other than proving criminal propensity or conforming conduct."); United States v. Cohen, 888 F.2d 770, 776 (11th Cir. 1989) (defense offered evidence of alleged co-conspirator's bad acts); United States v. McClure, 546 F.2d 670, 673 (5th Cir. 1977) ("Rule 404(b) is normally used by the government. But in the case before us it was the defendant who sought to introduce evidence of the informant's scheme. His right to present a vigorous defense required the admission of the proffered testimony.").

[49] *See* Dressler, Understanding Criminal Procedure ch. 28 (3d ed. 2002).

[50] Sorrells v. United States, 287 U.S. 435, 442 (1932) (emphasis added).

issue, and the defendant's prior criminal conduct becomes relevant. As the Supreme Court has stated, "If the defendant seeks acquittal by reason of entrapment he cannot complain of an appropriate and searching inquiry into his own conduct and predisposition as bearing upon that issue. If in consequence he suffers a disadvantage, he has brought it upon himself by reason of the nature of the defense."[51]

Thus, an entrapment defense raises issues concerning the defendant's character and commission of other-acts.[52] Although the commentators disagree on the theory of the admissibility, they do agree that the Federal Rules have not changed the prior law on the subject. The use of disposition evidence in the entrapment context could be considered as raising an issue of (1) other-acts evidence under Rule 404(b), (2) "character in issue," or (3) prosecution rebuttal to a defendant's raising a character issue under Rule 404(a)(1).[53] Nevertheless, this evidence rule has been characterized as the "greatest fault" of the subjective approach to the entrapment defense and an "indiscriminate attitude toward predisposition evidence is by no means a necessary feature of the subjective test."[54]

§ 11.08 Notice Requirement

Because of the prejudice associated with other-acts evidence, advance notice of the prosecution's intent to introduce this evidence is critical.[55] The rationale for notice is clear: "The major tactical advantage accruing to the prosecution is surprise since there is no requirement that the other crime be alleged in the pleadings and often the existence of such evidence cannot be determined through the limited discovery available in criminal cases."[56]

Justice Brennan wrote: "Only pretrial disclosure of such evidence will allow the defense adequate opportunity to investigate the claim of misconduct and to prepare objections to admission."[57] In 1991, Rule 404(b) was amended to include a notice provision.[58] Even before this amendment was

---

[51] *Id.* at 451–52.

[52] *See* 1 Imwinkelried, Uncharged Misconduct Evidence § 6.16 (rev. 1999) (affirmative defense of entrapment).

[53] *See* 22 Wright & Graham, Federal Practice and Procedure § 5235, at 372–79 (1978).

[54] Park, *The Entrapment Controversy*, 60 Minn. L. Rev. 163, 272 (1976).

[55] *See* Boyd v. United States, 142 U.S. 450, 458 (1892) ("No notice was given by the indictment of the purpose of the government to introduce proof of prior robberies.").

[56] 22 Wright & Graham, Federal Practice and Procedure § 5249, at 525 (1978).

[57] Brennan, *The Criminal Prosecution: Sporting Event or Quest for Truth? A Progress Report*, 68 Wash. U. L.Q. 1, 12 (1990). *See also* Imwinkelried, *The Worst Surprise of All: No Right to Pretrial Discovery of Prosecution's Uncharged Misconduct Evidence*, 56 Fordham L. Rev. 247 (1987).

[58] *See* United States v. Green, 275 F.3d 694, 701 (8th Cir. 2001) ("Factors to consider in determining the reasonableness of the government's pretrial notice of intent to introduce evidence of prior bad acts include: (1) the time when the government could have learned of the availability of the evidence through timely preparation for trial; (2) the extent of prejudice to defendant from lack of time to prepare; and (3) how significant the evidence is to the government's case.").

adopted, some courts had recommended this procedure.[59] Several states also have notice provisions, either by court rule[60] or decision.[61]

§ 11.09 Double Jeopardy & Collateral Estoppel

At one time the federal courts were divided over whether a prior acquittal precluded the admission of other-acts evidence.[62] The Supreme Court had ruled that the Double Jeopardy Clause encompasses the doctrine of collateral estoppel,[63] and some courts extended this principle to other-acts evidence.[64] The opposing view discerned a significant (and constitutional) difference between the evidentiary use of the other offense and standing trial a second time for that offense.[65]

In *Dowling v. United States*,[66] the Supreme Court rejected the double jeopardy and due process arguments. According to the Court, the prior acquittal meant only that the prosecution had failed to establish the defendant's guilt of the other crime beyond a reasonable doubt. The standard of admissibility for other-acts evidence is far less demanding.[67] The prosecution in a federal trial need only introduce sufficient evidence from which the jury could reasonably conclude that the accused committed the other act. Thus, collateral estoppel did not apply. In addition, the Court found nothing fundamentally unfair about introducing such evidence.[68]

---

[59] United States v. Foskey, 636 F.2d 517, 526 n.8 (D.C. Cir. 1980).

[60] *E.g.,* Minn. R. Crim. P. 706; Fla. Stat. § 90.404(2)(b)(1); Tex. R. Evid. 404(b).

[61] *E.g.,* State v. Gray, 643 P.2d 233, 236 (Mont. 1982) (prosecution must provide written notice, including a statement of purpose for which other-acts evidence will be offered).

[62] *Compare* United States v. Van Cleave, 599 F.2d 954, 957 (10th Cir. 1979) (evidence of another crime is not necessarily inadmissible by the fact of acquittal), *with* Albert v. Montgomery, 732 F.2d 865, 869-70 (11th Cir. 1984); United States v. Mespoulede, 597 F.2d 329, 334-35 (2d Cir. 1980) (collateral estoppel precludes admission of evidence of other crimes following an acquittal).

[63] *See* Ashe v. Swenson, 397 U.S. 436 (1970) (case did not involve other-acts evidence).

[64] *See* State v. Wakefield, 278 N.W.2d 307, 308–09 (Minn. 1979) ("It is a basic tenet of our jurisprudence that once the state has mustered its evidence against a defendant and failed, the matter is done. In the eyes of the law the acquitted defendant is to be treated as innocent and in the interests of fairness and finality made no more to answer for his alleged crime. It is our view that the admission into a trial of evidence of crimes of which the defendant has been acquitted prejudices and burdens the defendant in contravention of this basic principle and is fundamentally unfair.").

[65] *See* People v. Oliphant, 250 N.W.2d 443, 454 (Mich. 1976) ("Offering evidence of a prior crime, for which defendant has been acquitted, to a jury embarked on a distinct inquiry does not involve asking the second jury to convict defendant for the prior crime. It does not involve the second jury contradicting the first jury, since the first jury did not find that defendant did not commit the crime, only that the People had not proved that he had beyond a reasonable doubt."). *See generally* 2 Imwinkelried, Uncharged Misconduct Evidence §§ 10.03–.09 (rev. 1999).

[66] 493 U.S. 342 (1990).

[67] *See supra* § 11.05 (defendant's participation in the "other act").

[68] In United States v. Felix, 503 U.S. 378 (1992), the defendant was prosecuted for drug transactions that occurred in Oklahoma. At a prior trial for drug transactions in Missouri,

§ 11.10 Due Process

Several courts have indicated that the improper use of other-acts evidence may violate due process.[69] In *Estelle v. McGuire*,[70] the Supreme Court considered such a claim. McGuire was convicted of murdering his infant daughter. At trial, two physicians testified that the infant was a battered child, a finding based on prior injuries, some of which were discovered during the autopsy. McGuire argued that evidence of these prior injuries violated the rule prohibiting prior-crimes evidence. The Court disagreed, first noting that federal habeas was limited to a review of federal issues, typically federal constitutional issues, and does not extend to violations of state evidentiary rules.[71] Consequently, admission of the evidence had to be judged on due process grounds. The Court found the evidence relevant and therefore did not have to determine whether the admission of irrelevant evidence violates due process.[72]

McGuire also challenged the instruction, arguing that it permitted the jury to use propensity evidence in violation of due process. The Court disagreed with this interpretation of the instruction, finding that it did not violate the propensity rule. Rather, it presented an issue similar to an instruction on other-acts evidence under Federal Rule 404(b) — *i.e.*, evidence offered for some purpose other than character (propensity). The Court therefore had no reason to determine whether a propensity instruction would be unconstitutional.[73]

While unlikely in a routine case, the admissibility of other-acts evidence may violate due process in a particularly egregious case.

---

the Oklahoma crimes had been admitted as other-acts evidence. The Court held that the evidentiary use of the Oklahoma transactions was not the same as prosecuting the defendant for those offenses, and thus the Double Jeopardy Clause did not bar a later prosecution for those transactions. Citing *Dowling*, the Court recognized a "basic, yet important, principle that the introduction of relevant evidence of particular misconduct in a case is not the same thing as prosecution for that conduct." *Id.* at 387.

[69] *See* 2 Imwinkelried, Uncharged Misconduct Evidence ch. 10 (rev. 1999) (constitutional restrictions).

[70] 502 U.S. 62 (1991).

[71] *Id.* at 72 ("Nor do our habeas powers allow us to reverse McGuire's conviction based on a belief that the trial judge incorrectly interpreted the California Evidence Code in ruling that the prior injury evidence was admissible as bad acts evidence in this case."). *See also* Marshall v. Lonberger, 459 U.S. 422, 438 n.6 (1983) ("The Due Process Clause does not permit the federal courts to engage in a finely tuned review of the wisdom of state evidentiary rules.").

[72] 502 U.S. at 70 ("Concluding, as we do, that the prior injury evidence was relevant to an issue in the case, we need not explore further the apparent assumption of the Court of Appeals that it is a violation of the due process . . . for evidence that is not relevant to be received in a criminal trial.").

[73] *Id.* at 75 n.5 ("Because we need not reach the issue, we express no opinion on whether a state law would violate the Due Process Clause if it permitted the use of 'prior crimes' evidence to show propensity to commit a charged crime.").

§ 11.11   Other-acts Evidence in Civil Cases

Although other-acts evidence is most often used in criminal cases, Rule 404(b) applies in civil as well as criminal cases. [74] Professor Imwinkelried lists the following types of illustrative cases: antitrust suits, actions on promissory notes, assault and battery actions, civil discovery disputes, civil rights cases, civil fraud actions, contract lawsuits, insurance litigation, marriage dissolution proceedings, denaturalization proceedings, school desegregation suits, slander actions, attractive nuisance suits, copyright infringement proceedings, and product liability actions over food, aircraft, boats, industrial equipment, drugs, cosmetics, tobacco farm products, and containers. [75]

§ 11.12   Related Issues

Statute of limitations. Several cases have involved prior crimes for which the statute of limitations has expired. Most courts have held that this fact does not preclude admission of other-acts evidence, [76] finding that the reasons for statutes of limitations are inapposite in this context: "The statute of limitations is a defense to prosecution, not a rule of evidence. Therefore, once prosecution is timely instituted, the statute of limitations has no bearing on the admissibility of evidence. It would be a bizarre result indeed if a crime properly prosecuted within the limitations period could not be proven because an essential element, such as intent, could only be established by proof of incidents occurring outside the period." [77]

Exclusionary rule. The Fourth Amendment's exclusionary rule does not automatically preclude the use of other-acts evidence. [78]

§ 11.13   Key Issues

Common misconceptions. The terms "similar act" or "prior crime" are frequently used to describe this subject matter; these terms are misleading. Although often used to admit criminal acts, by its own terms, Rule 404(b) is not limited to crimes; it embraces "wrongs" and "acts" as well. The

---

[74] *E.g.,* Turley v. State Farm Mutual Auto Ins. Co., 944 F.2d 669, 672-75 (10th Cir. 1991) (evidence of prior insurance scams admissible); Doe v. New York City Dept. Soc. Services, 649 F.2d 134, 147 (2d Cir. 1981) (civil rights action).

[75] 2 Imwinkelried, Uncharged Misconduct Evidence § 7.01, at 2–3 (rev. 1999) (uncharged acts in civil cases).

[76] *E.g.,* United States v. DeFiore, 720 F.2d 757, 764 (2d Cir. 1983); United States v. Means, 695 F.2d 811, 816 (5th Cir. 1983); United States v. Blosser, 440 F.2d 697, 699 (10th Cir. 1971).

[77] United States v. Ashdown, 509 F.2d 793, 798 (5th Cir. 1975).

[78] *See* United States v. Hill, 60 F.3d 672, 679 (10th Cir. 1995) (exclusionary rule does apply to evidence offered under Rule 404(b), but "[w]here 'the connection between police misconduct and evidence of a crime is sufficiently attenuated,' . . . exclusion neither protects the constitutional principles the rule was designed to protect, nor advances deterrence enough to justify its costs."); United States v. Knight, 185 F. Supp. 2d 65, 69 (D.D.C. 2002) ("the exclusionary rule does not bar admission of Knight's July 2000 [illegal] arrest").

other-act also need not be "similar" to the charged offense nor have occurred prior to the charged offense; evidence of a *subsequent* act may be admissible.

Moreover, the accused may offer evidence under Rule 404(a) in an attempt to show another person committed the charged crime. Finally, Rule 404(b) is not limited to criminal cases; it applies in civil litigation as well.

Analysis. The application of Rule 404(b) requires three steps:

(1) Rule 401 — identify a material issue (other than character) for which the evidence is being offered to prove (*i.e.*, identity of perpetrator, mens rea, corpus delicti);

(2) Rule 403 — balance the probative value of the evidence against the risk that the jury will ignore the limiting instruction and make the prohibited character inference (unfair prejudice); and

(3) Rule 104(b) — determine whether there is prima facie evidence of accused's involvement in the other act.

In applying Rule 403, the trial court may consider whether the evidence is offered on a disputed issue, whether a stipulation has been proffered, and whether a cautionary instruction would be effective.

Chapter 12

HABIT EVIDENCE: FRE 406

§ 12.01 Introduction

What do you do when you first get up in the morning? Brush your teeth? Put on a pot of coffee? Do you travel to law school the same way each day? These are habits, and people are creatures of habit.

Evidence of the habit of a person or the routine practice of an organization when offered to prove that a person or organization acted in conformity with that habit or routine practice on a particular occasion may be admissible under Federal Rule 406. The phrase "routine practice of an organization" refers to the "habit" of an organization, commonly known as business practice, usage, or custom.

Some jurisdictions had limited the admissibility of habit evidence to situations in which there were no eyewitnesses. Other jurisdictions had required the corroboration of routine practices. Rule 406 rejects both conditions.

Rule 406 provides only that evidence of habit or routine practice as proof of conduct is relevant. Consequently, the rule must be read in conjunction with Rule 403.

§ 12.02 Habit & Character Distinguished

Evidence of habit must be distinguished from evidence of character because the former is admissible under Rule 406, whereas the latter is generally inadmissible under Rule 404(a).[1] The difference in treatment accorded habit and character evidence is based on the greater probative value of habit evidence.[2]

Rule 406, however, does not define habit. The definition is critical because habit is closely related to "character." The federal drafters quoted extensively from McCormick's description of habit and character: "A habit . . .

---

[1] *E.g.*, United States v. Angwin, 271 F.3d 786, 799 (9th Cir. 2001) ("Merely indicating that he takes a non-confrontational course of action in dangerous situations in general does not describe his conduct with sufficient particularity to be probative of whether he acted in conformity with that general practice on this particular occasion."). *See supra* chapter 10 (character evidence). *See also* Lewan, *The Rationale of Habit Evidence*, 16 Syracuse L. Rev. 39 (1964).

[2] *See* Jones v. Southern Pac. R., 962 F.2d 447, 449 (5th Cir. 1992) ("Habit evidence is superior to character evidence because the uniformity of one's response to habit is far greater than the consistency with which one's conduct conforms to character."); Loughan v. Firestone Tire & Rubber Co., 749 F.2d 1519, 1524 (11th Cir. 1985) ("Habit evidence is considered to be highly probative. . . .").

is the person's regular practice of meeting a particular kind of situation with a specific type of conduct, such as the habit of going down a particular stairway two stairs at a time, or of giving the hand-signal for a left turn, or of alighting from railway cars while they are moving. The doing of the habitual acts may become semi-automatic."[3] Other authorities also provide some guidance. Wigmore used the phrase "invariable regularity" of action.[4] The Model Code of Evidence defined habit as "a course of behavior of a person regularly repeated in like circumstances."[5] According to a leading treatise, "Character and habit are not synonymous. The former faces in the direction of Freud, the latter towards Pavlov."[6] Another treatise provides the following rule of thumb: "One could reasonably testify to having observed habitual behavior, but character is almost always a matter of opinion."[7] Okay, McCormick wins; bottom line: Habit is the "regular response to a repeated specific situation."

Relevant factors. The key elements in determining whether conduct constitutes habit are (1) specificity, (2) repetition, (3) duration, and (4) the semi-automatic nature of the conduct.[8]

Specificity. A person's general disposition as a careful or careless driver should be classified as character and excluded. On the other hand, evidence that a person always stopped her car at a particular intersection should be classified as habit due to its specificity.

Repetition. How many times has the person stopped the car at that intersection? Evidence that the person stopped at an intersection once a day is more probative of habit than a once-a-month occurrence.[9]

Duration. Evidence that the person has stopped at an intersection for five years is more probative than evidence of a two-month course of conduct. Evidence of a person's "habit" of traveling home from work by a certain route for years illustrates this point.

---

[3] *See also* Fed. R. Evid. 406 advisory committee's note (" 'Character and habit are close akin. Character is a generalized description of one's disposition, or of one's disposition in respect to a general trait, such as honesty, temperance, or peacefulness. "Habit," in modern usage, both lay and psychological, is more specific. It describes one's regular response to a repeated specific situation. If we speak of character for care, we think of the person's tendency to act prudently in all the varying situations of life, in business, family life, in handling automobiles and in walking across the street.' ") (quoting McCormick).

[4] 1A Wigmore, Evidence § 92, at 1608 (Tillers rev. 1983).

[5] Model Code of Evidence, Rule 307(1) (1942) (proposed by American Law Institute).

[6] 2 Weinstein & Berger, Weinstein's Evidence 40401, at 404–17 (1990).

[7] 22 Wright & Graham, Federal Practice and Procedure § 5233, at 354 (1978).

[8] *See* United States v. Angwin, 271 F.3d 786, 799 (9th Cir. 2001) ("(1) the degree to which the conduct is reflexive or semi-automatic as opposed to volitional; (2) the specificity or particularity of the conduct; and (3) the regularity or numerosity of the examples of the conduct.").

[9] *See* Mobil Exploration and Producing U.S., Inc. v. Cajun Const. Services, Inc., 45 F.3d 96, 99–100 (5th Cir. 1995) ("Evidence of the defendant's actions on only a few occasions or only in relation to the plaintiff are not enough; the plaintiff must show regularity over substantially all occasions or with substantially all other parties with whom the defendant has had similar business transactions.").

Semi-automatic conduct. Certain types of activities are done without thought — for example, braking a car with the right foot and locking the door of a house when departing. These types of activities, which are semi-automatic, are easily classified as habit. More volitional conduct is problematic, as illustrated by *Levin v. United States*,[10] which is cited by the federal drafters. In *Levin*, the defendant proffered evidence of his "habit" of observing the Sabbath in support of an alibi defense. The D.C. Circuit upheld the exclusion of this evidence, stating, "It seems apparent to us that an individual's religious practices would not be the type of activities which would lend themselves to the characterization of 'invariable regularity.' Certainly the very volitional basis of the activity raises serious questions as to its invariable nature, and hence its probative value."[11]

The *Levin* reasoning seems unpersuasive, and the federal cases seem to reject *Levin*[12] but not always.[13] Habit evidence is only circumstantial evidence, and the jury should have no problem appreciating the volitional aspects of the conduct. For example, in a murder prosecution, the defendant claimed that the victim was alive when he left her house. His fingerprints were found on a drinking glass. The court ruled habit evidence admissible: "Testimony that the victim was an immaculate housekeeper was relevant to show that she likely would have wiped the defendant's fingerprint off her glasses had he placed it there before the murder."[14] The point is not that this evidence is conclusive but that it is probative.

The admissibility of drinking habits has divided the federal courts.[15]

§ 12.03 Routine Business Practices

Rule 406 also permits the use of the routine practice of an organization to prove that the organization acted in conformity with that practice on a particular occasion. The phrase "routine practice of an organization" refers to the "habit" of an organization, commonly known as business practice,

---

[10] 338 F.2d 265 (D.C. Cir. 1964).

[11] *Id.* at 272.

[12] *E.g.,* Perrin v. Anderson, 784 F.2d 1040, 1045–46 (10th Cir. 1986) (decedent's habit of violent reaction to police officers); Loughan v. Firestone Tire & Rubber Co., 749 F.2d 1519, 1522–23 (11th Cir. 1985) (worker's habit of drinking on the job); Meyer v. United States, 638 F.2d 155, 156–58 (10th Cir. 1980) (regular practice of dentist to inform patients of risks prior to extractions).

[13] *E.g.,* United States v. Rangel-Arreola, 991 F.2d 1519, 1523 (10th Cir. 1993) (practice of truckers to accept jobs without checking fuel tanks not a habit).

[14] State v. Allen, 653 N.E.2d 675, 684 (Ohio 1995).

[15] *Compare* Loughan v. Firestone Tire & Rubber Co., 749 F.2d 1519, 1523 (11th Cir. 1985) (extensive drinking over a 6-year period, including proof that plaintiff regularly carried a cooler of beer on his truck, established habit); Keltner v. Ford Motor Co., 748 F.2d 1265, 1268–69 (8th Cir. 1984) (cross-examination of plaintiff under Rule 406 to the effect that he drank a six pack of beer four nights a week permitted), *with* Reyes v. Missouri Pacific R.R., 589 F.2d 791, 794 (5th Cir. 1979) ("The suggestion that the prior convictions constituted evidence of Reyes' 'habit' of excessive drinking is equally unpersuasive.").

usage, or custom.[16] Large businesses, of necessity, develop standard operating procedures (SOPs) such as a routine procedure for receiving and mailing documents. Hospitals have routine procedures for the operating room such as an instrument count before sewing up the patient. Because there is no risk of improper character being smuggled before the jury in this context, routine practice evidence should be readily admitted.[17]

[A] Custom to Establish Standard of Care

Rule 406 governs only one use of routine-practice evidence — the use of such evidence to show that an organization on a particular occasion acted in conformity with an established practice. The use of routine-practice evidence for some other purpose is not governed by the rule. For example, custom or routine practice is often used to establish the standard of care in negligence cases.[18] Such evidence is not offered to prove conduct, and therefore Rule 406 does not apply.[19]

§ 12.04 Determining Admissibility under Rule 403

Rule 406 provides only that evidence of habit or routine practice as proof of conduct is relevant, rather than admissible. Consequently, Rule 403 must be consulted to determine admissibility.[20] In making this determination, the trial court may consider the "compactness of proof." In other words, how many witnesses will be needed to establish the habit? "[T]estimony by W that on numerous occasions he had been with X when X crossed a railroad track and that on each occasion X had first stopped and looked in both directions" may be admitted but not the testimony "of 10 witnesses, each testifying to a different occasion."[21] The latter would simply be too time-consuming.

---

[16] The phrase "organization" is broader than the term "business." For purposes of the hearsay exception for business records, "business" is defined as an "institution, association, profession, occupation, and calling of every kind, whether or not conducted for profit" and includes the records of institutions and associations like schools, churches and hospitals. *See infra* § 33.10 (business records).

[17] *See* Mobil Exploration and Producing U.S., Inc. v. Cajun Const. Services, Inc., 45 F.3d 96, 100 (5th Cir. 1995) ("Mobil introduced evidence to show that Cajun invariably loaded its trucks in the same manner and to the same level when Cajun obtained limestone from a third-party supplier. Mobil provided weight scale tickets showing that Cajun typically loaded either approximately fourteen-ton or twenty-five-ton loads at third-party suppliers.").

[18] *See* Strum v. University of Cincinnati Med. Ctr., 739 N.E.2d 364, 368 (Ohio App. 2000) ("[W]hile not conclusive evidence of the proper standard of care, custom is evidence of what a reasonably prudent medical provider would do under similar circumstances. Thus, the customary practice provides further support for the standard of care advocated by Dr. Polesky and adopted by the court."). *See generally* Diamond, Levine & Madden, Understanding Torts § 7.02 (1996) (malpractice).

[19] *See* Morris, *Custom and Negligence*, 42 Colum. L. Rev. 1147 (1942).

[20] *See* proposed Fed. R. Evid. 406(b) advisory committee's note ("Proof by specific instances may be controlled by the overriding provisions of Rule 403 for exclusion on grounds of prejudice, confusion, misleading the jury, or waste of time."), 56 F.R.D. 225 (1972).

[21] *Id.*

Under Rule 104(a), the trial court determines whether evidence constitutes habit, and this determination will be reversed only for an abuse of discretion.[22]

§ 12.05 Methods of Proof

As proposed by the Supreme Court, Rule 406 contained a division (b), which governed the methods of proving habit. That provision read: "Habit or routine practice may be proved by testimony in the form of an opinion or by specific instances of conduct sufficient in number to warrant a finding that the habit existed or the practice was routine."[23] The House Judiciary Committee deleted this provision because "the method of proof of habit and routine practice should be left to the courts to deal with on a case-by-case basis."[24]

Even though proposed Rule 404(b) was not adopted by Congress, in most instances habit will be proved by opinion testimony or evidence of specific instances of conduct.[25] Hence, proposed Federal Rule 406(b) remains an appropriate guide.[26] The Uniform Rules adopted this provision.[27]

§ 12.06 Key Points

Habit or routine practice evidence may be admitted to prove that a person or organization acted in conformity with that habit or routine practice on a particular occasion. The phrase "routine practice of an organization" refers to the "habit" of an organization, commonly known as business practice, usage, or custom.

Character distinguished. Evidence of habit must be distinguished from evidence of character because the former is admissible under Rule 406, whereas the latter is generally inadmissible under Rule 404(a). The difference in treatment accorded habit and character evidence is based on the greater probative value of habit evidence.

---

[22] *See* United States v. Angwin, 271 F.3d 786, 798 (9th Cir. 2001) ("A district court's ruling on whether proffered evidence qualifies as habit evidence under Federal Rule of Evidence 406 is highly fact-specific. . . . Because factual matters predominate in determining whether certain evidence sought to be introduced at trial qualifies as habit under Rule 406, we will employ an abuse of discretion standard.").

[23] 56 F.R.D. 223 (1972).

[24] H.R. Rep. No. 650, 93d Cong., 1st Sess. (1973), reprinted in 1974 U.S.C.C.A.N. 7075, 7079.

[25] *See* Brokamp v. Mercy Hosp. Anderson, 726 N.E.2d 594, 605 (Ohio App. 1999)(Nurse "Barringer normally gave a shot in the outer quadrant of the buttocks, or, when a patient could not be turned to his side, in the middle portion of the thigh.").

[26] Proposed Fed. R. Evid. 406(b) advisory committee's note ("Permissible methods of providing habit or routine conduct include opinion and specific instances sufficient in number to warrant a finding that the habit or routine practice in fact existed. Opinion evidence must be 'rationally based on the perception of the witness' and helpful, under the provisions of Rule 701."), 56 F.R.D. 225 (1972).

[27] *See* Unif. R. 406(b) (rev. 1999).

Definition. Habit is the "regular response to a repeated specific situation." The key elements in determining whether conduct constitutes habit are (1) specificity, (2) repetition, (3) duration, and (4) the semi-automatic nature of the conduct.

Routine practice. The phrase "routine practice of an organization" refers to the "habit" of an organization. Rule 406 does not govern the use of routine-practice evidence for some other purpose. For example, custom or routine practice is often used to establish the standard of care in negligence cases. Such evidence is not offered to prove conduct, and therefore Rule 406 does not apply.

Rule 403. Rule 406 provides only that evidence of habit or routine practice as proof of conduct is relevant, rather than admissible. Consequently, Rule 403 must be consulted to determine admissibility. In making this determination, the trial court may consider the "compactness of proof."

Methods of proof. In most instances, habit will be proved by opinion testimony or evidence of specific instances of conduct.

Chapter 13

SUBSEQUENT REMEDIAL MEASURES: FRE 407

§ 13.01 Introduction

Suppose a sink hole develops overnight in front of the Ma and Pa General Store. Joe Klutz falls into the hole that morning and is injured. Ma and Pa fill in the hole that afternoon. Klutz sues and wants to introduce evidence about the repair, arguing that it tends to show an implied admission of negligence on the part of Ma and Pa. Should the evidence be admissible?

Federal Rule 407, sometimes known as the "repair rule," governs the admissibility of evidence of subsequent remedial measures. As discussed below, the phrase "subsequent remedial measure" is broader than the word "repair." The exclusionary rule embodied in Rule 407 applies only when evidence of subsequent remedial measures is offered to prove negligent or culpable conduct, including strict liability in federal courts. If the evidence is offered for some other purpose, such as proof of ownership, control, feasibility of precautionary measures, or impeachment, the rule does not apply.

Most courts have ruled that Rule 407 applies in diversity cases.[1]

§ 13.02 Rationale

Rule 407 rests on two grounds. The most important reason is "a social policy of encouraging people to take, or at least not discouraging them from taking, steps in furtherance of added safety."[2] The second ground is relevance: Is the repair probative of negligence, or maybe there are other motivations at work? In the above hypothetical, maybe Ma and Pa are humane do-gooders who do not want other people hurt. Or, maybe they are greedy entrepreneurs who realize it is difficult to sell goods to injured patrons. Here, the federal drafters quote Baron Bramwell: the rule rejects the notion that "because the world gets wiser as it gets older, therefore it

---

[1] *See* Kelly v. Crown Equip. Co., 970 F.2d 1273, 1278 (3d Cir. 1992) (Rule 407 "governs in this diversity action notwithstanding Pennsylvania law to the contrary. Our view is in accord with the majority of appellate courts that have considered the issue."); Flaminio v. Honda, Motor Co., 733 F.2d 463, 472 (7th Cir. 1984) ("But Rule 407 is not based on substantive considerations only. An important though not the primary reason for the rule was distrust of juries' ability to draw correct inferences from evidence of subsequent remedial measures. Although it was a mild distrust, as shown by the exceptions built into the rule, it is enough to establish the rule's constitutionality in diversity cases.").

[2] Fed. R. Evid. 407 advisory committee's note.

was foolish before." Given the lax definition of relevance in Rule 401, however, the relevancy argument would not result in the exclusion of this type of evidence.

Although the policy of encouraging remedial measures is salutary, one has to question whether an evidentiary rule effectuates that policy. First, it seems unlikely that most real people (*i.e.*, non-lawyers) are even aware of the evidentiary rule. The rules of evidence are the stock and trade of lawyers, not lay persons. Whatever Ma and Pa's motivation, you can be sure that Ma did not turn to Pa and say: "Pa. Remember Rule 407!" Second, even without an exclusionary rule, it seems arguable that most people would repair a known defect, if for no other reason than, in the event of a second accident, evidence of a prior accident would be admissible to prove notice of the defect.[3] If Ma and Pa consult an attorney, wouldn't the attorney say: "Make the repair because you are now on notice of a dangerous condition."[4]

§ 13.03 "Remedial Measures" Defined

Although known as the "repair rule" at common law, Rule 407 encompasses far more than subsequent repairs. It covers the "installation of safety devices, changes in company rules, and discharge of employees,"[5] as well as disciplinary action against the employee who caused the injury. Rule 407 also applies to subsequent changes in drug warnings[6] and modifications in product design.[7] In contrast, post-accident reviews or studies are generally not considered subsequent remedial measures.[8]

---

[3] *See* 23 Wright & Graham, Federal Practice and Procedure § 5282 (1980) ("The fear of further tort liability or other sanctions provides a substantial incentive for defendants to make repairs even if this will increase the likelihood of their being found liable for past accidents.").

[4] *See supra* § 9.06 (other accidents used to show notice).

[5] Fed. R. Evid. 407 advisory committee's note. *See also* First Sec. Bank v. Union Pac. R.R. Co., 152 F.3d 877, 881 (8th Cir. 1998) ("Rafferty's memorandum, issued several months subsequent to the accident, instructed Union Pacific employees to enforce a policy that discouraged, 'if possible,' the placement of cars within 250 feet of the crossing."); Bogosian v. Mercedes-Benz of N. Am., Inc.,104 F.3d 472, 481 (1st Cir. 1997) ("installation of park ignition interlocks on Mercedes-Benz vehicles apparently beginning with the 1990 model year"); Mehojah v. Drummon, 56 F.3d 1213, 1214 (10th Cir. 1995) (after accident a fence installed on the west side of the creek).

[6] *See* Wagner v. Roche Labs., 671 N.E.2d 252, 258 (Ohio 1996) ("To avoid the temptation of using 20/20 hindsight in this case, the trial court did not allow appellant to place evidence before the jury that, in 1984, both the package insert and the PDR Physicians' Desk Reference entry for Accutane an acne medication were supplemented to include a warning that Accutane used concomitantly with tetracycline therapy (*e.g.*, such as Minocin) could be associated with PTC pseudotumor cerebri. The trial court excluded this evidence under Evid. R. 407 as a subsequent remedial measure. The jury verdict thus focused on what appellees knew, or should have known, in 1982 [date of prescription].").

[7] *See* Flaminio v. Honda Motor Co., 733 F.2d 463 (7th Cir. 1984) (design change).

[8] *E.g.,* Prentiss & Carlisle Co. v. Koehring-Waterous Div., 972 F.2d 610 (1st Cir. 1992); Rocky Mountain Helicopters, Inc. v. Bell Helicopters Textron, 805 F.2d 907, 918 (10th Cir. 1986). *But see* Complaint of Consol. Coal Co., 123 F.3d 126, 136 (3d Cir. 1997) ("Consol objected that this [safety] memo was a subsequent remedial measure and thus inadmissible under Fed. R. Evid. 407, and the court agreed. While the dissent argues that the memo is not a subsequent

§ 13.04   Timing of Remedial Measures

The remedial measure must take effect *after* the accident or incident being litigated. A remedial measure that takes effect after purchase but before the accident that is the subject of litigation is not a subsequent measure.[9] In 1997, Rule 407 was amended; the phrase "an injury or harm allegedly caused by" was added to clarify that the rule applies only to post-event changes, not post-sale, pre-event remedial measures. Although not excluded by Rule 407, the evidence of pre-event measures must still be relevant.[10]

§ 13.05   Third-Party Remedial Measures

When a subsequent remedial measure is made by a third person, the policy of encouraging such measures is not implicated, and thus the rule does not apply.[11] In these cases, however, the relevance of the subsequent measure as an "admission by conduct" becomes doubtful and is subject to exclusion under Rules 401 and 403.[12] How is the repair an implied admission if the defendant did not make it?[13]

---

remedial measure within the meaning of Rule 407 because Newman only sought to admit the portion dealing with Consol's investigation of the accident, . . . there is authority supporting the exclusion of evidence of post-accident investigations under Rule 407.").

[9] *See* Trull v. Volkswagen of Am., Inc., 187 F.3d 88, 96 (1st Cir. 1999) ("Although evidence concerning subsequent remedial measures generally is not admissible at trial, see Fed. R. Evid. 407, measures that take place before the accident at issue do not fall within the prohibition."); Bogosian v. Mercedes-Benz of N. Am., 104 F.3d 472, 481 (1st Cir. 1997); Traylor v. Husqvarna Motor, 988 F.2d 729, 733 (7th Cir. 1993); Cates v. Sears, Roebuck & Co., 928 F.2d 679, 686 (5th Cir. 1991).

[10] *See* Bogosian v. Mercedes-Benz of N. Am., Inc., 104 F.3d 472, 481 (1st Cir. 1997) (Rule 407 "does not apply where, as here, the modification took place before the accident that precipitated the suit. In cases such as this, the district court may, if necessary, exclude evidence of the remedial modification by resort to its considerable discretion under Rule 403, which permits the exclusion of relevant evidence if its probative value is substantially outweighed by the danger of unfair prejudice or misleading the jury.").

[11] *E.g.,* Mehojah v. Drummond, 56 F.3d 1213, 1215 (10th Cir. 1995) (Rule 407 "does not apply to subsequent remedial measures by non-defendants."); TLT-Babcock, Inc. v. Emerson Elec. Co., 33 F.3d 397, 400 (4th Cir. 1994) ("Evidence of subsequent repairs may be admitted where those repairs have been performed by someone other than the defendant."); Dixon v. Int'l Harvester Co., 754 F.2d 573, 583 (5th Cir.1985) ("[Where] repairs were made by a non-defendant, Rule 407 does not bar the evidence.").

[12] *See* Raymond v. Raymond Corp., 938 F.2d 1518, 1524–25 (1st Cir. 1991) ("Rule 403 may be used to exclude evidence of subsequent third party actions which are felt to bear only marginally on the question of whether a product was unreasonably dangerous at the time of manufacture."); Gauthier v. AMF, Inc., 805 F.2d 337, 338 (9th Cir. 1986) ("Plaintiff's evidence of subsequent remedial measures by non-parties should have been excluded under Rule 403 as irrelevant."); Grenada Steel Indus., Inc. v. Alabama Oxygen Co., 695 F.2d 883, 889 (5th Cir. 1983).

[13] *See supra* § 9.07[A] (admissions by conduct).

§ 13.06 Required Remedial Measures

When a subsequent remedial measure is required by governmental regulation, the policy of encouraging such measures may not be implicated, and thus the application of Rule 407 in this context is drawn into question. Rule 407 has been held to apply only to remedial measures taken voluntarily by a defendant because required repairs will not be deterred by the rule of exclusion.[14] This does not mean, however, that admissibility is permissible; remedial measures required by the government are often of doubtful relevance as an implied admission.

§ 13.07 Strict Liability Cases

The applicability of the repair rule to strict liability cases is controversial, although a 1997 amendment to Rule 407 puts the issue to rest in the federal arena. In the leading case, *Ault v. Intn'l Harvester Co.*,[15] the California Supreme Court, interpreting section 1151 of the California Evidence Code, held that the exclusion of subsequent remedial measures did not extend to cases of strict liability and that, consequently, evidence of such measures was admissible. The Court based its decision on the differences between strict liability and negligence cases, believing that a large corporation, concerned about its public image and the distinct possibility of future lawsuits, would make the repair in any event.[16] Many states accept the *Ault* reasoning, holding their version of Rule 407 inapplicable in strict liability

---

[14] *See* O'Dell v. Hercules Inc., 904 F.2d 1194, 1204 (8th Cir. 1990) ("An exception to Rule 407 is recognized for evidence of remedial action mandated by superior governmental authority because the policy goal of encouraging remediation would not necessarily be furthered by exclusion of such evidence."); In re Aircrash in Bali, Indonesia, 871 F.2d 812, 817 (9th Cir. 1989) (FAA investigation) ("The purpose of Rule 407 is not implicated in cases involving subsequent measures in which the defendant did not voluntarily participate."); Chase v. General Motors Corp., 856 F.2d 17, 20–21 (4th Cir. 1988) (recall letter).

[15] 528 P.2d 1148 (Cal. 1974).

[16] The Court explained:

> When the context is transformed from a typical negligence setting to the modern products liability field, however, the "public policy" assumptions justifying this evidentiary rule are no longer valid. The contemporary corporate mass producer of goods, the normal products liability defendant, manufactures tens of thousands of units of goods; it is manifestly unrealistic to suggest that such a producer will forego making improvements in its product, and risk innumerable additional lawsuits and the attendant adverse effect upon its public image, simply because evidence of adoption of such improvement may be admitted in an action founded on strict liability for recovery on an injury that preceded the improvement. In the products liability area, the exclusionary rule of section 1151 does not affect the primary conduct of the mass producer of goods, but serves merely as a shield against potential liability. In short, the purpose of section 1151 is not applicable to a strict liability case and hence its exclusionary rule should not be gratuitously extended to that field.

Id. at 1152.

cases.[17] In some jurisdictions, this issue is explicitly addressed in the rule.[18]

Criticisms of *Ault* are varied. First, there is a problem of relevance. Under strict liability theory, a product's safety is determined at the time of manufacture but a subsequent remedial measure, by definition, occurs at a later date. Moreover, manufacturers modify product design for reasons other than to fix a defect. Thus, marginally relevant evidence may confuse the jury by diverting its attention away from the relevant time frame and perhaps causing the jurors to equate a subsequent design modification with an admission of a prior defective design.[19]

Second, the underlying premises of *Ault* have been attacked. For instance, *Ault*'s focus on large producers ignores the many small manufacturers whose "long-term prospects become highly suspect when faced with the losses of a single short-term products liability suit."[20]

Also, the differences between negligence and strict liability in this context may not be significant. If a manufacturer has to pay damages under either theory, the deterrent effect to taking remedial action is the same, *i.e.*, concern that the evidence may be used against the company.

Federal rule. Prior to 1997, a majority of the federal circuit courts had rejected *Ault*, holding that Rule 407 applied in strict liability cases,[21] and, in 1997, Federal Rule 407 was amended to codify this position. The phrase "a defect in a product or its design, or that a warning or instruction should have accompanied a product" was added to clarify this point.

---

[17] *See* Forma Scientific, Inc. v. Biosera, Inc., 960 P.2d 108, 115 (Colo. 1998); Motors Corp. v. Moseley, 447 S.E.2d 302, 310 (Ga. App. 1994), overruled on other grounds, Webster v. Boyett, 496 S.E.2d 459, 463 (Ga. 1998); Ford Motor Co. v. Fulkerson, 812 S.W.2d 119, 126 (Ky. 1991); D.L. v. Huebner, 329 N.W.2d 890 (Wis. 1983); Caldwell v. Yamaha Motor Co., 648 P.2d 519, 523 (Wyo. 1982). *But see* Duchess v. Langston Corp., 769 A.2d 1131, 1142 (Pa. 2001) ("[W]e conclude that the federal approach, extending the general rule excluding evidence of subsequent remedial measures to claims asserting product defect, represents the better view.").

[18] *Compare* Alaska Evid. R. 407; Hawaii Evid. R. 407; Me. Evid. R. 407; Tex. Evid. R. 407(a) (admitting subsequent remedial measures in strict liability cases), *with* Ariz. Rev. Stat. Ann. § 12-686(a); Neb. Rev. Stat. § 27-407 (excluding such evidence).

[19] There is also an inconsistency; if the reasons underlying *Ault* are correct, why not abolish the repair rule for negligence cases as well as strict liability suits?

[20] Cyr v. J.I. Case Co., 652 A.2d 685, 693 (N.H. 1994).

[21] *E.g.,* Wood v. Morbark Indus., Inc., 70 F.3d 1201, 1206–07 (11th Cir. 1995) ("Rule 407 does apply in strict products liability cases when the plaintiff alleges that a product is defective because the design is unreasonably dangerous. We are persuaded that Rule 407 is necessary in such cases to focus the jury's attention on the product's condition or design at the time of the accident."); Raymond v. Raymond Corp., 938 F.2d 1518, 1522 (1st Cir. 1991) (listing cases); Flaminio v. Honda, Motor Co., 733 F.2d 463, 469 (7th Cir. 1984) ("The analysis is not fundamentally affected by whether the basis of liability is the defendant's negligence or his product's defectiveness or inherent dangerousness. In either case, if evidence of subsequent remedial measures is admissible to prove liability, the incentive to take such measures will be reduced.").

§ 13.08 Admissibility for Other Purposes

Rule 407 excludes evidence of subsequent remedial measures *only* if offered to prove negligent or culpable conduct. The rule explicitly recognizes that this evidence may be admissible if offered for some other purpose, such as proof of ownership, control, feasibility of precautionary measures, or impeachment. The "other purposes" listed in Rule 407 are not exclusive. So long as evidence of remedial measures is not offered for the prohibited purpose, *i.e.*, to prove negligence or culpable conduct, exclusion is not required.

Evidence offered for some "other purpose" is not automatically admissible, however. The requirements of Rules 401 to 403 must be satisfied. As an added safeguard, Rule 407 requires that if evidence of remedial measures is offered for another purpose (except impeachment), that other purpose must involve a *"controverted"* issue. An offer to stipulate will often remove the issue from controversy.[22] If the evidence is admitted for another purpose, the trial judge must give an instruction limiting the use of the evidence to its proper purpose if a party so requests.[23]

[A] Ownership & Control

The exclusionary policy of Rule 407 is inapplicable where evidence of subsequent remedial measures is offered to prove ownership or control. If control and therefore responsibility of a party is controverted, a party's subsequent corrective action tends to show that they are the correct defendant. For example, in *Powers v. J. B. Michael & Co.*,[24] a highway contractor was sued for negligently failing to erect warning signs at a construction site over which the contractor and a state highway department had joint control. Evidence of the contractor's subsequent erection of warning signs was admitted to show control over the site by the contractor (but not for the purpose of showing negligence). Note that admissibility is not automatic; control must be a controverted issue,[25] and the requirements of Rule 403 must be satisfied.

---

[22] Fed. R. Evid. 407 advisory committee's note ("The requirement that the other purpose be controverted calls for automatic exclusion unless a genuine issue be present and allows the opposing party to lay the groundwork for exclusion by making an admission. Otherwise the factors of undue prejudice, confusion of issues, and misleading the jury remain for consideration under Rule 403.").

[23] *See* Fed. R. Evid. 105 (limiting instructions).

[24] 329 F.2d 674 (6th Cir. 1964) (cited by federal drafters). *See also* Clausen v. Sea-3, Inc., 21 F.3d 1181, 1190 (1st Cir. 1994) ("The parties agree that control of the ramp area where Clausen's injury occurred was a material issue in this case. According to the appellant, one aspect of the control issue arose because both Storage Tank and Sea-3 asserted that Goudreau was in control of the work site and was, therefore, responsible for clearing and sanding the area where the plaintiff fell.").

[25] *See* Hull v. Chevron U.S.A., Inc., 812 F.2d 584, 587 (10th 1987) ("Although Chevron insists the evidence at issue was critical to showing its lack of control of the forklift, we fail to see how this issue is controverted in the first instance.").

[B] Feasibility of Precautionary Measures

The exclusionary policy of Rule 407 is also inapplicable where evidence of subsequent remedial measures is offered to prove the feasibility of precautionary measures.[26] In many cases, however, the distinction between negligence and the feasibility of precautionary measures is almost nonexistent. Thus, courts must exercise care to ensure that this "exception" does not swallow the rule.[27]

The federal drafters cited *Boeing Airplane Co. v. Brown*[28] to illustrate the use of evidence of remedial measures to show the feasibility of precautionary measures. In *Boeing*, the crash of a B-52 bomber lead to a wrongful death action. The plaintiff was permitted to introduce evidence of a subsequent design modification in the alternator drive to show that the formerly used part was defectively designed. Admissibility was upheld on the theory of feasibility of alternative designs.

Recall, however, that admissibility is not automatic; the issue must be controverted,[29] and Rule 403 must be satisfied.

[C] Impeachment

Rule 407 is inapplicable where evidence of subsequent remedial measures is offered for impeachment.[30] For example, in *Dollar v. Long Mfg.*,[31] a defense witness testified that a backhoe was safe to operate while affixed to a rollbar-equipped tractor. He was impeached with a warning letter he had sent describing the "death dealing propensities" of the backhoe.

As explained above, evidence offered for some "other purpose" is not automatically admissible; the requirements of Rule 403 must be satisfied. There is a real concern that an expansive impeachment exception might

---

[26] *See* Duchess v. Langston Corp., 769 A.2d 1131, 1146–47 (Pa. 2001) ("[T]he feasibility exception has not been applied where a defendant merely suggests that an original design is acceptable, or argues about tradeoffs involved in taking precautionary measures. Where, however, a defendant's evidence and arguments are framed in categorical terms, are presented in the form of superlatives, or, more generally, upset the balance of fairness that Rule 407 seeks to maintain, courts have found the exceptions applicable.") (citations omitted).

[27] *See* Werner v. Upjohn Co., 628 F.2d 848 (4th Cir. 1980).

[28] 291 F.2d 310 (9th Cir. 1961).

[29] *See* Flaminio v. Honda, Motor Co., 733 F.2d 463, 468 (7th Cir. 1984) ("[D]efendants did not deny the feasibility of precautionary measures against wobble. Their argument was that there is a tradeoff between wobble and 'weave,' and that in designing the model on which Flaminio was injured Japanese Honda had decided that weave was the greater danger because it occurs at high speeds and because the Gold Wing model — what motorcycle buffs call a 'hog' — was designed for high speeds. The feasibility, as distinct from the net advantages, of reducing the danger of wobble was not in issue.").

[30] *E.g.,* Wood v. Morbark Indus., Inc., 70 F.3d 1201, 1208 (11th Cir. 1995) ("By referring to the seventeen-inch chute length as the 'safest' length possible, Morey opened the door for impeachment. Wood's counsel should have been allowed to ask why the supposedly safest design possible was modified after the accident involving Ginger Wood.").

[31] 561 F.2d 613, 618 (5th Cir. 1977).

eviscerate the rule.[32] If the evidence is admitted, a limiting instruction must be given upon the request of a party.[33]

§ 13.09 Key Points

Rule 407 excludes evidence of subsequent remedial measures when offered to prove negligent or culpable conduct, including strict liability cases in federal courts. Although known as the "repair rule" at common law, Rule 407 encompasses far more than subsequent repairs. It covers the installation of safety devices, changes in company rules, discharge of employees, disciplinary action against an employee, changes in drug warnings, and modifications in product design.

Rule 407 rests on two grounds. The most important reason is "a social policy of encouraging people to take, or at least not discouraging them from taking, steps in furtherance of added safety." The second ground is relevance: Is the repair probative of negligence or maybe there are other motivations at work?

Timing of repair. The remedial measure must take effect *after* the accident or incident being litigated. A remedial measure that takes effect after purchase but before the accident that is the subject of litigation is not a subsequent measure.

Third-party remedial measures. When a subsequent remedial measure is made by a third person, the policy of encouraging such measures is not implicated, and thus the rule does not apply. In these cases, however, the relevance of the subsequent measure becomes doubtful and is subject to exclusion under Rules 401 and 403.

Required remedial measures. When a subsequent remedial measure is required by governmental regulation, the policy of encouraging such measures is not be implicated. Consequently, Rule 407 does not apply. However, relevance issues remain, and the evidence may be excluded under Rules 401 and 403.

Strict liability. This is a controversial issue, but Federal Rule 407 applies in strict liability cases.

Other purposes. If the evidence is offered for some other purpose, such as proof of ownership, control, feasibility of precautionary measures, or impeachment, the rule does not apply. Rule 403 applies here, however.

---

[32] *See* Complaint of Consol. Coal Co., 123 F.3d 126, 136 (3d Cir. 1997) ("Yet a court must interpret the impeachment exception to Rule 407 circumspectly because 'any evidence of subsequent remedial measures might be thought to contradict and so in a sense impeach [a party's] testimony. . . .'") (quoting Flaminio v. Honda Motor Co., 733 F.2d 463, 468 (7th Cir. 1984). *See also* Kelly v. Crown Equip. Co., 970 F.2d 1273, 1278 (3d Cir. 1992) ("Dr. Watkins did not make a statement that the forklift's design was the best or the only one possible. He said only that it was an excellent and proper design. Thus, evidence of subsequent changes cannot serve to impeach his statements.").

[33] *See* Fed. R. Evid. 105 (limiting instructions).

Chapter 14

COMPROMISES & OFFERS: FRE 408

§ 14.01 Introduction

Federal Rule 408 excludes evidence of compromises and offers to compromise when offered to prove liability for or the invalidity of a claim or its amount. If the evidence is offered for some other purpose, however, the rule does not apply. Rule 408 also extends to statements made during the course of settlement negotiations. A different provision, Rule 410, governs the admissibility of offers to plead guilty or no contest in criminal cases.[1]

The trial court decides Rule 408 admissibility questions pursuant to Rule 104(a).[2]

§ 14.02 Rationale

Offers to settle lawsuits would quickly disappear if the other party could reject the offer but use it as evidence. It would be admissible as an admission of a party-opponent in the absence of a provision such as Rule 408.[3] As the drafters commented, it is the "promotion of the public policy favoring the compromise and settlement of disputes" that underlies Rule 408.[4]

A secondary rationale turns on relevancy: "The evidence is irrelevant, since the offer may be motivated by a desire for peace rather than from any concession of weakness of position. The validity of this position will vary as the amount of the offer varies in relation to the size of the claim and may also be influenced by other circumstances."[5] As this last sentence suggests, the relevancy argument would not justify a blanket rule such as Rule 408. In a million dollar lawsuit, a settlement offer of $12,000 may be an attempt to "buy peace" because it would cost far more to hire attorneys to litigate. However, a $800,000 offer suggests a real concern that the suit may be lost on the merits.

---

[1] *See infra* chapter 16 (criminal pleas & offers).

[2] *See* Pierce v. F.R. Tripler & Co., 955 F.2d 820, 827 (2d Cir. 1992) ("Under Fed. R. Evid.104(a) preliminary factual questions concerning the admissibility of evidence, such as whether an offer was made in the course of settlement negotiations, are to be determined by the court.").

[3] If the offer was made by the party, it would be an individual admission. Fed. R. Evid. 801(d)(2)(A). If made by the party's attorney, it would be an authorized admission. Fed. R. Evid. 801(d)(2)(C).

[4] Fed. R. Evid. 408 advisory committee's note.

[5] *Id.*

§ 14.03 Scope of Rule 408

Rule 408 applies to completed compromises as well as to offers of compromise. It covers disputes over the *amount* of the claim as well as its validity.[6] It applies even when the evidence is tendered by the person making the offer.[7] However, an unconditional offer may not be covered because the rule requires that the statement be made "in the course of compromise negotiations."[8]

[A] Statements

Rule 408 also excludes evidence of conduct or statements made during the course of compromise negotiations. This changes the common law, under which "independent statements of fact" made during settlement negotiations were admissible. The common law position was rejected because admitting statements made during negotiations had the effect of either inhibiting the negotiations or trapping the unwary negotiator (*e.g.*, failing to preface offers with words such as "hypothetically," "without prejudice," or "assuming").[9] In short, settlement negotiations involve communicating and the common law rule needlessly dampened or interrupted communications. In addition, such a rule raised controversies as to whether the proffered evidence constituted an independent statement of fact or was part of the offer.

[B] Criminal Cases

It is not uncommon for parallel civil and criminal suits to result from the same incident. Since a different provision, Rule 410, governs the admissibility of offers to plead guilty or no contest in criminal cases, one could argue that Rule 408 does not apply to criminal litigation.[10] Most

---

[6] *See Pierce*, 955 F.2d at 826–27 ("Evidence that demonstrates a failure to mitigate damages goes to the 'amount' of the claim and thus, if the offer was made in the course of compromise negotiations, it is barred under the plain language of Rule 408.").

[7] *See id.* at 827–28 ("[A]dmission into evidence of settlement offers, even by the offeror, could inhibit settlement discussions and interfere with the effective administration of justice. As the circumstances under which this issue arose in the district court suggest, widespread admissibility of the substance of settlement offers could bring with it a rash of motions for disqualification of a party's chosen counsel who would likely become a witness at trial.").

[8] *See* Lightfoot v. Union Carbide Corp., 110 F.3d 898, 909 (3d Cir. 1997) ("Lightfoot contends that under Rule 408 . . . the reinstatement letter should not have been considered. . . . By definition, an unconditional offer may not require the employee to abandon or modify his suit, and no such request was made by defendants. The offer therefore cannot be considered an offer of settlement or compromise.").

[9] *See* Fed. R. Evid. 408 advisory committee's note ("The practical value of the common law rule has been greatly diminished by its inapplicability to admissions of fact, even though made in the course of compromise negotiations. An inevitable effect is to inhibit freedom of communication with respect to compromise, even among lawyers.").

[10] *See infra* chapter 16 (criminal pleas & offers).

federal courts so hold.[11] Nevertheless, one could question whether admissibility undercuts the policy embedded in the rule.[12]

§ 14.04   "Dispute" Requirement

Rule 408 applies only if the claim or its amount is *disputed*. This is a critical but sometimes overlooked requirement. If there is no dispute, Rule 408 does not apply because the policy justification for the rule is absent. For example, assume I owe Schmedlap $5,000, and I do not dispute this debt. However, I tell Schmedlap that it will cost him $2,000 in litigation costs for him to collect the $5,000 in a lawsuit. Therefore, I offer him $3,000. This smacks more of a holdup than a good faith settlement offer, and the policies underlying Rule 408 "do not come into play when the effort is to induce a creditor to settle an admittedly due amount for a lesser sum."[13]

Because statements made *prior to* the existence of a controversy are not covered by the rule (no dispute), it is critical to identify the time at which a dispute arose.[14] Suppose I drive my Sentra into Schmedlap's Lexis (something that I would find rather appealing). If I immediately approach his car and say, "I am sorry. It was all my fault. I will pay for everything," there is no dispute; my statements are admissible. On the other hand, if I yell, "Fool! It's your fault! Where did you ever get a licence?" and he responds, "I beg to differ. I rather think it was your fault." Now we have a dispute, and if we agree to split the costs, that agreement and any related

---

[11] *E.g.,* United States v. Logan, 250 F.3d 350, 367 (6th Cir. 2001) ("[T]the plain language of Rule 408 makes it inapplicable in the criminal context. Although this conclusion arguably may have a chilling effect on administrative or civil settlement negotiations in cases where parallel civil and criminal proceedings are possible, we find that this risk is heavily outweighed by the public interest in prosecuting criminal matters."); Manko v. United States, 87 F.3d 50, 54–55 (2d Cir. 1996) ("[T]he policy that underlies Rule 408 does not apply to criminal prosecutions. The policy favoring the encouragement of civil settlements, sufficient to bar their admission in civil actions, is insufficient, in our view, to outweigh the need for accurate determinations in criminal cases where the stakes are higher. It makes no difference, in this regard, whether the settlement evidence is being offered by the government, . . . or by the defense, as in this case."); State v. Mead, 27 P.3d 1115, 1127 (Utah 2001) (Wife's death initially classified as an accident but her family sued; "During trial, the State asked Sultan, the attorney for Pamela Mead's family during the federal wrongful death action, if Mead offered to settle that case. She responded affirmatively. The State then asked, 'What did he propose to you?' Sultan responded, over Mead's objection, 'He told me that if I dropped the lawsuit, he would return the body to the family. And it sent chills down my spine.' ").

[12] *See* United States v. Hays, 872 F.2d 582 (5th Cir. 1989) (inadmissible); ABA Section of Litigation, Emerging Problems Under the Federal Rules of Evidence 70 (3d ed. 1998) ("Use of terms like 'liability' and 'claim' in the Rule have led some courts to hold it inapplicable in criminal proceedings. Despite the textual basis, this approach seems inconsistent with the Rules's policy to promote settlements negotiations and seems to encourage return to the trap for the unwary — 'hypothetical' negotiations — when parallel civil and criminal proceedings are possible.").

[13] Fed. R. Evid. 408 advisory committee's note.

[14] *See* Big O Tire Dealers, Inc. v. Goodyear Tire & Rubber Co., 561 F.2d 1365, 1373 (10th Cir. 1977) ("The discussions had not crystallized to the point of threatened litigation.").

statements are inadmissible. Note that litigation or the threat of litigation is not required, only a dispute.[15]

However, as the Second Circuit has noted, "It is often difficult to determine whether an offer is made 'in compromising or attempting to compromise a claim.'"[16] The timing of both the offer and the existence of a disputed claim are relevant to the determination.[17] Nevertheless, where a party is represented by counsel, threatens litigation, and has initiated the first administrative steps in that litigation, any offer made between attorneys will be presumed to be an offer within the scope of Rule 408.[18]

§ 14.05　Third-Party Compromises

Settlements between a litigant and a third party are excluded if offered to prove liability for or invalidity of a claim or its amount. For example, assume my car hits Schmedlap's car, in which Botz is a passenger. I settle with Botz, but I decide to defend against Schmedlap. Schmedlap wants to introduce the settlement with Botz. No can do. The policy of promoting settlements (here with Botz, the passenger) is operative.

Plaintiff as well as defendant third-party settlements are covered,[19] as are settlements that favor a party. The Fifth Circuit stated:

> While a principal purpose of Rule 408 is to encourage settlements by preventing evidence of a settlement (or its amount) from being

---

[15] *See* Affiliated Mfrs., Inc. v. Alum. Co. Am., 56 F.3d 521, 528 (3d Cir. 1995) ("[T]he meaning of 'dispute' as employed in the rule includes both litigation and less formal stages of a dispute.").

[16] *Pierce*, 955 F.2d at 827. *See also* Deere & Co. v. International Harvester Co., 710 F.2d 1551, 1557 (Fed. Cir. 1983) ("Rule 408, on its face, is limited to actual disputes over existing claims and, accordingly, cannot be applicable to an offer, albeit one ultimately rejected, to license an, as yet, uncontested patent."); Brazil, *Protecting the Confidentiality of Settlement Negotiations*, 39 Hastings L.J. 955, 960–66 (1988).

[17] *See* Cassino v. Reichhold Chemicals, 817 F.2d 1338, 1342–43 (9th Cir. 1987) (offer of severance pay conditioned on waiver of age discrimination claim made contemporaneous with discharge not protected by Rule 408); Big O Tire Dealers v. Goodyear Tire & Rubber Co., 561 F.2d 1365, 1372-73 (10th Cir. 1977) (correspondence between parties prior to the filing of an action held "business communications" rather than "offers to compromise" and thus outside scope of Rule 408).

[18] *Pierce*, 955 F.2d at 827.

[19] *See* McInnis v. A.M.F., Inc., 765 F.2d 240, 247 (1st Cir. 1985) ("In the context of settlements between a litigant and a third party, it is true that Rule 408 is more commonly invoked to bar the admission of agreements between a defendant and a third party to compromise a claim arising out of the same transaction as the one being litigated. . . . If the policies underlying Rule 408 mandate that settlements may not be admitted against a defendant who has recognized and settled a third party's claim against him, it is axiomatic that those policies likewise prohibit the admission of settlement evidence against a plaintiff who has accepted payment from a third party against whom he has a claim. The admission of such evidence would discourage settlements in either case. In addition, the relevance of the settlement to the validity of the claim cannot logically be considered stronger in the former instance than in the latter. . . . A number of recent federal cases have adopted this position, holding that Rule 408 bars evidence of settlements between plaintiffs and third party joint tortfeasors or former co-defendants.").

used against a litigant who was involved in a settlement, the rule is not limited by its terms to such a situation. Even where the evidence offered favors the settling party and is objected to by a party not involved in the settlement, Rule 408 bars the admission of such evidence unless it is admissible for a purpose other than "to prove liability for or invalidity of the claim or its amount."[20]

§ 14.06 Admissibility for Other Purposes

Rule 408 applies *only* if evidence of compromise is offered to prove liability for a claim or its amount. If the evidence is offered for some other purpose, the rule does not apply. The list of other purposes in Rule 408 — proving bias, negating a contention of undue delay, or proving obstruction of justice — is not exhaustive; such evidence may be offered for any other purpose.

Admissibility, however, is not automatic in this context; the trial court must still apply Rules 401 to 403.[21] If evidence of settlement is introduced for another purpose, a limiting instruction is required upon request of a party.[22]

[A] Bias

If a plaintiff sues defendants A and B, a settlement between the plaintiff and defendant A is inadmissible at B's trial if offered to prove liability. The policy of encouraging settlements is applicable in such a case. If, however, A testifies as a witness for the plaintiff at B's trial, evidence of the settlement between the plaintiff and A may be introduced to show bias.[23] The notion here is that the settlement may be a trade-off for the witness's favorable testimony, a classic example of impeachment by bias.[24]

As noted above, admissibility is not automatic; Rules 401 to 403 still apply. Furthermore, an impeachment argument should not be permitted to circumvent the policies underlying the rule.[25] An experienced cross-examiner can often "create" the opportunity for impeachment.

[B] Obstruction of Justice

Evidence of a compromise or an offer to compromise is also admissible if proffered to prove obstruction of a criminal investigation or prosecution.

---

[20] Kennon v. Slipstreamer, Inc., 794 F.2d 1067, 1069 (5th Cir. 1986).

[21] *See* Reichenbach v. Smith, 528 F.2d 1072, 1075 (5th Cir. 1976) ("The trial court must balance the policy of encouraging settlements with the need for evaluating the credibility of the witnesses.").

[22] *See* Fed. R. Evid. 105 (limiting instructions).

[23] *See* John McShain, Inc. v. Cessna Aircraft Co., 563 F.2d 632 (3d Cir. 1977).

[24] *See infra* § 22.04 (bias impeachment).

[25] *See* McInnis v. A.M.F., Inc., 765 F.2d 240, 251 (1st Cir. 1985) ("We cannot permit the defendants to avoid the policies of rule 408 by merely recasting the issue of who caused the injury as an issue of who the plaintiff believed caused it.").

An attorney not familiar with criminal litigation may fall into this trap. Sometimes the same conduct may result in parallel litigation, *i.e.*, both criminal and civil suits — for example, a drunk-driving accident that has caused property damage. Although there is nothing improper in attempting to settle the civil suit, care must be exercised in this context. If the damage amounts to $5,000 and you offer $6,000, hoping the criminal case disappears with the civil case, there may be a problem. "An effort to 'buy off' the prosecution or a prosecuting witness in a criminal case is not within the policy of the rule of exclusion."[26] Plea negotiations in criminal cases involve the prosecutor as the representative of the state; the civil plaintiff is *not a party* to the criminal prosecution (only a witness) and cannot settle a criminal matter. The prudent practice is to inform the prosecutor of attempts to settle a related civil suit.

[C] Prior Inconsistent Statements

In addition to bias, which was discussed above, impeachment may be by prior inconsistent statements.[27] The federal courts differ over whether a settlement statement can be used for this purpose. This type of impeachment would be "another purpose."[28] The underlying policy of Rule 408, however, may be undermined by impeachment,[29] especially if it is "a thinly veiled attempt to get the 'smoking gun' letters before the jury."[30]

§ 14.07 Discovery

Rule 408 specifically provides that evidence otherwise discoverable need not be excluded merely because it was presented during compromise negotiations. The Senate added this provision so attorneys would not attempt to "immunize" documents from discovery by disclosing them in settlement negotiations.[31] Thus, evidence produced through discovery

---

[26] Fed. R. Evid. 408 advisory committee's note.

[27] *See infra* § 22.10 (prior inconsistent statements, FRE 613).

[28] Cochenour v. Cameron Savings and Loan, 160 F.3d 1187, 1190 (8th Cir. 1998) ("Cameron offered Ms. Cochenour's statement regarding her plans to retire in order to rebut her earlier testimony that she had had no plans to retire and that Cameron's president had attempted to force her to retire early.").

[29] *See* 2 Saltzburg, Martin & Capra, Federal Rules of Evidence Manual 408-8-9 (8th ed. 2002) ("In most cases . . . the Court should decide against admitting statements made during settlement negotiations as impeachment evidence when they are used to impeach a party who tried to settle a case but failed. The philosophy of the Rule is to allow the parties to drop their guard and to talk freely and loosely without fear that a concession made to advance negotiations will be used at trial. Opening the door to prior inconsistent statement impeachment evidence on a regular basis may well result in more restricted — or more stilted, with every statement preceded by an 'assuming arguendo' — negotiations.").

[30] E.E.O.C. v. Gear Petroleum, Inc., 948 F.2d 1542, 1546 (10th Cir. 1991).

[31] S. Rep. No. 1277, 93d Cong., 2d Sess. (1974) ("This amendment adds a sentence to insure that evidence, such as documents, is not rendered inadmissible merely because it is presented in the course of compromise negotiations if the evidence is otherwise discoverable. A party should not be able to immunize from admissibility documents otherwise discoverable merely by offering them in a compromise negotiation.") reprinted in 1974 U.S.C.C.A.N. 7051, 7056.

procedures is not excludable under Rule 408. However, references to such evidence made during settlement negotiations are inadmissible.

§ 14.08 Key Points

Federal Rule 408 excludes evidence of compromises and offers to compromise when offered to prove liability for or the invalidity of a claim or its amount. A different provision, Rule 410, governs the admissibility of offers to plead guilty or no contest in criminal cases.

Rationale. Offers to settle lawsuits would quickly disappear if the other party could reject the offer but use it as evidence. Also, such evidence is of questionable relevance in some cases.

Statements. Rule 408's exclusionary policy also extends to statements made during the course of settlement negotiations.

Dispute requirement. Rule 408 applies only if the claim or its amount is *disputed*. Because statements made *prior to* the existence of a controversy are not covered by the rule (no dispute), it is critical to identify the time at which a dispute arose. Litigation or the threat of litigation is not required — only a dispute.

Third-party compromises. Settlements between a litigant and a third party are excluded if offered to prove liability for or invalidity of a claim or its amount.

Other purpose. If the evidence is offered for some other purpose, the rule does not apply. The list of other purposes in Rule 408 — proving bias, negating a contention of undue delay, or proving obstruction of justice — is not exhaustive.

Admissibility, however, is not automatic in this context; the trial court must still apply Rules 401 to 403. If evidence of settlement is introduced for another purpose, a limiting instruction is required upon request of a party.[32]

---

[32] *See* Fed. R. Evid. 105 (limiting instructions).

Chapter 15

MEDICAL PAYMENTS: FRE 409

§ 15.01 Introduction

You are in a traffic accident and accompany the other driver to the emergency room, where you offer to pay the expenses because the injured driver has no medical insurance. Later, the other driver sues you and wants to introduce the payment of medical expenses as proof of your negligence.

Federal Rule 409, sometimes known as the "Good Samaritan" rule, governs the admissibility of evidence of furnishing, offering, or promising to pay medical, hospital, or similar expenses.[1] Such evidence is inadmissible if offered to prove liability for the injury. However, if offered for some other purpose, the rule does not apply.

§ 15.02 Rationale

The policy underlying Rule 409 is straightforward — exclusion is based on the belief that "such payment or offer is usually made from humane impulses and not from an admission of liability, and that to hold otherwise would tend to discourage assistance to the injured person."[2]

Unlike Rule 408, which governs settlement offers, Rule 409 does not exclude statements that may accompany the payment of medical expenses. "This difference in treatment arises from fundamental differences in nature. Communication is essential if compromises are to be effected, and consequently broad protection of statements is needed. This is not so in cases of payments or offers or promises to pay medical expenses, where factual statements may be expected to be incidental in nature."[3] Rules 408 and 409 also differ in another respect; there need not be a "dispute" for Rule 409 to apply.

---

[1] *See* Quiel v. Wilson, 34 N.E.2d 590, 590 (Ohio App. 1940) ("If such evidence were to be considered admissible, it is manifest that no one, however kindly disposed to be of service in an emergency, would dare proffer his service or agree to be responsible for care and treatment without jeopardizing himself and by such acts furnish evidence through which he would be held to account for an injury for which he was in no way legally responsible. The Good Samaritan would have furnished evidence thus against himself for the injuries to the wayfarer who fell among thieves and robbers.").

[2] Fed. R. Evid. 409 advisory committee's note (quoting Annot., Admissibility of Evidence to Show Payment, or Offer or Promise of Payment, of Medical, Hospital, and Similar Expenses of an Injured Party by the Opposing Party, 20 A.L.R.2d 291, 293 (1951)).

[3] Fed. R. Evid. 409 advisory committee's note.

§ 15.03 Admissibility for Other Purposes

Unlike Rule 408, Rule 409 does not explicitly provide that evidence of medical payments may be admitted if offered for a purpose other than to prove liability. Nevertheless, that is the effect of the rule.[4] Rule 403 also applies.

§ 15.04 Key Point

Unlike Rule 408, which governs settlement offers, Rule 409 does not exclude statements that may accompany the payment of medical expenses. These rules also differ in another respect; there need not be a "dispute" for Rule 409 to apply.

---

[4] *See* Williams v. Mo. Pac. R.R., 11 F.3d 132, 135 (10th Cir. 1993) ("On retrial, to avoid possible confusion, the jury should be advised that past medical expenses, except for the $600.00 bill, have been paid and thus may not be estimated and added to the award. The jury may receive such information. See Fed.R.Evid. 409. Evidence of past medical expenses is inadmissible to prove liability, but liability will not be an issue on retrial [only damages]."); Savoie v. Otto Candies, Inc., 692 F.2d 363, 370 n.7 (5th Cir. 1982) ("Rule 409 only denies admissibility 'to prove liability for the injury.' Such evidence may be admissible to prove other facts, such as 'the status of the alleged tort-feasor as employer.' Here, the questioned evidence was not used to establish Candies' negligence, but only as circumstantial evidence of Savoie's status as a seaman. Were the only issue in the case the entitlement to medical or hospital or similar expenses, then proof of payment of a portion of such expenses might properly be labeled as going only to the issue of liability, and hence inadmissible under Rule 409. Even if there were some slight relevance on another issue, in a suit only for maintenance and cure the principles of Fed. R. Evid. 403 might still operate to exclude such evidence.") (citations omitted). *But see* 23 Wright & Graham, Federal Practice and Procedure § 5329 (1980) (the term "liability" in Rule 409 "precludes use to show ownership, control, and the like").

Chapter 16

CRIMINAL PLEAS & OFFERS: FRE 410

§ 16.01 Introduction

Federal Rule 410 governs the admissibility of evidence of (1) withdrawn pleas of guilty, (2) nolo contendere pleas, (3) statements made during proceedings to determine the voluntariness of the above pleas under Criminal Rule 11 or a comparable state procedure, and (4) certain statements made during plea bargaining discussions.[1]

The rule provides that evidence of all the above is inadmissible in both civil and criminal cases if offered *against the defendant* who made the offer, plea, or statement. There are two explicit exceptions: (1) perjury and false statement prosecutions, and (2) the rule of completeness. Other exceptions have been read into the rule.

The *key point* is that all the evidence covered by Rule 410 would be admissible as an admission of a party opponent in the absence of Rule 410.[2]

§ 16.02 Withdrawn Guilty Pleas

Rule 410(1) provides that a withdrawn guilty plea (and related statements) are inadmissible if offered against the defendant who made the plea.[3] Guilty pleas may be withdrawn under certain conditions. If the court permits a withdrawal, it makes no sense to allow the prosecutor to introduce the withdrawn plea at the subsequent trial.[4] This "would effectively set at naught the allowance of withdrawal and place the accused in a dilemma utterly inconsistent with the decision to award him a trial."[5] Moreover, admission of a withdrawn guilty plea would "compel the defendant to take the stand by way of explanation and to open the way for the prosecution to call the lawyer who had represented him at the time of entering the plea."[6]

---

[1] Rule 410 is identical to Federal Criminal Rule 11(e)(6).

[2] *See* Fed. R. Evid. 801(d)(2)(A) (individual admissions); Fed. R. Evid. 801(d)(2)(C) (authorized admissions).

[3] Fed. R. Crim. P. 11 governs guilty pleas in criminal cases.

[4] Note that pleas of guilty that are *not* withdrawn or rejected by the trial court are admissible as admissions of a party-opponent.

[5] Fed. R. Evid. 410 advisory committee's note (citing Kercheval v. United States, 274 U.S. 220 (1927)).

[6] *Id.* (citing People v. Spitaleri, 173 N.E.2d 35 (N.Y. 1961)).

§ 16.03　Nolo Contendere Pleas

Rule 410(2) provides that evidence of a nolo contendere plea (and related statements) are inadmissible if offered against the defendant who made the plea. Criminal Rule 11(a) permits an accused to plead nolo contendere. The exclusion of evidence of no-contest pleas is necessary to preserve the distinction between no contest and guilty pleas.[7] Stated another way: The *only* purpose of a nolo plea is to preclude its subsequent use in civil cases. In all other respects, a guilty plea and a no-contest plea are alike; a person can be sentenced and imprisoned based on a no contest plea.

Why have no-contest pleas? Assume parallel criminal and civil litigation — *e.g.*, car accident. In a jurisdiction without a no-contest plea, a defendant might contest a criminal charge for reckless driving *only* because of the fear that a guilty plea would be admissible in subsequent civil litigation involving personal injury and property damage.[8] The same rationale applies (big time) in criminal antitrust prosecutions, which may be followed by *treble* damage civil suits. The notion underlying no-contest pleas is that we do not want scarce prosecutorial resources expended in cases where the defendant does not want to contest the criminal charge. Nevertheless, court approval is required.[9]

Although Rule 410 precludes the admission of no-contest pleas, it does not preclude use of a *judgment of conviction* based on that plea. Rather, Rule 803(22) makes a judgment based on a no-contest plea inadmissible if offered in a civil case.[10] However, the use of a conviction based on a no-contest plea for impeachment under Rule 609 is not prohibited by either rule.[11]

§ 16.04　Criminal Rule 11 "Voluntariness" Statements

Under Rule 410(3), statements made during proceedings under Criminal Rule 11 or its state equivalent are inadmissible in cases involving *withdrawn guilty pleas or no-contest pleas*. Because an accused is giving up fundamental constitutional protections (*e.g.*, right to jury trial and privilege against self-incrimination), Criminal Rule 11 establishes detailed procedures for determining the voluntariness of pleas of guilty or no contest.

---

[7] Fed. R. Evid. 410 advisory committee's note (Rule 410 "gives effect to the principal traditional characteristic of the no contest plea, i.e., avoiding the admission of guilt which is inherent in pleas of guilty."). *See also* Lipsky v. Commonwealth United Corp., 551 F.2d 887 (2d Cir. 1976) (consent judgment considered the equivalent of a nolo plea).

[8] Because of speedy trial statutes, the criminal case will invariably be tried first.

[9] Fed. R. Crim. P. 11(b) ("A defendant may plead nolo contendere only with the consent of the court. Such a plea shall be accepted by the court only after due consideration of the views of the parties and the interest of the public in the effective administration of justice.").

[10] *See infra* § 33.17 (hearsay exception for a judgment of conviction).

[11] Fed. R. Evid. 609. *See infra* § 22.08 (impeachment by prior convictions).

Before accepting such a plea, the judge must determine that (1) the plea is voluntary (no coercion or improper inducements),[12] (2) the defendant understands the nature of the charged offense and the consequences of the plea, and (3) there is factual basis for the plea. This procedure usually requires the defendant to make incriminatory statements. Such statements are inadmissible if the plea itself is inadmissible under Rule 410.

§ 16.05 Plea Discussions

In some jurisdictions up to 90% of the criminal cases are resolved by a guilty plea, most often as a result of plea bargaining. Under Rule 410(4), plea bargaining statements involving a prosecutor are inadmissible. The policy underlying this exclusion is similar to the one underlying Rule 408, which governs compromise offers in civil cases: exclusion promotes the public policy of favoring the settlement of disputes.[13] Criminal Rule 11(f) recognizes that policy, and the Supreme Court has noted that "the guilty plea and the often concomitant plea bargain are important components of this country's criminal justice system."[14]

Determining when negotiations begin and end is important because Rule 410 does not apply before negotiations have commenced or after they have terminated.[15]

[A] Statements to Police

Several federal courts had read the original version of Rule 410 broadly to cover some "plea bargain" statements made during discussions between defendants and the police.[16] The rule was amended (1980) and is now

---

[12] Fed. R. Crim. P.11(d) ("The court shall not accept a plea of guilty or nolo contendere without first, by addressing the defendant personally in open court, determining that the plea is voluntary and not the result of force or threats or of promises apart from a plea agreement. The court shall also inquire as to whether the defendant's willingness to plead guilty or nolo contendere results from prior discussions between the attorney for the government and the defendant or the defendant's attorney.").

[13] Fed. R. Evid. 410 advisory committee's note ("As with compromise offers generally, free communication is needed, and security against having an offer of compromise or related statement admitted in evidence effectively encourages it.").

[14] Blackledge v. Allison, 431 U.S. 63, 71 (1977). See also Santobello v. New York, 404 U.S. 257, 260 (1971) ("Properly administered, it is to be encouraged."); Brady v. United States, 397 U.S. 742, 752 (1970) ("The correctional processes can begin immediately, and the practical burdens of a trial are eliminated.").

[15] E.g., United States v. Hays, 49 F.3d 447, 450 (8th Cir. 1997) ("Statements voluntarily offered either before any plea negotiation has begun or after a plea agreement has been reached cannot be considered statements made 'in the course of plea discussions' within the meaning of the exclusionary rules."); United States v. Lloyd, 43 F.3d 1183, 1186 (8th Cir. 1994) ("once a plea agreement has been reached, statements made thereafter are not entitled to [exclusion]"); United States v. White, 617 F.2d 1131, 1134 (5th Cir. 1980) (statements made as mere "cooperation negotiations" not subject to exclusion).

[16] See United States v. Herman, 544 F.2d 791, 795-99 (5th Cir. 1977); United States v. Brooks, 536 F.2d 1137, 1138–39 (6th Cir. 1976); United States v. Smith, 525 F.2d 1017, 1020–22 (10th Cir. 1975).

limited to statements made "in the course of plea discussions with an attorney for the prosecuting authority."[17] Only if the police are acting as the prosecutor's agents does the rule apply.[18]

A defendant's statements to the police, of course, must satisfy constitutional standards, such as the due process voluntariness test, the *Miranda* safeguards, and the Sixth Amendment right to counsel.[19]

[B] Broken Agreements

Since the policies under plea bargaining are undercut when a party reneges on the agreement, Rule 410 does not apply when a plea agreement is broken. In *United States v. Stirling*,[20] the defendant entered into a written agreement with the prosecution, under which the defendant would plead guilty and testify for the prosecution before the grand jury and at the trial of other defendants. After testifying before the grand jury, the defendant refused to perform his part of the agreement and plead not guilty. The Second Circuit upheld the admission of his grand jury testimony at his trial. The agreement specifically provided for use of information supplied by the defendant in the event the defendant reneged on the agreement. The same result was reached in *United States v. Davis*,[21] even though the agreement was silent on this issue.[22]

[C] Offered Against Prosecution

Rule 410, on its face, excludes evidence of offers to plead guilty or nolo contendere only when offered against the defendant who made the plea or offer. It does not appear to exclude such evidence when offered by the defendant against the prosecution, a possibility noted by the Supreme Court.[23] In *United States v. Verdoorn*,[24] however, the Eighth Circuit upheld

---

[17] *See* United States v. Lewis, 117 F.3d 980, 984 (7th Cir. 1997) ("Rule 410(4) and Rule 11(e)(6) only apply to statements made to government attorneys. They do not cover those made to law enforcement agents [IRS agent].").

[18] *See* United States v. Serna, 799 F.2d 842, 849 (2d Cir. 1986) ("We think the rule can be fairly read to require the participation of a Government attorney in the plea discussions, but not necessarily his physical presence when a particular statement is made to agents whom the attorney has authorized to engage in plea discussions. . . . Because the agents were acting under the AUSA's authority in determining whether Serna would in fact cooperate, Serna's statement was properly excluded.") (citation omitted).

[19] *See* Dressler, Understanding Criminal Procedure chs. 22–25 (3d ed. 2002).

[20] 571 F.2d 708, 730–32 (2d Cir. 1978).

[21] 617 F.2d 677 (D.C. Cir. 1979).

[22] The D.C. Circuit held that exclusion of "testimony made after and pursuant to the agreement would not serve the purpose of encouraging compromise. Indeed, such a rule would permit a defendant to breach his bargain with impunity; he could renounce the agreement and return to the status quo ante whenever he chose, even though the Government has no parallel power to rescind the compromise unilaterally." *Id.* at 685. *See also* United States v. Arroyo-Angulo, 580 F.2d 1137, 1147–49 (2d Cir. 1978).

[23] *See* United States v. Mezzanatto, 513 U.S. 196, 205 (1995) ("The Rules provide that state-

the exclusion of evidence of plea bargaining offered by the defendant to "challenge the credibility of the government's entire case, i.e., disclose the lengths to which the government went in attempting to obtain vital testimony." The court cited Rule 408 and Criminal Rule 11(e)(6), which is identical to Rule 410, to support its holding. This result seems correct. Admission of plea negotiation statements against the prosecution would hinder the policy of encouraging plea bargaining.

§ 16.06 Admissibility Against Third Parties

Rule 410 applies only if the evidence is offered *against the defendant who made the plea or offer*; it does not apply if the evidence is offered against a different person. "Limiting the exclusionary rule to use against the accused is consistent with the purpose of the rule, since the possibility of use for or against other persons will not impair the effectiveness of withdrawing pleas or the freedom of discussion which the rule is designed to foster."[25] For example, offers, pleas, and statements entered into between the prosecution and its own witnesses may be used for impeachment (bias) by a criminal defendant.[26] In this context, the evidence is not being offered against the defendant who made the offer, plea, or statement. Similarly, a defense witness may be impeached with prior inconsistent statements made during plea discussions because the statement is being admitted against a witness, not the "defendant."[27]

§ 16.07 Exceptions

There are two explicit exceptions in Rule 410, which are discussed below. Courts have read in others. For example, the rule does not apply if the defendant files a civil suit (*e.g.*, against the police[28] or his former criminal defense lawyer[29]) because, in the view of several courts, Rule 410 is a defensive, not an offensive, provision.

---

ments made in the course of plea discussions are inadmissible 'against' the defendant, and thus leave open the possibility that a defendant may offer such statements into evidence for his own tactical advantage.").

[24] 528 F.2d 103, 107 (8th Cir. 1976). *Accord* United States v. Greene, 995 F.2d 793, 798–99 (8th Cir. 1993). *See also* United States v. Biaggi, 909 F.2d 662, 690–91 (2d Cir. 1990) (accused's rejection of immunity offer admissible).

[25] Fed. R. Evid. 410 advisory committee's note. *See* United States v. Mathis, 550 F.2d 180, 182 (4th Cir. 1976).

[26] *See infra* § 22.04 (bias impeachment).

[27] *See* Fed. R. Evid. 613; United States v. Dortch, 5 F.3d 1056, 1067 (7th Cir. 1993).

[28] *See* Walker v. Schaeffer, 854 F.2d 138, 143 (6th Cir. 1988) ("Rule 410 was intended to protect a criminal defendant's use of the *nolo contendere* plea to defend himself from future civil liability. We decline to interpret the rule so as to allow the former defendants to use the plea offensively, in order to obtain damages, after having admitted facts which would indicate no civil liability on the part of the [defendant] police.").

[29] *See* Brown v. Theos, 550 S.E.2d 304, 307 n. 2 (S.C. 2001) (malpractice action against criminal defense attorneys; "Brown as a plaintiff is litigating whether his Attorneys' adequately advised him during his plea negotiations. Rule 410 . . . was never intended to cover this type of case.").

[A] Rule of Completeness

Rule 410 recognizes an exception in "any proceeding in which another statement made in the course of the same plea or plea discussions has been introduced and the statement should, in fairness, be considered contemporaneously with it."[30] This provision is comparable to Rule 106, which codifies the "rule of completeness."[31]

[B] Perjury & False Statement Prosecutions

Rule 410 also recognizes an exception for perjury and false statement prosecutions. In such cases, Rule 410 statements are admissible if they were made under oath, on the record, and in the presence of counsel. The Senate Judiciary Committee added this exception because without it "a defendant would be able to contradict his previous statements and thereby lie with impunity. To prevent such an injustice, the rule has been modified to permit the use of such statements in subsequent perjury or false statement prosecutions."[32]

[C] Impeachment

There is no impeachment exception to Rule 410.[33] Any doubt is removed when the legislative history of Rule 410 is considered. As enacted in 1975, Rule 410 contained an impeachment exception.[34] However, when the rule was subsequently amended later that year,[35] the impeachment exception had been deleted.

Note, however, an accused may waive the protections of the rule, and thereby subject himself to impeachment. Waiver is discussed in the next section. Furthermore, Rule 410 does not apply to statements made in connection with a guilty plea that is not withdrawn; thus, such statements are admissible for impeachment as well as substantively.[36]

---

[30] Fed. R. Crim. P. 11(e)(6) (1980) advisory committee's note ("For example, if a defendant upon a motion to dismiss a prosecution on some ground were able to admit certain statements made in aborted plea discussions in his favor, then other relevant statements made in the same plea discussions should be admissible against the defendant in the interest of determining the truth of the matter at issue.").

[31] *See infra* chapter 29 (rule of completeness).

[32] S. Rep. No. 1277, 93d Cong., 2d Sess., reprinted in 1974 U.S.C.C.A.N. 7051, 7057–58.

[33] *See* United States v. Acosta-Ballardo, 8 F.3d 1532, 1535–36 (10th Cir. 1993) (inadmissible for impeachment); United States v. Martinez, 536 F.2d 1107, 1108–09 (5th Cir. 1976).

[34] 65 F.R.D. 145 (1975) ("This rule shall not apply to the introduction of voluntary and reliable statements made in court on the record in connection with any of the foregoing pleas or offers where offered for *impeachment* purposes or in a subsequent prosecution of the declarant for perjury or false statement.") (emphasis added).

[35] *See* Act of December 12, 1975, Pub. L. No. 94-149, 89 Stat. 805.

[36] *See* United States v. Mathis, 550 F.2d 180, 182 (4th Cir. 1976).

§ **16.08 Waiver**

In *United States v. Mezzanatto*,[37] the Supreme Court ruled that an accused could waive the protections afforded by Rule 410. After his arrest for drug offenses, the defendant and his attorney requested a meeting with the prosecutor. As a condition to proceeding with discussions, the prosecutor required the defendant to agree that any statements he made during the meeting could be used to impeach any contradictory testimony he might give at trial if the case proceeded that far. After consulting with counsel, Mezzanatto agreed. The plea discussions eventually broke down, and the defendant was tried. When he took the stand to declare his innocence, the prosecutor used the plea discussion statements to impeach him during cross-examination.

Noting that evidentiary stipulations and the waiver of objections are common in litigation, the Court saw nothing wrong with this type of waiver:[38] "Evidentiary stipulations are a valuable and integral part of everyday trial practice. Prior to trial, parties often agree in writing to the admission of otherwise objectionable evidence, either in exchange for stipulations from opposing counsel or for other strategic purposes. . . . During the course of trial, parties frequently decide to waive evidentiary objections, and such tactics are routinely honored by trial judges."[39]

This holding is not limited to Rule 410; it has broader application, encompassing most evidence rules. The Court did recognize that there may be exceptions to the presumption of waivability, but the party seeking an exception bears the responsibility of identifying some affirmative basis for overriding this presumption. Note, however, that the waiver in *Mezzanatto* was voluntarily and knowingly made with the assistance of counsel.

§ **16.09 Key Points**

Federal Rule 410 excludes evidence of (1) withdrawn pleas of guilty, (2) nolo contendere pleas, (3) statements made during proceedings to determine the voluntariness of the above pleas under Criminal Rule 11 or a comparable state procedure, and (4) certain statements made during plea bargaining discussions with the prosecutor.

The rule applies only if the evidence is offered *against the defendant* who made the offer, plea, or statement.

---

[37] 513 U.S. 196 (1995).

[38] *Id.* at 203–04 ("Because the plea-statement Rules were enacted against a background presumption that legal rights generally, and evidentiary provisions specifically, are subject to waiver by voluntary agreement of the parties, we will not interpret Congress' silence as an implicit rejection of waivability.").

[39] *Id.* at 203. *See also* United States v. Burch 156 F.3d 1315, (D.C. Cir. 1998) ("[W]e believe these [waiver] principles do not countenance drawing any distinction in this case between permitting waivers for purposes of impeachment or rebuttal and permitting waivers for the prosecution's case-in-chief.").

There are two explicit exceptions: (1) perjury and false statement prosecutions, and (2) the rule of completeness. Other exceptions have been read into the rule.

The *key point* is that all the evidence covered by Rule 410 would be admissible as an admission of a party opponent in the absence of Rule 410.

Chapter 17

INSURANCE: FRE 411

§ 17.01 Introduction

Federal Rule 411 excludes evidence of liability insurance if offered to prove that a person carrying or failing to carry liability insurance acted negligently or otherwise wrongfully. If the evidence is offered for another purpose, such as proof of (1) agency, ownership or control, or (2) bias of a witness, the rule does not apply.

Scope of rule. Rule 411 was "drafted in broad terms so as to include contributory negligence or other fault of a plaintiff as well as fault of a defendant."[1] By its terms, the rule excludes evidence of the nonexistence as well as the existence of insurance.[2]

§ 17.02 Rationale

Evidence of liability insurance is simply irrelevant if offered to show negligence. Are people with liability insurance more likely to act negligently than those without insurance? In addition, there is a fear that the jury may unfairly penalize insurance companies because they have deep pockets.[3] Nevertheless, in traffic accident and malpractice cases juries probably assume insurance coverage, although the amount may be uncertain.[4]

---

[1] Fed . R. Evid. 411 advisory committee's note.

[2] Insurance agreements are discoverable, but discoverability is not the same as admissibility. *See* Fed. R. Civ. P. 26(a)(1)(D) ("for inspection and copying as under Rule 34 any insurance agreement under which any person carrying on an insurance business may be liable to satisfy part or all of a judgment which may be entered in the action or to indemnify or reimburse for payments made to satisfy the judgment."). The policy underlying Rule 411 may be defeated if prospective jurors are questioned during voir dire concerning possible connections (*e.g.*, employment) with insurance companies. Such questions, however, must be asked in good faith, and the trial court has discretion to control and limit the questioning.

[3] Fed . R. Evid. 411 advisory committee's note ("knowledge of the presence or absence of liability insurance would induce juries to decide cases on improper grounds").

[4] *See* Ede v. Atrium S. Ob-Gyn, Inc., 642 N.E.2d 365, 368 (Ohio 1994):

> Too often courts have a Pavlovian response to insurance testimony — immediately assuming prejudice. It is naive to believe that today's jurors, bombarded for years with information about health care insurance, do not already assume in a malpractice case that the defendant doctor is covered by insurance. The legal charade protecting juries from information they already know keeps hidden from them relevant information that could assist them in making their determinations.
>
> Given the sophistication of our juries, the first sentence of Evid. R. 411 does not merit the enhanced importance it has been given. Instead of juries knowing the truth about the existence and extent of coverage, they are forced to make assumptions which may have more prejudicial effect than the truth.

Indeed, for that reason, a party without insurance might like to inform the jury of this fact; however, the rule also excludes absence-of-insurance evidence.

The policy underlying Rule 411 does not apply in a criminal case (*e.g.*, arson) in which insurance proceeds are the motive for the crime.

§ 17.03 Admissibility for Other Purposes

Rule 411 does not apply if insurance evidence is offered for some other purposes — for example, bias, ownership or agency. The list of "other purposes" is illustrative, not exhaustive.[5] However, admissibility is not automatic in this context. The requirements of Rules 401 to 403 must still be satisfied.[6] Trial attorneys are rather creative when it comes to coming up with "proper" reasons for getting insurance evidence before a jury. Frequently, an offer to stipulate will remove an issue from controversy and preclude admissibility if the evidence is offered for some other purpose.

[A] Ownership & Agency

The fact that a party carried insurance that covered another person may be offered as tending to prove an agency relationship. Similarly, insurance coverage on certain premises is probative of a party's control over or ownership of those premises; people usually do not carry insurance on objects that they do not own.

[B] Bias

Evidence of insurance may also be admitted to prove bias or prejudice on the part of a witness.[7] The classic example is the insurance adjustor who interviews the other party and is called to impeach that party with a prior inconsistent statement. The adjustor herself is subject to bias impeachment because she is an employee of a company with a financial

---

[5] *See* Wheeling Pittsburgh Steel Corp. v. Beelman River Terminals, Inc., 254 F.3d 706, 716-17 (8th Cir. 2001) ("Whether his insurance covers the damage or not, we do not think that Sam Beelman's comments amount to an admission of legal liability or fault, but rather constitute an admission of responsibility for payment based on an erroneous view of what his insurance policy provided.").

[6] *See* Hunziker v. Scheidemantle, 543 F.2d 489, 595 n. 10 (3d Cir. 1976) (evidence of insurance coverage "may be admissible if offered for other relevant purposes and if its exclusion would be more prejudicial to the plaintiff here than its admission would be to the defendants").

[7] *E.g.,* Conde v. Starlight I, Inc., 103 F.3d 210, 214 (1st Cir. 1997) ("Rule 411 does permit mention of insurance coverage, not to prove negligence, but collaterally to show the possible 'bias or prejudice of a witness.'"); Charter v. Chleborad, 551 F.2d 246, 248 (8th Cir. 1977) ("[T]he fact that defendant's insurer employed [a witness] was clearly admissible to show possible bias of that witness."). *See infra* § 22.04 (bias impeachment).

interest in the litigation. Recall, however, that Rule 403 still operates in this context.[8]

§ 17.04 Key Points

Federal Rule 411 excludes evidence of liability insurance if offered to prove that a person carrying *or failing to carry* liability insurance acted negligently or otherwise wrongfully. Evidence of liability insurance is simply irrelevant if offered to show negligence. There is also a fear that the jury will unfairly penalize insurance companies because they have "deep pockets."

Other purposes. If the evidence is offered for another purpose, such as proof (1) of agency, ownership or control, or (2) bias of a witness, the rule does not apply, but Rule 403 does.

---

[8] *See* Granberry v. O'Barr, 866 F.2d 112, 114 (5th Cir. 1988) ("There is not the slightest shred of evidence that he had any knowledge as to whether the owner of the truck even had liability insurance, much less with the company with which he had in the past been associated, at the time he made those statements. Under these circumstances, we cannot conclude that the court abused its discretion in forbidding cross-examination as to the corporate connections of the witness Gregory and the existence of the liability insurance.").

Chapter 18

WITNESS COMPETENCY: FRE 601, 603, 605, 606

§ 18.01 Introduction

Witness competency concerns the witness's qualifications to testify.[1] Mental competence (capacity) involves the witness's ability to observe, recall, and relate.[2] Moral competence focuses on the witness's recognition of the duty to testify truthfully, which is fortified by the oath requirement. At one time, common law rules of incompetency or disqualification had immense impact on trials because there were so many categories, *including the parties*, whose testimony was deemed unreliable due to their interest in the case.

However, these rules have generally evolved over time into impeachment rules. Thus, the trend is to provide the jury with more information, both the testimony of persons who would have been disqualified at common law and the information needed to evaluate their credibility.[3] The following chart illustrates this point:

Common Law Disqualification Rule	*Current Impeachment Rule*
Interest (including parties and spouses)	Bias[4]
Infancy	Sensory or mental defect
Crime of infamy	Conviction of crime (Rule 609)
Insane, idiot, inebriate	Sensory or mental defect
Infidel	Oath (Rule 603 but see also Rule 610)

---

[1] The competency of a witness to testify differs from the competency of testimony. The latter typically concerns exclusionary rules in contradistinction to relevancy rules. Thus, under Rule 402, relevant evidence may be excluded due to the hearsay rule, a "competence" rule. *See supra* § 1.03 (law of evidence).

[2] Ladd, *Uniform Evidence Rules in the Federal Courts*, 49 Va. L. Rev. 692, 714 (1963) ("Competency of a witness is based upon the capacity of a witness to tell the truth, accompanied with a consciousness of the obligation to do so.").

[3] In 1918, the Supreme Court refused to be bound by "the dead hand of the common law rule of 1789" and wrote that it was "the conviction of our time that the truth is more likely to be arrived at by hearing the testimony of all persons of competent understanding who may seem to have knowledge of the facts involved in a case, leaving the credit and weight of such testimony to be determined by the jury or by the court." Rosen v. United States, 245 U.S. 467, 471 (1918).

[4] Moreover, the spousal privilege for testimony *against* a spouse in criminal cases has survived in many jurisdictions. *See infra* § 39.02 (spousal testimonial privilege).

211

In *Washington v. Texas*,[5] the Supreme Court struck down a witness disqualification rule as violative of the Sixth Amendment right to compulsory process: "The right to offer the testimony of witnesses, and to compel their attendance, if necessary, is in plain terms the right to present a defense, the right to present the defendant's version of the facts as well as the prosecution's to the jury so it may decide where the truth lies."[6]

Federal rules. Federal Rule 601 provides that all witnesses are competent, and the drafters stated that there are no competency requirements.[7] Nevertheless, some federal cases have suggested that a witness may be disqualified if he "does not have the capacity to recall, or that he does not understand the duty to testify truthfully."[8] In effect, this approach turns the competency issue into a Rule 403 issue.

A different rule, Rule 702, governs the competency or qualifications of expert witnesses. In addition, Rule 603 specifies an oath requirement, and Rules 605 and 606 deal, respectively, with the competency of jurors and the trial judge.

§ 18.02   Oath Requirement: FRE 603

Federal Rule 603 requires witnesses to swear or affirm to the truthfulness of their testimony prior to testifying.[9] According to Wigmore, the "true purpose of the oath is not to exclude any competent witness, but merely to add a stimulus to truthfulness wherever such a stimulus is feasible."[10] Moreover, a prosecution for perjury requires the taking of an oath.

The form of the oath or affirmation is not important, so long as it is "calculated to awaken the witness's conscience and impress the witness' mind with the witness' duty" to testify truthfully.[11] According to the federal

---

[5] 388 U.S. 14 (1967). Two state statutes precluded an accomplice from testifying in favor of a defendant.

[6] *Id.* at 19.

[7] Fed. R. Evid. 601 advisory committee's note ("no mental or moral qualifications for testifying as a witness are specified").

[8] United States v. Lightly, 677 F.2d 1027, 1028 (4th Cir. 1982). *See also* United States v. Phibbs, 999 F.2d 1053, 1069–70 (6th Cir. 1993) ("[T]he court had the additional authority, pursuant to Rule 403, to exclude their testimony in light of their past or present mental state. The court chose not to take any of these measures in the circumstances. Instead, it permitted defense counsel to use the psychiatric records of Parks and McKeehan, as well as other indicia of their mental capacity, to vigorously attack their credibility. . . . As long as a witness appreciates his duty to tell the truth, and is minimally capable of observing, recalling, and communicating events, his testimony should come in for whatever it is worth. It is then up to the opposing party to dispute the witness' powers of apprehension, which well may be impaired by mental illness or other factors.").

[9] Rule 610 limits the use of religious belief as a method of impeachment.

[10] 6 Wigmore, Evidence § 1827, at 413–14 (Chadbourn rev. 1976). *See also* Williams, *The Oath as an Aid in Securing Trustworthy Testimony*, 10 Tex. L. Rev. 64 (1931); Note, *A Reconsideration of the Sworn Testimony Requirement: Securing Truth in the Twentieth Century*, 75 Mich. L. Rev. 1681 (1977).

[11] *See* Moore v. United States, 348 U.S. 966, 966 (1955) (per curiam) (there "is no require-

drafters, "The rule is designed to afford the flexibility required in dealing with religious adults, atheists, conscientious objectors, mental defectives, and children. Affirmation is simply a solemn undertaking to tell the truth; no special verbal formula is required."[12]

Despite this flexibility in the form of the oath, "testimony taken from a witness who has not given an oath or affirmation to testify truthfully is inadmissible."[13] Unless there is an objection, however, the failure of a witness to swear or affirm is waived.[14]

§ 18.03 Mental Competency

Persons of "unsound mind" were automatically disqualified from testifying at common law.[15] This is not true today. A more sophisticated analysis is required because many mental conditions do not affect a person's ability to testify. Even those adjudged insane are not necessarily disqualified because the test for insanity differs from the standard for witness competency and focuses on a different point in time.[16] Civil commitment also does not automatically disqualify a person from testifying.[17] Expert testimony may be admitted on this issue.

---

ment that the word 'solemnly' be used in the affirmation"); United States v. Ward, 989 F.2d 1015 (9th Cir. 1992) ("Our cases have routinely held that it is reversible error for a district court to prevent a party from testifying solely on the basis of the party's religiously-based objections to the form of the oath."); Gordon v. Idaho, 778 F.2d 1397, 1400 (9th Cir. 1985) ("Courts that have considered issues involving oaths and affirmations have interpreted procedural rules flexibly to accommodate religious objections."); United States v. Looper, 419 F.2d 1405, 1047 n. 4 (4th Cir. 1969) ("With the sophistication derived from England's role as a world trader, its courts have permitted Chinese to break a saucer, a Mohammedan to bow before the Koran and touch it to his head and a Parsee to tie a rope around his waist to qualify them to tell the truth.").

[12] Fed. R. Evid. 603 advisory committee's note. Early common law cases which discuss the oath requirement in terms of belief in God or "superior being" are no longer controlling and are also constitutionally suspect.

[13] United States v. Hawkins, 76 F.3d 545, 551 (4th Cir. 1996).

[14] See United States v. Odom, 736 F.2d 104, 116 (4th Cir. 1984) (right to object waived when the objecting party voluntarily and knowingly refused at trial to object).

[15] Competence to testify should be distinguished from other types of mental conditions: (1) competency to stand trial, (2) insanity at the time of the crime, (3) competency for civil commitment, and (4) competence to make a will. These all use different tests, which is not surprising since they are directed at very different issues.

[16] See State v. Wildman, 61 N.E.2d 790, 793–94 (Ohio 1945) ("Under the trend of modern decisions the fact that the witness is insane does not necessarily exclude him from the witness stand. . . . . A person who is able to correctly state matters which have come within his perception, with respect to the issues involved, and appreciates and understands the nature and obligation of an oath is a competent witness, notwithstanding some unsoundness of mind.").

[17] See Andrews v. Neer, 253 F.3d 1052, 1062–63 (8th Cir. 2001) ("Pleas's status as an involuntarily committed schizophrenic was available for the appellants' use to challenge Pleas's credibility. But his status does not ipso facto render him incompetent to testify in federal district court . . . .").

Psychological examinations. The trial court has the authority to order a psychiatric or psychological examination of a potential witness who is challenged on mental competency grounds,[18] but few courts do so.[19]

§ 18.04   Ability to Communicate

On rare occasions, a witness's competency to testify has been challenged for lack of the ability to communicate. In *Byndom v. State*,[20] the Arkansas Supreme Court rejected such a challenge concerning a 25-year-old rape victim who suffered from cerebral palsy and mental retardation. The Court ruled that she was able to testify "by virtue of her gestures, facial expressions, ability to sign 'yes' and 'no,' and by the limited use of the yes/no function key on her Dynavox computer. To hold otherwise would render a segment of society incompetent merely because they cannot communicate as effectively and in the same manner as those who can speak through oral, written, or signed language."[21]

Except where the witness's disability precludes cross-examination,[22] the courts have permitted witnesses to testify through a variety of devices.[23]

§ 18.05   Child Competency & Testimony

Child abuse cases have had a substantial impact on the law of evidence in recent years, as will be seen in the chapters on hearsay and the right of confrontation. There are significant problems associated with the testimony of small children due to their suggestibility.[24] One court has noted

---

[18] *See* Conrad, *Mental Examination of Witnesses*, 11 Syracuse L. Rev. 149, 153–156 (1960); Weihofen, *Testimonial Competence and Credibility*, 34 Geo. Wash. L. Rev. 53, 55 (1964) ("[T]he judge has discretion to admit extrinsic evidence on the question [of competency] to use mental and psychological tests, and to hear opinion evidence of psychiatric experts.").

[19] *E.g.*, United States v. Gutman, 725 F.2d 417 (7th Cir. 1984); United States v. Heinlein, 490 F.2d 725 (D.C. Cir. 1973); United States v. Butler, 481 F.2d 531, 534 (D.C. Cir. 1973) ("[S]uch an examination 'may seriously impinge on a witness' right to privacy; . . . the examination itself could serve as a tool of harassment; and the likelihood of an examination could deter witnesses from coming forward. The resultant presumption against ordering an examination must be overcome by a showing of need.") (citation omitted).

[20] 39 S.W.3d 781 (Ark. 2001).

[21] *Id.* at 787. A Dynavox computer synthesizes speech for its users; it allows the user to "speak" the phrase or word indicated.

[22] *See* People v. White, 238 N.E.2d 389, 390 (Ill. 1968) (a partially paralyzed and bed-ridden person could communicate only by raising the right knee to answer affirmatively and remaining still to answer negatively; reversed).

[23] *E.g.*, People v. Spencer, 457 N.E.2d 473, 479 (Ill. App. 1983) (31-year-old deaf and speech-impaired rape victim who was mildly to moderately retarded could communicate through gestures and references to anatomically-correct dolls, picture symbols, numbers, colors, and the alphabet; defense objection on confrontation grounds rejected); People v. Vandiver, 468 N.E.2d 454, 458 (Ill. App. 1984) (affirming trial court's ruling that defendant's right to confront accuser was not violated where deaf and speech-impaired witness testified through the use of two sign language interpreters).

[24] *See* Ceci & Friedman, *The Suggestibility of Children: Scientific Research and Legal Implications*, 86 Cornell L. Rev. 33 (2000).

an "emerging consensus in the case law relies upon scientific studies to conclude that suggestibility and improper interviewing techniques are serious issues with child witnesses, and that expert testimony on these subjects is admissible."[25]

Competency is another issue that has received renewed interest.[26] Some jurisdictions continue the older approach of making children of ten years of age or older presumptively competent.[27] Children under 10 are often found competent, but generally a voir dire examination of the child by the trial court is required.[28] More recent statutes, focusing on child sexual abuse cases, limit or abolish competency rules,[29] including the oath requirement.[30] Rule 601 provides that every person is competent to be a witness, and a federal statute specifies that children are presumed to be competent to testify.[31]

---

[25] Washington v. Schriver, 240 F.3d 101, 112 (2d Cir. 2001).

[26] Child competency issues, of course, are not limited to abuse cases. *See* Evans v. State, 28 P.3d 498, 509 (Nev. 2001) (4-year-old witnessed murders, testified when 6 held competent; "Courts must evaluate a child's competency on a case-by-case basis, but relevant considerations include: (1) the child's ability to receive and communicate information; (2) the spontaneity of the child's statements; (3) indications of 'coaching' and 'rehearsing;' (4) the child's ability to remember; (5) the child's ability to distinguish between truth and falsehood; and (6) the likelihood that the child will give inherently improbable or incoherent testimony.").

[27] Many courts do not apply competency rules to hearsay statements, such as excited utterances. *See infra* § 33.05.

[28] *See* Ohio R. Evid. 601 ("Every person is competent to be a witness except: (A) . . . children under ten years of age, who appear incapable of receiving just impressions of the facts and transactions respecting which they are examined, or of relating them truly."); State v. Frazier, 574 N.E.2d 483, 487 (Ohio 1991) (During the voir dire examination, the "trial judge has the opportunity to observe the child's appearance, his or her manner of responding to the questions, general demeanor and any indicia of ability to relate the facts accurately and truthfully. Thus, the responsibility of the trial judge is to determine through questioning whether the child of tender years is capable of receiving just impressions of facts and events and to accurately relate them.").

[29] *See* Utah Code Ann. § 76-5-410 ("A child victim of sexual abuse under the age of ten is a competent witness and shall be allowed to testify without prior qualification in any judicial proceeding. The trier of fact shall determine the weight and credibility of the testimony."). *See also* State v. Webb, 779 P.2d 1108, 1113–14 (Utah 1989) (holding that trial court erred by assuming that an 18-month-old child was unavailable due to immaturity without interviewing the child or taking expert testimony regarding the capability of the child, then two years old, to testify in court).

[30] *See* Del. Code Ann. tit. 10, § 4302 ("No child under the age of 10 years may be excluded from giving testimony for the sole reason that such child does not understand the obligation of an oath. Such child's age and degree of understanding of the obligation of an oath may be considered by the trier of fact in judging the child's credibility."); N.Y. Crim. Proc. Law § 60.20(2) ("A witness less than nine years old may not testify under oath unless the court is satisfied that he or she understands the nature of an oath. If in either case the court is not so satisfied, the witness may nevertheless be permitted to give unsworn evidence if the court is satisfied that the witness possesses sufficient intelligence and capacity to justify the reception thereof. A witness understands the nature of an oath if he or she appreciates the difference between truth and falsehood, the necessity for telling the truth, and the fact that a witness who testifies falsely may be punished."); *id.* § 60.20(3) ("A defendant may not be convicted of an offense solely upon unsworn evidence given pursuant to subdivision two.").

[31] 18 U.S.C. § 3509(c)(2) ("A child is presumed to be competent.").

Procedure. It is not unusual for the trial judge to conduct a voir dire examination in order to decide competency. This interview may take place in chambers where defense counsel and the prosecutor have an opportunity to question the child. [32] Typically, the child is asked whether she knows the difference between telling the truth and telling a lie. Only in unusual circumstances will a child be subject to a psychological examination to determine competence. [33] Once the child is deemed competent to testify, the credibility of the child, like any other witness, is determined by the jury.

Another issue involves the method of receiving child testimony at trial. Such issues are often governed by Rule 611(a) — for example, one court permitted a child to testify while sitting on a relative's lap. [34]

[A] Close-Circuit Testimony

The right of confrontation includes the right to face your accusers at trial. Nevertheless, there are exceptions. [35] In *Maryland v. Craig*, [36] the Supreme Court upheld a statutory procedure that allowed the use of a one-way closed circuit television for a child witness in a sexual abuse case, where the trial court first determined, after a factfinding hearing, that requiring the child to testify in the presence of the defendant would result in severe emotional distress. There must be a fact-specific inquiry; a court or statute cannot assume that young children will be traumatized by testifying in the presence of the accused. [37] Typically, the accused can communicate with counsel via a telephone hookup. [38]

---

[32] *See* Kentucky v. Stincer, 482 U.S. 730 (1987) (ruling that the exclusion of the accused from a competency hearing did not violate the right of confrontation).

[33] A "competency examination regarding a child may be conducted only if the court determines, on the record, that compelling reasons exist," 18 U.S.C. § 3509(c)(4), and "only upon written motion and offer of proof of incompetency by a party." 18 U.S.C. § 3509(c)(3). Furthermore, "psychological and psychiatric examinations to assess the competency of a child witness shall not be ordered without a showing of compelling need." 18 U.S.C. § 3509(c)(9). *See* United States v. Snyder, 189 F.3d 640, 645 (7th Cir. 1999) ("As long as a witness has the capacity to testify truthfully, it is best left to the fact-finder to determine whether he in fact did so.").

[34] *See* State v. Johnson, 528 N.E.2d 567, 569 (Ohio App. 1986).

[35] *See infra* § 36.03 (face-to-face confrontation).

[36] 497 U.S. 836 (1990).

[37] *See* United States v. Rouse, 111 F.3d 561, 568 (8th Cir. 1997) ("Five-year-old J.R. was unable to speak when called to testify and stated in chambers that she was afraid to speak in front of her uncles. Considering this statement along with Kelson's pretrial testimony, the court found that defendants' presence in the courtroom would 'more than anything else prevent her from testifying.' The court made similar findings after questioning six-year-old R. R., who was found sobbing outside the courtroom and affirmed in chambers that she was crying out of fear of her uncles; and nine-year-old T. R., who became so fearful before testifying that 'the guardian ad litem would have had to physically pull her into the courtroom.' "; two other children testified in open court).

[38] See appendix for federal statute.

[B] Videotape Depositions

Another federal statute permits videotape depositions. [39] In *United States v. Miguel*, [40] the victim was allowed to give testimony via a videotaped deposition, while the defendant watched from another room by closed-circuit television. The judge, however, did not allow the defendant to communicate by telephone with counsel *during* the deposition, only during breaks. The Ninth Circuit reversed because the statute provided for "contemporaneous communication" with counsel "during the deposition."

In addition, a deposition is a type of former testimony, [41] and its use in a criminal case raises confrontation issues. [42]

§ 18.06   Dead Man Statutes

Dead Man statutes are intended to protect the estates of deceased or incompetent persons against fraudulent claims. While this is a noble aim, it is how these statutes accomplish this goal that is so troublesome. [43] Typically, they disqualify a surviving party from testifying if the other party dies. [44] Death need not be caused by the incident subject to litigation. Courts sometimes say "death has sealed the lips of one party, the law seals the lips of the other." (Poetic but rubbish.)

These statutes assume that a party-witness's interest in a case will result in fraudulent testimony which, because of death or legal incompetency, cannot be rebutted by the adverse party. This assumption is questionable. In addition, there are numerous other problems with Dead Man statutes. First, the statute is probably ineffective; it will not prevent a dishonest party from introducing false testimony through other witnesses. Second, the statute is unnecessary; the jury can easily comprehend the obvious bias of the party-witness and "cross-examination and other safeguards for truth are sufficient guarantee against frequent false decisions." [45] Third, because of innumerable exceptions and waiver options, these statutes are often

---

[39] 18 U.S.C. § 3509(b)(2).

[40] 111 F. 3d 666, 670 (9th Cir. 1997) ("Section 3509 represents a careful compromise of highly important rights. While the defendant loses the right to face to face confrontation, he retains "some of the protections inherent in the confrontation of witnesses.").

[41] Fed. R. Evid. 804(b)(1).

[42] *See infra* § 36.05 (hearsay and right of confrontation).

[43] The authorities have been virtually unanimous in their condemnation. *See* Ladd, *The Dead Man Statute*, 26 Iowa L. Rev. 207, 238 (1941); 2 J. Wigmore, Evidence § 65, at 697 (3d ed. 1940) (product of a "fallacious and exploded principle").

[44] There has never been a federal Dead Man's Statute. Such statutes vary considerably. Some cover transactions but not torts. *See* Ray, *Dead Man's Statutes*, 24 Ohio St. L.J. 89, 91 (1963) ("They vary greatly in their wording and coverage, and the attitudes of the courts differ as to their interpretation, even where similar provisions are involved. Consequently, precedents from one state may be of little value in another jurisdiction."). *See also* N.Y.C.P.L.R. § 4519.

[45] 2 J. Wigmore, Evidence § 65, at 696 (3d ed. 1940).

difficult to apply.[46] Fourth, and most important, the statute works an injustice upon an honest party who is disqualified. Finally, other mechanisms are available to protect the estates of deceased and legally incompetent persons.[47] For example, some jurisdictions recognize a hearsay exception for the statements of the deceased or incompetent person.[48] Such a provision, along with the abolition of the Dead Man's Statute, permits the jury to receive more information, not less, and avoids the injustices of the statute.

§ 18.07   Competency of Judge: FRE 605

Federal Rule 605 disqualifies the trial judge as a witness. It governs only cases in which the judge is presiding; a judge is not an incompetent witness in other cases.[49] The policy underlying Rule 605 is obvious: Can the judge be impartial after testifying? Or, appear impartial? What attorney will want to cross-examine? Who will rule on objections?[50]

Courts have extended Rule 605 to instances in which the judge does not take the witness stand[51] and to other court personnel — i.e., law clerks.[52] No objection is required to preserve the issue for appeal.[53]

Occasion to invoke Rule 605 should arise only in exceptional cases. If the trial judge knows in advance of trial that she may be a witness, the judge should recuse herself prior to trial.[54]

---

[46] *See* Morgan, *Foreword*, American Law Institute, Model Code of Evidence 16 (1942) (Dead Man's Statutes "have almost without exception been the source of much useless litigation.").

[47] Some jurisdictions require corroboration; others leave to trial judge discretion the decision to admit the survivor's testimony. *See* 5 J. Wigmore, Evidence § 1576 (Chadbourn rev. 1974).

[48] *E.g.*, Cal. Evid. Code §§ 1227, 1261; Ohio R. Evid. 804(B)(5).

[49] *See also* ABA Code of Judicial Conduct, Canon 2(b) (judge "should not testify voluntarily as a character witness").

[50] *See* Fed. R. Evid. advisory committee's note.

[51] *E.g.*, Lillie v. United States, 953 F.2d 1188, 1191 (10th Cir. 1992) (unauthorized view of traffic scene in bench trial); Cheeves v. Southern Clays, Inc., 797 F. Supp. 1570, 1582 (M.D. Ga. 1992) (deposition in connection with recusal motion).

[52] *E.g.*, Kennedy v. Great Atlantic & Pacific Tea Co., 551 F.2d 593 (5th Cir. 1977) (law clerk).

[53] This provision is an exception to Rule 103(a)(1), which generally requires an objection or motion to strike to preserve an error for appellate review. The federal drafters explained: "The rule provides an 'automatic' objection. To require an actual objection would confront the opponent with a choice between not objecting, with the result of allowing the testimony, and objecting, with the probable result of excluding the testimony but at the price of continuing the trial before a judge likely to feel that his integrity had been attacked by the objector." Fed. R. Evid. 605 advisory committee's note.

[54] *See* ABA Judicial Code, Canon 3(C)(1) ("A judge should disqualify himself in a proceeding in which his impartiality might reasonably be questioned, including but not limited to instances where: (a) he has a personal bias or prejudice concerning a party, or personal knowledge of disputed evidentiary facts concerning the proceeding.").

§ 18.08　Competency of Jurors: FRE 606

[A]　Juror as Witness

Rule 606(a) prohibits a juror from testifying in a case in which that juror is serving as a member of the jury. The rationale for the rule is straightforward. How can a juror remain impartial after testifying for one of the parties? The rule also avoids the problem that would face an opposing party attempting to impeach a juror and the adverse effects impeachment might have on other members of the panel. Occasion to invoke Rule 606(a) should arise only rarely because a person called as a juror may be challenged for cause if that person is a potential witness or has personal knowledge of the case. [55]

Objections. A party must object. The rule, however, requires that the party be provided an opportunity to object outside the presence of the jury. This avoids placing the party in the awkward position of objecting in front of the juror and other members of the panel.

[B]　Impeachment of Verdicts & Indictments

Under Rule 606(b), jurors are incompetent to testify about the validity of a verdict or an indictment if the subject of their testimony involves internal influences. [56] However, they are competent to testify concerning external influences.

Rationale. The rule attempts to accommodate several competing interests. "The values sought to be promoted by excluding the evidence include freedom of deliberation, stability and finality of verdicts, and protection of jurors against annoyance and embarrassment. On the other hand, simply putting verdicts beyond effective reach can only promote irregularity and injustice. The rule offers an accommodation between these competing considerations." [57]

Internal influences. A juror is not competent to testify about the internal operations or thought-processes of the jurors during the course of deliberations. The federal drafters justified this position by noting "the central focus has been upon insulation of the manner in which the jury reached its verdict, and this protection extends to each of the components of deliberation, including arguments, statements, discussions, mental and emotional reactions, votes, and any other feature of the process." [58] According to the

---

[55] *See supra* § 3.04 (jury selection & voir dire).

[56] Rule 606(b) applies to affidavits as well as to testimony.

[57] Fed. R. Evid. 606 advisory committee's note.

[58] *Id. See also* United States v. Jones, 132 F.3d 232, 245 (5th Cir. 1998) ("Jury deliberations entail delicate negotiations where majority jurors try to sway dissenting jurors in order to reach certain verdicts or sentences. An individual juror no longer exposed to the dynamic offered by jury deliberations often may question his vote once the jury has been dismissed. Such self-doubt would be expected once extrinsic influences bear down on the former jurors, especially in decisions of life and death. When polled, each juror affirmatively indicated that

Fifth Circuit, the rule "bars juror testimony regarding at least four topics: (1) the method or arguments of the jury's deliberations, (2) the effect of any particular thing upon an outcome in the deliberations, (3) the mind set or emotions of any juror during deliberations, and (4) the testifying juror's own mental process during the deliberations."[59]

Juror incompetence encompasses compromise verdicts, quotient verdicts, speculation about insurance coverage, misinterpretation of instructions,[60] mistakes in returning a verdict, and interpretation of a guilty plea by one defendant as implicating codefendants.[61] In *Tanner v. United States,*[62] the Supreme Court ruled that juror drunkenness was an internal, not external, influence.

External influences. A juror is competent to testify about extraneous prejudicial information that has been introduced into the jury deliberation process.[63] In addition, a juror is competent to testify about outside influences that have been improperly brought to bear on the deliberation process. "Thus a juror is recognized as competent to testify to statements by the bailiff or the introduction of a prejudicial newspaper account into the jury room."[64]

Substantive grounds. Rule 606(b) governs only the competency of jurors to testify; it does not specify the substantive grounds for setting aside verdicts or indictments.[65] Nevertheless, by precluding juror testimony on certain matters, the rule obviously affects, at least in some cases, the substantive grounds for reversing jury verdicts.

---

he had voted for the death penalty. We will not allow a juror to change his mind after the jury has rendered a verdict. In this situation, the outcome could just as easily have turned out the other way with the jurors not supporting the death sentence convincing the death-prone jurors to impose life without the possibility of release.") *aff'd,* 527 U.S. 373 (1999).

[59] 132 F.3d at 245.

[60] *See* United States v. Tran, 122 F.3d 670, 673 (8th Cir. 1997) ("Tran's failure to testify also was not 'extraneous prejudicial information' because it was known to the jurors as a result of their presence at the trial, not as a result of something disclosed to them that had not occurred in the courtroom.").

[61] Fed. R. Evid. 606 advisory committee's note.

[62] 483 U.S. 107 (1987). After the verdict, defense counsel received an unsolicited telephone call from a juror, stating that several of the other jurors had consumed alcohol during the lunch breaks, which caused them to sleep through the afternoons. In a post-verdict hearing, the trial court refused to admit the testimony concerning juror intoxication. A later affidavit by a second juror described further episodes of intoxication as well as marijuana and cocaine use.

[63] *See* United States v. Jones, 132 F.3d 232, 245 (5th Cir. 1998) ("An 'outside influence' refers to a factor originating outside of normal courtroom proceedings which influences jury deliberations, such as a statement made by a bailiff to the jury or a threat against a juror.").

[64] Fed. R. Evid. 606 advisory committee's note. *See also* Parker v. Gladden, 385 U.S. 363 (1966) (jury communications with bailiff violated right of confrontation).

[65] *See* Fed. R. Evid. 606 advisory committee's note ("This rule does not purport to specify the substantive grounds for setting aside verdicts for irregularity; it deals only with the competency of jurors to testify concerning those grounds.").

§ 18.09 Competency of Attorneys

Neither Rule 601 nor any other evidence rule makes an attorney incompetent to testify. Hence, an attorney may be called as a witness in a case in which the attorney is not acting as counsel. Of course, the attorney-client privilege would apply to confidential communications between attorney and a client.[66]

A problem arises in cases in which an attorney who is *acting as counsel* is called to testify. The rules of professional responsibility generally preclude an attorney from accepting employment or continuing to represent a client in such a case.[67] This issue can arise if counsel interviews adverse witnesses without a paralegal, investigator, or another attorney present. If the witness testifies differently at trial, counsel may want to impeach the witness with a prior inconsistent statement.[68] If the witness admits making the prior statement, the problem is avoided. But if the witness denies the statement, who can counsel call to introduce the statement?

The issue is illustrated by *United States v. Edwards,*[69] in which the prosecutor was involved in finding an item of evidence. Instead of taking the stand as a witness and recusing himself as prosecutor, he pursued a line of questioning that indicated his personal knowledge of the reliability of the evidence. The Ninth Circuit reversed: "[W]hen a prosecutor is personally involved in the discovery of a critical piece of evidence, when that fact is made evident to the jury, and when the reliability of the circumstances surrounding the discovery of the evidence is at issue, the prosecutor's participation in the trial of the defendant constitutes a form of improper vouching."[70]

§ 18.10 Choice of Law

The second sentence of Rule 601 provides: "However, in civil actions and proceedings, with respect to an element of a claim or defense as to which State law supplies the rule of decision, the competency of a witness shall be determined in accordance with State law." This phrase was added to the

---

[66] *See infra* chapter 38.

[67] *See* Model Rule 3.7(a) ("A lawyer shall not act as advocate at a trial in which the lawyer is likely to be a necessary witness except where: (a) the testimony relates to an uncontested issue; (b) the testimony relates to the nature and value of legal services rendered in the case; or (c) disqualification of the lawyer would work substantial hardship on the client.").

[68] *See infra* § 22.10 (prior inconsistent statements: FRE 613).

[69] 154 F.3d 915 (9th Cir.1998).

[70] *Id.* at 923. *Edwards* was distinguished in Walker v. State, 798 A.2d 1219, 1239-40 (Md. App. 2002) ("*Edwards* featured the prosecutor's direct involvement in the discovery of a highly incriminating piece of evidence — a 'smoking-gun.' . . . Unlike *Edwards,* here the prosecutor's implication that he had personal knowledge that Myrick said he had been threatened was called into doubt by Myrick's denial of this fact. Furthermore, Myrick's prior inconsistent statement implicating appellant was not of the same 'smoking gun' nature as the receipt in *Edwards.* Here, there was plenty of evidence linking appellant to the crime, even in the absence of Myrick's testimony.").

federal rule so that state Dead Man statutes would apply in federal courts in those cases in which state law supplies the rule of decision (*e.g.*, diversity cases).[71]

§ 18.11   Key Points

Witness competency concerns the witness's qualifications to testify. Mental competence (capacity) involves the witness's ability to observe, recall, and relate. Moral competence focuses on the witness's recognition of the duty to testify truthfully, which is fortified by the oath requirement. At one time, common law rules of incompetency or disqualification had immense impact on trials because there were so many categories, *including the parties*, whose testimony was deemed unreliable due to their interest in the case. These rules have generally evolved over time into impeachment rules. Thus, the trend is to provide the jury with more information, both the testimony of persons who would have been disqualified at common law and the information needed to evaluate their credibility.

Federal rule. Rule 601 provides that all witnesses are competent, and the drafters stated that there are no competency requirements. Nevertheless, some federal cases have suggested that the testimony of a witness who does not have the capacity to recall may be excluded under Rule 403.

Oath requirement. Rule 603 requires witnesses to swear or affirm to the truthfulness of their testimony. The purpose of the oath is merely to add a stimulus to truth-telling. Moreover, a perjury prosecution requires the taking of an oath. The form of the oath or affirmation is not important.

Mental competency. Persons of "unsound mind" were automatically disqualified from testifying at common law. This is not true today. Even those adjudged insane are not necessarily disqualified because the test for insanity differs the standard for witness competency and focuses on a different point in time. The trial court has the authority to order a psychiatric or psychological examination of a potential witness challenged on mental competency grounds, but few courts do so.

Ability to communicate. On rare occasions, a witness's competency to testify has been challenged for the lack of ability to communicate. Except where the witness's disability precludes cross-examination, the courts have permitted witnesses to testify through a variety of devices such as hand signals, language interpreters, and computers.

Child competency & testimony. Child abuse cases have had a substantial impact on the law of evidence, and competency has received renewed attention. Some jurisdictions continue the older approach of making children of ten years of age or older presumptively competent. Children under 10 are often found competent, but generally a voir dire examination of the

---

[71] *See* Lovejoy Electgronics, Inc. v. O'Berto, 873 F.2d 1001, 1005 (7th Cir. 1989) ("The legislative history of Rule 601 reveals that the purpose of this exception was, precisely, to preserve state dead man's laws in cases such as this where state law supplies the rule of decision"; Illinois statute).

child by the trial court is required. More recent statutes, focusing on child sexual abuse cases, limit or abolish competency rules, including the oath requirement in one state. Rule 601 provides that every person is competent to be a witness, and a federal statute specifies that children are presumed to be competent. Close-circuit testimony and videotape depositions are use in this context, but their use raises constitutional issues.

Dead Man Statutes. These statutes are intended to protect the estates of deceased or incompetent persons against fraudulent claims. While this is a noble aim, it is how these statutes accomplish this goal that is so troublesome. Typically, they disqualify a surviving party from testifying if the other party dies. Death need not be caused by the incident subject to litigation.

Competency of judge. Rule 605 disqualifies the presiding judge as a witness. No objection is required to preserve the issue for appeal. Occasion to invoke Rule 605 should arise only in exception cases. If the trial judge knows in advance of trial that she may be a witness, the judge should recuse herself prior to trial.

Competency of jurors. Rule 606(a) prohibits a juror from testifying in a case in which that juror is serving as a member of the jury. Occasion to invoke Rule 606(a) should arise only rarely because a person called as a juror may be challenged for cause if that person is a potential witness. A party must object to a juror testifying but an opportunity to do so outside the presence of the jury is provided.

Impeachment of verdicts & indictments. Under Rule 606(b), jurors are incompetent to testify about the validity of a verdict or an indictment if the subject of their testimony involves internal influences. The rule bars juror testimony regarding: (1) the method or arguments of the jury's deliberations, (2) the effect of any particular thing upon an outcome in the deliberations, (3) the mind set or emotions of jurors during deliberations, and (4) the testifying juror's own mental process during the deliberations. This would encompasses compromise verdicts, quotient verdicts, speculation about insurance coverage, misinterpretation of instructions, mistakes in returning a verdict, and interpretation of a guilty plea by one defendant as implicating codefendants.

However, a juror is competent to testify about extraneous prejudicial information that has come into the deliberation process — *e.g.*, statements by the bailiff or the introduction of a prejudicial newspaper account into the jury room. In addition, a juror is competent to testify about outside influences that have been improperly brought to bear on the deliberation process.

Competency of attorneys. Neither Rule 601 nor any other evidence rule makes an attorney incompetent to testify. Nevertheless, the rules of professional responsibility generally preclude an attorney from accepting employment or continuing to represent a client if the attorney will be a witness in the case. A difficulty can arise if counsel interviews adverse witnesses without another person present and counsel later wants to impeach that witness at trial with a prior inconsistent statement.

Choice of law. The second sentence of Rule 601 provides: "However, in civil actions and proceedings, with respect to an element of a claim or defense as to which State law supplies the rule of decision, the competency of a witness shall be determined in accordance with State law." This phrase was added to the federal rule so that state Dead Man statutes would apply in federal courts in those cases in which state law supplies the rule of decision (*e.g.*, diversity cases).

Chapter 19

SEQUESTRATION OF WITNESSES: FRE 615

§ 19.01 Introduction

We do not want witnesses hearing the testimony of other witnesses. Federal Rule 615, which governs the exclusion of witnesses, addresses this issue.[1] Often known simply as "the rule on witnesses," it is intended to preclude the "tailoring" of testimony.[2] "The efficacy of excluding or sequestering witnesses has long been recognized as a means of discouraging and exposing fabrication, inaccuracy, and collusion."[3]

Under Rule 615, the trial judge may exclude witnesses sua sponte. Upon request of a party, exclusion is mandatory. The rule may not apply to rebuttal witnesses, at least unexpected impeachment witnesses.[4] Several exceptions are discussed below.

§ 19.02 Exception: Parties

A party who is a natural person may not be excluded from the trial even though that party may be called as a witness. As the federal drafters noted, the exclusion of parties "would raise serious problems of confrontation and due process."[5] There is little question that excluding a criminal defendant from trial, in the absence of a waiver,[6] violates the right of confrontation.[7]

---

[1] The Civil Rules contain a provision on the separation of witnesses during discovery proceedings. Fed. R. Civ. P. 26(c)(5) (court may order "that discovery be conducted with no one present except person designated by the court").

[2] Geders v. United States, 425 U.S. 80, 87 (1976) ("The aim of imposing 'the rule on witnesses' is twofold. It exercises a restraint on witnesses 'tailoring' their testimony to that of earlier witnesses; and it aids in detecting testimony that is less than candid.").

[3] Fed. R. Evid. 615 advisory committee's note.

[4] See United States v. Hargrove, 929 F.2d 316, 320–21 (7th Cir. 1991) ("The testimony of Baker did not contravene [Rule 615's] purpose. Baker was a surprise witness whom the government did not intend to call until Michael Beckett testified that the police pressured him to falsely identify Hargrove as his source for cocaine. The government called Baker solely to testify to the lack of police coercion and not to the substance of what Michael Beckett had said about Hargrove. . . . Accordingly, its allowance was not an abuse of discretion.").

[5] Fed. R. Evid. 615 advisory committee's note.

[6] See infra § 36.02 (right to be present at trial).

[7] See Perry v. Leeke, 488 U.S. 272, 282 (1989) ("The defendant's constitutional right to confront the witnesses against him immunizes him from such physical sequestration."); Taylor v. United States, 414 U.S. 17 (1973); Illinois v. Allen, 397 U.S. 337, 338 (1970) ("One of the most basic of the rights guaranteed by the Confrontation Clause is the accused's right to be present in the courtroom at every stage of his trial."). See also Fed. R. Crim. P. 43(a) (defendant's presence at trial).

Comment on accused's presence. In *Portuondo v. Agard,*[8] the prosecutor, in her summation, called the jury's attention to the fact that the defendant had the opportunity to hear all other witnesses testify and to tailor his testimony accordingly. The defendant argued that these comments burdened his Sixth Amendment right to be present at trial and to be confronted with the witnesses against him, as well as his Fifth and Sixth Amendment rights to testify on his own behalf. The Supreme Court rejected these arguments, noting that it would not extend the rule in *Griffin v. California,*[9] which involved comments upon a defendant's refusal to testify. In *Griffin,* the trial court instructed the jury that it could consider the defendant's failure to deny or explain facts within his knowledge. The *Griffin* Court had held that such a comment, by "solemnizing the silence of the accused into evidence against him," unconstitutionally "cuts down on the privilege [against self-incrimination] by making its assertion costly."[10] The *Agard* Court distinguished *Griffin.* The "prosecutor's comments in [*Agard*], by contrast, concerned respondent's *credibility as a witness,* and were therefore in accord with our longstanding rule that when a defendant takes the stand, 'his credibility may be impeached and his testimony assailed like that of any other witness.'"[11]

§ 19.03 Exception: Designated Officers & Employees

Rule 615 provides that a designated officer or employee of a party which is not a natural person (*e.g.,* corporations, governmental entities) may not be excluded from the trial even though that person may be called as a witness. The representative is designated by the attorney.[12]

The Senate Judiciary Committee construed this exception to permit an "investigative agent" to remain during trial notwithstanding the possibility

---

[8] 529 U.S. 61 (2000).

[9] 380 U.S. 609 (1965). *See infra* § 43.05[A] (comment on failure to testify).

[10] *Id.* at 614.

[11] *Agard,* 529 U.S. at 69 (quoting Brown v. United States, 356 U.S. 148, 154 (1958)). Justice Ginsburg, in dissent, concluded that the "Court today transforms a defendant's presence at trial from a Sixth Amendment right into an automatic burden on his credibility." *Id.* at 76. "One evident explanation for the coherence of his testimony cannot be ruled out: Agard may have been telling the truth" and the "generic accusation that today's decision permits the prosecutor to make on summation does not serve to distinguish guilty defendants from innocent ones. Every criminal defendant, guilty or not, has the right to attend his trial." *Id.* at 77. "In addition to its incapacity to serve the individualized truth-finding function of trials, a generic tailoring argument launched on summation entails the simple unfairness of preventing a defendant from answering the charge." *Id.* at 80.

[12] *See* Fed. R. Evid. 615 advisory committee's note ("As the equivalent of the right of a natural-person party to be present, a party which is not a natural person is entitled to have a representative present. Most of the cases have involved allowing a police officer who has been in charge of an investigation to remain in court despite the fact that he will be a witness. Designation of the representative by the attorney rather than by the client may at first glance appear to be an inversion of the attorney-client relationship, but it may be assumed that the attorney will follow the wishes of the client, and the solution is simple and workable.") (citations omitted).

that the detective or case agent may be called as a witness.[13] Nevertheless, the trial judge has authority under Rule 611[14] to require the investigative agent to testify "at an early stage of the government's case if he remains the government's designated representative under Rule 615."[15] A court, however, does not have the same authority with respect to the testimony of a criminal defendant.[16]

§ 19.04　Exception: Essential Persons

Witnesses whose presence is essential to the presentation of the case may remain in court. This exception "contemplates such persons as an agent who handled the transaction being litigated or an expert needed to advise counsel in the management of the litigation."[17] Trial counsel often need an expert's advice when cross-examining the opponent's expert.[18]

The burden of establishing that a person is "essential" is on the party who desires that person's presence at trial.[19]

---

[13] S. Rep. No. 1277, 93d Cong., 2d Sess., reprinted in 1974 U.S.C.C.A.N. 7051, 7072 ("The investigative agent's presence may be extremely important to government counsel, especially when the case is complex or involves some specialized subject matter. The agent, too, having lived with the case for a long time, may be able to assist in meeting trial surprises where the best-prepared counsel would otherwise have difficulty."). *See also* United States v. Hickman, 151 F.3d 446, 453–54 (5th Cir. 1998) ("[W]e have approved the use of two case agents at trial, where a second agent's non-exclusion could be justified under the essential-presence exception of Rule 615(3). The Government argues that the complexity of this case justified a second case agent being excused from the Rule because two agents were essential to the presentation of the case. However, the prosecution did not invoke the third exemption at trial and the district court made no such finding. Further, we are not persuaded that this string of simple armed robberies falls within the ambit of Rule 615(3)'s complexity exception. Because neither the Government nor the district court has articulated a sound basis justifying the exemption of two agents from the requirements of Rule 615 and because, on review of the record, we can discern no such basis, we hold that the district court abused its discretion in overruling the Appellants' objection to the presence of both agents during the trial of this case.") (citation omitted).

[14] Fed. R. Evid. 611(a) ("The court shall exercise reasonable control over the mode and order of interrogating witnesses and presenting evidence. . . .").

[15] In re United States, 584 F.2d 666, 667 (5th Cir. 1978).

[16] *See* Brooks v. Tennessee, 406 U.S. 605, 613 (1972) (The defendant "was deprived of his constitutional rights when the trial court excluded him from the stand for failing to testify first" as required by statute.).

[17] Fed. R. Evid. 615 advisory committee's note.

[18] *See* Malek v. Federal Ins. Co., 994 F.2d 49, 53 (2d Cir. 1993) ("Under the circumstances revealed in this case, we find that the district court erred in sequestering [expert] Friedell. Our review of the record reveals that Redsicker's testimony differed from his reports: Redsicker testified that the fire was an 'intense fire' but did not make that specific finding anywhere in his report. Since this was an important finding bearing on the question of arson and was not made in Redsicker's reports, Friedell's presence in the courtroom was important to the presentation of the Maleks' case, and a ten-minute recess was not an adequate substitute for his presence.").

[19] *See* Opus 3 Ltd. v. Heritage Park, Inc., 91 F.3d 625, 628 (4th Cir. 1996) ("[T]he party seeking to avoid sequestration of a witness bears the burden of proving that a Rule 615 exemption applies."); Government of Virgin Islands v. Edinborough, 625 F.2d 472, 476 (3d Cir.

§ 19.05   Exception: Crime Victims

Federal Rule 615(4), which became effective in 1998, recognizes an exception to the sequestration rule when authorized by statute. This provision brought the Rule into conformity with the Victim's Rights and Restitution Act of 1990[20] and the Victim's Rights Clarification Act of 1997,[21] which permit a victim-witness to attend the trial unless the testimony at trial would materially affect the witness's testimony. Many state provisions are more specific.[22]

§ 19.06   Out-of-court Separation of Witnesses

Because the policy underlying Rule 615 would be defeated if, after testifying, a witness discussed her testimony with other witnesses,[23] courts often give an instruction "making it clear that witnesses are not only excluded from the courtroom but also that they are not to relate to other witnesses what their testimony has been and what occurred in the courtroom."[24] As the Supreme Court has noted, the "judge's power to control the progress and, within the limits of the adversary system, the shape of the trial includes broad power to sequester witnesses before, during, and after their testimony."[25]

Such an order may prohibit a spectator or witness from telling a prospective witness what has taken place in court. Thus, it is improper for a detective to telephone daily a prosecution witness, informing her of the testimony of witnesses who had preceded her.[26]

Attorneys. The trial court has inherent authority to prohibit attorneys from consulting with a witness during recesses if the witness is currently

---

1980) ("A party who believes that the presence of the witness is 'essential' must bear the burden of supporting that allegation and showing why the policy of the Rule in favor of automatic sequestration is inapplicable in that situation. The party desiring sequestration must then be given an opportunity to show why sequestration is needed. Finally, the trial court should explicate the factors considered if sequestration is denied.").

[20] 42 U.S.C. § 10606(b)(4).

[21] 18 U.S.C. § 3510.

[22] *See* Ala. R. Evid. 615 ("This rule does not authorize exclusion of . . . (4) a victim of a criminal offense or the representative of a victim who is unable to attend, when the representative has been selected by the victim, the victim's guardian, or the victim's family."); Fla. Stat. Ann. § 90.616(d) (recognizing an exception: "In a criminal case, the victim of the crime, the victim's next of kin, the parent or guardian of a minor child victim, or a lawful representative of such person, unless, upon motion, the court determines such person's presence to be prejudicial."). *See also* Mosteller, *The Unnecessary Victims' Rights Amendment*, 1999 Utah L. Rev. 443, 457–62 (discussing Rule 615 issues and victims' rights).

[23] *See* Perry v. Leeke, 488 U.S. 272, 281 (1989) ("It is a common practice for a judge to instruct a witness not to discuss his or her testimony with third parties until the trial is completed.").

[24] United States v. Johnston, 578 F.2d 1352, 1355 (10th Cir. 1978).

[25] Geders v. United States, 425 U.S. 80, 87 (1976).

[26] State v. Spirko, 570 N.E.2d 229, 246 (Ohio 1991).

being examined.[27] "Sequestering a witness over a recess called before testimony is completed serves the purpose of preventing improper attempts to influence the testimony in light of the testimony already given. Applied to nonparty witnesses who were present to give evidence, the orders were within sound judicial discretion."[28] As discussed in the next section, a different situation arises when the client is the witness.

§ 19.07 Out-of-court Separation of Attorney & Client

In *Geders v. United States*,[29] the Supreme Court held that an order precluding a defendant and his attorney from discussing evidence during an *overnight recess* violated the right to effective assistance of counsel. However, in *Perry v. Leeke*,[30] the Court upheld an order prohibiting the accused from talking with anyone, including his defense counsel, during a short break between direct and cross-examination. In the Court's view, once the accused takes the stand, he is subject to cross-examination and "cross-examination is more likely to elicit truthful responses if it goes forward without allowing the witness an opportunity to consult with third parties, including his or her lawyer."[31]

The Court distinguished *Geders* by pointing out that "an overnight recess would encompass matters that go beyond the content of the defendant's own testimony. It is the defendant's right to unrestricted access to his lawyer for advice on a variety of trial-related matters that is controlling in the context of a long recess."[32]

§ 19.08 Sanctions

Rule 615 does not specify what sanctions may be imposed if a witness violates an exclusion order. There are several possible remedies: (1) excluding the witness's testimony, (2) holding the witness in contempt, and

---

[27] *See* United States v. Rhynes, 218 F.3d 310, 316 (4th Cir. 2000) ("It is clear from the plain and unambiguous language of Rule 615 that lawyers are simply not subject to the Rule. This Rule's plain language relates only to 'witnesses,' and it serves only to exclude witnesses from the courtroom.").

[28] *Geders*, 425 U.S. at 87.

[29] 425 U.S. 80 (1976).

[30] 488 U.S. 272, 282 (1989) (Permitting consultation between direct and cross-examination "grants the witness an opportunity to regroup and regain a poise and sense of strategy that the unaided witness would not possess.").

[31] *Id.* at 282. The Court added: "[W]hen a defendant becomes a witness, he has no constitutional right to consult with his lawyer while he is testifying. He has an absolute right to such consultation before he begins to testify, but neither he nor his lawyer has a right to have the testimony interrupted in order to give him the benefit of counsel's advice." *Id.* at 281.

[32] *Id.* at 284.

(3) permitting comment to the jury on the witness's failure to obey the order.[33] Declaring a mistrial is a possible, but unlikely, sanction.

Although some cases indicate that exclusion of the witness's testimony lies within the trial court's discretion, courts are hesitant to employ this sanction in the absence of connivance.[34] The exclusion of defense witnesses in criminal cases implicates a defendant's right to compulsory process. While the Supreme Court has upheld the exclusion of defense witness's testimony as an appropriate sanction under some circumstances, the Court also indicated that exclusion is not always constitutional.[35]

§ 19.09 Key Points

Often known simply as "the rule on witnesses," Rule 615 is intended to preclude the "tailoring" of testimony. The trial judge may exclude witnesses sua sponte. Upon request of a party, exclusion is mandatory. There are several exceptions:

Exception: parties. A party who is a natural person may not be excluded from the trial even though that party may be called as a witness.

Exception: designated officers & employees. A designated officer or employee of a party which is not a natural person (*e.g.*, corporations, governmental entities) may not be excluded. In criminal cases, the "investigative agent" falls within this category. However, the trial judge has authority under Rule 611 to require the investigative agent to testify at an early stage of the government's case if he remains the government's designated representative.

Exception: essential persons. Trial counsel often need an expert's advice when cross-examining the opponent's expert. The burden of establishing that a person is "essential" is on the party who desires that person's presence at trial.

Exception: crime victims. The Victim's Rights and Restitution Act of 1990 and the Victim's Rights Clarification Act of 1997 permit a victim-witness to attend the trial unless the testimony at trial would materially affect the witness's testimony.

---

[33] *See* Holder v. United States, 150 U.S. 91, 92 (1893) (The witness's "testimony is open to comment to the jury by reason of his conduct."). *See also* Portuondo v. Agard, 529 U.S. 61 (2000) (permitting prosecutor to comment on the fact that the defendant had the opportunity to hear all other witnesses testify and to tailor his testimony accordingly).

[34] *See* United States v. Cropp, 127 F.3d 354, 363 (4th Cir. 1997) ("The remedy of exclusion is so severe that it is generally employed only when there has been a showing that a party or a party's counsel caused the violation. Because exclusion of a defense witness impinges upon the right to present a defense, we are quite hesitant to endorse the use of such an extreme remedy.").

[35] *See* Michigan v. Lucas, 500 U.S. 145 (1991) (exclusion of defense witness's testimony for failure to comply with a rape shield law's notice requirements not unconstitutional under certain circumstances); Taylor v. Illinois, 484 U.S. 400 (1988) (exclusion of defense witness's testimony for violating a discovery order not unconstitutional).

Out-of-court separation of witnesses. Because the policy underlying Rule 615 would be defeated if, after testifying, a witness discussed her testimony with other witnesses, courts often give an instruction "making it clear that witnesses are not only excluded from the courtroom but also that they are not to relate to other witnesses what their testimony has been and what occurred in the courtroom."

Out-of-court separation of attorney & client. In *Geders v. United States*,[36] the Supreme Court held that an order precluding a defendant and his attorney from discussing evidence during an *overnight recess* violated the right to effective assistance of counsel. However, in *Perry v. Leeke*,[37] the Court upheld a trial judge order prohibiting the accused from talking with anyone, including his defense counsel, during a short break between direct and cross-examination.

Sanctions. Rule 615 does not specify what sanctions may be imposed if a witness violates an exclusion order. There are several possible remedies: (1) excluding the witness's testimony, (2) holding the witness in contempt, and (3) permitting comment to the jury on the witness's failure to obey the order. Declaring a mistrial is a possible, but unlikely, sanction.

---

[36] 425 U.S. 80 (1976).
[37] 488 U.S. 272, 282 (1989).

Chapter 20

EXAMINATION OF WITNESSES: FRE 611

§ 20.01 Introduction

The examination of witnesses raises a host of issues: (1) the extent of judicial control of the trial, (2) the proper methods of eliciting testimony on direct examination, (3) the scope of cross-examination, (4) the purpose of redirect and recross examination, (5) the use of leading questions, and (6) the "coaching" of witnesses. There are, of course, many other issues. Refreshing recollection is discussed in the next chapter, while the privilege against self-incrimination[1] and the right of confrontation[2] are considered in later chapters.

§ 20.02 Judicial Control of Trial

Under Federal Rule 611(a), the trial judge may exercise reasonable control over the conduct of the trial, including the mode and order of examining witnesses and presenting evidence. In exercising this control, the court is to be guided by several objectives: (1) ascertaining the truth, (2) avoiding needless consumption of time, and (3) protecting witnesses from harassment and undue embarrassment.[3]

Rule 611(a) is written in broad terms. It covers the form of questioning (free narrative vs. specific questions), the order of calling witnesses, the use of demonstrative evidence, as well as "the many other questions arising during the course of a trial which can be solved only by the judge's common sense and fairness in view of the particular circumstances."[4] As discussed in chapter 3, rebuttal and surrebutal fall into this category, including the authority to reopen a case after a party has rested.[5] The trial court has inherent authority to alter the order of proof[6] such as changing the order

---

[1] See infra chapter 43.

[2] See infra chapter 36.

[3] These objectives are also stated in Rule 102, the purpose and construction provision, and Rule 403, which provides that the trial court may exclude relevant evidence if "its probative value is substantially outweighed by considerations of undue delay, waste of time, or needless presentation of cumulative evidence."

[4] Fed. R. Evid. 611 advisory committee's note.

[5] See United States v. Rodriguez, 43 F.3d 117, 125 (5th Cir. 1995).

[6] See Huddleston v. United States, 485 U.S. 681, 690 (1988) ("The trial court has traditionally exercised the broadest sort of discretion in controlling the order of proof at trial, and we see nothing in the Rules of Evidence that would change this practice.").

in which witnesses testify[7] and determining whether a witness may be recalled.[8]

The court's authority to consider motions in limine is encompassed by Rule 611.[9] In addition, authorizing special methods to deal with child witnesses[10] and setting time limits[11] come within the purview of the rule. The court's control also extends to jury issues, such as the use of exhibits in the jury room,[12] jury questioning,[13] and jury notetaking.[14]

[A] Harassment & Undue Embarrassment

Rule 611(a) authorizes the trial court to protect witnesses from harassment and undue embarrassment. The exercise of this authority "calls for a judgment under the particular circumstances. . . . Pertinent circumstances include the importance of the testimony, the nature of the inquiry, its relevance to credibility, waste of time, and confusion."[15] Nevertheless, "while the trial judge should protect the witness from questions which 'go beyond the bounds of proper cross-examination merely to harass, annoy or humiliate,' this protection by no means forecloses efforts to discredit the witness."[16]

---

[7] See Loinaz v. EG & G, Inc., 910 F.2d 1, 9 (1st Cir. 1990) ("[T]he general rule is that a party should be able to present his case and order that case as he sees fit. However, Rule 611 has carved out an exception to this general rule and requires the trial judge to control the presentation of evidence in the interest of ascertaining truth. The dynamics of a party's presentation may be compromised when the testimony of an opposing witness is allowed to interrupt that presentation, but Rule 611 recognizes that such an alteration in order may be necessary at times.").

[8] See United States v. Puckett, 147 F.3d 765, 770 (8th Cir. 1998) ("The witnesses testified about different subject matter each time they were called to the stand, the defendants were free to cross examine them about any of their testimony, and there is no indication that the government recalled the witnesses to bolster their credibility. While it may be preferable to have witnesses testify in a less interrupted manner, we cannot say the district court abused its discretion.").

[9] See supra § 6.04 (motions in limine).

[10] See supra § 18.05 (child competency & testimony).

[11] See United States v. Vest, 116 F.3d 1179, 1187 (7th Cir. 1997) ("In the past, we have explicitly approved the use of time limitations in civil trials, but we have warned that rigid hour limits may 'engender an unhealthy preoccupation with the clock.' Our concern about time limits is even greater in criminal cases where a defendant's Confrontation Clause rights may be threatened by an arbitrary cutoff of cross-examination. . . . Time limits are best used as guideposts rather than deadlines in criminal trials, and time limits are no substitute for involved trial judges who must always shepherd trials along, curtailing repetitive, irrelevant, and immaterial questioning.").

[12] See supra § 3.06[A] (exhibits in jury room).

[13] See supra § 2.06.

[14] See State v. Waddell, 661 N.E.2d 1043, 1048 (Ohio 1996) (trial court has discretion to permit notetaking).

[15] Fed. R. Evid. 611 advisory committee's note.

[16] Id.

[B]   Testimony in Narrative Form

Testimony may be elicited by specific interrogation (question and answer) or by free narrative.[17] Several advantages may be gained by a narrative presentation — the testimony may seem more natural, may be more accurate, and avoids leading questions.[18] On the other hand, specific interrogation may be more complete, save time, and provide initial confidence to a timid witness. The most cogent objection to free narrative is that there may be no opportunity to interpose objections.[19] Often counsel combine both methods, using specific questions on preliminary matters, followed by a narrative, and then followup questions. The trial court has discretion to preclude free narrative.[20]

[C]   Continuances

The trial court has discretion to grant continuances. However, in some cases denial of a continuance may violate due process.[21] In deciding whether a continuance is appropriate, courts consider factors such as the (1) length of the requested delay, (2) number of prior continuances requested, (3) inconvenience to litigants, witnesses, opposing counsel and the court, (4) reasons for request (whether it is dilatory or contrived), and (5) party's contribution to the circumstance giving rise to the request.

§ 20.03   Leading Questions

[A]   Direct Examination

Rule 611(c) follows the traditional practice of prohibiting leading questions on direct examination. Leading questions are prohibited on direct

---

[17] *See* United States v. Pless, 982 F.2d 1118, 1123 (7th Cir. 1992) ("Fed. R. Evid. 611(a) provides district judges with authority to allow testimony in narrative form rather than as answers to specific questions."); United States v. Garcia, 625 F.2d 162, 169 (7th Cir. 1980) ("[T]here is . . . nothing particularly unusual, or incorrect, in a procedure of letting a witness relate pertinent information in a narrative form as long as it stays within the bounds of pertinency and materiality").

[18] *See* Marshall, Marquis & Oskamp, *Effects of Kind of Question and Atmosphere of Interrogation in Accuracy and Completeness of Testimony*, 84 Harv. L. Rev. 1620 (1971); Tanford, *An Introduction to Trial Law*, 51 Mo. L. Rev. 623 (1986).

[19] *See* Northern Pac. R. Co. v. Charless, 51 F. 562, 570 (9th Cir. 1892) ("The court replied to this objection that the taking of the witness' testimony in the narrative form would be the best way of getting at what he knew or could state concerning the matter at issue; that it would save time to proceed in that way, and would perhaps furnish to the jury a more connected statement of the matter to be told as it occurred and took place.").

[20] *Id.* ("It was within the discretion of the court to allow the witness to give his testimony in a narrative form.").

[21] *See* Ungar v. Sarafite, 376 U.S. 575, 589 (1964) ("[T]here are no mechanical tests for deciding when a denial of a continuance is so arbitrary as to violate due process. The answer must be found in the circumstances . . . , particularly in the reasons presented [when] the request is denied.").

examination because it is thought that a witness is particularly susceptible to suggestion under questioning by the party calling the witness.[22] Here, again, the trial court has considerable discretion.[23]

A leading question is one that suggests the answer. A question that calls for a "yes" or "no" answer "may or may not be leading."[24] For example, the question, "Do you go to law school?" is not a leading question. Even a question in the alternative form may be leading.[25] For example:

> "State whether of not the defendant was the person in the brown pants, green shirt, red hair, wearing glasses and a beard, walking with a limp and speaking with an accent who robbed the bank?"

The specificity of detail makes it leading. A question may be leading because of its tone[26] or because of counsel's gestures.[27]

[1] Exceptions

Rule 611(c) recognizes several traditional exceptions to the prohibition against leading questions on direct examination. They are permitted (1) when necessary to develop a witness's testimony, (2) when the witness is "hostile," (3) when the witness is an adverse party, and (4) when the witness is identified with an adverse party.

---

[22] *See* Fed. R. Evid. 611 advisory committee's note ("The rule continues the traditional view that the suggestive powers of the leading question are as a general proposition undesirable.").

[23] *See* St. Clair v. United States, 154 U.S. 134, 150 (1894) (With leading questions "much must be left to the sound discretion of the trial judge who sees the witness and can, therefore, determine in the interest of truth and justice whether the circumstances justify leading questions to be propounded to a witness by the party producing him."); Fed. R. Evid. 611 advisory committee's note (this "matter clearly falls within the area of control by the judge over the mode and order of interrogation and presentation and accordingly is phrased in words of suggestion rather than command").

[24] 3 Wigmore, Evidence § 772(1), at 164 (Chadbourn rev. 1970). *See also* State v. Scott, 149 P.2d 152, 153 (Wash. 1944) ("Even though the question may call for a yes or a no answer, it is not leading for that reason, unless it is so worded that, by permitting the witness to answer yes or no, he would be testifying in the language of the interrogator rather than in his own.").

[25] 3 Wigmore, Evidence § 772(2), at 164 (Chadbourn rev. 1970) ("The alternative form of question ('State whether or not you said that you refused,' 'Did you or did you not refuse?') is free from this defect of form, because both affirmative and negative answers are presented for the witness' choice. Nevertheless, such a question may become leading, in so far as it rehearses lengthy details which the witness might not otherwise have mentioned, and thus supplies him with full suggestions which he incorporates without any effort, by the simple answer, 'I did,' or 'I did not.' Accordingly, the sound view is that such a question may or may not be improper, according to the amount of palpably suggestive detail which it embodies.").

[26] Example: "Was it or was it not, THE DEFENDANT who robbed the bank," the attorney asked, screaming the words "the defendant."

[27] *See* United States v. Warf, 529 F.2d 1170, 1173–74 (5th Cir. 1976) ("[W]ithout Hartman's testimony it was . . . a very dubious identification . . . The prosecutor assisted Hartman both verbally and by pointing. The explanation made to the District Court that he was pointing at the table where Warf was seated rather than at Warf individually is no explanation at all. The trial judge's statement that Hartman would have picked out Warf eventually was speculative, and, in any event, delay or indecision by Hartman in making an identification might have diminished the effect of his testimony.").

Necessity. Leading questions are often necessary when examining a child. "Or the adult with communication problems; the witness whose recollection is exhausted; and undisputed preliminary matters."[28] Leading questions are also permitted when the witness is "a non-English speaking witness testifying through a translator,"[29] suffers from mental retardation,[30] or is nervous.[31]

Hostile witnesses. Leading questions are also permissible when examining a hostile witness. Providing damaging testimony, by itself, does not make a witness hostile. Rather, the witness must be evasive, reluctant, or unwilling to testify.[32] The decision to declare a witness hostile rests with the trial judge.

Adverse party & associates. An adverse party as well as a witness identified with an adverse party are automatically considered "hostile" witnesses.[33] Persons identified with an adverse party include an employee,[34] girlfriend,[35] or investigating agent.[36]

[B] Cross-Examination

Leading questions typically are permitted on cross-examination. Here, the law assumes the witness is not as susceptible to suggestion. The term "ordinarily" in Rule 611(c) addresses situations where this assumption is not operative. For example, the plaintiff in a malpractice action often calls the defendant-physician to the stand to establish certain elements of the

---

[28] Fed. R. Evid. 611 advisory committee's note.

[29] United States v. Ajmal, 67 F.3d 12, 16 (2d Cir. 1995). *Accord* United States v. Rodriguez-Garcia, 983 F.2d 1563, 1570 (10th Cir. 1993) (use of leading questions in such a "language situation" was a permissible exercise of trial court's discretion).

[30] *E.g.,* United States v. Goodlow, 105 F.3d 1203, 1207 (8th Cir. 1997) ("In light of Robert Cook's mental retardation, Appellant does not dispute that leading questions were permissible pursuant to Fed. R. Evid. 611(c).").

[31] *E.g.,* United States v. Salameh, 152 F.3d 88, 128 (2d Cir. 1998) ("The challenged question was necessary to develop Igiri's testimony and elicit information from a nervous witness.").

[32] *See* United States v. Brown, 603 F.2d 1022, 1026 (1st Cir. 1979) ("The record does not bear out appellant's contention that witness Proulx was not adverse, evasive or hostile. Proulx and appellant were close friends. . . . Appellant talked to Proulx at length about the case right up to the trial. While Proulx was not hostile in the sense of being contemptuous or surly, he was both evasive and adverse to the government.").

[33] *See* Fed. R. Evid. 611 advisory committee's note ("The final sentence deals with categories of witnesses automatically regarded and treated as hostile.").

[34] *E.g.,* Chonich v. Wayne County Cmty. Coll., 874 F.2d 359, 368 (6th Cir. 1989) ("court designated Drs. Waters and Callaghan as witnesses identified with an adverse party under F.R.E. 611(c) and allowed plaintiffs' counsel to use leading questions on direct examination").

[35] *E.g.,* United States v. Hicks, 748 F.2d 854, 859 (4th Cir. 1984) (permitting government to ask two leading questions of girlfriend called as a government witness; "Clearly she was a person 'identified with an adverse party' so that interrogation by leading questions was permissible.").

[36] *E.g.,* United States v. Tsui, 646 F.2d 365, 368 (9th Cir. 1981) ("Tsui argues that he should have been allowed to ask leading questions of investigator Ono as an adverse witness. There is some merit to this contention.").

cause of action — *i.e.*, this was the doctor who performed the operation.[37] On cross-examination, leading questions by the physician's own attorney should not be permitted.[38]

§ 20.04　Scope of Cross-Examination

There are two principal rules on the scope of cross-examination: (1) the wide-open rule and (2) the restrictive rule. Federal Rule 611(b) adopts the restrictive rule. Under that rule, cross-examination is "limited to the subject matter of the direct examination and matters affecting the credibility of the witness." Credibility refers to impeachment, a subject often not raised on direct.[39] Determining what subjects were *raised* on direct examination is not always easy.[40] As with cross-examination generally, the trial court enjoys great latitude, and the rule permits the cross-examiner to "adopt" the witness as her own, which may result in the curtailment of the use of leading questions.[41]

Wide-open rule. In contrast, the wide open or English rule permits cross-examination on all relevant matters.[42] Even under the wide-open rule, the trial court has the authority to control and limit the scope of cross-examination.

The principal difference between the two rules is the order of proof. A party foreclosed on cross-examination from pursuing a topic because the judge ruled it beyond matters raised on direct examination may recall the witness later and elicit the desired information.[43]

---

[37] Note that in criminal cases, the privilege against self-incrimination prohibits the prosecutor from calling the accused as a witness. If called by the defense in its case-in-chief, the accused is waiving the privilege. *See infra* § 43.05 (accused's privilege at trial).

[38] Fed. R. Evid. 611 advisory committee's note ("The purpose of the qualification 'ordinarily' is to furnish a basis for denying the use of leading questions when the cross-examination is cross-examination in form only and not in fact, as for example the 'cross-examination' of a party by his own counsel after being called by the opponent (savoring more of re-direct) or of an insured defendant who proves to be friendly to the plaintiff.").

[39] *See infra* chapter 22.

[40] *See* United States v. Arnott, 704 F.2d 322, 324 (6th Cir. 1983) ("The subject matter of direct examination, for the purpose of cross-examination, is 'liberally construed to include all inferences and implications arising from such testimony.'").

[41] Fed. R. Evid. 611(b) ("The court may, in the exercise of discretion, permit inquiry into additional matters as if on direct examination."); United States v. Tomblin, 46 F.3d 1369, 1386 (5th Cir. 1995) ("Rule 611 allows, but does not require, the district court to permit cross-examination that exceeds the scope of direct examination.").

[42] There is also an intermediate view, under which the scope of cross-examination extends to all issues except those relating to affirmative defenses.

[43] The right to recall a witness, however, would not apply to the prosecutor when examining a criminal defendant. *See supra* note 37. In this situation, the prosecutor should be given some leeway, bound only by the extent of the Fifth Amendment waiver.

§ 20.05　Redirect & Recross-Examination

In theory, redirect examination is limited to new matters raised on cross-examination, and recross is limited to new matters raised on redirect. Because trials are rarely this neat,[44] the trial court has discretion to permit the elicitation of new matters on redirect and recross-examination.[45] Nevertheless, if new matters are raised on redirect or recross, further examination may be a matter of right under the Confrontation Clause.[46]

§ 20.06　Other Common Objections

There are numerous trial objections that are not specifically referenced in the Rules of Evidence.[47] Some of the more common are: (1) argumentative questions, (2) asked and answered,[48] (3) assuming facts not in evidence, (4) misleading questions,[49] (5) compound questions,[50] and (6) nonresponsive answers.

---

[44] *See* United States v. Riggi, 951 F.2d 1368, 1375 (3d Cir. 1991) ("The tradition in the federal courts has been to limit the scope of redirect examination to the subject matter brought out on cross-examination. Ideally, no new material should be presented on redirect, because litigants will in theory have presented all pertinent issues during the direct examination. In reality, however, new information may come out on redirect, when the trial court, in its discretion and in the interest of justice, determines that the information is relevant and admissible.") (citation omitted).

[45] *See* United States v. Vasquez, 267 F.3d 79, 86 (2d Cir. 2001) ("rebut an impression created during cross-examination"); United States v. Diaz, 176 F.3d 52, 80 (2d Cir. 1999) ("The scope of redirect examination is a matter entrusted to a trial judge's broad discretion. Such redirect may be used to rebut false impressions arising from cross-examination and the trial judge is in the best position to determine whether such a false impression was created.") (citations and internal quotation marks omitted).

[46] *See* United States v. Riggi, 951 F.2d 1368, 1375 (3d Cir. 1991) ("Recross is to redirect as cross-examination is to direct. To allow redirect examination on new material but deny recross on the same material is to violate both the Confrontation Clause and fundamental principles of fairness.").

[47] *See* Denbeaux & Risinger, *Questioning Questions: Objections to Form in the Interrogation of Witnesses*, 33 Ark. L. Rev. 439 (1980).

[48] *See* United States v. Collins, 996 F.2d 950, 952 (8th Cir. 1993) (The "defendant objected that the question had already been asked and answered. The trial court sustained the objection on that basis, but refused to instruct the jury to disregard the answer.").

[49] *See* United States v. Pantone, 609 F.2d 675, 681 (3d Cir. 1979) ("Pantone's counsel objected to this question as an inaccurate characterization of the direct testimony. That objection was well taken, since there is no hint in Pantone's prior testimony of a general denial of referrals. The district court nevertheless overruled the objection and permitted the government to elicit a denial of referrals.").

[50] *See* United States v. Kinnard, 465 F.2d 566, 578 n.7 (3d Cir. 1979) ("The question that led to the ruling was: 'Do you have any experience or any knowledge about the reliability of narcotic addicts, insofar as telling the truth or being reliable or being accurate or even caring who they hurt or don't hurt so long as they are not put in jail?' While this was objectionable in form as a compound question, its thrust is reasonably plain.).

§ 20.07 Preparation ("Coaching") of Witnesses

Under the adversary system as practiced in this country, counsel is allowed to interview witnesses prior to trial. Indeed, failure to interview an important witness may constitute incompetence, and in a criminal trial, a violation of the Sixth Amendment right to effective assistance of counsel. Thus, witness preparation, also known as "woodshedding" or "horse shedding" is an accepted feature of trial.[51] Nevertheless, there are important limits; an attorney cannot ethically assist in the fabrication of testimony. Model Rule 3.4(b) states that a lawyer shall not "falsify evidence, counsel or assist a witness to testify falsely, or offer an inducement to a witness that is prohibited by law."

§ 20.08 Key Points

Court control. Rule 611(a) is written in broad terms. Among other things, the trial judge has the authority to re-open the case, alter the order of proof, permit the recall of a witness, and grant continuances. In addition, the judge may authorize special methods to deal with child witnesses and set time limits for the presentation of evidence. The court's control also extends to jury issues, such as the use of exhibits in the jury room, jury questioning, and jury notetaking.

Narrative testimony. Testimony may be elicited by specific interrogation (question and answer) or by free narrative. The most cogent objection to free narrative is that there may be no opportunity to interpose objections. The trial court has discretion to preclude free narrative.

Leading questions. Leading questions are prohibited on direct examination because it is thought that a witness is particularly susceptible to suggestion under questioning by the party calling the witness. Here, again, the trial court has considerable discretion. A leading question is one that suggests the answer.

Exceptions. Rule 611(c) recognizes several traditional exceptions to the prohibition against leading questions on direct examination. They are permitted (1) when necessary to develop a witness's testimony, (2) when the witness is "hostile," (3) when the witness is an adverse party, and (4) when the witness is identified with an adverse party.

Scope of cross-examination. There are two principal rules on the scope of cross-examination: (1) the wide-open rule and (2) the restrictive rule. Federal Rule 611(b) adopts the restrictive rule. Under that rule, cross-examination is "limited to the subject matter of the direct examination and matters affecting the credibility of the witness."

Redirect & recross examination. In theory, redirect examination is limited to new matters raised on cross-examination, and recross is limited to new matters raised on redirect. Because trials are rarely this neat, the trial

---

[51] *The Horse Shed*, McElhaney's Trial Notebook 31 (2d ed. 1987).

court has discretion to permit the elicitation of new matters on redirect and recross-examination.

Chapter 21

REFRESHING RECOLLECTION: FRE 612

§ 21.01 Introduction

Witnesses, like the rest of us, sometimes forget things. If this occurs at trial, we permit them to refresh their recollection. This does not mean that the witness may simply read a document to the jury; in many cases that would raise hearsay issues. Instead, the witness is suppose to *testify* based on her memory, albeit refreshed by a document.

Federal Rule 612 operates differently depending on whether the witness's recollection is refreshed during or prior to trial. Production of the writing for inspection by the opposing party is *mandatory* in a case of trial refreshment; it is *discretionary* in a case of pretrial refreshment. Rule 612 is subject to an exception in criminal cases with respect to certain writings governed by the Jencks Act.

§ 21.02 Rationale

Rule 612 is based on necessity and the practicalities of trial practice.[1] In the heat of trial (actually, even without much heat) witnesses forget, they omit facts, they get momentarily confused — even concerning important matters and even when the attorneys have prepared them to testify.

Almost anything may be used to awaken a slumbering memory. One court said "a song, a face, or a newspaper item"[2] may be the source of the refreshment. Another court pointed out that it "may be a line from Kipling or the dolorous strain of the 'Tennessee Waltz'; a whiff of hickory smoke; the running of the fingers across a swatch of corduroy; the sweet carbonation of a chocolate soda; [or] the sight of a faded snapshot in a long-neglected album."[3] Okay, back to earth. It isn't going to be Kipling or the Tennessee Waltz. It isn't going to be Walt Whitman or the Beatles. It is going to be a document. The document need not have been prepared by the witness,[4] nor prepared contemporaneously with the event recorded.[5] It

---

[1] *See generally* Kalo, *Refreshing Recollection: Problems with Laying a Foundation*, 10 Rut.—Cam. L.J. 233 (1979); Maguire & Quick, *Testimony, Memory and Memoranda*, 3 How. L.J. 1 (1957); Hutchins & Slesinger, *Some Observations on the Law of Evidence—Memory*, 41 Harv. L. Rev. 860 (1928).

[2] Jewett v. United States, 15 F.2d 955, 956 (9th Cir. 1926).

[3] Baker v. State, 371 A.2d 699, 705 (Md. App. 1977).

[4] *See* United States v. Darden, 70 F.3d 1507, 1540 (8th Cir. 1995) ("As an informant, Parnell took part in many meetings with members of the enterprise during which the criminal activities of the enterprise were discussed. After those meetings, Parnell would meet with government agents to discuss what he had heard. Following each of these debriefing sessions,

doesn't even have to be accurate. For example, a witness's recollection could be refreshed by a newspaper account, even though the witness believes the account to be erroneous.

Several recognized safeguards, however, limit the use of writings used to refresh a faded memory.

Lack of memory requirement. The witness's memory must be exhausted, or nearly exhausted, before a writing may be used to refresh recollection. As an initial step, counsel could attempt to revive memory by leading questions.[6] If a document is used, it must, in fact, refresh the witness's recollection; the witness may not simply read aloud from a document. The trial court determines if the witness's memory has been sufficiently exhausted.

Admissibility: impeachment. A writing does not become admissible solely because it is used to refresh a witness's recollection. The opposing party, however, not only has the right to inspect the writing but also the right "to cross-examine the witness" on the writing and to introduce into evidence the parts that relate to the witness's testimony. In this situation, the writing is used to impeach the witness's credibility and not as substantive evidence. A limiting instruction under Rule 105 is required upon request.

Admissibility: hearsay. The writing may also be introduced in evidence if it is independently admissible. For example, the writing may qualify as an admission of a party-opponent,[7] or come within an exception to the hearsay rule, the most obvious of which is the recorded recollection exception.[8] Other exceptions are available, however.[9]

Misuse of writing. Rule 612 should not be used to circumvent the hearsay rule — by having the witness read aloud from the document. In *Douglas v. Alabama,*[10] the Supreme Court found a confrontation violation when this tactic was employed: "Under the guise of cross-examination to refresh Loyd's recollection, the Solicitor purported to read from the document, pausing after every few sentences to ask Loyd, in the presence of the jury, 'Did you make that statement?' Each time, Loyd asserted the privilege and refused to answer, but the Solicitor continued this form of questioning until the entire document had been read."[11]

---

a DEA report would be prepared detailing Parnell's account of his conversations. . . . Parnell reviewed these DEA reports in preparation for his testimony. The DEA reports in this case were based on Parnell's own accounts of conversations in which he took part. The District Court properly permitted him to refer to them in order to refresh his recollection of those conversations.").

[5] *See* United States v. Horton, 526 F.2d 884, 889 (5th Cir. 1976) ("[W]here the issue, as here, is one of present recollection revived, the doctrine of contemporaneity has little application.").

[6] *See* Fed. R. Evid. 611(c).

[7] Fed. R. Evid. 801(d)(2)

[8] Fed. R. Evid. 803(5). *See infra* § 21.07 (recorded recollection distinguished).

[9] *See* Fed. R. Evid. 803(6) (business records exception to hearsay rule).

[10] 380 U.S. 415 (1965).

[11] *Id.* at 416–17.

§ 21.03 Right of Inspection

The opposing party has the right to inspect *any* writing used during trial,[12] including those used to refresh memory. The right is mandatory for trial refreshment. Inspection is a safeguard against the misuse of writings (*e.g.*, direct examiner gives her witness a piece of paper telling the witness to answer "yes" to the next two questions).

If a party attempts to exercise the right of inspection and is met by an objection based on relevancy grounds, the trial court is required to examine the writing in camera and excise any parts not related to the witness's testimony.

[A] Pretrial Refreshment

Under Rule 612, the production of a writing used *prior to* trial to refresh a witness's recollection may be required "if the court in its discretion determines it is necessary in the interests of justice." As proposed by the Supreme Court, Rule 612 did not contain this limitation; production was mandatory.[13] Congress added the provision making inspection discretionary in order to preclude "fishing expeditions among a multitude of papers which a witness may have used in preparing for trial."[14]

In exercising this discretion, the judge should consider (1) the extent of the witness's reliance on that writing, (2) the importance of the information, (3) any resulting burden on another party, and (4) potential for disruption of the trial. The use of a writing "just before" the witness is called to testify is the sort of circumstance that should lead a trial court to require production — *i.e.*, reviewing a document in the courthouse corridor immediately prior to testifying should be treated like trial refreshment.[15]

§ 21.04 Jencks Act

Rule 612 does not apply to writings that are governed by the Jencks Act.[16] Currently, Criminal Rule 26.2 regulates this subject.[17] Like the

---

[12] *See also* Fed. R. Evid. 613(a) (prior written inconsistent statement used to impeach "shall be shown or disclosed to opposing counsel").

[13] *See* 56 F.R.D. 276 (1973).

[14] H.R. Rep. No. 650, 93d Cong., 1st Sess., reprinted in 1974 U.S.C.C.A.N. 7075, 7086.

[15] *See* ABA Section of Litigation, Emerging Problems Under the Federal Rules of Evidence, Rule 612, at 186 (3d ed. 1998) ("Most courts have ordered disclosure when it is clear that the witness has used a document to refresh memory and that the document has had at least some effect in restoring the memory of the witness.").

[16] 18 U.S.C. § 3500.

[17] Fed. R. Crim. P. 26.2(a) ("After a witness other than the defendant has testified on direct examination, the court, on motion of a party who did not call the witness, shall order the attorney for the government or the defendant and the defendant's attorney, as the case may be, to produce, for the examination and use of the moving party, any statement of the witness that is in their possession and that relates to the subject matter concerning which the witness has testified.").

Jencks Act, it limits discovery of witness's prior statements until after direct examination has been completed. In effect, it is a trial (rather than a pre-trial) discovery provision. The criminal rule applies to defense witnesses as well as prosecution witnesses.[18]

§ 21.05 Privileged Material; Work Product

Rule 612 does not address the issue of whether privileged material is excluded from required production. The rule provides only that matters not related to the subject matter of the witness's testimony shall be excised prior to production.[19] Whether the use of a writing to refresh a witness's memory constitutes a waiver of privilege, including the qualified work product privilege, is unsettled.[20] In-court refreshment has not caused a problem due to the waiver rule,[21] but pretrial refreshment is in a state of flux.[22]

§ 21.06 Sanctions

In a criminal case in which the prosecution fails to produce a writing used to refresh memory, the court shall either strike the testimony or, if the interests of justice require, declare a mistrial. If a criminal defendant or a party in a civil case fails to produce a writing, the "court shall make any order justice requires." This could include "contempt, dismissal, finding issues against the offender, and the like."[23]

"Dismissals" and "findings" against a criminal defendant, however, would raise constitutional problems. Striking a defense witness's testimony has been upheld under certain circumstances,[24] and permitting the prosecutor to comment on the defendant's refusal to produce a document also would be proper.

---

[18] The production of defense witness statements was upheld by the Supreme Court in United States v. Nobles, 422 U.S. 225 (1975).

[19] The House Judiciary Committee Report contains the following comment: "The Committee intends that nothing in the Rule be construed as barring the assertion of a privilege with respect to writings used by a witness to refresh his memory." H.R. Rep. No. 650, 93d Cong., 1st Sess. (1973), reprinted in 1974 U.S.C.C.A.N. 7075, 7086.

[20] See infra § 38.14 (work product privilege).

[21] See United States v. Nobles, 422 U.S. 225 (1975) (trial use of work product material constitutes a waiver).

[22] See ABA Section of Litigation, Emerging Problems Under the Federal Rules of Evidence, Rule 612, at 187 (3d ed. 1998) ("The majority of courts have permitted disclosure — or at least identification — of privileged materials used to refresh memory prior to testimony.").

[23] Fed. R. Evid. 612 advisory committee's note.

[24] See Michigan v. Lucas, 500 U.S. 145 (1991) (exclusion of defense witness's testimony for failure to comply with a rape shield law's notice requirements not unconstitutional under circumstances); Taylor v. Illinois, 484 U.S. 400 (1988) (exclusion of defense witness's testimony for violating a discovery order not violative of compulsory process under circumstances); United States v. Nobles, 422 US 225 (1975).

§ 21.07 Recorded Recollection Distinguished

Refreshing recollection (Rule 612) must be distinguished from the hearsay exception for recorded recollection (Rule 803(5)). [25] These rules are sometimes referred to as "present recollection revived" and "past recollection recorded." [26]

Under the hearsay exception, the *writing* is the evidence. In contrast, under Rule 612 the *testimony* of the witness whose recollection has been refreshed is the evidence. The writing itself is not admissible unless (1) introduced by the opposing party (only for impeachment) or (2) some other evidence rule applies.

The different requirements for the two rules are significant but often confused. [27] The recorded recollection exception, like other hearsay exceptions, is based on certain circumstantial guarantees of trustworthiness. Accordingly, Rule 803(5) requires a foundation showing that the witness, (1) based on firsthand knowledge, (2) made or adopted the record, (3) when the matter was fresh in the witness's memory, and (4) the record correctly reflects the witness's knowledge. In addition, the witness has to have "insufficient recollection to enable the witness to testify fully and accurately" about the matter recorded.

None of these requirements apply to refreshing recollection. The writing need not have been prepared or adopted by the witness, nor made when the matter was fresh in the witness's memory. Nor does the writing have to be accurate. [28]

§ 21.08 Key Points

The witness's memory must be exhausted, or nearly exhausted, before a writing may be used to refresh recollection.

Admissibility. A writing does not become admissible solely because it is used to refresh a witness's recollection. The opposing party, however, not only has the right to inspect the writing but also the right "to cross-examine the witness" on the writing and to introduce into evidence the parts that relate to the witness's testimony. In this situation, the writing is used to impeach the witness's credibility and not as substantive evidence.

Right of inspection. The right is mandatory for trial refreshment. The production of a writing used *prior to* trial to refresh a witness's recollection may be required "if the court in its discretion determines it is necessary in the interests of justice."

---

[25] *See infra* § 33.09 (recorded recollection).

[26] *See* 3 Wigmore, Evidence § 758, at 125 & 128 (Chadbourn rev. 1970).

[27] *See* 3 Wigmore, Evidence § 758, at 128 (Chadbourn rev. 1970) ("None of the limiting rules just examined for past recorded recollection has any bearing on the present subject. The confounding of the two has led to many misguided rulings.")

[28] In addition, the "best evidence" rule does not apply to refreshing recollection because the party is not attempting to prove the contents of the writing. *See infra* § 30.03 (proving contents).

Recorded recollection (Rule 803(5)). Refreshing recollection (Rule 612) must be distinguished from the hearsay exception for recorded recollection. This is critical. *See supra* § 21.07.

Chapter 22

WITNESS CREDIBILITY: FRE 607–609, 613

§ 22.01 Introduction

Credibility refers to a witness's worthiness of belief. Passing upon the credibility of a witness is a classic jury function. As one court remarked, "Sorting truth from fiction, of course, is for the jury."[1] In assessing credibility, the jury may consider a multitude of factors.[2]

[A] Stages of Credibility

Credibility may be viewed in three stages: (1) bolstering, (2) impeachment, and (3) rehabilitation. *Impeachment* involves attempts to diminish or attack a witness's credibility. There are also rules regulating attempts to support credibility. For example, as a general matter, a witness's credibility may not be *bolstered* (supported) prior to impeachment. Moreover, under certain circumstances a witness's credibility may be *rehabilitated* (supported) after impeachment. Thus, bolstering and rehabilitation both involve efforts to support credibility; the difference is one of timing.

[B] Types of Impeachment

Numerous factors may be considered in evaluating credibility, including a witness's demeanor while testifying. There are, however, five principal

---

[1] United States v. Jackson, 208 F.3d 633, 637 (7th Cir. 2000).

[2] Cal. Evid. Code § 780:

> General rule as to credibility. Except as otherwise provided by statute, the court or jury may consider in determining the credibility of a witness any matter that has any tendency in reason to prove or disprove the truthfulness of his testimony at the hearing, including but not limited to any of the following:

(a) His demeanor while testifying and the manner in which he testifies.
(b) The character of his testimony.
(c) The extent of his capacity to perceive, to recollect, or to communicate any matter about which he testifies.
(d) The extent of his opportunity to perceive any matter about which he testifies.
(e) His character for honesty or veracity or their opposites.
(f) The existence or nonexistence of a bias, interest, or other motive.
(g) A statement previously made by him that is consistent with his testimony at the hearing.
(h) A statement made by him that is inconsistent with any part of his testimony at the hearing.
(i) The existence or nonexistence of any fact testified to by him.
(j) His attitude toward the action in which he testifies or toward the giving of testimony.
(k) His admission of untruthfulness.

methods of impeachment: (1) bias or interest, (2) sensory or mental defects, (3) character for untruthfulness, which includes impeachment by reputation, opinion, prior convictions, and prior untruthful acts, (4) specific contradiction, and (5) prior inconsistent statements (self-contradiction). Moreover, Rule 610 prohibits the impeachment use of a witness's religious beliefs, and a special impeachment rule on learned treatises applies to experts. [3]

[C]   Extrinsic Evidence ("collateral matters")

Depending on the method, impeaching evidence may be elicited on cross-examination [4] or through other witnesses, which is known as *extrinsic evidence.* [5] The admissibility of extrinsic evidence depends on the type of impeachment — whether the method is considered "collateral." The word collateral is confusing; in this context, it is a conclusory label. [6] If impeachment is collateral, extrinsic evidence is prohibited. If not, extrinsic evidence is admissible. It would be better to avoid the word collateral and simply ask if extrinsic evidence is allowed.

There are some blanket rules in this context. Some types of impeachment, such as bias, are never collateral, and therefore extrinsic evidence is always admissible. [7] In contrast, other types of impeachment are always considered "collateral." For example, Rule 608(b) prohibits extrinsic evidence of specific instances of untruthful conduct not resulting in a conviction. The admissibility of extrinsic evidence of prior inconsistent statements and specific contradiction is more complicated. As explained later, sometimes extrinsic evidence is admissible and sometimes not.

Foundational requirements. The admissibility of extrinsic evidence for some types of impeachment is conditioned on the "laying" of a proper foundation during the examination of the witness. This means the cross-examiner must question the witness about the impeaching matter as a prerequisite to admitting extrinsic evidence through other witnesses. Some jurisdictions require such foundations for impeachment by bias and prior inconsistent statements.

---

[3] Fed. R. Evid. 803(18).

[4] Although Rule 611(b) adopts the restrictive view on the scope of cross-examination, it specifically permits impeachment matters. Fed. R. Evid. 611(b) ("Cross-examination should be limited to the subject matter of the direct examination and matters affecting the credibility of the witness.").

[5] Whether extrinsic evidence covers documents is unclear. Documentary evidence offered at the time the witness is impeached should not be considered extrinsic evidence because it does not consume much additional time (*e.g.*, record of conviction).

[6] The term differs depending on the context. Used with the best evidence rule, it means unimportant. *E.g.*, Fed. R. Evid. 1004(4).

[7] This is the common law view; Rule 403 may now control this issue.

§ 22.02 Prohibition on Bolstering

[A] General Rule

Generally, a witness's credibility may not be bolstered or supported with evidence relevant *only* for that purpose, until after impeachment.[8] Consumption of time and confusion of issues are the principal reasons for this rule.[9] There are two prominent examples: (1) a witness's good character for truthfulness is not admissible in the absence of an attack on character.[10] (2) Prior consistent statements are inadmissible before a witness's credibility has been attacked.[11]

Certain types of bolstering are permissible. Attorneys spend a good deal of time trying to bolster the credibility of their witnesses. Calling a witness "Doctor" rather than "Mister" (including a Ph.D); referring to FBI agents as "Special Agent" rather than "Mister." Offering several witnesses, each saying the same thing, bolsters each. Qualifying an expert is another type of permissible bolstering.

[B] Exceptions

At least two exceptions to the general prohibition against bolstering were recognized at common law. The major issue under the Federal Rules concerns plea bargaining agreements.

[1] Line-ups, Showups & Photo Displays

First, a witness's in-court identification of an accused as the person who committed the crime may be bolstered or corroborated by evidence of a prior out-of-court identification (*e.g.*, lineup, showup, or photo display). This rule is no longer as important as it once was because Rule 801(d)(1)(C) exempts prior identifications from the hearsay rule, making the identification admissible as substantive, rather than merely corroborative, evidence.[12]

[2] Fresh Complaints

The second exception was evidence of fresh complaints in rape trials.[13] The alleged rape victim's in-court testimony may be bolstered by the fact

---

[8] *See* United States v. Consentino, 844 F.2d 30, 32–33 (2d Cir. 1998) ("It is well settled that absent an attack, no evidence may be admitted to support a witness' credibility.").

[9] *See* United States v. LeFevour, 798 F.2d 977, 983 (3d Cir. 1986) ("To bolster a witness's credibility in advance is improper. It not only has the potential for extending the length of trials enormously, but asks the jury to take the witness's testimony on faith; it may therefore reduce the care with which jurors listen for inconsistencies and other signs of falsehood or inaccuracy.") (citation omitted).

[10] Fed. R. Evid. 608(a)(2).

[11] Fed. R. Evid. 801(d)(1)(B). Even after attack, they are not automatically admissible. *See infra* § 22.14[B]

[12] *See infra* § 32.04 (statements of identification).

[13] *See* Dunn v. State, 12 N.E. 826, 827–28 (Ohio 1887) ("[H]er declarations in relation to

that she made a complaint soon after the incident. [14] In short, a fresh complaint is a type of prior consistent statement. Frequently, resort to this theory of admissibility is unnecessary because the "fresh complaint" often qualifies as an excited utterance (hearsay exception) and therefore is admissible as substantive evidence. [15] Nevertheless, there may be situations in which the complaint is delayed and thus not admissible as an excited utterance, but nevertheless admissible under the bolstering theory, provided a sufficient explanation for the delay is offered. [16]

[3] Cooperation (Plea) Agreements

The admissibility of plea bargain agreements to *bolster* the testimony of a prosecution witness who testifies pursuant to such an agreement has divided the federal courts. The agreements are written and fairly elaborate, including provisions for perjury prosecutions if the witness testifies falsely. Such "deals" will inevitably be brought out on cross-examination as a type of bias impeachment — typically, the witness is receiving a sentence reduction or other benefit for the testimony. The prosecution, of course, would like to "draw the sting" on direct examination by preemptively bringing out the agreement.

This is all well and good and a traditional practice. However, introducing the *entire* agreement on direct examination is of more recent vintage. [17] This practice involves the risk that the agreement may convey the unspoken message that the prosecutor knows what the truth is and is assuring its revelation. Nevertheless, a majority of the federal circuits permit the prosecution on direct examination to introduce the cooperation agreement in its entirety. [18]

---

the injury, made immediately after it was inflicted, would be competent in corroboration of her statements made in court. . . . [Such complaints] are presumed to be the natural outburst of outraged feelings, and, if made at all, would naturally be made at the first opportunity, while the injury is yet fresh and aggravating.").

[14] Note that the "lack of a fresh complaint" is often not persuasive in light of the research on rape trauma syndrome, which shows that substantial numbers of rape victims make delayed complaints.

[15] *See* Fed. R. Evid. 803(2). *See infra* § 33.05 (excited utterances).

[16] *See* State v. Rolon, 777 A.2d 604, 625 (Conn. 2001) ("The constancy of accusation doctrine is well established in Connecticut. . . . [W]e restricted the doctrine so that a constancy of accusation witness could testify only to the fact and the timing of the victim's complaint. Even so limited, the evidence would be admissible solely for corroboration of the victim's testimony, and not for substantive purposes.").

[17] Not only is the agreement introduced but also the "proffer letter." A "proffer letter" is an interim agreement with a limited immunity attached. Such an agreement allows the prosecutor to determine whether the substance of the witness's information is sufficiently useful to proceed to a complete agreement. It is sometimes known as "Queen for a Day."

[18] *See* United States v. Spriggs, 996 F.2d 320, 323 (D.C. Cir. 1993) ("First, insofar as the agreement provides that if the witness lies the agreement is revokable, that the witness is liable to prosecution for perjury, and that his perjurious testimony may be used against him, it adds nothing to the law — as the defense is free to bring out upon cross-examination. . . . Furthermore, that the Government may (obviously) impose a sanction upon the witness if he lies does nothing to enhance the Government's ability to detect whether he is in fact lying;

The Fourth Circuit has provided guidelines: "To guard against such danger, . . . the government may elicit testimony regarding a plea agreement only if: (1) the prosecutor's questions do not imply that the government has special knowledge of the witness's veracity; (2) the trial judge instructs the jury on the caution required in evaluating the witness's testimony; and (3) the prosecutor's closing argument contains no improper use of the witness's promise of truthful cooperation."[19] In contrast, the Second Circuit has ruled that the prosecution may not introduce aspects of a cooperation agreement that could bolster the witness's credibility unless the defense attacks that credibility.[20]

§ 22.03 Impeachment of Own Witness: FRE 607

At common law, a party could not impeach its own witnesses. This was known as the *voucher rule* and was based on the theory that when a party produces a witness that party vouches for the witness's veracity — *i.e.*, a party should not hold the witness out as worthy of belief when the testimony is favorable and impeach credibility when it is adverse.[21] Several exceptions to the voucher rule were recognized: (1) A party who was *surprised* by a turncoat witness was permitted to impeach that witness; some jurisdictions added a second requirement — *affirmative damage.*[22] (2) The voucher rule did not apply to court-called witnesses.[23] (3) Compulsory witnesses were also exempt; a typical example would be a will statute requiring all witnesses to the will to be called in a will contest. (4) The voucher rule did not apply to the adverse party if called by the other side.

Rule 607 abolishes the "voucher rule." The rationale for the voucher rule was never persuasive because the firsthand knowledge rule requires percipient witnesses, and, thus the parties often have no choice concerning

---

again the terms of the cooperation agreement should do nothing to enhance the witness's credibility. Finally, at least in the present case there is nothing in the agreement or in the prosecutor's direct examination on that subject to 'imply that the government had special knowledge' of the witness's veracity.").

[19] United States v. Romer, 148 F.3d 359, 369 (4th Cir. 1998).

[20] *See* United States v. Edwards, 631 F.2d 1049, 1051–52 (2d Cir. 1980). *See also* United States v. Borello, 766 F.2d 46, 56–58 (2d Cir. 1985) (reversible error for trial court to have admitted full cooperation agreement in absence of prior attack on witness's credibility). *Accord* United States v. Wallace, 848 F.2d 1464, 1474 (9th Cir. 1988); United States v. Cruz, 805 F.2d 1464, 1479–80 (11th Cir. 1986).

[21] *See also* Chambers v. Mississippi, 410 U.S. 284, 296 (1973) ("Although the historical origins of the 'voucher' rule are uncertain, it appears to be a remnant of primitive English trial practice in which 'oath-takers' or 'compurgators' were called to stand behind a particular party's position in any controversy. Their assertions were strictly partisan and, quite unlike witnesses in criminal trials today, their role bore little relation to the impartial ascertainment of the facts.").

[22] Testimony that the witness could no longer remember was not considered *affirmative* damage. It may not help your case, but it also did not help the other side. Testimony that the light was red at the time of the accident when the witness had earlier said it was green is affirmative damage.

[23] *See* Fed. R. Evid. 614 (recognizing authority of trial court to call its own witnesses).

which witnesses to call. This is especially true with crimes or torts. If there are only a few witnesses who have personal knowledge, what choice do the parties have? Moreover, the continued validity of the voucher rule in criminal cases became suspect after *Chambers v. Mississippi,* [24] in which the Supreme Court held that the combined effect of Mississippi's voucher rule and hearsay rule precluded the admission of critical and reliable defense evidence and therefore violated due process.

[A] Problem: Prior Inconsistent Statements

The abolition of the voucher rule created one problem, which concerns impeachment with prior inconsistent statements. Prior inconsistent statements constitute hearsay (if offered for the truth) and thus are generally admissible only for the purpose of impeachment. [25] A party could call a witness for the sole purpose of disclosing the prior inconsistent statement (hearsay) to the jury. An instruction limiting the use of the statement to impeachment would likely be ineffective. In short, Rule 607 could be employed to circumvent the hearsay rule. [26]

Often, it is the prosecutor who attempts this after learning she has a turncoat witness on her hands. [27] The federal courts deal with this issue in a number of ways. Some focus on whether there is a subterfuge to get hearsay before the jury, while others use a Rule 403 analysis. [28]

§ 22.04 Bias Impeachment

A witness's bias, interest, partiality, or corruption [29] is always relevant for impeachment. Although the revised Uniform Rules of Evidence and

---

[24] 410 U.S. 284, 298 (1973) ("The 'voucher' rule, as applied in this case, plainly interfered with Chambers' right to defend against the State's charges.").

[25] There is an important exception in Fed. R. Evid. 801(d)(1)(A). *See infra* § 32.02 (prior inconsistent statements taken under oath and subject to penalty of perury are exempted from the hearsay rule).

[26] *See* ABA Section of Litigation, Emerging Problems Under the Federal Rules of Evidence, Rule 607, at 146 (3d ed. 1998) ("Accordingly, courts should be alert to the possibility that a party may called a known hostile witness and then try to impeach the witness with favorable statements merely 'as a stratagem to get before the jury otherwise inadmissible evidence.'") (quoting United States v. Gossett, 877 F.2d 901, 907 (11th Cir. 1989) (per curiam)).

[27] This problem arose because Congress changed the hearsay rule in Article VIII but overlooked its affect on Rule 607. *See* Graham, *Employing Inconsistent Statements for Impeachment and as Substantive Evidence: A Critical Review and Proposed Amendments of Federal Rules of Evidence 801(d)(1)(A), 613 and 607,* 75 Mich. L. Rev. 1565, 1617 (1977).

[28] *See* United States v. Logan, 121 F.3d 1172, 1174–75 (8th Cir. 1997) ("Although some courts focus on determining the 'true' purpose of the government in introducing testimony, we think that the relevant question is simply whether the evidence is admissible under Fed. R. Ev. 403. . . . Our assessment of the prior statements as creating a danger of unfair prejudice and jury confusion is reinforced by the fact that the government elicited, through the state police officer's testimony, additional inculpatory statements that Ms. Carlen allegedly made to the officer. . . . The only possible relevance that testimony could have had was as substantive evidence, yet it was clearly hearsay for those purposes. . . . It was therefore manifestly inadmissible.").

[29] Corruption would encompass, for example, a witness bribed to testify in a certain way.

several state jurisdictions have promulgated rules on bias,[30] there is *no rule on bias* in the Federal Rules.[31] However, a number of other rules mention bias,[32] and in *United States v. Abel*[33] the Supreme Court held that impeachment for bias was proper. According to the Court, "proof of bias is almost always relevant because the jury, as finder of fact and weigher of credibility, has historically been entitled to assess all evidence which might bear on the accuracy and truth of a witness' testimony."[34]

There are two broad categories of bias. First, a relationship between a witness and one of the parties may be evidence of bias.[35] The relationship may be a favorable one, such as a familial, employment, business, sexual,[36] or other relationship,[37] or it may be a hostile relationship, caused by prior fights and quarrels.[38] Fear may also be an impeaching factor.[39]

---

[30] *E.g.,* Unif. R. Evid. 616; Ohio R. Evid. 616(A); Utah R. Evid. 608(c).

[31] Why no rule on bias? (Also, none on sensory-mental defect impeachment.) The explanation is that some impeachment methods contain limitations on admissibility. Specific rules were needed to set forth these limitations (*e.g.,* Rules 608, 609, 613). Since no limitations were intended on bias impeachment, no rule was required. Rule 402 makes relevant evidence, such as bias, admissible in the absence of a rule of exclusion. Nevertheless, the omission of rules on all impeachment methods has caused some confusion.

[32] *See* Fed. R. Evid. 408 (settlement offers inadmissible except if offered for another purpose "such as proving bias or prejudice of a witness"); Fed. R. Evid. 411 (evidence of liability insurance is inadmissible except if offered for another purpose such as "bias or prejudice"); Fed. R. Evid. 801(d)(1)(B) (prior consistent statements admissible if "offered to rebut an express or implied charge . . . of recent fabrication or improper influence or motive"); Fed. R. Evid. 608(a) advisory committee's note ("corruption").

[33] 469 U.S. 45, 51 (1984) ("[T]he lesson to be drawn is that it is permissible to impeach a witness by showing his bias under the Federal Rules of Evidence just as it was permissible to do so before their adoption.").

[34] *Id.* at 52.

[35] *Id.* ("Bias is a term used in the 'common law of evidence' to describe the relationship between a party and a witness which might lead the witness to slant, unconsciously or otherwise, his testimony in favor of or against a party."). *See also* United States v. Booty, 621 F.2d 1291, 1299 n. 26 (5th Cir. 1980) ("relationships between a party and a witness are always relevant to a showing of bias, whether the relationship is based on ties of family, enmity or fear").

[36] *E.g.,* Olden v. Kentucky, 488 U.S. 227 (1988) (witness's current living arrangement with another witness relevant to impeachment).

[37] *E.g., Abel*, 469 U.S. at 52 ("A witness' and a party's common membership in an organization, even without proof that the witness or party has personally adopted its tenets, is certainly probative of bias.").

[38] *E.g, id.* at 52 ("Bias may be induced by a witness' like, dislike, or fear of a party, or by the witness' self-interest.").

[39] *See* United States v. Manske, 186 F.3d 770, 778 (7th Cir. 1999) (trial judge prevented defendant from asking witnesses about their fear of Pszeniczka and its relationship, if any, to their testimony against Manske; "This complete ban cut off an important avenue for the defendant to expose those individual's alleged bias and motive to testify as they did, leaving the jury short of potentially essential information."); United States v. Keys, 899 F.2d 983, 987 (10th Cir. 1990) ("Keys' statement that he controlled sixty soldiers in the prison system who would do him favors, including breaking the law, is relevant to show that Kinnison's and Ward's testimony might have been influenced by their fear of Keys and his gang.").

The Supreme Court in *Abel* pointed out that membership in a prison gang differed from membership in other groups: "If the prosecutor had elicited that both respondent and Mills belonged to the Book of the Month Club, the jury probably would not have inferred bias. The attributes of the Aryan Brotherhood — a secret prison sect sworn to perjury and self-protection — bore directly not only on the fact of bias but also the source and strength of Mills' bias. The tenets of this group showed that Mills had a powerful motive to slant his testimony towards respondent, or even commit perjury."[40]

Second, a relationship between a witness and the litigation also may be evidence of bias — such as a financial interest in the case, or a related case.[41] One of the most common examples is a prosecution witness who is offered immunity or a reduced charge in exchange for testifying against a defendant.

As with all types of impeachment, the examiner must have a good faith basis for a question.[42]

[A] Right of Confrontation

Substantial curtailment of a criminal defendant's efforts to establish bias on the part of prosecution witnesses is unconstitutional. In *Davis v. Alaska*,[43] the defense attempted to show that a key prosecution witness was a juvenile probationer and therefore had a motive — retention of his probationary status — to testify in a way favorable to the prosecution. The trial judge, based on a statute, excluded this evidence. The Supreme Court reversed: "The State's policy interest in protecting the confidentiality of a juvenile offender's record cannot require yielding of so vital a constitutional right as the effective cross-examination for bias of an adverse witness."[44]

---

[40] *Abel*, 469 U.S. at 54.

[41] *See* Clark v. Doe, 695 N.E.2d 276, 283 (Ohio App. 1997) ("An expert's bias and pecuniary interest are fair subjects for both cross-examination and argument. However, the permissible bounds of fair argument are not unlimited, and when they are crossed, the violation must be appropriately addressed. The expert did testify that he charged $1,000 per hour for his time, and that he arrived at that amount by trying to determine how much time he missed from taking care of patients and surgery, and what he missed in income. However, he also specifically stated that he only reviewed one or two legal cases each year. For defense counsel to argue that the expert would have to make $2,000,000 a year to charge $1,000 per hour, and that he was testifying because it was a 'money-making venture for him' crosses the line. These remarks were inappropriate and a deliberate attempt to discredit the expert's opinion by disparaging him.") (citations omitted).

[42] *See* United States v. Lin, 101 F.3d 760, 767–68 (D.C. Cir. 1997) ("The court denied the mistrial motion and explained that defense counsel was free to recall the witness if and when he provided the court with a proffer demonstrating that he had a good faith basis for the line of questioning.").

[43] 415 U.S. 308 (1974). *See also* Smith v. Illinois, 390 U.S. 129 (1968); Alford v. United States, 282 U.S. 687 (1931).

[44] *Davis*, 415 U.S. at 320. Similarly, in Delaware v. Van Arsdall, 475 U.S. 673 (1986), a murder defendant sought to cross-examine a prosecution witness about a possible agreement to dismiss charges against the witness. The trial court barred cross-examination, and the

Similarly, in *Olden v. Kentucky*,[45] a rape victim testified that Olden had tricked her into leaving a bar, raped her, and then drove her to the house of Bill Russell, where she was released. Russell, also a prosecution witness, testified that he had seen the victim leave Olden's car and that she had immediately complained of rape. The defense claimed consent, arguing that the victim and Russell were involved in an extramarital relationship and that the victim fabricated the rape story to explain to Russell why she was in the defendant's car. By the time of trial, the victim and Russell were living together, but the trial judge refused to permit cross-examination on this fact. The judge believed that this information would prejudice the jury against the victim because she was white and Russell was African-American. The Supreme Court reversed curiam: Olden had consistently maintained that the alleged victim lied because she feared jeopardizing her relationship with Russell. Thus, her current living arrangement with Russell was relevant to impeachment, and the foreclosure of this line of inquiry violated the right of confrontation.

[B] Foundational Requirement

Most jurisdictions require that a foundation be laid on cross-examination before extrinsic evidence of bias is admissible. Stated another way, the examiner must question the witness about the bias during the examination or be foreclosed from presenting the testimony of other witnesses (extrinsic evidence) on the issue. This requirement is fairer to the witness and saves time because the other side can attempt to rehabilitate on redirect examination rather than recalling the witness later in the trial. Moreover, there may be no need to introduce extrinsic evidence if the witness acknowledges the bias on cross-examination. Some courts have indicated that this is the federal practice.[46]

[C] Extrinsic Evidence

At common law, bias was not considered a "collateral matter," and thus extrinsic evidence of bias was always admissible.[47] Accordingly, the impeaching party was not limited to attempting to elicit the bias evidence during the examination of the witness; it could introduce other witnesses

---

Supreme Court reversed: "[A] criminal defendant states a violation of the Confrontation Clause by showing that he was prohibited from engaging in otherwise appropriate cross-examination designed to show a prototypical form of bias on the part of the witness, and thereby 'to expose to the jury the facts from which jurors . . . could appropriately draw inferences relating to the reliability of the witness.'" *Id.* at 680 (quoting *Davis*).

[45] 488 U.S. 227 (1988) (per curiam).

[46] *See* United States v. Betts, 16 F.3d 748, 764 (7th Cir. 1994) ("[T]he weight of authority supports the proposition that when a party seeks to prove bias through extrinsic evidence of a witness' prior statement, he must first give the witness the opportunity to explain or deny that statement. . . .").

[47] *See* United States v. Abel, 469 U.S. 45, 52 (1984) ("The 'common law of evidence' allowed the showing of bias by extrinsic evidence."). *See also supra* § 22.01[C].

on the issue. However, a recent Advisory Committee Note (dealing with another type of impeachment) indicates that Rule 403 should control in this context.[48] This makes sense where the witness admits the bias on cross-examination, thus eliminating the need for extrinsic proof.

§ 22.05 Impeachment: Sensory & Mental Defects

There is no federal rule on this type of impeachment. Any sensory or mental defect that might affect a witness's capacity to observe, recall,[49] or relate the events about which the witness has testified is admissible to impeach[50] — for example, a nearsighted person *sans* eyeglasses identifying a person at a distance, or a colorblind person testifying about whether a traffic light was red or green. Mental condition is sometimes relevant to credibility.[51] Often, however, it is not.[52] It depends on the condition's relationship to credibility.[53]

In addition, evidence that the witness was under the influence of alcohol or drugs at the time of the event *or* the trial falls within this category, but alcoholism or addiction generally does not.[54]

Extrinsic evidence. As for extrinsic evidence (*i.e.*, the testimony of other witnesses), there is probably no hard and fast rule. Sensory and mental defects often can be effectively disclosed through cross-examination, in

---

[48] Proposed Fed. R. Evid. 608(b) advisory committee's note (2001), 201 F.R.D. 729 (2001) ("By limiting the application of the Rule to proof of a witness' character for truthfulness, the amendment leaves the admissibility of extrinsic evidence offered for other grounds of impeachment (such as contradiction, prior inconsistent statement, *bias* and mental capacity) to Rules 402 and 403. . . . Rules 402 and 403 displace the common-law rules prohibiting impeachment on 'collateral' matters.") (emphasis added).

[49] *Cf.* Delaware v. Fensterer, 474 U.S. 15, 20 (1985) (defense counsel's cross-examination "demonstrated to the jury that [the expert] could not even recall the theory on which his opinion was based").

[50] *E.g.,* United States v. Ciocca, 106 F.3d 1079, 1082 (1st Cir. 1997) ("Ciocca was able to place before the jury ample evidence regarding Caporino's ability to remember the events that transpired prior to and after his accident.").

[51] *See* United States v. Gonzalez-Maldonado, 115 F.3d 9, 15 (1st Cir. 1997) ("It is well established that a witness' mental state can be relevant to the issue of the witness' credibility. . . . Dr. Fumero would have testified that Robles, as a result of his illness, was prone to exaggeration.").

[52] *E.g.,* United States v. Smith, 77 F.3d 511, 516 (D.C. Cir. 1996) ("Of course, a history of mental illness is not necessarily admissible as impeachment evidence."); Boggs v. Collins, 226 F.3d 728, 739 (6th Cir. 2000) ("While mental illness can indeed be relevant to a witness's credibility, courts hold that the decision of whether or not to allow in evidence of a witness's mental illness falls within the broad discretion of trial courts as they balance possible prejudice versus probative value.").

[53] *E.g.,* United States v. Sasso, 59 F.3d 341, 347–48 (2d Cir. 1995) (relevant factors are nature of the psychological problem, the temporal recency or remoteness of the condition, and whether the witness suffered from the condition at the time of the events to which she is to testify); United States v. Bari, 750 F.2d 1169, 1178–79 (2d Cir. 1984) (finding no abuse of discretion when trial judge would not permit cross-examination on witness's prior hospitalization for schizophrenia).

[54] *See* 3A Wigmore, Evidence §§ 931–35, 989–95 (Chadbourn rev. 1970).

which case the admissibility of extrinsic evidence should be regulated by the trial court pursuant to Rule 403.[55]

§ 22.06   Untruthful Character Impeachment: Overview

Recall from chapter 10 that character evidence is generally inadmissible under Rule 404(a). We saw, however, that there are some exceptions concerning the character of the accused and victim. A third exception deals with credibility.[56] Character is used circumstantially; a person with an untruthful character is more likely to testify untruthfully than a person with a truthful character.

Here again, there are three possibilities for methods of proof: (1) reputation evidence, (2) opinion evidence, and (3) specific acts. Rule 608(a) sanctions the use of reputation and opinion, which is consistent with the treatment of character on the merits under Rule 405(a). Specific acts are treated differently in this context. Rule 609 permits impeachment with prior convictions under some conditions. Rule 608(b) allows impeachment by specific acts that have not resulted in a conviction — under limited circumstances.

§ 22.07   Untruthful Character — Reputation & Opinion: FRE 608(a)

Rule 608(a) permits the use of opinion and reputation evidence to show a witness's untruthful character,[57] including that of the accused.[58] The limitation to veracity is intended "to sharpen relevancy, to reduce surprise, waste of time, and confusion, and to make the lot of the witness somewhat less unattractive."[59] The common law restricted this type of impeachment to reputation. In contrast, Rule 608(a) permits the use of opinion evidence as well.[60] This change is consistent with the treatment of opinion evidence in Rule 405(a). Although permitting opinion testimony raises the possibility

---

[55] See supra note 48.

[56] Fed. R. Evid. 404(a)(3) ("Evidence of the character of a witness, as provided in rules 607, 608, and 609.").

[57] See also Fed. R. Evid. 803(20) (recognizing a hearsay exception for reputation evidence concerning character). See infra § 33.18 (other hearsay exceptions).

[58] E.g., United States v. McMurray, 20 F.3d 831, 834 (8th Cir. 1994) ("The credibility of a defendant who testifies may be attacked in the same manner as that of any other witness. . . . The prosecutor asked Mrs. Carper whether she would believe McMurray's testimony under oath, based upon her opinion as to his truthfulness. This questioning is consistent with Rule 608(a).").

[59] Fed Fed. R. Evid. 608 advisory committee's note.

[60] See United States v. Malady, 960 F.2d 57, 58 (8th Cir. 1992) ("Assuming the sheriff had sufficient contact with Counts, Malady could have asked the sheriff for his general opinion of Counts's truthfulness. Instead, Malady asked the sheriff whether he believed Counts's story. Because this is an impermissible means of impeachment, the district court properly sustained the Government's objection.") (citations omitted).

of using expert witnesses, courts have been reluctant to admit expert testimony in this context.[61]

Foundational requirements. Before reputation evidence is permitted, a foundation must be laid showing that the character witness is acquainted with the principal witness's reputation in the community (*i.e.*, where the principal (fact) witness lives, works, or goes to school).[62] A similar foundation is required before a witness may express an opinion. This latter inquiry, however, focuses on the character witness's personal relationship with the principal witness rather than on community contacts.

§ 22.08 Untruthful Character — Prior Conviction: FRE 609

[A] Overview

Rule 609 governs the admissibility of evidence of prior convictions offered for impeachment *to show untruthful character*. The rule applies in both civil and criminal cases, and it applies to the impeachment of any witness, including a criminal defendant. When evidence of a prior conviction is admitted under Rule 609, a limiting instruction is required upon request.[63] A different rule, Rule 608(b), governs impeachment by specific instances of untruthful conduct that have *not* resulted in a conviction.

Convictions: other theories of admissibility. If prior conviction evidence is offered under an impeachment theory other than untruthful character or for reasons other than impeachment, Rule 609 does not apply. For example, evidence of a conviction may be admissible to show that a witness has received or expects to receive favorable treatment from the prosecution (*i.e.*, bias). Similarly, evidence of a conviction may be admissible under Rule 404(b) ("other acts") as proof of motive, opportunity, intent, and so forth.[64]

---

[61] *E.g.*, United States v. Cecil, 836 F.2d 1431, 1441 (4th Cir. 1988) ("[T]he authorities seem uniform that a psychiatrist may not testify to the credibility of a witness; that issue is one for the jury."); United States v. Barnard, 490 F.2d 907, 912–13 (9th Cir. 1973) ("It is now suggested that psychiatrists and psychologists have more of this expertise than either judges or juries, and that their opinions can be of value to both judges and juries in determining the veracity of witnesses. Perhaps. The effect of receiving such testimony, however, may be twofold: first, it may cause juries to surrender their own common sense in weighing testimony; second, it may produce a trial within a trial on what is collateral but still an important matter. For these reasons we, like other courts that have considered the matter, are unwilling to say that when such testimony is offered, the judge must admit it.").

[62] *E.g.*, Wilson v. City of Chicago, 6 F.3d 1233, 1239 (7th Cir. 1993) (reputation for untruthfulness among people who had worked with Coleman and members of his family; "Was this a 'community' within the meaning of the rule? We suppose so. Coleman is a peripatetic felon. He is not a member of any stable community, but that is true of a lot of law-abiding people in our mobile society, and a community doesn't have to be stable in order to qualify under the rule.").

[63] *See* Fed. R. Evid. 105 (limiting instruction).

[64] Note that Rule 404(b) does not require a conviction.

Also, if an accused testifies that he has "never committed a crime in my life," a prior conviction may be offered in rebuttal.[65] Finally, sometimes a prior conviction is *an element* of a subsequently tried offense, in which case the prior conviction must be proved.[66] Here, it is substantive, not impeachment, evidence.

[B] Conviction Defined; arrests; no-contest pleas

Rule 609 applies only to *convictions*. Under Rule 609, convictions based on no contest pleas should be admissible.[67] The policies underlying no contest pleas are not applicable in this context.[68] Arrests and indictments are not admissible under Rule 609.[69] The *conduct* that is the basis for the arrest or indictment may, however, be admissible pursuant to Rule 608(b) if it reflects untruthful character.

[C] Rationale

The theory of admissibility underlying Rule 609 corresponds to the theory underlying Rule 608 (reputation, opinion and specific acts): a person with an untruthful character is more likely to act in conformity with that character while testifying than a person without that character.[70]

Determining which crimes reflect untruthful character is the critical issue.[71] For example, should a prior conviction for driving while intoxicated be admissible? It reveals little about a person's character for truthfulness, although it may reveal other things about that person's character. Moreover, if convictions are automatically admissible, an accused with a prior criminal record may for that reason alone not testify, even if innocent. And

---

[65] *E.g.,* United States v. Bender, 265 F.3d 464, 471 (6th Cir. 2001) ("Bender's statements on direct examination that she had never sold drugs and did not begin using them until 1992 opened the door to bringing into evidence the nature of her prior conviction for conspiracy to distribute and possession with intent to distribute cocaine."); United States v. Norton, 26 F.3d 240, 244–45 (1st Cir. 1994). *See supra* § 10.4[A] (accused's character discussing personal history).

[66] *See* Old Chief v. United States, 519 U.S. 172 (1997) (possession of a firearm by a felon). *See supra* § 9.05[D][3] (stipulations).

[67] *E.g.,* United States v. Sonny Mitchell Center, 934 F.2d 77, 79 (5th Cir. 1991).

[68] Two other rules deal with no contest pleas. Fed. R. Evid. 410 & 803(23).

[69] This type of evidence often violates the prohibition against character evidence found in Rules 404(a) and 404(b).

[70] *See* Walden v. Georgia-Pacific Corp., 126 F.3d 506, 523 (3d Cir. 1997) ("Rule 609 is premised on 'the common sense proposition that one who has transgressed society's norms by committing a felony is less likely than most to be deterred from lying under oath.'") (citation omitted).

[71] Many jurisdictions have adopted impeachment rules based on the balancing approach of Federal Rule 609, although there are variations. Other jurisdictions have blanket rules, which also vary significantly. *Compare* Mont. R. Evid. 609 ("For the purpose of attacking the credibility of a witness, evidence that the witness has been convicted of a crime is not admissible."), *with* N.C. R. Evid. 609(a) (all felony and three classes of misdemeanors, including simple assault and even some speeding convictions, shall be admitted).

not taking the stand comes with its own risks; jurors naturally want to hear the defendant's side of the story, even though they will be instructed not to draw any adverse inferences from a failure to testify.[72]

The solution embedded in Rule 609 is to recognize the trial court's discretion to exclude prior convictions in some (but not all) circumstances. Thus, Rule 609(a) limits the types of convictions that are admissible to (1) crimes punishable by death or imprisonment in excess of one year ("felonies") and (2) crimes of dishonesty and false statement (crimen falsi), regardless of punishment. Additional restrictions are discussed later in this chapter.[73]

[D] Prior "Felony" Convictions of the Accused

Under Rule 609(a), prior convictions involving crimes punishable by death or imprisonment in excess of one year *may* be admissible against a criminal defendant.[74] The rule operates somewhat differently when used to impeach witnesses other than the accused. Note that the label "felony" is technically not correct and is used here only as a convenient shorthand label.[75] State as well as federal convictions fall within the rule. The *authorized maximum punishment*, rather than the actual punishment imposed, is determinative.

Discretion. Admissibility is not automatic, however; it is subject to the trial court's discretion. Only if the probative value of the prior conviction outweighs the unfair prejudice to the defendant is the evidence admissible. A number of factors should influence the trial court's admissibility determination.[76]

---

[72] *See infra* § 43.05[B] (Fifth Amendment).

[73] *Corporations.* Given the underlying rationale of the rule, it becomes clear that an employee of a corporation may not be impeached with the corporation's conviction, in which the witness did not participate. *See* Walden v. Georgia-Pacific Corp., 126 F.3d 506, 523–24 (3d Cir. 1997) ("Criminal acts are relevant to a witness' credibility only if that witness actually participated in the criminal conduct. It strains logic to argue that an employee's credibility is properly brought into question by the mere fact that he or she is presently employed by a corporation that in some unrelated manner was guilty of dishonest acts, no matter how egregious those acts may have been. There is no evidence that the individual witnesses who testified at trial had any involvement with Georgia-Pacific's tax evasion scheme, and thus that scheme could not possibly bear on the likelihood that those witnesses would testify truthfully.").

[74] Because Rule 609 deals with impeachment, either the defendant must testify at the trial or a hearsay statement of the defendant must be admitted before the defendant is subject to Rule 609 impeachment. *See* Fed. R. Evid. 806 (impeachment of hearsay declarants).

[75] Although the common law defined a felony as a crime punishable by death or imprisonment for more than one year, there is much variation throughout the states. Thus, a crime designated as a "misdemeanor" in a particular jurisdiction but punishable by imprisonment for more than one year satisfies the requirements of Rule 609(a).

[76] *See* United States v. Smith, 131 F.3d 685, 687 (7th Cir. 1997) ("Under this analysis, the district court should consider (1) the impeachment value of the prior crime; (2) the point in time of the conviction and the defendant's subsequent history; (3) the similarity between the past crime and the charged crime; (4) the importance of the defendant's testimony; and (5) the centrality of the credibility issue."); United States v. Alexander, 48 F.3d 1477, 1488 (9th Cir. 1995) (same).

[1] Relevant Factors

Nature of prior crime. A prior conviction that bears upon veracity has high probative value for reflecting untruthful character. In contrast, a crime of violence has little probative value for this purpose. Note, however, that crimes of dishonesty or false statement ("crimen falsi"), which are the most probative of veracity, are automatically admissible under Rule 609(a)(2), which is discussed below. Nevertheless, offenses falling outside the crimen falsi classification are not all alike; some reflect untruthful character more than others.[77] For example, burglary is more probative than assault.[78] One court suggested narcotic trafficking has similar probative value.[79]

Age of prior conviction (remoteness). A one-year-old conviction is more probative than an eight-year-old conviction.[80] The witness's criminal history after the prior conviction is also relevant; the remoteness theory does not apply if the defendant has been convicted in the interval between the prior conviction and the current trial. Convictions more than ten years old, however, are subject to the special limitations of Rule 609(b).

Similarity of crimes. The similarity between the prior offense and the charged offense is a relevant factor.[81] If a defendant is charged with a narcotics offense, evidence of a prior narcotics conviction is more unfairly prejudicial than a prior rape conviction. The jury is more likely to use the prior narcotics conviction as evidence of character to commit narcotics offenses rather than as evidence of untruthful character. In short, this factor focuses on the prejudicial impact of the prior conviction, not its probative value.

Need for accused's testimony. If the defendant is the only person who can provide defense evidence, the need for his testimony is greater, and the

---

[77] *E.g.,* United States v. Burston, 159 F.3d 1328, 1334 (11th Cir. 1998) ("Evidence of a murder conviction says something far different about a witness' credibility than evidence of a conviction for a minor drug offense, although both may constitute a prior felony conviction."); United States v. Alexander, 48 F.3d 1477, 1488 (9th Cir. 1995) ("'prior convictions for robbery are probative of veracity.' The same is true of prior convictions for drug offenses.") (citations omitted).

[78] United States v. Pritchard, 973 F.2d 905, 909 n. 6 (11th Cir. 1992) ("This circuit does not consider burglary a crime involving dishonesty or false statement, admissible under Rule 609(a)(2). However, the fact that a defendant has committed a burglary is relevant to the determination of whether he is likely to be truthful under oath.") (citations omitted).

[79] *See* United States v. Oritz, 533 F.2d 782, 784 (2d Cir. 1977) ("[A] narcotics trafficker lives a life of secrecy and dissembling in the course of that activity, being prepared to say whatever is required by the demands of the moment, whether the truth or a lie. From this he could rationally conclude that such activity in a witness' past is probative on the issue of credibility.").

[80] *See* United States v. Sanders, 964 F.2d 295, 298 (4th Cir. 1992) ("It was remote in time, almost falling within the presumptive bar of Rule 609(b).").

[81] *See Pritchard,* 973 F.2d at 909 ("[T]he prior burglary was not so similar to the charged robbery that it created an unacceptable risk that the jury would improperly consider the burglary as evidence that Pritchard committed the robbery."); United States v. Sanders, 964 F.2d 295, 297 (4th Cir. 1992) ("[A]lthough evidence of the prior convictions may be thought somehow generally probative of Sanders' lack of credibility, they were extremely prejudicial since they involved the exact type of conduct for which Sanders was on trial.").

argument for exclusion of the prior conviction is stronger. An entrapment defense is an example, as is a "home-alone" alibi.

Centrality of credibility at trial. If the case boils down to a "swearing contest" between two witnesses, one of whom is the accused, it is important for the jury to know of any evidence affecting credibility, and thus the argument for admission of the prior conviction is greater.[82] This is especially true if the prosecution witness has been impeached with a prior conviction.

Other factors. Additional factors include the length of the defendant's criminal record[83] and the circumstances surrounding the prior offense.

[2] Balancing of Factors

The factors discussed above may, in a particular case, cancel each other out — for example, the need for the accused's testimony may be offset by the centrality of credibility in the case.

The treatment of an accused under Rule 609(a)(1) differs in one important respect from that of other witnesses. Both involve balancing probative value against prejudice. However, impeachment of a witness other than an accused is more readily permitted — exclusion of the prior conviction is required only when probative value is *substantially* outweighed by unfair prejudice (Rule 403). The word "substantially" is not in Rule 609(a)'s internal balancing scheme, making admission more difficult.

Burden of proof. The prosecution bears the burden of showing that the probative value of the evidence outweighs the prejudicial impact.[84]

[E] "Felony" Convictions: Other Witnesses

Under Rule 609(a)(1), prior "felony" convictions of witnesses other than an accused may be admissible — *i.e.*, witnesses in civil cases and prosecution and other defense witnesses in criminal cases. Admissibility is not automatic; it is subject to the trial court's discretion under Rule 403. In making this determination, the court should consider factors such as the nature of the prior crime, the age of the conviction, and the centrality of credibility in the case.

---

[82] *See* United States v. Smith, 131 F.3d 685, 687 (7th Cir. 1997) ("[S]ince Smith's testimony on this point directly contradicted that of the bank teller, his credibility was a central issue.").

[83] *See* United States v. Burston, 159 F.3d 1328, 1334 (11th Cir. 1998) ("[E]vidence of fifteen murder convictions says something different about a witness' credibility than evidence of only one such conviction.") (citation omitted).

[84] *See* United States v. Meserve, 271 F.3d 314, 327–28 (1st Cir. 2001) ("[T]he government, as the party seeking to introduce evidence of a prior conviction for impeachment purposes under Rule 609, was obligated to have researched Kevin's prior offenses and to have determined that they were admissible.").

[F] Crimes of Dishonesty & False Statement ("crimen falsi")

Under Rule 609(a)(2), prior convictions involving crimes of dishonesty or false statement are *automatically* admissible. The trial court has no discretion to exclude these convictions.[85]

Definition. The principal problem in applying this rule is determining what crimes involve "dishonesty" or "false statement." The Conference Report indicated that these terms included *only* crimes such as perjury, subornation of perjury, false statement, criminal fraud, embezzlement, false pretenses, or "any other offense in the nature of *crimen falsi*, the commission of which involves some element of deceit, untruthfulness, or falsification bearing on the accused's propensity to testify truthfully."[86] In addition to the above crimes, forgery, counterfeiting, and tampering convictions are admissible under the rule[87] but assaults and drugs offenses are not.[88]

Although theft offenses are typically thought to involve "dishonesty," several federal courts have ruled them inadmissible.[89] These courts focus on the use of the term "crimen falsi" in the legislative history, which suggests deceit (*e.g.*, larceny by trick) and not simple larceny.

Going beyond the record. Another issue concerns whether the court may delve behind the record to determine whether an offense that on its face

---

[85] H.R. Rep. No. 1597, 93d Cong. 2d Sess. ("The admission of prior convictions involving dishonesty and false statement is not within the discretion of the Court. Such convictions are peculiarly probative of credibility and, under this rule, are always to be admitted."), reprinted in 1974 U.S.C.C.A.N. 7098, 7103. *See also* United States v. Tracy, 36 F.3d 187, 192 (1st Cir. 1994) ("The Government insists that under Fed. R. Evid. 609(a)(2) the district court had no discretion to exclude the evidence of Tracy's conviction for uttering a false prescription, as this was a crime of dishonesty offered to impeach Tracy's credibility as a witness. The Government is correct. A conviction for uttering a false prescription plainly involves dishonesty or false statement."); Cree v. Hatcher, 969 F.2d 34, 37 (3d Cir. 1992); United States v. Toney, 615 F.2d 277, 279 (5th Cir. 1980).

[86] H.R. Rep. No. 1597, 93d Cong. 2d Sess., reprinted in 1974 U.S.C.C.A.N. 7098, 7103.

[87] *E.g.,* United States v. Morrow, 977 F.2d 222, 228 (6th Cir. 1992) ("The term 'counterfeit' implies a sham or bogus act. To use counterfeit money is of necessity to trade on the inauthenticity and misrepresentative character of such currency. Counterfeit cash is a pretender to the real thing, and dishonesty is a core ingredient in the offense of counterfeiting."); Altobello v. Borden Confectionary Prod., Inc., 872 F.2d 215, 217 (7th Cir. 1989) ("An electric meter is not like a vending machine or a pay telephone, which you can jimmy to get out the coins. Tampering with an electric meter means altering the meter so that it records less use than the user is actually making of it. Meter tampering is necessarily a crime of deception; the goal is always to deceive the meter reader.").

[88] *See Meserve*, 271 F.3d at 328 (convictions for disorderly conduct and assault not admissible); Medrano v. City of Los Angeles, 973 F.2d 1499, 1507 (9th Cir. 1992) ("The misdemeanor convictions used for impeachment in this case were mainly drug use and shoplifting convictions. These convictions did not involve dishonesty or false statements.").

[89] *E.g.,* United States v. Mejia-Alaracon, 995 F.2d 982, 989–90 (10th Cir. 1993) ("crimes like burglary, robbery, and theft are not automatically admissible under Rule 609(a)(2)"); United States v. Grandmont, 680 F.2d 867, 871 (1st Cir. 1982) (robbery is not a crime of dishonesty absent a showing that the crime was committed by deceitful or fraudulent means); United States v. Glenn, 667 F.2d 1269 1273 (9th Cir. 1982) (crimes of violence, theft, or stealth do not involve dishonesty or false statement unless committed by fraudulent or deceitful means).

does not reflect deceitful conduct was committed in a deceitful manner. Some cases indicate that this is permissible.[90]

[G]   Ten-year Limit, FRE 609(b)

Evidence of a prior conviction that satisfies the criteria of Rule 609(a) is generally inadmissible if more than ten years has elapsed since the date of (1) conviction or (2) release from confinement, "whichever is the later date."[91] Remote convictions are not considered relevant in assessing a witness's credibility.[92]

Exception. An exception permits the use of convictions over 10-years old if (1) the proponent provides sufficient advance written notice to the adverse party and (2) the court determines, based upon "specific facts and circumstances," that the probative value of the evidence substantially outweighs its prejudicial effect.[93] Accordingly, unlike Rule 403, the balancing here is biased toward exclusion.[94] If the court decides to admit the conviction, findings indicating the "specific facts and circumstances" are required.[95]

Notice. The Conference Committee added the notice requirement:[96] "The Conferees anticipate that a written notice, in order to give the adversary

---

[90] *E.g.,* United States v. Payton, 159 F.3d 49, 56–57 (2d Cir. 1998) (courts "look beyond the elements of the offense to determine whether the conviction rested upon facts establishing dishonesty or false statement"); United States v. Mejia-Alaracon, 995 F.2d 982, 989–90 (10th Cir. 1993) ("[T]he trial court may look beyond the elements of an offense that is not considered a per se crime of dishonesty to determine whether the particular conviction rested upon facts establishing dishonesty or false statement.").

[91] Few courts have considered when the time period ends — date of indictment, date of trial, or date of testimony. *See* United States v. Daniel, 957 F.2d 162, 167 (5th Cir. 1002) ("within ten years of the date of Kunkle's testimony"). Since it is a witness's character at the time the witness testifies that is relevant, this position has merit.

[92] *See* H.R. Rep. No. 650, 93d Cong., 1st Sess. ("The Committee was of the view that after ten years following a person's release from confinement (or from the date of his conviction) the probative value of the conviction with respect to that person's credibility diminished to a point where it should no longer be admissible."), reprinted in 1973 U.S.C.C.A.N. 7075, 7085.

[93] The Senate Judiciary Committee added the exception to Rule 609(b) for the rare and exceptional situation: "Although convictions over ten years old generally do not have much probative value, there may be exceptional circumstances under which the conviction substantially bears on the credibility of the witness. . . . It is intended that convictions over 10 years old will be admitted very rarely and only in exceptional circumstances. The rules provide that the decision be supported by specific facts and circumstances thus requiring the court to make specific findings on the record as to the particular facts and circumstances it has considered in determining that the probative value of the conviction substantially outweighs its prejudicial impact." S. Rep. No. 1277, 93d Cong., 2d Sess., reprinted in 1974 U.S.C.C.A.N. 7051, 7061, 7062.

[94] *See* United States v. Bensisom, 172 F.3d 1121, 1125 (9th Cir. 1999) ("very rarely").

[95] *See id.* ("district court must make findings of specific facts and circumstances on the record."); United States v. Payton, 159 F.3d 49, 56–57 (2d Cir. 1998) ("A determination that the probative value of the conviction substantially outweighs its prejudicial effect must be made on-the-record and based on 'specific facts and circumstances.'").

[96] *See* United States v. Vgeri, 51 F.3d 876, 880 (9th Cir. 1995) ("Vgeri argues that he was unable to comply with the advance written notice requirement under Rule 609(b) because he

a fair opportunity to contest the use of the evidence, will ordinarily include such information as the date of the conviction, the jurisdiction, and the offense or statute involved."[97]

[H]   Pardon & Annulment, FRE 609(c)

If a pardon, annulment, or equivalent procedure is based on a finding of innocence, the impeachment value of the conviction is naught and Rule 609(c) so provides.[98] The rule goes beyond this, however, and also excludes where a pardon, annulment, certificate of rehabilitation, or other equivalent procedure is based on a "finding of rehabilitation," provided the witness has not been convicted of a subsequent crime punishable by death or imprisonment in excess of one year.[99]

[I]   Juvenile Adjudications, FRE 609(d)

Juvenile delinquency adjudications are generally not admissible to impeach.[100] Traditionally, juvenile records have been considered confidential.[101]

Rule 609 applies only to character impeachment. If the evidence is offered for some other purpose, the rule does not apply. For example, the Supreme

---

did not learn of Gogue's prior conviction until the Friday before trial. Gogue's testimony began on Wednesday, September 8, 1993. Vgeri had at least one full business day to provide the requisite written notice. It was not an abuse of discretion to deny Vgeri leave to cross-examine Gogue about the 18-year-old conviction.").

[97] H.R. Rep. No. 1597, 93d Cong., 2d Sess., reprinted in 1974 U.S.C.C.A.N. 7098, 7103. The Committee explained further: "In order to eliminate the possibility that the flexibility of this provision may impair the ability of a party-opponent to prepare for trial, the Conferees intend that the notice provision operate to avoid surprise."

[98] See Fed. R. Evid. 609 advisory committee's note ("A pardon or its equivalent granted solely for the purpose of restoring civil rights lost by virtue of a conviction has no relevance to an inquiry into character. If, however, the pardon or other proceeding is hinged upon a showing of rehabilitation the situation is otherwise. The result under the rule is to render the conviction inadmissible. The alternative of allowing in evidence both the conviction and the rehabilitation has not been adopted for reasons of policy, economy of time, and difficulties of evaluation. . . . Pardons based on innocence have the effect, of course, of nullifying the conviction ab initio.").

[99] See United States v. Swanson, 9 F.3d 1354, 1357 (8th Cir. 1993) ("The trial court properly held that it could not exclude evidence of the 1987 Incident based on Rule 609(c) because Swanson did not provide any evidence that the dismissal of the case was based on a finding of innocence or rehabilitation.").

[100] "Delinquency" refers to conduct that would be criminal if committed by an adult. It would not cover status offenses, variously called unruly, incorrigible, etc., that cover such conduct as habitual truancy or running away from home.

[101] See Smith v. Daily Mail Publ'g Co., 443 U.S. 97, 107 (1979) (concurring opinion) ("It is a hallmark of our juvenile justice system . . . that virtually from its inception at the end of the last century its proceedings have been conducted outside of the public's full gaze and the youths brought before our juvenile courts have been shielded from publicity. This insistence on confidentiality is born of a tender concern for the welfare of the child, to hide his youthful errors and 'bury them in the graveyard of the forgotten past'.").

Court found a confrontation violation in *Davis v. Alaska*,[102] where evidence of a prosecution witness's juvenile probationary status was excluded. *Davis* did not involve the use of a juvenile adjudication to show untruthful character; in *Davis*, the evidence was offered to show bias.

[J]   Pendency of Appeal, FRE 609(e)

The pendency of an appeal does not affect the admissibility of evidence of a prior conviction. Evidence that an appeal is pending, however, is admissible and may affect the weight accorded to the prior conviction.[103]

[K]   Methods of Proof

Typically, the prior conviction is elicited on cross-examination.[104] Generally, only the nature of the crime, time of conviction, and punishment are admissible[105] — aggravating circumstances are not. The rule does not bar counsel from bringing out the evidence on direct examination "for the purpose of lessening the import of these convictions upon the jury."[106] After *Ohler v. United States*,[107] which is discussed in next section, this tactic comes with a high price. A record of conviction may also be used.[108]

Explanation. Rule 609 does not specify whether the witness, once impeached with a prior conviction, may offer some type of explanatory comment. Offering an explanation is not without risks because some cases view the explanation as "opening the door" to rebuttal evidence, including cross-examination on the details of the crime.[109]

---

[102] 415 U.S. 308, 320 (1974) ("The State's policy interest in protecting the confidentiality of a juvenile offender's record cannot require yielding of so vital a constitutional right as the effective cross-examination for bias of an adverse witness."). *See supra* § 22.04[A] (bias).

[103] *See* Fed. R. Evid. 609 advisory committee's note ("The presumption of correctness which ought to attend judicial proceedings supports the position that pendency of an appeal does not preclude use of a conviction for impeachment. The pendency of an appeal is, however, a qualifying circumstance properly considerable.").

[104] The 1975 version of Rule 609(a) contained a phrase on methods of proof: prior convictions could be "elicited from [the witness] or established by public record during cross-examination." This was deleted by the 1990 amendment, but no change in practice was intended.

[105] *See* United States v. Burston, 159 F.3d 1328, 1336 (11th Cir. 1998) ("Rule 609(a)(1) requires a district court to admit evidence of the nature and number of a non-defendant witness' prior felony convictions."); United States v. Albers, 93 F.3d 1469, 1479 (10th Cir. 1996) ("well-established rule prohibiting examination into the underlying facts of prior convictions in recognition of the extremely high potential for unfair prejudice posed by such evidence").

[106] United States v. Bad Cob, 560 F.2d 877, 883 (8th Cir. 1977).

[107] 529 U.S. 753 (2000).

[108] Rule 803(21) recognizes a hearsay exception for judgments of previous convictions. A record of conviction also qualifies as a public record under Rule 803(8). This type of record is often self-authenticating, Rule 902, and certified copies are admissible under the best evidence rule. Fed. R. Evid. 1005 (public records).

[109] *E.g.,* United States v. Williams, 272 F.3d 845, 860 61 (7th Cir. 2001) ("Ordinarily, on cross-examination, the details of the prior convictions should not be exposed to the jury. However, where a defendant attempts to explain away the prior conviction during direct

[L] Motions in limine; Appeals

In *Luce v. United States*,[110] the Supreme Court ruled that "to raise and preserve for review the claim of improper impeachment with a prior conviction, a defendant must testify."[111] In *Ohler v. United States*,[112] the Court held that a defendant waived the right to appeal by introducing prior conviction evidence on direct-examination ("drawing the sting"). Both cases are discussed in chapter 6.

[M] Unconstitutional Convictions

In *Loper v. Beto*,[113] the Supreme Court held that the impeachment use of a conviction based upon a trial in which the defendant was denied the right to counsel violated due process. Once the validity of a prior conviction is raised, the prosecution has the burden of establishing that the right to counsel requirements were met.[114]

§ 22.09   Untruthful Character — Prior Acts: FRE 608(b)

Specific instances of conduct are admissible only if (1) the conduct reflects untruthful character, (2) its probative value outweighs the danger of unfair prejudice, (3) a good faith basis for the inquiry exists, and (4) the evidence is introduced on cross-examination (and not through extrinsic evidence — *e.g.*, other witnesses).

Truthfulness requirement. Only prior acts probative of untruthful character are admissible. Wigmore favored limiting admissibility to "only such misconduct as indicates a lack of veracity — fraud, forgery, perjury, and the like."[115] For example, a witness's falsification of an application for a marriage license, college admission, or unemployment benefits falls within this rule.[116] In contrast, drug use and assaults do not.[117]

---

examination by giving his own version of events, he has opened the door to impeachment by the prosecution on the details of the conviction.") (internal quotation marks omitted); United States v. Swanson, 9 F.3d 1354, 1357 (8th Cir. 1993) ("Although we acknowledge the general rule of impropriety of inquiry by the prosecutor into specific details surrounding prior convictions, [a] different situation is presented when an accused, on direct examination, attempts to explain away the effect of the conviction or to minimize his guilt. In such cases, the defendant may be cross-examined on any facts which are relevant to the direct examination.") (citation omitted).

[110] 469 U.S. 38 (1984).

[111] *Id.* at 43.

[112] 529 U.S. 753 (2000).

[113] 405 U.S. 473, 483 (1972) ("[T]he use of convictions constitutionally invalid under *Gideon v. Wainwright* to impeach a defendant's credibility deprives him of due process of law."). *See also* Nichols v. United States, 511 U.S. 738 (1994).

[114] *See* United States v. Lewis, 486 F.2d 217 (5th Cir. 1973).

[115] 3A Wigmore, Evidence § 983, at 840 (Chadbourn rev. 1970).

[116] *E.g.*, United States v. Chevalier, 1 F.3d 581, 584 (7th Cir. 1993) (bank fraud); United States v. 981 F.3d 799, 803 (5th Cir. 1993) (forgery).

[117] *E.g.*, United States v. Meserve, 271 F.3d 314, 328 (1st Cir. 2001) (witness's "status as

Rule 403. The admissibility of Rule 608(b) evidence is entrusted to the discretion of the trial judge per Rule 403.[118] The danger of unfair prejudice is acute if the witness is the criminal defendant.

Good faith basis-in-fact requirement. The party inquiring into specific instances of conduct must have a good faith basis-in-fact for asking the question. This is especially true in criminal cases where the unfair prejudice may be great. The Fourth Circuit, for example, found a due process violation where a prosecutor's questions concerning prior bad acts, offered to impeach the defendant, lacked a sufficient evidentiary foundation.[119]

Extrinsic evidence. Rule 608(b) explicitly prohibits extrinsic evidence in this context — for example, the testimony of other witnesses who had observed the conduct — even if the testifying witness denies the conduct on cross-examination.[120] This restriction is intended to avoid time-consuming and distracting mini-trials on purely credibility issues.

Other theories of admissibility. Rule 608(b) is not a bar to admissibility if the proffered evidence is relevant for some other purpose. In *United States v. Abel*,[121] the prosecution offered extrinsic evidence showing that the defendant and a defense witness were members of a secret prison gang, which had a creed requiring its members to lie for each other. The defendant argued, inter alia, that the evidence violated Rule 608(b) because it was not sufficiently probative of truthfulness and was introduced through extrinsic evidence. Without deciding the Rule 608(b) issue, the Supreme Court held the evidence admissible as impeachment by bias. According to the Court, "there is no rule of evidence which provides that testimony admissible for one purpose and inadmissible for another purpose is thereby rendered inadmissible; quite the contrary is the case."[122] A proposed amendment to Rule 608(b) is intended to clarify this point. It would substitute the phrase "character for untruthfulness" for the term "credibility" to eliminate any confusion on this score.[123]

---

a 'tough guy' and his reputation in the community for violence were completely irrelevant on the facts here to this jury's credibility determination"); United States v. Clemons, 32 F.3d 1504, 1511 (11st Cir. 1994) ("We do not agree that the question whether Smith ever used or sold drugs was probative of his credibility as a witness.").

[118] Fed. R. Evid. 608 advisory committee's note ("The overriding protection of Rule 403 requires that probative value not be outweighed by danger of unfair prejudice, confusion of issues, or misleading the jury, and that of Rule 611 bars harassment and undue embarrassment.").

[119] Watkins v. Foster, 570 F.2d 501 (4th Cir. 1978).

[120] *See* United States v. Abel, 469 U.S. 45, 55 (1984) ("If the answers received on cross-examination do not satisfy the examiner, it is said that the examiner is bound by or 'stuck' with the responses.").

[121] 469 U.S. 45, 56 (1984).

[122] *See supra* § 22.04 (bias).

[123] Proposed Fed. R. Evid. 608(b) advisory committee's note (2001) ("The amendment restores the Rule to its original intent, which was to impose an absolute bar on extrinsic evidence only if the sole purpose of offering the evidence was to prove the witness' character for veracity."), 201 F.R.D. 729 (2001). Prior to the amendment, the rule could have been read to prohibit extrinsic evidence on all issues of "credibility."

Self-incrimination privilege. The last sentence of Rule 608 recognizes a witness's right to claim the privilege against compelled self-incrimination "when examined with respect to matters which relate only to the witness's character for truthfulness."[124] Thus, a witness, including a criminal defendant, does not waive the constitutional privilege with respect to specific instances of conduct merely by taking the stand.[125]

Character witnesses. If a character witness testifies about the principal witness's character for truth and veracity pursuant to Rule 608(a), the character witness may be asked on cross-examination, subject to the trial court's discretion, about specific instances of conduct on the part of the principal witness.[126] The purpose of such inquiry is to test the character witness's qualifications to testify about the principal witness's character.[127] This type of cross-examination is comparable to that permitted by Rule 405(a) when a character witness testifies on the merits, except only specific instances relating to truthfulness are permissible here.

§ 22.10   Prior Inconsistent Statements: FRE 613

The underlying rationale for Rule 613 is self-contradiction.[128] Any prior statement, whether oral, taped, or written, and whether sworn or unsworn, may be used to impeach. It must, however, be the witness's statement, not a third party's statement.[129]

[A]   Hearsay Rule & Inconsistent Statements

At common law, prior inconsistent statements were admitted only for impeachment. The statement was offered to show the inconsistency between the witness's trial testimony and pretrial statements, rather than to show the truth of the assertions contained in the pretrial statement.[130]

---

[124] *See infra* § 45.05 (accused's privilege at trial).

[125] *See* 8 Wigmore, Evidence §§ 2275–77 (McNaughton rev. 1961).

[126] *See* Securities & Exch. Comm'n v. Peters, 978 F.2d 1162, 1169 (10th Cir. 1992) ("The district court noted, correctly, that a reputation character witness can be asked on cross-examination whether he has heard about a certain event.").

[127] *See supra* § 10.03[D] (specific instances: cross-examination).

[128] There is another impeachment method that involves contradiction ("specific contradiction"). It involves the testimony of one witness that conflicts with the testimony of another witness. *See infra* § 22.11 (specific contradiction).

[129] *See* United States v. Almonte, 956 F.2d 27, 29 (2d Cir. 1992) ("[I]n the absence of endorsement by the witness, a third party's notes of a witness's statement may not be admitted as a prior inconsistent statement unless they are a verbatim transcript of the witness's own words. The problem, in essence, is one of relevancy. If a third party's notes reflect only that note-taker's summary characterization of a witness's prior statement, then the notes are irrelevant as an impeaching prior inconsistent statement, and thus inadmissible.").

[130] The jury would be so instructed, although the efficacy of such an instruction may be doubted. *See* Fed. R. Evid. 105 (limited purpose instruction). However, the traditional view may result in a directed verdict if it is the only evidence linking a person with a crime. The prior inconsistent statement is not substantive evidence, and the judge does not consider credibility when ruling on such a motion.

The latter would violate the hearsay rule, which did not recognize an exception for inconsistent statements.[131]

In one important respect, the Federal Rules changed this. Under Rule 801(d)(1)(A), prior inconsistent statements taken under oath, subject to penalty of perjury, and made at certain proceedings are admitted as substantive evidence. In other words, there are two provisions on prior inconsistent statements: Rule 613 and Rule 801(d)(1)(A). The latter is considered in the hearsay materials.[132]

[B] Inconsistency Requirement

The prior statement must be inconsistent with the witness's trial testimony. The federal courts have adopted a liberal view of the inconsistency requirement.[133] A direct contradiction is not required. For example, in a traffic accident case, a witness's prior statement that the "boys were trying to beat the traffic" should be admitted to impeach trial testimony that the "boys crossed the street." Under this approach, the witness will have the opportunity to explain the inconsistency away and the jury, not the judge, determines credibility. A number of recurring situations are considered below:

Prior omission. If a witness's present testimony includes material facts that were omitted in the prior statement, the statement is inconsistent.[134] Example: Witness said, "I killed him," at time of arrest; at trial, "I killed him in self-defense."

Prior lack of knowledge. Prior statements that a witness had no knowledge about matters the witness is now testifying to are admissible under some circumstances.[135]

---

[131] Prior inconsistent statements that also qualified as admissions of a party-opponent were admissible as substantive evidence at common law. They still are under Rule 801(d)(2)(A).

[132] *See infra* § 32.02 (prior inconsistent statements).

[133] *See* United States v. Denetclaw, 96 F.3d 454, 458 (10th Cir. 1996) ("These statements could be understood as a denial of culpability as well as a denial that he inflicted the knife wounds on Hernandez and thus fair game for impeachment."); United States v. Gravely, 840 F.2d 1156, 1163 (4th Cir. 1988) ("The Federal Rules of Evidence, however, reject the view that the prior testimony must flatly contradict trial testimony. . . . It is enough if the 'proffered testimony, taken as a whole, either by what it says or by what it omits to say' affords some indication that the fact was different from the testimony of the witness whom it sought to contradict.").

[134] *See* United States v. Denetclaw, 96 F.3d 454, 458 (10th Cir. 1996) ("silence may qualify as a 'statement' in certain circumstances"); United States v. Strother, 49 F.3d 869, 874 (2d Cir. 1995) ("Under certain circumstances, a witness's prior silence regarding critical facts may constitute a prior inconsistent statement where 'failure to mention those matters . . . conflicts with that which is later recalled. Where the belatedly recollected facts merely augment that which was originally described, the prior silence is often simply too ambiguous to have any probative force. . . .' . . . It would have been 'natural' for Wollschleager to include Strother's request in her earlier statement.")(citations omitted).

[135] *See* United States v. Shoupe, 548 F.2d 636, 639 (6th Cir. 1977) ("Adkins credibility as a witness was also challenged by the defense. He was confronted with prior grand jury testimony in which he had stated unequivocally that he had no recollection of finding a ski

Current lack of memory. A witness's claim of a current lack of memory is more problematic. Witnesses often forget and such a memory lapse would not be an inconsistency. However, in some circumstances a claim of lack of memory is not credible.[136]

[C] Foundational Requirements

The two divisions of Rule 613 deal with different issues. Division (a) is concerned only with written statements. It provides that a prior written statement need not be shown to a witness as a prerequisite to an examination on that statement.[137] The rule provides, however, that the opposing counsel has a right to inspect the statement upon request,[138] a provision "designed to protect against unwarranted insinuations that a statement has been made when the fact is to the contrary."[139]

Rule 613(b) is the trickier provision. At common law, a witness must have been afforded an opportunity to explain or deny a prior inconsistent statement *before* extrinsic evidence of that statement was admissible. Typically, on cross-examination counsel would direct the witness's attention to the time when, the place where, and the person to whom the statement was made. This requirement is fairer to the witness and saves time because the other side can attempt to rehabilitate on redirect examination rather than recalling the witness later in the trial. Moreover, there may be no need to introduce extrinsic evidence if the witness acknowledges the inconsistency.

In contrast, Rule 613(b) does not require that the witness be afforded an opportunity to explain or deny *before* extrinsic evidence is introduced, so long as the witness is afforded such an opportunity *at some time* during the trial.[140] The federal drafters explained: "The traditional insistence that

---

mask included in the contents of the duffle bag and that his agreement with Willison called for him to receive a fee for the use of his apartment which differed from the sum which he mentioned at trial.").

[136] *See* United States v. Knox, 124 F.3d 1360, 1364 (10th Cir. 1997)("A well-settled body of case law holds that where a declarant's memory loss is contrived it will be taken as inconsistent with a prior statement for purposes of applying Rule 801(d)(1)(A)."); United States v. Grubbs, 834 F.2d 1277, 1282 (6th Cir. 1987) ("In essence, Causey argues that as Mrs. Jackson claimed only an inability to recall, the testimony of Agent Harrington was therefore not technically inconsistent with her statement. That contention is without merit. A trial judge has considerable discretion in determining whether testimony is inconsistent with prior statements, and inconsistencies can be found in changes.") (citations omitted).

[137] Thus, the rule abolishes the requirement imposed by Queen Caroline's Case, 129 Eng. Rep. 976 (1820). *See* Ladd, *Some Observations on Credibility: Impeachment of Witnesses*, 52 Cornell L. Q. 239, 246–47 (1967). *See also* Stern & Grosh, *A Visit With Queen Caroline: Her Trial and Its Rule*, 6 Capital U. L. Rev. 165 (1976).

[138] *See* United States v. Lawson, 683 F.2d 688, 694 (2d Cir. 1982) ("At least in the absence of a claim of privilege or confidentiality, Rule 613(a) does not allow for the exercise of discretion. It flatly commands disclosure of a document such as this to opposing counsel.").

[139] Fed. R. Evid. 613 advisory committee's note.

[140] *See* United States v. Hudson, 970 F.2d 948, 955 (1st Cir. 1992) (witness need only be available for recall to explain inconsistent statements). The word "prior" has been added before the phrase "opportunity to explain or deny" in some state rules to conform to the traditional practice. *See* Minn. R. Evid. 613(b); Ohio R. Evid. 613(B).

the attention of the witness be directed to the statement on cross-examination is relaxed in favor of simply providing the witness an opportunity to explain and the opposite party an opportunity to examine on the statement, with no specification of any particular time or sequence. Under this procedure, several collusive witnesses can be examined before disclosure of a joint prior inconsistent statement. Also, dangers of oversight are reduced."[141]

Thus, in federal practice a foundation need not be laid when the witness first testifies. However, some federal courts recognize a trial court's authority under Rule 611[142] to require a foundation.[143]

Exception. No foundation is required if the trial court finds that the "interests of justice" would be defeated by imposition of the foundational requirements. "In order to allow for such eventualities as the witness becoming unavailable by the time the statement is discovered, a measure of discretion is conferred upon the judge."[144]

[D]   Extrinsic Evidence ("collateral matters")

Even if a proper foundation had been laid on cross-examination, extrinsic evidence of a prior statement was admissible at common law *only* if it did not involve a "collateral matter." The collateral matter rule applied only to extrinsic evidence; it did not preclude inquiry on cross-examination so long as the examination was relevant to impeachment. The exact definition of what constituted a collateral matter was unclear.[145] Rule 403 should control.[146]

---

[141] Fed. R. Evid. 613 advisory committee's note (citations omitted).

[142] Fed. R. Evid. 611(a) ("The court shall exercise reasonable control over the mode and order of interrogating witnesses and presenting evidence. . . .").

[143] *See* United States v. Sutton, 41 F.3d 1257, 1260 (8th Cir. 1994) ("This testimony was not allowed because Mr. Smith was not given the opportunity to explain or deny having made a prior inconsistent statement while he was on the stand, which is normally the proper foundation for impeachment under Fed. R. Evid. 613(b). Mr. Sutton points out that the First Circuit has relaxed this requirement, requiring only that a witness be available to be recalled to explain inconsistent statements. However, this procedure is not mandatory, but is optional at the trial judge's discretion.") (citation omitted).

[144] Fed. R. Evid. 613 advisory committee's note.

[145] Extrinsic evidence was admissible when the subject matter of the statement was a material fact, and thus the statement was relevant substantively even in the absence of the contradiction. Extrinsic evidence was also admissible when the statement concerned a fact that could be proved by extrinsic evidence using other methods of impeachment, such as bias or evidence of sensory or mental defect. This was known as the "independently provable" rule. 3A Wigmore, Evidence § 1020 (Chadbourn rev. 1970); Attorney-General v. Hitchcock, 154 Eng. Rep. 38 (1847). However, some instances of apparently valid impeachment could not be explained by this rule. *E.g.,* Stephens v. People, 19 N.Y. 549, 572 (1859) (murder by poisoning with arsenic; defendant's witnesses testified that the arsenic was administered to rats in cellar where provisions kept; held proper for state to prove by another witness that no provisions were kept in cellar); Hartsfield v. Carolina Cas. Ins. Co., 451 P.2d 576 (Alaska 1969) (on issue whether insurance cancellation notice was sent to defendant by insurer where defendant denied receipt and also receipt of notice of cancellations of the insurance from two other sources; evidence of the mailing by the two latter sources held not collateral).

[146] *See supra* note 48.

[E] Statements in Opinion Form

Rule 701 governs the admissibility of lay opinion testimony. That provision adopts the modern view, which treats the opinion rule as a rule of preference as to the form of *trial* testimony. This view is inconsistent with the application of the opinion rule to extrajudicial statements. With an extrajudicial statement, counsel cannot ask the witness to be more specific. [147]

[F] Prior Inconsistent Conduct

Rule 613 does not govern impeachment by prior inconsistent conduct. [148] No federal rule prohibits this type of impeachment, however, and therefore such evidence is admissible for impeachment. Moreover, a party's inconsistent conduct may be introduced on the merits; admissions by the conduct of a party (sometimes known as "implied admissions") may be admissible substantively. [149]

[G] Impeachment by Silence

The constitutional issues concerning the use of an accused's silence are discussed in the next section. If there is no constitutional impediment, the relevance issue must be addressed. In *United States v. Hale*, [150] a robbery defendant was arrested and advised of his *Miranda* rights. When asked where he had obtained the $158 in cash that was seized from him, Hale did not respond. At trial, he testified that the money came from his wife. On cross-examination, the prosecutor asked whether Hale had informed the police of this when questioned shortly after his arrest. The Supreme Court did not decide the issue on constitutional grounds. Instead, the Court held that silence in these circumstances was, as a matter of federal evidence law, not inconsistent with a defendant's trial testimony and excluded the evidence.

---

[147] *See infra* § 23.02[E] (lay opinion rule).

[148] *See* Fed. R. Evid. 613 advisory committee's note ("Under principles of expression unius the rule does not apply to impeachment by evidence of prior inconsistent conduct.").

[149] *See supra* § 9.07 (adverse inferences).

[150] 422 U.S. 171, 177 (1975) ("At the time of arrest and during custodial interrogation, innocent and guilty alike — perhaps particularly the innocent — may find the situation so intimidating that they may choose to stand mute. A variety of reasons may influence that decision. In these often emotional and confusing circumstances, a suspect may not have heard or fully understood the question, or may have felt there was no need to reply. He may have maintained silence out of fear or unwillingness to incriminate another. Or the arrestee may simply react with silence in response to the hostile and perhaps unfamiliar atmosphere surrounding his detention. After *Miranda* warnings, his failure to offer an explanation during the custodial interrogation can as easily be taken to indicate reliance on the right to remain silent as to support an inference that the explanatory testimony was a later fabrication.") (citation omitted).

[H] Constitutional Issues

The Supreme Court has carved out an impeachment exception to the constitutionally derived exclusionary rule. In *Harris v. New York*,[151] the Court held that statements obtained in violation of the *Miranda* (Fifth Amendment) requirements may be used for impeachment. In *Michigan v. Harvey*,[152] the Court extended this exception to certain statements obtained in violation of the Sixth Amendment right to counsel. In contrast, involuntary (coercive) confessions cannot be used for impeachment.[153]

Similarly, the Court has permitted the impeachment use of evidence seized in violation of the Fourth Amendment's prohibition against unreasonable searches and seizures.[154] Although these statements may be used to impeach the accused, they cannot be used to impeach other defense witnesses.[155]

Impeachment by silence. In *Doyle v. Ohio*,[156] the Supreme Court held that the impeachment use of a defendant's silence after receiving *Miranda* warnings violated due process. According to the Court, "While it is true that the *Miranda* warnings contain no express assurance that silence will carry no penalty, such assurance is implicit to any person who receives the warnings. In such circumstances, it would be fundamentally unfair and a deprivation of due process to allow the arrested person's silence to be used to impeach an explanation subsequently offered at trial."[157] *Doyle* does not

---

[151] 401 U.S. 222, 225–26 (1971) ("Every criminal defendant is privileged to testify in his own defense, or to refuse to do so. But that privilege cannot be construed to include the right to commit perjury. Having voluntarily taken the stand, petitioner was under an obligation to speak truthfully and accurately, and the prosecution here did no more than utilize the traditional truth-testing devices of the adversary process. The shield provided by *Miranda* cannot be perverted into a license to use perjury by way of a defense, free from the risk of confrontation with prior inconsistent utterances."). *See also* Oregon v. Hass, 420 U.S. 714 (1975).

[152] 494 U.S. 344 (1990).

[153] Mincey v. Arizona, 437 U.S. 385 (1978). After a gunfight in which a police officer died, Mincey was taken to a hospital for the treatment of gunshot wounds. He was treated in the emergency room and then sent to the intensive care unit, where he was subsequently interrogated by the police. At trial, statements that he made during this interrogation were used to impeach him. The Supreme Court ruled that the statements were involuntary and that "due process of law requires that statements obtained as these were cannot be used in any way against a defendant at his trial." *Id.* at 402.

[154] United States v. Havens, 446 U.S. 620 (1980); Walder v. United States, 347 U.S. 62 (1954).

[155] James v. Illinois, 493 U.S. 307 (1990).

[156] 426 U.S. 610 (1976).

[157] *Id.* at 618. In Wainwright v. Greenfield, 474 U.S. 284 (1986), the prosecutor used the defendant's post-*Miranda* warnings silence as substantive evidence of the defendant's sanity. The Court reversed: "The point of the *Doyle* holding is that it is fundamentally unfair to promise an arrested person that his silence will not be used against him and thereafter to breach that promise by using the silence to impeach his trial testimony. It is equally unfair to breach that promise by using silence to overcome a defendant's plea of insanity." *Id.* at 292.

apply if the defendant decides to make a statement *after* receiving *Miranda* warnings. [158]

The Court clarified the limits of *Doyle* in subsequent cases. In *Jenkins v. Anderson*, [159] the Court held that a defendant's pre-arrest silence is admissible for impeachment purposes. In the Court's view, "no governmental action induced petitioner to remain silent before arrest. The failure to speak occurred before the petitioner was taken into custody and given *Miranda* warnings. Consequently, the fundamental unfairness present in *Doyle* is not present in this case."[160]

Doyle, which governs post-*Miranda* silence, and *Jenkins*, which governs pre-arrest silence, left one issue undecided. *Miranda* requires warnings only if there is "custodial interrogation." An arrest satisfies the custody requirement, but if there is no interrogation, warnings are not required. Consequently, a suspect could be arrested, remain silent, and never receive warnings. In *Fletcher v. Weir*, [161] the Court held that pre-*Miranda* silence could be used to impeach: "In the absence of the sort of affirmative assurances embodied in the *Miranda* warnings, we do not believe that it violates due process of law for a State to permit cross-examination as to postarrest silence when a defendant chooses to take the stand."[162]

§ 22.11 Specific Contradiction

Although there is no rule on the subject, the Federal Rules permit impeachment by specific contradiction. [163] For example, witness A may testify that he saw the defendant shoot the victim, but witness B, who was also present, may testify that she saw a different person shoot the victim. In this example, witness B's testimony, as an eyewitness, would be

---

[158] Anderson v. Charles, 447 U.S. 404, 408 (1980) ("*Doyle* does not apply to cross-examination that merely inquires into prior inconsistent statements. Such questioning makes no unfair use of silence because a defendant who voluntarily speaks after receiving Miranda warnings has not been induced to remain silent. As to the subject matter of his statements, the defendant has not remained silent at all.").

[159] 447 U.S. 231 (1980).

[160] *Id.* at 240.

[161] 455 U.S. 603 (1982). *See* Snyder, *A Due Process Analysis of the Impeachment Use of Silence in Criminal Trials*, 29 Wm. & Mary L. Rev. 285 (1988). *See infra* § 32.07[B] (adoptive admissions by silence).

[162] 455 U.S. at 607.

[163] *See* United States v. Castillo, 181 F.3d 1129, 1133 (9th Cir. 1999) ("Castillo's expansive and unequivocal denial of involvement with drugs on direct examination warranted the district court's decision to admit extrinsic evidence of the 1997 cocaine arrest as impeachment by contradiction."); United States v. Chu, 5 F.3d 1244, 1249 (9th Cir. 1993) (recognizing the distinction between evidence governed by Rule 608(b) and evidence offered to impeach by contradiction); United States v. Lopez, 979 F.2d 1024, 1034 (5th Cir. 1992) ("Extrinsic evidence is material, not collateral, if it contradicts 'any part of the witness's account of the background and circumstances of a material transaction, which as a matter of human experience he would not have been mistaken about if his story were true.'") (citations omitted).

admissible even in the absence of the incidental impeachment effect on the testimony of witness A.[164]

Extrinsic evidence. The problem arises when the *only* purpose of B's testimony is to contradict A's testimony, especially if the contradiction is on a minor point. Because we all make mistakes, the impeachment value is minimal. This situation gave rise to the so-called "collateral matters" rule. The common law rule did not prohibit a party from cross-examining on a "collateral matter." It prohibited only the introduction of extrinsic evidence on the issue. The policy underlying this rule is to avoid the dangers of surprise, jury confusion and wasted time.

The same issue arose with prior inconsistent statements,[165] and the same result should apply here — Rule 403 should govern.[166]

§ 22.12 Learned Treatise

At common law, impeachment by means of a learned treatise was permitted when an expert testified. Unlike the common law, Rule 803(18) recognizes a hearsay exception for this type of impeachment.[167]

§ 22.13 Religious Belief: FRE 610

Rule 610 provides that the "nature" of a witness's religious beliefs or opinions is not admissible either to *impeach* or *support* the witness's credibility. It is based on several premises: that religious beliefs or lack of such beliefs are simply not relevant to the issue of credibility, that such evidence may present issues of unfair prejudice and consumption of time, and that inquiry into religious beliefs infringes upon a witness's right to freedom of religion and privacy.

Rule 610 does not prohibit the introduction of evidence of religious beliefs under a different theory of impeachment — for example, by showing bias.[168]

§ 22.14 Rehabilitation

As a general rule, rehabilitation evidence must directly answer the impeachment evidence.

---

[164] There are two distinct methods of impeachment by contradiction. Self-contradiction involves the use of a witness's own statements to contradict that witness's present testimony. Rule 613 governs this method — prior inconsistent statements. *See supra* § 22.10.

[165] *See supra* § 22.10[D].

[166] *See supra* note 48.

[167] *See infra* § 33.16 (learned treatise).

[168] Fed. R. Evid. 610 advisory committee's note ("While the rule forecloses inquiry into the religious beliefs or opinions of a witness for the purpose of showing that his character for truthfulness is affected by their nature, an inquiry for the purpose of showing interest or bias because of them is not within the prohibition. Thus disclosure of affiliation with a church which is a party to the litigation would be allowable under the rule.").

[A]   Untruthful Character: FRE 608(a)(2)

Once a witness's character for truthfulness has been attacked, opinion and reputation evidence showing that the witness has a good character for truthfulness is admissible. The principal issue in applying this rule is determining what types of impeachment constitute attacks on character — thus, triggering the right to rehabilitate by evidence of truthful character. If the principal witness's character has been attacked under (1) Rule 608(a) (opinion or reputation); (2) Rule 608(b) (specific instances); or (3) Rule 609 (prior convictions), rebuttal evidence of truthful character is admissible. [169]

[B]   Prior Consistent Statements

Prior consistent statements do not rehabilitate impeachment by prior inconsistent statements because the inconsistency remains. However, in some circumstances a consistent statement may rehabilitate. Rule 801(d)(1)(B) permits the admission of consistent statements "to rebut an express or implied charge against the declarant of recent fabrication or improper influence or motive." The rule makes these consistent statements substantive evidence, rather than evidence merely affecting credibility. Some courts hold that statements not admissible under Rule 801 are nevertheless admissible for impeachment. [170]

§ 22.15   Key Points

Credibility may be viewed in three stages: (1) bolstering, (2) impeachment, and (3) rehabilitation. *Impeachment* involves attempts to diminish or attack a witness's credibility. There are also rules regulating attempts to support credibility. For example, as a general matter, a witness's credibility may not *be bolstered* (supported) prior to impeachment. Moreover, under certain circumstances a witness's credibility may be *rehabilitated* (supported) after impeachment. Thus, bolstering and rehabilitation both involve efforts to support credibility; the difference is one of timing.

Bolstering

Generally, a witness's credibility may not be bolstered or supported with evidence relevant *only* for that purpose, until after impeachment. Consumption of time and confusion of issues are the principal reasons for this rule. There are two prominent examples: (1) a witness's good character for truthfulness is not admissible in the absence of an attack on character. (2) Prior consistent statements are inadmissible before a witness's credibility is attacked.

---

[169] Fed. R. Evid. 608 advisory committee's note ("Opinion or reputation that the witness is untruthful specifically qualifies as an attack under the rule, and evidence of misconduct, including conviction of crime, and of corruption also fall within this category. Evidence of bias or interest does not.").

[170] *E.g., infra* § 32.03[B].

Pretrial identifications (*e.g.*, lineups), fresh complaints in rape cases, and cooperation agreements are common exceptions to the bolstering prohibition.

Voucher Rule

At common law, a party could not impeach its own witnesses. This was known as the *voucher rule* and was based on the theory that when a party produces a witness that party vouches for the witness's veracity —*i.e.*, a party cannot hold the witness out as worthy of belief when the testimony is favorable and impeach credibility when it is adverse. Rule 607 abolishes the "voucher rule." The rationale for the rule was never persuasive because the firsthand knowledge rule requires percipient witnesses, and, often the parties have no choice concerning which witnesses to call.

The abolition of the voucher rule created one problem, which concerns impeachment with prior inconsistent statements: Rule 607 could be employed to circumvent the hearsay rule. Some federal courts address this problem by focusing on whether the proffer is a subterfuge to get hearsay before the jury, while other courts apply Rule 403.

Methods of Impeachment

Numerous factors may be considered in evaluating credibility, including a witness's demeanor while testifying. There are, however, five principal methods of impeachment: (1) bias or interest, (2) sensory or mental defects, (3) character for untruthfulness, which includes impeachment by reputation, opinion, prior convictions, and prior untruthful acts; (4) specific contradiction, and (5) prior inconsistent statements (self-contradiction).[171]

Bias

A witness's bias is always relevant for impeachment. Although there is *no rule on bias* in the Federal Rules, in *United States v. Abel*[172] the Supreme Court held that impeachment of a witness for bias was proper. Most jurisdictions require that a foundation be laid on cross-examination before extrinsic evidence of bias is admissible; some courts have indicated that this is the federal position. At common law, bias was not considered a "collateral matter," and thus extrinsic evidence of bias was always admissible. However, a recent Advisory Committee Note (dealing with another type of impeachment) indicates that Rule 403 should control.

---

[171] Moreover, Rule 610 prohibits the impeachment use of a witness's religious beliefs, and a special impeachment rule on learned treatises applies to experts. Fed. R. Evid. 803(18).

[172] 469 U.S. 45, 51 (1984) ("[T]he lesson to be drawn is that it is permissible to impeach a witness by showing his bias under the Federal Rules of Evidence just as it was permissible to do so before their adoption.").

Sensory & Mental Defects

There is no federal rule on this type of impeachment, but there are numerous cases. Any sensory or mental defect that might affect a witness's capacity to observe, recall, or relate is admissible to impeach. As for extrinsic evidence (*i.e.*, the testimony of other witnesses), there is probably no hard and fast rule. Sensory and mental defects often can be effectively disclosed through cross-examination, in which case the admissibility of extrinsic evidence should be regulated by the trial court pursuant to Rule 403.

Untruthful Character: Overview

Recall from chapter 10 that character evidence is generally inadmissible under Rule 404(a). However, there are some exceptions concerning the accused and victims. A third exception deals with credibility. Character is used circumstantially; a person with an untruthful character is more likely to testify untruthfully than a person with a good character for truthfulness.

There are three possibilities for methods of proof: (1) reputation evidence, (2) opinion evidence, and (3) specific acts. Rule 608(a) sanctions the use of reputation and opinion, which is consistent with the treatment of character on the merits under Rule 405(a). Specific acts are treated differently in this context. Rule 609 permits impeachment with prior convictions under some conditions. Rule 608(b) allows impeachment by specific acts that have not resulted in a conviction — under limited circumstances.

Reputation & Opinion

Rule 608(a) permits the use of opinion and reputation evidence to show a witness's untruthful character, including that of the accused. Before reputation evidence is permitted, a foundation must be laid showing that the character witness is acquainted with the principal witness's reputation in the community (*i.e.*, where the principal witness lives, works, or goes to school). A similar foundation is required before a witness may express an opinion. This latter inquiry, however, focuses on the character witness's personal relationship with the principal witness rather than on community contacts.

Prior Convictions [173]

Under Rule 609(a)(1), prior convictions involving crimes punishable by death or imprisonment in excess of one year *may* be admissible against a criminal defendant. [174] Admissibility is not automatic. Only if the probative value of the prior conviction outweighs the unfair prejudice to the defendant is the evidence admissible. A number of factors should influence the trial court's admissibility determination: (1) nature of the prior crime, (2) age of the prior conviction (remoteness); (3) similarity between the prior and charged offenses, (4) need for accused's testimony, and (5) centrality of credibility at trial.

Other witnesses. Under Rule 609(a)(1), prior "felony" convictions of witnesses other than an accused is permitted — witnesses in civil cases and prosecution and other defense witnesses in criminal cases. Admissibility is not automatic; it is subject to the trial court's discretion under Rule 403. The balancing in this context differs from that applicable to the accused. Admissibility is more difficult in the latter situation because the term "substantially" has been omitted from the equation.

Crimes of dishonesty & false statement ("crimen falsi"). Under Rule 609(a)(2), prior convictions involving crimes of dishonesty or false statement are *automatically* admissible. The trial court has no discretion to exclude these convictions. The principal problem in applying this rule is determining what crimes involve "dishonesty" or "false statement." The Conference Report indicated that these terms included *only* crimes such as perjury, subornation of perjury, false statement, criminal fraud, embezzlement, false pretenses, or "any other offense in the nature of *crimen falsi*, the commission of which involves some element of deceit, untruthfulness, or falsification bearing on the accused's propensity to testify truthfully." Although theft offenses are typically thought to involve "dishonesty," several federal courts have ruled them inadmissible. Another issue concerns whether the court may delve behind the record to determine whether an offense that on its face does not reflect deceitful conduct was committed in a deceitful manner. Some cases indicate that this is permissible.

Ten-year limit, Rule 609(b). Evidence of a prior conviction that satisfies the criteria of Rule 609(a) is generally inadmissible if more than ten years

---

[173] *Convictions: other theories of admissibility.* If prior conviction evidence is offered under an impeachment theory other than untruthful character or for reasons other than impeachment, Rule 609 does not apply. For example, evidence of a conviction may be admissible to show that a witness has received or expects to receive favorable treatment from the prosecution (*i.e.*, bias). Similarly, evidence may be admissible under Rule 404(b) ("other acts") as proof of motive, opportunity, intent, and so forth. Also, if an accused testifies that he has "never committed a crime in my life," a prior conviction may be offered in rebuttal. Finally, sometimes a prior conviction is *an element* of a subsequently tried offense, in which case the prior conviction must be proved. Here, it is substantive, not impeachment, evidence.

[174] Note that the label "felony" is technically not correct and is used here only as a convenient shorthand label. State as well as federal convictions fall within the rule. The *authorized maximum punishment*, rather than the actual punishment imposed, is determinative.

has elapsed since the date of (1) conviction or (2) release from confinement, "whichever is the later date."

Prior Acts

Under Rule 608(b), specific instances of conduct are admissible only if (1) the conduct reflects untruthful character, (2) its probative value outweighs the danger of unfair prejudice, (3) a good faith basis for the inquiry exists, and (4) the evidence is introduced on cross-examination (and not through extrinsic evidence — *e.g.*, other witnesses).

Prior Inconsistent Statements

In one important respect, the Federal Rules change the common law. Under Rule 801(d)(1)(A), prior inconsistent statements taken under oath, subject to penalty of perjury, and made at certain proceedings are admitted as substantive evidence — *i.e.*, such statements are not hearsay. In other words, there are two provisions on prior inconsistent statements: Rule 613 and Rule 801(d)(1)(A).

Inconsistency. The federal courts have adopted a liberal view of the inconsistency requirement.

Foundation. Rule 613(b) does not require that the witness be afforded an opportunity to explain or deny *before* extrinsic evidence is introduced, so long as the witness is afforded such an opportunity *at some time* during the trial. However, some federal courts recognize a trial court's authority under Rule 611 to require the traditional foundation.

Extrinsic Evidence; "collateral matters." Even if a proper foundation had been laid on cross-examination, extrinsic evidence of a prior statement was admissible at common law *only* if it did not involve a "collateral matter." The exact definition of what constituted a collateral matter was unclear. Rule 403 should control.

Specific Contradiction

Although there is no rule on the subject, the Federal Rules permit impeachment by specific contradiction. A problem arises when the *only* purpose of witness B's testimony is to contradict A's testimony, especially if the contradiction is on a minor point. Because we all make mistakes, the impeachment value is minimal. This situation gave rise to the so-called "collateral matters" rule. The same issue arose with prior inconsistent statements (*see supra*), and the same result should apply here — leave the issue to Rule 403.

Methods of Impeachment Chart

	Cross-examination	Extrinsic evidence
A. Bias/interest	yes	yes with foundation (majority common law rule); FRE 403 now controls
B. Sensory/mental capacity	yes	yes (common law); FRE 403 now controls
C. Untruthful character		
— reputation, FRE 608(a)	not applicable	yes, character witness
— opinion, FRE 608(a)	not applicable	yes, character witness
— prior conviction, FRE 609	yes	yes, record of conviction
— prior acts, FRE 608(b)	yes	no
D. Prior inconsistent statement	yes	sometimes with foundation (common law: if not "collateral"); FRE 613(b) no foundation & FRE 403 controls extrinsic evidence
E. Specific contradiction	not applicable	sometimes (common law: if not "collateral"); FRE 403 now controls

Chapter 23

LAY WITNESSES: FRE 602 & 701

§ 23.01 Introduction

There are two rules relating to lay witnesses that do not apply to expert witnesses: (1) the firsthand knowledge rule and (2) the opinion rule.

§ 23.02 Firsthand Knowledge Rule: FRE 602

Federal Rule 602 requires that a witness have personal knowledge of the subject about which the witness testifies.[1] Firsthand knowledge is not limited to a witness's visual perception; it extends to all senses (*e.g.*, what the witness heard or smelled). Moreover, it is the witness's knowledge at the time of trial, not necessarily at the time of the event, that is determinative;[2] a witness could have gained new personal knowledge after an accident or crime.

Uncertainty. A witness's expression of uncertainty, such as "I think," "I believe," or "I'm not positive," is not grounds for exclusion so long as the witness "had an opportunity of personal observation and did get some impressions from this observation."[3] Accordingly, expressions of uncertainty affect the weight, not the admissibility, of the evidence.

Establishing firsthand knowledge. Typically, proof of firsthand knowledge is supplied by the witness. Rule 602 provides that such knowledge "may,

---

[1] *See* Kemp v. Balboa, 23 F.3d 211, 212 (8th Cir. 1994) ("C. Vicki Maness, a licensed practical nurse at the Center, testified that Kemp failed to pick up his medication from the prison infirmary on seven separate occasions. . . . As her testimony on cross examination brought out, however, she had no personal knowledge of these facts, since she was not on duty on the days on which she stated Kemp failed to pick up his medication. Her testimony was based not upon her personal knowledge of the facts about which she testified, but solely upon what she had read in the medical records prepared by others.").

[2] *See* Cleveland Terminal & Valley R.R. v. Marsh, 58 N.E. 821, 822 (Ohio 1900); Strickland Transp. Co. v. Ingram, 403 S.W.2d 192, 195 (Tex. App. 1966) ("A witness may testify in accordance with his knowledge at the time his testimony is offered; he is not restricted to his knowledge at the time the event occurred.").

[3] 2 Wigmore, Evidence § 658, at 894 (Chadbourn rev. 1979). *See also* M.B.A.F.B. Fed Credit Union v. Cumis Ins. Soc., 681 F.2d 930, 932 (4th Cir. 1982) ("It is true that Stowe did not state definitively that he personally discussed the purchase price with Montgomery — only that it was possible — and that much of his testimony in this respect was to the effect that he thought his attorney had told Montgomery. Rule 602, however, does not require that the witness' knowledge be positive or rise to the level of absolute certainty.").

but need not, consist of the witness's own testimony."[4] It also may be inferred from the testimony.[5]

[A]　Standard of Proof: Prima Facie

Frequently, it is difficult to distinguish between what a witness knows and what a witness thinks she knows. Suppose, for instance, that a witness testifies about observing an event a quarter-mile away through her rearview mirror. This is something better decided by the jury rather than the judge, because it comes close to credibility, a classic jury issue. Consequently, Rule 602 alters the judge's traditional function in applying the firsthand knowledge rule. The trial judge does not decide whether or not a witness has firsthand knowledge by a preponderance of evidence (the usual standard), but only whether sufficient evidence to support a finding of firsthand knowledge has been introduced, i.e., a *prima facie* standard. If sufficient evidence has been adduced, the witness may testify, and the jury decides whether or not the witness had firsthand knowledge.[6]

[B]　Relationship to Hearsay Rule

In many cases, the firsthand knowledge rule and the hearsay rule overlap. For example, if a witness's testimony that the defendant committed a bank robbery is based only on the statement of another person, both rules are violated. The witness has no personal knowledge of the robbery and is merely repeating the out-of-court declarant's statement.[7] The form of the testimony typically determines the proper objection. If the witness indicates that the basis of the testimony is the declarant's statement, the hearsay objection is proper. If, on the other hand, it appears that the witness was not present at the robbery, the lack of personal knowledge objection is proper.[8]

---

[4] *See* Fed. R. Evid. 602 advisory committee's note ("These foundation requirements may, of course, be furnished by the testimony of the witness himself; hence personal knowledge is not an absolute but may consist of what the witness thinks he knows from personal perception.").

[5] *See* United States v. Doe, 960 F.2d 221, 223 (1st Cir. 1992) ("Doe claims that the district court should have excluded the sports shop owner's testimony that he 'knows' Taurus pistols are 'manufactured in Brazil,' on the ground that the witness did not have 'personal knowledge' of that fact. Evidence proving personal knowledge may, however, 'consist of the witness' own testimony,' and that knowledge includes inferences and opinions, so long as they are grounded in personal observation and experience. . . . A reasonable trier of fact could believe that the sports shop owner had firsthand knowledge from which he could infer that the pistol was made outside of Massachusetts, indeed in Brazil, particularly since his testimony to this effect was unchallenged.") (citations omitted).

[6] Rule 602 is a specialized application of the conditional relevancy principle of Rule 104(b). By treating the firsthand knowledge rule as an aspect of conditional relevancy, the rule enlarges the jury's role. This approach poses little danger because if the jury finds that the witness did not possess firsthand knowledge, the jury will disregard the testimony. *See supra* § 7.03 (conditional relevancy).

[7] *See* Fed. R. Evid. 801 (hearsay defined).

[8] *See supra* note 1.

A different result is reached when the witness has personal knowledge of an admissible hearsay statement. For example, assume that the out-of-court *declarant* in the robbery example is the defendant. In this situation, the out-of-court statement is an admission of a party-opponent and is exempted from the hearsay rule.[9] Although the witness has no personal knowledge of the robbery, the witness does have personal knowledge that the statement was made, and the testimony concerning the statement is admissible.[10]

§ 23.03   Opinion Rule: FRE 701

[A]   Overview

What is the problem the opinion rule is intended to solve? Frequently, the opinion rule is difficult to understand, at least initially, because the terms "opinion, inference, and conclusion" can be used in a variety of ways in common parlance. In contrast, Rule 701 has a very narrow focus. We will use three hypotheticals to tease out the issue.

Hypothetical I: Firsthand knowledge. Suppose "that as the witness was leaving a room in which A, B and others remained, he saw A advance toward B with clenched fist, and on his return to the room later, he saw B wiping blood from his nose and lips and A with skinned knuckles[.] [H]is statement that A struck B would be the result of a conscious deduction from what he saw to what had happened."[11] What evidence rule governs this type of "conscious deduction," opinion, inference, or conclusion? Since the witness was out of the room at the time of the blow, the witness has no personal knowledge and Rule 602 governs.[12] There is no need to resort to Rule 701, although that rule also codifies the firsthand knowledge requirement by specifying that the opinion be "rationally based on the perception of the witness."

Hypothetical II: Expression of uncertainty. Suppose two bank customers, *both with firsthand knowledge*, testify as prosecution witnesses on the issue of identity in a bank robbery case as follows:

Witness A: "The defendant was the robber."

Witness B: "In my opinion, I believe that the defendant was the robber."

The difference between A and B's testimony may indicate that B did not get as good a look at the robber, but the difference may also be the result

---

[9] Fed. R. Evid. 801(d)(2)(A).

[10] Fed. R. Evid. 602 advisory committee's note ("Rule 602 does not govern the situation of a witness who testifies to a hearsay statement as such, if he has personal knowledge of the making of the statement. Rules 801 and 805 would be applicable. This rule would, however, prevent him from testifying to the subject matter of the hearsay statement, as he has no personal knowledge of it.").

[11] Morgan, Basic Problems of Evidence 216 (1962).

[12] The witness could testify about what she saw up until she left the room, and she could testify about what she saw upon returning.

of how two different people express themselves. Witness B may simply be more careful in her mode of expression. The phrase, "In my opinion, I believe" is implicit in Witness A's testimony.[13] In any event, assuming firsthand knowledge, a witness need not be positive.[14] Again, Rule 701 is not implicated.

Hypothetical III: The real issue. The following hypothetical illustrates the problem Rule 701 addresses. Assume a witness observes a bank robbery and is called by the defense in support of an insanity defense. The witness could testify in one of the following three ways:

(1) "The defendant acted like he was insane during the robbery."

(2) "The defendant acted in a bizarre manner and spoke incoherently."

(3) "The defendant was running around naked and screaming that he was the Governor of Arkansas."

Which statement is preferable? Number (1) is the most abstract and has an additional problem of containing a word (insanity) that has a specific legal meaning. Number (2) falls between (1) and (3). As a policy matter, we want the witness's primary sensory impressions rather than opinions, conclusions, or inferences drawn from those opinions. If the witness can give us (3), then (1) and (2) are superfluous.[15]

If opposing counsel objects to (1) or (2) and the judge strikes those statements, the offering party may rephrase the question and ask the witness to tell the jury specifically what the witness saw — *i.e.*, number (3). Accordingly, Rule 701 is not a rule of exclusion but a *rule of preference*; we strike (1) and (2) because we prefer (3). Of course, a good trial attorney will want to elicit (3) because it is the more convincing version. Moreover, cross-examination is available if either (1) or (2) is admitted. These are further reasons not to apply the opinion rule too strictly.

Is there a number (4)? Sometimes the witness is being as specific as possible, either (a) because the witness is not articulate or (b) because it is difficult for any of us to break down certain opinions without losing their meaning (*e.g.*, "The wood was rotten." or "The floor was slippery.").

---

[13] *See* Ladd, *Expert and Other Opinion Testimony*, 40 Minn. L. Rev. 437, 440 (1956) ("Not infrequently such precautionary statements may strengthen the testimony because they indicate that the witness does not want to overstate the facts. On the other hand, such statements may indicate that his recollection is poor which would weaken the testimony but not exclude it. Only when it appears that the witness has not personally perceived the matter about which he testifies will the testimony be excluded.").

[14] *E.g.,* United States v. Barker, 735 F.2d 1280, 1283 (11th Cir. 1984) (defendant's handwriting "similar to" handwriting on check); United States v. Freeman, 619 F.2d 1112, 1120 (5th Cir. 1980) ("Two witnesses testified about their 'impression' and 'understanding' of appellants' relationship to each other and to the different companies."); United States v. Young Buffalo, 591 F.2d 506, 513 (9th Cir. 1977) (witnesses' identification of defendant from bank robbery photographs was "somewhat equivocal").

[15] *See* 7 Wigmore, Evidence § 1918 (Chadbourn rev. 1978).

[B]   Common Law "Fact-Opinion" Formulation

At common law, lay witnesses could testify to *facts* and not opinions, inferences, or conclusions. The courts, however, recognized an exception, sometimes known as the "short-hand rendition" rule or "collective facts" exception.[16] This exception permitted opinions concerning the identity of persons, things, and handwriting; size, color, and weight of objects; times and distance; mental state or condition of another; insanity and intoxication; affection of one person for another; physical condition of another such as health or sickness; and values of property.[17]

Criticism. Despite its wide acceptance, the common law rule was sharply attacked.[18] Wigmore advocated its abolition.[19] There were several lines of criticism. First, the application of the traditional rule turned on an illusory fact-opinion categorization.[20] For example, a witness who testifies that a defendant had "slurred speech" and "staggered" when he walked is using inferences as much as the witness who testifies that the defendant was "intoxicated"; the difference is one of degree.

Second, witnesses frequently use inferences while testifying, since it is the natural way to tell a story. In some cases, it is the only way. "Opinions are constantly given. A case can hardly be tried without them. Their

---

[16] *See* United States v. Freeman, 514 F.2d 1184, 1191 (10th Cir. 1975) (opinion admissible as "a shorthand rendition of the witness's knowledge of the total situation and the collective facts"); Stone v. United States, 385 F.2d 713, 716 (10th Cir. 1967) ("Lay witnesses are frequently permitted to use so-called 'shorthand' descriptions, in reality opinions, in presenting to the court their impressions of what transpired."). The exception is sometimes used under the Federal Rules. *See* United States v. Thompson, 708 F.2d 1294, 1298 (8th Cir. 1983) (opinion that accused was involved in the conspiracy was admissible as a "shorthand rendition").

[17] *See* Ladd, *Expert Testimony*, 5 Vand. L. Rev. 414, 417 (1952) ("The appearance of persons or things, identity, the manner of conduct, competency of a person, feeling, degrees of light or darkness, sound, size, weight, distance and an endless number of things that cannot be described factually in words apart from inferences.").

[18] *See* Central R.R. v. Monahan, 11 F.2d 212, 214 (2d Cir. 1926) (L. Hand, J.) ("[T]he exclusion of opinion evidence has been carried beyond reason in this country, and . . . it would be a large advance if courts were to admit it with freedom. . . . It is a good rule as nearly as one can, to reproduce the scene as it was, and so to correct the personal equations of the witnesses. But one must be careful not to miss the forest for the trees, as generally happens, unless much latitude is allowed.").

[19] 7 Wigmore, Evidence § 1929, at 40 (Chadbourn rev. 1978). *See also id.* at 39 ("The opinion rule day by day exhibits its unpractical subtlety and its useless refinement to logic. Under this rule we accomplish little by enforcing it, and we should do no harm if we dispensed with it. We should do no harm, because, even when the final opinion or inference is admitted, the inference amounts in force usually to nothing unless it appears to be solidly based on satisfactory data, the existence and quality of which we can always bring out, if desirable, on cross-examination.").

[20] *See* Fed. R. Evid. 701 advisory committee's note ("The practical impossibility of determining by rule what is a 'fact,' demonstrated by a century of litigation of the question of what is a fact for purposes of pleading under the Field Code, extends into evidence also."). In a related context (the admissibility of public records containing factual findings under Rule 803(8)(C)), the Supreme Court referred to the "arbitrary distinction between 'fact' and 'opinion' " and an "inevitably arbitrary line between the various shades of fact/opinion." Beech Aircraft Corp. v. Rainey, 488 U.S. 153, 167, 169 (1988).

number is so vast, and their use so habitual, that they are not noticed as opinions distinguished from other evidence."[21] Consequently, a strict application of the opinion rule would stultify the presentation of testimony, "making it impossible for the witness to convey to the jury what he has observed."[22]

Third, the traditional rule is often unnecessary. The adversary system has built-in mechanisms that mitigate the undesirable effects of opinion testimony. Because "the detailed account carries more conviction than the broad assertion, and a lawyer can be expected to display his witness to the best advantage," counsel will tend to elicit concrete rather than abstract testimony.[23] Furthermore, opposing counsel can expose through cross-examination the weaknesses in opinion testimony.[24]

Finally, the opinion rule produced much unnecessary litigation, inviting "numberless trivial appeals and . . . many indefensible reversals."[25]

[C] Rule 701

Instead of codifying the common law fact-opinion dichotomy and an ill-defined exception, Rule 701 adopts a different formula — helpfulness.[26]

Requirements. Rule 701 provides that the opinion of a nonexpert is admissible if (1) rationally based on the perception of the witness (firsthand knowledge), (2) helpful to a clear understanding of the witness's testimony or the determination of a fact in issue, and (3) not based on scientific, technical or other specialized knowledge within the scope of Rule 702, which governs expert testimony.[27]

Factors. In deciding whether the opinion is *helpful*, the trial court should consider several factors. One is the ability of the witness to express

---

[21] State v. Pike, 49 N.H. 399, 423 (1870). *See* Maguire, Evidence: Common Sense and Common Law 24 (1947) ("In a way, all human assertions are opinions.").

[22] United States v. Schneiderman, 106 F. Supp. 892, 903 (S.D. Cal. 1952). *See also* Central R.R. v. Monahan, 11 F.2d 212, 214 (2d Cir. 1926) ("Every judge of experience in the trial of causes has again and again seen the whole story garbled, because of insistence upon a form with which the witness cannot comply, since, like most men, he is unaware of the extent to which inference enters into his perceptions. He is telling the 'facts' in the only way that he knows how, and the result of nagging and checking him is often to choke him altogether, which is, indeed, usually its purpose.").

[23] Fed. R. Evid. 701 advisory committee's note.

[24] There may be tactical reasons for not cross-examining the witness. "If a witness answers in terms of opinion rather than facts or if the question calls for such an answer, a wise opponent may choose not to urge the opinion objection because if sustained, a new question would be asked which would cause the witness to speak factually with much more telling effect than the expression of an opinion." Ladd, *supra* note 17, at 415–16.

[25] Morgan, *Foreword*, Model Code of Evidence 34 (1942).

[26] Admissibility under Rule 701 is entrusted to the trial judge's discretion. It is a preliminary issue under Rule 104(a).

[27] Several other rules also deal with opinion testimony. Rules 405(a) and 608(a) permit the use of opinion evidence to prove character but only when character evidence is admissible. Rule 901 allows use of opinion evidence with respect to the authentication of documents, tangible items, and speaker voices.

herself;[28] the more articulate the witness, the less need for an opinion — *i.e.*, whether the "jury could not be put in possession of all the facts necessary to its decision."[29] A second factor is the importance of the issue to which the opinion relates; the more critical the issue, the more important it is for the witness to supply, if possible, the underlying facts.[30] Finally, a witness's use of common terms that also have a specific legal meaning, such as "rape" and "insanity," should be explained or avoided.[31]

Cases decided under Rule 701 cover a wide-range of subjects, including lay opinion testimony on a person's insanity,[32] the identification of persons in bank surveillance videotapes,[33] a person's movements as "suspicious,"[34] and the identity of drugs.[35]

---

[28] *See* Government of Virgin Islands v. Knight, 989 F.2d 619, 629 (3d Cir. 1993) ("[A]n eyewitness' testimony that Knight fired the gun *accidentally* would be helpful to the jury. The eyewitness described the circumstances that led to his opinion. It is difficult, however, to articulate all of the factors that lead one to conclude a person did not intend to fire a gun. Therefore, the witness' opinion that the gunshot was accidental would have permitted him to relate the facts with greater clarity, and hence would have aided the jury.") (emphasis added).

[29] *See* United States v. Yazzie, 976 F.2d 1252, 1255–58 (9th Cir. 1992) ("In the case before us [statutory rape], the jurors could not themselves assess how old the minor looked at the time of the incident: by the time of the trial, the minor was almost seventeen years old, and her appearance was undoubtedly substantially different than it had been on the night in question, a year and a half earlier. Thus, the jurors were wholly dependent on the testimony of witnesses. Yet the witnesses were permitted to testify only to the minor's describable features and behavior. Their testimony was no substitute for a clear and unequivocal statement of their opinions. It did not tell the jury that these witnesses believed the minor to be at least sixteen years old at the time of the incident.").

[30] *See* United States v. Allen, 10 F.3d 405, 414 (7th Cir. 1993) ("[T]he relationship of the opinion to the issues in the case is important to determine helpfulness. 'The closer the subject of the opinion gets to critical issues the likelier the judge is to require the witness to be more concrete . . . because the jury is not sufficiently helped in resolving disputes by testimony which merely tells it what result to reach.'") (citation omitted).

[31] *See* United States v. Skeet, 665 F.2d 983, 985 (9th Cir. 1982) ("If it is impossible or difficult to reproduce the data observed by the witnesses, or the facts are difficult of explanation, or complex, or are of a combination of circumstances and appearances which cannot be adequately described and presented with the force and clearness as they appeared to the witness, the witness may state his impressions and opinions based upon what he observed. It is a means of conveying to the jury what the witness has seen or heard. If the jury can be put into a position of equal vantage with the witness for drawing the opinion, then the witness may not give an opinion.").

[32] *See* United States v. Anthony, 944 F.2d 780, 782–83 (10th Cir. 1991) ("'[B]efore a non-expert witness is competent to testify to the sanity or insanity of another person, he must show an acquaintance of such intimacy and duration as to clearly indicate that his testimony will be of value in determining the issue. . . . [A] lay witness should be required to testify regarding a person's unusual, abnormal or bizarre conduct before being permitted to express an opinion as to that person's insanity.'") (citation omitted).

[33] *See* United States v. Pierce, 136 F.3d 770, 774 (11th Cir. 1998) ("[L]ay opinion identification testimony may be helpful to the jury where, as here, 'there is some basis for concluding that the witness is more likely to correctly identify the defendant from the photograph than is the jury' . . . .") (citation omitted).

[34] United States v. Figuerona-Lopez, 125 F.3d 1241, 1246 (9th Cir. 1997).

[35] *See* United States v. Paiva, 892 F.2d 148, 157 (1st Cir. 1989) ("Although a drug user may

Even under this liberalized approach, there are limits. If "attempts are made to introduce meaningless assertions which amount to little more than choosing up sides, exclusion for lack of helpfulness is called for by the rule."[36] For example, an opinion as to fault should be excluded on this basis.

[D] Overlap Between Lay & Expert Opinions

In some cases there may be a permissible overlap between lay and expert testimony. For example, both lay witnesses and experts are permitted to give opinions about handwriting comparisons. Rule 901(b)(2) provides that nonexpert opinion testimony as to the genuineness of handwriting is sufficient to authenticate a document.[37] Similarly, both may testify on mental conditions in an insanity defense case.[38] There is, however, an important difference between these two types of opinions: "The lay witness is using his opinion as a composite expression of his observations otherwise difficult to state, whereas the expert is expressing his scientific knowledge through his opinions."[39]

Furthermore, a witness may testify as both a fact witness and an expert — e.g., a treating physician.

[E] Application to Out-of-Court Statements

As noted above, Rule 701, following the modern view, treats the opinion rule as a rule of preference as to the form of in-court testimony and not as a rule of exclusion. Under this view, the opinion rule should rarely be applied to extrajudicial statements, such as those that fall within a recognized hearsay exception or are used for impeachment. If an objection to trial testimony on the grounds of "opinion" is sustained, counsel can rephrase the question and usually elicit most of the information desired. For example, if a testifying witness says somebody was acting "crazy" and an objection is sustained, the examiner has the opportunity to adduce more specific information through follow-up questions.

If, however, an opinion is contained in an out-of-court statement and the declarant is unavailable, the application of the opinion rule operates as a rule of exclusion, rather than a rule of preference, because there will be

---

not qualify as an expert, he or she may still be competent, based on past experience and personal knowledge and observation, to express an opinion as a lay witness that a particular substance perceived was cocaine or some other drug.").

[36] Fed. R. Evid. 701 advisory committee's note.

[37] Fed. R. Evid. 901 advisory committee's note (The rule "states conventional doctrine as to lay identification of handwriting, which recognizes that a sufficient familiarity with the handwriting of another person may be acquired by seeing him write, by exchanging correspondence, or by other means, to afford a basis for identifying it on subsequent occasions.").

[38] A lay witness could testify that defendant's behavior appeared erratic, confused, different, and so forth. The lay witness would not be qualified to state a medical opinion, nor discuss the legal term insanity. *See supra* note 32.

[39] Ladd, *supra* note 17, at 419.

no opportunity to rephrase the question and elicit more concrete information.

§ 23.04   Key Points

Firsthand Knowledge Rule: FRE 602

Rule 602 requires that a witness have personal knowledge of the subject about which the witness testifies. A witness's expression of uncertainty, such as "I think," "I believe," or "I'm not positive," is not grounds for exclusion so long as the witness had an opportunity to observe. Typically, proof of firsthand knowledge is supplied by the witness.

Standard of proof. The trial judge does not decide whether or not a witness has firsthand knowledge by a preponderance of evidence (the usual standard), but only whether sufficient evidence to support a finding of firsthand knowledge has been introduced, *i.e.,* a *prima facie* standard. If sufficient evidence has been adduced, the witness may testify, and the jury decides whether or not the witness had firsthand knowledge. In effect, Rule 602 is a specialized application of the conditional relevancy principle of Rule 104(b).

Opinion Rule: FRE 701

Frequently, the opinion rule is difficult to understand, at least initially, because the terms "opinion, inference, and conclusion" can be used in different ways in common parlance. In contrast, Rule 701 has a very narrow focus.

Common law. At common law, lay witnesses could testify to *facts* and not opinions, inferences, or conclusions. The courts, however, recognized an exception, sometimes known as the "short-hand rendition" rule or "collective facts" exception. This exception permitted opinions concerning the identity of persons, things, and handwriting; size, color, and weight of objects; times and distance; mental state or condition of another; insanity and intoxication; affection of one person for another; physical condition of another such as health or sickness; and values of property.

Rule 701. Instead of codifying the common law fact-opinion dichotomy and an ill-defined exception, Rule 701 adopts a different formula. Rule 701 provides that the opinion of a nonexpert is admissible if (1) rationally based on the perception of the witness (firsthand knowledge), (2) helpful to a clear understanding of the witness's testimony or the determination of a fact in issue and, (3) not based on scientific, technical or other specialized knowledge within the scope of Rule 702, which governs expert testimony.

Factors. In deciding whether the opinion is *helpful,* the trial court should consider several factors. One is the ability of the witness to express herself; the more articulate the witness, the less need for an opinion. A second factor is the importance of the issue to which the opinion relates; the more critical the issue, the more important it is for the witness to supply, if possible, the underlying facts. Finally, a witness's use of common terms that also have a specific legal meaning, such as "rape" and "insanity," should be explained or avoided.

Cases decided under Rule 701 cover a wide-range of subjects, including lay opinion testimony on a person's insanity, the identification of persons in bank surveillance videotapes, a person's movements as "suspicious," and the identity of drugs. Even under the liberalized approach of the rule, there are limits. For example, an opinion as to fault should be excluded.

Chapter 24

EXPERT TESTIMONY: FRE 702, 704 & 706

§ 24.01 Introduction

The use of expert testimony raises two threshold issues. First, is the proffered testimony a proper subject matter for expert testimony? If the answer is "yes," the next question follows: Is this witness qualified in this subject matter? These issues are examined in this chapter, as well as some specific scientific techniques. The bases for expert testimony is discussed in the next chapter.

There is typically no requirement that an expert be called as a witness on a particular issue, except for malpractice cases which frequently require expert testimony to establish the standard of care.[1]

§ 24.02 Subject Matter Requirement: An Overview

Federal Rule 702 specifies the subject matter requirement for expert testimony. One commentator has noted this requirement raises two distinct issues: "The field of expertness is bounded on one side by the great area of the commonplace, supposedly within the ken of every person of moderate intelligence, and on the other by the even greater area of the speculative and uncertain."[2] A chart illustrates these two aspects of the subject matter requirement:

speculative-uncertain	expert testimony	commonplace
A		B

Boundaries A and B raise different issues, and thus the evidentiary standards for these two boundaries differ. We need to have one standard for instances where expertise is not needed —*i.e.*, the commonplace, and another standard for judging when the testimony is too unreliable or

---

[1] *See* Diamond, Levine & Madden, Understanding Torts § 7.02 (1996).

[2] Maguire, Evidence: Common Sense and Common Law 30 (1947). He also noted: "Of course both these boundaries constantly shift, as the former area enlarges and the latter diminishes. Only a few years ago it would have been necessary to take expert evidence on issues with respect to the operation of motor cars, airplanes, or radio which are now so completely inside the domain of popular understanding that such evidence would be rejected as superfluous. A century ago purportedly expert evidence on these topics would have been rejected as visionary." *Id.* X-rays are another example. A radiologist may be needed to interpret the x-ray and the technician may be necessary to establish the instrument was working properly, but we do not call a physicist to explain that there are such things as x-rays and why they penetrate skin but not bone.

uncertain. As enacted in 1975, Rule 702 dealt only with line B. Instead of adopting the common law formulation ("beyond the ken of a lay jury"), the Rule employs an "assist-the-jury" standard, which was thought to be somewhat more liberal in terms of admissibility. Because an evidentiary standard for line A was not included, the lower courts (and eventually the Supreme Court) were required to address the issue, *i.e., Daubert* and the 2000 amendment to Rule 702 which are discussed in § 24.04..

The trial judge decides whether a subject is a proper one for expert testimony.[3] The judge has "broad discretion in the matter of the admission or exclusion of expert evidence, and his action is to be sustained unless manifestly erroneous."[4] As the Supreme Court has noted, "The Rules of Evidence — especially Rule 702 — do assign to the trial judge the task of ensuring that an expert's testimony both rests on a reliable foundation and is relevant to the task at hand."[5]

§ 24.03   Subject Matter: Expertise Not Needed

Sometimes we do not need an expert because the jury can do perfectly well without one. For example, a jury does not require a witness with a Ph.D. in geology to tell them that the murder weapon, produced before them as a prosecution exhibit, is a rock. But we need a standard in this context, and Rule 702 sets forth an "assist-the-jury" standard: will the proposed testimony assist the jury in deciding the case?

The federal drafters quoted the test proposed by Dean Ladd: "There is no more certain test for determining when experts may be used than the common sense inquiry whether the untrained layman would be qualified to determine intelligently and to the best possible degree the particular issue without enlightenment from those having a specialized understanding of the subject involved in the dispute."[6] Rule 702 is also consistent with Wigmore's formulation of the test for expert testimony: "On this subject can a jury receive from this person appreciable help?"[7]

The standard adopted by Rule 702 — whether expert testimony will "assist the trier of fact" — is a more liberal formulation of the subject matter requirement than that found in many common-law opinions. The common law often phrased the requirement as whether the subject was beyond the comprehension of lay persons.[8]

---

[3] *See* Fed. R. Evid. 104(a).

[4] Salem v. United States Lines Co., 370 U.S. 31, 35 (1962). *Accord* Hamling v. United States, 418 U.S. 87, 108 (1974) ("The District Court has wide discretion in its determination to admit and exclude evidence, and this is particularly true in the case of expert testimony.").

[5] Daubert v. Merrell Dow Pharm., Inc., 509 U.S. 579, 597 (1993).

[6] Ladd, *Expert Testimony*, 5 Vand. L. Rev. 414, 418 (1952).

[7] 7 Wigmore, Evidence § 1923, at 29 (Chadbourn rev. 1978).

[8] *E.g.,* Fineberg v. United States, 393 F.2d 417, 421 (9th Cir. 1968) ("beyond the knowledge of the average layman"); Jenkins v. United States, 307 F.2d 637, 643 (D.C. Cir. 1962) ("beyond the ken of the average layman").

There are some controversial issues here. For example, many courts have excluded expert testimony concerning the unreliability of eyewitness identifications because "the trustworthiness in general of eyewitness observations [is] not beyond the ken of the jurors."[9] In *State v. Chapple,*[10] however, the Arizona Supreme Court ruled the trial judge erred in excluding such testimony. According to the court,

> [e]ven assuming that jurors of ordinary education need no expert testimony to enlighten them to the danger of eyewitness identification, the offer of proof indicated that [the expert's] testimony would have informed the jury that there are many specific variables which affect the accuracy of identification and which apply to the facts of this case.[11]

These variables may include cross-racial identifications, unconscious transference, the weak correlation between witness confidence and accuracy, as well as other factors.[12]

In contrast, police officer testimony on modus operandi is generally accepted. Testimony by police experts on the m.o. of various types of crimes, such as counterfeiting,[13] bookmaking,[14] pickpocketing,[15] fraud,[16] organized crime,[17] and gang-related crimes[18] has been admitted. The most frequent use of this type of testimony involves drug trafficking. Expert testimony has been introduced on the operation of clandestine laboratories,[19] the street value of drugs,[20] the quantity of drugs that is consistent

---

[9] State v. Porraro, 404 A.2d 465, 471 (R.I. 1979). Most appellate courts have upheld the discretion of a trial court to exclude expert testimony on this issue.

[10] 660 P.2d 1208 (Ariz. 1983).

[11] *Id.* at 1220.

[12] *See infra* § 24.13 (eyewitness identification).

[13] *See* United States v. Burchfield, 719 F.2d 356, 358 (11th Cir. 1983).

[14] *See* United States v. Scavo, 593 F.2d 837, 843–44 (8th Cir. 1979).

[15] *See* United States v. Jackson, 425 F.2d 574, 576–77 (D.C. Cir. 1970).

[16] *E.g.,* United States v. Alonso, 48 F.3d 1536, 1541 (9th Cir. 1995) (credit card fraud); United States v. Hutchins, 757 F.2d 11, 13 (2d Cir. 1985) (confidence schemes).

[17] *E.g.,* United States v. Amuso, 21 F.3d 1251, 1263 (2d Cir. 1994) (FBI agent's testimony concerning common cosa nostra terminology necessary to explain tape recorded evidence); United States v. Locascio, 6 F.3d 924, 936 (2d Cir. 1993) ("inner workings of the Gambino Family" in the John Gotti trial).

[18] *E.g.,* People v. Gardeley, 927 P.2d 713, 721 (Cal. 1996) ("The subject matter of the culture and habits of criminal street gangs, of particular relevance here, meets [the expert witness] criterion.").

[19] *See* United States v. Anderson, 61 F.3d 1290, 1297–98 (7th Cir. 1995) (clandestine PCP laboratory).

[20] *E.g.,* United States v. Nobles, 69 F.3d 172, 183 (7th Cir. 1995) (DEA agent "explained that the 774.9 grams of 94% pure cocaine that Nobles was carrying in his bag, when processed for retail sale, would result in approximately 3 kilograms of 24% pure cocaine, which would sell for roughly $300,000 on the street, and would be enough to provide over 24,000 individual doses of cocaine. [The agent] opined that this large quantity of cocaine could only have been intended for distribution, and not for personal use.").

with distribution rather than personal use,[21] strategies of deception,[22] as well as other aspects of the drug trade.[23] In addition, expert testimony on various tools of the drug trade, including the use of beepers,[24] code words,[25] weapons,[26] duct tape,[27] and the like,[28] has been accepted.

There are, of course, limitations on this type of testimony. For example, *United States v. Garcia*[29] involved the testimony of an FBI language specialist who translated ten telephone conversations and gave his opinion about the meaning of certain phrases used in the conversations. The specialist also testified that the phrase "your old man" referred to the defendant. The Tenth Circuit ruled this testimony improper: "Unlike [the expert's] opinion as to jargon used in the drug trade which may be explained by expert opinion testimony, . . . no specialized knowledge is necessary to understand the phrase 'your old man.' Therefore, expert testimony on this point was unnecessary."[30]

§ 24.04 Subject Matter: Reliability of Expert Evidence

As noted earlier, there are two boundaries that need to be defined in carving out the proper subject matter for expert testimony. We need a standard for instances where expertise is not needed, a topic discussed in the previous section. We now turn to the second boundary to determine the standard for judging when expert testimony is too unreliable or uncertain. But first some background.

---

[21] *E.g.,* United States v. Valle, 72 F.3d 210, 214 (1st Cir. 1995) (expert testified that "so large a quantity of crack was consistent with distribution as opposed to personal use . . . [and] listed the visible characteristics of the prototypical crack addict, and noted that the appellant manifested none of these symptoms").

[22] *E.g.,* United States v. Garcia, 86 F.3d 394, 400 (5th Cir. 1996) ("The average juror may not be aware that the presence of 166.9 kilograms of cocaine is indicative of a large drug trafficking organization, and may not be aware that large drug trafficking organizations commonly use 'car swaps,' 'stash houses' and conduct 'heat runs.'").

[23] *E.g.,* United States v. Boney, 977 F.2d 624, 631 (D.C. Cir. 1992) (police expert testimony about the roles and behavior of drug traffickers — who was a "runner," who was a "holder," and who was going to "make the sale" — admitted).

[24] *E.g.,* United States v. Solis, 923 F.2d 548, 550 (7th Cir. 1991).

[25] *E.g.,* United States v. Griffith, 118 F.3d 318, 321 (5th Cir. 1997) ("we now have, by one count, 223 terms for marijuana").

[26] *E.g.,* United States v. Conyers, 118 F.3d 755, 758 (D.C. Cir. 1997) (type of packaging used "consistent with distribution in District of Columbia" and ".357 Magnum is the revolver of choice among local drug dealers").

[27] *E.g.,* United States v. Moore, 104 F.3d 377, 384 (D.C. Cir. 1997) ("duct tape such as that found under the hood of Moore's car is often used by people in the drug world to bind hands, legs, and mouths of people who are either being robbed in the drug world or who need to be maintained").

[28] *E.g.,* United States v. Parker, 32 F.3d 395, 400 (8th Cir. 1994) (admitting agent's testimony that certain entries in a notebook were "drug notes").

[29] 994 F.2d 1499 (10th Cir. 1993).

[30] *Id.* at 1506 (evidence, however, admitted as lay opinion testimony).

The reliability of evidence derived from a scientific theory or principle depends upon three factors: (1) the validity of the underlying theory, (2) the validity of the technique applying that theory, and (3) the proper application of the technique on a particular occasion. In short, neither an invalid technique nor a valid technique improperly applied will produce reliable results.[31]

The first two factors — the validity of the underlying theory and the validity of the technique — are distinct issues. One could accept, for example, the validity of the premise underlying DNA profiling — the uniqueness of DNA (except for identical twins) — but still question whether a particular DNA technique can identify that uniqueness. Similarly, the underlying psychological and physiological principles of polygraph testing could be acknowledged without endorsing the proposition that a polygraph examiner can detect deception by means of the polygraph technique.

Methods of proof. The validity of a scientific principle and the validity of the technique applying that principle may be established through judicial notice, legislative recognition, stipulation, or the presentation of evidence, typically expert testimony.

Judicial notice. First, if the validity of a theory or technique has been sufficiently established, a court can take judicial notice of the technique's validity, thereby relieving the offering party of the burden of introducing expert testimony on this issue.[32] The principles underlying intoxication tests, fingerprint comparisons, and firearms identifications have all been judicially recognized in this fashion.[33]

Statutory recognition. Second, the validity of a scientific technique can be recognized legislatively. At an earlier time, most of the statutory provisions were limited to motor vehicle codes and paternity cases. Radar, intoxication tests, and blood tests are still often subject to legislative regulation. These techniques are typically subject to judicial notice as well. Like judicial notice, legislative "notice" or recognition relieves the proponent of the burden of introducing evidence on the validity issue. Frequently, these statutes specify additional requirements for admissibility, such as periodic testing as a prerequisite for introducing breathalyzer results in evidence.[34]

---

[31] Radar evidence illustrates this point. The reliability of evidence based on radar depends on (1) the validity of the underlying theory (*e.g.,* the Doppler effect), (2) the validity of the technique applying that theory (*e.g.,* the particular model of radar), and (3) the proper application of the technique on a particular occasion (*e.g.,* use of tuning forks to calibrate the instrument). Because stationary radar may satisfy the second prong, it does not necessarily mean that moving radar would. The application of the Doppler effect is more complicated for moving radar because the speed of the police cruiser must also be taken into account.

[32] *See infra* § 44.03[C] (judicial notice of accurately & readily determinable facts). *See also* Daubert v. Merrell Dow Pharm., Inc., 509 U.S. 579, 593 n. 11 (1993) ("Theories that are so firmly established as to have attained the status of scientific law, such as the laws of thermodynamics, properly are subject to judicial notice under Fed. Rule Evid. 201").

[33] *See* 1 Giannelli & Imwinkelried, Scientific Evidence § 1–2 (3d ed. 1999).

[34] *See* Ex parte Mayo, 652 So. 2d 201, 209 (Ala. 1994) (administrative rules concerning alcohol breath testing promulgated by Department of Public Health did not satisfy statute which required adoption by Department of Forensic Sciences).

More recent enactments, however, have extended legislative recognition to more controversial techniques — for example, polygraph,[35] hypnosis,[36] rape trauma syndrome,[37] and battered wife syndrome[38] evidence. Many of these techniques would not be subject to judicial notice because their validity is not indisputable. The most important of the newer statutes deal with DNA evidence.[39]

Stipulation. The third way to establish reliability is by stipulation. The most notable example is polygraph evidence. As one court has noted: "The primary effect of the stipulation is that it operates as a waiver of objection or challenge to the validity of the basic theory of polygraph testing and eliminates the necessity of or the opportunity for the parties to establish a foundation in each case to satisfy the trial court of the basic theory and validity of polygraphs."[40] Most jurisdictions reject the admissibility of polygraph results by stipulation.[41]

Evidentiary foundation. Finally, the validity of a particular scientific technique may be established by introducing evidence, including but not limited to expert testimony. At least three different approaches can be gleaned from the cases: (1) the *Frye* "general acceptance" test, (2) a relevancy approach, and (3) the Supreme Court's reliability approach, as set forth in *Daubert v. Merrell Dow Pharm., Inc.*[42]

[A] *Frye* "General Acceptance" Test

For most of this century, *Frye v. United States*[43] was the leading case on the admissibility of novel scientific evidence.[44] In rejecting the results of a precursor of the modern polygraph, the D.C. Circuit set forth what has come to be known as the "general acceptance" test:

> Just when a scientific principle or discovery crosses the line between the experimental and demonstrable stages is difficult to define. Somewhere in this twilight zone the evidential force of the principle must be recognized, and while courts will go a long way in admitting expert testimony deduced from a well-recognized scientific principle

---

[35] *E.g.,* Cal. Evid. Code § 351.1 (polygraph results admissible by stipulation); N.M. Evid. R. 707 (polygraph results admissible even without stipulation).

[36] *E.g.,* Cal. Evid. Code § 795; Or. Rev. Stat. § 136.675–.695.

[37] *E.g.,* Ill. Ann. Stat. ch. 38, § 115-7.2.

[38] *E.g.,* Mo. Ann. Stat. § 563.033; Ohio Rev. Stat. §§ 2901.06, 2945.39, 2945.392.

[39] *E.g.,* Ala. Code § 36-18-30; Va. Code Ann. § 19.2-270.5.

[40] State v. Dean, 307 N.W.2d 628, 637 (Wis. 1981).

[41] *See infra* § 24.08.

[42] 509 U.S. 579 (1993).

[43] 293 F. 1013 (D.C. Cir. 1923).

[44] *See* United States v. Skeens, 494 F.2d 1050, 1053 (D.C. Cir. 1974) (*Frye* "has been followed uniformly in this and other Circuits."); Reed v. State, 391 A.2d 364, 368 (Md. 1978) ("This criterion of 'general acceptance' in the scientific community has come to be the standard in almost all of the courts in the country which have considered the question of the admissibility of scientific evidence.").

or discovery, the thing from which the deduction is made must be sufficiently established to have gained general acceptance in the particular field in which it belongs.[45]

The court went on to hold that the polygraph had "not yet gained such standing and scientific recognition among physiological and psychological authorities."[46] The general acceptance standard was subsequently used to decide the admissibility of a plethora of techniques, including voiceprints, neutron activation analysis, gunshot residue tests, bite mark comparisons, psycholinguistics, truth serum, hypnosis, blood analysis, hair analysis, intoxication testing, and DNA profiling.[47]

The general acceptance test was justified on reliability grounds: "The requirement of general acceptance in the scientific community assures that those most qualified to assess the general validity of a scientific method will have the determinative voice."[48] Nevertheless, the *Frye* test was criticized on a number of grounds. First, there are problems associated with applying the *Frye* standard. For example, DNA analysis covers several fields. In which is general acceptance required? In addition, is acceptance by scientists rather than technicians required? If polygraph examiners are defined as the relevant field under *Frye*, polygraph results would be admissible because there is "general acceptance" in the community of polygraph examiners. Second, there is also a concern that reliable evidence would be excluded under *Frye* while courts awaited general acceptance in the scientific community. In short, the general acceptance standard is too conservative. Third, "[p]erhaps the most important flaw in the *Frye* test is that by focusing attention on the general acceptance issue, the test obscures critical problems in the use of a particular technique."[49] Each technique is different and a one-size-fits-all general acceptance test will overlook crucial issues.

Although *Frye* is no longer the majority rule, it is still followed in a dozen or so jurisdictions, including California, Florida, Illinois, Maryland, Michigan, Minnesota, New Jersey, New York, Pennsylvania, and Washington.[50] Because these are populous states and most crimes are prosecuted in state courts, *Frye* remains an important test.

---

[45] *Frye*, 293 F. at 1014.

[46] *Id.*

[47] *See* 1 Giannelli & Imwinkelried, *supra* note 33, § 1-5.

[48] United States v. Addison, 498 F.2d 741, 743–44 (D.C. Cir. 1974). *See also* People v. Barbara, 255 N.W.2d 171, 194 (1977) (*Frye* "permits the experts who know most about a procedure to experiment and to study it. In effect, they form a kind of technical jury, which must first pass on the scientific status of a procedure before the lay jury utilizes it in making its findings of fact.").

[49] Giannelli, *The Admissibility of Novel Scientific Evidence:* Frye v. United States, *a Half-Century Later*, 80 Colum. L. Rev. 1197, 1226 (1980).

[50] *See* 1 Giannelli & Imwinkelried, *supra* note 33, § 1-15.

[B] Relevancy Approach

In his 1954 text, Professor McCormick argued that a special test, such as general acceptance, was not needed and that the traditional evidentiary rules on relevancy and expert testimony should be applied in this context.[51] In effect, qualifying the expert presumptively qualifies the technique used by that expert. Since most trial judges do not possess the scientific background to determine relevance, the judge "will generally be forced to accept the probative value of the evidence as what a qualified expert testifies it to be."[52] This lax standard has its own drawbacks: "The major flaw in the relevancy analysis is its failure to recognize the distinctive problems of scientific evidence. The judge frequently is forced to defer to an expert, thereby permitting admissibility based on the views of a single individual in some cases."[53] Wisconsin follows this rule.[54] This approach was implicitly rejected by the Supreme Court in *Daubert*, which requires the trial judge to determine reliability in addition to relevancy.[55]

[C] *Daubert* Reliability Test

After the Federal Rules were adopted in 1975, the federal courts had divided over the continued validity of the general acceptance standard.[56] Some courts assumed *Frye* had survived the enactment of the Federal Rules, while other courts rejected this view. In *Daubert v. Merrell Dow Pharm., Inc.*,[57] the Supreme Court rejected the *Frye* test.[58] *Daubert* involved the

---

[51] McCormick, Evidence § 171, at 363–64 (1954) (" 'General scientific acceptance' is a proper condition upon the court's taking judicial notice of scientific facts, but not a criterion for the admissibility of scientific evidence. Any relevant conclusions which are supported by a qualified expert witness should be received unless there are other reasons for exclusion. Particularly, its probative value may be overborne by the familiar dangers of prejudicing or misleading the jury, unfair surprise and undue consumption of time.").

[52] Strong, *Questions Affecting the Admissibility of Scientific Evidence*, 1970 Ill. L. F. 1, 22.

[53] Giannelli, *supra* note 49, at 1250.

[54] *See* State v. Donner, 531 N.W.2d 369, 374 (Wis. App. 1995) ("[B]efore *Daubert*, the *Frye* test was not the law in Wisconsin. To that extent, Wisconsin law and *Daubert* coincide. Beyond that, Wisconsin law holds that 'any relevant conclusions which are supported by a qualified witness should be received unless there are other reasons for exclusion.' Stated otherwise, expert testimony is admissible in Wisconsin if relevant and will be excluded only if the testimony is superfluous or a waste of time.") (citations omitted).

[55] In one sense, all unreliable evidence is irrelevant. Nevertheless, evidence law often separates relevancy and reliability. For example, the judge decides relevancy (Rule 401), but the jury decides credibility, a reliability issue. In addition, relevancy and hearsay (reliability) are dealt with in two different rules.

[56] The *Frye* issue was not addressed in the Advisory Committee's Notes, the congressional committee reports, or the hearings on the Federal Rules. *See* Giannelli, Daubert: *Interpreting the Federal Rules of Evidence*, 15 Cardozo L. Rev. 1999 (1994).

[57] 509 U.S. 579 (1993).

[58] *Id.* at 589 ("Given the Rules' permissive backdrop and their inclusion of a specific rule on expert testimony that does not mention 'general acceptance,' the assertion that the Rules somehow assimilated *Frye* is unconvincing. *Frye* made 'general acceptance' the exclusive test for admitting expert scientific testimony. That austere standard, absent from and incompatible with the Federal Rules of Evidence, should not be applied in federal trials.").

admissibility of expert testimony concerning whether Bendectin, an anti-nausea drug, caused birth defects.[59]

The Court, however, also held that scientific evidence must satisfy a reliability test. Such a standard, in the Court's view, is derived from Rule 702 (since amended), which uses the terms "scientific" and "knowledge."[60] Under this analysis, the trial court must make an admissibility determination pursuant to Rule 104(a). This task "entails a preliminary assessment of whether the reasoning or methodology underlying the testimony is scientifically valid and of whether that reasoning or methodology properly can be applied to the facts in issue."[61] This has come to be known as the trial judge's "gatekeeper" role.

One of the more problematic passages in the opinion was the following admonition: "The focus, of course, must be solely on principles and methodology, not on the conclusions that they generate."[62] This statement implies a clear cut dichotomy between methods and conclusions. This assumption is drawn into question by the Court's later decisions in the *Daubert* trilogy: *General Elec. Co. v. Joiner*[63] and *Kumho Tire Co. v. Carmichael*.[64]

[1] *Daubert* Factors

In performing the *Daubert* "gatekeeping function," the trial court may consider a number of factors. The Supreme Court specified five nonexclusive factors.[65]

Testability. The first *Daubert* factor is whether the scientific theory or technique can be or has been tested.[66] Citing scientific authorities, the

---

[59] *Daubert* was a high profile case even before the Court handed down its opinion. There were 22 amicus briefs, including some by prominent scientists. This produced strange bedfellows: big business wanted higher admissibility standards (*e.g.*, *Frye*) as did criminal defense attorneys. In criminal cases, the prosecution is typically the party trying to introduce new scientific techniques, such as voiceprints, DNA, neutron activation analysis, etc. Big business found its voice in Huber, Galileo's Revenge: Junk Science in the Courtroom (1991). Huber attacked both the use of experts and the tort system. *See* Giannelli, *"Junk Science": The Criminal Cases*, 84 J. Crim. L. & Criminology 105 (1993). While the Court did not use the term "junk" science in *Daubert*, that case is often referred to as the "junk science" case. The Court later used the term in *General Elec. Co. v. Joiner. See infra.*

[60] 509 U.S. at 590 ("In order to qualify as 'scientific knowledge,' an inference or assertion must be derived by the scientific method. Proposed testimony must be supported by appropriate validation —*i.e.*, 'good grounds,' based on what is known. In short, the requirement that an expert's testimony pertain to 'scientific knowledge' establishes a standard of evidentiary reliability.").

[61] *Id.* at 592–93.

[62] *Id.* at 595.

[63] 522 U.S. 136 (1997).

[64] 526 U.S. 137 (1999).

[65] There are five *Daubert* factors, but because the Court combined two (error rate and maintenance of standards) in the same paragraph, it is sometimes said that there are four *Daubert* factors.

[66] 509 U.S. at 592 ("Ordinarily, a key question to be answered . . . will be whether [the technique or theory] can be (and has been) tested.").

Court noted that a hallmark of science is empirical testing. The Court quoted Hempel: "[T]he statements constituting a scientific explanation must be capable of empirical test."[67] And then Popper: "[T]he criterion of the scientific status of a theory is its falsifiability, or refutability, or testability."[68]

Peer review & publication. Second, whether a theory or technique has been subjected to peer review and publication is a relevant, though not dispositive, consideration in assessing validity. The peer review and publication process increases the likelihood that flaws in methodology will be detected. Despite its limitations,[69] peer review remains an important safeguard. Peer review means "refereed scientific journals." It is a screening mechanism and only the first step, followed by publication and then replication by other scientists.[70]

Error rate. Third, a technique's known or potential rate of error is also a relevant factor. While error rate is a significant factor, the *Daubert* Court unfortunately cited a voiceprint case, *United States v. Williams,*[71] in which

---

[67] Hempel, Philosophy of Natural Science 49 (1966).

[68] Popper, Conjectures and Refutations: The Growth of Scientific Knowledge 37 (5th ed. 1989). The term "falsifiability" needs to be explained. *See* Imwinkelried, *Evidence Law Visits Jurassic Park: The Far-Reaching Implication of the Daubert Court's Recognition of the Uncertainty of the Scientific Enterprise,* 81 Iowa L. Rev. 55, 62 (1995) ("Attempts to disprove [falsify] the hypothesis are more significant [than verification] in two respects. First, although a single outcome consistent with an hypothesis furnishes little proof of the truth of the hypothesis, a hypothesis phrased as a universal statement is disproved by even one singular inconsistent outcome. Second, even when there are an impressive number of consistent outcomes and no inconsistent outcomes, the hypothesis is not definitively confirmed because it is always possible that an empirical test will some day demonstrate the theory to be incorrect. The theoretical possibility of disproof remains.").

The term has an additional connotation: A proposition that cannot be falsified (tested) is not a "scientific" proposition. *See* Green, *Expert Witnesses and Sufficiency of Evidence in Toxic Substances Litigation: The Legacy of Agent Orange and Bendectin Litigation,* 86 Nw. U. L. Rev. 643, 645 (1992) ("Scientific methodology today is based on generating hypotheses and testing them to see if they can be falsified; indeed, this methodology is what distinguishes science from other fields of human inquiry.").

[69] An amici brief in *Daubert,* filed on behalf of several scientists, questioned the peer review system. Brief of Amici Curiae Daryl E. Chubin et al., Daubert v. Merrell Dow Pharm., Inc., 509 U.S. 579 (1993), at 28 ("[T]he peer review system should not be regarded as more rigorous and reliable than the jury system's use of cross-examination."). These scientists noted that the peer review system is not intended to yield "the truth" and publication does not mean that an article's content is "generally accepted" or represents a "consensus" position of the relevant academic community. In addition, they pointed out that peer review journals do not replicate or verify experiments; nor do they warrant that the information contained in an article is valid or otherwise amounts to "good science." They also observed that often only two referees are selected and that these individuals spend on average "2.4 hours" reviewing each manuscript.

[70] " 'Good science' is a commonly accepted term used to describe the scientific community's system of quality control which protects the community and those who rely upon it from unsubstantiated scientific analysis. It mandates that each proposition undergo a rigorous trilogy of publication, replication and verification before it is relied upon." Brief of the New England Journal of Medicine, et al., as Amici Curiae in Support of Respondent, Daubert v. Merrell Dow Pharm., Inc., 509 U.S. 579 (1993), at 2.

[71] 583 F.2d 1194 (2d Cir. 1978).

the Second Circuit recognized "the potential rate of error" as a reliability factor.[72] Citing a Michigan State study, the Second Circuit noted that the false identification error rate was 6.3%, a rate reduced to 2.4% when doubtful comparisons are eliminated. However, a subsequent National Academy of Sciences [NAS] Report concluded that the reported error rates were generally inadequate for forensic applications[73] and were not "valid over the range of conditions usually met in practice."[74] Thus, the question is not whether error rates are important, but rather how to determine whether they are valid. The Second Circuit accepted the proffered error rates without question.

Standards. Fourth, the *Daubert* Court identified the "existence and maintenance of standards controlling the technique's operation" as another indicia of trustworthiness, again citing the *Williams* case.[75] The certification procedures of the International Association of Voice Identification were cited in *Williams*. Most members of this group, however, were police officers, not scientists.[76] As the NAS Report later noted, this Association "as presently constituted does not possess the broad base of representation usually considered appropriate and perhaps essential for a national certifying board."[77] The Second Circuit simply did not appreciate that it was citing an association of technicians, rather than scientists.

General acceptance. Although the Court rejected "general acceptance" as the sole criterion for admissibility, it recognized its relevance in assessing the reliability of scientific evidence: "Widespread acceptance can be an important factor in ruling particular evidence admissible, and 'a known technique that has been able to attract only minimal support within the community' . . . may properly be viewed with skepticism."[78]

Other factors. These factors are neither dispositive nor exhaustive. Indeed, the Court emphasized that the standard is "a flexible one." After *Daubert*, other factors were judicially acknowledged as reliability factors. The Advisory Committee Note (2002) to amended Rule 702 lists a number

---

[72] *Id.* at 1198.

[73] National Research Council, On the Theory and Practice of Voice Identification 60 (1979) ("Estimates of error rates now available pertain to only a few of the many combinations of conditions encountered in real-life situations. These estimates do not constitute a generally adequate basis for a judicial or legislative body to use in making judgments concerning the reliability and acceptability of aural-visual voice identification in forensic applications.").

[74] "The presently available experimental evidence about error rates consists of results from a relatively small number of separate, uncoordinated experiments. These results alone cannot provide estimates of error rates that are valid over the range of conditions usually met in practice." *Id.* at 58.

[75] 509 U.S. at 594. *See* United States v. Williams, 583 F.2d 1194, 1198 (2d Cir. 1978) (noting professional organization's standards governing "voiceprints").

[76] Moenssens & Inbau, Scientific Evidence in Criminal Cases 580 (2d ed. 1978) ("Except for [Dr.] Tosi, no scientists were among its early members; the majority of them are still police officers who have been trained by either Kersta or Tosi to become 'voiceprint' technicians.").

[77] NAS Report, *supra* note 73, at 65.

[78] 509 U.S. at 594.

of these: (1) whether the underlying research was conducted independently of litigation,[79] (2) whether the expert unjustifiably extrapolated from an accepted premise to an unfounded conclusion,[80] (3) whether the expert has adequately accounted for obvious alternative explanations, (4) whether the expert was as careful as she would be in her professional work outside of paid litigation, and (5) whether the field of expertise claimed by the expert is known to reach reliable results.

[2] Appellate Review

General Elec. Co. v. Joiner[81] was the second opinion in the *Daubert* trilogy. In *Joiner*, the plaintiff alleged that exposure to PCBs had caused his cancer; the trial court had excluded the plaintiff's expert testimony on causation as unsupported speculation. The Supreme Court ruled that the proper standard for reviewing a trial court's admissibility decision under *Daubert* was an abuse-of-discretion.[82] The Court adopted this standard without even considering an alternative standard: de novo review.[83] The validity of scientific evidence — *e.g.*, the polygraph — is not going to change case to case, and therefore a de novo review standard is more appropriate. Moreover, an inevitable lack of consistency, one court finding polygraph evidence reliable and another finding the exact opposite, may result.

---

[79] On remand in *Daubert*, the Ninth Circuit excluded the plaintiff's evidence on the grounds that the underlying research had been conducted in anticipation of litigation and was therefore not valid. The court saw an important difference if experts were "proposing to testify about matters naturally and directly out of research they have conducted independent of the litigation, or whether they have developed their opinions expressly for purposes of testifying." Daubert v. Merrell Dow Pharm., Inc., 43 F.3d 1311, 1317 (9th Cir. 1995).

[80] *See* General Elec. Co. v. Joiner, 522 U.S. 136, 146 (1997) ("Trained experts commonly extrapolate from existing data. But nothing in either *Daubert* or the Federal Rules of Evidence requires a district court to admit opinion evidence that is connected to existing data only by the *ipse dixit* of the expert. A court may conclude that there is simply too great an analytical gap between the data and the opinion proffered.").

[81] 522 U.S. 136 (1997). The case also raises a causation issue not present in *Daubert*. There was no question that Mrs. Daubert had taken the drug Bendectin; the pharmacy prescription records supported her testimony (which is typical in a drug case). In *Joiner*, there was a question whether the plaintiff had sufficient exposure to PCBs. In ruling on the summary judgment motion, the District Court had held that there was a genuine issue of a material fact on the exposure issue.

[82] *Id.* at 146–47 ("We hold, therefore, that abuse of discretion is the proper standard by which to review a district court's decision to admit or exclude scientific evidence. We further hold that, because it was within the District Court's discretion to conclude that the studies upon which the experts relied were not sufficient, whether individually or in combination, to support their conclusions that Joiner's exposure to PCBs contributed to his cancer, the District Court did not abuse its discretion in excluding their testimony.").

[83] Other courts have taken a different approach to the standard of review issue. For example, the Massachusetts Supreme Judicial Court has stated that "[i]n considering the issue of scientific validity, our review is de novo because a trial judge's conclusion will have applicability beyond the facts of the case before him." Commonwealth v. Vao Sok, 683 N.E.2d 671, 677 (Mass. 1997). *See also* Faigman, *Appellate Review of Scientific Evidence Under Daubert and Joiner*, 48 Hastings L.J. 969 (1997); Jonakait, *The Standard of Appellate Review for Scientific Evidence: Beyond Joiner and Scheffer*, 32 U.C. Davis L. Rev. 289 (1999).

Several other aspects of *Joiner* deserve attention. First, the "methodology-conclusion" dichotomy, so prominent in *Daubert*, was drawn into question. The *Joiner* Court remarked that nothing in *Daubert* "requires a district court to admit opinion evidence that is connected to existing data only by the *ipse dixit* of the expert. A court may conclude that there is simply too great an analytical gap between the data and the opinion proffered."[84] In other words, the dichotomy is not as easy to apply as was suggested in *Daubert*.

Second, the Court stated that the *Daubert* approach may admit a "somewhat broader range of scientific testimony than would have been admissible under *Frye*."[85] There is language in *Daubert* suggesting that a lot more evidence would be admissible under *Daubert* than under *Frye*.[86] The "somewhat" language in *Joiner* significantly modified this view.

[3] Technical Expertise

The *Daubert* decision turned on the phrase "scientific knowledge" in Rule 702. The Supreme Court clarified the applicability of *Daubert* to expert testimony based on "technical or other specialized knowledge" (also used in Rule 702) in *Kumho Tire Co. v. Carmichael*.[87] The expert in that case was an engineer with a master's degree and ten years experience in the tire industry. The Court first extended *Daubert's* reliability requirement to non-scientific testimony.[88] In the aftermath of *Daubert*, litigators quickly understood that they might avoid the *Daubert* reliability requirement by simply relabeling their evidence from "scientific" to "technical." The Court had to shut this door or *Daubert's* impact would be restricted to a narrow category of cases.

Second, the Court acknowledged the relevance of the *Daubert* factors in determining reliability in this context.[89] In other words, these factors were

---

[84] 522 U.S. at 146.

[85] *Id.* at 142.

[86] *See supra* note 58.

[87] 526 U.S. 137 (1999).

[88] The Court concluded that *"Daubert's* general holding — setting forth the trial judge's general 'gatekeeping' obligation — applies not only to testimony based on 'scientific' knowledge, but also to testimony based on 'technical' and 'other specialized' knowledge." *Id.* at 141. To support its conclusion, the Court noted that (1) Rule 702 did not distinguish between between "scientific" knowledge and "technical" or "other specialized knowledge"; (2) *Daubert's* gatekeeping rationale was not limited to scientific knowledge; and (3) "it would prove difficult, if not impossible, for judges to administer evidentiary rules under which a gatekeeping obligation depended upon a distinction between 'scientific' knowledge and 'technical' or 'other specialized' knowledge." *Id.* at 148.

[89] In determining the admissibility of technical or other specialized knowledge, the Court held that the trial court "may consider one or more of the specific factors that *Daubert* mentioned when doing so will help determine that testimony's reliability." *Id.* at 141. The Court characterized the *Daubert* inquiry as "flexible" and noted:

> [W]e can neither rule out, nor rule in, for all cases and for all time the applicability of the factors mentioned in *Daubert*, nor can we now do so for subsets of cases

not limited to "scientific" evidence; they applied to all expert testimony in appropriate circumstances. This may turn out to be the most critical aspect of the case. Other courts had concluded that the reliability requirement applied to nonscientific expert testimony but had adopted extremely lenient standards for such evidence. For example, the Hawaii Supreme Court had ruled that "because the underlying scientific principles and procedures are of proven validity/reliability, it is unnecessary to subject technical knowledge to the same type of full-scale reliability determination required for scientific knowledge. Thus, although technical knowledge, like all expert testimony, must be both relevant and reliable, its reliability may be presumed."[90] Therefore, although the state court ruled that technical expert testimony must be reliable, it undercut the significance of that ruling by treating technical evidence as presumptively admissible. The court effectively shifted the burden of proof on the reliability requirement to the opposing party. *Kumho* rejects this approach.

Finally, the *Kumho* Court entrusted the trial judge with the task of determining which reliability factors were relevant to a particular technique: "whether *Daubert's* specific factors are, or are not, reasonable measures of reliability in a particular case is a matter that the law grants the trial judge broad latitude to determine."[91]

[4] Procedural Issues

The trial court is not required to hold a *"Daubert* hearing" every time expert testimony is challenged.[92] *Daubert* findings are generally required[93] but not necessarily a hearing.[94]

---

categorized by category of expert or by kind of evidence. *Daubert* itself is not to the contrary. It made clear that its list of factors was meant to be helpful, not definitive. Indeed, those factors do not all necessarily apply even in every instance in which the reliability of scientific testimony is challenged. It might not be surprising in a particular case, for example, that a claim made by a scientific witness has never been the subject of peer review, for the particular application at issue may never previously have interested any scientist. Nor, on the other hand, does the presence of *Daubert's* general acceptance factor help show that an expert's testimony is reliable where the discipline itself lacks reliability, as, for example, do theories grounded in any so-called generally accepted principles of astrology or necromancy.

Id. at 150–51.

[90] State v. Fukusaku, 946 P.2d 32, 43 (Haw. 1997).

[91] *Kumho*, 526 U.S. at 153.

[92] *See* Berger, *Procedural Paradigms for Applying the Daubert Test*, 78 Minn. L. Rev. 1345 (1994).

[93] *See* United States v. Velarde, 214 F.3d 1204, 1209 (10th Cir. 2000) ("While we recognize that the trial court is accorded great latitude in determining how to make *Daubert* reliability findings before admitting expert testimony, *Kumho* and *Daubert* make it clear that the court must, on the record, make some kind of reliability determination. . . . The record in this case reveals no such reliability determination."); People v. Shreck, 22 P.3d 68, 78 (Colo. 2001) ("[A] trial court's [Rule] 702 determination must be based upon specific findings on the record as to the helpfulness and reliability of the evidence proffered.").

[94] *See* United States v. Alatorre, 222 F.3d 1098, 1100, 1104 (9th Cir. 2000) ("[T]rial courts

[5]   Impact of *Daubert*

It would be difficult to overstate the impact of the *Daubert* decision. A number of states have explicitly adopted *Daubert*. [95] Other jurisdictions had rejected *Frye* before *Daubert* was handed down and most of those are now using the *Daubert* factors, [96] which often means an implicit shift from the relevancy approach to a more stringent reliability test.

Over the course of its three decisions, the Supreme Court has made *Daubert* a stringent standard. This was not obvious when *Daubert* was decided in 1993. At that time both sides claimed victory. The plaintiffs believed they had won because the Court had rejected *Frye* and adopted the methodology-conclusion dichotomy. In contrast, the defense saw in *Daubert* the structure for a "strict scrutiny" examination of scientific evidence. These differences in perception can be explained due to an inherent tension in the case. On the one hand, the *Daubert* Court referred to *Frye* as an "austere" test and cited its earlier cases, emphasizing the liberal thrust of Federal Rules. On the other hand, there was the "gatekeeper" language and "reliability requirement."

In any event, a decade later it is clear that *Daubert* erects a formidable barrier to the admissibility of expert testimony. As one district court stated, the Supreme Court in *Kumho* was "plainly inviting a reexamination even of 'generally accepted' venerable, technical fields."[97] Moreover, in *Weisgram v. Marley Co.*,[98] which involved a summary judgment in a wrongful death action against a manufacturer of an allegedly defective baseboard heater, the Court wrote: "Since *Daubert*, moreover, parties relying on expert evidence have had notice of the exacting standards of reliability such evidence must meet."[99] As amended in 2000, Rule 702 now contains an explicit reliability requirement.

---

are not compelled to conduct pretrial hearings in order to discharge the gatekeeping function."; "Here the court adopted a practical procedure, well within its discretion, when it allowed Alatorre to explore Jacobs's qualifications and the basis for his testimony at trial via voir dire and then, following voir dire, rejected his renewed objections to the testimony regarding wholesale and retail value [of drugs]."); United States v. Nichols, 169 F.3d 1255, 1263 (10th Cir. 1999) ("The trial court in this case did not abuse its discretion when it declined to hold a preliminary evidentiary hearing. The district court explained its decision by noting that 'the challenged evidence does not involve any new scientific theory and the testing methodologies are neither new nor novel. . . . The testing methodologies employed . . . are all well-known techniques routinely used by chemists to determine the elemental composition of unknown samples.' Rather, the court noted that the contentious issue was whether the test results were undercut by flaws in the laboratory tests, a matter involving the credibility of witnesses and weighing of the evidence, both of which were more suitable for resolution by the jury.").

[95] Alaska, Connecticut, Colorado, Idaho, Indiana, Kentucky, Massachusetts, Nebraska, New Hampshire, New Mexico, Oklahoma, South Dakota, Tennessee, and West Virginia. *See* 1 Giannelli & Imwinkelried, *supra* note 33, § 1-13.

[96] Arkansas, Delaware, Georgia, Iowa, Montana, North Carolina, Ohio, Oregon, Rhode Island, South Carolina, Texas, Utah, Vermont, and Wyoming. *See id.* § 1-14.

[97] United States v. Hines, 55 F. Supp. 2d 62, 67 (D. Mass. 1999) (limiting handwriting comparison testimony).

[98] 528 U.S. 440 (2000).

[99] *Id.* at 445.

§ 24.05 Qualifications Requirement

If the subject matter is a proper one for expert testimony, the next question is whether the proffered witness is qualified in that subject matter. Rule 702 provides that a witness may be qualified as an expert "by specialized knowledge, skill, experience, training, or education."[100] The trial judge determines this issue pursuant to Rule 104(a).[101]

The party offering a witness as an expert has the burden of establishing that the witness is qualified. There are some rules-of-thumb in this context. For example, the expert need not be the best witness on the subject, nor "an outstanding practitioner in the field in which he professes expertise."[102] The expert generally need not be licensed in his or her field, although this factor is relevant to the qualification issue. Nor must the expert's qualifications match those of the other side's experts.[103] Furthermore, the expert's qualifications should be based on the nature and extent of the witness's knowledge and not on the witness's "title."[104]

Practical experience. Experience alone may qualify a witness to express an opinion. There is no "degree" requirement, per se.[105] Wigmore stated it this way: The witness's expertise "may have been attained, so far as legal rules go, in any way whatever; all the law requires is that it should have been attained."[106] For example, a woodworker with 36 years experience could testify about the construction of chairs.[107] One case even involved

---

[100] *See* Fed. R. Evid. 702 advisory committee's note ("The expert is viewed, not in a narrow sense, but as a person qualified by 'knowledge, skill, experience, training or education.' Thus within the scope of the rule are not only experts in the strictest sense of the word, *e.g.* physicians, physicists, and architects, but also the large group sometimes called 'skilled' witnesses, such as bankers or landowners testifying to land values.").

[101] Fed. R. Evid. 104(a) ("Preliminary questions concerning the qualification of a person to be a witness shall be determined by the court.").

[102] United States v. Barker, 553 F.2d 1013, 1024 (6th Cir. 1977).

[103] *See* United States v. Madoch, 935 F. Supp. 965, 972 (N.D. Ill. 1996) ("[O]ne expert need not hold the exact same set of qualifications to rebut another expert's testimony. . . . This Court need not analyze, as Defendant contends it should, whether a psychologist or psychiatrist is more qualified to testify as to the psychological condition of a patient at the time of the offense.").

[104] *See* Jenkins v. United States, 307 F.2d 637, 643–44 (D.C. Cir. 1962) (reversing trial court's ruling that psychologists were not qualified to testify on the issue of insanity because they lacked medical training; "We must examine the reality behind the title 'psychologist.' ").

[105] *See* Davis v. United States, 865 F.2d 164,168 (8th Cir. 1988) ("Rule 702 does not state a preference for academic training over demonstrated practical experience.").

[106] 2 Wigmore, Evidence § 556, at 751 (Chadbourn rev. 1979).

[107] *See* McConnell v. Budget Inns, 718 N.E.2d 948, 955 (Ohio App. 1998) ("[The witness], a long-time owner of a woodworking company in New York, testified that he had approximately thirty-six years of woodworking experience that included the design, repair, manufacture, and construction of wood furniture, including wood chairs used in commercial settings and chairs of the type involved in the accident herein. These qualifications gave the witness knowledge of chair construction and mechanical failure therein superior to that possessed by the average juror."). *See also* United States v. Kunzman, 54 F.3d 1522, 1530 (10th Cir. 1995) ("Experience alone can qualify a witness to give expert testimony"; banker for 20 years interpreting numbers and bank stamps on checks to show they cleared interstate banking system).

an experienced "marijuana smoker."[108]

Testimony beyond expertise. An expert qualified on one subject may not be qualified on another (even a related) subject.[109] For example, a police officer may be qualified to operate a breathalyzer but not qualified to interpret the results. The training and experience needed to perform these two distinct functions are very different.[110] Similarly, a police officer may be qualified to conduct a horizontal gaze nystagmus test (an intoxication test) but not be qualified to interpret the results.[111] In other words, there is a difference between a scientist and a technician.

Hired gun. In civil litigation, there is what is known as the hired gun phenomenon. Some experts spend more time testifying than practicing in their field.[112]

§ 24.06 Court-Appointed Experts: FRE 706

A trial court has inherent authority to appoint expert witnesses and technical advisors. Federal Rule 706 recognizes this authority.[113] One

---

[108] *See* United States v. Johnson, 575 F.2d 1347, 1360 (5th Cir. 1978) (an experienced marijuana smoker was permitted to testify that certain marijuana came from Colombia; the witness "had smoked marijuana over a thousand times. . . . He based his identification upon the plant's appearance, its leaf, buds, stems, and other physical characteristics, as well as upon the smell and the effect of smoking it."). *See also* Hooten v. State, 492 So. 2d 948, 958 (Miss. 1986) (dissenting opinion) ("If this witness has indeed testified over 300 times as an *expert* on discovering spurious handwriting as she claimed, it is an astonishing indictment on the gullibility of lawyers and judges.").

[109] *See* Maguire, *supra* note 2, at 30–31 ("It goes without saying that an expert qualified to testify upon one topic may be completely unqualified to testify about another as to which he lacks special knowledge, skill, experience, or training, but some applications of this principle take the unwary by surprise.").

[110] *See* State v. James, 428 N.E.2d 876, 878 (Ohio App. 1980) (state trooper qualified as an expert in the operation of intoxilyzer but did not possess sufficient learning and knowledge about effects of alcohol consumption); State v. Priester, 391 S.E.2d 227, 228 (S.C. 1990) (lab toxicologist not qualified to testify about the effect of alcohol on the brain).

[111] *See* People v. Williams, 5 Cal. Rpt. 2d 130, 135 (Cal. App. 1992) ("[The officer's] opinion that appellant was under the influence of alcohol, to the extent it was based on the nystagmus test, rests on scientific principles well beyond his knowledge, training, or education. Without some understanding of the processes by which alcohol ingestion produces [eye] nystagmus, how strong the correlation is, how other possible causes might be masked, what margin of error has been shown in statistical surveys, and a host of other relevant factors, [the officer's] opinion on causation, notwithstanding his ability to recognize the symptom, was unfounded.").

[112] *See* In re Air Crash Disaster at New Orleans, 795 F.2d 1230, 1234 (5th Cir. 1986) ("experts whose opinions are available to the highest bidder have no place testifying in a court of law"); Chaulk v. Volkswagen of Am., Inc., 808 F.2d 639, 644 (7th Cir. 1986) ("There is hardly anything, not palpably absurd on its face, that cannot now be proved by some so-called 'experts.'"). For an insightful discussion of the "hired gun" problem, *see* Gross, *Expert Evidence*, 1991 Wis. L. Rev. 1113 (proposing changes to ensure the appointment of neutral experts).

[113] Fed. R. Evid. 706 advisory committee's note ("The inherent power of a trial judge to appoint an expert of his own choosing is virtually unquestioned."); Cecil & Willging, Court-Appointed Experts: Defining the Role of Experts Appointed under Federal Rule of Evidence 706 (Fed. Judicial Center 1993); Thorpe, Oelhafen & Arnold, *Court-Appointed Experts and Technical Advisors*, 26 Litigation 31 (Summer 2000); Note, *Improving Judicial Gatekeeping: Technical Advisors and Scientific Evidence*, 110 Harv. L. Rev. 941 (1997).

problem associated with this procedure is the risk that the witness may be cloaked with the authority of the court, at least in the eyes of the jury. The federal drafters acknowledged this problem: "court appointed experts [may] acquire an aura of infallibility to which they are not entitled . . . ."[114] Thus, the decision whether to disclose to the jury that the expert has been appointed by the court lies within the discretion of the trial judge.[115] The parties have the right to call their own experts, notwithstanding the appointment of an expert by the court.[116] Although not frequently used, Rule 706 has been employed in a variety of situations.[117]

§ 24.07 Right to Defense Experts

The appointment of an expert for an indigent criminal defendant may be required on constitutional grounds. In *Ake v. Oklahoma*,[118] the accused was charged with capital murder. At arraignment, his conduct was "so bizarre" that the trial judge ordered, sua sponte, a mental evaluation. Ake was found incompetent to stand trial but later recovered due to antipsychotic drugs. When the prosecution resumed, Ake's attorney requested a psychiatric evaluation at state expense to prepare an insanity defense. The trial court refused. Thus, although insanity was the only contested issue at trial, no psychiatrists testified on this issue, and Ake was convicted. In the penalty stage, the prosecution relied on state psychiatrists, who testified that Ake was "dangerous to society," in seeking the death sentence. This testimony stood unrebutted because Ake could not afford an expert.

The Supreme Court overturned Ake's conviction on due process grounds, commenting that "when a State brings its judicial power to bear on an indigent in a criminal proceeding, it must take steps to assure that the defendant has a fair opportunity to present his defense."[119] This fair opportunity mandates that an accused be provided with the "basic tools of an adequate defense." In another passage, the Court elaborated on what it meant by a "fair opportunity" and "basic tools" for an adequate defense: "We hold that when a defendant has made a preliminary showing that his sanity at the time of the offense is likely to be a significant factor at trial, the Constitution requires that a State provide access to a psychiatrist's assistance on this issue, if the defendant cannot otherwise afford one."[120]

While the *Ake* decision settled the core issue by recognizing a right to expert assistance, it left a number of important issues unresolved. Several

---

[114] Fed. R. Evid. 706 advisory committee's note.

[115] Fed. R. Evid. 706(c).

[116] Fed. R. Evid. 706(d).

[117] *See* Students of California School for the Blind v. Honig, 736 F.2d 538 (9th Cir. 1984) (seismic safety of new school campus for blind; after lengthy and conflicting evidence court appointed expert).

[118] 470 U.S. 68 (1985). *See* 1 Giannelli & Imwinkelried, *supra* note 33, ch. 4.

[119] *Ake,* 470 U.S. at 76.

[120] *Id.* at 74.

of these issues involved the scope of the right. One question was whether *Ake* extended to noncapital cases. While some early cases attempted to limit *Ake* to death penalty cases, the majority of courts have rejected this restriction.[121] The same pattern developed with *Ake's* application to nonpsychiatric experts, again with most courts declining to limit the opinion to psychiatric expertise.[122] Another issue involves the role of the expert — *i.e.,* whether an *Ake* expert is a "defense" (partisan) expert or a neutral expert. Here, the courts remain divided.[123]

Finally, the standard for appointment remains elusive. Some reasonable threshold showing is necessary because the system cannot afford defense experts on "demand." However, if the threshold standard is set too high, the defendant is placed in a "Catch-22" situation, in which the standard "demand[s] that the defendant possess already the expertise of the witness sought."[124]

Statutory provisions. The right to a defense expert is often implemented by statute. Under the Criminal Justice Act, an indigent person may obtain expert assistance in federal trials.[125] The Act limits expenses for expert services to $1,000.00 unless the court certifies that a greater amount is "necessary to provide fair compensation for services of an unusual character or duration." Until 1986 the maximum had been $300. Although many states have comparable provisions, the monetary limitations often pose problems.[126]

---

[121] *Compare* Isom v. State, 488 So. 2d 12, 13 (Ala. Crim. App. 1986) ("*Ake* does not reach noncapital cases."), *with* State v. Taylor, 939 S.W.2d 148, 152 (Tex. Crim. App. 1996) ("[W]e have also extended — at least implicitly — the due process protections recognized in *Ake* beyond the capital context.").

[122] *Compare* Ex parte Grayson, 479 So. 2d 76, 82 (Ala. 1985) ("[T]here is nothing contained in the *Ake* decision to suggest that the United States Supreme Court was addressing anything other than psychiatrists and the insanity defense."), *with* Little v. Armontrout, 835 F.2d 1240, 1243 (8th Cir. 1987) (en banc) (error to fail to appoint hypnotist; "[T]here is no principled way to distinguish between psychiatric and nonpsychiatric experts. The question in each case must be not what field of science or expert knowledge is involved, but rather how important the scientific issue is in the case, and how much help a defense expert could have given.").

[123] *Compare* Granviel v. Lynaugh, 881 F.2d 185, 191 (5th Cir. 1989) (a "court-appointed psychiatrist, whose opinion and testimony is available to both sides, satisfies [the accused's] rights."; "The state is not required to permit defendants to shop around for a favorable expert. . . . He has no right to the appointment of a psychiatrist who will reach biased or only favorable conclusions."), *with* United States v. Sloan, 776 F.2d 926, 929 (10th Cir. 1985) ("That duty [to appoint a psychiatrist] cannot be satisfied with the appointment of an expert who ultimately testifies contrary to the defense on the issue of competence. The essential benefit of having an expert in the first place is denied the defendant when the services of the doctor must be shared with the prosecution.").

[124] State v. Moore, 364 S.E.2d 648, 657 (N.C. 1988).

[125] 18 U.S.C. § 3006(A).

[126] *See* Ill. Stat. ch. 725, § 5-113-3(d) ($250 maximum in capital cases); Minn. Stat. Ann. § 611.21 ($1,000 maximum).

§ 24.08 Polygraph Evidence

The admissibility of polygraph evidence remains controversial.[127] Different types of polygraph tests are used depending on the purpose of the test.[128] The use of polygraph testing for pre-employment screening at one time was quite common. However, the Employee Polygraph Protection Act of 1988,[129] with limited exceptions, prohibits the use of polygraph tests for pre-employment screening or during the course of employment.

A different type of examination is used when the focus of the testing is a specific incident, criminal or otherwise. The most common test used in this context is the "control question" technique.[130] There are several different versions of this test as well as a number of methods for scoring the results: global evaluation, numerical scoring, and computerized scoring.

In *Frye v. United States*,[131] decided in 1923, the D.C. Circuit rejected the results of a precursor of the modern polygraph. The court held that the polygraph had "not yet gained such standing and scientific recognition among

---

[127] *See* 1 Giannelli & Imwinkelried, *supra* note 33, ch. 8 (polygraph).

[128] The physiological responses used in polygraph testing are changes in blood pressure-pulse, respiration, and galvanic skin resistance. The polygraph instrument simultaneously and continuously measures and records these physiological reactions on a graph or chart (polygram). Blood pressure-pulse is measured by a sphygmomanometer (blood pressure cuff) that is placed on the subject's arm; respiration is measured by pneumograph tubes that are fastened around the subject's abdomen and chest; and galvanic skin response is measured by electrodes that are attached to the subject's fingertips. A quality polygraph instrument can accurately measure and record these responses. The modern instruments are lap top computers. The instrument, however, detects neither deception nor the fear of detection; it provides only a recording of physiological responses. It is the examiner who, based on these recordings, infers deception.

[129] 29 U.S.C. §§ 2001–0929. The Department of Labor has promulgated regulations pursuant to the Act. 29 CFR pt 80129; 56 Fed. Reg. 9046 (1991). *See also* Note, *The Employee Polygraph Protection Act of 1988 — Should the Federal Government Regulate the Use of Polygraphs in the Private Sector?*, 58 Cin. L. Rev. 559 (1989); Note, *The Employee Polygraph Protection Act of 1988: A Balance of Interests*, 75 Iowa L. Rev. 539 (1990).

[130] The early examiners used the "relevant-irrelevant question" test. Relevant questions concern the subject matter under investigation. For example: "Did you take $100 from your employer's safe?" Irrelevant or neutral questions are used to obtain a subject's normal truthful reactions and chart tracings — *i.e.*, the examinee's physiological tracings while in a state of homeostasis or equilibrium. Examples of irrelevant questions are: "Is your name [subject's name]?" "Are you over 21 years of age?" Both types of questions must be answered "yes" or "no." The responses to the relevant questions are compared with the subject's responses to the irrelevant questions. The principal criticism of this test is its underlying assumption that an innocent person will not react to the relevant questions.

The control question technique was developed to improve the relevant-irrelevant exam. Control questions concern an act of wrongdoing to which the subject, in all probability, will lie. They are typically general and vague — for example, "After the age of 21, did you ever steal anything?" Control questions are designed as a stimulus for the truthful subject. Generally, the truthful person will respond more to the control questions than to the relevant questions because they represent a greater threat to that person. For the same reason, the deceptive person will respond more to the relevant questions than to the control questions. Therefore, the subject's *comparative* responses to the control and relevant questions are the key in this test.

[131] 293 F. 1013 (D.C. Cir. 1923). *See supra* § 24.04[A].

physiological and psychological authorities."[132] A majority of states still follow the traditional rule, holding polygraph evidence per se inadmissible. This exclusionary rule extends to evidence that a person was willing to take, took, or refused to take an examination. A substantial minority of jurisdictions admit polygraph results upon stipulation. A third group leaves the admissibility issue to the trial judge. At one time, most federal circuit courts followed the per se exclusion approach. However, the *Daubert* decision changed this result.[133] Nevertheless, most federal trial courts exercise their discretion to exclude polygraph evidence.[134]

Military Rule of Evidence 707 makes polygraph evidence inadmissible in court-martial proceedings. In *United States v. Scheffer*,[135] the Supreme Court held that this rule of per se exclusion did not violate the constitutional right of the defendant to present a defense. The Court stated: "Rule 707 serves several legitimate interests in the criminal trial process. These interests include ensuring that only reliable evidence is introduced at trial, preserving the jury's role in determining credibility, and avoiding litigation that is collateral to the primary purpose of the trial."[136]

Self-incrimination. In *Schmerber v. California*,[137] the Supreme Court indicated that compelled submission to a polygraph test would violate the Fifth Amendment's prohibition against compelled self-incrimination. Consequently, confessions obtained during or after the examination are subject to the *Miranda* requirements if the accused is in "custody."[138]

---

[132] *Id.* at 1014.

[133] *See* United States v. Posado, 57 F.3d 428, 429, 434 (5th Cir. 1995) ("[T]he rationale underlying this circuit's per se rule against admitting polygraph evidence did not survive *Daubert.* . . .").

[134] *See* 1 Giannelli & Imwinkelried, *supra* note 33, ch. 8 (polygraph evidence).

[135] 523 U.S. 303 (1998).

[136] *Id.* at 309. In his concurring opinion, Justice Kennedy pointed out that Federal Rule 704 abolishes the ultimate issue rule. Significantly, he also wrote that:

> I doubt that the rule of per se exclusion is wise, and some later case might present a more compelling case for introduction of the testimony than this one does. Though the considerable discretion given to the trial court in admitting and excluding scientific evidence is not a constitutional mandate, see *Daubert* . . . there is some tension between that rule and our holding today. And, as Justice Stevens points out in dissent, there is much inconsistency between the Government's extensive use of polygraph to make vital security determinations and the argument it makes here, stressing the inaccuracy of these tests.

Id. at 318.

[137] 384 U.S. 757, 764 (1966) ("Some tests seemingly directed to obtain 'physical evidence,' for example, lie detector tests measuring changes in body function during interrogation, may actually be directed to eliciting responses which are essentially testimonial. To compel a person to submit to testing in which an effort will be made to determine his guilt or innocence on the basis of physiological responses, whether willed or not, is to evoke the spirit and history of the Fifth Amendment.").

[138] *See* Wyrick v. Fields, 459 U.S. 42 (1982) (statements made by a defendant during a post-test interview were admissible where the defendant, represented by counsel, requested a polygraph examination and was informed of his *Miranda* rights; new warnings prior to the post-test interview were not required).

§ 24.09 Hypnotic Evidence

In 1897, the California Supreme Court wrote that the "law of the United States does not recognize hypnotism."[139] The issue did not resurface until the 1970s when the use of hypnosis in criminal cases increased significantly. In 1980, a New York trial court observed: "The past ten years have seen a dramatic rise in the use of hypnotism as an aid in criminal investigations."[140]

The principal evidentiary issues concerning hypnotic evidence involve: (1) the admissibility of out-of-court statements made by a person while hypnotized; (2) the admissibility of testimony of a witness whose memory has been "refreshed" by hypnosis; and (3) the admissibility of expert testimony concerning the accused's mental condition when based on an interview in which hypnosis was employed.

[A] Out-of-Court Hypnotic Statements

Courts uniformly have rejected the admissibility of statements made by a subject while hypnotized. Since these statements are made out of court and are offered for their truth, they are hearsay if offered by the accused. Moreover, "[m]ost experts agree that hypnotic evidence is unreliable because a person under hypnosis can manufacture or invent false statements. A person under a hypnotic trance is also subject to heightened suggestibility."[141] The prosecution's use of such statements raises similar reliability concerns. In *Leyra v. Denno*,[142] the Supreme Court ruled that a confession obtained by a "psychiatrist with considerable knowledge of hypnosis" was involuntary and thus violative of due process. The Court noted that the "suspect's ability to resist interrogation was broken to almost trancelike submission by use of the arts of a highly skilled psychiatrist."[143]

[B] Hypnotically-Refreshed Testimony

Courts are sharply divided over the admissibility of hypnotically-refreshed testimony. Some courts adopt a per se rule of exclusion, albeit, with some exceptions. Courts admitting hypnotically-refreshed testimony have taken three different positions: (1) a "credibility" approach which leaves the reliability issue to the jury, (2) a "discretionary admission" approach which entrusts the reliability issue to the trial judge, and (3) a "procedural safeguards" approach. In addition, constitutional concerns have played an influential role in some aspects of these cases.

---

[139] People v. Ebanks, 49 P. 1049, 1053 (Cal. 1897). *See* 1 Giannelli & Imwinkelried, *supra* note 33, ch. 12.

[140] People v. Lucas, 435 N.Y.S.2d 461, 462 (Sup. Ct. 1980).

[141] Greenfield v. Commonwealth, 204 S.E.2d 414, 419 (Va. 1974). *See also* Greenfield v. Robinson, 413 F. Supp. 1113 (W.D. Va. 1976).

[142] 347 U.S. 556 (1954).

[143] *Id.* at 559.

Per se exclusion. This position is based on the belief that hypnotically-refreshed testimony is unreliable.

Three general characteristics of hypnosis may lead to the introduction of inaccurate memories: the subject becomes "suggestible" and may try to please the hypnotist with answers the subject thinks will be met with approval; the subject is likely to "confabulate," that is, to fill in details from the imagination in order to make an answer more coherent and complete; and, the subject experiences "memory hardening," which gives him great confidence in both true and false memories, making effective cross-examination more difficult.[144]

Courts adopting the per se rule of exclusion, however, carve out an exception for testimony based on prehypnotic memory. For example, in *State ex rel. Collins v. Superior Court*,[145] several rape victims were hypnotized in an attempt to discover more information about the identity of their assailant. No new information developed from this process. The defense moved to disqualify the victims as witnesses. The Arizona Supreme Court initially reaffirmed its earlier position, ruling that the testimony of hypnotized witnesses is inadmissible. On a motion for rehearing, the court modified this ruling: "[A] witness will be permitted to testify with regard to those matters which he or she was able to recall and relate prior to hypnosis. Thus, for example, the rape victim would be free to testify to the occurrence of the crime, the lack of consent, the injury inflicted and the like, assuming that such matters were remembered and related to the authorities prior to use of hypnosis."[146] Otherwise, the prosecution would not have any witnesses to prove that a rape occurred.

A second exception for the testimony of the accused is required by *Rock v. Arkansas*.[147] In that case, the trial court excluded the defendant's testimony because she had previously been hypnotized, a ruling that was consistent with Arkansas's adoption of the per se rule of exclusion. The Supreme Court reversed. Initially, the Court recognized an accused's right to testify.[148] Although the right to testify is not without limitations, Arkansas applied a per se rule of inadmissibility, which precluded *Rock* from testifying that she did not have her finger on the gun when it fired. The Court recognized the problems associated with hypnotically-refreshed testimony but found the per se rule to be an arbitrary restriction on the defendant's right to testify. A less restrictive approach, however, might have satisfied constitutional guarantees.[149]

---

[144] Rock v. Arkansas, 483 U.S. 44, 59–60 (1987).

[145] 644 P.2d 1266 (Ariz. 1982).

[146] *Id.* at 1295.

[147] 483 U.S. 44 (1987).

[148] *Id.* at 49 ("At this point in the development of our adversary system, it cannot be doubted that a defendant in a criminal case has the right to take the witness stand and to testify in his or her own defense.").

[149] "The State would be well within its powers if it established guidelines to aid trial courts in the evaluation of posthypnosis testimony and it may be able to show that testimony in a

Procedural safeguards. A second approach is based on *State v. Hurd*,[150] in which the New Jersey Supreme Court adopted a number of procedural requirements. First, a psychiatrist or psychologist experienced in the use of hypnosis must conduct the session — not a police officer. Second, the hypnotist must be independent of and not regularly employed by the prosecutor, investigator, or defense. Third, any information provided to the hypnotist prior to the hypnotic session must be recorded. Fourth, before inducing hypnosis, the hypnotist must obtain from the subject a detailed description of the facts as the subject remembers them. Fifth, all contacts between the hypnotist and the subject must be recorded. According to the Court, the use of videotape is strongly encouraged but not mandatory. Sixth, only the hypnotist and the subject should be present during the hypnotic session, including the prehypnotic testing and the post-hypnotic interview. These requirements are designed to prevent suggestion, either intentional or unintentional, and to preserve a record for review.

Discretionary admissibility & credibility approach. The early cases adopted a "credibility" approach, which left the reliability issue to the jury. These cases have generally been displaced by a "discretionary admission" approach, which entrusts the judge with the task of determining the reliability issue. This is sometimes called the "totality of circumstances" approach, and many of the procedural safeguards enumerated in *Hurd* are considered relevant here.

[C] Mental Condition Testimony

The courts are divided on the admissibility of expert testimony concerning a defendant's mental state based on an hypnotic interview. For example, in *Morgan v. State*,[151] the Florida Supreme Court held that a criminal defendant who raised an insanity defense could present the testimony of a psychiatrist and a psychologist whose opinions were in part based on statements made by the defendant while under hypnosis. The court characterized hypnosis as "a medically approved diagnostic technique" and noted that testimony of mental health experts based on hypnotic statements was distinguishable from evidence of the hypnotic statements themselves when offered for their truth.[152] However, in *Adams v. State*,[153] the Alabama

---

particular case is so unreliable that exclusion is justified." *Id.* at 61. *See* Giuliana, *Between Rock and a Hurd Place: Protecting the Criminal Defendant's Right to Testify after Her Testimony Has Been Hypnotically Refreshed*, 65 Fordham L. Rev. 2151 (1997).

[150] 432 A.2d 86 (N.J. 1981).

[151] 537 So. 2d 973 (Fla. 1989). *See generally* Kline, *Defending the Mentally Ill: The Insanity Defense and the Role of Forensic Hypnosis*, 27 Int'l J. Clinical & Experimental Hypnosis 375 (1979).

[152] *Id.* at 976. *See also* People v. Santana, 604 N.Y.S.2d 1016, 1018 (Sup. Ct. 1993) ("While hypnosis may not be introduced as direct evidence of the truth of the matter asserted, a testifying psychiatrist may, nevertheless, rely on hypnosis for the purpose of assessing the subject's state of mind.").

[153] 484 So. 2d 1160 (Ala. Crim. App. 1985).

Court of Criminal Appeals held that "opinion testimony concerning the mental state of the accused, which is based upon statements of the accused while in hypnosis is inadmissible as a matter of law."[154]

§ 24.10 Fingerprint Evidence

In *United States v. Llera Plaza*,[155] the trial judge held that a fingerprint expert could not give an opinion that two sets of prints "matched" — that is, a positive identification to the exclusion of all other persons. And then, he reversed himself.[156] The prosecution had argued that latent fingerprint identification had been "tested" for nearly 100 years in adversarial proceedings with the highest possible stakes. However, *Llera Plaza I* pointed out that *Daubert* requires scientific, not judicial, testing:

> "[A]dversarial" testing in court is not, however, what the Supreme Court meant when it discussed testing as an admissibility factor. . . . It makes sense to rely on scientific testing, rather than "adversarial" courtroom testing, because to rely on the latter would be to vitiate the gatekeeping role of federal trial judges, thereby undermining the essence of Rule 702 as interpreted by the Court in *Daubert*. . . . Thus, even 100 years of "adversarial" testing in court cannot substitute for scientific testing when the proposed expert testimony is presented as scientific in nature.[157]

In *Llera Plaza II*, the prosecution offered evidence of the FBI's proficiency testing. There was one "false positive" in sixteen external tests taken by supervisory examiners. In addition, the

> internal tests taken over the seven years numbered 431. These tests generated three errors, two in 1995 and one in 2000. Each of the three errors was a missed identification — *i.e.*, a failure by the test taker to find a match between a latent print and a known exemplar which in fact existed; such an error is a "false negative" which, being

---

[154] *Id.* at 1164.

[155] 179 F. Supp. 2d 492 (E.D. Pa. 2002) (later withdrawn) [hereinafter *Llera Plaza I*].

[156] 188 F. Supp. 2d 549 (E.D. Pa. 2002) ("I have changed my mind.") [hereinafter *Plaza II*]. *See* Specter, *Do Fingerprints Lie? The Gold Standard of Forensic Science is Now Being Challenged*, 78 New Yorker 96 (May 27, 2002) (discussing case including interview with judge). *See also* United States v. Martinez-Cintron, 136 F. Supp. 2d 17, 20 (D. Puerto Rico 2001) (admitting fingerprint evidence).

[157] In United States v. Havvard 117 F. Supp. 2d 848 (S.D. Ind. 2000), *aff'd*, 260 F.3d 597 (7th Cir. 2001), the court, without citing any scientific research, ruled that fingerprint identification satisfied the standards announced in *Daubert* and *Kumho*: "First, the methods of latent print identification can be and have been tested. They have been tested for roughly 100 years. They have been tested in adversarial proceedings with the highest possible stakes — liberty and sometimes life. . . . Next, the methods of identification are subject to peer review. As just stated, any other qualified examiner can compare the objective information upon which the opinion is based and may render a different opinion if warranted. In fact, peer review is the standard operating procedure among latent print examiners." However, a second opinion by another examiner is a quality control mechanism, not peer review in a scientific journal as required by *Daubert*.

mistakenly exculpatory, is regarded by the FBI as considerably less serious than a false positive. In sum, the 447 proficiency tests administered in the seven years from 1995 through 2001 yielded four errors — a proficiency error rate of just under 1%.[158]

Nevertheless, defense experts were highly critical of the way in which the tests were conducted. A fingerprint examiner, who had worked for 25 years at New Scotland Yard, testified that the FBI tests were too easy: "It's not testing their ability. It doesn't test their expertise. I mean I've set these tests to trainees and advanced technicians. And if I gave my experts these tests, they'd fall about laughing."[159] Two other defense experts were not fingerprint examiners but experts on testing (psychometrics). Both were critical of the FBI proficiency tests: "The test materials and uninformative attendant literature, taken together with the ambiguity as to the conditions governing the taking of the tests (*e.g.,* may the test takers consult with one another? to what extent is taking the test perceived to be competitive with, or subordinated to, the performance of concurrent work assignments?), gave few clues as to what the test makers intended to measure."[160] Both experts believed that the "stratospheric" FBI success rate "was hardly reassuring; to the contrary, it raised 'red flags.' "[161]

In the end, the judge concluded, on the record before him, that the evidence should be admitted.[162] *Llera Plaza II* is far from a ringing endorsement. The judge recognized that the basic science (*i.e.,* empirical testing) is missing. Indeed, he invited the National Institute of Justice (NIJ) to sponsor such research. Actually, in March 2000, the NIJ had released a solicitation for "Forensic Friction Ridge (Fingerprint) Examination — Validation Studies."[163] Disturbingly, the FBI apparently caused the NIJ solicitation to be delayed due to a pending court challenge — presumably because it would have undercut its position.[164] Moreover, the FBI's

---

[158] *Plaza II*, 188 F. Supp. 2d at 556.

[159] *Id.* at 558.

[160] *Id.* at 559.

[161] *Id.*

[162] *Id.* at 572 ("[T]there is no evidence that certified FBI fingerprint examiners present erroneous identification testimony, and . . . there is no evidence that the rate of error of certified FBI fingerprint examiners is unacceptably high. With those findings in mind, I am not persuaded that courts should defer admission of testimony with respect to fingerprinting . . . until academic investigators financed by the National Institute of Justice have made substantial headway on a 'verification and validation' research agenda. For the National Institute of Justice, or other institutions both public and private, to sponsor such research would be all to the good. But to postpone present in-court utilization of this 'bedrock forensic identifier' pending such research would be to make the best the enemy of the good.").

[163] National Institute of Justice, Solicitation: Forensic Friction Ridge (Fingerprint) Examination Validation Studies (March 2000).

[164] *See* Epstein, *Fingerprints Meet Daubert: The Myth of Fingerprint "Science" Is Revealed,* 75 So. Cal. L. Rev. 605, 628 n. 122 (2002) ("Internal documents of the NIJ presently on file with the author . . . reveal that the Institute was ready to publish the Solicitation in September of 1999, but that at the FBI's request, publication was delayed until after Mitchell's trial.").

proficiency testing appears to be inadequate. Finally, several articles and books have questioned the lack of empirical support for fingerprint comparisons.[165]

§ 24.11   Questioned Documents; Handwriting

Questioned document examinations cover a wide range of analyses: handwriting, hand printing, typewriting, mechanical impressions, altered documents, obliterated writing, indented writing, and charred documents.[166] Rule 901(b)(3) provides that an item of evidence may be authenticated by comparison with specimens, which would include handwriting examinations by an expert witness.[167]

After *Daubert*, handwriting comparison testimony came under attack. In 1995, a district court in *United States v. Starzecpyzel*[168] concluded that "the testimony at the *Daubert* hearing firmly established that forensic document examination, despite the existence of a certification program, professional journals and other trappings of science, cannot, after *Daubert*, be regarded as 'scientific . . . knowledge.'"[169] The court further stated that "while scientific principles may *relate* to aspects of handwriting analysis, they have little or nothing to do with the day-to-day tasks performed by [Forensic Document Examiners]. . . . [T]his attenuated relationship does not transform the FDE into a scientist."[170] Nevertheless, the court did not exclude handwriting comparison testimony. Instead, it admitted the testimony as "technical" knowledge.

Later cases divided, with appellate courts upholding admissibility[171] and some district courts excluding the evidence.[172] In addition, some trial courts

---

[165] *See* Cole, Suspect Identities: A History of Fingerprinting and Criminal Identification (2001); Mnookin, *Fingerprint Evidence in an Age of DNA Profiling*, 67 Brooklyn L. Rev. 13 (2001); Stoney, *Fingerprint Identification* in Faigman et al., Modern Scientific Evidence ch. 27 (2d ed. 2002).

[166] 2 Giannelli & Imwinkelried, *supra* note 33, ch. 21.

[167] *See infra* § 28.05.

[168] 880 F. Supp. 1027 (S.D.N.Y. 1995).

[169] *Id.* at 1038.

[170] *Id.* at 1041. *See also* National Institute of Justice, Forensic Science: Review of Status and Needs 31 (1998) ("document examination . . . is currently in a state of upheaval; [c]ourts in several jurisdictions recently questioned the scientific basis of handwriting identifications.").

[171] *See* United States v. Jolivet, 224 F.3d 902, 906 (8th Cir. 2000) (affirming admission of expert testimony that it was likely that defendant wrote the questioned documents and finding such opinion reliable because the expert was well-qualified in handwriting analysis and that his testimony "may be properly characterized as offering the jury knowledge beyond their own and enhancing their understanding of the evidence before them"); United States v. Paul, 175 F.3d 906, 911 (11th Cir. 1999); United States v. Jones, 107 F.3d 1147, 1160 (6th Cir. 1997) ("In short, expert handwriting analysis is a field of expertise under the Federal Rules of Evidence. This decision, however, does not guarantee the reliability or admissibility of this type of testimony in a particular case.").

[172] *E.g.,* United States v. Saelee, 162 F. Supp. 2d 1097, 1103 (D. Alaska 2001) ("There is little known about the error rates of forensic document examiners. The little testing that has

permit expert testimony about the similarities and dissimilarities between exemplars but not opinions that the same person wrote both.[173] This controversy has been exhaustively covered in several articles.[174]

In *United States v. Gricco*,[175] a district court admitted handwriting comparison testimony. The court cited several new studies to support its decision that the procedure had been tested.[176] Furthermore, standards have been developed.[177] In addition, the court noted that "Dr. Kam's studies show a professional document analyst error rate of 6.5 percent, and this rate does not take into account the second review performed by Ms. Bolsover's colleague."[178]

§ 24.12   DNA Profiling

DNA profiling was first reported in 1985 by Dr. Alec Jeffreys of the University of Leicester, England. The initial reports on DNA evidence were

---

been done raises serious questions about the reliability of methods currently in use. As to some tasks, there is a high rate of error and forensic document examiners may not be any better at analyzing handwriting than laypersons. This is illustrated not only in the Kam studies relied on by Mr. Cawley, but also in a series of proficiency tests carried out by Collaborative Testing Service under the supervision of the Forensic Sciences Foundation."); United States v. Fujii, 152 F. Supp. 2d 939, 940 (N.D. Ill. 2000) (expert testimony concerning Japanese handprinting inadmissible; "Handwriting analysis does not stand up well under the *Daubert* standards. Despite its long history of use and acceptance, validation studies supporting its reliability are few, and the few that exist have been criticized for methodological flaws.").

[173] *See* United States v. Rutherford, 104 F. Supp. 2d 1190, 1194 (D. Neb. 2000) ("[T]he Court concludes that FDE Rauscher's testimony meets the requirements of Rule 702 to the extent that he limits his testimony to identifying and explaining the similarities and dissimilarities between the known exemplars and the questioned documents. FDE Rauscher is precluded from rendering any ultimate conclusions on authorship of the questioned documents and is similarly precluded from testifying to the degree of confidence or certainty on which his opinions are based."); United States v. Hines, 55 F. Supp. 2d 62, 67 (D. Mass. 1999) (expert testimony concerning the general similarities and differences between a defendant's handwriting exemplar and a stick up note admissible but not the specific conclusion that the defendant was the author, because such an opinion lacked empirical validation).

[174] Risinger et al., *Brave New "Post-Daubert World" — A Reply to Professor Moenssens*, 29 Seton Hall L. Rev. 405 (1998); Moenssens, *Handwriting Identification Evidence In the Post-Daubert World*, 66 UMKC L. Rev. 251 (1997); Risinger et al., *Exorcism of Ignorance as a Proxy for Rational Knowledge: The Lessons of Handwriting Identification "Expertise,"* 137 U. Pa. L. Rev. 731, 738 (1989).

[175] 2002 WL 746037 (E.D. Pa. 2002) ("Most recently, document analysts conducted a study in which they undertook to validate the hypothesis that handwriting is individualistic and that handwriting analysis is reliable.").

[176] *See* Kam et al., *Signature Authentication by Forensic Document Examiners*, 46 J. Forensic Sci. 884 (2001) (finding that laypersons classified "nongenuine" signatures as genuine 13 times more often than forensic document examiners); Srihari et al., *Individuality of Handwriting*, 47 J. Forensic Sci. (May, 2002).

[177] United States v. Gricco, 2002 WL 746037 (E.D. Pa. 2002) ("Ms. Bolsover testified that she follows the methodology that is universally accepted in the handwriting analysis field, most recently promulgated by the Scientific Working Group Documents for Forensic Document Examination ('SWGDOC') which developed protocols for conducting handwriting analysis.").

[178] *Id.*

dramatic. One judge wrote that it was the "single greatest advance in the 'search for truth' since the advent of cross-examination."[179] There is little dispute that the basic science upon which DNA testing rests is valid. Nevertheless, questions concerning the methods used and the interpretation of the results have arisen.

[A]　DNA Technology

DNA (deoxyribonucleic acid) is a chemical messenger of genetic information, a code that gives both common and individual characteristics to people.[180] Except for identical twins, no two individuals share the same DNA pattern. DNA is found in every body cell with a nucleus, and with few exceptions, DNA does not vary from cell to cell. Each cell contains the entire genetic code, although each cell reads only the part of the code that it needs to perform its job. Thus, blood obtained from a suspect can be compared with semen or saliva cells from a crime scene.

DNA is composed of a chain of nucleotide bases twisted into a double helix structure, resembling a twisted ladder. Each rung of the helix is a "base pair." The order of the base pairs on the DNA ladder is known as the DNA sequence; it constitutes the "genetic code." In other words, these base pairs provide specific instructions to the cell; a sequence of base pairs that is the source for a particular trait is called a gene.[181] It is the area of base pair variation that is used in DNA analysis. These base pairs are called "polymorphisms."

DNA profiling involves two fields: molecular biology and population genetics. The analysis involves two corresponding steps — first, determining whether the genetic characteristics at several loci on the DNA strand "match," and second, assuming a match at each loci, calculating the population frequency for these matches. *Any* non-match at *any* loci in the first step means the suspect is excluded as a source of the evidence DNA. In other words, it is much easier to exclude a suspect than to include. A possible "inclusion" will be reported as a statistic of a random match — what are the chances that a person with the same genetic characteristics as in the evidence DNA would be found in the population? Thus, while the validity of DNA testing (molecular biology) does not hinge on population statistics, the interpretation of multiple "matches" at different loci does. For the calculations to be reliable, all the DNA characteristics tested must be independent of each other. For this assumption to be true, individuals must reproduce randomly so that distinct subgroups (population substructure) are absent.

Three generations of DNA profiling procedures have been used in forensic cases. The first was based on Restriction Fragment Length Polymorphism

---

[179] People v. Wesley, 533 N.Y.S.2d 643, 644 (Sup. Ct. 1988).

[180] *See* 1 Giannelli & Imwinkelried, *supra* note 33, ch. 18.

[181] Approximately 99% of the base pairs found in humans are the same. A single DNA molecule contains roughly three billion base pairs. If unraveled, it would measure approximately six feet.

(RFLP). This was followed by polymerase chain reaction (PCR) analysis for specific alleles.[182] The newest technique is called Short Tandem Repeats (STR). Mitochondrial DNA, which is present outside the cell nucleus, is used when STR profiling is not possible — *i.e.*, hair without roots and bones without marrow.

[B] Admissibility

DNA evidence was first introduced in an American court in 1986. The first reported appellate case was *Andrews v. State*,[183] a Florida decision. The most publicized case rejecting DNA evidence was *People v. Castro*,[184] where the court wrote: "In a piercing attack upon each molecule of evidence presented, the defense was successful in demonstrating to this court that the testing laboratory failed in its responsibility to perform the accepted scientific techniques and experiments."[185] The ruling in *Castro*, however, was limited. The court accepted the general validity of DNA evidence; it ruled only that the results in that case were inadmissible. Today, DNA evidence is admitted in all courts, although some questions about new technologies and the interpretation of statistics continue.

Numerous decisions applied *Daubert* to DNA profiling, including RFLP,[186] different types of PCR analysis,[187] STRs,[188] mitochondrial DNA,[189] statistical probabilities,[190] and so forth.[191]

§ 24.13 Eyewitness Identifications

The reliability of eyewitness identifications has long been a concern. As the Supreme Court wrote in a lineup case, "The vagaries of eyewitness

---

[182] PCR is essentially DNA amplification or molecular photocopying. It allows a scientist to take an insufficient forensic sample and amplify it until enough DNA is present for further analysis. The distinct advantage of PCR is that smaller, older samples can be used.

[183] 533 So. 2d 841 (Fla. App. 1988) (no defense experts).

[184] 545 N.Y.S.2d 985 (Sup. Ct. 1989).

[185] *Id.* at 996.

[186] *E.g.*, Taylor v. State, 889 P.2d 319, 328 (Okla. Crim. App. 1995) (RFLP match and statistical calculations admissible).

[187] *E.g.*, United States v. Beasley, 102 F.3d 1440, 1448 (8th Cir. 1996) (DQ-alpha and Poly-markers); United States v. Hicks, 103 F.3d 837, 844–46 (9th Cir. 1996); United States v. Gaines, 979 F. Supp. 1429 (S.D. Fla. 1997) (DQ-alpha, Polymarkers, D1S80, and amelogenin); Smith v. State, 702 N.E.2d 668, 672 (Ind. 1998) ("PM and D1S80 tests are scientifically reliable.").

[188] *E.g.*, Commonwealth v. Rosier, 685 N.E.2d 739 (Mass. 1997).

[189] *E.g.*, State v. Underwood, 518 S.E.2d 231 (N.C. App. 1999); State v. Council, 515 S.E.2d 508, 518 (S.C. 1999).

[190] *E.g.*, United States v. Davis, 40 F.3d 1069, 1075 (10th Cir. 1994) (FBI method and statistical probability evidence admitted); United States v. Chischilly, 30 F.3d 1144, 1153 (9th Cir. 1994) (FBI statistics based on its Native American database admissible, even though defendant's Navajo tribe may be underrepresented).

[191] *E.g.*, United States v. Black Cloud, 101 F.3d 1258, 1261 (8th Cir. 1996) (DNA for paternity admitted); United States v. Lowe, 954 F. Supp. 401 (D. Mass. 1996) (RFLP chemiluminescence admitted).

identification are well-known; the annals of criminal law are rife with instances of mistaken identification."[192] Several factors have been identified
as causing misidentifications. First, cross-racial identifications present
special problems.[193] Dr. Elizabeth Loftus, a prominent researcher in this
field, noted that people "have greater difficulty in recognizing faces of
another race than faces of their own race. This cross-racial identification
problem is not due to the fact that people have greater prejudices or less
experience with members of the other race."[194] Second, "unconscious
transference" may lead to misidentifications.[195] A witness who has seen
an innocent suspect at an earlier time may misidentify that suspect because
he "looks familiar." For example, a witness may view a photographic display
that includes a picture of an innocent suspect. No identification is made.
Later, the witness picks the suspect out of a lineup, unconsciously remem-
bering the face from the photo display. Third, research indicates that the
relationship between the accuracy of an identification and a witness's
confidence in the identification is not strong.[196] Indeed, two researchers
have concluded that "the eyewitness accuracy-confidence relationship is
weak under good laboratory conditions and functionally useless in forensically representative settings."[197]

Despite the mounting evidence of eyewitness misidentifications, most
courts exclude expert testimony concerning their unreliability because "the
trustworthiness in general of eyewitness observations is not beyond the ken
of the jurors."[198] This may be changing.[199]

The present status of expert testimony on this subject is summed up in
a recent decision as follows:

> The use of expert testimony in regard to eyewitness identification
> is a recurring and controversial subject. Trial courts have tradition-
> ally hesitated to admit expert testimony purporting to identify flaws
> in eyewitness identification. Among the reasons given to exclude
> such testimony are that the jury can decide the credibility issues

---

[192] United States v. Wade, 388 U.S. 218, 228 (1967).

[193] *See* Platz & Hosch, *Cross Racial/Ethnic Eyewitness Identification: A Field Study*, 18
J. Applied Soc. Psychol. 972 (1988); Johnson, *Cross-Racial Identification Errors in Criminal
Cases*, 69 Cornell L. Rev. 934, 938–39 (1984) ("The impairment in ability to recognize black
faces is substantial.").

[194] Loftus, Eyewitness Testimony 139 (1979).

[195] *Id.* at 142–51.

[196] *See* Cutler & Penrod, *Forensically Relevant Moderators of the Relation Between Eyewit-
ness Identification Accuracy and Confidence*, 74 J. Applied Psychol. 650 (1989); Deffenbacher,
Eyewitness Accuracy and Confidence: Can We Infer Anything About Their Relationship?, 4 Law
& Hum. Behav. 243, 250–57 (1980).

[197] Wells & Murray, *Eyewitness Confidence*, in Eyewitness Testimony: Psychological
Perspectives 155, 165 (Wells & Loftus eds. 1984).

[198] State v. Porraro, 404 A.2d 465, 471 (R.I. 1979).

[199] *E.g.,* United States v. Moore, 786 F.2d 1308, 1312 (5th Cir. 1986); United States v. Down-
ing, 753 F.2d 1224, 1231–32 (3d Cir. 1985); United States v. Smith, 736 F.2d 1103, 1106–07
(6th Cir. 1984); People v. McDonald, 690 P.2d 709 (Cal. 1984).

itself; that experts in this area are not much help and largely offer rather obvious generalities; that trials would be prolonged by a battle of experts; and that such testimony creates undue opportunity for confusing and misleading the jury.

Several courts, however, including our own, have suggested that such evidence warrants a more hospitable reception. *See United States v. Smithers* (holding that "the district court abused its discretion in excluding [the eyewitness identification expert's] testimony, without first conducting a hearing pursuant to *Daubert*") . . . . Moreover, such testimony has been allowed in with increasing frequency where the circumstances include "cross-racial identification, identification after a long delay, identification after observation under stress, and [such] psychological phenomena as . . . unconscious transference." Nonetheless, each court to examine this issue has held that the district court has broad discretion in, first, determining the reliability of the particular testimony, and, second, balancing its probative value against its prejudicial effect. [200]

Although a trend toward admissibility may be developing, the overwhelming number of cases involve upholding trial court decisions to exclude such evidence. [201]

§ 24.14 Battered Woman Syndrome

[A] Research

The battered woman syndrome (BWS) describes a pattern of violence inflicted on a woman by her mate. [202] Dr. Lenore Walker, the principal researcher in this field, describes a battered woman as follows:

A battered woman is a woman who is repeatedly subjected to any forceful physical or psychological behavior by a man in order to coerce her to do something he wants her to do without any concern for her rights. Battered women include wives or women in any form of intimate relationships with men. [203]

---

[200] United States v. Langan, 263 F.3d 613, 621 (6th Cir. 2001) (citations omitted). *See also* People v. Lee, 750 N.E.2d 63, 66 (N.Y. 2001) ("Despite the fact that jurors may be familiar from their own experience with factors relevant to the reliability of eyewitness observation and identification, it cannot be said that psychological studies regarding the accuracy of an identification are within the ken of the typical juror."); In re Thomas, 733 N.Y.S.2d 591, 593 (Sup. Ct. 2001) ("Psychologists speculate that in a simultaneous lineup the viewer subconsciously believes that he or she should select the person that most resembles the perpetrator.").

[201] *See* Mosteller, *Syndromes and Politics in Criminal Trials and Evidence Law*, 46 Duke L. J. 461, 495 (1996) ("[D]espite lip service to the inherent weakness of eyewitness identification evidence, courts do not believe that innocent defendants are frequently convicted as a result of such evidence. The greater perceived danger is that such expert testimony would too often produce acquittals of the guilty; this fear has led to its general exclusion.").

[202] *See* 1 Giannelli & Imwinkelried, *supra* note 33, § 9-3; Schneider, Battered Woman and Feminist Lawmaking (2000).

[203] Walker, The Battered Woman xv (1979).

Cycle of violence. This type of violence is neither constant nor random. It follows a pattern according to Dr. Walker, who has posited a three stage cycle of violence. The first stage is the "tension building" phase, during which small abusive episodes occur. These episodes gradually escalate over a period of time. The tension continues to build until the second stage — the "acute battering" phase — erupts. During this phase, in which most injuries occur, the battering is out of control. Psychological abuse in the form of threats of future harm is also prevalent. The third phase is a calm loving period in which the batterer is contrite, seeks forgiveness, and promises to reform. This phase provides a positive reinforcement for the woman to continue the relationship in the hope that the violent behavior will not recur. The cycle then repeats itself.[204]

Walker's research has not been free of criticism: "The syndrome, first proposed in the 1970's and based on the clinical observations of a single researcher, has yet to be corroborated by serious and rigorous empirical work. . . . Given the lack of a scientific basis and its failure to achieve specific political and policy goals, the battered woman syndrome can be expected to soon pass from the legal scene."[205] This seems unlikely, however. A 1992 review of the research literature indicated that BWS had attained, to a large extent, scientific acceptance. Citing a survey of experts in the field,[206] Schuller and Vidmar concluded: "The degree of expert consensus shown in the Dodge and Greene survey tends to suggest that the scientific literature bearing on a battered woman's circumstances and situation is sound. There are, however, some aspects of the testimony — the cycle pattern of violence and the development of learned helplessness — that are not universal across battering relationships."[207]

[B] Admissibility

The admissibility of BWS evidence initially divided the courts. In *State v. Thomas*,[208] the Ohio Supreme Court was one of the first courts to consider the issue, and it rejected BWS evidence. Later decisions began to gradually accept BWS evidence. According to one court, "only by understanding these unique pressures that force battered women to remain with

---

[204] *Id.* at 55–70.

[205] Faigman & Wright, *Battered Woman Syndrome in the Age of Science*, 39 Ariz. L. Rev. 67, 114 (1997). They also wrote that the research is seriously flawed. The experiments were designed to prove/confirm set ideas, rather than to objectively test a given hypothesis. Further, based on the research done, "[i]t is not obvious that the psychological profile of most battered women generalizes to the small number of battered women who kill." *Id.* at 79. "[L]earned helplessness as a psychological construct, is fundamentally at odds with a situation in which a woman has exercised the degree of control reflected in the act of self defense, [killing]." *Id.* at 82.

[206] Dodge & Greene, *Jurors and Expert Conceptions of Battered Women*, 6 Victims & Violence 271 (1991) (eighteen-item survey of forty-five professionals who had published in the field).

[207] Schuller & Vidmar, *Battered Woman Syndrome Evidence in the Courtroom: A Review of the Literature*, 16 Law & Hum. Behav. 273, 281 (1992).

[208] 423 N.E.2d 137, 140 (Ohio 1981), *overruled by*, State v. Koss, 51 N.E.2d 907 (Ohio 1990).

their mates, despite their long-standing and reasonable fear of severe bodily harm and the isolation that being a battered woman creates, can a battered woman's state of mind be accurately and fairly understood."[209] Another court put it this way:

> [T]he battered person syndrome is not a separate defense, but . . . evidence of battered person syndrome is relevant in a proper case as a component of justifiable homicide by self-defense. . . . [E]vidence that a defendant suffered from battered person syndrome is only another circumstance which, if believed by the jury, would authorize a finding that a reasonable person, who had experienced prior physical abuse such as was endured by the defendant, would reasonably believe that the use of force against the victim was necessary, even though that belief may have been, in fact, erroneous.[210]

The recent cases involve extending the use of BWS evidence beyond self-defense to support a duress defense[211] or to permit its use by the prosecution.[212]

§ 24.15 Rape Trauma Syndrome

[A] Research

Burgess and Holmstrom coined the phrase rape trauma syndrome (RTS), to describe the behavioral, somatic, and psychological reactions of rape and attempted rape victims.[213] They found that victims usually progress through a two-phase process — an acute phase and a long-term reorganization phase. Many victims react in the acute phase either with an "expressed style" in which fear, anger, and anxiety are manifested, or a "controlled style" in which these feelings are masked by a composed or subdued behavior. Other reactions include humiliation, embarrassment, anger, revenge, and self-blame. The second phase, the reorganization phase, typically begins two to six weeks after the attack and is a period in which the victim

---

[209] State v. Kelly, 478 A.2d 364, 372 (N.J. 1984). *See also* People v. Torres, 488 N.Y.S.2d 358, 363 (Sup. Ct. 1985) ("The theory underlying the battered woman's syndrome has indeed passed beyond the experimental stage and gained a substantial enough scientific acceptance to warrant admissibility. Numerous articles and books have been published about the battered woman's syndrome; and recent findings of researchers in the field have confirmed its presence and thereby indicated that the scientific community accepts its underlying premises.").

[210] State v. Smith, 486 S.E.2d 819, 822 (Ga. 1997).

[211] *See* Dunn v. Roberts, 963 F.2d 308 (10th Cir. 1992) (accused entitled to expert assistance to raise duress defense).

[212] *See* Arcoren v. United States, 929 F.2d 1235 (8th Cir. 1991) (defendant charged with aggravated sexual abuse; his estranged wife reported the assault but then recanted her grand jury testimony at trial; BWS evidence admissible to explain recantation); Barrett v. State, 675 N.E.2d 1112 (Ind. App. 1996) (BWS evidence relevant to a neglect-of-dependent charge).

[213] Burgess & Holmstrom, *Rape Trauma Syndrome*, 131 Am. J. Psychiatry 981 (1974). *See also* Burgess, *Rape Trauma Syndrome*, 1 Behav. Sci. & Law 97 (Summer 1983).

attempts to re-establish her life. In this period, the victim often changes residences, switches telephone numbers, or visits family members. Nightmares, dreams, and rape-related phobias are common.

"Subsequent research, which is much more rigorous, conceptualizes rape trauma in terms of specific symptoms rather than more general stages of recovery."[214] RTS is now recognized as a type of post-traumatic stress disorder (PTSD), and these disorders are included in the most recent edition of the American Psychiatric Association's Diagnostic and Statistical Manual of Mental Disorders.[215]

The focus of much of the research was on understanding the victim's reactions in order to provide assistance to the victim. The focus was not on evaluating a victim's reactions in order to establish the fact that a rape had occurred, which is how RTS evidence is sometimes used at trial. There is an accepted body of research concerning the aftereffects of rape. The critical issue, however, is how the research is used in court.[216]

[B] Admissibility

RTS evidence may be offered at trial for several different purposes: (1) to prove lack of consent by the alleged victim, or (2) to explain post-incident conduct by a victim that a jury might perceive as inconsistent with the claim of rape. The courts divide over the first use but generally accept the second use.

Lack of consent. In 1982, the Kansas Supreme Court concluded that the "literature clearly demonstrates that the so-called 'rape trauma syndrome'

---

[214] Frazier & Borgida, *Rape Trauma Syndrome: A Review of the Case Law and Psychological Research*, 16 Law & Hum. Behav. 293, 299 (1992). *See generally* Mosteller, *Legal Doctrines Governing the Admissibility of Expert Testimony Concerning Social Framework Evidence*, 52 Law & Contemp. Probs. 85, 125–28 (Autumn 1989); Comment, *Making the Woman's Experience Relevant to Rape: The Admissibility of Rape Trauma Syndrome in California*, 39 UCLA L. Rev. 251 (1991).

[215] A 1992 review of the literature by Frazier and Borgida concluded:

> In our opinion, although early studies were plagued by numerous methodological problems, several studies have since been conducted that are much more sophisticated methodologically. These studies have assessed victim recovery at several points after the assault using standardized assessment measures and have employed carefully matched control groups. This research has established that rape victims experience more depression, anxiety, fear, and social adjustment and sexual problems than women who have not been victimized. Research on PTSD among rape victims is more recent but consistently suggests that many victims experience PTSD symptoms following an assault. Initially high symptom levels generally abate by 3 to 4 months postassault, although significant levels of distress continue for many victims.

Frazier & Borgida, *supra* note 214, at 301.

[216] *Id.* at 304–05 ("In sum, experts in recent cases have described a broad range of symptoms and behaviors as consistent with RTS, some of which do not appear to be based on research. Testimony that is not research based often seems to be prompted by a defendant's claims that a complainant's behavior was inconsistent with having been raped. If virtually any victim behavior is described as consistent with RTS, the term soon will have little meaning. Indeed, some critics have argued that this already is the case.").

is generally accepted to be a common reaction to sexual assault. As such, qualified expert psychiatric testimony regarding the existence of rape trauma syndrome is relevant and admissible in a case such as this where the defense is consent."[217] A psychiatrist, who examined the victim two weeks after the attack, testified that the victim had suffered a "frightening assault" and was "suffering from the post-traumatic stress disorder known as rape trauma syndrome." Other courts followed this precedent but imposed a variety of limitations. Some courts permit the expert to testify that the victim's behavior was consistent with RTS but not that the victim had been raped. Others prohibit (1) comment on the credibility of the alleged victim, (2) use of the term "rape trauma syndrome," or (3) any reference to the accused.[218]

Courts rejecting RTS as proof of lack of consent dispute the scientific validity of the syndrome when offered for this purpose. In *People v. Bledsoe*,[219] the California Supreme Court noted that "rape trauma syndrome was not devised to determine the 'truth' or 'accuracy' of a particular past event — *i.e.*, whether, in fact, a rape in the legal sense occurred — but rather was developed by professional rape counselors as a therapeutic tool, to help identify, predict and treat emotional problems experienced by the counselors' clients or patients."[220] Thus, according to the court, although generally accepted by the scientific community for a therapeutic purpose, expert testimony on RTS was not generally accepted to prove that a rape in fact occurred. As a rule, "rape counselors do not probe inconsistencies in their clients' descriptions of the facts of the incident, nor do they conduct independent investigations to determine whether other evidence corroborates or contradicts their clients' renditions. Because their function is to help their clients deal with the trauma they are experiencing, the historical accuracy of the clients' descriptions of the details of the traumatizing events is not vital in their task."[221]

Explaining behavior. Although the Court rejected RTS evidence when offered to prove lack of consent, it approved its use where the defendant suggests to the jury that the victim's conduct after the incident is inconsistent with the claim of rape. In this situation, the Court wrote, "expert testimony on rape trauma syndrome may play a particularly useful role by disabusing the jury of some widely held misconceptions about rape and rape victims, so that it may evaluate the evidence free of the constraints of popular myths."[222] For example, expert testimony has been admitted to explain a victim's (1) passive resistance during a rape, (2) delay in reporting the crime, and (3) calm demeanor after an attack.[223]

---

[217] State v. Marks, 647 P.2d 1292, 1299 (Kan. 1982).

[218] 1 Giannelli & Imwinkelried, *supra* note 33, § 9-4.

[219] 681 P.2d 291 (Cal. 1984).

[220] *Id.* at 300.

[221] *Id.*

[222] *Id.* at 298.

[223] 1 Giannelli & Imwinkelried, *supra* note 33, § 9-4.

§ 24.16   Child Sexual Abuse Accommodation Syndrome

[A]   Research

The typical responses of child sexual abuse victims are counter-intuitive in many respects. Delayed disclosure, conflicting statements, and retraction suggest fabrication unless an explanation is offered for this anomalous behavior. Dr. Roland Summit coined the phrase "Child Sexual Abuse Accommodation Syndrome" (CSAAS) in 1983 to describe five aspects of child sexual abuse.[224] The first two are preconditions to child sexual abuse; the last three are "sequential contingencies" that vary in both form and degree. The factors are: (1) secrecy,[225] (2) helplessness,[226] (3) entrapment and accommodation,[227] (4) delayed, conflicting, and unconvincing disclosure,[228] and (5) retraction.[229]

Dr. Summit developed the "syndrome" to assist professionals in treating abused children. The syndrome is not a diagnostic tool[230] and the term syndrome should be avoided as misleading.

Sexually abused children do react in a variety of ways, including anxiety, depression, nightmares, enuresis, regression, and acting out. Many of these responses, however, are also associated with other psychological problems unrelated to sex abuse. Some reactions are strongly suggestive of abuse: "Examples of behaviors that have greater specificity for sexual abuse include age-inappropriate knowledge of sexual acts or anatomy, sexualization of play and behavior in young children, the appearance of genitalia in young children's drawings, and sexually explicit play with anatomically detailed dolls."[231]

---

[224] Summit, *The Child Sexual Abuse Accommodation Syndrome*, 7 Child Abuse & Neglect 177 (1983).

[225] The child receives the message, either explicitly through threats or admonishments or implicitly, that the subject is to be kept secret.

[226] The imbalance of power that exists between child and adult makes the child feel powerless to resist. The feeling of helplessness is increased when the abuser is a trusted friend or family member.

[227] The child who does not seek or receive intervention learns to live with the sexual abuse in order to survive. In addition to submission, other survival mechanisms include turning to imaginary friends, developing multiple personalities, taking refuge in altered states of consciousness or substance abuse, running away, promiscuity, hysterical phenomena, delinquency, sociopathy, projection of rage, and self-mutilation.

[228] Rarely will the child report incidents of sexual abuse immediately upon their occurrence. Because of the time lapse before report occurs and the emotional upheaval experienced by the child, the disclosure is likely to contain contradictions and misstatements. Often the disclosure is greeted by disbelief.

[229] Particularly if the abuser is a family member, the child will attempt to undo the disintegration of the family caused by the disclosure. "Whatever a child says about sexual abuse, she is likely to reverse it." Summit, *supra* note 224, at 188.

[230] "The syndrome does not detect sexual abuse. Rather, it assumes the presence of abuse, and explains the child's reactions to it. Thus, CSAAS is not the sexual abuse analogue of battered child syndrome, which is diagnostic of physical abuse." Myers, et al., *Expert Testimony in Child Sexual Abuse Litigation*, 68 Neb. L. Rev. 1, 67 (1989).

[231] *Id.* at 62–63.

[B] Admissibility

Expert testimony on child sexual abuse may be offered for several distinct purposes: (1) as substantive evidence to prove that the child has been abused; (2) to explain conduct of the child that a jury might perceive as inconsistent with a claim of abuse; or (3) to bolster or impeach the child's credibility. Moreover, the form of the testimony may vary. For example, expert testimony offered to establish abuse could take three different forms: (1) general testimony about the behavioral characteristics of abused children; (2) testimony that a particular child's behavior is consistent with that of abused children; or (3) an opinion that a particular child has been abused.[232]

Fact of abuse. Some courts permit expert testimony "regarding the behavioral and emotional indicia of child sexual abuse victims" as well as testimony that "an alleged victim exhibits behavior consistent with such a profile."[233] Other courts reject the substantive use of expert testimony to prove the fact of abuse, questioning the scientific basis of this type of evidence.[234]

Explaining behavior. Virtually all courts admit evidence derived from research on child sexual abuse when offered in response to a defense suggestion that specific behavior is inconsistent with a claim of abuse. For example, courts have admitted expert testimony to explain why a sexually abused child would delay making an accusation, retract an accusation, make inconsistent statements, or remain with the offender.[235] Commentators have pointed out that such "expert testimony is needed to disabuse jurors of commonly held misconceptions about child sexual abuse, and to explain the emotional antecedents of abused children's seemingly self-impeaching behavior."[236]

Credibility. Most courts prohibit expert testimony concerning the credibility of the child: "Opinion evidence on who is telling the truth in cases such as this is nothing more than the expert's opinion on how the case should be decided. Such testimony is inadmissible, both because it usurps the jury's traditional functions and roles and because, when given insight into the behavioral sciences, the jury needs nothing further from the expert."[237]

---

[232] 1 Giannelli & Imwinkelried, *supra* note 33, § 9-5.

[233] State v. Edward Charles L., 398 S.E.2d 123 (W. Va. 1990). *See generally* McCord, *Expert Psychological Testimony About Child Complainants in Sexual Abuse Prosecutions: A Foray Into the Admissibility of Novel Psychological Evidence*, 77 J. Crim. L. & Criminology 1 (1986).

[234] *See* State v. Rimmasch, 775 P.2d 388, 401 (Utah 1989) ("Not only is there lack of any consensus about the ability of the profile to determine abuse, but the scientific literature raises serious doubts as to the reliability of profile testimony when used for forensic purposes to demonstrate that abuse actually occurred.").

[235] *See* United States v. Bighead, 128 F.3d 1329, 1330 (9th Cir. 1997) (In rebuttal, an expert "testified about 'delayed disclosure' and 'script memory,' which are typical characteristics she has observed among the more than 1300 persons she has interviewed who say they are victims of child abuse.").

[236] Myers et al., *supra* note 230, at 89.

[237] State v. Lindsey, 720 P.2d 73, 76 (Ariz. 1986).

§ 24.17   Ultimate Issue Rule: FRE 704

Rule 704 abolishes the "ultimate issue" prohibition, under which a witness was precluded from giving an opinion on the ultimate issues in a case. Abolition of the rule prohibiting opinions, lay or expert, on ultimate issues does not mean that all such opinions are admissible. It means only that admissibility is governed by Rule 701, requiring lay opinions to be "helpful," and Rule 702, requiring expert opinions to "assist the trier of fact."[238]

The ultimate issue prohibition was justified on the ground that opinions on ultimate issues "invade the province of the jury" or "usurp the function of the jury." For a number of reasons, this rationale was never persuasive. First, difficult questions of application are involved in distinguishing "ultimate facts" from other "facts." Second, the witness can never usurp the function of the jury. The jury is not bound by an opinion, even one by an expert, and is instructed that it may disregard the opinion of witnesses, including those of experts. Of course, there is a danger that the jury may be unduly influenced by the opinion of a particular witness, especially an expert, but this problem exists whether the witness is offering an opinion or testifying about observed facts.[239]

Finally, the principal defect in the ultimate issue rule is that it establishes the wrong standard for the admissibility of opinion testimony. The issue should be whether the opinion, lay or expert, assists the jury, and not whether the opinion relates to the ultimate issues in the case. In many instances, the jury needs an opinion on issues that could be classified as "ultimate." For example, in a forgery case the only contested issue may be whether the defendant forged a check. A handwriting expert, based on training and experience, may be able to answer that question. In such a case, an opinion on the "ultimate issue" is both desirable and necessary. The expert, however, should not be permitted to testify that the defendant was "guilty"; the expert, based on an examination of the exemplars, may testify on whether the known exemplars and the check were written by the same person.

Limitations. As noted above, abolition of the ultimate issue rule does not mean that all opinions on ultimate issues are now admissible. Rather, it means that the admissibility of such opinions is determined by the standards set forth in Rule 701 and Rule 702. The federal drafters commented:

> The abolition of the ultimate issue rule does not lower the bars so as to admit all opinions. Under Rules 701 and 702, opinions must be helpful to the trier of fact, and Rule 403 provides for exclusion

---

[238] *See* Fed. R. Evid. 704 advisory committee's note ("The basic approach to opinions, lay and expert, in these rules is to admit them when helpful to the trier of fact. In order to render this approach fully effective and to allay any doubt on the subject, the so-called *ultimate issue* rule is specifically abolished.").

[239] *See* Note, *Opinion Testimony "Invading the Province of the Jury,"* 20 U. Cin. L. Rev. 484, 488 (1951).

of evidence which wastes time. These provisions afford ample assurances against the admission of opinions which would merely tell the jury what result to reach, somewhat in the manner of the oath-helpers of an earlier day. They also stand ready to exclude opinions phrased in terms of inadequately explored legal criteria. Thus the question, "Did T have sufficient mental capacity to make a will?" would be excluded, while the question, "Did T have sufficient mental capacity to know the nature and extent of his property and the natural objects of his bounty and to formulate a rational scheme of distribution?" would be allowed.[240]

One court has observed: "No witness should be permitted to give his opinion directly that a person is guilty or innocent, or is criminally responsible or irresponsible."[241] Moreover, the Tenth Circuit has properly noted: "Caution should be the watchword in receiving such evidence in criminal cases."[242]

[A] Mental States

In 1984 Congress amended Rule 704 by adding subdivision (b). This amendment was part of the Comprehensive Crime Control Act of 1984, one aspect of which dealt with the insanity defense in federal prosecutions. In "reforming" the insanity defense, Congress did not limit itself to changing the substantive law of insanity. It also restricted expert testimony on the insanity defense, by amending Rule 704. The Senate Judiciary Committee Report comments:

> The purpose of this amendment is to eliminate the confusing spectacle of competing expert witnesses testifying to directly contradictory conclusions as to the ultimate legal issue to be found by the trier of fact. Under this proposal, expert psychiatric testimony would be limited to presenting and explaining their diagnoses, such as whether the defendant had a severe mental disease or defect and what the characteristics of such a disease or defect, if any, may have been.[243]

As support for this position, the committee cited the position of the American Psychiatric Association, which had questioned whether psychiatrists were competent to address some aspects of the insanity defense.[244]

---

[240] Fed. R. Evid. 704 advisory committee's note.

[241] Grismore v. Consolidated Prods. Co., 5 N.W.2d 646, 663 (Iowa 1942).

[242] United States v. Gutierrez, 576 F.2d 269, 275 (10th Cir. 1978).

[243] S. Rep. No. 225, 98th Cong., 2nd Sess. (1984), reprinted in 1984 U.S.C.C.A.N. 3182, 3412-13.

[244] The committee quoted the following:

> [I]t is clear that psychiatrists are experts in medicine, not the law. As such, it is clear that the psychiatrist's first obligation and expertise in the courtroom is to "do psychiatry," i.e., to present medical information and opinion about the defendant's mental state and motivation and to explain in detail the reason for his medical-

Moreover, the committee noted that "the rationale for precluding ultimate opinion psychiatric testimony extends beyond the insanity defense to any ultimate mental state of the defendant that is relevant to the legal conclusion sought to be proven. The Committee has fashioned its Rule 704 provision to reach all such *ultimate* issues, *e.g.*, premeditation in a homicide case, or lack of predisposition in entrapment."[245]

The federal rule still requires trial courts to engage in line-drawing. For example, one federal court ruled that testimony in terms of a legal conclusion — whether a defendant was able to appreciate the wrongfulness of his conduct — was improper. In contrast, testimony that the defendant suffered from a mental disease or whether such a mental disease would affect a person's ability to appreciate his actions is acceptable.[246] Another court stated the rule this way:

> [E]xpert testimony . . . may address the mental illness of Defendant and the characteristics, if any, of that mental illness. Expert testimony may not be introduced, however, with respect to an expert's inference or opinion that, at the time of the alleged crimes, Defendant was (1) sane; (2) insane; (3) lacked substantial capacity to know the wrongfulness of his conduct; or (4) lacked substantial capacity to conform his conduct to the requirements of the law which he is charged with violating.[247]

---

psychiatric conclusions. When, however, "ultimate issue" questions are formulated by the law and put to the expert witness who must then say "yea" or "nay," then the expert witness is required to make a leap in logic. He no longer addresses himself to medical concepts but instead must infer or intuit what is in fact unspeakable, namely, the probable relationship between medical concepts and legal or moral constructs such as free will. These impermissible leaps in logic made by expert witnesses confuse the jury. [Footnote omitted.] Juries thus find themselves listening to conclusory and seemingly contradictory psychiatric testimony that defendants are either "sane" or "insane" or that they do or do not meet the relevant legal test for insanity. This state of affairs does considerable injustice to psychiatry and, we believe, possibly to criminal defendants. In fact, in many criminal insanity trials both prosecution and defense psychiatrists do agree about the nature and even the extent of mental disorder exhibited by the defendant at the time of the act.

Psychiatrists, of course, must be permitted to testify fully about the defendant's diagnosis, mental state and motivation (in clinical and commonsense terms) at the time of the alleged act so as to permit the jury or judge to reach the ultimate conclusion about which they and only they are expert. Determining whether a criminal defendant was legally insane is a matter for legal fact-finders, not for experts.

[245] S. Rep. No. 225, 98th Cong., 2nd Sess. (1984), reprinted in 1984 U.S.C.C.A.N. 3182, 3412-13.

[246] United States v. Kristiansen, 901 F.2d 1463, 1466 (8th Cir. 1990). *See also* United States v. Brown, 32 F.3d 236, 240 (7th Cir. 1994) (In an insanity case, "Rule 704(b) clearly excludes expert opinion as to the defendant's appreciation for his acts. The testimony in this case, though, is not specific to Brown's mental state, but concerns the characteristics of his mental disorder, which is permitted by Rule 704(b).").

[247] United States v. Pickett, 604 F. Supp. 407, 410-11 (S.D. Ohio 1985), *aff'd*, 790 F.2d 35 (6th Cir. 1986).

§ 24.18 Key Points

The use of expert testimony raises two threshold issues. First, is the proffered testimony a proper subject matter for expert testimony? If the answer is "yes," the next question follows: Is this witness qualified in this subject matter? There is typically no requirement that an expert be called as a witness on a particular issue. Malpractice cases, however, frequently require expert testimony to establish the standard of care.

Subject Matter Requirement

Expert testimony is bounded on one side by the unreliable and on the other side by the commonplace. Thus, courts developed one standard for instances where expertise is not needed — *i.e.,* the commonplace, and another standard for judging when the testimony is too unreliable.

Commonplace. The standard adopted by Rule 702 — whether expert testimony will "assist the trier of fact" — is a more liberal formulation of the subject matter requirement than that found in many common-law opinions, which phrased the requirement as whether the subject was beyond the ken of lay persons.

Unreliable. At least three different approaches can be gleaned from the cases: (1) the *Frye* "general acceptance" test, (2) a relevancy approach, and (3) the Supreme Court's reliability approach, as set forth in *Daubert v. Merrell Dow Pharm., Inc.*

Frye test. Although *Frye* is no longer the majority rule, it is still followed in a dozen or so jurisdictions, including California, Florida, Illinois, Maryland, Michigan, Minnesota, New Jersey, New York, Pennsylvania, and Washington. Because these are populous states and most crimes are prosecuted in state courts, *Frye* remains an important test.

Relevancy approach. In his 1954 text, McCormick argued that a special test, such as general acceptance, was not needed and that the traditional evidentiary rules on relevancy and expert testimony should be applied in this context. In effect, qualifying the expert presumptively qualifies the technique used by that expert. This is the most lax standard, and only a few states presently follow it. This approach was implicitly rejected by the Supreme Court in *Daubert*, which requires the trial judge to determine reliability in addition to relevancy.

Reliability test. In *Daubert*, the Supreme Court rejected the *Frye* test and substituted a reliability approach. In performing the *Daubert* "gatekeeping function," the trial court may consider a number of nonexclusive factors. First, a judge ought to determine whether the scientific theory or technique can be and has been tested. Science's distinctive methodology is controlled experimentation. Second, whether a theory or technique has been subjected to peer review and publication is a relevant consideration. Third, a technique's known or potential rate of error is a pertinent factor. Fourth, the existence and maintenance of standards controlling the technique's operation are indicia of trustworthiness. Finally, "general acceptance" remains an important consideration. General acceptance is no longer the test; it has been demoted to the status of a mere relevant factor.

General Elec. Co. v. Joiner was the second opinion in the *Daubert* trilogy. The Court ruled that the proper standard for reviewing a trial court's admissibility decision under *Daubert* was an abuse-of-discretion.

In *Kumho Tire Co. v Carmichael,* the Court extended *Daubert's* reliability requirement to non-scientific testimony under Rule 702. In addition, the Court acknowledged the relevance of the *Daubert* factors in determining reliability in this context.

Qualifications

Rule 702 provides that a witness may be qualified as an expert "by specialized knowledge, skill, experience, training, or education." The expert need not be the best witness on the subject, nor an outstanding practitioner in the field. The expert generally need not be licensed in the field, although this factor is relevant to the qualification issue. Nor must the expert's qualifications match those of the other side's expert. Experience alone may qualify a witness to express an opinion. There is no "degree" requirement, per se.

Court-Appointed Experts

A trial court has inherent authority to appoint expert witnesses and technical advisors. Rule 706 recognizes this authority.

Right to Defense Experts

The appointment of an expert for an indigent criminal defendant may be required on due process grounds. In *Ake v. Oklahoma,* the Supreme Court held that "when a State brings its judicial power to bear on an indigent in a criminal proceeding, it must take steps to assure that the defendant has a fair opportunity to present his defense."

Chapter 25

BASES OF EXPERT TESTIMONY: FRE 703 & 705

§ 25.01 Introduction

The last chapter discussed the subject matter and qualification requirements for expert testimony. This chapter considers the *bases* of expert testimony.

To be relevant, the expert's opinion must be *based* on the facts in the particular case. Moreover, if the jury rejects those facts (and they may be disputed), the jury should also reject the opinion.

Expert's Opinion

Facts or Data

How does the expert get those facts? Rule 703 recognizes three bases for expert testimony:[1]

Firsthand knowledge. The expert may have personal knowledge of the relevant facts. For example, the treating physician who set a broken bone may testify that the patient had a compound fracture (*i.e.*, bone protruding through the skin). The Doc was there. The Doc saw it. The Doc fixed it.

Hypothetical question. If the bases were limited to firsthand knowledge, our use of experts would be greatly restricted. Therefore, the common law developed the hypothetical question, in which we give the relevant facts to the expert (*e.g.*, "Doctor. Assume that a patient had a compound fracture. Do you have an opinion as to the proper course of treatment?") Such facts, however, must be adduced through other witnesses. They are called "*record facts*" because they must be in the *record of trial*. Thus, at common law,

---

[1] *See* Fed. R. Evid. 703 advisory committee's note ("Facts or data upon which expert opinions are based may, under the rule, be derived from three possible sources. The first is the firsthand observation of the witness with opinions based thereon traditionally allowed. A treating physician affords an example. . . . The second source, presentation at the trial, also reflects existing practice. The technique may be the familiar hypothetical question or having the expert attend the trial and hear the testimony establishing the facts. . . . The third source contemplated by the rule consists of presentation of data to the expert outside of court and other than by his own perception.").

there were generally two bases for expert testimony: (1) personal knowledge and (2) assumed record facts (*i.e.,* hypothetical question).

Opinions based on nonrecord facts. Federal Rule 703 adds a third basis: facts not in the record "if of a type reasonably relied upon by experts in the particular field in forming opinions or inferences upon the subject." This innovation is controversial because it means that the expert may base an opinion on facts not admitted in evidence. Indeed, the facts may be inadmissible — *e.g.,* hearsay.

Rule 705. Rule 703 must be read in conjunction with Rule 705, which permits an expert to give an opinion before disclosing the underlying bases. This also changes the common law. By its very nature, the hypothetical question requires disclosure of the facts (*i.e.,* the assumed facts) upon which the opinion is based prior to the rendition of the opinion.

§ 25.02   Opinion Based on Personal Knowledge

Rule 703 provides that an expert may base an opinion on facts or data that are "perceived" (*i.e.,* firsthand knowledge). Typical examples are the forensic chemist who analyzes and testifies about the nature of a controlled substance (*i.e.,* heroin) or the treating physician who testifies about the cause and extent of an injury. Similarly, a forensic pathologist who expresses an opinion about the cause of death in a homicide case, after conducting an autopsy, is basing her opinion on personal observation.

§ 25.03   Opinion Based on Admitted Evidence ("record facts")

Under Rule 703, an expert may base an opinion on facts or data "made known to the expert" at the hearing (*i.e.,* hypothetical question). Although this method of eliciting expert opinion is still available,[2] the Federal Rules do not require its use.

If the expert has personal knowledge of data, there is no need to resort to a hypothetical question. Experts, however, frequently testify based on both personal knowledge and assumed facts. For example, the pathologist has personal knowledge of what she saw during an autopsy but not of the toxicologist's findings. In a poisoning case, the pathologist could testify that she observed the cherry red color of the skin that suggests the presence

---

[2] *E.g.,* Iconco v. Jensen Constr. Co., 622 F.2d 1291, 1300–01 (8th Cir. 1980) (dispute over government contract; "Johnson was asked to assume that the low bidder on the Saylorville contract was not a small business, that the second low bidder was and submitted a bid which was reasonable in amount (roughly 50% of the amount estimated by the [Army Corps of Engineers] as necessary to perform the contract), that the second low bidder could obtain a performance bond and had successfully completed in its ten years experience several other similar contracts, and that it met other requirements of the pre-award survey in terms of financial ability, licensing, organization, experience, equipment, integrity, and reputation. Assuming these facts, Colonel Johnson [the expert] was asked for an opinion about whether the contract would have been awarded to the second low bidder.").

of carbon monoxide and that no other cause of death was apparent. These two facts are based on firsthand knowledge gained at the autopsy. The trial attorney could also ask the pathologist to *assume* toxicological findings of a lethal dose of carbon monoxide (hypothetical question) as well as the personally observed facts at the autopsy and then ask for an opinion as to the cause of death: carbon monoxide poisoning. The attorney would still need to have the toxicological findings admitted into evidence at some point in the trial.

In addition to the standard hypothetical question, a "modified" hypothetical (my term) may be used.

[A] Hypothetical Questions

During direct examination, the attorney may ask the expert to *assume* certain facts as true and then ask if the expert has formed an opinion based on those *assumed* facts. If the expert replies "yes," an opinion may be given.[3] Recall that the assumed facts must be adduced through other evidence at some point during the trial; these facts must be in the record.[4]

The hypothetical question serves two purposes. First, it expands the parties' access to expert testimony because they are no longer limited to experts with personal knowledge. Outside experts can be brought into the case and supplied with the relevant facts through hypothetical questions. Second, the hypothetical question compels the expert to disclose the bases before giving the opinion, thus informing the jury of the facts upon which the opinion rested. These facts are often controverted. If the jury rejects these facts, the jury should also reject the opinion. Hypothetical questions provide the opposing party with an opportunity to object if the bases includes facts not admitted in evidence (*i.e.,* nonrecord facts).

Material facts. Some jurisdictions require that the hypothetical question contain all the "material" facts. Otherwise, there is a risk that the jury may be misled because the offering party — by omitting some facts — could elicit

---

[3] *E.g.,* United States v. Mancillas, 183 F.3d 682, 705 (7th Cir. 1999) (prosecutor posed a hypothetical question to a DEA agent, regarding a person possessing a plastic bag containing 400 grams of marijuana, a slip of paper bearing the notation "420 g," a handgun, a scale, two pagers, a cellular phone, and $2440 in cash. After setting forth these hypothetical facts, the prosecutor "asked the agent whether, in his opinion, the marijuana was being held for distribution or personal consumption. The agent testified that in his opinion, the marijuana was being held for distribution.").

[4] *See* Toucet v. Maritime Overseas Corp., 991 F.2d 5, 10 (1st Cir. 1993) ("Maritime asserts that the trial court erred by allowing the plaintiff's expert witness, Dr. Jaun Llompart, to answer a hypothetical question that improperly assumed facts not in evidence. Specifically, plaintiff's counsel asked Dr. Llompart to assume, in part, that a hypothetical seaman was injured after pulling a hose and butterworth out of 12 tank openings. Maritime asserts that this assumption was contrary to the evidence introduced at trial, which revealed that Toucet was injured after only 4 tank openings were cleaned. While a hypothetical should include only those facts supported by the evidence, the record here indicates that sufficient facts existed to support the challenged hypothetical.") (citation omitted); *Iconco,* 622 F.2d at 1301 ("hypothetical should include only such facts as are supported by the evidence").

an opinion grounded on a faulty basis. However, many courts reject this requirement. Instead, they deal with the issue by allowing the cross-examiner to change the hypothetical question by including additional facts. The trial judge, of course, retains discretion to require the examiner to rephrase an unfair or misleading hypothetical question.[5]

Disputed bases. A dispute concerning underlying facts that are assumed in the hypothetical question does not preclude admissibility. Typically, this dispute involves a jury issue. In the above hypothetical, was there a cherry red hue to the skin? Was there no other cause of death?

Criticism of hypothetical questions. Although it has advantages, the hypothetical question has been extensively criticized. Wigmore noted that "its abuses have become so obstructive and nauseous that no remedy short of extirpation will suffice. It is a logical necessity, but a practical incubus; and here logic must be sacrificed."[6] Other critics attacked the hypothetical question rule "as encouraging partisan bias, affording an opportunity for summing up in the middle of the case, and as complex and time consuming."[7] Finally, some have questioned whether the hypothetical question actually inhibits the intelligent use of expert testimony by artificially cabining the expert's answer.[8]

---

[5] *See* Piotrowski v. Southworth Prods. Corp., 15 F.3d 748, 753 (8th Cir. 1994) ("Southworth urges that the district court erred in admitting the testimony of Piotrowski's treating physician. According to Southworth, a hypothetical question posed to the doctor did not include all of the facts regarding Piotrowski's medical history. The form of a hypothetical question is left largely to the trial court's discretion. . . . The fact that the hypothetical question posed to Piotrowski's physician did not include a reference to Piotrowski's visit to a chiropractor on one or two occasions approximately four years prior to this accident is not a material omission. We find that the hypothetical, taken as a whole, fairly and accurately presented Piotrowski's condition."); *Iconco*, 622 F.2d at 1301 ("Jensen argues that the hypothetical omitted some of the findings material to the determination of responsibility by the contracting officer, but we think the question fairly characterized the material considerations.").

[6] 2 Wigmore, Evidence § 686, at 962 (Chadbourn rev. 1979).

[7] Fed. R. Evid. 705 advisory committee's note.

[8] *See* Rabata v. Dohner, 172 N.W.2d 409, 417 (Wis. 1969) ("Rather than inducing a clear expression of expert opinion and the basis for it, the hypothetical question inhibits the expert and forecloses him from explaining his reasoning in a manner that is intelligible to a jury."). *See also* Dieden & Gasparich, *Psychiatric Evidence and Full Disclosure in the Criminal Trial*, 52 Cal. L. Rev. 543, 556 (1964) ("Unfortunately the hypothetical question has been the traditionally accepted method of adducing expert testimony. It even has been characterized as one of the truly scientific features of the rules of evidence in that it is designed to reveal all of the pertinent facts in the most logical order to support the expert opinion. In fact, its objectives have never been realized and the method has been uniformly criticized by the authorities, as well as the California courts which have commented on the undue length and complexity of hypothetical questions and the slanting of their hypotheses. Medical men have also been outspoken in expressing their disdain for the technique."); Maguire & Hahesy, *Requisite Proof of Basis for Expert Opinion*, 5 Vand. L. Rev. 432 (1952); Rheingold, *The Basis of Medical Testimony*, 15 Vand. L. Rev. 473 (1962).

[B] "Modified" Hypothetical Questions

An expert present during the testimony of other witnesses may base an opinion on that testimony.[9] The expert is simply asked to *assume* that the overheard testimony was true.[10] In general, this procedure is practicable only when the case is simple and the testimony concerning the underlying data is not disputed; otherwise the jury may not know upon what data the opinion is based.

§ 25.04 Opinion Based on Nonrecord Facts: "Reasonable Reliance" Requirement

In addition to personal knowledge and hypothetical questions, Rule 703 permits an expert to give an opinion based on information supplied to the expert outside the record (nonrecord facts), if of a type reasonably relied upon by experts in the particular field. Rule 705 provides that disclosure of the underlying basis of the opinion need not precede the answer. The drafters of the Federal Rules wanted to bring the courtroom use of expert testimony into conformity with how information is used in practice by experts. A physician, for example, will frequently arrive at a diagnosis (a type of opinion) based on radiology and toxicology reports.[11]

The drafters believed that the "reasonable reliance" requirement would ensure the reliability of this type of expert testimony, noting that the requirement would exclude "the opinion of an 'accidentologist' as to the point of impact in an automobile collision based on statements of bystanders since this requirement is not satisfied."[12] Nevertheless, Rule 703 has its detractors.[13]

---

[9] *See* United States v. Crabtree, 979 F.2d 1261, 1270 (7th Cir. 1992) ("Rule 703 of the Federal Rules of Evidence specifically states that an expert can base his opinion on the facts and data learned from attending the trial and listening to testimony. That is precisely what Agent Turner did; there is little if any difference between counsel disclosing prior testimony [in the form of a hypothetical question] to an expert and having an expert listen to such testimony in the courtroom.").

[10] The sequestration rule, Rule 615, recognizes an exception for "essential" witnesses, which typically means experts. *See supra* § 19.02[C] (exception for essential persons).

[11] *See* Fed. R. Evid. 703 advisory committee's note ("[T]he rule is designed to broaden the basis for expert opinions beyond that current in many jurisdictions and to bring the judicial practice into line with the practice of the experts themselves when not in court. Thus a physician in his own practice bases his diagnosis on information from numerous sources and of considerable variety, including statements by patients and relatives, reports and opinions from nurses, technicians and other doctors, hospital records, and X rays. Most of them are admissible in evidence, but only with the expenditure of substantial time in producing and examining various authenticating witnesses. The physician makes life-and-death decisions in reliance upon them. His validation, expertly performed and subject to cross-examination, ought to suffice for judicial purposes.").

[12] *Id.*

[13] *See* ABA Section of Litigation, Emerging Problems Under the Federal Rules of Evidence, Rule 703, at 224 (3d ed. 1998) ("Rule 703 was a controversial rule when enacted, and it remains controversial.").

In effect, Rule 703 permits an expert to base an opinion on hearsay evidence. In *United States v. Lundy,* [14] an arson expert testified that a fire had been purposefully set. His opinion was based on his firsthand inspection of the scene and on *interviews with witnesses at the scene.* The Seventh Circuit ruled the testimony admissible because such interviews "are a standard investigatory technique in cause and origin inquiries." [15] Another court addressed the policy supporting Rule 703: "The rationale in favor of the admissibility of expert testimony based on hearsay is that the expert is fully capable of judging for himself what is, or is not, a reliable basis for his opinion. This relates directly to one of the functions of the expert witness, namely to lend his special expertise to the issue before him." [16]

Criticisms. There are several problems with this aspect of Rule 703. First, it assumes extensive pretrial discovery. Such discovery is often not available in criminal cases, and thus the opponent may not know the bases of the opinion until cross-examination. [17] Second, the jury may not understand the bases for the opinion because Rule 705 does not require prior disclosure of the bases. If the jury rejects the bases, it should reject the opinion upon which it is based. [18]

[A] Determining Admissibility: Judge's Role

There are two different approaches to the judge's role in determining "reasonable reliance." One approach (often referred to as the "restrictive" approach) requires the trial court to make an *independent* assessment of the reasonableness of the expert's reliance. [19] In contrast, other courts

---

[14] 809 F.2d 392 (7th Cir. 1987).

[15] *Id.* at 395. *See also* In Ferrara & DiMercurio v. St. Paul Mercury Ins. Co., 240 F.3d 1, 8 (1st Cir. 2001) (Expert "had visited the fire scene and examined the evidence there . . . Besides looking at burn patterns and studying the electrical system, he took measurements and photographs and wrote his own report. He also interviewed the vessel's engineer. . . . [H]e testified that he read [another expert's] report in preparation for his expert testimony, along with the report of the local fire department. But the opinion he rendered was his own. . . .").

[16] United States v. Sims, 514 F.2d 147, 149 (9th Cir. 1975). *See also* Soden v. Freightliner Corp., 714 F.2d 498, 502–03 (5th Cir. 1983) (The inquiry under Rule 703 "must be made on a case-by-case basis and should focus on the reliability of the opinion and its foundation rather than on the fact that it was based, technically speaking, upon hearsay.").

[17] The drafters specifically mentioned discovery in civil cases but ignored the lack of the same discovery in criminal cases. *See* Fed. R. Evid. 705 advisory committee's note ("If the objection is made that leaving it to the cross-examiner to bring out the supporting data is essentially unfair, the answer is that he is under no compulsion to bring out any facts or data except those unfavorable to the opinion. The answer assumes that the cross-examiner has the advance knowledge which is essential for effective cross-examination. This advance knowledge has been afforded, though imperfectly, by the traditional foundation requirement. Rule 26(b)(4) of the Rules of Civil Procedure, as revised, provides for substantial discovery in this area, obviating in large measure the obstacles which have been raised in some instances to discovery of findings, underlying data, and even the identity of the experts.").

[18] The hypothetical question ameliorates these problems to a certain extent; the bases is disclosed in the question itself and the opinion follows immediately.

[19] *E.g.,* In re "Agent Orange" Prod. Liab. Litig., 611 F. Supp. 1221, 1245 (E.D.N.Y. 1985)

(adopting a "liberal" approach) limit the judge's role to determining what experts in the field consider reasonable. According to the Third Circuit, the "proper inquiry is not what the court deems reliable, but what experts in the relevant discipline deem it to be."[20] In short, the trial court is not suppose to substitute its view of what constitutes reasonable reliance for that of the experts in the relevant field. This does not mean, of course, that the judge must rely only on the testifying expert to determine what other experts rely upon. The court may consider the testimony of other experts, consult learned treaties,[21] or take judicial notice.[22]

The Third Circuit, however, changed positions after the Supreme Court decided *Daubert*.[23] The court noted that its "former view is no longer tenable in light of *Daubert*."[24]

[B] Hearsay Use

Although Rule 703 permits an expert to base an opinion on hearsay information, it does not recognize a hearsay exception for this information. Thus, the jury may consider the information only in evaluating the expert's opinion; it cannot use the information substantively, *i.e.,* for the truth of the assertions contained therein. But should the hearsay basis be excluded or subject only to a limiting instruction per Rule 105?[25] In order to deal with this problem, a sentence was added to Rule 703 in 2000: "Facts or data that are otherwise inadmissible shall not be disclosed to the jury by the proponent of the opinion or inference unless the court determines that their

---

("The court may not abdicate its independent responsibilities to decide if the bases meet minimum standards of reliability as a condition of admissibility. If the underlying data are so lacking in probative force and reliability that no reasonable expert could base an opinion on them, an opinion which rests entirely upon them must be excluded."), *aff'd*, 818 F.2d 204 (2d Cir. 1987).

[20] In re Japanese Elec. Prod. Antitrust Litig., 723 F.2d 238, 276 (3d Cir. 1983), *rev'd on other grounds sub nom.* Matsushita Elec. Indus. Co. v. Zenith Radio Corp., 475 U.S. 574 (1986).

[21] Fed. R. Evid. 803(18) (learned treatise exception to hearsay rule). *See infra* § 33.16

[22] Fed. R. Evid. 201. *See infra* § 44.03[C] (judicial notice of "accurately & readily determinable" facts).

[23] *Daubert* is discussed in chapter 24.

[24] In re Paoli R.R. Yard PCB Litig., 35 F.3d 717, 748 (3d Cir. 1994) ("It is the judge who makes the determination of reasonable reliance, and for the judge to make the factual determination under Rule 104(a) that an expert is basing his or her opinion on a type of data reasonably relied upon by experts, the judge must conduct an independent evaluation into reasonableness. The judge can of course take into account the particular expert's opinion that experts reasonably rely on that type of data, as well as the opinions of other experts as to its reliability, but the judge can also take into account other factors he or she deems relevant.").

[25] *See* Brennan v. Reinhart Inst. Foods, 211 F.3d 449, 451 (8th Cir. 2000) ("In facing this apparent contradiction between Fed. R. Evid. 703 and the inadmissibility of hearsay reports, this court has reconciled the issue by allowing an expert to testify about facts and data outside of the record for the limited purpose of exposing the factual basis of the expert's opinion. Effective cross-examination can then highlight the weaknesses in the expert's opinion. Obviously, it is helpful when trial courts instruct juries as to the limited applicability of the hearsay evidence by informing the jury that the hearsay is inadmissible as substantive evidence to prove the truth of the fact asserted.").

probative value in assisting the jury to evaluate the expert's opinion substantially outweighs their prejudicial effect."

[C] Right of Confrontation

In criminal trials, the use of hearsay evidence as a basis for expert opinion testimony raises confrontation issues. Confrontation challenges have typically been rejected unless the testifying witness is a *mere conduit* for another expert's opinion — *i.e.,* merely summarizing the views of others.[26]

§ 25.05 Expert Opinions & "Background" Hearsay

There are two distinct hearsay issues relating to the use of expert testimony. One issue involves the use of hearsay as a basis for expert testimony in a particular case, an issue governed by Rule 703 and discussed in the preceding section. The other issue concerns the expert's use of hearsay in forming an opinion, even though the basis for the opinion is personal knowledge or facts in the record. The confusion between these two issues is common.

Viewing expert testimony as a syllogism may obviate the confusion between these two issues.[27] For example, a forensic pathologist may testify that a homicide victim had been shot at close range. The major premise is a general proposition: powder burns on a gunshot victim indicate a close-range (6–18 inches) entrance wound. The minor premise is the finding of such powder burns during the autopsy. The conclusion as stated above is derived from these two premises.

Major premise:	Powder burns on a gunshot victim indicate a close-range entrance wound (Rule 702 issue).
Minor premise:	Powder burns were found on the victim's chest during the autopsy (Rule 703 issue).
Conclusion:	Victim in this case had been shot at close range.

Facts in a particular case. Rule 703 concerns only the minor premise, which it refers to as the facts or data "in the particular case."

Background hearsay. The major premise is the general proposition (powder burns on a gunshot victim indicate a close-range entrance wound),

---

[26] *See* United States v. Smith, 869 F.2d 348, 355 (7th Cir. 1989) (voiceprints admitted; "The confrontation clause does not forbid reliance at trial by experts upon material prepared by others. It requires, however, that the defendant have access to such material, in order that she has an adequate opportunity to prepare her cross-examination. It is, of course, true that an expert witness may not simply summarize the out-of-court statements of others as his testimony. That is not, however, what Dr. Nakasone did in this case. He was not merely an 'understudy' for Lieutenant Smrkovski."). *See also* United States v. Wright, 783 F.2d 1091, 1101 (D.C. Cir. 1986) ("Confrontation Clause concerns arise where the rules governing expert testimony are misused in order to bring otherwise inadmissible evidence before the jury without the opportunity for effective cross-examination.").

[27] *See* Imwinkelried, *The "Bases" of Expert Testimony: The Syllogistic Structure of Scientific Testimony*, 67 N.C. L. Rev. 1 (1988).

an issue governed by Rule 702. This premise is gleaned from the expert's experience and learning in forensic pathology. In one sense, most expert testimony is based, in part, on hearsay. The extrajudicial statements of colleagues, textwriters, and teachers are all used by experts in forming opinions. This use of texts and lectures contribute to the expert's qualifications. Professor Maguire stated it this way:

> Progress of expert knowledge demands reliance upon the learning of the past. Almost invariably this learning is recorded in hearsay form. No individual can ever make himself into an expert without absorbing much hearsay — lectures by his teachers, statements in textbooks, reports of experiments and experiences of others in the same field.[28]

There is nothing wrong with relying on this type of background hearsay; indeed, the witness would probably not be an expert without it. Thus, an expert who has consulted books or spoken to other experts is acting properly, and Rule 703 does not address this use of hearsay information. There are, however, limitations. The witness may state that she consulted the standard texts and other experts in the field, but the witness may not repeat what these sources stated. If the text or consulted expert's opinion is offered at trial for the truth, it is hearsay. Rule 803(18), which recognizes a hearsay exception for learned treatises, may be the basis for admitting a standard text, but that rule does not extend to the oral statements of other experts.

Wells v. Miami Valley Hosp.[29] provides an illustration. A physician testified that Wells "probably died of a cardiac tamponade." This expert "indicated that the factual basis of his testimony was his review of the medical records and the autopsy report." He also read "scholarly medical articles on cardiac tamponade risks from CVP catheter placement." The patient's medical records and the autopsy report were the "facts or data in the particular case" (the minor premises), and Rule 703 controls. The scholarly articles read by the expert during his research are not governed by Rule 703 because they are "background" hearsay.

§ 25.06　Opinion Based Upon Opinion

Some courts have held that the opinion of an expert witness cannot be predicated either in whole or in part upon the opinions, inferences, or conclusions of others, whether expert or lay witnesses. Commentators have harshly criticized this rule. Wigmore called the rule unsound: "There is no mysterious logical fatality in basing 'one expert opinion upon another'; it is done every day in business and in applied science."[30] For example, physicians frequently base diagnostic opinions on the reports of specialists such as radiologists and pathologists (laboratory reports). These can all be

---

[28] Maguire, Evidence: Common Sense and Common Law 29 (1947).

[29] 631 N.E.2d 642, 654 (Ohio App. 1993).

[30] 2 Wigmore, Evidence § 682, at 957 (Chadbourn rev. 1979).

considered "opinions." There is nothing wrong with this type of testimony — provided the jury understands the basis for the physician's opinion. Indeed, this type of opinion testimony is often very helpful.

§ 25.07 Key Points

To be relevant, an expert's opinion must be *based* on the facts in the particular case. Moreover, if the jury rejects those facts (they may be disputed), the jury should also reject the opinion.

Rule 703 recognizes three bases for expert testimony: (1) firsthand knowledge of the expert (*e.g.,* treating physician), (2) assumed facts that are in the record, typically in the form of a hypothetical question, (3) nonrecord facts if of a type reasonably relied upon by experts in the field.

Hypothetical Questions Based on Record Facts

Material facts. Some jurisdictions require that the hypothetical question contain all the "material" facts. Otherwise, there is a risk that the jury may be misled because the offering party — by omitting some facts — could elicit an opinion grounded on a faulty basis. However, many courts reject this requirement. Instead, they deal with the issue by allowing the cross-examiner to change the hypothetical question by including additional facts.

"Modified" hypothetical questions. An expert present during the testimony of other witnesses may base an opinion on that testimony. The expert is simply asked to *assume* that the overheard testimony was true. In general, this procedure is practicable only when the case is simple and the testimony concerning the underlying data is not disputed; otherwise the jury may not know upon what data the opinion is based.

Opinion Based on Nonrecord Facts: "Reasonable Reliance" Requirement

In addition to personal knowledge and hypothetical questions, Rule 703 permits an expert to give an opinion based on information supplied to the expert outside the record (nonrecord facts), *if of a type reasonably relied upon by experts in the particular field.* Rule 705 provides that disclosure of the underlying basis of the opinion need not precede the answer. The drafters of the Federal Rules wanted to bring the courtroom use of expert testimony into conformity with how information is used in practice by experts.

Determining admissibility — judge's role. There are two different approaches to the judge's role in determining "reasonable reliance." One approach ("restrictive" approach) requires the trial court to make an *independent* assessment of the reasonableness of the expert's reliance. In contrast, other courts ("liberal" approach) limit the judge's role to determining what experts in the field consider reasonable.

Hearsay use. Although Rule 703 permits an expert to base an opinion on hearsay information, it does not recognize a hearsay exception for this information. In order to deal with this issue, a sentence was added to Rule 703 in 2000: "Facts or data that are otherwise inadmissible shall not be disclosed to the jury by the proponent of the opinion or inference unless the court determines that their probative value in assisting the jury to evaluate the expert's opinion substantially outweighs their prejudicial effect."

Right of confrontation. In criminal trials, the use of hearsay evidence as a basis for expert opinion testimony raises confrontation issues. Confrontation challenges have typically been rejected unless the testifying witness is a *mere conduit* for another expert's opinion — *i.e.,* merely summarizing the views of others.

Chapter 26

REAL & DEMONSTRATIVE EVIDENCE

§ 26.01 Introduction

Real evidence (*e.g.*, murder weapon) must be identified as a prerequisite to admissibility. The term "real evidence" is used to describe tangible evidence that is *historically connected* with a case, as distinguished from evidence, such as a model, which is merely illustrative. The latter is often called demonstrative evidence, although there is no agreed upon terminology in this area.

§ 26.02 Real Evidence

There are two principal methods of identifying real evidence: (1) establishing that the evidence is "readily identifiable" and (2) establishing a "chain of custody."[1] These methods are discussed below.

[A] Condition of Object

Sometimes more than mere identification is involved, however. The condition of an object may also be important. In such cases, the offering party must show that the object has retained its relevant evidentiary characteristics. Alteration of the item may reduce or negate its probative value and may mislead the jury. Thus, before physical objects are admissible at trial the offering party must establish that they are in "substantially the same condition" as at the time of the crime or accident.

Determining what changes are "substantial" depends on how the changes affect the relevance of the evidence.[2] For example, in *State v. Wilkins*,[3] a rape victim identified pants that she had worn at the time of the rape; the pants were admissible even though they had been laundered; the evidentiary value had not been affected.

[B] Readily Identifiable Objects: FRE 901(b)(4)

If an item of evidence is readily identifiable, it is often not necessary to establish a chain of custody. Rule 901(b)(4) provides for the identification

---

[1] *See* Giannelli, *Chain of Custody and the Handling of Real Evidence*, 20 Am. Crim. L. Rev. 527 (1983); 1 Giannelli & Imwinkelried, Scientific Evidence ch. 7 (3d ed. 1999).

[2] *See* Comment, *Preconditions for Admission of Demonstrative Evidence*, 61 Nw. L. Rev. 472, 484 (1966) ("Even though the object is not in exactly the same condition at trial as at the time in issue — or even in substantially the same condition — the exhibit may still be admitted if the changes can be explained, and they do not destroy the evidentiary value of the object.").

[3] 415 N.E.2d 303 (Ohio 1980).

of evidence with "distinctive characteristics."[4] Items imprinted with serial numbers,[5] inscribed with a police officer's initials,[6] or possessing other distinctive aspects[7] may be authenticated in this manner.[8] The item does not have to be positively identified to gain admission into evidence.[9]

[C]   Chain of Custody: FRE 901(b)(1)

Real evidence may also be identified by means of a chain of custody.[10] As noted above, establishing a chain of custody is but one means of identifying real evidence. However, a chain of custody may be required under certain circumstances. First, a chain of custody is often required for fungible evidence because these items have no unique characteristics. The proper handling of fungible evidence — e.g., using lock-sealed envelopes or containers which custodians then mark and initial — makes the evidence readily identifiable and eliminates most problems of misidentification and contamination.[11]

Second, if the relevance of an exhibit depends on its laboratory analysis, identification by police markings made at the scene does not provide a sufficient foundation. The markings establish that the exhibit in court was the item seized by the police, but a chain of custody may be necessary to establish that the item seized was the one analyzed at the crime laboratory.[12]

---

[4] See State v. Conley, 288 N.E.2d 296, 300 (Ohio App. 1971) ("If an exhibit is directly identified by a witness as the object which is involved in the case, then that direct identification is sufficient. Such is the case with many objects which have special identifying characteristics, such as a number or mark, or are made to have such identifying characteristics by special marks.").

[5] E.g., United States v. Douglas, 964 F.2d 738, 742 (8th Cir. 1992) ("Smith and Wesson with serial number 79515").

[6] E.g., United States v. Ricco, 52 F.3d 58, 61 (4th Cir. 1995) (detective "identified the vials [of cocaine] using his initials and the case number"); United States v. Madril, 445 F.2d 827, 828 (9th Cir. 1971) (pistol), vacated on other grounds, 404 U.S. 1010 (1972); Dixon v. State, 189 N.E.2d 715, 716 (Ind. 1963) (shotgun); Almodovar v. State, 464 N.E.2d 906, 911 (Ind. 1984) (initials scratched on shell casing).

[7] E.g., United States v. Reed, 392 F.2d 865, 867 (7th Cir. 1968)) ("unusual looking hat"); Reyes v. United States, 383 F.2d 734, 734 (9th Cir. 1967) (holdup note "was unique and readily identifiable").

[8] See also 1 Giannelli & Imwinkelried, supra note 1, ch. 7 (citing cases involving firearms, bullets, currency, laboratory slides, and sundry other objects).

[9] E.g., Howland v. State, 186 N.W.2d 319, 323 (Wis. 1971) ("lack of certitude does not preclude admissibility").

[10] This means of identification is an illustration of Rule 901(b)(1) — authentication by a witness with knowledge. The federal drafters explicitly cited chain of custody as an example under Rule 901(b)(1). See Fed. R. Evid. 901 advisory committee's note (The rule "contemplates a broad spectrum ranging from testimony of a witness who was present at the signing of a document to testimony establishing narcotics as taken from an accused and accounting for custody through the period until trial, including laboratory analysis.").

[11] 1 Giannelli & Imwinkelried, supra note 1, at 343–44.

[12] For example, in Robinson v. Commonwealth, 183 S.E.2d 179 (Va. 1971), the court reversed a rape conviction due to a break in the chain of custody: "The mere fact that the blouse and

Third, if the condition of the object, not merely its identity, is the relevant issue, a chain of custody may be required to establish that the object had not been altered during police custody.

[1] Length of Chain of Custody

The "length" of the chain of custody depends on the purpose for which the evidence is offered. This point is illustrated by *State v. Conley*,[13] which involved a prosecution for the illegal sale of LSD. The drugs were purchased with marked bills whose serial numbers had been recorded. The defendant objected to the admissibility of both the bills and the LSD. The court wrote:

> To identify a particular item as being part of a pertinent incident in the past usually requires the showing of a continuous chain of custodians up to the material moment. When a chemical analysis is involved the material moment is the moment of analysis, since this provides the basis for the expert testimony and makes that testimony relevant to the case. In the case of many other items, the material moment occurs at the trial.[14]

The court went on to hold that the chain of custody for the marked bills ran from the time the bills were marked until the trial, at which time they were identified. The chain of custody for the drugs differed; it ran from the time of seizure to the time of chemical analysis.

As a matter of relevancy, this approach is sound. The loss or destruction of drugs after chemical analysis would not affect the relevance of the expert's testimony concerning the nature of the drugs.[15] Moreover, the prosecution generally is not required to introduce real evidence to prove its case.[16] Even when evidence is available, it need not be physically offered. "Thus, the grand larceny of an automobile may be established merely on competent testimony describing the stolen vehicle without actually producing the automobile before the trier of fact."[17]

---

the panties were identified [by the victim at trial] did not prove the chain of possession necessary to validate the F.B.I. analysis of them." *Id.* at 181. *See also* United States v. Ladd, 885 F.2d 954, 957 (1st Cir. 1989) ("In short, there was no competent proof to indicate that the sample extracted from Massey's corpse was the one which CSL tested. An important step in the custodial pavane was omitted."); Graham v. State, 255 N.E.2d 652, 655–56 (Ind. 1970) (wrapper containing white powder initialed at time police took possession but break in chain of custody prior to chemical analysis resulted in reversal).

[13] 288 N.E.2d 296 (Ohio App. 1971).

[14] *Id.* at 300.

[15] *E.g.,* United States v. Bailey, 277 F.2d 560, 565 (7th Cir. 1960) ("Even if the exhibits, including the heroin, had not been introduced in evidence the testimony of the witnesses and the stipulation as to the chemical analysis were sufficient.").

[16] The best evidence rule applies only to writings, recordings, and photographs, not to real evidence. *See* Fed. R. Evid. 1002.

[17] Holle v. State, 337 A.2d 163, 166–67 (Md. App. 1975) (stolen marked currency). *Accord* United States v. Figueroa, 618 F.2d 934, 941 (2d Cir. 1980) (heroin); Chandler v. United States, 318 F.2d 356, 357 (10th Cir. 1963) (whiskey bottles).

Nevertheless, the loss or destruction of the evidence after laboratory analysis may affect a defendant's right to reexamine the evidence, which could result in the exclusion of expert testimony based on the prior laboratory examination. [18]

[2] Links in Chain of Custody

The "links" in the chain of custody are those persons who had physical custody of the object. Persons who had access to, but not possession of, the evidence are not links. [19] Failure to account for the evidence during possession by a custodian may constitute a critical break in the chain of custody. [20] A few courts have indicated that all the links in the chain of custody must testify at trial. [21] Most courts, however, hold that "the fact of a missing link does not prevent the admission of real evidence, so long as there is sufficient proof that the evidence is what it purports to be." [22] Thus, while a custodian in the chain of possession need not testify under all circumstances, the evidence should be accounted for during the time it was under that custodian's control. [23]

Postal employees who handle evidence sent to a crime laboratory by mail are custodial links. They rarely, if ever, testify at trial, however. A rule requiring every custodian to testify would necessitate calling all postal employees who handled the evidence and "place an impossible burden upon the state." [24] Controlled drug buys are similar. [25] Another category of cases

---

[18] See 1 Giannelli & Imwinkelried, *supra* note 1, ch. 3.

[19] See Gallego v. United States, 276 F.2d 914, 917 (9th Cir. 1960) ("There is no rule requiring the prosecution to produce as witnesses all persons who were in a position to come into contact with the article sought to be introduced in evidence."). *Accord* Reyes v. United States, 383 F.2d 734, 734 (9th Cir. 1967) (per curiam) ("[T]he Government was under no obligation to produce as witnesses all persons who may have handled exhibit 1.").

[20] *E.g.*, United States v. Panczko, 353 F.2d 676, 679 (7th Cir. 1965) ("There is no evidence as to where or from whom Lieutenant Remkus got the keys."); Novak v. District of Columbia, 160 F.2d 588, 589 (D.C. Cir. 1947) (evidence failed "to identify the sample from which the [urine] analyses were made as being that sample taken from appellant").

[21] *E.g.*, People v. Connelly, 316 N.E.2d 706, 708 (N.Y. 1974) ("Admissibility generally requires that all those who have handled the item identify it and testify to its custody and unchanged condition.") (citation omitted).

[22] United States v. Howard-Arias, 679 F.2d 363, 366 (4th Cir. 1982). *See also* United States v. Harrington, 923 F.2d 1371, 1374 (9th Cir. 1991) ("The prosecution was not required to call the custodian of the evidence."); United States v. Cardenas, 864 F.2d 1528, 1532 (10th Cir. 1989) ("There is no rule that the prosecution must produce *all* persons who had custody of the evidence to testify at trial.").

[23] See Cooper v. Eagle River Mem. Hosp., Inc., 270 F.3d 456, 463 (7th Cir. 2001) ("[A]n uninterrupted chain of custody is not a prerequisite to admissibility. Instead, gaps in the chain go to the weight of the evidence, not its admissibility.").

[24] Trantham v. State, 508 P.2d 1104, 1107 (Okla. Crim. App. 1973). Courts often invoke the presumption of delivery of items sent in the mail to fill the gap.

[25] See United States v. Beal, 279 F.3d 567, 572 (8th Cir. 2002) ("While the officers monitoring the controlled buy may not have been able to see the actual transaction occur within the car, the otherwise complete surveillance supports the conclusion that, within a reasonable probability, Booker had no opportunity to retrieve the evidence from a body cavity or to change or tamper with the evidence.").

involves what may be called "minor links" — intermediate custodians who had possession for a short period of time and merely passed the evidence along to another link. This category includes not only laboratory personnel, but also police officers who receive evidence from a seizing officer and mail or transport it to a laboratory for analysis.[26] In short, "accounting for" all the links in the chain of custody does not necessarily mean all the links need testify at trial.

[D] Standard of Proof

The burden of proving the chain of custody rests with the party offering the evidence. Prior to the adoption of the Federal Rules, the courts described the standard of proof in various ways. The most common expression of the standard was that the offering party had to establish the identity and condition of the exhibit by a "reasonable probability."[27] In contrast, Rule 901(a) requires only that the offering party introduce "evidence sufficient to support a finding that the matter in question is what its proponent claims." In other words, the offering party need only make a "prima facie" showing of authenticity to gain admissibility, and the jury decides whether the evidence has been sufficiently identified.[28]

Nevertheless, in criminal cases admissibility may not be enough. For example, in a controlled substance trial, the prosecution needs to prove to the jury that the item seized was the same item analyzed beyond a reasonable doubt.

In establishing the chain of custody, the offering party typically presents the testimony of persons with firsthand knowledge. In addition, habit[29] and documentary[30] evidence may be used.

---

[26] *See* 1 Giannelli & Imwinkelried, *supra* note 1, ch. 7 (listing cases).

[27] *E.g.,* United States v. Brown, 482 F.2d 1226, 1228 (8th Cir. 1973) ("reasonable probability the article has not been changed in any important respect"); United States v. Capocci, 433 F.2d 155, 157 (1st Cir. 1970).

[28] *See* In re Exxon Valdez, 270 F.3d 1215, 1249 (9th Cir. 2001) ("If a witness offers testimony from which a reasonable juror could find in favor of authenticity, the trial court may properly admit the evidence to allow the jury to decide what probative force it has."); United States v. Johnson, 637 F.2d 1224, 1247 (9th Cir. 1980); United States v. Goichman, 547 F.2d 778, 784 (3d Cir. 1976).

[29] The routine procedures used by the police and crime laboratory are admissible for this purpose. *See* Fed. R. Evid. 406 (habit & routine practice evidence).

[30] *See* United States v. Brown, 9 F.3d 907, 911 (11th Cir. 1993) ("Before introducing the property receipt into evidence, the government established that its regular and customary procedure was to fill out a property receipt for any type of evidence. The police custodian testified that for every piece of evidence, he filled out a property receipt containing the case number, date, location the property was found, and a description of the evidence. Brown's argument that the government must establish that it was customary to list the make and serial number of the gun takes the foundation requirement to unwarranted extremes."). *See also* Fed. R. Evid. 803(6) (business records exception to hearsay rule).

§ 26.03　Charts, Models & Maps

Diagrams, models, maps, blueprints, sketches, and other exhibits used to illustrate and explain testimony may be admissible if they are substantially accurate representations of what the witness is endeavoring to describe.[31] For example, a replica shotgun could be used as illustrative evidence, provided the jury understood that it was not the actual weapon used in the crime.[32] This issue is left to the discretion of the trial judge under Rule 403.[33]

In recent years, so-called "anatomically correct dolls" have been used in child sex abuse cases. The use of these dolls solely as demonstrative evidence to help a child witness explain what had happened may be justifiable.[34] To use them as evidence of abuse is an entirely different matter.[35]

§ 26.04　In-Court Exhibitions

Another type of "real" evidence involves an exhibition before the jury, often of a physical condition in a personal injury action. For example, a plaintiff might show scars or amputated limps to the jury on the issue of damages.[36]

Control of this issue rests with the trial judge under Rules 403 and 611(a). For reasons of propriety, some exhibitions should be conducted out of court

---

[31] See Joseph, Modern Visual Evidence ch. 9 (1999) (diagrams, charts, graphs & models).

[32] United States v. Aldaco, 201 F.3d 979, 986 (7th Cir. 2000) ("The government introduced the replica to illustrate what Officer Sanchez saw when he observed Aldaco holding the shotgun in order that the jury might properly determine whether the events happened as Officer Sanchez testified. This Court has frequently approved the use of this type of demonstrative evidence to establish that objects of this nature were actually used in the commission of a crime."). See also United States v. Humphrey, 279 F.3d 372, 376–77 (6th Cir. 2002) (no abuse of discretion in bank embezzlement trial to admit 107 coin bags (most filled with stryofoam) as demonstrating what that much cash would look like); United States v. Salerno, 108 F.3d 730, 742–43 (7th Cir. 1997) (no abuse of discretion to use a scale model of a crime scene as demonstrative evidence); United States v. Towns, 913 F.2d 434, 446 (7th Cir. 1990) (no abuse of discretion in allowing admission of a gun and ski mask identified by eyewitnesses "as being similar to those possessed by the robbers" for "the limited demonstrative purpose of providing examples of the gun and ski mask" used in the robbery).

[33] See Roland v. Langlois, 945 F.2d 956, 963 (7th Cir. 1991) ("There is no requirement that demonstrative evidence be completely accurate, however, and the evidence was admitted only on the express condition that the jury be alerted to the perceived inaccuracies. . . . [W]e agree with the district court that the benefits from the use of a life-size model were not substantially outweighed by the danger of unfair prejudice.").

[34] See Reyna v. State, 797 S.W.2d 189, 193 (Tex. Crim. App. 1990) (dolls were "not used as a scientific method of proof, but merely as a tool to aid the jury with the witness' testimony").

[35] See United States v. Spotted War Bonnet, 882 F.2d 1360, 1370 (8th Cir. 1989) ("empirical literature clearly reflects a concern that repeated use of the dolls can be highly suggestive"), vacated on other grounds, 497 U.S. 1021 (1990) See also 1 Giannelli & Imwinkelried, supra note 1, ch. 9 (discussing issue).

[36] E.g., Allen v. Seacoast Prod., Inc., 623 F.2d 355, 365 n. 23 (5th Cir. 1980) (demonstration of the removal and replacement of artificial eye in front of the jury; trial judge "did not abuse his discretion in determining that the demonstration's probative value (in showing the daily regimen which Allen must endure) outweighed its prejudicial effect").

and then described to the jury through a witness.[37] In a criminal case, the trial court may require the defendant to exhibit identifying physical characteristics or speak for identification. The privilege against self-incrimination extends only to "testimonial," and not physical, evidence.[38]

§ 26.05   In-Court Demonstrations

In-court demonstrations, which go beyond mere physical exhibition, involve other considerations. For example, demonstrations of pain can easily be faked. This is a Rule 403 issue. In some cases demonstrations are helpful. In one case, for example, the prosecution conducted a demonstration using nylon stockings as a mask over a person's head to illustrate the extent to which a stocking would distort facial features.[39]

§ 26.06   Jury Views

Jury views are a well-established trial procedure.[40] In some jurisdictions, a jury view is not considered evidence because it cannot be recorded. This makes little sense; the only reason to take the jury to the scene is for the jury to use what they observe in deciding the case.[41] Moreover, "demeanor" evidence (observing a witness in determining credibility) is also not recorded but is always recognized as admissible.[42]

The trial court has discretion to permit a jury view.[43] Views are time-consuming and difficult to control so that unauthorized comments, hearsay,

---

[37] See State v. Minkner, 637 N.E.2d 973, 976 (Ohio App. 1994) (rape prosecution; "Under these circumstances, we conclude that his request to designate an impartial person to conduct a visual examination and testify concerning the findings of that examination [whether accused had a surgical scar or mark on his penis] was a reasonable request.").

[38] See United States v. Wade, 388 U.S. 218, 222 (1967) (compelling an accused to exhibit his person for observation was compulsion "to exhibit his physical characteristics, not compulsion to disclose any knowledge he might have" and thus not proscribed by the privilege.). See infra § 43.04 ("testimonial-real" evidence distinction).

[39] State v. Jackson, 621 N.E.2d 710, 711 (Ohio App. 1993) ("the state did not claim that Exhibit A was the stocking used in the robbery").

[40] See Fed. R. Evid. 401 advisory committee's note ("Evidence which is essentially background in nature is universally offered and admitted as an aid to understanding. Charts, photographs, views of real estate, murder weapons, and many other items of evidence fall in this category."). See generally Wendorf, Some Views on Jury Views, 15 Baylor L. Rev. 379 (1963).

[41] See United States v. Lillie, 953 F.2d 1188, 1190 (10th Cir. 1992) ("We disagree . . . that a view sometimes is not evidence. We acknowledge that jurisdictions vary as to whether a view is treated as evidence or simply as an aid to help the trier of fact understand the evidence. However, we believe such a distinction is only semantic, because any kind of presentation to the jury or the judge to help the fact finder determine what the truth is and assimilate and understand the evidence is itself evidence.")

[42] See supra § 22.01.

[43] E.g., United States v. Culpepper, 834 F.2d 879, 883 (10th Cir. 1987) ("Whether the jury is permitted to view evidence outside the courtroom is a matter for the discretion of the trial court."); Stokes v. Delcambre, 710 F.2d 1120, 1129 (5th Cir. 1983) ("Whether a trial is to be

or other occurrences do not infect the process.[44] "With respect to taking a jury for a view, the disruption and confusion likely to result closely resembles that associated with taking a third grade class to a firehouse."[45]

§ 26.07 Key Points

Real evidence (*e.g.*, murder weapon) must be identified as a prerequisite to admissibility. The term "real evidence" is used to describe tangible evidence that is *historically connected* with a case, as distinguished from evidence, such as a model, which is merely illustrative. The latter is often called demonstrative evidence, although there is no agreed upon terminology in this area.

Real Evidence

Condition of object. Sometimes more than mere identification is involved. The condition of an object may also be important. Before physical objects are admissible, the offering party must establish that they are in "substantially the same condition" as at the time of the crime or accident.

There are two principal methods of identifying real evidence: (1) establishing that the evidence is "readily identifiable" and (2) establishing a "chain of custody."

Chain of custody. The "links" in the chain of custody are those persons who had physical custody of the object. Persons who had access to, but not possession of, the evidence are not links. Most courts hold that "the fact of a missing link does not prevent the admission of real evidence, so long as there is sufficient proof that the evidence is what it purports to be."[46] Rule 901(a) requires only that the offering party introduce "evidence sufficient to support a finding that the matter in question is what its proponent claims" —*i.e.*, a "prima facie" showing of authenticity.

Demonstrative Evidence

Diagrams, models, maps, blueprints, sketches, and other exhibits used to illustrate and explain testimony may be admissible if they are substantially accurate representations of what the witness is endeavoring to describe.

---

interrupted and suffer the inconvenience and risk attendant upon a jury view are matters for the discretion of the trial court and are reviewable only for abuse. We find no abuse here. A trial judge would understandably be reluctant to halt a trial and cause the jurors to be transported to the jail for a view. The security problems are not small and the risk of comment by the prisoners is not insubstantial. While it may well have been helpful there was an abundance of evidence at trial as to the layout of the jail. The trial judge was on the scene and balanced these concerns.").

[44] Statutes often provide for the accused's right to be present at the view, although this right may be waived. Whether this right is constitutionally based is uncertain. *See* Snyder v. Massachusetts, 291 U.S. 97 (1934) (5-4 decision that an accused did not have a due process right to be present at a view).

[45] 1 Graham, Handbook of Federal Evidence § 401.11, at 280 n. 4 (5th ed. 2001).

[46] United States v. Howard-Arias, 679 F.2d 363, 366 (4th Cir. 1982).

In-court exhibitions. Another type of "real" evidence involves an exhibition before the jury, often of a physical condition in a personal injury action. For example, a plaintiff might show scars or amputated limps to the jury on the issue of damages. Control of this issue rests with the trial judge under Rules 403 and 611(a).

In-court demonstrations. In-court demonstrations, which go beyond mere physical exhibition, involve other considerations. For example, demonstrations of pain can easily be faked. This is also a Rule 403 issue.

Jury views. In some jurisdictions, a jury view is not considered evidence because it cannot be recorded. This makes little sense; the only reason to take the jury to the scene is for the jury to use what they observe in deciding the case. The trial court has discretion to permit a jury view. Views are time-consuming and difficult to control so that unauthorized comments, hearsay, or other occurrences do not infect the process.

Chapter 27

PHOTOGRAPHS, TAPES & VOICE IDENTIFICATIONS

§ 27.01 Introduction

Photographic evidence raises different issues depending on how it is used. [1] Sometimes photographs play a pivotal role at trial; at other times they are used merely as background evidence. [2] The use of digital photographs and videotapes is now quite common. Computer animations and simulations are but the latest technological development being adapted to courtroom use.

Speaker identification presents different issues. However, because it often involves sound recordings (which require a foundation similar to videotapes), it is included in this chapter.

§ 27.02 Photographs

[A] "Pictorial Communication" Theory

A foundation for the admissibility of photographs is laid by establishing that the photograph is an "accurate and faithful representation" of the scene or object depicted. [3] The foundational witness need not be the photographer — anyone who saw the scene depicted can testify. [4] These foundational requirements are based on what is known as the "pictorial testimony" theory of admissibility. [5] Under this theory, the authenticating witness *adopts*

---

[1] *See generally* Scott, Photographic Evidence (2d ed. 1969); Fischnaller, *Technical Preparation and Exclusion of Photographic Evidence*, 8 Gonz. L. Rev. 292 (1973); Paradis, *The Celluloid Witness*, 37 Colo. L. Rev. 235 (1965).

[2] *See* Fed. R. Evid. 401 advisory committee's note ("Evidence which is essentially background in nature is universally offered and admitted as an aid to understanding. Charts, photographs, views of real estate, murder weapons, and many other items of evidence fall in this category.").

[3] *See* United States v. Paterson, 277 F.3d 709, 713 (4th Cir. 2002) ("The necessary foundation for the introduction of a photograph is most commonly established through eyewitness testimony that the picture accurately depicts the scene in question or expert testimony that the picture was generated by a reliable imaging process."); United States v. Clayton, 643 F.2d 1071, 1073 (5th Cir. 1981) (photographs were "identified by all the bank employees present at the robbery as accurate depictions of the scene").

[4] *See* United States v. Clayton, 643 F.2d 1071, 1074 (5th Cir. 1981) ("A witness qualifying a photograph need not be the photographer or see the picture taken; it is sufficient if he recognizes and identifies the object depicted and testifies that the photograph fairly and correctly represents it.").

[5] Wigmore wrote: "The use of maps, models, diagrams, and photographs as testimony to the objects represented rests fundamentally on the theory that they are the pictorial communications of a qualified witness who uses this method of communication instead of or in addition to some other method." Quotation from third edition; later edition deletes the words "photographs" and "pictorial." 3 Wigmore, Evidence § 793 (Chadbourn rev. 1970).

the photograph as her own testimony.[6] In other words, the witness could have described the scene depicted in the photograph in her testimony but, instead, the witness adopts the photograph in lieu of that description.

[B] "Silent Witness" Theory

One shortcoming with the "pictorial testimony" theory is that it does not work with X-rays. Nor with surveillance photographs or any type of photograph where no witness saw the scene or object depicted. Here, nobody can testify that the photograph accurately reflects that scene. Consequently, a second theory of admissibility was recognized: the "silent witness" theory, by which the process that produced the photo is authenticated.[7] This theory is consistent with Rule 901(b)(9), which recognizes the authentication of a result produced by an accurate process. Surveillance tapes[8] and ATM photographs[9] have been authenticated in this way. Photographs may also be authenticated circumstantially.[10]

[C] Posed Scenes

Photographs of reconstructed scenes sometimes raise problems. If there is no dispute about the staged or posed scene reflected in the photograph, admissibility is the rule. If the photograph represents a one-sided version

---

[6] The best evidence rule does not apply because the offering party is not attempting to prove the contents of a photograph but rather the scene itself. *See infra* § 30.03 (proving contents).

[7] *See* Gardner, *The Camera Goes to Court*, 24 N.C. L. Rev. 233 (1956); McNeal, *Silent Witness Evidence in Relation to the Illustrative Evidence Foundation*, 37 Okla. L. Rev. 219 (1984).

[8] *E.g.,* United States v. Taylor, 530 F.2d 639, 641–42 (5th Cir. 1076) (photographs from bank camera sufficiently authenticated when testimony established the manner in which the film was used, how the camera was activated, that the film was removed immediately after the robbery, and the chain of possession of the film and the development of the prints); Fisher v. State, 643 S.W.2d 571, 575 (Ark. App. 1982) (grocery store surveillance videotapes; "In adopting the 'silent witness' theory, we join the overwhelming majority of other jurisdictions that have decided this issue").

[9] *E.g.,* United States v. Rembert, 863 F.2d 1023, 1028 (D.C. Cir. 1988) ("the circumstantial evidence provided by the victim witnesses as to the occurrences at the ATM machines, together with the testimony of Wohlfarth as to the loading of the cameras and the security of the film, coupled with the internal indicia of date, place, and event depicted in the evidence itself provide ample support" for admission); State v. Henderson, 669 P.2d 736, 737–38 (N.M. App. 1983). ("The [ATM] is a 'silent witness' which tells us that on a certain date, at a certain time, the defendant was dressed a certain way.").

[10] *E.g.,* United States v. Stearns, 550 F.2d 1167, 1170–71 (9th Cir. 1977) ("A critical part of the foundation, that relating to time, is derived only by referring to one of the photographs. In this respect the case is rather unusual, for that photograph by itself establishes a necessary element of its authenticity. No witness testified explicitly, during the Government's case in chief, where or when the pictures were taken or what they represented. . . . [T]he Sea Wind could not have been equipped with the Iola's [distinctive red] net until its return voyage to Hawaii. The picture showing the red net on the Sea Wind and its absence on the Iola thus establish that the photograph was taken on the return voyage.").

of the case, it may be objectionable as misleading, an issue for trial court discretion under Rule 403.[11]

[D] Digital Enhancement

Digital photography presents additional issues because electronic data can be manipulated and detection is difficult. The advantage is that such photographs can be enhanced. For example, in one case computer enhancement of digital photographs of a bloody handprint on a bed sheet were admitted at trial.[12]

[E] Internet Downloading

Internet downloading poses some new problems because manipulation of electronic data is relatively simple. Moreover, data posted on a Web site may have been posted by anyone, with or without the owner's consent.[13] Often, traditional methods of authentication may assist,[14] even with material downloaded from chat rooms.[15]

[F] Gruesome Photographs

A properly authenticated photograph may nevertheless be inadmissible if its probative value is outweighed by other considerations — for example,

---

[11] See Johnson v. Matlock, 771 F.2d 1432, 1432 (10th Cir. 1985) (photographs depicting expert's reconstruction of the accident scene; "photographs are admissible both to demonstrate mechanical principles relative to the vehicle and as a visual summary of the expert's opinion. When offered for the later purpose they are admissible within the discretion of the trial court so long as they are carefully drawn and executed and accurately represent the theory the expert proposed. Of course, it must be pointed out that the photos represent only that view of the facts which the witness is seeking to establish. This, however, was done in the present case both by the defendant's expert and by the court in its instructions to the jury.").

[12] State v. Hayden, 950 P.2d 1024, 1028 (Wash. App. 1998). See also Nooner v. State, 907 S.W.2d 677, 686 (Ark. 1995) ("Reliability must be the watchword in determining the admissibility of enhanced videotape and photographs, whether by computer or otherwise. . . . [T]he original videotape was introduced into evidence and viewed by the circuit court and jury, and the reliability of the enhanced photographs was attested to by multiple witnesses. There was no evidence of distortion to any photograph of the suspect."); English v. State, 422 S.E.2d 924, 924 (Ga. App. 1992) (same).

[13] See United States v. Jackson, 208 F.3d 633, 638 (7th Cir. 2000) ("Jackson needed to show that the web postings in which the white supremacist groups took responsibility for the racist mailings actually were posted by the groups', as opposed to being slipped onto the groups' web sites by Jackson herself, who was a skilled computer user.").

[14] See ACTONet, Ltd. v. Allou Health & Beauty Care, 219 F.3d 836, 848 (8th Cir. 2000) ("HTML [hypertext markup language] codes are similar enough to photographs to apply the criteria for admission of photographs to the admission of HTML codes.").

[15] See United States v. Stimpson, 152 F.3d 1241, 1250 (10th Cir. 1998) ("In the printout of the chat room discussion, the individual using the identity 'Stavron' gave Detective Rehman his name as B. Simpson and his correct street address. The discussion and subsequent e-mail exchanges indicated an e-mail address which belonged to Simpson. And the pages found near the computer in Simpson's home and introduced as evidence as Plaintiff's Exhibit 6 contain a notation of the name, street address, e-mail address, and telephone number that Detective Rehman gave to the individual in the chat room.") (citations omitted).

the photograph may be misleading or unduly prejudicial. This is a Rule 403 issue and often involves gruesome crime scene photographs.[16] More often than not such photographs are admissible.[17]

Photographs that illustrate a coroner's testimony or depict the number and location of stab wounds, which are indicative of purposeful conduct, have more probative value than the run-of-the-mill crime scene pictures.[18] The number of photos and their cumulative nature are also important factors under Rule 403. An offer to stipulate to the cause of death does not result in automatic exclusion, especially if the photographs are relevant to issues in dispute beyond defense counsel's stipulation.

§ 27.03 Videotapes & Movies

The admissibility of videotapes and movies depends on their use. First, parts of a trial, including the testimony of witnesses, may be presented to the jury through videotape — i.e., prerecorded videotaped trial.[19] Second, a videotaped deposition may be offered as a prior inconsistent statement[20] or as former testimony if the declarant is unavailable to testify at trial.[21] Third, an out-of-court experiment may be videotaped and proffered at trial.[22] Fourth, videotaped reenactments may be introduced in evidence.[23]

---

[16] See supra § 9.05[B][1] (unfair prejudice).

[17] See People v. Long, 113 Cal. Rptr. 530, 536–37 (Cal. App. 1974) ("(1) murder is seldom pretty, and pictures, testimony and physical evidence in such a case are always unpleasant; and (2) many attorneys tend to underestimate the stability of the jury. A juror is not some kind of a dithering nincompoop, brought in from never-never land and exposed to the harsh realities of life for the first time in the jury box. There is nothing magic about being a member of the bench or bar which makes these individuals capable of dispassionately evaluating gruesome testimony which, it is often contended, will throw jurors into a paroxysm of hysteria. Jurors are our peers, often as well educated, as well balanced, as stable, as experienced in the realities of life as the holders of law degrees. The average juror is well able to stomach the unpleasantness of exposure to the facts of a murder without being unduly influenced. The supposed influence on jurors of allegedly gruesome or inflammatory pictures exists more in the imagination of judges and lawyers than in reality."); State v. Ruebke, 731 P.2d 842, 861 (Kan. 1987) ("What Ruebke is claiming is that an individual may commit a murder so gruesome that photographs of victims and the murder scene must be kept from the jury to insure that the defendant receives a fair trial. We do not agree or adopt his reasoning."); State v. Adams, 458 P.2d 558, 563 (Wash. 1969) ("A bloody, brutal crime cannot be explained to a jury in a lily-white manner to save the members of the jury the discomforture of hearing and seeing the results of such criminal activity.").

[18] See State v. Chapple, 660 P.2d 1208, 1215 (Ariz. 1983) ("photographs of a corpse may be admitted in a homicide prosecution: to prove the corpus delicti, to identify the victim, to show the nature and location of the fatal injury, to help determine the degree or atrociousness of the crime, to corroborate state witnesses, to illustrate or explain testimony, and to corroborate the state's theory of how and why the homicide was committed.").

[19] See Ohio R. Civ. P. 40 (pre-recorded testimony).

[20] Fed. R. Evid. 613 (prior inconsistent statements).

[21] Fed. R. Evid. 804(b)(1) (former testimony). See also Joseph, Modern Visual Evidence chs. 2 & 3 (1999) (videotaped depositions).

[22] See supra § 9.09 (out-of-court experiments).

[23] See Note, Videotaped Reenactments in Civil Trials: Protecting Probate Evidence from the Trial Judge's Unbridled Discretion, 24 J. Marshall L. Rev. 433 (1991).

[A] Videotape Evidence

Videotapes may also be used in the same way that photographs are — to depict a scene or an object.[24] Videotapes of the commission of a crime, the confession of an accused, the conduct of an intoxicated driver at the time of arrest, or an allegedly incapacitated plaintiff playing basketball may be admitted upon a showing that they accurately depict the scene which they purport to portray.[25]

Other evidence rules may also apply — for example, the rule of completeness[26] and the best evidence rule.[27] Moreover, the audio part of the tape may contain inadmissible hearsay.

[B] "Day-in-the-life" Videotapes

What are known as "day-in-the-life" tapes are offered to show the daily struggles of an injured party, typically offered on the issue of damages.[28] They raise the following concerns: (1) "whether the videotape fairly represents the facts with respect to the impact of the injuries on the plaintiff's day-to-day activities," (2) the possibility of self-serving behavior because of plaintiff's self-awareness of the purpose of the videotape, (3) "the dominating nature of film evidence," and (4) jury distraction "because the benefit of effective cross-examination is lost."[29] These are Rule 403 issues.

§ 27.04 Computer Animations & Simulations

There are several different types of computer-generated evidence. For example, computer-generated business or public records are quite common; they are generally judged by the same hearsay standards as hard copy

---

[24] See Joseph, Modern Visual Evidence chs. 4 & 5 (1999) (real & demonstrative videotape evidence).

[25] See Saturn Mfg., Inc. v. Williams Patent Crusher & Pulverizer Co., 713 F.2d 1347, 1357 (8th Cir. 1983) ("Dan Burda, who was present at the making of both movies, testified that the Saturn shredder movie was a true and accurate representation of the Saturn shredder he observed, that the shredder depicted was manufactured and sold by Saturn in 1976, and that the shredder had all the features shown in Claims 8 and 10 of the Saturn patent.").

[26] Fed. R. Evid. 106. See infra chapter 29 (rule of completeness).

[27] See infra § 30.03[B] (proving contents).

[28] See Grimes v. Employers Mut. Liab. Ins. Co., 73 F.R.D. 607, 610 (D. Alaska 1977). See also Note, Beyond Words: The Evidentiary Status of "Day in the Life" Films, 66 B.U. L. Rev. 133 (1986); Note, Day-in-the-Life Films: The Celluloid Witness Comes to the Aid of the Plaintiff, 33 S.C. L. Rev. 577 (1982); Note, Plaintiffs' Use of "Day in the Life" Films: A New Look at the Celluloid Witness, 49 UMKC L. Rev. 179 (1981).

[29] Bannister v. Noble, 812 F.2d 1265, 1269 (10th Cir. 1987) (citing Bolstridge v. Cent. Maine Power Co., 621 F. Supp. 1202 (D. Me. 1985)). See also Watkins v. Cleveland Clinic Found., 719 N.E.2d 1052, 1069 (Ohio App. 1998) ("The third example cited by the defense of an appeal to inflame the passion of the jury was plaintiffs showing the videotape of Watkins, in which she is seen exhibiting a painful reflex during the suctioning of her airway. The images depicted in this videotape were relevant to demonstrate that Watkins could experience pain and suffering and corroborated the plaintiffs' testimony in that regard.").

business and public records.[30] More recent uses involve animations and simulations.

[A] Computer Animations

An animation is merely a moving series of drawings, such as the Saturday morning cartoons.[31] They are often used in conjunction with expert testimony. Some computer-generated animations fall into this category. Here, the fair-and-adequate portrayal requirement applies.

There is a difference between computer-generated animations used as *illustrative* evidence and those used as recreations of the event at issue. One court explained the difference as follows

> Although defendant argues that there is no practical difference between recreating an accident and re-creating an expert's theory of the accident, the difference is both real and significant; it is the difference between a jury believing that they are seeing a repeat of the actual event and a jury understanding that they are seeing an illustration of someone else's opinion of what happened. So long as that distinction is made clear to them there is no reason for them to credit the illustration any more than they credit the underlying opinion.[32]

The court further noted: "It is also because of that distinction that tests or experiments that merely illustrate a theory or scientific principle are not required to possess as high a degree of similarity to the actual event as are purported re-creations of the event."[33]

Under either theory, Rule 403 applies. As the Tenth Circuit has observed: "Video animation adds a new and powerful evidentiary tool to the trial scene. Because of its dramatic power, trial judges should carefully and meticulously examine proposed animation evidence for proper foundation, relevancy and the potential of undue prejudice.[34] In *Sommervold v. Grevlos*,[35] the South Dakota Supreme Court affirmed a trial court's decision to

---

[30] *See* Fed. R. Evid. 803(6) (business records); Fed. R. Evid. 803(8) (public records).

[31] *See* People v. Hood, 62 Cal. Rptr.2d 137, 140 (Cal. App. 1997) ("The prosecution and defense computer animations were tantamount to drawings by the experts from both sides to illustrate their testimony. We view them as a mechanized version of what a human animator does when he or she draws each frame of activity. . . ."); People v. McHugh, 476 N.Y.S.2d 721, 722 (Sup. Ct. 1984) ("Whether a diagram is hand drawn or mechanically drawn by means of a computer is of no importance."; animation admitted to illustrate defense position in a homicide case).

[32] Datskow v. Teledyne Cont. Motors Aircraft Prod., 826 F. Supp. 677, 686 (W.D. N.Y. 1993).

[33] *Id.* at 686. *See* State v. Farner, 66 S.W.3d 188, 209 (Tenn. 2001) ("Because the jury may be so persuaded by its life-like nature that it becomes unable to visualize an opposing or differing version of the event, the requirement that the animation fairly and accurately portray the event is particularly important when the evidence at issue is a computer animated recreation of an event.").

[34] Robinson v. Missouri Pac. R.R., 16 F.3d 1083, 1088 (10th Cir. 1994).

[35] 518 N.W.2d 733, 738 (S.D. 1994). *See also* Clark v. Cantrell, 504 S.E.2d 605, 614 (S.C.

exclude a computer-generated video animation offered to illustrate the testimony of an accident reconstruction expert on the ground that it was more prejudicial than probative. The court noted the special risk of computer-generated animations, even when offered to illustrate an expert's testimony: "'a video recreation of an accident . . . stands out in the jury's mind. So it emphasizes that evidence substantially over ordinary spoken testimony.'"[36] As with any party's staged reproduction of facts, there is the risk that the resulting product might be more like a Hollywood version of an event than anything resembling an fair depiction of that event.[37]

[B] Computer Simulations

Computer simulations differ from animations. They are a type of scientific evidence. "Simulations are recreations or experiments based upon scientific principles and data. In a simulation, data is entered into a computer, which is programmed to analyze and draw conclusions from it. The validity of the conclusions drawn depends on proper application of scientific principles. Because the results of the simulation are dependent upon the application of scientific principles for the purpose of admission, simulations are treated like other scientific tests."[38]

In simulations, mathematical models are used to predict and reconstruct an event for the trier of fact.[39] Foundational concerns for simulations can

---

1998) ("The video animation, however, is inconsistent with this testimony. Among other inaccuracies, the video did not accurately portray Cantrell's speed. It also depicted Anderson turning directly in front of Cantrell, which, as indicated by the eighty feet of skid marks, inaccurately depicts the physical evidence and expert testimony. The animation, therefore, was neither relevant nor authentic because (1) it would not have aided the jury in understanding the expert's prior testimony and (2) did not fairly and accurately reflect the evidence to which it relates."); State v. Clark, 655 N.E.2d 795 (Ohio App. 1995) (crime scene reconstruction expert allowed to use a computer drafting program to illustrate his opinion that the shooting, which had taken place in a bathroom, could not have been accidental).

[36] 518 N.W.2d at 738 (quoting the opinion of the trial court).

[37] See also What Computes in Court, Nat'l L. J, at C1, Sept. 11, 1995 (statement of Gregory Joseph) ("These exhibits often re-create events as to which there is no eyewitness—which raises the risk that they may be taken by the jury to be representations of photo-like accuracy when they could be the product of a creative lawyer or expert's imagination.").

[38] People v. Cauley, 32 P.3d 602, 606–07 (Colo. App. 2001) (shaken baby syndrome). The court added: "In contrast to a simulation, an animation is demonstrative evidence used to illustrate a witness' testimony. . . . However, an animation is distinguishable from a simulation because it is demonstrative, rather than scientific, and the validity of the conclusion does not depend on proper application of scientific principles. Within the category of animations, courts have distinguished between experiments or demonstrations that purport to recreate an event and illustrations of a general principle." Id. See also State v. Farner, 66 S.W.3d 188, 208 (Tenn. 2001) ("In contrast, a simulation is based on scientific or physical principles and data entered into a computer, which is programmed to analyze the data and draw a conclusion from it, and courts generally require proof to show the validity of the science before the simulation evidence is admitted.").

[39] The leading text is Joseph, Modern Visual Evidence ch. 8 (1999) (computer generated animations). See also Cerniglia, Computer-Generated Exhibit—Demonstrative, Substantive or Pedagogical — Their Place in Evidence, 18 Am. J. Trial Advoc. 1, 5 (1994) ("Empirical or

be broken down generally into input, processing, and output. Input concerns the probative value and admissibility of the underlying data used, the integrity of that data, and the proper physical insertion of the data into the computer. Processing involves the assurance that both the hardware and software of the computer are functioning properly. Software includes both the operating system, which controls the overall operation of the machine, and the specific application to a particular use. The output of the simulation must be consistent with the earlier foundational testimony.[40]

Pretrial notice to the opposing side, with an opportunity for that party to view and scrutinize the simulation, should be required in this context.[41]

§ 27.05   Voice Identification: FRE 901(b)(5)

Sometimes we need to identify a person's voice in order to make evidence relevant.[42] For example, an accused may make threats or obscene remarks over the telephone, or leave them on voicemail. In a racketeering prosecution, FBI eavesdropping tapes may be offered as evidence. So too, an accused's confession may be taped.[43] Rule 901(b)(5) provides for the identification of a person's voice by someone familiar with that voice.[44] Enhancement of the sound quality is permissible.[45]

---

recorded data, such as size and shape of an object, time, altitude, and velocity are entered into a computer program from several different sources. The data is then processed according to formulae programmed into the computer and the relative paths of all objects throughout the pertinent time period are independently plotted. The computer tracks and accurately depicts each object relative to all other objects throughout the time span. It moves all objects in x, y, and z coordinates, taking into account known laws of physics, such as gravity, inertia, friction and drag."); Note, *Lights, Camera, Action: Computer-Animated Evidence Gets Its Day in Court*, 34 B.C. L. Rev. 1087 (1993); Comment, *Digital Litigation: The Prejudicial Effects of Computer-Generated Animation in the Courtroom*, 9 High Tech L. J. 337 (1994).

[40] Joseph, *A Simplified Approach to Computer-Generated Evidence and Animations*, 156 F.R.D. 327 (1994).

[41] *See* Md. R. Civ. P. 2-504.3 (generally requiring 90 day notice).

[42] *See* Clifford, *Memory for Voices: The Feasibility and Quality of Earwitness Evidence,* in Evaluating Witness Evidence 189, 214 (Lloyd-Bostock & Clifford eds. 1983) ("While voice memory is a demonstrable fact, good voice memory under all but super-optimal conditions of encoding, storage, and retrieval, is the exception rather than the rule. The implication for the criminal justice system is thus fairly straightforward: voice identification by a witness concerning a stranger should be treated with the utmost caution, both in its informational and its evidential aspects.").

[43] *E.g.,* United States v. Lance, 853 F.2d 1177, 1181 (5th Cir. 1988) ("Pettitt identified the Lances' voices, testifying that he knew them well.").

[44] *See* United States v. Puentes, 53 F.3d 1567, 1577 (11th Cir. 1995) ("Rule 901(b)(5) does not require Inspector Perez to have been familiar with Puentes's voice prior to commencing the wiretapping activity. At trial, Inspector Perez testified that he became familiar with Puentes's voice during the two-month wiretap surveillance.").

[45] *E.g.,* Narvaiz v. State, 840 S.W.2d 415, 431 (Tex. Crim. App. 1992) ("F.B.I. signal processing analyst Barbara Colus then testified that she electronically copied and enhanced the marked portion of exhibit 223A [911 tape], that exhibit 226 was the enhanced copy in question, and that the enhancement removed only 'a hiss' and did not alter any of the voices on the tape in any way.").

Voice recognition is only one method of identifying a speaker's voice. For example, Rule 901(b)(6), which is discussed in the next section, recognizes a special rule for telephone conversations. In addition, Rule 901(b)(4) recognizes speaker identification by content — for example, a "telephone conversation may be shown to have emanated from a particular person by virtue of its disclosing knowledge of facts known peculiarly to him."[46]

Criminal cases. The characteristics of a person's voice fall outside the purview of the privilege against self-incrimination, which covers testimonial, not physical, evidence.[47] Consequently, voice exemplars may be obtained prior to trial for comparative purposes without violating the Fifth Amendment, although there may be Fourth Amendment[48] and other constitutional issues implicated.[49] In addition, a person may be required to speak for identification at trial.[50] Moreover, a defendant's refusal to provide in-court voice exemplars of specific words is a proper subject of a jury instruction or prosecutorial comment.[51]

---

[46] Fed. R. Evid. 901 advisory committee's note. *See also* Van Riper v. United States, 13 F.2d 961, 968 (2d Cir. 1926) (Learned Hand, J.) ("The chance that these circumstances should unite in the case of some one [other than the defendant] seems . . . so improbable that the speaker was sufficiently identified.").

[47] *See infra* § 43.04 (testimonial-real evidence distinction).

[48] Exemplars obtained during an illegal arrest or seizure may be suppressed. Exemplars, however, may be obtained by use of a grand jury subpoena, which does not require probable cause. In United States v. Dionisio 410 U.S. 1 (1973), the Supreme Court stated, "Compulsion exerted by a grand jury subpoena differs from the seizure effected by an arrest or even an investigative 'stop'" and therefore is not a "seizure" within the meaning of the Fourth Amendment. The Court also held that "the physical characteristics of a person's voice, its tone and manner, as opposed to the content of a specific conversation, are constantly exposed to the public. Like a man's facial characteristics, or handwriting, his voice is repeatedly produced for others to hear. No person can have a reasonable expectation that others will not know the sound of his voice, any more than he can reasonably expect that his face will be a mystery to the world." *Id.* at 14. Accordingly, there was no search.

[49] If a voice identification is made at a lineup or other pretrial identification procedure, due process and right to counsel issues may arise. *See* Government of Virgin Islands v. Sanes, 57 F.3d 338, 341 (3rd Cir. 1995) ("Although voice identification obviously differs from eyewitness identification we conclude that the due process eyewitness identification test, adapted to voice identification, provides a standardized source of guidance to district courts for assessing the reliability of voice identification as well."); Sobel, Eyewitness Identification: Legal and Practical Problems § 5.6 (1991) (voice identification); Yarmey, Yarmey & Yarmey, *Face and Voice Identifications in Showups and Lineups*, 8 Appl. Cognitive Psych. 453 (1994).

[50] *See* Hopkins v. State, 721 A.2d 231, 236 (Md. 1998) ("We discern little difference in a Fifth Amendment analysis of whether the voice exemplar was testimonial in nature because of the context in which it was given, here during the trial. That petitioner was required to give an exemplar in court as opposed to pre-trial is of no consequence; his statement was not testimonial because it was used for identification purposes only.").

[51] *See* State v. Hubanks, 496 N.W.2d 96 (Wis. App. 1992). Since the defendant does not have a privilege against self-incrimination in this context, commenting on the refusal to speak does not penalize the exercise of a constitutional right.

§ 27.06   Telephone Conversations: FRE 901(b)(6)

Rule 901(b)(6) provides for the authentication of telephone conversations. Outgoing and incoming calls must be distinguished.

[A]   Outgoing Calls

The rule applies only to telephone calls made by the witness to the person or number in question (*i.e.*, outgoing calls). In the drafters' view, the "calling of a number assigned by the telephone company reasonably supports the assumption that the listing is correct and that the number is the one reached."[52]

[B]   Incoming Calls

Incoming telephone calls are not covered by this rule. The "mere assertion of his identity by a person talking on the telephone is not sufficient evidence of the authenticity of the conversation and . . . additional evidence of his identity is required."[53] Caller identification systems alter this result.[54] Furthermore, other ways to identify the speaker of an incoming call may apply. Incoming (as well as outgoing) calls may be authenticated by identification of the speaker's voice,[55] by the content of the conversation,[56] or by the reply technique.[57]

---

[52] Fed. R. Evid. 901 advisory committee's note. They also extended the rule to agents: "If the number is that of a place of business, the mass of authority allows an ensuing conversation if it relates to business reasonably transacted over the telephone, on the theory that the maintenance of the telephone connection is an invitation to do business without further identification. The authorities divide on the question whether the self-identifying statement of the person answering suffices. Example (6) answers in the affirmative on the assumption that usual conduct respecting telephone calls furnish adequate assurances of regularity, bearing in mind that the entire matter is open to exploration before the trier of fact." *Id.* (citations omitted).

[53] Fed. R. Evid. 901 advisory committee's note. *See also* United States v. Kahn, 53 F.3d 507, 516 (2d Cir. 1995) ("self-identification by a person who makes a call, alone, is insufficient for authentication purposes").

[54] *E.g.*, Culbreath v. State, 667 So.2d 156, 162 (Ala. Crim. App.1995) ("the caller ID display is based on computer generated information and not simply the repetition of prior recorded human input or observation") (internal quotations omitted); People v. Caffey, 2001 WL 1243638 (Ill. 2001) ("only requirement necessary for the admission of caller ID evidence is that the caller ID device be proven reliable"); State v. Schuette, 44 P.3d 459, 463 (Kan. 2002) ("The foundation requirement of reliability is satisfied through witness testimony that the caller ID device is or has in the past been operating properly.").

[55] Fed. R. Evid. 901(b)(5).

[56] Fed. R. Evid. 901(b)(4). *See also* United States v. Garrison, 168 F.3d 1089, 1092 (8th Cir. 1999) ("While the mere assertion by a person talking on the telephone of his or her identity is not sufficient evidence of the authenticity of the conversation, the requisite additional evidence 'need not fall in any set pattern.' Indeed, a 'telephone conversation may be shown to have emanated from a particular person by virtue of its disclosing knowledge of facts known peculiarly to him.' ") (citing Fed. R. Evid. 901 advisory committee's note).

[57] Fed. R. Evid. 901(b)(4). *See* Noriega v. United States, 437 F.2d 435, 436 (9th Cir. 1971) (call made by defendant authenticated where defendant provided witness with a number, witness left message for defendant, and defendant returned the call). *See infra* § 28.05[A] (reply rule).

§ 27.07 Sound Recordings

Audiotapes may be admissible under several theories. Rule 901(b)(5) specifies voice recognition by a witness familiar with a person's voice as a method of authentication, "whether heard firsthand or through mechanical or electronic transmission or recording."[58] A sound recording may also be authenticated under Rule 901(b)(9), if the process or system used to produce the recording is shown to be reliable.[59]

[A] Inaudibility

Audiotapes that are inaudible are commonly encountered. Their use at trial raises questions best addressed under Rules 403 and 611(a).[60] The main problem is misleading the jury. Sometimes, however, more serious problems are raised. For example, in *United States v. Patrick*,[61] a defense expert testified that a tape had been "dubbed." A prosecution expert disagreed. The court ruled that "tape authentication is a subject of scientific knowledge" and that the prosecution expert was qualified in this field.[62] If a foundation is laid and the opponent is afforded the opportunity to cross-examine the witnesses, the jurors can decide for themselves what is on the tape.

[B] Transcripts

Even when a tape is audible, the proponent might still want to provide the jury with a transcript. This is permissible so long as there are no material differences between the tape and transcript which is given to the jury as a listening aid. The jury should be instructed that the tapes are merely an aid to facilitate listening and that if jurors find differences between the tape and transcript, they should disregard the transcript.[63]

---

[58] *See* United States v. Lance, 853 F.2d 1177, 1181 (5th Cir. 1988) ("Pettitt and the law enforcement agents who participated in the taped conversations testified that, according to their memories, the audio and video tapes contained accurate recordings of the conversations that occurred.").

[59] *See infra* § 28.08 (process or system). *See also* Williams v. Butler, 746 F.2d 431, 441 (8th Cir. 1984) ("The proponent of the tapes must establish that: (1) the recording device was capable of taking the conversation offered into evidence; (2) the operator of the device was competent to operate the device; (3) the recording is authentic and correct; (4) changes, additions, or deletions have not been made; (5) the recording has been preserved in a manner that is shown to the court; (6) the speakers are identified, and (7) the conversation elicited was made voluntarily and in good faith, without any kind of inducement.").

[60] *See* United States v. Carbone, 798 F.2d 21 (1st Cir. 1986).

[61] 6 F. Supp. 2d 51 (D. Mass. 1998).

[62] *Id.* at 55.

[63] *See* State v. Mason, 694 N.E.2d 932, 950 (Ohio 1998). The rule of completeness (Rule 106) and the best evidence rule (Rule 1001) may also apply to tape recordings. Moreover, the tape may contain inadmissible hearsay or double hearsay.

§ 27.08 Key Points

Photographs

"Pictorial communication" theory. A foundation for the admissibility of a photograph is laid by establishing that the photograph is an "accurate and faithful representation" of the scene or object depicted. The photographer is not required. Anyone who has firsthand knowledge may lay the foundation.

"Silent witness" theory. The process that produced the photograph may be used to authenticate. This theory is consistent with Rule 901(b)(9), which recognizes the authentication of a result produced by an accurate process. X-rays, surveillance tapes, and ATM photographs have been authenticated in this way.

Videotapes. Like photographs, videotapes are authenticated upon a showing that they accurately depict the scene which they purport to portray. What are known as "day-in-the-life" tapes are offered to show the daily struggles of an injured party, typically offered on the issue of damages.

Computer Animations

An animation is merely a moving series of drawings. Some computer-generated animations fall into this category. Here, the fair-and-adequate portrayal requirement applies. Rule 403. There is a difference between computer-generated animations used as *illustrative* evidence and those used as *recreations* of the event at issue. A higher burden must be met for recreations.

Computer Simulations

Computer simulations differ from animations. They are a type of scientific evidence. In simulations, mathematical models are used to predict and reconstruct an event for the trier of fact.

Voice Identification

Rule 901(b)(5) provides for the identification of a person's voice by someone familiar with that voice.

Telephone Conversations

Rule 901(b)(6) provides for the authentication of telephone conversations. Outgoing and incoming calls must be distinguished. The rule applies only to telephone calls made by the witness to the person or number in question (*i.e.*, outgoing calls). Incoming calls are not covered by this rule. Caller identification systems alter this result. Furthermore, other ways to identify the speaker of an incoming telephone call may apply. Incoming (as well as outgoing) calls may be authenticated by identification of the speaker's voice, by the content of the conversation, or by the reply technique.

Sound Recordings

Audiotapes may be admissible under several theories. Rule 901(b)(5) specifies voice recognition by a witness familiar with a person's voice as a method of authentication, "whether heard firsthand or through mechanical or electronic transmission or recording." A sound recording may also be authenticated under Rule 901(b)(9), if the process or system used to produce the recording is shown to be reliable.

Chapter 28

AUTHENTICATION OF WRITINGS: FRE 901–903

§ 28.01 Introduction

Documents are generally not self-authenticating — *i.e.*, a confession purportedly signed by the accused may not be admitted simply based on the signature. An authenticating witness (*e.g.*, the detective who took the confession) must testify that she saw the accused sign the document. This is known as "laying the foundation" for admissibility.

Federal Rule 901 governs the authentication of documents, the identification of real evidence, and the verification of a speaker's voice. The latter two issues are examined in chapters 26 and 27. A different rule, Rule 902, provides for the *self-authentication* of certain types of documents. Rule 903 makes the testimony of subscribing witnesses unnecessary unless required by the law of the appropriate jurisdiction.[1]

Rule 901 deals only with authentication. A document properly authenticated under Rule 901 may nevertheless be inadmissible because it fails to satisfy the requirements of the hearsay rule[2] or the best evidence rule,[3] or because its probative value is substantially outweighed by its prejudicial effect under Rule 403.

§ 28.02 General Rule

The authentication requirement imposes on the offering party the burden of proving that an item of evidence is genuine — that it is what the proponent says it is. Rule 901(a) is the general provision governing authentication. Rule 901(b) presents examples of traditional methods of authentication. These examples are merely illustrative.[4] Different methods of authentication may be used by themselves or in combination.

Reliability (truthfulness). The authentication rule is not concerned with the truthfulness of the contents of a document, a task left to the hearsay rule. Thus, an authentic (genuine) document may contain errors and even lies — for example, a newspaper article may contain erroneous information.

---

[1] *See infra* § 28.12

[2] Fed. R. Evid. 802.

[3] Fed. R. Evid. 1002.

[4] *See* United States v. Simpson, 152 F.3d 1241, 1249–50 (10th Cir. 1998) ("The specific examples of authentication referred to by Simpson are merely illustrative, however, and are not intended as an exclusive enumeration of allowable methods of authentication.").

[A] Standard of Proof: Prima Facie

Rule 901(a) represents a special application of the conditional relevance doctrine of Rule 104(b).[5] The trial court does not decide whether the evidence is authentic by a preponderance of evidence, which is the typical standard of proof.[6] Instead, the court decides only whether sufficient evidence has been introduced to support a finding of authenticity. In short, only a prima facie showing is required. If sufficient evidence has been adduced, the evidence is admitted, and the jury decides whether the evidence is authentic. Of course, the opposing party may introduce evidence to dispute authenticity.[7]

[B] Relationship with Civil Rules

Because of the availability of pretrial discovery procedures, authentication is rarely a significant problem in civil cases.[8] For example, Civil Rule 36(a) provides for requests for admissions as to the genuineness of documents. In addition, pretrial conferences under Civil Rule 16 are designed, in part, to obtain stipulations "regarding the authenticity of documents."[9]

§ 28.03 Witness with Knowledge: FRE 901(b)(1)

A witness with personal knowledge may authenticate a document.[10] This is nothing more than an application of the firsthand knowledge rule.[11] The authenticating witness need not be the author of the document, nor in most cases a subscribing witness.[12] For example, anyone who observed an accused sign a confession could authenticate the confession. Similarly, anybody present when a contract was signed could be the authenticating witness.

§ 28.04 Nonexpert Opinion on Handwriting: FRE 901(b)(2)

In some cases, a lay witness may testify to the genuineness of handwriting.[13] The rule "states conventional doctrine as to lay identification of

---

[5] *See supra* § 7.03 (conditional relevancy).

[6] *See supra* § 7.02[B] (burden of proof on preliminary issues).

[7] *See* Fed. R. Evid. 104(e) (recognizing right to attack admissible evidence before the jury).

[8] *See* ABA Section of Litigation, Emerging Problems Under the Federal Rules of Evidence, Rule 901, at 380 (3d ed. 1998) ("Article IX issues in civil cases are routinely handled before trial *via* the discovery process, especially request to admit, and the pre-trial housekeeping orders (often Draconian) used by the federal courts to eliminate as many contested issues as possible."). *See supra* § 3.02[C][3].

[9] Fed. R. Civ. P. 16(c)(3). *See supra* § 3.02[B].

[10] *See* Fed. R. Evid. 901 advisory committee's note (The rule "contemplates a broad spectrum ranging from testimony of a witness who was present at the signing of a document to testimony establishing narcotics as taken from an accused and accounting for custody through the period until trial, including laboratory analysis.").

[11] *See also* Fed. R. Evid. 602 (firsthand knowledge rule).

[12] *See* Fed. R. Evid. 903 (subscribing witnesses). *See infra* § 28.13.

[13] *See* Fed. R. Evid. 701 (lay opinion testimony).

handwriting, which recognizes that a sufficient familiarity with the handwriting of another person may be acquired by seeing him write, by exchanging correspondence, or by other means, to afford a basis for identifying it on subsequent occasions."[14] The offering party must establish that the witness is *sufficiently familiar* with the handwriting to offer a valid opinion concerning its authenticity. For example, my spouse, secretary, and coauthors could all identify my writing. There is one limitation: Familiarity with the handwriting of another acquired "for purposes of the litigation" is precluded.

§ 28.05   Comparison by Trier or Expert: FRE 901(b)(3)

A document may be authenticated by comparison with known specimens of a writing — by either the trier of fact or an expert witness.[15]

Double authentication. The handwriting exemplars (*i.e.*, "known" documents) that are used for comparative purposes must themselves be authenticated. In other words, the rule raises a "double authentication" problem. The common law tradition placed the responsibility for determining the authenticity of the known exemplars upon the trial court. Rule 901 changes this approach, treating authentication of exemplars the same as authentication of the questioned document. The trial court decides only whether there is sufficient evidence to support a jury finding of authenticity of the exemplars. The jury decides whether the exemplars are, in fact, authentic.[16]

Criminal cases. Compelling an accused to provide handwriting exemplars does not violate the privilege against self-incrimination, which is limited to testimonial, not real, evidence.[17] Exemplars obtained during an illegal arrest or seizure, however, may be suppressed.[18]

---

[14] Fed. R. Evid. 901 advisory committee's note.

[15] *See also supra* § 24.05 (qualifications of experts); § 24.11 (questioned documents).

[16] Fed. R. Evid. 901 advisory committee's note ("While explainable as a measure of prudence in the process of breaking with precedent in the handwriting situation, the reservation to the judge of the question of the genuineness of exemplars and the imposition of an unusually high standard of persuasion are at variance with the general treatment of relevancy which depends upon fulfillment of a condition of fact. Rule 104(b). No similar attitude is found in other comparison situations, *e.g.*, ballistics comparison by jury, or by experts, and no reason appears for its continued existence in handwriting cases. Consequently Example (3) sets no higher standard for handwriting specimens and treats all comparison situations alike to be governed by Rule 104(b).") (citations omitted).

[17] *See* United States v. Euge, 444 U.S. 707, 718 (1980) ("Compulsion of handwriting exemplars is not testimonial evidence protected by the Fifth Amendment privilege against self incrimination."); United States v. Mara, 410 U.S. 19, 22 n. * (1973); Gilbert v. California, 388 U.S. 263, 266–67 (1967) (Compelled production of a "mere handwriting exemplar, in contrast to the content of what is written, like the voice or body itself, is an identifying physical characteristic outside the Fifth Amendment's protection."). *See infra* § 43.04 (testimonial-real evidence distinction).

[18] *See* Davis v. Mississippi, 394 U.S. 721 (1969) (fingerprints obtained during illegal detention suppressed). Exemplars, however, may be obtained by grand jury subpoena, which does not require probable cause. *See* United States v. Dionisio, 410 U.S. 1, 10 (1973) ("compulsion

§ 28.06   Distinctive Characteristics: FRE 901(b)(4)

The "appearance, contents, substance, internal patterns, or other distinctive characteristics, taken in conjunction with circumstances" may satisfy the authentication requirement.[19] In short, any circumstantial method of proof may be used — e.g., postmark, letterhead, contents, and circumstances of discovery.[20] One case listed the following circumstances:

> The written materials were found in an isolated and remote area where law enforcement agents observed no one other than Harvey. The materials were within Harvey's campsite; indeed, they were next to Harvey's own bed. The writings also make numerous references to Harvey's beloved dog, Drigo. These distinctive characteristics and circumstances are sufficient to support a finding that the materials were written by Harvey.[21]

In another case, an e-mail message was authenticated in this manner.[22]

[A]   Reply Rule

The federal drafters specifically mentioned the reply doctrine as a method of authentication under Rule 901(b)(4). It works this way: I properly address

---

exerted by a grand jury subpoena differs from the seizure effected by an arrest or even an investigative 'stop'" and therefore is not a seizure within the meaning of the Fourth Amendment). *See also* United States v. Euge, 444 U.S. 707, 718 (1980) ("Compulsion of handwriting exemplars is neither a search or seizure subject to Fourth Amendment protections."); United States v. Mara, 410 U.S. 19, 21 (1973) ("Handwriting, like speech, is repeatedly shown to the public, and there is no more expectation of privacy in the physical characteristics of a person's script than there is in the tone of his voice.").

[19] Fed. R. Evid. 901 advisory committee's note ("The characteristics of the offered item itself, considered in the light of circumstances, afford authentication techniques in great variety. Thus a document or telephone conversation may be shown to have emanated from a particular person by virtue of its disclosing knowledge of facts known peculiarly to him; similarly, a letter may be authenticated by content and circumstances indicating it was in reply to a duly authenticated one. Language patterns may indicate authenticity or its opposite.") (citations omitted).

[20] *E.g.*, United States v. Smith, 918 F.2d 1501, 1510 (11th Cir. 1990) ("[t]he government may authenticate a document solely through the use of circumstantial evidence, including the document's own distinctive characteristics and the circumstances surrounding its discovery"); United States v. Helmel, 769 F.2d 1306 (8th Cir. 1985) (illegal gambling; ledgers reflecting intimate acquaintance with organization found at one of defendants' homes held authenticated); United States v. Sutton, 426 F.2d 1202, 1210 (D.C. Cir. 1969) ("[T]he aggregated circumstances forged such links between the questioned writings and appellant as reasonably to enable findings by the jury that he was a prior possessor of the note from 'Arthur' and the author of the remainder.").

[21] United States v. Harvey, 117 F.3d 1044, 1049 (7th Cir. 1997).

[22] United States v. Siddiqui, 235 F.3d 1318, 1322 (11th Cir. 2000) ("[A] number of factors support the authenticity of the e-mail. The e-mail sent to Yamada and von Gunten each bore Siddiqui's e-mail address . . . at the University of South Alabama. This address was the same as the e-mail sent to Siddiqui from Yamada as introduced by Siddiqui's counsel in his deposition cross-examination of Yamada. Von Gunten testified that when he replied to the e-mail apparently sent by Siddiqui, the 'reply-function' on von Gunten's e-mail system automatically dialed Siddiqui's e-mail address as the sender.").

and mail a letter to a person or company. My letter is not returned though I included my return address. Then, in due course, I receive a letter back purportedly from the person to whom I wrote, responding to the content of my letter. The return letter is authenticated circumstantially by the reply rule. Not foolproof, but few people would have knowledge of the content of my letter. Besides, authentication only requires a prima facie showing.

§ 28.07   Public Records & Reports: FRE 901(b)(7)

Public (government) records may be authenticated by showing they were retrieved from the correct place of custody — *i.e.*, the governmental repository for that type of record. The federal drafters noted: "Public records are regularly authenticated by proof of custody, without more. The rule extends the principle to include data stored in computers ["data compilations"] and similar methods."[23]

This rule deals with only one method of authenticating public records. Many public records are self-authenticating under Rule 902. In addition, Rule 901(b)(10) provides that any method of authentication recognized by statute or rule may be used, and the authentication of public records is often addressed in statutes. The Federal Rules also recognize hearsay[24] and best evidence rule[25] exceptions for public records. You will rarely see an original public record used at trial. Instead, *certified copies* are used.

§ 28.08   Ancient Documents: FRE 901(b)(8)

The rule provides a method for authenticating ancient documents, including computer data compilations.[26] Authentication is accomplished by showing that the document "(A) is in such condition as to create no suspicion concerning its authenticity, (B) was in a place where it, if authentic, would likely be, and (C) has been in existence twenty years or more at the time it is offered." The rule reduces the common law time period from 30 to *20 years*.

Another provision, Rule 803(16), recognizes a hearsay exception for ancient documents. Although the rule originated as an authentication rule, not as a hearsay exception, a number of jurisdictions recognized a hearsay exception. The rationale underlying the exception is that the "danger of mistake is minimized by authentication requirements, and age affords assurance that the writing antedates the present controversy."[27] Moreover, few authenticating witnesses will be available after a 20-year time lapse.

---

[23] Fed. R. Evid. 901 advisory committee's note.

[24] Fed. R. Evid. 803(8) (public records); Fed. R. Evid. 803(9) (vital statistics).

[25] Fed. R. Evid. 1005.

[26] *See* United States v. Kairys, 782 F.2d 1374 (7th Cir. 1986) (in denaturalization proceeding on grounds that defendant was ineligible for citizenship because he had served as a Nazi camp guard during World War II; a German Waffen SS identity card produced from the depository for German SS documents in Soviet Union archives admitted).

[27] Fed. R. Evid. 803 advisory committee's note.

§ 28.09 Process or System: FRE 901(b)(9)

Evidence describing a process or system used to produce an accurate result suffices to authenticate evidence derived from that process or system — *e.g.*, computer-generated documents.[28] Since Rule 901 is not limited to writings, this provision may also be used to authenticate sound recordings,[29] X-rays,[30] and surveillance camera photographs.[31] If the process or system is not an appropriate subject of judicial notice,[32] expert testimony may be required to establish its accuracy.[33]

§ 28.10 Statute or Rule Methods: FRE 901(b)(10)

The rule recognizes any method of authentication provided by statute or rule. Numerous statutes have provisions on public records and sometimes on hospital records. Both the Civil and Criminal Rules also contain authentication provisions.[34]

§ 28.11 Self-Authenticating Documents: FRE 902

[A] General Rule

Certain types of documents are self-authenticating. They are presumed to be genuine and therefore require no extrinsic proof of authenticity — *e.g.*, an authenticating witness. The opposing party, of course, may introduce evidence before the jury attacking the authenticity.[35] A document that fails to satisfy the requirements of Rule 902 may nevertheless achieve admissibility under Rule 901, the general rule on authentication.

[B] Domestic Public Documents with Seal

Under Rule 902(1), a document bearing (1) the seal of a governmental entity or agency and (2) a signature purporting to be an attestation or

---

[28] Fed. R. Evid. 901 advisory committee's note (The rule "is designed for situations in which the accuracy of a result is dependent upon a process or system which produces it. X rays afford a familiar instance. Among more recent developments is the computer. The rule does not, of course, foreclose taking judicial notice of the accuracy of the process or system.").

[29] *See supra* § 27.07 (sound recordings).

[30] *See supra* § 27.02[B] (silent witness theory).

[31] *E.g.*, United States v. Taylor, 530 F.2d 639, 641–42 (5th Cir. 1976) (surveillance camera photographs). *See supra* § 27.02[B] (silent witness theory).

[32] *See* Fed. R. Evid. 201 (judicial notice).

[33] Fed. R. Evid. 702 (expert testimony). *See supra* chapter 24.

[34] Fed. R. Civ. P. 44 (authentication of official & foreign records); Fed. R. Civ. P. 36 (admissions); Fed. R. Crim. P. 27 ("An official record or an entry therein or the lack of such a record or entry may be proved in the same manner as in civil actions.").

[35] *See* Fed. R. Evid. 104(e) (recognizing right to attack admissible evidence before the jury); Fed. R. Evid. 902 advisory committee's note ("In no instance is the opposite party foreclosed from disputing authenticity.").

execution is self-authenticating. [36] The rule applies to both federal and state documents. Several other rules also deal with the authentication of domestic public records. [37] The most important is Rule 902(4), which provides for the admissibility of certified copies of records admissible under the present rule. [38] A different rule governs foreign public records. [39] In addition, the Rules of Evidence recognize hearsay [40] and best evidence rule [41] exceptions for public records.

[C] Domestic Public Documents Without Seal

Domestic public documents without a seal purportedly signed by an official are self-authenticating under Rule 902(2) if accompanied by an authentication certificate: (1) signed under seal by a public officer having a seal and (2) certifying that the first officer has the official capacity claimed and that the signature is genuine. [42] In others, an authenticating certificate is attached to the original document, and, since the former is under seal, it authenticates the latter.

[D] Foreign Public Documents

Foreign birth and marriage certificates are sometimes authenticated under Rule 902(3). [43] A foreign public document is self-authenticating under two conditions. [44] First, the document must purport to have been executed or attested by a person, in an official capacity, authorized by the laws of a foreign country to make the execution or attestation — *i.e.*, a foreign official. Second, it must be accompanied by a final certificate of authentication, which may be signed by United States diplomatic personnel serving in the foreign country or by diplomatic personnel of the foreign country

---

[36] Fed. R. Evid. 902 advisory committee's note ("The acceptance of documents bearing a public seal and signature, most often encountered in practice in the form of acknowledgments or certificates authenticating copies of public records, is actually of broad application. Whether theoretically based in whole or in part upon judicial notice, the practical underlying considerations are that forgery is a crime and detection is fairly easy and certain.").

[37] *See* Fed. R. Evid. 902(2) (domestic public records without seal); Fed. R. Evid. 901(b)(7) (specifying additional methods of authenticating public records). *See also* Fed. R. Civ. P. 44 (a)(1) (domestic official records with seal); Fed. R. Crim. P. 27 (adopting the civil rule).

[38] *See infra* § 28.11[E] (certified copies of public records).

[39] Fed. R. Evid. 902(3).

[40] Fed. R. Evid. 803(8) (public records); Fed. R. Evid. 803(10) (absence of public record); Fed. R. Evid. 803(9) (vital statistics).

[41] Fed. R. Evid. 1005.

[42] Fed. R. Evid. 902 advisory committee's note ("While statutes are found which raise a presumption of genuineness of purported official signatures in the absence of an official seal, the greater ease of effecting a forgery under these circumstances is apparent. Hence this paragraph of the rule calls for authentication by an officer who has a seal.").

[43] *See* 7 Wigmore, Evidence § 2163 (Chadbourn rev. 1978).

[44] The rule is consistent with Civil Rule 44(a)(2) but more expansive, as it includes foreign public documents as well as foreign public records. Criminal Rule 27 adopts the civil rule for criminal prosecutions.

assigned or accredited to the United States. The court may waive final certification where all the parties have had a reasonable opportunity to investigate the authenticity of the foreign document and good cause is shown.

[E] Certified Copies of Public Records

This is the most important self-authentication rule for official records because it is the one used most frequently.[45] Under Rule 902(4), copies of official records, official reports, and recorded documents are self-authenticating under two conditions.[46] First, the copy must be certified as correct by the custodian or other authorized person. Second, the copy must be accompanied by an authentication certificate complying with: (a) the prior rules (Rules 902(1), (2), or (3))[47] ; (b) an Act of Congress; or (c) a rule prescribed by the Supreme Court.[48]

Public records do not leave their place of custody. Instead, a copy certified as correct by a government official is used at trial.

[F] Official Publications

Books, pamphlets, or other publications purporting to be issued by public authorities are self-authenticating under Rule 902(5).[49] For example, the South Dakota Driver's License Manual, containing a chart projecting blood

---

[45] *See* Fed. R. Evid. 902 advisory committee's note ("The common law and innumerable statutes have recognized the procedure of authenticating copies of public records by certificate. The certificate qualifies as a public document, receivable as authentic when in conformity with paragraph (1), (2), or (3). Rule 44(a) of the Rules of Civil Procedure and Rule 27 of the Rules of Criminal Procedure have provided authentication procedures of this nature for both domestic and foreign public records.").

[46] *E.g.,* United States v. Huffhines, 967 F.2d 314, 320 (9th Cir. 1992) ("Copies of judgments certified by the Texas Department of Corrections custodian of records are admissible under Texas law. Moreover, they are admissible in federal court under Federal Rule of Evidence 902(4).") (citation omitted); United States v. Darveaux, 830 F.2d 124, 126 (8th Cir. 1987); United States v. Dancy, 861 F.2d 77, 79 (5th Cir. 1988) (copy of prior criminal judgment prepared and certified by official of California Department of Corrections).

[47] Note that the types of materials covered by this rule is narrower than what is covered in the first three rules (records, reports and recorded documents, rather than all official documents). *See* Fed. R. Evid. 902 advisory committee's note ("It will be observed that the certification procedure here provided extends only to public records, reports, and recorded documents, all including data compilations, and does not apply to public documents generally. Hence documents provable when presented in original form under paragraphs (1), (2), or (3) may not be provable by certified copy under paragraph (4).").

[48] *See* Fed. R. Civ. P. 44(a)(1) (domestic official records with seal); Fed. R. Crim. P. 27 (adopting the civil rule).

[49] Fed. R. Evid. 902 advisory committee's note ("Dispensing with preliminary proof of the genuineness of purportedly official publications, most commonly encountered in connection with statutes, court reports, rules, and regulations, has been greatly enlarged by statutes and decisions. . . . Paragraph (5), it will be noted, does not confer admissibility upon all official publications; it merely provides a means whereby their authenticity may be taken as established for purposes of admissibility.").

alcohol levels based upon weight, number of drinks consumed, and rates of alcohol absorption over various periods of time, is a self-authenticating document under this provision.[50]

[G] Newspapers & Periodicals

Newspapers or periodicals, including notices and advertisements contained therein, are self-authenticating per Rule 902(6). Thus, the N.Y. Times, Wall Street Journal, or other publications may be admitted in evidence without an authenticating witness.[51] Note that the rule deals only with authentication. A newspaper account may be inadmissible because of some other evidentiary rule, such as the hearsay rule.

[H] Trade Inscriptions & the Like

Rule 902(7) rejects the result reached in *Keegan v. Green Giant Co.*,[52] where the plaintiff's attorney did not lay a proper foundation for a can of peas with the *Green Giant* label — the big green guy. Can of peas not admissible; case over. Under Rule 902, the can would have been self-authenticating: "inscriptions, signs, tags, or labels purporting to have been affixed in the course of business and indicating ownership, control, or origin" are self-authenticating. Several factors support this rule: the "risk of forgery is minimal. Trademark infringement involves serious penalties. Great efforts are devoted to inducing the public to buy in reliance on brand names, and substantial protection is given them."[53]

[I] Acknowledged Documents

Rule 902(8) provides that documents "accompanied by a certificate of acknowledgment executed in the manner provided by law by a notary public or other officer authorized by law to take acknowledgments" are self-authenticating.[54]

---

[50] State v. Machmuller, 630 N.W.2d 495 (S.D. 2001).

[51] Fed. R. Evid. 902 advisory committee's note ("The likelihood of forgery of newspapers or periodicals is slight indeed. Hence no danger is apparent in receiving them. Establishing the authenticity of the publication may, of course, leave still open questions of authority and responsibility for items therein contained.").

[52] 110 A.2d 599 (Me. 1954).

[53] *See* Fed. R. Evid. 902 advisory committee's note ("Cattle brands have received similar acceptance in the western states.").

[54] *See* Fed. R. Evid. 902 advisory committee's note ("In virtually every state, acknowledged title documents are receivable in evidence without further proof. Statutes are collected in 5 Wigmore § 1676. If this authentication suffices for documents of the importance of those affecting titles, logic scarcely permits denying this method when other kinds of documents are involved.").

[J] Commercial Paper & Related Documents

Commercial paper, signatures thereon, and related documents to the extent provided by general commercial law are self-authenticating per Rule 902(9) — *i.e.*, Uniform Commercial Code.[55]

[K] Presumptions Created by Law

Under Rule 902(10), any signature, document, or other matter declared by Congress to be presumptively (prima facie) genuine is self-authenticating.[56]

[L] Certified Domestic Business Records

Rule 902(11) covers certified domestic business records.[57] It is new and important because it will be used more than any other provision in the rule. An original or duplicate admissible under the hearsay exception for business records[58] is self-authenticating if accompanied by a certification prepared by its custodian or other qualified person.

The certification must state that the record (1) was made at or near the time of the event recorded, (2) based on firsthand knowledge (or from information transmitted by such a person), (3) was kept in the course of the regularly conducted activity; and (4) was made as a regular practice. These are the foundational requirements for the business records exception, which covers nonprofit records as well.[59] The party must provide written notice to adverse parties and make the record and certification available for inspection sufficiently in advance of trial to give those parties a fair opportunity to challenge them.

[M] Certified Foreign Business Records

Rule 902(12) covers certified foreign business records.[60] To a large extent, it tracks the prior rule. In a civil case, the original or a duplicate admissible

---

[55] For example, one provision makes bills of lading, insurance policies, insurance certificates, official weigher's certificates, official inspector's certificates, consular invoices, or any other document authorized or required by the contract to be issued by a third party, prima facie authentic. Another provision makes a negotiable instrument signature admissible unless specifically denied in the pleadings. U.C.C. §§ 1-202, 3-307, 3-510.

[56] *E.g.*, 15 U.S.C. § 77f(a) (signature on SEC registration presumed genuine); 26 U.S.C. § 6064 (signature on tax return prima facie genuine).

[57] Fed. R. Evid. 902 advisory committee's note (2000) ("A declaration that satisfies 28 U.S.C. § 1746 would satisfy the declaration requirement of Rule 902(11), as would any comparable certification under oath. The notice requirement in Rules 902(11) and (12) is intended to give the opponent of the evidence a full opportunity to test the adequacy of the foundation set forth in the declaration.").

[58] Fed. R. Evid. 803(6).

[59] *See infra* § 33.10 (business records exception).

[60] Fed. R. Evid. 902 advisory committee's note (2000) ("18 U.S.C. § 3505 currently provides a means for certifying foreign records of regularly conducted activity in criminal cases, and this amendment is intended to establish a similar procedure for domestic records, and for foreign records offered in civil cases.").

under the business records exception to the hearsay rule, Rule 803(6), is self-authenticating if accompanied by a written certification by its custodian or other qualified person.[61]

The declaration must be signed in a manner that, if falsely made, would subject the maker to criminal penalty under the laws of the country where the certification is signed. The party must provide written notice to adverse parties and make the record and declaration available for inspection sufficiently in advance of trial to provide those parties with a fair opportunity to challenge them.

§ 28.12   Subscribing Witnesses: FRE 903

Rule 903 makes the testimony of subscribing witnesses unnecessary unless required by the law of the appropriate jurisdiction. Some states require the witnesses to a will to testify, if available, when a will is contested.

§ 28.13   Key Points

Documents are generally not self-authenticating — *i.e.*, a confession purportedly signed by the accused may not be admitted simply based on the signature. An authenticating witness (*e.g.*, the detective who took the confession) must testify that she saw the accused sign the document. This is known as "laying the foundation" for admissibility. Rule 901 governs the authentication generally, and Rule 902 provides for the *self-authentication* of certain types of documents.

Rule 901 deals only with authentication. A document properly authenticated under Rule 901 may nevertheless be inadmissible because it fails to satisfy the requirements of the hearsay rule or the best evidence rule, or because its probative value is substantially outweighed by its prejudicial effect under Rule 403.

General rule. Rule 901(a) imposes on the offering party the burden of proving that an item of evidence is genuine — that it is what the proponent says it is. Rule 901(b) presents examples of traditional methods of authentication. These examples are merely illustrative. Different methods of authentication may be used by themselves or in combination.

Standard of proof. Only a prima facie showing is required.

Illustrations. Most of the illustrations are not difficult once you have gone through once. Two are worth special attention:

Reply rule. The federal drafters specifically mentioned the reply rule as a method of authentication under Rule 901(b)(4). Assume that I properly

---

[61] The certification must state that the record (1) was made at or near the time of the event recorded, (2) based on firsthand knowledge (or from information transmitted by such a person), (3) was kept in the course of the regularly conducted activity; and (4) was made as a regular practice. These are the foundational requirements for the business records exception, which covers nonprofit records as well. *See infra* § 33.10 (business records exception).

address and mail a letter to a person or company. My letter is not returned though I included my return address. Then, in due course, I receive a letter back purportedly from the person to whom I wrote, responding to the content of my letter. The return letter is authenticated circumstantially by the reply rule.

Ancient documents. Under Rule 901(b)(8), a document may be authenticated by showing that the document "(A) is in such condition as to create no suspicion concerning its authenticity, (B) was in a place where it, if authentic, would likely be, and (C) has been in existence twenty years or more at the time it is offered." Another provision, Rule 803(16), recognizes a hearsay exception for ancient documents.

Self-authentication. The most important rules concern *certified copies* of public records[62] and business records.[63] Other provisions cover newspapers, notarized documents, and commercial documents under the U.C.C.

---

[62] Fed. R. Evid. 902(4).

[63] Fed. R. Evid. 902(11).

Chapter 29

RULE OF COMPLETENESS: FRE 106

§ 29.01 Introduction

The refrain "My statements were taken out of context" is frequently heard. In evidence law, the "rule of completeness" is designed to deal with this problem.[1] For example, suppose the accused's written confession contains the following passage: "Yes, I killed him. But I did it in self-defense." However, the prosecution introduces the first but not the second sentence. Under Rule 106, which codifies the rule of completeness, the defense has the right to introduce the second sentence *immediately*.[2]

In addition to writings, the rule also covers recorded statements. It does not apply to oral statements.

§ 29.02 Rationale

Rule 106 is based on two considerations. "The first is the misleading impression created by taking matters out of context. The second is the inadequacy of repair work when delayed to a point later in the trial."[3] It is the second consideration that is the key to the rule. In most trial situations, a party wishing to put the opposing party's evidence in context must wait until cross-examination or the next stage of trial at which that party is entitled to introduce evidence. Rule 106 defines a special exception for documents and recorded statements, permitting a party to place the opposing party's evidence "in context" immediately. (The rule uses the phrase "contemporaneously with it"). The rule "does not in any way circumscribe the right of the adversary to develop the matter on cross-examination or as part of his own case."[4]

§ 29.03 Oral Conversations

Rule 106 does not apply to oral conversations unless they are taped.[5] A

---

[1] *See also* Fed. R. Evid. 410(b)(1) (adopting a "rule of completeness" for statements made during certain types of pleas and plea discussions); Fed. R. Civ. P. 32(a)(4) ("If only part of a deposition is offered in evidence by a party, an adverse party may require the offeror to introduce any other part which ought in fairness to be considered with the part introduced, and any party may introduce any other parts."); Fed. R. Crim. P. 15(f).

[2] *See* United States v. Jamar, 561 F.2d 1103, 1108 (4th Cir. 1977) (Rule 106's purpose is "to permit the contemporaneous introduction of recorded statements that place in context other writings admitted into evidence which, viewed alone, may be misleading.").

[3] Fed. R. Evid. 106 advisory committee's note.

[4] *Id.*

[5] *See Id.* ("For practical reasons, the rule is limited to writings and recorded statements and does not apply to conversations."); United States v. Terry, 702 F.2d 299, 314 (2d Cir. 1983).

party who wishes to elicit additional parts of a conversation to put the conversation in context must wait until a later stage in the proceeding — typically, cross-examination or redirect examination. The trial court, however, has authority under Rule 611(a) to apply the rule of completeness to conversations.[6]

However, Rule 106 does apply when a witness is questioned about a *writing*, which is tantamount to the introduction of the writing in evidence.[7]

§ 29.04 "Ought in fairness" Standard

A second document or recording may be required to "(1) explain the admitted portion, (2) place the admitted portion in context, (3) avoid misleading the trier of fact, or (4) insure a fair and impartial understanding."[8] The party invoking in the rule must specify which parts of the document are needed to place the writing in context.[9] Although Rule 106 recognizes the right of a party to invoke the rule of completeness, decisions concerning the application of the rule fall within the discretion of the trial court.[10]

---

[6] *See* Fed. R. Evid. 611(a) ("The court shall exercise reasonable control over the mode and order of interrogating witnesses and presenting evidence. . . ."); United States v. Li, 55 F.3d 325, 329 (7th Cir. 1995) ("We have recently refused to extend this rule to oral statements but have held that Fed. R. Evid. 611(a) grants district courts the same authority regarding oral statements which Fed. R. Evid. 106 grants regarding written and recorded statements."); United States v. Castro, 813 F.2d 571, 576 (2d Cir. 1987) ("Whether we operate under Rule 106's embodiment of the rule of completeness, or under the more general provision of Rule 611(a), we remain guided by the overarching principle that it is the trial court's responsibility to exercise common sense and a sense of fairness.").

[7] *See* Rainey v. Beech Aircraft Corp., 784 F.2d 1523, 1529 n.11 (11th Cir. 1986) ("Technically, Rule 106 is limited in its application to instances when a party introduces a writing or recorded statement into evidence. Here, we find the defendant's questions concerning Rainey's letter tantamount to the introduction of the letter into evidence. We therefore apply the concerns of the Rule — fairness and completeness — to this case."), *vacated*, 791 F.2d 833 (11th Cir.1986), *reinstated en banc*, 827 F.2d 1498 (11th Cir. 1987), *modified*, 488 U.S. 153, 172 (1988) ("Clearly the concerns underlying Rule 106 are relevant here.").

[8] United States v. Soures, 736 F.2d 87, 91 (3d Cir. 1984). *Accord* United States v. Branch, 91 F.3d 699, 727 (5th Cir. 1996) ("Although different circuits have elaborated Rule 106's 'fairness standard in different ways, common to all is the requirement that the omitted portion be relevant and 'necessary to qualify, explain, or place into context the portion already introduced.'") (citations omitted); United States v. Li, 55 F.3d 325, 329–30 (7th Cir. 1995) ("A trial judge need not admit every portion of a statement but only those needed to explain portions previously received.").

[9] *See* United States v. Sweiss, 814 F.2d 1208, 1212 (7th Cir. 1987) ("To lay a sufficient foundation at trial for a rule of completeness claim, the offeror need only specify the portion of the testimony that is relevant to the issue at trial and that qualifies or explains portions already admitted. This is a minimal burden that can be met without unreasonable specificity.") (citation omitted).

[10] *See* Beech Aircraft Corp. v. Rainey, 488 U.S. 153, 172 (1988) ("The District Court's refusal to admit the proffered completion evidence was a clear abuse of discretion."); United States v. Branch, 91 F.3d 699, 727 (5th Cir. 1996) ("We review the district court's decision for abuse of discretion.").

Accused's statements. When the statement introduced is that of a criminal defendant, other considerations support the rule of completeness. The Fifth Amendment precludes the prosecution from calling the accused as a witness.[11] Thus, the prosecution typically introduces the accused's incriminatory statements through the police. Selective admission of the accused's statements is not uncommon; why should the prosecution offer evidence helpful to the accused? Some courts question this practice,[12] while others believe the rule of completeness should not be extended beyond its limited purpose: "We acknowledge the danger inherent in the selective admission of post-arrest statements. Neither the Constitution nor Rule 106, however, requires the admission of the entire statement once any portion is admitted in a criminal prosecution."[13]

§ 29.05 "Inadmissible Evidence" Problem

Does Rule 106 authorize the admission of otherwise inadmissible evidence (*e.g.*, hearsay)? Although Rule 106 does not expressly include a requirement that the evidence be otherwise admissible,[14] a number of federal courts have imposed this requirement.[15] The problem with this limitation is that an inadmissible part, say hearsay, of a document may be needed to put the document "in context."

This problem can sometimes be remedied by limiting the purpose for which the remainder of the document is admitted, *i.e.*, the document is not

---

[11] *See infra* § 43.05 (accused's privilege at trial).

[12] United States v. Walker, 652 F.2d 708, 713 (7th Cir. 1981):

> The Advisory committee's note indicates that Rule 106 is primarily designed to affect the order of proof. In criminal cases where the defendant elects not to testify, as in the present case, more is at stake than the order of proof. If the Government is not required to submit all relevant portions of prior testimony which further explain selected parts which the Government has offered, the excluded portions may never be admitted. Thus there may be no "repair work" which could remedy the unfairness of a selective presentation later in the trial of such a case. While certainly not as egregious, the situation at hand does bear similarity to "(f)orcing the defendant to take the stand in order to introduce the omitted exculpatory portions of (a) confession (which) is a denial of his right against self-incrimination."

[13] United States v. Branch, 91 F.3d 699, 729 (5th Cir. 1996). The court added: "We do not doubt the exculpatory nature of the excluded statement, but that does not require its admission under Rule 106." *Id.* at 728.

[14] *See* ABA Section of Litigation, Emerging Problems Under the Federal Rules of Evidence 26 (3d ed. 1998) ("Some cases and commentators question whether Rule 106 also has independent evidentiary authority for admitting otherwise inadmissible evidence. The Rule does not address this issue, and unlike other Federal Rules of Evidence, does not contain the 'except as otherwise provided' language which acts to reinforce the mandates of other evidentiary provisions.").

[15] *See* United States v. LeFevour, 798 F.2d 977, 981 (7th Cir. 1986) ("Rule 106 was not intended to override every privilege and other exclusionary rule of evidence in the legal armamentarium, so there must be cases where if an excerpt is misleading the only cure is to exclude it rather than to put in other excerpts."); United States v. Terry, 702 F.2d 299, 314 (2d Cir. 1983) ("Rule 106 does not render admissible evidence that is otherwise inadmissible."). *But see* United States v. Sutton, 801 F.2d 1346, 1368 (D.C. Cir. 1986).

offered for its truth but only for the purpose of placing the document in context (a nonhearsay purpose).[16] Also, the doctrine of "fighting fire with fire" (curative admissibility) may also justify admission.[17] The Supreme Court has indicated that relevancy is automatically satisfied in this context. In commenting on Rule 106, the Court in *Beech Aircraft Corp v. Rainey*[18] wrote: "When one party has made use of a portion of a document, such that misunderstanding or distortion can be averted only through presentation of another portion, the material required for completeness is ipso facto relevant and therefore admissible under Rules 401 and 402."[19]

§ 29.06 Key Points

Under Rule 106, which codifies the rule of completeness, the other party has the right to introduce a second document immediately to place the first document in context. It is the "immediately" requirement that makes Rule 106 important; the party does not have to wait either for cross-examination or until it can introduce evidence. The rule applies to parts of documents as well as to recordings.

Oral statements. Rule 106 does not apply to oral conversations unless they are taped. The trial court, however, has authority under Rule 611(a) to apply the rule of completeness to conversations.

"Ought in fairness" standard. A second document or recording may be required to (1) explain the admitted portion, (2) place the admitted portion in context, (3) avoid misleading the trier of fact, or (4) insure a fair and impartial understanding. The party invoking the rule must specify which parts of the document are needed to place the writing in context.

Inadmissible evidence. Whether Rule 106 authorizes the admission of otherwise inadmissible evidence (*e.g.*, hearsay) is an issue that has divided the courts.

---

[16] *See* Beech Aircraft Corp. v. Rainey, 488 U.S. 153, 173 n.18 (1988) ("Nor would a hearsay objection have been availing. Although the question called for Rainey to testify to an out-of-court statement, that statement was not offered 'to prove the truth of the matter asserted.' Rule 801(c). Rather, it was offered simply to prove what Rainey had said about the accident six months after it happened, and to contribute to a fuller understanding of the material the defense had already placed in evidence."); United States v. LeFevour, 798 F.2d 977, 981 (7th Cir. 1986) ("If otherwise inadmissible evidence is necessary to correct a misleading impression, then either it is admissible for this limited purpose by force of Rule 106 or, if it is inadmissible (maybe because of privilege), the misleading evidence must be excluded too."); Fed. R. Evid. 105 (limiting instructions).

[17] *See supra* § 6.08 (fighting fire with fire).

[18] 488 U.S. 153 (1988).

[19] *Id.* at 172.

Chapter 30

"BEST EVIDENCE" RULE: FRE 1001-1008

§ 30.01 Introduction

To prove the contents of a writing, the "best evidence" rule requires that the original be introduced in evidence unless an exception applies. The label "best evidence rule" is misleading. The rule applies *only* to writings, recordings, and photographs (and only when proving their *contents*). There is no general rule requiring the "best evidence." A party generally is not required to introduce real evidence in order to prove its case.[1] You can prove a theft case without introducing the stolen property. You can even prove a drug possession case without introducing the drugs.[2] Thus, a more apt description of the rule is the "original writing" rule.[3]

§ 30.02 Rationale

The nature of writings gives rise to their being singled out for special treatment. The copying of a writing is especially susceptible to the introduction of inaccuracies, and even a minor mistake may have significant legal consequences — for example, in wills, deeds, and contracts.[4] Although prevention of fraud has been identified as an additional purpose of the original writing rule,[5] this view has been challenged.[6]

---

[1] *See* Holle v. State, 337 A.2d 163, 166–67 (Md. App. 1975) (stolen marked currency; "It is not always necessary that tangible evidence be physically admitted at a trial. . . . Even when evidence is available it need not be physically offered. Thus, the grand larceny of an automobile may be established merely on competent testimony describing the stolen vehicle without actually producing the automobile before the trier of fact."). *Accord* United States v. Figueroa, 618 F.2d 934, 941 (2d Cir. 1980) (heroin); Chandler v. United States, 318 F.2d 356, 357 (10th Cir. 1963) (whiskey bottles).

[2] All you need is two witnesses. For example, an arresting officer testifies that she found the defendant holding a package that looked like it contained a controlled substance. She seized it and took it to the crime lab. The second witness is the chemist who testifies that he received this package from the arresting officer and when tested, the substance was revealed to be heroin. Of course, tactically, it is always better to introduce the drugs, but legally it is not required.

[3] *See* United States v. Duffy, 454 F.2d 809, 811 (5th Cir. 1972) ("Although the phrase 'Best Evidence Rule' is frequently used in general terms, the 'Rule' itself is applicable only to the proof of the contents of a writing.").

[4] *See* Seiler v. Lucasfilm, Ltd., 808 F.2d 1316, 1319 (9th Cir. 1986) ("The modern justification for the rule has expanded from prevention of fraud to a recognition that writings occupy a central position in the law. . . . [T]he importance of the precise terms of writings in the world of legal relations, the fallibility of the human memory as reliable evidence of the terms, and the hazards of inaccurate or incomplete duplication are the concerns addressed by the best evidence rule.").

[5] *See id.* at 1319.

[6] *See* 4 Wigmore, Evidence § 1181 (Chadbourn rev. 1972).

Think Bob Cratchit or some medieval monk laboriously copying documents by hand. At the time the rule developed, this was the type of secondary evidence that was of concern. Perhaps worst was the testimony of a witness who had read a document sometime in the past and attempted to recount at trial what he had read (another type of secondary evidence).

§ 30.03 Proving Contents

The rule applies *only* when a party attempts to prove the contents of a writing or recording. Typically, this occurs when (1) the event to be proved is a written transaction or (2) a party chooses a written method of proof.

[A] Written Events; Independent Events

Some events and transactions, such as those involving deeds, contracts, and judgments, are written transactions, and the rule requires production of the original writing when the contents are sought to be proved.

Independent events recorded. Rule 1002 does not apply when the event sought to be proved existed independently of a writing, even if that event has been recorded. This is counter-intuitive.[7] For example, if an accused makes an oral confession which is recorded or subsequently reduced to writing, the rule does *not* apply. The prosecution is not attempting to prove the contents of the recording or writing but rather the independent event (oral confession) that happened to have been recorded. Other examples include proof of the existence of a marriage, payment of a debt or a purchase, perjured testimony,[8] conversations,[9] as well as earnings in an account.[10]

The trial court, however, has authority to require production of the writing or recording pursuant to Rule 611(a).[11]

---

[7] Fed. R. Evid. 1002 advisory committee's note ("an event may be proved by nondocumentary evidence, even though a written record of it was made").

[8] *See* United States v. Myers, 171 F.2d 800, 812 (D.C. Cir. 1948) ("Here there was no attempt to prove the contents of a writing; the issue was what Lamarre had said, not what the transcript contained. The transcript made from shorthand notes of his testimony was, to be sure, evidence of what he had said, but it was not the only admissible evidence concerning it. Rogers' testimony was equally competent, and was admissible. . . . Statements alleged to be perjurious may be proved by any person who heard them, as well as by a reporter who recorded them in shorthand.").

[9] *See* United States v. Branham, 97 F.3d 835, 853 (6th Cir. 1996); United States v. Martin, 920 F.2d 393, 397 (6th Cir. 1990) (government informant taped conversations with defendant concerning a cocaine purchase; Rule 1002 "is not relevant to this situation" because the "intention here is not to prove the content of a recording but rather to corroborate a conversation which the government claims to have occurred.").

[10] Fed. R. Evid. 1002 advisory committee's note ("For example, payment may be proved without producing the written receipt which was given. Earnings may be proved without producing books of account in which they are entered.").

[11] Fed. R. Evid. 611(a) ("The court shall exercise reasonable control over the mode and order of interrogating witnesses and presenting evidence. . . .").

[B] Written Method of Proof

If a party chooses to introduce a writing to prove a fact, the original must be produced.[12] Thus, in the confession hypothetical cited above, if the prosecution chose to use the writing to prove the confession, it would have to offer the original writing.[13] The rule would also apply to a witness who had *read* the confession and testifies to the contents of the *written* confession. (This differs from a witness who *heard* the *oral* confession.)

[C] Related Issues

Absence of a writing. The federal drafters noted that the original writing rule does not apply "to testimony that books or records have been examined and found not to contain any reference to a designated matter."[14]

Recordings. The discussion in the preceding sections also applies to recordings. Recordings, however, raise an additional issue: whether the original writing rule applies to transcripts that are provided to jurors to aid in following tape recordings played at trial.[15]

Photographs. The original photograph is required to prove the contents of the photograph.[16] In most cases, however, photographs are not offered to prove their contents.[17] Photographs are typically admitted in evidence under what is known as the "pictorial testimony" theory of admissibility. A foundation for the admissibility of photographs is laid by establishing

---

[12] It does not matter that the fact could have been proved without the writing —*i.e.*, a fact that existed independently of the writing. If the party chooses a written method of proof, the rule applies.

[13] *See* Fed. R. Evid. 1002 advisory committee's note ("If . . . the event is sought to be proved by the written record, the rule applies.").

[14] *Id. Accord* State v. Nano, 543 P.2d 660, 662 (Or. 1975) ("In the present case the witness testified to what the document did not contain; that is, the sales records did not show any sales of the calculators. Literally, this is not proof of the terms of a document. More importantly, this is not testimony in which 'the smallest variation in words may be of importance.' ") (citing Wigmore).

[15] The answer is no. The transcripts are merely a guide. The recording is the evidence and trumps the transcript if there is a conflict. *See supra* § 27.07 (sound recordings).

[16] Rule 1001(2) defines photographs to include X-ray films, videotapes, and motion pictures. In addition, Rule 1001(3) provides that the original of a photograph "includes the negative or any print therefrom."

[17] "The assumption should not be made that the rule will come into operation on every occasion when use is made of a photograph in evidence. On the contrary, the rule will seldom apply to ordinary photographs. In most instances a party wishes to introduce the item and the question raised is the propriety of receiving it in evidence. Cases in which an offer is made of the testimony of a witness as to what he saw in a photograph or motion picture, without producing the same, are most unusual. The usual course is for a witness on the stand to identify the photograph or motion picture as a correct representation of events which he saw or of a scene with which he is familiar. In fact he adopts the picture as his testimony, or, in common parlance, uses the picture to illustrate his testimony. Under these circumstances, no effort is made to prove the contents of the picture, and the rule is inapplicable." Fed. R. Evid. 1002 advisory committee's note (citing Paradis, *The Celluloid Witness*, 37 Colo. L. Rev. 235, 249–51 (1965)).

that the photograph is an "accurate and faithful representation" of the scene or object depicted.[18] Under this theory, the authenticating witness adopts the photograph as his own testimony. The original writing rule does not apply because the offering party is not attempting to prove the contents of a photograph but rather the scene depicted, an independent event.

There are, of course, cases in which the proponent is trying to prove the contents of a picture. Copyright cases, defamation cases, and cases involving invasion of privacy by photograph fall into this category. Obscene pictures also come within this category.[19] In addition, when the picture has independent value, such as the photograph of a bank robber by a surveillance camera or an X-ray in a personal injury case, the rule also applies. These cases involve attempts to prove the contents of the picture.

§ 30.04   Definition of "Writing" & "Original"

[A]   "Writings" Defined

Rule 1001(1) defines writings and recordings broadly. This definition is intended to include writings produced from modern photographic and computer systems.[20] The term writing also encompasses artwork, engineering drawings, and architectural designs.[21] In addition, inscribed chattels (*e.g.*, tombstones) come within the definition of a writing, but, because of their nature, the trial court has more discretion in determining whether the original need be produced.[22]

---

[18] *See supra* § 27.02[A] ("pictorial communication" theory).

[19] *See* United States v. Levine, 546 F.2d 658, 668 (5th Cir. 1977) ("Whether a motion picture film is obscene must be adjudged upon viewing it in its entirety. The contents of the film are what is sought to be proved. Thus, the 'best evidence' standard embodied in rule 1002 applies to the introduction of the film.") (citation omitted).

[20] Fed. R. Evid. 1001 advisory committee's note ("Present day techniques have expanded methods of storing data, yet the essential form which the information ultimately assumes for usable purposes is words and figures. Hence the considerations underlying the rule dictate its expansion to include computers, photographic systems, and other modern developments.").

[21] Seiler v. Lucasfilm, Ltd., 808 F.2d 1316, 1320 (9th Cir. 1986).

[22] *See* United States v. Duffy, 454 F.2d 809, 812 (5th Cir. 1972) ("When the disputed evidence, such as the shirt in this case, is an object bearing a [laundry] mark or inscription, and is, therefore, a chattel *and* a writing, the trial judge has discretion to treat the evidence as a chattel or as a writing. In reaching his decision, the trial judge should consider the policy-consideration behind the 'Rule'. In the instant case, the trial judge was correct in allowing testimony about the shirt without requiring the production of the shirt. Because the writing involved in this case was simple, the inscription 'D—U—F', there was little danger that the witness would inaccurately remember the terms of the 'writing'. Also, the terms of the 'writing' were by no means central or critical to the case against Duffy. The crime charged was not possession of a certain article, where the failure to produce the article might prejudice the defense. The shirt was collateral evidence of the crime. Furthermore, it was only one piece of evidence in a substantial case against Duffy.") (citations omitted); United States v. Marcantoni, 590 F.2d 1324 (5th Cir. 1979) (two $10 bills found but not seized during a search of the defendants' residence and bearing serial numbers included in the list of "bait money" taken in a robbery fell within best evidence rule).

[B] "Originals" Defined

Rule 1001(3) defines an original as the writing or recording itself or any "counterpart intended to have the same effect by a person executing or issuing it." The rule employs an *intent* test to determine whether a writing is an original.

In most instances, what is an original will be self-evident. Note, however, that there may be more than one original.[23] "A carbon copy of a contract executed in duplicate becomes an original, as does a sales ticket carbon copy given to a customer."[24] In addition, "what is an original for some purposes may be a duplicate for others. Thus a bank's microfilm record of checks cleared is the original as a record. However, a print offered as a copy of a check whose contents are in controversy is a duplicate."[25] If, for example, a defendant charged with submitting fraudulent expense vouchers used photocopies of expense receipts to support the reimbursement claim, the photocopies are the originals because they are the relevant documents.[26]

Computer records. Rule 1001(3) contains a specific provision on computer-generated writings: "any printout or other output readable by sight, shown to reflect the data accurately, is an 'original.'"[27]

Photographs. Rule 1001(3) provides that the original of a photograph "includes the negative or any print therefrom."[28] The federal drafters justified this definition by noting that "[w]hile strictly speaking the original of a photograph might be thought to be only the negative, practicality and common usage require that any print from the negative be regarded as an original."[29]

---

[23] *See* Greater Kansas City Laborers Pension Fund v. Thummel, 738 F.2d 926, 928 (8th Cir. 1984) ("There was evidence that the contract was executed in quadruplicate, and that the second, third and fourth copies were not always signed individually, but were usually placed under the top copy and separated by sheets of carbon paper. This is sufficient to qualify a carbon copy as an original, and we see no error in its admission."); United States v. Rangel, 585 F.2d 344, 346 (8th Cir. 1978) (bank copy, merchant copy, and customer copy of Master Charge credit card forms are all originals).

[24] Fed. R. Evid. 1001 advisory committee's note.

[25] *Id.*

[26] United States v. Rangel, 585 F.2d 344, 346 (8th Cir. 1978) ("The government had to prove the contents of the photocopy of the altered receipt since the photocopy, not the altered receipt, was identified as the document Rangel had submitted to support his demand for payment. Thus the photocopies were admitted as originals."). *See also* Cartier v. Jackson, 59 F.3d 1046, 1049 (10th Cir. 1995) ("Ms. Cartier was not trying to prove the contents of the rented master tape. She was trying to show Mr. [Michael] Jackson had access to her version of 'Dangerous' through her demo tapes. Therefore, she had to show what was on the demo tapes. In trying to prove the contents of these cassettes, the demo tapes themselves are the originals or best evidence.").

[27] Fed. R. Evid. 1001 advisory committee's note ("practicality and usage confer the status of original upon any computer printout") (citing Transport Indem. Co. v. Seib, 132 N.W.2d 871 (Neb. 1965)).

[28] *See supra* § 30.03[C] (the original writing rule rarely applies to photographs).

[29] Fed. R. Evid. 1001 advisory committee's note.

§ 30.05   Exception — Duplicates: FRE 1003 ("Xerox" Rule)

Rule 1003, sometimes known as the "Xerox" rule, says duplicates are generally admissible. This represents a major change from the common law. Under the common law, the offeror had the burden of establishing an adequate excuse for failing to produce the original before secondary evidence was admissible. Rule 1003 reverses this burden with respect to duplicates as defined in Rule 1001(4).

In sum, duplicates are generally as admissible as originals. If the principal concern of the best evidence rule is the reliability of secondary evidence, the accuracy of modern technology should be taken into account. [30] Thus, duplicates are admissible unless (1) a genuine question of the authenticity of the original is raised, or (2) fairness requires production of the original.

[A]   "Duplicates" Defined

Not all copies qualify as "duplicates." Rule 1001(4) defines a duplicate as a counterpart produced by a process "which accurately reproduce[s] the original." Thus, handwritten copies are not duplicates. [31] Recall, however, if a counterpart, no matter how produced, is intended by the person executing or issuing it to have the same effect as the original, the counterpart is an original under Rule 1001(3). A counterpart, therefore, may be either an original or a duplicate, depending on the intent of the person executing or issuing it. [32]

[B]   Exceptions to Duplicate Rule

Authenticity question. Duplicates are not admissible if there is a genuine question about the authenticity of the original — for example, when it is "barely legible" [33] or otherwise suspect. [34]

---

[30] *See* United States v. Haddock, 956 F.2d 1534, 1545 (10th Cir. 1992) ("Rule 1003 is part of a broadened set of evidentiary rules that reflect the fact that, due to modern and accurate reproduction techniques, duplicates and originals should normally be treated interchangeably."); Fed. R. Evid. 1003 advisory committee's note ("When the only concern is with getting the words or other contents before the court with accuracy and precision, then a counterpart serves equally as well as the original, if the counterpart is the product of a method which insures accuracy and genuineness. By definition in Rule 1001(4), *supra*, a 'duplicate' possesses this character.").

[31] Fed. R. Evid. 1001 advisory committee's note ("Copies subsequently produced manually, whether handwritten or typed, are not within the definition. It should be noted that what is an original for some purposes may be a duplicate for others. Thus a bank's microfilm record of checks cleared is the original as a record. However, a print offered as a copy of a check whose contents are in controversy is a duplicate.").

[32] *See supra* § 30.04[B] (originals defined).

[33] Lozano v. Ashcroft, 258 F.3d 1160, 1166 (10th Cir. 2001). The House Judiciary Committee approved the federal rule "with the expectation that the courts would be liberal in deciding that a 'genuine question is raised as to the authenticity of the original.'" H.R. Rep. No. 650, 93d Cong., 1st Sess. (1973), reprinted in 1974 U.S.C.C.A.N. 7075, 7090.

Unfairness. Fairness is jeopardized "when only a part of the original is reproduced and the remainder is needed for cross-examination or may disclose matters qualifying the part offered or otherwise useful to the opposing party."[35] The federal note cites two cases. In one, the Fourth Circuit held it error to admit an incomplete photocopy of the check in a prosecution for theft of a Social Security check.[36] In the other, the Second Circuit ruled it proper to exclude photocopies of portions of business records in a civil fraud case when the originals were in Japan and the defendant had no opportunity to determine whether omitted portions might be relevant.[37] Exclusion of a photocopy is also proper where "the most critical part of the original . . . is not completely reproduced in the 'duplicate.'"[38]

Procedural issues. A party seeking to exclude a "duplicate" under Rule 1003 has the burden of demonstrating that the duplicate should not be admitted. This issue is entrusted to the discretion of the judge.[39]

§ 30.06 Exception — Original Lost or Destroyed: FRE 1004(1)

Secondary evidence is admissible if the originals are lost or destroyed, provided that the offering party has acted in good faith.[40] The trial court determines whether the proponent has established loss or destruction and the absence of bad faith under Rule 104(a).[41] The test is subjective — mere negligence is not bad faith.[42] It is not uncommon for businesses to have

---

[34] *See Haddock*, 956 F.2d at 1545–46 (The evidence indicated that "only Haddock could recall ever seeing either the original or a copy of these documents. Except for Haddock, no one including in some cases persons who allegedly typed the document and persons to whom the original allegedly was sent — was familiar with the contents of the photocopies. In addition, witnesses testified that several of the documents bore markings and included statements that did not comport with similar documents prepared in the ordinary course of business at the Bank of White City and at the Bank of Herington.").

[35] Fed. R. Evid. 1003 advisory committee's note.

[36] United States v. Alexander, 326 F.2d 736 (4th Cir. 1964).

[37] Toho Bussan Kaisha, Ltd. v. Am. President Lines, Ltd., 265 F.2d 418 (2d Cir. 1959).

[38] Amoco Prod. Co. v. United States, 619 F.2d 1383, 1391 (10th Cir. 1980).

[39] Fed. R. Evid. 104(a).

[40] *See Cartier*, 59 F.3d at 1049 ("The 'original' for which Ms. Cartier is trying to demonstrate the contents was the demo tape. Therefore, according to Rule 1004(1), she must show that the demo tapes, and not the rented master tape, had been lost or destroyed."). *See also* H. R. Rep. No. 650, 93d Cong., 1st Sess. (1973) ("loss or destruction of an original by another person at the instigation of the proponent should be considered as tantamount to loss or destruction in bad faith by the proponent himself."), reprinted in 1974 U.S.C.C.A.N. 7075, 7090

[41] *See* Fed. R. Evid. 1008 advisory committee's note ("[T]he question whether the loss of the originals has been established . . . is for the judge."); Seiler v. Lucasfilm, Ltd., 808 F.2d 1316, 1319 (9th Cir. 1986).

[42] *E.g.,* Estate of Gryder v. Comm'r., 705 F.2d 336, 338 (8th Cir. 1983) ("[T]he Commissioner was unable to produce the originals of many corporate records, including journals and check-stub books. These records were destroyed by employees of the Internal Revenue Service after Cordial's criminal trial. The Tax Court's finding that these documents were destroyed negligently but not in bad faith is not clearly erroneous; thus, the Commissioner could seek to prove their contents by secondary evidence.").

document destruction policies in order to avoid being swamped with paper.[43] If secondary evidence is admitted, an adverse inference instruction may be appropriate in some cases.[44]

§ 30.07   Exception — Original Not Obtainable: FRE 1004(2)

If an original cannot be obtained by any available judicial process or procedure, secondary evidence is admissible.[45] The territorial limits of a subpoena duces tecum in civil cases is 100 miles, while it is nationwide in criminal cases.[46]

§ 30.08   Exception — Original in Opponent's Possession: FRE 1004(3)

Secondary evidence is admissible if the opposing party fails to produce the original at trial, despite having been put on notice, while the original was under his control, that it would be subject to proof at trial.[47] Notice may be by the pleadings or otherwise. A different provision, Rule 1007, governs admissions by an opposing party.

Discovery. Rule 1004(3) is not a discovery rule.[48] If a party in a civil case wants the original produced, it should be sought through discovery.[49]

---

[43] *See* United States v. Workinger, 90 F.3d 1409, 1415 (9th Cir. 1996) (The "tape was not available because it had been erased by its owner, Mr. Johnson, prior to the trial. That had been done in the ordinary course of his business and not at the behest of the government.").

[44] *See* Vodusek v. Bayliner Marine Corp., 71 F.3d 148, 156 (4th Cir. 1995) ("Even if a court determines not to exclude secondary evidence, it may still permit the jury to draw unfavorable inferences against the party responsible for the loss or destruction of the original evidence. An adverse inference about a party's consciousness of the weakness of his case, however, cannot be drawn merely from his negligent loss or destruction of evidence; the inference requires a showing that the party knew the evidence was relevant to some issue at trial and that his willful conduct resulted in its loss or destruction."). *See supra* § 9.07 (adverse inferences).

[45] *See* Fed. R. Evid. 1004 advisory committee's note ("When the original is in the possession of a third person, inability to procure it from him by resort to process or other judicial procedure is a sufficient explanation of nonproduction. Judicial procedure includes subpoena duces tecum as an incident to the taking of a deposition in another jurisdiction. No further showing is required.").

[46] Fed. R. Civ. P. 45(b)(2); Fed. R. Crim. P. 17(e). *See also* Fed. R. Civ. P. 28(a) and 45 (deposition duces tecum nationwide).

[47] Fed. R. Evid. 1004 advisory committee's note ("A party who has an original in his control has no need for the protection of the rule if put on notice that proof of contents will be made. He can ward off secondary evidence by offering the original.").

[48] *Id.* ("The notice procedure here provided is not to be confused with orders to produce or other discovery procedures, as the purpose of the procedure under this rule is to afford the opposite party an opportunity to produce the original, not to compel him to do so.").

[49] Fed. R. Civ. P. 34 (production of documents). Discovery in criminal cases is often limited to documents that will be admitted at trial, or in the case of defense discovery, documents that are material. Fed. R. Crim. P. 16.

§ 30.09   Exception — Collateral Matters: FRE 1004(4)

If the document is not important, the rule doesn't apply. Documents are often referred to during trials, and it would be disruptive and time-consuming to apply the best evidence rule every time a witness alludes to a writing.[50] Collateral matters are "not closely related to a controlling issue."[51] While collateral matters are "difficult to define with precision, . . . situations arise in which no good purpose is served by production of the original. Examples are the newspaper in an action for the price of publishing defendant's advertisement"[52] and "the streetcar transfer of plaintiff claiming status as a passenger."[53]

§ 30.10   Exception — Public Records: FRE 1005

Once again, public records get favorable treatment.[54] Rule 1005 provides for the admissibility of copies of official records and recorded documents, thus recognizing an automatic dispensation from the requirements of the original writing rule. "Public records call for somewhat different treatment. Removing them from their usual place of keeping would be attended by serious inconvenience to the public and to the custodian."[55] The trade-off is that only a specific class of secondary evidence is admissible — certified copies.[56] Note that "the mere fact that a document is kept in a working file of a governmental agency does not automatically qualify it as a public record."[57]

---

[50] *See* Jackson v. Crews, 873 F.2d 1105, 110 (8th Cir. 1989) ("Even if Jackson had been trying to prove the content of the flyer, he would have been exempted from producing the flyer because the issue was collateral to the principal issue in the trial.").

[51] *See* United States v. Duffy, 454 F.2d 809, 812 (5th Cir. 1972) ("[T]he terms of the 'writing' [laundry mark on shirt] were by no means central or critical to the case against Duffy. The crime charged was not possession of a certain article, where the failure to produce the article might prejudice the defense. The shirt was collateral evidence of the crime. Furthermore, it was only one piece of evidence in a substantial case against Duffy.").

[52] Fed. R. Evid. 1004 advisory committee's note (citing Foster-Holcomb Inv. Co. v. Little Rock Publ'g Co., 236 S.W. 597 (Ark. 1922)).

[53] *Id.* (citing Chicago City Ry. Co. v. Carroll, 68 N.E. 1087 (Ill. 1903)).

[54] Rule 1005 deals only with the best evidence rule. Hearsay and authentication rules may also need to be satisfied for admissibility. Many public records are self-authenticating, however. Rule 902. In addition, Rules 803(8) to (10) recognize hearsay exceptions for public records.

[55] Fed. R. Evid. 1005 advisory committee's note (citing McCormick, Evidence § 204; 4 Wigmore, Evidence §§ 1215–28).

[56] Fed. R. Evid. 1005 advisory committee's note ("This blanket dispensation from producing or accounting for the original would open the door to the introduction of every kind of secondary evidence of contents of public records were it not for the preference given certified or compared copies. Recognition of degrees of secondary evidence in this situation is an appropriate quid pro quo for not applying the requirement of producing the original.").

[57] Amoco Prod. Co. v. United States, 619 F.2d 1383, 1390 n. 7 (10th Cir. 1980) ("[I]t is the actual record maintained by the public office which is the object of Rule 1005, not the original deed from which the record is made. If the original deed is returned to the parties after it is recorded, it is not a public record as contemplated by Rule 1005.").

§ 30.11   Exception — Summaries: FRE 1006

Sometimes there are simply too many records. Rule 1006 permits them to "be presented in the form of a chart, summary, or calculation."[58] The summary itself may be presented as a tangible exhibit or through the testimony of a witness. The underlying materials that are summarized, however, must be a writing, recording, or photograph. The rule does not encompass a summary of verbal statements.[59] The summary must also be distinguished from the originals. For example, printouts of a business ledger kept on computer are the actual records, not summaries; Rule 803(6), the hearsay exception for business records, controls, not Rule 1006.[60]

"Voluminous" requirement. While the writings that are summarized must be voluminous, convenicnce (not necessity) is the standard in this context.[61]

Right of inspection. Rule 1006 explicitly provides that the underlying materials must be made available for inspection and copying by the other parties.[62] Inspection is only possible with advance notice.[63] Consequently, discovery procedures and pretrial hearings are important.

Production of originals. Rule 1006 explicitly authorizes the trial judge to order in-court production of the originals or duplicates. This decision is left to the judge's discretion.[64]

Admissibility of underlying documents. Although not explicitly stated in the rule, a summary is not admissible if the originals upon which it is based are inadmissible.[65] In other words, Rule 1006 is not an exception to the hearsay rule.

---

[58] Fed. R. Evid. 1006 advisory committee's note (The "admission of summaries of voluminous books, records, or documents offers the only practicable means of making their contents available to judge and jury. The rule recognizes this practice, with appropriate safeguards.").

[59] *See* United States v. Goss, 650 F.2d 1336, 1344 n. 5 (5th Cir. 1981) ("[T]here is no provision for the admission of summaries of the testimony of out-of-court witnesses.").

[60] *See* United States v. Catabran, 836 F.2d 453, 457 (9th Cir. 1988); United States v. Draiman, 784 F.2d 248, 256 n. 6 (7th Cir. 1986) (properly kept business records under Rule 803(6) are not subject to Rule 1006 even if they are a summary of other records); United States v. Sanders, 749 F.2d 195, 199 (5th Cir. 1984) (data stored on a computer, as opposed to a selective compilation of random pieces of data, are not summaries).

[61] *See* United States v. Briscoe, 896 F.2d 1476, 495 (7th Cir. 1990); United States v. Possick, 849 F.2d 332, 339 (8th Cir. 1988) ("Rule 1006 does not require that it be literally impossible to examine all the underlying records, but only that in-court examination would be an inconvenience.").

[62] *See* Coates v. Johnson & Johnson, 756 F.2d 524, 549-50 (7th Cir. 1985) (right of inspection limited to underlying materials and not the summary itself).

[63] *See* Air Safety, Inc. v. Roman Catholic Archbishop of Boston, 94 F.3d 1, 7 (1st Cir. 1996) ("Common sense dictates that this guaranteed access, designed to give the opponent the ability to check the summary's accuracy and prepare for cross-examination, must include unequivocal notice of the other party's intent to invoke Rule 1006. It seemingly was the lack of such notice that gave rise to the misunderstanding and confusion here.") (citations omitted); Fla. Stat. Evid. Code § 90.956 (requiring pretrial notice).

[64] *See* United States v. Bakker, 925 F.2d 728, 736 (4th Cir. 1991); United States v. Strissel, 920 F.2d 1162, 1163 (4th Cir. 1990).

[65] *See* United States v. Pelullo, 964 F.2d 193, 204 (3d Cir. 1992); State Office Sys., Inc. v. Olivetti Corp. of Am., 762 F.2d 843, 845 (10th Cir. 1985); Paddack v. Dave Christensen, Inc., 745 F.2d 1254, 1259 (9th Cir. 1984).

Accuracy requirement. Although not explicitly stated, a summary must "fairly represent and be taken from" the originals.[66] In one case, a summary of medical articles was ruled inadmissible because the expert who prepared the summary had not read all the articles.[67] In another case, summaries of figures were excluded because "there was virtually no documentation."[68]

Experts. The use of summaries often requires expert testimony, in which case the expert must be qualified.[69] Expert testimony, however, is not always required.[70]

Summaries as pedagogic devices. The use of summaries as evidence must be distinguished from the use of summaries and charts as pedagogical devices. A summary admitted under Rule 1006 is itself *evidence* and should go to the jury room along with other exhibits.[71] Charts and other visual aids that merely summarize or organize testimony or documents that have already been admitted in evidence are not themselves evidence and should not be sent to the jury room.[72]

§ 30.12   Exception — Opponent Admission: FRE 1007

Where the party against whom the writing is offered admits the contents, the original need not be produced. Rule 1007 is limited to written or transcribed admissions; oral admissions do not qualify.[73] Oral admissions, however, may be admissible pursuant to another exception to the original document rule.[74]

---

[66] Gomez v. Great Lakes Steel Div., Nat'l Steel Corp., 803 F.2d 250, 257 (6th Cir. 1986). *Accord* United States v. Drougas, 748 F.2d 8, 25 (1st Cir. 1984) ("Charts and summaries are . . . inadmissible if they contain information not present in the original or duplicate materials on which they are based."), *modified sub nom.* United States v. Piper, 35 F.3d 611 (1st Cir. 1994).

[67] Needham v. White Labs, Inc., 639 F.2d 394, 403 (7th Cir. 1981).

[68] United States v. Sorrentino, 726 F.2d 876, 884 (1st Cir. 1984).

[69] *See* United States v. Kaatz, 705 F.2d 1237, 1245 (10th Cir. 1983). Fed. R. Evid. 702 governs the qualifications of experts.

[70] *See* United States v. Jennings, 724 F.2d 436, 443 (5th Cir. 1984) ("[W]hen a chart does not contain complicated calculations requiring the need of an expert for accuracy, no special expertise is required in presenting the chart.").

[71] *See supra* § 3.06[A] (exhibits in jury room).

[72] *See* United States v. Possick, 849 F.2d 332, 339 (8th Cir. 1988); Pierce v. Ramsey Winch Co., 753 F.2d 416, 431 (5th Cir. 1985). *See supra* § 26.03 (diagrams, maps & models).

[73] Fed. R. Evid. 1007 advisory committee's note ("While the parent case, Slatterie v. Pooley, 6 M. & W. 664, 151 Eng. Rep. 579 (Exch.1840), allows proof of contents by evidence of an oral admission by the party against whom offered, without accounting for nonproduction of the original, the risk of inaccuracy is substantial and the decision is at odds with the purpose of the rule giving preference to the original.").

[74] *Id.* (The rule "does not call for excluding evidence of an oral admission when nonproduction of the original has been accounted for and secondary evidence generally has become admissible.").

§ 30.13 Function of Judge & Jury: FRE 1008

Under most circumstances, the trial court decides preliminary questions concerning the applicability of the original writing rule pursuant to Rule 104(a). The judge decides whether a writing is an original or a duplicate. Similarly, the judge decides if a party is attempting to prove the contents of a writing or recording. The court also decides the applicability of the exceptions.[75] The offering party has the burden of establishing admissibility by a preponderance of evidence.[76]

However, there are three circumstances where the jury should play an expanded role:[77] (1) when there is a question whether a writing ever existed; (2) when another writing is claimed to be the original; and (3) when the issue is whether other evidence correctly reflects the contents of the original. This represents a specialized application of Rule 104(b) on conditional relevancy.[78] The court determines only whether evidence sufficient to support a finding by a reasonable jury has been admitted. The third circumstance, allocating to the jury the responsibility of determining whether secondary evidence correctly reflects the contents of the original, does not apply until the court has excused nonproduction of the original.[79]

§ 30.14 Degrees of Secondary Evidence

Some of the exceptions to the original writing rule specify what type of secondary evidence is admissible. Under Rule 1003, "duplicates" have a precise meaning.[80] Under Rule 1005, only *certified copies* of public records are admissible. By its own terms, Rule 1006 is limited to summaries.

---

[75] *See* Fed. R. Evid. 1008 advisory committee's note ("Most preliminary questions of fact in connection with applying the rule preferring the original as evidence of contents are for the judge, under the general principles announced in Rule 104, supra. Thus, the question whether the loss of the originals has been established, or of the fulfillment of other conditions specified in Rule 1004, supra, is for the judge.").

[76] *See supra* § 7.02[B].

[77] Fed. R. Evid. 1008 advisory committee's note ("[Q]uestions may arise which go beyond the mere administration of the rule preferring the original and into the merits of the controversy. For example, plaintiff offers secondary evidence of the contents of an alleged contract, after first introducing evidence of loss of the original, and defendant counters with evidence that no such contract was ever executed. If the judge decides that the contract was never executed and excludes the secondary evidence, the case is at an end without ever going to the jury on a central issue. The latter portion of the instant rule is designed to insure treatment of these situations as raising jury questions. The decision is not one for uncontrolled discretion of the jury but is subject to the control exercised generally by the judge over jury determinations. See Rule 104(b), supra.")(citations omitted). *See generally* Morgan, *The Law of Evidence, 1941–45*, 59 Harv. L. Rev. 481, 490–91 (1946).

[78] *See supra* § 7.03 (conditional relevancy).

[79] *See* Seiler v. Lucasfilm, Ltd., 808 F.2d 1316, 1321 (9th Cir. 1986) ("Rule 1008 states, in essence, that when the admissibility of evidence other than the original depends upon the fulfillment of a condition of fact, the trial judge generally makes the determination of that condition of fact.").

[80] Fed. R. Evid. 1001(4) (defining duplicates).

Other exceptions differ. If any of the conditions specified in Rule 1004 are satisfied, the rule does not prescribe the type of secondary evidence that must be produced.[81] For example, if an original is lost, secondary evidence in the form of a copy or in the form of the testimony of a witness is permitted. The copy is not preferred. The notion is that attorneys, for the most part, will proffer the most persuasive proof and thus there is no need for further regulation.[82]

§ 30.15   Key Points

The term "best evidence rule" is misleading. The rule applies *only* to writings, recordings, and photographs (and only when proving their *contents*). There is no general rule requiring the "best evidence." A party generally is not required to introduce real evidence in order to prove its case.

Rationale. The nature of writings gives rise to their being singled out for special treatment. The copying of a writing is especially susceptible to the introduction of inaccuracies, and even a minor mistake may have significant legal consequences — for example, in wills, deeds, and contracts.

"Proving contents." The rule applies *only* when a party attempts to prove the contents of a writing or recording. Typically, this occurs when (1) the event to be proved is a written transaction or (2) a party chooses a written method of proof.

Written events; independent events. Some events and transactions, such as those involving deeds, contracts, and judgments, are written transactions, and the rule requires production of the original writing when the contents are sought to be proved. In contrast, Rule 1002 does not apply when the event sought to be proved existed independently of a writing, even if that event has been recorded. For example, if an accused makes an oral confession which is recorded or subsequently reduced to writing, the rule does *not* apply. The prosecution is not attempting to prove the contents of the recording or writing but rather the independent event (oral confession) that happened to have been recorded. Other examples include proof of the existence of a marriage, the payment of a debt or a purchase, perjured testimony, conversations, as well as earnings in an account.

---

[81] *See* United States v. Billingsley, 160 F.3d 502, 505 n. 2 (8th Cir. 1998) ("Because the district court in this case could admit any form of secondary testimony once the tape was destroyed and because there is no evidence of bad faith, the agent's oral testimony was properly admitted.").

[82] Fed. R. Evid. 1004 advisory committee's note ("The rule recognizes no 'degrees' of secondary evidence. While strict logic might call for extending the principle of preference beyond simply preferring the original, the formulation of a hierarchy of preferences and a procedure for making it effective is believed to involve unwarranted complexities. Most, if not all, that would be accomplished by an extended scheme of preferences will, in any event, be achieved through the normal motivation of a party to present the most convincing evidence possible and the arguments and procedures available to his opponent if he does not.") (citing McCormick, Evidence § 207). *See also* United States v. Gerhart, 538 F.2d 807, 809 (8th Cir. 1976).

Written method of proof. If a party chooses to introduce a writing to prove a fact, the original must be produced. Thus, in the confession hypothetical cited above, if the prosecution chose to use the writing to prove the confession, it would have to offer the original writing.

"Xerox" rule. Rule 1003 says duplicates are generally admissible. This represents a major change from the common law. Duplicates are admissible unless (1) a genuine question about the authenticity of the original is raised, or (2) fairness requires production of the original.

Rule 1004 recognizes four exceptions: (1) original lost or destroyed, (2) original not obtainable, (3) original in opponent's possession, and (4) collateral matters. If one of these exceptions applies, there are no "degrees" of secondary evidence; thus, oral testimony concerning the contents of the original are admissible as well as a written copy.

Public records. Rule 1005 provides for the admissibility of copies of official records and recorded documents, thus recognizing an automatic dispensation from the requirements of the original writing rule.

Summaries. In lieu of voluminous writings, Rule 1006 permits the use of summaries "in the form of a chart, summary, or calculation." Although not explicitly stated in the rule, a summary is not admissible if the originals upon which it is based are inadmissible. The use of summaries as evidence must be distinguished from the use of summaries and charts as pedagogical devices. Rule 1006 does not govern the latter.

Chapter 31

HEARSAY RULE: FRE 801(a)-(c), 805, 806

§ 31.01 Overview of Article VIII

In the absence of an exception or exemption, Federal Rule 802 bars hearsay evidence. Rule 802 must be read in conjunction with Rule 801, which defines hearsay.

Exceptions. The exceptions to the hearsay rule are found in three rules.[1] Rule 803 specifies twenty-three exceptions that apply whether or not the declarant is available.[2] Rule 804 specifies five exceptions that apply *only* if the declarant is unavailable.[3] Rule 807 recognizes a residual or "catch all" exception, under which some hearsay statements may be admitted on an ad hoc basis.[4]

Exemptions. In addition to the exceptions, there were two categories of hearsay statements that the drafters wanted to admit into evidence.[5] However, for theoretical reasons, the drafters choose not to classify them as exceptions. Instead, these statements were simply defined out of the definition of hearsay in Rule 801(d). In order to distinguish these categories from the exceptions, they are often called "exemptions" or "exclusions." Note that the exemptions function like exceptions; statements falling within them are not barred by the hearsay prohibition.

The first category of exemptions involves prior statements of a witness. Rule 801(d)(1) provides that certain prior inconsistent statements, prior consistent statements, and statements of identification are not hearsay. This represents a change from the common law. The second category, Rule 801(d)(2), covers admissions of a party-opponent.[6] Under the common law, admissions were characterized as exceptions to the hearsay rule. The Federal Rules do not change this result; admissions are still admissible — albeit under a different theory.

Multiple hearsay. Rule 805 governs the admissibility of multiple hearsay — *i.e.,* hearsay within hearsay. If each part of a double hearsay statement falls within an exception, the statement is admissible.[7]

---

[1] Rule 802 states that an exception recognized by a procedural rule prescribed by the Supreme Court may also be the basis for admission — *e.g.,* Civil Rule 32 on depositions. In addition, as discussed in a later section, admissibility of hearsay statements may be required by the Due Process Clause. *See infra* § 31.08 (constitutional issues).

[2] *See infra* chapter 33.

[3] *See infra* chapter 34.

[4] *See infra* chapter 35.

[5] *See infra* chapter 32.

[6] There are five types of admissions: (1) individual admissions, (2) adoptive admissions, (3) authorized admissions, (4) agent admissions, and (5) coconspirator admissions.

[7] *See infra* § 31.10 (double hearsay).

Impeachment of hearsay declarants. Rule 806 regulates the calling of hearsay declarants as well as the impeachment and rehabilitation of declarants. In effect, a hearsay declarant is a witness and generally may be impeached in the same manner as trial witnesses.[8]

Admissibility. Evidence that falls within one of the exceptions or exemptions is not automatically admissible. The statement must also satisfy the requirements of other evidentiary rules. For example, evidence must be relevant, and must not be excludable for some other reason, such as being unfairly prejudicial (Rule 403), or failing to satisfy the requirements of authentication[9] or "best evidence" rules.[10]

§ 31.02 Rationale for Hearsay Rule

Cross-examination is the key to understanding the hearsay rule.[11] Suppose a witness testifies at trial as follows: "I saw the accused shoot the victim." The accuracy of this testimony depends upon the witness's perception,[12] memory,[13] and narration,[14] as well as the witness's sincerity.[15] These four factors may be explored and tested on cross-examination. In addition, the witness is under oath, and the jury has an opportunity to observe the demeanor of the witness while testifying.[16]

Now change the hypothetical. The trial witness testifies that another person (called a declarant) told the witness that he (the declarant) "saw the accused shoot the victim." There is no cross-examination of the *real* witness, the declarant, to test perception, memory, narration, and sincerity.[17] If this out-of-court statement is offered to prove that the accused shot

---

[8] *See infra* §§ 31.11 & .12.

[9] Fed. R. Evid. 901.

[10] Fed. R. Evid. 1002.

[11] *But see* Park, *A Subject Matter Approach to Hearsay Reform,* 86 Mich. L. Rev. 51, 77 (1987) (arguing that cross-examination by itself cannot justify the hearsay rule; other considerations such as surprise and the use of trained investigators to exact statements by trickery and offers of immunity also play a part). *See also* Swift, *Abolishing the Hearsay Rule,* 75 Cal. L. Rev. 495, 514 (1987); Swift, *A Foundation Fact Approach to Hearsay,* 75 Cal. L. Rev. 1339 (1987).

[12] What if the witness had only a split second opportunity to observe the shooting, was at a far distance, or was not wearing prescribed eyeglasses?

[13] Perhaps the shooting occurred five years before, or the witness was later present when other witnesses gave their accounts, thus introducing new information into the witness's "memory" of the shooting.

[14] Narration is the traditional term. Communicative ability is perhaps a better one. Was the witness able to convey what she intended to convey? For example, a witness testifying about the time of a robbery may use the term "two o'clock" meaning "a.m" but some jurors may interpret it to mean "p.m."

[15] In this context, sincerity refers to intentional lying.

[16] In the hearsay context, the oath and observation of demeanor are secondary safeguards to cross-examination. Even when they are present, a statement may still be hearsay. For example, an affidavit taken under oath is hearsay, as is testimony taken at a former trial. Moreover, statements recorded on videotape, which would provide some opportunity to observe demeanor, are nevertheless hearsay.

[17] *See* Williamson v. United States, 512 U.S. 594, 598 (1994) ("The hearsay rule, Fed. Rule

the victim (*i.e.,* offered for its truth), it is the credibility of the declarant, not the witness, that is critical to an assessment of the statement's reliability.[18] In sum, we have the "hearsay dangers" but *no* cross-examination.[19]

§ 31.03 Hearsay Definitions

[A] Declarant-focused Definition

Given the above analysis, we can define hearsay as an out-of-court statement whose probative value depends on the credibility of the declarant.[20] Such a "declarant-focused" definition highlights the underlying policy of the hearsay rule. There is, however, a competing definition.

[B] Assertion-focused Definition

A different definition defines hearsay as an out-of-court statement offered for the truth of its assertion. In most cases, the same result is reached under either definition. But not always. For example, what if the declarant says, "Did you bring my gun?" A question is not an assertion, so it cannot be offered for its truth. Correct? Not so fast. Isn't there an "implied assertion" (that the declarant owns a gun) in the question? A declarant-oriented definition would underscore this point and might lead a court to exclude the statement. An assertion-oriented definition might not.

Evid. 802, is premised on the theory that out-of-court statements are subject to particular hazards. The declarant might be lying; he might have misperceived the events which he relates; he might have faulty memory; his words might be misunderstood or taken out of context by the listener. And the ways in which these dangers are minimized for in-court statements — the oath, the witness' awareness of the gravity of the proceedings, the jury's ability to observe the witness' demeanor, and, most importantly, the right of the opponent to cross-examine — are generally absent for things said out of court."); California v. Green, 399 U.S. 149, 154 (1970) (noting "the usual reasons that have led to the exclusion of hearsay statements: the statement may not have been made under oath; the declarant may not have been subjected to cross-examination when he made the statement; and the jury cannot observe the declarant's demeanor at the time he made the statement").

[18] This is not to say that the credibility of the *witness* will never be an issue —*i.e.,* whether the witness actually heard the declarant make the statement. But the witness is on the stand and can be cross-examined on this point.

[19] Perception, memory, narration, and sincerity are called the "hearsay" dangers. Morgan, *Hearsay Dangers and the Application of the Hearsay Concept,* 62 Harv. L. Rev. 177 (1948). Note that these are the same "testimonial" dangers associated with any witness's live testimony. They are called "hearsay" dangers because, unlike a testifying witness, they cannot be probed through cross-examination.

[20] *See* Park, *McCormick on Evidence and the Concept of Hearsay: A Critical Analysis Followed by Suggestions to Law Teachers,* 65 Minn. L. Rev. 423, 424 (1981) ("Definitions of hearsay are commonly either assertion-oriented or declarant-oriented. An assertion-oriented definition focuses on whether an out-of-court assertion will be used to prove the truth of what it asserts, while a declarant-oriented definition focuses on whether the use of the utterance will require reliance on the credibility of the out-of-court declarant.").

It is this difference in definition that causes many of the more difficult hearsay problems.[21] The "assertion-oriented" definition is used in practice and is embodied in the Federal Rules — at least in the view of most commentators. From the beginning, it is worth noting that a "perfect hearsay definition is unattainable"[22] and a prominent scholar once wrote an article entitled "The Borderland of Hearsay."[23] On the other hand, most hearsay issues are readily grasped — at least by the second time through the material.

§ 31.04 "Declarant" Defined: FRE 801(b)

Rule 801(b) defines "declarant" as a "person who makes a statement." This definition makes clear that the hearsay rule does not apply to devices, such as radar, or to tracking dogs.[24] The principal objection to hearsay is the lack of cross-examination. It makes no sense to demand cross-examination of a machine or a dog. This is not to say, however, that this type of evidence does not raise reliability concerns. Nevertheless, those concerns are better addressed as problems of scientific proof.[25]

§ 31.05 "Out-of-Court" (extrajudicial) Requirement

Rule 801(c) defines hearsay as a "statement, *other than one made by the declarant while testifying at the trial or hearing.*" Hence, an out-of-court (extrajudicial) statement does not lose its hearsay character simply because the declarant later becomes a witness at trial and testifies about the statement. For example, if an eyewitness to an accident makes a statement at the time of the accident and later testifies at trial, the prior statement is hearsay if offered for its truth; to be admissible, it must fall within an exception or exemption. The witness, of course, may testify about what she saw; only the witness's prior statement is hearsay.

This result has been questioned since the witness is on the stand, under oath, is now subject to cross-examination, and the jury can observe the witness's demeanor. The only problem is that the statement was not subject to cross-examination at the time it was made. In the case of prior inconsistent statements, however, practitioners have argued that *delayed* cross-examination is not effective and, therefore, such statements should be classified as hearsay, which is the traditional approach.[26]

---

[21] For a helpful discussion, see Tribe, *Triangulating Hearsay,* 87 Harv. L. Rev. 957 (1974).

[22] Park, *"I Didn't Tell Them Anything About You": Implied Assertions as Hearsay Under the Federal Rules of Evidence*, 74 Minn. L. Rev. 783, 784 (1990).

[23] McCormick, *The Borderland of Hearsay*, 39 Yale L.J. 489 (1930).

[24] Computer-generated records may also fall into this category if they do not contain an assertion of a person — *e.g.*, telephone logs.

[25] *See supra* § 24.04 (admissibility of scientific evidence).

[26] *See* Mueller, *Post-Modern Hearsay Reform: The Importance of Complexity*, 76 Minn. L. Rev. 367, 386–87 (1992) ("Practitioners say cross-examination can expose falsehood and error in live testimony, but not in prior statements. The witness may be friendly or neutral, and

§ 31.06   Statements Offered for Their Truth

Rule 801(c) defines hearsay as a statement offered in evidence to prove the truth of the matter asserted. If the relevance of an out-of-court statement is that the statement was made, rather than the truth of the assertion contained therein, the statement is not hearsay. For example, suppose my son telephones me from Chicago and says, "I am broke, send more money." If offered to show that he was broke, the statement is hearsay — *i.e.*, "I am broke" offered to prove he's broke. In contrast, if the same statement is offered to prove that the telephone system was operating on that day, it is not hearsay. Or, to prove he was alive that day, the statement is not hearsay. Or, to prove he had the ability to speak English — not hearsay. In sum, if the statement is offered for *any* purpose other than for its truth, it is not hearsay. This means that the hearsay character of a statement cannot be determined until we know what the statement is being offered to prove — *i.e.*, its relevancy.[27] In other words, Rule 801 must be read along with Rule 401 (defining relevancy).

Rule 403. In addition to Rule 401, Rule 403 plays an important role here. If the proponent of the evidence comes forward with a *nonhearsay (i.e.,* not for its truth) purpose, the hearsay rule does not bar admissibility.[28] A limiting instruction, of course, must be given on request.[29] This does not, however, guarantee admissibility. It may be that the probative value of the statement for the nonhearsay purpose is substantially outweighed (Rule 403) by the risk of unfair prejudice — *i.e.,* that the jury will make the prohibited hearsay inference despite the limiting instruction. Hence, the statement may be excluded pursuant to Rule 403.

Examples. Courts and commentators have recognized a number of recurring situations where statements are *not* offered for their truth content. These are discussed below. Note, however, this is not an exhaustive list.

[A]   To Show Effect on Listener

In many cases a person's state of mind — *e.g.,* knowledge, belief, good faith, reasonableness — is an issue.[30] A statement offered to show its effect on the state of mind of the person who heard it is *not* hearsay.

---

lawyer cannot come at him full bore as an enemy in an attempt to burst the balloon of credibility, but must find a way to deflate the prior statement while leaving the live testimony intact, floating above the fray.").

[27] As with any item of evidence, it is the offering party who decides the purpose of the evidence.

[28] Knowing of this rule, lawyers often respond to a hearsay objection by claiming a nonhearsay purpose — "Your Honor, we are not offering the statement for the truth of the assertion." This response obviates the hearsay objection — *provided the nonhearsay purpose is a relevant issue in the case*. Often it is not.

[29] Fed. R. Evid. 105.

[30] *See* 6 Wigmore, Evidence § 1789 (Chadbourn rev. 1976) ("[T]he hearsay rule interposes no obstacle to the use of letters, notices, oral information, reputation, or any other form of verbal utterances by one person, as circumstantial evidence that another person had

To prove reasonableness. If an accused claims self-defense, her reasonable fear of the victim becomes an issue. Accordingly, statements made to her regarding the victim's dangerous or violent character are relevant to show her subjective state of mind (fear) as well as the reasonableness of this fear. For example, suppose a friend told her that the victim had recently stabbed three people. Here, the statement is not offered to show that the victim actually stabbed three people but rather to show that such information was communicated to the defendant and thus reasonably induced fear.[31] The statement is not hearsay.

To prove notice. Statements offered to show that a person received notice of a fact, condition, or event are not offered for their truth. For example, in *Koury v. Follo*,[32] a patient sued a pediatrician for prescribing an excessive amount of a drug. The label on the bottle of the drug, which stated, "Not for Pediatric Use," was admitted for a nonhearsay purpose — notice.[33] Similarly, in *Smedra v. Stanek*,[34] the court upheld the admissibility of the following statement on the same grounds: "Dr. Stanek had been told by someone in the operating room that the sponge count did not come out right."[35] Other common examples: A mechanic tells a driver that her brakes are worn; if the statement if offered to show only that the driver had notice of this condition (not that the brakes were worn), it is not hearsay. An owner of a fleet of trucks is told that one of his drivers is a very careless driver; if offered to show notice (not that driver is careless), the statement is not hearsay.

To prove good or bad faith. In an income tax evasion case, the defendant offered love letters of the deceased to establish her good faith belief that the things he gave her were gifts, rather than income. The Seventh Circuit ruled the letters were not hearsay:

> These letters were hearsay if offered for the truth of the matters asserted — that Kritzik did in fact love Harris, enjoyed giving her things, wanted to take care of her financial security, and gave her

---

knowledge or belief as to the violent character or intentions of the deceased in a homicide case, the incompetence of an employee, the vicious nature of an animal, the dangerous condition of a place or a machine, the insolvency or lunacy of a vendor, the character of stolen goods bought, the falsity of representations made, the guilt of an arrested person or the dangerous intentions of a mob or riotous assemblage.").

[31] The statement would be relevant for this purpose even if it was untrue.

[32] 158 S.E.2d 548 (N.C. 1968).

[33] *Id.* at 556–57 ("The Hearsay Rule does not apply where the purpose of offering the extrajudicial statement is not to prove the truth of the statement, but merely to prove the fact that it was made and that the circumstances under which it was made were such as should reasonably have made it known to the litigant. . . . [T]he label on the bottle was properly admitted in evidence. It is not proof that [the drug] was unsafe for use upon a child. It is evidence of a warning which the physician disregards at his peril, and his disregard of it is relevant upon the issue of his use of reasonable care, where other evidence shows the drug is, in fact, dangerous to a child."). Other evidence that the drug was not suitable for children would have to be admitted.

[34] 187 F.2d 892 (10th Cir. 1951).

[35] *Id.* at 893.

the jewelry at issue as a gift. But the letters were not hearsay for the purpose of showing what Harris believed, because her belief does not depend on the actual truth of the matters asserted in the letters. Even if Kritzik were lying, the letters could have caused Harris to believe in good faith that the things he gave her were intended as gifts. [36]

To explain behavior. Sometimes a statement is offered to explain someone's conduct in response to the statement and not for its truth content — for example, to explain why a search warrant was executed or other police conduct. [37] Unless there is some need to explain such behavior, however, such evidence is subject to exclusion under Rule 403. [38]

[B] Verbal Acts

Statements that constitute verbal acts or operative acts are not hearsay because they are not offered for the truth. In other words, the uttering of certain words has independent legal significance under the substantive law — *e.g.,* words of a contract, slander, threats, and the like. Thus, we only care that these words were *said*, not that they are *true*.

Some of these instances are easily understood. Suppose Schmedlap tells a third party that "Botz is a liar." If Botz sues for defamation, he will need to introduce the defamatory statement uttered by Schmedlap — *i.e.,* the

---

[36] United States v. Harris, 942 F.2d 1125, 1130 (7th Cir. 1991). *See also* United States v. Castro, 887 F.2d 988, 1000 (9th Cir. 1989) ("The [credit] reports were introduced to show what information was available to Castro at the time he approved the loans, and to illustrate his reckless disregard for the Bank's interests by failing to act in response to the information disclosed by the reports. The credit reports were not introduced for the truth of their contents. They were not hearsay.").

[37] *E.g.,* United States v. Aguwa, 123 F.3d 418, 421 (6th Cir. 1997) ("In an effort simply to account for the events leading up to their chance encounter with the defendant, DEA agents testifying at trial recounted several statements made by the informant. Specifically, they testified that the informant told them that the original target of the investigation was not in the restaurant, that she recognized Tiger who was across the street standing by a set of pay phones, and that Tiger was making phone calls to individuals who might supply the heroin. . . . The statements were not offered 'for the truth of the matter asserted,' *see* Fed.R.Evid.* 801(c), but only to provide background information and to explain how and why the agents even came to be involved with this particular defendant."); United States v. Levy, 904 F.2d 1026, 1030 (6th Cir. 1990) (police officer testified that, as a result of a tip, he was looking for a new yellow Cadillac on a certain street; court held testimony was not hearsay because it "was not offered to prove the truth of the informant's remarks, and none of the officers testified about the contents and details of the tip").

[38] *See* United States v. Cass, 127 F.3d 1218, 1223 (10th Cir. 1997) ("Courts and commentators have recognized that out-of-court statements should not be admitted to explain why a law enforcement agency began an investigation if the statements present too great a danger of prejudice."); Garrett v. United States, 78 F.3d 1296, 1302 (8th Cir. 1996) ("fairness demands that the government find a way to get the background into evidence without the hearsay"); United States v. Hernandez, 750 F.2d 1256 (5th Cir. 1985) (referral by U.S. Customs of defendant as a drug smuggler inadmissible to explain motivation behind DEA investigation); United States v. Escobar, 674 F.2d 469 (5th Cir. 1982) (error to allow officer to testify that he ran the defendant's name through a computer and the resulting printout read "suspected" narcotics smuggler).

verbal act. Botz is obviously not offering the statement for its truth content — that he is in fact a liar. Instead, he wants the jury to believe the opposite.

Other examples are not as easy to understand when first encountered. In a contract case, the statement "I accept your offer" is a verbal act under the objective theory of contract law. We care only that it was said, not that it was true. But isn't it also offered for its truth?[39] Think of it this way. In criminal law, culpability requires an act (actus reus), but some words may satisfy the act requirement. There are verbal crimes —*e.g.*, perjury, solicitation, fraud, gambling,[40] or threatening another person.[41] Statements constituting these crimes have independent legal significance as the actus reus; they are crimes if accompanied by the requisite mental state. The same is true of the statement "I accept your offer." It has independent legal significance under contract law.[42]

[C] Verbal Parts of Acts

Verbal parts of acts are closely related to verbal acts. Indeed, they may be understood as a subcategory rather than a separate category. Such statements are offered in evidence only to show that the statements were made and to explain an otherwise ambiguous act. For example, words of donative intent accompanying the transfer of diamonds[43] or statements made in

---

[39] *See* Mueller, *supra* note 26, at 415 ("Words have both performative and assertive aspects, as all recognize in the example of 'I'm alive' offered to prove that the declarant was alive. It follows that sometimes words are both hearsay and nonhearsay when offered for a single purpose."); Park, *The Definition of Hearsay: To Each Its Own*, 16 Miss. Coll. L. Rev. 125, 133 (1995) ("The concept of performative utterances is indeed helpful in explaining the law's treatment of legal operative language. Suppose that the proponent offers the utterance 'I accept your offer' to show acceptance of a contract offer. A hearsay novice might think that the statement is offered for the truth of what it asserts. One way of explaining why the language is not hearsay is to say that it is not assertive but performative. The words are not offered for what they say, but for what they do.").

[40] *See* United States v. Boyd, 566 F.2d 929, 937 (5th Cir. 1978) ("In the case at bar, the government introduced the tape recordings to show the scope of the gambling operation in which Boyd and Wright were involved. The recordings were not offered to prove . . . the truth of the contents of any of the conversations, but merely to prove that the conversations occurred. The conversations are not hearsay but constitute verbal acts and can be considered part of the offense in question.").

[41] *See* United States v. Jones, 663 F.2d 567, 571 (5th Cir. 1981) (prosecution for threatening court officers; "Only the language containing the actual threats . . . was admitted into evidence as an exhibit for the jury during its deliberation. . . . The statement at issue is paradigmatic nonhearsay; it was offered because it contains threats made against officers of the federal courts, *i.e.*, it contains the operative words of this criminal action. It was not 'offered in evidence to prove the truth of the matter asserted,'. . . .").

[42] *See* West Coast Truck Lines, Inc. v. Arcata Cmty. Recycling Ctr., Inc., 846 F.2d 1239, 1246 n. 5 (9th Cir. 1988) ("West Coast argues on appeal that evidence regarding an oral agreement to charge the reduced rates was inadmissible hearsay. . . . Evidence of an oral agreement is not offered to prove the truth of the matter stated. Rather, such evidence is offered simply to show that the statement was made. It is well established that statements which may themselves affect the legal rights of the parties are not considered hearsay under the Federal Rules of Evidence.").

[43] The law of gifts requires donative intent and an act of transfer.

connection with handing over a bag of money as a bribe come within this category. [44] The conduct to be explained should be relevant, equivocal, and contemporaneous with the statements. Most importantly, the conduct must have independent legal significance. [45]

[D] Prior Inconsistent Statements for Impeachment

The common law admitted prior inconsistent statements *only* for impeachment. Under this approach, the prior statement is offered to show the inconsistency between the witness's trial testimony and pretrial statements, rather than to show the truth of the assertions contained in the pretrial statement. [46] The latter use would violate the hearsay rule, which did not recognize an exception for such statements. For instance, suppose the witness testifies at trial that the robber wore a red shirt during a bank robbery, but at the scene immediately following the robbery the same witness told the police that the shirt was blue. The prior statement (blue shirt) is not being offered to prove that the shirt was blue but only that a statement about the color of the shirt was made and it contradicts the witness's trial testimony. [47] Such self-contradiction affects the witness's credibility.

[E] To Circumstantially Prove Declarant's State of Mind

A person's mental state is often a material issue. If that person makes a statement that manifests her state of mind, the statement is relevant. Frequently, such statements are hearsay but fall within the exception for presently existing state of mind. [48] In other cases, the statement shows the

---

[44] The conduct of handing over the money is ambiguous. It could be salary for a job, the repayment of a loan, or a gift.

[45] According to Wigmore, the verbal parts of act concept applies when four conditions are met: (1) The conduct to be characterized by the words must be independently material to the issue; (2) The conduct must be equivocal; (3) The words must aid in giving legal significance to the conduct; and (4) The words must accompany the conduct. 6 Wigmore, Evidence § 1772, at 268 (Chadbourn rev. 1976).

[46] The jury would be so instructed, although the efficacy of such an instruction may be doubted. *See* Fed. R. Evid. 105 (limited purpose instruction). Sometimes the traditional view resulted in a directed verdict because the prior inconsistent statement was not substantive evidence but was the only evidence linking a person with a crime. As an example, suppose a witness, when arrested at the scene of a fire, told police that the defendant had paid him $800 to torch the building. At trial, the witness claims a lack of memory concerning both the statement and the fire.

[47] In general, the Rules of Evidence maintain this position. There is, however, an important exception. Under Rule 801(d)(1)(A), some prior inconsistent statements taken under oath and subject to penalty of perjury may be admitted as substantive evidence. Recognizing a hearsay exemption under these circumstances changed the law. *See infra* § 32.02 (prior inconsistent statements). Moreover, prior inconsistent statements that qualify as admissions of a party-opponent under Rule 801(d)(2) are also admissible as substantive evidence, as they were at common law. Other hearsay exceptions, such as excited utterances, Fed. R. Evid. 803(2), may also be applicable, in which case the statement could be admitted substantively.

[48] Fed. R. Evid. 803(3). *See infra* § 33.06 (present mental condition).

declarant's state of mind only circumstantially. Suppose in a wrongful death action, a husband claims damages for loss of companionship for the death of his wife. The defendant in rebuttal offers statements of the wife made a week before her death — *e.g.,* "My husband is the cruelest man in the world." The statement is not being offered to prove that the husband, in fact, is the cruelest person in the world, but rather to establish circumstantially how the wife felt about the husband. Under an assertion-oriented definition (Rule 801), the statement is not hearsay.[49] But the wife was making an assertion about his cruelty and doesn't this implicate her credibility as the declarant? This would be an argument for classifying the statement as hearsay under a declarant-oriented definition.

A common example involves statements of a defendant offered to establish insanity — *e.g.,* "I am the Emperor of Africa." The statement is offered not to prove that the defendant is the Emperor of Africa, but rather as evidence of the defendant's insane delusions. As such, it would not appear to invoke the hearsay prohibition. This analysis, however, has been criticized because it ignores sincerity problems (an issue implicating the declarant's credibility). Moreover, is there a difference between saying "I am the Emperor of Africa" and "I believe I am the Emperor of Africa"? The latter would be hearsay if offered to prove that belief.[50] Nevertheless, sincerity issues are not always implicated, and the jury is capable of dealing with these problems. In any event, such statements are admissible under Rule 803(3), which recognizes an exception for statements of present mental state.[51]

[F] To Prove Personal Knowledge

In *Bridges v. State,*[52] the accused was charged with taking indecent liberties with a seven-old, named Sharon. Before the defendant's house was identified as the place where the offense took place, Sharon made statements describing the entrance to the house, a room, and a number items in that room. The Wisconsin Supreme Court ruled that her statements were not hearsay because they were not offered for their truth but rather as circumstantial evidence of her knowledge.[53] Here, the argument is that the statement was offered merely to show that she had such knowledge (and other evidence was offered to establish that she had no other way of gaining

---

[49] *See supra* § 31.03 (hearsay definitions).

[50] *See* Hinton, *States of Mind and the Hearsay Rule,* 1 U. Chi. L. Rev. 394, 398 (1934) ("If the statement had taken the form, 'I believe that I am Napoleon,' and were offered to prove that the [declarant] so believed, it would be generally conceded that the statement was hearsay, and receivable only because of an exception to the rule [Rule 803(3)]. The former assertion is simply a short method of stating the speaker's opinion or belief.").

[51] *See infra* § 33.06.

[52] 19 N.W.2d 529 (Wis. 1945).

[53] For other examples of this kind, see United States v. Muscato, 534 F. Supp. 969 (E.D.N.Y. 1982); State v. Galvan, 297 N.W.2d 344 (Iowa 1980); Kinder v. Commonwealth, 306 S.W.2d 265 (Ky. App. 1957).

that knowledge).[54] Once again, the analysis depends on which hearsay definition controls — an assertion-focused definition or a declarant-focused definition.[55]

§ 31.07 "Statement" Defined; "Implied Assertions" — FRE 801(a)

Rule 801(a) defines a "statement" as "(1) an oral or written assertion or (2) nonverbal conduct of a person, if it is intended by the person as an assertion." The first part of this definition is not controversial. Oral and written assertions clearly present the hearsay dangers — lack of cross-examination concerning a declarant's perception, memory, narration, and sincerity. Tape recordings, including the audio part of a video tape, come within this definition.

Conduct, however, is problematic. The critical distinction under the Federal Rules is between assertive and nonassertive conduct.

[A] Assertive Conduct

Sometimes people use conduct to communicate — *e.g.,* a hearing impaired person employing sign language. Suppose a police officer asks: "Did Jones rob you?" You reply by nodding your head. You intend to communicate; the nod is hearsay. It is the same as if the officer asked the question: "Who robbed you?" And you said, "Jones." If the officer asks the same question and you point to Jones, your conduct in pointing is hearsay.

Rule 801(a) treats conduct intended as an assertion (assertive conduct) as hearsay.[56] The above examples illustrate why such conduct is considered hearsay.[57] They present the hearsay dangers inherent in perception, memory, narration, and sincerity untested by cross-examination.

[B] Nonassertive Conduct

Conduct that is not intended by the declarant to be an assertion is far more troublesome. The topic is often labeled "implied assertions," but this term itself is somewhat misleading.[58] The issue has sparked a lively debate

---

[54] *But see* Graham, *"Stickperson Hearsay": A Simplified Approach to Understanding the Rule Against Hearsay,* 1982 U. Ill. L. Rev. 887, 917 ("[A]ll four hearsay risks are present.").

[55] *See supra* § 31.03.

[56] *See* Fed. R. Evid. 801 advisory committee's note ("Some nonverbal conduct, such as the act of pointing to identify a suspect in a lineup, is clearly the equivalent of words, assertive in nature, and to be regarded as a statement.").

[57] *See* United States v. Caro, 569 F.2d 411, 416 n. 9 (5th Cir. 1978) (Asked which vehicle was the source of drugs: " 'It was pointed out by Mr. Casillas and we stopped the vehicle.' It is plain that assertive conduct, like an oral declaration, is subject to the hearsay rule. Fed.R.Evid. 801(a)(2). Mr. Casillas' 'pointing out' constitutes such assertive conduct.").

[58] Perhaps "inferred" assertions would be a more apt phrase. *See* Mueller, *supra* note 26, at 418 n. 153 ("But 'implied assertion' is a singularly inept and artificial umbrella term. It

among evidence scholars for many years,[59] and the Federal Rules only further fueled the debate.[60]

The leading case is *Wright v. Doe D' Tatham*.[61] It involved the competency of John Marsden to make a will. To prove his testamentary capacity to do so, the beneficiary under the will (Wright) offered letters that had been written to Marsden by a cousin, a vicar, and a curate. If these letters had stated, "Dear Marsden, you old competent testator," they would have been hearsay. Instead, these letters merely discussed everyday affairs.[62] Thus, they did not say that Marsden was competent, but they indicated that the letter-writers (the declarants) believed that he was mentally competent, and from this belief, Wright wanted the triers-of-fact to infer that indeed Marsden was competent. The House of Lords ruled the letters inadmissible hearsay,[63] *a position rejected by the Federal Rules.*

The judges in *Wright* offered several examples, which often find their way into evidence classes: (1) a person's election to high office as evidence of that person's sanity and (2) the conduct of a sea captain who, after examining a ship, embarks on it with his family as evidence of the vessel's seaworthiness. In the first example, the voters did not intend to make a statement about sanity, and in the second, the sea captain did not intend to make a statement about seaworthiness.

---

requires us to understand 'imply' in the weak sense of 'suggest' or 'indicate,' not in the ususal strong sense of describing what a person means to convey. It divorces 'assertion' from normal usage, making it mean essentially 'evidence' and severing it from expressive or communicative purpose."); Park, *supra* note 22, at 788 ("The term 'implied assertion' has become a term of art for hearsay writers, who tend to give it a meaning somewhat broader than that which it may connote to many readers. To say an utterance is offered as an 'implied assertion' is not say that the declarant intended to insinuate the fact the proponent is trying to prove. It merely means the trier is being asked to infer that fact from the declarant's utterance.").

[59] *See* Falknor, *The Hearsay Rule as a "See-Do" Rule: Evidence of Conduct*, 33 Rocky Mtn. L. Rev. 133 (1961); Finman, *Implied Assertions as Hearsay: Some Criticisms of the Uniform Rules of Evidence*, 14 Stan. L. Rev. 682 (1962); McCormick, *The Borderland of Hearsay*, 39 Yale L.J. 489 (1930); Morgan, *supra* note 19.

[60] *See* Callen, *Hearsay and Informal Reasoning*, 47 Vand. L. Rev. 43 (1994); Graham, *supra* note 54; Rice, *Should Unintended Implications of Speech Be Considered Nonhearsay? The Assertive/Nonassertive Distinction Under Rule 801(a) of the Federal Rules of Evidence*, 65 Temple L. Rev. 529 (1992); Wellborn, *The Definition of Hearsay in the Federal Rules of Evidence*, 61 Tex. L. Rev. 49 (1982).

[61] 112 Eng. Rep. 488 (1837). *See* Maguire, *The Hearsay System: Around and Through the Thicket*, 14 Vand. L. Rev. 741 (1961) (detailed account of case).

[62] All the letter writers had died by the time of the trial. One letter was from a cousin concerning his voyage to American and what he found there. The cousin later wrote a second letter. A third letter was from a vicar and involved a legal controversy. The fourth was an ingratiating letter from a curate.

[63] One opinion concluded "that proof of a particular fact, which is not of itself a matter in issue, but which is relevant only as implying a statement or opinion of a third person on the matter in issue, is inadmissible in all cases where such a statement or opinion not on oath would be of itself inadmissible; and, therefore, in this case the letters which are offered only to prove the competence of the testator, that is the truth of the implied statements therein contained, were properly rejected, as the mere statements or opinion of the writer would certainly have been inadmissible."

Other common examples are (1) a person observing the opening of an umbrella as evidence that it is raining and (2) a driver moving from a stop position at a traffic light as evidence that the light had changed from red to green.[64] Once again, the actor does not intend to make a statement about the weather in the first example; she intends only to keep dry. Nevertheless, the hearsay danger of perception is present and cross-examination would aid in probing its dimensions. Perhaps the umbrella was opened merely to test its operation or the actor needed to be protected from direct sunlight due to some skin ailment. Under a declarant-focused definition of hearsay, these acts should be hearsay because their probative value depends on the credibility of the declarant.[65]

Federal rule. Although the federal drafters recognized that nonassertive conduct may present some hearsay dangers, they believed that such conduct did not present a substantial risk of *insincerity* and should, therefore, not be classified as hearsay.[66] That is to say, if a person does not intend to make an assertion, insincerity issues are significantly reduced or eliminated. Moreover, "actions speak louder than words." What is more trustworthy: a sea captain who tells you that a ship is seaworthy or one who gets on the ship as it is leaving port? In any event, that is the argument that won the day as far as the federal drafters were concerned.[67] The fact that the hearsay objection is often overlooked by lawyers in this context is cited as a supporting rationale for this position.[68]

[1] Nonverbal & Verbal Conduct

Note that nonassertive conduct may be verbal as well as nonverbal. The facts of *Wright* involved verbal conduct but the hypotheticals (*e.g.,* the sea

---

[64] *See* Falknor, *supra* note 59.

[65] *See supra* § 31.03 (definitions of hearsay).

[66] Fed. R. Evid. 801 advisory committee's note ("Admittedly evidence of this character is untested with respect to the perception, memory, and narration (or their equivalents) of the actor, but the Advisory Committee is of the view that these dangers are minimal in the absence of an intent to assert and do not justify the loss of the evidence on hearsay grounds. No class of evidence is free of the possibility of fabrication, but the likelihood is less with nonverbal than with assertive verbal conduct. The situations giving rise to the nonverbal conduct are such as virtually to eliminate questions of sincerity.").

[67] *See id.* ("The effect of the definition of 'statement' is to exclude from the operation of the hearsay rule all evidence of conduct, verbal or nonverbal, not intended as an assertion. The key to the definition is that nothing is an assertion unless intended to be one. . . . When evidence of conduct is offered on the theory that it is not a statement, and hence not hearsay, a preliminary determination will be required to determine whether an assertion is intended. The rule is so worded as to place the burden upon the party claiming that the intention existed; ambiguous and doubtful cases will be resolved against him and in favor of admissibility.").

[68] Falknor, *supra* note 59, at 135 ("And there is a cogent practical argument for such a rule in the circumstance that experience has shown that very often, probably more often than not, and understandably, the hearsay objection to evidence of non-assertive conduct is overlooked in practice with the result the present doctrine operates very unevenly."); Park, *supra* note 22, at 791 ("Rules excluding nonverbal conduct would be applied sporadically and arbitrarily. This abiding practical obstacle may be the strongest reason for not seeking doctrinal refinement.").

captain and voters) involve nonverbal conduct, as does the umbrella example. Some commentators have thought this distinction significant.[69]

[2] Intent-Based Definition

As noted earlier, the Federal Rules adopt an assertion-focused definition.[70] Nevertheless, a literalistic interpretation of this definition would lead to absurd results. Under such an approach, metaphorical statements would *not* qualify as assertions: (1) "It is raining cats and dogs."; or (2) "The sky is on fire."[71] Thus, an "intent-based" test makes sense: Did the declarant intend to make an assertion?[72] The person making the "cats and dogs" comment intended to assert that it was raining hard.

Suppose, however, that during a police raid of an illegal gambling operation, the telephone rings and a detective answers it. The caller says, "Put $50 on Diggie in the fourth at Belmont." Under the Federal Rules, the statement is not hearsay, even if offered by the prosecution to prove the location was used for illegal betting.[73] The cases hold that the caller did not intend to make an assertion that the place was being used for gambling.[74]

---

[69] *See* Wellborn, *supra* note 60 at 67 ("[I]t is the nature of speech — unlike acts — to convey thought and information; this possibility of concealed assertive intent, while perhaps remote in the case of much nonverbal conduct offered to show belief, must be regarded as far more significant in the ordinary case of apparently nonassertive words.").

[70] *See supra* § 31.03.

[71] Comment, *Hearsay: the Threshold Question*, 9 U.C. Davis L. Rev. 1, 14 n. 48 (1976).

[72] *See also* United States v. Reynolds, 715 F.2d 99, 103 (3d Cir. 1983) (in the presence of postal inspectors, declarant said to defendant, "I didn't tell them anything about you."; "As the government uses it, the statement's probative value depends on the truth of an assumed fact it implies. Unless the trier assumes that the statement implies that [the declarant] did not tell the postal inspectors that [defendant] was involved in the conspiracy to defraud, even though [defendant] was in fact involved, the statement carries no probative weight for the government's case."). *See also* Park, *"I Didn't Tell Them Anything About You"; Implied Assertions Under the Federal Rules of Evidence*, 74 Minn. L. Rev. 783 (1990); Milich, *Re-Examining Hearsay Under the Federal Rules: Some Method for the Madness*, 39 U. Kan. L. Rev. 893 (1991).

[73] This issue can be approached in several ways. A literalist approach might conclude that a command is not an assertion and stop there. A second approach might conclude that the statement is a verbal act. *See supra* § 31.06[B]. A third approach would treat the statement as an assertion, but one that is implied and thus not hearsay under the Federal Rules.

[74] *See* United States v. Zenni, 492 F. Supp. 464 (E.D. Ky. 1980) (while searching the location of an illegal bookmaking operation, police received telephone calls from persons attempting to place bets; "The unknown callers stated directions for the placing of bets on various sporting events. The government proposes to introduce this evidence to show that the callers believed that the premises were used in betting operations."; "[T]his court holds that the utterances of the betters telephoning in their bets were nonassertive verbal conduct, offered as relevant for an implied assertion to be inferred from them, namely that bets could be placed at the premises being telephoned. . . . As an implied assertion, the proffered evidence is expressly excluded from the operation of the hearsay rule by Rule 801 . . . and the objection thereto must be overruled."). *See also* United States v. Long, 905 F.2d 1572, 1579–80 (D.C. Cir. 1990) ("During the search of Mayfield's apartment, the telephone rang, and a police officer answered it. An unidentified female voice asked to speak with 'Keith.' The officer replied that Keith was

[3] Silence

Can silence ever be an assertion? In *Silver v. New York Cent. Ry. Co.*,[75] a passenger claimed to have suffered circulatory problems due to a four hour train stop in Cleveland during the winter. The defendant railroad company proffered the testimony of the porter that other passengers had not complained about frigid temperatures.[76] Here, the issue is whether silence is an assertion and therefore hearsay.[77] Under the Federal Rules, it is not hearsay because a passenger by remaining silent does not intend to make an assertion. There are, of course, relevance issues — was the porter available to receive complaints and would any complaints have been made to the porter rather than to the conductor or some other person?

[4] Questions

One might conclude that, "because a true question or inquiry is by its nature incapable of being proved either true or false and cannot be offered 'to prove the truth of the matter asserted,' it does not constitute hearsay."[78] And this is the traditional analysis.[79] Questions may, however, raise the

---

busy. The caller then asked if Keith 'still had any stuff.' The officer asked the caller what she meant, and the caller responded a 'fifty' [$50 crack bag].'"; "The caller's words, thus, cannot be characterized as an 'assertion,' even an implied one, unless the caller intended to make such an assertion. While Long's criticism of a rigid dichotomy between express and implied assertions is not without merit, it misses the point that the crucial distinction under rule 801 is between intentional and unintentional messages, regardless of whether they are express or implied. It is difficult to imagine any question, or for that matter any act, that does not in some way convey an implicit message. One of the principal goals of the hearsay rule is to exclude declarations when their veracity cannot be tested through cross-examination. When a declarant does not intend to communicate anything, however, his sincerity is not in question and the need for cross-examination is sharply diminished. Thus, an unintentional message is presumptively more reliable.").

[75] 105 N.E.2d 923 (Mass. 1952).

[76] *See* Falknor, *Silence as Hearsay*, 89 U. Pa. L. Rev. 192 (1940).

[77] *See also* Landfield v. Albiani Lunch Co., 168 N.E. 160 (Mass. 1929) (restaurant sued for serving bad food; other diners did not complain).

[78] State v. Carter, 651 N.E.2d 965, 971 (Ohio 1995). *See also* State v. Stojetz, 705 N.E.2d 329, 341 (Ohio 1999) (Testimony of witness that declarant asked, "What are you going to do now?" was not hearsay "since the declarant in this instance was clearly not making an assertion.").

[79] *See* United States v. Jackson, 88 F.3d 845, 848 (10th Cir. 1996) ("The question, 'Is this Kenny?' cannot reasonably be construed to be an intended assertion, either express or implied. Were we to construe this question completely in Mr. Jackson's favor, it might be possible to imply that the declarant believed Mr. Jackson was in possession of the pager and therefore he was the person responding by telephone to the declarant's message. The mere fact, however, that the declarant conveyed a message with her question does not make the question hearsay."); United States v. Lewis, 902 F.2d 1176, 1179 (5th Cir. 1990) ("Later that day, at the police station, the pager associated with Lewis began beeping. Officer Jerry Price called the number displayed on the pager and identified himself as Lewis. The person on the other end asked Price 'Did you get the stuff?' Price answered affirmatively. The unidentified person then asked 'Where is Dog?' . . . The questions asked by the unknown caller, like most questions and inquiries, are not hearsay because they do not, and were not intended to, assert anything.").

"implied assertion" issue. Common illustrations would be: "Has it stopped raining?" and "Did you find my umbrella?"[80]

§ 31.08 Constitutional Issues

The Due Process Clause may require the admissibility of hearsay in limited circumstances.[81] The leading case is *Chambers v. Mississippi*,[82] in which the Supreme Court held that state evidentiary rules that precluded the admission of critical and reliable evidence denied the defendant due process. One of the rules in *Chambers* which made defense evidence inadmissible was the hearsay rule.[83] According to the Court, "In these circumstances, where constitutional rights directly affecting the ascertainment of guilt are implicated, the hearsay rule may not be applied mechanistically to defeat the ends of justice."[84]

In a later case, the Court again overturned a conviction because the application of the hearsay rule precluded the admission of defense evidence. The Court commented: "Regardless of whether the proffered testimony comes within Georgia's hearsay rule, under the facts of this case its exclusion constituted a violation of the Due Process Clause of the Fourteenth Amendment. The excluded testimony was highly relevant to a critical issue in the punishment phase of trial and substantial reasons existed to assume its reliability."[85]

§ 31.09 Procedural Issues

The trial judge decides the admissibility of hearsay evidence under Rule 104(a).[86] Failure to raise the hearsay objection in a timely manner waives the issue,[87] and the evidence may be considered by the jury for whatever probative value the jury wishes to give it.

---

[80] *See also* Weissenberger, *Unintended Implications of Speech and the Definition of Hearsay*, 65 Temple L. Rev. 857 (1992); Seligman, *An Exception to the Hearsay Rule*, 26 Harv. L. Rev. 146, 150–51 n. 13 (1912).

[81] *See generally* Westen, *The Compulsory Process Clause*, 73 Mich. L. Rev. 71, 149–59 (1974); Clinton, *The Right to Present a Defense: An Emergent Constitutional Guarantee in Criminal Trials*, 9 Ind. L. Rev. 711 (1976).

[82] 410 U.S. 284 (1973).

[83] Mississippi at that time did not recognized an exception for declarations against penal interests, which was the traditional rule. However, the Federal Rules take a different approach. *See infra* § 34.05[B] (declarations against penal interests).

[84] 410 U.S. at 302.

[85] Green v. Georgia, 442 U.S. 95, 97 (1979).

[86] *See* Bourjaily v. United States, 483 U.S. 171, 175 (1987) ("Petitioner and the Government agree that the existence of a conspiracy and petitioner's involvement in it are preliminary questions of fact that, under Rule 104, must be resolved by the court.").

[87] *See* Fed. R. Evid. 103 (objections).

§ 31.10 Double Hearsay: FRE 805

Rule 805 governs the admissibility of multiple hearsay. The rule permits the admission of hearsay within hearsay if each part of the hearsay chain falls within an exception.[88] Multiple hearsay issues often arise in connection with the public[89] and business records exceptions.[90] Those exceptions encompass a double-hearsay principle if both declarants are under a business duty[91] or an official duty.[92] In this situation, there is no need to resort to Rule 805.

If, however, only the entrant is under such a duty, the statement is inadmissible in the absence of another hearsay exception. Here Rule 805 comes into play. The federal drafters provided several examples:

> Thus a hospital record might contain an entry of the patient's age based on information furnished by his wife. The hospital record would qualify as a regular entry except that the person who furnished the information was not acting in the routine of the business. However, her statement independently qualifies as a statement of pedigree (if she is unavailable) or as a statement made for purposes of diagnosis or treatment, and hence each link in the chain falls under sufficient assurances. Or, further to illustrate, a dying declaration may incorporate a declaration against interest by another declarant.[93]

Other examples are found in the cases,[94] including one involving triple hearsay.[95]

§ 31.11 Calling Hearsay Declarants: FRE 806

Under Rule 806, if a party against whom a hearsay statement is admitted calls the declarant as a witness, that party may examine the declarant "as if under cross-examination." This provision provides an automatic exception

---

[88] *See* Fed. R. Evid. 805 advisory committee's note ("On principle it scarcely seems open to doubt that the hearsay rule should not call for exclusion of a hearsay statement which includes a further hearsay statement when both conform to the requirements of a hearsay exception.").

[89] Fed. R. Evid. 803(8).

[90] Fed. R. Evid. 803(6).

[91] *See infra* § 33.10 (business records; double hearsay).

[92] *See infra* § 33.12[B] (public records; matters observed-legal duty).

[93] Fed. R. Evid. 805 advisory committee's note.

[94] *E.g.,* United States v. Steele, 685 F.2d 793, 809 (3d Cir. 1982) (conspirator admission within recorded recollection exception); United States v. Diez, 515 F.2d 892, 895–96 n. 2 (5th Cir. 1975) (state of mind statement within conspirator admission).

[95] *See* United States v. Portsmouth Paving Corp., 694 F.2d 312, 321–23 (4th Cir. 1982) (Immediately following a telephone conversation, (1) the declarant told the witness (2) what a party's secretary said that (3) the party had said to her. The first link is a present sense impression under Rule 803(1). The secretary's statement to the declarant qualifies as an admission by an agent under Rule 801(d)(2)(D). The party's statement to the secretary is an individual admission under Rule 801(d)(2)(A)).

to Rule 611(c), which generally prohibits the use of leading questions on direct examination.[96]

§ 31.12   Impeachment of Declarants: FRE 806

Rule 806 also governs the admissibility of evidence relating to the credibility of hearsay declarants and persons who make representative admissions.[97] As the federal drafters explained, "The declarant of a hearsay statement which is admitted in evidence is in effect a witness. His credibility should in fairness be subject to impeachment and support as though he had in fact testified."[98] Accordingly, declarants may be impeached by showing bias, defects in mental or sensory capacity, untruthful character, and so forth as discussed in the credibility chapter.

Due to differences between the context in which live witnesses and hearsay declarants are impeached several issues have arisen.

Prior convictions. If, for example, the hearsay statement of a declarant is admitted into evidence, Rule 806 applies and the declarant may be impeached with evidence of a conviction under Rule 609. Thus, an accused may be impeached even though he never testified.[99] Rule 806 has even been

---

[96] *See supra* § 20.03 (leading questions).

[97] *See* Fed. R. Evid. 801(d)(2)(C) (authorized admissions); Fed. R. Evid. 801(d)(2)(D) (agent admissions); Fed. R. Evid. 801(d)(2)(E) (coconspirator admissions).

[98] Fed. R. Evid. 806 advisory committee's note. *See* United States v. Finley, 934 F.2d 837, 839 (7th Cir. 1991) ("Still, that rule does not allow the use of evidence made inadmissible by some other rule. Rule 806 extends the privilege of impeaching the declarant of a hearsay statement but does not obliterate the rules of evidence that govern how impeachment is to proceed. It says the opposite — that counsel may use 'any evidence which would be admissible . . . if declarant had testified as a witness.'"); United States v. Moody, 903 F.2d 321, 328–29 (5th Cir. 1990) ("Thus, a hearsay declarant is deemed to be a witness whose credibility is subject, in fairness, to impeachment. Impeachment of out-of-court declarants may be accomplished, for example, by testimony of prior convictions, reputation, or prior inconsistent statements. We note, however, that rule 806 is not an invitation to the defense to revisit, ad nauseam, the sordid history of the hearsay declarants in order to disparage their credibility. The scope of impeachment parallels that available if the declarant had testified in court, since rule 806 treats the physical location of the testifying declarant, for impeachment purposes, as legally insignificant. Thus, Moody is free to elicit from his in-court witnesses, especially former CIJL associates, opinion testimony to the effect that Pabst and Beaudreau had earned an abysmal reputation for truthfulness.") (citation omitted).

[99] *See* United States v. Noble, 754 F.2d 1324, 1330–31 (7th Cir. 1985) (impeached by prior conviction); United States v. Lawson, 608 F.2d 1129, 1130 (6th Cir. 1979); Cordray, *Evidence Rule 806 and the Problem of Impeaching the Nontestifying Declarant*, 56 Ohio St. L.J. 495, 503–04 (1995) ("Where, in an effort to advance his case, the defendant offers his own hearsay statements, it seems well within the intended scope of Rule 609 to allow the prosecutor to impeach the defendant's credibility. Rule 609 reflects Congress's determination that it is fair to allow the prosecutor to impeach a testifying defendant with prior convictions in order to prevent him from appearing as one who has led an exemplary life. It seems equally fair to allow the prosecutor to impeach a nontestifying defendant with his prior convictions, where the defendant has chosen to tell his story through his own hearsay statements rather than by taking the witness stand. Indeed, it is arguably more important to allow impeachment in this context, because the defendant has avoided the rigors of cross-examination by introducing his hearsay statements rather than testifying.").

held to permit impeachment of a defendant whose out-of-court statements were offered by the prosecution or a codefendant,[100] and thus has done nothing to put his credibility at issue. This result has been justifiably criticized.[101]

Specific acts reflecting untruthful character. Rule 608(b) restricts impeachment with specific instances reflecting untruthful character to cross-examination; extrinsic evidence is prohibited.[102] If the hearsay declarant does not testify, application of the ban on extrinsic evidence would preclude this method of impeachment. One court has interpreted Rule 806 to permit impeachment of a hearsay declarant with extrinsic evidence in this context. In *United States v. Friedman*,[103] the Second Circuit stated: "Rule 806 applies, of course, when the declarant has not testified and there has by definition been no cross-examination, and resort to extrinsic evidence may be the only means of presenting such evidence to the jury."[104]

Inconsistent statements. The second sentence of Rule 806 establishes a special rule for impeachment by evidence of inconsistent statements: "Evidence of a statement or conduct by the declarant at any time, inconsistent with the declarant's hearsay statement, is not subject to any requirement that declarant's may have been afforded an opportunity to deny or explain." Hence, Rule 613(b), which requires that a witness be provided an opportunity to explain or deny an inconsistent statement as a condition for the admissibility of extrinsic evidence, does not extend to the impeachment of hearsay declarants. Moreover, inconsistent statements made subsequent to the hearsay statement are admissible.[105]

Rehabilitation. Once the declarant is impeached, rehabilitation evidence may be admissible.[106]

---

[100] *See* United States v. Bovain, 708 F.2d 606, 613 (11th Cir. 1983).

[101] *See* Cordray, *supra* note 99, at 512 (arguing that impeachment of a criminal defendant whose hearsay statement is offered by the prosecution or another defendant should not be permitted under Rule 806 because the defendant in such a case "has not affirmatively placed his credibility in issue").

[102] *See supra* § 22.09 (specific-acts impeachment).

[103] 854 F.2d 535 (2d Cir. 1988).

[104] *Id.* at 570 n. 8. *See also* Cordray, *supra* note 99, at 529 ("Rule 806 should direct the trial court to use its discretion in determining whether to allow the attacking party to use extrinsic evidence when she seeks to impeach a nontestifying declarant with specific instances of conduct pursuant to Rule 608(b).").

[105] Fed. R. Evid. 806 advisory committee's note ("The principal difference between using hearsay and an actual witness is that the inconsistent statement will in the case of the witness almost inevitably of necessity in the nature of things be a prior statement, which it is entirely possible and feasible to call to his attention, while in the case of hearsay the inconsistent statement may well be a subsequent one, which practically precludes calling it to the attention of the declarant. The result of insisting upon observation of this impossible requirement in the hearsay situation is to deny the opponent, already barred from cross-examination, any benefit of this important technique of impeachment.").

[106] *See supra* § 22.14 (rehabilitating credibility).

§ 31.13 "Res Gestae"

The Federal Rules avoid the use of the term "res gestae," a confusing phrase which encompasses both evidence that is not hearsay and evidence that is hearsay but falls within one of several exceptions to the hearsay rule. Wigmore believed that the "phrase res gestae has long been not only entirely useless, but even positively harmful."[107] Many courts have agreed. "As for . . . 'res gestae', if it means anything but an unwillingness to think at all, what it covers cannot be put in less intelligible terms."[108]

§ 31.14 Key Points

Overview of Article VIII

In the absence of an exception or exemption, Rule 802 bars hearsay evidence. Rule 802 must be read in conjunction with Rule 801, which defines hearsay.

Exceptions. The exceptions are found in three rules. Rule 803 specifies twenty-three exceptions that apply whether or not the declarant is available. Rule 804 specifies five exceptions that apply *only* if the declarant is unavailable. Rule 807 recognizes a residual or "catch all" exception, under which some hearsay statements may be admitted on an ad hoc basis.

Exemptions. In addition to the exceptions, there were two categories of hearsay statements that the drafters wanted to admit into evidence. However, for theoretical reasons, the drafters choose not to classify them as exceptions. Instead, these statements were simply defined out of the definition of hearsay in Rule 801(d). The first category of exemptions (Rule 801(d)(1)) involves prior statements of a witness: it provides that certain prior inconsistent statements, prior consistent statements, and statements of identification are not hearsay. The second category, Rule 801(d)(2), covers admissions of a party-opponent. Note that the exemptions function like exceptions; statements falling within them are not barred by the hearsay prohibition.

---

[107] 6 Wigmore, Evidence § 1767, at 255 (Chadbourn rev. 1976). *See also* Morgan, *A Suggested Classification of Utterances Admissible as Res Gestae*, 31 Yale L.J. 229, 229 n. 7 (1922) ("The marvelous capacity of a Latin phrase to serve as a substitute for reasoning, and the confusion of thought inevitably accompanying the use of inaccurate terminology, are nowhere better illustrated than in the decisions dealing with the admissibility of evidence as 'res gestae.' It is probable that this troublesome expression owes its existence and persistence in our law of evidence to an inclination of judges and lawyers to avoid the toilsome exertion of exact analysis and precise thinking."); Sir Frederick Pollock, 2 Holmes-Pollock Letters 284–85 (M. Howe ed. 1941) ("I am reporting, with some reluctance, a case on the damnable pretended doctrine of res gestae, and wishing some high authority would prick that bubble of verbiage; the unmeaning term merely fudges the truth that there is no universal formula for all the kinds of relevancy.").

[108] United States v. Matot, 146 F.2d 197, 198 (2d Cir. 1944) (Learned Hand, J.). *See also* In re Estate of Gleason, 130 P. 872, 875 (Cal. 1913) ("Definitions of res gestae are as numerous as prescriptions for the cure of rheumatism and generally about as useful.").

Multiple hearsay. Rule 805 governs the admissibility of multiple hearsay —*i.e.,* hearsay within hearsay. If each part of a double hearsay statement falls within an exception, the statement is admissible.

Impeachment of hearsay declarants. Rule 806 regulates the calling of hearsay declarants as well as the impeachment and rehabilitation of declarants. In effect, a hearsay declarant is a witness and generally may be impeached in the same manner as trial witnesses.

Admissibility. Evidence that falls within one of the exceptions or exemptions is not automatically admissible. The statement must also satisfy the requirements of other evidentiary rules. For example, evidence must be relevant, and must not be excludable for some other reason, such as being unfairly prejudicial (Rule 403), or failing to satisfy the requirements of authentication or "best evidence" rules.

Hearsay Rule

Rationale. Cross-examination is the key to understanding the hearsay rule. With hearsay, there is no cross-examination of the *real* witness, the declarant, to test perception, memory, narration, and sincerity. (The oath and observation of demeanor are secondary safeguards to cross-examination.)

Definitions. Hearsay can be defined as an out-of-court statement whose probative value depends on the credibility of the declarant. Such a "declarant-focused" definition highlights the underlying policy of the hearsay rule. There is, however, a competing definition, an "assertion-focused" definition: Hearsay is an out-of-court statement offered for the truth of its assertion. In most cases, the same result is reached under either definition. But not always —*i.e.,* implied assertions. The Federal Rules adopt the latter definition.

Declarant defined. Rule 801(b) defines "declarant" as a "person who makes a statement." This definition makes clear that the hearsay rule does not apply to devices, such as radar, or to tracking dogs.

"Out-of-Court" (extrajudicial) requirement. Rule 801(c) defines hearsay as a "statement, other than one made by the declarant while testifying at the trial or hearing." Hence, an out-of-court (extrajudicial) statement does not lose its hearsay character simply because the declarant later becomes a witness at trial and testifies about the statement.

Statements Offered for Their Truth

If the statement is offered for *any* purpose other than for its truth, it is not hearsay. This means that the hearsay character of the statement cannot be determined until we know what the statement is being offered to prove —*i.e.,* its relevancy. In other words, Rule 801 must be read along with Rule 401 (defining relevancy).

Rule 403. In addition to Rule 401, Rule 403 plays an important role here. If the proponent of the evidence comes forward with a *nonhearsay* (*i.e.,* not for its truth) purpose, the hearsay rule does not bar admissibility. A limiting instruction, of course, must be given on request. This does not, however, guarantee admissibility. It may be that the probative value of the statement for the nonhearsay purpose is substantially outweighed (Rule 403) by the risk of unfair prejudice — *i.e.,* that the jury will make the prohibited hearsay inference despite the limiting instruction. Hence, the statement may be excluded under Rule 403.

Examples. Courts and commentators have recognized a number of recurring situations where the statements are *not* offered for their truth. These are discussed below. Note, however, this is not an exhaustive list.

To show effect on listener. A statement offered to show its effect on the state of mind of the person who heard it is *not* hearsay — *e.g.,* to prove knowledge, good faith, or reasonableness.

Verbal acts. Statements that constitute verbal acts or operative acts are not hearsay because they are not offered for the truth. In other words, the uttering of certain words has independent legal significance under the substantive law — *e.g.,* words of a contract, slander, threats, and the like. Thus, we only care that these words were *said*, not that they are *true*.

Verbal parts of acts. Verbal parts of acts are closely related to verbal acts. Such statements are offered in evidence only to show that the statements were made and to explain an otherwise ambiguous act. For example, words of donative intent accompanying the transfer of diamonds or statements made in connection with handing over a bag of money as a bribe come within this category. Most importantly, the conduct must have independent legal significance.

Prior inconsistent statements for impeachment. The common law admitted prior inconsistent statements *only* for impeachment. Under this approach, the prior statement is offered to show the inconsistency between the witness's trial testimony and pretrial statements, rather than to show the truth of the assertions contained in the pretrial statement.[109]

To circumstantially prove declarant's state of mind. A person's mental state is often a material issue. If that person makes a statement that manifests her state of mind, the statement is relevant. Frequently, such statements are hearsay but fall within the exception for presently existing state of mind.[110] In other cases, the statement shows the declarant's state of mind only circumstantially. Suppose in a wrongful death action, a husband claims damages for loss of companionship for the death of his wife. The defendant in rebuttal offers statements of the wife made a week before her death — *e.g.,* "My husband is the cruelest man in the world." The

---

[109] In general, the Rules of Evidence maintain this position. There is, however, an important exception. Under Rule 801(d)(1)(A), some prior inconsistent statements taken under oath and subject to penalty of perjury may be admitted as substantive evidence.

[110] Fed. R. Evid. 803(3). *See infra* § 33.06 (present mental condition).

statement is not being offered to prove that the husband, in fact, is the cruelest person in the world, but rather to establish circumstantially how the wife felt about the husband. Under an assertion-oriented definition as in Rule 801, the statement is not hearsay.

"Statement" Defined; "Implied Assertions"

Rule 801(a) defines a "statement" as "(1) an oral or written assertion or (2) nonverbal conduct of a person, if it is intended by the person as an assertion." Conduct is problematic. The critical distinction under the Federal Rules is between assertive and nonassertive conduct.

Assertive conduct. Sometimes people use conduct to communicate — *e.g.,* a hearing impaired person employing sign language. Nodding the head and pointing a finger are other examples. Rule 801(a) treats conduct intended as an assertion (assertive conduct) as hearsay.

Nonassertive conduct. Conduct that is not intended by the declarant to be an assertion ("implied assertions) has divided courts and commentators. In *Wright v. Doe D' Tatham*, the House of Lords declared such conduct hearsay, a position rejected by the Federal Rules. Although the federal drafters recognized that nonassertive conduct may present some hearsay dangers, they believed that such conduct did not present a substantial risk of *insincerity* and should, therefore, not be classified as hearsay. That is to say, if a person does not intend to make an assertion, insincerity issues are significantly reduced or eliminated. Moreover, "actions speak louder than words."

Chapter 32

HEARSAY EXEMPTIONS: FRE 801(d)

§ 32.01 Introduction

Rule 801(d) defines some statements as nonhearsay. There are two categories: (1) certain prior statements and (2) admissions of a party-opponent. The first category includes prior inconsistent statements, prior consistent statements, and statements of identification. The second category encompasses five types of admissions.

§ 32.02 Prior Inconsistent Statements: FRE 801(d)(1)(A)

Rationale. With prior statements, the witness and declarant are the same person. At trial, the witness-declarant is under oath, subject to cross-examination, and her demeanor is observable by the jury. The only deficiency in trial safeguards is that the cross-examination is delayed; it occurs at trial rather than at the time the statement was made. In these circumstances, the policies supporting the exclusion of hearsay do not seem to apply. If this is so, all prior inconsistent statement should be admitted, which is what the federal drafters proposed. Congress balked at such an extensive rejection of the common law position and limited admissibility to only a narrow category of statements as reflected in Rule 801(d)(1)(A).[1]

At common law, prior inconsistent statements were admissible only for impeachment; such statements were not offered for their truth but only to show that the statement was made and was inconsistent with the witness's trial testimony.[2] In other words, the statement was admitted for credibility (impeachment) and not as substantive evidence. Prior inconsistent statements that do not satisfy the requirements of Rule 801(d)(1)(A) are still admissible for impeachment purposes; Rule 613 governs the admissibility of these statements.

Four conditions must be satisfied for admissibility: (1) the declarant must testify, subject to cross-examination, at the current trial; (2) the prior statement must be inconsistent with the witness's trial testimony;[3] (3) the

---

[1] *See* Mueller, *Post-Modern Hearsay Reform: The Importance of Complexity*, 76 Minn. L. Rev. 367, 386–87 (1992) ("Practitioners say cross-examination can expose falsehood and error in live testimony, but not in prior statements. The witness may be friendly or neutral, and lawyer cannot come at him full bore as an enemy in an attempt to burst the balloon of credibility, but must find a way to deflate the prior statement while leaving the live testimony intact, floating above the fray.").

[2] *See supra* § 22.10[A] (hearsay rule & inconsistent statements).

[3] *See supra* § 22.10[B] (inconsistency requirement). *See* United States v. Gajo, 290 F.3d 922,

prior statement must have been given under oath subject to penalty of perjury; and (4) the prior statement must have been made "at a trial, hearing, or other proceeding, or in a deposition."

"Other proceedings" defined. Statements made at a prior trial, a suppression hearing, a preliminary hearing, a deposition, or any other proceeding at which testimony is taken under oath and subject to penalty of perjury, qualify under Rule 801(d)(1)(A). Grand jury testimony also qualifies.[4] Stationhouse statements to the police or affidavits to government officials are not admissible under the rule.[5] Formalized proceedings with transcripts are typically required.

Cross-examination defined. The rationale underlying the rule requires only that the witness have been *subject* to examination. The Supreme Court has taken the position that no more is required where a witness could not remember.[6] However, the statement of a witness who asserts the privilege against self-incrimination is not admissible under this rule because such a witness has not been subject to cross-examination.[7]

§ 32.03   Prior Consistent Statements: FRE 801(d)(1)(B)

The common law generally viewed prior inconsistent statements with suspicion because they are easily manufactured before trial and typically have little rehabilitative power. Nevertheless, prior consistent statements were admissible if offered to rebut a charge of recent fabrication. The statement, however, could be considered for rehabilitative purposes but not as substantive evidence.[8] Under Rule 801(d)(1)(B), such statements are substantively admissible.[9] The witness must be subject to cross-

---

931 (7th Cir. 2002) ("a lack of memory is inconsistent with the description of specific details before the grand jury"); United States v. DiCaro, 772 F.2d 1314, 1321 (7th Cir. 1985) ("Particularly in a case of manifest reluctance to testify if a witness has testified to certain facts before a grand jury and forgets them at trial, his grand jury testimony falls squarely within Rule 801(d)(1)(A).") (internal quotation marks omitted).

[4] *E.g., Gajo,* 290 F.3d at 931.

[5] *See* United States v. Williams, 272 F.3d 845, 859 (7th Cir. 2001) ("[W]hen an affidavit is taken under an oath administered by an IRS special agent, the investigative interview that generated the affidavit was not shown to be a 'proceeding' for the purposes of the rule, and the affidavit was therefore not admissible under this rule."); United States v. Day, 789 F.2d 1217, 1222–23 (6th Cir. 1986).

[6] United States v. Owens, 484 U.S. 554, 561 (1988) ("Ordinarily a witness is regarded as 'subject to cross-examination' when he is placed on the stand, under oath, and responds willingly to questions."). *See infra* § 32.04[A] for a discussion of *United States v. Owens.*

[7] United States v. Torrez-Ortega, 184 F.3d 1128, 1132 (10th Cir. 1999) (witness asserting Fifth Amendment was "not subject to cross-examination").

[8] *See supra* § 22.14[B] (rehabilitating credibility). Because the statement was made *before* the improper motive could have influenced it, the statement corroborates the truthfulness of the trial testimony.

[9] Fed. R. Evid. 801(d)(1)(B) advisory committee's note ("Prior consistent statements traditionally have been admissible to rebut charges of recent fabrication or improper influence or motive but not as substantive evidence. Under the rule they are substantive evidence. The prior statement is consistent with the testimony given on the stand, and, if the opposite party

examination at trial.[10] Thus, the statement of a witness who asserts the privilege against self-incrimination is not admissible.[11]

[A] "Premotive" Requirement

In *Tome v. United States*,[12] the Supreme Court held that Rule 801(d)(1)(B) applies only when the statements "were made before the charged recent fabrication or improper influence or motive."[13] The Court found that the phrase "offered to rebut an express or implied charge of recent fabrication or improper influence or motive" connoted a temporal requirement that "the consistent statements must have been made *before* the alleged influence, or motive to fabricate arose."[14] In the Court's view, a consistent statement that predates the improper influence or motive to fabricate forcefully refutes a charge of improper influence or motive, whereas a consistent statement made after the alleged improper influence or motive to fabricate had arisen has far less probative force in refuting the charge.

[B] Rehabilitation

Another issue is whether prior consistent statements not admissible under this rule are nevertheless admissible for rehabilitation — *i.e.*, to support credibility rather than as substantive evidence. Some federal courts have concluded that a prior consistent statement must satisfy the requirements of Rule 801(d)(1)(B) or it is inadmissible for any purpose,[15] whereas others have held that a statement's inadmissibility under the rule precludes substantive use but not rehabilitative use.[16] Even if admission is

---

wishes to open the door for its admission in evidence, no sound reason is apparent why it should not be received generally. In contrast to the rule on prior inconsistent statements, Rule 801(d)(1)(A), a prior consistent statement need not have been given under oath, subject to penalty of perjury, and subject to cross-examination.").

[10] *Owens*, 484 U.S. at 561 ("Ordinarily a witness is regarded as 'subject to cross-examination' when he is placed on the stand, under oath, and responds willingly to questions."). *See infra* § 32.04[A] for a discussion of *United States v. Owens*.

[11] *Torrez-Ortega*, 184 F.3d at 1132 (witness asserting Fifth Amendment was "not subject to cross-examination").

[12] 513 U.S. 150 (1995).

[13] *Id.* at 167.

[14] *Id.* at 158 (emphasis added).

[15] *See* United States v. Miller, 874 F.2d 1255, 1273 (9th Cir. 1989) ("A prior consistent statement offered for rehabilitation is either admissible under Rule 801(d)(1)(B) or it is not admissible at all.").

[16] *See* United States v. Simonelli, 237 F.3d 19, 27 (1st Cir. 2001) ("We now join the majority view, that 'where prior consistent statements are not offered for their truth but for the limited purpose of rehabilitation, . . . Rule 801(d)(1)(B) and its concomitant restrictions do not apply.' When the prior statements are offered for credibility, the question is not governed by Rule 801.") (citations omitted); United States v. Brennan, 798 F.2d 581, 587–88 (2d Cir. 1986) ("Prior consistent statements may be admissible for rehabilitation even if not admissible under Rule 801(d)(1)(B).").

permissible for rehabilitative purposes, the "[p]rior consistent statements still must meet at least the standard of having 'some rebutting force beyond the mere fact that the witness has repeated on a prior occasion a statement consistent with his trial testimony.'"[17]

§ 32.04   Statements of Identification: FRE 801(d)(1)(C)

A witness's prior statement of identification of a person after "perceiving" that person is admissible as substantive evidence.[18] In effect, the rule recognizes that the standard in-court identification of the accused as the prepetrator of the charged offense is more "show" than substance and that a prior identification is more reliable.[19] For example, an identification made at a lineup, show-up (one-on-one confrontation), photographic display, or prior hearing falls within the rule, i.e., "That's the person who did it." The rule, however, is not restricted to "formal" identification procedures.[20]

The use of prior identifications only as corroborative, rather than substantive, evidence was recognized in many jurisdictions before the enactment of the Federal Rules.[21] Under the corroboration (bolstering) theory, the witness had to make an in-court identification before evidence of a prior identification could be admitted. Stated another way, there first needed to be an "identification" in order for it to be bolstered.

In contrast, prior identifications are admissible as substantive evidence under the rule. Thus, the rule applies whether or not the witness makes an in-court identification.[22] So long as the witness is "subject to cross-examination concerning the statement" at trial, the testimony of other witnesses who were present at the time of the identification is admissible.[23]

---

[17] *Simonelli*, 237 F.3d at 27 (citation omitted).

[18] Even though statements of identification are usually a type of prior consistent statement, the limitations of Rule 801(d)(1)(B) do not apply to such statements. Indeed, in some cases the identification has not been consistent.

[19] *See* United States v. Lewis, 565 F.2d 1248, 1251 (2d Cir. 1977) ("Congress has recognized, as do most trial judges, that identification in the courtroom is a formality that offers little in the way of reliability and much in the way of suggestibility. The experienced trial judge gives much greater credence to the out-of-court identification.").

[20] In United States v. Lopez, 271 F.3d 472, 483 (3d Cir. 2001), a government witness subpoenaed to testify told the police, on the day after the crime, that he had seen three of the defendants in the area during the time the homes were invaded. On the day he was called to testify, he failed to appear in court. Once apprehended by United States Marshals and brought to court, he denied making any such statement to the police and was declared a hostile witness. Statement admitted.

[21] *See supra* § 22.02[B][1] (eyewitness identifications).

[22] *See* United States v. Brink, 39 F.3d 419, 426 (3d Cir. 1994) (evidence admitted under Rule 801(d)(1)(C) "when a witness has identified the defendant in a lineup or photospread, but forgets, or changes, his testimony at trial"); United States v. O'Malley, 796 F.2d 891, 899 (7th Cir. 1986) (prior identification repudiated); United States v. Jarrad, 754 F.2d 1451, 1456 (9th Cir. 1985) (prior identification denied).

[23] *See* United States v. Anglin, 169 F.3d. 154, 159 (2d Cir. 1999) ("Crowl's testimony to that effect was properly admitted, even if he could not identify Anglin in court."); United States v. Salameh, 152 F.3d. 88, 125 (2d Cir. 1998) (per curiam) ("A prior identification is admissible under Fed. R. Evid. 801(d)(1)(C), regardless of whether the witness confirms the identification in-court.").

For example, a robbery victim may have identified the robber at a lineup, at which time the robber wore a beard. If the victim cannot positively identify the defendant at trial because the beard had been shaved, the lineup identification is nevertheless admissible through the testimony of a police officer who was present.[24]

[A] Cross-examination Requirement

In *United States v. Owens*,[25] a hospitalized witness, who had suffered a fractured skull, identified Owens as his attacker and picked his picture from an array of photographs. At trial, the witness testified about the attack, including his identification of Owens while in the hospital. On cross-examination, however, he admitted that he could not remember seeing his assailant. The Supreme Court held that Rule 801(d)(1)(C)'s requirements had been satisfied. The witness had been subjected to cross-examination "concerning the statement." He took the stand and responded willingly to questions. The witness's impaired memory did not mean that cross-examination was lacking. The Court also ruled that the Confrontation Clause did not bar this evidence. According to the Court, the Clause guarantees only an opportunity for effective cross-examination. This right is satisfied when the defendant has the opportunity to bring out such matters as a bad memory during the examination.[26]

[B] Constitutional Requirements

Rule 801(d)(1)(C) covers only the hearsay aspects of pretrial identifications. In criminal cases, identification evidence also must satisfy Sixth Amendment and due process requirements. The Sixth Amendment requires the presence of counsel at some types of identification procedures.[27] Due process requires that identification evidence be reliable.[28]

§ 32.05 Admissions of Party-opponents: Overview

Rule 801(d)(2) exempts admissions of a party-opponent from the hearsay rule by defining admissions as nonhearsay. Under the common law, an admission was classified as an exception to the hearsay rule. The Federal

---

[24] *See also* United States v. Lewis, 565 F.3d 1248, 1250 (2d Cir. 1977) ("At trial, Mrs. Sharpe was unable to identify appellant in the courtroom and mistakenly picked out a Deputy United States Marshal instead.").

[25] 484 U.S. 554 (1988).

[26] *See infra* § 36.04[A] (limitations on cross-examination).

[27] *See* Moore v. Illinois, 434 U.S. 220 (1977) (right to counsel applicable at identification made at preliminary hearing); United States v. Ash, 413 U.S. 300 (1973) (right to counsel not applicable at photographic display); Kirby v. Illinois, 406 U.S. 682 (1972) (right to counsel attaches at commencement of judicial adversary proceedings, not at time of arrest); United States v. Wade, 388 U.S. 218 (1967). *See generally* Dressler, Understanding Criminal Procedure ch. 27 (3d ed. 2002).

[28] *See* Manson v. Brathwaite, 432 U.S. 98 (1977); Neil v. Biggers, 409 U.S. 188 (1972).

Rules do not change this result; admissions are admissible, although under a different theory. The rule recognizes five types of party admissions: (1) individual admissions, (2) adoptive admissions, (3) authorized admissions, (4) agent admissions, and (5) coconspirator admissions.

In addition, statements or conduct that could be classified as "admissions" may be regulated by other rules. For example, Rule 408 excludes compromises and offers of compromise[29] and Rule 410 excludes certain pleas, offers to plead, and statements in criminal cases.[30]

[A] Rationale

An admission of a party-opponent is treated as nonhearsay rather than as an exception to the hearsay rule for two reasons. First, the principal objection to hearsay evidence is that the party against whom the hearsay statement is offered has been denied the opportunity to cross-examine the declarant. A party-opponent cannot object on this ground, however, "because he does not need to cross-examine himself."[31]

Second, all hearsay exceptions are based on some guarantee of trustworthiness.[32] There is no circumstantial guarantee of trustworthiness for party admissions. The firsthand knowledge rule does not apply. The opinion rule does not apply. And, the statement need not be against interest when made. Instead, party admissions "are excluded from the category of hearsay on the theory that their admissibility in evidence is the result of the adversary system rather than satisfaction of the conditions of the hearsay rule."[33] In other words, the adversary system imposes upon a party the burden of explaining her prior statements. In any event, although the theory of admissibility is changed by the Federal Rules, the result is generally the same as under prior law.

[B] Evidential & Judicial Admissions Distinguished

Rule 801(d)(2) deals with evidential admissions. It does not govern the use of judicial admissions, such as admissions in pleadings[34] or in stipulations.[35] Unlike evidential admissions which can be rebutted at trial,[36] a

---

[29] See supra chapter 14.

[30] See supra chapter 16.

[31] 4 Wigmore, Evidence § 1048, at 4 (Chadbourn rev. 1972). Accord Morgan, Basic Problems of Evidence 266 (1962) ("A party can hardly object that he had no opportunity to cross-examine himself or that he is unworthy of credence save when speaking under sanction of an oath.").

[32] See infra § 33.02 (rationale for hearsay exceptions).

[33] Fed. R. Evid. 801 advisory committee's note.

[34] See Fed. R. Civ. P. 8(d) (failure to deny averment in pleadings); Fed. R. Civ. P.36 (requests for admissions). See supra § 3.02.

[35] See infra chapter 45 (stipulations).

[36] For example, an accused may challenge the reliability of his confession after it is admitted. See supra § 7.06 (weight & credibility).

party is bound by its judicial admissions. Thus, a judicial admission, unless allowed by the court to be withdrawn, is conclusive in the case, whereas an evidentiary admission is not binding and is subject to contradiction or explanation.

[C] Firsthand Knowledge & Opinion Rules

Neither the firsthand knowledge rule[37] nor the opinion rule[38] applies to admissions of a party-opponent. Assume, for instance, that the police telephone me and say my kid was in an automobile accident. I reply: "Oh. I am sure it was his fault." That statement — in opinion form and without any personal knowledge — is admissible if I am sued for the accident. This result follows from the underlying theory of party admissions, which is based on the adversary system and not on the reliability of these statements. Parties should not be able to exclude their own statements on the grounds that they did not have the opportunity to cross-examine themselves when they made the statement — whether or not they lacked firsthand knowledge or spoke in opinion terms. They are free to take the stand and explain this to the jury.

§ 32.06   Individual Admissions: FRE 801(d)(2)(A)

Statements, oral or written, of a party, in either her individual or representative capacity, are admissible as substantive evidence if offered *against* that party. A party cannot introduce her own statements under this rule.

An individual admission may be defined as any statement made by a party that is inconsistent with that party's position at trial. Stated another way, *any* statement made by a party at *any* time is admissible as an admission if (1) relevant and (2) offered by the opposing party, ranging from deposition testimony to casual statements made to friends.

[A] Pleas of Guilty

A plea of guilty in a criminal case is an admission and thus is admissible against a party-opponent in a subsequent case. Rule 410, however, precludes the admissibility of guilty pleas that are subsequently withdrawn, pleas of no contest, offers to plead guilty or no contest, and statements made in connection with such pleas and offers.[39] In addition, judgments of prior convictions, whether based upon a guilty plea or jury verdict, may be admissible under Rule 803(22).[40]

---

[37] Fed. R. Evid. 602.

[38] Fed. R. Evid. 701.

[39] *See supra* chapter 16.

[40] *See infra* § 33.17 (judgment of previous conviction; withdrawn guilty pleas and no contest pleas are excluded).

[B] Confessions

The confession of a criminal defendant is an admission of a party-opponent. Some common law cases distinguish confessions and admissions, characterizing confessions as a complete acknowledgment of guilt and admissions as something less. The distinction is not important. Both confessions and admissions are admissible under Rule 801(d)(2)(A).[41] The rule governs only the hearsay aspects of admissions. It is not concerned with the constitutional requirements surrounding the obtaining of statements from defendants by the police.[42]

[C] "Privity" Admissions

Prior to the adoption of the Rules of Evidence, common law cases admitted against a party statements of persons who were in privity of estate or interest with that party. Privity admissions are not admissible under Rule 801(d)(2). No provision encompasses such statements, and they are therefore excluded as hearsay under Rule 802. Such statements, of course, may be admissible under a different rule — for example, as statements against interest[43] or agent admissions.[44]

[D] "Declarations Against Interest" Distinguished

Party admissions are often confused with the hearsay exception relating to declarations against interest, which is governed by Rule 804(b)(3). There are several differences between the two rules. First, as noted above, the firsthand knowledge rule does not apply to admissions, but it does apply to declarations against interest.

Second, admissions need not have been against the interest of the declarant when made. Thus, a statement that is self-serving when made by a party may later be introduced at trial by an opposing party, whereas the declaration against interest exception turns on the adverse nature of the statement when made. For example, I tell the Cleveland police, who are investigating a bank robbery, that I was in New York on August 1, the day of the robbery. That statement is not against my interest, but it can be admitted against me as a party admission if I am later charged with a New York murder that occurred on August 1.

---

[41] Moreover, the Supreme Court has held the distinction irrelevant when a statement obtained from a defendant by the police is challenged on constitutional grounds. *See* Miranda v. Arizona, 384 U.S. 436, 476–77 (1966) ("No distinction can be drawn between statements which are direct confessions and statements which amount to 'admissions' of part or all of an offense. The privilege against self-incrimination . . . does not distinguish degrees of incrimination.").

[42] *See* Miranda v. Arizona, 384 U.S. 436, 476–77 (1966) (Fifth Amendment requirements); Brewer v. Williams, 430 U.S. 387 (1977) (right to counsel requirements). *See generally* Dressler, Understanding Criminal Procedure ch. 22–25 (3d ed. 2002).

[43] Fed. R. Evid. 804(b)(3).

[44] Fed. R. Evid. 801(d)(2)(D).

Third, the declarant need not be unavailable for an admission to be introduced. In contrast, a declaration against interest is not admissible unless the declarant is unavailable at the time of trial. Finally, declarations against interest need not be made by a party.

§ 32.07 Adoptive Admissions: FRE 801(d)(2)(B)

A statement "adopted" by a party is admissible as substantive evidence if offered against that party.[45] A party may expressly adopt the statement of a third person.[46] More difficult issues arise when the adoption is circumstantial.[47]

[A] Adoption by Use

Mere possession of a document is not an adoption of the contents of the document. Use of the document, however, is different. Wigmore wrote: "The party's use of a document made by a third person will frequently amount to an approval of its statements as correct, and thus it may be received against him as an admission by adoption."[48] For example, in *Wagstaff v. Protective Apparel Corp. of Am., Inc.*,[49] the Tenth Circuit found that newspaper reprints had been adopted by a party: "By reprinting the newspaper articles and distributing them to persons with whom defendants were doing business, defendants unequivocally manifested their adoption of the inflated statements made in the newspaper articles."[50]

Similarly, in *Price v. Cleveland Clinic Found.*,[51] a malpractice action for negligently performing blood grouping tests, the plaintiff offered three

---

[45] The firsthand knowledge and opinion rules do not apply to admissions. *See supra* § 32.05[C] (firsthand knowledge & opinion rules).

[46] Fed. R. Evid. 801 advisory committee's note ("Under established principles an admission may be made by adopting or acquiescing in the statement of another. Adoption or acquiescence may be manifested in any appropriate manner."). *See also* United States v. Jinadu, 98 F.3d. 239, 245 (6th Cir. 1996) ("The evidence, thus, indicates that there is sufficient indicia of reliability that Hein's statements were made in defendant's presence, that defendant understood the statements, and that he had an opportunity to deny them, but instead answered, 'yes,' indicating his acquiescence in the truth of the questions he was being asked.").

[47] *See* United States v. Hove, 52 F.3d 233, 237 (9th Cir. 1995) ("declining an invitation to testify in front of the grand jury simply does not constitute an admission by silence").

[48] 4 Wigmore, Evidence § 1073, at 138 (Chadbourn rev. 1972).

[49] 760 F.2d 1074 (10th Cir. 1985). *See also* Pilgrim v. Trustees of Tufts Coll., 118 F.3d. 864, 870 (1st Cir. 1997) ("[H]is acceptance of the contents of the Report and his implementation of its recommendations, without disclaimer, served as an adoption of the Report for the purposes of Rule 801(d)(2)(B)."); Computer Sys. Eng'g., Inc. v. Qantel Corp., 740 F.2d 59 (1st Cir. 1984) (Qantel's vice president gave a one-page document to plaintiff; adoptive admission of document); Pekelis v. Transcontinental & Western Air, Inc., 187 F.2d 122, 128 (2d Cir. 1951) (report of accident investigating board used by defendant as a basis for remedial measures and also filed with CAB is an adoptive admission); Oxley v. Linnton Plywood Assn., 284 P.2d 766, 776–77 (Or. 1955) (by including a timber report in preparing a registration statement filed with the SEC, defendant adopted it as his own).

[50] *Id.* at 1078.

[51] 515 N.E.2d 931 (Ohio App. 1986).

scientific papers as evidence. The court ruled the papers were admissible as adoptive admissions: "[T]he defendants used all of them to train their own personnel at seminars. Thus, they were statements made or adopted by the defendants and were not hearsay when the adverse party offered them as evidence."[52]

[B] Adoption by Silence

A party may adopt the statement of a third person by failing to deny or correct under circumstances in which it would be *natural to deny or correct the truth* of the statement. It is not sufficient that the statement was merely made in the presence of a party.[53] In other words, silence is not equivalent to assent. It needs to occur in circumstances where it would be natural to respond by denying or correcting the statement.[54]

In criminal cases, "troublesome questions have been raised by decisions holding that failure to deny is an admission: the inference is a fairly weak one, to begin with; silence may be motivated by advice of counsel or realization that 'anything you say may be used against you'; unusual opportunity is afforded to manufacture evidence; and encroachment upon the privilege against self-incrimination seems inescapably to be involved."[55] In *United States v. Hale*,[56] the Supreme Court stated that "in most circumstances silence is so ambiguous that it is of little probative force."[57]

In addition to the evidentiary issue, constitutional issues are involved when a suspect is *Mirandized*.[58]

[C] Correspondence

The adoption-by-silence rule may apply to correspondence, that is, the failure to answer or correct statements in a letter may be considered to be an adoption if, under the circumstances, it would have been natural to answer or object to the contents of the letter. As in all cases of adoption by silence, the surrounding circumstances are critical. Justice Holmes once wrote that a person

---

[52] *Id.* at 937.

[53] *See* United States v. Beckham, 968 F.2d 47, 52 (D.C. Cir. 1992) ("When Monroe told Officer Dunston that he could get another rock of crack from 'my buddy', Beckham immediately got up from his chair, walked over to a stash of crack that was packaged for distribution, and began to open it. By that action, Beckham indicated his endorsement of Monroe's statement.").

[54] *See* United States v. Henke, 222 F.3d 633, 642 (9th Cir. 2002) ("[C]ourt properly admitted Desaigoudar's out-of-court response — 'next question please' — to an accusation in a press conference that the defendants were 'cooking the books.' The district court found . . . that, under the circumstances, the natural response to such an accusation would be to address or deny it. It therefore admitted the statement as an adoptive admission.").

[55] Fed. R. Evid. 801 advisory committee's note.

[56] 422 U.S. 171 (1975).

[57] *Id.* at 176.

[58] For a discussion of these issues, *see supra* § 22.10[H] (constitutional issues — prior inconsistent statements).

cannot make evidence for himself by writing a letter containing the statements that he wishes to prove. He does not make the letter evidence by sending it to the party against whom he wishes to prove the facts. He no more can impose a duty to answer a charge than he can impose a duty to pay by sending goods. Therefore a failure to answer such adverse assertions in the absence of further circumstances making an answer requisite or natural has no effect as an admission.[59]

§ 32.08   Authorized Admissions: FRE 801(d)(2)(C)

Statements made by a person authorized by a party to speak for it are admissible as substantive evidence if offered against that party.[60] The rule governs only statements by agents who have *speaking authority* — *e.g.,* attorneys, partners, and corporate officers.[61] A different rule governs the admissibility of statements by agents who do not have speaking authority: Rule 801(d)(2)(D). (*See infra.*)

In-house statements. The rule covers statements made by agents to their principals ("in-house" statements) as well as statements made by agents to third persons.[62]

Proof of authority. At common law, before statements of an agent were admissible, the authority of the agent to speak must have been established by independent evidence.[63] In other words, this authority could not be proved by the statements themselves. In 1997, the federal rule was amended, rejecting this position: "The contents of the statement shall be considered but are not alone sufficient to establish the declarant's authority under subdivision (C). . . ."

---

[59] A.B. Leach & Co. v. Peirson, 275 U.S. 120, 128 (1927). *See also* Southern Stone Co. v. Singer, 665 F.2d 698, 703 (5th Cir. 1982) ("The mere failure to respond to a letter does not indicate an adoption unless it was reasonable under the circumstances for the sender to expect the recipient to respond and to correct erroneous assertions.").

[60] The firsthand knowledge and opinion rules do not apply to admissions. *See supra* § 32.05[C] (firsthand knowledge, competency & opinion rules).

[61] *See* Mahlandt v. Wild Canid Survival & Research Ctr., Inc., 588 F.2d 626, 631 (8th Cir. 1978) ("As to the entry in the records of a corporate meeting, the directors as primary officers of the corporation had the authority to include their conclusions in the record of the meeting. So the evidence would fall within 801(d)(2)(C) as to Wild Canid Survival and Research Center, Inc., and be admissible.").

[62] *See* Fed. R. Evid. 801 advisory committee's note ("No authority is required for the general proposition that a statement authorized by a party to be made should have the status of an admission by the party. However, the question arises whether only statements to third persons should be so regarded, to the exclusion of statements by the agent to the principal. The rule is phrased broadly so as to encompass both. While it may be argued that the agent authorized to make statements to his principal does not speak for him, communication to an outsider has not generally been thought to be an essential characteristic of an admission. Thus, a party's books or records are usable against him, without regard to any intent to disclose to third persons.") (citation omitted). *See also Mahlandt,* 588 F.2d at 631 (admitting in-house statements).

[63] *See* 4 Wigmore, Evidence § 1078 (Chadbourn rev. 1972).

§ 32.09 Agent Admissions: FRE 801(d)(2)(D)

Because a corporation can speak only through its employees, statements by corporate officials are considered admissions by a corporate defendant. Many common law cases had held, however, that statements of an agent without "speaking authority" were inadmissible on the ground that the agent had no authority to make admissions detrimental to the interests of her employer.[64] Rule 801(d)(2)(D) changes this result.[65] Statements by agents or servants (1) concerning a matter within the scope of their agency or employment and (2) made during the existence of the agency or employment relationship are admissible as substantive evidence if offered against the party.[66]

Within scope of agency or employment. The statement must relate to the declarant's employment responsibilities.[67] A truck driver's statements about a truck accident in which he was involved are admissible but not statements about a SEC investigation.

During time of employment. Statements by disgruntled employees after discharge are not admissible. They are not considered reliable.

Unidentified agent-declarant. If the agency relationship is established, the statement is admissible even if the agent remains unidentified.[68]

"In-house" statements. The rule applies to statements made by agents to their principals ("in-house" statements) as well as statements made to third persons.[69] Statements of an employee are sometimes admissible against

---

[64] A related provision, discussed in the preceding section, governs the admissibility of statements of agents who have "speaking authority." Virtually all statements admissible as authorized admissions under that provision are also admissible under this rule; the reverse, however, is not true.

[65] The firsthand knowledge and opinion rules do not apply to admissions. *See supra* § 32.05[C] (firsthand knowledge, competency & opinion rules). *See also Mahlandt,* 588 F.2d at 631 (firsthand knowledge not required).

[66] *See* Lippay v. Christos, 996 F.2d 1490, 1497 (3d Cir. 1993) ("Because the Federal Rules of Evidence do not define 'agent' or 'servant,' we believe that Congress intended Rule 801(d)(2)(D) 'to describe the traditional master-servant relationship as understood by common law agency doctrine.' Furthermore, given Congress' intent that the Federal Rules of Evidence have uniform nationwide application, we apply federal common law rules of agency, rather than relying on the agency law of the forum in determining whether Philbin's statement comes within the Rule.") (citation omitted).

[67] United States v. Photogrammetric Data Serv., Inc., 259 F.3d 229, 242–43 (4th Cir. 2001) ("There is no dispute that the statements Webb made to the government informant (a co-employee) and to the law enforcement agents concerned Webb's billing practices and procedures at PDS while he was employed as the manager of the photogram department. Thus, the statements concerned matters within the scope of Webb's employment with PDS, made during the existence of the employment relationship, and were admissible against PDS under Rule 801(d)(2)(D).").

[68] *See* Davis v. Mobil Oil Exploration and Prod. Southeast, Inc., 864 F.2d 1171, 1173–74 (5th Cir. 1989).

[69] *See also Mahlandt,* 588 F.2d at 630 (admitting in-house statements).

another employee,[70] provided the employee supervises the declarant's work.[71]

Proof of agency. In 1997, the federal rule was amended. The following sentence was added: "The contents of the statement shall be considered but are not alone sufficient to establish . . . the agency or employment relationship and scope thereof under subdivision (D)."

[A] Admissions by Police

Courts have held that statements by law enforcement officers are generally are not admissible against the prosecution under Rule 801(d)(1)(D).[72] "[C]ourts faced with this issue have refused to apply this provision to government employees testifying in criminal trials based on the rationale that no individual can bind the sovereign."[73] This rationale is unpersuasive, and the result is difficult to justify when viewed in light of the expansive exemption for coconspirator statements, which is discussed in the next section. It is difficult to distinguished the two situations, except in terms of who gains. Indeed, one commentator questioned whether equal protection rights are violated in this context.[74] In one case, however, the Sixth Circuit accepted the argument that a paid government informant was in essence an agent of a party opponent.[75]

[B] Admissions by Attorneys

The statement of an attorney may be admissible against the client as either an authorized admission, because the attorney usually has "speaking authority," or as an agent admission.[76]

---

[70] *See* Zaken v. Boerer, 964 F.2d 1319, 1323 (2d Cir. 1992) ("When the factors proving an agency relationship are present, the testimony should not be excluded simply because it is offered against a corporate employee rather than the company itself.").

[71] *See Lippay*, 996 F.2d at 1498 ("[F]ederal courts will not impute the statements of a declarant to a party-opponent who is merely the declarant's co-employee. Instead, an agency relationship is established only where the party-opponent personally 'directed [the declarant's] work on a continuing basis.'").

[72] *E.g.,* United States v. Kampiles, 609 F.2d 1233, 1246 (7th Cir. 1979) ("Because the agents of the Government are supposedly disinterested in the outcome of a trial and are traditionally unable to bind the sovereign, their statements seem less the product of the adversary process and hence less appropriately described as admissions of a party.") (citations omitted); United States v. Santos, 372 F.2d 177 (2d Cir. 1967).

[73] United States v. Prevatte, 16 F.3d. 767, 779 n. 9 (7th Cir. 1994).

[74] *See* Imwinkelried, *Of Evidence and Equal Protection: The Unconstitutionality of Excluding Government Agents Statements Offered as Vicarious Admissions Against the Prosecution,* 71 Minn. L. Rev. 269 (1986).

[75] United States v. Branham, 97 F.3d 835, 851 (6th Cir. 1996) ("Arguably, Cordle conversed with Branham on a regular basis in order to establish a trusting relationship. Whatever Cordle said during these conversations was in furtherance of that goal, and thus within the scope of the existing agency.").

[76] *See* United States v. GAF Corp., 928 F.2d 1253, 1259 (2d Cir. 1991).

In *United States v. McKeon*,[77] a prosecution expert concluded that a xerox machine located at the accused's wife's place of employment made photocopies associated with a conspiracy to export firearms. In opening statement, defense counsel stated that a defense expert would testify that this machine did not make these copies. The trial terminated in a mistrial during the prosecution case-in-chief, and the defense expert subsequently learned that his former teacher would be a prosecution expert at the retrial. At the retrial, the defense position had changed significantly. The defense opening statement in the earlier trial, was admitted as an admission against the accused.

> The expert testimony about the xerox machine promised by Kennedy defense counsel in the opening statement at the earlier trial was in support of a factual claim that Olive McKeon [the wife] had not copied the documents. Kennedy's opening argument at the later trial, stating that Olive McKeon had indeed copied the documents at the request of her husband, was facially and irreconcilably at odds with the earlier assertion.[78]

Prosecutors. The rule also applies to the prosecuting attorney.[79] In addition to agent admissions, these statements may also be adoptive admissions. In *United States v. Kattar*,[80] the First Circuit ruled that a government brief in a civil case, which contradicted a government witness, constituted an adoptive admission:

> The Justice Department here has, as clearly as possible, manifested its belief in the substance of the contested documents; it has submitted them to other federal courts to show the truth of the matter contained therein. We agree with Justice (then Judge) Stevens that the assertions made by the government in a formal prosecution (and, by analogy, a formal civil defense) "establish the position of the United States and not merely the views of its agents who participated therein."[81]

Other examples include affidavits,[82] search warrants,[83] bills of

---

[77] 738 F.2d 26 (2d Cir. 1984).

[78] *Id.* at 33.

[79] *See* United States v. Morgan, 581 F.2d 933, 937 n. 10 (D.C. Cir. 1978 ("The Federal Rules clearly contemplate that the federal government is a party-opponent of the defendant in criminal cases.").

[80] 840 F.2d 118 (1st Cir. 1988).

[81] *Id.* at 131. *See also* United States v. Blood, 806 F.2d 1218, 1221 (4th Cir. 1986) (statements by prosecution during voir dire would be binding against the government if they had constituted a clear and unambiguous admission).

[82] *See Morgan*, 581 F.2d at 938 ("Where the government has indicated in a sworn affidavit to a judicial officer that it believes particular statements are trustworthy, it may not sustain an objection to the subsequent introduction of those statements on grounds that they are hearsay.").

[83] *See* United States v. Ramirez, 894 F.2d 565, 570 (2d Cir. 1990) ("When the government advances a statement of its agent in a judicial proceeding to obtain a search warrant, the government has adopted the content of the statement, and a criminal defendant may introduce the statement as a party admission under Fed. R. Evid. 801(d)(2)(B).").

particulars,[84] and government manuals.[85]

[C] Admissions by Experts

In *Collins v. Wayne Corp.,*[86] the deposition testimony of an expert employed by a bus manufacturer to investigate an accident was admitted under Rule 801(d)(2)(C). The Fifth Circuit held that in giving the deposition, the expert was performing the function that the manufacturer had employed him to perform. A later case disagreed with this analysis.[87] Extending the rule to experts is troublesome because in theory, at least, the expert is suppose to provide an independent opinion.

§ 32.10   Coconspirator Admissions: FRE 801(d)(2)(E)

A conspirator's statement made during and in furtherance of the conspiracy is admissible as substantive evidence if offered against another conspirator.[88]

Rationale. Commentators have criticized the theory underlying the coconspirator exemption, a rationale that "is not altogether easy to grasp."[89] One went so far as to state that, "in terms of theory, the rule is an embarrassment. It seems to have been created by accident, and the one traditional explanation which survives does not convince."[90] Unlike other hearsay exceptions at common law, coconspirator statements were not "regarded as carrying some particular guarantee of trustworthiness."[91] The agency theory — "partners in crime" — is a fiction. The federal drafters acknowledged this but failed to provide an alternative theory to justify admissibility.[92]

---

[84] *See* United States v. GAF Corp., 928 F.2d 1253, 1260–61 (2d Cir. 1991) ("Confidence in the justice system cannot be affirmed if any party is free, wholly without explanation, to make a fundamental change in its version of the facts between trials, and then conceal this change from the final trier of the facts. A bill of particulars is prepared, reviewed, and presented by an agent of the United States.").

[85] *See* United States v. Van Griffin, 874 F.2d 634, 638 (9th Cir. 1989) ("We do not say that every publication of every branch of government can be treated as a party admission by the United States under Fed. R. Evid. 801(d)(2)(D).").

[86] 621 F.2d 777, 782 (5th Cir. 1980).

[87] Kirk v. Raymark Indust., Inc., 61 F.3d 147, 164 n. 20 (3d Cir. 1995) ("To the extent that *Collins* holds that an expert witness who is hired to testify on behalf of a party is automatically an agent of that party who called him and consequently his testimony can be admitted as non-hearsay in future proceedings, we reject this rule.").

[88] *See supra* § 32.05[C] (firsthand knowledge & opinion rules).

[89] Johnson, *The Unnecessary Crime of Conspiracy,* 61 Cal. L. Rev. 1137, 1183 (1973).

[90] Mueller, *The Federal Coconspirator Exception: Action, Assertion, and Hearsay,* 12 Hofstra L. Rev. 323, 324 (1984).

[91] Johnson, *supra* note 89, at 1183.

[92] Fed. R. Evid. 801(d)(2) advisory committee's note. *See also* Davenport, *The Confrontation Clause and the Co-Conspirator Exception in Criminal Prosecutions: A Functional Analysis,* 85 Harv. L. Rev. 1378, 1384 (1972) ("The co-conspirator exception has usually been supported by a variety of theories unrelated to the trustworthiness of the evidence itself.").

Coconspirator admissions are sometimes against the penal interest of the declarant, but nothing in the rule requires that the statement be against interest when made.[93] Moreover, Rule 804(b)(3) now recognizes an exception for statements against penal interest, and thus there is no need for a separate coconspirator exemption if the "against interest" notion is the underlying rationale. That exception, however, is more demanding than the coconspirator exemption because it requires the unavailability of the declarant.

Some commentators candidly admit that the principal justification for the exception is "necessity,"[94] but necessity may exist in the absence of reliability, which may mean that the most crucial evidence is the least trustworthy. In any event, what is clear is that the evidence rule is heavily influenced by the substantive crime of conspiracy.[95]

Confrontation. The Supreme Court has ruled that coconspirator admissions do not violate the Confrontation Clause.[96] These decisions are discussed in Chapter 36.

Requirements. There are three conditions for admissibility: (1) there must have been a conspiracy in which the defendant and declarant participated; (2) the statement must have been made during the course of the conspiracy; and (3) the statement must have been in furtherance of the conspiracy. If the statement was part of the initial agreement (the actus reus of conspiracy), the statement may be admissible under the verbal acts doctrine, and resort to this rule is unnecessary.[97]

[A] Proof of Conspiracy

Conspiracy charge. The crime of conspiracy need not be charged in the indictment.[98] Indeed, the rule also applies in civil cases.[99] In addition, an

---

[93] Johnson, *supra* note 89, at 1184 ("The authorities agree that admissions of the agent are admissible whether or not he thought the statements to be against his or his principal's interest at the time he made them.").

[94] *See* Levie, *Hearsay and Conspiracy: A Reexamination of the Co-Conspirators' Exception to the Hearsay Rule*, 52 Mich. L. Rev. 1159, 1166 (1954) ("Conspiracy is a hard thing to prove. Conspirators' declarations are admitted out of necessity.").

[95] *See generally* Dressler, Understanding Criminal Law ch. 29 (3d ed. 2001).

[96] Bourjaily v. United States, 483 U.S. 171 (1987); United States v. Inadi, 475 U.S. 387 (1986).

[97] *See supra* § 31.06[B] (verbal acts).

[98] *See* United States v. Lara, 181 F.3d. 183, 196 (1st Cir. 1999) ("Subject to relevancy and similar considerations, out-of-court statements of a declarant coconspirator, if made during and in furtherance of a conspiracy, are admissible for the truth of the matter asserted, regardless of whether the conspiracy furthered is charged or uncharged, and regardless of whether it is identical to or different from the crime that the statements are offered to prove.") (citations omitted). *See also* United States v. Marino, 277 F.3d 11, 26 (1st Cir. 2002) ("We have already ruled that another conspiracy, larger than the one charged at trial, may provide the basis for the admission of the coconspirator's statements.").

[99] *See* S. Rep. No. 1277, 93d Cong., 2d Sess. ("While the rule refers to a co-conspirator, it is this committee's understanding that the rule is meant to carry forward the universally

acquittal of the conspiracy charge does not affect admissibility.[100]

Rule 801(d)(2)(E) applies only if the offering party establishes the existence of a conspiracy, which requires an agreement between two or more persons (the actus reus) with an intent to commit a crime. With one exception, the statement must have been made while both the declarant and the defendant were members of the conspiracy.[101] Hence, if the defendant withdraws from the conspiracy before the objectives are achieved or abandoned, statements made by other conspirators after the withdrawal are not admissible against the defendant. Moreover, the arrest of the declarant usually terminates his participation in the conspiracy and makes his post-arrest statements to the police inadmissible against the defendant.[102] Similarly, the defendant's arrest usually terminates his participation in the conspiracy and makes subsequent statements by coconspirators inadmissible against him.[103]

[B] "During the course" Requirement

Rule 801(d)(2)(E) requires that the statement be made "during the course" of the conspiracy, a requirement recognized at common law. Statements of coconspirators made after the conspiracy ends (i.e., "concealment phase" statements) are not admissible. In other words, statements made after the objectives have been achieved, but while the conspirators are attempting to avoid detection are inadmissible.[104] There is some leeway for the prosecutor to define the objectives of the conspiracy. For example, "unlike most other criminal conspiracies, concealment is actually one of the main criminal objectives of an arson-for-profit scheme, because it facilitates

---

accepted doctrine that a joint venturer is considered as a coconspirator for the purposes of this rule even though no conspiracy has been charged."), reprinted in 1974 U.S.C.C.A.N. 7051, 7073.

[100] See United States v. Peralta, 941 F.2d 1003, 1005–07 (9th Cir. 1991).

[101] The exception involves the defendant who joins an on-going conspiracy, in which case the defendant is deemed to have adopted or ratified all prior statements made by the other conspirators. See United States v. United States Gypsum Co., 333 U.S. 364, 393 (1948); United States v. Lampley, 68 F.3d. 1296, 1301 (11th Cir. 1995) ("Although Lampley did not join the conspiracy until Tarver contacted him, which was sometime after December 7, 1990, all of the tapes were admissible because a 'declaration of one co-conspirator is admissible against members of the conspiracy who joined after the statement was made.' . . . Thus, the statements on all of the tapes were properly admitted because a conspiracy existed when the statements were made and Lampley subsequently joined that conspiracy.") (citations omitted); United States v. Brown, 943 F.2d 1246, 1255 (10th Cir. 1991) (concluding that the "prevailing view among the circuits is that previous statements made by co-conspirators are admissible against a defendant who subsequently joins the conspiracy").

[102] See Wong Sun v. United States, 371 U.S. 471 (1963); Fiswick v. United States, 329 U.S. 211 (1946).

[103] A conspiracy, however, could continue even while a defendant is incarcerated.

[104] Fed. R. Evid. 801 advisory committee's note ("The rule is consistent with the position of the Supreme Court in denying admissibility to statements made after the objectives of the conspiracy have either failed or been achieved.") (citing Krulewitch v. United States, 336 U.S. 440 (1949); Wong Sun v. United States, 371 U.S. 471, 490 (1963)). See also Anderson v. United States, 417 U.S. 211, 218 (1974); Dutton v. Evans, 400 U.S. 74, 81 (1970).

the primary objective of fraudulently acquiring insurance proceeds."[105] In other words, the conspiracy does not end with arson; it continues until the insurance is collected.

This rule does not govern the admissibility of *acts* engaged in during the concealment phase. Such acts may be admissible if relevant to prove the existence of the conspiracy.[106]

FIGURE 32-1

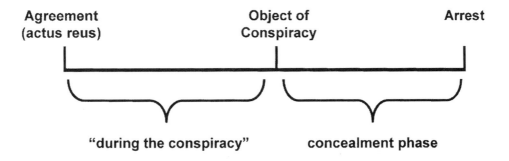

[C] **"In furtherance" Requirement**

The statement must be made "in furtherance of the conspiracy." Statements that are only casual admissions or merely inform the listener of the declarant's activities are not made in furtherance of the conspiracy.[107] Statements that provide assurance, serve to maintain trust and cohesiveness among the conspirators, or inform each conspirator of the current status of the conspiracy do *further* the ends of the conspiracy and are admissible. Similarly, statements that seek to induce someone into joining the conspiracy or assisting the conspirators in meeting their objectives are in furtherance of the conspiracy.

[D] **Procedure Issues**

Independent proof. At common law, the conspiracy had to have been established by independent proof — *i.e.*, the statement itself could not be used to determine whether a conspiracy existed. However, in *Bourjaily v. United States*,[108] the Supreme Court ruled that Rule 104(a) abolished the independent proof requirement. A 1997 amendment codified this ruling: "The contents of the statement shall be considered but are not alone

---

[105] United States v. Gajo, 290 F.3d 922, 928 (7th Cir. 2002).

[106] Anderson v. United States, 417 U.S. 211, 219–22 (1974); Lutwak v. United States, 344 U.S. 604, 617 (1953).

[107] *See Gajo*, 290 F.3d at 929 ("We consider statements to be 'in furtherance of' the conspiracy when they promote the conspiracies objectives, *i.e.,* when the statements are 'part of the information flow between conspirators to help each perform a role.'") (citations omitted).

[108] 483 U.S. 171 (1987).

sufficient to establish . . . the existence of the conspiracy and the participation therein of the declarant and the party against whom the statement is offered under subdivision (E)." The defendant's own admissions (admissible under Rule 801(d)(2)(A)), are independent evidence and thus may be used to establish the conspiracy.

Standard of proof. In *Bourjaily*, [109] the Supreme Court also ruled that the trial court in determining the admissibility of coconspirator admissions must use the "preponderance of the evidence" standard of proof.

Jury's role. Even if the statement is admitted, a conspiracy defendant still may introduce evidence before the jury challenging the existence of the conspiracy. [110] There is no reason for the jury to be informed of the judge's admissibility decision; the jury simply hears the evidence. [111] The jury, of course, must apply the beyond-a-reasonable-doubt standard when deciding whether the accused has committed the crime of conspiracy if charged.

Order of proof. The existence of the conspiracy, as well as the defendant's and declarant's participation in it, should be established before a coconspirator statement is admitted, [112] but this is not required. However, if the evidence is not introduced by the end of the prosecution's case, a mistrial may be required. [113]

§ 32.11 Key Points

Rule 801(d) defines some statements as nonhearsay. There are two categories: (1) certain prior statements and (2) admissions of a party-opponent.

Prior Inconsistent Statements: FRE 801(d)(1)(A)

There are two types of prior inconsistent statements in the Federal Rules. Prior inconsistent statements that do not satisfy the requirements of Rule

---

[109] 483 U.S. at 171–72.

[110] *See supra* § 7.06 (weight & credibility).

[111] *See* United States v. Hartley, 678 F.2d 961, 975 (11th Cir. 1982) ("It would have been improper for the judge to have done so. 'Such an instruction can serve only to alert the jury that the judge has determined that a conspiracy involving the defendant has been proven by a preponderance of the evidence.' ").

[112] *See* United States v. Centracchio, 265 F.3d 518, 522 n. 1 (7th Cir. 2001) ("The court has a duty to screen proposed co-conspirator statements for admissibility. A recognized way of bringing such issues to the court's attention is through the filing of a pre-trial proffer pursuant to United States v. Santiago, 582 F.2d 1128 (7th Cir. 1978)."); United States v. Sinclair, 109 F.3d 1527, 1533 (10th Cir. 1997) ("the 'strongly preferred order of proof' in determining the admissibility of an alleged coconspirator's statement is to first hold a hearing outside the presence of the jury to determine whether the party offering the statements has established the existence of a conspiracy by a preponderance of the evidence").

[113] *See* United States v. Wood, 851 F.2d 185, 187 (8th Cir. 1988) (trial court may declare a mistrial unless a cautionary instruction to the jury to disregard the statement would suffice to cure any prejudice).

801(d)(1)(A) are still admissible for impeachment; Rule 613 governs the admissibility of these statements. Four conditions must be satisfied for admissibility under Rule 801: (1) the declarant must testify, subject to cross-examination, at the current trial; (2) the prior statement must be inconsistent with the witness's trial testimony; (3) the prior statement must have been given under oath subject to penalty of perjury; and (4) the prior statement must have been made "at a trial, hearing, or other proceeding, or in a deposition."

"Other proceedings" defined. Statements made at a prior trial, a suppression hearing, a preliminary hearing, a deposition, or any other proceeding at which testimony is taken under oath and subject to penalty of perjury qualify under Rule 801(d)(1)(a). Grand jury testimony also qualifies. In contrast, stationhouse statements to the police or affidavits to government officials are not admissible. Formalized proceedings with transcripts are typically required.

Prior Consistent Statements: FRE 801(d)(1)(B)

Prior consistent statements are admissible as *substantive* evidence if "offered to rebut an express or implied charge of recent fabrication or improper influence or motive." The witness must be subject to cross-examination at trial. In *Tome v. United States*, the Supreme Court held that the rule applies only when the statements are made before the alleged fabrication or improper influence or motive arose — premotive requirement.

Statements of Identification: FRE 801(d)(1)(C)

A witness's prior statement of identification of a person after "perceiving" that person is admissible as substantive evidence. An identification made at a lineup, show-up (one-on-one confrontation), photographic display, or prior hearing falls within the rule, *i.e.,* "That's the person who did it." Because prior identifications are admissible as substantive evidence, the rule applies whether or not the witness makes an in-court identification. So long as the witness is "subject to cross-examination concerning the statement" at trial, the testimony of other witnesses who were present at the time of the identification is admissible. For example, a robbery victim may have identified the robber at a lineup, at which time the robber wore a beard. If the victim cannot positively identify the defendant at trial because the beard had been shaved, the lineup identification is nevertheless admissible through the testimony of a police officer who was present.

Admissions of Party-opponents: Overview

Rule 801(d)(2) exempts admissions of a party-opponent from the hearsay rule by defining admissions as nonhearsay. Under the common law, an admission was classified as an exception to the hearsay rule. The Federal Rules do not change this result; admissions are admissible, although under a different theory. The rule recognizes five types of party admissions: (1) individual admissions, (2) adoptive admissions, (3) authorized admissions, (4) agent admissions, and (5) coconspirator admissions.

Evidential & judicial admissions distinguished. Rule 801(d)(2) does not govern the use of judicial admissions, such as admissions in pleadings or in stipulations. Unlike evidential admissions which can be rebutted at trial, a party is bound by its judicial admissions.

Firsthand knowledge & opinion rules. Neither the firsthand knowledge nor opinion rule applies to admissions of a party-opponent.

Individual Admissions: FRE 801(d)(2)(A)

Statements of a party, in either her individual or representative capacity, are admissible as substantive evidence if offered *against* that party. A party cannot introduce her own statements under this rule. An individual admission is *any* statement made by a party at *any* time if (1) relevant and (2) offered by the opposing party — *e.g.*, guilty pleas, confessions, deposition testimony, or statements to friends.

"Declarations against interest" distinguished. Party admissions are often confused with the hearsay exception relating to declarations against interest, Rule 804(b)(3). There are several differences between the two rules. First, the firsthand knowledge rule does not apply to admissions but does to declarations against interest. Second, admissions need not have been against the interest of the declarant when made. Thus, a statement that is self-serving when made by a party may later be introduced at trial by an opposing party, whereas the declaration against interest exception turns on the adverse nature of the statement when made. Third, the declarant need not be unavailable for an admission to be introduced. In contrast, a declaration against interest is not admissible unless the declarant is unavailable at the time of trial. Finally, declarations against interest need not be made by a party.

Adoptive Admissions: FRE 801(d)(2)(B)

A statement that a party "adopts" is admissible as substantive evidence if offered against that party — *e.g.*, adoption by use.

Adoption by Silence. A party may adopt the statement of a third person by failing to deny or correct under circumstances in which it would have been *natural to deny or correct the truth* of the statement. It is not sufficient that the statement was merely made in the presence of a party.

Authorized Admissions: FRE 801(d)(2)(C)

Statements made by a person authorized by a party to speak of it are admissible as substantive evidence if offered against that party. The rule governs only statements by agents who have *speaking authority* — *e.g.*, attorneys, partners, and corporate officers. In-house statements are included. "The contents of the statement shall be considered but are not alone sufficient to establish the declarant's authority under subdivision (C)."

Agent Admissions: FRE 801(d)(2)(D)

Statements by agents or servants (1) concerning a matter within the scope of their agency or employment and (2) made during the existence of the agency or employment relationship are admissible as substantive evidence if offered against the party. In-house statements are included.

Courts have held that statements by law enforcement officers are generally not admissible against the prosecution under the rule. However, statements of an attorney may be admissible against the client as either authorized admissions, because the attorney usually has "speaking authority," or as agent admissions.

Coconspirator Admissions: FRE 801(d)(2)(E)

A conspirator's statement made during and in furtherance of the conspiracy is admissible as substantive evidence if offered against another conspirator. To be admissible, three conditions must be satisfied: (1) there must have been a conspiracy in which the defendant and declarant participated; (2) the statement must have been made during the course of the conspiracy; and (3) the statement must have been in furtherance of the conspiracy.

Chapter 33

HEARSAY EXCEPTIONS: FRE 803

§ 33.01 Introduction

Exceptions to the hearsay rule are found in Rules 803, 804, and 807. This chapter discusses Rule 803, which specifies twenty-three exceptions that apply whether or not the declarant is available. Rule 804 specifies five exceptions that apply only if the declarant is unavailable; it is examined in the next chapter. Rule 807, the residual exception, is considered in chapter 35. In addition, exemptions to the hearsay rule, which function like exceptions, are explored in chapter 32.

There is no need to look for an exception until you first determine that the statement is in fact hearsay. In practice, always argue in the alternative — *e.g.*, "Your Honor. The statement is not hearsay, but if it is, it falls within the excited utterance exception." The same is true of the exceptions — argue in the alternative. There is an overlap between many of the exceptions, so a statement may fall in more than one. Moreover, the residual exception (Rule 807) is always a possible backup argument, but it requires notice.

§ 33.02 Rationale for Hearsay Exceptions

Hearsay exceptions are based on some *circumstantial guarantee of trustworthiness* that is thought to warrant admissibility notwithstanding the lack of cross-examination. Recall the hearsay dangers: perception, memory, narration, and sincerity risks.[1] The reduction or elimination of one or more of these risks typically supports an exception. Sincerity dangers, for example, are reduced or eliminated with excited utterances (Rule 803(2)) because the declarant's faculties are suspended while under the influence of a startling event.[2] There may be more than one justification for an exception. For instance, there is also not much of a memory risk with excited utterances because the statement closely follows the event. The rationale for each exception is critical because the requirements of an exception track its rationale.

Most exceptions are also supported by a necessity or practical convenience argument.[3] The necessity rationale is clearly present in the Rule 804

---

[1] *See supra* § 31.02 (rationale for hearsay rule).

[2] Reduced sincerity risks also support the exceptions for (1) present sense impression (Rule 803(1)), (2) dying declarations (Rule 804(b)(2)), and (3) declarations against interest (Rule 802(b)(3)), among others.

[3] Wigmore argued that all exceptions were based on these two considerations: "a circumstantial probability of trustworthiness, and a necessity, for the evidence." 5 Wigmore, Evidence § 1420, at 251 (Chadbourn rev. 1974). According to Wigmore, the guarantee of trustworthiness

exceptions, because the unavailability of the declarant is required as a condition of admissibility. The Rule 803 exceptions, however, also may be justified upon a modified necessity argument, that is, the hearsay statement is thought to be superior to the declarant's trial testimony.[4] Business[5] and public records[6] are examples; the possibility that the person who made the records will remember the record is typically remote.

§ 33.03   Firsthand Knowledge & Opinion Rules

Several of the exceptions recognized in Rule 803 specifically require firsthand knowledge on the part of the declarant.[7] For other exceptions, the rule is silent. Nevertheless, firsthand knowledge is generally a requirement for all exceptions.[8]

The application of the opinion rule to hearsay statements is discussed with Rule 701.[9] In a nutshell, it makes no sense to apply the opinion rule to out-of-court statements.

§ 33.04   Present Sense Impressions: FRE 803(1)

Rationale. The reliability of present sense impressions rests upon the declarant's *lack of time to fabricate*, which reduces the risk of insincerity.[10] Prior to the Federal Rules, this was not a well-recognized exception. In one of the few pre-Rules cases, *Houston Oxygen Co. v. Davis*,[11] the court held

---

for every exception is based upon some "practicable substitute for the ordinary test of cross-examination. We see that under certain circumstances the probability of accuracy and trustworthiness of statement is practically sufficient, if not quite equivalent to that of statements tested in the conventional manner. This circumstantial probability of trustworthiness is found in a variety of circumstances sanctioned by judicial practice; and it is usually from one of these salient circumstances that the exception takes its name." *Id.* at 253.

[4] Wigmore explained that the "assertion may be such that we cannot expect, again, or at this time, to get evidence of the same value from the same or other sources. This appears more or less fully in the exception for spontaneous declarations [excited utterances], for reputation, and in part elsewhere. Here we are not threatened with the entire loss of a person's evidence, but merely of some valuable source of evidence. The necessity is not so great; perhaps hardly a necessity, only an expediency or convenience, can be predicated." 5 Wigmore, Evidence § 1421, at 253 (Chadbourn rev. 1974).

[5] Fed. R. Evid. 803(6).

[6] Fed. R. Evid. 803(8).

[7] *E.g.,* Fed. R. Evid. 803(1) (present sense impressions); Fed. R. Evid. 803(6) (business records).

[8] *See* Fed. R. Evid. 803 advisory committee's note ("In a hearsay situation, the declarant is, of course, a witness, and neither this rule nor Rule 804 dispenses with the requirement of firsthand knowledge. It may appear from his statement or be inferable from circumstances.") (citing Fed. R. Evid. 602).

[9] *See supra* § 23.03[E] (application to out-of-court statements).

[10] Fed. R. Evid. 803 advisory committee's note ("The underlying theory of Exception (1) is that substantial contemporaneity of event and statement negative the likelihood of deliberate or conscious misrepresentation."). *See* Waltz, *The Present Sense Impression Exception to the Rule Against Hearsay: Origins and Attributes,* 66 Iowa L. Rev. 869 (1981).

[11] 161 S.W.2d 474 (Tex. 1942). As plaintiff's car past declarant's car, the declarant said:

that the statement was "sufficiently spontaneous to save it from the suspicion of being manufactured evidence. There was no time for a calculated statement." In addition, the time requirement — "substantial contemporaneity" — eliminates any problem associated with defects in the declarant's ability to remember the event.

Rule 803(1) requires: (1) a statement describing or explaining an event or condition, (2) about which the declarant had firsthand knowledge,[12] and (3) made at the time the declarant was perceiving the event or immediately thereafter.[13] The trial court decides admissibility under Rule 104(a).

[A] Time Requirement

The statement must have been made "while the declarant was perceiving the event or condition, or immediately thereafter." In other words, the statement must be nearly contemporaneous with the perception of the event.[14] As the federal drafters noted, "With respect to the time element, Exception (1) recognizes that in many, if not most, instances precise contemporaneity is not possible, and hence a slight lapse is allowable."[15] We are talking "minutes" here.

"They must have been drunk, we will find them somewhere on the road wrecked if they keep that rate of speed up." Shortly thereafter declarant came to a traffic accident, in which plaintiff's car was involved.

[12] See Hynes v. Coughlin, 79 F.3d 285, 294 (2d Cir. 1996) (Exception "inapplicable because, inter alia, LaBoy did not see the start of the Green Haven incident. Further, even had she seen it, there was no indication that the report was made at, or immediately after, the time of the event as is required for admission as a present-sense impression."); Bemis v. Edwards, 45 F.3d 1369, 1373–74 (9th Cir. 1995) ("Estep's proximity to the scene at the time of the incident provided some circumstantial evidence of firsthand knowledge, which ordinarily may be sufficient to satisfy the foundational requirement in the context of a statement by a phone caller. . . . The district court, however, correctly noted that the record in this case gives an articulable basis to suspect that Estep did not witness the events he described, but instead had relayed to the 911 operator descriptions by other people who had been observing from the windows of Estep's house. Not only did Estep admit at one point that he could not describe what was happening outside, but he also could be heard repeating the words of an unidentified voice in the background."). See supra § 33.03 (firsthand knowledge & opinion rules).

[13] See United States v. Ruiz, 249 F.3d 643, 646 (7th Cir. 2001) ("Courts have agreed on three principal criteria for the admission of statements pursuant to this rule: (1) the statement must describe an event or condition without calculated narration; (2) the speaker must have personally perceived the event or condition described; and (3) the statement must have been made while the speaker was perceiving the event or condition, or immediately thereafter.").

[14] See United States v. Hawkins, 59 F.3d 723, 730 (8th Cir. 1995) ("Ms. Hawkins' 911 call was placed with sufficient contemporaneity to the underlying events to be admissible under Rule 803(1). The occupants of apartment 204 placed a 911 call at approximately 1:07 a.m. complaining about a disturbance in apartment 304. Ms. Hawkins placed her 911 call at approximately 1:14 a.m. from a nearby SuperAmerica convenience store. Further, Ms. Hawkins stated that 'my husband *just* pulled a gun out on me.' "), vac'd on other grounds, 516 U.S. 1168 (1996); United States v. Cain, 587 F.2d 678, 681 (5th Cir. 1979) ("The distances and time lapses involved make it impossible to determine whether the declaration by the 'CB'er' was made immediately following the observation or not, but the chances that it was are slim.").

[15] Fed. R. Evid. 803 advisory committee's note. See also Hilyer v. Howat Concrete Co., 578 F.2d 422, 426 n. 7 (D.C. Cir. 1978) (45 minute time lapse too long).

[B] Subject Matter Requirement

Under Rule 803(1), the statement must describe or explain an event or condition. This requirement follows from the theory underlying the exception — lack of time to fabricate. Statements beyond descriptions or explanations indicate that the declarant has had sufficient time to think about the event.

[C] Verification

One of the guarantees of trustworthiness upon which the present sense impression exception was originally thought to be based was verification, *i.e.,* the person to whom the statement was made (the testifying witness) would be in a position to verify the statement. But if the witness heard the statement but did not perceive the event, this safeguard is not present — *e.g.,* a 911 telephone conversation unless the 911 operator can hear the event (*e.g.,* fight) in the background. There is no verification requirement in Rule 803(1).

§ 33.05 Excited Utterances: FRE 803(2)

The excited utterance exception had long been recognized by the common law, although rarely by that name; early cases treated such statements as res gestae,[16] and the later cases used the term "spontaneous exclamations."[17]

Rationale. The reliability of excited utterances is based upon the declarant's *lack of capacity to fabricate*: "a condition of excitement which temporarily stills the capacity of reflection and produces utterances free of conscious fabrication."[18] In addition, reduced memory risk is a secondary justification. Nevertheless, the stress of an exciting event, especially if the declarant is a participant rather than merely an eyewitness, often enhances the risk of misperception.[19]

Rule 803(2) requires: (1) a startling event; (2) a statement relating to that event; (3) made by a declarant with firsthand knowledge; and (4) made while the declarant was under the stress of the excitement caused by the event. The differences between this exception and the present sense

---

[16] *See supra* § 31.14 (res gestae).

[17] *See* Slough, *Res Gestae,* 2 Kan. L. Rev. 41 (1954); Hutchins & Slesinger, *Some Observations on the Law of Evidence — Spontaneous Exclamations,* 28 Colum. L. Rev. 432 (1928).

[18] Fed. R. Evid. 803 advisory committee's note (citing 6 Wigmore, Evidence § 1747, at 135 (Chadbourn rev. 1976)).

[19] The federal drafters acknowledged this criticism. Fed. R. Evid. 803 advisory committee's note ("excitement impairs accuracy of observation as well as eliminating conscious fabrication"). *See also* Hutchins & Slesinger, *supra,* note 17 at 439 ("What the emotion gains by way of overcoming the desire to lie, it loses by impairing the declarant's power of observation."). *See also* Loftus, Eyewitness Testimony 33 (1979) (discussing the effect of stress on perception); Stewart, *Perception, Memory, and Hearsay: A Criticism of Present Law and the Proposed Federal Rules of Evidence,* 1970 Utah L. Rev. 1, 27.

impression exception are examined below. The trial court determines the admissibility of excited utterances under Rule 104(a).

[A] "Startling Event" Requirement

The startling event requirement follows from the theory underlying the exception — without a startling event, the declarant's capacity to reflect and fabricate will not be suspended. In other words, there must be some occurrence startling enough to still reflective faculties.[20] Merely being "upset" is not sufficient. Assaults and traffic accidents are typical examples.[21] In some cases the revival of a memory of a startling event results in a stressful excitement. For example, in one case, a child-witness's return, three days later, to the scene where he witnessed his brother's murder "was a startling event which produced in him a nervous excitement and . . . this nervous excitement stilled his reflective faculties."[22]

Proof. Proof of the startling event may consist of extrinsic evidence of the event, including the condition and appearance of the declarant.[23] In addition, the utterance itself may establish the existence of a startling event.[24] Consideration of the statement for this purpose is permissible under Rule 104(a).[25]

---

[20] *See* United States v. Brown, 254 F.3d 454, 459 (3d Cir. 2001) ("observation of a man wielding a firearm qualified as a startling occasion"); David v. Pueblo Supermarket, 740 F.2d 230, 235 (3d Cir. 1984) (statement at time of slip and fall accident was "I told them to clean it up about two hours ago — an hour and a half ago."; Declarant "saw a woman who was eight months pregnant fall directly on her stomach. This would reasonably qualify as a 'startling occasion.' Second, the substance of her statement was a matter of sensory perception, it was unsolicited and it was made within seconds of the fall. It was therefore reasonable for the trial court to conclude that Jacobs' statement was made before she had time to fabricate.").

[21] *See* United States v. Moore, 791 F.2d 566, 571 n. 2 (7th Cir. 1986) ("Although startling events are frequently totally unexpected happenings such as an accident or act of criminal conduct, they need not be, so long as the event actually has a startling impact on the declarant.").

[22] State v. Brown, 679 N.E.2d 361, 373 (Ohio App. 1996). The court also noted that the child's statements were made "within minutes" of arriving back at the crime scene.

[23] *See Brown*, 254 F.3d at 459 ("Academic commentators tend to agree that the hearsay statement itself is sufficient proof of the exciting event without resort to independent corroborating evidence, in both theory and practice. Most jurisdictions also find the statement in itself sufficient. Similarly, many courts have held that the appearance, behavior and condition of the declarant may establish, without other independent evidence, that a startling event occurred."); *Moore*, 791 F.2d at 570–71 ("The appearance, behavior and condition of the declarant may establish that a startling event occurred. Further, the declaration itself may establish that a startling event occurred.") (citations omitted).

[24] Fed. R. Evid. 803 advisory committee's note ("Whether proof of the startling event may be made by the statement itself is largely an academic question, since in most cases there is present at least circumstantial evidence that something of a startling nature must have occurred. Nevertheless, on occasion the only evidence may be the content of the statement itself, and rulings that it may be sufficient are described as 'increasing.' ") (citing Slough, *Spontaneous Statements and State of Mind*, 46 Iowa L. Rev. 224, 246 (1961)).

[25] Fed. R. Evid. 803 advisory committee's note ("the judge is not limited by the hearsay rule in passing upon preliminary questions of fact"). *See supra* § 7.02[A] (application of evidence rules to preliminary questions of admissibility).

[B] "Under Stress" Requirement

The statement must have been made "while the declarant was under the stress of excitement caused by the event or condition." This requirement follows from the underlying theory of the exception; unless the declarant is speaking while under the influence of the event, her capacity to reflect and fabricate will not be suspended. The statement itself may indicate that the declarant was under the stress of excitement.[26] Many courts apply a more expansive interpretation of the rule in child abuse cases.[27] Several factors should be considered: "(1) The lapse of time between the event and the declarations; (2) the age of the declarant; (3) the physical and mental state of the declarant; (4) the characteristics of the event; (5) the subject matter of the statements."[28]

Time requirement. There is no explicit "time element" for the rule.[29] The statement may be admissible even if not contemporaneous with its exciting cause.[30] Statements made after a substantial time has elapsed may be admissible so long as the declarant remained under the influence of the exciting event. "[A] period of unconsciousness, even an extended period, does not necessarily destroy the effect of a startling event upon the mind of the declarant for the purpose of satisfying the excited-utterance exception to the hearsay rule."[31]

Response to questioning. A statement made in response to a question may fit within the exception if made under the stress of the startling event.[32]

---

[26] *See Brown*, 254 F.3d at 459 ("[B]ecause the declarants appeared to be 'very excited,' 'very nervous' and 'hopping around,' and given that approximately one minute had passed between the startling occasion and the declarants' statements to Officer Hughes . . ., such statements were made without the opportunity to reflect and fabricate."); *Moore*, 791 F.2d at 571 ("just like jumping up and down" and talking "[a]s if she had won a million dollars in a lottery").

[27] *See* Haggins v. Warden, Fort Pillow State Farm, 715 F.2d 1050, 1058 (6th Cir. 1983) ("[A] court must take into account other factors that could affect spontaneity. For example, the declarant's age or physical or mental condition might indicate that a statement is not the result of reflection even if it was made some time after the exciting event. . . . In this case, the hearsay statements were made by a four year old child an hour to an hour and a half after she suffered very serious injuries [rape]. There is testimony that at the time the statements were made, she was still suffering from the effects of the event. She was bleeding and in critical condition.").

[28] *See* Morgan v. Foretich, 846 F.2d 941, 947 (4th Cir. 1988).

[29] "Under Exception (2) the standard of measurement is the duration of the state of excitement. 'How long can excitement prevail? Obviously there are no pat answers and the character of the transaction or event will largely determine the significance of the time factor.'" Fed. R. Evid. 803 advisory committee's note (quoting Slough, *Spontaneous Statements and State of Mind*, 46 Iowa L. Rev. 224, 243 (1961)).

[30] *See* United States v. Scarpa, 913 F.2d 993, 1017 (2d Cir. 1990) ("There is little doubt that at the time Leon gave the statements to Detective Rodenburg [five or six hours later], he was still under the stress of excitement caused by his beating at the candy store, and by his sister's screams when DeCarlo appeared at the hospital.").

[31] State v. Wallace, 524 N.E.2d 466, 470 (Ohio 1988) (statement made 15 hours after the event during which time declarant was unconscious).

[32] *See* United States v. Joy, 192 F.3d 761, 767 (7th Cir. 1999) ("The fact that Paul Joy was

In one case, nods by a victim who was intubated and therefore unable to speak were held admissible.[33]

[C]   Declarants; "Unidentified" Declarants

The declarant may be a participant in the event — for example, the victim of an assault or the driver in an automobile accident. The declarant may also be a bystander.[34] If the bystander-declarant is unidentified, admissibility of the statement requires close scrutiny.[35] For example, the firsthand knowledge rule must be satisfied,[36] although the opportunity to observe may be inferred from the circumstances. The federal drafters noted, "[W]hen declarant is an unidentified bystander, the cases indicate hesitancy in upholding the statement alone as sufficient, a result which would under appropriate circumstances be consistent with the rule."[37]

This issue is sometimes known as the "phantom" witness problem. This term can be used in two different ways. A different problem arises if trial counsel is challenging the existence of a declarant, not just the declarant's

---

answering questions, rather than giving a spontaneous narrative, does not indicate that he was not excited when he provided the answers. . . . On the contrary, it is possible for someone to be too excited to volunteer pertinent information (as Paul Joy appeared to be), and thus the inherent 'guarantee of truthfulness' supporting the admission of excited utterances applies equally to declarations made in response to an inquiry. Importantly, there is no 'absolute spontaneity' requirement to the excited utterance exception to the hearsay rule.") (citation omitted); Territory of Guam v. Cepeda, 69 F.3d 369, 372 (9th Cir. 1995) ("The fact that a statement is made in response to a question is one factor to weigh in considering the statement's admissibility, but it does not per se bar admission. Instead, we must also consider various other factors, including timing, age of the declarant, characteristics of the event, and the subject matter of the statements.").

[33] State v. Simko, 644 N.E.2d 345 (Ohio 1994). She was questioned by a police detective, who testified to her nods. The Court stated: "Given that the victim was unable to speak because of the intubation in her throat, the questions posed to her by the detective could certainly be characterized as leading. However, the questioning by the detective does not appear to be coercive, and the victim could have readily shook her head 'no' to any of the questions, since the detective described her as being 'alert' and 'aware of what was going on.' " Id. at 352.

[34] See Fed. R. Evid. 803 advisory committee's note ("Participation by the declarant is not required.").

[35] See Miller v. Keating, 754 F.2d 507, 510 (3d Cir. 1985) ("We do not conclude, however, that statements by unidentified declarants are ipso facto inadmissible under Fed. R. Evid. 803(2). Such statements are admissible if they otherwise meet the criteria of 803(2). [However,] the unidentifiability of the declarant is germane to the admissibility determination. A party seeking to introduce such a statement carries a burden heavier than where the declarant is identified to demonstrate the statement's circumstantial trustworthiness. At minimum, when the declarant of an excited utterance is unidentified, it becomes more difficult to satisfy the established case law requirements for admission of a statement under Fed. R. Evid. 803(2). . . . Partly because the declarant is unidentified, however, problems arise with . . . personal knowledge and spontaneity.").

[36] See supra § 33.03 (firsthand knowledge & opinion rules).

[37] Fed R. Evid. 803 advisory committee's note. See also Miller, 754 F.2d at 510 ("The circumstances external to the statement itself not only fail to demonstrate that the declarant was in a position to have seen what happened, they also fail to show that the declarant was excited when he spoke.").

identity. This is not a *hearsay* problem because counsel can cross-examine the witness who is claiming to be relating the hearsay statement. In other words, if counsel is attacking the credibility of the witness, not the declarant, there is no hearsay issue. The witness can be cross-examined.

[D] Subject Matter Requirement

Rule 803(2) requires that the statement "relate" to a startling event.[38] This requirement is simply a refinement of the "under the stress of the excitement" requirement discussed previously. Statements that do not "relate" to the startling event indicate that the declarant is no longer speaking while under the influence of the event. The D.C. Circuit explained it this way:

> As soon as the excited utterance goes beyond description of the exciting event and deals with past facts or with the future it may tend to take on a reflective quality. In other words, the very fact that the utterance is not descriptive of the exciting event is one of the factors which the trial court must take into account in the evaluation of whether the statement is truly a spontaneous, impulsive expression excited by the event.[39]

[E] Present Sense Impressions Distinguished

Although present sense impressions and excited utterances often overlap, there are significant distinctions between the two exceptions. The reliability of present sense impressions rests upon the declarant's *lack of time* to fabricate. The reliability of excited utterances is based upon the declarant's *lack of capacity* to fabricate. This difference in theory explains the different requirements for each exception. For example, a startling event is required for the excited utterance exception but not for the present sense impression exception. In addition, the time requirement is more stringent for present sense impressions than for excited utterances. An excited utterance could be made 30 minutes (sometimes hours) after the exciting event, so long as the declarant is under the influence of the excitement caused by the event at the time the statement is made.[40] In contrast, a present sense impression must be nearly contemporaneous with the event.

The subject matter requirement also differs. A present sense impression must *describe or explain* the event. The subject matter of an excited

---

[38] *See* David v. Pueblo Supermarket, 740 F.2d 230, 235 (3d Cir. 1984) (statement at time of slip and fall was "I told them to clean it up about two hours ago — an hour and a half ago."; "[I]t is undisputed that Jacobs' statement directly concerned the 'circumstance' surrounding the occurrence.").

[39] Murphy Auto Parts Co. v. Ball, 249 F.2d 508, 511 (D.C. Cir. 1957), cited in Fed. R. Evid. 803 advisory committee's note. *See also* Territory of Guam v. Cepeda, 69 F.3d 369, 372 (9th Cir. 1995) ("Here, the declarant's statement that the robber had tattoos clearly related to the startling event, the robbery. We see no basis for excluding that statement on the basis of its subject matter.").

[40] *See* Fed. R. Evid. 803 advisory committee's note ("Under Exception (2) excited utterances the standard of measurement is the duration of the state of excitement.").

utterance is not so circumscribed — statements "relating to a startling event" are admissible.[41] *Murphy Auto Parts Co. v. Ball,*[42] a case cited by the federal drafters, illustrates this difference. In that case the statement of a driver who was involved in an accident was admitted as an excited utterance. The statement revealed that the driver was acting as an agent at the time of the accident. This statement could not qualify as a present sense impression because it did not explain or describe the event (the accident). The statement did qualify as an excited utterance because it "related" to the event.

§ 33.06 Present Mental Condition: FRE 803(3)

Rule 803(3) recognizes a hearsay exception for statements of *present* physical or mental condition, including statements of intent, plan, motive, design, emotion, or mental feeling.[43] Statements of physical condition are discussed in the next section.

Rationale. The spontaneity of the statement reduces the risk of conscious fabrication. In addition, there are no memory problems because the statement is made contemporaneously with the mental condition, and the statement is often more reliable than later trial testimony.[44] Necessity is also a factor; a person's state of mind is often a material fact under the substantive law, and a statement concerning that state of mind may be the only evidence of that subjective mental state.

Nonhearsay. Frequently, statements regarding the mental state of the declarant are not hearsay because they are not offered for the truth. For example, a declarant's statement in a homicide prosecution, "John Doe is the most despicable person I know," offered to prove motive (and ultimately intent), is not offered to prove the truth of the assertion and is, therefore, not hearsay. In contrast, the statement, "I will kill John Doe," offered to prove intent is hearsay but falls within the exception of Rule 803(3).[45]

Types of statements. For purposes of analysis, the discussion is divided into three categories: (1) statements of present state of mind offered to prove

---

[41] Fed. R. Evid. 803 advisory committee's note ("Permissible subject matter of the statement is limited under Exception (1) to description or explanation of the event or condition, the assumption being that spontaneity, in the absence of a startling event, may extend no farther. In Exception (2) excited utterances, however, the statement need only "relate" to the startling event or condition, thus affording a broader scope of subject matter coverage.").

[42] 249 F.2d 508 (D.C. Cir. 1957).

[43] *See* Hinton, *States of Mind and the Hearsay Rule,* 1 U. Chi. L. Rev. 394 (1934); Rice, *The State of Mind Exception to the Hearsay Rule: A Response to "Secondary Relevance,"* 14 Duq. L. Rev. 219 (1976); Seidelson, *The State of Mind Exception to the Hearsay Rule,* 13 Duq. L. Rev. 251 (1974).

[44] *See* Mutual Life Ins. Co. v. Hillmon, 145 U.S. 285, 295 (1892) (The declarant's "own memory of his state of mind at a former time is no more likely to be clear and true than a bystander's recollection of what he then said.").

[45] *See supra* § 31.06[E] (to circumstantially prove declarant's state of mind). If the declarant is the person on trial, these statements are also party admissions.

that state of mind, (2) statements of present state of mind offered to prove future conduct, and (3) statements reflecting belief about past events. These categories are discussed in subsequent sections.

[A] To Prove a State of Mind that is a Material Fact

Under Rule 803(3), statements of presently existing state of mind are excepted from the hearsay rule [46] — for example, the statement "I am depressed" in a suicide case. Statements made by an accused may be offered under this exception to show that the accused did not have the requisite mens rea. [47] Prosecutors do not need to resort to this exception because any statement made by the accused and offered by the prosecution qualifies as an admission of a party-opponent. [48]

Victim's state of mind. In some cases, statements concerning a homicide victim's fear of the defendant have been admitted — *e.g.,* "I am afraid of Botz." These decisions are problematic. The statement does reflect the victim's state of mind and thus satisfies Rule 803(3). However, the victim's state of mind is rarely a material issue. [49] The defendant's, not the victim's, state of mind is an element in a homicide case. [50] Consequently, the statement is ordinarily irrelevant, and its use may circumvent the hearsay rule because the obvious inference is that a past threat was made or other conduct produced the fear.

[B] To Prove Future Conduct: *Hillmon* Doctrine

Statements of present state of mind are also admissible to prove that the declarant subsequently acted in accordance with that state of mind. For

---

[46] *See* Hong v. Children's Memorial Hosp., 993 F.2d 1257, 1265 (7th Cir. 1993) (The rule "does not authorize receipt of a statement by one person as proof of another's state of mind.").

[47] *See* United States v. Peak, 856 F.3d 825, 833 (7th Cir. 1988) ("While the government was attempting to show that Bennie had the specific intent to conspire in a drug scheme, Bennie's reply to Buford on the telephone tends to show that his intent was to help 'capture' Hackney."); United States v. Harris, 733 F.2d 994, 1003–05 (2d Cir. 1984); United States v. DiMaria, 727 F.2d 265, 270–71 (2d Cir. 1984) ("It was not offered to prove that the cigarettes were not stolen cigarettes but only to show that DiMaria did not think they were. . . . It was a statement of what he was thinking in the present.").

[48] *See supra* § 32.06 (individual admissions).

[49] Fear is, however, an element of some crimes, and statements of the victim's fear of the defendant would be properly admitted under Rule 803(3) in these cases. *See* United States v. Collins, 78 F.3d 1021, 1036 (6th Cir. 1996) ("In a prosecution based upon extortion through fear of economic loss, the state of mind of the victim of extortion is highly relevant."); United States v. Adcock, 558 F.2d 397, 404 (8th Cir. 1977); State v. Denis, 690 N.E.2d 955, 958 (Ohio App. 1997) (domestic violence: no person "by threat of force, shall knowingly cause a family or household member to believe that the offender will cause imminent physical harm to the family or household member").

[50] *See* United States v. Joe, 8 F.3d 1488, 1492–93 (10th Cir. 1993) ("Ms. Joe's statement to Dr. Smoker, though indicating her state of mind, also included a statement of why she was afraid (*i.e.,* because she thought her husband might kill her). This portion of Ms. Joe's statement is clearly a 'statement of memory or belief' expressly excluded by the Rule 803(3) exception.").

example, a declarant's statement, "I will revoke my will," is admissible to prove that the declarant subsequently revoked that will. Such statements are less reliable proof of future conduct than of present intent because people frequently do not or cannot carry out their intentions. This, however, is a relevancy concern which is left to the jury in this context.[51]

The leading case is *Mutual Life Ins. Co. v. Hillmon*,[52] in which the insurance company argued that a body found at Crooked Creek was that of Walters, not the insured, Hillmon. Letters in which Walters (the declarant) stated that he intended to travel from Wichita to Crooked Creek with Hillmon were offered in evidence. The Supreme Court upheld their admissibility:

> The letters were competent not as narratives of facts communicated to the writer by others, nor yet as proof that he actually went away from Wichita, but as evidence that, shortly before the time when other evidence tended to show that he went away, he had the intention of going, and of going with Hillmon, which made it more probable both that he did go and that he went with Hillmon than if there had been no proof of such intention.[53]

In terms of the hearsay dangers, there were no perception or memory problems associated with Walters' statements; admissibility makes sense under the state of mind exception. The problem is one of relevancy. How probative are such statements as proof of future conduct?

Joint conduct problem. Statements offered to prove that a person other than the declarant also engaged in the intended conduct (*e.g.*, that Hillmon accompanied the declarant to Crooked Creek) are problematic. It is one thing to admit the statement to show the declarant's (Walters') future conduct, but to use it to prove a third party's conduct (Hillmon's) is something else. Suppose, for instance, that a murder victim said that she was going out with the accused on the night of the killing. Because admissibility is stretching (breaking?) the *Hillmon* rule, some courts admitting this type

[51] *See* Shelden v. Barre Belt Granite Employer Union Pension Fund, 25 F.3d 74, 79 (2d Cir. 1996) ("It is well settled that the existence of a plan to do a given act is relevant to show that thereafter the act was in fact done, and under a long-established exception to the hearsay rule, the existence of the plan or intention may be proven by evidence of 'the person's own statements as to its existence.' ") (citation omitted).

[52] 145 U.S. 285 (1892). The plaintiff claimed that Hillmon (the insured) was killed, but the insurance company believed that the dead body was that of Walters, not Hillmon. The trial court excluded letters written by Walters that stated his intention of going to Crooked Creek (where the body at issue was found) with Hillmon. *See generally* Maguire, *The Hillmon Case — Thirty-Three Years After*, 38 Harv. L. Rev. 709 (1925); McFarland, *Dead Men Tell Tales: Thirty Times Three Years of the Judicial Process After Hillmon*, 30 Vill. L. Rev. 1 (1985); Payne, *The Hillmon Case — An Old Problem Revisited*, 41 Va. L. Rev. 1011 (1955); Hutchins & Slesinger, *Some Observations on the Law of Evidence — State of Mind to Prove an Act*, 38 Yale L.J. 283 (1929); Weissenberger, *Hearsay Puzzles: An Essay on Federal Evidence Rule 803(3)*, 64 Temp. L. Rev. 145 (1991). *See also* Wigmore, The Science of Judicial Proof 970 (3d ed. 1937) (history of *Hillmon* case); MacCracken, *The Case of the Anonymous Corpse*, 19 American Heritage 51 (No. 4, June, 1968).

[53] 145 U.S. at 295–96.

of statement require limiting instructions and corroboration.[54] Although the House Judiciary Committee Report attempted to limit the rule in this respect,[55] some federal cases have admitted such statements.[56] Several state cases are in accord.[57]

[C] To Prove Past Conduct: *Shepard v. United States*

Rule 803(3) excludes statements of memory or belief to prove the fact remembered or believed except in cases involving the declarant's will. In contrast to statements that look forward as in *Hillmon*, statements that look backwards raise all the hearsay dangers: perception, memory, narration, and sincerity. The rule adopts the Supreme Court's position in *Shepard v. United States*,[58] in which the Court refused to extend the *Hillmon* rule to statements looking backward into the past. The murder victim-declarant in *Shepard* had stated that "Dr. Shepard has poisoned me." Justice Cardozo distinguished *Hillmon*:

> Declarations of intention, casting light upon the future, have been sharply distinguished from declarations of memory, pointing

---

[54] *See* People v. Alcalde, 148 P.2d 627 (Cal. 1944).

[55] H.R. Rep. No. 650, 93d Cong., 1st Sess. (1973) ("The Committee intends that the Rule be construed to limit the doctrine of *Mutual Life Insurance Co. v. Hillmon* so as to render statements of intent by a declarant admissible only to prove his future conduct, not the future conduct of another person."), reprinted in 1974 U.S.C.C.A.N.7075,7087. Other parts of the legislative history are ambiguous.

[56] *See* United States v. Pheaster, 544 F.2d 353, 376 n. 14 (9th Cir. 1976) ("Even where no actions by other parties are necessary in order for the intended act to be performed, a myriad of contingencies could intervene to frustrate the fulfillment of the intention. The fact that the cooperation of another party is necessary if the intended act is to be performed adds another important contingency, but the difference is one of degree rather than kind. The possible unreliability of the inference to be drawn from the present intention is a matter going to the weight of the evidence which might be argued to the trier of fact, but it should not be a ground for completely excluding the admittedly relevant evidence."). *But see* United States v. Delvecchio, 816 F.2d 859, 862–63 (2d Cir. 1987).

[57] *See* People v. Malizia, 460 N.Y.S.2d 23, 27 (App. Div. 1983) ("Everyday experience confirms that people frequently express an intent to see another under circumstances that make it extremely likely that such a meeting will occur. Indeed, it is not uncommon for such expressions of intent to be more trustworthy evidence that the meeting took place than many statements of intent with regard to the performance of acts not involving any inference with regard to another person."); State v. Terrovona, 716 P.2d 295, 300 (Wash. 1986) (en banc) ("The decedent's statements, made before leaving his house, about the phone call from the defendant and his intention to go help him, constituted the State's strongest evidence of the defendant's guilt. Neither this defendant's nor the decedent's states of mind were at issue in the trial. Under the '*Hillmon* doctrine', however, the decedent's intentions were admissible to infer that he acted according to those intentions, and that he acted with the person he mentioned. The conduct of the decedent and the defendant after the phone call was definitely at issue in the trial. The decedent's statements under the circumstances here created a trustworthy inference that the defendant met him on 116th Street where he was killed within a half hour of receiving the phone call and leaving his home. Those statements were properly admitted into evidence, the weight of such evidence being for the jury.").

[58] 290 U.S. 96 (1933). The case also involved the dying declaration exception. *See infra* § 34.04[A].

backwards to the past. There would be an end, or nearly that, to the rule against hearsay if the distinction were ignored.

The testimony now questioned faced backward and not forward. This at least it did in its most obvious implications. What is even more important, it spoke to a past act, and more than that, to an act by some one not the speaker.[59]

Echoing Cardozo, the federal drafters inserted this limitation as "necessary to avoid the virtual destruction of the hearsay rule which would otherwise result from allowing state of mind, provable by a hearsay statement, to serve as the basis for an inference of the happening of the event which produced the state of mind."[60] Their concern was that almost any statement of past events could be rephrased as a statement reflecting present state of mind — *i.e.,* "My present belief is that Dr. Shepard has poisoned me."[61]

FIGURE 33-1

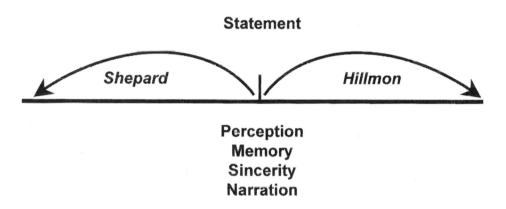

Statement

Shepard   **Hillmon**

Perception
Memory
Sincerity
Narration

[1] Exception for Will Cases

Statements of memory or belief that are offered to prove the fact remembered or believed are admissible if the statements relate to the execution, revocation, identification, or terms of a testator-declarant's will. This

---

[59] *Id.* at 106. Even in *Hillmon,* however, a looking-backward aspect was implicit. To write that he was going to Crooked Creek with Hillmon, Walters must have spoken to him in the past. In effect, Walters was saying, "I have spoken with Hillmon (past), and I am going to Crooked Creek with him (future)." This point was not an issue in the case; there was no dispute that Hillmon went to Crooked Creek.

[60] Fed. R. Evid. 803 advisory committee's note.

[61] Cardozo wrote that *Hillmon* "marks the high-water line beyond which courts have been unwilling to go. . . . Declarations of intention, casting light upon the future, have been sharply distinguished from declarations of memory, pointing backward to the past. There would be an end, or nearly that, to the rule against hearsay if the distinction were ignored." 290 U.S. at 105–06.

exception rests "on practical grounds of necessity and expediency rather than logic."[62]

§ 33.07　Present Physical Condition: FRE 803(3)

Rule 803(3) covers statements of present *physical* condition in addition to mental condition. The reliability of these statements (*e.g.,* "My back hurts"; "I feel great"; "I'm in pain.") rests on the spontaneity of the statement, which reduces the risk of conscious fabrication. There is also a reduced memory risk because the statement is made contemporaneously with the condition. In addition, this exception may be justified on the grounds that the out-of-court statement is often more reliable than in-court testimony, which takes place after litigation has commenced and motivations are more suspect.

Present [not past] conditions. The critical requirement is that the statement relate to a present condition and not to past conditions, pains, or symptoms. It must be contemporaneous with the condition, not the event which caused the condition. The statement, "My back hurts," is admissible because it concerns a *present* physical condition, even though the condition may have been caused by a car accident six months earlier.

Statements of *past* physical conditions are governed by Rule 803(4), which requires that such statements be made for the purposes of medical treatment or diagnosis. This requirement is not found in Rule 803(3); a statement of present physical condition may be made to any person for any reason. Rules 803(3) and 803(4) overlap *only* when a statement of present physical condition is made for the purpose of medical treatment or diagnosis.

§ 33.08　Medical Treatment-Diagnosis: FRE 803(4)

Rule 803(4) recognizes a hearsay exception for statements made for purposes of medical diagnosis or treatment, including a description of medical history, past or present symptoms, pain, sensations, and the inception or general character of the cause or external source if reasonably pertinent to diagnosis or treatment. Such statements are often part of a hospital or medical record and thus may present double hearsay problems.[63]

Rationale. The reliability of statements made for the purpose of medical treatment rests on the belief that the declarant will not fabricate under these circumstances because the effectiveness of the treatment depends on the accuracy of the statement. However, Rule 803(4) is not limited to statements made for the purpose of medical treatment. It also covers statements made for the *purpose of diagnosis, i.e.,* statements made to a

---

[62] Fed. R. Evid. 803 advisory committee's note.

[63] *See* Fed. R. Evid. 805 (multiple hearsay). *See also supra* § 31.10.

physician solely for the purpose of presenting expert testimony at trial.[64] Such statements were inadmissible at common law.

Statements made to expert witnesses in anticipation of trial are not validated on a reliability rationale.[65] This aspect of the rule rests on a pragmatic assessment of the use of expert testimony at trial. A physician, consulted only for the purpose of testifying as an expert, may state an opinion; the opinion is often based, in part, on medical history provided by the patient. Although the medical history was not admissible as substantive evidence at common law, it was admissible to show the basis of the expert's opinion.[66] The federal drafters believed that a jury instruction limiting the testimony to this nonhearsay use would in all likelihood be ineffective.[67] They were probably correct, and in any event, most jurors appreciate the self-serving nature of these statements.

[A] Subject Matter Requirement

Rule 803(4) is limited to statements that describe "medical history, or past or present symptoms, pain, or sensations, or the inception or general character of the cause or external source thereof insofar as reasonably pertinent to diagnosis or treatment."[68] The provision relating to "causes" represents an extension of the common law.

Statements of fault. Statements relating to the cause of an injury do not include statements of fault.[69] "Thus a patient's statement that he was struck by an automobile would qualify but not his statement that the car was driven through a red light."[70] Under this rule, the fact that a declarant had been sexually attacked would be admissible but not the identity of the

---

[64] *See* United States v. Iron Shell, 633 F.2d 77, 82 (8th Cir. 1980) ("[T]he rule abolished the distinction between the doctor who is consulted for the purpose of treatment and an examination for the purpose of diagnosis only; the latter usually refers to a doctor who is consulted only in order to testify as a witness.").

[65] Some courts recognize a reliability rationale for the rule — that such statements are reasonably relied on by the medical profession. In other words, the expertise of physicians in evaluating the accuracy of these statements is a safeguard against false statements.

[66] *See supra* § 25.03 (bases of expert testimony).

[67] Fed. R. Evid. 803 advisory committee's note ("Conventional doctrine has excluded from the hearsay exception, as not within its guarantee of truthfulness, statements to a physician consulted only for the purpose of enabling him to testify. While these statements were not admissible as substantive evidence, the expert was allowed to state the basis of his opinion, including statements of this kind. The distinction thus called for was one most unlikely to be made by juries. The rule accordingly rejects the limitation.").

[68] *See Iron Shell*, 633 F.2d at 82 ("[T]he rule adopted an expansive approach by allowing statements concerning past symptoms and those which related to the cause of the injury.").

[69] *See* Robers v. Hollocher, 664 F.2d 200, 205 (8th Cir. 1981) ("While a statement that the injuries resulted from 'force' or 'trauma' might be admissible in some circumstances, the conclusion that 'excessive force' was used was properly excluded here.").

[70] Fed. R. Evid. 803 advisory committee's note.

perpetrator.[71] A physician would need the former, but not the latter, information to treat the patient.

Child abuse cases. The use of Rule 803(4) in child abuse cases (*e.g.,* incest) has been controversial.[72] Unlike child abuse by a stranger, abuse by a household member is considered relevant to treatment.[73] A physician, so the argument runs, does not want to return the child to the abuse.[74] Courts also offer an additional rationale for the exception — that such statements are reasonably relied on by the medical profession — to support the rule.[75]

---

[71] *See Iron Shell*, 633 F.2d at 84 ("It is important to note that the statements concern what happened rather than who assaulted her. The former in most cases is pertinent to diagnosis and treatment while the latter would seldom, if ever, be sufficiently related. . . . Dr. Hopkins explained in detail the relevancy of his questions to the task of diagnosis and treatment. He testified that a discussion of the cause of the injury was important to provide guidelines for his examination by pinpointing areas of the body to be examined more closely and by narrowing his examination by eliminating other areas. . . . The fact that in this case the discussion of the cause of the injury did not lead to a fundamentally different exam does not mean that the discussion was not pertinent to diagnosis. It is enough that the information eliminated potential physical problems from the doctor's examination in order to meet the test of 803(4)."); State v. Cruz, 792 A.2d 823, 826–27 (Conn. 2002) ("[T]he medical treatment exception to the hearsay rule applies to statements made by a sexual assault victim to a social worker who is acting within the chain of medical care, as long as those statements are made for the purpose of obtaining medical diagnosis or treatment and are pertinent to the diagnosis or treatment sought."). *See also* Flores v. State, 69 S.W.3d 864, 874 (Ark. 2002) ("[T]hat part of Karen Stephens's statement that identifies Flores as the culprit in throwing Victor against the wall has no pertinence to his diagnosis and treatment and is inadmissible hearsay. Identifying the perpetrator had nothing to do with medical treatment and could well have been blame-shifting by someone who was soon to be charged as a co-defendant.").

[72] *See* Mosteller, *Child Sexual Abuse and Statements for the Purpose of Medical Diagnosis or Treatment*, 67 N.C. L. Rev. 257 (1989).

[73] *See* United States v. Longie, 984 F.2d 955, 959 (8th Cir. 1996) ("The defense argues that the victim's statements to Dr. Fahey that she was sexually abused are exceptions to the hearsay rule as valid statements of causation relating to medical diagnosis or treatment. However, the defense contends, the victim's further statements to Dr. Fahey that her father was the abuser are statements of fault which are not within the hearsay exception. We disagree. The crucial question is whether the victim's statements identifying her father as the abuser are 'reasonably pertinent' to medical diagnosis or treatment. This court has developed a two-part test to answer this question. First, the declarant's motive in making the statement must be consistent with the purpose of promoting treatment; and second, the content of the statement must be such as is reasonably relied on by a doctor in treatment or diagnosis. . . . The identity of the abuser is particularly important as it affects the physician's treatment and recommendation for counseling.") (citations omitted).

[74] *See* United States v. Renville, 779 F.2d 430, 438 (8th Cir. 1985); Garrett v. Commonwealth, 48 S.W.3d 6, 11 (Ky. 2001) ("[S]tatements identifying the perpetrator have been held 'reasonably pertinent' to diagnosis and treatment of a child sexual abuse victim where the treatment was for psychological injuries and the abuser lived with the child, the theory being that the abuse would likely continue as long as the child remained in the same household with the abuser.").

[75] *See Iron Shell*, 633 F.2d at 84 ("This principle recognizes that life and death decisions are made by physicians in reliance on such facts and as such should have sufficient trustworthiness to be admissible in a court of law. . . . Thus, two independent rationales support the rule and are helpful in its application. A two-part test flows naturally from this dual rationale: first, is the declarant's motive consistent with the purpose of the rule; and second, is it reasonable for the physician to rely on the information in diagnosis or treatment.")

In other words, the expertise of physicians in evaluating the accuracy of these statements is a safeguard against false statements.

[B] Statements to Nonphysicians

Although the rule requires the statement be made for medical diagnosis or treatment, the statement need not be made to a physician. "Statements to hospital attendants, ambulance drivers, or even members of the family might be included."[76] In one case, the Eighth Circuit upheld the admissibility of statements made by a victim's mother to a nurse; the daughter could not communicate orally or in writing on her own and was being examined by a medical professional in connection with allegations of sexual abuse by the father.[77] The exception does not extend to statements by the physician.[78]

§ 33.09 Recorded Recollection: FRE 803(5)

Suppose a witness sees a car flee from the scene of a bank robbery and writes down the license plate number. Months or years later at trial, the witness cannot remember the number but testifies that she accurately wrote it down at the time of the robbery. Recorded recollection is the hearsay exception that the prosecutor will use to admit the writing.

Rationale. The trustworthiness of recorded recollection "is found in the reliability inherent in a record made while events were still fresh in mind and accurately reflecting them."[79] A writing accurately recording an event near in time to the event will have reduced memory risks. In any case, the lack of present memory compels us to choose between such a writing or nothing. The exception for recorded recollection should be distinguished from the practice of refreshing recollection, which does not involve hearsay evidence and is governed by Rule 612. The distinction between the two rules is discussed with Rule 612.[80]

---

[76] Fed. R. Evid. 803 advisory committee's note. *E.g.,* United States v. Newman, 965 F.2d 206, 210 (7th Cir. 1992) (clinical psychologist).

[77] Lovejoy v. United States, 92 F.3d 628, 632 (8th Cir. 1996) ("The District Court did not abuse its discretion in deciding the mother's motive in making these statements was consistent with promoting the treatment of her daughter."; "This information would aid the medical professionals examining the victim by 'pinpointing areas of the body to be examined more closely and by narrowing [the] examination by eliminating other areas.' 'Discovering what is not injured is equally as pertinent to treatment and diagnosis as finding what is injured.'") (citations omitted).

[78] *See* Bombard v. Fort Wayne Newspaper, Inc., 92 F.3d 560, 564 (7th Cir. 1996) ("Rule 803(4) does not purport to except, nor can it reasonably be interpreted as excepting, statements by the person providing the medical attention to the patient.").

[79] Fed. R. Evid. 803 advisory committee's note. *See also* Blakely, *Past Recollection Recorded: Restrictions on Use as Exhibit and Proposals for Change,* 17 Hous. L. Rev. 411 (1980); Morgan, *The Relation Between Hearsay and Preserved Memory,* 40 Harv. L. Rev. 712, 720 (1927).

[80] *See supra* § 21.07 (recorded recollection distinguished).

The rule requires that the witness (1) made or adopted a record, (2) based on firsthand knowledge,[81] (3) when the matter recorded was fresh in the witness's memory, and (4) the record correctly reflected the witness's knowledge. Finally, (5) the witness at trial must have insufficient recollection to testify "fully and accurately" about the matter recorded.[82]

[A]　Time Requirement

The record must have been made or adopted close to the time of the event. This requirement is designed to ensure the reliability of the record by reducing memory risks. Common law cases required the record be prepared "at or near the time of the event." In contrast, the rule requires that the record have been prepared "when the matter was fresh in the witness's memory." This formulation follows Wigmore's view that the "at or near the time" requirement was too restrictive and arbitrary.[83]

[B]　Preparation Requirement; Joint Records

Rule 803(5) requires that the record "have been made or adopted by the witness." As with the time requirement, this requirement is designed to ensure the reliability of the record. If a witness makes a statement to a third person who prepares a record, the record is admissible if the witness verified the accuracy of the record ("adopted") at a time when the event was fresh in memory.

Joint (cooperative) records. Even if the observer did not verify the record, the record may be admissible if the recorder testifies that the record contains an accurate account of the witness's statement. In short, two witnesses must testify. According to the federal drafters, such "multiple person involvement in the process of observing and recording is entirely consistent with the exception."[84]

---

[81] *See supra* § 33.03 (firsthand knowledge & opinion rules).

[82] In some cases a writing qualifying as recorded recollection under Rule 803(5) will itself contain hearsay, in which case admissibility is governed by Rule 805 (multiple hearsay). The trial court decides admissibility pursuant to Rule 104(a).

[83] *See* 3 Wigmore, Evidence § 745, at 94 (Chadbourn rev. 1970).

[84] Fed. R. Evid. 803 advisory committee's note. *See* United States v. Lewis, 954 F.2d 1386, 1394 (7th Cir. 1992) ("Jones testified the events were fresher in his memory when he was interviewed, and that he told Staedtler the truth. Staedtler testified he accurately transcribed his notes of the interview when he prepared the report, and that Jones adopted it during a pre-trial meeting."); United States v. Booz, 451 F.2d 719, 725 (3d Cir. 1971) ("If Agent Bass can verify the accuracy of his transcription and if Kulp can testify he related an accurate recollection of the [license] number to Agent Bass, we believe that, even though Kulp may not have read the report, sufficient indicia of its accuracy exist to let the evidence go to the jury."). *See also* Morgan, The *Relation Between Hearsay and Preserved Memory*, 40 Harv. L. Rev. 712, 720 (1927).

[C] Accuracy Requirement

Under Rule 803(5), the record must reflect the witness's "knowledge correctly." This, of course, is also designed to ensure the reliability of the record. The accuracy requirement may be satisfied by testimony that the witness routinely makes accurate records of the type involved in the case or would not have signed the document unless she believed it was accurate.[85]

[D] Memory Lapse Requirement

Recollection of the matter recorded must be insufficient for the witness to testify "fully and accurately" at trial.[86] This requirement relaxes the common law rule, which often required a complete lack of recollection. Unlike the other requirements, however, this one does not relate to the accuracy of the record. Rather, it is aimed at avoiding abuse of the exception. "The absence of the requirement, it is believed, would encourage the use of statements carefully prepared for purposes of litigation under the supervision of attorneys, investigators, or claim adjusters."[87]

[E] Trial Use

Rule 803(5) provides that, if a record qualifies as recorded recollection, "the memorandum or record may be read into evidence but may not itself be received as an exhibit unless offered by an adverse party." This provision is intended to avoid the risk that the record will be given undue weight.

§ 33.10 Business Records: FRE 803(6)

Rule 803(6) recognizes a hearsay exception for records of regularly conducted activities.[88] Rule 803(7) recognizes an exception for the *absence*

---

[85] *See* United States v. Porter, 986 F.2d 1014, 1017 (6th Cir. 1993) ("It is not a *sine qua non* of admissibility that the witness actually vouch for the accuracy of the written memorandum. Admissibility is, instead, to be determined on a case-by-case basis upon a consideration, as was done by the district court in this case, of factors indicating trustworthiness, or the lack thereof.").

[86] *See* Vicksburg & Meridian R.R. v. O'Brien, 119 U.S. 99, 102 (1886) ("[A]t the time the witness testified he had, without even looking at his written statement, a clear, distinct recollection of every essential fact stated in it. If he had such present recollection, there was no necessity whatever for reading that paper to the jury."); United States v. Humphrey, 279 F.3d 372, 377 (6th Cir. 2002) ("In this case, Peeks stated that he remembered the events in question."); United States v. Felix-Jerez, 667 F.2d 1297, 1301 (9th Cir. 1982) ("Witness Hardeman did not testify that he now had an insufficient recollection as to the matters contained in the statement so as to be able to testify regarding them. In fact, he was not even asked if he now had an insufficient recollection as to such matters. The proper predicate was not laid for the introduction of the statement. Hardeman was on the witness stand and, as far as the record shows, he could have testified about the facts contained in the statement.").

[87] Fed. R. Evid. 803 advisory committee's note.

[88] Rules 901& 902(11) govern the authentication of business records, and Rules 1001 to 1008 specify the best evidence rule.

of such records. Many public records also satisfy the requirements of the business records exception; the opposite, however, is not true.[89]

Rationale. The exception is based on an assumption of self-interest; most businesses cannot operate for long without accurate records. The federal drafters echoed this rationale, writing that the reliability of business records "is said variously to be supplied by systematic checking, by regularity and continuity which produce habits of precision, by actual experience of business in relying upon them, or by a duty to make an accurate record as part of a continuing job or occupation."[90] The exception began as the common law "shop book" rule[91] and later was codified by statute[92] — for example, the Uniform Business Records as Evidence Act. The federal rule builds on prior codification efforts.

Rule 803(6) requires: (1) a record of an act, event, or condition, (2) made at or near that time, (3) by, or from information transmitted by, a person with knowledge, (4) which was kept in the course of a regularly conducted business activity, (5) if it was the regular practice to make such record, (6) as shown by the testimony of the custodian or other qualified witness or as provided by Rules 902(11), 902(12), or statute, (7) unless the source of information or the method or circumstances of preparation indicate a lack of trustworthiness.

"Business" defined. The rule defines a business expansively to include an "institution, association, profession, occupation, and calling of every kind, whether or not conducted for profit." The term encompasses not for profit entities, such as "schools, churches and hospitals."[93] The records of an individual may be admissible if regularly kept and not merely a personal or household record.[94]

"Records" defined. Memoranda, reports, records, or data compilations in any form qualify. The federal drafters anticipated the widespread use of computer-generated records[95] and the federal cases routinely admit them.[96]

---

[89] *See infra* § 33.12[E] (business & public records compared).

[90] Fed. R. Evid. 803 advisory committee's note.

[91] *See* Tracy, *The Introduction of Documentary Evidence*, 24 Iowa L. Rev. 436 (1939).

[92] *See* Hallen, *The Uniform Evidence Acts*, 6 Ohio St. L.J. 25 (1939); Polasky & Paulson, *Business Entries*, 4 Utah L. Rev. 327 (1955).

[93] H. R. Rep. No. 1597, 93d Cong., 2d Sess., reprinted in 1974 U.S.C.C.A.N. 7098, 7104 (Conference Report).

[94] *See* Keogh v. Comm'r of Internal Revenue, 713 F.2d 496, 499–500 (9th Cir. 1983) (casino employee's personal diary listing wages and tips admitted).

[95] Fed. R. Evid. 803 advisory committee's note ("The expression 'data compilation' is used as broadly descriptive of any means of storing information other than the conventional words and figures in written or documentary form. It includes, but is by no means limited to, electronic computer storage."). Similarly, the "best evidence" rule contains a provision on computers: "If data are stored in a computer or similar device, any printout or other output readable by sight, shown to reflect the data accurately, is an 'original.'" Fed. R. Evid. 1001(3).

[96] *E.g.,* United States v. Briscoe, 896 F.2d 1476, 1494 (7th Cir. 1990) ("It is well established that computer data compilations are admissible as business records.") (computerized telephone

[A]　Regular Practice; "Routine" Records

The rule requires that the record be the product of "the regular practice of that business activity."[97] This typically means that the record is the product of a routine practice. A document "not a part of any system of recording events of business" is not admissible.[98] Records prepared for a criminal enterprise may qualify under Rule 803(6).[99]

[B]　Events, Opinions & Diagnoses

Rule 803(6) requires that the record concern "acts, events, conditions, opinions, or diagnoses." Including "opinions and diagnoses" expanded upon the rule's statutory predecessors. A medical diagnosis must have been made by a qualified person.[100] Inevitably, the federal courts had to draw a line between diagnosis and speculation. An opinion that would not be admissible at trial under Rule 702, which governs expert testimony, should not be admitted only because it was written in a medical record. A compound fracture diagnosis is one thing, the cause of some cancers is another.

[C]　Time Requirement

Under Rule 803(6), the record must have been "made at or near the time" of the event. The time requirement is one of the conditions that ensures the reliability of business records.[101] It is satisfied if the data was recorded

---

records in drug conspiracy case); United States v. Young Bros. Inc., 728 F.2d 682, 693 (5th Cir. 1984) (rejecting claim that computer records "are less reliable than other kinds of business records because they depend on the accuracy of software").

[97] See Shelton v. Consumer Prod. Safety Com'n, 277 F.3d 99, 1010 (8th Cir. 2002) ("It is undisputed that the CPSC tests fireworks in the course of its regularly conducted activity. It is further undisputed that every time the CPSC tests fireworks, the data is recorded in the same way, reviewed for accuracy in the same way, and stored in the same way.") (citations omitted).

[98] See Timberlake Constr. Co. v. U.S. Fidelity & Guaranty Co., 71 F.3d 335, 342 (10th Cir. 1995) ("None are a record made in the 'regular practice' of the construction business. Instead, his letters have all the earmarks of being motivated and generated to further Timberlake's interest, with litigation actually not far around the corner. The same holds true for the October 13 letter from Abowitz, Timberlake's counsel, to James, counsel for Fidelity, demanding that Fidelity cover Timberlake's loss."); Waddell v. C.I.R., 841 F.2d 264, 267 (9th Cir. 1988) ("We find no indication in the record that Comp-U-Med obtained appraisals of this sort as a 'regular practice' of its business. There is thus no foundation for admitting it as Comp-U-Med's business record.").

[99] See United States v. Hedman, 630 F.2d 1184, 1197–98 (7th Cir. 1980) (diary recording payoffs to city building inspector admissible); United States v. Foster, 711 F.2d 871, 882–83 (9th Cir. 1983) (ledger of number of heroin balloons distributed and amount of money received admissible).

[100] See Evid. R. Evid. 702 (qualifications of expert witnesses).

[101] See 5 Wigmore, Evidence § 1526 (Chadbourn rev. 1974).

near the time of the event recorded; the time at which a computer printout is produced does not matter.[102]

[D] Firsthand Knowledge

The record must have been made (1) by a person with knowledge of the matter recorded or (2) from information transmitted by a person with such knowledge. This provision does not require that the "person with knowledge" be produced at trial or even identified. Moreover, the witness (*e.g.,* custodian) who lays the foundation for admissibility at trial is not required to have firsthand knowledge of either the recording or the underlying event. (*See infra.*)

Multiple-person records. The firsthand knowledge requirement presents no problem when the person making the record had personally observed the event. The difficultly arises when the supplier of information does not make the record but transmits the information to another person (the recorder) who makes the record.[103] If both the supplier and recorder are part of the business, the record is admissible; the supplier is under a business duty to transmit the information and the recorder is under a duty to make the record. The recorder need not have firsthand knowledge of the event. Stated another way, the exception incorporates a *double hearsay* component.

[E] Business Duty Requirement

If the supplier is *not* under a duty to transmit the information, the record is inadmissible.[104] The trustworthiness guarantee that supports the exception is missing. Although the business duty requirement is not explicitly stated in the rule, it is consistent with the underlying rationale of the rule — accuracy is assumed only for persons under a business duty.[105]

---

[102] *See* United States v. Briscoe, 896 F.2d 1476, 1494 n. 13 (7th Cir. 1990) ("We note that the fact that the actual computer printouts presented at trial were prepared specifically for this case, thus not in the regular course of Illinois Bell's business, does not preclude their admissibility under Rule 803(6)."); United States v. Sanders, 749 F.2d 195, 198 (5th Cir. 1984) ("The printouts themselves may have been made in preparation for litigation, but the data contained in the printouts was not so prepared. That information was recorded in Medicaid claim forms by Sanders or his employees shortly after Sanders supposedly filled the prescriptions, and Southwestern promptly recorded the information in a form acceptable to TDHR computers.").

[103] *See* United States v. Lieberman, 637 F.2d 95, 100 (2d Cir. 1980) ("In light of the complexities of modern business, direct proof of actual knowledge of the person making the record or providing the information is not required, and the requisite knowledge may be inferred from the fact that it was someone's business to obtain such information.").

[104] Fed. R. Evid. 803 advisory committee's note (If "the supplier of the information [an outsider] does not act in the regular course, an essential link is broken; the assurance of accuracy does not extend to the information itself, and the fact that it may be recorded with scrupulous accuracy is of no avail. An illustration is the police report incorporating information obtained from a bystander: the officer qualifies as acting in the regular course but the informant does not.").

[105] *See* United States v. Ismoila, 100 F.3d 380, 392 (5th Cir. 1996) ("The [credit] cardholders

Furthermore, the federal drafters cited the leading case on the issue, *Johnson v. Lutz,* [106] which held that an accident report prepared by a police officer based on information supplied by bystanders was inadmissible. [107]

Verification. Some decisions permit admissibility for information supplied by a person without a business duty if the business enterprise verifies the information. [108]

Double hearsay: Rule 805. If the supplier is not under a duty to transmit the information, the record may nevertheless be admissible if the supplier's statement falls within another hearsay exception. This situation presents a double hearsay problem, and admissibility is governed by Rule 805. For example, if the statement by the supplier is made for the purpose of medical treatment and is recorded in a hospital record, the statement may qualify under Rules 803(4) and 803(6). [109]

[F]　Lack of Trustworthiness Clause

Litigation records. A record that satisfies the requirements of Rule 803(6) may nevertheless be excluded if "the source of information or the method or circumstances of preparation indicate lack of trustworthiness." The leading case is *Palmer v. Hoffman,* [110] a pre-Rules decision, in which the

---

statements do not qualify as business records of the cardholders because the business records exception 'applies only if the person who makes the statement "is himself acting in the regular course of business.'" As the Appellants correctly point out, it is not the regular course of business for credit cardholders to fill out affidavits or otherwise give information to their banks regarding stolen credit cards.") (citations omitted).

[106] 170 N.E. 517 (N.Y. 1930). In a wrongful death action involving a motorcycle and truck crash, the police report was offered as a business record under a New York statute; it contained the statements of bystanders, which were held inadmissible.

[107] Fed. R. Evid. 803 advisory committee's note ("The rule follows this lead in requiring an informant with knowledge acting in the course of the regularly conducted activity.").

[108] *See* United States v. Reyes, 157 F.3d 949, 952 (2d Cir. 1998) ("[T]his and other circuits have recognized an exception to the general rule: The person making the record need not have a duty to report so long as someone has a duty to verify the information reported. Tellingly, nearly all of these cases involve reporting arrangements that resemble the [prison] sign-in for the Cape Vincent logbook in certain critical respects: Customers or other non-employees provide their names and (sometimes) their addresses to entities that demand ID verification as a regular practice of their business. So long as the regular practice of verification is established, the cases allow the names into evidence under the business records exception."); United States v. Lieberman, 637 F.2d 95, 100–01 (2d Cir. 1980) (hotel registration card; "Lieberman's objection to the admission of the hotel guest card was that the lines showing the guest's name and address had been filled in by the guest, not the hotel's employee. This objection missed the mark. We do not view the applicability of the business records exception as depending on the purely formal matter of whether the guest supplies the information by writing it on the card, or by stating it so that it may be written on the card by the employee. The latter process would not suffice to make the business records exception applicable to prove the identity of the guest unless the employee were able in some way to verify the information provided . . . . By the same token, however, if such verification is obtained by the employee, we see no reason why the guest card that has been filled in by the guest himself would not qualify as a business record and thus be admissible for the truth of its statements.").

[109] *See supra* § 31.10 (double hearsay).

[110] 318 U.S. 109 (1943).

Supreme Court interpreted the then-federal business records statute as excluding an accident report prepared by an employee of the defendant-railroad company (*i.e.,* the engineer who was at the throttle at the time of the accident). The report was excluded because it was not made "in the regular course of business." According to the Court, the primary use of the report was "in litigating, not in railroading."[111] *Palmer v. Hoffman* has been criticized because accident reports are often prepared for legitimate business reasons, such as safety concerns and insurance liability. Nevertheless, a record prepared with an eye toward litigation raises reliability concerns, and the federal drafters decided to deal explicitly with the problem of unreliable records by including the "lack of trustworthiness" clause.[112]

The trustworthiness clause is not limited to litigation records. Other deficiencies in the way in which a record is prepared may make that record untrustworthy. However, proof of one error in an account record does not render the record inadmissible. "[O]nce the offering party has met its burden of establishing the foundational requirements of the business records exception, the burden shifts to the party opposing admission to prove inadmissibility by establishing sufficient indicia of untrustworthiness."[113]

[G] Foundation Requirements for Business Records

The foundation for the admissibility of business records may be shown by the testimony of the custodian or other qualified witness or as provided by Rules 902(10) and (11), which make business records self-authenticating.[114]

The foundational witness must be sufficiently acquainted with the records management system to establish that the requirements of the exception have been satisfied.[115] The custodian or *other qualified person* may lay the foundation.[116] The foundational witness is not required to have

---

[111] *Id.* at 114.

[112] *See* Scheerer v. Hardee's Food Systems, Inc., 92 F.3d 702, 706 (8th Cir. 1996) ("Here, the incident report shows on its face that it was prepared in anticipation of litigation and not in the ordinary course of Hardee's usual restaurant business operations.").

[113] Shelton v. Consumer Prod. Safety Comm'n, 277 F.3d 998, 1010 (8th Cir. 2002).

[114] Under Rule 902(11), a certification must state that the record was (1) made at or near the time of the event recorded, (2) based on firsthand knowledge (or from information transmitted by such a person), (3) kept in the course of the regularly conducted activity, and (4) prepared as a regular practice. The party must provide written notice to adverse parties and make the record and certification available for inspection sufficiently in advance of trial to give those parties a fair opportunity to challenge them. *See supra* § 28.10[L] (certified domestic business records).

[115] *See* S. Rep. No. 1277, 93d Cong., 2d Sess. ("It is the understanding of the committee that the use of the phrase 'person with knowledge' is not intended to imply that the party seeking to introduce the memorandum, report, record, or data compilation must be able to produce, or even identify, the specific individual upon whose first-hand knowledge the memorandum, report, record or data compilation was based."), reprinted in 1974 U.S.C.C.A.N. 7051, 7063-64.

[116] *See* United States v. Linn, 880 F.2d 209, 216 (9th Cir. 1989) (no special foundation

firsthand knowledge of the particular entry. Indeed, in most instances the witness will not have personal knowledge.

§ 33.11 Absence of Business Records: FRE 803(7)

In some situations, it is the absence of a business record that is important.[117] Rule 803(7) recognizes a hearsay exception for absence of a business record. The rule must be read in conjunction with Rule 803(6).[118] The drafters observed: "Failure of a record to mention a matter which would ordinarily be mentioned is satisfactory evidence of its nonexistence. While probably not hearsay as defined in Rule 801, decisions may be found which classify the evidence not only as hearsay but also as not within any exception. In order to set the question at rest in favor of admissibility, it is specifically treated here."[119]

§ 33.12 Public Records: FRE 803(8)

The Federal Rules use the term "public records" to refer to governmental records, sometimes also known as official records. The term "public" can be misleading because these records need not be "open" to the public.

Rationale. "Justification for the exception is the assumption that a public official will perform his duty properly and the unlikelihood that he will remember details independently of the record."[120]

Rule 803(8) recognizes three types of public records: (1) those setting forth the activities of the office or agency, (2) those recording matters observed

---

required for computer records); S. Rep. No. 1277, 93d Cong., 2d Sess. (Foundation may be laid "in the case of a computer printout, upon a report from the company's computer programmer or one who has knowledge of the particular record system."), reprinted in 1974 U.S.C.C.A.N. 7051, 7063-64.

[117] *See* United States v. De Georgia, 420 F.2d 889, 893 (9th Cir. 1969) (Hertz rent-a-car computer record showing no record of vehicle being rented during time stolen); "[T]his same circumstance offers a like assurance that if a business record designed to note every transaction of a particular kind contains no notation of such a transaction between specified dates, no such transaction occurred between those dates. Moreover, in our opinion, that assurance is not likely to be enhanced by the only other means of proving such a negative; that is by bringing into court all of the documents involving similar transactions during the period in question to prove that there was no record of the transactions alleged not to have occurred, and calling as witnesses all company personnel who had the duty of entering into transactions of that kind during the critical period and inquiring whether the witnesses remembered any additional transactions for which no record had been produced.").

[118] A comparable provision for public records is found in Rule 803(10). *See infra* § 33.13.

[119] Fed. R. Evid. 803 advisory committee's note.

[120] Fed. R. Evid. 803 advisory committee's note. *See also* Chesapeake & Delaware Canal Co. v. United States, 250 U.S. 123, 128–29 (1919) ("Thus, their character as public records required by law to be kept, the official character of their contents, entered under the sanction of public duty, the obvious necessity for regular contemporaneous entries in them, and the reduction to a minimum of motive on the part of public officials and employees to either make false entries or to omit proper ones, all unite to make these books admissible as unusually trustworthy sources of evidence.").

pursuant to a legal duty, and (3) investigative reports. The rule contains two limitations. First, public records that are otherwise admissible may be excluded if the "sources of information or other circumstances indicate lack of trustworthiness." Second, certain types of police records are inadmissible in criminal cases.

Related rules. Several other hearsay exceptions deal with specific types of public records.[121] Moreover, other rules also deal with different aspects of public records. Rule 1005, by permitting the use of certified copies, recognizes an exception to the "best evidence" rule for public records. Authentication of public records is governed by Rules 901(b) and 902. Under the latter rule, many public records are self-authenticating and thus admissible without any need to produce an authenticating witness. All these provisions combine to make admissibility quite easy to achieve.

[A] Activities of Agency

Rule 803(8)(A) provides for the admission of records setting forth the "activities of the office or agency."[122] This is the most straightforward division in the rule. Although division (A) contains no explicit firsthand knowledge requirement, that requirement is implicit. As with business records, the person making the record need not have firsthand knowledge so long as the official transmitting the information had such knowledge.

[B] Matters Observed Per Legal Duty

Rule 803(8)(B) governs records setting forth "matters observed pursuant to duty imposed by law as to which matters there was a duty to report, excluding, however, in criminal cases matters observed by police officers and other law enforcement personnel." As illustrations, the federal drafters cited cases admitting (1) a letter from an induction officer to a District Attorney, pursuant to army regulations, stating facts and circumstances of the accused's refusal to be inducted into the military, (2) an affidavit of a White House personnel officer that the search of records showed no employment of an accused charged with fraudulently representing himself as an envoy of the President, (3) Weather Bureau records of rainfall, and (4) a map prepared by a government engineer from information furnished

---

[121] *See* Fed. R. Evid. 803(9) (vital statistics); Fed. R. Evid. 803(10) (absence of a public record); Fed. R. Evid. 803(14) (documents affecting an interest in property); Fed. R. Evid. 803(22) (judgments of previous conviction); Fed. R. Evid. 803(23) (judgments as to personal, family, general history, or boundaries).

[122] *E.g.,* Chesapeake & Delaware Canal Co. v. United States, 250 U.S. 123 (1919) (Treasury Department records of accounts receivable); Fed. R. Evid. 803 advisory committee's note (citing cases involving General Land Office and Pension Office records); United States v. Johnson, 722 F.2d 407, 410 (8th Cir. 1983) (Bureau of Alcohol, Tobacco & Firearms firearm serial number record).

by men working under his supervision.[123] A more recent case involved a chain-of-custody receipt.[124]

Official duty; double hearsay. The firsthand observations of the official making the report or those of another official *with a duty* to report come within the exception. However, hearsay statements by third persons are not admissible merely because they are included in a public record.[125]

[1] Police Records Exclusion

The rule specifically excludes police reports in criminal cases. According to the Senate Committee Report, the police records exclusion was based on the belief that "observations by police officers at the scene of the crime or the apprehension of the defendant are not as reliable as observations by public officials in other cases because of the adversarial nature of the confrontation between the police and the defendant in criminal cases."[126] In addition, the legislative history indicates that Congress was concerned with the Confrontation Clause problems raised by the use of police records in criminal trials.[127]

Routine nonadversarial records. Most federal courts have adopted a flexible approach, holding that the police records exclusion does not apply to all police records. For example, the Ninth Circuit has held that "Congress did not intend to exclude police records of routine, nonadversarial matters."[128] The court focused on the Senate Committee Report's language

---

[123] Fed R. Evid. 803 advisory committee's note.

[124] *See* United States v. Brown, 9 F.3d 907, 911 (11th Cir. 1993) ("Before introducing the property receipt into evidence, the government established that its regular and customary procedure was to fill out a property receipt for any type of evidence. The police custodian testified that for every piece of evidence, he filled out a property receipt containing the case number, date, location the property was found, and a description of the evidence. Brown's argument that the government must establish that it was customary to list the make and serial number of the gun takes the foundation requirement to unwarranted extremes.").

[125] *See* United States v. Mackey, 117 F.3d 24, 28 (1st Cir. 1997) ("The FBI report, however, did not find or conclude that Mackey had won $ 60,000, but merely that Munichiello had made that statement. In line with the advisory committee note to Rule 803(8), decisions in this and other circuits squarely hold that hearsay statements by third persons such as Munichiello are not admissible under this exception merely because they appear within public records.").

[126] S. Rep. No. 1277, 93d Cong., 2d Sess. 17, reprinted in 1974 U.S.C.C.A.N. 7051, 7064.

[127] *See* United States v. Oates, 560 F.2d 45, 78 (2d Cir. 1977) ("The pervasive fear of the draftsmen and of Congress that interference with an accused's right to confrontation would occur was the reason why in criminal cases law enforcement reports were expressly denied the benefit to which they might otherwise be entitled under FRE 803(8)."). *See infra* chapter 36 (right of confrontation).

[128] United States v. Orozco, 590 F.2d 789, 793 (9th Cir. 1979) (customs officer's recording of license plate numbers admissible). *See also* United States v. Loyola-Dominguez, 125 F.3d 1315, 1318 (9th Cir. 1997) (warrants for deportation generally admissible and not subject to the law enforcement exception); United States v. Brown, 9 F.3d 907, 911 (11th Cir. 1993) ("[P]roperty receipt in the instant case is not the type of evidence contemplated by the exclusion of Rule 803(8)(B). . . . Many courts . . . have drawn a distinction between police records prepared in a routine, non-adversarial setting and those resulting from a more subjective investigation and evaluation of a crime. . . . The police custodian in the instant case had no

concerning the "adversarial nature of the confrontation" between the police and the defendant "at the scene of the crime or the apprehension of the defendant."[129] The "factors likely to cloud the perception of an official engaged in the more traditional law enforcement functions of observation and investigation of crime are simply not present. Due to the lack of any motivation on the part of the recording official to do other than mechanically register an unambiguous factual matter, such records are, like other public documents, inherently reliable."[130] A computer report containing identification numbers of stolen vehicles,[131] a state prison fingerprint card,[132] and a Customs Service computer printout of license plates of cars crossing the border have all been admitted as routine, nonadversarial records.[133]

[2] Business Records

If a record is excluded because it involves a matter observed by law enforcement personnel, the question remains whether the record may be admitted under the business records exception. As noted below, there is often an overlap between the two exceptions. In *United States v. Oates*,[134] the Second Circuit answered the question in the negative. Other courts, however, have reached the opposite result if the declarant testifies,[135] which makes the declarant subject to cross-examination.

[3] Offered by Defense

On its face, Rule 803(8)(B) is absolute — excluding police records when offered by the *defense* as well as the prosecution. However, the D.C. Circuit rejected this interpretation, realizing that it was probably a congressional oversight.[136] The police records exclusion was added by Congress specifically to deal with prosecution use of these records.

---

incentive to do anything other than mechanically record the relevant information on the property receipt. We believe that this is the type of reliable public record envisioned by the drafters of Rule 803(8).") (citations omitted).

[129] *Orozco*, 590 F.2d at 793 (quoting S. Rep. No. 1277, 93d Cong., 2d Sess. 17, reprinted in 1974 U.S.C.C.A.N. 7051, 7064).

[130] United States v. Quezada, 754 F.2d 1190, 1194 (5th Cir. 1985).

[131] United States v. Enterline, 894 F.2d 287, 289–91 (8th Cir. 1990).

[132] United States v. Dancy, 861 F.2d 77, 79–80 (5th Cir. 1988).

[133] United States v. Puente, 826 F.2d 1415, 1417–18 (5th Cir. 1987).

[134] 560 F.2d 45 (2d Cir. 1977). *Accord* United States v. Brown, 9 F.3d 907, 911 (11th Cir. 1993) ("Rule 803(6) cannot be used as a back door to admit evidence excluded by Rule 803(8)(B).").

[135] *See* United States v. Sokolow, 91 F.3d 396, 405 (3d Cir. 1996) ("Although we have not specifically addressed this issue, the Seventh and Tenth Circuits have held that Rule 803(8)(C) does not compel the exclusion of documents properly admitted under Rule 803(6) where the author testifies. The *Hayes* court stated that the *Oates* rule does not apply in such circumstances 'because such [investigator] testimony protects against the loss of an accused's confrontation rights, the underlying rationale for Rule 803(8) and the basis of the court's concern in *Oates*.' We reach the same conclusion here.") (citing United States v. Hayes, 861 F.2d 1225, 1230 (10th Cir. 1988)).

[136] United States v. Smith, 521 F.2d 957 (D.C. Cir. 1975) (interpreting the federal rule to admit these records if offered by the defense).

[C]   Investigative Reports

Rule 803(8)(C) governs investigative or evaluative records, which are admissible in civil actions and against the prosecution in criminal cases. The underlying theory is that reports, for example, dealing with the causes of mine disasters issued by the Bureau of Mines or airplane crashes issued by the FAA are sufficiently reliable.[137] A fire marshal's report concluding that the cause of a fire was arson is another illustration. These types of reports are typically prepared by officials with special expertise who are often the first on the scene. These officials moreover are not partisan. In some cases, findings are based on hearings.[138]

In *Beech Aircraft Corp. v. Rainey*,[139] the Supreme Court resolved a split in the circuits by adopting a liberal view of admissibility: "factually based conclusions or opinions are not on that account excluded from the scope of Rule 803(8)(C)."[140] The case involved a Navy report of a service-related air crash during a training flight, which concluded that pilot error was probably the cause of the crash. Although this was an opinion, it was based on a factual investigation. The Supreme Court held that a

> broad approach to admissibility under Rule 803(8)(C) . . . is . . . consistent with the Federal Rules' general approach of relaxing the traditional barriers to "opinion" testimony. Rules 702–705 permit experts to testify in the form of an opinion, and without any exclusion of opinions on "ultimate issues." And Rule 701 permits even a lay witness to testify in the form of opinions or inferences drawn from her observations when testimony in that form will be helpful to the trier of fact. We see no reason to strain to reach an interpretation of Rule 803(8)(C) that is contrary to the liberal thrust of the Federal Rules.[141]

---

[137] In re Air Disaster at Lockerbie Scotland, 37 F.3d 804, 828 (2d Cir. 1994) (conclusion that bomb was placed in unaccompanied bag admitted; "The investigation was timely, Henderson was an experienced and skilled investigator, and no bias may be presumed in the Scottish investigation.").

[138] *See* Fed. R. Evid. 803 advisory committee's note ("Factors which may be of assistance in passing upon the admissibility of evaluative reports include: (1) the timeliness of the investigation; (2) the special skill or experience of the official, (3) whether a hearing was held and the level at which conducted; (4) possible motivation problems . . .").

[139] 488 U.S. 153 (1988).

[140] *Id.* at 162. Lt. Cmdr. Barbara Rainey, a Navy training pilot, crashed with a student pilot. Her husband sued, and the issue was whether the crash was due to pilot error or from "roll back" due to a defect in the fuel control system. Lt. Cmdr. Morgan prepared a report on the accident.

[141] *Id.* at 169. *See also id.* at 167 n. 11 ("The Advisory Committee proposed a nonexclusive list of four factors it thought would be helpful in passing on this question: (1) the timeliness of the investigation; (2) the investigator's skill or experience; (3) whether a hearing was held; and (4) possible bias when reports are prepared with a view to possible litigation").

[D] Trustworthiness Clause

Public records otherwise admissible under Rule 803(8) may be excluded if the "sources of information or other circumstances indicate lack of trustworthiness." This provision is identical to the one found in the business records exception and serves the same purpose.[142] This provision is less important here than with business records because the police records exclusion discussed above covers many, if not most, litigation records.

[E] Business Records Compared

Many public records also satisfy the requirements of the business records exception; the opposite, however, is not true. The public records exception does not require that the record be prepared at or near the time of the event recorded.[143] In other words, *delayed* entries may be admissible. Nor does a public record need to be a regular or routine record.[144] Recall also, however, that records that are inadmissible under the police records exclusion of the public records exception are also not admissible as business records.

§ 33.13 Absence of Public Records: FRE 803(10)

Sometimes the absence of a public record is the critical issue — *e.g.,* failure to file an income tax return, or failure to register a firearm. Rule 803(10) addresses this issue and is comparable to Rule 803(7), which governs the absence of a business record. The two exceptions, however, are not identical. Admissibility under Rule 803(10) requires a showing "that diligent search failed to disclose" the record.

§ 33.14 Ancient Documents: FRE 803(16)

Rule 803(16) recognizes a hearsay exception for "statements in a document in existence twenty years or more the authenticity of which is established." The rule must be read in conjunction with Rule 901(b)(8), which governs the authentication of ancient documents. Both the hearsay exception and the authentication requirement are discussed with that rule.[145]

---

[142] *See* Harveston v. State, 798 So. 2d 638, 641 (Miss. App. 2001) ("Because the necessary predicate was not laid showing how registration information on motor vehicles is compiled and made available by computer connection to law enforcement authorities, we conclude that, in this case, the [National Crime Information Computer printout purporting to reveal ownership of the particular motor vehicles in question did not demonstrate the necessary indications of trustworthiness to be admitted over a hearsay objection.").

[143] *See* United States v. Versaint, 849 F.2d 827, 832 (3d Cir. 1988) ("Fed. R. Evid. 803(8) does not require that a report be made at or near the time of the event it is describing.").

[144] *See* In re Oil Spill by the Amoco Cadiz, 954 F.2d 1279, 1308 (7th Cir. 1992) ("The public-document exception to the hearsay rule does not contain the requirement of the business records exception (Rule 803(6)) that the documents be kept in the course of a regularly conducted activity.").

[145] *See supra* § 28.07 (ancient documents).

§ 33.15 Market Reports; Commercial Lists: FRE 803(17)

Rule 803(17) recognizes a hearsay exception for "market quotations, tabulations, lists, directories, or other published compilations" if they are "generally used and relied upon by the public or by persons in particular occupations." The rule goes beyond compilations prepared for professions and trades to include "newspaper market reports, telephone directories, and city directories."[146] Mortality tables are also admissible. These records are believed to be trustworthy due to "general reliance by the public or by a particular segment of it, and the motivation of the compiler to foster reliance by being accurate."[147]

§ 33.16 Learned Treatises: FRE 803(18)

Learned treatises were admissible at common law but only for the impeachment of experts.[148] Rule 803(18) changes this result, making the treatise admissible as substantive evidence, not merely for credibility. According to the federal drafters, the "hearsay objection must be regarded as unimpressive when directed against treatises since a high standard of accuracy is engendered by various factors: the treatise is written primarily and impartially for professionals, subject to scrutiny and exposure for inaccuracy, with the reputation of the writer at stake."[149]

The common law cases divided over the requirement for impeachment —i.e, whether the expert had to *rely* on the treatise in arriving at her opinion or whether recognition of the treatise as an authoritative text by the expert was sufficient even if there was no reliance.[150] Experts, of course, know of the rule and tailor their testimony accordingly —i.e., not recognizing any text as authoritative. To avoid this tactic, Rule 803(18) permits the authoritativeness to be established by another expert or by judicial notice (e.g., judicially noticing *Gray's Anatomy*).

Limitations. Two limitations appear in the rule. First, a treatise may be used substantively only when an expert is on the stand.[151] This requirement provides an important safeguard because it ensures that a knowledgeable person is available "to explain and assist in the application of the

---

[146] Fed. R. Evid. 803 advisory committee's note.

[147] *Id.*

[148] Some jurisdictions still follow the traditional rule. *E.g.,* Mich. R. Evid. 707 (treatises "admissible for impeachment purposes only"); Ohio R. Evid. 706 (impeachment only).

[149] Fed. R. Evid. 803 advisory committee's note.

[150] *See id.* ("In all jurisdictions an expert may be impeached with a learned treatise. There is, however, disagreement as to the conditions under which a treatise may be used for this purpose. Some jurisdictions allow this method of impeachment only when the expert *relies* on the treatise in reaching her opinion. . . . Other jurisdictions permit impeachment if the expert *recognizes* the treatise as an authoritative work, even though the expert did not rely on it. Still other jurisdictions permit impeachment if the treatise is established as a recognized authority *by any means,* including the testimony of other experts or by judicial notice.").

[151] *See* United States v. An Article of Drug, 661 F.3d 742, 745 (9th Cir. 1981) (treatise read by expert during direct examination).

treatise."[152] Second, the treatise may be read to the jury but not received as an exhibit, thus precluding its misuse in the jury room.[153]

§ 33.17 Judgment of Previous Conviction: FRE 803(22)

Rule 803(22) recognizes a hearsay exception for judgments of previous criminal convictions when offered "to prove any fact essential to sustain the judgment."[154] The rule also provides that the "pendency of an appeal may be shown but does not affect admissibility."

Rationale. This exception rests on the high degree of reliability which attends a criminal judgment. Either the defendant pleaded guilty in conformity with the procedural safeguards surrounding the acceptance of guilty pleas or was convicted (beyond a reasonable doubt) after a trial.

Rebuttal. If evidence of a previous criminal judgment is admitted, rebuttal evidence, typically in the form of an explanation, may also be admissible. As an example the federal drafters cited *North River Ins. Co. v. Militello*,[155] a case "in which the jury found for plaintiff on a fire policy despite the introduction of his conviction for arson."[156]

Convictions. Rule 803(22) applies only to criminal judgments, including convictions in federal and state courts. A civil judgment is not admissible under the rule. Neither is evidence of an acquittal admissible. The rule limits the types of convictions that are admissible to those involving "a crime punishable by death or imprisonment in excess of one year."[157] The maximum punishment for the offense, not the actual punishment imposed, is controlling.[158]

No contest plea. A conviction based upon a "plea of no contest or the equivalent plea from another jurisdiction" is inadmissible. This limitation is consistent with Rule 410, which provides that pleas of no contest are not admissible.[159] Precluding admission of pleas of no contest but permitting

---

[152] Fed. R. Evid. 803 advisory committee's note. *See also* United States v. Turner, 104 F.3d 217, 221 (8th Cir. 1997) ("In the present case, there was no expert testimony establishing the texts as authoritative.").

[153] *See* Graham v. Wyeth Labs., 906 F.2d 1399, 1414 (10th Cir. 1990) (permitting treatise in jury room raises danger that jurors will be unduly impressed by treatise).

[154] The rule deals only with the hearsay aspects of previous conviction evidence; it does not modify substantive rules of res judicata or collateral estoppel. *See* Fed. R. Evid. 803 advisory committee's note ("The rule does not deal with the substantive effect of the judgment as a bar or collateral estoppel."). In effect, the rule operates in cases in which the doctrines of res judicata and collateral estoppel are not applicable.

[155] 88 P.2d 567 (Colo. 1939).

[156] Fed. R. Evid. 803 advisory committee's note.

[157] *See id.* ("Practical considerations require exclusion of convictions of minor offenses, not because the administration of justice in its lower echelons must be inferior, but because motivation to defend at this level is often minimal or nonexistent.").

[158] In addition to the conviction, a guilty plea itself is admissible as an admission of a party-opponent. *See supra* § 32.06 [A] (individual admissions — pleas of guilty).

[159] *See supra* § 16.03 (nolo contendere pleas).

admission of evidence of a conviction based on such a plea would undercut the usefulness of no contest pleas.

"Essential fact" requirement. Evidence of a previous criminal judgment is admissible only if it "proves any fact essential to sustain the judgment." As the Supreme Court recognized in *Emich Motors Corp. v. General Motors Corp.*,[160] a pre-Rules case, this requirement may prove troublesome:

> The difficult problem, of course, is to determine what matters were adjudicated in the antecedent suit. A general verdict of the jury or judgment of the court without special findings does not indicate which of the means charged in the indictment were found to have been used in effectuating the conspiracy. And since all of the facts charged need not be proved for conviction such a verdict does not establish that the defendants used all of the means charged or any particular one. Under these circumstances what was decided by the criminal judgment must be determined by the trial judge hearing the treble-damage suit, upon an examination of the record, including the pleadings, the evidence submitted, the instructions under which the jury arrived at its verdict, and any opinions of the court.[161]

Criminal cases. The limitation to impeachment[162] in criminal cases is based on constitutional concerns. In *Kirby v. United States*,[163] the defendant was charged with possessing stolen postage stamps and the only evidence of theft was the record of conviction of the thieves. The use of the record deprived Kirby of his right of confrontation.[164] This limitation does not preclude an accused from introducing judgments against third persons.[165]

§ 33.18   Other Exceptions

There are a bunch of other exceptions in Rule 803. Many are codifications of the common law that are not as important today. For example, a number of exceptions deal with pedigree, *i.e.,* births, deaths, legitimacy, marriage, and family relationships. While these issues are still important today, better recording systems make resort to the family Bible[166] and community

---

[160] 340 U.S. 558 (1951).

[161] *Id.* at 569.

[162] *See* Fed. R. Evid. 609 (impeachment by prior conviction).

[163] 174 U.S. 47 (1899).

[164] Fed. R. Evid. 803 advisory committee's note ("The exception does not include evidence of the conviction of a third person, offered against the accused in a criminal prosecution to prove any fact essential to sustain the judgment of conviction. A contrary position would seem clearly to violate the right of confrontation. . . . The situation is to be distinguished from cases in which conviction of another person is an element of the crime, *e.g.* 15 U.S.C. § 902(d), interstate shipment of firearms to a known convicted felon, and, as specifically provided, from impeachment.").

[165] *See* Fed. R. Evid. 404(b) (admissibility of prior crimes, wrongs, or acts).

[166] Fed. R. Evid. 803(13).

reputation [167] rare. [168] Indeed, Rule 803(9) recognizes a hearsay exception for records of vital statistics.

Another group of exceptions deal with real property — *i.e.*, who owns Blackacre? [169]

§ 33.19 Key Points

There is no need to look for an exception until you first determine that the statement is in fact hearsay. In practice, always argue in the alternative — *e.g.,* "Your Honor. The statement is not hearsay, but if it is, it falls within the excited utterance exception." The same is true of the exceptions — argue in the alternative. There is an overlap between many of the exceptions, so a statement may fall in more than one. Moreover, the residual exception (Rule 807) is always a possible backup argument, but it requires notice.

Rationale. Hearsay exceptions are based on some circumstantial guarantee of trustworthiness that is thought to warrant admissibility notwithstanding the lack of cross-examination, oath, and personal appearance of the declarant. Recall the hearsay dangers: perception, memory, narration, and sincerity risks. Each exception is thought to reduce one or more of these risks. Most exceptions are also supported by a necessity or practical convenience argument. The necessity rationale is clearly present in the exceptions specified in Rule 804, because the unavailability of the declarant is required as a condition of admissibility.

Firsthand knowledge rule. Several of the exceptions recognized in Rule 803 specifically require firsthand knowledge on the part of the declarant. For other exceptions, the rule is silent. Nevertheless, firsthand knowledge is generally a requirement for all exceptions.

Opinion rule. The application of the opinion rule to hearsay statements is discussed with Rule 701. [170] In a nutshell, it makes no sense to apply the opinion rule to out-of-court statements.

Present Sense Impressions: FRE 803(1)

The reliability of present sense impressions rests upon the declarant's *lack of time to fabricate*, which reduces the risk of insincerity. Rule 803(1) requires: (1) a statement describing or explaining an event or condition, (2) about which the declarant had firsthand knowledge, and (3) made at the time the declarant was perceiving the event or immediately thereafter.

---

[167] Fed. R. Evid. 803(19).

[168] *See also* Fed. R. Evid. 803(11) (records of religious organizations); Fed. R. Evid. 803(12) (marriage & baptismal certificates); Fed. R. Evid. 803(23) (judgments concerning personal/family history). Another exception is found in Rule 804. Fed. R. Evid. 804(b)(4) (statements of personal/family relationship).

[169] *See* Fed. R. Evid. 803(14) (recording statutes, interest in property); Fed. R. Evid. 803(15) (statements in documents); Fed. R. Evid. 803(20) (reputation concerning boundaries & general history); Fed. R. Evid. 803(23) (judgments concerning boundaries & general history).

[170] *See supra* § 23.03[E] (application to out-of-court statements).

Excited Utterances: FRE 803(2)

The reliability of excited utterances is based upon the declarant's lack of capacity to fabricate. Rule 803(2) requires: (1) a startling event; (2) a statement relating to that event; (3) made by a declarant with firsthand knowledge; and (4) made while the declarant was under the stress of the excitement caused by the event.

Present sense impressions distinguished. Although present sense impressions and excited utterances often overlap, there are significant distinctions between the two exceptions. The reliability of present sense impressions rests upon the declarant's *lack of time* to fabricate. The reliability of excited utterances is based upon the declarant's *lack of capacity* to fabricate. This difference in theory explains the different requirements for each exception. For example, a startling event is required for the excited utterance exception but not for the present sense impression exception. In addition, the time requirement is more stringent for present sense impressions than for excited utterances. The subject matter requirement also differs. A present sense impression must *describe or explain* the event. The subject matter of an excited utterance is not so circumscribed — statements "relating to a startling event" are admissible.

Present Mental Condition: FRE 803(3)

Rationale. The spontaneity of the statement reduces the risk of conscious fabrication. In addition, there are no memory problems because the statement is made contemporaneously with the mental condition, and the statement is often more reliable than later trial testimony. Necessity is also a factor; a person's state of mind is often a material fact under the substantive law, and a statement concerning that state of mind may be the only evidence of that subjective mental state.

Nonhearsay. Frequently, statements regarding the mental state of the declarant are not hearsay because they are not offered for the truth.

Types of statements. Rule 803(3) can be divided into three categories of mental state evidence: (1) statements of present state of mind offered to prove that state of mind, (2) statements of present state of mind offered to prove future conduct, and (3) statements reflecting belief about past events.

To prove a state of mind that is a material fact. Statements made by an accused may be offered under this exception to show that the accused did not have the requisite mens rea.[171] In some cases, statements concerning a homicide victim's fear of the defendant have been admitted — *e.g.,* "I am afraid of Botz." These decisions are problematic. The statement does reflect the victim's state of mind and thus satisfies Rule 803(3). However, the victim's state of mind is rarely a material issue.

---

[171] Prosecutors do not need to resort to this exception because any statement made by the accused and offered by the prosecution qualifies as an admission of a party-opponent.

To Prove Future Conduct: Hillmon Doctrine. Statements of present state of mind are also admissible to prove that the declarant subsequently acted in accordance with that state of mind. For example, a declarant's statement, "I will revoke my will," is admissible to prove that the declarant subsequently revoked that will. A controversial issue is whether the *Hillmon* rule should extend to joint conduct. Statements offered to prove that a person other than the declarant also engaged in the intended conduct (*e.g.,* that Hillmon accompanied the declarant to Crooked Creek) are problematic. Most courts have permitted such use.

To Prove Past Conduct: Shepard v. United States. Rule 803(3) excludes statements of memory or belief to prove the fact remembered or believed except in cases involving the declarant's will. In contrast to statements that look forward as in *Hillmon*, statements that look backwards raise all the hearsay dangers: perception, memory, narration, and sincerity. The rule adopts the Supreme Court's position in *Shepard v. United States*, in which the Court refused to extend the *Hillmon* rule to statements looking backward into the past.

Present Physical Condition: FRE 803(3)

Rule 803(3) covers statements of present *physical* condition in addition to mental condition. The reliability of these statements (*e.g.,* "My back hurts.") rests on the spontaneity of the statement, which reduces the risk of conscious fabrication. There is also a reduced memory risk because the statement is made contemporaneously with the condition. The critical requirement is that the statement relate to a present condition and not to past conditions, pains, or symptoms. The statement must be contemporaneous with the condition, not the event which caused the condition.

Statements of *past* physical conditions are governed by Rule 803(4), which requires that such statements be made for the purposes of medical treatment or diagnosis. This requirement is not found in Rule 803(3); a statement of present physical condition may be made to any person for any reason. Rules 803(3) and 803(4) overlap *only* when a statement of present physical condition is made for the purpose of medical treatment or diagnosis.

Medical Treatment-Diagnosis: FRE 803(4)

The exception rests on the belief that the declarant will not fabricate under these circumstances because the effectiveness of the treatment depends on the accuracy of the statement. However, Rule 803(4) is not limited to statements made for the purpose of medical treatment. It also covers statements made for the *purpose of diagnosis, i.e.,* statements made to a physician solely for the purpose of presenting expert testimony at trial. Such statements were inadmissible at common law. Statements relating to the cause of an injury do not include statements of fault. Although the rule requires the statement be made for medical diagnosis or treatment, the statement need not be made to a physician.

Recorded Recollection: FRE 803(5)

The rule requires that the witness (1) made or adopted a record, (2) based on firsthand knowledge, (3) when the matter recorded was fresh in the witness's memory, and (4) the record correctly reflected the witness's knowledge. Finally, (5) the witness at trial must have insufficient recollection to testify "fully and accurately" about the matter recorded. Joint (cooperative) records are admissible. The exception for recorded recollection should be distinguished from the practice of refreshing recollection, which does not involve hearsay evidence and is governed by Rule 612.[172]

Business Records: FRE 803(6)

The exception is based on an assumption of self-interest; most businesses cannot operate for long without accurate records. Rule 803(6) requires: (1) a record of an act, event, or condition, (2) made at or near in time, (3) by, or from information transmitted by, a person with knowledge, (4) which was kept in the course of a regularly conducted business activity, (5) if it was the regular practice to make such record, (6) as shown by the testimony of the custodian or other qualified witness or as provided by Rules 902(11), 902(12), or statute, (7) unless the source of information or the method or circumstances of preparation indicate a lack of trustworthiness.

"Business" defined. The rule defines a business expansively to include an "institution, association, profession, occupation, and calling of every kind, whether or not conducted for profit." The term encompasses not for profit entities, such as "schools, churches and hospitals." The records of an individual may be admissible if regularly kept and not merely a personal or household record.

Opinions & diagnoses. Including "opinions and diagnoses" expanded upon the rule's statutory predecessors. Inevitably, the federal courts had to draw a line between diagnosis and speculation. An opinion that would not be admissible at trial under Rule 702, which governs expert testimony, should not be admitted only because it was written in a medical record. A compound fracture diagnosis is one thing, the cause of some cancers is another.

Business duty requirement. If both the supplier and recorder are part of the business, the record is admissible; the supplier is under a business duty to transmit the information and the recorder is under a duty to make the record. The recorder need not have firsthand knowledge of the event. Stated another way, the exception incorporates a *double hearsay* component.

If the supplier is *not* under a duty to transmit the information, the record is inadmissible as a business record. This situation presents a double

---

[172] *See supra* § 21.07 (recorded recollection/refreshing recollection distinguished).

hearsay problem, and admissibility is governed by Rule 805. For example, if the statement by the supplier is made for the purpose of medical treatment and is recorded in a hospital record, the statement may qualify under Rules 803(4) and 803(6).

Lack of trustworthiness clause. A record that satisfies the requirements of Rule 803(6) may nevertheless be excluded if "the source of information or the method or circumstances of preparation indicate lack of trustworthiness." Records prepared in anticipation of litigation are an example.

Foundational requirements. The foundation for the admissibility of business records may be shown by the testimony of the custodian or other qualified witness or as provided by Rules 902(10) and (11), which make business records self-authenticating. The foundational witness must be sufficiently acquainted with the records management system to establish that the requirements of the exception have been satisfied, but the witness is not required to have firsthand knowledge of the particular entry. Indeed, in most instances the witness will not have personal knowledge.

Absence of business records. Rule 803(7) recognizes a hearsay exception for absence of a business record.

Public Records: FRE 803(8)

Rule 803(8) recognizes three types of public records: (1) those setting forth the activities of the office or agency, (2) those recording matters observed pursuant to a legal duty, and (3) investigative reports.[173] The rule contains two limitations. First, public records that are otherwise admissible may be excluded if the "sources of information or other circumstances indicate lack of trustworthiness." Second, certain types of police records are inadmissible in criminal cases.

Police records exclusion. The rule specifically excludes police reports in criminal cases. Most federal courts have adopted a flexible approach, holding that the police records exclusion does not apply to all police records — *i.e.,* routine, nonadversarial matters. If a record is excluded because it involves a matter observed by law enforcement personnel, it is also inadmissible under the business records exception unless the declarant testifies. On its face, Rule 803(8)(B) is absolute — excluding police records when offered by the *defense* as well as the prosecution. However, the courts have read in an exemption when the records are offered by the defense.

Investigative reports. Rule 803(8)(C) governs investigative or evaluative records, which are admissible in civil actions and against the prosecution in criminal cases. The underlying theory is that reports, for example,

---

[173] Other rules also deal with different aspects of public records. Rule 1005, by permitting the use of certified copies, recognizes an exception to the "best evidence" rule for public records. Authentication of public records is governed by Rules 901(b) and 902. Under the latter rule, many public records are self-authenticating and thus admissible without any need to produce an authenticating witness. All these provisions combine to make admissibility quite easy to achieve.

dealing with the causes of mine disasters issued by the Bureau of Mines or airplane crashes issued by the FAA are sufficiently reliable. These types of reports are typically prepared by officials with special expertise who are often the first on the scene. These officials moreover are not partisan. In some cases, findings are based on hearings.

Business records compared. Many public records also satisfy the requirements of the business records exception; the opposite, however, is not true. The public records exception does not require that the record be prepared at or near the time of the event recorded. Nor does a public record need to be a regular or routine record.

Ancient Documents: FRE 803(16)

Rule 803(16) recognizes a hearsay exception for "statements in a document in existence twenty years or more the authenticity of which is established." The rule must be read in conjunction with Rule 901(b)(8), which governs the authentication of ancient documents.

Market Reports; Commercial Lists: FRE 803(17)

The rule recognizes a hearsay exception for "market quotations, tabulations, lists, directories, or other published compilations" if they are "generally used and relied upon by the public or by persons in particular occupations." The rule goes beyond compilations prepared for professions and trades to include newspaper market reports, telephone directories, and city directories.

Learned Treatises: FRE 803(18)

Learned treatises were admissible at common law but only for the impeachment of experts. Rule 803(18) changes this result, making the treatise admissible as substantive evidence. Rule 803(18) permits the authoritativeness to be established by another expert or by judicial notice.

Limitations. First, a treatise may be used substantively only when an expert is on the stand. This requirement provides an important safeguard because it ensures that a knowledgeable person is available "to explain and assist in the application of the treatise." Second, the treatise may be read to the jury but not received as an exhibit, thus precluding its misuse in the jury room.

Judgment of Previous Conviction: FRE 803(22)

Rule 803(22) recognizes a hearsay exception for judgments of previous criminal convictions when offered "to prove any fact essential to sustain the judgment."

Chapter 34

HEARSAY EXCEPTIONS — UNAVAILABLE DECLARANT: FRE 804

§ 34.01 Introduction

Rule 804 specifies five hearsay exceptions that require a showing that the declarant is unavailable to testify at trial.[1] In contrast, the exceptions enumerated in Rule 803 do not depend on the unavailability of the declarant. Unlike the Rule 803 exceptions, here we prefer live testimony and resort to these exceptions only when testimony is not available.[2]

One might be tempted to label the Rule 804 exceptions as "second class" exceptions. This would be questionable, at least for former testimony which could be considered the most reliable exception since the opportunity for cross-examination is required for that exception. The reasons for requiring unavailability for this exception do not involve its unreliability (*see* § 34.03 *infra*).

§ 34.02 Unavailability

Rule 804(a) contains five conditions of unavailability. The list is illustrative, not exclusive.[3] By adopting a uniform rule of unavailability for all the Rule 804(b) exceptions, the rule changes the common law, under which each exception had developed its own conditions of unavailability. For example, the common law unavailability requirements for former testimony, dying declarations, and declarations against interest were not identical.[4]

The unavailability of the declarant's *testimony*, rather than the unavailability of the declarant, is determinative. Thus, if the declarant is present in court but claims a valid privilege, refuses to testify, or suffers a lack of memory, the declarant's testimony is unavailable, and the Rule 804(b) exceptions apply. A witness is not "unavailable" under Rule 804(a) if the circumstances that would constitute unavailability were due to the procurement or other wrongdoing of the proponent of the statement.[5]

---

[1] There is no Rule 804(b)(5). That provision previously contained a residual exception but was deleted when the residual exception was moved to Rule 807 in 1997.

[2] The theory underlying exceptions to the hearsay rule is discussed with Rule 803. *See supra* § 33.02 (rationale for exceptions).

[3] *See* Gregory v. North Carolina, 900 F.2d 705, 707 n. 6 (4th Cir. 1990) (declarant who was "incompetent due to immaturity" was unavailable).

[4] While there was only one common law unavailability condition for a dying declaration (*i.e.,* death of declarant), several conditions satisfied the former testimony and declaration against interest exceptions.

[5] *See also* Fed. R. Evid. 804(b)(6); *infra* § 34.06 (forfeiture by wrongdoing).

Once there is an objection, the burden of establishing unavailability rests on the party offering the evidence.

[A]   Claim of Privilege: FRE 804(a)(1)

A declarant is unavailable if exempted by a court ruling on the ground of privilege.[6] The most common example is a witness who claims the Fifth Amendment privilege against self-incrimination.[7]

[B]   Refusal to Testify: FRE 804(a)(2)

If the court decides a claim of privilege is invalid but the witness persists in refusing to testify, Rule 804(a)(2) applies and the unavailability requirement is met. A ruling by the trial judge on the claim of privilege is required.[8] If the court rules the claim invalid, continued refusal to testify may result in holding the witness in contempt. The rule does not, however, require the imposition of contempt as a condition for finding the declarant unavailable — only an order to testify is required.[9]

[C]   Lack of Memory: FRE 804(a)(3)

If the declarant testifies to a lack of memory, the declarant is unavailable. The rationale is straightforward: "If the claim is successful, the practical effect is to put the testimony beyond reach, as in the other instances."[10] Nevertheless, the rule was somewhat controversial because of a concern about fabricated claims of lack of memory. In response, the drafters observed: "In this instance, however, it will be noted that the lack of memory must be established by the testimony of the witness himself, which clearly contemplates his production and subjection to cross-examination."[11] Stated another way, the trial judge can eyeball the witness and "may choose to disbelieve the declarant's testimony as to his lack of memory."[12]

---

[6] Rule 501 governs the law of privilege. *See infra* chapters 37–43.

[7] *See* United States v. Williams, 927 F.3d 95, 99 (2d Cir. 1991) ("Appellants have suggested no reason why Judge Griesa should not have believed the representations of the attorneys for the incarcerated defendants concerning their clients' intentions to rely on their Fifth Amendment privileges. The law does not require the doing of a futile act."). *See infra* § 43.06 (witness's privilege).

[8] *See* Fed. R. Evid. 804 advisory committee's note ("A ruling by the judge is required, which clearly implies that an actual claim of privilege must be made.").

[9] *See also* United States v. Zappoloa, 646 F.2d 48, 54 (2d Cir. 1981) (actual court order to testify required).

[10] Fed. R. Evid. 804 advisory committee's note.

[11] *Id.*

[12] H. R. Rep. No. 650, 93d Cong., 1st Sess. (1973), reprinted in 1974 U.S.C.C.A.N. 7075, 7088.

[D]　Death or Illness: FRE 804(a)(4)

A declarant is unavailable if unable to testify because of death or then-existing physical or mental illness or infirmity.[13] A continuance may resolve problems associated with a temporary infirmity.[14] Moreover, the Confrontation Clause imposes stricter unavailability standards, at least for former testimony.[15]

[E]　Unable to Procure Testimony: FRE 804(a)(5)

A declarant is unavailable if the proponent has been unable to procure the declarant's attendance. The rule governs situations in which the declarant's present whereabouts are unknown or the declarant is beyond the subpoena power of the court.[16]

Depositions required. In the case of most of the Rule 804(b) exceptions, the rule requires that the *testimony* as well as the attendance of the witness be unavailable,[17] which refers to the deposition of the declarant.[18] This provision does not apply to former testimony because a deposition is a type of former testimony. In contrast, deposition evidence is thought superior to dying declarations and declarations against interest.

"Other reasonable means." In addition to showing that the declarant's testimony is beyond judicial process, the offering party must also show that the testimony could not have been obtained by "other reasonable means" such as attempting to secure the witness's voluntary attendance at trial. This should include offering to pay reasonable witness expenses and travel fees, especially in criminal cases where unavailability is governed by constitutional principles.[19] Of course, the "question of reasonable means cannot be divorced from the significance of the witness to the proceeding

---

[13] *See also* Fed. R. Civ. P. 32(a)(3) (deposition admissible due to deponent's death, "age, sickness, infirmity"); Fed. R. Crim. P. 15(f) (deposition admissible due to deponent's death, "sickness or infirmity").

[14] *See supra* § 20.02 (continuances).

[15] *See infra* chapter 36.

[16] *See* Fed. R. Civ. P. 45 (subpoenas); Fed. R. Crim. P. 17 (same).

[17] *See* Campbell v. Coleman Co., 786 F.2d 892, 896 (8th Cir. 1986) ("This subsection is concerned with the absence of testimony, rather than the physical absence of the declarant. Hayes was absent from the trial, but his testimony was available. Coleman had taken his deposition on July 5, 1984, eight months before trial. Since Hayes was not unavailable within the meaning of Rule 804(a)(5) and (b), his hearsay statements could not be admitted under the 'statement against interest' exception in Rule 804(b)(3).") (citations omitted).

[18] H. R. Rep. No. 650, 93d Cong., 1st Sess. (1973) (Judiciary Committee inserted the "parenthetical expression '(or, in the case of a hearsay exception under subdivision (b)(2), (3), or (4), his attendance or testimony)'. The amendment is designed primarily to require that an attempt be made to depose a witness (as well as seek his attendance) as a precondition to the witness being deemed unavailable."), reprinted in 1974 U.S.C.C.A.N. 7075, 7088.

[19] Federal courts are authorized to issue subpoenas to United States nationals and residents who are in foreign countries in order to compel their attendance at state trials. *See* 28 U.S.C. § 1783(a); Mancusi v. Stubbs, 408 U.S. 204, 222 (1972) (Marshall, J., dissenting).

at hand, the reliability of the former testimony, and whether there is reason to believe that the opposing party's prior cross exam was inadequate."[20]

§ 34.03   Former Testimony: FRE 804(b)(1)

Former testimony, sometimes called prior testimony, has a long common law history.[21] Note also that prior testimony may be admissible under other rules.[22]

Rationale. Unlike other hearsay exceptions, former testimony is not based on any trustworthiness guarantee that is considered an adequate substitute for cross-examination. The exception requires an opportunity for cross-examination as well as testimony under oath. The only trial safeguard missing is the opportunity for the jury to observe the demeanor of the witness while testifying, and this could be supplied if the prior testimony has been videotaped. "Hence it may be argued that former testimony is the strongest hearsay and should be included under Rule 803."[23]

Nevertheless, the federal drafters placed the exception in Rule 804, thereby imposing an unavailability requirement. They justified this position by noting that the "opportunity to observe demeanor is what in a large measure confers depth and meaning upon oath and cross-examination."[24] In addition, many hearsay exceptions typically involve one or two statements — often a phrase or sentence. In contrast, former testimony may involve days of previous testimony.

---

[20] United States v. Johnson, 108 F.3d 919, 922 (8th Cir. 1997).

[21] *See* Falknor, *Former Testimony and the Uniform Rules: A Comment,* 38 N.Y.U. L. Rev. 651 (1963). *See also* Martin, *The Former—Testimony Exception in the Proposed Federal Rules of Evidence,* 57 Iowa L. Rev. 547 (1972); Weissenberger, *The Former Testimony Hearsay Exception: A Study in Rulemaking, Judicial Revisionism, and the Separation of Powers,* 67 N.C. L. Rev. 295 (1989).

[22] For example, the former testimony of a party is admissible against that party as an admission of a party-opponent. *See* Fed. R. Evid. 801(d)(2)(A). In addition, former testimony may be used as a prior inconsistent statement. *See* Fed. R. Evid. 801(d)(1)(A).

[23] Fed. R. Evid. 804 advisory committee's note ("Former testimony does not rely upon some set of circumstances to substitute for oath and cross-examination, since both oath and opportunity to cross-examine were present in fact. The only missing one of the ideal conditions for the giving of testimony is the presence of trier and opponent ('demeanor evidence'). This is lacking with all hearsay exceptions."). Wigmore was a leading proponent of the view that prior testimony should not even be classified as hearsay. 5 Wigmore, Evidence § 1370 (Chadbourn rev. 1974).

[24] Fed. R. Evid. 804 advisory committee's note ("Thus in cases under Rule 803 demeanor lacks the significance which it possesses with respect to testimony. In any event, the tradition, founded in experience, uniformly favors production of the witness if he is available. The exception indicates continuation of the policy. This preference for the presence of the witness is apparent also in rules and statutes on the use of depositions, which deal with substantially the same problem."). *See also* United States v. Inadi, 475 U.S. 387, 394 (1986) ("former testimony often is only a weaker substitute for live testimony").

[A] Type of Proceeding

Under Rule 804(b)(1), testimony given at another hearing or in a deposition may be admitted. In addition to depositions, former testimony includes testimony given at a prior trial. If a motion for a new trial is granted by the trial judge or a judgment is overturned on appeal, the case may be retried. Preliminary hearing testimony is often admissible under this rule in criminal cases.[25] Testimony given at an administrative proceeding may also qualify, and in some cases, testimony at a motion to suppress would qualify.[26]

Grand jury. Grand jury testimony is not admissible against a criminal defendant under this rule because the opportunity to examine the declarant is lacking. Neither the defendant nor a defense attorney is permitted in the grand jury room.[27] In contrast, the prosecution is provided that opportunity, and some cases have ruled that grand jury testimony may be admissible against the government. The issue is whether there is a similar motive at the trial and grand jury (*see* § [E] *infra*).

[B] Opportunity to Examine

The rule requires *only* an "opportunity" to examine, not actual examination. Failure to examine the declarant for tactical reasons does not affect admissibility.[28] Moreover, an opportunity for "direct" or "redirect" examination suffices; cross-examination is not required.[29]

---

[25] *See* Fed. R. Crim. P. 5; *supra* § 3.03[B] (preliminary hearing). Admitting preliminary hearing testimony in a criminal trial, however, still raises confrontation issues. *See infra* chapter 36.

[26] *See* United States v. Poland, 659 F.2d 884, 896 (9th Cir. 1981) (testimony offered at hearing on defendant's motion to suppress identification evidence admissible at trial since motive for cross-examination at hearing was to challenge the central issue of reliability of the identification).

[27] *See supra* § 3.03[C] (grand jury proceedings).

[28] *E.g.,* United States v. Mann, 161 F.3d 840, 861 (5th Cir. 1998) (discovery deposition in related civil case admissible in criminal case; rule "does not require that the party against whom the prior testimony is offered had a compelling tactical or strategic incentive to subject the testimony to cross-examination, only that an opportunity and similar motive to develop the testimony existed"); United States v. Koon, 34 F.3d 1416, 1427 & n. 4 (9th Cir. 1994) ("The failure of a defendant to discover potentially useful evidence at the time of the former proceeding does not constitute a lack of opportunity to cross-examine. . . . It is that opportunity, rather than the scope or efficacy of its employment, which is important under Rule 804(b)(1)."), *aff'd in part, rev'd in part on other grounds,* 518 U.S. 81 (1996); Hendrix v. Raybestos-Manhattan, Inc., 776 F.2d 1492, 1506 (11th Cir. 1985) ("As a general rule, a party's decision to limit cross-examination in a discovery deposition is a strategic choice and does not preclude his adversary's use of the deposition at a subsequent proceeding."); United States v. Zurosky, 614 F.2d 779, 793 (1st Cir. 1979) ("Defense counsel made a tactical decision not to question Smith at the suppression hearing; this does not mean they were denied an opportunity to do so.").

[29] *See* Fed. R. Evid. 804 advisory committee's note (The drafters treated "direct and redirect examination of one's own witness as the equivalent of cross-examining an opponent's witness. Allowable techniques for dealing with hostile, double-crossing, forgetful, and mentally deficient witnesses leave no substance to a claim that one could not adequately develop his own witness at the former hearing.").

[C] "Against Whom" Requirement

The rule does not require "identity of parties," as had some common law cases. As long as the party *against whom* the former testimony is offered (or a predecessor in interest) had an opportunity to examine the witness at the former hearing, the rule is satisfied.

Accordingly, only one of the parties has to have participated in the prior proceeding. For example, assume that defendant injures A and B in an automobile accident. In the first trial, A sues defendant and witness X testifies. X dies prior to the second trial, in which B sues defendant. X's testimony at the first trial is admissible in the second trial against defendant because he had an opportunity to examine X. X's testimony, however, is not admissible against B because B had no opportunity to examine X at the first trial:

> *First trial:*   Plaintiff A v. defendant — witness X testifies.
> *Second trial:*   Plaintiff B v. defendant — X's former testimony proffered.

Only if A is considered a "predecessor in interest" would X's testimony be admissible against B. However, given the expansive definition of that term by the federal courts, the former testimony may indeed be admissible against B.

[D] "Predecessor in Interest"

History. As proposed by the Supreme Court, Rule 804(b)(1) would have also permitted admission of former testimony if the witness had been examined at a prior hearing by a person *"with motive and interest similar to those of the party against whom the testimony is now offered."*[30] (Plaintiff B in the above example.) Congress rejected this provision as unfair to the party in the second trial (plaintiff B) who was never given an opportunity to examine the declarant at the first trial. Consequently, Congress struck the above quoted language and substituted the "predecessor in interest" language.[31]

Predecessor-in-interest defined. Although Congress did not define the term "predecessor in interest," the most plausible reading would be that "privity" or some of sort of legal relationship between the parties at the two trials was required. The federal courts, however, have interpreted the

---

[30] 56 F.R.D. 321 (1973).

[31] H.R. Rep. No. 650, 93d Cong., 1st Sess. (1973) ("Rule 804(b)(1) as submitted by the Court allowed prior testimony of an unavailable witness to be admissible if the party against whom it is offered or a person 'with motive and interest similar' to his had an opportunity to examine the witness. The Committee considered that it is generally unfair to impose upon the party against whom the hearsay evidence is being offered responsibility for the manner in which the witness was previously handled by another party. The sole exception to this, in the Committee's view, is when a party's predecessor in interest in a civil action or proceeding had an opportunity and similar motive to examine the witness. The Committee amended the Rule to reflect these policy determinations."), reprinted in 1974 U.S.C.C.A.N. 7075, 7088.

phrase "predecessor in interest" expansively. A leading case, *Lloyd v. American Export Lines, Inc.*,[32] held that a "party having like motive to develop the testimony about the same material facts is, in the final analysis, a predecessor in interest to the present party."[33] This interpretation seems to adopt the Supreme Court's version of the rule, one specifically rejected by Congress, and collapses this aspect of the rule into the similar motive requirement. Nevertheless, federal courts have continued to follow *Lloyd*.[34]

Civil actions defined. A dispute has arisen over whether the phrase "in a civil action" in Rule 804(b)(1) applies to the case in which the former testimony is offered and to the case in which the testimony was originally given, or only to the latter. In *United States v. McDonald*,[35] a criminal defendant charged with mail fraud offered former testimony of a witness given in a civil action brought by the fraud victim. The Fifth Circuit found that "Rule 804(b)(1) is not per se inapplicable to criminal cases."[36] The Rule requires in such a case that "a party in a civil case and the government in a later criminal case have sufficiently similar incentives to develop the testimony."[37] The court found, however, that the plaintiff in the civil action for fraud and the government in the criminal case did not have similar incentives to develop the witness's testimony.[38]

In contrast, in *United States v. North*,[39] the D.C. Circuit held that, in a criminal case, the rule requires that "the party against whom the testimony is now offered" must have been a party to the case in which the former testimony was originally given. This result followed from the plain language of the rule, according to the court.[40] The Tenth Circuit has agreed with this analysis.[41]

---

[32] 580 F.2d 1179 (3d Cir. 1978).

[33] *Id.* at 1187.

[34] *E.g.,* Supermarket of Marlinton, Inc. v. Meadow Gold Dairies, Inc., 71 F.3d 119, 128 (4th Cir. 1995) (" 'Instead, the party against whom the [testimony] is offered must point up distinctions in her case not evident in the earlier litigation that would preclude similar motives of witness examination.' Like the party opposing admission of the evidence in [a prior case], the dairies offer no sufficient distinction here. Moreover, even if privity was a concern in the analysis under Rule 804(b)(1), it would present little problem here because the individual defendants in the prior criminal case were officials of one of the defendant dairy companies in the present civil suit.") (citation omitted); New England Mut. Life Ins. Co. v. Anderson, 888 F.2d 646, 651 (10th Cir. 1989); Dykes v. Raymark Indus., Inc., 801 F.2d 810, 816 (6th Cir. 1986) ("[T]he fact of being a predecessor in interest is not limited to a legal relationship, but is also to be determined by the second aspect of the test under the rule: whether the defendant had an opportunity and similar motive to develop the testimony by cross-examination.").

[35] 837 F.2d 1287 (5th Cir. 1988).

[36] *Id.* at 1291.

[37] *Id.* at 1293.

[38] *Id.*

[39] 910 F.2d 843 (D.C. Cir. 1990).

[40] *Id.* at 907.

[41] *See* United States v. Harenberg, 732 F.2d 1507, 1516 (10th Cir. 1984) ("The United States had no opportunity to examine the witnesses during the course of the civil depositions" and therefore the depositions were inadmissible under Rule 801(b)(1).); United States v. Kapnison,

[E] Similar Motive Requirement

There is no explicit requirement for "identity of issues" in both proceedings.[42] Nevertheless, a substantial identity of issues is an aspect of the similar motive requirement.[43] If the issues are not substantially the same, the motive in examining the witness will often not be similar.[44] Several factors are used in determining whether a similarity of motive exists: "(1) the type of proceeding in which the testimony is given, (2) trial strategy, (3) the potential penalties or financial stakes, and (4) the number of issues and parties."[45]

Grand jury. The admissibility of grand jury testimony against the prosecution raises a significant issue. In *United States v. Salerno*,[46] two immunized witnesses testified before a grand jury investigating racketeering. They testified that neither they nor the defendants had participated in the alleged scheme. When the defense called these witnesses at trial,

---

743 F.2d 1450, 1459 (10th Cir. 1984) ("Since the government, as the 'party against whom the testimony is now offered,' has never had the 'opportunity to develop the testimony of the witness by direct, cross or redirect examination,' the district court correctly refused to allow the introduction of the deposition."). *See also* United States v. Jackson-Randolph, 282 F.3d 369, 382 (6th Cir. 2002) ("We are aware of only one circuit that has applied the 'predecessor in interest' clause to a criminal prosecution.") (citing *McDonald*).

[42] Fed. R. Evid. 804 advisory committee's note ("The common law did not limit the admissibility of former testimony to that given in an earlier trial of the same case, although it did require identity of issues as a means of insuring that the former handling of the witness was the equivalent of what would now be done if the opportunity were presented. Modern decisions reduce the requirement to 'substantial' identity. . . . Since identity of issues is significant only in that it bears on motive and interest in developing fully the testimony of the witness, expressing the matter in the latter terms is preferable.").

[43] *E.g.,* United States v. Koon, 34 F.3d 1416, 1427 & n. 4 (9th Cir. 1994) ("The operative facts and legal issues in the state and federal trials were substantially similar, and appellants do not challenge the district court's finding to this effect. Appellants thus had every reason to develop Briseno's testimony in the state trial with an eye to undermining his credibility and casting into doubt his statements about their behavior.") (citing United States v. Salerno, 504 U.S. 317 (1992) (Blackmun, J., concurring) (" 'similar motive' does not mean 'identical motive' "), *aff'd in part, rev'd in part on other grounds*, 518 U.S. 81 (1996); Supermarket of Marlinton, Inc. v. Meadow Gold Dairies, Inc., 71 F.3d 119, 127 (4th Cir. 1995) ("[T]o be admissible under Rule 804(b)(1), the party against whom the testimony was admitted in the prior proceeding need only have had a 'similar motive,' not an 'identical motive,' to the party in the second proceeding. Here, the defendants' motivation in questioning French in the criminal trial — to show the conspiracy never occurred — although not identical, is substantially similar to the dairies' motivation . . .") (citing *Salerno*); United States v. Miller, 904 F.2d 65, 68 (D.C. Cir. 1990); United States v. Licavoli, 725 F.2d 1040, 1048 (6th Cir. 1984) ("Here the issues in the cases were nearly identical, since in the state cases the defendants were charged with murder and conspiracy to commit murder, and in the RICO prosecution these two acts constituted the predicate acts for the RICO conviction.").

[44] *See* United States v. Jackson-Randolph, 282 F.3d 369, 382 (6th Cir. 2002) ("Fraud and embezzlement were not issues at the hearing. No criminal violations were alleged. Thus, the department hearing and the criminal trial had significantly different issues, the State Attorney General and the United States Attorney had different motives in the proceedings, and different outcomes were at stake.").

[45] United States v. Feldman, 761 F.2d 380, 385 (7th Cir. 1985).

[46] 505 U.S. 317 (1992).

they asserted the Fifth Amendment privilege. The defense then offered their grand jury testimony as former testimony, arguing that the prosecution had had an opportunity to cross-examine them before the grand jury. The Second Circuit ruled that the prosecutor's motive was not critical where the government obtains immunized testimony in a grand jury proceeding from a witness who refuses to testify at trial. According to the court, "adversarial fairness" required admission of the grand jury testimony. The Supreme Court disagreed, finding that courts had no authority to disregard the congressional language in order to achieve "adversarial fairness." The Court did not, however, decide the "similar motive" issue because the court of appeals had not considered the issue. Accordingly, the Court remanded the case on this issue. On remand, the Second Circuit ruled that the motives were not the same. [47]

Several other appellate courts have addressed the issue. "Three Circuits have suggested and the District of Columbia Circuit has affirmatively ruled that the government has the same motive to develop a witness' testimony during a grand jury proceeding as it does at trial." [48] In *United States v. Omar*, [49] the First Circuit agreed that grand jury testimony may fall within the purview of the former testimony rule in some cases. [50] The court, however, also issued a caution because the prosecution's motive is often different at the grand jury. The court wrote:

> Grand juries present a different face. Often, the government neither aims to discredit the witness nor to vouch for him. The prosecution may want to secure a small piece of evidence as part of an ongoing investigation or to compel an answer by an unwilling witness or to "freeze" the position of an adverse witness. In particular, discrediting a grand jury witness is rarely essential, because the government has a modest burden of proof, selects its own witnesses, and can usually call more of them at its leisure. [51]

---

[47] United States v. DiNapoli, 8 F.3d 909 (2d Cir. 1993) (Salerno had died by this time). The court wrote: "The proper approach . . . in assessing similarity of motive under Rule 804(b)(1) must consider whether the party resisting the offered testimony at a pending proceeding had at a prior proceeding an interest of substantially similar intensity to prove (or disprove) the same side of a substantially similar issue. The nature of the two proceedings — both what is at stake and the applicable burden of proof — and, to a lesser extent, the cross-examination at the prior proceeding — both what was undertaken and what was available but forgone — will be relevant though not conclusive on the ultimate issue of similarity of motive." *Id.* at 914–15.

[48] United States v. Foster, 128 F.3d 949, 955 (6th Cir. 1997). *See also* United States v. Miller, 904 F.2d 65, 68 (D.C. Cir. 1990).

[49] 104 F.3d 519 (1st Cir. 1997).

[50] *Id.* at 523 ("There has been confusion on this issue in the circuits. No one knows whether the drafters of the rule had grand jury proceedings in mind. In fact, it is likely to be very difficult for defendants offering grand jury testimony to satisfy the 'opportunity and similar motive' test; and the reasons why this is so probably underlie the doubts courts have expressed as to whether the rule should ever apply to grand jury testimony. But the government concedes that it could in principle apply and (yielding to *Salerno*) we agree, if and when the quoted condition is met.") (citation omitted).

[51] *Id.*

While this argument has merit, the defense could make a comparable argument concerning preliminary hearing testimony, and yet such testimony has been admitted, even in face of a confrontation challenge.[52]

[F] Method of Proof

A transcript of the former proceeding is the typical method of proof,[53] but neither Rule 804 nor the "best evidence" rule requires a transcript's use.[54] Nevertheless, the trial court has the authority pursuant to Rule 611(a) to require the use of a transcript if available.[55] Former testimony also may be proved by the testimony of a witness who was present at the time the testimony was given.

§ 34.04 Dying Declarations: FRE 804(b)(2)

Rationale. The exception for dying declarations is based on (1) necessity (*i.e.,* the unavailability of the declarant) and (2) a circumstantial guarantee of trustworthiness.[56] The theory is that people would not want to die with a lie upon their lips. As an early English case put it: Dying declarations "are made in extremity, when the party is at the point of death, and when every hope of this world is gone; when every motive to falsehood is silenced, and the mind is induced, by the most powerful consideration, to speak the truth. A situation so solemn and so awful is considered by the law as creating an obligation equal to that which is imposed by a positive oath administered in a court of justice."[57]

Unavailability. In contrast to the common law, admissibility is not conditioned on the declarant's death. Any of the conditions of unavailability specified in Rule 804(a) is sufficient. In other words, a person could make the statement believing that death was near but later recover. If that person is in France at the time of trial and refuses to return, the unavailability requirement is satisfied.

Firsthand knowledge. As with all hearsay exceptions, the firsthand knowledge rule applies.[58] The federal drafters noted that "continuation of

---

[52] *See infra* § 36.05[B] (right of confrontation).

[53] *See* Fed. R. Evid. 803(8) (hearsay exception for public records).

[54] Rule 1002, the best evidence rule, does not apply when the event sought to be proved existed independently of a writing, even if that event has been recorded. The federal drafters commented that "an event may be proved by nondocumentary evidence, even though a written record of it was made." Fed. R. Evid. 1002 advisory committee's note. Here, it is the testimony, an independent event, that is sought to be proved. *See* Meyers v. United States, 171 F.2d 800 (D.C. Cir. 1948).

[55] Fed. R. Evid. 611(a) ("The court shall exercise reasonable control over the mode and order of interrogating witnesses and presenting evidence. . . .").

[56] *See generally* Jaffee, *The Constitution and Proof by Dead or Unconfrontable Declarants*, 33 Ark. L. Rev. 227 (1979); Quick, *Some Reflections on Dying Declarations*, 6 How. L.J. 109, 111–12 (1960).

[57] Rex v. Woodcock, 168 Eng. Rep. 352, 353 (K.B. 1789).

[58] *See supra* § 33.03 (firsthand knowledge & opinion rules).

a requirement of first-hand knowledge is assured by Rule 602."[59] Such knowledge, however, may be inferred from the circumstances.

[A] "Imminent Expectation of Death" Requirement

The statement must be made while believing death was "imminent." This requirement follows from the theory underlying the exception; a declarant who does not believe that death is near may not feel compelled to speak truthfully. In *Shepard v. United States*,[60] Justice Cardozo stated that the declarant must have spoken "without hope of recovery and in the shadow of impending death" and "with the consciousness of a swift and certain doom."[61] In another passage, he wrote that the statement must be "made under a sense of impending death, excluding from the mind of the dying person all hope or expectation of recovery."[62]

Proof. In *Shepard*, Cardozo also commented that "the state of mind must be exhibited in the evidence, and not left to conjecture."[63] The declarant's belief of impending death may be established by the declarant's own statements or it may be shown circumstantially.[64]

[B] Subject Matter Requirement

Only statements concerning the cause or circumstances of what the declarant believed to be his or her impending death are admissible. This requirement follows from the theory underlying the exception — statements beyond cause and circumstances indicate that the declarant may no longer be acting under an expectation of imminent death — *e.g*, "Bolz shot me, and he also cheats on his income tax." Statements identifying the assailant who caused the injury are admissible, as are statements describing the events leading up to the injury.[65]

---

[59] *See* Fed. R. Evid. 804 advisory committee's note.

[60] 290 U.S. 96 (1933).

[61] *Id.* at 99–100.

[62] *Id.*

[63] *Id.* at 100.

[64] *See* State v. Kotowicz, 9 N.E.2d 1003, 1005 (Ohio App. 1937) ("One declarant might say: 'Well, I am shot and I'm going to die'; another, of a different temperament, nationality, educational qualifications and manner of speech, might say: 'Well, they got me right this time.' These words were spoken by the deceased within a half hour after the shooting, he having repeatedly called to his wife to get a doctor while he was still at the store, and the words were spoken while in the receiving room at the hospital and ready to be taken to the operating room, and the nurses had told the officers that their interview would have to be 'very short.' His outer clothing had been removed; he was bleeding profusely; the doctor testified that at that time his condition was very grave; he was ashen-gray in color, very cold, pulse weak, with a 45-caliber bullet hole through his right upper abdomen; the bullet had penetrated the large bowel twice and severed the blood supply to the right kidney, which later was removed, and caffeine had been administered to stimulate his heart.").

[65] *See* 5 Wigmore, Evidence § 1434, at 282 (Chadbourn rev. 1974) ("facts leading up to or causing or attending the injurious act").

[C] Type of Case

At common law, dying declarations were admissible only in homicide cases. Under Rule 804, dying declarations are admissible in civil actions as well. They remain inadmissible in criminal trials other than homicide cases. This limitation seems indefensible; if such declarations are deemed reliable enough for homicide prosecutions, including death penalty cases, and civil actions, why are they not considered sufficiently reliable in other types of criminal prosecutions? For example, one court ruled inadmissible a dying declaration of the victim in a rape prosecution, though death resulted from a fever following the birth of a child conceived during the rape.[66]

§ 34.05 Statements Against Interest: FRE 804(b)(3)

At common law, the declaration had to be against the declarant's *pecuniary* or *proprietary* interest to be admissible. Courts gradually interpreted "pecuniary interest" expansively to include statements that would subject declarants to civil liability.[67] Declarations against penal interest were not admissible — Rule 804(b)(3) changes this.

Rationale. Declarations against interest are based on (1) necessity (*i.e.,* the unavailability of the declarant) and (2) a circumstantial guarantee of trustworthiness that eliminates the risk of insincerity. The Supreme Court put it this way: "Rule 804(b)(3) is founded on the commonsense notion that reasonable people, even reasonable people who are not especially honest, tend not to make self-inculpatory statements unless they believe them to be true."[68]

Firsthand knowledge. Although not explicitly mentioned in the rule, firsthand knowledge on the part of the declarant is required.[69]

Social interest. As proposed by the Supreme Court, the federal rule also covered declarations against social interest, that is, a statement making the declarant "an object of hatred, ridicule, or disgrace."[70] Congress rejected this provision, but some states adopted it.

---

[66] Hansel v. Commonwealth, 84 S.W.2d 68, 69 (Ky. 1935).

[67] *See generally* Goodman & Waltuch, *Declarations Against Penal Interest: The Majority Has Emerged*, 28 N.Y.L. Sch. L. Rev. 51 (1983); Jefferson, *Declarations Against Interest: An Exception to the Hearsay Rule*, 58 Harv. L. Rev. 1 (1944); Morgan, *Declarations Against Interest*, 5 Vand. L. Rev. 451 (1952); Tague, *Perils of the Rulemaking Process: The Development, Application, and Unconstitutionality of Rule 804(b)(3)'s Penal Interest Exception*, 69 Geo. L.J. 851 (1981); Note, *Declarations Against Penal Interest: Standards of Admissibility Under an Emerging Majority Rule*, 56 B.U. L. Rev. 148 (1976).

[68] Williamson v. United States, 512 U.S. 594, 599 (1994). *See also* Fed. R. Evid. 804 advisory committee's note ("The circumstantial guaranty of reliability for declarations against interest is the assumption that persons do not make statements which are damaging to themselves unless satisfied for good reason that they are true.").

[69] *See supra* § 33.03 (firsthand knowledge & opinion rules).

[70] 56 F.R.D. 321 (1972).

Party admissions. Statements of the parties are admissible as admissions of party-opponents under Rule 801(d)(2). The differences between party admissions and statements against interest are discussed with Rule 801.[71] The two rules rarely overlap, and the term "admission against interest" is hopelessly confusing.

[A] "Against Interest" Requirement

The "against interest" requirement focuses on the declarant's situation and motives *at the time the statement was made.*[72] This is the critical requirement, which follows from the underlying theory of the rule. Determining whether the statement is, in fact, against interest requires an examination of the context in which the statement was made. For example, a statement acknowledging a debt of $500 would, under most circumstances, be a statement against the declarant's pecuniary interest. If, however, the declarant made the statement while disputing a $1000 debt (and the statement is offered to prove the debt was *only* $500), the statement is not against interest. By its terms, the rule requires the "against interest" standard to be judged from the perspective of a "reasonable" person.

[B] Declarations Against Penal Interests

At common law, declarations against penal interest were not admissible. This position rested upon a concern about collusive arrangements between defendants and declarants to fabricate confessions exonerating the defendant. The declarant would "confess" to the crime that the defendant was charged with and then disappear.[73] If the statement were admitted as a declaration against interest, the defendant may be acquitted, in which case the Double Jeopardy Clause would preclude a retrial — even if the declarant returned and repudiated the "confession."

Nevertheless, the federal drafters, following the position of Wigmore[74] and Justice Holmes,[75] rejected the common law position but then added

---

[71] *See supra* § 32.06[E] (declarations against interest distinguished).

[72] *See* Fed. R. Evid. 804 advisory committee's note ("Whether a statement is in fact against interest must be determined from the circumstances of each case. Thus a statement admitting guilt and implicating another person, made while in custody, may well be motivated by a desire to curry favor with the authorities and hence fail to qualify as against interest. On the other hand, the same words spoken under different circumstances, *e.g.,* to an acquaintance, would have no difficulty in qualifying.").

[73] If the declarant were on trial, the statement would be admissible as an admission of a party-opponent and resort to the declaration against interest exception would not be needed.

[74] *See* 5 Wigmore, Evidence § 1477, at 359–60 (Chadbourn rev. 1974) ("The only practical consequences of this unreasoning limitation are shocking to the sense of justice. It is therefore not too late to discard this barbarous doctrine, which would refuse to let an innocent accused vindicate himself.").

[75] *See* Donnelly v. United States, 228 U.S. 243, 278 (1913) ("no other statement is so much against interest as a confession of murder") (Holmes, J., dissenting).

a corroboration requirement as a safeguard against fabricated confessions.[76] The rejection of the common law rule is also supported by *Chambers v. Mississippi*,[77] in which the Supreme Court held that the exclusion
of declarations against penal interest offered by a criminal defendant for
the purpose of exculpation violated due process under the facts of that case.
The *Chambers* case went beyond the rule because the declarant in *Chambers* was not unavailable.[78]

[1] Corroboration Requirement

Rule 804(b)(3) imposes a corroboration rule when declarations against
penal interest are offered in criminal cases to exculpate the accused. The
federal cases, however, have applied the corroboration requirement to
inculpatory statements as well — *i.e.*, when offered by the prosecution.[79]
A 2002 proposed amendment would make clear that the corroboration
requirement applied to the prosecution, as well as in civil cases.[80]

The federal cases specify a number of relevant factors in determining
whether the corroboration requirement has been satisfied:

> (1) whether the declarant had at the time of making the statement
> pled guilty or was still exposed to prosecution for making the
> statement, (2) the declarant's motive in making the statement and
> whether there was a reason for the declarant to lie, (3) whether the
> declarant repeated the statement and did so consistently, (4) the
> party or parties to whom the statement was made, (5) the relation-
> ship of the declarant with the accused, and (6) the nature and

---

[76] Fed. R. Evid. 804 advisory committee's note ("The refusal of the common law to concede
the adequacy of a penal interest was no doubt indefensible in logic, but one senses in the
decisions a distrust of evidence of confessions by third persons offered to exculpate the accused
arising from suspicions of fabrication either of the fact of the making of the confession or in
its contents, enhanced in either instance by the required unavailability of the declarant.
Nevertheless, an increasing amount of decisional law recognizes exposure to punishment for
crime as a sufficient stake. The requirement of corroboration is included in the rule in order
to effect an accommodation between these competing considerations. The requirement of
corroboration should be construed in such a manner as to effectuate its purpose of circumvent-
ing fabrication.").

[77] 410 U.S. 284 (1973). *See supra* § 31.08 (constitutional issues).

[78] *See also* Green v. Georgia, 442 U.S. 95 (1979).

[79] *See* United States v. Costa, 31 F.3d 1073, 1077 (11th 1994); United States v. Candoli,
870 F.2d 496, 509 (9th Cir. 1989) ("When a statement is against the declarant's penal interest
and is offered to inculpate the defendant, many circuits have held that the statement must
be corroborated by circumstances which indicate trustworthiness."); United States v. Alvarez,
584 F.2d 694 (5th Cir. 1978).

[80] At the time the Rules were enacted, the declaration against penal interest provision was
thought to be a "defense" rule —*i.e.*, that it would be used to exculpate. This is probably why
the corroboration requirement applied only to exculpatory statements. Prosecutors, however,
quickly learned how valuable this exception could be. It is this use that gave rise to the
Williamson case discussed in the next section.

strength of independent evidence relevant to the conduct in question.[81]

[C] Collateral Statements

The admissibility of collateral statements — those that are not directly
against the declarant's interest — has proved controversial. Wigmore
argued that the entire passage should be scrutinized, and if it, as a whole,
was against the declarant's interest, the statement should be admitted.[82]
For example, the statement "Botz and I shot Schmedlap" is admissible
under this view, even though the collateral statement about Botz is not
directly against the declarant's interest. Other commentators disagreed,
urging that only the part explicitly against the declarant's interest be
admitted.[83] Under this view, the phrase about Botz would not be admissible. A third view, a compromise position, distinguished between "collateral
neutral" statements and "collateral self-serving" statements.[84] For example, in the statement "Botz and I shot Schmedlap," the phrase "Botz and"
is neutral and thus is admissible under this approach. In contrast, the
statement "Botz, not I, did the actual shooting" is a collateral self-serving
statement and not admissible.

In *Williamson v. United States*,[85] the Supreme Court addressed this
issue. After the declarant was arrested for possession of cocaine, he
implicated Williamson as a cocaine distributor. When the declarant asserted his privilege against self-incrimination at Williamson's trial, the
prosecution offered the declarant's out-of-court confessions as declarations
against interest pursuant to Rule 804(b)(3). The declarant's statements
implicating himself in cocaine trafficking were clearly against his penal
interest. However, the statements concerning Williamson's involvement
(collateral statements) were not explicitly against the declarant's penal
interest, and these, of course, were the critical statements in Williamson's

---

[81] United States v. Bumpass, 60 F.3d 1099, 1102 (4th Cir. 1995). *See also* United States
v. Garcia, 986 F.2d. 1135, 1140 (7th Cir. 1993) (factors include: (1) the relationship between
the confessing party and the exculpated party: Did the confessor fabricate his story for the
benefit of a friend? If the two involved parties do not have a close relationship, "one important
corroborating circumstance exists," (2) "the confessor made a voluntary statement after being
advised of his *Miranda* rights," and (3) "there was no evidence that his statement was made
in order to curry favor with authorities"); United States v. One Star, 979 F.2d 1319, 1322 (8th
Cir. 1992) ("(1) whether there is any apparent motive for the out-of-court declarant to
misrepresent the matter, (2) the general character of the speaker, (3) whether other people
heard the out-of-court statement, (4) whether the statement was made spontaneously, (5) the
timing of the declaration and the relationship between the speaker and the witness") (citation
omitted).

[82] 5 Wigmore, Evidence § 1465, at 341 (Chadbourn rev. 1974).

[83] Jefferson, *Declarations Against Interest: An Exception to the Hearsay Rule*, 58 Harv. L.
Rev. 1, 62–63 (1944).

[84] McCormick, Evidence § 256, at 552–53 (1954).

[85] 512 U.S. 594 (1994).

trial. The Court, in a divided opinion, adopted a strict interpretation of the federal rule.[86]

The Court noted that the rationale underlying the exception does not necessarily apply to collateral statements: "The fact that a person is making a broadly self-inculpatory confession does not make more credible the confession's non-self-inculpatory parts. One of the most effective ways to lie is to mix falsehood with truth, especially truth that seems particularly persuasive because of its self-inculpatory nature."[87] Accordingly, the exception "does not allow admission of non-self-inculpatory statements, even if they are made within a broader narrative that is generally self-inculpatory."[88] This approach makes admissibility more difficult to achieve but not impossible.[89]

---

[86] Justice O'Connor, who wrote the lead opinion, wanted the case remanded for a "fact-intensive inquiry, which would require careful examination of all the circumstances surrounding the criminal activity involved." *Id.* at 604. Justice Scalia agreed. Justice Ginsburg, and three other Justices, disagreed only with the remand. They believed that the declarant's statements were inadmissible: "The declarant's arguably inculpatory statements are too closely intertwined with his self-serving declarations to be ranked as trustworthy. The declarant was caught red-handed with 19 kilos of cocaine — enough to subject even a first-time offender to a minimum of 12 ½ years' imprisonment. The declarant admitted involvement, but did so in a way that minimized his own role and shifted blame to petitioner Fredel Williamson (and a Cuban man named Shawn)." *Id.* at 608.

Justice Kennedy, along with two other Justices, concurred in the remand but offered a different analysis. He argued that a trial court should first determine whether the statement contained a fact against the declarant's interest. If so, all collateral statements relating to the precise statement against penal interest should be admitted, subject to two limitations. First, courts should exclude "a collateral statement that is so self-serving as to render it unreliable (if, for example, it shifts blame to someone else for a crime the defendant could have committed)." Second, "where the statement was made under circumstances where it is likely that the declarant had a significant motivation to obtain favorable treatment, as when the government made an explicit offer of leniency in exchange for the declarant's admission of guilt, the entire statement should be inadmissible." *Id.* at 620.

[87] *Id.* at 599–60.

[88] *Id.* at 600-01.

[89] *See also* United States v. Barone, 114 F.3d 1284, 1295-96 (1st Cir. 1997) ("[A] statement inculpating both the declarant and the defendant may be sufficiently reliable as to be admissible in the circumstances that obtain here —*i.e.,* where the statement is made in a non-custodial setting to an ally, rather than to a law enforcement official, and where the circumstances surrounding the portion of the statement that inculpates the defendant provide no reason to suspect that this portion of the statement is any less trustworthy than the portion that inculpates the declarant."); United States v. Paguio, 114 F.3d 928, 933 (9th Cir. 1997) ("*Williamson* does not mean that the trial judge must always parse the statement and let in only the inculpatory part. It means that the statement must be examined in context, to see whether as a matter of common sense the portion at issue was against interest and would not have been made by a reasonable person unless he believed it to be true. Sometimes that requires exclusion of part of the statement, sometimes not. A reasonable man caught with a trunk full of cocaine, like the unavailable declarant in *Williamson*, might well imagine that he could advance his own penal interest by fingering someone else. But Paguio Sr.'s statement that 'my son had nothing to do with it' was not an attempt to 'shift blame or curry favor.' ").

[D] Right of Confrontation

The Court's disposition of *Williamson* on evidentiary grounds allowed it to avoid addressing the confrontation argument. Subsequently, in *Lilly v. Virginia,*[90] the Court decided that issue. An accomplice gave a statement to the police in which he admitted his participation in a burglary and several robberies but implicated his brother, the defendant, in the murder of the victim. The Virginia Supreme Court affirmed the trial court's decision to admit the statement under Virginia's hearsay exception for declarations against penal interest.[91]

The United States Supreme Court overturned the conviction on confrontation grounds. The Court first concluded that the state's hearsay exception for declarations against penal interest as interpreted by the Virginia Supreme Court was not a "firmly rooted" hearsay exception, a critical Confrontation Clause issue.[92] In examining the reliability of the statements, the Court voiced several concerns. First, the statements "'are not unambiguously adverse to the penal interest of the declarant' but instead are likely to be attempts to minimize the declarant's culpability."[93] In addition, such statements may be attempts to make a deal with the prosecution, even in "the absence of an express promise of leniency."[94] Finally, the statement was obtained while the declarant was in custody and was "obviously obtained for the purpose of creating evidence that would be useful at a future trial."[95]

§ 34.06   Forfeiture by Wrongdoing: FRE 804(b)(6)

In 1997, a new subsection was added to Rule 804(b) for statements offered against a party who causes the unavailability of the declarant by wrongdoing — *e.g.,* killing or scaring a witness.[96] The rule applies when the party against whom the statement is offered has "engaged or acquiesced in wrongdoing" that procured the declarant's unavailability.[97]

---

[90] 527 U.S. 116 (1999).

[91] The declarant was unavailable because he invoked his privilege against self-incrimination when called to testify. The statement would not be admissible under Rule 804(b)(3) as interpreted in *Williamson,* because the part of the declarant's statement implicating the defendant in the murder was not self-inculpatory.

[92] *See infra* § 36.05[C][1] ("firmly rooted" exceptions). The Court did not decide whether an exception construed consistently with *Williamson* would be a firmly rooted hearsay exception, but "noted the presumptive unreliability of the 'non-self-inculpatory' portions of the statement." *Lilly,* 527 U.S. at 133.

[93] *Id.* at 132 (quoting Lee v. Illinois, 476 U.S. 530, 541 (1986)).

[94] *Id.* at 139.

[95] *Id.* at 125.

[96] Fed. R. Evid. 804(b)(6). *See* Steele v. Taylor, 684 F.2d 1193, 1202 (6th Cir. 1982); Comment, *The Admission of Hearsay Evidence Where Defendant Misconduct Causes the Unavailability of a Prosecution Witness,* 43 Am. U. L. Rev. 995, 1014 (1994).

[97] Under some circumstances, a party's mere inaction has been held to result in forfeiture.

Several cases had examined this issue before the rule was adopted. For example, in *United States v. Carlson*,[98] the court admitted grand jury testimony. On the night prior to trial, the declarant advised a DEA agent that he would not testify because he feared reprisals. The witness was equivocal about the source of his change of mind, even though he had previously testified before the grand jury. He said he would not have a "chance" if he testified. The next day with counsel, the witness refused to testify, although he said that he had testified truthfully to the grand jury. When called as a witness the next day, he asserted the Fifth Amendment. When given immunity, he still refused, was held in contempt, and sentenced to six months imprisonment. The grand jury testimony was admitted under the residual exception. As for the Sixth Amendment, the court relied on waiver: "To permit the defendant to profit from such conduct would be contrary to public policy, common sense and the underlying purpose of the confrontation clause."[99]

In *United States v. Mastraneglo*,[100] the Second Circuit wrote: "If the District Court finds that Mastrangelo was in fact involved in the death of Bennett through knowledge, complicity, planning or in any other way, it must hold his objections to the use of Bennett's testimony waived. Bare knowledge of a plot to kill Bennett and a failure to give warning to appropriate authorities is sufficient to constitute a waiver."[101]

In *United States v. Cherry*,[102] the Tenth Circuit held that if a murder is reasonably foreseeable to a conspirator and within the scope and in

---

[98] 547 F.2d 1346 (8th Cir. 1976).

[99] *Id.* at 1359. *See also* United States v. White, 116 F.3d 903, 912 (D.C. Cir. 1997) ("The forfeiture principle, as distinct from the confrontation clause, is designed to prevent a defendant from thwarting the normal operation of the criminal justice system."; informant murdered; eyewitnesses identified several of the defendants); United States v. Thevis, 665 F.2d 616, 630 (5th Cir. 1982) (murder of declarant, grand jury testimony admitted; "[A] defendant who causes a witness to be unavailable for trial for the purpose of preventing that witness from testifying also waives his right to confrontation. . . ."); United States v. Balano, 618 F.2d 624, 629 (10th Cir. 1979) (declarant told FBI agent that defendant had made threats; "[B]efore permitting the admission of grand jury testimony of witnesses who will not appear at trial because of the defendant's alleged coercion, the judge must hold an evidentiary hearing in the absence of the jury and find by a preponderance of the evidence that the defendant's coercion made the witness unavailable.").

[100] 693 F.2d 269 (2d Cir. 1982) (grand jury testimony of murdered witness; tape recording of conversation between defendant and witness easily read as a threat; witness killed on day of his testimony; mistrial declared).

[101] *Id.* at 273–74. *See also* United States v. Miller, 116 F.3d 641, 668 (2d Cir. 1997) ("We have never indicated that *Mastrangelo* did not apply to a defendant's procurement of the unavailability of the declarant unless there was an ongoing proceeding in which the declarant was scheduled to testify, and we see no reason to do so now."); United States v. Thai, 29 F.3d 785 (2d Cir. 1994) (unsworn statements made to detective prior to declarant's murder by defendant); United States v. Aguiar, 975 F.2d 45, 47 (2d Cir. 1992) (declarant refused to cooperate and withdrew plea agreement; threatening letters found; "Although *Mastrangelo* involved sworn grand jury testimony, we did not there, and do not here, limit its rationale to such testimony. A defendant who procures a witness's absence waives the right of confrontation for all purposes with regard to that witness, not just to the admission of sworn hearsay statements.").

[102] 217 F.3d 811 (10th Cir. 2000).

furtherance of the conspiracy, the conspirator waives his right to confront that witness just as if he killed the witness himself.[103] The Second Circuit has found that there is no subject matter limitation under the rule.[104] The preponderance of evidence standard applies.[105]

§ 34.07　Key Points

Unavailability: FRE 804(a)

Rule 804(a) contains five conditions of unavailability. The list is illustrative, not exclusive. By adopting a uniform rule of unavailability for all the Rule 804(b) exceptions, the rule changes the common law, under which each exception had developed its own conditions of unavailability.

Claim of privilege. The most common example is a witness who claims the privilege against self-incrimination.

Refusal to testify. If the court decides a claim of privilege is invalid but the witness persists in refusing to testify, the unavailability requirement is met. A ruling by the trial judge on the claim of privilege is required.

Lack of memory. The rule was somewhat controversial because of a concern about fabricated claims of lack of memory. The judge, however, can eyeball the witness and may choose to disbelieve the declarant's testimony as to his lack of memory.

Death or illness. A continuance may resolve problems associated with a temporary infirmity.

Unable to procure testimony. The rule governs situations in which the declarant's present whereabouts are unknown or the declarant is beyond the subpoena power of the court. In the case of most of the Rule 804 exceptions, the rule requires that the *testimony* as well as the attendance of the witness be unavailable, which refers to the deposition of the declarant. This provision does not apply to former testimony because a deposition is a type of former testimony.

---

[103] *See also* United States v. Thompson, 286 F.3d 950, 963 (7th Cir. 2002) ("Although we believe that *Cherry* is well-reasoned, we find that Willis's murder was not reasonably foreseeable to these defendants.").

[104] United States v. Dhinsa, 243 F.3d 635, 653 (2d Cir. 2001) ("In sum, based on the plain language of Rule 804(b)(6) and the strong policy reasons favoring application of the waiver-by-misconduct doctrine to prevent a party from profiting from his wrongdoing, we hold that Rule 804(b)(6) places no limitation on the subject matter of the declarant's statements that can be offered against the defendant at trial to prove that the defendant murdered the declarant.").

[105] United States v. Zlatogur, 271 F.3d 1025, 1028 (11th Cir. 2001) (adopting "the preponderance of the evidence standard for determining whether a defendant, through his own misconduct in procuring the unavailability of a witness, has waived his right to object to evidence on hearsay grounds under Rule 804(b)(6)").

Former Testimony: FRE 804(b)(1)

Rationale. Unlike other hearsay exceptions, former testimony is not based on any trustworthiness guarantee that is considered an adequate substitute for cross-examination. The exception requires an opportunity for cross-examination as well as testimony under oath. The only trial safeguard missing is the opportunity for the jury to observe the demeanor of the witness while testifying, and this could be supplied if the prior testimony has been videotaped.

Type of proceeding. Former testimony includes testimony given at a deposition, prior trial, preliminary hearing, and administrative proceeding.

Opportunity to examine. The rule requires only an "opportunity" to examine, not actual examination. Failure to examine the declarant for tactical reasons does not result in exclusion. Moreover, an opportunity for "direct" or "redirect" examination suffices.

"Against whom" requirement. The rule does not require "identity of parties," as had some common law cases. As long as the party against whom the former testimony is offered (or a predecessor in interest) had an opportunity to examine the witness at the former hearing, the rule is satisfied.

Predecessor-in-interest defined. Although Congress did not define the term "predecessor in interest," the most plausible reading would require privity or some of sort of legal relationship. The federal courts, however, have interpreted the phrase "predecessor in interest" expansively — a "party having like motive to develop the testimony about the same material facts is, in the final analysis, a predecessor in interest to the present party."

Similar motive requirement. There is no explicit requirement for "identity of issues." Nevertheless, this is an aspect of the similar motive requirement if modified to require only an substantial identity of issues. If the issues are not substantially the same, the motive in examining the witness will often not be similar.

Dying Declarations: FRE 804(b)(2)

Rationale. The exception for dying declarations is based (1) on necessity (*i.e.,* the unavailability of the declarant) and (2) on a circumstantial guarantee of trustworthiness. The theory is that people would not want to die with a lie upon their lips.

Unavailability. In contrast to the common law, admissibility is not conditioned on the declarant's death. Any of the conditions of unavailability specified in Rule 804(a) is sufficient. In other words, a person could make the statement believing that death was near but later recover. If they are in France at the time of trial and refuse to return, the unavailability requirement is satisfied.

Firsthand knowledge. As with all hearsay exceptions, the firsthand knowledge rule applies.

"Imminent expectation of death" requirement. This requirement follows from the theory underlying the exception; a declarant who does not believe that death is near may not feel compelled to speak truthfully. The declarant's belief of impending death may be established by the declarant's own statements. In addition, it may be established circumstantially by the apparent fatal quality of the wound, by the statements made to the declarant by doctors or others of the hopelessness of the condition, or by other circumstances.

Subject matter requirement. Only statements concerning the cause or circumstances of what the declarant believed to be his or her impending death are admissible. This requirement also follows from the theory underlying the exception — statements beyond cause and circumstances indicate that the declarant may no longer be acting under an expectation of imminent death.

Type of case. At common law, dying declarations were admissible only in homicide cases. Under Rule 804, dying declarations are admissible in civil actions as well. They remain inadmissible in criminal trials other than homicide cases.

Statements Against Interest: FRE 804(b)(3)

At common law, the declaration had to be against the declarant's pecuniary or proprietary interest to be admissible. Courts gradually interpreted "pecuniary interest" expansively to include statements that would subject declarants to civil liability. Declarations against penal interest were not admissible — Rule 804(b)(3) changes this.

Rationale. Declarations against interest are based (1) on necessity (*i.e.,* the unavailability of the declarant) and (2) a circumstantial guarantee of trustworthiness that eliminates the risk of insincerity.

Firsthand knowledge. Although not explicitly mentioned in the rule, firsthand knowledge on the part of the declarant is required.

Corroboration requirement. Rule 804(b)(3) imposes a corroboration rule when declarations against penal interest are offered in criminal cases when offered to exculpate the accused. The federal cases, however, have applied the corroboration requirement to inculpatory statements. A 2002 proposed amendment would make clear that the corroboration requirement applied to the prosecution, as well as in civil cases.

Collateral statements. The admissibility of collateral statements — those that are not directly against the declarant's interest — have often proved controversial. In *Williamson v. United States*, the Supreme Court adopted a strict interpretation of the federal rule: the non-self-inculpatory portions are not against interest.

Forfeiture by Wrongdoing: FRE 804(b)(6)

In 1997, a new subsection was added to Rule 804(b) for statements offered against a party when the unavailability of the declarant is due to the wrongdoing of the party — *e.g.*, killing a witness. The rule applies when the party against whom the statement is offered has "engaged or acquiesced in wrongdoing" that procured the unavailability of the declarant as a witness.

Chapter 35

RESIDUAL EXCEPTION: FRE 807

§ 35.01 Introduction

Rule 807 recognizes a residual hearsay exception — variously described as the catch-all, open-ended, or garbage exception. When the Federal Rules were enacted, there were two residual exceptions — Rule 803(24) and Rule 804(b)(5). In 1997, they were transferred to Rule 807 because they were basically redundant.

§ 35.02 Rationale

There are reliable hearsay statements that do not fall within any of the exceptions specified in Rules 803 and 804. The residual exception is a way to recognize this by giving the trial judge ad hoc authority to admit trustworthy hearsay in a particular case.[1] In addition, the drafters did not want to codify the status quo. They included the residual exceptions because it would "be presumptuous to assume that all possible desirable exceptions to the hearsay rule have been catalogued and to pass the hearsay rule to oncoming generations as a closed system."[2]

The drafters cited *Dallas County v. Commercial Union Assurance Co.*,[3] as support for the residual exception. In that case, the plaintiffs contended that a courthouse collapsed because it was struck by lightening. Evidence of charred timbers was offered to support this theory. The defendant insurance company, however, argued that structural deterioration caused the collapse and proffered a 1901 newspaper account of a fire in the courthouse to explain the charring. The Fifth Circuit upheld the admissibility of the newspaper account, even though it constituted hearsay and did not fall within a recognized exception, because it was reliable: "[I]t is inconceivable to us that a newspaper reporter in a small town would report a fire in the dome of the new courthouse — if there had been no fire."[4] In short, charred timbers suggested lightening but the newspaper account provided an alternative explanation.

Dallas County demonstrates the value of a residual exception; the newspaper account was both reliable and necessary for a fair determination of the case. Even if the declarant [journalist] had been available after all

---

[1] Moreover, in the absence of a residual exception, a judge faced with reliable hearsay either would have to exclude it or torture a recognized exception to get the statement admitted.

[2] Fed. R. Evid. 803 advisory committee's note.

[3] 286 F.2d 388 (5th Cir. 1961).

[4] *Id.* at 397.

these years had passed, the newspaper account would in all likelihood be more reliable than the reporter's memory.

Nevertheless the residual exceptions ran into opposition in Congress because of their open-ended nature.[5] While the House deleted these provisions,[6] the Senate restored them with qualifications.[7] Before such a statement is admissibile, the trial judge has to make three determinations: (A) the statement must be offered as evidence of a material fact; (B) the statement must be more probative on the point for which it is offered than any other evidence which the proponent can procure through reasonable efforts; and (C) the general purposes of the Federal Rules and the interests of justice must be served by admission. The first and third requirements are redundant. Rule 401 also requires materiality, and Rule 102, the purpose and construction clause, requires the doing of justice, among other things. In contrast, the second requirement is an important qualification — a sort of "best evidence" provision.[8]

Notice. In conference, the Senate version was adopted with a further qualification: the offering party was required to provide advance notice of its intention to use the residual exceptions, including the name and address of the declarant.[9] As enacted, the residual exceptions seemed an acceptable compromise — hearsay exceptions would not be frozen, but safeguards had been added. Nevertheless, they remain controversial, especially in criminal cases where significant confrontation issues arise.

§ 35.03 "Equivalent Guarantee of Trustworthiness" Requirement

Rule 807 requires a finding of reliability. However, requiring that the statement have "equivalent circumstantial guarantees of trustworthiness" as the exceptions in Rules 803 and 804 is not particularly helpful because those exceptions vary widely. While various reliability factors are discussed

---

[5] The drafters stated that these provisions "do not contemplate an unfettered exercise of judicial discretion. . . ." Fed. R. Evid. 803 advisory committee's note.

[6] H.R. Rep. No. 650, 93d Cong., 1st Sess. 5-6 (1973), reprinted in [1974] U.S.C.C.A.N. 7075, 7079.

[7] S. Rep. No. 1277, 93d Cong., 2d Sess. 18-20, reprinted in [1974] U.S.C.C.A.N. 7051, 7065–66.

[8] *See* Noble v. Alabama Dept. of Envtl. Mgmt., 872 F.2d 361, 366 (11th Cir. 1989) ("[I]t was not unreasonable to expect appellees to call the writers of the letters themselves to testify about the context of their statements as well as their qualifications to evaluate the competence of CET graduates instead of admitting the hearsay evidence. Noble is correct in arguing that one of the purposes of Rule [807] is to allow admission of hearsay . . . under special conditions of hardship when the evidence would be unreasonably difficult to get from a declarant. When the evidence is not unreasonably difficult to obtain directly from a declarant, Rule [807] does not apply.").

[9] H.R. Rep. No. 1597, 93d Cong., 2d Sess. 11-12, reprinted in [1974] U.S.C.C.A.N. 7098, 7105. *See also* United States v. Williams, 272 F.3d 845, 858 (7th Cir. 2001) ("Williams gave the government no notice at all, and did not even obtain the documents until the trial was well under way. Moreover, he has never identified the proponent of the log pages he submitted.").

below, an initial question needs to be addressed — what is known as the "near-miss" theory.

[A]　"Near Miss" Issue

Rule 807 requires that the statement not be "specifically" covered by another hearsay exception. From this requirement, the argument runs, any statement close (a "near miss") to a recognized exception should be excluded because the recognized exception "covers the field," so to speak.[10] The federal courts for the most part have rejected this theory.[11] Indeed, some courts have found that classification as a "near miss" favors admissibility.[12]

[B]　Grand Jury Testimony

The most prominent illustration of Rule 807 is grand jury testimony,[13] which is frequently admitted. While it is not automatically admissible, courts frequently find enough reliability factors to admit such testimony despite the lack of defense cross-examination.[14]

---

[10] *See* United States v. Deeb, 13 F.3d 1532, 1536 (11th Cir. 1994) (The "near miss" theory "maintains that a hearsay statement that is close to, but that does not fit precisely into, a recognized hearsay exception is not admissible under [the residual hearsay exception].").

[11] *See* United States v. Laster, 258 F.3d 525, 530 (6th Cir. 2001) ("Although some courts have held that if proffered evidence fails to meet the requirements of the Fed. R. Evid. 803 hearsay exception, it cannot qualify for admission under the residual exception, the court declines to adopt this narrow interpretation of Fed.R.Evid. 807. . . ."); United States v. Earles, 113 F.3d 796, 800 (8th Cir. 1997) (holding that "the phrase 'specifically covered' [by a hearsay exception] means only that if a statement is admissible under one of the [FRE 803] exceptions such subsection should be relied upon instead of the residual exception"); United States v. Ismoila, 100 F.3d 380, 393 (5th Cir. 1996) (holding that where hearsay statements do not qualify under the business records exception, they may properly be admitted under the residual exception).

[12] *See* United States v. Valdez-Soto, 31 F.3d 1467, 1471 (9th Cir. 1994) ("[T]he existence of a catchall hearsay exception is a clear indication that Congress did not want courts to admit hearsay only if it fits within one of the enumerated exceptions. And the reference to guarantees of trustworthiness equivalent to those in the enumerated exceptions strongly suggests that almost fitting within one of these exceptions cuts in favor of admission, not against.").

[13] *See* United States v. McHan, 101 F.3d 1027, 1038 (4th Cir. 1996) ("Grand jury testimony is given in the solemn setting of the grand jury, under oath and the danger of perjury, and in the presence of jurors who are free to question witnesses and assess their credibility and a court reporter who prepares an official transcript of the testimony. The nature of grand jury testimony thus provides some indicia of trustworthiness."); United States v. Zanniono, 895 F.2d 1, 6 (1st Cir. 1990) ("[O]ur sister circuits have uniformly admitted uncrossexamined grand jury testimony into evidence at a subsequent trial where the declarant is no longer available and the requisite indicia of reliability exist.").

[14] *E.g., McHan*, 101 F.3d at 1038 ("First, Cunningham testified before the grand jury voluntarily. Second, because Cunningham had participated with McHan in the narcotics offenses, he testified from personal knowledge. Third, when Cunningham gave his grand jury testimony, he had already been sentenced pursuant to a plea bargain that granted him immunity. Fourth, Cunningham was gravely ill, and expected to die within two years. Finally, and perhaps most importantly, McHan acknowledged that Cunningham's grand jury testimony, with a few exceptions mostly pertaining to dates, was 'fairly accurate' and 'close enough.'") (citations omitted).

[C] Reliability Factors

There are numerous factors that a court may consider in judging reliability under Rule 807, and the trial court is accorded "considerable discretion" in this determination.[15] An obvious starting point are the hearsay dangers — "the declarant's perception, memory, narration, or sincerity concerning the matter asserted."[16] It is the reduction or elimination of one or more of these dangers that underlies the exceptions in Rules 803 and 804. The same should be true here.

Although it was decided on constitutional, rather than evidentiary, grounds,[17] *Idaho v. Wright*[18] listed several factors as indicative of reliability: (1) the spontaneity of the statement; (2) the consistency of the statement; (3) the lack of motive to fabricate or lack of bias; (4) the reason the declarant cannot testify; (5) the voluntariness of the statement, *i.e.,* whether it was made in response to leading questions or made under undue influence; (6) the personal knowledge of the declarant about the matter on which he spoke; (7) the person to whom the statement was made, *e.g.,* a police officer who was likely to investigate further; and (8) the time frame within which the statement was made.

Additional factors are whether the statement was taken under oath, whether the declarant ever recanted the statement, whether other evidence suggested the declarant was unreliable, and whether extrinsic evidence seriously undermined the declarant's version of the events.[19]

Corroboration. Independent corroboration is another factor,[20] except when the statement is offered against the accused in a criminal case and the declarant does not testify. *Idaho v. Wright* held that corroborating circumstances could not be considered in judging reliability under the Confrontation Clause.[21]

§ 35.04 Key Points

There are reliable hearsay statements that do not fall within any of the exceptions specified in Rules 803 and 804. The residual exception is a way

---

[15] United States v. Singleton, 125 F.3d 1097, 1106 (7th Cir. 1997).

[16] United States v. Friedman, 593 F.2d 109, 119 (9th Cir.1979). *See supra* § 31.02 (rationale for hearsay rule).

[17] *See infra* § 36.05[B][1][b] (particularized guarantees of trustworthiness). *Wright* involved a confrontation challenge to a state residual exception.

[18] 497 U.S. 805, 814 (1990).

[19] *See* United States v. Donlon, 909 F.2d 650, 654 (1st Cir. 1990).

[20] *See* United States v. Valdez-Soto, 31 F.3d 1467, 1471 (9th Cir. 1994) ("corroborating evidence is a valid consideration in determining the trustworthiness of out-of-court statements for purposes of the residual exceptions"); Larez v. City of Los Angeles, 946 F.2d 630, 643 n. 6 (9th Cir.1991) (declarants' out-of-court statements were "especially reliable" because they corroborated one another).

[21] *See Valdez-Soto,* 31 F.3d at 1470 ("We are aware of no Supreme Court case, or any other case, which holds that introduction of hearsay evidence can violate the Confrontation Clause where the putative declarant is in court, and the defendants are able to cross-examine him.").

to recognize this by giving the trial judge ad hoc authority to admit trustworthy hearsay in a particular case.

The residual exception requires: (1) the statement have "equivalent circumstantial guarantees of trustworthiness" as the exceptions in Rules 803 and 804; (2) the statement must be offered as evidence of a material fact; (3) the statement must be more probative on the point for which it is offered than any other evidence which the proponent can procure through reasonable efforts; (4) the general purposes of the Federal Rules and the interests of justice must be served by admission; and (5) notice must be given to the other party.[22]

The courts have rejected the "near miss" theory and have also frequently admitted grand jury testimony. Numerous factors are relevant to determining reliability. Consider first the hearsay dangers — perception, memory, narration, or sincerity problems.

---

[22] Two of these requirements are redundant. Rule 401 requires materiality, and Rule 102, the purpose and construction clause, requires the doing of justice, among other things.

Chapter 36

RIGHT OF CONFRONTATION

§ 36.01 Introduction

The Sixth Amendment provides that "in all criminal prosecutions, the accused shall enjoy the right to be confronted with the witnesses against him." The Confrontation Clause was held binding upon the states in *Pointer v. Texas*.[1]

There are several aspects to this constitutional guarantee. First, the right of confrontation includes the right of the accused to be present at trial. Second, it guarantees the accused the right to face adverse witnesses ("face-to-face" confrontation). Third, the defendant also has the right to cross-examine these witnesses. Any significant limitation of this right raises serious confrontation issues. Finally, the hearsay rule often permits the admission of evidence without the opportunity to cross-examine the hearsay declarant, thus raising confrontation issues.

§ 36.02 Right to be Present at Trial

At the very least, the right of confrontation guarantees an accused the right to be present during trial. The Supreme Court has written: "One of the most basic of the rights guaranteed by the Confrontation Clause is the accused's right to be present in the courtroom at every stage of his trial."[2] This right is fortified by Criminal Rule 43.[3]

Whether an accused has a right to attend all in camera proceedings is unclear.[4] In *Kentucky v. Stincer*,[5] the defendant, charged with child sexual abuse, was excluded from a hearing to determine the competency of two child witnesses. At the hearing, the children, ages 7 and 8, were questioned by the prosecutor and defense counsel, and were found to be competent by the trial court. Stincer challenged his exclusion from the hearing on confrontation grounds. The Supreme Court rejected his argument. Two factors influenced the Court's decision. First, the competency hearing had

---

[1] 380 U.S. 400 (1965).

[2] Illinois v. Allen, 397 U.S. 337, 338 (1970). *See also* Perry v. Leeke, 488 U.S. 272, 281 (1989) ("The defendant's constitutional right to confront the witnesses against him immunizes him from such physical sequestration."); Taylor v. United States, 414 U.S. 17 (1973).

[3] Fed. R. Crim. P. 43(a) ("The defendant shall be present at the arraignment, at the time of the plea, at every stage of the trial including the impaneling of the jury and the return of the verdict, and at the imposition of sentence, except as otherwise provided by this rule.").

[4] *See* Fed. R. Crim. P. 43(c)(3) (accused's presence not required "when the proceeding involves only a conference or hearing upon a question of law").

[5] 482 U.S. 730 (1987).

a limited function. It was intended to determine whether the child was capable of observing, recollecting, and narrating facts to the jury and whether the child appreciated the obligation to tell the truth. Accordingly, the children were asked background questions such as their names, where they went to school, and how old they were. They were also asked whether they knew what a lie was and whether they knew what happens when one tells a lie. Thus, the issues raised at the hearing were unrelated to the basic issues of the trial.

Second, the primary function of the Confrontation Clause is to safeguard the right of cross-examination. Stincer was provided with the opportunity to cross-examine both children at trial. Some of the same questions that were asked at the hearing were again asked at trial. Moreover, the defense had the opportunity to ask whatever questions it wished on the competency issue because that issue remained open throughout the trial. In light of these two factors, the Court found against Stincer.

Stincer's due process argument fared no better. The Court acknowledged that "a defendant is guaranteed the right to be present at any stage of the criminal proceeding that is critical to its outcome if his presence would contribute to the fairness of the procedure."[6] Given the particular nature of the competency hearing, however, the Court could find no reason "that his presence . . . would have been useful in ensuring a more reliable determination as to whether the witnesses were competent to testify."[7]

[A] Forfeiture by Disruptive Behavior

A defendant's right to be present may be forfeited by disruptive behavior. In *Illinois v. Allen*,[8] the trial judge warned Allen about his disruptive conduct but Allen persisted to the point where it became difficult to conduct the trial. The judge ordered Allen removed from the courtroom and continued the trial without him, over his objection. The issue was whether the defendant's Sixth Amendment right to be present at his own trial was absolute. The Supreme Court held that, while the defendant has the right to be present at his trial, the right may be lost where a defendant is so disorderly that the trial cannot continue with his presence. The trial judge has discretion in choosing appropriate measures in such a situation. For example, the Court pointed out, the judge may order the defendant to be gagged or removed or held in contempt.[9] The court may also take appropriate steps to communicate the proceedings (*i.e.*, close-circuit TV) to the defendant.

---

[6] *Id.* at 745.

[7] *Id.* at 747.

[8] 397 U.S. 337 (1970).

[9] *See* Fed. R. Crim. P. 43(b)(3) (accused may be removed "after being warned by the court that disruptive conduct will cause the removal of the defendant from the courtroom, persists in conduct which is such as to justify exclusion from the courtroom").

[B]   Forfeiture by Voluntary Absence

Forfeiture may also result from the accused's voluntary absence — once the trial has commenced. In *Taylor v. United States*,[10] the Supreme Court held that the defendant's voluntary absence from the courtroom can be construed as a waiver of the right of confrontation, even without a warning from the court. When a defendant absents himself by choice, the court may proceed without him after balancing the defendant's right of confrontation against various factors including (1) the waste and expense of suspending the trial; (2) the inconvenience to the court, prosecution, codefendants, and witnesses if the trial does not proceed; (3) the public interest in having the matter resolved; and (4) the court's duty under the Speedy Trial Clause to resolve the matter with dispatch.[11]

§ 36.03   Right to "Face-to-Face" Confrontation

In several early cases, the Supreme Court indicated in dicta that the right of confrontation required "face-to-face" confrontation. For example, in *Kirby v. United States*,[12] the Court wrote: "[A] fact which can be primarily established only by witnesses cannot be proved against an accused . . . except by witnesses who confront him at the trial, upon whom he can look while being tried, who he is entitled to cross-examine."[13]

In 1988, the Court confronted the issue directly in *Coy v. Iowa*,[14] holding that the "Confrontation Clause guarantees the defendant a face-to-face meeting with the witnesses appearing before the trier of fact."[15] The defendant was charged with sexually assaulting two 13-year old girls. At trial, the prosecution moved to have the girls testify either by closed-circuit television or from behind a screen. Both procedures were authorized by statute. The trial court opted to use a large screen. The Supreme Court found that face-to-face confrontation was essential to the fairness and integrity of the fact-finding process: "It is always more difficult to tell a lie about a person 'to his face' than 'behind his back.' In the former context, even if the lie is told, it will often be told less convincingly."[16] In the Court's view, the importance of this right outweighed its drawbacks:

---

[10] 414 U.S. 17 (1973).

[11] In Crosby v. United States, 506 U.S. 255 (1993), the Supreme Court construed Criminal Rule 43 to require that the defendant be present at the commencement of trial before the trial may proceed in his absence. In other words, the Court precluded a trial in absentia. *See* Fed. R. Crim. P. 43(b)(1) (trial may proceed if accused "is voluntarily absent after the trial has commenced (whether or not the defendant has been informed by the court of the obligation to remain during the trial)").

[12] 174 U.S. 47 (1899).

[13] *Id.* at 55. *See also* Pennsylvania v. Ritchie, 480 U.S. 39, 51 (1987) ("The Confrontation Clause provides two types of protection for a criminal defendant: the right physically to face those who testify against him, and the right to conduct cross-examination.").

[14] 487 U.S. 1012 (1988).

[15] *Id.* at 1017.

[16] *Id.*

[F]ace-to-face presence may, unfortunately, upset the truthful rape victim or abused child; but by the same token it may confound and undo the false accuser, or reveal the child coached by a malevolent adult. It is a truism that constitutional protections have costs.[17]

Although the Court declined to determine whether an exception to face-to-face confrontation would pass constitutional muster, Justice O'Connor, in a concurring opinion, wrote:

I agree with the Court that appellant's rights under the Confrontation Clause were violated in this case. I write separately only to note my view that those rights are not absolute but rather may give way in an appropriate case to other competing interests so as to permit the use of certain procedural devices designed to shield a child witness from the trauma of courtroom testimony.[18]

She added: "[I]f a court makes a case-specific finding of necessity, as is required by a number of state statutes, our cases suggest that the strictures of the Confrontation Clause may give way to the compelling state interest of protecting child witnesses."[19]

The situation envisioned by Justice O'Connor presented itself in *Maryland v. Craig*.[20] The Court upheld a statutory procedure that allowed the use of one-way closed circuit television for the testimony of a child witness in a sexual abuse case, where the trial court first determined, after a fact-finding hearing, that requiring the child to testify in the presence of the defendant would result in the child's suffering severe emotional distress. Unlike *Coy*, the trial court in *Craig* had made a fact-specific inquiry to determine whether the child would be traumatized by testifying.[21]

§ 36.04 Right to Cross-Examination

Every party has the right to cross-examine witnesses called by other parties or by the court.[22] Wigmore wrote that "it is beyond any doubt the greatest legal engine ever invented for the discovery of truth."[23] In criminal cases, this right is guaranteed by the right of confrontation. As the Supreme Court has noted: "Our cases construing the confrontation clause hold that a primary interest secured by it is the right of cross-examination."[24] The

---

[17] *Id.* at 1019.

[18] *Id.* at 1022.

[19] *Id.* at 1025 (citations omitted).

[20] 497 U.S. 836 (1990).

[21] For a discussion of the federal statute, *see supra* § 18.05[A] (child testimony via close-circuit testimony).

[22] *See supra* § 2.03 (court-called witnesses).

[23] *See* 5 J. Wigmore, Evidence § 1367, at 32 (Chadbourn rev. 1974) ("[C]ross-examination, not the trial by jury, is the great and permanent contribution of the Anglo-American system of law to improved methods of trial procedure.").

[24] Douglas v. Alabama, 380 U.S. 415, 418 (1965). *See also* Olden v. Kentucky, 488 U.S. 227 (1988) (per curiam); Delaware v. Van Arsdall, 475 U.S. 673 (1986); Davis v. Alaska, 415 U.S. 308 (1974); Smith v. Illinois, 390 U.S. 129 (1968); Brookhart v. Janis, 384 U.S. 1 (1966).

Court, however, has recognized some limitations on this right: "It does not follow, of course, that the Confrontation Clause of the Sixth Amendment prevents a trial judge from imposing any limits on defense counsel's inquiry into the potential bias of a prosecution witness. On the contrary, trial judges retain wide latitude insofar as the Confrontation Clause is concerned to impose reasonable limits on such cross-examination based on concerns about, among other things, harassment, prejudice, confusion of the issues, the witness' safety, or interrogation that is repetitive or only marginally relevant."[25]

[A] Supreme Court Cases

Sometimes cross-examination is seriously impeded, if not completely frustrated, by an exclusionary statute or trial court ruling.[26] The Court's principal cases on this issue are discussed in this section.

Bias. In *Davis v. Alaska*,[27] a defendant was prohibited from cross-examining a prosecution witness concerning that witness's status as a juvenile probationer. This curtailment of cross-examination was based on a state statute designed to protect the confidentiality of juvenile adjudications. The Supreme Court reversed: "The State's policy interest in protecting the confidentiality of a juvenile offender's record cannot require yielding of so vital a constitutional right as the effective cross-examination for bias of an adverse witness."[28]

In *Delaware v. Van Arsdall*,[29] a murder defendant sought to cross-examine a prosecution witness about a possible agreement to dismiss charges against the witness. The trial court barred any cross-examination, citing Delaware Rule 403. The Supreme Court reversed: "A criminal defendant states a violation of the Confrontation Clause by showing that he was prohibited from engaging in otherwise appropriate cross-examination designed to show a prototypical form of bias on the part of the witness, and thereby 'to expose to the jury the facts from which jurors could appropriately draw inferences relating to the reliability of the witness.'"[30]

---

[25] Delaware v. Van Arsdall, 475 U.S. 673, 679 (1986). *See also* Alford v. United States, 282 U.S. 687, 694 (1931) ("The extent of cross-examination with respect to an appropriate subject of inquiry is within the sound discretion of the trial court. It may exercise a reasonable judgment in determining when the subject is exhausted."); Stevens v. Bordenkircher, 746 F.2d 342, 346 (6th Cir. 1984) ("[A] balance must be struck between permitting a trial court to exercise its sound discretion and affording a criminal defendant the opportunity to expose bias and prejudice.").

[26] For example, one obstacle to cross-examination is the rape-shield law, which contains evidentiary restrictions designed to protect the privacy of rape victims. Fed. R. Evid. 412. *See supra* § 10.07 (Rape Shield Law).

[27] 415 U.S. 308 (1974).

[28] *Id.* at 320. *See also* Smith v. Illinois, 390 U.S. 129 (1968); Alford v. United States, 282 U.S. 687, 694 (1931).

[29] 475 U.S. 673 (1986).

[30] *Id.* at 680 (quoting *Davis*).

In *Olden v. Kentucky*,[31] an alleged rape victim testified that Olden had tricked her into leaving a bar, raped her, and then drove her to the house of Bill Russell, where she was released. Russell, also a prosecution witness, testified that he had seen the victim leave Olden's car and that she had immediately complained of rape. The defense claimed consent, arguing that the victim and Russell were involved in an extramarital relationship and that the victim fabricated the rape story to explain to Russell why she was in the defendant's car. By the time of trial, the victim and Russell were living together, but the trial judge refused to permit cross-examination on this fact. The judge believed that this information would prejudice the jury against the victim because she was white and Russell was African American. The Supreme Court reversed per curiam. Olden had consistently maintained that the alleged victim lied because she feared jeopardizing her relationship with Russell. Thus, her current living arrangement with Russell was relevant to impeachment, and the foreclosure of this line of inquiry violated the right of confrontation.

Lack of memory. In *United States v. Owens*,[32] a hospitalized witness, suffering from a fractured skull, identified Owens as his attacker and picked his picture from a photo array. At trial, the witness testified about the attack, including his hospital identification of Owens. On cross-examination, however, he admitted that he could not remember seeing his assailant. The Supreme Court held that the witness's impaired memory did not deprive Owens of the right of cross-examination. According to the Court, the Confrontation Clause guarantees only an opportunity for effective cross-examination. This right is satisfied when the defendant has the opportunity to bring out such matters as a witness's faulty memory.[33]

In *Delaware v. Fensterer*,[34] the prosecution contended that Fensterer had strangled the victim in their apartment with a cat leash. Two hairs on the leash were similar to the victim's hair, and an FBI analyst testified that one of the two hairs had been "forcibly removed" but he could not remember what method he had used to reach this conclusion.[35] The Court upheld the conviction, commenting that "the Confrontation Clause guarantees an opportunity for effective cross-examination, not cross-examination that is effective in whatever way, and to whatever extent, the defense might wish."[36] The Court also wrote: "The Confrontation Clause is generally satisfied when the defense is given a full and fair opportunity to probe and expose infirmities through cross-examination, thereby calling to the attention of the factfinder the reasons for giving scant weight to the witness'

---

[31] 488 U.S. 227 (1988) (per curiam).

[32] 484 U.S. 554 (1988).

[33] *See supra* § 32.04[A] (cross-examination requirement).

[34] 474 U.S. 15 (1985) (per curiam).

[35] At trial, he testified: "As to the exact manner in which this particular hair was forcibly removed, I don't know. I have no indication in my notes other than the fact it was forcibly removed." State v. Fensterer, 493 A.2d 959, 963 (Del. 1985).

[36] *Fensterer*, 474 U.S. at 20.

testimony."[37] The Court went on to hold that a sufficient opportunity had been provided at trial because the defense counsel's cross-examination "demonstrated to the jury that the expert could not even recall the theory on which his opinion was based."[38]

[B] Fifth Amendment Conflicts

A party's right to cross-examine may be defeated by a witness's claim of privilege. This problem is especially troublesome in criminal cases in which a prosecution witness claims the privilege against self-incrimination during cross-examination, thereby creating a conflict between the witness's Fifth Amendment right and the defendant's Sixth Amendment right.[39] In this situation, the defendant may be severely prejudiced by an inability to uncover flaws in the adverse testimony. There may be no choice but to strike the direct testimony from the record.[40] Requiring the witness to invoke the privilege in front of the jury is also permissible.[41] Fifth Amendment claims may also be avoided by granting immunity to the witness, after which the witness could testify fully without fear of incrimination.[42]

§ 36.05   Confrontation & Hearsay

Since a hearsay declarant is, in effect, a witness, a literal application of the Confrontation Clause would preclude the prosecution from introducing any hearsay statement, notwithstanding the applicability of a recognized

---

[37] *Id.* at 22.

[38] *Id.* at 20 ("We need not decide whether there are circumstances in which a witness' lapse of memory may so frustrate any opportunity for cross-examination that admission of the witness' direct testimony violates the Confrontation Clause.").

[39] *See* Douglas v. Alabama, 380 U.S. 415 (1965).

[40] *See* United States v. Berrior-Londono, 946 F.2d 158, 160-61 (1st Cir. 1991) ("In determining whether a witness's refusal to answer questions posed during cross-examination constitutes a denial of the defendant's confrontation rights and requires striking the witness's testimony, a distinction must be drawn between direct and collateral matters. If the subject of the inquiry is closely related to the commission of the crime or the witness's testimony with respect to a material issue, striking the witness's testimony may be warranted. On the other hand, if the inquiry involves only collateral matters or cumulative material concerning credibility, a cautionary instruction as to the weight to be given to the witness's testimony normally will suffice."); United States v. Cardillo, 316 F.2d 606, 612 (2d Cir. 1963) (the determination whether a defendant has been denied the right to confront and cross-examine a witness requires an "analysis of the purpose of the inquiry and the role which the answer, if given, might have played in the defense").

[41] *See* United States v. Kaplan, 832 F.2d 676, 684 (1st Cir. 1987) (defense sought to cross-examine prosecution witness within the scope of his direct but witness asserted the privilege to some questions; "We hold that the district court's refusal to force Alan Brown to assert his fifth amendment privilege before the jury was error. None of the permissible reasons for circumscribing the scope of a criminal defendant's constitutional right to cross-examination — harassment, prejudice, confusion, repetitiveness, marginal relevance, for example — warranted such a ruling."). *See infra* § 43.06 (witness's Fifth Amendment privilege).

[42] *See infra* § 43.03[B] (immunity).

hearsay exception.[43] The Supreme Court has never adopted such an extreme view.[44]

The Clause also could be interpreted as requiring only the right to cross-examine *in-court* witnesses and not out-of-court declarants. Under this view, all hearsay exceptions would satisfy constitutional requirements. The Supreme Court also has rejected this view, writing that although the Confrontation Clause and the hearsay rule "stem from the same roots," the Court "has never equated the two."[45] In a later case, the Court noted: "We have been careful 'not to equate the Confrontation Clause's prohibitions with the general rule prohibiting the admission of hearsay statements.' "[46]

Instead of either of these two approaches, the Court has attempted to steer a middle course, a task that has often proved elusive.[47] Indeed, the Court is still attempting to define the relationship between the Confrontation Clause and the hearsay rule. The Court has found a confrontation violation by the admission of evidence that fell within a traditional hearsay exception.[48] In other cases, it has upheld the admissibility of evidence that did not fall within a traditional exception.[49]

---

[43] The confrontation issues that arise in joint trials are discussed *supra* § 8.03 (evidence admissible against one party, discussing *Bruton v. United States*).

[44] *See* Ohio v. Roberts, 448 U.S. 56, 63 (1980) (Such an interpretation "would abrogate virtually every hearsay exception, a result long rejected as unintended and too extreme.").

[45] Dutton v. Evans, 400 U.S. 74, 86 (1970). In California v. Green, 399 U.S. 149, 155 (1970), the Court commented: "While it may readily be conceded that hearsay rules and the Confrontation Clause are generally designed to protect similar values, it is quite a different thing to suggest that the overlap is complete and that the Confrontation Clause is nothing more or less than a codification of the rules of hearsay and their exceptions as they existed historically at common law.").

[46] White v. Illinois, 502 U.S. 346, 352 (1992) (quoting Idaho v. Wright, 497 U.S. 805, 814 (1990)). *But see* White v. Illinois, 502 U.S. 346, 365 (1992) (Thomas, J., concurring with Scalia, J.) (suggesting that perhaps only extrajudicial statements contained in "formalized testimonial materials, such as affidavits, depositions, prior testimony, or confessions" implicate confrontation values).

[47] There does appear to be general agreement that the Confrontation Clause was originally intended to preclude trial by affidavit. In an early confrontation case, the Court wrote: "The primary purpose of the constitutional provision was to prevent depositions or ex parte affidavits being used against the prisoner in lieu of a personal examination and cross-examination of the witnesses." Mattox v. United States, 156 U.S. 237, 242 (1895). *See also* Dutton v. Evans, 400 U.S. 74, 94 (1970) (Harlan, J., concurring) (The "paradigmatic evil the Confrontation Clause was aimed at was "trial by affidavit."); California v. Green, 399 U.S. 149, 156 (1970) ("It is sufficient to note that the particular vice that gave impetus to the confrontation claim was the practice of trying defendants on (evidence) which consisted solely of ex parte affidavits or depositions."); Westen, *Confrontation and Compulsory Process: A Unified Theory of Evidence for Criminal Cases*, 91 Harv. L. Rev. 567, 574-75 (1978) ("Yet it has been understood since the earliest confrontation cases that the prohibition of trials by affidavit lies at the very core of our notions of confrontation.").

[48] *See* Barber v. Page, 390 U.S. 719 (1968) (unavailability requirement for the former testimony hearsay exception).

[49] *See* Dutton v. Evans, 400 U.S. 74 (1970) (state coconspirator exception included concealment phase statements); California v. Green, 399 U.S. 149 (1970) (substantive use of prior inconsistent statements).

The cases can be divided into two categories — those in which the declarant testifies at trial and those in which the declarant does not testify.

[A] Available Declarant: Cross-Examination at Trial

The existence of an opportunity to cross-examine the hearsay declarant at trial usually satisfies the Confrontation Clause.[50] In *California v. Green*,[51] the Supreme Court reviewed the substantive use of prior inconsistent statements under a statute that rejected the common law approach of limiting the use of such statements to impeachment.[52] The Court found that the witness-declarant's presence in court obviated any confrontation concerns:

> Viewed historically, then, there is good reason to conclude that the Confrontation Clause is not violated by admitting a declarant's out-of-court statements, as long as the declarant is testifying as a witness and subject to full and effective cross-examination.
>
> This conclusion is supported by comparing the purposes of confrontation with the alleged dangers in admitting an out-of-court statement. Confrontation: (1) insures that the witness will give his statements under oath — thus impressing him with the seriousness of the matter and guarding against the lie by the possibility of a penalty for perjury; (2) forces the witness to submit to cross-examination . . .; (3) permits the jury that is to decide the defendant's fate to observe the demeanor of the witness in making his statement, thus aiding the jury in assessing his credibility.[53]

In the Court's view, cross-examination of the witness-declarant at trial satisfied all these conditions, rejecting the notion "that contemporaneous cross-examination before the ultimate trier of fact is so much more effective than subsequent examination that it must be made the touchstone of the Confrontation Clause."[54]

---

[50] *See* United States v. Valdez-Soto, 31 F.3d 1467, 1470 (9th Cir. 1994) ("We are aware of no Supreme Court case, or any other case, which holds that introduction of hearsay evidence can violate the Confrontation Clause where the putative declarant is in court, and the defendants are able to cross-examine him.").

[51] 399 U.S. 149 (1970).

[52] *See supra* § 22.10[A] (hearsay rule & inconsistent statements).

[53] 399 U.S. at 158.

[54] *Id.* at 161. The Court observed: "It may be true that a jury would be in a better position to evaluate the truth of the prior statement if it could somehow be whisked magically back in time to witness a gruelling cross-examination of the declarant as he first gives his statement. But the question as we see it must be not whether one can somehow imagine the jury in 'a better position,' but whether subsequent cross-examination at the defendant's trial will still afford the trier of fact a satisfactory basis for evaluating the truth of the prior statement." *Id.* at 160–61. In Nelson v. O'Neil, 402 U.S. 622 (1971), the availability at trial of the hearsay declarant remedied any *Bruton* problems that might have existed. *See supra* § 8.03.

[B] Unavailable Declarants: *Ohio v. Roberts'* Two-Pronged Test

In cases where the declarant does not testify at trial, the Supreme Court has not developed a consistent framework for analysis. In *Ohio v. Roberts*,[55] the Court identified two values underlying the Confrontation Clause: the "Framers' preference for face-to-face accusation" and an "underlying purpose to augment accuracy in the factfinding process."[56] From these values, the Court derived a two-pronged analysis that focused on (1) the unavailability of the declarant and (2) the reliability of the hearsay statement. The Court wrote:

> In sum, when a hearsay declarant is not present for cross-examination at trial, the Confrontation Clause normally requires a showing that he is unavailable. Even then, his statement is admissible only if it bears adequate "indicia of reliability." Reliability can be inferred without more in a case where the evidence falls within a firmly rooted hearsay exception. In other cases, the evidence must be excluded, at least absent a showing of particularized guarantees of trustworthiness.[57]

Although both the unavailability and indicia of reliability requirements were independently recognized in prior cases, the combination of the two as stated in *Roberts* was groundbreaking — especially the unavailability requirement.[58] Later cases, however, cut back significantly on an expansive reading of *Roberts* in this regard (*see infra*).

[1] Reliability Requirement

As *Roberts* indicates, the reliability requirement may be satisfied in either of two ways: (1) showing that the statement fell within a "firmly rooted" hearsay exception, which makes it presumptively reliable; or (2) demonstrating that the statement possessed particularized guarantees of trustworthiness.[59]

[a] "Firmly Rooted" Exceptions

In *Bourjaily v. United States*,[60] the Supreme Court ruled that statements falling within the coconspirator exception automatically satisfied the

---

[55] 448 U.S. 56 (1980).

[56] *Id.* at 65–66.

[57] *Id.* at 66.

[58] *See* Jonakait, *Restoring the Confrontation Clause to the Sixth Amendment*, 35 UCLA L. Rev. 557, 558 (1988) (The *Roberts* "framework was immediately controversial."); Lilly, *Notes on the Confrontation Clause and Ohio v. Roberts*, 36 Fla. L. Rev. 207, 224 (1984) ("Beneath *Roberts's* apparently orthodox disposition lies an interpretation of possibly far-reaching significance.").

[59] In Lilly v. Virginia, 527 U.S. 116 (1999), the Court adhered to the general framework summarized in *Roberts*: Hearsay statements are admissible only when (1) the statement falls within a "firmly rooted" hearsay exception or (2) it contains "particularized guarantees of trustworthiness."

[60] 483 U.S. 171 (1987).

reliability requirement.[61] Tracing the judicial history of the coconspirator exception back over a century and a half, the Court found the exception "firmly enough rooted in our jurisprudence."[62] The Court looked only at longevity without analyzing whether the exception was supported by a persuasive reliability argument, thereby ignoring the extensive criticism of the rule.[63]

The Court took the same approach in *White v. Illinois*,[64] which involved the excited utterance and medical diagnosis exceptions in a child sex abuse prosecution. The Court concluded that there "can be no doubt" that the excited utterance and medical diagnosis hearsay exceptions are "firmly rooted."[65] Again, the Court's automatic acceptance of "firmly rooted" hearsay exceptions is problematic. Although the Court noted that the excited utterance exception had been recognized for "at least two centuries" and the Federal Rules and nearly "four-fifths" of the states had adopted it,[66] the Court failed to acknowledge that the exception has long been criticized.[67] In addition, the Court's treatment of the medical diagnosis exception is flawed. As one commentator noted, this exception "is not a centuries' old exception, since it was firmly adopted only eighteen years ago in the Federal Rules of Evidence. The *White* opinion does not mention this."[68] The Court's definition of the exception "would seem to include anything the patient chooses to talk about with a doctor!"[69]

In *Lilly v. Virginia*,[70] the Court scrutinized the hearsay exception — declarations against interest — more closely. An accomplice gave a statement to the police in which he admitted his participation in a burglary and several robberies but also implicated the accused in the murder of the victim. The United States Supreme Court held that the exception for declarations against penal interest, at least as interpreted by the Virginia Supreme Court, was not a firmly rooted hearsay exception. The Court observed: "The decisive fact, which we make explicit today, is that accomplices' confessions that inculpate a criminal defendant are not within a firmly rooted exception to the hearsay rule as that concept has been defined in our Confrontation Clause jurisprudence."[71]

---

[61] *See* Fed. R. Evid. 801(d)(2)(E).

[62] 483 U.S. at 183.

[63] *See supra* § 32.10 (coconspirator admissions).

[64] 502 U.S. 346 (1992).

[65] *Id.* at 356 n. 8.

[66] *Id.*

[67] *See* Swift, *Smoke and Mirrors: The Failure of the Supreme Court's Accuracy Rationale in* White v. Illinois *Requires a New Look at Confrontation*, 22 Capital U. L. Rev. 145, 154 (1993) ("What the opinion does not say is that, despite this pedigree, such spontaneous or excited statements are viewed as one of the least reliable types of admissible hearsay."). *See also supra* § 33.05 (excited utterances).

[68] *Swift, supra* note 67, at 155.

[69] *Id.* at 157.

[70] 527 U.S. 116 (1999).

[71] *Id.* at 134.

[b] Particularized Guarantees of Trustworthiness

According to the Court in *Roberts*, a statement that does not fall within a "firmly rooted" hearsay exception may nevertheless satisfy Confrontation Clause demands if it possesses particularized guarantees of trustworthiness. The Court addressed this issue in *Idaho v. Wright*, [72] a case involving the admissibility of a child's statement under the Idaho residual hearsay exception. [73] In this context, the trustworthiness requirement involves a case-by-case approach that considers the "totality of the circumstances" *at the time* the statement was made. The relevant factors include spontaneity, consistency of repetition, the mental state of the declarant, use of terminology unexpected of a child of similar age, and lack of motivation to lie.

The Court also ruled that after-the-fact corroboration cannot be considered: "The relevant circumstances include only those that surround the making of the statement and that render the declarant particularly worthy of belief."[74] In rejecting reliance on corroborating proof, the Court wrote:

> The use of corroborating evidence to support a hearsay statement's "particularized guarantees of trustworthiness" would permit admission of a presumptively unreliable statement by bootstrapping on the trustworthiness of other evidence at trial, a result we think at odds with the requirement that hearsay evidence admitted under the Confrontation Clause be so trustworthy that cross-examination of the declarant would be of marginal utility. [75]

The Court in *Lilly v. Virginia* (discussed above) reviewed an accomplice's incriminatory statement to police which also implicated the accused. After concluding that the declaration against penal interest exception, as interpreted by the state court, was not a "firmly rooted" exception, the Court looked for particularized guarantees of trustworthiness and found them wanting:

> It is abundantly clear that neither the words that Mark [the declarant] spoke nor the setting in which he was questioned provides any basis for concluding that his comments regarding petitioner's guilt were so reliable that there was no need to subject them to adversarial testing in a trial setting. Mark was in custody for his involvement in, and knowledge of, serious crimes and made his statements under the supervision of governmental authorities. He was primarily responding to the officers' leading questions, which were asked without any contemporaneous cross-examination by adverse parties. Thus, Mark had a natural motive to attempt to exculpate himself as much as possible. [76]

---

[72] 497 U.S. 805, 806 (1990).

[73] *See supra* chapter 35 (residual exception).

[74] 497 U.S. at 819.

[75] *Id.* at 823.

[76] 527 U.S. at 139.

In other words, the statements "'are not unambiguously adverse to the penal interest of the declarant' but instead are likely to be attempts to minimize the declarant's culpability."[77] In addition, such statements may be attempts to make a deal with the prosecution, even in "the absence of an express promise of leniency."[78] Finally, the Court noted that the statement was obtained while the declarant was in custody and was "obviously obtained for the purpose of creating evidence that would be useful at a future trial."[79]

[2] Unavailability Requirement

The second prong of *Ohio v. Roberts* focuses on the unavailability of the declarant. At the time *Roberts* was decided, this requirement suggested a demanding standard. The test for unavailability had been set forth in *Barber v. Page*,[80] in which the Court had held that this requirement is satisfied only if "the prosecutorial authorities have made a good-faith effort to obtain" the presence of the declarant at trial.[81] According to the Court in *Barber*, a good-faith effort required more than a showing that the declarant is beyond the subpoena power of the trial court. The Court in *Roberts* reaffirmed this test and provided the following explanation:

> The law does not require the doing of a futile act. Thus, if no possibility of procuring the witness exists (as, for example, the witness' intervening death), "good faith" demands nothing of the prosecution. But if there is a possibility, albeit remote, that affirmative measures might produce the declarant, the obligation of good faith may demand their effectuation. "The lengths to which the prosecution must go to produce a witness is a question of reasonableness." The ultimate question is whether the witness is unavailable despite good-faith efforts undertaken prior to trial to locate and present that witness. As with other evidentiary proponents, the prosecution bears the burden of establishing this predicate.[82]

Later cases demonstrate that the *Roberts'* unavailability requirement will not be strictly applied. In *United States v. Inadi*,[83] which involved the admissibility of coconspirator admissions, the Supreme Court limited *Roberts* to cases involving former testimony,[84] explaining that *Roberts* cannot be read "to stand for the radical proposition that no out-of-court statement can be introduced by the government without a showing that the declarant is unavailable."[85] The Court reaffirmed this position in *White*

---

[77] *Id.* at 132 (quoting Lee v. Illinois, 476 U.S. 530, 541 (1986)).

[78] *Id.* at 139.

[79] *Id.* at 125.

[80] 390 U.S. 719 (1968).

[81] *Id.* at 725.

[82] *Roberts*, 448 U.S. at 74–75.

[83] 475 U.S. 387 (1986).

[84] *See supra* § 34.03 (former testimony).

[85] *Inadi,* 475 U.S. at 394. The Court also wrote: "*Roberts* should not be read as an abstract

v. Illinois,[86] which involved the excited utterance and medical diagnosis exceptions in a child sex abuse prosecution. Again, the Court ruled that "*Roberts* stands for the proposition that unavailability analysis is a necessary part of the Confrontation Clause inquiry only when the challenged out-of-court statements were made in the course of a prior judicial proceeding."[87]

Thus, despite the language in *Roberts*, a showing of unavailability is not always demanded. Indeed, *Inadi* and *White* establish blanket rules dispensing with the unavailability requirement for some hearsay exceptions — the coconspirator admissions in *Inadi* and the excited utterance and medical diagnosis exceptions in *White*. One commentator has suggested that eventually "the former testimony exception [as in *Roberts*] will likely stand practically alone as to the requirement that the prosecution demonstrate the hearsay declarant's unavailability."[88]

"Better evidence" argument. The Court offered two rationales for these rulings. First, the Court reasoned that the coconspirator, excited utterance, and medical diagnosis exceptions differ from the former testimony exception at issue in *Roberts*. According to the *Inadi* Court, unlike former in-court testimony, coconspirator statements "provide evidence of the conspiracy's context that cannot be replicated, even if the declarant testifies to the same matters in court."[89] Similarly, the *White* Court noted that excited utterances and statements made for the purpose of medical diagnosis had substantial probative value that "could not be duplicated simply by the declarant later testifying in court."[90] In short, the Court believed that the out-of-court statement was "better evidence" than the in-court testimony. "When two versions of the same evidence are available, longstanding principles of the law of hearsay, applicable as well to Confrontation Clause analysis, favor the better evidence."[91]

This argument is flawed because it presupposes that the out-of-court statement *or* the in-court testimony may be introduced at trial, but not both. There is no reason, however, why both cannot be admitted in evidence in most trials. Under the hearsay rule, statements falling within these exceptions are admissible even if the declarant testifies.

---

answer to questions not presented in that case, but rather as a resolution of the issue the Court said it was examining: 'the constitutional propriety of the introduction in evidence of the preliminary hearing testimony of a witness not produced at the defendant's subsequent state criminal trial.'" *Id.* at 392–93 (quoting *Roberts*, 448 U.S. at 58).

[86] 502 U.S. 346 (1992).

[87] *Id.* at 354.

[88] Haddad, *The Future of Confrontation Clause Developments: What Will Emerge When the Supreme Court Synthesizes the Diverse Lines of Confrontation Decisions?*, 81 J. Crim. L. & Criminology 77, 82 (1990). *See also Swift, supra* note 67, at 146 (*White* represents a "blanket rejection of an unavailability requirement in most cases.").

[89] *Inadi,* 475 U.S. at 395.

[90] *White,* 502 U.S. at 356.

[91] *Inadi,* 475 U.S. at 394.

"Unnecessary burden" argument. The second reason noted in these cases involved what the Court believed to be an unnecessary burden on the prosecution. The prosecution subpoenas the witnesses it needs, and the defense is guaranteed the same opportunity under the Compulsory Process Clause. An unavailability rule would operate only in those cases in which neither side wanted to call the witness. In the Court's view, the benefit of an unavailability rule is therefore marginal. At the same time, keeping track of additional witnesses would impose "substantial additional burdens" because the "prosecution would be required to repeatedly locate and keep continuously available each declarant."[92]

Once, again, the Court's opinions are not persuasive. The prosecution has to keep track of the state's witnesses. Typically, this means retaining a witness's name, address, telephone number, and place of employment, and issuing subpoenas when necessary. The incremental burden of keeping track of additional witnesses would often be minimal. The declarant in *Inadi* failed to appear because of car trouble, a rather unimpressive excuse.

[C] Summary

Despite the Supreme Court's disclaimers, some of its decisions suggest that the right of confrontation has been "deconstitutionalized" into the hearsay rule. "Firmly rooted" exceptions are presumptively reliable, and the test for classifying an exception as "firmly rooted" is not rigorous. Most of the hearsay exceptions considered by the Supreme Court have been held to be "firmly rooted," except for the residual exception and Virginia's expansive version of the exception for declarations against interest. The unavailability requirement has been applied only to former testimony. Yet, traditional hearsay law always required unavailability as a prerequisite for the use of this exception.[93] As one commentator has written: "The confrontation clause is no longer a constitutional right protecting the accused, but essentially a minor adjunct to evidence law."[94]

Nevertheless, the Court has not formally adopted this position,[95] and commentators continue to search for the proper interpretation of the

---

[92] *White*, 502 U.S. at 355.

[93] *See supra* § 34.03 (former testimony).

[94] Jonakait, *Restoring the Confrontation Clause to the Sixth Amendment*, 35 UCLA L. Rev. 557, 558 (1988). *See also* Berger, *The Deconstitutionalization of the Confrontation Clause: A Proposal for a Prosecutorial Restraint Model*, 76 Minn. L. Rev. 557, 557 (1992) (The Supreme Court "has transformed a constitutional guarantee into an evidentiary doctrine 'generally designed to protect similar values,' as the hearsay rule."); Haddad, *supra* note, at 88 ("Because of these rules, the confrontation clause offers little protection beyond that afforded by domestic hearsay law.").

[95] *See generally* Graham, *The Confrontation Clause, the Hearsay Rule, and Child Sexual Abuse Prosecutions: The State of the Relationship*, 72 Minn. L. Rev. 523 (1988); Kirkpatrick, *Confrontation and Hearsay: Exemptions from the Constitutional Unavailability Requirement*, 70 Minn. L. Rev. 665 (1986); Kirst, *The Procedural Dimension of Confrontation Doctrine*, 66 Neb. L. Rev. 485 (1987); Westen, *The Future of Confrontation*, 77 Mich. L. Rev. 1185 (1979); Westen, *Confrontation and Compulsory Process: A Unified Theory of Evidence for Criminal Cases*, 91 Harv. L. Rev. 567 (1978).

Confrontation Clause. One has argued: "Hearsay statements procured by agents of the prosecution or police should stand on a different footing than hearsay created without governmental intrusion. The Confrontation Clause should bar hearsay statements elicited by governmental agents unless the declarant is produced at trial or unless special procedures are followed."[96] Another has written: "The confrontation clause gives the accused the right to exclude all out-of-court statements when the declarant is not produced except when the prosecutor establishes the lack of a reasonable probability that the accused's cross-examination of the declarant would have led the jury to weigh the evidence more favorably to the accused."[97]

§ 36.06 Key Points

There are several aspects to the Confrontation Clause. First, the right of confrontation includes the right of the accused to be present at trial. Second, it guarantees the accused the right to face adverse witnesses ("face-to-face" confrontation). Third, the defendant also has the right to cross-examine these witnesses. Finally, the hearsay rule by permitting the admission of evidence without the cross-examination of the declarant, raises confrontation issues.

Right to be present at trial. The right of confrontation guarantees an accused the right to be present during trial, a right that may be forfeited by disruptive behavior or the accused's voluntary absence after the trial has commenced.

Right to "face-to-face" confrontation. The Supreme Court has held that the right of confrontation requires "face-to-face" confrontation. However, this right is not absolute. In *Maryland v. Craig,* the Court upheld a statutory procedure that allowed the use of one-way closed circuit television to provide the testimony of a child witness in a sexual abuse case. Significantly, the trial court made a fact-specific inquiry to determine whether the child would be traumatized by testifying in the presence of the accused.

Right to cross-examination. On more than one occasion, the Supreme Court has stated that the primary interest secured by the Confrontation Clause is the right of cross-examination. Many of the Court's cases have involved limitations on the elicitation of bias impeachment on cross-examination. These limitations have invariably been struck down.

---

[96] Berger, *supra* note 94, at 561-62. *See also* Swift, *Abolishing the Hearsay Rule,* 75 Cal. L. Rev. 495, 514 (1987) ("The crucial point about Burden-Shifting Declarants is that their systematic use allows plaintiffs and prosecutors to present hearsay statements, often in documentary form, without simultaneously producing a witness knowledgeable about the declarant, the statement, or any of her testimonial qualities or circumstances. Burden-shifting is a tactical choice.").

[97] Jonakait, *supra* note 94, at 622.

Confrontation & Hearsay

Since a hearsay declarant is, in effect, a witness, a literal application of the Confrontation Clause would preclude the prosecution from introducing any hearsay statement, notwithstanding the applicability of a recognized hearsay exception. The Supreme Court has never adopted such an extreme view. The Clause also could be interpreted as requiring only the right to cross-examine in-court witnesses and not out-of-court declarants. Under this view, all hearsay exceptions would satisfy constitutional requirements. The Supreme Court also has rejected this view. Instead of either of these two approaches, the Court has attempted to steer a middle course. The cases can be divided into two categories — those in which the declarant testifies at trial and those in which the declarant does not testify.

Available declarant: Cross-examination at trial. The existence of an opportunity to cross-examine the hearsay declarant at trial usually satisfies the demands of the Confrontation Clause.

Unavailable declarant: Two-pronged test. In *Ohio v. Roberts*, the Court set forth a two-pronged analysis that focused on (1) the unavailability of the declarant and (2) the reliability of the hearsay statement.

Reliability requirement. The reliability requirement may be satisfied in either of two ways: (1) showing that the statement falls within a "firmly rooted" hearsay exception, which makes the statement presumptively reliable; or (2) demonstrating that the statement possesses particularized guarantees of trustworthiness.

"Firmly rooted" exceptions include the coconspirator exception,[98] as well as the excited utterance and medical diagnosis exceptions.[99] The Court took a closer look at this requirement in *Lilly v. Virginia*,[100] ruling that the exception for declarations against penal interest, as interpreted by the Virginia Supreme Court, was not a firmly rooted exception.

If a statement does not fall within a "firmly rooted" hearsay exception, it may nevertheless satisfy Confrontation Clause demands if it possesses particularized guarantees of trustworthiness. In *Idaho v. Wright*,[101] a case involving the admissibility of a child's statement under a residual hearsay exception, the Court held that the trustworthiness requirement involves a case-by-case approach that considers the "totality of the circumstances" *at the time* the statement was made. The relevant factors include spontaneity, consistency of repetition, the mental state of the declarant, use of terminology unexpected of a child of similar age, and lack of motivation to lie.

---

[98] Bourjaily v. United States, 483 U.S. 171 (1987).

[99] White v. Illinois, 502 U.S. 346 (1992).

[100] 527 U.S. 116 (1999).

[101] 497 U.S. 805, 806 (1990).

Chapter 37

PRIVILEGES: FRE 501

§ 37.01 Introduction

There are different types of privileges. Probably the most familiar are those concerning confidential communications: attorney-client, clergy-penitent, husband-wife, doctor-patient, psychotherapist-patient, and accountant-client (few jurisdictions). There are also privileges governing specified topics such as trade secrets[1] or political vote.[2] Still other privileges cover only the identity of the source of information — *i.e.*, informant and journalist privileges. Some privileges are private, while others are governmental, *e.g.*, state secrets.

§ 37.02 Federal Rule 501

Rule 501 is the only provision in the Rules of Evidence that governs the law of privilege.[3] The Supreme Court originally proposed thirteen rules of privilege — a general rule, nine specific privileges, and three procedural rules.[4] Privileges proved to be the most controversial part of the Federal Rules; they delayed enactment for two years. As one scholar has noted, "The testimonial privilege rules in the Proposed Rules of Evidence submitted to Congress by the United States Supreme Court in 1972 almost doomed the total project. The presence of those rules became a rallying point for general opposition to the entire proposal and a symbol for all that was perceived to be wrong with the rules as a whole."[5] Fifty percent of the complaints

---

[1] *See* Proposed Fed. R. Evid. 508 advisory committee's note ("While sometimes said not to be a true privilege, a qualified right to protection against disclosure of trade secrets has found ample recognition, and indeed, a denial of it would be difficult to defend.").

[2] *See* Proposed Fed. R. Evid. 507 advisory committee's note ("Secrecy in voting is an essential aspect of effective democratic government, insuring free exercise of the franchise and fairness in elections. Secrecy after the ballot has been cast is as essential as secrecy in the act of voting.").

[3] However, the rules on subsequent remedial measures (Rule 407), offers of compromise (Rule 408 and Rule 410), and payment of medical expenses (Rule 409) may be considered quasi-privileges.

[4] *See* Proposed Fed. R. Evid. 502 (required reports); Proposed Fed. R. Evid. 503 (attorney-client); Proposed Fed. R. Evid. 504 (psychotherapist-patient); Proposed Fed. R. Evid. 505 (husband-wife); Proposed Fed. R. Evid. 506 (clergy-penitent); Proposed Fed. R. Evid. 507 (political vote); Proposed Fed. R. Evid. 508 (trade secrets); Proposed Fed. R. Evid. 509 (state secrets); Proposed Fed. R. Evid. 510 (informant); Proposed Fed. R. Evid. 511 (waiver by voluntary disclosure); Proposed Fed. R. Evid. 512 (disclosure under compulsion or without opportunity to claim privilege); Proposed Fed. R. Evid. 513 (comment on assertion of privilege), reprinted at 56 F.R.D. 230–61 (1972).

[5] Broun, *Giving Codification a Second Chance —Testimonial Privileges and the Federal Rules*

before Congress concerned privileges. Given the value judgments inherent in this area of law, this controversy is not surprising. In the Watergate era, the state secrets and official information privilege was attacked as too broad. The spousal privilege was criticized as too narrow. Journalists, doctors, and accountants received no privileges.

Congress rejected the proposed rules on privilege, substituting a general provision, which left the law of privilege unchanged. Unless specified by statute or court rule, "the privilege of a witness, person, government, State, or political subdivision thereof shall be governed by the principles of common law as they may be interpreted by the courts of the United States in the light of reason and experience."[6]

Several general observations can be made about Rule 501 and how the Supreme Court has interpreted it. First, Congress did not intend to take a stand on the merits of the specific rules proposed by the Supreme Court. The Senate Report commented: "It should be clearly understood that, in approving this general rule as to privileges, the action of Congress should not be understood as disapproving any . . . of the enumerated privileges contained in the Supreme Court rules. Rather, our action should be understood as reflecting the view that the recognition of a privilege based on a confidential relationship and other privileges should be determined on a case-by-case basis."[7]

Second, the Supreme Court has viewed its role in this context as evolutionary.[8] The Court has observed: "In rejecting the proposed Rules and enacting Rule 501, Congress manifested an affirmative intention not to freeze the law of privilege. Its purpose rather was to 'provide the courts with the flexibility to develop rules of privilege on a case-by-case basis,' and to leave the door open to change."[9] In another case, the Court wrote: "Rule 501's direction to look to 'the principles of the common law as they may be interpreted by the courts of the United States in the light of reason and

---

of Evidence, 53 Hastings L.J. 769, 769 (2002). He went on to note: "Not only was the substance of the posed privilege rules vigorously attacked by scholars, practitioners, judges and members of Congress, the idea that the federal law of privilege should be codified was rejected by many. Many academics and practicing lawyers preferred an uncodified federal law of privilege, and, in particular, one that relied upon state privilege law. There was especially widespread criticism of a federal law of privilege insofar as it would govern diversity cases." *Id.*

[6] Fed. R. Evid. 501.

[7] S. Rep. No. 1277, 93rd Cong., 2d Sess. 4, reprinted in 1974 U.S.C.C.A.N. 7051, 7059.

[8] As proposed by the Supreme Court, Rule 501 did not recognize a common law of privilege. Only privileges based on the Constitution, statute, or those specified in the Federal Rules were recognized.

[9] Trammel v. United States, 445 U.S. 40, 47 (1980) (quoting 120 Cong. Rec. 40891 (1974) (remarks of Rep Hungate)). *See also* Jaffee v. Redmond, 518 U.S. 1, 8–9 (1996) ("The Rule thus did not freeze the law governing the privileges of witnesses in federal trials at a particular point in our history, but rather directed federal courts to 'continue the evolutionary development of testimonial privileges.' ") (quoting *Trammel*).

experience' does not mandate that a rule, once established, should endure for all time."[10]

Third, the Court has looked to state law more in this context than in any other part of evidence law.[11]

Finally, the Court has stated that it would eschew "balancing" tests in this context.[12] "[I]f the purpose of the privilege is to be served, the participants in the confidential conversation 'must be able to predict with some degree of certainty whether particular discussions will be protected. An uncertain privilege, or one which purports to be certain but results in widely varying applications by the courts, is little better than no privilege at all.'"[13]

In some ways the Court's approach to Rule 501 is difficult to characterize. It has rejected some new privileges.[14] However, in *Jaffee v. Redmond*,[15] the Court recognized a psychotherapist-patient privilege for the first time when the lower courts were divided over the issue, and then the Court extended it to cover social workers, a rather broad interpretation of that privilege. In *Swidler & Berlin v. United States*,[16] the Court refused to cut back on the attorney-client privilege; instead, the Court held that the privilege, in accord with the traditional view, survived the death of the client. In *Upjohn Co. v. United States*,[17] the Court adopted an expansive view of the attorney-client privilege in the corporate context by rejecting

---

[10] Swidler & Berlin v. United States, 524 U.S. 399, 410–11 (1998) (citing Funk v. United States, 290 U.S. 371, 381 (1933) ("And, since experience is of all teachers the most dependable, and since experience also is a continuous process, it follows that a rule of evidence at one time thought necessary to the ascertainment of truth should yield to the experience of a succeeding generation whenever that experience has clearly demonstrated the fallacy or unwisdom of the old rule.")). *See also* In re Grand Jury Investigation, 918 F.2d 374, 379 (3d Cir. 1990) ("The Rule dictates the evolution and application of a federal common law of privilege in federal criminal cases.").

[11] *See* Jaffee v. Redmond, 518 U.S. 1, 12-13 (1996) ("That it is appropriate for the federal courts to recognize a psychotherapist privilege under Rule 501 is confirmed by the fact that all 50 States and the District of Columbia have enacted into law some form of psychotherapist privilege. We have previously observed that the policy decisions of the States bear on the question whether federal courts should recognize a new privilege or amend the coverage of an existing one.").

[12] *See id.* at 17–18 (1996) ("We part company with the Court of Appeals on a separate point. We reject the balancing component of the privilege implemented by that court and a small number of States. Making the promise of confidentiality contingent upon a trial judge's later evaluation of the relative importance of the patient's interest in privacy and the evidentiary need for disclosure would eviscerate the effectiveness of the privilege.").

[13] *Id.* (citing *Upjohn*).

[14] *E.g.,* University of Pennsylvania v. EEOC, 493 U.S. 182 (1990) (privilege against disclosure of academic peer review materials); United States v. Gillock, 445 U.S. 360, 367-68 (1980) (Rule 501 does not include a state legislative privilege).

[15] 518 U.S. 1 (1996). *See infra* § 40.03 (psychotherapist-patient privilege).

[16] 524 U.S. 399, 410 (1998) ("[H]ere we deal with one of the oldest recognized privileges in the law. And we are asked, not simply to 'construe' the privilege, but to narrow it, contrary to the weight of the existing body of case law."). *See infra* § 38.10 (duration of the privilege).

[17] 449 U.S. 383 (1981). *See infra* § 38.08 (clients & their agents defined).

the "control group" test. In contrast, in *Trammel v. United States*,[18] the Court cut back on the spousal testimonial privilege, but not radically, and at the same time implicitly recognized the spousal communication privilege, a privilege rejected by the Advisory Committee when drafting the Federal Rules.[19]

§ 37.03 Rationale for Privileges

Privileges differ from most other rules of evidence. They are intended to promote some policy that is external to the goals of a trial. Most other evidence rules are designed to enhance the search for truth and thus the fact-finding process. Privileges hinder that goal by excluding relevant and reliable evidence.[20]

Because privileges are inconsistent with the judicial goal of truth seeking, the Supreme Court has not been particularly receptive to new privileges, writing in one case that, "[w]hatever their origins, these exceptions to the demand for every man's evidence are not lightly created nor expansively construed, for they are in derogation of the search for truth."[21] In another case, the Court again emphasized this point: "Testimonial exclusionary rules and privileges contravene the fundamental principle that the public has a right to every man's evidence. As such, they must be strictly construed and accepted only to the very limited extent that permitting a refusal to testify or excluding relevant evidence has a public good transcending the normally predominant principle of utilizing all rational means for ascertaining truth."[22]

Interestingly, when upholding a privilege, the Court has noted that the loss-of-evidence argument has to be tempered somewhat because without the privilege there may not have been "any evidence" — *i.e.,* the party may not have spoken.[23]

There are two main theories underlying the law of privilege. The first is a utilitarian or instrumental justification: If you want clients to speak

---

[18] 445 U.S. 40, 47 (1980). *See infra* § 39.02[C] (holder of spousal testimonial privilege).

[19] There are two spousal privileges. The spousal *testimonial* privilege provides that a spouse may not be compelled to testify against a defendant-spouse in a *criminal* prosecution. A second privilege involves *confidential communications* between spouses and applies in both civil and criminal cases.

[20] For this reason, the rules on subsequent remedial measures (Rule 407), offers of compromise (Rule 408 and Rule 410), and payment of medical expenses (Rule 409) are often considered quasi-privileges.

[21] United States v. Nixon, 418 U.S. 683, 710 (1974). *See also* Branzburg v. Hayes, 408 U.S. 665 (1972).

[22] *Trammel,* 445 U.S. at 50 (internal quotation marks and citations omitted). *See also Jaffee,* 518 U.S. at 18-19 (Scalia, J., dissenting) (The majority "has not mentioned the purchase price: occasional injustice. That is the cost of every rule which excludes reliable and probative evidence — or at least every one categorical enough to achieve its announced policy objective.").

[23] *See Swidler & Berlin,* 524 U.S. at 408 ("[T]he loss of evidence admittedly caused by the privilege is justified in part by the fact that without the privilege, the client may not have made such communications in the first place.").

to lawyers, patients to therapists, or penitents to the clergy, provide encouragement by recognizing a privilege for such communications. The second theory is based on the notion of privacy.

[A] Instrumental Justification

The instrumental rationale requires a cost-benefit analysis, mostly based on speculation.[24] Does the spousal testimonial privilege really save viable marriages? And, is the cost in loss of evidence worth whatever benefit that may be derived from the privilege?

The Supreme Court's opinions in *Jaffee v. Redmond*,[25] which recognized the therapist-patient privilege, illustrate this analysis. The majority explained the important private and public interests served by the privilege:

> Effective psychotherapy depends upon an atmosphere of confidence and trust in which the patient is willing to make a frank and complete disclosure of facts, emotions, memories, and fears. Because of the sensitive nature of the problems for which individuals consult psychotherapists, disclosure of confidential communications made during counseling sessions may cause embarrassment or disgrace. For this reason, the mere possibility of disclosure may impede development of the confidential relationship necessary for successful treatment. By protecting confidential communications between a psychotherapist and her patient from involuntary disclosure, the proposed privilege thus serves important private interests.[26]

In dissent, Justice Scalia vigorously attacked this reasoning:

> When is it, one must wonder, that the psychotherapist came to play such an indispensable role in the maintenance of the citizenry's mental health? For most of history, men and women have worked out their difficulties by talking to, inter alios, parents, siblings, best friends, and bartenders — none of whom was awarded a privilege against testifying in court. Ask the average citizen: Would your mental health be more significantly impaired by preventing you from seeing a psychotherapist, or by preventing you from getting advice from your mom? I have little doubt what the answer would be. Yet there is no mother-child privilege. How likely is it that a person will be deterred from seeking psychological counseling, or

---

[24] Adopting the instrumental rationale, Professor Wigmore listed four conditions that he deemed fundamental to the establishment of a privilege against disclosure of communications: "(1) The communications must originate in a confidence that they will not be disclosed. (2) This element of confidentiality must be essential to the full and satisfactory maintenance of the relation between the parties. (3) The relation must be one which in the opinion of the community ought to be sedulously fostered. (4) The injury that would inure to the relation by the disclosure of the communications must be greater than the benefit thereby gained for the correct disposal of litigation." 8 Wigmore, Evidence § 2285, at 527 (McNaughton rev. 1961).

[25] 518 U.S. 1 (1996).

[26] *Id.* at 10.

from being completely truthful in the course of such counseling, because of fear of later disclosure in litigation? And even more pertinent to today's decision, to what extent will the evidentiary privilege reduce that deterrent? The Court does not try to answer the first of these questions; and it cannot possibly have any notion of what the answer is to the second, since that depends entirely upon the scope of the privilege, which the Court amazingly finds it "neither necessary nor feasible to delineate," . . . If, for example, the psychotherapist can give the patient no more assurance than "A court will not be able to make me disclose what you tell me, unless you tell me about a harmful act," I doubt whether there would be much benefit from the privilege at all. That is not a fanciful example, at least with respect to extension of the psychotherapist privilege to social workers.[27]

Nor was the Justice content to leave it at that. Instead, he also criticized the cost-benefit balancing undertaken by the majority.

Even where it is certain that absence of the psychotherapist privilege will inhibit disclosure of the information, it is not clear to me that that is an unacceptable state of affairs. Let us assume the very worst in the circumstances of the present case: that to be truthful about what was troubling her, the police officer who sought counseling would have to confess that she shot without reason, and wounded an innocent man. If (again to assume the worst) such an act constituted the crime of negligent wounding under Illinois law, the officer would of course have the absolute right not to admit that she shot without reason in criminal court. But I see no reason why she should be enabled both not to admit it in criminal court (as a good citizen should), and to get the benefits of psychotherapy by admitting it to a therapist who cannot tell anyone else. And even less reason why she should be enabled to deny her guilt in the criminal trial — or in a civil trial for negligence — while yet obtaining the benefits of psychotherapy by confessing guilt to a social worker who cannot testify. It seems to me entirely fair to say that if she wishes the benefits of telling the truth she must also accept the adverse consequences. To be sure, in most cases the statements to the psychotherapist will be only marginally relevant, and one of the purposes of the privilege (though not one relied upon by the Court) may be simply to spare patients needless intrusion upon their privacy, and to spare psychotherapists needless expenditure of their time in deposition and trial. But surely this can be achieved by means short of excluding even evidence that is of the most direct and conclusive effect.[28]

The parent-child privilege, which is not recognized by the federal courts nor by most states, offers another example. One court gave the following

---

[27] *Id.* at 22–23.

[28] *Id.* at 23–24.

reasons for rejecting this privilege: "First, confidentiality — in the form of a testimonial privilege — is not essential to a successful parent-child relationship. . . . A privilege should be recognized only where such a privilege would be indispensable to the survival of the relationship that society deems should be fostered. . . . [I]t is not clear whether children would be more likely to discuss private matters with their parents if a parent-child privilege were recognized than if one were not. It is not likely that children, or even their parents, would typically be aware of the existence or non-existence of a testimonial privilege covering parent-child communications."[29] The court went on to state that, "even assuming *arguendo* that children and their parents generally are aware of whether or not their communications are protected from disclosure, it is not certain that the existence of a privilege enters into whatever thought processes are performed by children in deciding whether or not to confide in their parents. Indeed, the existence or nonexistence of a parent-child privilege is probably one of the least important considerations in any child's decision as to whether to reveal some indiscretion, legal or illegal, to a parent."[30]

Another court expressed a more sympathetic view, even though it did not need to address the critical issue of recognition of this privilege: "There may be much to commend a testimonial privilege in connection with the testimony of or against a minor child to preserve the family unit which is so much under stress in today's society. The tangible and intangible benefits of keeping families intact often seem to be forgotten in today's willingness to enact laws that readily authorize the fracture of the family or that provide incentives for doing so."[31]

[B] Privacy Rationale

There has long been a competing theory to the instrumental rationale — one based on privacy.[32] According to Professor Louisell, privileges constitute "a right to be let alone, a right to unfettered freedom, in certain narrowly prescribed relationships, from the state's coercive or supervisory powers and from the nuisance of its eavesdropping."[33] Indeed, many of the attacks on the Supreme Court's proposed Article V were based on the privacy rationale. For example, one commentator wrote that "it is not a farfetched view that personal evidentiary privileges go to the heart of the modern American citizen's need for a right to privacy."[34] In criticizing the

---

[29] In re Grand Jury Proceedings, 103 F.3d 1140, 1152 (3d Cir. 1997).

[30] *Id.* at 1153.

[31] United States v. Dunford, 148 F.3d 385, 391 (4th Cir. 1998).

[32] *See* Imwinkelried, *The Historical Cycle in the Law of Evidentiary Privileges: Will Instrumentalism Come In Conflict With The Modern Humanistic Theories?*, 55 Ark. L. Rev. 241 (2002).

[33] Louisell, *Confidentiality, Conformity and Confusion: Privileges in Federal Court Today*, 31 Tulane L. Rev. 101 (1956).

[34] Krattenmaker, *Testimonial Privileges in Federal Courts: An Alternative to the Proposed Federal Rules of Evidence*, 62 Geo. L.J. 61 (1963) ("[T]he right of privacy is not simply a very

drafters failure to include a spousal communication privilege in the proposed Rules,[35] another wrote a letter to Congress containing the following observations:

> [H]owever intimate, however private, however embarrassing may be a disclosure by one spouse to another, or some fact discovered, within the privacies of marriage, by one spouse about another, that disclosure or fact can be wrung from the spouse under penalty of being held in contempt of court, if it is thought barely relevant to the issues in anybody's lawsuit for breach of contract to sell a carload of apples. It ought to be enough to say of such a rule that it could easily — even often — force any decent person — anybody any of us would want to associate with — either to lie or to go to jail. No rule can be good that has that consequence — that compels the decent and honorable to evade or to disobey.[36]

§ 37.04 Source of Privileges

There are several sources for the law of privilege. Some privileges, such as the Fifth Amendment privilege against compulsory self-incrimination, are constitutional.[37] Others are based on federal statutes. In addition, the Civil and Criminal Rules recognize a qualified work product privilege.[38] As noted above, much of the federal law of privilege rests on common law developments. In the states, however, privileges are often statutory.

§ 37.05 Procedural Issues

[A] Standing to Assert & Waive Privileges

The identity of the holder of a privilege is critical to an understanding of the purpose of a privilege. For example, the holder of the attorney-client privilege is the client, not the lawyer.[39] The government is the holder of the informant's privilege, not the informant.[40]

---

important means to highly valued but distinct ends. Rather privacy is further an end in itself — an essential condition of political liberty and our very humanity."). *See also* Krattenmaker, *Interpersonal Testimonial Privileges Under the Federal Rules of Evidence: A Suggested Approach*, 64 Geo. L.J. 613 (1976).

[35] As discussed in chapter 39, there are two spousal privileges. The spousal *testimonial* privilege provides that a spouse may not be compelled to testify against a defendant-spouse in a *criminal* prosecution. A second privilege involves *confidential communications* between spouses and applies in both civil and criminal cases. The drafters proposed only the former.

[36] Black, *The Marital and Physician Privileges — A Reprint of a Letter to a Congressman*, 1975 Duke L.J. 45, 48.

[37] *See infra* chapter 43 (self-incrimination).

[38] Fed. R. Civ. P. 26(b)(3); Fed. R. Crim. P.16(b)(2) & (c)(2). *See infra* § 38.14 (work product).

[39] *See infra* § 38.03 (holder of attorney-client privilege).

[40] *See infra* § 42.02[A] (holder of informant's privilege).

Only the holder may waive a privilege. While a privilege may be waived by voluntary disclosure,[41] involuntary disclosure raises far more difficult issues.[42]

[B] Appeals

If the holder is *not* a party and the privilege is improperly breached at trial, a party does not have standing to object. The party, as opposed to the holder, has suffered no legal harm. If a privilege is incorrectly applied, party could appeal because relevant evidence has been excluded (but not as a holder of the privilege).

[C] Burden of Proof

Generally, the burden of persuasion is on the person claiming a privilege.[43]

[D] In Camera Inspection

In *United States v. Zolin*,[44] the Supreme Court held, as a matter of federal common law, that the trial judge could review in camera allegedly privileged communications to determine whether they fell within the crime-fraud exception to the attorney-client privilege. To obtain in camera review, the party opposing the privilege "must present evidence sufficient to support a reasonable belief that in camera review may yield evidence that establishes the exception's applicability."[45] The Court also held that, under Rule 104(a), the trial court may consider the allegedly privileged communications in determining whether the threshold showing for in camera review

---

[41] *See* Proposed Fed. R. Evid. 511 advisory committee's note ("The central purpose of most privileges is the promotion of some interest or relationship by endowing it with a supporting secrecy or confidentiality. It is evident that the privilege should terminate when the holder by his own act destroys this confidentiality.").

[42] *See* Proposed Fed. R. Evid. 512 advisory committee's note ("Confidentiality, once destroyed, is not susceptible of restoration, yet some measure of repair may be accomplished by preventing use of the evidence against the holder of the privilege. The remedy of exclusion is therefore made available when the earlier disclosure was compelled erroneously or without opportunity to claim the privilege. . . . Illustrative possibilities are disclosure by an eavesdropper, by a person used in the transmission of a privileged communication, by a family member participating in psychotherapy, or privileged data improperly made available from a computer bank.").

[43] In re Grand Jury Proceedings (Gregory P. Violette), 183 F.3d 71, 73 (1st Cir. 1999) ("As a general matter, a party asserting a privilege has the burden of showing that the privilege applies. . . . To do so, the proponent of the privilege must set forth facts sufficient to establish all the elements of the claimed privilege.").

[44] 491 U.S. 554, 568 (1989) ("We see no basis for holding that the tapes in this case must be deemed privileged under Rule 104(a) while the question of crime or fraud remains open.").

[45] *Id.* at 574–75.

has been satisfied.[46] In camera review is not limited to the attorney-client privilege.[47]

[E] Comment on Exercise of a Privilege

Proposed Federal Rule 513(a) provided: "The claim of a privilege, whether in the present proceeding or upon a prior occasion, is not a proper subject of comment by judge or counsel. No inference may be drawn therefrom."[48] Another provision stated that "[u]pon request, any party against whom the jury might draw an adverse inference from a claim of privilege is entitled to an instruction that no inference may be drawn therefrom."[49]

§ 37.06 Choice of Law

Federal Rule 501 provides that "in civil actions and proceedings, with respect to an element of a claim or defense as to which State law supplies the rule of decision, the privilege of a witness, person, government, State, or political subdivision thereof shall be determined in accordance with State law." Congress adopted this provision to address the choice-of-law concerns raised by *Erie R.R. Co. v. Tompkins.*[50] This provision may present problems where a case involves both federal and state claims. In this situation, the Third Circuit has written;

> In general, federal privileges apply to federal law claims, and state privileges apply to claims arising under state law. The present case, however, presents the complexity of having both federal and state law claims in the same action. The problems associated with the application of two separate privilege rules in the same case are readily apparent, especially where, as here, the evidence in dispute is apparently relevant to both the state and the federal claims. This court has resolved this potential conflict in favor of federal privilege law.[51]

In an earlier case, the court had stated that "applying two separate disclosure rules with respect to different claims tried to the same jury would

---

[46] *Id.* at 568 ("[D]isclosure of allegedly privileged materials to the district court for purposes of determining the merits of a claim of privilege does not have the legal effect of terminating the privilege.").

[47] *See infra* § 42.02[D] (in camera inspection & informant's privilege).

[48] Proposed Fed. R. Evid. 513 advisory committee's note ("Hence the present subdivision forbids comment upon the exercise of a privilege, in accord with the weight of authority. . . . Thus, the calling of a witness in the presence of the jury and subsequently excusing him after a sidebar conference may effectively convey to the jury the fact that a privilege has been claimed, even though the actual claim has not been made in their hearing. Whether a privilege will be claimed is usually ascertainable in advance and the handling of the entire matter outside the presence of the jury is feasible.").

[49] Proposed Fed. R. Evid. 513(c).

[50] 304 U.S. 64 (1938).

[51] Pearson v. Miller, 211 F.3d 57, 66 (3d Cir. 2000).

be unworkable."[52] The court went on to hold that "when there are federal law claims in a case also presenting state law claims, the federal rule favoring admissibility, rather than any state law privilege, is the controlling rule."[53]

§ 37.07 Key Points

Privileges differ from most other rules of evidence. They are intended to promote some policy that is external to the goals of a trial. Most other evidence rules are designed to enhance the search for truth and thus the fact-finding process. Privileges hinder that goal by excluding relevant and reliable evidence.

Rule 501 is the only provision in the Rules of Evidence that governs the law of privilege. The Supreme Court originally proposed thirteen rules of privilege — a general rule, nine specific privileges, and three procedural rules. Privileges proved to be the most controversial part of the Federal Rules; they delayed enactment for two years. Congress rejected these rules, substituting Rule 501, which left the law of privilege unchanged. Unless specified by statute or court rule, "the privilege of a witness, person, government, State, or political subdivision thereof shall be governed by the principles of common law as they may be interpreted by the courts of the United States in the light of reason and experience."

Rationales. There are two main theories underlying the law of privilege. The first is the utilitarian or instrumental justification: If you want clients to speak to lawyers, patients to therapists, or penitents to the clergy, provide encouragement by recognizing a privilege for such communications. The second theory is based on the notion of privacy.

Procedural issues. Only the holder may waive a privilege. Generally, the burden of persuasion is on the person claiming a privilege. In *United States v. Zolin*, the Supreme Court held, as a matter of federal common law, that the trial judge could review in camera allegedly privileged communications to determine whether they fell within the crime-fraud exception to the attorney-client privilege.

Choice of Law. Rule 501 provides that "in civil actions and proceedings, with respect to an element of a claim or defense as to which State law supplies the rule of decision, the privilege of a witness, person, government, State, or political subdivision thereof shall be determined in accordance with State law."

---

[52] Wm. T. Thompson Co. v. General Nutrition Corp., 671 F.2d 100, 104 (3d Cir. 1982).
[53] *Id.*

Chapter 38

ATTORNEY-CLIENT PRIVILEGE

§ 38.01 Introduction

The attorney-client privilege is "the oldest of the privileges for confidential communications known to the common law."[1] A separate qualified privilege for work-product has also been recognized.[2]

The attorney-client privilege is intended to permit clients to receive informed legal advice and effective representation, which depends on "full and frank communication between attorneys and their clients."[3] This, in turn, is thought to "promote broader public interests in the observance of law and administration of justice. The privilege recognizes that sound legal advice or advocacy serves public ends and that such advice or advocacy depends upon the lawyer's being fully informed by the client."[4] In criminal cases, the Sixth Amendment right to the effective assistance of counsel also supports the privilege.[5]

The privilege is not without detractors.[6] What would happen without the privilege? Would clients really cease talking to their attorneys? Would attorney's preface all remarks with "hypothetically speaking"? Would opposing parties call the other side's lawyer as their first witness?

---

[1] Upjohn Co. v. United States, 449 U.S. 383, 389 (1981). *See also* Swidler & Berlin v. United States, 524 U.S. 399, 403 (1998) ("The attorney-client privilege is one of the oldest recognized privileges for confidential communications."); Rice, Attorney-Client Privilege in the United States (1999); Hazard, *An Historical Perspective on the Attorney-Client Privilege*, 66 Cal. L. Rev. 1061 (1978); *Developments in the Law — Privileged Communications*, 98 Harv. L. Rev. 1450, 1455–58 (1985).

[2] *See infra* § 38.14 (work product privilege).

[3] *Upjohn Co.*, 449 U.S. at 389. *See also* Hunt v. Blackburn, 128 U.S. 464, 470 (1888) ("The rule which places the seal of secrecy upon communications between client and attorney is founded upon the necessity, in the interest and administration of justice, of the aid of persons having knowledge of the law and skilled in its practice, which assistance can only be safely and readily availed of when free from the consequences or the apprehension of disclosure.").

[4] *Upjohn Co.*, 449 U.S. at 389. *See also* United States v. Trammel, 445 U.S. 40, 51 (1980) ("The lawyer-client privilege rests on the need for the advocate and counselor to know all that relates to the client's reasons for seeking representation if the professional mission is to be carried out."); Fisher v. United States, 425 U.S. 391, 403 (1976) ("The purpose of the privilege is to encourage clients to make full disclosure to their attorneys.").

[5] *See* Parler & Wobber v. Miles & Stockbridge, 756 A.2d 526, 526 (Md. 2000) ("[W]hile never granted express constitutional lineage in criminal cases, the privilege is linked to the constitutional guarantee of effective assistance of counsel and that strict limitations on its application could undermine this basic guarantee.").

[6] *See* Fischel, *Lawyers and Confidentiality*, 65 U. Chi. L. Rev. 1 (1998); 5 Bentham, Rationale of Judicial Evidence 302 (Mill ed. 1827).

As with all confidential communication privileges, the issues can be broken down into the following components: (1) Who are the proper parties (*e.g.*, who is a client and who is an attorney?); (2) What constitutes a communication?; (3) Was the communication made incident to the professional relationship? Not everything said to a lawyer is privileged; (4) Was the communication intended to be confidential?; (5) What are the exceptions?; and (6) How is the privilege waived? This last question requires us to identify the "holder" of the privilege.

As drafted by the Supreme Court, proposed Federal Rule 503 recognized the attorney-client privilege.[7] However, Congress deleted all the proposed privilege rules when it substituted the general federal rule on privileges.[8] Thus, the attorney-client privilege in federal practice is a common law rule. Some federal courts cite proposed Rule 503 as guidance in developing the contours of the privilege. In many states, the privilege is statutory.

§ 38.02   Professional Responsibility Distinguished

The attorney-client privilege should be distinguished from an attorney's obligations under the rules governing professional responsibility. Model Rule 1.6(a) states that lawyers "shall not reveal information relating to representation of a client," with only two narrow exceptions: (1) To prevent a client from committing a criminal act likely to result in imminent death or substantial bodily harm, or (2) where there is a dispute concerning the attorney's conduct. The confidentiality rule goes beyond the evidentiary privilege: "The rule of client-lawyer confidentiality applies in situations other than those where evidence is sought from the lawyer through compulsion of law. The confidentiality rule applies not merely to matters communicated in confidence by the client but also to all information relating to the representation, whatever its source."[9]

In short, the attorney-client privilege is limited to *communications*, the ethical rule covers all information obtained as a result of the representation. Moreover, an evidentiary privilege applies only in *legal* proceedings, the ethical rule applies outside legal proceedings.[10]

---

[7] *See* 56 F.R.D. 244, 245 (1973).

[8] Fed. R. Evid. 501. For a discussion of the congressional action, *see supra* § 37.02 (Federal Rule 501).

[9] Model Rule 1.6, Comment. *See also* Code of Professional Responsibility E.C. 4-4 ("The attorney-client privilege is more limited than the ethical obligation of a lawyer to guard the confidences and secrets of his client. This ethical precept, unlike the evidentiary privilege, exists without regard to the nature or source of information or the fact that others share the knowledge."); Zacharia, *Privilege and Confidentiality in California*, 28 U.C. Davis L. Rev. 367 (1995).

[10] Legal proceedings include congressional hearings and administrative proceedings.

§ 38.03 Holder

The holder of the privilege is the client and not the attorney. Accordingly, only the client has the right to invoke and waive the privilege.[11] The attorney may, however, claim the privilege on behalf of the client.[12] The privilege applies even if the holder is not a party to the lawsuit in which the privilege is invoked.

If the holder is not a party and the trial court incorrectly breaches the privilege, the parties lack standing to appeal on the privilege issue (but not the holder in a separate action). If the judge excludes evidence based on the erroneous assertion of the privilege, a party who is not the holder could appeal on the grounds that relevant evidence was excluded, which gives that party standing.

§ 38.04 Professional Relationship Requirement

The attorney-client privilege applies only where the communication is made for the purpose of receiving legal advice.[13] It protects a client against disclosure of facts revealed in non-litigious as well as in litigious consultation[14] — *e.g.,* preparing a contract or will. The privilege extends to communications made to an attorney by a person seeking legal services, even if

---

[11] *See* Hunt v. Blackburn, 128 U.S. 464, 470 (1888) ("But the privilege is that of the client alone, and no rule prohibits the latter from divulging his own secrets."); In re von Bulow, 828 F.2d 94, 100 (2d Cir. 1987) ("[T]he privilege belongs solely to the client and may only be waived by him. An attorney may not waive the privilege without his client's consent. Hence, absent a client's consent or waiver, the publication of confidential communications by an attorney does not constitute a relinquishment of the privilege by the client.") (citation omitted).

[12] *See* Fisher v. United States, 425 U.S. 391, 402 n. 8 (1976) ("The only privilege of the taxpayer involved here is the attorney-client privilege, and it is universally accepted that the attorney-client privilege may be raised by the attorney."); Code of Professional Responsibility E.C. 4-4 ("lawyer owes an obligation timely to assert the privilege unless it is waived by the client").

[13] *See Upjohn*, 449 U.S. at 393 ("The communications at issue were made by Upjohn employees to counsel for Upjohn acting as such, at the direction of corporate superiors in order to secure legal advice from counsel."); In re Sealed Case, 737 F.2d 94, 98–99 (D.C. Cir. 1984) (privilege applies only if the person to whom the communication was made is "a member of the bar of a court" who "in connection with th[e] communication is acting as a lawyer" and the communication was made "for the purpose of securing primarily either (i) an opinion on law or (ii) legal services or (iii) assistance in some legal proceeding") (quoting United States v. United Shoe Machinery Corp., 89 F. Supp. 357, 358–59 (D. Mass. 1950)); Proposed Fed. R. Evid. 503 advisory committee's note ("All these communications must be specifically for the purpose of obtaining legal services for the client; otherwise the privilege does not attach.").

[14] *See Swidler & Berlin*, 524 U.S. at 407–08 ("Clients consult attorneys for a wide variety of reasons. . . . Many attorneys act as counselors on personal and family matters, where, in the course of obtaining the desired advice, confidences about family members or financial problems must be revealed in order to assure sound legal advice. The same is true of owners of small businesses who may regularly consult their attorneys about a variety of problems arising in the course of the business."); Proposed Fed. R. Evid. 503 advisory committee's note ("The client need not be involved in litigation: the rendition of legal service or advice under any circumstances suffices.").

the attorney decides not to represent that person.[15] It applies to attorneys serving pro bono as well as to in-house counsel.

If an attorney is consulted for reasons unrelated to legal services (*e.g.,* as a friend or business advisor), the privilege does not apply.[16] It also does not extend to lobbying the President for pardons.[17] The person asserting the privilege has the burden of establishing that the attorney was consulted for legal services.[18]

§ 38.05   Communications Defined

Generally, only the communication is covered and not the facts that are the subject of the communication.[19] For example, a client who has been involved in a traffic accident may be required to testify about that accident but not about what that client told her attorney about the accident. Stated another way, the communication, but not the client's knowledge, is protected by the privilege.[20] Communications by the attorney to the client are

---

[15] *See* United States v. Dennis, 843 F.2d 652, 656-57 (2d Cir. 1988) ("[I]nitial statements made while Pilgrim intended to employ Gerace [lawyer] were privileged even though the employment was not accepted. But the privilege may have ended . . . when Gerace told Pilgrim he would not represent him. . . . The key, of course, to whether an attorney/client relationship existed is the intent of the client and whether he reasonably understood the conference to be confidential.") (citations omitted); Proposed Fed. R. Evid. 503 advisory committee's note ("The definition also extends the status of client to one consulting a lawyer preliminarily with a view to retaining him, even though actual employment does not result.").

[16] *See* In re Lindsey, 158 F.3d 1263, 1270 (D.C. Cir. 1998) ("Lindsey's advice on political, strategic, or policy issues, valuable as it may have been, would not be shielded from disclosure by the attorney-client privilege."); Proposed Fed. R. Evid. 503 advisory committee's note ("The services must be professional legal services: purely business or personal matters do not qualify.").

[17] *See* In re Grand Jury Subpoenas, 179 F. Supp. 2d 270, 291 (S.D.N.Y. 2001) ("Communications about non-legal issues such as public relations, the solicitation of prominent individuals or persons with access to the White House (such as Denise Rich and Beth Dozoretz) to support the [pardon] Petition, and strategies for persuading the President to grant the petition are not privileged (or protected by the work product doctrine). The lawyers' reports to the clients on these non-legal items and lobbying efforts are not privileged (or protected by the work product doctrine).") .

[18] *See In re Lindsey*, 158 F.3d at 1270 ("Recognizing that a government attorney-client privilege exists is one thing. Finding that the Office of the President is entitled to assert it here is quite another. It is settled law that the party claiming the privilege bears the burden of proving that the communications are protected.").

[19] *See Upjohn*, 449 U.S. at 395 ("The privilege only protects disclosure of communications; it does not protect disclosure of the underlying facts by those who communicated with the attorney."); United States v. Trammel, 445 U.S. 40, 51 (1980) ("The privilege[] between . . . attorney and client . . . limit[s] protection to private communications.").

[20] *See* Proposed Fed. R. Evid. 511 advisory committee's note ("[T]he fact that a client has discussed a matter with his lawyer does not insulate the client against disclosure of the subject matter discussed, although he is privileged not to disclose the discussion itself. Therefore a client, merely by disclosing a subject which he had discussed with his attorney, would not waive the applicable privilege; he would have to make disclosure of the communication itself in order to effect a waiver.").

probably covered as a practical matter, although there is some dispute on this issue.[21]

[A]　Documents

The privilege may encompass written communications between attorney and client — *e.g.*, letter containing a legal opinion about a proposed course of conduct. However, pre-existing documents do not become privileged merely because they are transmitted to an attorney.[22] For example, if a client consults an attorney for advice on tax matters and gives financial records to the attorney, those records, which existed prior to the consultation, are not privileged. The attorney's legal advice based on those documents, however, is protected.

[B]　Client Identity; Fee Arrangements

Generally, a client's identity, the fact of consultation with or employment of an attorney, and fee arrangements do not fall within the protection of the attorney-client privilege.[23] Such information is not usually intended to be confidential, and in most instances, the client's name or identity is not one of the facts about which the client seeks legal assistance.

However, some courts extend the privilege's protection to the name and address of the client under certain circumstances.[24] Such information is privileged if "the revelation of the identity of the client along with information regarding the fee arrangement would reveal a confidential

---

[21] *See* Sprague v. Thorn Americas, Inc.,129 F.3d 1355, 1370–71 (10th Cir. 1997) ("A dichotomy in treatment of the attorney-client privilege has been noted in several cases. . . . Under a narrower approach, the attorney-client privilege is held not to protect from disclosure a legal opinion and advice communicated in confidence by an attorney to his client where that opinion and advice do not reveal client confidences."; the "broader approach" protects "an attorney's communications to his client without the qualification that the communications must contain confidential matters revealed by the client earlier to the attorney").

[22] *See* Fisher v. United States, 425 U.S. 391, 403–04 (1976) ("Pre-existing documents which could have been obtained by court process from the client when he was in possession may also be obtained from the attorney by similar process following transfer by the client in order to obtain more informed legal advice.").

[23] *See* United States v. Goldberger & Dubin, P.C., 935 F.2d 501, 505 (2d Cir. 1991) ("[D]isclosure of fee information and client identity is not privileged even though it might incriminate the client."); In re Grand Jury Investigation No. 83-2-35 (Durant), 723 F.2d 447, 450 (6th Cir. 1983) ("The federal forum is unanimously in accord with the general rule that the identity of a client is, with limited exceptions, not within the protective ambit of the attorney-client privilege.").

[24] Baird v. Koerner, 279 F.2d 623 (9th Cir. 1960), is the seminal case. In *Baird*, the IRS received a letter from an attorney stating that an enclosed check in the amount of $12,706 was being tendered for additional amounts due from undisclosed taxpayers. When the IRS summoned the attorney to ascertain the identity of the delinquent taxpayers, the attorney refused to disclose the client's identity, asserting the attorney-client privilege. The Ninth Circuit, applying California law, recognized an exception to the general rule that client identity is not privileged. This "legal advice" exception has been recognized by other federal circuits. *See Developments in the Law — Privileged Communications*, 98 Harv. L. Rev. 1450, 1522–24 (1985) (criticizing rule).

communication between attorney and client."[25] These cases often seem questionable. Many involve attempts by clients to manipulate the legal system in some way.

Other cases tie the privilege to whether disclosure of the client's identity would provide the "last link" in the incrimination of the client.[26] This rationale, however, has little to do with the policies underlying the attorney-client privilege — encouraging communications.[27]

[C] Physical Evidence

A difficult problem arises when a client delivers tangible evidence to the attorney or provides the attorney with information necessary to retrieve the evidence. Here, the privilege applies to the communication itself. The attorney may not, however, take possession and hide the evidence;[28] this would amount to an obstruction of justice. Nor, for the same reason, may the attorney tell the client to destroy the evidence.

Once the attorney takes possession, some decisions hold that the evidence must be turned over to the prosecution.[29] A further question arises because the prosecution will often have difficulty authenticating the evidence at trial. Without the means to authenticate the evidence, the item loses its

---

[25] In re Grand Jury Proceeding (Cherney), 898 F.2d 565, 568 (7th Cir. 1990). *See also* Vingelli v. United States, Drug Enforcement Ageny, 992 F.2d 449, 452 (2d Cir. 1993) ("Currently most circuits considering the issue have found special circumstances warranting a privilege when the disclosure of the information would be tantamount to revealing a confidential communication.").

[26] *See* In re Grand Jury Proceedings (Pavlick), 680 F.2d 1026, 1027 (5th Cir. 1982) ("limited and narrow exception to the general rule, one that obtains when the disclosure of the client's identity by his attorney would have supplied the last link in an existing chain of incriminating evidence likely to lead to the client's indictment").

[27] *See* In re Grand Jury Investigation No. 83-2-35 (Durant), 723 F.2d 447, 454 (6th Cir. 1983) (The "last link" exception "is simply not grounded upon the preservation of confidential communications and hence not justifiable to support the attorney-client privilege. Although the last link exception may promote concepts of fundamental fairness against self-incrimination, these concepts are not proper considerations to invoke the attorney-client privilege. Rather, the focus of the inquiry is whether disclosure of the identity would adversely implicate the confidentiality of communications."); In re Grand Jury Empanelled February 14, 1978 (Markowitz), 603 F.2d 469, 473 n. 4 (3d Cir. 1979) (it is the link between the client and the communication, rather than the link between the client and the possibility of potential criminal prosecution, which serves to bring the client's identity within the protective ambit of the attorney-client privilege). *See also* Goode, *Identity, Fees, and the Attorney-Client Privilege*, 59 Geo. Wash. L. Rev. 307 (1991).

[28] *See* In re Ryder, 263 F. Supp. 360 (E.D. Va. 1967), *aff'd*, 381 F.2d 713 (4th Cir. 1967).

[29] *E.g.,* Morrell v. State, 575 P.2d 1200, 1210 (Alaska 1978) (recognizing "the rule that a criminal defense attorney must turn over to the prosecution real evidence that the attorney obtains from the client"); State v. Carlin, 640 P.2d 324, 328 (Kan. App. 1982) ("Since the appellant's attorney had a duty to turn over the evidence, there was no error in the court ordering him to do so."); Saltzburg, *Communications Falling Within the Attorney-Client Privilege*, 66 Iowa L. Rev. 811, 837 (1981) ("Some decided cases hold that a lawyer who takes possession of criminal evidence has an obligation to turn it over to the government after examining it.").

probative value. [30] Thus, authentication should be permitted. [31] In lieu of the attorney's testimony, a stipulation could be used to authenticate the evidence.

§ 38.06　Confidentiality Requirement

The attorney-client privilege covers only *confidential* communications. [32] Thus, where the information communicated is intended to become public, the privilege does not apply. [33] Similarly, information concerning a defendant's obligation to appear for sentencing is not "of a confidential nature" and thus not covered by the privilege. [34] When a client communicates with the attorney in a public place, such as an elevator or hallway of a courthouse, and the client fails to take precautionary measures to ensure confidentiality, it is presumed that the client did not intend the communication to be confidential.

[A]　Presence of Third-Parties

The privilege does not apply when the client's actions are inconsistent with an intention of confidentiality — for example, if the communication is made in the presence of a third person. The presence of a third party indicates that confidentiality was not intended. Confidentiality will be considered preserved, however, where the third person is assisting in the legal consultation, such as the case with legal secretaries, investigators, and paralegal assistants. In some cases the privilege is retained when a spouse, parent, or business associate is present. [35]

---

[30] *See* People v. Meredith, 631 P.2d 46 (Cal. 1981).

[31] *See* Saltzburg, *supra* note 29. *But see* Lefstein, *Incriminating Physical Evidence, The Defense Attorney's Dilemma, and the Need for Rules*, 64 N.C. L. Rev. 897 (1986).

[32] *See* Upjohn, 449 U.S. at 395 ("[T]he communications were considered 'highly confidential' when made . . . and have been kept confidential by the company."); United States v. Trammel, 445 U.S. 40, 51 (1980) ("The privileges between priest and penitent, attorney and client, and physician and patient limit protection to private communications.").

[33] *See* Proposed Fed. R. Evid. 503 advisory committee's note ("A communication made in public or meant to be relayed to outsiders or which is divulged by the client to third persons can scarcely be considered confidential. The intent is inferable from the circumstances. Unless intent to disclose is apparent, the attorney-client communication is confidential. Taking or failing to take precautions may be considered as bearing on intent.").

[34] *See* United States v. Gray, 876 F.2d 1411, 1415 (9th Cir. 1989); United States v. Freeman, 519 F.2d 67, 68 (9th Cir. 1975) (Lawyer's testimony regarding the fact that the client was informed of the hearing date "simply relate[s] to whether [the attorney] advised his client of the court's order to appear.").

[35] *See* Proposed Fed. R. Evid. 503 advisory committee's note ("Practicality requires that some disclosure be allowed beyond the immediate circle of lawyer-client and their representatives without impairing confidentiality. Hence the definition allows disclosure to persons 'to whom disclosure is in furtherance of the rendition of professional legal services to the client,' contemplating those in such relation to the client as 'spouse, parent, business associate, or joint client.' ").

[B] Eavesdroppers

As long as the client did not know of the presence of an eavesdropper when the communication took place, and the client took reasonable steps to preserve confidentiality, the privilege is preserved and the eavesdropper may be prohibited from testifying about what was overheard.[36]

§ 38.07 Attorneys & Their Agents Defined

Proposed Rule 503 defined "lawyer" as "a person authorized, or reasonably believed by the client to be authorized, to practice law in any state or nation."[37] A "representative of the lawyer" was defined as "one employed to assist the lawyer in the rendition of professional legal services."[38] Agents who assist in providing legal services, such as associates and secretaries, are included. When determining whether the privilege applies to communications between a client and an agent of the attorney, "what is vital is that the communication be made in confidence for the purpose of obtaining legal advice from the lawyer."[39] Extending the privilege to cover communications between a client and the attorney's agent is necessary for "the effective operation of the privilege of client and lawyer under conditions where the lawyer needs outside help."[40]

Insurance companies. Some courts hold that communications from an insured to a representative of her insurance company come within the privilege.[41] Other courts take a more restrictive view, requiring that "the

---

[36] *See* Proposed Fed. R. Evid. 503 advisory committee's note ("Substantial authority has in the past allowed the eavesdropper to testify to overheard privileged conversations and has admitted intercepted privileged letters. Today, the evolution of more sophisticated techniques of eavesdropping and interception calls for abandonment of this position. The rule accordingly adopts a policy of protection against these kinds of invasion of the privilege.").

[37] Proposed Fed. R. Evid. 503(a)(2), 56 F.R.D. 236 (1972). *See also* Proposed Fed. R. Evid. 503 advisory committee's note ("There is no requirement that the licensing state or nation recognize the attorney-client privilege, thus avoiding excursions into conflict of laws questions. 'Lawyer' also includes a person reasonably believed to be a lawyer.").

[38] Proposed Fed. R. Evid. 503(a)(3), 56 F.R.D. 236 (1972). *See also* Proposed Fed. R. Evid. 503 advisory committee's note ("The definition of 'representative of the lawyer' recognizes that the lawyer may, in rendering legal services, utilize the services of assistants in addition to those employed in the process of communicating. Thus the definition includes an expert employed to assist in rendering legal advice. It also includes an expert employed to assist in the planning and conduct of litigation, though not one employed to testify as a witness. The definition does not, however, limit 'representative of the lawyer' to experts. Whether his compensation is derived immediately from the lawyer or the client is not material.").

[39] United States v. Kovel, 296 F.2d 918, 922 (2d Cir. 1961).

[40] *Id. Accord* United States v. Schwimmer, 892 F.2d 237, 243 (2d Cir. 1989), *modified,* 924 F.2d 443 (2d Cir. 1991).

[41] *See* People v. Ryan, 197 N.E.2d 15, 17 (Ill. 1964) ("We believe that the same salutory reasons for the privilege as exist when the communication is directly between the client and attorney were present when Della Emberton [the insured] made her statement to the investigator for her insurer.").

dominant purpose of the communication" be for the insured's defense and that the insured have a "reasonable expectation of confidentiality."[42]

Experts. Two different uses of experts must be distinguished. First, an expert may be retained for the purpose of testifying at trial. In this situation, any privilege is waived.[43] A "party ought not to be permitted to thwart effective cross-examination of a material witness whom he will call at trial merely by invoking the attorney-client privilege to prohibit pretrial discovery."[44]

Second, an expert may be retained for the purpose of consultation; that is, to provide the attorney with information needed to determine whether a scientific defense is feasible. If such an expert provides an adverse opinion and the defense nevertheless desires to proceed with the defense, typically through the use of other experts, the question arises whether the attorney-client privilege precludes the prosecution from calling the defense-retained expert as a government witness.[45]

Numerous courts have held that the attorney-client privilege covers communications made to an attorney by an expert retained for the purpose of providing information necessary for proper representation.[46] This appears to be the majority view.[47] The argument supporting this rule rests on the attorney's need to obtain expert advice. As one court has stated: "Only a foolhardy lawyer would determine tactical and evidentiary strategy in a case with psychiatric issues without the guidance and interpretation of psychiatrists and others skilled in this field."[48] An attorney, however,

---

[42] Cutchin v. State, 792 A.2d 359, 366 (Md. App. 2002). *See also* State v. Pavin, 494 A.2d 834, 837-38 (N.J. App. 1985).

[43] *See* United States v. Alvarez, 519 F.2d 1036, 1046-47 (3d Cir. 1975); Pouncy v. State, 353 So. 2d 640, 642 (Fla. App. 1977); State v. Mingo, 392 A.2d 590, 595 (N.J. 1978). *See also* United States v. Nobles, 422 U.S. 225, 239 (1975) ("Respondent, by electing to present the investigator as a witness, waived the [work product] privilege with respect to matters covered in his testimony.").

[44] Friedenthal, *Discovery and Use of an Adverse Party's Expert Information,* 14 Stan. L. Rev. 455, 464–65 (1962). *See also* Graham, *Discovery of Experts Under Rule 26(b)(4) of the Federal Rules of Civil Procedure: Part One, An Analytical Study,* 1976 U. Ill. L. F 895, 897 & n. 12.

[45] *See generally* Imwinkelried, *The Applicability of the Attorney-Client Privilege to Non-Testifying Experts: Reestablishing the Boundaries Between the Attorney-Client Privilege and the Work Product Protection,* 68 Wash. L.Q. 19, 21-23 (1990); Saltzburg, *Privileges and Professionals: Lawyers and Psychiatrists,* 66 Va. L. Rev. 597 (1980); Note, *Discovery of Attorney-Expert Communications: Current State of, and Suggestions for, Federal and Missouri Practice,* 57 Mo. L. Rev. 247 (1992) (civil rules); Note, *Protecting the Confidentiality of Pretrial Psychiatric Disclosures: A Survey of Standards,* 51 N.Y.U. L. Rev. 409 (1976).

[46] *E.g.,* United States v. Alvarez, 519 F.2d 1036, 1046–47 (3d Cir. 1975) (psychiatrist); United States v. Kovel, 296 F.2d 918, 921–22 (2d Cir. 1961) (accountant); United States v. Layton, 90 F.R.D. 520, 525 (N.D. Cal. 1981) (psychiatrist); Bailey v. Meister Brau, Inc., 57 F.R.D. 11, 13 (N.D. Ill. 1972) (financial expert); Houston v. State, 602 P.2d 784, 791 (Alaska 1979) (psychiatrist); People v. Lines, 531 P.2d 793, 802-03 (Cal. 1975) (psychiatrist); Miller v. District Court, 737 P.2d 834 (Colo. 1987) (psychiatrist); Pouncy v. State, 353 So. 2d 640, 642 (Fla. App. 1977) (psychiatrist); People v. Knippenberg, 362 N.E.2d 681, 684 (Ill. 1977) (investigator).

[47] *See* State v. Pratt, 398 A.2d 421, 423 (Md. 1979) (This view is "almost universally accepted").

[48] United States *ex rel.* Edney v. Smith, 425 F. Supp. 1038, 1047 (E.D.N.Y. 1976), *aff'd,* 556 F.2d 556 (2d Cir. 1977).

might not seek such assistance if an expert's adverse opinion could be introduced by the prosecution: "Breaching the attorney-client privilege . . . would have the effect of inhibiting the free exercise of a defense attorney's informed judgment by confronting him with the likelihood that, in taking a step obviously crucial to his client's defense, he is creating a potential government witness who theretofore did not exist."[49]

Other courts have rejected the extension of the privilege in this context, although their reasons vary. First, some courts limit the privilege to communications between the attorney and client. Under this view, experts and other agents are not covered by the privilege.[50] Second, other courts hold that the privilege extends only to confidential communications and thus does not apply to experts who do not rely on the client's communications in reaching their opinions. Under this view, a psychiatrist may be protected by the privilege[51] but not a fingerprint examiner,[52] handwriting expert,[53] or pathologist.[54] Third, still other courts hold that the privilege is waived when the defense introduces scientific evidence. Accordingly, a defendant who raises an insanity defense waives the privilege with respect to all psychiatrists who have examined the defendant.

In addition to the attorney-client privilege, defendants have argued that the Sixth Amendment right to effective assistance of counsel precludes the prosecution use of defense-retained experts. Several courts have accepted this argument:

---

[49] *Pratt*, 398 A.2d at 426.

[50] *E.g.,* State v. Carter, 641 S.W.2d 54, 57 (Mo. 1982); State v. Hamlet, 944 P.2d 1026, 1031 (Wash. 1997) ("[N]either the attorney-client privilege nor the Sixth Amendment right to counsel is violated by the ordered disclosure of the name of the nontestifying expert retained by the defense for purposes of a diminished capacity defense . . . nor by the State calling that expert as a State's witness to rebut evidence of a diminished capacity defense"). *See also* State v. Schaaf, 819 P.2d 909, 918 (Ariz. 1991) ("Even if defendant had not waived this right, we find it to be within the trial court's broad discretion to determine whether an expert witness will be required to testify, even if it was the other party who initially retained the expert witness").

[51] In People v. Knuckles, 650 N.E.2d 974 (Ill. 1995), the crime was committed nine years before the trial, and the defense psychiatrist was the only expert who had examined the accused at that time. First, the court ruled that the attorney-client privilege covered a mental health professional. Second, the court rejected an automatic waiver rule, under which the privilege is waived if the defendant "puts his mental state in issue." The court held that the privilege is waived only with respect to the testimony and reports of those experts who will testify. Third, the court rejected creating a "public interest" exception for this case.

[52] *See* People v. Speck, 242 N.E.2d 208, 221 (Ill. 1968).

[53] *See* United States v. Pipkins, 528 F.2d 559, 563–64 (5th Cir. 1976) (handwriting exemplars given to expert by attorney not within privilege). *See also* Morris v. State, 477 A.2d 1206, 1211 (Md. App. 1984).

[54] Rose v. State, 591 So. 2d 195, 197 (Fla. App. 1991) (medical examiner initially hired by the defense) ("[T]he assertion of the privilege in the psychiatric witness cases is based on the confidential communications which may be made to the psychiatrist"). *See also* State v. Richey, 595 N.E.2d 915, 922 (Ohio 1992) ("Although the prosecutor's use of a defense expert may violate an accused's attorney-client privilege, [the arson expert] did not disclose or rely upon any confidential communications here.").

A defense attorney should be completely free and unfettered in making a decision as fundamental as that concerning the retention of an expert to assist him. Reliance upon the confidentiality of an expert's advice itself is a crucial aspect of a defense attorney's ability to consult with and advise his client. If the confidentiality of that advice cannot be anticipated, the attorney might well forego seeking such assistance, to the consequent detriment of his client's cause. [55]

Similarly, a commentator has argued that a "rule allowing any incriminating information developed during defense preparation to be used against the defendant would impair both a vigorous defense effort, which is central to the adversary system, and the defendant-counsel relationship." [56] Notwithstanding the persuasiveness of this argument, some courts have rejected it. [57]

§ 38.08 Clients & Their Agents Defined

The definition of client includes governmental bodies and corporations. [58] Extending the privilege to governmental entities is supported by the underlying policy of the attorney-client privilege; governmental entities, like individuals, need legal services.

Corporations. The privilege extends to a firm, partnership, or corporation. There is often a problem in determining whether the attorney represents only the corporation or also the corporate officers. "The default assumption is that the attorney only represents the corporate entity, not the individuals within the corporate sphere, and it is the individuals' burden to dispel that presumption." [59]

A corporation, as a legal fiction, can only communicate through its agents. An issue arises when a lower-level employee communicates with the corporation attorney about some corporate-related issue in which the employee was involved — for example, a traffic accident in which the employee drove the corporation's truck. Some courts apply the "control group" test, which covers only communications between the attorney and a corporate agent who possesses the authority to control or act on the legal advice. [60] This rule excludes the truckdriver mentioned above because he

---

[55] State v. Mingo, 392 A.2d 590, 595 (N.J. 1978) (handwriting expert). *See also* United States v. Alvarez, 519 F.2d 1036, 1046 (3d Cir. 1975) (psychiatrist); Perez v. People, 745 P.2d 650, 652 (Colo. 1987) (handwriting expert); Hutchinson v. People, 742 P.2d 875, 881 (Colo. 1987) (handwriting expert) ("[A] defense counsel's access to expert assistance is a crucial element in assuring a defendant's right to effective legal assistance."); People v. Knippenberg, 362 N.E.2d 681, 684-85 (Ill. 1977) (investigator). *See* 1 Giannelli & Imwinkelried, Scientific Evidence ch. 5 (3d ed. 1999).

[56] *See* Mosteller, *Discovery Against the Defense: Tilting the Adversarial Balance*, 74 Cal. L. Rev. 1567, 1668 (1986).

[57] *See* Noggle v. Marshall, 706 F.2d 1408, 1414–15 (6th Cir. 1983); Granviel v. Estelle, 655 F.2d 673, 683 (5th Cir. 1981); State v. Richey, 595 N.E.2d 915, 922 (Ohio 1992).

[58] Proposed Fed. R. Evid. 503 advisory committee's note.

[59] In re Grand Jury Subpeona, 274 F.3d 563, 571 (1st Cir. 2001).

[60] *See* Consolidation Coal Co. v. Bucyrus-Erie Co., 432 N.E.2d 250, 257 (Ill. 1982.) ("The

is not part of the "control group." Only the top echelon of the corporate pyramid can act on behalf of the corporation.

In *Upjohn Co. v. United States*,[61] the Supreme Court rejected the "control group" test as a matter of federal common law.[62] With individual clients, the client typically provides the attorney with the relevant information and then the attorney responds with the legal advice. The corporate context is different. The control group, which can act on the advice, does not necessarily have the relevant information.[63] The truckdriver has that information in the above example. For this reason, the Court adopted a different test, the critical factors of which include: (1) whether the employee communicated with the attorney in her capacity as corporate counsel, (2) whether both were acting at the behest of their corporate superiors, (3) whether the communication was made to enable the corporation to obtain legal advice and the employee was aware of this, (4) whether the communication concerned matters within the employee's duties, and (5) whether the communications were considered confidential when made.

Numerous other issues arise in the corporate context. For example, does the privilege belong to the stockholders or management?[64] If the stockholders are the holders of the privilege, then they can waive it. In *Garner v. Wolfinbarger*,[65] a leading case, the Fifth Circuit held that in a stockholders suit against the corporation and its officers the privilege remained with management but could be overcome by a showing of good cause.[66]

---

control-group test appears to us to strike a reasonable balance by protecting consultations with counsel by those who are the decisionmakers or who substantially influence corporate decisions and by minimizing the amount of relevant factual material which is immune from discovery.").

[61] 449 U.S. 383 (1981).

[62] *Id.* at 392 ("The control group test adopted by the court below . . . frustrates the very purpose of the privilege by discouraging the communication of relevant information by employees of the client to attorneys seeking to render legal advice to the client corporation. The attorney's advice will also frequently be more significant to noncontrol group members than to those who officially sanction the advice, and the control group test makes it more difficult to convey full and frank legal advice to the employees who will put into effect the client corporation's policy.").

[63] *Id.* at 391 ("In the case of the individual client the provider of information and the person who acts on the lawyer's advice are one and the same. In the corporate context, however, it will frequently be employees beyond the control group as defined by the court below — 'officers and agents . . . responsible for directing [the company's] actions in response to legal advice' — who will possess the information needed by the corporation's lawyers. Middle-level — and indeed lower-level — employees can, by actions within the scope of their employment, embroil the corporation in serious legal difficulties, and it is only natural that these employees would have the relevant information needed by corporate counsel if he is adequately to advise the client with respect to such actual or potential difficulties.").

[64] *See* In re Occidental Petroleum Corp., 217 F.3d 293 (5th Cir. 2000) (employee-participants in stock plan who sue management for breach of fiduciary duty).

[65] 430 F.2d 1093 (5th Cir. 1970).

[66] *See* Friedman, *Is The* Garner *Qualification of the Corporate Attorney-Client Privilege Viable After* Jaffee v. Redmond?, 55 Bus. Law. 243 (1999); Saltzburg, *Corporate Attorney-Client Privilege in Shareholder Litigation and Similar Cases:* Garner *Revisited*, 12 Hofstra L. Rev. 817 (1984).

§ 38.09   Joint Defense Agreements

The privilege may apply in "joint defense" situations,[67] those in which attorneys for different clients confer for the purpose of advancing the same defense.[68] Because the privilege may apply outside the litigation context, it is more aptly termed the "common interest" or "pooled information" rule.[69] Client-to-client communications in the absence of attorneys, as John Gotti found out, are not covered by this rule.[70] "Even when that rule applies, however, a party always remains free to disclose his own communications. Thus, the existence of a joint defense agreement does not increase the number of parties whose consent is needed to waive the attorney-client privilege; it merely prevents disclosure of a communication made in the course of preparing a joint defense by the third party to whom it was made."[71]

This rule must be distinguished from the joint-clients issue discussed below.

§ 38.10   Duration of the Privilege

In *Swidler & Berlin v. United States*,[72] the Supreme Court held that the federal attorney-client privilege survives the death of the client. The majority justified the result by reference to the purpose of the privilege:

> Knowing that communications will remain confidential even after death encourages the client to communicate fully and frankly with counsel. While the fear of disclosure, and the consequent withholding of information from counsel, may be reduced if disclosure is limited to posthumous disclosure in a criminal context, it seems unreasonable to assume that it vanishes altogether. Clients may be concerned about reputation, civil liability, or possible harm to

---

[67] *See* Proposed Fed. R. Evid. 503 advisory committee's note ("The rule does not apply to situations where there is no common interest to be promoted by a joint consultation, and the parties meet on a purely adversary basis.").

[68] *E.g.,* In re Grand Jury Subpoenas 89-3 and 89-4, 902 F.2d 244, 248–49 (4th Cir. 1990) ("common interest" privilege); United States v. Schwimmer, 892 F.2d 237, 243–44 (2d Cir. 1989), *modified,* 924 F.2d 443 (2d Cir. 1991); United States v. Bay State Ambul. & Hosp. Rental Serv., Inc., 874 F.2d 20, 28 (1st Cir. 1989) ("The joint defense privilege protects communications between an individual and an attorney for another when the communications are 'part of an ongoing and joint effort to set up a common defense strategy.'"); United States v. Stotts, 870 F.2d 288, 290 (5th Cir. 1989) (privilege applied to accused's statements made in a conference with his attorney, a codefendant and his attorney, and a third codefendant).

[69] *See* United States v. Schwimmer, 892 F.2d 237, 243 (2d Cir. 1989), *modified,* 924 F.2d 443 (2d Cir. 1991).

[70] United States v. Gotti, 771 F. Supp. 535, 545 (E.D.N.Y. 1991).

[71] In re Grand Jury Subpeona, 274 F.3d 563, 572–73 (1st Cir. 2001). *See also* Proposed Fed. R. Evid. 503 advisory committee's note ("But, if for reasons of his own, a client wishes to disclose his own statements made at the joint conference, he should be permitted to do so, and the rule is to that effect.").

[72] 524 U.S. 399 (1998).

friends or family. Posthumous disclosure of such communications may be as feared as disclosure during the client's lifetime.[73]

In addition, the Court noted that "the loss of evidence admittedly caused by the privilege is justified in part by the fact that without the privilege, the client may not have made such communications in the first place. This is true of disclosure before and after the client's death."[74] The Court also rejected a proposed exception for criminal cases because "a client may not know at the time he discloses information to his attorney whether it will later be relevant to a civil or a criminal matter."[75]

§ 38.11 Exceptions

There are several well-recognized exceptions to the attorney-client privilege.

[A] Crime-Fraud Exception

The privilege does not apply to communications concerning future criminal or fraudulent acts.[76] "It is the purpose of the crime-fraud exception to the attorney-client privilege to assure that the 'seal of secrecy,' between lawyer and client does not extend to communications 'made for the purpose of getting advice for the commission of a fraud' or crime."[77] It is the client's intent, not the attorney's, that is determinative.[78]

When a party opposing the assertion of the privilege alleges that the attorney-client communication involved future illegal acts, the trial court must decide if the crime-fraud exception applies. The Supreme Court, in

---

[73] *Id.* at 407.

[74] *Id.* at 408 (citations omitted).

[75] *Id.* at 409.

[76] *See* Proposed Fed. R. Evid. 503 advisory committee's note ("The privilege does not extend to advice in aid of future wrongdoing. The wrongdoing need not be that of the client. The provision that the client knew or reasonably should have known of the criminal or fraudulent nature of the act is designed to protect the client who is erroneously advised that a proposed action is within the law. No preliminary finding that sufficient evidence aside from the communication has been introduced to warrant a finding that the services were sought to enable the commission of a wrong is required."). *See also* Clark v. United States, 289 U.S. 1, 15 (1933) ("We turn to the precedents in the search for an analogy, and the search is not in vain. There is a privilege protecting communications between attorney and client. The privilege takes flight if the relation is abused. A client who consults an attorney for advice that will serve him in the commission of a fraud will have no help from the law."); In re Richard Roe, Inc., 68 F.3d 38, 40 (2d Cir. 1995) ("Although there is a societal interest in enabling clients to get sound legal advice, there is no such interest when the communications or advice are intended to further the commission of a crime or fraud.").

[77] United States v. Zolin, 491 U.S. 554, 563 (1989).

[78] *See* In re BankAmerica Corp. Securities Litig., 270 F.3d 639, 642 (8th Cir. 2001) ("Because the attorney-client privilege benefits the client, it is the client's intent to further a crime or fraud that must be shown. Both the attorney's intent, and the attorney's knowledge or ignorance of the client's intent, are irrelevant."). *See also* Subin, *The Lawyer as Superego: Disclosure of Client Confidences to Prevent Harm*, 70 Iowa L. Rev. 1091 (1985).

United States v. Zolin,[79] held as a matter of federal common law that the trial judge could review in camera allegedly privileged communications to determine whether they fell within the crime-fraud exception. To obtain such review, the party opposing the privilege "must present evidence sufficient to support a reasonable belief that in camera review may yield evidence that establishes the exception's applicability."[80] The Court also held that, under Rule 104(a), the trial court may consider the allegedly privileged communications in determining whether the threshold showing for in camera review has been satisfied.[81] The quantum of evidence needed to overcome the privilege was left undecided by the Court.[82]

[B] Joint Clients

An exception for joint representation is widely recognized in situations where two clients subsequently disagree and litigation ensues — *e.g.,* Schmedlap and Botz retain an attorney to draw up a partnership agreement, and they later have a dispute that results in a lawsuit. The privilege does not apply in later litigation between the joint clients; in that situation, one client's interest in the privilege is counterbalanced by the other's interest in being able to waive it. The communications, however, remain privileged from disclosure at the instance of outsiders.[83]

Joint defense. This exception should be distinguished from "joint defense" situations, in which attorneys for two different clients confer for the purpose of advancing the same defense.[84]

[C] Breach of Duty by Attorney or Client

In some cases, a client's assertion of a claim, counterclaim, or affirmative defense that places an otherwise privileged matter at issue may be deemed a limited exception ("waiver").[85] Often, a malpractice suit against the attorney or an incompetence of counsel claim in post-conviction criminal

---

[79] 491 U.S. 554, 568 (1989) ("We see no basis for holding that the tapes in this case must be deemed privileged under Rule 104(a) while the question of crime or fraud remains open.").

[80] *Id.* at 574–75.

[81] *Id.* at 568 (The "disclosure of allegedly privileged materials to the district court for purposes of determining the merits of a claim of privilege does not have the legal effect of terminating the privilege.").

[82] *Id.* at 563 n. 7. *See also* In re BankAmerica Corp. Securities Litig., 270 F.3d 639, 644 (8th Cir. 2001) (noting that other circuits had adopted different standards regarding the quantum of proof required to satisfy the crime-fraud exception — *e.g.,* reasonable cause, probable cause, and evidence that will suffice until contradicted by other evidence; also noting that *Zolin* dictates a higher standard of proof for public disclosure than for in camera review).

[83] FDIC v. Ogden Corp., 202 F.3d 454, 461 (1st Cir. 2000).

[84] *See supra* § 38.09 (joint defense agreements).

[85] *See* Proposed Fed. R. Evid. 503 advisory committee's note ("The exception is required by considerations of fairness and policy when questions arise out of dealings between attorney and client, as in cases of controversy over attorney's fees, claims of inadequacy of representation, or charges of professional misconduct.").

cases comes within this exception.[86] The privilege also does not apply in an action by an attorney against the client for the collection of legal fees.

[D] Claimant Through Same Deceased Client

"Normally the privilege survives the death of the client and may be asserted by his representative. When, however, the identity of the person who steps into the client's shoes is in issue, as in a will contest, the identity of the person entitled to claim the privilege remains undetermined until the conclusion of the litigation. The choice is thus between allowing both sides or neither to assert the privilege, with authority and reason favoring the latter view."[87]

[E] Document Attested by Lawyer

The privilege does not apply where the attorney also acted as a subscribing witness.[88] When a testator uses his attorney as a subscribing witness to his will, the attorney should be treated like any other subscribing witness. The only purpose a testator has in requesting any person to witness his will is to assure its legal execution.

§ 38.12 Waiver

The privilege may be waived in several ways. A "corporation's attorney-client privilege may be waived by current management."[89] The Supreme Court has noted that "when control of a corporation passes to new management, the authority to assert and waive the corporation's attorney client privilege passes as well."[90] Moreover, "a corporation may unilaterally waive the attorney-client privilege with respect to any communications made by a corporate officer in his corporate capacity, notwithstanding the existence of an individual attorney-client relationship between him and the corporation's counsel."[91]

---

[86] See Johnon v. Alabama, 256 F.3d 1156, 1178 (11th Cir. 2001) ("By alleging that his attorneys provided ineffective assistance of counsel in their choice of a defense strategy, Johnson put at issue — and thereby waived — any privilege that might apply to the contents of his conversations with those attorneys to the extent those conversations bore on his attorneys' strategic choices.").

[87] See Proposed Fed. R. Evid. 503 advisory committee's note. See also United States v. Osborn, 561 F.2d 1334, 1340 n. 11 (9th Cir. 1977) ("The rationale behind the exception to the general rule is that the privilege itself is designed for the protection of the client, and it cannot be said to be in the interests of the testator, in a controversy between parties all of whom claim under the testator, to have those confidential communications of the testator and attorney excluded which are necessary to a proper fulfillment of the testator's intent.").

[88] Proposed Fed. R. Evid. 503 advisory committee's note ("When the lawyer acts as attesting witness, the approval of the client to his so doing may safely be assumed, and waiver of the privilege as to any relevant lawyer-client communications is a proper result.").

[89] In re Grand Jury Subpeona, 274 F.3d 563, 571 (1st Cir. 2001).

[90] CFTC v. Weintraub, 471 U.S. 343, 349 (1985).

[91] In re Grand Jury Subpeona, 274 F.3d 563, 573 (1st Cir. 2001).

[A]   Client's or Attorney's Testimony

If the client testifies or elicits testimony from the attorney concerning the communication, the privilege is waived.[92] There is no waiver if only the underlying facts are elicited during examination and the communication is not referred to. In short, there is no subject-matter waiver. Any other rule would result in the waiver of the privilege in virtually every case in which a client testifies (on the assumption that clients discuss their testimony with their attorneys prior to trial).[93] Once the client testifies, the client's attorney could be called as a witness by the other party and compelled to divulge what the client had said about the case.

[B]   Putting the Communication in Issue

The privilege may also be waived by putting the attorney's advice in issue.[94] For example, in *United States v. Workman*,[95] the accused claimed that he relied on his former attorney's advice in cashing certain checks. The Eighth Circuit found an implicit waiver of the privilege: "Workman cannot selectively assert the privilege to block the introduction of information harmful to his case after introducing other aspects of his conversations with Levad [attorney] for his own benefit. The attorney client privilege cannot be used as both a shield and a sword, and Workman cannot claim in his defense that he relied on Levad's advice without permitting the prosecution to explore the substance of that advice."[96]

[C]   Voluntary Disclosure

The voluntary disclosure of privileged information to a third party waives the privilege.[97] For example, in *In re von Bulow*,[98] the client acquiesced

---

[92] *See* Hunt v. Blackburn, 128 U.S. 464, 470–71 (1888) ("When Mrs. Blackburn entered upon a line of defense which involved what transpired between herself and Mr. Weatherford, and respecting which she testified, she waived her right to object to his giving his own account of the matter."); In re von Bulow, 828 F.2d 94, 101 (2d Cir. 1987) ("[W]hen the client waives the privilege by testifying about what transpired between her and her attorney, she cannot thereafter insist that the mouth of the attorney be shut."); International Tel. & Tel. Corp. v. United Tel. Co. of Fla., 60 F.R.D. 177, 185–86 (M.D. Fla. 1973) ("[I]f the client or his attorney at his instance takes the stand and testifies to privileged communications in part this is a waiver as to the remainder . . . about the same subject.").

[93] *See* United States v. Billmyer, 57 F.3d 31, 36 (1st Cir. 1995) ("[T]his rule protects testimony given by the client in court, in order that the right to testify should not come at the price of one's ability to consult privately with counsel.").

[94] *See* Chevron Corp. v. Pennzoil Co., 974 F.2d 1156, 1162 (9th Cir. 1992) (The "privilege which protects attorney-client communications may not be used both as a sword and a shield. Where a party raises a claim which in fairness requires disclosure of the protected communication, the privilege may be implicitly waived.").

[95] 138 F.3d 1261 (8th Cir. 1998).

[96] *Id.* at 1263–64 (citations omitted).

[97] *See* United States v. Workman, 138 F.3d 1261, 1263 (8th Cir. 1998) ("Voluntary disclosure of attorney client communications expressly waives the privilege . . . . The waiver covers any information directly related to that which was actually disclosed."); Weil v. Investment/

in and encouraged the publication of a book, *Reversal of Fortune*, about his former criminal trial, thus partly waiving his attorney-client privilege. The issue then becomes the extent of the waiver. Generally, "disclosure of information resulting in the waiver of the attorney-client privilege constitutes waiver 'only as to communications about the matter actually disclosed.' "[99]

[D] Inadvertent Waiver

Modern technology makes inadvertent waiver more common — *e.g.,* sending fax to the wrong number or sending wrong computer disk in response to a discovery request. Courts have generally followed one of three approaches to waiver based on inadvertent disclosure: (1) the lenient approach, (2) the "middle of the road" approach, and (3) the strict approach.[100] Under the lenient approach,[101] the privilege must be knowingly waived by the client because it exists for the benefit of the client.[102] In contrast, under the strict test, any document, intentionally or otherwise, disclosed loses its privileged status with the possible exception of situations where all precautions had been taken to preserve confidentiality. Once waiver has occurred, it extends "to all other communications relating to the same subject matter."[103]

The intermediate test is based on *Hydraflow, Inc. v. Enidine Inc.*[104] Under this approach, waiver depends on five factors: (1) the reasonableness

---

Indicators, Research & Mmgt., 647 F.2d 18, 24 (9th Cir. 1981) (voluntary disclosure of a privileged communication to a third party waives privilege); Proposed Fed. R. Evid. 511 ("A person upon whom these rules confer a privilege against disclosure of the confidential matter or communication waives the privilege if he or his predecessor while holder of the privilege voluntarily discloses or consents to the disclosure of any significant part of the matter or communication. This rule does not apply if the disclosure is itself a privilege communication."), 56 F.R.D. 244, 245 (1973).

[98] 828 F.2d 94, 101 (2d Cir. 1987).

[99] *Chevron Corp.*, 974 F.2d at 1162.

[100] Pavlik v. Cargill, Inc., 9 F.3d 710, 713 (8th Cir. 1993).

[101] *See* Georgetown Manor, Inc. v. Ethan Allen, Inc., 753 F. Supp. 936, 938 (S.D. Fla. 1991); Mendenhall v. Barber-Greene Co., 531 F. Supp. 951, 954 (N.D. Ill. 1982) (holding that the better rule is that mere inadvertent production does not waive attorney-client privilege).

[102] *But see* Gray v. Bicknell, 86 F.3d 1472, 1483-84 (8th Cir. 1996) ("The lenient test creates little incentive for lawyers to maintain tight control over privileged material. While the lenient test remains true to the core principle of attorney-client privilege, which is that it exists to protect the client and must be waived by the client, it ignores the importance of confidentiality. To be privileged, attorney-client communications must remain confidential, and yet, under this test, the lack of confidentiality becomes meaningless so long as it occurred inadvertently.").

[103] In re Sealed Case, 877 F.2d 976, 981 (D.C. Cir. 1989) (citation omitted). "The courts will grant no greater protection to those who assert the privilege than their own precautions warrant." *Id.* at 980. *But see Gray*, 86 F.3d at 1483–84 ("There is an important societal need for people to be able to employ and fully consult with those trained in the law for advice and guidance. The strict test would likely impede the ability of attorneys to fill this need by chilling communications between attorneys and clients. If, when a document stamped 'attorney-client privileged' is inadvertently released, it and all related documents lose their privileged status, then clients will have much greater hesitancy to fully inform their attorney.").

[104] 145 F.R.D. 626 (W.D.N.Y. 1993).

of the precautions taken to prevent inadvertent disclosure in view of the extent of document production, (2) the number of inadvertent disclosures, (3) the extent of the disclosures, (4) the promptness of measures taken to rectify the disclosure, and (5) whether the interests of justice would be served by relieving the party of its error.[105]

§ 38.13 Procedural Issues

[A] Burden of Proof

As with all privileges, the burden of persuasion generally rests with the person asserting the privilege.[106]

[B] In Camera Hearings

In *United States v. Zolin*,[107] the Supreme Court held that the applicability of the crime-fraud exception can be resolved by an in camera inspection of the allegedly privileged material.

§ 38.14 Work Product Privilege

The attorney-client privilege should be distinguished from the work-product doctrine, a *qualified* privilege recognized in both the Civil and Criminal Rules.[108] In *Hickman v. Taylor*,[109] the Supreme Court rejected "an attempt, without purported necessity or justification, to secure written statements, private memoranda and personal recollections prepared or formed by an adverse party's counsel in the course of his legal duties."[110] In applying the work-product rule to criminal cases, the Court wrote:

---

[105] *Id.* at 637. *See also Gray*, 86 F.3d at 1484 ("This test strikes the appropriate balance between protecting attorney-client privilege and allowing, in certain situations, the unintended release of privileged documents to waive that privilege. The middle test is best suited to achieving a fair result. It accounts for the errors that inevitably occur in modern, document-intensive litigation, but treats carelessness with privileged material as an indication of waiver. The middle test provides the most thoughtful approach, leaving the trial court broad discretion as to whether waiver occurred and, if so, the scope of that waiver. It requires a detailed court inquiry into the document practices of the party who inadvertently released the document.").

[106] *See In re Grand Jury Proceedings*, 219 F.3d 175, 182 (2d Cir. 2000); In re Lindsey, 158 F.3d 1263, 1270 (D.C. Cir. 1998) ("It is settled law that the party claiming the privilege bears the burden of proving that the communications are protected."); In re Grand Jury Investigation No. 83-2-35 (Durant), 723 F.2d 447, 450 (6th Cir. 1983) ("The burden of establishing the existence of the privilege rests with the person asserting it.").

[107] 491 U.S. 554 (1989). *See supra* § 37.05[D] for a further discussion of *Zolin*.

[108] Fed. R. Civ. P. 26(b)(3); Fed. R. Crim. P.16(b)(2) (prosecution); Fed. R. Crim. P. 16(c)(2) (defense counsel). *See* Feldman, *Work Product in Criminal Practice and Procedure*, 50 Cin. L. Rev. 495 (1981).

[109] 329 U.S. 495 (1947).

[110] *Id.* at 510. The Court further commented that "it is essential that a lawyer work with a certain degree of privacy" and if discovery of the material sought were permitted "much of what is now put down in writing would remain unwritten. An attorney's thoughts, heretofore

At its core, the work-product doctrine shelters the mental processes of the attorney, providing a privileged area within which he can analyze and prepare his client's case. But the doctrine is an intensely practical one, grounded in the realities of litigation in our adversary system. One of those realities is that attorneys often must rely on the assistance of investigators and other agents in the compilation of materials in preparation for trial. It is therefore necessary that the doctrine protect material prepared by agents for the attorney as well as those prepared by the attorney himself.[111]

The work-product doctrine generally protects a broader range of materials than does the attorney-client privilege. The former protects materials prepared in anticipation of trial, while the latter is limited to communications.

However, the protection for work product is not absolute; it may be overcome if the party seeking discovery shows that it has a "substantial need" for the materials and is unable without "undue hardship" to obtain the substantial equivalent of the materials by other means.[112]

Work product privilege can also be waived.[113]

§ 38.15 Key Points

Professional responsibility distinguished. The attorney-client privilege should be distinguished from an attorney's obligations under the rules governing professional responsibility. Model Rule 1.6(a) states that lawyers "shall not reveal information relating to representation of a client," with only two narrow exceptions. The attorney-client privilege is limited to *communications*, whereas the ethical rule covers all information obtained as a result of the representation. Moreover, an evidentiary privilege applies only in *legal* proceedings; the ethical rule applies outside legal proceedings.

---

inviolate, would not be his own. Inefficiency, unfairness and sharp practices would inevitably develop in the giving of legal advice and in the preparation of cases for trial. The effect on the legal profession would be demoralizing. And the interests of the clients and the cause of justice would be poorly served." *Id.* at 511.

[111] United States v. Nobles, 422 U.S. 225, 238–39 (1975).

[112] Fed. R. Civ. P. 26(b)(3). *See also* Upjohn v. United States, 449 U.S. 383, 400 (1981) ("Rule 26 accords special protection to work product revealing the attorney's mental processes. The Rule permits disclosure of documents and tangible things constituting attorney work product upon a showing of substantial need and inability to obtain the equivalent without undue hardship. . . . Although this language does not specifically refer to memoranda based on oral statements of witnesses, the *Hickman* court stressed the danger that compelled disclosure of such memoranda would reveal the attorney's mental processes. It is clear that this is the sort of material the draftsmen of the Rule had in mind as deserving special protection.").

[113] *See* In re Grand Jury Subpoena, 274 F.3d 563, 574–75 (1st Cir. 2001) ("Although a valid joint defense agreement may protect work product, one party to such an agreement may not preclude disclosure of work product by another party on whose behalf the work originally was performed. Nor can the parties, by agreement, broaden the scope of the privilege that the law allows. Such an agreement would contravene public policy (and, hence, would be unenforceable).") (citations omitted).

Holder. The holder of the privilege is the client and not the attorney. Accordingly, only the client has the right to invoke and waive the privilege. The attorney may, however, claim the privilege on behalf of the client.

Professional Relationship Requirement

The attorney-client privilege applies only where the communication is made for the purpose of receiving legal advice. It protects a client against disclosure of facts revealed in non-litigious as well as in litigious consultation. The privilege extends to communications made to an attorney by a person seeking legal services, even if the attorney decides not to represent that person. If an attorney is consulted for reasons unrelated to legal services (*e.g.,* as a friend or business advisor), the privilege does not apply.

Communications Defined

Generally, only the communication is covered and not the facts that are the subject of the communication. Stated another way, the communication, but not the client's knowledge, is protected by the privilege.

Documents. The privilege may encompass written communications between attorney and client — *e.g.,* letter containing a legal opinion about a proposed course of conduct. However, pre-existing documents do not become privileged merely because they are transmitted to an attorney.

Client identity & fee arrangements. Generally, a client's identity, the fact of consultation with or employment of an attorney, and fee arrangements do not fall within the protection of the attorney-client privilege. However, some courts extend the privilege's protection to the name and address of the client under certain circumstances — *e.g.,* where the revelation of the identity of the client would reveal a confidential communication.

Physical evidence. A difficult problem arises when a client delivers tangible evidence to the attorney or provides the attorney with information necessary to retrieve the evidence. Here, the privilege applies to the communication itself. The attorney may not, however, take possession and hide the evidence; this would amount to an obstruction of justice. Nor, for the same reason, may the attorney tell the client to destroy the evidence. Once the attorney takes possession, some decisions hold that the evidence must be turned over to the prosecution.

Confidentiality Requirement

Where the information communicated is intended to become public, the privilege does not apply.

Presence of third-parties. The privilege is also inapplicable when the client's actions are inconsistent with an intention of confidentiality — for example, if the communication is made in the presence of a third person. Confidentiality will be considered preserved, however, where the third person is necessary to the legal consultation such as the case with legal secretaries, investigators, and paralegal assistants. In some cases the privilege is retained when a spouse, parent, or business associate is present.

Eavesdroppers. As long as the client did not know of the presence of an eavesdropper when the communication took place, and the client took reasonable steps to preserve confidentiality, the privilege is preserved and the eavesdropper may be prohibited from testifying about what was overheard.

Attorneys & Their Agents Defined

Agents who assist in providing legal services, such as paralegals and secretaries, are included.

Insurance companies. Some courts hold that communications from an insured to a representative of her insurance company come within the privilege. Other courts take a more restrictive view, requiring that the dominant purpose of the communication be for the insured's defense and that the insured have a "reasonable expectation of confidentiality."

Experts. Two different uses of experts must be distinguished. First, an expert may be retained for the purpose of testifying at trial. In this situation, the privilege is waived. Second, an expert may be retained for the purpose of consultation; that is, to provide the attorney with information needed to determine whether a scientific defense is feasible. Numerous courts have held that the attorney-client privilege covers communications made to an attorney by an expert retained for the purpose of providing information necessary for proper representation. Other courts have rejected the extension of the attorney-client privilege in this context, although their reasons vary.

Clients & Their Agents Defined

The definition of client includes governmental bodies and corporations. There is often a problem in determining whether the attorney represents only the corporation or also the corporate officers.

Control group test. In *Upjohn Co. v. United States*, the Supreme Court rejected the "control group" test as a matter of federal common law. The Court adopted a different test, the critical factors of which include: (1) whether the employee communicated with the attorney in her capacity as corporate counsel, (2) whether both were acting at the behest of their corporate superiors, (3) whether the communication was made to enable the corporation to obtain legal advice and the employee was aware of this, (4) whether the communication concerned matters within the employee's duties, and (5) whether the communications were considered confidential when made.

Exceptions

There are several well-recognized exceptions to the attorney-client privilege: (1) crime-fraud, (2) joint clients (distinguished from "joint defense" situations), (3) breach of duty by attorney or client, (4) claimant through same deceased client, and (5) document attested by lawyer.

Waiver

The privilege may be waived in several ways: (1) client testifies about communication or attorney testifies about communication at client's behest, (2) client puts the communication in issue, (3) voluntary disclosure, and (4) inadvertent waiver (sometimes).

Procedural Issues

Burden of proof. Burden of persuasion generally rests with the person asserting the privilege.

In camera hearings. In *United States v. Zolin*, the Supreme Court held that the applicability of the crime-fraud exception can be resolved by an in camera inspection of the allegedly privileged material.

Work Product Privilege

The attorney-client privilege should be distinguished from the work-product doctrine, a *qualified* privilege recognized in both the Civil and Criminal Procedure Rules. The work product doctrine generally protects a broader range of materials than does the attorney-client privilege. The former protects materials prepared in anticipation of trial, while the latter is limited to communications. However, the protection for work product is not absolute; it may be overcome if the party seeking discovery shows that it has a "substantial need" for the materials and is unable without "undue hardship" to obtain the substantial equivalent of the materials by other means.

Chapter 39

SPOUSAL & FAMILY PRIVILEGES

§ 39.01 Introduction

There are two spousal privileges. The spousal *testimonial* privilege provides that a spouse may not be compelled to testify against a defendant-spouse in *criminal* prosecutions. A second privilege involves *confidential communications* between spouses and applies in both civil and criminal cases. There are exceptions to both. Some jurisdictions have both privileges while others have one or the other.

As drafted by the Supreme Court, proposed Federal Rule 505 recognized only the testimonial privilege.[1] However, Congress deleted all the proposed privilege rules when it substituted the general federal rule on privileges.[2] Nevertheless, federal cases recognize both privileges.[3] There is no federal parent-child privilege.[4]

§ 39.02 Spousal Testimonial Privilege

The spousal testimonial privilege, which is sometimes known as the anti-marital fact privilege,[5] is based on the policy of protecting the marital relationship from "dissension" and the "natural repugnance" for convicting a defendant upon the testimony of his or her "intimate life partner."[6] Criticism of the rule has a long history.[7] Bentham argued that the privilege

---

[1] *See* 56 F.R.D. 244, 245 (1973).

[2] Fed. R. Evid. 501. For a discussion of the congressional action, *see supra* § 37.02 (Federal Rule 501).

[3] *See* United States v. Singleton, 260 F.3d 1295, 1297 (11th Cir. 2001) ("There are two recognized types of marital privilege: the marital confidential communications privilege and the spousal testimonial privilege."); United States v. Bahe, 128 F.3d 1440, 1441–42 (10th Cir. 1997) ("The marital privilege as recognized in the federal courts has two aspects: the testimonial privilege which permits one spouse to decline to testify against the other during the marriage, and the marital communications privilege which either spouse may assert to prevent the other from testifying to confidential communications made during the marriage.").

[4] *See infra* § 39.04 (parent-child privilege).

[5] *See also* United States v. Morris, 988 F.2d 1335, 1339 (4th Cir. 1993) ("The marital privilege is conferred upon witnesses by the Congress and not by the Constitution. See Fed. R. Evid. 501."); Port v. Heard, 764 F.2d 423, 430 (5th Cir. 1985) ("[T]he marital privilege has never been placed on a constitutional footing.").

[6] 8 Wigmore, Evidence § 2228, at 216–17 (McNaughton rev. 1961). *See also* Trammel v. United States, 445 U.S. 40, 44 (1980) ("The modern justification for this privilege against adverse spousal testimony is its perceived role in fostering the harmony and sanctity of the marriage relationship.").

[7] This rule is sometimes called spousal incompetency because it was initially tied to the

goes far beyond making "every man's house his castle" and permits a person to convert his house into "a den of thieves."[8] As with all privileges, a cost-benefit analysis, mostly based on speculation, is required in order to assess the validity of the privilege. Does the privilege really save viable marriages? And, is the cost in loss of evidence worth whatever benefit that may be derived from the privilege?

[A] Type of Case

Unlike the confidential communication privilege, the testimonial privilege applies only in criminal cases. If the testimonial privilege is inapplicable, the confidential communication privilege remains in tact in those jurisdictions that have both.[9]

[B] Scope & Duration of Privilege

The testimonial privilege is determined as of the time of trial. If there is a valid marriage,[10] the privilege applies and all testimony, including testimony concerning events that predated the marriage, is excluded.[11] Thus, if the defendant and witness marry after the crime has been committed but before trial, the witness's testimony becomes privileged.[12] This "marry-the-witness" tactic is viable in many jurisdictions.[13]

---

common law spousal disqualification rule; it also has the effect of keeping the spouse off the witness stand altogether. Nevertheless, it is better understood as a privilege. *See* Ladd, *Uniform Evidence Rules in the Federal Courts*, 49 Va. L. Rev. 692, 714 (1963) ("Competency of a witness is based upon the capacity of a witness to tell the truth, accompanied with a consciousness of the obligation to do so. . . . Privileges, on the other hand, are established to serve a policy purpose other than truth-testing. Here the objective is to accomplish a social end, even though truthful evidence may be suppressed.").

[8] 5 Bentham, Rationale of Judicial Evidence 340 (Mill ed. 1827).

[9] *See* Wolfle v. United States, 291 U.S. 7, 14 (1934) ("Hence it is that the privilege with respect to communications extends to the testimony of husband or wife even though the different [testimonial] privilege, excluding the testimony of one against the other, is not involved.").

[10] *See* United States v. Lustig, 555 F.2d 737, 747 (9th Cir. 1977) (neither the marital communications privilege nor the testimonial privilege applies where the marriage is not valid under state law, though the couple have lived together as man and wife for years). Common-law marriages are recognized if valid under the applicable state law.

[11] *See* United States v. Lofton, 957 F.2d 476, 477 (7th Cir. 1992) ("The testimonial privilege, should the witness assert it, applies to all testimony against a defendant-spouse, including testimony on nonconfidential matters and matters which occurred prior to the marriage.").

[12] *See* State v. Gianakos, 644 N.W.2d 409, 411–12 (Minn. 2002) (holding the privilege applicable even though "both admitted the marriage was at least partially motivated by their desire to take advantage of the privilege against adverse spousal testimony with respect to their anticipated robbery charges, ultimately filed against them on February 27, 1997").

[13] The federal drafters attempted to preclude this result. *See* Proposed Fed. R. Evid. 505 advisory committee's note ("The second exception renders the privilege inapplicable as to matters occurring prior to the marriage. This provision eliminates the possibility of suppressing testimony by marrying the witness.").

Once the marriage ceases, so does the privilege.[14] Moreover, the parties
are not considered spouses if the marriage was a sham.[15] In addition, the
privilege does not necessarily apply to out-of-court statements by the
spouse.[16] Some federal courts have held the privilege inapplicable where the
marriage is no longer viable.[17]

[C] Holder

In some jurisdictions, both spouses may assert the privilege.[18] In others,
only the witness-spouse holds the privilege. Because the privilege is based
on the policy of protecting the marital relationship from conflict, its
application can be questioned where one spouse is willing to testify against
the other spouse.[19] The Supreme Court in *Trammel v. United States*[20]
observed:

> When one spouse is willing to testify against the other in a criminal
> proceeding — whatever the motivation — their relationship is
> almost certainly in disrepair; there is probably little in the way of
> marital harmony for the privilege to preserve. In these circum-
> stances, a rule of evidence that permits an accused to prevent
> adverse spousal testimony seems far more likely to frustrate justice
> than to foster family peace.[21]

Trammel modified the common law rule "so that the witness-spouse alone
has a privilege to refuse to testify adversely; the witness may be neither

---

[14] *See* Pereira v. United States, 347 U.S. 1, 6 (1954) ("[W]hile divorce removes the bar of
incompetency [testimonial privilege], it does not terminate the privilege for confidential marital
communications.").

[15] *See* Lutwak v. United States, 344 U.S. 604, 612–13 (1953) (prosecution for violating the
War Brides Act by bringing foreign spouses into country; privilege not applicable where "the
relationship was entered into with no intention of the parties to live together as husband and
wife but only for the purpose of using the marriage ceremony in a scheme to defraud"); United
States v. Saniti, 604 F.2d 603, 604 (9th Cir. 1979) ("there is a narrow exception to the husband-
wife privilege when the marriage is not entered into in good faith"); United States v. Mathis,
559 F.2d 294, 298 (5th Cir. 1977) ("It is well established that an exception to the husband-wife
privilege exists if the trial judge determines that the marriage is a fraud.").

[16] *See* United States v. Chapman, 866 F.2d 1326, 1332–33 (11th Cir. 1989) ("Chapman essentially argues that the marital privilege excludes not only the in-court testimony of the spouse
who claims the privilege, but also any out-of-court statements attributed to that spouse by
a testifying third party or by other documentary evidence. . . . We adopt the view held by
the Fifth and other circuits that extrajudicial statements are not excludable on the basis of
the spousal privilege.").

[17] *See* United States v. Cameron, 556 F.2d 752, 756 (5th Cir. 1977) ("[W]here the evidence
supported a finding that the marriage was no longer viable and its members had little hope
or desire for reconciliation, reason, experience and common sense indicate that the traditional
policy reasons for the privilege are non-existent.").

[18] *See* State v. Gianakos, 644 N.W.2d 409 (Minn. 2002).

[19] *See* 8 Wigmore, Evidence § 2228, at 218 (McNaughton rev. 1961). In Locke v. State, 169
N.E. 833 (Ohio App. 1929), the husband shot at his wife and mother-in-law, killing the latter.
The husband asserted the privilege to keep the wife from testifying in the murder trial.

[20] 445 U.S. 40 (1980).

[21] *Id.* at 52.

compelled to testify nor foreclosed from testifying."[22] In short, the witness-spouse is the holder in federal courts.

[D] Exceptions

[1] Crimes Against Spouse or Child

If the charged offense involves a crime against the other spouse[23] or their children, the privilege typically does not apply.[24] In such a case, the decision to testify is not optional; the witness-spouse can be compelled to testify.[25] This rule has a significant impact in domestic violence cases where spouses sometimes change their minds about prosecution, often due to fear. If the crime is against both a spouse and a third party, the exception applies and the spouse may testify.[26]

[2] Joint Participation in Crime

Some federal courts have engrafted a "joint participant" exception onto the common law privilege.[27] The policy of preserving family harmony is not thought sufficient to permit a criminal to enlist his or her spouse as an accomplice without fear of creating an adverse witness. In addition, the rehabilitative effect of a marriage, which in part justifies the privilege, is diminished when both spouses are participants in the crime.[28] This exception is not recognized in many jurisdictions.[29]

---

[22] *Id.* at 53. *See* Lempert, *A Right to Every Woman's Evidence*, 66 Iowa L. Rev. 725 (1981) (disagreeing with *Trammel*); Mullane, *Trammel v. United States: Bad History, Bad Policy, and Bad Law*, 47 Me. L. Rev. 105 (1995); Regan, *Spousal Privilege and the Meanings of Marriage*, 81 Va. L. Rev. 2045 (1995). *But see* Medine, *The Adverse Testimony Privilege: Time to Dispose of a Sentimental Relic*, 67 Or. L. Rev. 519 (1988).

[23] *See* Wyatt v. United States, 362 U.S. 525 (1960) (privilege does not apply in Mann Act prosecution — transporting woman across state lines for immoral purposes).

[24] *See* United States v. Bahe, 128 F.3d 1440, 1446 (10th Cir. 1997) ("We see no significant difference, as a policy matter, between a crime against a child of the married couple, against a stepchild living in the home or, as here, against an eleven-year-old relative visiting in the home."); United States v. Allery, 526 F.2d 1362, 1365 (8th Cir. 1975) (testimonial privilege did not apply to attempted rape of daughter and sexual abuse of couple's children); Proposed Fed. R. Evid. 505 advisory committee's note ("The need of limitation upon the privilege in order to avoid grave injustice in cases of offenses against the other spouse or a child of either can scarcely be denied.").

[25] *See Wyatt*, 362 U.S. at 530 (spouse can be compelled to testify).

[26] *See* People v. Sinohui, 47 P.3d 629, 633–34 (Cal. 2002) (interpreting state statutory exception for crimes against spouse to include crimes against a third person if part of a continuous course of criminal conduct and there is some logical relationship between the crimes).

[27] *E.g.,* United States v. Clark, 712 F.2d 299, 301 (7th Cir. 1983) ("[A] joint participants exception is consistent with the general policy of narrowly construing the privilege."). The federal cases on the confidential communication privilege also recognize this exception. *See infra* § 39.03[F][2].

[28] *See* United States v. Van Drunen, 501 F.2d 1393, 1396 (7th Cir. 1974) ("Today's holding . . . limits the privilege to those cases where it makes most sense, namely, where a spouse who is neither a victim nor a participant observes evidence of the other spouse's crime.").

[29] *E.g.,* Gianakos, 644 N.W.2d at 420 (rejecting joint participation exception; such a change, if made, should be done legislatively).

[E] Waiver

Failure to object to a spouse's testimony at trial waives the privilege, as does voluntary disclosure to a third party.[30] The privilege may also be waived by the holder or spouse testifying.[31]

[F] Procedural Issues

Generally, the prosecution should not call a spouse as a witness and force the spouse to invoke the privilege in front of the jury if the prosecutor knows the privilege will be asserted.[32] In other words, the defendant should not be penalized when a spouse exercises a valid privilege. This does not mean, however, that the spouse may not be called as a witness outside the jury's presence had to determine if the spouse will in fact assert the privilege. Moreover, the prosecutor should not be permitted to ask a spouse at trial whether she had invoked the privilege when summoned before the grand jury.[33]

§ 39.03   Spousal Communication Privilege

The second spousal privilege concerns confidential communications.[34] The purpose of this rule is to promote marital discourse, an instrumental rationale.[35] The efficacy of this privilege, however, may be questioned. Most married couples do not know of the privilege, and thus it cannot encourage spousal communications. In addition, the existence non vel of such a

---

[30] *See* Proposed Fed. R. Evid. 511 ("A person upon whom these rules confer a privilege against disclosure of the confidential matter or communication waives the privilege if he or his predecessor while holder of the privilege voluntarily discloses or consents to the disclosure of any significant part of the matter or communication. This rule does not apply if the disclosure is itself a privileged communication."), 56 F.R.D. 244, 245 (1973).

[31] *See* United States v. Lofton, 957 F.2d 476, 477 (7th Cir. 1992) ("[T]he district court found that Lofton's wife waived her privilege by giving a voluntary statement to law enforcement officers and by testifying at a pre-trial suppression hearing without objection or claim of privilege.").

[32] *See* United States v. Chapman, 866 F.2d 1326, 1333 (11th Cir. 1989) ("The record supports Chapman's claim that the court and the parties knew before Mrs. Chapman was called to the stand that she would claim her privilege and refuse to testify. And, we are mindful that as a general matter it is improper to permit a witness to claim a testimonial privilege in front of the jury where the witness's intention not to testify is known beforehand.").

[33] *See* United States v. Morris, 988 F.2d 1335, 1340 (4th Cir. 1993) ("The inference that a wife remained silent before the grand jury because she knew information that would inculpate her husband is one the jury is likely to draw. The Government must not be allowed to try its case by the use of improper inferences.").

[34] Although the Supreme Court in *Trammel* dealt only with the testimonial privilege, it cited the communication privilege. 445 U.S. at 45 n. 5 ("This Court recognized just such a confidential marital communications privilege in Wolfle v. United States, 291 U.S. 7 (1934), and in Blau v. United States, 340 U.S. 332 (1951).").

[35] *See* United States v. Leas, 249 F.3d 632, 641 (7th Cir. 2001) ("We encourage married people to confide in each other by protecting their statements from later scrutiny in court."). For a discussion of the instrumental justification, *see supra* § 37.03 (rationale for privileges).

privilege probably wouldn't affect their conduct one way or the other.[36] Marital privacy is probably a better rationale[37] but one that raises other issues — e.g., whether the privilege should be extended to parents, children, partners, or perhaps others.[38]

As with all confidential communication privileges, the issues can be broken down into the following components: (1) Who are the proper parties (e.g., are they spouses?); (2) What is a communication? Are acts covered?; (3) Was the communication intended to be confidential?; (4) What are the exceptions?; and (5) How is the privilege waived?

[A] Type of Case

Unlike the testimonial privilege which applies only in criminal prosecutions, the confidential communication privilege applies in both civil and criminal cases. If the testimonial privilege is inapplicable, the confidential communication privilege remains in tact in those jurisdictions that have both.[39]

[B] Scope & Duration of Privilege

The privilege applies only to communications made during coverture.[40] Communications made prior to marriage are not covered,[41] and those made after the termination of the marriage (e.g., divorce) are also not protected.[42]

---

[36] The federal drafters rejected this privilege for these reasons. See Proposed Fed. R. Evid. 505 advisory committee's note ("Nor can it be assumed that marital conduct will be affected by a privilege for confidential communications of whose existence the parties in all likelihood are unaware. The other communication privileges, by the way of contrast, have as one party a professional person who can be expected to inform the other of the existence of the privilege. Moreover, the relationships from which those privileges arise are essentially and almost exclusively verbal in nature, quite unlike marriage.").

[37] See Black, The Marital and Physician Privileges — A Reprint of a Letter to a Congressman, 1975 Duke L.J. 45, 48 ("[H]owever intimate, however private, however embarrassing may be a disclosure by one spouse to another, or some fact discovered, within the privacies of marriage, by one spouse about another, that disclosure or fact can be wrung from the spouse under penalty of being held in contempt of court, if it is thought barely relevant to the issues in anybody's lawsuit for breach of contract to sell a carload of apples. It ought to be enough to say of such a rule that it could easily — even often — force any decent person — anybody any of us would want to associate with — either to lie or to go to jail. No rule can be good that has that consequence — that compels the decent and honorable to evade or to disobey.").

[38] See Levinson, Testimonial Privileges and the Preferences of Friendship, 1984 Duke L.J. 631.

[39] See Wolfle, 291 U.S. at 14 ("Hence it is that the privilege with respect to communications extends to the testimony of husband or wife even though the different [testimonial] privilege, excluding the testimony of one against the other, is not involved.").

[40] See United States v. Leas, 249 F.3d 632, 641 (7th Cir. 2001) ("The privilege . . . applies only to communications made in confidence between the spouses during a valid marriage.").

[41] See Pereira v. United States, 347 U.S. 1, 6-7 (1954) ("Much of her testimony related to matters occurring prior to the marriage.").

[42] See id. at 6 ("[W]hile divorce removes the bar of incompetency [testimonial privilege], it does not terminate the privilege for confidential marital communications.").

However, the privilege survives the termination of the marriage to the extent that communications made *during* the marriage remain confidential even after the marriage ceases. Thus, conversations that occur during coverture continue to be privileged after divorce or death.

The federal courts have curtailed the reach of this privilege by holding that it does not apply to permanently separated couples.[43] In making this determination, courts focus on several factors: "(1) Was the couple cohabiting?; (2) if they were not cohabiting, how long had they been living apart?; and (3) had either spouse filed for divorce? A district court may, of course, consider other objective evidence of the parties' intent or lack of intent to reconcile."[44] This development illustrates the courts' general hostility to privileges.

[C] Holder

The privilege is personal to the husband and wife and may not be invoked by a third party. As between the spouses, it could be argued that only the communicating spouse should be able to assert the privilege. Nevertheless, the privilege often is held to extend to both spouses.[45]

[D] Communications & Acts

The privilege applies to confidential communications and includes acts intended as communications.[46] Whether the privilege extends to conduct in addition to communications depends on the jurisdiction.[47]

---

[43] *See* United States v. Singleton, 260 F.3d 1295, 1299 (11th Cir. 2001) ("[S]ociety's interest in protecting the confidentiality of the relationships of permanently separated spouses is outweighed by the need to secure evidence in the search of truth that is the essence of a criminal trial, and that proof of permanent separated states at the time of the communication between the defendant and the defendant's spouse renders the communications privilege automatically inapplicable."); United States v. Porter, 986 F.2d 1014, 1018–19 (6th Cir. 1993) ("While the privilege is said to apply to confidential communications made during marriage, an exception to the privilege has been recognized by the Second, Seventh, Eighth and Ninth Circuits where the evidence consists of statements made by one spouse after the spouses have permanently separated, even though they may not have been legally divorced.").

[44] *Singleton*, 260 F.3d at 1300.

[45] *See* United States v. Leas, 249 F.3d 632, 641 (7th Cir. 2001) (privilege "can be asserted by either spouse"); United States v. Bahe, 128 F.3d 1440, 1441–42 (10th Cir. 1997) ("either spouse may assert to prevent the other from testifying to confidential communications made during the marriage").

[46] *See* United States v. Estes, 793 F.2d 465, 467 (2d Cir. 1986) ("Testimony concerning a spouse's conduct can be precluded upon the spouse's challenge only in the rare instances where the conduct was intended to convey a confidential message from the actor to the observer."); United States v. Robinson, 763 F.2d 778, 783 (6th Cir. 1985) (same).

[47] *Compare Pereira*, 347 U.S. at 6 ("The privilege, generally, extends only to utterances, and not to acts. . . . [The] acts of Pereira which did not amount to communications, trips taken with third parties, and her own acts."); United States v. Lofton, 957 F.2d 476, 477 (7th Cir. 1992) ("Because acts observed by Lofton's wife are not privileged, any testimony regarding her observation of his use of cocaine or her knowledge whether the package at issue was for him was properly admitted."); United States v. Esters, 793 F.2d 465, 467 (2d Cir. 1986) (act

[E] Confidentiality

The spousal privilege applies *only* to communications that are intended to be confidential.[48] It generally does not apply if the conversation took place in the known presence of a third person.[49] Sometimes the presence of children defeats the privilege.[50] In the absence of a third party, confidentiality is presumed.[51] Spousal communications over a jail phone, however, do not satisfy the confidentiality requirement.[52]

[F] Exceptions

[1] Crimes Against Spouse or Child

As with the testimonial privilege, the communication privilege does not apply in prosecutions for crimes against the spouse[53] or their children.[54]

---

of bringing home a bag of money not covered; "Normally, the confidential communication privilege extends only to utterances and not to acts."), *with* Shepherd v. State, 277 N.E.2d 165, 168 (Ind. 1971) ("[I]it is not merely written or verbal communications that are privileged as between husband and wife, but the imparting of information, however conveyed, when done in reliance upon the inviolate nature of the marital relationship. Clearly participation in the crime was a matter of confidence between the defendant and the witness. The operation of the vehicle was the witness' role; and in this context, it was information imparted in confidence.").

[48] United States v. Leas, 249 F.3d 632, 642 (7th Cir. 2001) ("necessary element of confidentiality is lost when a spouse divulges to a third party the communication which he or she seeks to exclude from evidence").

[49] *See Pereira*, 347 U.S. at 6 ("The presence of a third party negatives the presumption of privacy. So too, the intention that the information conveyed be transmitted to a third person. . . . A review of Mrs. Joyce's testimony reveals that it involved primarily statements made in the presence of Brading or Miss Joyner, or both. . . .") (citations omitted).

[50] *See Wolfle*, 291 U.S. at 17 (noting the "uniform ruling that communications between husband and wife, voluntarily made in the presence of their children, old enough to comprehend them, or other members of the family within the intimacy of the family circle, are not privileged"); People v. Sanders, 457 N.E.2d 1241, 1244 (Ill. 1983) (conversation took place in the presence of her sons who were 13, 10, and 8 at the time; "great weight of authority is that the presence of children of the spouses destroys confidentiality unless they are too young to understand what is being said").

[51] *See* Blau v. United States, 340 U.S. 332, 333–34 (1951) ("marital communications are presumptively confidential"); *Wolfle*, 291 U.S. at 14 ("Communications between the spouses, privately made, are generally assumed to have been intended to be confidential, and hence they are privileged. . . .").

[52] *See* United States v. Madoch, 149 F.3d 596, 602 (7th Cir. 1998); United States v. Harrelson, 754 F.2d 1153, 1169–70 (5th Cir. 1985) (no privilege during prison visit where eavesdropping could reasonably be expected).

[53] *See* People v. Dudley, 248 N.E.2d 860, 863 (N.Y. 1969) ("There can be no doubt that the record fully supports the factual findings of the courts below that defendant held their marriage together solely by fear and domination — and that no confidential relationship, therefore, existed between the spouses at the time of Mrs. Vella's murder.").

[54] *See* United States v. White, 974 F.2d 1135, 1137 (9th Cir. 1992) (no privilege where defendant accused of murdering his stepdaughter).

[2] Joint Participation in Crime

Like the testimonial privilege, a joint crime exception has been carved out by the federal courts. However, the "government must produce evidence of a spouse's complicity in the underlying, on-going criminal activity before the district court may admit testimony regarding confidential communications between the defendant and the spouse. The spouse's involvement in the criminal activity . . . need not be particularly substantial to obviate the privilege."[55]

[G] Waiver

Failure to object at trial to disclosure of a privileged communication waives the privilege. It may also be waived by offering the testimony of a witness concerning the privileged communication. In addition, voluntary communication to a third party is a waiver.[56]

§ 39.04 Parent-Child Privilege

Although some courts[57] and legislatures[58] have recognized a parent-child privilege, most have not.[59] Why?[60] One court gave the following reasons:

"First, confidentiality — in the form of a testimonial privilege — is not essential to a successful parent-child relationship . . . . A privilege should be recognized only where such a privilege would be indispensable to the survival of the relationship that society deems should be fostered. . . . [I]t is not clear whether children would be more likely to discuss private matters with their parents if a parent-child privilege were recognized than if one were not. It is not likely that children, or even their parents, would

---

[55] United States v. Bey, 188 F.3d 1, 5 (1st Cir. 1999).

[56] See United States v. Bahe, 128 F.3d 1440, 1441–42 (10th Cir. 1997) ("a waiver requires an intentional disclosure of the content of the confidential communication by the party seeking to invoke the privilege"); Proposed Fed. R. Evid. 511 ("A person upon whom these rules confer a privilege against disclosure of the confidential matter or communication waives the privilege if he or his predecessor while holder of the privilege voluntarily discloses or consents to the disclosure of any significant part of the matter or communication. This rule does not apply if the disclosure is itself a privileged communication."), 56 F.R.D. 244, 245 (1973).

[57] See In re Agosto, 553 F. Supp. 1298 (D. Nev. 1983); In re Application of A. and M., 403 N.Y.S.2d 375 (App. 1978); People v. Fitzgerald, 422 N.Y.S.2d 309 (Sup. Ct. 1979).

[58] See Idaho Codes § 9-203(7); Minn. Stat. Ann. § 595.02(j); Mass. Gen. L. ch. 233, § 20.

[59] See Jaffee v. Redmond, 518 U.S. 1, 22 (1996) (dissenting opinion) ("Yet there is no mother-child privilege."); In re Grand Jury Proceedings, 103 F.3d 1140 (3d Cir. 1997); In re Grand Jury Proceedings, 842 F.2d 244 (10th Cir. 1988); Port v. Heard, 764 F.2d 423 (5th Cir. 1985); United States v. Ismail, 756 F.2d 1253 (6th Cir. 1985); In re Terry W., 130 Cal. Rptr. 913 (App. 1976); State v. DeLong, 456 A.2d 877 (Me. 1983); Three Juveniles v. Commonwealth, 455 N.E.2d 1203 (Mass. 1983).

[60] See generally Watts, The Parent-Child Privileges: Hardly a New or Revolutionary Concept, 28 Wm. & Mary L. Rev. 583 (1987); Note, Parent-Child Loyalty and Testimonial Privilege, 100 Harv. L. Rev. 910 (1987); Note, Making Form Follow Function: Considerations in Creating and Applying a Statutory Parent-Child Privilege, 1990 U. Ill. L. Rev. 879.

typically be aware of the existence or non-existence of a testimonial privilege covering parent-child communications."[61]

The court went on to state that "even assuming *arguendo* that children and their parents generally are aware of whether or not their communications are protected from disclosure, it is not certain that the existence of a privilege enters into whatever thought processes are performed by children in deciding whether or not to confide in their parents. Indeed, the existence or nonexistence of a parent-child privilege is probably one of the least important considerations in any child's decision as to whether to reveal some indiscretion, legal or illegal, to a parent"[62]

§ 39.05   Key Points

The spousal testimonial and confidential communication privileges need to be distinguished. Some jurisdictions have both privileges while others have one or the other.

Type of case. The testimonial privilege applies only in criminal prosecutions; the confidential communication privilege applies in civil and criminal cases alike. If the witness-spouse elects to testify as permitted by the testimonial privilege in some jurisdictions, the confidential communication privilege is still applicable.

Effect of rule. The testimonial rule precludes a spouse from testifying at all; the confidential communication privilege precludes a spouse from testifying *only* about communications (which may include acts depending on the jurisdiction).

Scope & duration. The spousal testimonial privilege is determined as of the time of trial. If it applies, all testimony, including testimony concerning events that predated the marriage, is excluded. Once the marriage ceases, the privilege no longer applies. In contrast, the confidential communication privilege survives the termination of the marriage but does not apply to "communications" made either before or after the marriage.

Holder. The witness-spouse is the holder of the testimonial privilege in federal trials. Either spouse may be the holder of the communication privilege. Only the holder may waive a privilege.

---

[61] In re Grand Jury Proceedings, 103 F.3d 1140, 1152 (3d Cir. 1997).

[62] *Id.* at 1153. *But see* United States v. Dunford, 148 F.3d 385, 391 (4th Cir. 1998) ("There may be much to commend a testimonial privilege in connection with the testimony of or against a minor child to preserve the family unit which is so much under stress in today's society. The tangible and intangible benefits of keeping families intact often seem to be forgotten in today's willingness to enact laws that readily authorize the fracture of the family or that provide incentives for doing so. . . . This case does not present the circumstances through which to address whether to recognize a parent-child testimonial privilege for minor children.").

Chapter 40

DOCTOR & PSYCHOTHERAPIST PRIVILEGES

§ 40.01 Introduction

The doctor-patient and psychotherapist-patient privileges have much in common. Although the doctor-patient privilege is the older of the two, the psychotherapist-patient privilege has been more extensively adopted. For example, the federal courts do not recognize a doctor-patient privilege.[1] In contrast, the Supreme Court recognized the psychotherapist-patient privilege in *Jaffee v. Redmond*.[2] As drafted by the Supreme Court, proposed Federal Rule 504 recognized the psychotherapist, but not the physician, privilege.[3] Congress deleted all the proposed privilege rules when it substituted the general federal rule on privileges.[4]

As with all confidential communication privileges, the issues can be broken down into the following components: (1) Who are the proper parties (*e.g.,* who is a patient and who is psychotherapist?); (2) What is a communication?; (3) Was the communication made incident to the professional relationship? Everything said to a doctor or therapist is not privileged; (4) Was the communication intended to be confidential?; (5) What are the exceptions?; and (6) How is the privilege waived? This last question requires us to identify the "holder" of the privilege.

§ 40.02 Physician-Patient Privilege

In contrast to federal practice, most states recognize a physician-patient privilege.[5] A few have expanded the privilege to include dentists in order

---

[1] *See* Whalen v. Roe, 429 U.S. 589, 602 n. 28 (1977) ("The physician-patient evidentiary privilege is unknown to the common law. In States where it exists by legislative enactment, it is subject to many exceptions and to waiver for many reasons."); Gilbreath v. Guadalupe Hosp. Found., Inc., 5 F.3d 785, 791 (5th Cir. 1993) ("there is no physician-patient privilege under federal law"); Hancock v. Dodson, 958 F.2d 1367, 1373 (6th Cir. 1992) ("A decision in this case based on considerations of the physician-patient relationship would, in effect, expand the scope of the 'federal common law.' This we decline to do."); United States v. Bercier, 848 F.2d 917, 920 (8th Cir. 1988) ("Because no physician-privilege existed at common law, federal courts do not recognize the physician-patient privilege in federal criminal proceedings.") (citation omitted).

[2] 518 U.S. 1 (1996).

[3] *See* 56 F.R.D. 240–41 (1973).

[4] Fed. R. Evid. 501. For a discussion of the congressional action, *see supra* § 37.02 (Federal Rule 501).

[5] Proposed Article V advisory committee's notes ("physician-patient privilege is the most widely recognized privilege not found in the proposed rules"), 56 F.R.D. 234 (1972).

to protect communications concerning HIV and AIDS.[6] In those jurisdictions that have adopted the physician-patient privilege, there is wide variation in the type of exceptions recognized and the conditions for waiver.

The privilege is intended to encourage disclosure by patients so as to aid in the effective treatment of disease and injury without fear that such information will later become public: "the physician must know all that a patient can articulate in order to identify and to treat disease; barriers to full disclosure would impair diagnosis and treatment."[7]

Nevertheless, proposed Article V of the Federal Rules (which was not enacted) did not include a provision for a physician-patient privilege. Why? First, the instrumental justification seems weak; even without a privilege, patients will disclose information to their physicians. Indeed, how many people know that there is no federal physician-patient privilege? Now that you know, will you stop telling your physician what she needs to know to treat you? If patient privacy is the rationale, there are alternative protections, such as the physician's ethical duty and tort actions for breach of privacy, to effectuate this goal.[8] The privilege, in any event, only functions in a legal proceeding. Finally, the exceptions to the privilege often gut its protections. For example, the California Evidence Code excepts *inter alia* (1) all criminal proceedings, (2) cases in which the patient places her condition in issue ("patient-litigant" rule), (3) will contests, (4) malpractice cases, and (5) disciplinary proceedings.[9]

[A] Holder

The holder of the privilege is the patient, not the physician.[10] Only the

---

[6] *See* Ohio Rev. Stat. § 2317.02(B); *Developments in the Law — Privileged Communications,* 98 Harv. L. Rev. 1450, 1533 (1985).

[7] Trammel v. United States, 445 U.S. 40, 51 (1980) (dictum in case on spousal privilege).

[8] *But see* Black, *The Marital and Physician Privileges — A Reprint of a Letter to a Congressman,* 1975 Duke L.J. 45, 48:

> The question here is not only whether people might be discouraged from making full communication to physicians, though it seems flatly impossible that this would not sometimes happen — a consideration which would in itself be enough to make incomprehensible the absolute subordination of this privacy interest to any trivial interest arising in litigation. But evaluation of a rule like this entails not only a guess as to what conduct it will motivate, but also an estimate of its intrinsic decency. All of us would consider it indecent for a doctor, in the course, say, of a television interview, or even a textbook, to tell all he knows, naming names, about patients who have been treated by him. Why does this judgment of decency altogether vanish from sight, sink to absolute zero, as soon as somebody files any kind of a non-demurrable complaint in a federal court? Here, again, can a rule be a good one when the ethical doctor *must* violate it, or hedge, or evade?

[9] Cal. Evid. Code §§ 996–1007. *See also* Proposed Fed. R. Evid. 504 advisory committee's note ("While many states have by statute created the privilege, the exceptions which have been found necessary in order to obtain information required by the public interest or to avoid fraud are so numerous as to leave little if any basis for the privilege.").

[10] *See* Unif. R. Evid. 503(c) (1999) ("The privilege under this rule may be claimed by the patient, the patient's guardian or conservator, or the personal representative of a deceased patient. The person who was the [physician or psychotherapist] at the time of the communication is presumed to have authority to claim the privilege, but only on behalf of the patient.").

patient has the right to invoke and waive the privilege.[11]

[B] Physician Defined

Depending on the statute, the privilege many apply to doctors of medicine, doctors of osteopathic medicine, doctors of podiatric medicine, and dentists. Sometimes nurses are also included. Often, other medical personnel who work under a doctor's direction fall within the privilege's protection.

[C] Professional Relationship Requirement

The communication to the physician must be made while seeking medical treatment.[12] The privilege does not apply where a person is examined by a physician for purposes other than treatment. Court-ordered physical examinations or those required for worker's compensation are examples.[13]

[D] Communications

The privilege covers communications made to a physician by a patient and often advice given by the physician to a patient.[14] Matters other than communications and advice do not fall within the privilege, and a treating physician may be compelled to testify about such other matters. Thus, the privilege does not prevent testimony by a physician as to the fact of professional consultation by a person on a certain date. However, some jurisdictions define "communication" broadly to include any medical, dental, or hospital communication "such as a record, chart, letter, memorandum, laboratory test and results, x-ray, photograph, financial statement, diagnosis, or prognosis."[15] Moreover, exhibition of the body to a physician for examination is typically covered.

---

[11] See DeWitt, *Privileged Communications Between Physician and Patient*, 10 CWRU L. Rev. 488 (1959).

[12] See Unif. R. Evid. 503(b) (1999) ("A patient has a privilege to refuse to disclose and to prevent any other person from disclosing confidential communications made for the purpose of diagnosis or treatment of the patients's [physical,] mental[,] or emotional condition, including addiction to alcohol or drugs, among the patient, the patient's [physician or psychotherapist] and persons, including members of the patient's family, who are participating in the diagnosis or treatment under the direction of the [physician or psychotherapist."). The rule is written as optional.

[13] See Unif. R. Evid. 503(d)(2) (1999).

[14] See Trammel v. United States, 445 U.S. 40, 51 (1980) ("The privilege[] between . . . physician and patient limit[s] protection to private communications."); Varghese v. Royal Maccabees Life Ins. Co., 181 F.R.D. 359, 362 (S.D. Ohio 1998) (privilege applies to "any communication made to a physician by his patient in that relation or a physician's advice to his patient").

[15] Ohio Rev. Code § 2317.02(B)(3).

[E] Confidentiality

The physician-patient privilege covers only *confidential* communica-tions.[16] Thus, where the information communicated is intended to become public, the privilege does not apply.

[F] Exceptions

The privilege is subject to numerous exceptions, the scope of which depends on the particular jurisdictions.[17] The privilege, for example, may not apply to (1) required reports of gunshot, stab, or other wounds,[18] (2) required reports of suspected child abuse and neglect,[19] (3) required reports of abuse of mentally retarded persons,[20] and (4) test results showing the presence of alcohol or drugs in a criminal suspect's body.[21] As mentioned earlier, the California Evidence Code excepts *inter alia* (1) all criminal proceedings, (2) cases in which the patient places her condition in issue ("patient-litigant" rule), (3) will contests, (4) malpractice cases, and (5) disci-plinary proceedings.[22]

[G] Waiver

One of the principal waiver rules is the patient-litigant rule. This rule prevents a plaintiff from filing a suit against a physician or hospital, thereby putting his medical condition at issue, and then refusing to answer questions about this condition based on the privilege.[23]

---

[16] *See* Unif. R. Evid. 503(a)(1) (1999) ("A communication is 'confidential' if it is not intended to be disclosed to third persons, except those present to further the interest of the patient in the consultation, examination, or interview, those reasonably necessary for the transmission of the communication, and persons who are participating in the diagnosis and treatment of the patient under the direction of [physician or psychotherapist], including members of the patient's family.").

[17] Proposed Fed. R. Evid. 504 advisory committee's note ("Among the exclusions from the statutory privilege, the following may be enumerated; communications not made for purposes of diagnosis and treatment; commitment and restoration proceedings; issues as to wills or otherwise between parties claiming by succession from the patient; actions on insurance policies; required reports (venereal diseases, gunshot wounds, child abuse); communications in furtherance of crime or fraud; mental or physical condition put in issue by patient (personal injury cases); malpractice actions; and some or all criminal prosecutions.").

[18] Ohio Rev. Code § 2921.22(B).

[19] Ohio Rev. Code § 2151.421.

[20] Ohio Rev. Code § 5123.61.

[21] Ohio Rev. Code § 2317.02(B)(1)(b).

[22] Cal. Evid. Code §§ 996–1007. *See also* Proposed Fed. R. Evid. 504 advisory committee's note ("While many states have by statute created the privilege, the exceptions which have been found necessary in order to obtain information required by the public interest or to avoid fraud are so numerous as to leave little if any basis for the privilege.").

[23] Note, *The Ohio Physician-Patient Privilege: Modified, Revised, and Defined*, 49 Ohio St. L.J. 1147, 1157 (1989) ("[A] patient should not have the right to use the figurative sword by commencing an action based on personal injuries, yet at the same time shield himself from discovery mechanisms by using the physician-patient privilege.").

Failure to object to the physician's testimony at trial waives the privilege, as does voluntary disclosure to a third party.[24] The privilege may also be waived by the holder testifying about the communication.

§ 40.03 Psychotherapist-Patient Privilege

Many jurisdictions recognize a psychotherapist-patient privilege.[25] In *Jaffee v. Redmond*,[26] the therapist was a licensed clinical social worker who had counseled a police officer after she shot and killed a man while on duty. In the lawsuit filed by the victim's family against the officer, the family sought to discover the social worker's notes to use in cross-examining the officer. The Supreme Court concluded that the communications were protected by the psychotherapist-patient privilege. Explaining the important private and public interests served by the privilege, the Court wrote:

> Effective psychotherapy depends upon an atmosphere of confidence and trust in which the patient is willing to make a frank and complete disclosure of facts, emotions, memories, and fears. Because of the sensitive nature of the problems for which individuals consult psychotherapists, disclosure of confidential communications made during counseling sessions may cause embarrassment or disgrace. For this reason, the mere possibility of disclosure may impede development of the confidential relationship necessary for successful treatment. By protecting confidential communications between a psychotherapist and her patient from involuntary disclosure, the proposed privilege thus serves important private interests.[27]

The overarching purpose of the privilege is the public interest in facilitating treatment for individuals suffering the effects of a mental or emotional problem.[28] Justice Scalia found the Court's analysis of the need for the psychotherapist-patient privilege "insufficiently convincing."[29] He found

---

[24] *See* Proposed Fed. R. Evid. 511 ("A person upon whom these rules confer a privilege against disclosure of the confidential matter or communication waives the privilege if he or his predecessor while holder of the privilege voluntarily discloses or consents to the disclosure of any significant part of the matter or communication. This rule does not apply if the disclosure is itself a privileged communication."), 56 F.R.D. 244, 245 (1973).

[25] *See* Jaffee v. Redmond, 518 U.S. 1, 12–13 (1996) ("That it is appropriate for the federal courts to recognize a psychotherapist privilege under Rule 501 is confirmed by the fact that all 50 States and the District of Columbia have enacted into law some form of psychotherapist privilege. We have previously observed that the policy decisions of the States bear on the question whether federal courts should recognize a new privilege or amend the coverage of an existing one."). If a jurisdiction also has a physician-patient privilege, then psychiatric treatment would be covered by that privilege when rendered by a physician.

[26] 518 U.S. 1 (1996).

[27] *Id.* at 10.

[28] *Id.* at 11 ("The psychotherapist privilege serves the public interest by facilitating the provision of appropriate treatment for individuals suffering the effects of a mental or emotional problem. The mental health of our citizenry, no less than its physical health, is a public good of transcendent importance.").

[29] *Id.* at 22 (Scalia, J., dissenting). For a further discussion of Justice Scalia's views, *see* *supra* § 37.03[A] (rationale for privileges).

the Court's explanation for its decision to extend the privilege to licensed social workers "even less persuasive."[30]

The Court commented that, since *Jaffee* was "the first case in which we have recognized a psychotherapist privilege, it is neither necessary nor feasible to delineate its full contours in a way that would 'govern all conceivable future questions in this area.'"[31] Consequently, the lower courts have had to address these issues as a matter of federal common law. The scope of the state statutes differs from each other as well as from the federal case law.[32]

[A] Holder

The holder of the privilege is the patient, not the therapist.[33] Only the patient has the right to invoke and waive the privilege.

[B] Psychotherapist Defined

Proposed Rule 504 limited the term psychotherapist to physicians and licensed psychologists.[34] In *Jaffee*, however, the Court extended the federal privilege to clinical social workers:

> The reasons for recognizing a privilege for treatment by psychia-
> trists and psychologists apply with equal force to treatment by a
> clinical social worker. Today, social workers provide a significant
> amount of mental health treatment. Their clients include the poor
> and those of modest means who could not afford the assistance of
> a psychiatrist or psychologist, but whose counseling sessions serve
> the same public goals.[35]

In addition, the Court also noted that most states had extended the privilege to social workers. The Ninth Circuit has extended the privilege

---

[30] *Id.* at 27.

[31] *Id.* at 18.

[32] *See* Amann & Imwinkelried, *The Supreme Court's Decision to Recognize a Psychotherapist Privilege in* Jaffee v. Redmond: The Meaning of "Experience" and the Role of "Reason" Under Federal Rule of Evidence 501, 65 Cin. L. Rev. 1019 (1997); Poulin, *The Psychotherapist-Patient Privilege After* Jaffee v. Redmond: *Where Do We Go From Here?*, 76 Wash. U. L. Q. 1341 (1998); Note, *Rationales for the Confidentiality of Psychotherapist -Patient Communications: Testimonial Privilege and the Constitution*, 35 Hous. L. Rev. 187 (1998).

[33] *See* Unif. R. Evid. 503(c) (1999) ("The privilege under this rule may be claimed by the patient, the patient's guardian or conservator, or the personal representative of a deceased patient. The person who was the [physician or psychotherapist] at the time of the communication is presumed to have authority to claim the privilege, but only on behalf of the patient.").

[34] Proposed Fed. R. Evid. 504 advisory committee's note ("The requirement that the psychologist be in fact licensed, and not merely be believed to be so, is believed to be justified by the number of persons, other than psychiatrists, purporting to render psychotherapeutic aid and the variety of their theories.").

[35] *Jaffee*, 518 U.S. at 15–16 (footnotes omitted).

to unlicensed counselors[36] and another court to a case in which the patient believed the person was a social worker.[37]

[C] Professional Relationship Requirement

The communication to the therapist must be made while seeking psychological treatment.[38] The privilege does not apply where a person is examined for purposes other than treatment. Court-ordered psychological examinations or those required for worker's compensation fall into this category.

[D] Communications

The privilege covers communications made to a therapist by a patient and advice given by a therapist to a patient. Matters other than communications and advice do not fall within the privilege, and a treating therapist may be compelled to testify about such other matters. For example, the privilege does not prevent testimony by a therapist as to the fact of professional consultation by a person on a certain date.[39]

---

[36] Oleszko v. State Compensation Ins. Fund, 243 F.3d 1154, 1159 (9th Cir. 2001) (Fund's Employee Assistance Program; "EAPs work to address serious national problems, from substance abuse and depression to workplace and domestic violence. Given the importance of the public and private interests EAPs serve, the necessity of confidentiality in order for EAPs to function effectively, and the importance of protecting this gateway to mental health treatment by licensed psychiatrists, psychologists, and social workers, we hold that the psychotherapist-patient privilege recognized in *Jaffee v. Redmond* extends to communications with EAP personnel."). *But see* United States v. Schwensow, 151 F.3d 650, 657 (7th Cir. 1998) (statements made to volunteer telephone operators at an Alcoholics Anonymous office were not protected by the psychotherapist-patient privilege because the volunteers did not act or hold themselves out as counselors, were not licensed or trained in counseling, and did not confer in a fashion resembling a psychotherapy session); Carman v. McDonnell Douglas Corp., 114 F.3d 790, 791 (8th Cir. 1997) (communications to an ombudsman employed to resolve workplace disputes without litigation were not protected by the psychotherapist-patient privilege).

[37] Speaker ex rel. Speaker v. County of San Bernardino, 82 F. Supp. 2d 1105, 1110 (C.D. Cal. 2000) ("[T]he psychotherapist/patient privilege applies when the patient reasonably, but mistakenly, believes that he or she was being counseled by a licensed psychologist or social worker.").

[38] *See* In re Grand Jury Proceedings (Gregory P. Violette), 183 F.3d 71, 73 (1st Cir. 1999) ("between a licensed psychotherapist and her patient . . . in the course of diagnosis or treatment"); Proposed Fed. R. Evid. 504(b) ("A patient has a privilege to refuse to disclose and to prevent any other person from disclosing confidential communications, made for the purposes of diagnosis or treatment of his mental or emotional condition, including drug addiction, among himself, his psychotherapist, or persons who are participating in the diagnosis or treatment under the direction of the psychotherapist, including members of the patient's family.").

[39] *See* In re Zuniga, 714 F.2d 632, 640 (6th Cir. 1983) ("The appellants argue with some force, however, that the *identity* alone of the patient must be privileged to maintain the effective psychotherapist-patient relationship the general privilege seeks to promote. . . . [Nevertheless, the] essential element of the psychotherapist-patient privilege is its assurance to the patient that his innermost thoughts may be revealed without fear of disclosure. Mere disclosure of the patient's identity does not negate this element. Thus, the Court concludes that, as a general rule, the identity of a patient or the fact and time of his treatment does not fall within the scope of the psychotherapist-patient privilege.").

[E] Confidentiality

The therapists-patient privilege covers only *confidential* communications.[40] Thus, where the information communicated is intended to become public, the privilege does not apply.[41]

[F] Exceptions

The exceptions to the privilege must be determined under the law of the jurisdiction in which the issue arises. There is significant variation in the state statutes, and the federal privilege is only beginning to be fleshed out. There are some common exceptions. For example, proposed Rule 504 recognized three: (1) civil commitment proceedings,[42] (2) court-ordered examinations,[43] and (3) the patient-litigant rule.[44] Since *Jaffee,* a crime-fraud exception has been upheld.[45]

---

[40] *See* In re Grand Jury Proceedings (Gregory P. Violette), 183 F.3d 71, 73 (1st Cir. 1999) ("a party asserting the psychotherapist-patient privilege must show that the allegedly privileged communications were made . . . confidentially"); Proposed Fed. R. Evid. 504(a)(3) ("A communication is 'confidential' if not intended to be disclosed to third persons other than those present to further the interest of the patient in the consultation, examination, or interview, or persons reasonably necessary for the transmission of the communication, or persons who are participating in the diagnosis and treatment under the direction of the psychotherapist, including members of the patient's family.").

[41] *See* Barrett v. Vojtas, 182 F.R.D. 177, 179 (W.D. Pa. 1998) ("The Court's reasoning clearly shows that confidentiality is the foundation upon which the psychotherapist-patient privilege rests. Indeed, a crucial element of any testimonial privilege is an intent to keep a communication confidential. . . . Although we have found no cases on point in which the *Jaffee* privilege has been asserted, communications that are intended to be disclosed to third parties are generally not protected by a testimonial privilege. There would be no reasonable expectation of confidentiality, and therefore no confidential intent, if a party to a conversation was aware that the other party may report on the conversation to a third party.").

[42] *See* Proposed Fed. R. Evid. 504 advisory committee's note ("The interests of both patient and public call for a departure from confidentiality in commitment proceedings. Since disclosure is authorized only when the psychotherapist determines that hospitalization is needed, control over disclosure is placed largely in the hands of a person in whom the patient has already manifested confidence. Hence damage to the relationship is unlikely.").

[43] *See Barrett*, 182 F.R.D. at 181 ("Vojtas did not seek treatment, but was ordered [by public official] to see Dr. Guinn and Dr. Pass. More importantly, Vojtas had no expectation of confidentiality in this treatment, as it was known that Dr. Guinn and Dr. Pass would report back to Brentwood on the results of their examinations. Thus, the conversations and the notes taken during counseling sessions with Dr. Guinn and Dr. Pass are not protected by the psychotherapist-patient privilege."); Proposed Fed. R. Evid. 504 advisory committee's note ("In a court ordered examination, the relationship is likely to be an arm's length one, though not necessarily so. In any event, an exception is necessary for the effective utilization of this important and growing procedure. The exception, it will be observed, deals with a court ordered examination rather than with a court appointed psychotherapist.").

[44] *See* Proposed Fed. R. Evid. 504 advisory committee's note ("By injecting his condition into litigation, the patient must be said to waive the privilege, in fairness and to avoid abuses. Similar considerations prevail after the patient's death.").

[45] In re Grand Jury Proceedings (Gregory P. Violette), 183 F.3d 71, 77 (1st Cir. 1999) ("[C]ommunications that are intended to further a crime or fraud will rarely, if ever, be allied with bona fide psychotherapy and, thus, protecting such communications will not promote mental health. In this regard, it is important to emphasize that the crime-fraud exception will apply only when the patient's purpose is to promote a particular crime or fraud.").

A "duty to warn" exception has been engrafted onto the privilege in a number of jurisdictions.[46] The leading case is *Tarasoff v. Regents of the University of California*,[47] in which the California Supreme Court held that "once a therapist does in fact determine, or under applicable professional standards reasonably should have determined, that a patient poses a serious danger of violence to others, he bears a duty to exercise reasonable care to protect the foreseeable victim of that danger."[48]

In *Jaffee,* the Supreme Court dropped a footnote touching on this subject: "Although it would be premature to speculate about most future developments in the federal psychotherapist privilege, we do not doubt that there are situations in which the privilege must give way, for example, if a serious threat of harm to the patient or to others can be averted only by means of a disclosure by the therapist."[49] Citing this footnote, the Eleventh Circuit indicated the existence of such an exception.[50] However, the Sixth Circuit took a different tack[51] — noting that a duty to warn is not the same as permitting court testimony.

[G] Waiver

Failure to object to the therapist's testimony at trial waives the privilege, as does voluntary disclosure to a third party.[52] The privilege may also be waived by the patient testifying about the communication.

---

[46] *E.g.,* Estates of Morgan v. Fairfield Family Counseling Ctr., 673 N.E.2d 1311, 1328–29 (Ohio 1997) ("[W]hen a psychotherapist knows or should know that his or her patient represents a substantial risk of harm to others, the therapist is under a duty to exercise his or her best professional judgment to prevent such harm from occurring.").

[47] 551 P.2d 334 (Cal. 1976).

[48] *Id.* at 345.

[49] 518 U.S. at 18 n. 19.

[50] United States v. Glass, 133 F.3d 1356, 1357 (10th Cir. 1998). *See also* Guerrier v. State, 811 So. 2d 852, 855–56 (Fla. App. 2002) ("We find that the goal of victim protection extends to eliciting from the psychiatrist relevant evidence (the threat) that will facilitate the prosecution of a crime committed against the victim by the dangerous patient. Thus when the Legislature enacted section 456.059, the Legislature intended to allow admission of the psychiatrist's testimony in a subsequent prosecution of the dangerous patient for offenses committed against the victim.").

[51] United States v. Hayes, 227 F.3d 578, 583–84 (6th Cir. 2000) ("We see only a marginal connection, if any at all, between a psychotherapist's action in notifying a third party (for his own safety) of a patient's threat to kill or injure him and a court's refusal to permit the therapist to testify about such threat (in the interest of protecting the psychotherapist/patient relationship) in a later prosecution of the patient for making it. State law requirements that psychotherapists take action to prevent serious and credible threats from being carried out serve a far more immediate function than the proposed 'dangerous patient' exception. Unlike the situation presented in *Tarasoff*, the threat articulated by a defendant such as Hayes is rather unlikely to be carried out once court proceedings have begun against him.").

[52] *See* Proposed Fed. R. Evid. 511 ("A person upon whom these rules confer a privilege against disclosure of the confidential matter or communication waives the privilege if he or his predecessor while holder of the privilege voluntarily discloses or consents to the disclosure of any significant part of the matter or communication. This rule does not apply if the disclosure is itself a privileged communication."), 56 F.R.D. 244, 245 (1973).

[H] Procedural Issues

Like other privileges, "the burden of proof for the psychotherapist/patient privilege is on the party seeking to establish that the privilege applies."[53]

§ 40.04 Key Points

Doctor-patient privilege. Although most states recognize a doctor-patient privilege, the federal courts do not. The privilege is intended to encourage disclosure by patients in order to aid in the effective treatment of disease and injury without fear that such information will later become public. The holder of the privilege is the patient, not the physician; only the patient has the right to invoke and waive the privilege.

In those jurisdictions that have adopted the privilege, there is wide variation in the type of exceptions recognized and the conditions for waiver. The privilege, for example, may not apply to (1) required reports of gunshot, stab, or other wounds, (2) required reports of suspected child abuse and neglect, (3) required reports of abuse of mentally retarded persons, and (4) test results showing the presence of alcohol or drugs in a criminal suspect's body. The California Evidence Code excepts *inter alia* (1) all criminal proceedings, (2) cases in which the patient places her condition in issue ("patient-litigant" rule), (3) will contests, (4) malpractice cases, and (5) disciplinary proceedings.

Psychotherapist-patient privilege. The Supreme Court recognized the psychotherapist-patient privilege in *Jaffee v. Redmond*: "Effective psychotherapy depends upon an atmosphere of confidence and trust in which the patient is willing to make a frank and complete disclosure of facts, emotions, memories, and fears." The holder of the privilege is the patient, not the therapist; only the patient has the right to invoke and waive the privilege. In *Jaffee*, the Court extended the federal privilege not only to psychiatrists and psychologists, but also to clinical social workers.

The communication to the therapist must be made while seeking psychological treatment. Court-ordered psychological examinations or those required for worker's compensation are not covered. Matters other than communications and advice also do not fall within the privilege.

The exceptions to the privilege must be determined under the law of the jurisdiction in which the issue arises. There is significant variation in the state statutes, and the federal privilege is only beginning to be fleshed out. Common exceptions include: (1) civil commitment proceedings, (2) court-ordered examinations, and (3) the patient-litigant rule. Since *Jaffee*, a crime-fraud exception has been upheld. Moreover, a "duty to warn" exception has been engrafted onto the privilege in a number of jurisdictions. The leading case is *Tarasoff v. Regents of the University of California*, in which the California Supreme Court held that "once a therapist does in fact

---

[53] Speaker ex rel. Speaker v. County of San Bernardino, 82 F. Supp. 2d 1105, 1110 (C.D. Cal. 2000).

determine, or under applicable professional standards reasonably should have determined, that a patient poses a serious danger of violence to others, he bears a duty to exercise reasonable care to protect the foreseeable victim of that danger."

Chapter 41

OTHER PRIVATE PRIVILEGES

§ 41.01 Introduction

There are numerous other privileges. Two of the most important are the clergy-penitent and journalist privileges.

§ 41.02 Clergy-Penitent Privilege

Every jurisdiction recognizes a clergyman-penitent privilege.[1] As drafted by the Supreme Court, proposed Federal Rule 506 recognized this privilege.[2] Although Congress deleted all the proposed privilege rules when it substituted the general federal rule on privileges,[3] the federal cases continue to acknowledge this privilege.[4]

The encouragement of the communicant to disclose troubling matters is the immediate goal. The overarching purpose is the recognition of "the human need to disclose to a spiritual counselor, in total and absolute confidence, what are believed to be flawed acts or thoughts and to receive priestly consolation and guidance in return."[5]

---

[1] *See generally* Mitchell, *Must Clergy Tell? Child Abuse Reporting Requirements Versus the Clergy Privilege and Free Exercise of Religion*, 71 Minn. L. Rev. 723 (1987); Reece, *Confidential Communications to the Clergy*, 24 Ohio St. L.J. 55 (1963); Yellin, *The History and Current Status of the Clergy-Penitent Privilege*, 23 Santa Clara L. Rev. 95 (1983); *Developments in the Law — Privileged Communications*, 98 Harv. L. Rev. 1450, 1556 (1985) (all fifty states grant some form of privilege to clergy-communicant communications").

[2] *See* 56 F.R.D. 244, 245 (1973).

[3] Fed. R. Evid. 501. For a discussion of the congressional action, *see supra* § 37.02 (Federal Rule 501).

[4] *See* In re Grand Jury Investigation, 918 F.2d 374, 377 (3d Cir. 1990) ("[W]e hold that a clergy-communicant privilege does exist. We further hold that this privilege protects communications to a member of the clergy, in his or her spiritual or professional capacity, by persons who seek spiritual counseling and who reasonably expect that their words will be kept in confidence. As is the case with the attorney-client privilege, the presence of third parties, if essential to and in furtherance of the communication, does not vitiate the clergy-communicant privilege."); United States v. Mohanlal, 867 F. Supp. 199, 200 (S.D.N.Y. 1994) ("It is clear that one of the privileges to be recognized under Fed. R. Ev. 501 is the clergy-communicant privilege."); In re Verplank, 329 F. Supp. 433, 435 (C.D. Cal. 1971) ("As the Government asserts, the clergyman-communicant privilege was not generally recognized at common law. However, modern law, nurtured in a climate of religious freedom and tolerance, has given sanction to such a privilege. It has been established by statute in nearly two-thirds of the states and has also been recognized by court decision. . . .") (citations omitted). *See also* United States v. Nixon, 418 U.S. 683, 709 (1974) ("[G]enerally, an attorney or a priest may not be required to disclose what has been revealed in professional confidence."); Totten v. United States, 92 U.S. 105, 107 (1876) ("suits cannot be maintained which would require a disclosure of the confidences of the confessional").

[5] Trammel v. United States, 445 U.S. 40, 51 (1980) (dictum, case concerned marital privilege).

As with all confidential communication privileges, the issues can be broken down into the following components: (1) Who are the proper parties (*e.g.,* who is a member of the clergy and who is a communicant?); (2) What is a communication?; (3) Was the communication made incident to the clergy-penitent relationship? Everything said to the clergy is not privileged; (4) Was the communication intended to be confidential?; (5) What are the exceptions?; and (6) How is the privilege waived?

Holder. The proposed federal rule made the communicant the holder of the privilege.[6] Some state statutes permit the clergy member to refuse to testify even when the penitent has expressly consented, if "the disclosure of the information is in violation of his sacred trust."[7] First Amendment Free Exercise issues are obviously implicated in this context.

Clergyperson defined. Proposed Rule 506(a)(1) defined "clergyman" as "a minister, priest, rabbi, or other similar functionary of a religious organization, or an individual reasonably believed so to be by the person consulting him." The drafters noted that this definition was "not so broad as to include all self-denominated 'ministers.' A fair construction of the language requires that the person to whom the status is sought to be attached be regularly engaged in activities conforming at least in a general way with those of a Catholic priest, Jewish rabbi, or minister of an established Protestant denomination, though not necessarily on a full-time basis. No further specification seems possible in view of the lack of licensing and certification procedures for clergymen."[8]

Professional relationship. The communication must be made for the purpose of obtaining spiritual guidance.[9] Consultations for other reasons do not fall within the privilege.[10]

---

[6] *See* Proposed Fed. R. Evid. 506 advisory committee's note ("Subdivision (c) makes clear that the privilege belongs to the communicating person. However, a prima facie authority on the part of the clergyman to claim the privilege on behalf of the person is recognized. The discipline of the particular church and the discreetness of the clergyman are believed to constitute sufficient safeguards for the absent communicating person.").

[7] Ohio Rev. Code § 2317.02(C).

[8] Proposed Fed. R. Evid. 506 advisory committee's note. *See also* In re Verplank, 329 F. Supp. 433, 436 (C.D. Cal. 1971) ("Under the circumstances here concerned, it would appear that the activities of the other counselors at the McAlister Center conform 'at least in a general way' with a significant portion of the activities of a minister of an established Protestant denomination, to the extent necessary to bring them within the privilege covering communications to clergymen.").

[9] *See* In re Grand Jury Investigation, 918 F.2d 374, 377 (3d Cir. 1990) (The "privilege protects communications to a member of the clergy, in his or her spiritual or professional capacity, by persons who seek spiritual counseling and who reasonably expect that their words will be kept in confidence."); Proposed Fed. R. Evid. 506(b) ("A person has a privilege to refuse to disclose and to prevent another from disclosing a confidential communication by the person to a clergyman in his professional character as spiritual adviser.").

[10] *E.g.,* United States v. Dube, 820 F.2d 886 (7th Cir. 1987) (acknowledging existence of clergy-penitent privilege, but holding that privilege did not apply to communications made ᵐman to obtain assistance in avoiding tax obligations, not spiritual relief); United States on, 655 F.2d 478 (2d Cir. 1981) (holding that defendant's business communications st he employed in a nonreligious capacity were not protected by priest-penitent

Communications. "The privilege[] between priest and penitent . . . limit[s] protection to private communications."[11] However, the modern privilege is not limited to "confessions" in the doctrinal religious sense.[12] Restricting the privilege to confessions would raise First Amendment issues.[13]

In *United States v. Mohanlal*,[14] a minister was asked whether the accused knew right from wrong in an insanity defense case. The court ruled that the responding answer did not violate the privilege:

> Rev. Enquist did not testify to any communication to himself on the part of defendant, . . . His testimony concerning his conclusion as to defendant's mental state, although no doubt based upon communications to him by defendant, as well as observations of defendant, including observations as to the manner of defendant's communications, did not reveal, or suggest, the content of any communication by defendant.[15]

Confidentiality. Like other communication privileges, the privilege requires confidentiality.[16] The presence of a third party cuts against an intent of confidentiality.[17]

---

privilege); United States v. Wells, 446 F.2d 2, 4 (2d Cir. 1971) (noting absence of any indication that letter was confidential or that "its purpose was to obtain religious or other counsel, advice, solace, absolution or ministration").

[11] *Trammel*, 445 U.S. at 51.

[12] *See* Proposed Fed. R. Evid. 506 advisory committee's note ("The choice between a privilege narrowly restricted to doctrinally required confessions and a privilege broadly applicable to all confidential communications with a clergyman in his professional character as spiritual adviser has been exercised in favor of the latter. Many clergymen now receive training in marriage counseling and the handling of personality problems."), 56 F.R.D. 248 (1972); *Developments, supra* note 1, at 1558 ("Strictly applied, the requirement that confidentiality be mandated by church doctrine could remove the protection of the privilege from communications made to Protestant and Jewish clergy because, for the most part, their religious doctrines neither mandate confession nor prohibit subsequent disclosure of confidential communications.").

[13] *See* In re Grand Jury Investigation, 918 F.2d 374, 385 n. 14 (3d Cir. 1990) ("Indeed, the prospect of restricting the privilege to Roman Catholic penitential communications raises serious first amendment concerns.") (citing Larsen v. Valente, 456 U.S. 228, 245–46 (1982) (emphasizing that the establishment clause articulates a "principle of denominational neutrality" and holding that state law "granting a denominational preference" is subject to strict scrutiny)).

[14] 867 F. Supp. 199 (S.D.N.Y. 1994).

[15] *Id.* at 200–01.

[16] *See* Proposed Fed. R. Evid. 506 (a)(2) ("A communication is 'confidential' if made privately and not intended for further disclosure except to other persons present in furtherance of the purpose of the communication.").

[17] *See In re Grand Jury Investigation*, 918 F.2d at 386 ("As is the case with consultations between attorneys and clients, the presence of multiple parties, unrelated by blood or marriage, during discussions with a member of the clergy may, but will not necessarily, defeat the condition that communications be made with a reasonable expectation of confidentiality in order for the privilege to attach").

Exceptions. The federal drafters saw no need to specify a crime-fraud exception because the "nature of what may reasonably be considered spiritual advice makes it unnecessary to include in the rule a specific exception for communications in furtherance of crime or fraud."[18] Other jurisdictions recognize other exceptions, such as for child abuse.[19]

Waiver. Failure to object to clergy testimony at trial waives the privilege, as does voluntary disclosure to a third party.[20] The privilege may also be waived by the holder testifying concerning the communication.

§ 41.03 Journalist's Privilege

Numerous states recognize a journalist's privilege,[21] which is intended to encourage the flow of information to newspapers and the electronic media.[22] The privilege is limited to the identity of the source.[23]

In *Branzburg v. Hayes*,[24] the Supreme Court held that the First Amendment guarantee of freedom of the press did not require the recognition of a journalist's privilege.[25] In a concurring opinion, Justice Powell observed:

---

[18] Proposed Fed. R. Evid. 506 advisory committee's note.

[19] Ohio Rev. Stat. § 2151.421(A)(1) (requiring clergy, as well as other professionals, to report suspected child abuse).

[20] *See* Proposed Fed. R. Evid. 511 ("A person upon whom these rules confer a privilege against disclosure of the confidential matter or communication waives the privilege if he or his predecessor while holder of the privilege voluntarily discloses or consents to the disclosure of any significant part of the matter or communication. This rule does not apply if the disclosure is itself a privileged communication."), 56 F.R.D. 244, 245 (1973).

[21] *See* N.J. Stat. Ann. § 2A:84A-21.1. *See also* Henderson v. People, 879 P.2d 383, 393 (Colo. 1994) ("Although the newsperson's privilege is broad, the statute also sets forth several situations in which the privilege does not apply. For instance, section 13-90-119(2)(a) through (d) provides that the privilege of nondisclosure does not apply to information that is: (1) received at a press conference; (2) published or broadcast; (3) based on a newsperson's personal observation of a crime, when such information cannot be reasonably obtained through other means; and (4) based on a newsperson's observations of a class 1, 2, or 3 felony.").

[22] *Developments, supra* note 1, at 1601 ("Proponents of the privilege observe that media sources often provide valuable information only on the condition that their identities or a portion of the information they reveal remain confidential. Thus, requiring journalists to disclose such confidences would deter future sources from communicating with the news media and would hinder media efforts to collect and disseminate information. This hinderance to the media is particularly worrisome when the sources in question provide information on matters of public concern such as official misconduct or criminal activities.").

[23] *See generally* Morele, *Evidentiary Privilege for Journalists' Sources: Theory and Statutory Protection*, 51 Mo. L. Rev. 1 (1986); Note, *Journalist's Privilege: When Deprivation is a Benefit*, 108 Yale L.J. 1449 (1999).

[24] 408 U.S. 665 (1972).

[25] The Court did not accept the argument that sources of information would vanish without a privilege:

> Reliance by the press on confidential informants does not mean that all such sources will in fact dry up because of the later possible appearance of the newsman before a grand jury. The reporter may never be called and if he objects to testifying, the prosecution may not insist. Also, the relationship of many informants to the press is a symbiotic one which is unlikely to be greatly inhibited by the threat of subpoena:

If a newsman believes that the grand jury investigation is not being conducted in good faith he is not without remedy. Indeed, if the newsman is called upon to give information bearing only a remote and tenuous relationship to the subject of the investigation, or if he has some other reason to believe that his testimony implicates confidential source relationship without a legitimate need of law enforcement, he will have access to the court on a motion to quash and an appropriate protective order may be entered. The asserted claim to privilege should be judged on its facts by the striking of a proper balance between freedom of the press and the obligation of all citizens to give relevant testimony with respect to criminal conduct. The balance of these vital constitutional and societal interests on a case-by-case basis accords with the tried and traditional way of adjudicating such questions.[26]

A number of federal courts, focusing on Justice Powell's concurring opinion, have recognized a qualified journalist's privilege.[27] This qualified privilege requires a balancing of interests, which in criminal cases may implicate a defendant's right to a fair trial. Other courts have rejected even this qualified privilege.[28]

---

quite often, such informants are members of a minority political or cultural group that relies heavily on the media to propagate its views, publicize its aims, and magnify its exposure to the public. Moreover, grand juries characteristically conduct secret proceedings, and law enforcement officers are themselves experienced in dealing with informers, and have their own methods for protecting them without interference with the effective administration of justice. There is little before us indicating that informants whose interest in avoiding exposure is that it may threaten job security, personal safety, or peace of mind, would in fact be in a worse position, or would think they would be, if they risked placing their trust in public officials as well as reporters. We doubt if the informer who prefers anonymity but is sincerely interested in furnishing evidence of crime will always or very often be deterred by the prospect of dealing with those public authorities characteristically charged with the duty to protect the public interest as well as his.

Id. at 694–95.

[26] *Id.* at 710.

[27] *E.g.,* Shoen v. Shoen, 5 F.3d 1289, 1292 (9th Cir. 1993) ("[W]hen facts acquired by a journalist in the course of gathering the news become the target of discovery, a qualified privilege against compelled disclosure comes into play."); LaRouche v. National Broadcasting Co., 780 F.2d 1134, 1139 (4th Cir. 1986) ("In determining whether the journalist's privilege will protect the source in a given situation, it is necessary for the district court to balance the interests involved. To aid in the balancing of these interests, courts have developed a three part test: (1) whether the information is relevant, (2) whether the information can be obtained by alternative means, and (3) whether there is a compelling interest in the information.") (citation omitted); United States v. Cuthbertson, 651 F.2d 189, 195 (3d Cir. 1981) ("We have held that to overcome the media's federal common law qualified privilege the seeker of the information must demonstrate that his only practical means of access to the information sought is through the media."); Miller v. Transamerican Press, 621 F.2d 721, 725 (5th Cir. 1980).

[28] *See* In re Grand Jury Proceedings, 5 F.3d 397, 400 (9th Cir. 1993) ("This reading of *Branzburg,* however, is at odds with the majority opinion itself, and with the manner in which we have applied it in our own cases. It is important to note that Justice White's opinion is not a plurality opinion. Although Justice Powell wrote a separate concurrence, he also signed Justice White's opinion, providing the fifth vote necessary to establish it as the majority opinion

§ 41.04 Miscellaneous Privileges

New privileges are always being proposed. Federal courts have rejected an academic peer-review privilege[29] and an accountant's privilege.[30] Some have recognized a privilege for critical self-analysis, at least under limited circumstances.[31]

§ 41.05 Key Points

Clergy-penitent privilege. Every jurisdiction recognizes a clergyman-penitent privilege. The proposed federal rule made the communicant the holder of the privilege. Some state statutes permit the clergy member to refuse to testify even when the penitent has expressly consented, if "the disclosure of the information is in violation of his sacred trust." First Amendment Free Exercise issues obviously are implicated in this context.

The communication must be made for the purpose of obtaining spiritual guidance; consultations for other reasons do not fall within the privilege. The modern privilege is not limited to "confessions" in the doctrinal religious sense; restricting the privilege to confessions would raise First Amendment issues. Like other communication privileges, the privilege requires confidentiality, and the presence of a third party cuts against an intent of confidentiality.

Journalist's privilege. Numerous states recognize a journalist's privilege, which is intended to encourage the flow of information to newspapers and the electronic media. The privilege is limited to the identity of the source. In *Branzburg v. Hayes*, the Supreme Court held that the First Amendment guarantee of freedom of the press did not require the recognition of a journalist's privilege. However, a number of federal courts, focusing on Justice Powell's concurring opinion in *Branzburg*, have recognized a qualified journalist's privilege. This qualified privilege requires a balancing of interests, which in criminal cases may implicate the defendant's right to a fair trial. Other courts have rejected even this qualified privilege.

---

of the court."); In re Grand Jury Proceedings, 810 F.2d 580, 584–85 (6th Cir. 1987) ("[W]e decline to join some other circuit courts. . . . Generally, these circuits indicate that their positions are based, at least in part, upon [a] portion of Justice Powell's concurring opinion. . . . That portion of Justice Powell's opinion certainly does not warrant the rewriting of the majority opinion to grant a first amendment testimonial privilege to news reporters. . . .").

[29] *See* University of Pennsylvania v. Equal Employment Opportunity Comm'n, 493 U.S. 182 (1990).

[30] *See* Couch v. United States, 409 U.S. 322, 335 (1973) ("no confidential accountant-client privilege exists under federal law"); In re Grand Jury Proceedings, 220 F.3d 568, 571 (7th Cir. 2000) ("There is no accountant-client privilege."); United States v. Frederick, 182 F.3d 496, 500 (7th Cir. 1999); In re International Horizons, Inc., 689 F.2d 996, 1004 (11th Cir. 1982) ("Since *Couch*, the notion that the federal courts should recognize a general accountant-client privilege has been consistently rejected."). *See also* United States v. Arthur Young & Co., 465 U.S. 804 (1984) (rejecting work product privilege for accountants).

[31] *See* Dowling v. American Hawaii Cruises, Inc., 971 F.2d 423, 425–27 (9th Cir. 1992) (noting cases that have recognized such a privilege).

Chapter 42

GOVERNMENTAL PRIVILEGES

§ 42.01 Introduction

The privileges discussed in the preceding chapters were private privileges. In some circumstances, they may apply to the government, such as the attorney-client privilege. This chapter examines privileges that *only* the government may assert.

As drafted by the Supreme Court, proposed Federal Rule 509 recognized a state secrets and official information privilege and proposed Rule 510 recognized an informant's privilege.[1] However, Congress deleted all the proposed privilege rules when it substituted the general federal rule on privileges.[2] Nevertheless, federal cases recognize these privileges as well as others.

§ 42.02 Informant's Privilege

All jurisdictions recognize a qualified privilege that permits the prosecution to withhold the identity of an informer.

Rationale. This common law privilege is intended to protect "the public interest in effective law enforcement. The privilege recognizes the obligation of citizens to communicate their knowledge of the commission of crimes to law-enforcement officials and, by preserving their anonymity, encourages them to perform that obligation."[3] One commentary explained the purpose of the informant's privilege as follows:

> It is founded on the rationale that information provided by informants is critical to law enforcement efforts — especially in the area of "victimless" crimes such as drug trafficking, prostitution, and illegal trading in weapons — and that the promise of confidentiality is necessary to maintain this flow of information. Informants are frequently targets of economic or physical retaliation that may, in the extreme, include murder. In addition, many informants have

---

[1] *See* 56 F.R.D. 244, 245 (1973).

[2] Fed. R. Evid. 501. For a discussion of the congressional action, *see supra* § 37.02 (Federal Rule 501).

[3] Roviaro v. United States, 353 U.S. 53, 59 (1957). *See also* McCray v. Illinois, 386 U.S. 300, 307 (1967) (informants are a "vital part of society's defense arsenal"); Proposed Fed. R. Evid. 510 advisory committee's note ("The rule recognizes the use of informers as an important aspect of law enforcement, whether the informer is a citizen who steps forward with information or a paid undercover agent. . . . The public interest in law enforcement requires that the privilege be that of the government, state, or political subdivision, rather than that of the witness.").

ongoing relationships with government officials, and disclosure of their identities would render them useless in future law enforcement efforts. Finally, unlike beneficiaries of other privileges whose communications are often made without the expectation of litigation, informants are fully aware that the government uses their information in order to prosecute criminals who will almost certainly attempt to learn their identities during trial.[4]

[A] Holder

The holder of the privilege is the government, not the informant.[5] Thus, the government may waive the privilege over the informant's objection.

[B] Scope of Privilege

The privilege covers only the identity of the informant and not necessarily the content of the communication.[6] If "revealing the informant's communication will not reveal the informant's identity, that communication is not privileged."[7] The privilege applies in civil as well as in criminal cases.[8]

[C] Exceptions

There are two exceptions to the privilege. First, once the identity of the informant becomes known, the privilege ceases.[9]

Second, if the identity of the informant would provide substantial assistance to the defense at trial, the state is required to reveal the identity

---

[4] *Developments in the Law — Privileged Communications*, 98 Harv. L. Rev. 1450, 1596–97 (1985).

[5] *See Roviaro*, 353 U.S. at 59 ("What is usually referred to as the informer's privilege is in reality the Government's privilege to withhold from disclosure the identity of persons who furnish information of violations of law to officers charged with enforcement of that law."); United States v. Sanchez, 988 F.2d 1384, 1391 (5th Cir. 1993) (privilege "in actuality is the Government's privilege.").

[6] *See* Proposed Fed. R. Evid. 510 advisory committee's note ("Only identity is privileged; communications are not included except to the extent that disclosure would operate also to disclose the informer's identity."); *Roviaro*, 353 U.S. at 60 ("Thus, where the disclosure of the contents of a communication will not tend to reveal the identity of an informer, the contents are not privileged.").

[7] United States v. Sanchez, 988 F.2d 1384, 1391 (5th Cir. 1993). *See also Roviaro*, 353 U.S. at 60 ("where the disclosure of the contents of a communication will not tend to reveal the identity of an informer, the contents are not privileged").

[8] *See* Hoffman v. Reali, 973 F.2d 980, 987 (1st Cir. 1992) ("Where as here the privilege was raised in a civil action, it was Hoffman's burden to establish a clear need and relevance before he could force the state, over its objection, to reveal the informers' identities and further particulars as to the information they had provided. He failed to show the degree of necessity and urgency required.").

[9] *See Roviaro*, 353 U.S. at 60 ("[O]nce the identity of the informer has been disclosed to those who would have cause to resent the communication, the privilege is no longer applicable."); *Sanchez*, 988 F.2d at 1391 ("[I]f the informant's identity has already been revealed . . ., the identity may be disclosed.").

of the informant or dismiss the prosecution. In *Roviaro v. United States*,[10] the accused was charged with the sale and transportation of narcotics. According to the prosecution's evidence, the informer had been an active participant in the crime. He "had taken a material part in bringing about the possession of certain drugs by the accused, had been present with the accused at the occurrence of the alleged crime, and might be a material witness as to whether the accused knowingly transported the drugs as charged."[11] Nevertheless, the trial judge denied a defense motion to compel the prosecution to disclose the informer's identity. The Supreme Court held that where disclosure "is relevant and helpful to the defense of an accused, or is essential to a fair determination of a cause, the privilege must give way. In these situations the trial court may require disclosure and, if the Government withholds the information, dismiss the action."[12]

The Court went on to state: "We believe that no fixed rule with respect to disclosure is justifiable. The problem is one that calls for balancing the public interest in protecting the flow of information against the individual's right to prepare his defense. Whether a proper balance renders nondisclosure erroneous must depend on the particular circumstances of each case, taking into consideration the crime charged, the possible defenses, the possible significance of the informer's testimony, and other relevant factors."[13]

The Court then reviewed the circumstances of Roviaro's trial, pointing out that the informer's possible testimony was highly relevant — *i.e.*, it might have disclosed an entrapment defense, thrown doubt upon the accused's identity, the identity of the package, and possible lack of knowledge. Moreover, the informer was the sole participant, other than the accused, in the transaction charged. The Court concluded that, "under these circumstances, the trial court committed prejudicial error in permitting the Government to withhold the identity of its undercover employee in the face of repeated demands by the accused for his disclosure."[14]

According to the Fifth Circuit, whether disclosure of the informant's identity or communication is required depends on "1) the informant's degree of involvement in the crime, 2) the helpfulness of the disclosure to the defense, and 3) the Government's interest in nondisclosure."[15] The key factors are whether the informant was a participant[16] or the sole witness

---

[10] 353 U.S. 53 (1957).

[11] *Id.* at 55.

[12] *Id.* at 60–61.

[13] *Id.* at 62.

[14] *Id.* at 65.

[15] *Sanchez*, 988 F.2d at 1391. *See also* Proposed Fed. R. Evid. 510 advisory committee's note ("If the informer becomes a witness for the government, the interests of justice in disclosing his status as a source of bias or possible support are believed to outweigh any remnant of interest in nondisclosure which then remains.").

[16] *See* United States v. Mendoza-Salgado, 964 F.2d 993, 1001 (10th Cir. 1992) ("Unlike *Roviaro*, the informer here did not actively participate in the transaction which generated the charge. Instead, the record indicates the informer merely spread the word about Agent Gallo's interest in large quantities of cocaine, later informed the DEA that defendant could supply

to the crime.[17] But, by themselves, these factors may not be sufficient to require disclosure; the informant's testimony must also be material to the defense.[18] In contrast, a "mere tipster" without personal knowledge of the crime usually can not provide crucial defense evidence.[19]

[D] In Camera Proceedings

The trial court may use an in camera proceeding to determine the privilege's application.[20] The Ninth Circuit has observed:

> From the defendant's standpoint, an *in camera* hearing may provide many of the same benefits as disclosure itself, particularly where defendant's counsel is allowed to participate under an order not to reveal any information disclosed in chambers. However, unlike actual disclosure, an *in camera* hearing bears little risk of disclosing the identity of the informant and does not jeopardize the government's future use of that individual. Consequently, there is ordinarily no governmental interest to balance against the defendant's in deciding whether to hold an *in camera* hearing.[21]

---

the drug, and accompanied Agent Gallo during the introductory meeting with defendant's supplier, Mr. Sierra. Nothing in the record suggests the informer participated in the actual sale of cocaine.").

[17] *See* United States v. Martinez, 922 F.2d 914, 920 (1st Cir. 1991) ("[W]hen the government informant is not an actual participant or a witness to the offense, disclosure is required only in those exceptional cases where the defendant can point to some concrete circumstance that might justify overriding both the public interest in encouraging the flow of information, and the informant's private interest in his or her own safety.").

[18] *See* DiBlasio v. Keane, 932 F.2d 1038, 1042 (2d Cir. 1991) ("While we agree that the informant's testimony was not material to the state's case, the same cannot be said regarding the entrapment defense. . . . [W]hen the defendant raises the defense of entrapment, or claims that he did not have the requisite state of mind for the offense charged, testimony about events preceding and in between these crimes may be as material as that detailing their actual commission, or more so."); United States v. Saa, 859 F.2d 1067, 1073 (2d Cir. 1988) ("Thus, if his testimony would have been material, his identity should have been revealed to the defense. But the defendants other than Esperanza Saa have made no showing that Robert's potential testimony was material to their defense.").

[19] *See* United States v. Whitely, 734 F.2d 1129, 1138 (6th Cir. 1984) ("[T]he record indicates that the informant, Bob, was not a major participant in the drug transaction. His role was that of merely introducing Agent Best to appellant Whitley. He was not involved in any other phase of the price negotiations or discussions regarding the drugs. Nor was he present when the actual drug transaction occurred at the Holiday Inn. This very limited involvement in the transactions of this case is inconsistent with the role played by the informant in *Roviaro*.").

[20] *See* United States v. Spires, 3 F.3d 1234, 1238 (9th Cir. 1993) ("Our precedents demonstrate that in disclosure cases an *in camera* hearing is favored procedure. Other circuits have also noted the advantages of that procedure.") (citations omitted); Proposed Fed. R. Evid. 510 advisory committee's note ("A hearing *in camera* provides an accommodation of these conflicting interests. The limited disclosure to the judge avoids any significant impairment of secrecy, while affording the accused a substantial measure of protection against arbitrary police action.").

[21] *Spires*, 3 F.3d at 1238.

The defense must make an initial showing to trigger the right to an in camera proceeding,[22] although the showing need not be substantial.[23] In some cases, defense counsel have been allowed to participate in the hearing.[24]

[E] Burden of Proof

In determining this issue, the burden of persuasion rests with the defendant, and the trial court is given some latitude.[25]

[F] Suppression Hearings

Disclosure of an informant's identity is rarely required during a suppression hearing because, unlike a trial, guilt or innocence is not at issue. In *McCray v. Illinois*,[26] the Supreme Court distinguished *Rovario*, noting that the "issue is the preliminary one of probable cause, and guilt or innocence is not at stake."[27] The Court rejected both due process and confrontation arguments put forth by the defendant:

---

[22] *See* United States v. Amdor-Galvan, 9 F.3d 1414, 1417 (9th Cir. 1993) ("The district court, in exercising its discretion on whether to conduct an *in camera* hearing on the defendant's need for a confidential informant's identity or testimony, must hold such a hearing where the defendant has shown that the information would be 'relevant and helpful.' Although Amador-Galvan and Molina showed the potential relevance and helpfulness to their defense of discovering the identity of the confidential informants, the district court denied the request on the ground that the defendants did not have any evidence independent of the informants themselves to support the claim that the driver was not Amador-Galvan. Given that the Government's theory of prosecution hinges on the assumption that Amador-Galvan was the driver of the car in question, one or more of these four informants could have provided evidence weakening the Government's case. For example, if they were percipient witnesses, these informants could provide eyewitness testimony; if not, they might still be able to provide information which might lead to a firsthand source or circumstantial evidence. Any such evidence would clearly be 'relevant and helpful' to preparing Amador-Galvan's defense.").

[23] *See Spires*, 3 F.3d at 1238 ("While an *in camera* hearing need not be held whenever there is a request for the identity of an informant, we have previously approved the holding of such a hearing where the defendant makes a 'minimal threshold showing' that disclosure would be relevant to at least one defense. We now hold that under those circumstances a hearing is required.").

[24] *See* United States v. Henderson, 241 F.3d 638, 645 (9th Cir. 2000) ("defense counsel may participate under an order not to reveal any information disclosed during the hearing").

[25] *See Amdor-Galvan*, 9 F.3d at 1417 ("The defendant bears the burden of demonstrating a need for disclosure of a confidential informant's identity. He must show that he has more than a 'mere suspicion' that the informant has information which will prove 'relevant and helpful' or will be essential to a fair trial.") (citation omitted).

[26] 386 U.S. 300 (1967). *See also* United States v. Raddatz, 447 U.S. 667, 679 (1980) ("Although the Due Process Clause has been held to require the Government to disclose the identity of an informant at trial, provided the identity is shown to be relevant and helpful to the defense, it has never been held to require the disclosure of an informant's identity at a suppression hearing.").

[27] *Id.* at 311. *See also* Lewis v. United States, 385 U.S. 206, 210 (1966) (a rule virtually prohibiting the use of informers would "severely hamper the Government in enforcement of the narcotics laws").

We find no support for the petitioner's position in either of those constitutional provisions. The arresting officers in this case testified, in open court, fully and in precise detail as to what the informer told them and as to why they had reason to believe his information was trustworthy. Each officer was under oath. Each was subjected to searching cross-examination. The judge was obviously satisfied that each was telling the truth, and for that reason he exercised the discretion conferred upon him by the established law of Illinois to respect the informer's privilege.[28]

§ 42.03 Surveillance Location Privilege

In *United States v. Green*,[29] the D.C. Circuit, reasoning by analogy to the informer's privilege, recognized a privilege for the location of a surveillance location:

Like confidential informants, hidden observation posts may often prove to be useful law enforcement tools, so long as they remain secret. Just as the disclosure of an informer's identity may destroy his future usefulness in criminal investigations, the identification of a hidden observation post will likely destroy the future value of that location for police surveillance. The revelation of a surveillance location might also threaten the safety of police officers using the observation post, or lead to adversity for cooperative owners or occupants of the building. Finally, the assurance of nondisclosure of a surveillance location may be necessary to encourage property owners or occupants to allow the police to make such use of their property.[30]

Green involved a suppression hearing. The privilege was extended to trial in *United States v. Harley*.[31] There, however, the officers who conducted the surveillance were not essential witnesses for the prosecution. Harley was charged with engaging in a drug transaction with a different officer, and that officer identified him at trial. Moreover, the surveillance was recorded on videotape.

In contrast, in *United States v. Foster*,[32] the police officer claiming the privilege and the accuracy of his identification of Foster were critical. Fifteen other people were in the vicinity at the time, some playing basketball, others moving about in the open area. Another officer, who arrived on the scene in response to the surveillance officer's call describing Foster, arrested someone else, who was later released. The defense wanted to cross-examine the officer about his estimate of the distance between himself and Foster, the angle of his view, and his line of sight. Without knowing the

---

[28] *Id.* at 313.

[29] 670 F.2d 1148 (D.C. Cir. 1981).

[30] *Id.* at 1155.

[31] 682 F.2d 1018 (D.C. Cir. 1982).

[32] 986 F.2d 541, 542–44 (D.C. Cir. 1993).

location of the observation post, the defense could not effectively probe the officer's memory or veracity about these subjects and therefore the privilege should have given way to the right of confrontation.

Some state courts have recognized this privilege,[33] while others have rejected it.[34]

§ 42.04   State Secrets & Executive Privilege

Proposed Federal Rule 509 recognized a state secrets privilege.[35] The government was the holder.[36] The proposed rule was based on *United States v. Reynolds*,[37] a federal Tort Claims Act case against the Government involving the deaths of civilians in the crash of a B-29 airplane. The plane was testing secret electronic equipment. The Supreme Court wrote: "It may be possible to satisfy the court, from all the circumstances of the case, that there is a reasonable danger that compulsion of the evidence will expose military matters which, in the interest of national security, should not be divulged. When this is the case, the occasion for the privilege is appropriate, and the court should not jeopardize the security which the privilege is meant to protect by insisting upon an examination of the evidence, even by the judge alone, in chambers."[38]

Proposed Rule 509(c) required the chief officer of the government agency or department to assert the privilege and also provided for in chambers procedures, including ex parte in camera inspection at the government's request.[39] The Classified Information Procedures Act[40] was later enacted to deal with classified information in criminal prosecutions.[41]

In *United States v. Nixon*,[42] the Supreme Court recognized a limited presidential privilege, although it also found that the privilege had to give

---

[33] *See* Commonwealth v. Lugo, 548 N.E.2d 1263 (Mass. 1990); State v. Garcia, 618 A.2d 326 (N.J. 1993).

[34] *See* State v. Darden, 41 P.3d 1189, 1197 (Wash. 2002) ("[W]e stand without authority from Washington statutes or common law to recognize a surveillance location privilege.").

[35] Proposed Fed. R. Evid. 509(b) ("The government has a privilege to refuse to give evidence and to prevent any person from giving evidence upon a showing of reasonable likelihood of danger that the evidence will disclose a secret of state or official information, as defined in this rule."); Proposed Fed. R. Evid. 509(a)(1) ("A 'secret of state' is a governmental secret relating to the national defense or the international relations of the United States.").

[36] Proposed Fed. R. Evid. 509 advisory committee's note ("The rule vests the privileges in the government where they properly belong rather than a party or witness.").

[37] 345 U.S. 1 (1953).

[38] *Id.* at 10.

[39] *See also* Monarch Assurance P.L.C. v. United States, 244 F.3d 1356, 1357–60 (Fed. Cir. 2001) (CIA status); Bareford v. General Dynamics Corp., 973 F.2d 1138 (5th Cir. 1992) (weapons systems); Northrop Corp. v. McDonnell Douglas Corp., 751 F.2d 395, 401 (D.C. Cir. 1984); Ellsberg v. Mitchell, 709 F.2d 51 (D.C. Cir. 1983).

[40] 18 U.S.C. App. 3 § 1 et seq.

[41] *See* United States v. Noriega, 117 F.3d 1206, 1215–17 (11th Cir. 1997); United States v. Ho Lee, 90 F. Supp. 2d 1234 (D.N.M. 2000).

[42] 418 US. 683 (1974).

way in that case: "In this case we must weigh the importance of the general privilege of confidentiality of Presidential communications in performance of the President's responsibilities against the inroads of such a privilege on the fair administration of criminal justice. The interest in preserving confidentiality is weighty indeed and entitled to great respect. However, we cannot conclude that advisers will be moved to temper the candor of their remarks by the infrequent occasions of disclosure because of the possibility that such conversations will be called for in the context of a criminal prosecution."[43]

§ 42.05 Miscellaneous Governmental Privileges

Proposed Federal Rule 509 also recognized an official information privilege, which covered several different categories of governmental information.[44] Sometimes disclosure is controlled by the Freedom of Information Act.[45] The secrecy of grand jury proceedings is also frequently litigated.[46]

§ 42.06 Key Points

Informant's privilege. All jurisdictions recognize a qualified privilege that permits the prosecution to withhold the identity of an informer. This common law privilege is intended to protect the public interest in effective law enforcement by protecting the identity of informants. The holder is the government, not the informant. The privilege covers only the identity of the informant. Thus, if revealing the informant's communication will not reveal the informant's identity, the communication is not privileged.

There are two exceptions to the privilege. First, once the identity of the informant becomes known, the privilege ceases. Second, if the identity of the informant would provide substantial assistance to the defense at trial, the state may be required to reveal the identity of the informant or dismiss the prosecution. The trial court may use an in camera proceeding to determine the privilege's application. Disclosure of an informant's identity is

---

[43] *Id.* at 711–12. *See also* In re Sealed Case, 211 F.3d 729 (D.C. 1997) (White House assertion of privilege against Office of Independent Counsel).

[44] *See* Proposed Fed. R. Evid. 509(a)(2) (" 'Official information' is information within the custody or control of a department or agency of the government the disclosure of which is shown to be contrary to the public interest and which consists of: (A) intragovernmental opinions or recommendations submitted for consideration in the performance of decisional or policymaking functions, or (B) subject to the provisions of 18 U.S.C. § 3500, investigatory files complied for law enforcement purposes and not otherwise available, or (C) information within the custody or control of a governmental department or agency whether initiated within the department or agency or acquired by it in its exercise of its official responsibilities and not otherwise available to the public pursuant to 5 U.S. C. § 552.").

[45] 5 U.S. C. § 552(b)(7). *See also* Department of Interior and Bureau of Indian Affairs v. Klamath Water Users Protective Ass'n, 532 U.S. 1 (2001).

[46] *See* Douglas Oil Co. v. Petrol Stops Northwest, 441 U.S. 211, 219 (1979); United States v. Sells Engineering, Inc., 463 U.S. 418 (1983) (court must always be reluctant to conclude that breach of secrecy has been authorized).

rarely required during a suppression hearing because, unlike a trial, guilt or innocence is not at issue.

Chapter 43

PRIVILEGE AGAINST SELF-INCRIMINATION

§ 43.01 Introduction

The Fifth Amendment to the United States Constitution prohibits compulsory self-incrimination: "No person . . . shall be compelled in any criminal case to be a witness against himself." In *Malloy v. Hogan*,[1] the Supreme Court held the privilege applicable in state trials. Many state constitutions also guarantee the right against self-incrimination.

Although the privilege applies in other contexts, this chapter examines the Fifth Amendment as it applies to trials.[2] There are several components to the Self-Incrimination Clause: (1) *compulsion* to provide (2) *testimonial* evidence (3) that would subject the person to *criminal liability*.

§ 43.02 "Compulsion" Requirement

The Fifth Amendment does not prohibit self-incrimination; it prohibits only *compulsory* self-incrimination.[3] For example, the compulsion issue was critical in the *Miranda* decision, where the Court determined that custodial interrogation amounted to "compulsion" within the meaning of the privilege.[4] For present purposes, a subpoena requiring a person to testify at trial is the paradigmatic example of compulsion.

§ 43.03 "Criminal Liability" Requirement

The Fifth Amendment protects only against incriminatory statements that subject the speaker to *criminal* prosecution. As the Supreme Court has observed: "The privilege cannot . . . be asserted by a witness to protect others from possible criminal prosecution. Nor can it be invoked simply to protect the witness' interest in privacy."[5] Moreover, once the possibility of criminal prosecution no longer exists, the privilege ceases. For example, if the statute of limitations for the offense has expired, there is no Fifth

---

[1] 378 U.S. 1 (1964).

[2] *See generally* Dressler, Understanding Criminal Procedure ch. 26 (3d ed. 2002); Whitebread & Slobogin, Criminal Procedure ch. 15 (4th ed. 1999); Langbein, *The Historical Origins of the Privilege Against Self-Incrimination at Common Law*, 92 Mich. L. Rev. 1047 (1994); Moglen, *Taking the Fifth: Reconsidering the Origins of the Constitutional Privilege Against Self-Incrimination*, 92 Mich. L. Rev. 1086 (1994).

[3] *See* United States v. Washington, 431 U.S. 181, 188 (1977) ("The constitutional guarantee is *only* that the witness be not compelled to give self-incriminating testimony.").

[4] *See generally* Dressler, Understanding Criminal Procedure ch. 24 (3d ed. 2002).

[5] United States v. Mandujano, 425 U.S. 564, 572 (1976) (citations omitted).

Amendment privilege. Similarly, because the Double Jeopardy Clause precludes a second trial (whether or not the first trial ended in an acquittal or conviction), there is no longer a privilege for that offense.[6] Thus, after an acquittal for murder, the defendant may be required to testify in a civil action for wrongful death based on the murder.

[A] Civil Trials & Other Proceedings

It is the exposure to possible criminal liability, rather than the forum in which the privilege is asserted, that is determinative. In *Lefkowitz v. Turley*,[7] for example, the Supreme Court held that the Fifth Amendment privilege applies in any proceeding "civil or criminal, formal or informal, where the answers might incriminate [a person] in future criminal proceedings."[8] Similarly, in *Minnesota v. Murphy*,[9] the Court stated that the privilege "not only permits a person to refuse to testify against himself at a criminal trial in which he is a defendant, but also 'privileges him not to answer official questions put to him in any other proceeding, civil or criminal, formal or informal, where the answers might incriminate him in future criminal proceedings."[10] Accordingly, the privilege may be asserted during civil depositions, congressional hearings, or administrative proceedings.

[B] Immunity

Immunity from prosecution is used to elicit testimony from witnesses who assert the privilege against self-incrimination.[11] In effect, immunity takes away the Fifth Amendment privilege because persons receiving immunity can no longer "incriminate" themselves. Once granted immunity, a witness who refuses to answer questions may be held in contempt.[12]

[1] Scope of Immunity

There are two types of immunity: (1) transactional immunity and (2) use and derivative use immunity. The latter is more limited than the former. Transactional immunity precludes the state from prosecuting the witness for the offense about which the witness testifies. Use and derivative use

---

[6] Mistrials are different. A second trial is generally permitted after a mistrial is declared. *See generally* Dressler, Understanding Criminal Procedure ch. 32 (3d ed. 2002) (Double Jeopardy Clause).

[7] 414 U.S. 70 (1973).

[8] *Id.* at 77. *See also* McCarthy v. Arndstein, 266 U.S. 34, 40 (1924).

[9] 465 U.S. 420 (1984).

[10] *Id.* at 426 (quoting *Lefkowitz*, 414 U.S. at 77).

[11] *See Mandujano*, 425 U.S. at 576 ("Immunity is the Government's ultimate tool for securing testimony that otherwise would be protected.").

[12] *Id.* at 575 ("If immunity is sought by the prosecutor and granted by the presiding judge, the witness can then be compelled to answer, on pain of contempt, even though the testimony would implicate the witness in criminal activity.").

immunity precludes only the use of the witness's testimony; it does not preclude prosecution if other evidence is available.

In *Kastigar v. United States*,[13] the Supreme Court held that the federal statute[14] that provided only use and derivative use immunity satisfied Fifth Amendment demands: "such immunity from use and derivative use is co-extensive with the scope of the privilege against self-incrimination, and therefore is sufficient to compel testimony over a claim of the privilege."[15] Consequently, a jurisdiction is not constitutionally compelled to provide transactional immunity, although it is free to do so.

[2] Trial Use

With use and derivative use immunity, if the witness is subsequently tried, the prosecution must establish by clear and convincing evidence that its evidence is not derived, either directly or indirectly, from the immunized testimony. In *Kastigar,* the Court wrote: "This burden of proof . . . is not limited to a negation of taint; rather, it imposes on the prosecution the affirmative duty to prove that the evidence it proposes to use is derived from a legitimate source wholly independent of the compelled testimony."[16] Moreover, a defendant may not be impeached by a prior statement given pursuant to a grant of immunity.[17]

The difficulty of establishing an independent source that is untainted by the immunized testimony is illustrated by *United States v. North*.[18] Ollie North received immunity from Congress during the Iran-Contra hearings. In a subsequent criminal prosecution, the Independent Counsel in a "taint" hearing, was required to show that the prosecution's evidence had an independent source. The court ruled that the Fifth Amendment is violated if any witness studied, reviewed, or was exposed to the immunized testimony (*i.e.,* watched North on TV). It is not enough for the prosecutor to show that the witnesses had an independent basis for the testimony; the prosecutor must also demonstrate that the immunized testimony in no way

---

[13] 406 U.S. 441 (1972).

[14] 18 U.S.C. § 6002.

[15] 406 U.S. at 453.

[16] *Id.*

[17] *See* New Jersey v. Portash, 440 U.S. 450 (1979):

Testimony given in response to a grant of legislative immunity is the essence of coerced testimony. In such cases there is no question whether physical or psychological pressures overrode the defendant's will; the witness is told to talk or face the government' coercive sanctions, notably, a conviction for contempt. . . . The Fifth and Fourteenth Amendments provide a privilege against *compelled* self-incrimination. Balancing of interests was thought to be necessary in *Harris* and *Hass* when the attempt to deter unlawful police conduct collided with the need to prevent perjury. Here, by contrast, we deal with the constitutional privilege against compulsory self-incrimination in its most pristine form. Balancing, therefore, is not simply unnecessary. It is impermissible.

Id. at 459. The Supreme Court had carved out an impeachment exception to *Miranda* in *Harris* and *Haas. See supra* § 22.10 [H] (prior inconsistent statements — constitutional issues).

[18] 910 F.2d 843 (D.C. Cir. 1990); United States v. North, 920 F.2d 940 (D.C. Cir. 1990).

influenced the testimony. The prosecution could not meet this burden and the case was dismissed.[19]

§ 43.04 "Testimonial-Real" Evidence Distinction

The Supreme Court has held that the application of the privilege turns on the distinction between testimonial or communicative evidence and real or physical evidence. Justice Holmes in *Holt v. United States*[20] wrote that the compelled modeling of a blouse found at the crime scene fell outside the scope of the privilege: "[T]he prohibition of compelling a man in a criminal court to be witness against himself is a prohibition of the use of physical or moral compulsion to extort communications from him, not an exclusion of his body as evidence when it may be material."[21]

Schmerber v. California[22] subsequently became the leading case on this issue. Schmerber was arrested for driving under the influence of alcohol after being treated at a hospital for injuries sustained in an automobile collision. At the direction of the investigating police officer, a physician obtained a blood sample from Schmerber. Although the defendant objected to this procedure on the advice of counsel, his blood was extracted and analyzed for alcoholic content. Schmerber argued that the extraction of blood violated the privilege against self-incrimination. Rejecting this argument, the Court held that the privilege covers only communicative or testimonial evidence, not physical or real evidence. According to the Court:

> It is clear that the protection of the privilege reaches an accused's communications, whatever form they might take. . . . On the other hand, both federal and state courts have usually held that it offers no protection against compulsion to submit to fingerprinting, photographing, or measurements, to write or speak for identification, to appear in court, to stand, to assume a stance, to walk, or to make a particular gesture. The distinction which has emerged, often expressed in different ways, is that the privilege is a bar against compelling "communications" or "testimony," but that compulsion which makes a suspect or accused the source of "real or physical evidence" does not violate it.[23]

In *United States v. Wade*,[24] a line-up case, the Court held that compelling an accused to exhibit his person for observation was compulsion "to exhibit his physical characteristics, not compulsion to disclose any knowledge he

---

[19] *See* N.Y. Times, Sept. 12, 1991, at 1 (reporting that the prosecutors were surprised by Robert McFarlane's testimony that his testimony was "inevitably" colored by North's testimony before Congress. Prosecutors had spent several days preparing McFarlane and accused him of "torpedoing" the prosecution.).

[20] 218 U.S. 245 (1910).

[21] *Id.* at 252–53.

[22] 384 U.S. 757 (1966).

[23] *Id.* at 763–64.

[24] 388 U.S. 218 (1967).

might have" and thus not proscribed by the privilege.[25] In *Gilbert v. California*,[26] the Court concluded that the compelled production of a "mere handwriting exemplar, in contrast to the content of what is written, like the voice or body itself, is an identifying physical characteristic outside [the Fifth Amendment's] protection."[27] Similarly, in *United States v. Dionisio*,[28] the Court ruled that compelling a defendant to speak for the purpose of voice analysis did not violate the Fifth Amendment because the "voice recordings were to be used solely to measure the physical properties of the witnesses' voices, not for the testimonial or communicative content of what was to be said."[29]

The Court also applied this distinction in *Pennsylvania v. Muniz*,[30] holding that evidence of an arrestee's slurred speech and lack of muscular coordination during sobriety tests involved nontestimonial physical evidence. Muniz was requested to perform a horizontal gaze nystagmus test, a "walk and turn" test, and a "one leg stand test." A videotape of his performance was shown at trial. The Court wrote:

> Under *Schmerber* and its progeny, . . . any slurring of speech and other evidence of lack of muscular coordination revealed by Muniz's responses to Officer Hosterman's direct questions constitute nontestimonial components of those responses. Requiring a suspect to reveal the physical manner in which he articulates words, like requiring him to reveal the physical properties of the sound produced by his voice, see *Dionisio* . . ., does not, without more, compel him to provide a "testimonial" response for purposes of the privilege.[31]

The Court also held that routine booking questions fell outside the protection of the Fifth Amendment.[32] Muniz's inability to answer when requested to state the date of his sixth birthday, however, amounted to a testimonial response and should have been excluded.[33]

---

[25] *Id.* at 222.

[26] 388 U.S. 263 (1967).

[27] *Id.* at 266–67. *Accord* United States v. Euge, 444 U.S. 707, 718 (1980) ("Compulsion of handwriting exemplars . . .[is not] testimonial evidence protected by the Fifth Amendment privilege against self incrimination."); United States v. Mara, 410 U.S. 19, 22 n. * (1973) (same).

[28] 410 U.S. 1 (1973).

[29] *Id.* at 7. *See also* Fisher v. United States, 425 U.S. 391, 408 (1976).

[30] 496 U.S. 582 (1990).

[31] *Id.* at 592. *See also* Doe v. United States, 487 U.S. 201, 210 (1988) ("[I]n order to be testimonial, an accused's communication must itself, explicitly or implicitly, relate a factual assertion or disclose information.").

[32] Muniz was asked his name, address, height, weight, eye color, date of birth, and current age. Four Justices stated that these routine booking questions were not testimonial. Four other Justices disagreed but believed routine booking questions fell within an exception to the Fifth Amendment *Miranda* requirements.

[33] When asked if he knew the date of his sixth birthday, Muniz responded: "No, I don't." 496 U.S. at 586 (1990).

Under *Schmerber*, obtaining evidence for most types of scientific techniques is free from Fifth Amendment concerns because these techniques involve physical, not testimonial, evidence. Thus, the lower courts have applied *Schmerber* to cases involving handwriting, fingerprints, voice exemplars, dental impressions, urine samples, gunshot residues, and other techniques.[34] The *Schmerber* rule is also important at trial; it means the trial judge can require the accused to speak for identification[35] or put on a ski mask so a robbery witness can make an identification.

In other contexts, however, the Supreme Court has noted that "the distinction between real or physical evidence, on the one hand, and communications or testimony, on the other, is not readily drawn."[36] The *Schmerber* Court, for example, commented on the Fifth Amendment aspects of polygraph examinations:

> Some tests seemingly directed to obtain "physical evidence," for example, lie detector tests measuring changes in body function during interrogation, may actually be directed to eliciting responses which are essentially testimonial. To compel a person to submit to testing in which an effort will be made to determine his guilt or innocence on the basis of physiological responses, whether willed or not, is to evoke the spirit and history of the Fifth Amendment.[37]

§ 43.05 Accused's Privilege at Trial

A defendant in a criminal case cannot be compelled to be a witness, which means the prosecution cannot call the accused as an adverse witness in the government's case-in-chief. If the defendant voluntarily takes the witness stand in the defense case-in-chief, the privilege against self-incrimination is waived. The Supreme Court has observed: "A defendant who chooses to testify waives his privilege against compulsory self-incrimination with respect to the testimony he gives, and that waiver is no less effective or complete because the defendant may have been motivated to take the witness stand in the first place only by reason of the strength of the lawful evidence adduced against him."[38]

The extent of the waiver, however, is not as clear. One position is that the defendant has waived the privilege to all relevant matters, including matters affecting credibility. In contrast, a second position limits the waiver

---

[34] *See* 1 Giannelli & Imwinkelried, Scientific Evidence ch. 2 (3d ed. 1999).

[35] *See supra* § 27.05 (voice identification).

[36] South Dakota v. Neville, 459 U.S. 553, 561 (1983).

[37] *Schmerber*, 384 U.S. at 764. *See supra* § 24.08.

[38] Harrison v. United States, 392 U.S. 219, 222 (1968). *See also* Brown v. United States, 356 U.S. 148, 155–56 (1958); Raffel v. United States, 271 U.S. 494, 496–97 (1926) (The "immunity from giving testimony is one which the defendant may waive by offering himself as a witness. . . . When he takes the stand in his own behalf, he does so as any other witness, and within the limits of the appropriate rules he may be cross-examined as to the facts in issue.").

to those matters about which the accused testified on direct examination. As the drafters of the Federal Rules noted, the constitutional issue is not resolved by the evidence rule — Rule 611(b).[39] As a matter of federal constitutional law, however, the issue remains clouded.[40]

[A] Comment Upon Failure to Testify

In *Griffin v. California*,[41] the Supreme Court held that the Fifth Amendment prohibits the use of an accused's failure to testify as evidence of guilt. The Court wrote:

> [Comment on the refusal to testify] is a penalty imposed by courts for exercising a constitutional privilege. It cuts down on the privilege by making its assertion costly. It is said, however, that the inference of guilt for failure to testify as to facts peculiarly within the accused's knowledge is in any event natural and irresistible, and that comment on the failure does not magnify that inference into a penalty for asserting a constitutional privilege. What the jury may infer, given no help from the court, is one thing. What it may infer when the court solemnizes the silence of the accused into evidence against him is quite another.[42]

Accordingly, the Court held that the privilege "forbids either comment by the prosecution on the accused's silence or instructions by the court that such silence is evidence of guilt."[43]

The Court limited *Griffin* in *United States v. Robinson*,[44] a mail fraud case. The prosecution introduced a number of out-of-court statements made by Robinson, who did not testify. In closing argument, Robinson's counsel tried to minimize the prior statements by suggesting that his client had not been given the opportunity to explain his actions. In response, the prosecutor told the jury: "He could have taken the stand and explained it to you. The United States of America has given him, throughout, the opportunity to explain."[45] The Court in *Robinson* distinguished *Griffin*:

> Where the prosecutor on his own initiative asks the jury to draw an adverse inference from a defendant's silence, *Griffin* holds that the privilege against compulsory self-incrimination is violated. But where as in this case the prosecutor's reference to the defendant's

---

[39] *See* Fed. R. Evid. 611 advisory committee's note ("The rule does not purport to determine the extent to which an accused who elects to testify thereby waives his privilege against self-incrimination. . . . [T]he extent of the waiver . . . ought not to be determined as a by-product of a rule on scope of cross-examination.").

[40] *See* Carlson, *Cross-Examination of the Accused*, 52 Cornell L. Q. 705 (1967).

[41] 380 U.S. 609 (1965).

[42] *Id.* at 614.

[43] *Id.* at 615. *See also* United States v. Hastings, 461 U.S. 499 (1983) (applying harmless error doctrine to a *Griffin* violation).

[44] 485 U.S. 25 (1988).

[45] *Id.* at 28.

opportunity to testify is a fair response to a claim made by defendant or his counsel, we think there is no violation of the privilege.[46]

In short, it is one thing to use the Fifth Amendment as a shield; it is quite another thing to use it as a sword.

[B] Jury Instructions

Notwithstanding the accused's right to not take the witness stand, jurors frequently wonder why a silent defendant has not come forward and probably penalize a defendant for this silence. In an attempt to overcome that reaction, a defendant has the right, upon request, to an instruction explaining the defendant's constitutional right to remain silent and admonishing the jury not to speculate on the defendant's reasons for not testifying. As the Supreme Court has noted: "The defendant is not compelled to testify and the fact that he does not cannot be used as an inference of guilt and should not prejudice him in any way."[47]

Some defense attorneys, however, believe that the instruction is more harmful than helpful since it calls the jurors' attention to the defendant's silence. Nonetheless, it is not error to give the instruction over the defendant's objection.[48]

An adverse inference may be drawn against a non-testifying party in a civil proceeding.[49]

§ 43.06   Other Witness's Privilege

In contrast to the accused, other witnesses may be subpoenaed and compelled to testify at trial. These witnesses, however, retain the privilege — in both criminal and civil trials.[50]

A witness may refuse to answer any question that would subject that witness to criminal liability.[51] The test is whether there is an appreciable risk that the answer could subject the witness to criminal prosecution, state or federal.[52] The privilege "embraces those [answers] which would furnish

---

[46] *Id.* at 32.

[47] Carter v. Kentucky, 450 U.S. 288, 289 (1981).

[48] Lakeside v. Oregon, 435 U.S. 333 (1978).

[49] Baxter v. Palmigiano, 425 U.S. 308, 318 (1976) (privilege against self-incrimination does not forbid drawing adverse inferences from an inmate's failure to testify at his own disciplinary proceedings; privilege "does not preclude the inference where the privilege is claimed by a party to a civil cause"); Pagel, Inc. v. Securities and Exchange Comm'n, 803 F.2d 942, 946 (1986).

[50] *See supra* § 43.03.

[51] Counselman v. Hitchcock, 142 U.S. 547 (1892).

[52] In Murphy v. Waterfront Comm'n, 378 U.S. 52 (1964), the Court rejected the "separate sovereign" doctrine, ruling that a witness is entitled to assert the Fifth Amendment in federal grand jury proceeding if the answer would subject the witness to state prosecution. The privilege protects "a state witness against incrimination under federal as well as state law and a federal witness against incrimination under state as well as federal law." *Id.* at 78. The separate sovereign doctrine had permitted a witness to be "whipsawed into incriminating himself under both state and federal law." *Id.* at 55.

a link in the chain of evidence needed to prosecute the claimant for a . . . crime."[53] The privilege, however, must be asserted to each specific question;[54] the trial court may separate incriminating questions from those that are not incriminating and require the witness to answer the latter. Moreover, when the witness "asserts the privilege, questioning need not cease, except as to the particular subject to which the privilege has been addressed."[55]

Generally, a party may not call a witness for the sole purpose of having the witness claim the privilege in front of the jury.[56]

§ 43.07 Key Points

There are several components to the Self-Incrimination Clause: (1) *compulsion* to provide (2) *testimonial* evidence (3) that would subject the person to *criminal liability*.

Compulsion requirement. A subpoena requiring a person to testify at trial is the paradigmatic example of compulsion within the meaning of the Fifth Amendment.

Criminal liability requirement. Two points deserve attention. First, it is the exposure to possible criminal liability, rather than the forum in which the privilege is asserted, that is determinative. Thus, a witness can assert the privilege in civil trials, congressional hearings, or administrative proceedings. Second, immunity is used to elicit testimony from witnesses who assert the privilege against self-incrimination. In effect, immunity takes away the Fifth Amendment privilege because persons receiving immunity can no longer "incriminate" themselves.

---

[53] Hoffman v. United States, 341 U.S. 479, 486 (1951) (witness properly refused to answer questions about current occupation and contacts with fugitives). *See also* Malloy v. Hogan, 378 U.S. 1 (1964).

[54] United States v. Mandujano, 425 U.S. 564, 572 (1976) ("Under settled principles, the Fifth Amendment does not confer an absolute right to decline to respond in a grand jury inquiry; the privilege does not negate the duty to testify but simply conditions that duty.").

[55] *Id.* at 581.

[56] *See* United States v. Deutsch, 987 F.2d 878, 883 (2d Cir. 1993) ("The district court has the discretion to prevent a party from calling a witness solely to have him or her invoke the privilege against self-incrimination in front of the jury. Most of the circuits which have addressed this issue have held it not to be error for a district court to bar such a witness from testifying."); United States v. Victor, 973 F.2d 975, 978 (1st Cir. 1992) ("Where the government has sufficient reason to believe that a witness may invoke his or her Fifth Amendment rights in response to questioning, the better practice requires that the prosecutor so inform the court, thus allowing for a voir dire to be conducted out of the presence of the jury to determine 'reliably that the witness will claim the privilege and the extent and validity of the claim.' This is so for the simple reason that the refusal of a witness to answer a specific question, particularly in the context of cross-examination, could lead a jury to draw impermissible inferences from which neither side has a right to benefit. Not every failure to follow this procedure, however, creates reversible error.") (citations omitted); United States v. Johnson, 488 F.2d 1206, 1211 (1st Cir. 1973) (If "a witness intends to claim the privilege as to essentially all questions, the court may, in its discretion, refuse to allow him to take the stand.").

"Testimonial-real" evidence distinction. The Supreme Court has held that the privilege applies to testimonial or communicative evidence, not real or physical evidence. Thus, a person may be compelled to provide specimens of blood, handwriting, fingerprints, voice, dental impressions, and urine without violating the privilege.

Accused's privilege at trial. A defendant in a criminal case cannot be compelled to be a witness by the prosecution. If the defendant voluntarily takes the witness stand in the defense case-in-chief, the privilege against self-incrimination is waived.

Comment upon failure to testify. In *Griffin v. California*, the Supreme Court held that the Fifth Amendment prohibits the use of an accused's failure to testify as evidence of guilt.

Jury instructions. A defendant has the right, upon request, to an instruction explaining the defendant's constitutional right to remain silent and admonishing the jury not to speculate on the defendant's reasons for not testifying.

Other witness's privilege. In contrast to the accused, other witnesses may be subpoenaed and compelled to testify at trial. These witnesses must assert the privilege to each question that would subject them to criminal prosecution. The test is whether there is an appreciable risk that the answer could subject the witness to criminal prosecution, state or federal.

Chapter 44

JUDICIAL NOTICE: FRE 201

§ 44.01 Introduction

In a prosecution for selling liquor on Sunday, the prosecutor must show that the day alleged in the indictment, *e.g.*, May 21, was a Sunday. Producing a calendar, the prosecutor asks the trial court to take *judicial notice* that May 21 was a Sunday in the relevant year.

Judicial notice is a short-cut. The party with the burden of proving an adjudicative fact typically must introduce evidence to establish that fact. If, however, a fact is indisputable, the court may, and in some instances must, accept the fact as established (judicially noticed) and thereby dispense with the requirement of evidentiary proof.

Judicial notice of adjudicative facts serves two functions. First, it expedites the trial, thus conserving both time and expense. Second, it prevents a jury from reaching an absurd result; the jury is precluded from denying the indisputable.[1]

Rule 201 is the only provision in the Federal Rules on judicial notice. It specifies the kinds of facts that are subject to judicial notice as well as the procedural aspects of taking judicial notice.

Caution. The term "judicial notice" is used to describe a number of related but different concepts, and Rule 201 deals only with one of them — judicial notice of *adjudicative facts*. There are two other concepts that need to be understood: (1) judicial notice of law and (2) judicial notice of *legislative facts*.

§ 44.02 Adjudicative & Legislative Facts: FRE 201(a)

Rule 201 applies only to judicial notice of adjudicative facts. The term "adjudicative fact" is used in contradistinction to the term "legislative fact." These terms were coined by Professor Davis.

Adjudicative facts. Davis described adjudicative facts as follows: "[A]djudicative facts are those to which the law is applied in the process of adjudication. They are the facts that normally go to the jury in a jury case."[2] In other words, adjudicative facts are what we normally think of

---

[1] *See* Keeffe, Landis & Shaad, *Sense and Nonsense About Judicial Notice*, 2 Stan. L. Rev. 664, 670 (1950) ("[I]t makes a mockery of a court of justice to permit a jury to accept or reject in accordance with their prejudices a fact capable of exact scientific determination.").

[2] Davis, *Judicial Notice*, 55 Colum. L. Rev. 945, 952 (1955) ("When a court or an agency finds facts concerning the immediate parties — who did what, where, when, how, and with what motive or intent — the court or agency is performing an adjudicative function, and the

when we talk about the "facts of a case."[3] For example, if an accused is charged with grand theft, the prosecution is required to prove that the value of the property was $5,000.00 or more if that is the statutory amount specified for grand theft. The value of the property is an adjudicative fact; it is a "fact of the case" that would normally be decided by a jury.

Legislative facts. In contrast, legislative facts are those facts "which have relevance to legal reasoning and the lawmaking process, whether in the formulation of a legal principle or ruling by a judge or court or in the enactment of a legislative body."[4] According to Davis, when a court "develops law or policy, it is acting legislatively. . . . Legislative facts are those which help the tribunal to determine the content of law and policy and to exercise its judgment or discretion in determining what course of action to take."[5] You have seen legislative facts in every law school class you have taken, although probably not by that name.

Legislative facts, then, are used in lawmaking. Courts, as well as legislatures and administrative agencies, perform a lawmaking function. In developing constitutional principles,[6] interpreting statutes, and creating the common law, courts, of necessity, make factual assumptions — historical, scientific, economic, and political. In this context, judicial notice is a broad concept, rather than a narrow evidentiary rule.[7]

Common law example. The federal drafters cited *Hawkins v. United States*[8] to illustrate judicial notice of legislative facts. In *Hawkins*, the Supreme Court decided to retain the common law testimonial privilege for spouses in criminal cases. The Court's decision rested on a factual assumption: that "[a]dverse testimony given in criminal proceedings would . . . be likely to destroy almost any marriage."[9] This factual assumption had nothing to do with the facts of the case (adjudicative facts); the defendant was charged with a violation of the Mann Act, which proscribes the interstate transportation of a female for immoral purposes. Instead, the Court used the factual assumption quoted above as the basis for a common law evidence rule that it applied in the proceedings.

Constitutional law examples. Constitutional adjudication also frequently rests on legislative facts. For example, in *Turner v. United States*,[10] the

---

facts so determined are conveniently called adjudicative facts."). *See also* Davis, *An Approach to Problems of Evidence in the Administrative Process*, 55 Harv. L. Rev. 364, 402 (1942).

[3] *See* Fed. R. Evid. 201 advisory committee's note ("Adjudicative facts are simply the facts of the particular case.").

[4] Fed. R. Evid. 201 advisory committee's note.

[5] Davis, *Judicial Notice*, 55 Colum. L. Rev. 945, 952 (1955).

[6] *See* Karst, *Legislative Facts in Constitutional Litigation*, 1960 Sup. Ct. Rev. 75.

[7] Roberts, *Preliminary Notes Toward a Study of Judicial Notice*, 52 Cornell L. Q. 210, 236 (1967) ("[J]udicial notice is not a distinct doctrine like the hearsay rule or best evidence; rather, judicial notice is the art of thinking as practiced within the legal system. Indeed, the fundamental error lies in teaching judicial notice as an aspect of Evidence.").

[8] 358 U.S. 74 (1958). This rule was later modified by the Court. *See supra* § 39.02 (spousal testimonial privilege).

[9] *Id.* at 78.

[10] 396 U.S. 398, 408 (1970).

Supreme Court relied on nonrecord facts in deciding whether a criminal presumption of knowledge of illegal importation based on possession of heroin satisfied constitutional standards. The Court upheld the presumption because it concluded that heroin was not produced domestically. To support this factual conclusion, the Court cited numerous sources that were not part of the trial record.[11]

Judicially noticed legislative facts need not be indisputable. The factual assumption about marriages upon which the Court rested its decision in *Hawkins* was debatable. In addition, judicially noticed legislative facts need not be, and frequently are not, supported by evidence in the record. Indeed, such evidence may be totally absent from the record.[12] For example, in *Miranda v. Arizona*,[13] the Supreme Court relied extensively on extra-record facts — texts on police interrogation practices — to support its conclusion that the "process of in-custody interrogation of persons suspected or accused of a crime contains inherently compelling pressures which work to undermine the individual's will to resist and to compel him to speak where he would not otherwise do so freely."[14]

Rule 201 does *not* govern judicial notice of legislative facts.[15] Thus, a court need not comply with the procedural requirements imposed by the rule, such as the opportunity to be heard, when noticing legislative facts. While the distinction between legislative and adjudicative facts may be obvious in many cases, in other cases it is not.[16]

§ 44.03   Types of Facts Subject to Notice: FRE 201(b)

Two kinds of adjudicative facts are subject to judicial notice: (1) facts generally known within the territorial jurisdiction of the trial court; and (2) facts capable of accurate and ready determination by resort to sources

---

[11] The Court relied on previous cases, official reports, and other sources. *Id.* at 407–19 n. 7–38. "[T]he massive statistics cited in the Supreme Court's opinion [in *Turner*] were undoubtedly brought into the case through appellate briefs or by judicial notice." United States v. Gonzalez, 442 F.2d 698, 707 n. 4 (2d Cir. 1971). The presentation of legislative facts in appellate briefs is commonly called the Brandeis-brief technique.

[12] Roberts, *supra* note 7, at 233 ("Courts seen as superlegislatures must be allowed to roam far and wide and must at all costs not be inhibited by any requirement that the facts with which they deal must be either found in the record or attributable to common knowledge or sources of indisputable accuracy. The law, in short, must be seen as a creative process and the rules of judicial notice recast to expedite this creativity."). *See also* Woolhandler, *Rethinking the Judicial Reception of Legislative Facts*, 41 Vand. L. Rev. 111 (1988).

[13] 384 U.S. 436 (1966).

[14] *Id.* at 467. "An understanding of the nature and setting of this in-custody interrogation is essential to our decisions today." *Id.* at 445.

[15] Fed. R. Evid. 201 advisory committee's note ("No rule deals with judicial notice of 'legislative' facts.").

[16] *See* 1 Graham, Handbook of Federal Evidence § 201.1, at 132 (5th ed. 2001) ("[C]onsider the determination of whether cocaine hydrochloride is a derivative of the coca leaf so as to come within the comprehensive Drug Abuse Prevention and Control Act of 1970. Is it a legislative fact in the sense of interpretation of a statute or is it adjudicative in the sense that it clearly and immediately affects the parties?").

whose accuracy cannot be reasonably questioned. Facts that fit these two categories, however, are proper subjects for judicial notice *only* if they are "not subject to reasonable dispute."[17]

[A] Indisputability Requirement

Morgan view. By limiting judicial notice to indisputable facts,[18] Rule 201 adopts Professor Morgan's view of judicial notice, which is based on the judicial function of resolving disputes.[19] For example, in a bail-jumping case the Ninth Circuit ruled that the trial court improperly took judicial notice that the defendant was absent from the jurisdiction for approximately seven months. According to the court, this fact was not indisputable.[20] In another case, the First Circuit upheld a trial court's refusal to judicially notice that "Rastafarians use marijuana as part of their religion" because this fact was not indisputable.[21]

Two consequences follow from Morgan's theory. First, once a fact is judicially noticed by the court, evidence tending to establish or rebut that fact is inadmissible. Second, in civil cases the jury must accept the judicially noticed fact and is so instructed.

Wigmore-Davis view. In contrast to the Morgan theory, the theory of judicial notice advocated by Dean Wigmore[22] and Professor Davis[23] is based on procedural convenience: "Proving facts with evidence takes time and effort. Noticing facts is simpler, easier, and more convenient."[24] Under

---

[17] *See* Fed. R. Evid. 201 advisory committee's note ("A high degree of indisputability is the essential prerequisite.").

[18] *See* Kaggen v. IRS, 71 F.2d 1018, 1020 (2d Cir. 1995) ("That banks send customers monthly statements which inform customers to whom their money was paid and in what amounts is not reasonably subject to dispute. . . ."); United States v. Jones, 29 F.3d 1549, 1553 (11th Cir. 1994) ("In order for a fact to be judicially noticed under Rule 201(b), indisputability is a prerequisite."); Hardy v. Johns-Manville Sales Corp., 681 F.2d 334, 347–48 (5th Cir. 1982) ("[J]udicial notice applies to self-evident truths that no reasonable person could question, truisms that approach platitudes or banalities. The proposition that asbestos causes cancer, because it is inextricably linked to a host of disputed issues — e.g., can mesothelioma arise without exposure to asbestos, is the sale of asbestos insulation products definitely linked to carcinoma in the general population, was this manufacturer reasonably unaware of the asbestos hazards in 1964 — is not at present so self-evident a proposition as to be subject to judicial notice."); United States v. Bourque, 541 F.2d 290, 296 (1st Cir. 1976) (whether IRS ever loses tax returns is not a subject for judicial notice).

[19] Morgan, *Judicial Notice*, 57 Harv. L. Rev. 269, 273 (1944) (A court "cannot adjust legal relations among members of society and thus fulfill the sole purpose of its creation if it permits the parties to take issue on, and thus secure results contrary to, what is so notoriously true as not to be the subject of reasonable dispute, or what is capable of immediate and accurate demonstration by resort to sources of indisputable accuracy easily accessible to men in the situation of members of the court.").

[20] United States v. Wilson, 631 F.2d 118, 119–20 (9th Cir. 1980).

[21] United States v. Simon, 842 F.2d 552, 555 (1st Cir. 1988).

[22] *See* 9 Wigmore, Evidence § 2567 (3d ed. 1940).

[23] Davis, *Judicial Notice*, 1969 Law & Social Order 513.

[24] *Id.* at 515 ("The ultimate principle is that extra-record facts should be assumed whenever

this theory, facts that are probably true may be judicially noticed, even though they are not indisputable. Moreover, evidence controverting a judicially noticed fact is admissible,[25] and the jury is not bound to accept the judicially noticed fact.[26]

As noted above, Rule 201 reflects the Morgan view, limiting judicial notice to indisputable facts. The rule deviates from the Morgan theory in one respect. Division (g) of the rule provides that in criminal cases the jury shall be instructed that it is not bound to accept a judicially noticed fact.[27]

[B] "Generally Known Facts"

An adjudicative fact, not subject to reasonable dispute, may be judicially noticed if generally known.[28] Facts in this category need only be generally known within the "territorial jurisdiction" of the court. Knowledge within a trade or subclass is not subject to notice.[29]

United States v. Bello[30] involved the fact that a particular prison was within the territorial jurisdiction of the United States. The First Circuit ruled that judicial notice of this fact was improper:

> Although the label "federal penitentiary" might suggest to the average person that MDC-Guaynabo is under the jurisdiction of the United States, it is unlikely that the "reasonable person" has any familiarity with MDC-Guaynabo at all, let alone its jurisdictional status. Hence, Rule 201(b)(1) cannot supply a basis for judicially noticing the jurisdictional fact in this case.[31]

The category of generally known facts includes many kinds of information. Courts have taken judicial notice: (1) "that a social security check is sent out by first class mail and bears on its envelope not only a return address but a written direction that if the addressee is deceased it is to be returned to the sender"[32] ; (2) "that federal officers do not patrol the interstate highways or the streets en route; there are no federal jails in the states; and committing magistrates are conveniently available"[33] ; (3)

---

it is convenient to assume them, except that convenience should always yield to the requirement of procedural fairness that parties should have an opportunity to meet in the appropriate fashion all facts that influence the disposition of the case.").

[25] *See* 9 Wigmore, Evidence § 2567, at 535 (3d ed. 1940) ("[T]he opponent is not prevented from disputing the matter by evidence.").

[26] *See also* McNaughton, *Judicial Notice — Excerpts Relating to the Morgan-Wigmore Controversy*, 14 Vand. L. Rev. 779 (1961).

[27] *See infra* § 44.04[D] (jury instructions).

[28] Sundry labels have been used to describe this category. *See* 9 Wigmore, Evidence § 2571(1) (3d ed. 1940) ("notorious" facts); Unif. R. Evid. 9(1) (1953) ("universally known" facts).

[29] *See* United States v. Bramble, 641 F.2d 681, 683 (9th Cir. 1981) (that twenty-one marijuana plants make up a commercial crop for inference of "intent to sell").

[30] 194 F.3d 18, 22 (1st Cir. 1999).

[31] *Id.* at 23.

[32] Ross v. United States, 374 F.2d 97, 103 (8th Cir. 1967).

[33] United States v. Chadwick, 415 F.2d 167, 171 (10th Cir. 1969).

"that 7:30 P.M. in July . . . is daytime in Dallas during Daylight Savings Time"[34] ; (4) "that contraband is smuggled into custodial institutions";[35] that Southwestern Bell Telephone System is involved in interstate communications[36] ; (5) that "New York has no firearms manufacturers";[37] and (6) that the United States has authority over Puerto Rico.[38]

In addition, federal courts have cited Rule 201 when judicially noticing that "Citibank . . . is an FDIC-insured bank and . . . engages in interstate and foreign commerce";[39] that the Klan "is a white hate group";[40] and that dietary laws are important to orthodox Judaism.[41] Courts have also taken judicial notice of foreign events.[42]

Personal knowledge of judge. "Generally known facts," for purposes of Rule 201(b), must be distinguished from facts that a judge personally knows; only the former are properly the subject of judicial notice.[43] For example, in *Government of Virgin Islands v. Gereau,*[44] the Third Circuit reversed a conviction because the trial judge relied on his "personal subjective belief about the needs and motives"[45] of a witness whose credibility was an issue in a motion for a new trial.

---

[34] United States v. Wilson, 451 F.2d 209, 214 (5th Cir. 1971).

[35] Mathis v. Superior Court, 105 Cal. Rpt. 126, 127 (App. 1972).

[36] United States v. Deckard, 816 F.2d 426, 428 (8th Cir. 1987).

[37] United States v. Ramirez, 910 F.2d 1069, 1071 (2d Cir. 1990).

[38] United States v. Rodriquez, 803 F.2d 318, 321 (7th Cir. 1986).

[39] United States v. Helgesen, 513 F. Supp. 209, 219 (E.D.N.Y. 1981), *aff'd and remanded,* 669 F.2d 69 (2d Cir. 1982).

[40] United Klans of Am. v. McGovern, 453 F. Supp. 836, 839 (N.D. Ala. 1978), *aff'd,* 621 F.2d 152 (5th Cir. 1980). *See also* Marshall v. Bramer, 828 F.2d 355, 358 (6th Cir. 1987) ("The nature of the Ku Klux Klan, and its historic commitment to violence against blacks in particular, is generally known throughout this country and is not subject to reasonable dispute.").

[41] United States v. Kahane, 396 F. Supp. 687, 692 (E.D.N.Y.), *modified,* 527 F.2d 492 (2d Cir. 1975).

[42] *E.g.,* Gafoor v. INS, 231 F.3d 645, 656 (9th Cir. 2000) ("We do not exceed our authority by taking judicial notice of dramatic foreign developments. . . ."); Quinn v. Robinson, 783 F.2d 776, 797 n.18 (9th Cir. 1986) ("American courts generally will take judicial notice of a state of uprising."); Ivezaj v. INS, 84 F.3d 215, 219 (6th Cir. 1996) (taking judicial notice of persecution of Albanians by Serbs); Kaczmarczyk v. INS, 933 F.2d 588, 594 n. 4 (7th Cir. 1991) ("We exercise our discretion to take judicial notice of further changes in Polish politics that occurred between the time of the BIA's decision and our review."); Dawood-Haio v. INS, 800 F.2d 90, 91(6th Cir. 1986) (taking judicial notice of the Iran-Iraq war).

[43] *See* 9 Wigmore, Evidence § 2569(a), at 539 (3d ed. 1940) ("There is a real but elusive line between the judge's personal knowledge as a private man and [those] matters of which he takes judicial notice as a judge. The latter does not necessarily include the former; as a judge, indeed, he may have to ignore what he knows as a man, and contrariwise.").

[44] 523 F.2d 140 (3d Cir. 1975).

[45] *Id.* at 147. Another finding of the trial judge "was based solely on the judge's personal knowledge of the soundproofing in his chambers." *Id.* at 148. *See also* United States v. Sorrells, 714 F.2d 1522, 1527 n.6 (11th Cir. 1983) ("The trial judge's conclusion that his personal knowledge could cure an otherwise defective affidavit is contrary to Fed. R. Evid. 201(b)."); Furtado v. Bishop, 604 F.2d 80, 90 (1st Cir. 1979) (trial judge's knowledge of witness as a "very honorable man" not a proper subject of judicial notice).

Jury notice. Judicial notice of generally known facts should also be distinguished from what is known as "jury knowledge" — the common knowledge and experience that jurors bring with them and use in deciding cases.[46]

[C] "Accurately & Readily Determinable" Facts

Historical, geographic, physical, political, statistical, and scientific facts have all been noticed as verifiably certain.[47] Courts have taken judicial noticed that: (1) "human blood groupings are . . . not subject to change"[48] ; (2) "cocaine is a derivative of coca leaves"[49] ; (3) "the United States was at war" on certain dates[50] ; (4) "the moon on that night [when the crime was committed] rose at 10:57 P.M."[51] ; and (5) "Fort Rucker is "a military enclave under Title 18."[52]

Court records. Courts have also judicially noticed court records.[53] For example, the Fifth Circuit has stated: "[T]he trial judge was warranted in

---

[46] *See* Mansfield, *Jury Notice*, 74 Geo. L.J. 395 (1985); Morgan, *Judicial Notice*, 57 Harv. L. Rev. 269, 272 (1944).

[47] *See generally* United States v. Bello, 194 F.3d 18, 23 (1st Cir. 1999) ("Indeed, 'geography has long been peculiarly susceptible to judicial notice for the obvious reason that geographic locations are facts which are not generally controversial and thus it is within the general definition contained in Fed.R.Evid. 201(b). . . .' "); Shahar v. Bowers, 120 F.3d 211, 214 (11th Cir. 1997) ("For example, the kinds of things about which courts ordinarily take judicial notice are (1) scientific facts: for instance, when does the sun rise or set; (2) matters of geography: for instance, what are the boundaries of a state; or (3) matters of political history: for instance, who was president in 1958."); United States v. Southard, 700 F.2d 1, 25 (1st Cir. 1983) (court may judicially notice a fact such as the driving time between New Haven and Rhode Island); Newman v. Village of Hinsdale, 592 F. Supp. 1307, 1309 (N.D. Ill. 1984) (judicial notice of amount of snow fall on a particular day based on records of the National Oceanic and Atmospheric Administration), *aff'd,* 767 F.2d 925 (7th Cir. 1995).

[48] Graves v. Beto, 301 F. Supp. 264, 265 (D.C. Tex. 1969), *aff'd,* 424 F.2d 524 (5th Cir. 1970). *See also* Hines v. Secretary of Health & Human Servs., 940 F.2d 1518, 1526 (Fed. Cir. 1991) (incubation period of measles is the type of well-known medical fact subject to judicial notice).

[49] United States v. Umentum, 401 F. Supp. 746, 748 (E.D. Wis. 1975), *aff'd,* 547 F.2d 987 (7th Cir. 1976). *Accord* United States v. Gould, 536 F.2d 216, 220 (8th Cir. 1976).

[50] Seebach v. United States, 262 F. 885, 888 (8th Cir. 1919).

[51] People v. Mayes, 45 P. 860, 862 (Cal. 1896).

[52] United States v. Benson, 495 F.2d 475, 482 (5th Cir. 1974). *See also* United States v. Piggie, 622 F.2d 486, 487 (10th Cir. 1980)) (Leavenworth Penitentiary within special territorial jurisdiction of U.S.); United States v. Anderson, 528 F.2d 590, 591–92 (5th Cir. 1976) (judicial notice that Federal Correction Institute at Tallahassee, Florida, is within special territorial jurisdiction of U.S.).

[53] *E.g.,* Opoka v. INS, 94 F.3d 392, 394 (7th Cir. 1996) ("[I]t is a well-settled principle that the decision of another court or agency, including the decision of an administrative law judge, is a proper subject of judicial notice."); Colonial Penn Ins. Co. v. Coil, 887 F.2d 1236, 1239 (4th Cir. 1989) (judicial notice of guilty pleas in related criminal case); United States v. Estep, 760 F.2d 1060, 1063 (10th Cir. 1985) (judicial notice of court records of prior proceedings in the same case); *See also* United States v. Aluminum Co., 148 F.2d 416, 446 (2d Cir. 1945) (L. Hand, J.) (judicial notice of congressional committee report as an official statement proper but not truth of statement contained therein).

taking judicial notice of immutable geographic and physical facts adjudi-cated in a previous proceeding."[54] In another case, the Third Circuit upheld the trial court's judicial notice of a defendant's prior conviction for purposes of impeachment.[55]

Scientific facts. Courts have also taken judicial notice of scientific facts.[56] The principles underlying intoxication tests, fingerprint comparisons, and firearms identification have all been judicially noticed.[57] According to the Supreme Court, "[T]heories that are so firmly established as to have attained the status of scientific law, such as the laws of thermodynamics, properly are subject to judicial notice under Fed. Rule Evid. 201."[58]

Authoritative sources. In deciding whether a fact is capable of ready and accurate determination, a court may rely only upon sources "whose accuracy cannot reasonably be questioned." The source itself need not be admissible in evidence.[59] Almanacs, encyclopedias, and other standard reference works are acceptable, so long as the source is recognized as authoritative and reliable. According to Wigmore, "any source whatever that suffices to satisfy [the judge's] mind in making a ruling" is acceptable.[60]

§ 44.04 Procedural Issues

[A] Discretionary & Mandatory Notice: FRE 201(c) & (d)

Rule 201(c) permits a court to take judicial notice sua sponte, notwith-standing the absence of a request by either party.[61] Rule 201(d) requires

---

[54] United States v. Alvarado, 519 F.2d 1133, 1135 (5th Cir. 1975).

[55] Government of Virgin Islands v. Testamark, 528 F.2d 742, 743 (3d Cir. 1976).

[56] *See supra* § 24.04 (reliability of scientific evidence). Judicial notice of scientific principles, however, usually arises in the context of decisions concerning the admissibility of evidence. Rule 104(a) excepts admissibility decisions from the Rules of Evidence (except the law of privilege); thus, Rule 201 would not apply to these situations.

[57] *See* 1 Giannelli & Imwinkelried, Scientific Evidence ch. 1 (3d ed. 1999).

[58] Daubert v. Merrell Dow Pharm., Inc., 509 U.S. 579, 593 n. 11 (1993).

[59] *See* Fed. R. Evid. 104(a). *See also* Morgan, Basic Problems of Evidence 10 (1961) ("If the issue is whether a matter falls within the scope of judicial notice, neither judge nor counsel will be hampered by the rules of evidence.").

[60] 9 Wigmore, Evidence § 2568a, at 538 (3d ed. 1940) (listing "official records, encyclopedias, any books or articles" as examples). *See also* Cal. Evid. Code § 454(a)(1) ("Any source of pertinent information, including the advice of persons learned in the subject matter, may be consulted or used. . . ."); United States v. Bello, 194 F.3d 18, 24 (1st Cir. 1999) ("The government submitted to the court official government maps, letters from Army officials, and various legislative acts of Puerto Rico, all tending to show that MDC-Guaynabo was within the jurisdiction of the United States. . . . To be sure, the trial court's decision to judicially recognize a fact upon which testimony had already been presented and subjected to cross-examination before the jury was unusual. Nonetheless, the existence of independent and undisputed documentary evidence in the form of government maps, official letters, and public laws provided a sufficient basis for judicial notice under Rule 201(b)(2), irrespective of Lopez's testimony.").

[61] *See also* United States v. Mentz, 840 F.2d 315, 322 (6th Cir. 1988) (When a trial court

the court to take judicial notice if one of the parties so requests. If the fact is one capable of accurate and ready determination, the requesting party must also supply the court with sources whose accuracy cannot reasonably be questioned.[62]

[B] Opportunity to be Heard: FRE 201(e)

Rule 201(e) entitles a party, upon timely request, to an opportunity to be heard concerning both the propriety of taking judicial notice and the tenor of the matter to be noticed. The hearing should be held outside the presence of the jury.[63] When there is no advance indication that judicial notice will be taken, the parties are entitled to be heard after the court has judicially noticed the fact.[64]

The provision requiring the opportunity to be heard is constitutionally mandated by due process. The federal drafters wrote: "Basic considerations of procedural fairness demand an opportunity to be heard on the propriety of taking judicial notice and the tenor of the matter noticed."[65]

---

takes judicial notice, "there will normally be a record of this. . . . This facilitates intelligent appellate review, and is particularly necessary when the fact noticed is an essential element of the crime charged"); Colonial Leasing Co. Of New England v. Logistics Control Group Int'l., 762 F.2d 454, 459 (5th Cir. 1985) ("Care should be taken by the court to identify the fact it is noticing, and its justification for doing so.").

[62] See United States v. Sorenson, 504 F.2d 406, 410 (7th Cir. 1974) ("[T]he government . . . supplied the court with no information regarding the fact to be noticed."). See also Morgan, supra note 19, at 274–75 ("Whether or not the truth of a given proposition is disputable may itself be the subject of dispute among reasonable men.").

[63] See Fed. R. Evid. 103(c) & 104(c).

[64] "No formal scheme of giving notice is provided. An adversely affected party may learn in advance that judicial notice is in contemplation, either by virtue of being served with a copy of a request by another party under subdivision (d) that judicial notice be taken, or through an advance indication by the judge. Or he may have no advance notice at all. The likelihood of the latter is enhanced by the frequent failure to recognize judicial notice as such. And in the absence of advance notice, a request made after the fact could not in fairness be considered untimely." Fed. R. Evid. 201 advisory committee's note. See also United States v. Garcia, 672 F.2d 1349, 1356 n. 9 (11th Cir. 1982) ("Ordinarily, when a judge takes judicial notice of a fact other than at the request of a party (i.e. 'discretionary judicial notice'), he should notify the parties that he is doing so and afford them an opportunity to be heard. . . . Indeed, where failure to do so deprives an accused in a criminal trial of knowledge of the evidence on which he is being convicted and of an opportunity to challenge the facts relied on, due process requires that the defendant be informed.").

[65] Fed. R. Evid 201 advisory committee's note. More forceful language is found in Garner v. Louisiana, 368 U.S. 157, 173 (1961): "[U]nless an accused is informed at the trial of the facts of which the court is taking judicial notice, not only does he not know upon what evidence he is being convicted, but, in addition, he is deprived of any opportunity to challenge the deductions drawn from such notice or to dispute the notoriety or truth of the facts allegedly relied upon. Moreover, there is no way by which an appellate court may review the facts and law of a case and intelligently decide whether the findings of the lower court are supported by the evidence where that evidence is unknown. Such an assumption would be a denial of due process." See also Ohio Bell Tel. Co. v. Public Util. Comm'n, 301 U.S. 292 (1937).

[C] Time of Taking Judicial Notice: FRE 201(f)

A court may take judicial notice of adjudicative facts at any time during the proceeding — *e.g.,* motions for directed verdicts, motions to dismiss for failure to state a claim upon which relief can be granted, or motions for summary judgment.

Appeals. Judicial notice may also be taken on appeal.[66] An important limitation on this use of judicial notice is imposed on criminal appeals. Where no evidence on an ultimate fact (essential element) has been introduced at trial, an appellate court may not supply the missing fact on appeal through the use of judicial notice. The Court has observed: "To extend the doctrine of judicial notice to the length pressed by the respondent would require us to allow the prosecution to do through argument to this Court what it is required by due process to do at the trial, and would be 'to turn the doctrine into a pretext for dispensing with a trial.'"[67] Other courts have echoed this view.[68]

This issue is not limited to criminal cases. The Fifth Circuit has ruled that taking judicial notice after trial in a civil case is improper if it deprives a party of the opportunity to adduce evidence on a critical fact placed in issue by the court's action.[69]

[D] Jury Instructions: FRE 201(g)

Rule 201(g) governs jury instructions of judicially noticed facts. In civil cases, the court must instruct the jury "to accept as conclusive any fact

---

[66] *E.g.,* United States v. Herrera-Ochoa, 245 F.3d 495, 501(5th Cir. 2001) ("An appellate court may take judicial notice of facts, even if such facts were not noticed by the trial court.").

[67] Garner v. Louisiana, 368 U.S. 157, 173 (1961) (quoting *Ohio Bell Tel. Co.,* 301 U.S. at 302).

[68] United States v. Dior, 671 F.2d 351, 358 n. 11 (9th Cir. 1982) (government failed to enter Canadian-American exchange rate into evidence to establish value of transported property):

> [T]o take judicial notice of an adjudicative fact after a jury's discharge in a criminal case would cast the court in the role of a fact-finder and violate defendant's Sixth Amendment right to trial by jury . . . Indeed, for a trial court (in a post-verdict motion) or an appellate court to take judicial notice of an adjudicative fact in a criminal case would frustrate the policies Congress sought to achieve in providing in F.R.Evid. 201(g) that a jury is not required to accept as conclusive a judicially noticed fact. These policies are to preserve the jury's traditional prerogative, in a criminal case, to ignore even uncontroverted facts in reaching a verdict and to prevent the trial court from violating the spirit of the Sixth Amendment . . . by directing a partial verdict as to facts.

See also United States v. Jones, 580 F.2d 219, 224 (6th Cir. 1978) ("As enacted by Congress, Rule 201(g) plainly contemplates that the jury in a criminal case shall pass upon facts which are judicially noticed. This it could not do if this notice were taken for the first time . . . on appeal.") (status of phone company as "common carrier" not established at trial).

[69] Colonial Leasing Co. v. Logistics Control Group Int'l, 762 F.2d 454, 461 (5th Cir. 1985) ("[W]hen Logistics declined to produce evidence, it relied on Colonial's failure to establish its prima facie case. When the district court subsequently took notice of the only fact necessary to complete Colonial's prima facie proof, Logistics was deprived of the opportunity to adduce evidence on a critical fact.").

judicially noticed." Criminal prosecutions, however, are treated differently. Rule 201(g) directs the court to instruct the jury in a criminal case that it "may, but is not required to, accept as conclusive any fact judicially noticed."[70]

Congress added the provision on jury instructions in criminal cases. According to the House Judiciary Committee Report, adoption of this provision was based on the belief that a "mandatory instruction to a jury in a criminal case to accept as conclusive any fact judicially noticed is inappropriate because [it is] contrary to the spirit of the Sixth Amendment right to jury trial."[71] In effect, judicial notice operates as a permissive inference in a criminal case; the jury may, but need not, find the judicially noticed fact. There is some case support for this position,[72] but there is also a contrary view.[73]

§ 44.05 Criminal Cases

Several unique issues concerning judicial notice arise in criminal cases. As noted in the previous section, the jury instructions in criminal and civil cases are different. Rule 201, however, specifically resolves this issue. Two other issues are not explicitly addressed: (1) whether a trial court may take judicial notice of an ultimate fact or element of a crime, and (2) whether a defendant in a criminal prosecution may introduce rebuttal evidence.

Elements of offense. By its own terms, Rule 201 seems to permit a court to take judicial notice of all adjudicative facts not subject to reasonable dispute, including ultimate facts. Some courts, however, have indicated that judicial notice of an essential element is improper.[74] However, other courts

---

[70] *See* United States v. Bello, 194 F.3d 18, 24 (1st Cir. 1999) (Trial court instructed the jury as follows: "As with any fact presented in the case, however, the final decision whether or not to accept it is for you to make and you are not required to agree with me."); United States v. Dickered, 816 F.2d 426, 428 (8th Cir. 1987).

[71] H.R. Rep. No. 650, 93d Cong., 1st Sess. (1973), reprinted in [1974] U.S.C.C.A.N. 7075, 7080.

[72] In State v. Lawrence, 234 P.2d 600 (Utah 1951), the prosecution failed to introduce evidence to establish that the value of a car exceeded the minimum statutory amount ($50.00) for grand larceny. Instead, at the prosecutor's request, the court took judicial notice of the value of the car and instructed the jury that the car had a value in excess of $50. In reversing, the appellate court reasoned: " 'The provision of our State Constitution which grants accused persons the right to a trial by jury extends to each and all of the facts which must be found to be present to constitute the crime charged, and such right may not be invaded by the presiding judge indicating to the jury that any of such facts are established by the evidence.' . . . If a court can take one important element of an offense from the jury and determine the facts for them because such facts seems [sic] plain enough to him, then which element cannot be similarly taken away, and where would the process stop?" *Id.* at 603 (quoting State v. Estrada, 227 P.2d 247, 248 (Utah 1951).

[73] A number of states have rejected this view, providing that the jury in criminal cases is bound by judicially noticed facts. *E.g.,* Del. R. Evid. 201(g); Me. R. Evid. 201(g); N.D. R. Evid. 201(g). "It would be as absurd to allow jurors to consider, for example, on the basis of their individual recollection or speculation, whether December 4, 1972, actually fell on a Monday as the court had instructed them." Me. R. Evid. 201 advisor's note.

[74] *See* United States v. Herrera-Ochoa, 245 F.3d 495, 502 (5th Cir. 2001) ("Taking judicial

have noticed facts about geography and distances, which are jurisdictional facts.[75]

Rebuttal evidence. Another issue concerns the accused's right to introduce rebuttal evidence. There is little dispute that such evidence is inadmissible in civil cases.[76] Nevertheless, the congressional change in the criminal jury instruction, Rule 201(g), could be interpreted to recognize a right to offer rebuttal evidence to the jury in criminal cases.[77] For example, the Sixth Circuit has ruled that "in criminal cases, the parties may contest facts judicially noticed."[78] The contrary view is that "the right of jury trial does not extend to matters which are beyond reasonable dispute"[79] and "accepting what [is] plainly true could not abridge any Sixth Amendment right to confront witnesses."[80]

§ 44.06 Judicial Notice of Law

Rule 201 is limited to judicial notice of adjudicative facts. There is no provision in the Rules of Evidence that governs judicial notice of law. According to the drafters, "the manner in which law is fed into the judicial process is never a proper concern of the rules of evidence but rather the rules of procedure."[81]

The term "judicial notice of law" can be understood only from an historical perspective. The trial judge is responsible for finding the applicable law to be applied in the case. This law is not subject to proof. Accordingly, it became commonplace to speak of this judicial knowledge of law by using judicial notice terminology: "A trial judge must take judicial notice of the

---

notice of the trial court record arguably infringes on Herrera's Sixth Amendment right to confront witnesses. . . . Taking judicial notice in this case of an essential element of the crime, however, potentially infringes on Herrera's right to have each element proved beyond a reasonable doubt.").

[75] *E.g.,* United States v. Deckard, 816 F.2d 426, 428 (8th Cir. 1987) (trial court judicially noticed interstate character of Southwestern Bell Telephone System); United States v. Rodriquez, 803 F.2d 318, 321 (7th Cir. 1986) (trial court took judicial notice of United States authority over Puerto Rico).

[76] Fed. R. Evid. 201 advisory committee's note.

[77] United States v. Horn, 185 F. Supp. 2d 530, 549 n. 34 (D. Md. 2002) ("Implicitly, the rule would permit a defendant in a criminal case to offer evidence to rebut any adjudicative fact noticed by the Court. Thus, if a Court took judicial notice of the reliability and general acceptance of the HGN test, the defendant initially could object to it doing so under Rule 201(e).").

[78] United States v. Garland, 991 F.2d 328, 333 (6th Cir. 1993) (court took judicial notice of existence, not truthfulness, of findings of facts by foreign court). Some commentators have argued that the exclusion of evidence rebutting a judicially noticed fact violates the defendant's rights to confrontation and jury trial. Comment, *The Presently Expanding Concept of Judicial Notice,* 13 Vill. L. Rev. 528, 541–50 (1968).

[79] Fed. R. Evid. 201 advisory committee's note. 51 F.R.D. 335 (1971) (revised draft). The provision to which this section of the Note refers was subsequently changed by Congress.

[80] United States v. Alvarado, 519 F.2d 1133, 1135 (5th Cir. 1975) (court may judicially notice "immutable geographic and physical facts adjudicated in a previous proceeding").

[81] Fed. R. Evid. 201 advisory committee's note.

domestic law of the jurisdiction of which he is a judicial officer."[82] The assumption of judicial knowledge of law, however, generally did not extend to the laws of other states and foreign countries (laws of another forum). These were initially treated as questions of fact to be pleaded and proved like other facts. Over time, however, the law changed and viewed the law of another forum as an issue of "law" and not fact. Under this view, this topic is not controlled by the rules of evidence, but rather by the rules of procedure.

Judicial notice of law is governed by the Rules of Civil and Criminal Procedure.[83] Some states, however, include provisions on judicial notice of law in the rules of evidence.[84]

§ 44.07 Key Points

Rule 201 applies only to judicial notice of adjudicative facts. The term "adjudicative fact" is used in contradistinction to the term "legislative fact." Adjudicative facts are what we normally think of when we talk about the "facts of a case."

Two kinds of adjudicative facts are subject to judicial notice under Rule 201(b): (1) facts generally known within the territorial jurisdiction of the trial court; and (2) facts capable of accurate and ready determination by resort to sources whose accuracy cannot be reasonably questioned. Facts that fit these two categories, however, are proper subjects for judicial notice *only* if they are "not subject to reasonable dispute."

Generally known facts, for purposes of Rule 201(b), must be distinguished from facts that a judge personally knows; only the former are properly the subject of judicial notice.

Accurate & readily determined facts. Historical, geographic, physical, political, statistical, and scientific facts have all been noticed as verifiably certain. In deciding whether a fact is capable of ready and accurate determination, a court may rely only upon sources "whose accuracy cannot reasonably be questioned." The source itself need not be admissible in evidence.

Procedural issues. Rule 201(c) permits a court to take judicial notice sua sponte. Rule 201(d) requires the court to take judicial notice if one of the parties so requests. Rule 201(e) entitles a party, upon timely request, to an opportunity to be heard concerning both the propriety of taking judicial notice and the tenor of the matter to be noticed. Judicial notice may be taken at any time, including on appeal.

Jury instructions. In civil cases, the court must instruct the jury "to accept as conclusive any fact judicially noticed." In contrast, Rule 201(g) directs

---

[82] Morgan, Basic Problems of Evidence 1 (1962).

[83] Fed. R. Civ. P. 44.1(a); Fed. R. Crim. P. 27.

[84] *E.g.,* Alaska R. Evid. 202; Del. R. Evid. 202; Hawaii R. Evid. 202; Mont. R. Evid. 202; Okla. Stat. Ann. tit. 12, § 2220; Wis. Stat. Ann. § 902.02.

the court to instruct the jury in a criminal case that it "may, but is not required to, accept as conclusive any fact judicially noticed.

Judicial notice of law. There is no provision in the Rules of Evidence that governs judicial notice of law. Judicial notice of law is covered in the rules of procedure.

A diagram based on a syllogism may help distinguish different types of judicial notice: (1) judicial notice of law, (2) judicial notice of adjudicative facts, and (3) judicial notice of legislative facts.

Syllogistic diagram

Major premise (applicable law): (judge's function)	A person who negligently causes harm to another must pay damages.
Minor premise (adjudicative facts): (jury's function)	Defendant negligently harmed plaintiff.
Conclusion (verdict): (jury's function)	Defendant must pay X amount of damages.

The major premise is the judge's responsibility (law-finding function — *i.e.* judicial notice of law). The minor premise and verdict are jury functions. The minor premise involves the facts of the case — *i.e.*, adjudicative facts. If these facts are indisputable, they may be the subject of judicial notice under Rule 201. Judicial notice of law can be distinguished from judicial notice of legislative facts, a "law making" function, which can be considered an aspect of law-finding.

Chapter 45

STIPULATIONS

§ 45.01 Introduction

A stipulation is a voluntary agreement between the opposing parties concerning the disposition of some matter before the court. Stipulations range from informal, impromptu oral concessions made during trial to complicated written agreements developed in the pretrial process. The primary function of a stipulation is to expedite the trial, a goal that has been endorsed in a number of cases.[1] As one court put it: "In this day of crowded dockets and crushing case loads, stipulations should be favored, if not encouraged."[2] Indeed, one of the recognized purposes of pretrial conferences is to encourage stipulations.[3]

Stipulations also are used for tactical reasons. Frequently, defense counsel offers to stipulate in order to minimize the impact of unfavorable evidence, or to eliminate the prosecution's bona fide need to resort to a particular item of damaging evidence such as other-acts evidence offered under Rule 404(b). Thus, counsel may offer to stipulate to: a defendant's prior convictions when they could be established easily by court records;[4] the identity of a seized substance such as heroin to prevent the trial from focusing on the "most damning part of the evidence;"[5] or the cause of death when the prosecutor attempts to introduce gruesome photographs of the victim.[6]

Opposing counsel sometimes offer to stipulate to the qualifications of an expert. These offers are often rejected because the stipulation deprives the jury of information that makes the expert's opinion more persuasive. In *State v. Colwell*,[7] the trial court required the defense counsel to accept the prosecution's offer to stipulate to the qualifications of the defense pathologist. Consequently, the jury was deprived of learning the credentials of the

---

[1] *See* People v. Morris, 285 N.E.2d 247, 250 (Ill. App. 1972) ("[T]he use of a stipulation to waive necessity of proof is an accepted and established, as well as an essential, method of expediting the trial of criminal cases."); State v. Murchinson, 96 S.E.2d 540, 541 (N.C. App. 1973) ("The making of stipulations as to facts about which there can be no dispute is to be encouraged as a proper means of expediting trials.").

[2] James v. State, 305 So. 2d 829, 830 (Fla. App. 1975).

[3] *See* Fed. R. Civ. P. 16(c)(3); Fed. R. Crim. P. 17.1 ("At the conclusion of a conference the court shall prepare and file a memorandum of the matters agreed upon.").

[4] Cox v. State, 513 S.W.2d 798, 801 (Ark. 1974).

[5] People v. Chasco, 80 Cal. Rptr. 667, 669 (App. 1970).

[6] Beagles v. State, 273 So. 2d 796 (Fla. App. 1973); State v. Poe, 441 P.2d 512, 518–19 (Utah 1968) (dissenting opinion).

[7] 790 P.2d 430 (Kan. 1990).

expert, who had a "national reputation" in the field of forensic pathology. In contrast, eleven pages of the transcript were needed to record the qualifications of the prosecution's expert. The Kansas Supreme Court reversed:

> We conclude that an offer by the State to stipulate to the qualifications of an expert witness called by the defendant is merely an offer unless accepted by the defendant. Absent such acceptance, the defendant has the right to present the witness' qualifications to the jury.[8]

There are three types of stipulations: (1) stipulations of fact, (2) stipulations of expected testimony, and (3) stipulations concerning procedural and evidentiary rules.

§ 45.02 Stipulations of Fact

A trial judge will usually accept stipulations of fact between the parties. In an extraordinary case, however, when the purported stipulation of fact is either irrelevant or amounts to a conclusion of law, the judge may reject the stipulation.[9] If the judge accepts the stipulation, the party who has the burden of proof on the stipulated fact is relieved of the responsibility of establishing that fact through the introduction of formal proof. In this respect, a stipulation serves a function similar to that of judicial notice.

After the parties stipulate to a fact and the judge accepts the stipulation, controverting evidence is inadmissible; and the jury will be instructed to accept the fact as established.[10] As one court has remarked, a stipulation is considered "an express waiver . . . conceding for the purposes of the trial the truth . . . of some alleged fact. . . . [A] stipulation of facts when entered into is in lieu of testimony or evidence . . . [It is] conclusive upon both the parties and the tribunal."[11] Moreover, even parties who did not enter into the stipulation may use it as an admission.[12] Stipulations are a type of judicial admission.[13]

---

[8] *Id.* at 434.

[9] *See* United States v. Navarro-Varelas, 541 F.2d 1331, 1334 (9th Cir. 1976) (irrelevant); Houston v. Deshotel, 585 S.W.2d 846, 849 (Tex. Civ. 1979) (legal conclusion).

[10] *See* Guidroz v. Lynaugh, 852 F.2d 832, 838 (5th Cir. 1988) (in summation, the prosecutor improperly urged the jury to ignore a stipulation). *But see* United States v. James, 987 F.2d 648, 655 (9th Cir. 1993) ("[T]here is simply no constitutional requirement that a stipulation be read to the jury in order to remove an undisputed element from the case. No federal court has held that it is prejudicial error for a trial judge to fail to instruct a jury that the parties have stipulated to an element of a crime.").

[11] *See* Faught v. State, 319 N.E.2d 843, 846–47 (Ind. App. 1974) (citations omitted). *Accord* Osborne v. United States, 351 F.2d 111, 120 (8th Cir. 1965) ("Stipulations of fact fairly entered into are controlling and conclusive and courts are bound to enforce them."); Barnes v. State, 354 A.2d 499, 505 (Md. App. 1976) ("Under an agreed statement of facts both State and defense agree as to the ultimate facts. Then the facts are not in dispute, and there can be, by definition, no factual conflict."); Spindell v. State Bar of California, 530 P.2d 168, 173 (Cal. 1975) (parties cannot contradict stipulated facts).

[12] *See* Turner Gas Co. v. Workmen's Comp. Appeals Bd., 120 Cal. Rptr. 663, 666 (App. 1975).

[13] *See supra* § 32.05[B] (evidential & judicial admissions distinguished).

Of course, a party is bound only by the facts specified in the stipulation. For instance, in *State v. Saunders*,[14] the defendant stipulated merely that a government chemist had examined plant material and had found the material to be marijuana. The trial judge erroneously assumed that the defense had stipulated that the marijuana had been sold by the defendant. The judge's instruction conveying that erroneous impression to the jury constituted reversible error.

Counsel may be unwilling to stipulate because a "colorless admission" will often lack the probative force of the available evidence.[15] For this reason, courts often do not require the parties, typically the prosecutor, to accept an offer to stipulate; when a defendant pleads not guilty, "the State [has] the right to prove every element of the crime charged and [is] not obligated to rely on the defendant's stipulation."[16] Similarly, a defendant may reject a codefendant's offer to stipulate.[17]

Nevertheless, there are risks in rejecting a defense offer to stipulate. In *United States v. White*,[18] for example, the defendant "was willing to stipulate at a crucial stage of the trial that he had typed and signed a letter on the same typewriter used to write other letters" involved in a mail fraud scheme.[19] In spite of the offer to stipulate, the government presented a probation officer's testimony to prove that the defendant had typed the letter — a method of proof that revealed the defendant's otherwise inadmissible prior conviction to the jury. In reversing the conviction, the appellate court emphasized that the probation officer's testimony was "unnecessary" in view of the offer to stipulate.[20] Likewise, in *Beagles v. State*,[21] the court held it error to admit gruesome photographs of a murder victim after the defendant "had admitted the victim's death, how her death occurred, her identity and that a bullet went into her brain and did not come out."[22] The court commented: "There was no fact or circumstance in issue which necessitated or justified the admission of the numerous gruesome photographs in question."[23]

As discussed in chapter 9, however, the Supreme Court's opinion in *Old Chief v. United States*[24] suggests that a prosecutor often need not accept a defense stipulation.[25]

---

[14] 241 S.E.2d 351 (N.C. App. 1978).

[15] 9 Wigmore, Evidence § 2591 (3d ed. 1940).

[16] People v. Speck, 242 N.E.2d 208, 221 (Ill. 1968), *rev'd on other grounds*, 403 U.S. 946 (1971). *See also* Juan Alire v. United States, 313 F.2d 31, 34 (10th Cir. 1962); People v. McClellan, 457 P.2d 871, 876 (Cal. 1969).

[17] United States v. Caldwell, 543 F.2d 1333 (D.C. Cir. 1974).

[18] 355 F.2d 909 (7th Cir. 1966).

[19] *Id.* at 911.

[20] *Id.*

[21] 273 So. 2d 796 (Fla. App. 1973).

[22] *Id.* at 799.

[23] *Id.*

[24] 519 U.S. 172 (1997).

[25] *See supra* § 9.05[D][3] (stipulations).

§ 45.03 Stipulations of Expected Testimony

In addition to stipulations of fact, the parties may stipulate to the expected testimony of a witness who will not attend the trial or to the contents of a document that will not be produced at trial. By entering into such an agreement, the parties do not accept the admissibility or factual accuracy of the stipulated testimony: "[W]hen evidence is offered by way of stipulation, there is no agreement as to the facts which the evidence seeks to establish. Such a stipulation only goes to the content of the testimony of a particular witness if he were to appear and testify. The agreement is to what the evidence will be, not to what the facts are."[26]

Hence, by entering into a stipulation of expected testimony, a party is not precluded from raising independent evidentiary objections to the content of the stipulated testimony or from introducing rebuttal evidence.

The problems associated with stipulations of expected testimony are illustrated by *People v. Maurice*,[27] a prosecution for illegally dispensing heroin. "The entire case for the prosecution was contained in a stipulation entered into between the parties."[28] The stipulated testimony, however, failed to show that the drugs analyzed by the state's expert were the same drugs that had been seized from the defendant. Because there was no evidence connecting the analyzed and seized drugs, the appellate court reversed.

§ 45.04 Stipulations Concerning Procedural & Evidentiary Rules

Stipulations also include agreements between the parties about procedural and evidentiary rules. As the Supreme Court has noted, "[e]videntiary stipulations are a valuable and integral part of everyday trial practice. Prior to trial, parties often agree in writing to the admission of otherwise objectionable evidence, either in exchange for stipulations from opposing counsel or for other strategic purposes. . . . During the course of trial, parties frequently decide to waive evidentiary objections, and such tactics are routinely honored by trial judges."[29]

Civil Rule 29 explicitly permits the parties to change discovery procedures by stipulation. In addition, counsel often stipulate to the authenticity of documents under Rule 901, the accuracy of copies of documents under Rule 1001, or the admissibility of evidence. In effect, by stipulating, counsel waives the foundational prerequisites required by the rules of evidence.

Although courts generally favor this type of agreement, they have rejected such stipulations on occasion. The courts often assert that

---

[26] Barnes v. State, 354 A.2d 499, 505 (Md. App. 1976). *See also* Stewart v. State 681 S.W.2d 774 (Tex. App. 1984).

[27] 202 N.E.2d 480 (Ill. 1964).

[28] *Id.* at 481.

[29] United States v. Mezzanatto, 513 U.S. 196, 203 (1995).

stipulations relating to procedure and evidence are not binding on the judge.[30] For example, they have divided over the admissibility of the results of polygraph examinations offered pursuant to a stipulation. Courts excluding the evidence reason that the stipulation does not establish the validity of the polygraph technique; the agreement "does nothing to enhance the reliability of such evidence."[31] In contrast, courts admitting stipulated polygraph results take the position that the parties should control this issue. As one court has noted: "[T]he primary effect of the stipulation is that it operates as a waiver of objection or challenge to the validity of the basic theory of polygraph testing and eliminates the necessity of or the opportunity for the parties to establish a foundation in each case to satisfy the trial court of the basic theory and validity of polygraphs."[32]

§ 45.05　Enforceability of Stipulations

Once the trial judge has accepted a stipulation, both parties generally are entitled to enforcement of the agreement. A party cannot escape the effect of a stipulation simply by retaining new counsel.[33] A trial stipulation can be binding at the later sentencing phase.[34] Further, in many jurisdictions, a stipulation accepted in the first trial is enforceable and binding at a subsequent retrial.[35]

There are special problems with the enforceability of stipulations in criminal cases. In *James v. State*,[36] for instance, the prosecution stipulated before trial that the state would not elicit in-court identification testimony without first affording the defendant an opportunity for a lineup. The appellate court reversed the defendant's conviction because the prosecution breached the agreement. The court's decision rested on policy grounds: "Agreements between counsel must be enforceable if the courts are to retain the respect and confidence of the public."[37]

In exceptional circumstances, the judge may relieve a party from the effects of a stipulation. The judge may do so on the grounds of mistake of fact, mistake of law, fraud, misrepresentation, change of circumstance, excusable neglect, or some special circumstance creating a possibility of manifest injustice.[38] Suppose, for instance, that the stipulation is

---

[30] United States v. Dyer, 752 F.2d 591, 595 (11th Cir. 1985).

[31] Romero v. State, 493 S.W.2d 206, 213 (Tex. Crim. App. 1973).

[32] State v. Dean, 307 N.W.2d 628, 637 (Wis. 1981). *See supra* § 24.08 (polygraph evidence).

[33] Marden v. International Ass'n of Machinists & Aerospace Workers, 576 F.2d 576, 580 (5th Cir. 1978).

[34] United States v. Dailey, 918 F.2d 747, 748 (8th Cir. 1990).

[35] Willis v. State, 374 N.E.2d 520, 522 (Ind. 1978).

[36] 305 So. 2d 829 (Fla. App. 1975).

[37] *Id.* at 830.

[38] Federal Credit Union v. Delbonis, 72 F.3d 921, 928 (1st Cir. 1995) (on the one hand, litigants may not set aside their stipulations at will; on the other hand, a litigant may be relieved of a stipulation made under clear mistake, especially when the mistake concerns a legal conclusion); Marshall v. Emersons Ltd., 593 F.2d 565, 568 (4th Cir. 1979); Commonwealth v. Daniels, 387 A.2d 861, 864 (Pa. 1978).

ambiguous; it excludes statements made by an accused to police officers but does not clearly indicate that it also excludes statements to private persons. The trial judge decides that the stipulation should be construed as reaching those statements as well, but the judge finds that the prosecutor mistakenly assumed that the stipulation did not apply. In this situation, one court indicated that this mistake would constitute good cause warranting relief from the stipulation.[39] To obtain the relief, the prosecutor should file a motion to vacate the stipulation.[40]

§ 45.06   Key Points

A stipulation is a voluntary agreement between the opposing parties concerning the disposition of some matter before the court. Stipulations range from informal, impromptu oral concessions made during trial to complicated written agreements developed in the pretrial process.

There are three types of stipulations: (1) stipulations of fact, (2) stipulations of expected testimony, and (3) stipulations concerning procedural and evidentiary rules.

Generally, an offer to stipulate is just that — an offer. The other side does not have to accept the offer.

---

[39] People v. Williams, 396 N.W.2d 805 (Mich. App. 1986).
[40] *Id.* at 808.

APPENDIX A

FEDERAL RULES OF EVIDENCE

Effective July 1, 1975, as amended to December 1, 2001

ARTICLE I. GENERAL PROVISIONS

Rule 101. Scope

These rules govern proceedings in the courts of the United States and before the United States bankruptcy judges and United States magistrate judges, to the extent and with the exceptions stated in rule 1101.

(As amended Mar. 2, 1987, eff. Oct. 1, 1987; Apr. 25, 1988, eff. Nov. 1, 1988; Apr. 22, 1993, eff. Dec. 1, 1993.).

Rule 102. Purpose and Construction

These rules shall be construed to secure fairness in administration, elimination of unjustifiable expense and delay, and pro-motion of growth and development of the law of evidence to the end that the truth may be ascertained and proccedings justly determined.

Rule 103. Rulings on Evidence

(a) Effect of erroneous ruling.— Error may not be predicated upon a ruling which admits or excludes evidence unless a substantial right of the party is affected, and

(1) Objection.—In case the ruling is one admitting evidence, a timely objection or motion to strike appears of record, stating the specific ground of objection, if the specific ground was not apparent from the context; or

(2) Offer of proof.—In case the ruling is one excluding evidence, the substance of the evidence was made known to the court by offer or was apparent from the context within which questions were asked.

Once the court makes a definitive ruling on the record admitting or excluding evidence, either at or before trial, a party need not renew an objection or offer of proof to preserve a claim of error for appeal.

(b) Record of offer and ruling.—The court may add any other or further statement which shows the character of the evidence, the form in which it was offered, the objection made, and the ruling thereon. It may direct the making of an offer in question and answer form.

(c) Hearing of jury.—In jury cases, proceedings shall be conducted, to the extent practicable, so as to prevent inadmissible evidence from being suggested to the jury by any means, such as making statements or offers of proof or asking questions in the hearing of the jury.

(d) Plain error.—Nothing in this rule precludes taking notice of plain errors affecting substantial rights although they were not brought to the attention of the court.

(As amended Apr. 17, 2000, eff. Dec. 1, 2000.).

Rule 104.   Preliminary Questions

(a) Questions of admissibility generally.—Preliminary questions concerning the qualification of a person to be a witness, the existence of a privilege, or the admissibility of evidence shall be determined by the court, subject to the provisions of subdivision (b). In making its determination it is not bound by the rules of evidence except those with respect to privileges.

(b) Relevancy conditioned on fact.—When the relevancy of evidence depends upon the fulfillment of a condition of fact, the court shall admit it upon, or subject to, the introduction of evidence sufficient to support a finding of the fulfillment of the condition.

(c) Hearing of jury.—Hearings on the admissibility of confessions shall in all cases be conducted out of the hearing of the jury.

Hearings on other preliminary matters shall be so conducted when the interests of justice require, or when an accused is a witness and so requests.

(d) Testimony by accused.—The accused does not, by testifying upon a preliminary matter, become subject to cross-examination as to other issues in the case.

(e) Weight and credibility.—This rule does not limit the right of a party to introduce before the jury evidence relevant to weight or credibility.

(As amended Mar. 2, 1987, eff. Oct. 1, 1987.).

Rule 105.   Limited Admissibility

When evidence which is admissible as to one party or for one purpose but not admissible as to another party or for another purpose is admitted, the court, upon request, shall restrict the evidence to its proper scope and instruct the jury accordingly.

Rule 106.   Remainder of or Related Writings or Recorded Statements

When a writing or recorded statement or part thereof is introduced by a party, an adverse party may require the introduction at that time of any other part or any other writing or recorded statement which ought in fairness to be considered contemporaneously with it.

(As amended Mar. 2, 1987, eff. Oct. 1, 1987.).

ARTICLE II. JUDICIAL NOTICE

Rule 201.   Judicial Notice of Adjudicative Facts

(a) Scope of rule.—This rule governs only judicial notice of adjudicative facts.

(b) Kinds of facts.—A judicially noticed fact must be one not subject to reasonable dispute in that it is either (1) generally known within the territorial jurisdiction of the trial court or (2) capable of accurate and ready determination by resort to sources whose accuracy cannot reasonably be questioned.

(c) When discretionary.—A court may take judicial notice, whether requested or not.

(d) When mandatory.—A court shall take judicial notice if requested by a party and supplied with the necessary information.

(e) Opportunity to be heard.—A party is entitled upon timely request to an opportunity to be heard as to the propriety of taking judicial notice and the tenor of the matter noticed. In the absence of prior notification, the request may be made after judicial notice has been taken.

(f) Time of taking notice.—Judicial notice may be taken at any stage of the proceeding.

(g) Instructing jury.—In a civil action or proceeding, the court shall instruct the jury to accept as conclusive any fact judicially noticed. In a criminal case, the court shall instruct the jury that it may, but is not required to, accept as conclusive any fact judicially noticed.

ARTICLE III. PRESUMPTIONS IN CIVIL ACTIONS AND PROCEEDINGS

Rule 301.   Presumptions in General in Civil Actions and Proceedings

In all civil actions and proceedings not otherwise provided for by Act of Congress or by these rules, a presumption imposes on the party against whom it is directed the burden of going forward with evidence to rebut or meet the presumption, but does not shift to such party the burden of proof in the sense of the risk of non-persuasion, which remains throughout the trial upon the party on whom it was originally cast.

Rule 302. Applicability of State Law in Civil Actions and Proceedings

In civil actions and proceedings, the effect of a presumption respecting a fact which is an element of a claim or defense as to which State law supplies the rule of decision is determined in accordance with State law.

ARTICLE IV. RELEVANCY AND ITS LIMITS

Rule 401. Definition of "Relevant Evidence"

"Relevant evidence" means evidence having any tendency to make the existence of any fact that is of consequence to the determination of the action more probable or less probable than it would be without the evidence.

Rule 402. Relevant Evidence Generally Admissible; Irrelevant Evidence Inadmissible

All relevant evidence is admissible, except as otherwise provided by the Constitution of the United States, by Act of Congress, by these rules, or by other rules prescribed by the Supreme Court pursuant to statutory authority. Evidence which is not relevant is not admissible.

Rule 403. Exclusion of Relevant Evidence on Grounds of Prejudice, Confusion, or Waste of Time

Although relevant, evidence may be excluded if its probative value is substantially outweighed by the danger of unfair prejudice, confusion of the issues, or misleading the jury, or by considerations of undue delay, waste of time, or needless presentation of cumulative evidence.

Rule 404. Character Evidence Not Admissible To Prove Conduct; Exceptions; Other Crimes

(a) Character evidence generally.—Evidence of a person's character or a trait of character is not admissible for the purpose of proving action in conformity therewith on a particular occasion, except:

(1) Character of accused.—Evidence of a pertinent trait of character offered by an accused, or by the prosecution to rebut the same, or if evidence of a trait of character of the alleged victim of the crime is offered by an accused and admitted under Rule 404(a)(2), evidence of the same trait of character of the accused offered by the prosecution;

(2) Character of alleged victim.—Evidence of a pertinent trait of character of the alleged victim of the crime offered by an accused, or by the prosecution to rebut the same, or evidence of a character trait of

peacefulness of the alleged victim offered by the prosecution in a homicide case to rebut evidence that the alleged victim was the first aggressor;

(3) Character of witness.—Evidence of the character of a witness, as provided in rules 607, 608, and 609.

(b) Other crimes, wrongs, or acts.—Evidence of other crimes, wrongs, or acts is not admissible to prove the character of a person in order to show action in conformity therewith. It may, how-ever, be admissible for other purposes, such as proof of motive, opportunity, intent, preparation, plan, knowledge, identity, or absence of mistake or accident, provided that upon request by the accused, the prosecution in a criminal case shall provide reasonable notice in advance of trial, or during trial if the court excuses pretrial notice on good cause shown, of the general nature of any such evidence it intends to introduce at trial.

(As amended Mar. 2, 1987, eff. Oct. 1, 1987; Apr. 30, 1991, eff. Dec. 1, 1991; Apr. 17, 2000, eff. Dec. 1, 2000.).

Rule 405. Methods of Proving Character

(a) Reputation or opinion.—In all cases in which evidence of character or a trait of character of a person is admissible, proof may be made by testimony as to reputation or by testimony in the form of an opinion. On cross-examination, inquiry is allowable into relevant specific instances of conduct.

(b) Specific instances of conduct.—In cases in which character or a trait of character of a person is an essential element of a charge, claim, or defense, proof may also be made of specific instances of that person's conduct.

(As amended Mar. 2, 1987, eff. Oct. 1, 1987.).

Rule 406. Habit; Routine Practice

Evidence of the habit of a person or of the routine practice of an organization, whether corroborated or not and regardless of the presence of eyewitnesses, is relevant to prove that the conduct of the person or organization on a particular occasion was in conformity with the habit or routine practice.

Rule 407. Subsequent Remedial Measures

When, after an injury or harm allegedly caused by an event, measures are taken that, if taken previously, would have made the injury or harm less likely to occur, evidence of the subsequent measures is not admissible to prove negligence, culpable conduct, a defect in a product, a defect in a product's design, or a need for a warning or instruction. This rule does not require the exclusion of evidence of subsequent measures when offered for another pur-pose, such as proving ownership, control, or feasibility of pre-cautionary measures, if controverted, or impeachment.

(As amended Apr. 11, 1997, eff. Dec. 1, 1997.).

Rule 408. Compromise and Offers to Compromise

Evidence of (1) furnishing or offering or promising to furnish, or (2) accepting or offering or promising to accept, a valuable consideration in compromising or attempting to compromise a claim which was disputed as to either validity or amount, is not admissible to prove liability for or invalidity of the claim or its amount. Evidence of conduct or statements made in compromise negotiations is likewise not admissible. This rule does not require the exclusion of any evidence otherwise discoverable merely because it is presented in the course of compromise negotiations. This rule also does not require exclusion when the evidence is offered for another purpose, such as proving bias or prejudice of a witness, negativing a contention of undue delay, or proving an effort to obstruct a criminal investigation or prosecution.

Rule 409. Payment of Medical and Similar Expenses

Evidence of furnishing or offering or promising to pay medical, hospital, or similar expenses occasioned by an injury is not admissible to prove liability for the injury.

Rule 410. Inadmissibility of Pleas, Plea Discussions, and Related Statements

Except as otherwise provided in this rule, evidence of the following is not, in any civil or criminal proceeding, admissible against the defendant who made the plea or was a participant in the plea discussions:

(1) a plea of guilty which was later withdrawn;

(2) a plea of nolo contendere;

(3) any statement made in the course of any proceedings under Rule 11 of the Federal Rules of Criminal Procedure or comparable state procedure regarding either of the foregoing pleas; or

(4) any statement made in the course of plea discussions with an attorney for the prosecuting authority which do not result in a plea of guilty or which result in a plea of guilty later withdrawn. However, such a statement is admissible (i) in any proceeding wherein another statement made in the course of the same plea or plea discussions has been introduced and the statement ought in fairness be considered contemporaneously with it, or (ii) in a criminal proceeding for perjury or false statement if the statement was made by the defendant under oath, on the record and in the presence of counsel.

(As amended Dec. 12, 1975; Apr. 30, 1979, eff. Dec. 1, 1980.).

Rule 411. Liability Insurance

Evidence that a person was or was not insured against liability is not admissible upon the issue whether the person acted negligently or otherwise wrongfully. This rule does not require the exclusion of evidence of insurance against liability when offered for another purpose, such as proof of agency, ownership, or control, or bias or prejudice of a witness.

(As amended Mar. 2, 1987, eff. Oct. 1, 1987.).

Rule 412. Sex Offense Cases; Relevance of Alleged Victim's Past Sexual Behavior or Alleged Sexual Predisposition

(a) Evidence Generally Inadmissible.—The following evidence is not admissible in any civil or criminal proceeding involving alleged sexual misconduct except as provided in subdivisions (b) and (c):

(1) Evidence offered to prove that any alleged victim engaged in other sexual behavior.

(2) Evidence offered to prove any alleged victim's sexual predisposition.

(b) Exceptions.

(1) In a criminal case, the following evidence is admissible, if otherwise admissible under these rules:

(A) evidence of specific instances of sexual behavior by the alleged victim offered to prove that a person other than the accused was the source of semen, injury or other physical evidence;

(B) evidence of specific instances of sexual behavior by the alleged victim with respect to the person accused of the sexual misconduct offered by the accused to prove consent or by the prosecution; and

(C) evidence the exclusion of which would violate the constitutional rights of the defendant.

(2) In a civil case, evidence offered to prove the sexual behavior or sexual predisposition of any alleged victim is admissible if it is otherwise admissible under these rules and its probative value substantially outweighs the danger of harm to any victim and of unfair prejudice to any party. Evidence of an alleged victim's reputation is admissible only if it has been placed in controversy by the alleged victim.

(c) Procedure To Determine Admissibility.

(1) A party intending to offer evidence under subdivision (b) must—

(A) file a written motion at least 14 days before trial specifically describing the evidence and stating the purpose for which it is offered unless the court, for good cause requires a different time for filing or permits filing during trial; and

(B) serve the motion on all parties and notify the alleged victim or, when appropriate, the alleged victim's guardian or representative.

(2) Before admitting evidence under this rule the court must conduct a hearing in camera and afford the victim and parties a right to attend and be heard. The motion, related papers, and the record of the hearing must be sealed and remain under seal unless the court orders otherwise.

(As added Oct. 28, 1978, eff. Nov. 28, 1978; amended Nov. 18, 1988; Apr. 29, 1994, eff. Dec. 1, 1994; Sept. 13, 1994, eff. Dec. 1, 1994.).

Rule 413.   Evidence of Similar Crimes in Sexual Assault Cases

(a) In a criminal case in which the defendant is accused of an offense of sexual assault, evidence of the defendant's commission of another offense or offenses of sexual assault is admissible, and may be considered for its bearing on any matter to which it is relevant.

(b) In a case in which the Government intends to offer evidence under this rule, the attorney for the Government shall disclose the evidence to the defendant, including statements of witnesses or a summary of the substance of any testimony that is expected to be offered, at least fifteen days before the scheduled date of trial or at such later time as the court may allow for good cause.

(c) This rule shall not be construed to limit the admission or consideration of evidence under any other rule.

(d) For purposes of this rule and Rule 415, "offense of sexual assault" means a crime under Federal law or the law of a State (as defined in section 513 of title 18, United States Code) that involved—

(1) any conduct proscribed by chapter 109A of title 18, United States Code;

(2) contact, without consent, between any part of the defendant's body or an object and the genitals or anus of another person;

(3) contact, without consent, between the genitals or anus of the defendant and any part of another person's body;

(4) deriving sexual pleasure or gratification from the infliction of death, bodily injury, or physical pain on another person; or

(5) an attempt or conspiracy to engage in conduct described in paragraphs (1)–(4).

(Added Sept. 13, 1994, eff. July 9, 1995.).

Rule 414.   Evidence of Similar Crimes in Child Molestation Cases

(a) In a criminal case in which the defendant is accused of an offense of child molestation, evidence of the defendant's commission of another offense or offenses of child molestation is admissible, and may be considered for its bearing on any matter to which it is relevant.

(b) In a case in which the Government intends to offer evidence under this rule, the attorney for the Government shall disclose the evidence to the defendant, including statements of witnesses or a summary of the substance of any testimony that is expected to be offered, at least fifteen days before the scheduled date of trial or at such later time as the court may allow for good cause.

(c) This rule shall not be construed to limit the admission or consideration of evidence under any other rule.

(d) For purposes of this rule and Rule 415, "child" means a person below the age of fourteen, and "offense of child molestation" means a crime under Federal law or the law of a State (as defined in section 513 of title 18, United States Code) that involved—

(1) any conduct proscribed by chapter 109A of title 18, United States Code, that was committed in relation to a child;

(2) any conduct proscribed by chapter 110 of title 18, United States Code;

(3) contact between any part of the defendant's body or an object and the genitals or anus of a child;

(4) contact between the genitals or anus of the defendant and any part of the body of a child;

(5) deriving sexual pleasure or gratification from the infliction of death, bodily injury, or physical pain on a child; or

(6) an attempt or conspiracy to engage in conduct described in paragraphs (1)–(5).

(Added Sept. 13, 1994, eff. July 9, 1995.).

Rule 415. Evidence of Similar Acts in Civil Cases Concerning Sexual Assault or Child Molestation

(a) In a civil case in which a claim for damages or other relief is predicated on a party's alleged commission of conduct constituting an offense of sexual assault or child molestation, evidence of that party's commission of another offense or offenses of sexual assault or child molestation is admissible and may be considered as provided in Rule 413 and Rule 414 of these rules.

(b) A party who intends to offer evidence under this Rule shall disclose the evidence to the party against whom it will be offered, including statements of witnesses or a summary of the substance of any testimony that is expected to be offered, at least fifteen days before the scheduled date of trial or at such later time as the court may allow for good cause.

(c) This rule shall not be construed to limit the admission or consideration of evidence under any other rule.

(Added Sept. 13, 1994, eff. July 9, 1995.).

ARTICLE V. PRIVILEGES

Rule 501. General Rule

Except as otherwise required by the Constitution of the United States or provided by Act of Congress or in rules prescribed by the Supreme Court pursuant to statutory authority, the privilege of a witness, person, government, State, or political subdivision thereof shall be governed by the principles of the common law as they may be interpreted by the courts of the United States in the light of reason and experience. However, in civil actions and proceedings, with respect to an element of a claim or defense as to which State law supplies the rule of decision, the privilege of a witness, person, government, State, or political subdivision thereof shall be determined in accordance with State law.

ARTICLE VI. WITNESSES

Rule 601. General Rule of Competency

Every person is competent to be a witness except as otherwise provided in these rules. However, in civil actions and proceedings, with respect to an element of a claim or defense as to which State law supplies the rule of decision, the competency of a witness shall be determined in accordance with State law.

Rule 602. Lack of Personal Knowledge

A witness may not testify to a matter unless evidence is introduced sufficient to support a finding that the witness has personal knowledge of the matter. Evidence to prove personal knowledge may, but need not, consist of the witness' own testimony. This rule is subject to the provisions of rule 703, relating to opinion testimony by expert witnesses.

(As amended Mar. 2, 1987, eff. Oct. 1, 1987; Apr. 25, 1988, eff. Nov. 1, 1988.).

Rule 603. Oath or Affirmation

Before testifying, every witness shall be required to declare that the witness will testify truthfully, by oath or affirmation administered in a form calculated to awaken the witness' conscience and impress the witness' mind with the duty to do so.

(As amended Mar. 2, 1987, eff. Oct. 1, 1987.).

Rule 604. Interpreters

An interpreter is subject to the provisions of these rules relating to qualification as an expert and the administration of an oath or affirmation to make a true translation.

(As amended Mar. 2, 1987, eff. Oct. 1, 1987.).

Rule 605.   Competency of Judge as Witness

The judge presiding at the trial may not testify in that trial as a witness. No objection need be made in order to preserve the point.

Rule 606.   Competency of Juror as Witness

(a) At the trial.—A member of the jury may not testify as a witness before that jury in the trial of the case in which the juror is sitting. If the juror is called so to testify, the opposing party shall be afforded an opportunity to object out of the presence of the jury.

(b) Inquiry into validity of verdict or indictment.—Upon an inquiry into the validity of a verdict or indictment, a juror may not testify as to any matter or statement occurring during the course of the jury's deliberations or to the effect of anything upon that or any other juror's mind or emotions as influencing the juror to assent to or dissent from the verdict or indictment or concerning the juror's mental processes in connection therewith, except that a juror may testify on the question whether extraneous prejudicial information was improperly brought to the jury's attention or whether any outside influence was improperly brought to bear upon any juror. Nor may a juror's affidavit or evidence of any statement by the juror concerning a matter about which the juror would be precluded from testifying be received for these purposes.

(As amended Dec. 12, 1975; Mar. 2, 1987, eff. Oct. 1, 1987.)

Rule 607.   Who May Impeach

The credibility of a witness may be attacked by any party, including the party calling the witness.

(As amended Mar. 2, 1987, eff. Oct. 1, 1987.).

Rule 608.   Evidence of Character and Conduct of Witness

(a) Opinion and reputation evidence of character.—The credibility of a witness may be attacked or supported by evidence in the form of opinion or reputation, but subject to these limitations: (1) the evidence may refer only to character for truthfulness or un-truthfulness, and (2) evidence of truthful character is admissible only after the character of the witness for truthfulness has been attacked by opinion or reputation evidence or otherwise.

(b) Specific instances of conduct.—Specific instances of the conduct of a witness, for the purpose of attacking or supporting the witness' credibility, other than conviction of crime as provided in rule 609, may not be proved by extrinsic evidence. They may, however, in the discretion of the court, if probative of truthfulness or untruthfulness, be inquired into on cross-examination of the witness (1) concerning the witness' character for truthfulness or un-truthfulness, or (2) concerning the character for truthfulness or untruthfulness of another witness as to which character the witness being cross-examined has testified.

The giving of testimony, whether by an accused or by any other witness, does not operate as a waiver of the accused's or the witness' privilege against self-incrimination when examined with respect to matters which relate only to credibility.

(As amended Mar. 2, 1987, eff. Oct. 1, 1987; Apr. 25, 1988, eff. Nov. 1, 1988.).

Rule 609. Impeachment by Evidence of Conviction of Crime

(a) General rule.—For the purpose of attacking the credibility of a witness,

(1) evidence that a witness other than an accused has been convicted of a crime shall be admitted, subject to Rule 403, if the crime was punishable by death or imprisonment in excess of one year under the law under which the witness was convicted, and evidence that an accused has been convicted of such a crime shall be admitted if the court determines that the probative value of admitting this evidence outweighs its prejudicial effect to the accused; and

(2) evidence that any witness has been convicted of a crime shall be admitted if it involved dishonesty or false statement, regardless of the punishment.

(b) Time limit.—Evidence of a conviction under this rule is not admissible if a period of more than ten years has elapsed since the date of the conviction or of the release of the witness from the confinement imposed for that conviction, whichever is the later date, unless the court determines, in the interests of justice, that the probative value of the conviction supported by specific facts and circumstances substantially outweighs its prejudicial effect. However, evidence of a conviction more than 10 years old as calculated herein, is not admissible unless the proponent gives to the adverse party sufficient advance written notice of intent to use such evidence to provide the adverse party with a fair opportunity to contest the use of such evidence.

(c) Effect of pardon, annulment, or certificate of rehabilitation.— Evidence of a conviction is not admissible under this rule if (1) the conviction has been the subject of a pardon, annulment, certificate of rehabilitation, or other equivalent procedure based on a finding of the rehabilitation of the person convicted, and that person has not been convicted of a subsequent crime which was punishable by death or imprisonment in excess of one year, or (2) the conviction has been the subject of a pardon, annulment, or other equivalent procedure based on a finding of innocence.

(d) Juvenile adjudications.—Evidence of juvenile adjudications is generally not admissible under this rule. The court may, however, in a criminal case allow evidence of a juvenile adjudication of a witness other than the accused if conviction of the offense would be admissible to attack the credibility of an adult and the court is satisfied that admission in evidence is necessary for a fairdetermination of the issue of guilt or innocence.

(e) Pendency of appeal.—The pendency of an appeal therefrom does not render evidence of a conviction inadmissible. Evidence of the pendency of an appeal is admissible.

(As amended Mar. 2, 1987, eff. Oct. 1, 1987; Jan. 26, 1990, eff. Dec. 1, 1990.).

Rule 610.   Religious Beliefs or Opinions

Evidence of the beliefs or opinions of a witness on matters of religionis not admissible for the purpose of showing that by reason of their nature the witness' credibility is impaired or enhanced.

(As amended Mar. 2, 1987, eff. Oct. 1, 1987.).

Rule 611.   Mode and Order of Interrogation and Presentation

(a) Control by court.—The court shall exercise reasonable control over the mode and order of interrogating witnesses and presenting evidence so as to (1) make the interrogation and presentation effective for the ascertainment of the truth, (2) avoid needless consumption of time, and (3) protect witnesses from harassment or undue embarrassment.

(b) Scope of cross-examination.—Cross-examination should be limited to the subject matter of the direct examination and matters affecting the credibility of the witness. The court may, in the exercise of discretion, permit inquiry into additional matters as if on direct examination.

(c) Leading questions.—Leading questions should not be used on the direct examination of a witness except as may be necessary to develop the witness' testimony. Ordinarily leading questions should be permitted on cross-examination. When a party calls a hostile witness, an adverse party, or a witness identified with an adverse party, interrogation may be by leading questions.

(As amended Mar. 2, 1987, eff. Oct. 1, 1987.)

Rule 612.   Writing Used To Refresh Memory

Except as otherwise provided in criminal proceedings by section 3500 of title 18, United States Code, if a witness uses a writing to refresh memory for the purpose of testifying, either—

(1) while testifying, or

(2) before testifying, if the court in its discretion determines it is necessary in the interests of justice,

an adverse party is entitled to have the writing produced at the hearing, to inspect it, to cross-examine the witness thereon, and to introduce in evidence those portions which relate to the testimony of the witness. If it is claimed that the writing contains matters not related to the subject matter of the testimony the court shall examine the writing in camera, excise any portions not so related, and order delivery of the remainder to the party entitled thereto. Any portion withheld over objections shall be preserved and made available to the appellate court in the event of an appeal. If a writing is not produced or delivered pursuant to order under this rule, the court shall make any order justice requires, except that in criminal cases when the prosecution elects not to comply, the order shall be one striking the testimony or, if the court in its discretion determines that the interests of justice so require, declaring a mistrial.

(As amended Mar. 2, 1987, eff. Oct. 1, 1987.).

Rule 613. Prior Statements of Witnesses

(a) Examining witness concerning prior statement.—In examining a witness concerning a prior statement made by the witness, whether written or not, the statement need not be shown nor its contents disclosed to the witness at that time, but on request the same shall be shown or disclosed to opposing counsel.

(b) Extrinsic evidence of prior inconsistent statement of witness.—Extrinsic evidence of a prior inconsistent statement by a witness is not admissible unless the witness is afforded an opportunity to explain or deny the same and the opposite party is afforded an opportunity to interrogate the witness thereon, or the interests of justice otherwise require. This provision does not apply to admissions of a party-opponent as defined in rule 801(d)(2).

(As amended Mar. 2, 1987, eff. Oct. 1, 1987; Apr. 25, 1988, eff. Nov. 1, 1988.).

Rule 614. Calling and Interrogation of Witnesses by Court

(a) Calling by court.—The court may, on its own motion or at the suggestion of a party, call witnesses, and all parties are entitled to cross-examine witnesses thus called.

(b) Interrogation by court.—The court may interrogate witnesses, whether called by itself or by a party.

(c) Objections.—Objections to the calling of witnesses by the court or to interrogation by it may be made at the time or at the next available opportunity when the jury is not present.

Rule 615.   Exclusion of Witnesses

At the request of a party the court shall order witnesses excluded so that they cannot hear the testimony of other witnesses, and it may make the order of its own motion. This rule does not authorize exclusion of (1) a party who is a natural person, or (2) an officer or employee of a party which is not a natural person designated as its representative by its attorney, or (3) a person whose presence is shown by a party to be essential to the presentation of the party's cause, or (4) a person authorized by statute to be present.

(As amended Mar. 2, 1987, eff. Oct. 1, 1987; Apr. 25, 1988, eff. Nov. 1, 1988; Nov. 18, 1988; Apr. 24, 1998, eff. Dec. 1, 1998.).

ARTICLE VII. OPINIONS AND EXPERT TESTIMONY

Rule 701.   Opinion Testimony by Lay Witnesses

If the witness is not testifying as an expert, the witness' testimony in the form of opinions or inferences is limited to those opinions or inferences which are (a) rationally based on the perception of the witness, and (b) helpful to a clear understanding of the witness' testimony or the determination of a fact in issue, and (c) not based on scientific, technical, or other specialized knowledge within the scope of Rule 702.

(As amended Mar. 2, 1987, eff. Oct. 1, 1987; Apr. 17, 2000, eff. Dec. 1, 2000.).

Rule 702.   Testimony by Experts

If scientific, technical, or other specialized knowledge will assist the trier of fact to understand the evidence or to determine a fact in issue, a witness qualified as an expert by knowledge, skill, experience, training, or education, may testify thereto in the form of an opinion or otherwise, if (1) the testimony is based upon sufficient facts or data, (2) the testimony is the product of reliable principles and methods, and (3) the witness has applied the principles and methods reliably to the facts of the case.

(As amended Apr. 17, 2000, eff. Dec. 1, 2000.).

Rule 703.   Bases of Opinion Testimony by Experts

The facts or data in the particular case upon which an expert bases an opinion or inference may be those perceived by or made known to the expert at or before the hearing. If of a type reasonably relied upon by experts in the particular field in forming opinions or inferences upon the subject, the facts or data need not be admissible in evidence in order for the opinion or inference to be admitted. Facts or data that are otherwise inadmissible shall not be disclosed to the jury by the proponent of the opinion or inference unless the court determines that their probative value in assisting the jury to evaluate the expert's opinion substantially outweighs their prejudicial effect.

(As amended Mar. 2, 1987, eff. Oct. 1, 1987; Apr. 17, 2000, eff. Dec. 1, 2000.).

Rule 704.   Opinion on Ultimate Issue

(a) Except as provided in subdivision (b), testimony in the form of an opinion or inference otherwise admissible is not objectionable because it embraces an ultimate issue to be decided by the trier of fact.

(b) No expert witness testifying with respect to the mental state or condition of a defendant in a criminal case may state an opinion or inference as to whether the defendant did or did not have the mental state or condition constituting an element of the crime charged or of a defense thereto. Such ultimate issues are matters for the trier of fact alone.

(As amended Oct. 12, 1984.).

Rule 705.   Disclosure of Facts or Data Underlying Expert Opinion

The expert may testify in terms of opinion or inference and give reasons therefor without first testifying to the underlying facts or data, unless the court requires otherwise. The expert may in any event be required to disclose the underlying facts or data on cross-examination.

(As amended Mar. 2, 1987, eff. Oct. 1, 1987; Apr. 22, 1993, eff. Dec. 1, 1993.).

Rule 706.   Court Appointed Experts

(a) Appointment.—The court may on its own motion or on the motion of any party enter an order to show cause why expert witnesses should not be appointed, and may request the parties to submit nominations. The court may appoint any expert witnesses agreed upon by the parties, and may appoint expert witnesses of its own selection. An expert witness shall not be appointed by the court unless the witness consents to act. A witness so appointed shall be informed of the witness' duties by the court in writing, a copy of which shall be filed with the clerk, or at a conference in which the parties shall have opportunity to participate. A witness so appointed shall advise the parties of the witness' findings, if any; the witness' deposition may be taken by any party; and the witness may be called to testify by the court or any party. The witness shall be subject to cross-examination by each party, including a party calling the witness.

(b) Compensation.—Expert witnesses so appointed are entitled to reasonable compensation in whatever sum the court may allow. The compensation thus fixed is payable from funds which may be provided by law in criminal cases and civil actions and proceedings involving just compensation under the fifth amendment. In other civil actions and proceedings the compensation shall be paid by the parties in such proportion and at such time as the court directs, and thereafter charged in like manner as other costs.

(c) Disclosure of appointment.—In the exercise of its discretion, the court may authorize disclosure to the jury of the fact that the court appointed the expert witness.

(d) Parties' experts of own selection.—Nothing in this rule limits the parties in calling expert witnesses of their own selection.

(As amended Mar. 2, 1987, eff. Oct. 1, 1987.).

ARTICLE VIII. HEARSAY

Rule 801. Definitions

The following definitions apply under this article:

(a) Statement.—A "statement" is (1) an oral or written assertion or (2) nonverbal conduct of a person, if it is intended by the person as an assertion.

(b) Declarant.—A "declarant" is a person who makes a statement.

(c) Hearsay.—"Hearsay" is a statement, other than one made by the declarant while testifying at the trial or hearing, offered in evidence to prove the truth of the matter asserted.

(d) Statements which are not hearsay.—A statement is not hearsay if—

(1) Prior statement by witness.—The declarant testifies at the trial or hearing and is subject to cross-examination concerning the statement, and the statement is (A) inconsistent with the declarant's testimony, and was given under oath subject to the penalty of perjury at a trial, hearing, or other proceeding, or in a deposition, or (B) consistent with the declarant's testimony and is offered to rebut an express or implied charge against the declarant of recent fabrication or improper influence or motive, or (C) one of identification of a person made after perceiving the person; or

(2) Admission by party-opponent.—The statement is offered against a party and is (A) the party's own statement, in either an individual or a representative capacity or (B) a statement of which the party has manifested an adoption or belief in its truth, or (C) a statement by a person authorized by the party to make a statement concerning the subject, or (D) a statement by the party's agent or servant concerning a matter within the scope of the agency or employment, made during the existence of the relationship, or (E) a statement by a coconspirator of a party during the course and in furtherance of the conspiracy. The contents of the statement shall be considered but are not alone sufficient to establish the declarant's authority under subdivision (C), the agency or employment relationship and scope thereof under subdivision (D), or the existence of the conspiracy and the participation therein of the

declarant and the party against whom the statement is offered under subdivision (E).

(As amended Oct. 16, 1975, eff. Oct. 31, 1975; Mar. 2, 1987, eff. Oct. 1, 1987; Apr. 11, 1997, eff. Dec. 1, 1997.).

Rule 802. Hearsay Rule

Hearsay is not admissible except as provided by these rules or by other rules prescribed by the Supreme Court pursuant to statutory authority or by Act of Congress.

Rule 803. Hearsay Exceptions; Availability of Declarant Immaterial

The following are not excluded by the hearsay rule, even though the declarant is available as a witness:

(1) Present sense impression.—A statement describing or explaining an event or condition made while the declarant was perceiving the event or condition, or immediately thereafter.

(2) Excited utterance.—A statement relating to a startling event or condition made while the declarant was under the stress of excitement caused by the event or condition.

(3) Then existing mental, emotional, or physical condition.—A statement of the declarant's then existing state of mind, emotion, sensation, or physical condition (such as intent, plan, motive, design, mental feeling, pain, and bodily health), but not including a statement of memory or belief to prove the fact remembered or believed unless it relates to the execution, revocation, identification, or terms of declarant's will.

(4) Statements for purposes of medical diagnosis or treatment.— Statements made for purposes of medical diagnosis or treatment and describing medical history, or past or present symptoms, pain, or sensations, or the inception or general character of the cause or external source thereof insofar as reasonably pertinent to diagnosis or treatment.

(5) Recorded recollection.—A memorandum or record concerning a matter about which a witness once had knowledge but now has insufficient recollection to enable the witness to testify fully and accurately, shown to have been made or adopted by the witness when the matter was fresh in the witness'memory and to reflect that knowledge correctly. If admitted, the memorandum or record may be read into evidence but may not itself be received as an exhibit unless offered by an adverse party.

(6) Records of regularly conducted activity.—A memorandum, report, record, or data compilation, in any form, of acts, events, conditions, opinions, or diagnoses, made at or near the time by, or from information transmitted by, a person with knowledge, if kept in the course of a regularly conducted business activity, and if it was the regular practice

of that business activity to make the memorandum, report, record or data compilation, all as shown by the testimony of the custodian or other qualified witness, or by certification that complies with Rule 902(11), Rule 902(12), or a statute permitting certification, unless the source of information or the method or circumstances of preparation indicate lack of trustworthiness. The term "business" as used in this paragraph includes business, institution, association, profession, occupation, and calling of every kind, whether or not conducted for profit.

(7) Absence of entry in records kept in accordance with the provisions of paragraph (6).—Evidence that a matter is not included in the memoranda reports, records, or data compilations, in any form, kept in accordance with the provisions of paragraph (6), to prove the nonoccurrence or nonexistence of the matter, if the matter was of a kind of which a memorandum, report, record, or data compilation was regularly made and preserved, unless the sources of information or other circumstances indicate lack of trustworthiness.

(8) Public records and reports.—Records, reports, statements, or data compilations, in any form, of public offices or agencies, setting forth (A) the activities of the office or agency, or (B) matters observed pursuant to duty imposed by law as to which matters there was a duty to report, excluding, however, in criminal cases matters observed by police officers and other law enforcement personnel, or (C) in civil actions and proceedings and against the Government in criminal cases, factual findings resulting from an investigation made pursuant to authority granted by law, unless the sources of information or other circumstances indicate lack of trustworthiness.

(9) Records of vital statistics.—Records or data compilations, in any form, of births, fetal deaths, deaths, or marriages, if the report thereof was made to a public office pursuant to requirements of law.

(10) Absence of public record or entry.—To prove the absence of a record, report, statement, or data compilation, in any form, or the nonoccurrence or nonexistence of a matter of which a record, report, statement, or data compilation, in any form, was regularly made and preserved by a public office or agency, evidence in the form of a certification in accordance with rule 902, or testimony, that diligent search failed to disclose the record, report, statement, or data compilation, or entry.

(11) Records of religious organizations.—Statements of births, marriages, divorces, deaths, legitimacy, ancestry, relationship by blood or marriage, or other similar facts of personal or family history, contained in a regularly kept record of a religious organization.

(12) Marriage, baptismal, and similar certificates.—Statements of fact contained in a certificate that the maker performed a marriage or other ceremony or administered a sacrament, made by a clergyman, public official, or other person authorized by the rules or practices of a religious organization or by law to perform the act certified, and purporting to have been issued at the time of the act or within a reasonable time thereafter.

(13) Family records.—Statements of fact concerning personal or family history contained in family Bibles, genealogies, charts, engravings on rings, inscriptions on family portraits, engravings on urns, crypts, or tombstones, or the like.

(14) Records of documents affecting an interest in property.— The record of a document purporting to establish or affect an interest in property, as proof of the content of the original recorded document and its execution and delivery by each person by whom it purports to have been executed, if the record is a record of a public office and an applicable statute authorizes the recording of documents of that kind in that office.

(15) Statements in documents affecting an interest in property.— A statement contained in a document purporting to establish or affect an interest in property if the matter stated was relevant to the purpose of the document, unless dealings with the property since the document was made have been inconsistent with the truth of the statement or the purport of the document.

(16) Statements in ancient documents.—Statements in a document in existence twenty years or more the authenticity of which is established.

(17) Market reports, commercial publications.—Market quotations, tabulations, lists, directories, or other published compilations, generally used and relied upon by the public or by persons in particular occupations.

(18) Learned treatises.—To the extent called to the attention of an expert witness upon cross-examination or relied upon by the expert witness in direct examination, statements contained in published treatises, periodicals, or pamphlets on a subject of history, medicine, or other science or art, established as a reliable authority by the testimony or admission of the witness or by other expert testimony or by judicial notice. If admitted, the statements may be read into evidence but may not be received as exhibits.

(19) Reputation concerning personal or family history.—Reputation among members of a person's family by blood, adoption, or marriage, or among a person's associates, or in the community, concerning a person's birth, adoption, marriage, divorce, death, legitimacy, relationship by blood, adoption, or marriage, ancestry, or other similar fact of personal or family history.

(20) Reputation concerning boundaries or general history.— Reputation in a community, arising before the controversy, as to boundaries of or customs affecting lands in the community, and reputation as to events of general history important to the community or State or nation in which located.

(21) Reputation as to character.—Reputation of a person's character among associates or in the community.

(22) Judgment of previous conviction.—Evidence of a final judgment, entered after a trial or upon a plea of guilty (but not upon a plea of nolo

contendere), adjudging a person guilty of a crime punishable by death or imprisonment in excess of one year, to prove any fact essential to sustain the judgment, but not including, when offered by the Government in a criminal prosecution for purposes other than impeachment, judgments against persons other than the accused. The pendency of an appeal may be shown but does not affect admissibility.

(23) Judgment as to personal, family, or general history, or boundaries.—Judgments as proof of matters of personal, family or general history, or boundaries, essential to the judgment, if the same would be provable by evidence of reputation.

(24) [Other exceptions.] [Transferred to Rule 807]

(As amended Dec. 12, 1975; Mar. 2, 1987, eff. Oct. 1, 1987; Apr. 11, 1997, eff. Dec. 1, 1997; Apr. 17, 2000, eff. Dec. 1, 2000.)

Rule 804. Hearsay Exceptions; Declarant Unavailable

(a) Definition of unavailability.—"Unavailability as a witness" includes situations in which the declarant—

(1) is exempted by ruling of the court on the ground of privilege from testifying concerning the subject matter of the declarant's statement; or

(2) persists in refusing to testify concerning the subject matter of the declarant's statement despite an order of the court to do so; or

(3) testifies to a lack of memory of the subject matter of the declarant's statement; or

(4) is unable to be present or to testify at the hearing because of death or then existing physical or mental illness or infirmity; or

(5) is absent from the hearing and the proponent of a statement has been unable to procure the declarant's attendance (or in the case of a hearsay exception under subdivision (b)(2), (3), or (4), the declarant's attendance or testimony) by process or other reasonable means.

A declarant is not unavailable as a witness if exemption, refusal, claim of lack of memory, inability, or absence is due to the procurement or wrongdoing of the proponent of a statement for the purpose of preventing the witness from attending or testifying.

(b) Hearsay exceptions.—The following are not excluded by the hearsay rule if the declarant is unavailable as a witness:

(1) Former testimony.—Testimony given as a witness at another hearing of the same or a different proceeding, or in a deposition taken in compliance with law in the course of the same or another proceeding, if the party against whom the testimony is now offered, or, in a civil action or proceeding, a predecessor in interest, had an opportunity and similar motive to develop the testimony by direct, cross, or redirect examination.

(2) Statement under belief of impending death.—In a prosecution for homicide or in a civil action or proceeding, a statement made by a

declarant while believing that the declarant's death was imminent, concerning the cause or circumstances of what the declarant believed to be impending death.

(3) Statement against interest.—A statement which was at the time of its making so far contrary to the declarant's pecuniary or proprietary interest, or so far tended to subject the declarant to civil or criminal liability, or to render invalid a claim by the declarant against another, that a reasonable person in the declarant's position would not have made the statement unless believing it to be true. A statement tending to expose the declarant to criminal liability and offered to exculpate the accused is not admissible unless corroborating circumstances clearly indicate the trustworthiness of the statement.

(4) Statement of personal or family history.—(A) A statement concerning the declarant's own birth, adoption, marriage, divorce, legitimacy, relationship by blood, adoption, or marriage, ancestry, or other similar fact of personal or family history, even though declarant had no means of acquiring personal knowledge of the matter stated; or (B) a statement concerning the foregoing matters, and death also, of another person, if the declarant was related to the other by blood, adoption, or marriage or was so intimately associated with the other's family as to be likely to have accurate information concerning the matter declared.

(5) [Other exceptions.] [Transferred to Rule 807]

(6) Forfeiture by wrongdoing.—A statement offered against a party that has engaged or acquiesced in wrongdoing that was intended to, and did, procure the unavailability of the declarant as a witness.

(As amended Dec. 12, 1975; Mar. 2, 1987, eff. Oct. 1, 1987; Nov. 18, 1988; Apr. 11, 1997, eff. Dec. 1, 1997.).

Rule 805. Hearsay Within Hearsay

Hearsay included within hearsay is not excluded under the hearsay rule if each part of the combined statements conforms with an exception to the hearsay rule provided in these rules.

Rule 806. Attacking and Supporting Credibility of Declarant

When a hearsay statement, or a statement defined in Rule 801(d)(2)(C), (D), or (E), has been admitted in evidence, the credibility of the declarant may be attacked, and if attacked may be supported, by any evidence which would be admissible for those purposes if declarant had testified as a witness. Evidence of a statement or conduct by the declarant at any time, inconsistent with the declarant's hearsay statement, is not subject to any requirement that the declarant may have been afforded an opportunity to deny or explain. If the party against whom a hearsay statement has been admitted calls the declarant as a witness, the party is entitled to examine the declarant on the statement as if under cross-examination.

(As amended Mar. 2, 1987, eff. Oct. 1, 1987; Apr. 11, 1997, eff. Dec. 1, 1997.)

Rule 807. Residual Exception

A statement not specifically covered by Rule 803 or 804 but having equivalent circumstantial guarantees of trustworthiness, is not excluded by the hearsay rule, if the court determines that (A) the statement is offered as evidence of a material fact; (B) the statement is more probative on the point for which it is offered than any other evidence which the proponent can procure through reasonable efforts; and (C) the general purposes of these rules and the interests of justice will best be served by admission of the statement into evidence. However, a statement may not be admitted under this exception unless the proponent of it makes known to the adverse party sufficiently in advance of the trial or hearing to provide the adverse party with a fair opportunity to prepare to meet it, the proponent's intention to offer the statement and the particulars of it, including the name and address of the declarant.

(Added Apr. 11, 1997, eff. Dec. 1, 1997.)

ARTICLE IX. AUTHENTICATION AND IDENTIFICATION

Rule 901. Requirement of Authentication or Identification

(a) General provision.—The requirement of authentication or identification as a condition precedent to admissibility is satisfied by evidence sufficient to support a finding that the matter in question is what its proponent claims.

(b) Illustrations.—By way of illustration only, and not by way of limitation, the following are examples of authentication or identification conforming with the requirements of this rule:

(1) Testimony of witness with knowledge.—Testimony that a matter is what it is claimed to be.

(2) Nonexpert opinion on handwriting.—Nonexpert opinion as to the genuineness of handwriting, based upon familiarity not acquired for purposes of the litigation.

(3) Comparison by trier or expert witness.—Comparison by the trier of fact or by expert witnesses with specimens which have been authenticated.

(4) Distinctive characteristics and the like.—Appearance, contents, substance, internal patterns, or other distinctive characteristics, taken in conjunction with circumstances.

(5) Voice identification.—Identification of a voice, whether heard firsthand or through mechanical or electronic transmission or recording,

by opinion based upon hearing the voice at any time under circumstances connecting it with the alleged speaker.

(6) Telephone conversations.—Telephone conversations, by evidence that a call was made to the number assigned at the time by the telephone company to a particular person or business, if (A) in the case of a person, circumstances, including self-identification, show the person answering to be the one called, or (B) in the case of a business, the call was made to a place of business and the conversation related to business reasonably transacted over the telephone.

(7) Public records or reports.—Evidence that a writing authorized by law to be recorded or filed and in fact recorded or filed in a public office, or a purported public record, report, statement, or data compilation, in any form, is from the public office where items of this nature are kept.

(8) Ancient documents or data compilation.—Evidence that a document or data compilation, in any form, (A) is in such condition as to create no suspicion concerning its authenticity, (B) was in a place where it, if authentic, would likely be, and (C) has been in existence 20 years or more at the time it is offered.

(9) Process or system.—Evidence describing a process or system used to produce a result and showing that the process or system produces an accurate result.

(10) Methods provided by statute or rule.—Any method of authentication or identification provided by Act of Congress or by other rules prescribed by the Supreme Court pursuant to statutory authority.

Rule 902. Self-authentication

Extrinsic evidence of authenticity as a condition precedent to admissibility is not required with respect to the following:

(1) Domestic public documents under seal.—A document bearing a seal purporting to be that of the United States, or of any State, district, Commonwealth, territory, or insular possession thereof, or the Panama Canal Zone, or the Trust Territory of the Pacific Islands, or of a political subdivision, department, officer, or agency thereof, and a signature purporting to be an attestation or execution.

(2) Domestic public documents not under seal.—A document purporting to bear the signature in the official capacity of an officer or employee of any entity included in paragraph (1) hereof, having no seal, if a public officer having a seal and.having official duties in the district or political subdivision of the officer or employee certifies under seal that the signer has the official capacity and that the signature is genuine.

(3) Foreign public documents.—A document purporting to be executed or attested in an official capacity by a person authorized by the laws of a foreign country to make the execution or attestation, and accompanied by a final certification as to the genuineness of the signature and official

position (A) of the executing or attesting person, or (B) of any foreign official whose certificate of genuineness of signature and official position relates to the execution or attestation or is in a chain of certificates of genuineness of signature and official position relating to the execution or attestation. A final certification may be made by a secretary of an embassy or legation, consul general, consul, vice consul, or consular agent of the United States, or a diplomatic or consular official of the foreign country assigned or accredited to the United States. If reasonable opportunity has been given to all parties to investigate the authenticity and accuracy of official documents, the court may, for good cause shown, order that they be treated as presumptively authentic without final certification or permit them to be evidenced by an attested summary with or without final certification.

(4) Certified copies of public records.—A copy of an official record or report or entry therein, or of a document authorized by law to be recorded or filed and actually recorded or filed in a public office, including data compilations in any form, certified as correct by the custodian or other person authorized to make the certification, by certificate complying with paragraph (1), (2), or (3) of this rule or complying with any Act of Congress or rule prescribed by the Supreme Court pursuant to statutory authority.

(5) Official publications.—Books, pamphlets, or other publications purporting to be issued by public authority.

(6) Newspapers and periodicals.—Printed materials purporting to be newspapers or periodicals.

(7) Trade inscriptions and the like.—Inscriptions, signs, tags, or labels purporting to have been affixed in the course of business and indicating ownership, control, or origin.

(8) Acknowledged documents.—Documents accompanied by a certificate of acknowledgment executed in the manner provided by law by a notary public or other officer authorized by law to take acknowledgments.

(9) Commercial paper and related documents.—Commercial paper, signatures thereon, and documents relating thereto to the extent provided by general commercial law.

(10) Presumptions under Acts of Congress.—Any signature, document, or other matter declared by Act of Congress to be presumptively or prima facie genuine or authentic.

(11) Certified domestic records of regularly conducted activity.— The original or a duplicate of a domestic record of regularly conducted activity that would be admissible under Rule 803(6) if accompanied by a written declaration of its custodian or other qualified person, in a manner complying with any Act of Congress or rule prescribed by the Supreme Court pursuant to statutory authority, certifying that the record—

(A) was made at or near the time of the occurrence of the matters set forth by, or from information transmitted by, a person with knowledge of those matters;

(B) was kept in the course of the regularly conducted activity; and

(C) was made by the regularly conducted activity as a regular practice.

A party intending to offer a record into evidence under this paragraph must provide written notice of that intention to all adverse parties, and must make the record and declaration available for inspection sufficiently in advance of their offer into evidence to provide an adverse party with a fair opportunity to challenge them.

(12) Certified foreign records of regularly conducted activity.— In a civil case, the original or a duplicate of a foreign record of regularly conducted activity that would be admissible under Rule 803(6) if accompanied by a written declaration by its custodian or other qualified person certifying that the record—

(A) was made at or near the time of the occurrence of the matters set forth by, or from information transmitted by, a person with knowledge of those matters;

(B) was kept in the course of the regularly conducted activity; and

(C) was made by the regularly conducted activity as a regular practice. The declaration must be signed in a manner that, if falsely made, would subject the maker to criminal penalty under the laws of the country where the declaration is signed. A party intending to offer a record into evidence under this paragraph must provide written notice of that intention to all adverse parties, and must make the record and declaration available for inspection sufficiently in advance of their offer into evidence to provide an adverse party with a fair opportunity to challenge them.

(As amended Mar. 2, 1987, eff. Oct. 1, 1987; Apr. 25, 1988, eff. Nov. 1, 1988; Apr. 17, 2000, eff. Dec. 1, 2000.)

Rule 903. Subscribing Witness' Testimony Unnecessary

The testimony of a subscribing witness is not necessary to authenticate a writing unless required by the laws of the jurisdiction whose laws govern the validity of the writing.

ARTICLE X. CONTENTS OF WRITINGS, RECORDINGS, AND PHOTOGRAPHS

Rule 1001. Definitions

For purposes of this article the following definitions are applicable:

(1) Writings and recordings.—"Writings" and "recordings" consist of letters, words, or numbers, or their equivalent, set down by handwriting, typewriting, printing, photostating, photographing, magnetic impulse, mechanical or electronic recording, or other form of data compilation.

(2) Photographs.—"Photographs" include still photographs, Xray films, video tapes, and motion pictures.

(3) Original.—An "original" of a writing or recording is the writing or recording itself or any counterpart intended to have the same effect by a person executing or issuing it. An "original" of a photograph includes the negative or any print therefrom. If data are stored in a computer or similar device, any printout or other output readable by sight, shown to reflect the data accurately, is an "original".

(4) Duplicate.—A "duplicate" is a counterpart produced by the same impression as the original, or from the same matrix, or by means of photography, including enlargements and miniatures, or by mechanical or electronic rerecording, or by chemical reproduction, or by other equivalent techniques which accurately reproduces the original.

Rule 1002. Requirement of Original

To prove the content of a writing, recording, or photograph, the original writing, recording, or photograph is required, except as otherwise provided in these rules or by Act of Congress.

Rule 1003. Admissibility of Duplicates

A duplicate is admissible to the same extent as an original unless (1) a genuine question is raised as to the authenticity of the original or (2) in the circumstances it would be unfair to admit the duplicate in lieu of the original.

Rule 1004. Admissibility of Other Evidence of Contents

The original is not required, and other evidence of the contents of a writing, recording, or photograph is admissible if—

(1) Originals lost or destroyed.—All originals are lost or have been destroyed, unless the proponent lost or destroyed them in bad faith; or

(2) Original not obtainable.—No original can be obtained by any available judicial process or procedure; or

(3) Original in possession of opponent.—At a time when an original was under the control of the party against whom offered, that party was put on notice, by the pleadings or otherwise, that the contents would be a subject of proof at the hearing, and that party does not produce the original at the hearing; or

(4) Collateral matters.—The writing, recording, or photograph is not closely related to a controlling issue.

(As amended Mar. 2, 1987, eff. Oct. 1, 1987.)

Rule 1005. Public Records

The contents of an official record, or of a document authorized to be recorded or filed and actually recorded or filed, including data compilations in any form, if otherwise admissible, may be proved by copy, certified as correct in accordance with rule 902 or testified to be correct by a witness who has compared it with the original. If a copy which complies with the foregoing cannot be obtained by the exercise of reasonable diligence, then other evidence of the contents may be given.

Rule 1006. Summaries

The contents of voluminous writings, recordings, or photographs which cannot conveniently be examined in court may be presented in the form of a chart, summary, or calculation. The originals, or duplicates, shall be made available for examination or copying, or both, by other parties at reasonable time and place. The court may order that they be produced in court.

Rule 1007. Testimony or Written Admission of Party

Contents of writings, recordings, or photographs may be proved by the testimony or deposition of the party against whom offered or by that party's written admission, without accounting for the nonproduction of the original.

(As amended Mar. 2, 1987, eff. Oct. 1, 1987.)

Rule 1008. Functions of Court and Jury

When the admissibility of other evidence of contents of writings, recordings, or photographs under these rules depends upon the fulfillment of a condition of fact, the question whether the condition has been fulfilled is ordinarily for the court to determine in accordance with the provisions of rule 104. However, when an issue is raised (a) whether the asserted writing ever existed, or (b) whether another writing, recording, or photograph produced at the trial is the original, or (c) whether other evidence of contents correctly reflects the contents, the issue is for the trier of fact to determine as in the case of other issues of fact.

ARTICLE XI. MISCELLANEOUS RULES

Rule 1101. Applicability of Rules

(a) Courts and judges. These rules apply to the United States district courts, the District Court of Guam, the District Court of the Virgin Islands, the District Court for the Northern Mariana Islands, the United States courts of appeals, the United States Claims Court,[1] and to United States bankruptcy judges and United States magistrate judges, in the actions, cases, and proceedings and to the extent hereinafter set forth. The terms "judge" and "court" in these rules include United States bankruptcy judges and United States magistrate judges.

(b) Proceedings generally.—These rules apply generally to civil actions and proceedings, including admiralty and maritime cases, to criminal cases and proceedings, to contempt proceedings except those in which the court may act summarily, and to proceedings and cases under title 11, United States Code.

(c) Rule of privilege.—The rule with respect to privileges applies at all stages of all actions, cases, and proceedings.

(d) Rules inapplicable.—The rules (other than with respect to privileges) do not apply in the following situations:

(1) Preliminary questions of fact.—The determination of questions of fact preliminary to admissibility of evidence when the issue is to be determined by the court under rule 104.

(2) Grand jury.—Proceedings before grand juries.

(3) Miscellaneous proceedings.—Proceedings for extradition or rendition; preliminary examinations in criminal cases; sentencing, or granting or revoking probation; issuance of warrants for arrest, criminal summonses, and search warrants; and proceedings with respect to release on bail or otherwise.

(e) Rules applicable in part. In the following proceedings these rules apply to the extent that matters of evidence are not provided for in the statutes which govern procedure therein or in other rules prescribed by the Supreme Court pursuant to statutory authority: the trial of misdemeanors and other petty offenses before United States magistrate judges; review of agency actions when the facts are subject to trial de novo under section 706(2)(F) of title 5, United States Code; review of orders of the Secretary of Agriculture under section 2 of the Act entitled "An Act to authorize association of producers of agricultural products" approved February 18, 1922 (7 U.S.C. 292), and under sections 6 and 7(c) of the Perishable Agricultural Commodities Act, 1930 (7 U.S.C. 499f, 499g(c)); naturalization and revocation of naturalization under sections 310–318 of the Immigration and Nationality Act (8 U.S.C. 1421–1429); prize proceedings in admiralty under sections 7651–7681 of title 10, United States Code; review of orders of the Secretary of the Interior under section 2 of the Act entitled "An Act authorizing associations of producers of aquatic products" approved June 25, 1934 (15 U.S.C. 522); review of orders of petroleum control boards under section 5 of the Act entitled "An Act to regulate interstate and foreign commerce in petroleum and its products by prohibiting the shipment in such commerce

---

[1] Pub. L. 102-572, title IX, § 902(b)(1), Oct. 29, 1992, 106 Stat. 4516, provided that reference in any other Federal law or any document to the "United States Claims Court" shall be deemed to refer to the "United States Court of Federal Claims".

of petroleum and its products produced in violation of State law, and for other purposes", approved February 22, 1935 (15 U.S.C. 715d); actions for fines, penalties, or forfeitures under part V of title IV of the Tariff Act of 1930 (19 U.S.C. 1581–1624), or under the AntiSmuggling Act (19 U.S.C. 1701–1711); criminal libel for condemnation, exclusion of imports, or other proceedings under the Federal Food, Drug, and Cosmetic Act (21 U.S.C. 301–392); disputes between seamen under sections 4079, 4080, and 4081 of the Revised Statutes (22 U.S.C. 256–258); habeas corpus under sections 2241–2254 of title 28, United States Code; motions to vacate, set aside or correct sentence under section 2255 of title 28, United States Code; actions for penalties for refusal to transport destitute seamen under section 4578 of the Revised Statutes (46 U.S.C. 679);[2] actions against the United States under the Act entitled "An Act authorizing suits against the United States in admiralty for damage caused by and salvage service rendered to public vessels belonging to the United States, and for other purposes", approved March 3, 1925 (46 U.S.C. 781–790), as implemented by section 7730 of title 10, United States Code.

(As amended Dec. 12, 1975; Nov. 6, 1978, eff. Oct. 1, 1979; Apr. 2, 1982, eff. Oct. 1, 1982; Mar. 2, 1987, eff. Oct. 1, 1987; Apr. 25, 1988, eff. Nov. 1, 1988; Nov. 18, 1988; Apr. 22, 1993, eff. Dec. 1, 1993.).

Rule 1102. Amendments

Amendments to the Federal Rules of Evidence may be made as provided in section 2072 of title 28 of the United States Code. (As amended Apr. 30, 1991, eff. Dec. 1, 1991.)

Rule 1103. Title

These rules may be known and cited as the Federal Rules of Evidence.

STATUTORY AUTHORITY FOR PROMULGATION OF EVIDENCE RULES

TITLE 28 UNITED STATES CODE

§ 2072. Rules of procedure and evidence; power to prescribe

(a) The Supreme Court shall have the power to prescribe general rules of practice and procedure and rules of evidence for cases in the United States district courts (including proceedings before magistrates thereof) and courts of appeals.

---

[2] Repealed and reenacted as 46 U.S.C. 11104(b)–(d) by Pub. L. 98-89, §§ 1, 2(a), 4(b), Aug. 26, 1983, 97 Stat. 500.

(b) Such rules shall not abridge, enlarge or modify any substantive right. All laws in conflict with such rules shall be of no further force or effect after such rules have taken effect.

(c) Such rules may define when a ruling of a district court is final for the purposes of appeal under section 1291 of this title.

(Added Pub. L. 100-702, title IV, § 401(a), Nov. 19, 1988, 102 Stat. 4648, eff. Dec. 1, 1988; amended Pub. L. 101-650, title III, § 315, Dec. 1, 1990, 104 Stat. 5115.)

§ 2073   Rules of procedure and evidence; method of prescribing

(a)(1) The Judicial Conference shall prescribe and publish the procedures for the consideration of proposed rules under this section.

(2) The Judicial Conference may authorize the appointment of committees to assist the Conference by recommending rules to be prescribed under sections 2072 and 2075 of this title. Each such committee shall consist of members of the bench and the professional bar, and trial and appellate judges.

(b) The Judicial Conference shall authorize the appointment of a standing committee on rules of practice, procedure, and evidence under subsection (a) of this section. Such standing committee shall review each recommendation of any other committees so appointed and recommend to the Judicial Conference rules of practice, procedure, and evidence and such changes in rules proposed by a committee appointed under subsection (a)(2) of this section as may be necessary to maintain consistency and otherwise promote the interest of justice.

(c)(1) Each meeting for the transaction of business under this chapter by any committee appointed under this section shall be open to the public, except when the committee so meeting, in open session and with a majority present, determines that it is in the public interest that all or part of the remainder of the meeting on that day shall be closed to the public, and states the reason for so closing the meeting. Minutes of each meeting for the transaction of business under this chapter shall be maintained by the committee and made available to the public, except that any portion of such minutes, relating to a closed meeting and made available to the public, may contain such deletions as may be necessary to avoid frustrating the purposes of closing the meeting.

(2) Any meeting for the transaction of business under this chapter, by a committee appointed under this section, shall be preceded by sufficient notice to enable all interested persons to attend.

(d) In making a recommendation under this section or under section 2072 or 2075, the body making that recommendation shall provide a proposed rule, an explanatory note on the rule, and a written report explaining the body's action, including any minority or other separate views.

(e) Failure to comply with this section does not invalidate a rule prescribed under section 2072 or 2075 of this title.

(Added Pub. L. 100-702, title IV, § 401(a), Nov. 19, 1988, 102 Stat. 4649, eff. Dec. 1, 1988; amended Pub. L. 103-394, title I, § 104(e), Oct. 22, 1994, 108 Stat. 4110.)

§ 2074 Rules of procedure and evidence; submission to Congress; effective date

(a) The Supreme Court shall transmit to the Congress not later than May 1 of the year in which a rule prescribed under section 2072 is to become effective a copy of the proposed rule. Such rule shall take effect no earlier than December 1 of the year in which such rule is so transmitted unless otherwise provided by law. The Supreme Court may fix the extent such rule shall apply to proceedings then pending, except that the Supreme Court shall not require the application of such rule to further proceedings then pending to the extent that, in the opinion of the court in which such proceedings are pending, the application of such rule in such proceedings would not be feasible or would work injustice, in which event the former rule applies.

(b) Any such rule creating, abolishing, or modifying an evidentiary privilege shall have no force or effect unless approved by Act of Congress.

(Added Pub. L. 100-702, title IV, § 401(a), Nov. 19, 1988, 102 Stat. 4649, eff. Dec. 1, 1988.)

HISTORICAL NOTE

The Supreme Court prescribes Federal Rules of Evidence pursuant to section 2072 of Title 28, United States Code, as enacted by Title IV "Rules Enabling Act" of Pub. L. 100-702 (approved November 19, 1988, 102 Stat. 4648), effective December 1, 1988, and section 2075 of Title 28. Pursuant to section 2074 of Title 28, the Supreme Court transmits to Congress (not later than May 1 of the year in which a rule prescribed under section 2072 is to become effective) a copy of the proposed rule. The rule takes effect no earlier than December 1 of the year in which the rule is transmitted unless otherwise provided by law.

Public Law 93-595 (approved January 2, 1975, 88 Stat. 1926) enacted the Federal Rules of Evidence proposed by the Supreme Court, with amendments made by Congress, to be effective July 1, 1975.

APPENDIX B

§ 3509 Child victims' and child witnesses' rights

(a) Definitions. For purposes of this section—

(1) the term "adult attendant" means an adult described in subsection (i) who accompanies a child throughout the judicial process for the purpose of providing emotional support;

(2) the term "child" means a person who is under the age of 18, who is or is alleged to be—

(A) a victim of a crime of physical abuse, sexual abuse, or exploitation; or

(B) a witness to a crime committed against another person;

(3) the term "child abuse" means the physical or mental injury, sexual abuse or exploitation, or negligent treatment of a child;

(4) the term "physical injury" includes lacerations, fractured bones, burns, internal injuries, severe bruising or serious bodily harm;

(5) the term "mental injury" means harm to a child's psychological or intellectual functioning which may be exhibited by severe anxiety, depression, withdrawal or outward aggressive behavior, or a combination of those behaviors, which may be demonstrated by a change in behavior, emotional response, or cognition;

(6) the term "exploitation" means child pornography or child prostitution;

(7) the term "multidisciplinary child abuse team" means a professional unit composed of representatives from health, social service, law enforcement, and legal service agencies to coordinate the assistance needed to handle cases of child abuse;

(8) the term "sexual abuse" includes the employment, use, persuasion, inducement, enticement, or coercion of a child to engage in, or assist another person to engage in, sexually explicit conduct or the rape, molestation, prostitution, or other form of sexual exploitation of children, or incest with children;

(9) the term "sexually explicit conduct" means actual or simulated—

(A) sexual intercourse, including sexual contact in the manner of genital-genital, oral-genital, anal-genital, or oral-anal contact, whether between persons of the same or of opposite sex; sexual contact means the intentional touching, either directly or through clothing, of the genitalia, anus, groin, breast, inner thigh, or buttocks of any person with an intent to abuse, humiliate, harass, degrade, or arouse or gratify sexual desire of any person;

(B) bestiality;

(C) masturbation;

(D) lascivious exhibition of the genitals or pubic area of a person or animal; or

(E) sadistic or masochistic abuse;

(10) the term "sex crime" means an act of sexual abuse that is a criminal act;

(11) the term "negligent treatment" means the failure to provide, for reasons other than poverty, adequate food, clothing, shelter, or medical care so as to seriously endanger the physical health of the child; and

(12) the term "child abuse" does not include discipline administered by a parent or legal guardian to his or her child provided it is reasonable in manner and moderate in degree and otherwise does not constitute cruelty.

(13) [Redesignated]

(b) Alternatives to live in-court testimony.

(1) Child's live testimony by 2-way closed circuit television.

(A) In a proceeding involving an alleged offense against a child, the attorney for the Government, the child's attorney, or a guardian ad litem appointed under subsection (h) may apply for an order that the child's testimony be taken in a room outside the courtroom and be televised by 2-way closed circuit television. The person seeking such an order shall apply for such an order at least 5 days before the trial date, unless the court finds on the record that the need for such an order was not reasonably foreseeable.

(B) The court may order that the testimony of the child be taken by closed-circuit television as provided in subparagraph (A) if the court finds that the child is unable to testify in open court in the presence of the defendant, for any of the following reasons:

(i) The child is unable to testify because of fear.

(ii) There is a substantial likelihood, established by expert testimony, that the child would suffer emotional trauma from testifying.

(iii) The child suffers a mental or other infirmity.

(iv) Conduct by defendant or defense counsel causes the child to be unable to continue testifying.

(C) The court shall support a ruling on the child's inability to testify with findings on the record. In determining whether the impact on an individual child of one or more of the factors described in subparagraph (B) is so substantial as to justify an order under subparagraph (A), the court may question the minor in chambers, or at some other comfortable place other than the courtroom, on the record for a reasonable period of time with the child attendant, the prosecutor, the child's attorney, the guardian ad litem, and the defense counsel present.

(D) If the court orders the taking of testimony by television, the attorney for the Government and the attorney for the defendant not including an attorney pro se for a party shall be present in a room outside the courtroom with the child and the child shall be subjected to direct and cross-examination. The only other persons who may be permitted in the room with the child during the child's testimony are—

(i) the child's attorney or guardian ad litem appointed under subsection (h);

(ii) persons necessary to operate the closed-circuit television equipment;

(iii) a judicial officer, appointed by the court; and

(iv) other persons whose presence is determined by the court to be necessary to the welfare and well-being of the child, including an adult attendant.

The child's testimony shall be transmitted by closed circuit television into the courtroom for viewing and hearing by the defendant, jury, judge, and public. The defendant shall be provided with the means of private, contemporaneous communication with the defendant's attorney during the testimony. The closed circuit television transmission shall relay into the room in which the child is testifying the defendant's image, and the voice of the judge.

(2) Videotaped deposition of child.

(A) In a proceeding involving an alleged offense against a child, the attorney for the Government, the child's attorney, the child's parent or legal guardian, or the guardian ad litem appointed under subsection (h) may apply for an order that a deposition be taken of the child's testimony and that the deposition be recorded and preserved on videotape. (

B) (i) Upon timely receipt of an application described in subparagraph (A), the court shall make a preliminary finding regarding whether at the time of trial the child is likely to be unable to testify in open court in the physical presence of the defendant, jury, judge, and public for any of the following reasons:

(I) The child will be unable to testify because of fear.

(II) There is a substantial likelihood, established by expert testimony, that the child would suffer emotional trauma from testifying in open court.

(III) The child suffers a mental or other infirmity.

(IV) Conduct by defendant or defense counsel causes the child to be unable to continue testifying.

(ii) If the court finds that the child is likely to be unable to testify in open court for any of the reasons stated in clause (i), the court shall order that the child's deposition be taken and preserved by videotape.

(iii) The trial judge shall preside at the videotape deposition of a child and shall rule on all questions as if at trial. The only other persons who may be permitted to be present at the proceeding are—

(I) the attorney for the Government;

(II) the attorney for the defendant;

(III) the child's attorney or guardian ad litem appointed under subsection (h);

(IV) persons necessary to operate the videotape equipment;

(V) subject to clause (iv), the defendant; and

(VI) other persons whose presence is determined by the court to be necessary to the welfare and well-being of the child. The defendant shall be afforded the rights applicable to defendants during trial, including the right to an attorney, the right to be confronted with the witness against the defendant, and the right to cross-examine the child.

(iv) If the preliminary finding of inability under clause (i) is based on evidence that the child is unable to testify in the physical presence of the defendant, the court may order that the defendant, including a defendant represented pro se, be excluded from the room in which the deposition is conducted. If the court orders that the defendant be excluded from the deposition room, the court shall order that 2-way closed circuit television equipment relay the defendant's image into the room in which the child is testifying, and the child's testimony into the room in which the defendant is viewing the proceeding, and that the defendant be provided with a means of private, contemporaneous communication with the defendant's attorney during the deposition.

(v) Handling of videotape. The complete record of the examination of the child, including the image and voices of all persons who in any way participate in the examination, shall be made and preserved on video tape in addition to being stenographically recorded. The videotape shall be transmitted to the clerk of the court in which the action is pending and shall be made available for viewing to the prosecuting attorney, the defendant, and the defendant's attorney during ordinary business hours.

(C) If at the time of trial the court finds that the child is unable to testify as for a reason described in subparagraph (B)(i), the court may admit into evidence the child's videotaped deposition in lieu of the child's testifying at the trial. The court shall support a ruling under this subparagraph with findings on the record.

(D) Upon timely receipt of notice that new evidence has been discovered after the original videotaping and before or during trial, the court, for good cause shown, may order an additional videotaped deposition. The testimony of the child shall be restricted to the matters specified by the court as the basis for granting the order.

(E) In connection with the taking of a videotaped deposition under this paragraph, the court may enter a protective order for the purpose of protecting the privacy of the child.

(F) The videotape of a deposition taken under this paragraph shall be destroyed 5 years after the date on which the trial court entered its judgment, but not before a final judgment is entered on appeal including Supreme Court review. The videotape shall become part of the court record and be kept by the court until it is destroyed.

(c) Competency examinations.

(1) Effect of Federal Rules of Evidence. Nothing in this subsection shall be construed to abrogate rule 601 of the Federal Rules of Evidence.

(2) Presumption. A child is presumed to be competent.

(3) Requirement of written motion. A competency examination regarding a child witness may be conducted by the court only upon written motion and offer of proof of incompetency by a party.

(4) Requirement of compelling reasons. A competency examination regarding a child may be conducted only if the court determines, on the record, that compelling reasons exist. A child's age alone is not a compelling reason.

(5) Persons permitted to be present. The only persons who may be permitted to be present at a competency examination are—

(A) the judge;

(B) the attorney for the Government;

(C) the attorney for the defendant;

(D) a court reporter; and

(E) persons whose presence, in the opinion of the court, is necessary to the welfare and well-being of the child, including the child's attorney, guardian ad litem, or adult attendant.

(6) Not before jury. A competency examination regarding a child witness shall be conducted out of the sight and hearing of a jury.

(7) Direct examination of child. Examination of a child related to competency shall normally be conducted by the court on the basis of questions submitted by the attorney for the Government and the attorney for the defendant including a party acting as an attorney pro se. The court may permit an attorney but not a party acting as an attorney pro se to examine a child directly on competency if the court is satisfied that the child will not suffer emotional trauma as a result of the examination.

(8) Appropriate questions. The questions asked at the competency examination of a child shall be appropriate to the age and developmental level of the child, shall not be related to the issues at trial, and shall focus on determining the child's ability to understand and answer simple questions.

(9) Psychological and psychiatric examinations. Psychological and psychiatric examinations to assess the competency of a child witness shall not be ordered without a showing of compelling need.

(d) Privacy protection.

(1) Confidentiality of information.

(A) A person acting in a capacity described in subparagraph (B) in connection with a criminal proceeding shall—

(i) keep all documents that disclose the name or any other information concerning a child in a secure place to which no person who does not have reason to know their contents has access; and

(ii) disclose documents described in clause (i) or the information in them that concerns a child only to persons who, by reason of their participation in the proceeding, have reason to know such information.

(B) Subparagraph (A) applies to—

(i) all employees of the Government connected with the case, including employees of the Department of Justice, any law enforcement agency involved in the case, and any person hired by the Government to provide assistance in the proceeding;

(ii) employees of the court;

(iii) the defendant and employees of the defendant, including the attorney for the defendant and persons hired by the defendant or the attorney for the defendant to provide assistance in the proceeding; and

(iv) members of the jury.

(2) Filing under seal. All papers to be filed in court that disclose the name of or any other information concerning a child shall be filed under seal without necessity of obtaining a court order. The person who makes the filing shall submit to the clerk of the court—

(A) the complete paper to be kept under seal; and

(B) the paper with the portions of it that disclose the name of or other information concerning a child redacted, to be placed in the public record.

(3) Protective orders.

(A) On motion by any person the court may issue an order protecting a child from public disclosure of the name of or any other information concerning the child in the course of the proceedings, if the court determines that there is a significant possibility that such disclosure would be detrimental to the child.

(B) A protective order issued under subparagraph (A) may—

(i) provide that the testimony of a child witness, and the testimony of any other witness, when the attorney who calls the witness has reason to anticipate that the name of or any other information concerning a child may be divulged in the testimony, be taken in a closed courtroom; and

(ii) provide for any other measures that may be necessary to protect the privacy of the child.

(4) Disclosure of information. This subsection does not prohibit disclosure of the name of or other information concerning a child to the defendant, the attorney for the defendant, a multidisciplinary child abuse team, a guardian ad litem, or an adult attendant, or to anyone to whom, in the opinion of the court, disclosure is necessary to the welfare and well-being of the child.

(e) Closing the courtroom. When a child testifies the court may order the exclusion from the courtroom of all persons, including members of the press, who do not have a direct interest in the case. Such an order may be made if the court determines on the record that requiring the child to testify in open court would cause substantial psychological harm to the child or would result in the child's inability to effectively communicate. Such an order shall be narrowly tailored to serve the Government's specific compelling interest.

(f) Victim impact statement. In preparing the presentence report pursuant to rule 32(c) of the Federal Rules of Criminal Procedure, the probation officer shall request information from the multidisciplinary child abuse team and other appropriate sources to determine the impact of the offense on the child victim and any other children who may have been affected. A guardian ad litem appointed under subsection (h) shall make every effort to obtain and report information that accurately expresses the child's and the family's views concerning the child's victimization. A guardian ad litem shall use forms that permit the child to express the child's views concerning the personal consequences of the child's victimization, at a level and in a form of communication commensurate with the child's age and ability.

(g) Use of multidisciplinary child abuse teams.

(1) In general. A multidisciplinary child abuse team shall be used when it is feasible to do so. The court shall work with State and local governments that have established multidisciplinary child abuse teams designed to assist child victims and child witnesses, and the court and the attorney for the Government shall consult with the multidisciplinary child abuse team as appropriate.

(2) Role of multidisciplinary child abuse teams. The role of the multidisciplinary child abuse team shall be to provide for a child services that the members of the team in their professional roles are capable of providing, including—

(A) medical diagnoses and evaluation services, including provision or interpretation of x-rays, laboratory tests, and related services, as needed, and documentation of findings;

(B) telephone consultation services in emergencies and in other situations;

(C) medical evaluations related to abuse or neglect;

(D) psychological and psychiatric diagnoses and evaluation services for the child, parent or parents, guardian or guardians, or other caregivers, or any other individual involved in a child victim or child witness case;

(E) expert medical, psychological, and related professional testimony;

(F) case service coordination and assistance, including the location of services available from public and private agencies in the community; and

(G) training services for judges, litigators, court officers and others that are involved in child victim and child witness cases, in handling child victims and child witnesses.

(h) Guardian ad litem.

(1) In general. The court may appoint a guardian ad litem for a child who was a victim of, or a witness to, a crime involving abuse or exploitation to protect the best interests of the child. In making the appointment, the court shall consider a prospective guardian's background in, and familiarity with, the judicial process, social service programs, and child abuse issues. The guardian ad litem shall not be a person who is or may be a witness in a proceeding involving the child for whom the guardian is appointed.

(2) Duties of guardian ad litem. A guardian ad litem may attend all the depositions, hearings, and trial proceedings in which a child participates, and make recommendations to the court concerning the welfare of the child. The guardian ad litem may have access to all reports, evaluations and records, except attorney's work product, necessary to effectively advocate for the child. (The extent of access to grand jury materials is limited to the access routinely provided to victims and their representatives.) A guardian ad litem shall marshal and coordinate the delivery of resources and special services to the child. A guardian ad litem shall not be compelled to testify in any court action or proceeding concerning any information or opinion received from the child in the course of serving as a guardian ad litem.

(3) Immunities. A guardian ad litem shall be presumed to be acting in good faith and shall be immune from civil and criminal liability for complying with the guardian's lawful duties described in paragraph (2).

(i) Adult attendant. A child testifying at or attending a judicial proceeding shall have the right to be accompanied by an adult attendant to provide emotional support to the child. The court, at its discretion, may allow the adult attendant to remain in close physical proximity to or in contact with the child while the child testifies. The court may allow the adult attendant to hold the child's hand or allow the child to sit on the adult attendant's lap throughout the course of the proceeding. An adult attendant shall not provide the child with an answer to any question directed to the child during the course of the child's testimony or otherwise prompt the child. The image of the child attendant, for the time the child is testifying or being deposed, shall be recorded on videotape.

(j) Speedy trial. In a proceeding in which a child is called to give testimony, on motion by the attorney for the Government or a guardian ad litem, or on its own motion, the court may designate the case as being of special public importance. In cases so designated, the court shall, consistent with these rules, expedite the proceeding and ensure that it takes precedence over any other. The court shall ensure a speedy trial in order to minimize the length of time the child must endure the stress of involvement with the criminal process. When deciding whether to grant a continuance, the court shall take into consideration the age of the child and the potential adverse impact the delay may have on the child's well-being. The court shall make written findings of fact and conclusions of law when granting a continuance in cases involving a child.

(k) Stay of civil action. If, at any time that a cause of action for recovery of compensation for damage or injury to the person of a child exists, a criminal action is pending which arises out of the same occurrence and in which the child is the victim, the civil action shall be stayed until the end of all phases of the criminal action and any mention of the civil action during the criminal proceeding is prohibited. As used in this subsection, a criminal action is pending until its final adjudication in the trial court.

(l) Testimonial aids. The court may permit a child to use anatomical dolls, puppets, drawings, mannequins, or any other demonstrative device the court deems appropriate for the purpose of assisting a child in testifying.

APPENDIX C

§ 3510   Rights of victims to attend and observe trial

(a) Non-capital cases. Notwithstanding any statute, rule, or other provision of law, a United States district court shall not order any victim of an offense excluded from the trial of a defendant accused of that offense because such victim may, during the sentencing hearing, make a statement or present any information in relation to the sentence.

(b) Capital cases. Notwithstanding any statute, rule, or other provision of law, a United States district court shall not order any victim of an offense excluded from the trial of a defendant accused of that offense because such victim may, during the sentencing hearing, testify as to the effect of the offense on the victim and the victim's family or as to any other factor for which notice is required under section 3593(a).

(c) Definition. As used in this section, the term "victim" includes all persons defined as victims in section 503(e)(2) of the Victims' Rights and Restitution Act of 1990 [42 USCS ù 10607(e)(2)].

APPENDIX D

§ 10606   Victims' rights

(a) Best efforts to accord rights. Officers and employees of the Department of Justice and other departments and agencies of the United States engaged in the detection, investigation, or prosecution of crime shall make their best efforts to see that victims of crime are accorded the rights described in subsection (b).

(b) Rights of crime victims. A a crime victim has the following rights:

(1) The right to be treated with fairness and with respect for the victim's dignity and privacy.

(2) The right to be reasonably protected from the accused offender.

(3) The right to be notified of court proceedings.

(4) The right to be present at all public court proceedings related to the offense, unless the court determines that testimony by the victim would be materially affected if the victim heard other testimony at trial.

(5) The right to confer with [the] attorney for the Government in the case.

(6) The right to restitution.

(7) The right to information about the conviction, sentencing, imprisonment, and release of the offender.

(c) No cause of action or defense. This section does not create a cause of action or defense in favor of any person arising out of the failure to accord to a victim the rights enumerated in subsection (b).

TABLE OF CASES

[References are to page numbers]

[References are to page numbers]

[References are to page numbers]

[References are to page numbers]

[References are to page numbers]

[References are to page numbers]

[References are to page numbers]

[References are to page numbers]

[References are to page numbers]

[References are to page numbers]

[References are to page numbers]

[References are to page numbers]

[References are to page numbers]

[References are to page numbers]

INDEX

[References are to page numbers.]

[References are to page numbers.]

C

[References are to page numbers.]

[References are to page numbers.]

[References are to page numbers.]

[References are to page numbers.]

[References are to page numbers.]

[References are to page numbers.]

[References are to page numbers.]

[References are to page numbers.]

[References are to page numbers.]

[References are to page numbers.]

[References are to page numbers.]

P

[References are to page numbers.]

[References are to page numbers.]

[References are to page numbers.]

[References are to page numbers.]

[References are to page numbers.]